JUVENILE DELINQUENCY

THEORY, PRACTICE AND LAW

FIFTH EDITION

JUVENILE DELINQUENCY

THEORY, PRACTICE AND LAW

FIFTH EDITION

Larry J. Siegel, PH.D.

UNIVERSITY OF MASSACHUSETTS—LOWELL

Joseph J. Senna, M.S.W., J.D.

NORTHEASTERN UNIVERSITY

WEST PUBLISHING COMPANY

St. Paul   New York   Los Angeles   San Francisco

Composition: Carlisle Communications, Ltd.
Copyediting: Marilynn Taylor
Cover Painting: City Figures #8 by Irene Moss, with permission from Reece Galleries
Index: Linda Buskus/Northwind Editorial Services
Text Design: Kristin Weber
Color Insert: Nancy Wirsig McClure/Hand to Mouse Arts
Production, prepress, printing, and binding: West Publishing Company

WEST'S COMMITMENT TO THE ENVIRONMENT

In 1906, West Publishing Company began recycling materials left over from the production of books. This began a tradition of efficient and responsible use of resources. Today, up to 95 percent of our legal books and 70 percent of our college and school texts are printed on recycled, acid-free stock. West also recycles nearly 22 million pounds of scrap paper annually—the equivalent of 181,717 trees. Since the 1960s, West has devised ways to capture and recycle waste inks, solvents, oils, and vapors created in the printing process. We also recycle plastics of all kinds, wood, glass, corrugated cardboard, and batteries, and have eliminated the use of Styrofoam book packaging. We at West are proud of the longevity and the scope of our commitment to the environment.

 PRINTED ON 10% POST CONSUMER RECYCLED PAPER

Library of Congress Cataloging-in-Publication Data

Siegel, Larry J.
    Juvenile delinquency : theory, practice, and law / Larry J.
Siegel, Joseph J. Senna.—5th ed.
        p.   cm.
    Includes index.
    ISBN 0-314-02673-8
    1. Juvenile delinquency—United States. 2. Juvenile justice,
Administration of—United States.   I. Senna, Joseph J.   II. Title.
HV9104.S53 1994
364.3'6'0973—dc20   93-30593
                                                                CIP

PHOTO CREDITS

CHAPTER ONE
3 Jeff Isaac Greenburg/Photo Researchers
5 AP/Wide World
10 Bill Freeman/PhotoEdit
17 Richard Hutchings/PhotoEdit
22 Jim Tynan/Impact Visuals
CHAPTER TWO
27 Barry Lewis/Network Matrix

32 Mark Richards/PhotoEdit
33 Rob Crandall/Stock Boston
34 Dorothy Littell/Stock Boston
40 AP/Wide World
44 Joel Gordon
48 AP/Wide World
CHAPTER THREE
53 Tony Freeman/PhotoEdit

Photo credits continue following the index.

To my wife Therese J. Libby and my children,
Julie, Andrew, Eric, and Rachel.

L.J.S.

To my wife Janet and my children, Christian,
Stephen, Peter, and Joseph.

J.J.S.

CONTENTS

CHAPTER 3
DELINQUENCY THROUGH THE LIFE COURSE   53

PART II THEORIES OF DELINQUENCY   89

CHAPTER 4
FOCUS ON THE INDIVIDUAL
CHOICE, BIOSOCIAL AND PSYCHOLOGICAL THEORIES   91

CHAPTER 5
SOCIAL STRUCTURE THEORIES
DISORGANIZATION, STRAIN, AND

CULTURAL DEVIANCE   139

CHAPTER 8
THEORIES OF FEMALE DELINQUENCY   241

CHAPTER 10
PEERS AND DELINQUENCY
JUVENILE GANGS AND GROUPS   311

CHAPTER 11
SCHOOLS AND DELINQUENCY   343

CHAPTER 12
DRUGS AND DELINQUENCY   375

CHAPTER **14**

AN OVERVIEW OF THE JUVENILE JUSTICE SYSTEM AND ITS GOALS   441

PART V   **CONTROLLING JUVENILE OFFENDERS**   473

CHAPTER **15**

POLICE WORK WITH JUVENILES   475

PART VI   **JUVENILE CORRECTIONS**   585

CHAPTER **18**
**JUVENILE PROBATION AND COMMUNITY
TREATMENT**   587

CHAPTER **19**

INSTITUTIONS FOR JUVENILES 615

PREFACE

The events of the past few years have heightened interest in the study of juvenile delinquency appreciably. The media has focused on incidents involving youth gangs, violence in schools, and teenage substance abuse. Adolescents seem more violent today than ever before. And while the justice system seems incapable of controlling youth crime, the general public demands that police guarantee community safety and the courts rigorously punish dangerous adolescent offenders.

Because these issues are so critical to the quality of life in the United States, an on-going effort has been made to study and understand the causes of delinquent behavior and to devise strategies to control or eliminate its occurrence.

We enjoy updating this text because, as university professors who have taught this course over the past twenty years, we realize that the study of juvenile delinquency is a dynamic, ever-changing field of scientific inquiry. The theories, concepts and processes of this area of study are constantly evolving. We have therefore updated *Juvenile Delinquency, Theory, Practice and Law* to reflect the changes that have taken place in the study of delinquent behavior during the past few years. The fifth edition includes a review of recent legal cases, research studies and policy initiatives. It provides a groundwork for the study of juvenile delinquency by analyzing and describing the nature and extent of delinquency, the suspected causes of delinquent behavior, and the environmental influences on youthful misbehavior. This edition also identifies the agencies of juvenile justice and the procedures used to treat juvenile offenders. It covers what most experts believe are the critical issues in juvenile delinquency and analyzes crucial policy issues including the death penalty for juveniles, shock incarceration, and the courtroom testimony of children in sexual abuse cases.

GOALS AND OBJECTIVES

Our primary goals in writing this fifth edition remain as they have been for previous editions:

1. To be as objective as possible, presenting the many diverse views and perspectives that characterize the study of juvenile delinquency and reflect its interdisciplinary nature.
2. To contain a balance of theory, law, policy, and practice. It is essential that a text on delinquency not solely be a theory book without presenting the juvenile justice system or contain sections on current policies without examining legal issues and cases.
3. To be as thorough and up-to-date as possible. We have attempted to include the most current data and information available.
4. To make the study of delinquency interesting as well as informative. We want to make readers as interested as possible in the study of delinquency so that they will pursue it on an undergraduate or graduate level.

We have tried to provide a text which is both scholarly and informative, comprehensive yet interesting, well organized and objective yet provocative and thought provoking.

ORGANIZATION OF THE TEXT

The fifth edition is divided into five main sections.

Part I examines the concept of delinquency and status offending, the measurement of delinquency, and trends and patterns in the delinquency rate. Chapter 1 now contains material on the current crisis faced by adolescents as well as material on delinquency in foreign countries. Chapter 2 covers recent trends in teen violence and includes material on hate crimes. Chapter 3 has been significantly revamped and retitled. Its content reflects the life-course view of delinquency and contains sections on problem behavior syndrome and the turning points of crime.

Part II describes the various theoretical models which have been used to explain the onset of delinquent behavior. Chapter 4 covers recent findings on choice, biological and psychological theories. Chapter 5 looks at environmental influences and has new sections on strain theory. Chapter 6 focuses on socialization and contains analysis of the general theory of crime. Chapter 7 on social reaction theories has been updated to reflect recent research on labeling and conflict theory. Chapter 8 has been revised to reflect recent writing on the relationship between gender and delinquency. Included is a section on the sexualization of female delinquency.

Part III covers the environmental influences on delinquency. All the chapters in part III have been updated because there have been so many changes in the area of family (chapter 9), gangs (chapter 10), schools (chapter 11), and drugs (chapter 12). Chapter 13 reviews the history of childhood and the emergence of state control over children in need. Emphasis has been placed on reporting the latest changes in child abuse data, the relationship between abuse and delinquency, court testimony of child abuse victims, emerging patterns of school achievement, crime in schools, and trends in teenage drug abuse.

Part IV on juvenile justice advocacy contains material on both the history of juvenile justice and the philosophy and practice of today's juvenile justice system. Chapter 14 gives extensive coverage to the role of the federal government in the juvenile justice system, a review of theoretical models of juvenile justice, extensive coverage of the legal rights of children including a new time line of Constitutional cases.

Part V on controlling juvenile offenders contains three chapters on the police and court process. Chapter 15 on police has been updated with the major court decisions on school searches and *Miranda* rights of juveniles. It also contains new material on race and gender effects on police discretion. Chapter 16 on early court process, has new information on plea bargaining in juvenile court, the use of detention and transfer to adult jails. It now contains an analysis of the critical factors which influence the waiver decision. Chapter 17 on the juvenile trial and sentencing has been extensively revised, and contains new sections on special problems faced by juvenile court judges such as substance abuse cases and gangs. It reviews the role of the public defender and federal prosecutor in juvenile court.

Part VI contains two chapters on the juvenile correctional system. Chapter 18 on community based treatments has been updated with material on probation innovations including the increased use of restitution. A new survey on public attitudes toward community corrections is discussed. How does the public view probation for violent juvenile offenders? Chapter 19 on closed institutions reflects the continued expansion of the juvenile correctional population including the disturbing increase in the number of minorities in that population.

Once again the book closes with a brief overview of significant findings found within the text.

LEARNING TOOLS

The text contains the following features designed to help students learn and comprehend the material:

1. Each chapter begins with an outline.
2. The book contains more than 200 photos, tables and charts.
3. **Case In Point** Every chapter contains boxed inserts on intriguing issues concerning juvenile delinquency policy or processes. Within the boxed inserts are critical thinking sections which help students conceptualize problems of concern to juvenile delinquency.
4. **Focus on Delinquency** As in previous editions, these boxed inserts focus attention on topics of special importance and concern. They also include major Supreme Court cases that influence and control the juvenile justice system—for example, *In Re Gault,* which defines the concept of due process for youthful offenders.
5. **Key Terms** At the end of each chapter is a list of key terms used throughout the chapter. Every effort has been made to include the key terms within the glossary which concludes the book.
6. **Discussion Questions** Each chapter ends with thought provoking discussion questions.
7. A glossary is included which sets out and defines key terms used in the text.

ACKNOWLEDGMENTS

The preparation of this text would not have been possible without the aid of our colleagues who helped by reviewing the text and giving us material to use in its preparation. These include: Professor Aric Steven Frazier, Vincennes University;

Professor David M. Horton, St. Edward's University; Professor Harold W. Osborne, Baylor University; Professor Barbara Owen, California State University–Fresno; Professor Ray Paternoster, University of Maryland; Professor Stanley L. Swart, University of North Florida; Professor Pamela Tontodonato, Kent State University; Professor Kim Weaver, Ferris State University.

In addition, important information was provided by the following individuals and institutions: Joan McDermott, Helene Raskin White, Joe Sanborn, Jim Inciardi, Vic Streib, Eve Buzawa, Chris Marshall, Meda Chesney-Lind, Gerald Hotaling, Marv Zalman, John Laub, Rob Sampson, David Farrington, G. David Curry, Larry Sherman, James A. Fox, Jack McDevitt, Alan Lincoln, Lee Ellis, and the staff at the Institute for Social Research at the University of Michigan; the National Center For State Courts; the Police Foundation; the Sentencing Project; Kathleen Maguire and the staff of the Hindelang Research Center at State University of New York—Albany; James Byrne of the Criminal Justice Research Center at the University of Massachusetts–Lowell; Kristina Rose and Janet Rosenbaum of the National Criminal Justice Reference Service; Deborah Daro and Karen McCurdy of the National Committee for Prevention of Child Abuse; Terence Thornberry, Margaret Farnworth, Marvin Krohn, Alan Lizotte and the researchers at the Rochester Youth Study, Albany, New York. We extend a special thanks to Dr. Lynn Sametz for providing most of the timeline data.

And, of course, our colleagues at West Publishing did their usual outstanding job of aiding us in the preparation of the text. Mary Schiller, our senior executive editor, whom we consider a non-attributed co-author, did her usually superb job of guiding us through another edition. Debra Meyer, our production editor on the project, was thoroughly professional and creative and helped make this a very attractive text. We extend special thanks to Barbara Fuller for completing the production work.

I

THE CONCEPT OF DELINQUENCY

■■■

The field of juvenile delinquency has been an important area of study since the turn of the century. Academicians, practitioners, policymakers, and legal scholars have devoted their attention to basic questions about the nature of youth crime: Who commits delinquent acts? How much delinquency occurs each year? Is the rate of delinquent activity increasing or decreasing? How should delinquency be defined? What can we do to prevent delinquency?

Part I reviews these basic questions in detail. Chapter 1 shows how the definition of delinquency has become quite complex. While society has chosen to treat adult and juvenile law violators separately, it has also expanded the definition of youthful misbehaviors eligible for social control; these are referred to as status offenses. Status offenses include such behaviors as truancy, running away, and incorrigibility. Critics suggest that juveniles' noncriminal behavior is probably not a proper area of concern for law enforcement agencies.

The remaining two chapters in this section examine the nature and extent of delinquent behavior. Chapter 2 discusses how social scientists gather information on juvenile delinquency and provides an overview of some of the major trends on juvenile crime. Chapter 3 examines the factors related to delinquency—race, gender, class, and age—and links them to an important theme in the study of delinquency: the maintenance of a delinquent career over the life course. Why do some kids continually get in trouble with the law, escalate the seriousness of their offenses, and become adult criminals? Why do others desist from delinquent activities? These are the major themes of the newly emerging life course view of delinquency. ■

OUTLINE

THE NATURE OF DELINQUENCY

You might have read about the following incidents in the press.

On February 12, 1993, 2-year-old James Bulger was abducted from a shopping mall in Liverpool, England, dragged half mile away to a construction site, beaten to death, and left on a railroad track to be run over by a train. His abductors were two 10-year-old boys whose actions were captured by mall security cameras. Angry crowds tried to attack the suspects while they were in police custody. This was especially shocking because Britain's murder rate is only one tenth as great as that of the United States.[1]

On July 10, 1992, a Florida judge ruled that a boy could sue to obtain his freedom from his biological parents so he could be adopted by his foster family. The boy, Gregory K., claimed he was neglected and abused by his biological parents and had spent all but seven months of the past eight years in state or foster care. Gregory requested in court that he have no further contact with Rachel K., his biological mother. Gregory was granted his petition to remain with his foster parents. The press sensationalized the case by claiming that Gregory in effect had "divorced" his parents.[2]

In what the media referred to as the *"Home Alone"* case, David and Sharon Schoo were arrested at Chicago's O'Hare Airport after they returned from a nine-day Acapulco vacation. They had left their two daughters, 9-year-old Nicole and 4-year-old Diana, alone at home while they were gone. The children had called 911 when a smoke alarm went off, alerting authorities to their plight. When police arrived, Nicole told them, "For a long time, I was feeling really lonely and wondering what they were doing." Police found a note instructing the children in what to eat and when to go to bed. Nicole and Diana were left to fend for themselves despite the fact that their paternal grandmother lived in a neighboring town. Upon their return, the Schoos seemed surprised by all the fuss being made over their vacation.[3]

On January 11, 1992, four teenage girls lured 12-year-old Shanda Renee Sharer into their car, drove her down a country road where they tortured, sodomized, slashed, and finally covered her with gasoline and burned her to death. One of the girls had accused Sharer of stealing away her girlfriend in a homoerotic relationship. The crime occurred in Madison, Indiana, a quiet town of thirteen thousand people. The girls, who later plead guilty, were given the maximum sentence allowed by law.[4]

On October 20, 1992, Chicago police began shutting down four buildings in the Cabrini-Green housing project after a sniper killed 7-year-old Dantrell Davis as his mother walked him to school. Cabrini-Green has been described as "the most crime-infested 70 acres in the country." Experts consider inner-city housing projects to be places that concentrate "poverty, misery, drugs, alcoholism, people with mental disabilities, and people [who are] unemployable."[5]

While these cases are extremes (they would not have been reported in the press otherwise), they are by no means extraordinary or unique. They illustrate the problems adolescents face in modern American society. Many live below the poverty line in dangerous, deteriorated inner-city areas. The Tufts University Center on Hunger, Poverty, and Nutrition Policy estimates that child poverty effects 14.3 million adolescents in 1993; the Tufts researchers estimate that by the year 2012, 20.7 million, or 28 percent, of all minor children will be living in poverty.[6] Research shows that children in the United States are being polarized into two distinct economic groups: those born into affluent, two-earner, married couple households and those residing in impoverished, single-parent households.[7]

The destructive environment of deteriorated urban areas prevents too many adolescents from having productive, fulfilling, or happy lives. Many face an early death from random bullets and drive-by shootings. Violence also threatens adolescents in small towns and rural areas.

■ ■ ■ ■ ■ ■ ■ ■ ■ ■ ■ ■ ■ ■ ■ ■

More than 14 million American youths are living in poverty. Many are homeless and lack proper nutrition and health care.

Even those who escape poverty may be enduring a destructive and dysfunctional family life. Some are physically and sexually abused, while others are abandoned and neglected. It is not surprising then that teenage violence has increased during the past few decades. A recent study by James Alan Fox indicates that the number of homicides involving juvenile offenders more than doubled from 1984 to 1989, while during the same period of time the number of adult offenders committing homicide increased less than 5 percent.[8]

Crime and violence are by no means the only problems faced by youth in the United States. Millions are also at risk of physical abuse and neglect, substance abuse, poverty, and death (see Table 1.1). The U.S. educational system lags behind other developed nations in critical such areas as science and mathematics achievement. The United States, the richest and most powerful country in the world, has higher infant and preschool-age mortality rates than nineteen other countries.

The problems of youth in modern society have become a major national concern and an important subject for academic study. This text focuses on one area of particular concern: **juvenile delinquency:** *criminal behavior committed by minors.* The study of juvenile delinquency is important both because of the damage suffered by its victims and the problems faced by its perpetrators. Juveniles who engage in criminal acts are placed under the control of law

■■ **TABLE 1.1**   Is This the Best America Can Do?

■ Every 12 seconds of the school day, a child drops out of school (380,000 a year).

■ Every 13 seconds, a child is reported abused or neglected (2.7 million a year).

■ Every 26 seconds, a child runs away from home (1.2 million a year).

■ Almost every minute, an American teenager has a baby.

■ Every 9 minutes, a child is arrested for a drug offense.

■ Every 40 minutes, a child is arrested for drunken driving.

■ Every 53 minutes a child dies from poverty.

■ Every 3 hours, a child is murdered.

The United States Has:

■ A higher infant mortality rate than 19 other countries.

■ A higher infant mortality rate for black infants than the overall rates of 31 other nations, including Cuba, Bulgaria, and Kuwait.

■ A death rate among preschool children worse than 19 other nations.

■ A worse low-birthweight rate than 30 other nations.

■ A low-birthweight rate among blacks worse than the overall rates of 73 other countries.

■ A ranking of 12 out of 14 among industrialized nations in science achievement among 13-year-olds.

■ A ranking of 13 out of 14 among industrialized nations in mathematics achievement among all 13-year-olds.

■ A higher child poverty rate than seven other industrialized Western countries.

■ An estimated 2.4 million children involved in prostitution each year.

■ The highest rate of working children among affluent countries.

■ The highest rate of teen drug use of any nation in the industrialized world.

■ The record of being one of only seven countries carrying out the capital punishment of juvenile offenders within the past decade. At least 145 nations ban such executions.

Source: Adapted from Children's Defense Fund, *The State of America's Children,* 1992 (Washington, D.C. Children's Defense Fund, 1992).

enforcement, court, and correctional agencies that comprise the **juvenile justice system.** They may be taken into custody by the police, have their cases heard in a juvenile or family court, and be placed in a residential facility that treats troubled children.

During the 1990s, more than 1.5 million youths have been arrested each year for crimes ranging in seriousness from murder to loitering.[9] Though most juvenile law violations are minor, some young offenders are extremely dangerous and violent. More than 250,000 youths belong to street gangs and groups that can put fear into an entire city. Youths involved in multiple serious criminal acts—referred to as life-style, repeat, or **chronic delinquent** offenders—are now recognized as a serious social problem. State juvenile authorities must deal with these offenders, along with responding to a range of other social problems, including child abuse and neglect, school crime and vandalism, family crises, and drug abuse.

THE STUDY OF DELINQUENCY

Given the diversity and gravity of these problems, it is essential to study delinquency in an orderly and scientific manner. It would be difficult, if not impossible, to devise strategies to combat such a complex social phenomenon as juvenile delinquency if its fundamental dimensions were unknown. Is delinquency a function of psychological abnormality? A collective reaction by youths against destructive social conditions? The product of a disturbed home life and disrupted socialization? Does serious delinquent behavior occur only in large urban areas among lower-class youths? Or is it spread throughout the entire social structure? What impact do family life, substance abuse, school experiences, and peer relations have on youth and their law-violating behaviors? We know that most youthful law violators do not go on to become adult criminals (what is known as the **aging-out process**). Yet we do not know why some youths become *chronic career offenders* whose delinquent career begins early and persists into their adulthood. Why does the onset of delinquency begin so early in some children? Why does the severity of their offenses escalate? What factors predict the *persistence*, or continuation, of delinquency, and conversely, what are the factors associated with its *desistance*, or termination? Unless these questions are answered, developing effective prevention and control efforts will be difficult.

The study of delinquency also involves the analysis of the agencies designed to treat youthful offenders who fall into the arms of the law—known collectively as the *juvenile justice system*. How should police deal with minors who violate the law? What are the legal rights of children? For example, should minors who commit murder receive the death penalty? What kind of correctional programs are most effective with delinquent youths? How effective are educational, community, counseling, and vocational development programs? Is it true, as some critics claim, that most efforts to rehabilitate young offenders are doomed to failure?[10] Should we adopt a punishment or a treatment orientation to combat delinquency, or something in between?

In sum, the scientific study of delinquency requires understanding the nature, extent, and cause of youthful law violations and the methods devised for their control. It also involves the study of important environmental and social issues associated with delinquent behavior, including substance abuse, child abuse and neglect, education, and peer relations. Because of these requirements, this text attempts to provide a comprehensive look at the problem of delinquency by reviewing its nature, extent, cause, and influences and the efforts being made to treat problem youths and prevent the spread of delinquency.

An Interdisciplinary Study

Because these problems are so complex, the study of delinquency is *interdisciplinary*. Most experts on the subject are *criminologists*, originally trained as sociologists, whose interests and experience allow them to conduct detailed studies of the social factors related to crime and delinquency—environment, schools, family, peer relations, and so on. Consequently, most research efforts and resulting theoretical models used to explain the cause of delinquent behavior have a decidedly sociological bent.

Members of many other academic disciplines have made significant contributions to our understanding of delinquent behavior. Psychologists have directed their efforts toward determining whether psychological factors can predict delinquent behavior. For example, they have attempted to identify the personality traits of young offenders and have studied the association between delinquency and mental processes. Similarly, biologists and medical doctors have explored the neurological, biochemical, and genetic influences on violence and other forms of antisocial behavior.

Political scientists, historians, and legal scholars have also become involved in delinquency research. They have attempted to analyze how governments deal with the problem of youthful misconduct: How do legislative bodies implement juvenile law? How do sociopolitical institutions, such as the educational and welfare systems, organize their activities? How does the system of juvenile justice operate? How have these institutions evolved?

Experts in law and criminal justice have also made delinquency an area of study. Their concern is usually directed at the operations of the police, the courts, and the correctional agencies, which are designed to treat, control, and process juvenile offenders.

Finally, those in the helping professions who are interested in treatment of young offenders—including educators, religious leaders, social workers, counselors, and mental health professionals—have made a significant effort to devise rehabilitation and treatment programs and to monitor their success.

So the study of delinquent behavior is not the province of any one group. It is a multidisciplinary field involving social scientists, the helping professions, and legal scholars. Students interested in the study of delinquent behavior can specialize in one of a number of different academic disciplines or professions.

THE ADOLESCENT DILEMMA

Adolescence is unquestionably a time of transition. During this period the self, or basic personality, is still undergoing a metamorphosis and is vulnerable to a host of external determinants as well as internal physiological changes.[11]

Delinquency is a function of the trials facing many adolescents in modern American society. By the time they reach 15, a significant number of teenagers are approaching adulthood unable to adequately meet the requirements and

1967

President's Commission on Law Enforcement recognizes the problems of the juvenile justice system.

1967

In re Gault, a U.S. Supreme court decision that establishes that juveniles have the right to counsel, notice, confrontation of witnesses, and the avoidance of self-incrimination. The decision also applies procedural due process to juveniles in the adjudicatory phase of a hearing and if loss of liberty is threatened. In general, the court holds that Fourteenth Amendment due process applies to the juvenile justice system, specifically in adjudicatory hearings.

1968

Ginsberg v. New York establishes that it is unlawful to sell pornography to a minor.

1969

Tinker v. Des Moines School District establishes that the First Amendment applies to juveniles and protects their constitutional right to free speech.

1969

Hirschl publishes *Causes of Delinquency.*

1970

In re Winship establishes that proof beyond a reasonable doubt is necessary in the adjudicatory phase of a juvenile hearing. A juvenile can appeal on the ground of insufficiency of the evidence if the offense alleged is an act that would be a crime in an adult court.

1970

White House Conference on Children.

1971

McKeiver v. Pennsylvania establishes that a jury trial is not constitutionally required in a juvenile hearing but states can permit one if they wish.

1971

The Twenty-sixth Amendment to the Constitution is passed, granting the right to vote to 18-year-olds.

1972

Wisconsin v. Yoder gives parents the right to impose their religion on their children.

1972

Wolfgang publishes *Delinquency in a Birth Coh*

1973

In re Snyder gives minors the ri proceedings against their paren

1973

San Antonio Independent School Rodriguez establishes that diffe education based on wealth we sarily discriminatory.

1974

Federal Child A Act.

1974

Buckley Amenc Education Act c Family Educatic Privacy Act. Stu right to see thei parental consen

1974

Juvenile Justice Prevention Act.

1975

G fa p

1954
- *Brown v. Board of*
- *Education,* a major
- school desegregation
  decision.

1959
- Standard Family
- Court Act of National
- Council on Crime
- and Delinquency
- establishes that juve-
- nile hearings are to
- be informal.

1966
- *Kent v. United*
- *States*—initial
- decision to
- establish due
- process protec-
- tions for juvenile
- at transfer
  proceedings.

studies are conducted by
Kay.

924
Federal Probation Act.

1930
- Children's Charter.

1930   1940   1950   1960

A History of Children's Rights
in the United States

rt.

ght to bring
ts.

District v.
ences in
e not neces-

1977
- Report of the Committee of the Judiciary, especially concerning the rights of the unborn and the right of 18-year-olds to vote.

1977
- Juvenile Justice Amendment of 1977.

1977
- *Ingraham v. Wright* establishes that corporal punishment is permissible in public schools and is not a violation of the Eighth Amendment.

1977
- American Bar Association, Standards on Juvenile Justice.

1977
- Washington State amends its sentencing policy.

1982
- Efforts to decarcerate status offenders escalate.

1983
- The Federal G
  its attention o

1

1979
- International Year of the Child.

1980
- National concern over child abuse and neglect.

1981
- *Fare v. Michael C.* defines *Miranda* rights of

buse Prevention

ment to the
f 1974, the
n Rights and
dents have the
r own files with
t.

and Delinquency

oss v. Lopez establishes that a student
cing suspension has the right to due
ocess, prior notice, and an open hearing.

1980

1875–1900

Case Law begins to deal with protective statutes.

1897

Ex Parte Becknell, a California decision that reverses the sentence of a juvenile who has not been given a jury trial.

1881

Michigan begins child protection with the Michigan Public Acts of 1881.

1899

Illinois Juvenile Court Act.

1884

The state assumes the authority to take neglected children and place them in an institution. See *Reynolds v. Howe,* 51 Conn. 472, 478 (1884).

1903–1905

Many other states pass juvenile court acts.

1905

Commonwealth v. Fisher—Pennsylvania Supreme Court upholds the constitutionality of the Juvenile Court Act.

establishes that
ower over chil-
whose parents

1886

First neglect case is heard in Massachusetts.

the Fourteenth
ent to the U.S.
on.

1906

Massachusetts passes an act to provide for the treatment of children not as criminals but as children in need of guidance and aid.

1889

Board of children's guardians is established in Indiana and given jurisdiction over neglected and dependent children.

ois Supreme Court
ses Dan
nnell's vagrancy
ence to the Chicago
rm School due to
of due process
edures in *People v.*
er.

1908

Ex Parte Sharpe defines more clearly the role of the juvenile court to include *parens patriae.*

1890

Children's Aid Society of Pennsylvania, a foster home for the juvenile delinquent used as an alternative to reform schools, is established.

1910

Compulsory school acts.

1918

Chicago area
Shaw and M

1891

Supreme Court of Minnesota establishes the doctrine of parental immunity.

1880   1890   1900   1910   1920

A History of Children's Rights
in the United States

1838
Ex Parte Crouse—Parens patriae concept relied on. The right of the parent is not inalienable.

1841
John Augustus, first official probation officer in the United States, begins work in Boston.

1847
State institutions for juvenile delinquents open in Boston and New York.

1850
The House of Refuge in Philadelphia closes.

1851
The first adoption act in the United States is passed in Massachusetts.

1853
New York Juvenile Asylum started by the Children's Aid Society.

1866
Massachusetts the state has p dren under 16 are "unfit."

1868
Passage o Amendm Constitut

1870
Illin reve O'C sent Refo lack proc *Turn*

1825
New York House of Refuge is founded.

1828
Boston House of Refuge is founded.

820   1830   1840   1850   1860   1870

1988
Re-emergence of nationwide gang problem.

1989
Supreme Court upholds death penalty for children over 16.

1990
Maryland v. Craig allows child abuse victims to testify on closed-circuit television.

overnment focuses
n chronic offenders.

84
Schall v. Martin allows states to use preventive detention with juvenile offenders.

1985
New Jersey v. T.L.O. allows teachers to search students without a warrant or probable cause.

1985
Wilson and Herrnstein publish *Crime and Human Nature,* focusing attention on biological causes of delinquency.

1986
Juvenile offenders waived to adult court are executed, focusing attention on the death penalty for children.

inors.

1987
Conservative trends result in 10,000 juvenile waivers to adult courts.

1991
Juvenile violence rate hits an all-time high at 430 acts per 100,000 adolescents.

1992
The Gregory K. case focuses national attention on the issues of custody and adolescent self-determination.

1993
Tufts University study finds that 14 million American youth live in poverty; 21 million will be poor by 2012.

1985

1990

responsibilities of the workplace, family, and neighborhood. Many suffer from health problems, are educational underachievers, and are already skeptical about their ability to enter the American mainstream.[12]

Adolescence is a time of trial and uncertainty for many youths. They may become extremely vulnerable to emotional turmoil and experience anxiety, humiliation, and mood swings. Adolescents also undergo a period of biological development that proceeds at a far faster pace than at any other time in their lives except infancy. Over a period of a few years, their height, weight, and sexual characteristics change dramatically. The average age at which girls reach puberty today is 12.5 years; a hundred and fifty years ago, girls matured sexually at age 16. But while they may become biologically mature and capable of having children as early as 14, many youngsters remain emotionally and intellectually immature.[13] Because of this, the problem of teenage pregnancy is a growing concern.

In later adolescence (ages 16 to 18), youths may experience a life crisis that famed psychologist Erik Erikson labeled **ego identity** versus **role diffusion.** Ego identity is formed when youths develop a firm sense of who they are and what they stand for; role diffusion occurs when they experience personal uncertainty, spread themselves too thin, and place themselves at the mercy of leaders who promise to give them a sense of identity they cannot mold for themselves.[14] Psychologists also find that late adolescence is a period dominated by the yearning for independence from parental domination.[15] Given this explosive mixture of biological change and desire for autonomy, it should not be surprising that the teenage years are a time of rebelliousness and conflict with authority at home, at school, and in the community.

Is Adolescent Crisis a Recent Development?

Worry over youthful rebellion is not a recent phenomenon. In the 1950s, social commentators were concerned about the development of a postwar youth culture.[16] The American teenager was viewed as a rebellious troublemaker influenced by cult figures (especially James Dean and Elvis Presley), comic books, movies, and advertising. Teens spoke a separate language ("blast," "drag," "shook up"), had their own dress code (jeans and "duck tail" haircuts) and listened to the new rock and roll music, which sounded quite alien to their parents, who were part of the "swing generation." And though the delinquency rate was still relatively low, an increase in youth crime between 1950 and 1956 prompted angry public outbursts against a "generation gone sour"; *New York Times* reporter Harrison Salisbury called teens in the '50s the "shook up generation."[17]

These concerns prompted a U.S. Senate subcommittee headed by Estes Kefauver to look into the delinquency problem. Psychologist Frederic Wertham published *The Seduction of the Innocent,* which named comic books with a violent theme as a cause of delinquency; the resulting public outrage forced the comic book industry to adopt a code of standards.[18]

Forty years later, many of these problems have not diminished, and some have increased in severity. Many American youths live in neighborhoods where they fear walking to school in the morning and where it is common to begin experimenting with drugs and alcohol at an early age. They live in a country whose leaders tell them to practice sexual abstinence yet also tell them that if they "do it," they should practice "safe sex"; they are bombarded with media campaigns based on the premise that sex sells. The number of teenage pregnancies has increased sharply, and many children born to underage mothers have low birth weights and are extremely vulnerable to health problems. Teenage mothers are more likely to drop out of school and face economic disadvantages that hinder their future.[19] Early sexual experimentation has also increased the proportion of youth who contract a sexually transmitted disease, increasing the threat of AIDS for millions of American youth.[20]

While 1950s youths were reading comic books, 1990s teens are listening to heavy metal rock bands, such an Guns' N Roses and Metallica, whose songs dwell on satanism, drug use, and racial hatred. They watch TV shows and movies that rely on graphic scenes of violence as their main theme. Such films as those in the *Friday the Thirteenth* and *Nightmare on Elm Street* series depict brutish acts, such as decapitation and dismemberment; their ghoulish main characters, Jason Voorhees and Freddy Kreuger, have become familiar icons to a whole generation of Americans.

American youths also live in families undergoing tremendous strain. Divorce strikes about half of all new marriages; many families sacrifice time with each other to afford better housing and life-styles.

Although all young people face stress as they mature, the risks are greatest for the poor, members of racial and ethnic minorities, and recent immigrants. These children usually attend the most underfunded schools, receive inadequate health care, and have the fewest opportunities to achieve conventional success. For example, the rate of *retention*—being forced to repeat a grade—is far higher among minority youths than among whites. Retention rates are associated with another major educational problem—dropping out. It is estimated that about 15

■ ■ ■ ■ ■ ■ ■ ■ ■ ■ ■ ■ ■ ■ ■

The youth culture stresses rebelliousness, freedom and searching for new identities.

percent of all eligible youths do not finish high school; about 45 percent of all Hispanic youths aged 18–21 do not have a high school diploma.[21]

Considering these problems, it should not be surprising that measures of teenage stress are on the rise: the teenage suicide rate has doubled since 1980, and more than half of all high school seniors report having experimented with drugs and over 90 percent have tried alcohol.[22]

Adolescent Crisis and Delinquency

Problems in the home, the school, and the neighborhood, coupled with health and developmental hazards, have placed a significant portion of American youth "at risk." Though it is impossible to precisely determine the number of *at-risk youth* in the United States, one estimate is that 7 million or 25 percent of the population under 17, are extremely vulnerable to the negative consequences of school failure, substance abuse, and early sexuality, while another 7 million can be classified as at "moderate risk."[23]

Clearly, the adolescent period is a time when children are extremely vulnerable to pressures caused by social problems as well as their own sense of uncertainty and frustration. Some may turn to drugs and alcohol and join with other like-minded kids in becoming heavily involved in substance abuse. Others may join a teenage gang that provides a sense of belonging, achievement, and peer support. Others may engage in individual acts of mindless destruction and vandalism, such as painting Nazi signs on synagogues and churches or desecrating cemeteries.

As the following Focus on Delinquency shows, youth crime is not restricted to the United States. Still, it remains an enduring American social problem whose control and elimination deserves attention, study, and concern. It is to this end that the study of juvenile delinquency is devoted.

THE CONCEPT OF DELINQUENCY

Before meaningful analysis of the nature, cause, and treatment of juvenile delinquency can be attempted, how this concept evolved into its present form and how it is interpreted in today's society must be understood.

Before the twentieth century, little distinction was made between adult and juvenile offenders. Although judges considered the age of an offender when deciding punishments, both adults and children were often eligible for the same forms of punishment—prison, corporal punishment, and even the death penalty. In fact, children were treated with extreme cruelty at home, at school, and by the law.[24] Over the years, this treatment changed, as society became aware of the special needs of children.

The current treatment of juvenile delinquents is a by-product of the development of a national consciousness of the problems of youth. The designation *delinquent* became popular toward the end of the nineteenth century, when the first separate juvenile courts were instituted. Advocates of a separate legal status for youths believed that treating minors and adults equivalently violated the humanitarian ideals of American society. Consequently, the newly emerging juvenile justice system operated under the **parens patriae** philosophy (literally, the state is the father). This doctrine views minors who engage in extralegal

FOCUS ON DELINQUENCY

International Delinquency

Youth crime, substance abuse, and delinquency are considered major social problems in the United States. Are other nations similarly plagued by juvenile delinquency? The killing of 2-year-old James Bulger in Great Britain by two 10-year-old boys in 1993 was evidence that delinquency is not unique to the United States.

Recent research from a few representative nations indicates that youth crime is an international problem. For example, Alison Hatch and Curt Griffiths examined the problem of delinquency in Canada. Though Canada has a lower aggregate crime rate than the United States and less per capita violence, it too has its share of problems. Youth crime has been on the rise since 1956. Between 1980 and 1990, the number of youths charged with violent crimes doubled (though the increase in adolescent violence lagged that of adults). About one-third of all property crimes are committed by juvenile offenders.

Hatch and Griffiths also identified some of the specific types of youth crime emerging in Canada. They found reports of violent, thrill-seeking behavior (looting, rioting, "wilding") by middle-class youths. Youth gangs are becoming a common feature in larger cities, such as Vancouver and Toronto. Some of these gangs are made up of Canada's burgeoning population of ethnic minorities; for example, Jamaican gangs are involved in the drug trade. Severe economic problems have resulted in the overrepresentation of aboriginal (native Canadians such as Inuits in Arctic region) youths in crime and substance abuse.

Canada is not the only nation experiencing youth crime. Germany has been wracked by well-publicized outbursts of violence against immigrants and minorities by youth gangs of "skinheads." The "skins" are reacting to unemployment and competition for jobs between Germans and immigrants. Some skins are neo-Nazis whose violence is fueled by racial hatred, while others are apolitical youths whose violence is motivated by the anger of poverty and ignorance. In addition to these fascist outbursts, juveniles have been involved in about 20 percent of all violent crime in Germany and one-third of all property offenses. Drug abuse is also a common problem. More than 10 percent of German youth have had experience with drugs; Germany has more than one hundred thousand drug addicts today.

Paul Friday reports that crime in Sweden, a country known for its liberal social welfare programs, is also on the increase. Crime patterns in Sweden seem similar to those in the United States: the majority of offenders are young males, and a few chronic offenders are responsible for a majority of all known offenses. The factors that cause delinquency in Sweden seem similar to those found in the United States—peer influence, alienation, and lack of attachment to society.

These and other studies show that delinquency is not a problem confined to the United States. After reviewing problems of youth crime and substance abuse around the world, Galan Janeksela concludes that juvenile behavior is quite complex and resistant to simple explanation, that most juveniles are not committed to a life of crime and are amenable to treatment. ■

Source: Alison Hatch and Curt Griffiths, "Youth Crime in Canada: Observations for Cross-Cultural Analysis," *International Journal of Comparative and Applied Criminal Justice* 16: 165–79 (1992); Gunther Kaiser, "Juvenile Delinquency in the Federal Republic of Germany," *International Journal of Comparative and Applied Criminal Justice* 16: 185–97 (1992); Marie Douglas, "Auslander Raus! Nazi Raus! An Observation of German Skins and Jugendgangen," *International Journal of Comparative and Applied Criminal Justice* 16: 129–33 (1992); Paul Friday, "Delinquency in Sweden: Current Trends and Theoretical Implications," *International Journal of Comparative and Applied Criminal Justice* 16: 231–44 (1992); Galan Janeksela, "The Significance of Comparative Analysis of Juvenile Delinquency and Juvenile Justice," *International Journal of Comparative and Applied Criminal Justice* 16: 137–47 (1992), on p. 146.

behavior as victims of improper care, custody, and treatment at home. Illegal behavior is a sign that the state should step in and take control of the youths before they commit more serious crimes. The state, through its juvenile authorities, should act in the **best interests of the child.** This means that children should not be punished for their misdeeds but instead should be given the care and custody necessary to remedy and control wayward behavior. It makes no sense to find children guilty of specific crimes, such as burglary or petty larceny, because that stigmatizes them and labels them as thieves or burglars. Instead, the catch-all term *juvenile delinquency* should be used since it indicates that the child needs the care, custody, and treatment of the state.

Legal Issues

The development of the legal status of "juvenile delinquent" can be traced to the roots of our Anglo-Saxon legal tradition. Early English jurisprudence held that children under the age of 7 were legally incapable of committing crimes. Children between the ages of 7 and 14 were responsible for their actions, but their age might be used to excuse or lighten their punishment. Our legal system still recognizes that many young people are incapable of making mature judgments and that responsibility for their acts should be limited. Children can intentionally steal cars and know full well that the act is illegal, but they may be incapable of fully understanding the consequences of their behavior and the harm it may cause. Therefore, the law does not punish a youth as it would an adult, and it sees youthful misconduct as evidence of unreasoned or impaired judgment.

Today, the legal status of "juvenile delinquent" refers to a minor child who has been found to have violated the penal code. Most states define "minor child" as an individual who falls under a statutory age limit, most commonly 17 or 18 years of age. Because of their minority status, juveniles are usually kept separate from adults and receive different consideration and treatment under the law. For example, most large police departments employ officers whose sole responsibility is youth crime and delinquency. Every state has some form of separate juvenile court with its own judges, probation department, and other facilities. Terminology is also different: Adults are tried in court; children are adjudicated. Adults can be punished; children are treated. If treatment is mandated, children can be sent to secure detention facilities; they cannot normally be committed to adult prisons.

Children also have their own unique legal status. Minors apprehended for a criminal act are usually charged with being a "juvenile delinquent" regardless of the crime they commit. These charges are usually confidential, trial records are kept secret, and the name, behavior, and background of delinquent offenders are sealed. Eliminating specific crime categories and maintaining secrecy are efforts to shield children from the stigma of a criminal conviction and to prevent youthful misdeeds from becoming a lifelong burden.

Legal Responsibility

The *parens patriae* doctrine places the juvenile delinquent somewhere between criminal and civil law. Criminal laws prohibit activities that are injurious to the well-being of society and threaten the social order, for example, drug use, theft, and rape; they are legal actions brought by state authorities against private citizens. Civil laws, on the other hand, control interpersonal or private activities and are usually initiated by individual citizens. The ownership and transfer of property, contractual relationships, and personal conflicts (torts) are the subject of the civil law. Also covered under the civil law are provisions for the care and custody of those people who cannot care for themselves—the mentally ill, incompetent, or infirm.

Under *parens patriae*, delinquent acts are not considered criminal violations, nor are delinquents considered "criminals." Children cannot be found "guilty" of a crime and punished like adult criminals; the legal action against them is considered more similar (though not identical) to a civil action that determines their "need for treatment." This legal theory recognizes that children who violate the law are in need of the same care and treatment as are law-abiding citizens who cannot care for themselves and require state intervention into their lives.

Today, the juvenile delinquency concept occupies a legal status falling somewhere between the criminal and the civil law. While we would like to think that youthful offenders are only taken into state custody for purposes of benign care and treatment, they are in fact also subject to arrest, trial, and incarceration. Their legal predicament has prompted the courts to grant them many of the same legal protections enjoyed by adults accused of criminal offenses. These legal protections include the right to consult an attorney, to be free from self-incrimination, and to be protected from illegal searches and seizures.

While appreciation of the "criminal" nature of the delinquency concept has helped increase the legal rights of minors, it has also allowed state authorities to declare that some offenders are "beyond control" and cannot be treated as children. This recognition has prompted the policy of **waiver,** or transferring legal jurisdiction over the most serious and experienced juvenile offenders to the adult court for criminal prosecution. So while the *parens patriae* concept is still applied to children whose law violations are considered not to be serious, the more serious juvenile offenders can be declared "legal adults" and placed outside the jurisdiction of the juvenile court.

STATUS OFFENDERS

A child can also become subject to state authority because of conduct that is illegal only because the child is under age. Such acts are known as **status offenses.** Figure 1.1 illustrates some typical status offenses.

State control over a child's noncriminal behavior is considered consistent with the *parens patriae* philosophy and is used to protect the best interests of the child. Usually, status offenders are put in the hands of the juvenile court when it is determined that their parents are unable or unwilling to care for or control them and that their behavior will eventually hurt themselves and society.

A historical basis exists for status offense statutes. It was common practice early in the nation's history to place disobedient or runaway youths in orphan asylums, residential homes, or houses of refuge.[25] When the first juvenile courts were established in Illinois, the Chicago Bar Association described part of their purpose as follows:

The whole trend and spirit of the [1889 Juvenile Court Act] is that the State, acting through the Juvenile Court, exercises that tender solicitude and care over its neglected, dependent wards that a wise and loving parent would exercise with reference to his own children under similar circumstances.[26]

Until relatively recently, however, almost every state treated status offenders exactly like juvenile delinquents, referring to them as either **wayward minors** or **delinquent children.** A trend begun in the 1960s has resulted in the creation of separate status offense categories—children, minors, persons, youths, or juveniles in need of supervision (CHINS, MINS, PINS, YINS, or JINS)—in different states. The purpose of creating separate status offender categories was to shield noncriminal youths from the stigma attached to the label "juvenile

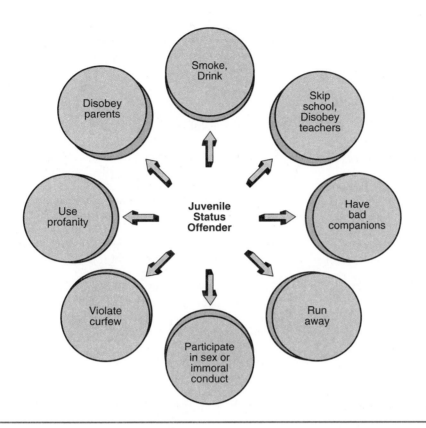

delinquent" and to signify that they were troubled youths who had special needs and problems (see Table 1.2).

A survey by the National Center for Juvenile Justice found that forty-two states now have separate categories for juvenile conduct that would not be considered criminal if committed by an adult; these sometimes pertain to neglected or dependent children as well.[27] Of these, eleven states use the term "child in need of supervision," while the remainder use such terms as "unruly child," "incorrigible child," and "minor in need of supervision." The other eight states either place status offenses within the definition of delinquency, use separate but unlabeled categories, or include them in a general jurisdictional category that establishes the court's control over all children who engage in criminal and specified noncriminal behavior.[28]

Even where there are separate legal categories for delinquents and status offenders, the distinction between them has become blurred. Some noncriminal conduct may be included in the definition of delinquency, and some less serious criminal offenses occasionally may be included within the status offender definition. Also, research shows that there are very few "pure" status offenders who have had no prior involvement in delinquency.[29]

In some states, the juvenile court judge is granted discretion to substitute a status offense for a delinquency charge.[30] Substitution of charges can be used as a bargaining chip to encourage youths originally charged with delinquency to admit to the charges against them in return for a promise of being included in the less stigmatized status offense category and receiving less punitive treatment.

LOUISIANA

"Child in need of supervision" means a child who   needs care or rehabilitation because:

1. Being subject to compulsory school attendance, he is habitually truant from school or willfully violates the rules of the school;
2. He habitually disobeys the reasonable and lawful demands of his parents, and is ungovernable and beyond their control;
3. He absents himself from his home or usual place of abode without the consent of his parent;
4. He purposefully, intentionally and willfully deceives, or misrepresents the true facts to, any person holding a retail dealer's permit, or his agent, associate, employee or representative, for the purposes of buying or receiving alcoholic beverages or beer, or visiting or loitering in or about any place where such beverages are the principal commodities sold or handled;
5. His occupation, conduct, environment or associations are injurious to his welfare; or
6. He has committed an offense applicable only to children.

WISCONSIN

The court has exclusive original jurisdiction over a child alleged to be in need of protection or services which can be ordered by the court, and:

1. Who is without a parent or guardian;
2. Who has been abandoned;
3. Who has been the victim of sexual or physical abuse including injury which is self-inflicted or inflicted by another by other than accidental means;
4. Whose parent or guardian signs the petition requesting jurisdiction and states that he or she is unable to care for, control or provide necessary special care or special treatment for the child;
5. Who has been placed for care or adoption in violation of law;
6. Who is habitually truant from school, *after evidence is provided by the school attendance officer that the activities under s. 118.16(5) have been completed;*
7. Who is habitually truant from home and either the child or a parent, *guardian or a relative in whose home the child resides signs* the petition requesting jurisdiction and attests in court that reconciliation efforts have been attempted and have failed;
8. Who is receiving inadequate care during the period of time a parent is missing, incarcerated, hospitalized or institutionalized;
9. Who is at least age 12, signs the petition requesting jurisdiction and attests in court that he or she is in need of special care and treatment which the parent, guardian or legal custodian is unwilling to provide;
10. Whose parent, guardian or legal custodian neglects, refuses or is unable for reasons other than poverty to provide necessary care, food, clothing, medical or dental care or shelter so as to seriously endanger the physical health of the child;
11. Who is suffering emotional damage for which the parent or guardian is unwilling to provide treatment, which is evidenced by one or more of the following characteristics, exhibited to a severe degree: anxiety, depression, withdrawal or outward aggressive behavior;
12. Who, being under 12 years of age, has committed a delinquent act as defined in s. 48.12;
13. Who has not been immunized as required by s. 140.05(16) and not exempted under s. 140.05(16)(c); or
14. Who has been determined, under s. 48.30(5)(c), to be not responsible for a delinquent act by reason of mental disease or defect.

Source: LA. Code Juv.Proc.Ann. art. 13 § 12 (West 1979, amended 1987) and Wis.Stat.Ann. § 48.13 (West 1979, amended 1987).

The Status Offender in the Juvenile Justice System

Separate status offense categories may avoid some of the stigma associated with the delinquency label, but they can have relatively little practical effect on the child's treatment. Youths in either category can be picked up by the police and brought to a police station. They can be petitioned to the same juvenile court, where they have a hearing before the same judge and come under the supervision of the probation department, the court clinic, and the treatment staff. At a hearing, status offenders may see little difference between the treatment they receive and the treatment of the delinquent offenders sitting across the room.

The most recent data (1989) developed by the National Center for Juvenile Justice indicates that about seventy-seven thousand status offense cases are annually petitioned to the juvenile court. The most common offense involves the possession and use of alcohol (24,400) followed by truancy (20,900), running

■ ■ ■ ■ ■ ■ ■ ■ ■ ■ ■ ■ ■ ■ ■
Status offenses include
drinking, precocious sex,
disobeying parents and
running away. A majority
of runaways are adolescent
girls.

away (11,800), and ungovernability (11,000). With the exception of alcohol offenses, which rose 57 percent, the number of status offenses petitioned to juvenile court declined between 1985 and 1989.[31]

Status offenders do in fact receive juvenile justice system processing that, although more lenient, in many ways parallels the treatment of delinquent offenders. As Figure 1.2 shows, about 63 percent of the status offenders petitioned to juvenile court are adjudicated and receive some form of judicial disposition. Of these, almost nine thousand (18 percent) are given out-of-home placements in a residential facility; 65 percent are placed on probation.

The status offense concept was created to limit the stigma and onus of a delinquency label. The fact that nearly one in five adjudicated status offenders is placed in a private or public treatment center and two-thirds are monitored by a probation officer may limit this stated purpose of the status offense concept.

Aiding the Status Offender

Efforts have been ongoing to reduce the penalties and stigma borne by status offenders. For the past decade, the federal government's **Office of Juvenile**

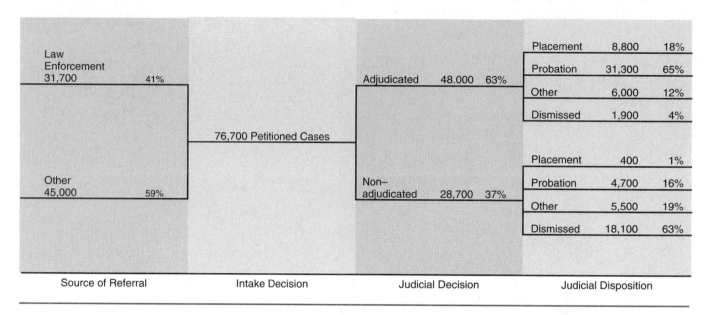

Source of Referral	Intake Decision	Judicial Decision	Judicial Disposition		
Law Enforcement 31,700 41%		Adjudicated 48.000 63%	Placement	8,800	18%
	76,700 Petitioned Cases		Probation	31,300	65%
			Other	6,000	12%
			Dismissed	1,900	4%
Other 45,000 59%		Non–adjudicated 28,700 37%	Placement	400	1%
			Probation	4,700	16%
			Other	5,500	19%
			Dismissed	18,100	63%

■■ **FIGURE 1.2**

Juvenile court processing of
petitioned status offense cases

*1989 data

Source: Jeffrey Butts and Melissa
Sickmund, *Offenders in Juvenile Court*
(Washington, D.C.: Office of Juvenile
Justice and Delinquency Prevention,
1992), p. 9.

Justice and Delinquency Prevention (OJJDP), an agency created to identify
the needs of youths and fund policy initiatives in the juvenile justice system, has
made it a top priority to encourage the removal of status offenders from secure
lockups, detention centers, and postdisposition treatment facilities that also
house delinquent offenders. Evaluations indicate that this has been a highly
successful policy initiative.[32] In the past ten years, the number of status offenders
who are kept in secure pretrial detention has dropped significantly. The latest
available data (1989) indicates that about sixty-five hundred status offenders
were detained before trial, a decline of 50 percent in five years.[33]

Despite this mandate, juvenile court judges in many states can still detain
status offenders in secure lockups if the youths are found in "contempt of court."
The act that created the OJJDP was amended in 1987 to allow status offenders to
be detained and incarcerated for violations of "valid court orders."[34] Children
have been detained for such behaviors as wearing shorts to court, throwing paper
on the floor, and, in one Florida case involving a pregnant teenager, for not
keeping a doctor's appointment.[35] Activists have attempted to outlaw the
practice because it puts noncriminal youth in jeopardy; the Florida State
Supreme Court forbade the practice in the case of *A.A. v. Rolle (1992).* [36] It
remains to be seen whether other jurisdictions will follow suit.

Change in the treatment of status offenders reflects the current attitude toward
children who violate the law. On the one hand, there appears to be a national
movement to severely sanction youths who commit serious, violent offenses. On
the other hand, a great effort has been made to remove nonserious cases, such as
those involving status offenders, from the official agencies of justice and place
these youth in informal, community-based treatment programs. New York state
has experimented with the mandatory diversion or removal of status offenders
from the jurisdiction of the juvenile court. Before status offense cases are brought
before the juvenile court, they must first be referred to community treatment
centers; only those deemed treatment "failures" wind up in juvenile court.[37]

Reforming Status Offense Laws

A number of national commissions seeking to reform the treatment of status offenders have called for the abolition of the authority that juvenile courts have over status offenders. For example, the American Bar Association's *National Juvenile Justice Standards Project,* designed to promote significant improvements in the way children are treated by the police and the courts, has called for the end of juvenile court jurisdiction over status offenders. In its standard for dealing with noncriminal youth, the project states: "A juvenile's acts of misbehavior, ungovernability or unruliness which do not violate the criminal law should not constitute a ground for asserting juvenile court jurisdiction over the juvenile committing them."[38]

One of the more influential critiques of the status offense concept has been made by the National Advisory Commission on Criminal Justice Standards and Goals. In 1976, a task force of the commission proposed a national policy for the treatment of status offenders that, in essence, held: "The only conduct that should warrant family court intervention is conduct that is clearly self-destructive or otherwise harmful to the child." To meet this standard, the commission suggested that the nation's juvenile courts confine themselves to controlling five status offenses: habitual truancy, repeated disregard for parental authority, repeated running away, repeated use of intoxicating beverages, and delinquent acts by youths under the age of 10.[39] A number of jurisdictions, including New York state, are experimenting with replacing juvenile court jurisdiction over most status offenders with community-based treatment programs.[40] A few states, such as Maine, Delaware, Idaho, and Washington, have attempted to eliminate status offense laws, though they still retain limited legal jurisdiction over status type offenders.[41]

Those who favor removing status offenders from juvenile court authority charge that their experience with the legal system further stigmatizes these already troubled youths, exposes them to the influence of "true" delinquents, and enmeshes them in a system that cannot really afford to help them.[42] Reformer Ira Schwartz, for one, argues that status offenders "should be removed from the jurisdiction of the courts altogether."[43] Schwartz maintains that status offenders would best be served not by juvenile courts but by dispute resolution and mediation programs designed to strengthen family ties since "status offense cases are often rooted in family problems."[44]

Those in favor of retaining the status offense category point to society's responsibility to care for troubled youths. For example, Lawrence Martin and Phyllis Snyder suggest that the failure of the courts to take control over wayward youths neglects the rights of concerned parents who are not able to control their children:[45]

The court would be abdicating its responsibility if it did not attempt to support these parents with its authority and thus speak for the society that will soon confer adult status on these children. Though the behavior of status offenders may not be criminal, it is unlawful. Unless we believe that truancy and waywardness are good for children, we ought to concern ourselves with all avenues of service that might change such behavior.[46]

Judge Lindsay Arthur supports this position, suggesting that the status offense should remain a legal category so that juvenile courts can "force" a youth into receiving treatment.[47] While he recognizes the stigma associated with a court appearance, Judge Arthur counters that the stigma may be less important than the need for treatment.[48]

Today, all fifty states still retain at least *some* sort of control over status offenders.

Are They Really Different?

Court jurisdiction over status offenders may be defended if in fact their offending patterns are similar to those of delinquents. Is their current offense only the tip of an antisocial "iceberg," or are they actually noncriminal youths who need only the loving hand of a substitute parent-figure interested in their welfare?

A number of studies have attempted to answer this question, but their results are at best inconclusive. Thomas Kelley analyzed the offense patterns of two thousand juveniles appearing before a large urban court over a five-year period.[49] He found that status offenders have different offense careers than delinquents and are less likely to be **recidivists** (repeat offenses). His conclusion: status offenders are a different type of offender than a juvenile delinquent and deserve different treatment.

In contrast, Charles Thomas employed a sample of youths referred to the juvenile court in Virginia and found that many who appeared on status offense charges had previous experiences as delinquents.[50] Similarly, using a large sample (sixty-nine thousand) of court-processed youths in Utah and Arizona, Howard Snyder found that over half of all status offenders also had prior delinquency referrals; one-quarter of all delinquents had prior status offense charges.[51] The Thomas and Snyder studies indicate that delinquents and status offenders may be quite similar and deserving of equivalent legal process.

These disparate findings may be explained in part by the fact that there may be different "types" of status offenders, some similar to delinquents and others who are quite different. In one study, Randall Shelden, John Horvath, and Sharon Tracy found that status offenders petitioned to court as "runaways" or "unmanageables" were less likely to also experience delinquency charges than status offenders referred to juvenile court for truancy, curfew, or liquor law violations.[52] Similarly, in an evaluation of eight juvenile court programs, Solomon Kobrin and his associates found that status offenders could actually be divided into three groups: (1) first offenders, (2) those with prior status offenses, and (3) those with both a delinquent record and a status offense record.[53] While first-time offenders typically did not become recidivists, those youths with prior status offense charges were quite likely to progress to more serious delinquent offenses. The fact that many young offenders had mixed delinquent-status offender records indicates that these legal categories are not entirely independent.

The predominate view today is that many status offenders and delinquents share similar social and developmental problems and that consequently both categories should fall under the jurisdiction of the juvenile court. Not surprisingly, research does show that the legal processing of delinquents and status offenders remains quite similar.[54] It is now recognized that some "pure" first-time status offenders are quite different from delinquents and that a juvenile court experience can be harmful to them and escalate the frequency and seriousness of their law-violating behaviors.[55] The removal of these status offenders from the juvenile court is an issue that continues to be debated. The following Case in Point explores this question.

You have just been appointed by the governor as chairperson of a newly formed group charged with overhauling the state's juvenile justice system.

One primary concern is the treatment of status offenders. Kids charged with being runaways, truants, or incorrigible are petitioned to juvenile court under an existing status offense statute. Those adjudicated as minors in need of supervision are usually placed with the county probation department. In serious cases, they may be removed from the home and placed in foster care or a state or private custodial institution.

At an open hearing, advocates of the current system argue that many families cannot provide the care and control needed to keep kids out of trouble and that it is therefore important for the state to maintain control. They contend that many status offenders have histories of drug and delinquency problems and are little different from kids arrested on criminal charges. Control by the juvenile court is necessary if the youths are ever to get needed treatment.

Another vocal group argues that it is a mistake for a system that deals with criminal youth to also handle troubled adolescents whose problems usually are the result of child abuse and neglect. They believe that the current statute should be amended to give the state's Department of Social Welfare (DSW) jurisdiction over all noncriminal youths who are in need of assistance. These opponents of the current law point out that even though status offenders and delinquents are held in separate facilities, those who violate the rules or run away can be transferred to correctional facilities that house criminal youths. Furthermore, the whole process of lawyers, trials, and court proceedings helps convince these troubled youth that they are "bad kids" and social outcasts and not youths who need a helping hand. If necessary, the DSW could place needy children in community mental health clinics or with foster parents; they would, however, be totally removed from the justice system.

Should status offenders be treated differently than juvenile delinquents?

Should distinctions be made between different types of status offenders?

Are status-type problems best handled by social service agencies?

THE "DILEMMA" OF DELINQUENCY

The reaction to juvenile delinquency can be very troubling to the American public. People are concerned about the problems of youths and want to insulate young people from a life of crime and drug abuse. Research evidence suggests that a majority of the American public still favors policies mandating of rehabilitation and treatment of known offenders.[56] Evidence also exists that many at-risk youths can be successfully helped with the proper treatment and care.[57]

On the other hand, the general public is wary of teenage hoodlums and gangs and their violent way of life. How can we control their behavior and protect innocent people? Should we embrace a "get tough" policy in which violent teens are locked up or even face the death penalty? Or should we continue to treat delinquents as troubled teens who need a helping hand from a "wise parent."

The term delinquency refers to underage minors who violate the law. Delinquents may be subject to arrest and prosecution in a manner not dissimilar from adults.

This tension pervades every aspect of the legal treatment of youths. For example, the creation of delinquency statutes and an independent juvenile court at the turn of the century is evidence that society recognizes that children are distinctly different from adults and therefore should be treated separately and with more compassion. At the same time, statutes that allow the transfer of delinquents to adult legal jurisdictions show that the legal system is ready and willing to get tough with juveniles. Despite the lip service paid to society's obligation to help at-risk children, prosecutors appear to be exercising their right to waive youths to the adult justice system more frequently today than in the past.[58] Similarly, the Supreme Court has legalized the death penalty for children once they reach age 16.[59] While the American public is generally in favor of the death penalty, surveys indicate that a substantial majority oppose capital punishment for minor offenders.[60] Still, more than thirty people are on death row for crimes committed in their minority.

The value conflict in our current response to juvenile delinquency is a potent theme in American jurisprudence.[61] Throughout the country are programs to treat, help, and rehabilitate minor offenders. Existing side-by-side are efforts to control, incarcerate, and punish youths who violate the law. Some critics have warned that our treatment of juveniles is becoming more and more intrusive and involved in the justice process, a condition referred to as **widening the net.**[62]

To many experts, our inability to overcome these goal conflicts has resulted in the failure to develop a coherent and effective delinquency control policy. As policy expert Ira Schwartz states:

. . . the abuses and mistreatment of children that helped give rise to the child-saver movement at the turn of the century and subsequently led to the creation of the juvenile court continue to exist.[63]

While Schwartz remains optimistic that positive change can be effected, it has been more than nine decades since the first separate juvenile court was created, and conflict still exists over the proper treatment of delinquent youths and their place in modern society.[64]

■■■■■■■■■■■■■■■■

SUMMARY

The study of delinquency is concerned with a number of different issues: the nature and extent of the criminal behavior of youths; the causes of youthful law violations; the legal rights of juveniles; and prevention and treatment techniques. It is an interdisciplinary field, populated by sociologists, psychologists, political scientists, historians, legal scholars, and members of the helping professions.

Studying the problems of youth is especially important when the dynamic nature of adolescence and the stress American youth are under are considered. Drugs, pregnancy, suicide, and social conflict are all taking their toll on youths.

The concept of delinquency was developed in the early twentieth century. Before that, criminal youths and adults were treated in almost the same fashion. A group of reformers, referred to as child savers, helped create a separate delinquency category to insulate juvenile offenders from the influence of adult criminals. A separate juvenile court was established in Chicago in 1899 and was soon followed by juvenile courts in all states. Today, the juvenile justice system handles cases involving minors who commit criminal offenses.

The juvenile justice concept is predicated on the *parens patriae* philosophy, which holds that children have the right to care and custody and that if parents are not capable of providing that care, the state must.

Juvenile courts also have jurisdiction over noncriminal, status offenders. Status offenses are illegal only because of the minority status of the offender. They include such misbehaviors as truancy, running away, and sexual misconduct. Some experts have called for an end to juvenile court control over status offenders, charging that it merely further stigmatizes already troubled youths. Some research indicates that status offenders are harmed by juvenile court processing. Other efforts indicate that status offenders and delinquents are actually quite similar.

The treatment of juveniles is an ongoing dilemma in American society. Still uncertain is whether young law violators respond better to harsh punishments or benevolent treatment.

KEY TERMS

juvenile delinquency
juvenile justice system
chronic delinquent
aging-out process
ego identity
role diffusion
parens patriae
best interests of the child

waiver
status offenses
wayward minors
delinquent children
Office of Juvenile Justice and Delinquency
    Prevention (OJJDP)
recidivists
widening the net

Questions for Discussion

1. Is it fair to have a separate legal category for youths? Does this unfairly penalize adults?
2. Are juveniles incapable of understanding the serious consequences of their actions?
3. Is it fair to institutionalize a minor simply for being truant or running away from home?
4. Should delinquency proceedings be secretive? Does the public have the right to know who juvenile criminals are?
5. Can a "get tough" policy help control juvenile misbehavior, or should *parens patriae* remain the standard?
6. Should juveniles who commit felonies such as rape or robbery be treated as adults?

Notes

1. "What Kind of Child Would Kill a Child," *Newsweek,* 1 March 1993, p. 56.
2. Ike Flores, "Boy Allowed to Seek 'Divorce' from Parents," *Boston Globe,* 10 July 1992, p. 3.
3. Cliff Edwards, "Pair Held for Leaving Children Home Alone," *Boston Globe,* 30 December 1992, p. 3.
4. Bob Lewis, "Cruel Killing Stuns Small Town," *Houston Chronicle,* 17 June 1992, p. 6A.
5. David Dishneau, "Chicago Shuts Four Project High-Rises," *Boston Globe,* 21 October 1992, p. 3.
6. John Cook and Larry Brown, *Two Americas: Alternative Future for Child Poverty in America* (Medford, Mass.: Tufts University Center on Hunger, Poverty and Nutrition, 1993).
7. David Eggebeen and Daniel Lichter, "Race, Family Structure, and Changing Poverty among American Children," *American Sociological Review* 56: 801–17 (1991).
8. James Alan Fox, "Teenage Males Are Committing Murder at an Increasing Rate," Press Release, College of Criminal Justice, Northeastern University, November 1, 1992, p. 1.
9. Federal Bureau of Investigation, *Crimes in the United States, 1991* (Washington, D.C.: Government Printing Office, 1992), p. 174.
10. John Whitehead and Steven Lab, "A Meta-Analysis of Juvenile Correctional Treatment," *Journal of Research in Crime and Delinquency* 26: 276–95 (1989).
11. Susan Crimmins and Michael Foley, "The Threshold of Violence in Urban Adolescents" (Paper presented at the annual meeting of the American Society of Criminology, Reno, Nevada, November 1989).
12. Task Force on Education of Young Adolescents, *Turning Points, Preparing American Youth for the 21st Century* (New York: Carnegie Council on Adolescent Development, 1989). (Hereinafter cited as *Turning Points*).
13. Ibid., p. 21.
14. Erik Erikson, *Childhood and Society* (New York: W. H. Norton, 1963).
15. Roger Gould, "Adult Life Stages: Growth toward Self-Tolerance," *Psychology Today* 8:74–8 (1975).
16. This section leans heavily on James Gilbert, *A Cycle of Outrage, America's Reaction to the Juvenile Delinquent in the 1950's* (New York: Oxford University Press, 1986).
17. Harrison Salisbury, *The Shook-Up Generation* (New York: Harper, 1958).
18. Frederic Wertham, *Seduction of the Innocent* (Port Washington, N.Y.: Kennikat Press, 1953).
19. *Turning Points,* p. 24.
20. Ibid.
21. Children's Defense Fund, *The State of America's Children, 1991* (Washington, D.C.: Children's Defense Fund, 1991), p. 76.
22. Lloyd Johnson, Patrick O'Malley, and Jerald Bachman, *Illicit Drug Use, Smoking and Drinking by America's High School Students, College Students and Young Adults, 1975–1987* (Washington, D.C.: Government Printing Office, 1988).
23. *Turning Points,* p. 27.
24. Graeme Newman, *The Punishment Response* (Philadelphia: J. B. Lippincott, 1978), pp. 53–79; Philipp Aries, *Centuries of Childhood* (New York: Knopf, 1962). The history of childhood juvenile justice is discussed in detail in Chapter 13.
25. See, generally, David Rothman, *The Discovery of the Asylum* (Boston: Little, Brown, 1971).
26. Reports of the Chicago Bar Association Committee, 1899, cited in Anthony Platt, *The Child Savers,* (Chicago: University of Chicago Press, 1969) p. 119.
27. John L. Hutzler, *Juvenile Court Jurisdiction over Children's Conduct: 1982 Comparative Analysis of Juvenile and Family Codes and National Standards* (Pittsburgh: National Center for Juvenile Justice, 1982), p. 2.
28. Ibid.
29. Susan Datesman and Mikel Aickin, "Offense Specialization and Escalation among Status Offenders," *Journal of Criminal Law and Criminology* 75:1246–75 (1985).

30. Ibid.
31. Jeffrey Butts and Melissa Sickmund, *Offenders in Juvenile Court, 1989,* Juvenile Justice Bulletin, OJJDP Update on Statistics (Washington, D.C.: Office of Juvenile Justice and Delinquency Prevention, November 1992).
32. See, generally, Solomon Kobrin and Malcolm Klein, *National Evaluation of the Deinstitutionalization of Status Offender Programs—Executive Summary* (Los Angeles: Social Science Research Institute, University of Southern California, 1982).
33. Barry Krisberg and Ira Schwartz, "Rethinking Juvenile Justice," *Crime and Delinquency* 29:333–64 (1983).
34. 42 U.S.C.A. 5601–5751 (1983 & Supp. 1987).
35. Claudia Wright, "Contempt No Excuse for Locking Up Status Offenders, Says Florida Supreme Court," *Youth Law News* 13:1–3 (1992).
36. *A.A. v. Rolle,* 604 So. 2d 813 (1992).
37. Martin Rouse, "The Diversion of Status Offenders, Criminalization, and the New York Family Court" (Revised version of the paper presented at the American Society of Criminology, Reno, Nevada, November 1989).
38. American Bar Association Joint Commission on Juvenile Justice Standards, *Summary and Analysis* (Cambridge, Mass.: Ballinger, 1977), sect. 1.1.
39. National Advisory Commission on Criminal Justice Standards and Goals, *Juvenile Justice and Delinquency Prevention* (Washington, D.C.: Government Printing Office, 1977), p. 311.
40. Rouse, "The Diversion of Status Offenders, Criminalization, and the New York Family Court," p. 12.
41. Marc Miller, "Changing Legal Paradigms in Juvenile Justice," in Peter Greenwood, ed., *The Juvenile Rehabilitation Reader* (Santa Monica, Calif.: Rand Corporation, 1985) p. V.44.
42. Thomas Kelley, "Status Offenders Can Be Different: A Comparative Study of Delinquent Careers," *Crime and Delinquency* 29:365–80 (1983).
43. Ira Schwartz, *(In) Justice for Juveniles: Rethinking the Best Interests of the Child* (Lexington, Mass: Lexington Books, 1989), p. 171.
44. Ibid.
45. Lawrence Martin and Phyllis Snyder, "Jurisdiction over Status Offenses Should Not Be Removed from the Juvenile Court," *Crime and Delinquency* 22:44–47 (1976).
46. Ibid., p. 45.
47. Lindsay Arthur, "Status Offenders Need a Court of Last Resort," *Boston University Law Review* 57:631–44 (1977).
48. Ibid.
49. Kelley, "Status Offenders Can Be Different."
50. Charles Thomas, "Are Status Offenders Really So Different?" *Crime and Delinquency* 22:438–55 (1976).
51. Howard Snyder, *Court Careers of Juvenile Offenders* (Washington, D.C.: Office of Juvenile Justice and Delinquency Prevention, 1988), p. 65.
52. Randall Shelden, John Horvath, and Sharon Tracy, "Do Status Offenders Get Worse? Some Clarifications on the Question of Escalation," *Crime and Delinquency* 35:202–16 (1989).
53. Solomon Kobrin, Frank Hellum, and John Peterson, "Offense Patterns of Status Offenders," in D. Schichor and D. Kelly, eds., *Critical Issues in Juvenile Delinquency* (Lexington, Mass.: Lexington Books, 1980), pp. 203–35.
54. Chris Marshall, Ineke Marshall, and Charles Thomas, "The Implementation of Formal Procedures in Juvenile Court Processing of Status Offenders," *Journal of Criminal Justice* 11:195–211 (1983).
55. Schwartz, *(In) Justice for Juveniles,* pp. 378–79.
56. Francis Cullen, Sanda Evans Skovron, Joseph Scott, and Velmer Burton, "Public Support for Correctional Treatment: The Tenacity of Rehabilitative Ideology," *Criminal Justice and Behavior* 17:6–18 (1990).
57. Rhena Izzo and Robert Ross, "Meta-Analysis of Rehabilitation Programs for Juvenile Delinquents," *Criminal Justice and Behavior* 17:134–42 (1990).
58. Dean Champion, "Teenage Felons and Waiver Hearing: Some Recent Trends, 1980–1988," *Crime and Delinquency* 35:577–85 (1989).
59. *Stanford v. Kentucky,* and *Wilkins v. Missouri,* 109 S.Ct. 2969 (1989).
60. Sandra Skovron, Joseph Scott, and Francis Cullen, "The Death Penalty for Juveniles: An Assessment of Public Support," *Crime and Delinquency* 35:546–61 (1989).
61. See, generally, Edmund McGarrell, *Juvenile Correctional Reform: Two Decades of Policy and Procedural Change* (Albany, N.Y.: State University of New York Press, 1988); Barry Krisberg, Ira Schwartz, Paul Litsky, and James Austin, "The Watershed of Juvenile Justice Reform," *Crime and Delinquency* 32:5–38 (1986), at 34.
62. Mark Ezell, "Juvenile Arbitration: Net Widening and Other Unintended Consequences," *Journal of Research in Crime and Delinquency* 26:358–77 (1990).
63. Schwartz, *(In) Justice for Juveniles,* p. 17.

OUTLINE

MEASURING
JUVENILE
DELINQUENCY

How common is juvenile delinquency? Who commits delinquent acts, and where are they most likely to occur? Is the juvenile crime rate increasing or decreasing? These are some of the most important questions in the study of juvenile delinquency. Without answers to them, it would be impossible to determine the actual causes of delinquency and then devise effective strategies for its control. Therefore, criminologists and delinquency experts have long struggled to create valid methods of measuring the nature and extent of delinquency. Three separate methods currently enjoy widespread acceptance and use: official data, self-report data, and victimization data.

Official data refers to information collected about crimes reported to the police. "Official delinquents" are youths who have been formally arrested. In contrast, *self-report data* comes from juvenile offenders themselves. It is collected in anonymous surveys or interviews, conducted in schools or juvenile institutions, that are directed at uncovering illegal activities that have gone undetected by the police. Self-reports allow researchers to determine the extent of unrecorded juvenile delinquency, the so-called *dark figures of crime,* and compare the personal characteristics of official delinquents with youths who have escaped detection. *Victim surveys* ask those who have witnessed crime firsthand about their experiences. They can provide important information on such subjects as the rate of juvenile victimization and the percentage of all crimes in which victims claim they were preyed upon by a juvenile.

The sections below describe each of these methods in some detail and examine the information they provide on the nature and extent of delinquency. In the following chapter, these data sources will be used to analyze the social forces that influence delinquency.

OFFICIAL STATISTICS

The term *official statistics* refers to the records of youths whose illegal activities have come to the attention of law enforcement agencies.[1] Youths with a public record are official delinquents; their actions are considered official delinquency. In contrast, "unofficial" delinquency is that which remains hidden and unknown. A youngster arrested by police for shoplifting has an official record; one thousand youths who bought crack without getting arrested by police are unofficial or secret delinquents.

The accuracy of official statistics has been the source of much debate. For more than thirty years, critics have charged that official data can lead to a spurious view of delinquency, one dominated by the biases of police.[2] For one thing, many victims do not report crime to the police, so official data may underestimate the total crime problem; victim surveys indicate that up to half of all crimes are not reported. Police departments themselves may choose not to report crime (to get the crime rate down), or conversely, they may inflate crime data (in order to justify more funding). Arrest data may be equally biased. It has been alleged that local police departments make it a policy to arrest the poor and minority group members while letting middle-class white youths go with a warning.[3] If these allegations are true, the nature and extent of official delinquency is more reflective of police behavior than youthful misbehavior.[4]

In contrast to these views, some criminologists believe that the accuracy of official statistics may be improving.[5] After more than twenty years of efforts to increase the sensitivity of police officers to civil rights, arrest statistics may now be less class- and race-biased and, consequently, a more valid indicator of the actual participation in delinquent acts.[6]

Regardless of which position is correct, official statistics continue to be widely used because they are one of the few sources of information on the nature and extent delinquency. And even if this kind of data has some built-in inaccuracies, the flaws are probably consistent over time, so that *trends* in delinquent behavior can be charted. That is, even if inaccurate, official statistics may be stable enough to show year-to-year changes in the amount of delinquent behavior and the delinquency rate.

The standard source of official crime and delinquency statistics has been the annual effort of the U.S. Justice Department's **Federal Bureau of Investigation (FBI)** to accumulate information gathered by the nation's police departments on the number of criminal acts reported by citizens and the number of persons arrested each year for criminal and delinquent activity. Called the *Uniform Crime Report (UCR),* the FBI's effort constitutes our best known and most widely used source of national crime and delinquency statistics.[7]

Uniform Crime Reports

The FBI's Uniform Crime Report is an annual survey of crime compiled from statistics sent to the FBI from more than sixteen thousand police departments serving a majority of the population of the United States. Its major unit of analysis involves the *index crimes,* also known as **Part I offenses:** homicide and nonnegligent manslaughter, forcible rape, robbery, aggravated assault, burglary, larceny, arson, and motor vehicle theft (see Table 2.1). A record is compiled by cooperating police agencies every time one of these offenses is reported by a victim or witness. The FBI receives quarterly tallies of these offenses and annually publishes the results. Data is broken down by city, county, standard metropolitan statistical area (SMSA), and geographical divisions of the United States. In addition to these statistics, the UCR provides information on the number and characteristics of individuals who have been arrested for these and all other criminal offenses (known as **Part II offenses**). The arrest data includes age, sex, and race.

The UCR expresses crime data in three ways. First, the number of crimes reported to the police and arrests made are given as raw figures (for example, 1,661,738 motor vehicle thefts occurred in 1991). Second, percent changes in the amount of crime between years are computed (for example, motor vehicle theft increased 1.6 percent between 1990 and 1991). Finally, crime rates per one hundred thousand people are computed. That is, when the UCR indicates that the murder rate was 9.8 in 1991, it means that about 10 people in every 100,000 fell victim to murder between January 1 and December 31 of 1991. The equation used is:

Number of reported crimes ÷ total U.S. population X 100,000 = rate per 100,000

All three methods will be used in the following discussion, which reviews some of the most significant trends reported by the UCR.

TABLE 2.1   UCR Crimes and Definitions

CRIME	DEFINITION
Homicide	Causing the death of another person without legal justification or excuse.
Rape	Unlawful sexual intercourse with a female, by force or without legal or factual consent.
Robbery	Unlawful taking or attempted taking of property that is in the immediate possession of another, by force or threat of force.
Assault	Unlawful intentional inflicting, or attempted inflicting, of injury upon the person of another. *Aggravated assault* is the unlawful intentional inflicting of serious bodily injury or unlawful threat or attempt to inflict bodily injury or death by means of a deadly or dangerous weapon with or without actual infliction of injury. *Simple assault* is the unlawful intentional inflicting of less than serious bodily injury without a deadly or dangerous weapon or an attempt or threat to inflict bodily injury without a deadly or dangerous weapon.
Burglary	Unlawful entry of any fixed structure, vehicle, or vessel used for regular residence, industry, or business, with or without force, with the intent to commit a felony or larceny.
Larceny (Theft)	Unlawful taking or attempted taking of property other than a motor vehicle from the possession of another, by stealth, without force and without deceit, with intent to permanently deprive the owner of the property.
Motor Vehicle Theft	Unlawful taking or attempted taking of a self-propelled road vehicle owned by another, with the intent of depriving the owner of it permanently or temporarily.
Arson	Intentional damaging or destruction or attempted damaging or destruction by means of fire or explosion of the property without the consent of the owner, or of one's own property or that of another by fire or explosives with or without the intent to defraud.

CRIME TRENDS IN THE UNITED STATES

Crime continues to be one of the leading social problems in the United States. The crime rate skyrocketed between 1960, when about 3.3 million crimes were reported to police agencies, and 1981, when 13.4 million were recorded. Then, after four years of decline (1981 to 1984), the rate went up in 1985 and has continued to increase for more than five years. In 1992 the FBI estimated that about 14 million serious crimes were reported to police annually, a rate of almost 6,000 per 100,000 inhabitants.[8] Some encouraging signs were that the overall crime rate dipped 4 percent between 1991–1992, and the murder rate declined 6 percent. Less encouraging were 2 percent increases in the numbers of rapes and assaults between 1991–1992.

A number of possible explanations are given for the fluctuations in the crime rate over the past decade. The decrease in the number of reported crimes during the early 1980s was attributed to the decline in the teenage population. The U.S. population is steadily aging—the so-called graying of America. Since young people are believed to be involved in much more criminal behavior than older people, the shift in the population was used to explain the declining crime rate in the early 1980s. Research indicates that changes in the age structure of U.S. society account for approximately 40 percent of the changes in the crime rate.[9] Consequently, crime rates should parallel the number of teens in the population.[10]

The increase in the violent crime rate, that began in 1984 is more of a puzzle, since the teenage population has not suddenly begun to soar. One possible explanation is that the nations' drug abuse problem is responsible for an increased crime rate. Evidence is consistent that substance abusers commit a significant portion of all serious crimes and that inner-city drug abuse problems may in part account for the recent escalation in the violent crime rate.[11] Violence may also be a function of urban problems and the economic deterioration in the nation's inner cities.[12] Youths who at one time might have obtained low-skill jobs in factories and shops may find these legitimate economic opportunities no longer exist. Low-skill manufacturing jobs have been dispersed to overseas plants. Lack of economic opportunity may encourage drug dealing, theft, and violence.[13]

Increases in the violent crime rate (up 29 percent between 1987 and 1992) account for a significant portion of the overall increase in the crime rate. Access to handguns and firearms may help explain this increase in violence; about two-thirds of all murders are committed with handguns and other firearms.

Another explanation is that the actual number of crimes committed is relatively stable but the public may now be more willing to cooperate with the police and report crime. Many jurisdictions have established citizens' crime councils, neighborhood watch groups, and community patrols. Recent increases in the crime rate may be more a matter of victim reporting practices than an actual change in crime patterns. While reporting practices may certainly affect the rates of some crimes, such as property offenses, they are less likely to be an explanation of others, such as the increase in the murder rate.

Crime Patterns

The Uniform Crime Reports also tells us something about the nature of violent and property crime patterns in the United States. First, there is a strong association between crime and population density. Urban areas have much higher violence and property crime rates than rural counties. Cities of 250,000 or more are considerably more violence-prone than small towns.

Regional differences also exist in crime rates. Western and southern regions have higher property crime rates than midwestern and northeastern regions; the violence rate in the West is the highest, followed by those in the Northeast and the South.

Violence is more likely to occur in warmer climates and during the hot summer months of July and August. And there is usually an upsurge of murder and robbery during the New Year's season. Property-crime trends follow a similar temperature and seasonal pattern.

The Uniform Crime Reports show that the cost of crime is high. For example, in 1991, some $16.1 billion worth of property was stolen, an average of $1,243 per offense.[14]

They also show that the police consistently solve, or clear, about 20 percent of all reported crimes (a *clearance* is recorded when a person is arrested, charged,

Crime rates are highest in urban areas, during the summer months and in Western and Southern states.

and turned over for prosecution). Serious violent crimes are much more likely to be cleared than property crimes. For example, 67 percent of reported murders are cleared, while only 14 percent of motor vehicle crimes are similarly resolved. Police are probably more successful in solving the most serious crimes because they are willing to devote more resources to violent personal crimes and because the majority of these offenses involve a victim and an assailant who were acquainted with or related to one another.

The existence of consistent and enduring social and ecological patterns in the crime rate is quite important to the study of delinquency. They indicate that *social forces* influence crime and delinquency patterns. If crime were a result of an individual trait alone, such as low intelligence, crime rates would be spread more evenly across time and geographic boundaries. There is no reason to believe that people in Kansas and North Dakota have higher IQs than residents of New York and California, yet the crime rates are higher in these latter states. The fact that crime rates are higher in urban areas than in rural counties and higher in some seasons and lower in others tells us that social forces must be operating at times in these congested metropolitan areas that produce and sustain criminality.

Measuring Official Delinquency

Because the UCR's arrest statistics are **disaggregated** (broken down) by suspect's age, they can be used to estimate adolescent participation in the official crime rate. Arrest data must be interpreted with caution, however. First, the number of teenagers arrested does not represent the actual number of youths who have committed delinquent acts but only those caught and officially processed by the police. Some offenders are never counted because they are never caught. Others are counted more than once since multiple arrests of the same individual for different crimes are counted separately in the UCR. Conse-

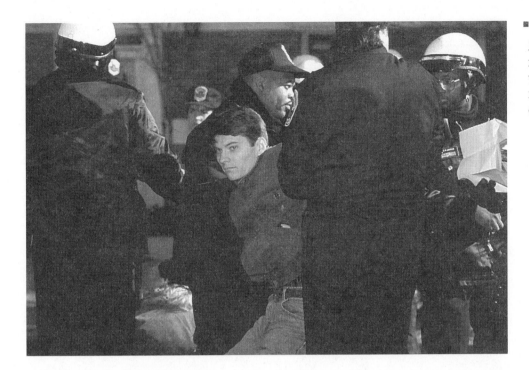

More than 1.5 juvenile arrests have been made each year during the 1990's, more than 600,000 for serious felony crimes.

quently, the total number of arrests does not equal the number of people who have been arrested. Put another way, if 2 million arrests of youths under 18 years of age were made in a given year, we could not be sure if 2 million individuals had been arrested once or if five hundred thousand chronic offenders had been arrested four times each.

The official statistics also cannot tell us the proportion of delinquent offenders who get caught. Though police generally solve about 20 percent of all crimes, there is no guarantee that the clearance rate is stable across age categories. It cannot be determined if the number of youths arrested represents a high proportion of their total criminal behavior, a low proportion, or one that is similar to that of people in other age categories. In other words, if the FBI reports that 1 million youths were arrested, we could not be certain if they represent 20 percent, 50 percent, or 100 percent of all delinquents. Teenagers may face a greater apprehension probability than adults because they are easier targets than older, more experienced criminals.

In addition, arrest patterns are influenced by jurisdictional variations in police practices, use of discretion, and other law enforcement factors. Some police agencies may practice full enforcement, arresting all teens who violate the law, while others may follow a policy of discretion that encourages unofficial handling of juvenile matters through social service agencies. This, too, can influence the arrest data.

With these issues in mind, what does the UCR tell us about delinquency?

Official Delinquency

Table 2.2 illustrates the number and percentage of arrests for serious crimes disaggregated by the legal status of the offender. In 1991, about 3 million arrests

	JUVENILE	ADULT	% JUVENILE	% ADULT	RATIO
Murder	2,626	16,028	9%	91%	1:10
Rape	4,766	25,844	15%	85%	1:6
Robbery	35,632	103,550	25%	75%	1:3
Assault	52,653	315,830	14%	86%	1:6
Burglary	109,965	218,825	33%	67%	1:2
Larceny	369,227	846,076	30%	70%	1:2
Auto Theft	70,659	90,969	44%	56%	1:1
Arson	6,940	9,976	40%	60%	1:1.5
Violence	95,677	460,992	17%	83%	1:5
Property	556,791	1,163,846	32%	68%	1:2
Total	652,468	1,624,838	39%	71%	1:2

Source: FBI, *Uniform Crime Reports, Crime in the United States, 1991*, p. 223.

■■■■■■■■■■■■■■

Many juveniles are taken into custody for status type offenses such as running away from home. Life is treacherous for these two runaways living under a freeway in Hollywood, California. Prostitution is common because sometimes individuals, such as the boy holding the sign in this picture, have no choice.

were made for serious crimes. Jurisdictions that report the age of arrestees to the FBI indicate that about 29 percent are juveniles; more than 650,000 juveniles were arrested for serious crimes in 1991.

According to UCR data, it appears that crime is a young person's game: property crime activity peaks at age 16, and the peak age for violent crime arrests is 18. Age-level crime rates continue unabated until age 30 (see Figure 2.1).[15] Both the violent and property crime arrest rates decline dramatically in the over-30-year-old population. Adolescent participation in the crime rate is underscored by the arrests of very young children for violent crimes. More than five hundred youths under 12 years of age were arrested for rape in 1991; of these, eighty-one were less than 10 years old.

In addition to collecting information on the arrests made for serious crime, the FBI also examines the additional 11 million arrests made for other (Part II) criminal offenses, ranging from forgery to suspicion. Some of these Part II crimes correspond to status (juvenile) offenses—curfew violations, running away, and drinking. In all, about *1.1 million juvenile arrests were made for Part II offenses.*

Table 2.3 lists some of the Part II crimes that youths are most likely to commit. As might be expected, all 135,000 arrests for running away and curfew violations

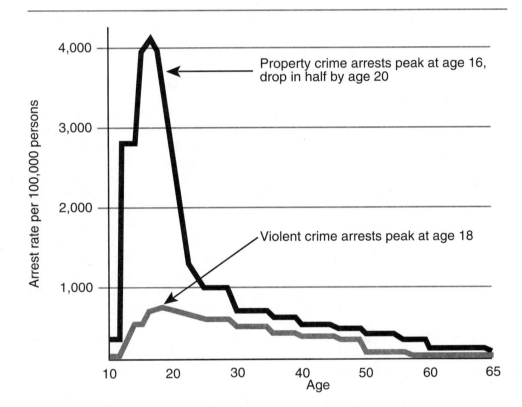

■ ■ FIGURE 2.1

The relationship between age and serious crime arrests.

Source: FBI, *Uniform Crime Reports, 1991,* pp. 178–79.

■ ■ TABLE 2.3   Arrests for Minor Crimes by Age

	JUVENILE	ADULT	% JUVENILE	% ADULT	RATIO
Vandalism	107,890	144,579	42%	58%	1:1
Sex offenses	14,417	67,811	17%	83%	1:5
Drug abuse	60,428	720,822	11%	89%	1:8
Liquor laws	104,210	349,597	25%	75%	1:3
Drunkenness	16,372	640,747	2%	98%	1:49
Disorderly conduct	99,322	469,992	14%	86%	1:6
Curfew violation	73,125	————			
Running away	135,471	————			

involve youths under 18 years of age. Youths also made up a significant portion of those arrested for vandalism, minor assaults, and liquor law violations.

In contrast, adults were arrested disproportionately for the crime of driving while intoxicated: While more than 1.2 million adults were arrested in 1991 for driving under the influence, only thirteen thousand youths under 18 were arrested for this crime.

Juvenile Crime Trends

What are the recent trends in juvenile crime? The number of juveniles arrested by police has actually declined during the past twenty years, and the percentage of crimes cleared in which a juvenile was arrested has similarly decreased. For example, in 1972, 27 percent of offenses known to police and cleared by arrest involved an arrest of a minor under 18; by 1991, this juvenile share of the clearance rate had decreased to about 19 percent. And while the percentage of violent offenses known to the police and cleared by an arrest of a person (or persons) under 18 years of age has been moving upward in the past few years, it is still somewhat lower than it was in the 1970s.

While these data seem encouraging, they are probably more representative of population trends than crime rate reductions: there are simply fewer teenagers in the population today than 20 years ago. In 1970, about 26 percent of the population was between age 5 and 18; today, that number is about 18 percent; there are 6 million fewer adolescents aged 5 to 18 today than there were in 1970.

Considering the changes in the age makeup of the population, what are the trends in juvenile delinquency? While the juvenile property crime arrest rate has been stable (increasing 3 percent between 1982 and 1991), there has been a disturbing increase in the number of youths 18 and under arrested for violent crimes (an increase of 41 percent between 1982 and 1991). While juvenile arrest rates for property crimes, such as robbery and larceny, peaked in the 1970s, arrest rates for rape, murder, and assault have been climbing. As Figure 2.2 shows, the juvenile violent crime arrest rate is now at its highest peak, about 430 per 100,000.

Most disturbing are increases in the most serious offenses, including rape and murder. The nation's juvenile forcible rape arrest rate has more than doubled since 1965. In that year, about 11 kids in every 100,000 were arrested for rape; by 1991, 22 per 100,000 were arrested for sexual assault. And as Figure 2.3 shows, the juvenile murder arrest rate has also climbed significantly. The overall rate increased 332 percent between 1965 and 1990, from 2.8 to 12.1 per 100,000.

Table 2.4, prepared by criminologists Glen Pierce and James Alan Fox, shows the changes in arrest rates for criminal homicide per 100,000 males within selected age groups. While the murder arrest rate for adolescents ages 18 and under was increasing at a breakneck pace, the rate for adults 30 and over was declining. Clearly, these data indicate that young Americans are becoming more violent.[16]

Why Is Teenage Violence Increasing?

Why is teenage violence increasing? A number of independent reasons probably account for the escalation of the teenage violent crime arrest rate. One important factor may be the proliferation of weapons in the hands of teens. Between 1982

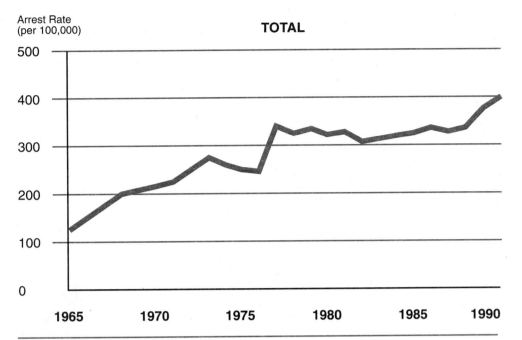

Arrest Rate (per 100,000)

TOTAL

■■FIGURE 2.2

Juvenile Violent Crime Arrest Rates: United States, 1965–1990

Source: FBI, *Uniform Crime Reports, 1991,* p. 280.

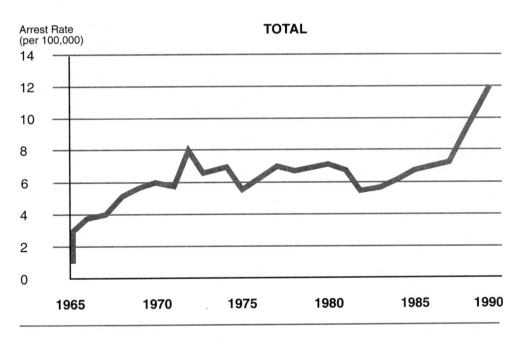

Arrest Rate (per 100,000)

TOTAL

■■FIGURE 2.3

Juvenile Murder Arrest Rates: United States, 1965–1990

Source: FBI, *Uniform Crime Reports, 1991,* p. 281.

and 1991, the number of kids under 18 arrested on weapons charges rose 78 percent. In 1990, 151 teens per 100,000 were arrested on weapons charges, the highest rate in history. Between 1990 and 1991 alone, the number of kids 15 and under arrested on weapons charges rose almost 28 percent and those 18 and under increased 18 percent; in contrast, arrests of people over 18 remained

Arrest Rates for Criminal Homicide per 100,000 Males within Selected Age Groups

	1970	1975	1980	1985	1990	1991	% CHANGE 85–91
12 & Under	0.2	0.2	0.1	0.1	0.1	0.2	100%
13–14	4.2	3.6	4.4	4.0	8.8	9.6	140%
15	17.2	14.9	13.5	11.8	31.0	37.4	217%
16	26.8	24.9	24.6	22.4	56.5	57.7	158%
17	32.9	29.2	38.2	34.5	72.4	76.1	121%
18–20	44.5	43.4	46.4	41.8	73.5	89.0	113%
21–24	45.6	45.4	44.3	39.0	49.4	54.7	40%
25–29	36.1	36.9	34.4	30.4	31.4	31.2	3%
30-34	27.7	26.5	28.0	22.3	21.2	21.5	−4%
35-44	19.5	19.5	19.4	15.4	13.9	12.9	−16%
45–54	11.8	9.6	9.8	8.5	7.7	7.1	−16%
55–64	7.1	6.0	5.4	4.9	3.8	3.3	−33%
65 & Over	3.5	3.2	2.5	2.1	1.7	1.6	−24%

Source: Glenn Pierce and James Alan Fox, *Recent Trends in Violent Crime: A Closer Look* (Boston: National Crime Analysis Program, Northeastern University, 1992).

constant. Adolescents are now possessing handguns at an unprecedented rate and using them in violent crimes: 62 percent of the homicides committed by juveniles involve firearms.[17]

Another factor may be the explosive growth in teenage gangs. Surveys indicate that there are more than 250,000 gang members in the United States. The FBI estimates that 317 youths were killed in juvenile gang killings in 1987; by 1991, that number had more than doubled, to 838.[18] A large and growing number of juveniles who kill do so in groups of two or more; multiple-offender killings have doubled since the mid-1980s.[19] Gangs will be discussed in Chapter 10.

Though the numbers are still uncertain, there is little question that numerous acts of teenage aggression are the result of seemingly unmotivated, random street violence. Some of these incidents may find their root cause in hatred or bias. **Hate crimes** are the subject of the following Focus on Delinquency.

In sum, fewer delinquents are being arrested today than 20 years ago because of a decline in the number of adolescents in the United States population. Though property crime rates have remained stable, the teenage violent crime rate has increased for the past ten years. There may be fewer teens today, but they are more violent then at any other time in recent history.

SELF-REPORTS

The validity of official statistics has been a serious issue.[20] In addition to their problematic accuracy, official data have only limited ability to measure particular crime patterns, such as recreational drug use and alcohol abuse. They do not tell us much about the personality, attitudes, and behavior of individual delinquents. Official statistics are useful for the examination of general trends in the relative frequency of delinquent behavior and geographic patterns of youth crime, but they are an inadequate source of individual-level information, such as the personality characteristics of delinquents. To address these deficiencies, criminol-

Hate Crimes

Violence trends may also be explained in part by an increase in random street crime. In an important new book, sociologists Jack Levin and Jack McDevitt analyze a newly recognized source of violence: hate crimes. According to Levin and McDevitt, many of the thousands of hate crimes committed each year are perpetrated by young people and are usually one of three types:

1. *Thrill-seeking hate crimes.* In the same way that some kids like to get together to "shoot hoops," hate mongers join forces to have fun by bashing minorities or destroying property. Inflicting pain on others gives them a sadistic thrill.
2. *Reactive hate crimes.* Perpetrators of these crimes rationalize criminal behavior as a defensive stand taken against "outsiders" who are threatening their community or way of life. A gang of teens that attacks a new family in the neighborhood because they are the "wrong" race are committing a reactive hate crime.
3. *Mission hate crime.* Some disturbed individuals see it as their duty to rid the world of evil. Those on a "mission" may seek to eliminate people who threaten their religious beliefs because they belong to a different faith. Others seek to maintain "racial purity" by attacking minorities.

While it is difficult to determine the influence of hate crime on teen violence, McDevitt estimates that fifty thousand hate crimes are committed each year, 70 percent by teens. ■

Source: Jack Levin and Jack McDevitt, *Hate Crimes: The Rising Tide of Bigotry and Bloodshed* (New York: Plenum, 1993); personal communication, 4 April 1993.

ogists have sought to develop alternative sources of delinquency statistics, of which the most commonly used are *self-reports* of delinquent behavior.

Self-report studies are designed to let youthful subjects reveal information about their violations of the law. A number of formats have been used: youths arrested by police are interviewed at the station house; an anonymous survey is simultaneously distributed to every student in a high school; boys in a youth detention center are asked to respond to a survey; youths randomly selected from the population of teenagers are questioned in the privacy of their homes. Self-report studies can be conducted one to one between the researcher and the subject through an interview or a self-administered questionnaire, but more commonly, they are done through a mass distribution of questionnaires. The subjects can be asked their identity or remain anonymous.

While the format can vary, the basic benefits and assumptions of self-report surveys remain constant: they can include all segments of the population (*cross-sectional data*) to avoid the class bias of official data; they can measure behavior that is rarely detected by police, such as drug abuse; and the promise of anonymity allows youths to describe their illegal activities honestly.

An example of self-report questions would be as illustrated in Table 2.5. Subjects check the appropriate spaces to indicate how many times they have participated in illegal or deviant behavior. Other formats allow subjects to write in the precise number of times they engaged in each delinquent activity. Note that the sample survey limits the reporting period to the past twelve months, thereby focusing on relatively recent behavior; other surveys can question lifetime involvement.

■■ TABLE 2.5   Self-Report Survey Questions

PLEASE INDICATE HOW OFTEN IN THE PAST 12 MONTHS YOU DID EACH ACT.
(CHECK THE BEST ANSWER.)

	NEVER DID ACT	ONE TIME	2–5 TIMES	6–9 TIMES	10+ TIMES
Stole something worth less than $50	_____	_____	_____	_____	_____
Stole something worth more than $50	_____	_____	_____	_____	_____
Used cocaine	_____	_____	_____	_____	_____
Been in a fistfight	_____	_____	_____	_____	_____
Carried a weapon such as a gun or knife	_____	_____	_____	_____	_____
Fought someone using a weapon	_____	_____	_____	_____	_____
Stole a car	_____	_____	_____	_____	_____
Used force to steal	_____	_____	_____	_____	_____
(For boys) Forced a girl to have sexual relations against her will	_____	_____	_____	_____	_____

■■■■■■■■■■■■■■■

While property crime rates have been stable, violence rates have increased sharply. Hate crime may be one reason for the increase in violence.

Surveys measuring self-reported delinquency are also likely to contain items not directly related to delinquent activity—for example, items requesting information on such diverse topics as subjects' self-image, intelligence, personality, and attitudes toward family, friends, and school; leisure activities; and school activities. Self-report surveys also gather personal information on subjects' family background, social status, race, and sex. Reports of delinquent acts can then be used with this information to create a much more complete picture of delinquent offenders than official statistics can provide.

In sum, criminologists have used self-report studies of delinquency frequently for more than forty years.[21] They are a valuable source of information on the delinquent activities of youths who have had formal contact with the juvenile justice system and those who have escaped official notice of their delinquent acts; the latter are the "dark figures of crime."

Self-Report Data

Most self-report studies indicate that the number of children who break the law is far greater than previously believed.[22] In fact, when truancy, alcohol consumption, petty theft, and soft drug use are included in self-report scales, delinquency appears almost universal.

Self-report studies indicate that the most common offenses are truancy, drinking alcohol, using a false ID, shoplifting or larceny under five dollars, fighting, using marijuana, and damaging the property of others.[23] In Chapter 12, self-report data will be used to gauge trends in adolescent drug abuse.

Table 2.6 contains data from a national survey of juvenile misbehavior conducted annually by researchers at the University of Michigan's Institute for Social Research (ISR). This survey is one of the most methodologically sound and important sources of self-report data since it is conducted nationally and involves a sample of more than three thousand youths.[24]

▨▨TABLE 2.6   Self-Reported Delinquent Acts, High School Class of 1992*

| | PERCENT WHO COMMITTED ACT | | | | |
DELINQUENT ACT	NEVER	ONCE	TWICE	3 OR 4 TIMES	5 OR MORE TIMES
Serious fight	82%	10%	4%	2%	1%
Gang or group fight	79%	11%	4%	3%	2%
Hurt someone badly	87%	8%	2%	1%	1%
Used a weapon	97%	2%	0.6%	0.3%	0.9%
Stealing less $50	68%	14%	7%	4%	6%
Stealing more $50	90%	5%	2%	2%	2%
Shoplifting	69%	12%	7%	5%	7%
Car theft	94%	3%	1%	0.1%	0.7%
Joyriding	94%	3%	1%	0.6%	1%
Breaking and entering	76%	11%	7%	3%	3%
Arson	98%	1%	0.4%	0.1%	0.5%
Damaged school property	87%	6%	3%	1%	2%
Damaged work property	93%	3%	1%	0.8%	1%

*2,627 students completed survey.

Source: Jerald Bachman, Lloyd Johnston, and Patrick O'Malley, Monitoring the Future, 1992 (Ann Arbor, Mich.: University of Michigan, Institute for Social Research, 1993.

A number of important conclusions can be drawn from the ISR data. First, a surprising number of these "typical" teenagers reported involvement in serious criminal behavior during the twelve months before the survey: about 11 percent reported hurting someone bad enough so that the victim needed medical care (1 percent said they did this five times or more); about 32 percent reported stealing something worth less than fifty dollars, and 10 percent stole something worth more (about 2 percent said they did this five times or more); 32 percent reported shoplifting from a store; 13 percent had damaged school property. Of the youths reporting, about 23 percent said they got into trouble with the police for something they did.

The juvenile crime problem is much greater than what the UCR leads us to believe if the ISR data accurately represents the national distribution of delinquent activities. There are approximately 54 million youths between the ages of 5 and 17. If 2 percent committed more than five theft offenses per year, that alone would amount to 5 million thefts. The 1 percent claiming five or more serious assaults (in which the victim needed medical attention) account for 2.8 million assaults.

While these disturbing statistics show that the delinquency problem is far greater than indicated by the national arrest statistics, there is also little evidence that the delinquency rate is climbing. A recent analysis by ISR statisticians indicates that with the exception of assault, patterns of self-reported delinquency have been rather stable since 1975.[25] Property crime rates, most notably shoplifting, may actually be in decline.

When the results of the ISR surveys are compared with various studies conducted over a twenty-year period, a uniform pattern emerges: teenager participation in theft, violence, and damage-related crimes seems to be stable. Although a self-reported crime wave has not occurred, neither has there been any visible reduction in teenage delinquency. And some research efforts indicate that these trends may actually have originated more than thirty years ago, since self-report statistics collected in the late 1970s are little changed from similar data obtained in the 1960s.[26] Though self-report data suggests a stable teenage crime rate, it typically does not focus on such crimes as murder and rape, which official statistics show are increasing.

Validating Self-Reports

Critics of self-report studies frequently suggest that it is not feasible to expect young people to admit illegal acts candidly. They have nothing to gain, and those taking the greatest risk are the ones with official records. On the other hand, some young people may exaggerate their delinquent acts, forget some of them, or be confused. In addition, many self-reports may not use representative samples, while others contain items that are trivial and without real interest to police ("used a false ID"). For these reasons, the use of self-reports has been criticized.

The most common technique for validating self-reports is to compare the answers that youths give on them with official police records. A typical approach is to ask youths if they have ever been arrested for or convicted of a delinquent act and then check their official records against their self-reported responses. A number of studies using this method have found a remarkable degree of uniformity between self-reported answers and official records.[27]

Other methods of testing the validity of self-reports are used:

1. The "known group method" compares incarcerated youths with "normal" groups to see whether the former report more delinquency.[28]
2. Peer informants—friends who can verify the honesty of a subject's answers—are used.[29]
3. Subjects are tested twice to see if their answers remain the same (testing across time).
4. Questions are designed to identify those who are lying—for example, "I have never done anything wrong in my life."[30]
5. Subjects are asked to take a polygraph to verify their answers.[31]

In general, these efforts have been supportive of self-report techniques.

In what is considered the most thorough analysis of self-report validity, Michael Hindelang, Travis Hirschi, and Joseph Weis made use of data gathered in Seattle and other sites.[32] They concluded that the problems of accuracy in self-reports are "surmountable," that self-reports are more accurate than most criminologists believe, and that self-reports and official statistics are quite compatible. They state:

> the method of self-reports does not appear from these studies to be fundamentally flawed. Reliability measures are impressive and the majority of studies produce validity coefficients in the moderate to strong range.[33]

Despite the clean bill of health given self-reports by these preeminent sociologists, some serious questions about the true accuracy of the technique have recently emerged. Most damaging is the charge leveled by Stephen Cernkovich, Peggy Giordano, and Meredith Pugh that self-reports typically exclude the most serious chronic offenders in the teenage population.[34] Cernkovich, Giordano, and Pugh base their finding on comparisons made between samples of incarcerated youth and youths selected from the general population of a north-central SMSA. The researchers found significant differences in the offending patterns between the incarcerated youth and the neighborhood sample. They found that "institutionalized youth are not only more delinquent than the 'average kid' in the general youth population, but also considerably more delinquent than the most delinquent youth identified in the typical self-report survey."[35] Their conclusion is that self-reports may be measuring only nonserious, occasional delinquents while ignoring hard-core chronic offenders who may be institutionalized and unavailable for self-reports.

The Cernkovich, Giordano, and Pugh research implies that self-reports are limited in their ability to provide data that can be used to accurately assess the delinquency problem. Despite these criticisms, self-reports continue to be used as a standard method of delinquency research.[36] This usage has been supported by studies that indicate that the patterns and trends evident in official delinquency are also contained in self-report data.[37] These findings have encouraged the continued use of self-reports in delinquency research.

VICTIMIZATION DATA

While the UCR and self-reports focus on the perpetrators of crime, efforts are also being made to look at crime victims.[38] The most important of these is a cooperative effort of the Bureau of Justice Statistics of the U.S. Department of Justice and the U.S. Census Bureau, called the National Crime Victimization

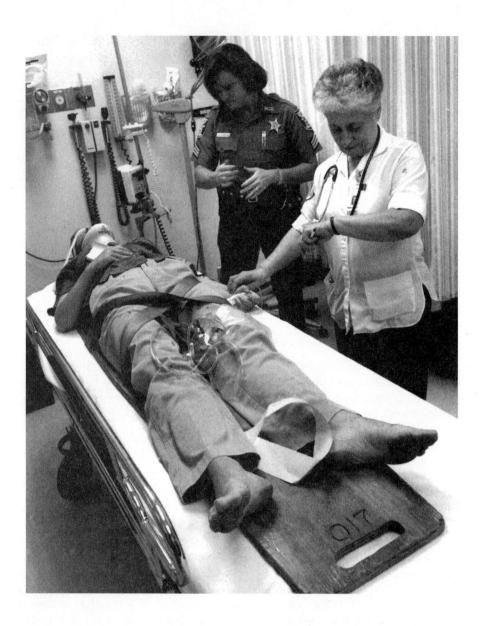

Survey (NCVS). The NCVS is a massive, annual household survey of the victims
of criminal behavior in the United States that measures the nature of the crime
and the personal characteristics of victims.

The total annual sample size of the NCVS has been about fifty thousand
households containing about one hundred thousand individuals. The sample is
broken down into subsamples of ten thousand household (about twenty thousand individuals), and each group is interviewed twice a year; for example,
people interviewed in January will be recontacted in July. The NCVS has been
conducted annually for more than 15 years.

Victimization in the United States

The National Crime Victimization Survey provides yearly estimates of the total
amount of personal-contact crimes (such as assault, rape, and robbery) and

household **victimizations** (such as burglary, larceny, and vehicle theft). According to victims' reports, about 34.7 million crimes occurred in the United States in 1991 (the last available data), an increase of less than 1 percent from the previous year.[39] This includes about 6 million crimes of violence, 14 million personal thefts, and 15.8 million household crimes, such as burglary.

While at first glance these figures seem overwhelming, victimization rates seem to be stable or declining for most crime categories. As Figure 2.4 shows, estimates of criminal activity in the United States for the years 1973 to 1991 indicate that the crime rate seems to have peaked in the early 1980s. As was found in the UCR, the violence rate climbed in the past few years, increasing almost 6 percent between 1990 and 1991; the personal theft rate declined about 4 percent, and the household crime rate was essentially stable.

Many of the differences between the NCVS data and official statistics can be attributed to the fact that many victims do not report their victimizations to police. About 50 percent of the crimes of violence, 72 percent of the personal crimes of theft, and 60 percent of household crimes go unreported. However, as the crime rate has declined, the reporting rate has slowly increased; today, more than half of all violent offenses are reported to law enforcement agencies.

Young Victims

The National Crime Victimization Survey data indicate that young people are much more likely to be the victims of crime than adults.[40] While it is common for the media to portray the elderly as particularly vulnerable to violent personal crime, it is actually teenagers who have the greatest risk of victimization.

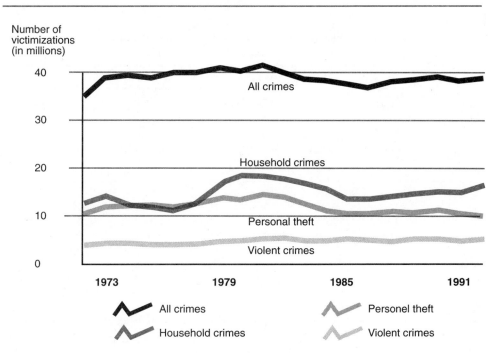

■■ FIGURE 2.4

Victimization trends, 1973–91

Source: Linda Bastian, *Criminal Victimization, 1991* (Washington, D.C.: Bureau of Justice Statistics, 1992), p. 1.

Table 2.7 shows the victimization rates for crimes of violence and theft by age group.[41] Here, we can see that the chance of victimization declines with age. Young teens are about ten times more likely to be the victim of violent crime and six times more likely to be the victim of theft than people over 65. What is both surprising and shocking is that this pattern holds for such serious crimes as rape, aggravated assault, and robbery; juvenile victimization is not just a matter of minor schoolyard assaults.

In addition to these age patterns, NCVS data show that male teenagers had a significantly higher (about two to one) chance of becoming victims than female teens. Black teens had a greater chance of becoming the victim of violent crimes than teenagers of other racial groups; in contrast, white teens maintained the highest theft victimization rates.

Considering these findings, it is somewhat ironic that, in general, older women are the most likely to have a generalized fear of crime, while teenage males and females are usually found to be the least fearful. While fear of crime is often difficult to measure, there are some indications that those who actually have the lowest risk of crime victimization are the most fearful of crime.[42]

Victim Patterns

NCVS data can also tell us something about the relationship between victims and offenders. This information is available because victims of violent personal crimes, such as assault and robbery, can identify the age, sex, and race of their attackers.

In general, youths tend to be victimized by their peers: a majority of teens were victimized by other teens, while victims aged 20 and over identified their attackers as being 21 or older. However, people in almost all age groups who were victimized by groups of offenders identified their attackers as teenagers.

The NCVS data also tell us that victimization is intraracial: black teens tended to be victimized by other black teenagers and whites by whites. And while most

■■ TABLE 2.7   Victimization Rates for Persons Age 12 or Older, by Type of Crime and Age, 1991

		VICTIMIZATIONS PER 1,000 PERSONS AGE 12 OR OLDER					
		CRIMES OF VIOLENCE					
					Assault		
	Total	Total* Violence	Robbery	Total	Aggravated	Simple	Crimes of theft
AGE							
12–15	163.9	62.7	10.0	51.6	12.9	38.7	101.2
16–19	185.1	91.1	8.3	79.2	25.5	53.8	94.1
20–24	189.4	74.6	13.9	59.0	23.0	36.0	114.8
25–34	106.3	34.9	7.2	26.6	8.3	18.3	71.4
35–49	75.5	20.0	4.0	15.4	3.9	11.4	55.6
50–64	45.0	9.6	1.8	7.6	2.4	5.2	35.4
65 or older	23.2	3.8	1.9	1.8	.9	.9	19.5

*Totals may vary because of rounding.

Source: Linda Bastian, *Criminal Victimization,* 1991, (Washington, D.C.: National Institute of Justice, 1992), p. 6.

offenders were males, about one-third of teenage girls reported their attackers to be other females.

Teens also were victimized by people they knew or were acquainted with, and their victimization was more likely to occur during the day. In contrast, adults were more often victimized by strangers and at night. One explanation for this pattern was that many teenage victimizations occurred at school. For example, about one-third of all the violent acts directed against those aged 12 to 15 occurred on school grounds. These teens tend to be victimized in public places, such as schools and parks, by peers of the same sex, race, and age.

Children Killed by Strangers

Though victim surveys tell us that youths are most likely to be victimized by people their own age, national concern has been growing over that most frightening of crimes: children who are abducted and killed by strangers. Public fears about this phenomenon have been fanned by some well-publicized cases, such as Wayne Gacy's serial killing of more than forty teenage runaways and the Adam Walsh abduction-murder case, which was the subject of a well-received TV docudrama starring Daniel J. Travanti. The fear that there are human beings who will kidnap and kill children is enough to keep parents up at night devising ways to protect their young ones.

Despite the magnitude of public concern, relatively little information has been available until recently on the incidence of stranger abduction homicides. At one time, it was believed that thousands of children were kidnapped and murdered each year by strangers. However, Gerald Hotaling and David Finkelhor analyzed data from the FBI's supplemental homicide reports to obtain a clearer picture of the problem.[43] They found that the problem of child abduction and murder is less severe than had been thought. Each year, there are an average of 52 cases in which the researchers are reasonably sure that a child was abducted and feloniously killed by a stranger and another 106 in which the surrounding circumstances remain unknown except that a child was killed by a stranger, for a total of about 158 stranger homicides a year. The research indicates that 14- to 17-year-old kids account for nearly two out of three victims, a risk nearly seven times greater than that faced by children 9 years old and younger. Girls were twice as likely as boys to be the victim of known stranger homicides, a pattern that contrasts with general homicide rates, which indicate that boys are more than twice as likely to be victims as girls (however, boys are more likely to be the victims in cases where the circumstances were undetermined). While a greater number of white children fall victim to strangers each year, the rate of minority victimization is significantly higher (6.46 per million black children compared to 1.79 per million white children). Finally, the research indicates another pattern that contradicts what we know about general murder patterns: stranger abduction homicides are greater in the northeast and lowest in southern states.

What does this data tell us about children abducted and murdered by strangers? First, while the problem is not as common as previously believed, it is still an important social issue: every week in the United States, as many as three children are abducted and killed by strangers. These horrible crimes permanently scar the victims' family and friends and probably take a greater toll on the general public than any other crime.

Victims surveys show that sometime during their lifetime about 80 percent of all teens will become victims of violent crimes. In the past 10 years the number of kids under 18 arrested for possession of a weapon increased 78 percent.

The Lifetime Likelihood of Victimization

Analysis of the National Crime Victimization Survey data indicates that sometime during their lifetime, about 80 percent of the 12-year-old kids in the United States will become victims of completed or attempted violent crimes, 99 percent will experience theft, and 40 percent will be injured during the course of the crime.[44] Even more startling is the finding that 52 percent of the 12 year olds will become the casualty of multiple acts of violence, and 95 percent will fall prey to multiple thefts.

As might be expected, personal characteristics also influence one's lifetime chances of becoming a crime victim. For example, while the probability of someday being a victim of robbery is about 30 percent, about 50 percent of black youths will become victims, as opposed to only 25 percent of white youths. Similarly, the lifetime chances of being the victim of rape is estimated to be one in twelve for white females and one in nine for black females. Males have a much higher probability of being the victims of violent crimes, and African-Americans in general can expect to be victimized more frequently than whites. It also appears that living in an urban environment significantly increases one's lifetime chances of becoming a victim. The following Case in Point explores this issue.

The lifetime prevalence rates mirror the annual rates supplied by the NCVS. They indicate that crime and delinquency is a basic social issue, because like it or not, most of us will feel its impact.

■ ■ ■ ■ ■ ■ ■ ■ ■ ■ ■ ■ ■ ■ ■

CASE IN POINT

You are a male aged 17. Your parents announce that they are interested in getting new jobs and trying to start their lives over again. They want to move to a new home in a different section of the country and seek a new life-style.

While at first you find this proposal startling, you accept the inevitable and try to make the best of a bad situation. You tell your parents that you are up for the move but that, as a teenager, you are the one who faces the greatest risk of being a crime victim. Therefore, you will be the one most deeply affected by where and how they choose to live. Your parents are surprised by this information and claim they want to relocate to an environment that offers you the most safety. They tell you that since you are so well-informed about crime, you should give them input on where to move and what life-style is the safest.

To what type of area would you advise them to move?

What kind of life-style seems to be the safest?

What are your chances of being a crime victim in that area?

Are Delinquents and Victims One and the Same?

How can we explain the close association in personal characteristics between the victims and the perpetrators of teenage crime? One view is that both live within close proximity of one another and are therefore likely to have similar personal characteristics. Yet, middle-aged and the elderly live in these areas, and they have lower victimization rates than teens. Another view, therefore, is that since offenders must have easy access to their victims, they must by design share a similar life-style. It should not come as a surprise, then, that delinquents find it easier to prey upon their peers than members of any other age group.

A more intriguing view is that offenders and victims are so much alike because, in reality, they are the same people. For example, Joan McDermott found that the young victims of school crime were likely to strike back at other students in order to regain lost possessions or recover their self-respect.[45] In another study, Simon Singer found that the victims of violent assault were those most likely to become offenders themselves.[46] And a number of studies show that youths who are the victims of child abuse are quite likely to later victimize their own children and families.[47] Gary Jensen and David Brownfield conclude:

. . . for personal victimizations those most likely to be the victims of crime are those who have been most involved in crime; and the similarity of victims and offenders reflects that association.[48]

Consequently, it may be foolish to separate delinquents and their victims into separate categories; the conditions that create delinquency may be present in all people at some time in their lives.[49]

SUMMARY

Official delinquency refers to youths who are arrested by police agencies. What is known about official delinquency comes from the FBI's Uniform Crime Reports (UCR), an annual tally of crimes reported to police by citizens. In addition, the FBI gathers arrest statistics from local police departments. From these, it is possible to determine the number of youths who are arrested each year, along with their age, race, and gender.

In 1991, about 1.7 million youths were arrested by police. A disturbing trend has been an increase in the number of juveniles arrested for violent crimes, especially rape and murder. Though it is not certain why this trend has developed, possible explanations include involvement in gang activity, drug abuse, and participation in hate crimes.

Dissatisfaction with the validity of the UCR has prompted criminologists to develop other means of measuring the true amount of delinquent behavior. Self-reports are surveys of youth in which subjects are asked to tell about their misbehavior. While self-reports indicate that many more crimes are committed than are known to the police, they also show that the delinquency rate is rather stable.

The third method of gathering information on delinquency involves the use of victim surveys. The National Crime Victimization Survey is an annual national survey of the victims of crime conducted by agencies of the federal government. It also indicates that the crime problem is far greater than official statistics indicate. Teenagers seem much more likely to become the victims of crime than people in other age groups.

All three sources of crime statistics agree on one thing, however: young people commit more crime than adults.

KEY TERMS

official data
self-report data
dark figures of crime
victim surveys
Federal Bureau of Investigation (FBI)
Part I offenses

Part II offenses
clearance
disaggregated
hate crimes
victimizations

QUESTIONS FOR DISCUSSION

1. Have you ever been the victim of crime or delinquency and failed to report it to the police? If so, why?
2. Do you believe that the police treat certain ethnic and racial groups in a discriminatory fashion?
3. Do you believe that self-reports can be accurate?
4. Why are violence rates higher in cities than in rural or suburban areas?
5. Do you think that police alter crime statistics?
6. Why are young people committing violent crime at a higher rate than at any time in U.S. history? Are there social forces, such as violent TV shows or family breakup, that promote violence?
7. What can you do to reduce your lifetime risk of victimization?

NOTES

1. The most commonly used statistics are the Federal Bureau of Investigation's annual compilation of crime data, referred to as the Uniform Crime Reports. The latest volume at the time of this writing is *Crime in the* *United States: Uniform Crime Reports, 1991* (Washington, D.C.: Government Printing Office, 1992). (Hereafter cited as *Uniform Crime Reports, 1991*.)

2. Patrick Jackson, "Assessing the Validity of Official Data on Arson," *Criminology* 26:181–95 (1988); for an early criticism of official data, see Ronald Beattie, "Criminal Statistics in the United States," *Journal of Criminal Law, Criminology, and Police Science* 51:49–53 (1960).

3. For an important study, see Terence Thornberry, "Race, Socioeconomic Status, and Sentencing in the Juvenile Justice System," *Journal of Criminal Law and Criminology* 64:90–98 (1973).

4. See, for example, Irving Piliavin and Scott Briar, "Police Encounters with Juveniles," *American Sociological Review* 70:206 (1964).

5. For the most complete review, see Michael Hindelang, Travis Hirschi, and Joseph Weis, *Measuring Delinquency* (Beverly Hills, Calif.: Sage, 1981).

6. Walter Gove, Michael Hughes, and Michael Geerken, "Are Uniform Crime Reports a Valid Indicator of the Index Crimes? An Affirmative Answer with Minor Qualifications," *Criminology* 23:451–501 (1985); Michael Hindelang; Travis Hirschi, and Joseph Weis, "Correlates of Delinquency: The Illusion of Discrepancy between Self-Report and Official Data," *American Sociological Review* 44:995–1014 (1979).

7. *Uniform Crime Reports, 1991.*

8. FBI, Press Release, data used here comes from April 25, 1993. Other data is from Federal Bureau of Investigation, *Crime in the United States, 1991* (Washington, D.C.: Government Printing Office, 1992).

9. Darrell Steffensmeir, "Is the Crime Rate Really Falling? An 'Aging' U.S. Population and Its Impact on the Nation's Crime Rate, 1980–1984," *Journal of Research in Crime and Delinquency* 24:23–48 (1987).

10. Ibid., pp. 38–39.

11. *Drug Use Forecasting Update, 1991* (Washington, D.C.: National Institute of Justice, 1992).

12. National Research Council, *Common Destiny: Blacks and American Society* (Washington, D.C.: National Research Council, 1989).

13. William Julius Wilson, "Studying Inner-City Social Dislocations: The Challenge of Public Agenda Research," *American Sociological Review* 56:1–14 (1991).

14. *Uniform Crime Reports, 1991,* p. 36.

15. *Report to the Nation on Crime and Justice* (Washington, D.C.: Bureau of Justice Statistics, 1988), p. 32. (Hereafter cited as *Report to the Nation.)*

16. Glenn Pierce and James Alan Fox, *Recent Trends in Violent Crime: A Closer Look* (Boston: National Crime Analysis Program, Northeastern University, 1992).

17. James Alan Fox, *Teenage Males Are Committing Murder at an Increasing Rate* (Boston: Northeastern University, 1992).

18. *Uniform Crime Reports, 1991,* p. 21.

19. Fox, *Teenage Males Are Committing Murder at an Increasing Rate,* p. 3.

20. Roger Hood and Richard Sparks, *Key Issues in Criminology* (New York: McGraw-Hill, 1970), p. 72.

21. A pioneering effort of self-report research is A. L. Porterfield's *Youth in Trouble* (Fort Worth, Texas: Leo Potishman Foundation, 1946). For a review, see Robert Hardt and George Bodine, *Development of Self-Report Instruments in Delinquency Research: A Conference Report* (Syracuse, N.Y.: Syracuse University Youth Development Center, 1965). See also Fred Murphy, Mary Shirley, and Helen Witmer, "The Incidence of Hidden Delinquency," *American Journal of Orthopsychiatry* 16:686–96 (1946).

22. For example, the following studies have noted the great discrepancy between official statistics and self-report studies: Maynard Erickson and LaMar Empey, "Court Records, Undetected Delinquency, and Decision-Making," *Journal of Criminal Law, Criminology, and Police Science* 54:456–69 (1963); Martin Gold, "Undetected Delinquent Behavior," *Journal of Research in Crime and Delinquency* 3:27–46 (1966); James Short and F. Ivan Nye, "Extent of Unrecorded Delinquency, Tentative Conclusions," *Journal of Criminal Law, Criminology, and Police Science* 49:296–302 (1958).

23. In addition to the studies listed above, see David Farrington, "Self-Reports of Deviant Behavior: Predictive and Stable?" *Journal of Criminal Law and Criminology* 64:99–110 (1973); Michael Hindelang, "Causes of Delinquency: A Partial Replication and Extension," *Social Problems* 20:471–87 (1973).

24. The latest in this yearly series is Jerald Bachman, Lloyd Johnston, and Patrick O'Malley, *Monitoring the Future: Questionnaire Responses from the Nation's High School Seniors, 1990* (Ann Arbor, Mich.: University of Michigan's Institute for Social Research, 1991).

25. D. Wayne Osgood, Patrick O'Malley, Jerald Bachman, and LLoyd Johnston, "Time Trends and Age Trends in Arrests and Self-Reported Illegal Behavior," *Criminology* 27:389–417 (1989).

26. Rosemary Sarri, "Gender Issues in Juvenile Justice," *Crime and Delinquency* 29:381–97 (1983).

27. Erickson and Empey, "Court Records, Undetected Delinquency, and Decision Making"; H.B. Gibson, Sylvia Morrison, and D.J. West, "The Confession of Known Offenses in Response to a Self-Reported Delinquency Schedule," *British Journal of Criminology* 10:277–80 (1970); and John Blackmore, "The Relationship between Self-Reported Delinquency and Official Convictions amongst Adolescent Boys," *British Journal of Criminology* 14:172–76 (1974).

28. Farrington, "Self-Reports of Deviant Behavior."

29. Gold, "Undetected Delinquent Behavior."

30. David Farrington, "Self-Reports of Deviant Behavior;" F. Ivan Nye and James Short, "Scaling Delinquent Behavior," *American Sociological Review* 22:326–31 (1957).

31. John Clark and Larry Tifft, "Polygraph and Interview Validation of Self-Reported Deviant Behavior," *American Sociological Review* 31:516–23 (1966).

32. Hindelang, Hirschi, and Weis, *Measuring Delinquency.*

33. Ibid., p. 114.
34. Stephen Cernkovich, Peggy Giordano, and Meredith Pugh, "Chronic Offenders: The Missing Cases in Self-Report Delinquency Research," *Journal of Criminal Law and Criminology* 76:705–32 (1985).
35. Ibid., p. 706.
36. Hindelang, Hirschi, and Weis, *Measuring Delinquency*.
37. Douglas Smith and Laura Davidson, "Interfacing Indicators and Constructs in Criminological Research: A Note on the Comparability of Self-Report and Violence Data for Race and Sex Groups," *Criminology* 24:473–87 (1986); Robert Sampson, "Sex Differences in Self-Reported Delinquency and Official Records: A Multiple Group Structural Modeling Approach," *Journal of Quantitative Criminology* 23:345–68 (1985).
38. The most recent data available are included in Linda Bastian, *Criminal Victimization, 1991* (Washington, D.C.: Bureau of Justice Statistics, 1992).
39. Ibid.
40. Joan Johnson, *Criminal Victimization in the United States* (Washington, D.C.: Bureau of Justice Statistics, 1992).
41. Data in this section comes from Catherine Whitaker, *Teenage Victims* (Washington, D.C.: Bureau of Justice Statistics, 1986).
42. Randy LaGrange and Kenneth Ferraro, "Assessing Age and Gender Differences in Perceived Risk and Fear of Crime," *Criminology* 27:697–719 (1989).
43. Gerald Hotaling and David Finkelhor, "Estimating the Number of Stranger Abduction Homicides of Children: A Review of Available Evidence," *Journal of Criminal Justice* 18:385–99 (1990).
44. Herbert Koppel, *Lifetime Likelihood of Victimization* (Washington, D.C.: Bureau of Justice Statistics, Technical Report, 1987).
45. Joan McDermott, "Crime in the School and in the Community: Offenders, Victims and Fearful Youth," *Crime and Delinquency* 29:270–83 (1983).
46. Simon Singer, "Homogeneous Victim-Offender Populations: A Review and Some Research Implications," *Journal of Criminal Law and Criminology* 72:779–99 (1981).
47. Ross Vasta, "Physical Child Abuse: A Dual Component Analysis," *Developmental Review* 2:128–35 (1982).
48. Gary Jensen and David Brownfield, "Gender, Lifestyles and Victimization: Beyond Routine Activities," *Violence and Victims*, 1:85–101 (1986).
49. Jeffrey Fagan, Elizabeth Piper, and Yu-Teh Cheng, "Contributions of Victimization to Delinquency in Inner Cities," *Journal of Criminal Law and Criminology* 78:586–613 (1987).

OUTLINE

DELINQUENCY THROUGH THE LIFE COURSE

The various sources of delinquency data—official records, self-report surveys, victim interviews—tell a great deal about the personal and social factors associated with delinquent behavior. Who are delinquents? What are their personal characteristics: Old? Young? Male? Female? Rich? Poor? What offending patterns are routine? Is delinquency typically a singular act, or is it more likely to be a part of a repeated, **chronic** activity that persists over time? How does delinquency evolve as an adolescent moves through the **life course?**

Measurement of the personal traits and social characteristics associated with adolescent misbehavior is essential for the study of delinquency. If, for example, a strong association exists between delinquent behavior and limited social status, then poverty and economic deprivation must be considered in any explanation of the onset of delinquent behavior. If the crime-poverty association is not found, then forces independent of the socioeconomic structure may be responsible for the onset of youthful law violations. It would be fruitless to concentrate delinquency control efforts in such areas as job creation and vocational training if social status were found to be unrelated to delinquent behavior. Similarly, if only a handful of delinquents are responsible for much of all serious crime, then crime control policies might be made more effective by identifying and treating these persistent offenders.

This chapter will review the most important social and personal variables that have been linked to delinquent behavior: gender, race, class, and age. Then it will analyze the concept of the chronic or life-style delinquent offender and discuss the patterns of delinquency throughout the life cycle.

GENDER AND DELINQUENCY

Crime and delinquency have long been considered male-dominated phenomena. To early criminologists, the female offender was an aberration who engaged in crimes that usually had a sexual connotation—prostitution, running away (which presumably leads to sexual misadventure), engaging in premarital sex, incorrigibility, and, later, crimes of passion (killing a boyfriend or husband).[1] Delinquency experts often ignored female offenders, assuming either that they rarely violated the law or, if they did, that their illegal acts were status-type offenses. Of course, these archaic views are no longer taken seriously. As gender roles have evolved, so too has interest in female delinquency. There is now considerble interest in such issues as female gangs, sexual abuse, and gender differences in the crime rate.

Official arrest statistics, victim data, and self-reports indicate that boys are significantly more delinquent than girls. While the number and rate of female arrests increased faster than those for male arrests in the 1970s and early 1980s, they have leveled off since 1987. Between 1987 and 1991, the number of arrests of males and females under 18 both increased about 9 percent. Today, the UCR results typically show that the gender ratio for serious violent crime arrests is approximately eight to one, and for property crime approximately four to one, in favor of males.[2] Figure 3.1 compares representation of boys and girls in serious crime arrests. Overall, the ratio of male arrests to female arrests is about four to one.

These patterns are not unique to the United States. Similar findings have been observed in self-report and official record studies in Great Britain. A 1990 Home Office study found that the overall male-female offense ratio was about five to

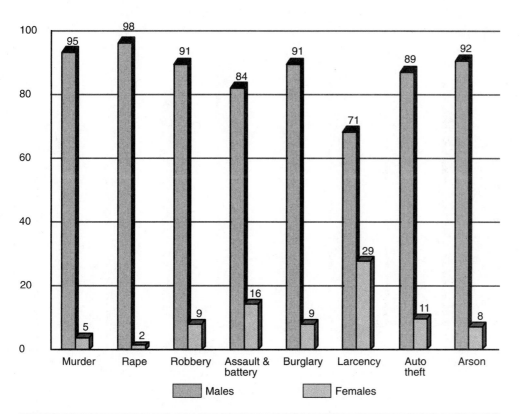

■■ FIGURE 3.1

Gender ratios in delinquency
arrests

Source: FBI, *Uniform Crime Reports, 1991,*
p. 239

one at ages 10 to 13 and four to one at ages 14 to 16. The ratio was much higher
for serious crimes; for example, for burglary, it was about seventeen to one.[3]

Figure 3.2 illustrates the male-female arrest patterns for some selected status-
type offenses. Although males also maintain a significant edge in arrests for these
acts, one relationship does reverse this general pattern: girls are actually more
likely than boys to be arrested for being runaways. There are two explanations
for this. First, girls could simply be more likely than boys to run away from home.
Or police may view the female runaway as the more serious problem and
therefore be more likely to process females through official justice channels. This
may reflect paternalistic attitudes toward troubled girls, who are viewed by police
as likely candidates for "getting in trouble."[4]

What have been the trends in female criminality in the past decade? While the
total number of female arrests increased almost 36 percent between 1982-1991,
the number of girls under 18 who were arrested increased about 15 percent, a
pattern similar to that of male offenders. This probably reflects the decreasing
number of youths in the 10-to-18-year-old age bracket, rather than any change
in offending patterns.

Self-report data seems to show that the incidence of female delinquency is
much higher than previously expected and that, overall, the pattern of delinquency committed by males and females is quite similar. That is, the crimes most
males commit are also the ones most females commit.[5] Still, boys are more likely
than girls to be "frequently delinquent," and males are more likely than females
to engage in serious felony-type acts; gender ratios in official and self-report data

Gender ratios in status arrests

Source: FBI, *Uniform Crime Reports, 1991,* p. 239

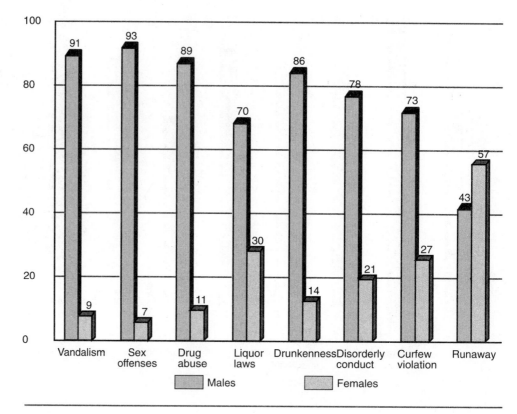

are quite similar.[6] So while self-report studies indicate that female delinquency is more prevalent than reflected in the official statistics and the content of girls' delinquency is similar to that of boys, the few adolescents who report frequently engaging in violent crime are predominantly male.[7]

A number of factors have been suggested as explanations for the gender differences in the delinquency rate. These include biosocial, sex role, and socialization differences. Because of the importance of this issue, female delinquency will be discussed in detail in Chapter 8.

RACIAL AND ETHNIC PATTERNS IN DELINQUENCY

The FBI also collects information on the race and ethnic origins of people arrested. The data show that racial minorities are disproportionately represented in the arrest statistics. While African-Americans make up about 12 percent of the population, they account for about 28 percent of all arrests and 37 percent of index crime arrests. Figure 3.3 presents the relative involvement of black and white juveniles in the arrest data. It shows that black youths are arrested for a disproportionate number of serious crimes—murder, rape, and robbery. Overall-,black youths account for about 26 percent of the juvenile arrests. The racial gap in the violent crime arrest rate has widened during the past decade. Particularly disturbing are the rates for murder arrests. For example, as Figure 3.4 shows, while the number of white youths arrested for murder between 1980 and 1990

■ ■ ■ ■ ■ ■ ■ ■ ■ ■ ■ ■ ■ ■ ■

Experts suspect that girls
involved in delinquency are
the product of troubled
homes and disrupted family
life. Teenage pregnancy is
on the increase. This may
explain why the female
runaway rate is higher
than the male rate.

remained stable at about five per 100,000, the number of black youths doubled over the same period, to more than forty per 100,000.

Figure 3.5 illustrates arrest patterns for minor and status offenses by race. White youths are more likely than black youths to be arrested for such crimes as liquor law violations and vandalism, while blacks are more heavily represented in the disorderly conduct and sex offenses categories, perhaps because police are more likely to use formal measures to handle black youths whose attitude and demeanor are not deferential to police authority.

Self-Report Differences

Official statistics show that minority youths are much more likely than white youths to be arrested for serious criminal behavior and that race is an important predictor of delinquent behavior. To many delinquency experts, this pattern merely reflects racism and discrimination in the juvenile justice system. In other words, black youths show up in the official statistics more often because they are more likely to be formally arrested by the police, who, in contrast, will treat white youths informally.

Index arrests by race

Source: Uniform Crime Reports, 1991,
p. 240

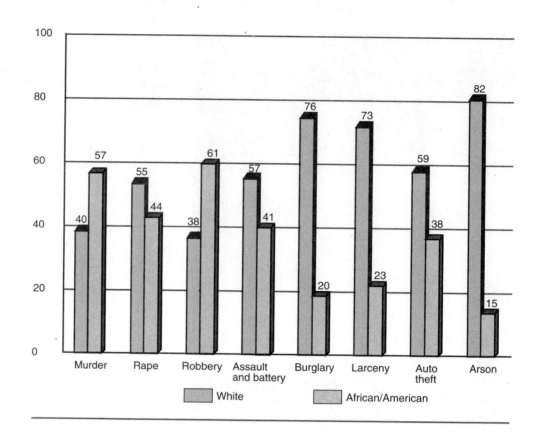

Arrest rate for murder by race

Source: FBI, Crime in the United States,
1991, p. 381

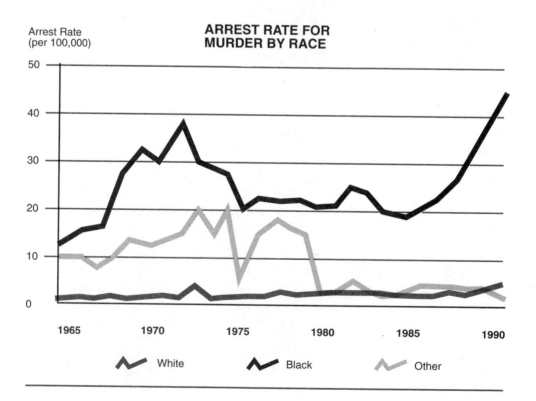

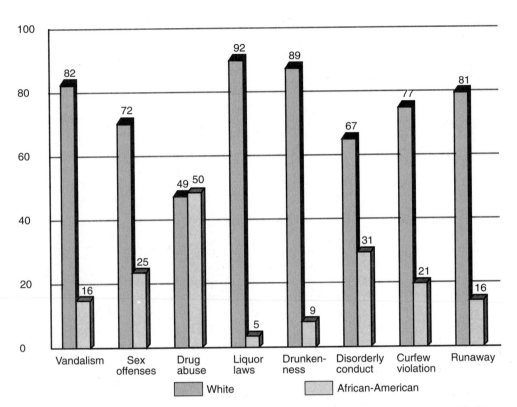

■■ **FIGURE 3.5**

Status arrests by race

Source: FBI, *Uniform Crime Reports, 1991,* p. 240

One way to examine this issue is to compare the racial differences in self-reported data with those found in the official delinquency records. Charges of racial discrimination in the arrest process would be supported by an insignificant racial difference in self-report data.

Early efforts by Leroy Gould in Seattle, Harwin Voss in Honolulu, and Ronald Akers in Seven midwestern states found that relationship between race and self-reported delinquency was virtually nonexistent.[8] These research efforts confirmed that racial differences in the official crime data may be a function of law enforcement practices.

Two recent self-report studies that use large national samples of youth have also found little evidence of racial disparity in offending. One conducted by the Institute for Social Research at the University of Michigan found that black youth self-report less delinquent behavior than whites.[9] And social scientists at the Behavioral Science Institute in Boulder, Colorado, found that while a few racial differences did exist in the delinquency rate, black youths simply have a much greater chance of being arrested and officially processed.[10] Self-report studies seem to indicate that the delinquent behavior rates of black and white teenagers are generally similar and that differences in arrest statistics may indicate a differential selection policy by police.[11]

Explaining Racial Patterns

Racial patterns in the delinquency rate have long been the subject of considerable controversy. One view is that the disproportionate amount of black official delinquency is a result of juvenile justice system bias. According to this view, police are more likely to arrest and officially process black youths while treating white offenders in a more charitable manner.[12] As Donna Bishop and Charles Frazier have found, possession of a prior record, even if it is the product of bias, increases the likelihood that upon subsequent contact, police will formally arrest a suspect rather than release the individual with a warning or take some other "unofficial" action.[13]

Those who challenge this view find that while some bias in the justice system does exist, there is enough similarity between official and self-report data to conclude that racial differences in the crime rate are real and not a result of a racially biased juvenile justice system.[14]

A number of attempts have been made to explain racial differences in the official crime data. One view, summarized by Daniel Georges-Abeyie, maintains that if in fact the racial differences in the delinquency rate recorded by official data *are valid,* they are a function of the ecological differences in American society: African-Americans reside in "natural areas" of crime, which are characterized by (1) deteriorated housing; (2) limited or nonexistent legitimate employment and recreational opportunities; (3) anomic behavior patterns; (4) a local criminal tradition that actually predates the current black ethnic group in residence; (5) an abnormally high incidence of transient or pychopathological individuals; (6) a disproportionate number of opportunities to engage in criminal behavior or form delinquent subcultures; and (7) poverty being the norm rather than the exception.[15]

Another view is that racial bias has produced a black culture that is separate and in opposition to conventional white middle-class values. Located in inner-city ghettos, the black subculture has been solidified by unduly harsh economic conditions; there seems little cause for optimism that this will change in the 1990s because most minority youth still see few prospects for economic success.[16] Sociologist Troy Duster found the existence of a permanent black teenage underclass whose members lack the basic job skills needed to enter the social mainstream: African-Americans are more than three times as likely to be poor as whites; their median income is only half that of whites; their net worth is only one-twelfth that of whites; and black men are twice as likely to be jobless as white men.[17] Duster concludes that the lack of economic opportunity for African-Americans has directly influenced their crime and delinquency rates.[18]

In sum, official data indicate that black youth are arrested for more serious crimes than whites. However, a number of self-report studies conducted by some of the nation's most respected criminologists show that the differences between the races is insignificant and that official differences, therefore, are an artifact of bias in the justice system: police are more likely to arrest and courts more likely to convict young African-Americans.[19] If the official data is valid, the participation of black youth in serious criminal behavior is generally viewed as a function of their socioeconomic position and the racism they face.

SOCIAL CLASS AND DELINQUENCY

One of the most enduring debates among criminologists is over the relationship between economic status and delinquent behavior. This relationship is a key element of delinquency theory. If delinquency is purely a lower-class phenomenon, then its cause must be rooted in the social forces that are to be found solely in lower-class areas: poverty, unemployment, social disorganization, culture conflict, and alienation.[20] If delinquent behavior is spread throughout the social structure, then its cause must be related to some noneconomic factor: intelligence, personality, socialization, family dysfunction, educational failure, or peer influence.

At first glance, the relationship between class and crime should be clear-cut: Youths who lack wealth or social standing, who live in deteriorated inner-city areas, and who rightfully perceive few legitimate opportunities also should be the ones most likely to use criminal means to achieve their goals. Despite the inherent logic of this observation, available research data does not consistently support his relationship. Many indicators of poverty and economic deprivation do not correlate with delinquency. For example, little, if any, consistent evidence exists that unemployment rates are associated with crime rates.[21] And while many lower-class people live conventional and law-abiding lives, a great number of middle-class people are delinquents and criminals.

Research on Social Class and Delinquency

Research on the class-crime relationship has been confusing and contradictory. Those who use official delinquency data persistently find *social class* to be a significant predictor of delinquency. Juvenile arrest rates are highest in areas that are economically deprived and socially disorganized.[22] Theorists who have based their efforts on official police statistics maintain that those who think delinquency is spread throughout the social classes are just "wishful thinkers"; to many experts, "real" delinquency is a lower-class phenomenon.[23]

■ ■ ■ ■ ■ ■ ■ ■ ■ ■ ■ ■ ■ ■ ■

If there is a relationship between class and crime then delinquency may reflect efforts by lower class kids to obtain desired material goods which they cannot otherwise afford. If a class-crime relationship does not exist then the cause of delinquency may exclude economic factors.

However, the first few self-report studies, specifically those conducted by James Short and F. Ivan Nye, did not find a direct relationship between social class and delinquency.[24] They found that socioeconomic class was related to official processing (chances of arrest and incarceration) by police, court, and correctional agencies but not to the actual commission of delinquent acts.

The pioneering work of Nye and Short sparked numerous self-report studies in the 1960s and 1970s, most of which supported their view of a weak or nonexistent relationship between class and delinquency.[25] Some of the most important work was conducted by sociologist Martin Gold. Although in his first few studies, Gold found that delinquents were predominantly lower-class youth, his later work with Jay Williams showed no significant self-reported differences among economic classes.[26] The only statistically significant relationship indicated that higher-status white males were more seriously delinquent than other white males!

In sum, the widespread use of self-reports in the 1960s and 1970s uncovered the rather startling fact that upper- and middle-class youth were as delinquent as their lower-class peers. Most researchers did conclude that lower-class youths were more likely to receive official notice from the justice system. Therefore, they appeared to be overrepresented as official delinquents. Middle-class delinquency, on the other hand, remained hidden.

Estimating Class Differences

Is there a relationship between social class and delinquency? This issue is still critical for the study of delinquency. Little question exists that the aggregate crime and delinquency rates of inner-city areas are much higher than those of wealthier, suburban areas.[27] Surveys of prison inmates show conclusively that the majority were raised in economically and socially deprived homes. Yet, cross-sectional self-report surveys show little clear-cut evidence of class differences in the delinquency rate. Class differences found using official data may, therefore, be more reflective of selective enforcement and sentencing policy than of actual crime involvement.

In the most widely cited research on this issue, Charles Tittle, Wayne Villemez, and Douglas Smith reviewed thirty-five studies containing 363 separate estimates of the relationship between class and crime.[28] Their conclusion was that little, if any, support exists for the position that delinquency is primarily a lower-class phenomenon. Tittle and his associates argue forcefully that official statistics probably reflect class bias in the processing of lower-class youths. A follow-up study (1991) conducted by Tittle and Robert Meier once again found an insignificant association between delinquency and a variety of social-class measures.[29] These reviews are usually cited by delinquency experts as the strongest refutation of the assertion that lower-class youths are disproportionately delinquent.[30]

Those who find fault with Tittle's conclusions usually point to the inclusion of trivial offenses, for example, using a false ID, in most self-report instruments. Although middle- and upper-class youths may appear to be as delinquent as those in the lower class, it is because they engage in significant amounts of what are actually status offenses. In a cross-sectional survey of 1,726 youths ages 11 to 17, Delbert Eliott and Suzanne Ageton found lower-class youths to be much more likely than middle-class youths to engage in serious delinquent acts, such as burglary, assault, robbery, sexual assault, and vandalism.[31] Lower-class youths were much more likely than middle-class youths to have committed "numerous" (more than two hundred) serious personal and property crimes. These findings forced Eliott and Ageton to conclude that self-report data give findings about class and crime that are actually similar to those of official data. Furthermore, the authors charge that studies showing middle- and lower-class youths to be equally delinquent rely on measures weighted toward minor crimes (for example, using a false ID or skipping school). When serious crimes, such as burglary and assault, are used in the comparison, lower-class youths are significantly more delinquent.

Reassessing the Class-Crime Controversy

After more than thirty years of research efforts, the true relationship between social class and delinquency remains elusive. Adding to the confusion is the fact that the manner in which research is conducted produces significantly different outcomes. **Aggregate** measures of delinquency, which compare the delinquency rates in poor neighborhoods with those in wealthier areas (such as those using the *Uniform Crime Reports* and census tract data), usually show that adolescents in lower-class areas are the more delinquent. In contrast, studies using individual-level data, such as self-reports, show few class distinctions in the delinquency rate: middle-class kids report as much crime and drug abuse as those in the lower classes. However, when the analysis of self-reported behavior is restricted to serious "street crimes," such as burglary and robbery, an inverse relationship between class and delinquency has been found.[32]

How the concept of "social class" is measured has also been found to significantly influence research findings. While some researchers use parental income and education as measures of social-class affiliation, others use occupation, employment status, welfare status, and housing quality; these differences have been found to have a major effect on findings.[33] For example, Simon Singer and Susyan Jou found that while parents' income, education, and wealth (based on assessed housing values) and other measures of social class were unrelated to delinquent behavior, parental occupational prestige was significantly related to adolescent offense rate.[34] In contrast, Margaret Farnworth and her associates found that if class is measured on the basis of parental occupational prestige or status, the association between class and delinquency is insignificant. When Farnworth divided her subjects into "upper-class" and "under-class" groups (those whose parents are unemployed or on welfare), a significant class-crime relationship was found. Such conflicting results have helped obscure the true relationship between social class and delinquency.

AGE AND DELINQUENCY

Age is generally agreed to be inversely related to criminality.[35] Official statistics tell us that young people are arrested at a disproportionate rate to their numbers in the population, and victim surveys generate similar findings for crimes in which the age of the assailant can be determined. Table 3.1 illustrates arrests for people at various age levels compared to their percentage of the population. This is graphic proof of the age-crime relationship. While youths 15 to 19 collectively make up about 7 percent of the total U.S. population, they account for about 28

■■ TABLE 3.1   Arrests by Age Distribution of the United States

AGE	% OF POPULATION	% OF ARRESTS	% OF INDEX ARRESTS
under 10	15%	.4	.8
10-14	7%	4.9	10.9
15-19	7%	20.0	27.5
20-24	8%	21.0	17.5
25-29	8%	17.0%	14.1
30-34	9%	14.0%	11.6
35-39	8%	9.6%	7.7
40-44	7%	6.0%	4.5
45-49	6%	3.2%	2.2
50-54	4%	1.8%	1.3%
55-59	4%	1.1%	.8
60-64	4%	0.7%	.5
65+	12%	0.7%	.8

Source: FBI, *Uniform Crime Reports, 1991*, pp. 223–24; Census Bureau, *1990 Census without Modification,* (Washington, D.C.: Government Printing Office, 1991).

percent of the index crime arrests and 20 percent of the arrests for all crimes.[36] As a general rule, the peak age for property crime is believed to be 16 and for violence, 18. In contrast, adults 45 and older, who make up 30 percent of the population, account for only 5 percent of the index crime arrests.

Self-report data collected by the Institute of Social Research also indicates that people commit less crime as they mature. The results of a six-year, nationwide survey of high school seniors found that the self-reported rates for such crimes as assault, gang fighting, robbery, stealing, and trespass decline substantially between ages 17 to 23.[37] As Table 3.2 shows, this pattern held for both males and females for property, violent, and total crimes.

Victim data can also be used to evaluate the age-crime relationship. It is possible to derive some estimates of rates of offending by age for the violent

■■ TABLE 3.2   Self-Reported Illegal Behavior by Age and Gender: Percent Reporting One or More Offenses*

	AGE						
	17	**18**	**19**	**20**	**21**	**22**	**23**
MALES	%	%	%	%	%	%	%
Violence	35	28	22	21	14	17	09
Property	69	60	48	46	42	31	28
Any Crime	74	65	55	53	46	41	30
FEMALES	%	%	%	%	%	%	%
Violence	20	15	15	09	09	05	09
Property	45	35	29	28	19	23	17
Any Crime	51	40	36	32	25	25	24

Source: D. Wayne Osgood, Patrick O'Malley, Jerald Bachman, and Lloyd Johnston, "Time Trends and Age Trends in Arrests and Self-Reported Illegal Behavior," *Criminology* 27:398(1989).

personal crimes measured by the National Crime Victimization Survey because victims had the opportunity to view their attacker and estimate their age. Research by the Hindelang Research Center in Albany, New York, shows that the estimated rate of offending for youths aged 18 to 20 is about three times greater than the estimated rate for adults 21 and older; youths 12 to 17 offended at a rate twice that of adults.[38] This relationship is even more pronounced when some specific crimes, such as robbery and personal larceny, are considered; for these offenses, the youthful offending rate is almost six times the adult rate.

Age-Crime Controversy

The relationship between age and crime is highly important to delinquency experts. One of the major criticisms leveled against theories of delinquency causation is that they fail to adequately explain why many youngsters forgo delinquent behavior as they mature, a process referred to as **aging out, desistance,** or **spontaneous remission.** That is, well-known theories that

Crime rates decline with age. The peak age for property crimes, such as larceny, is 16; violent crimes peak at age 18. Crime rates drop off dramatically after age 30.

account for the *start* or onset of delinquency rarely bother to explain why people *stop* committing crime as they mature. This theoretical failure is the subject of considerable academic debate.

One position, championed by respected criminologists Travis Hirschi and Michael Gottfredson, is that the age-crime relationship is a *constant* and therefore irrelevant to the study of crime. They find that regardless of race, sex, social class, intelligence, or any other social variable, people commit less crime as they age.[39] In fact, they argue that even the most chronic juvenile offenders will commit less crime as they age.[40] Since all people commit less crime as they age, age is irrelevant to the study of crime.

The Hirschi-Gottfredson concept of age and crime can be best understood through an example. Let's assume that children who drop out of high school will commit more delinquent acts than youths who are committed to their education. (See Figure 3.6) According to Hirschi and Gottfredson, members of both groups will commit less crime as they age, but the crime rate of the dropouts will remain relatively higher than the rate of the high school graduates at any given point in their respective life cycles: the observed differences in the respective crime rates of dropouts and graduates, which first appeared in early childhood, will remain constant as they mature. By implication, it would be possible to compare the relative difference in the crime rate of dropouts and graduates (or any other two groups) by measuring their criminal activity at any single point in their lifetime.

Those who oppose the Hirschi-Gottfredson view of the age-crime relationship suggest that while age is an *important* determinant of crime, other factors directly associated with a person's life-style also affect offending rates.[41] For example, David Farrington has shown that crime patterns may evolve over a person's life

■■**FIGURE 3.6**

Crime by age: Dropouts versus graduates

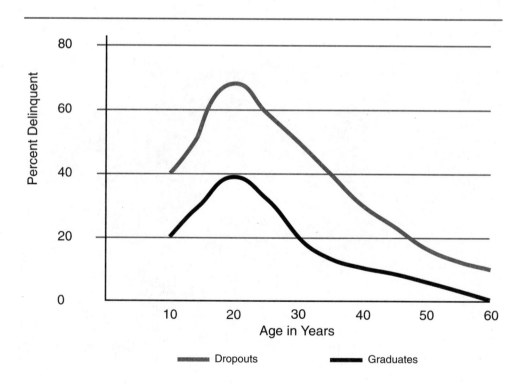

Part I   The Concept of Delinquency

course. The probability that a person may become a persistent "career criminal" may be influenced by a number of personal and environmental factors.[42] Evidence exists, for example, that the **age of onset** of a delinquent career has an important effect on its length: those who demonstrate antisocial tendencies at a very early age are more likely to commit more crime for a longer duration. According to this "life course" view, it is important to follow delinquents over their life cycle (**longitudinal studies**) to fully understand the factors that influence offending patterns.[43]

In sum, some criminologists believe that youths who get involved with delinquency at a very early age and who acquire an official record will be the ones most likely to become career criminals; to them, age is a key determinant of delinquency.[44] Those opposed to this view find that the age of onset is irrelevant and that all people commit less crime as they age; the relationship between age and crime is constant and therefore inconsequential to the study of delinquency.[45]

The true role of the age variable in the production of criminal careers has been the focus of many lively debates in the literature of crime and delinquency.[46] The research evidence indicates that there is a generalized decline in criminal activity as a person matures but that the incidence of some illegal acts, such as substance abuse, fraud, gambling, and drunkenness, may increase.[47] In addition, a small segment of the chronic delinquent population may exist whose criminal behavior remains intact as they reach adulthood. The age crime association is discussed in the following Focus on Delinquency.

THE LIFE CYCLE OF DELINQUENCY

Conclusions drawn from the ongoing analyses of age and other patterns in the delinquency data have convinced some researchers that the **life history** of youths must be studied to fully understand their careers in crime. It has been suggested that as adolescents move through their life course, the nature, frequency, severity, and variety of their antisocial behavior patterns change. Criminogenic traits or conditions may emerge that from that time forward influence the direction of behavior. Some, such as family dysfunction or personality development, may occur very early on in childhood and be related to the onset of delinquent activity. Other conditions, such as school failure, marriage, or unemployment, may be the products of social interactions that occur in late adolescence or even adulthood; despite their late onset, these too can profoundly effect behavior choices.

Delinquency experts who study the life cycle of crime assume that people vary in their behaviors as they mature. As both the official and unofficial data sources indicate, some youths begin early in crime and then continue at a high rate into their adulthood. Others engage in delinquency and then quit or *desist,* only to begin again. Many questions still need to be addressed: Why do some kids begin committing antisocial acts? Why do they stop or desist? Why do some escalate the severity of their delinquency, that is, go from shoplifting to armed robbery, while others de-escalate, committing serious crimes at first and then becoming petty criminals as they age? If they stop committing delinquent acts, what causes them to begin again? Why do some delinquents specialize in certain types of crime, such as robbery, while others are generalists engaging in a variety of

Aging out of Crime

The debate over the age-crime relationship is a fierce one. But the fact remains that after the mid-teens, the crime rate declines. Research indicates that youths who quit committing crime rarely take it up again in their adulthood. What causes this decline?

A number of explanations are offered for the aging out or desistance phenomenon. As people grow older, they go through biological changes that, in effect, slow them down. Offending patterns have been linked to testosterone levels, which increase during adolescence, then level off and decline into adulthood.

As adolescents enter adulthood, they simply may have fewer opportunities for crime. Research by Edward Mulvey and John LaRosa found that desistance was linked to youths' realization that they were "going nowhere" and had better change if they were going to become successful as adults. Similarly, Neal Shover and Carol Thompson found that desistance increases when offenders perceive that their chances of achieving "friends, money, autonomy and happiness" from criminal activities are decreasing.

According to James Q. Wilson and Richard Herrnstein, the aging out process is a function of the natural history of the human life cycle. Adolescent criminality coincides with the emergence of major sources of reinforcement for delinquent behavior—money, sex, and peers who defy conventional morality. At the same time, the child is becoming more independent of parents and other adults who enforce conventional standards. The new sense of energy and strength, a lack of economic and social skills, and relationships with peers who are similarly vigorous and frustrated combine to create the conditions needed for a rise in criminality.

Why does the crime rate then decline? Wilson and Herrnstein found that small gains from petty crime lose their power to reinforce criminal behavior as youths mature and develop legitimate sources of money, sex, alcohol, and status. As adults, former delinquents develop increasingly powerful ties to conventional society, not the least of which is the acquisition of a family. Adult peers will further make crime an unattractive choice by expressing opinions in opposition to risk taking and law violation ("you're acting childishly"). According to Wilson and Herrnstein, the typical person also turns "from the egocentric and hedonistic focus of childhood to more abstract and principled guidelines to action." Along with this sense of maturity comes the ability to delay gratification and forgo the immediate gains that illegal activities bring.

The life course view is supported in part by research conducted by Alicia Rand. Using data gathered from a group of delinquent males followed over time, Rand found that some personal factors predicted desistance, while others were correlated with persistent offending patterns. Youths who got married early, earned a high school diploma, and received vocational training within the armed services were the most likely to desist. In contrast, delinquent offenders who lived with a woman persisted in their criminal behavior almost four years longer than those who had never done so. And, as might be expected, delinquents who joined gangs were more likely to continue in their delinquency than those who remained unaffiliated. Rand also found that some expected associations between life-transition events and criminality did not exist: fatherhood, going to college, and joining the military were not related to desistance. In sum, youths who choose a more conventional life-style marked by marriage and productive military service are the most likely to forgo criminal careers.

Research conducted by Barry Glassner, Margaret Ksander, Bruce Berg, and Bruce Johnson found that aging out of crime might also be linked to a very practical consideration: the fear of punishment. According to Glassner and his associates, youths are well aware that once they reach legal majority, punishment takes a decidedly more serious turn. They are no longer protected by the kindly arms of the juvenile justice system. As one teenage boy told them:

When you're a teenager, you're rowdy. Nowadays you aren't rowdy. You know, you want to settle down because you can go to jail now. [When] you are a boy, you can be put into a detention home. But you can go to jail now. Jail ain't no place to go.

Of course, not all juvenile criminals desist as they age; many go on to be chronic offenders as adults. Yet, even people who actively remain in a criminal career will eventually slow down as they age. Crime is too dangerous, physically taxing, and unrewarding, and punishments too harsh and long-lasting, to become a long-term way of life for most people. ■

Source: Neal Shover and Carol Thompson, "Age, Differential Expectations, and Crime Desistance," *Criminology* 30:89-104 (1992); Kimberly Kempf, "Delinquency: Do the Dropouts Drop Back in?", *Youth and Society* 20:269-89 (1989); Alicia Rand, "Transitional Life Events and Desistance from Delinquency and Crime," in Marvin Wolfgang, Terence Thornberry, and Robert Figlio, eds., *From Boy to Man, from Delinquency to Crime* (Chicago: University of Chicago Press, 1987), pp. 134-63; Edward Mulvey and John LaRosa, "Delinquency Cessation and Adolescent Development: Preliminary Data," *American Journal of Orthopsychiatry* 56:212-24 (1986); James Q. Wilson and Richard Herrnstein, *Crime and Human Nature* (New York: Simon and Schuster, 1985), pp. 126-47; Barry Glassner, Margaret Ksander, Bruce Berg, and Bruce Johnson, "A Note on the Deterrent Effect of Juvenile vs. Adult Jurisdiction," *Social Problems* 31:219-21 (1983), at p. 219.

antisocial behavior?[48] To truly understand delinquency, we must find out why people behave the way the do at different points in their life cycle.

Current interest in persistent delinquent careers has two sources, both of which are discussed below.

THE GLUECK LEGACY

In the 1930s, Sheldon Glueck and Eleanor Glueck of Harvard University popularized research on the life cycle of delinquent careers. In a series of longitudinal research studies, they followed the careers of known delinquents in order to determine the factors that predicted persistent offending.[49] A key characteristic of the Glueck research was the use of multiple measures to calculate research findings. They used both self-reports and official data to measure delinquency and interviewed not only adolescent subjects but also their teachers and parents. The Gluecks also made extensive use of existing records in their elaborate comparisons of delinquents and nondelinquents. In their most well-known study, *Unraveling Juvenile Delinquency,* they carefully matched a sample of five hundred delinquent youths with five hundred nondelinquents to ascertain the personal characteristics that predict antisocial behavior.

The Gluecks focused on the early onset of delinquency as a harbinger of a criminal career: "the deeper the roots of childhood maladjustment, the smaller the chance of adult adjustment."[50] They also noted the stability of offending careers: children who are antisocial early in life are the ones most likely to continue their offending careers into adulthood.

Their research findings convinced the Gluecks that a number of personal factors present early in life were the most significant predictors of delinquent careers. They identified a variety of social factors related to persistent offending, the most important of which, family relations, included the quality of discipline and emotional ties with parents. The adolescent raised in a large, single-parent family of limited economic means and educational achievement was the one most vulnerable to delinquency.

The Gluecks did not restrict their analysis to social variables. They measured such biological and psychological traits as body type, intelligence, and personality and found that physical and mental factors also played a role in determining behavior. Children with low intelligence, a background of mental disease, and a powerful physique were the ones most likely to become persistent offenders.

The Gluecks' research was virtually ignored for nearly thirty years as the study of crime and delinquency shifted almost exclusively to social factors, such as poverty, neighborhood deterioration, cultural values, interpersonal relations, and social learning. The Gluecks' methodology and their integration of biological, psychological, and social factors were heavily criticized by the sociologists who dominated the field.[51] During the past decade, as delinquency experts began to appreciate the importance of age and other individual-level variables in the criminal process (see above), the Glueck legacy was "rediscovered." In a series of papers, John Laub and Robert Sampson reconsidered the Gluecks' research and directed attention to their multimeasure, multifactor concept of criminal career formation.[52] The Gluecks' method of giving equal weight to social, biological, and psychological traits seemed to jibe with current thinking on the formation of criminal careers.

The Chronic Juvenile offender

Current interest in the delinquent life cycle was also prompted by the "discovery" in the 1970s of the *chronic delinquent offender*. According to this view, a relatively few youthful offenders commit a significant percentage of all serious crimes in the community, and many of these same offenders grow up to become chronic adult criminals who are responsible for a large share of the total adult crime rate.

Chronic offenders can be distinguished from conventional delinquent youths. The latter are youthful law violators who may be apprehended for a single instance of criminal behavior, usually of relatively minor seriousness—shoplifting, joyriding, petty larceny, and so on. The chronic offender begins his or her delinquent career at a relatively young age (under 10 years old; referred to as "early onset"), has serious and persistent brushes with the law, is building a career in crime, and may be excessively violent and destructive. Moreover, chronic offenders do not age out of crime but continue their law-violating behavior into adulthood.[53] The important conclusion is: *early and repeated delinquent activity is the best predictor of future adult criminality.*

A number of important research efforts have set out to chronicle the careers of serious delinquent offenders. The following sections describe these initiatives.

Delinquency in a Birth Cohort

The concept of the chronic career offender is most closely associated with the research efforts of *Marvin Wolfgang* and his associates at the University of Pennsylvania.[54] In 1972, Wolfgang, Robert Figlio, and Thorsten Sellin published a landmark study, *Delinquency in a Birth Cohort*, that has profoundly influenced the very concept of the delinquent offender.

Wolfgang, Figlio, and Sellin used official records to follow the delinquent careers of a *cohort* of 9,945 boys, born in Philadelphia in 1945, until they reached 18 years of age. Data was obtained from police files and school records; socioeconomic status was determined by locating the residence of each member of the cohort and assigning him the median family income for that area.

Findings of the Cohort Study

About one-third of the boys (3,475) had some police contact. The remaining two-thirds (6,470) had none. Those boys with at least one contact with the police during their minority committed a total of 10,214 offenses. Race was found to be the most significant predictor of eventual police contact. Of the 2,902 nonwhite subjects, 1,458 had police contact (50.24 percent); of the 7,043 white youths, 2,017 (28.64 percent) had similar records. Wolfgang and his associates also noted that minority youths tended to fall in the lower-class category (84.2 percent of nonwhites and 30.8 percent of whites were from lower socioeconomic levels). However, when youths from the same socioeconomic levels were compared, nonwhites still had a higher level of police contact. After further analysis, the researchers were forced to conclude that no single variable predicted juvenile police contact better than race.

Wolfgang found that school-related variables were significantly associated with delinquent behavior. For one thing, the types of schools youths attended influenced whether they would eventually be picked up by police. A greater proportion of delinquents spent most of their school years in public schools, and fewer delinquents than nondelinquents attended parochial schools. Furthermore, 4 percent of delinquents, compared with 1 percent of nondelinquents, attended a public disciplinary institution. Nondelinquents received more education than delinquents (11.24 years completed versus 9.96). While this relationship was consistent across racial lines, it was equally apparent that nonwhites received significantly less schooling than whites.

Another school-related factor, IQ, also distinguished delinquents from nondelinquents (see Chapter 4). The average IQ for nondelinquents was 107.87; for delinquents, it was 100.95. Again, this relationship was consistent across racial lines.

Similarly, school achievement levels were significantly related to delinquent activities: 12.8 percent of nondelinquents were rated "very low" on school achievement; 27.46 percent of delinquents received such negative ratings. Conversely, 19.48 percent of nondelinquents received a "very high" rating, while only 5.63 percent of delinquent youths received that rating. However, the researchers found major differences in school achievement between the races, with nonwhites doing considerably less well.

Chronic Offenders

The most well-known discovery of Wolfgang and his associates was that of the so-called "chronic offender." The cohort data indicated that 54 percent (1,862) of the sample's delinquent youths were repeat offenders, while the remaining 46 percent (1,613) were one-time offenders. However, the repeaters could be further categorized as nonchronic recidivists and **chronic recidivists.** The former were 1,235 youths who had been arrested more than once but fewer than five times and who made up 35.6 percent of all delinquents. The latter were 627 boys arrested *five times or more* and who accounted for 18 percent of the delinquents and 6 percent of the total sample of 9,945.

It was the chronic offenders (known today as "the chronic 6 percent") who were involved in the most delinquent behavior; they were responsible for *5,305 offenses, or 51.9 percent of all offenses.* Even more striking was their involvement in serious criminal acts. Of the entire sample, chronic offenders committed 71 percent of the homicides, 73 percent of the rapes, 82 percent of the robberies, and 69 percent of the aggravated assaults.

Wolfgang and his associates found that arrest and juvenile court experience did little to deter the chronic offenders. In fact, disposition was inversely related to chronic delinquency—the greater the punishment, the more likely they were to engage in repeat delinquent behavior. Strict punishment dispositions also increased the probability that further court action would be taken. Two factors stood out as encouraging recidivism: the seriousness of the original offense and the severity of the disposition. The researchers concluded that the efforts of the juvenile justice system to control or eliminate delinquent behavior may be futile because not only do a greater proportion of those who receive a severe disposition violate the law, but their violations are serious and frequent.

Birth Cohort Follow-up

In a subsequent analysis, Wolfgang and his associates followed a 10 percent sample of the original cohort (974 subjects) through their adulthood to age 30.[55]

They divided the sample into three groups: those who had been juvenile offenders only; those who were adult offenders only; and persistent offenders (those who had offenses in both time periods). Those classified as chronic juvenile offenders in the original birth cohort made up 70 percent of the "persistent" group. They had an 80 percent chance of becoming adult offenders and a 50 percent chance of being arrested four or more times as adults. In comparison, subjects with no juvenile arrests had only an 18 percent chance of getting arrested as an adult. The chronic offenders also continued to engage in the most serious crimes. Though they accounted for only 15 percent of the follow-up sample, the former chronic delinquents were involved in 74 percent of all arrests and 82 percent of all serious crimes, such as homicide, rape, and robbery.

Although persistent delinquency was related to adult criminality, offensive behavior dropped substantially from the juvenile period to the adult period.[56] For example, more than half of the boys arrested twice as juveniles were never arrested as adults. While desistance was common, those youth who did commit crime as adults were likely to escalate the seriousness of their offenses.

Birth Cohort II

The juveniles who made up Wolfgang's original birth cohort were born in 1945. How have the behavior patterns of youths changed in subsequent years? To answer this question, Wolfgang and his associates Paul Tracy and Robert Figlio conducted a new, larger birth cohort study (Birth Cohort II) of youths born in Philadelphia in 1958 and followed them until their maturity.[57] Larger than the original, the 1958 cohort had 27,160 youths, of which 13,160 were males and 14,000 female.

What did this second cohort study reveal about delinquent behavior? For one thing, the proportion of delinquent youths in the second cohort (1,159 offenses per 1,000 subjects) was larger than that in the 1945 cohort (1,027). And those in the larger sample were involved in a total of 15,248 delinquent acts up to the age 18. However, the overall offending patterns in both cohorts were relatively similar; for example, about one third of the boys in both samples has at least one police contact before their eighteenth birthday.

The racial differences so apparent in the first cohort were less significant in the second. While a greater percentage of minority youth (42 percent) than white youth (23 percent) were delinquent, the differences between the two had declined (by 2 percent) since the earlier cohort data was analyzed. The violent crime ratio, which was fifteen to one in the first cohort, had declined to about six to one in the second. In addition, the number of white chronic delinquents increased substantially (by 5 percent), while the number of chronic nonwhite offenders declined (by 2 percent).

Since the second cohort contained female subjects, it allowed for a comparison between male and female delinquency patterns. As might be expected, males were two and a half times more likely to become involved in delinquent behavior than females. In addition, females who did get in trouble with the law were much more likely to be one-time offenders and less likely to be chronic delinquents. However, about 7 percent of the delinquent females were classified as chronic recidivists (147 girls).

Of the males in the sample, chronic delinquents (five or more arrests) made up 7.5 percent of the 1958 cohort (compared with 6.3 percent in 1945) and 23 percent of all delinquent offenders (compared with 18 percent in 1945). Chronic male delinquents continued to be responsible for a disproportionate amount of criminal behavior. The 982 chronic male delinquents accounted for 9,240 offenses, or 61 percent of the total. They also committed a disproportionate amount of the most serious crimes: 61 percent of the homicides, 76 percent of the rapes, 73 percent of the robberies, and 65 percent of the aggravated assaults. The chronic female offender was less likely to be involved in serious crime.

It is interesting to note that the 1958 cohort, as a group, was involved in significantly more serious crime than the 1945 group. They committed more serious crimes (455 per 1,000) than the subjects in the first cohort (274 per 1,000); the violent crime ratio between the two samples was three to one.

The 1945 cohort study found that chronic offenders dominate the total juvenile crime rate and continue their law-violating careers as adults. The newer cohort study showed that the chronic delinquent syndrome was being maintained in a group of subjects who were born thirteen years later than the original cohort and, if anything, were more violent than their older brothers. Finally, the efforts of the justice system seemed to have little preventive effect on the behavior of chronic offenders.

Tracking the Chronic Offender

Wolfgang's pioneering effort to identify the chronic career offender has been supplemented by a number of other important research studies.[58] Lyle Shannon also used the cohort approach to investigate career delinquency patterns.[59] He employed three cohorts totaling 6,127 youths born in 1942, 1949, and 1955 in Racine, Wisconsin. Shannon also encountered the phenomenon of the chronic career offender who engages in a disproportionate amount of delinquent behavior and later becomes involved in adult criminality. He found that less than 25 percent of each cohort's male subjects had five or more nontraffic offenses but accounted for 77 percent to 83 percent of all police contacts (by males) in their cohort. Similarly, from 8 percent to 14 percent of the persons in each cohort were responsible for all the serious felony offenses. According to Shannon, if one wished to identify the persons responsible for about 75 percent of the felonies and much of the other crimes—then approximately 5 percent of each cohort— the persons with two or three felony contacts would be the target population. Shannon also found that involvement with the justice system did little to inhibit criminality. Though most youths eventually desisted, the few who continued their offending careers as adults had been arrested as teenagers.

A number of other studies have taken somewhat different approaches to track the chronic offender. For example, Franklyn Dunford and Delbert Eliott employed a nationally selected sample of 1,725 youths to study the self-reported delinquency of chronic offenders who had remained undetected by police.[60] They were able to identify within their sample a **serious career offender type,** which they defined as a youth committing at least three serious felonies (such as aggravated or sexual assault, gang fighting, car theft, or strong-arm robbery) two or more years in a row. In all, seventy of the subjects were classified as serious career offenders. Dunford and Eliott found that only 24 percent of the serious career offenders had ever been arrested, indicating that the problem of the chronic delinquent offender may actually be much greater than that found by studies that use police records exclusively to measure delinquent behavior.

Most studies of the chronic offender rely on police data records. In a departure from this model, Howard Snyder of the National Center for Juvenile Justice examined the records of sixty-nine thousand youth who were referred to juvenile court in Arizona and Utah.[61] Snyder found the majority of youths (59 percent) were referred to juvenile court only once. Of the remaining 41 percent who were recidivists, the majority were males whose first offense was robbery and aggravated assault. Conversely, those least likely to be recidivists were females referred for underage drinking, truancy, shoplifting, or drug law violations.

The court-processed chronic offenders began their careers at a relatively early age (9, 10, or 11), and they were more likely than others in the study to have been referred to the court for a serious violent crime. Of these, the 16 percent most chronic offenders with four or more court referrals accounted for over half of all petitions to juvenile court. Importantly, youths under 16 who had already been sent to juvenile court at least twice *had about a 70 percent chance* of becoming recidivists. Snyder suggests that persistent offenders can be identified with a degree of certainty early in their offending careers—by age 15, if they have been to court at least twice. Rather than waiting for a fourth or fifth offense before classifying these youths as chronic offenders, juvenile justice officials could develop programs to focus resources on these youth very early in their offending careers.[62]

DELINQUENCY THROUGH THE LIFE COURSE

These research efforts on the relationship of age, gender, and other personal traits to delinquency and the discovery of the chronic offender have prompted research on the **life cycle of crime:** what causes the onset of delinquency, and what sustains it over the life course? A number of themes are now emerging. One view is that multiple social, personal, and economic factors can influence delinquency and that as these factors change and evolve over time, so too does criminal involvement. In an important paper, Robert Sampson and John Laub describe how delinquency and drug abuse evolves over the life course. They found that events and experiences encountered as a child matures influence the direction and frequency of antisocial behavior.[63] For example, delinquents who later manage to find stable work and maintain intact marriages as adults are the ones most likely to desist from crime. In contrast, those who have adverse experiences with the justice system (arrest, incarceration) are stigmatized with negative labels that interfere with family relations and inhibit employment opportunities; these factors heighten criminal liability.[64] A number of factors that encourage delinquency during the life course have been identified, including educational failure and family relations. Joan McCord found that fathers who undermine their wives, who are aggressive, and who fight with their families produce children who later become adult offenders. Criminality, she concludes, cannot be attributed to a single type of cause, nor does it represent a single underlying tendency.[65]

Another opposing theme that has developed is that there is a single underlying criminal propensity that is present at birth or soon after. This yet unidentified disposition or trait is established early in life and remains stable over time. The positive association between past and future criminality reflects the presence of this underlying criminogenic trait; what causes crime early in life also is

Part I   The Concept of Delinquency

responsible for antisocial behavior in adulthood.[66] Fluctuations in offending rates may reflect changes in criminal and delinquent opportunities and not the propensity to commit crime.[67] For example, the propensity to be violent is constant, but opportunities for violence fluctuate over time. The violence rate declines with age simply because teenagers have more opportunity for violent confrontation than do older adults. Proponents of this view, such as Michael Gottfredson and Travis Hirschi (whose work is discussed more fully in Chapter 6) and James Q. Wilson and Richard Herrnstein (Chapter 4), believe that criminal tendencies are quite stable over the life course because their underlying cause develops early in life.[68]

While these two views seem irreconcilable, they do have a degree of commonality. Both indicate that crime and delinquency can be viewed as a passage along which people travel, that a criminal career has a beginning and end, and that events and life circumstances influence the journey. In the sections below, some of the most recent research on the factors influencing the onset, maintenance, and termination of a delinquent career is discussed in some detail.

Pathways to Delinquency

What is the natural history of a delinquent way of life? What causes some kids to begin a delinquent career? Why do some sustain and even escalate their antisocial behavior patterns? Richard Jessor identified a number of factors that lead to what he labels "health/life compromising outcomes." As Figure 3.7 shows, some of these are biological, others are environmental, and still others rest on personality traits. Each of these factors may act alone or in concert to affect risk-taking behaviors, including delinquency and substance abuse, which eventually lead to a destructive adult life-style characterized by low self-esteem, disease, unemployment, and suicide.[69]

Jessor's views coincide with a number of significant research projects being conducted on delinquent life-styles. Using data taken from a longitudinal cohort study conducted in Pittsburgh, Rolf Loeber and his associates are now beginning to formulate the **pathways** to crime traveled by at-risk youth.[70] Loeber and his associates found that three paths to a delinquent career can be identified:

1. The authority conflict pathway begins at an early age with stubborn behavior, leading to defiance (doing things own way, refusing to do things, disobedience) and then to authority avoidance (staying out late, truancy, and running away). Defiance of parents and authority avoidance leads to more serious offenses including drug use.
2. The covert pathway begins with minor under-handed behavior (lying, shoplifting) which leads to property damage (setting fires, damaging property) and eventually escalating to more serious forms of delinquency ranging from joyriding, pickpocketing, larceny and fencing to bad checks, bad credit cards, car theft, drug dealing, and breaking and entering.
3. The overt pathway consists of an escalation of aggressive acts beginning with aggression (annoying others, bullying) leading to physical fighting (fighting and gang fighting) to violence (attacking someone, strong-arming, forced theft).

The Loeber research indicates that each of these paths may lead a youth into a sustained deviant career. Some enter two and even three paths simultaneously:

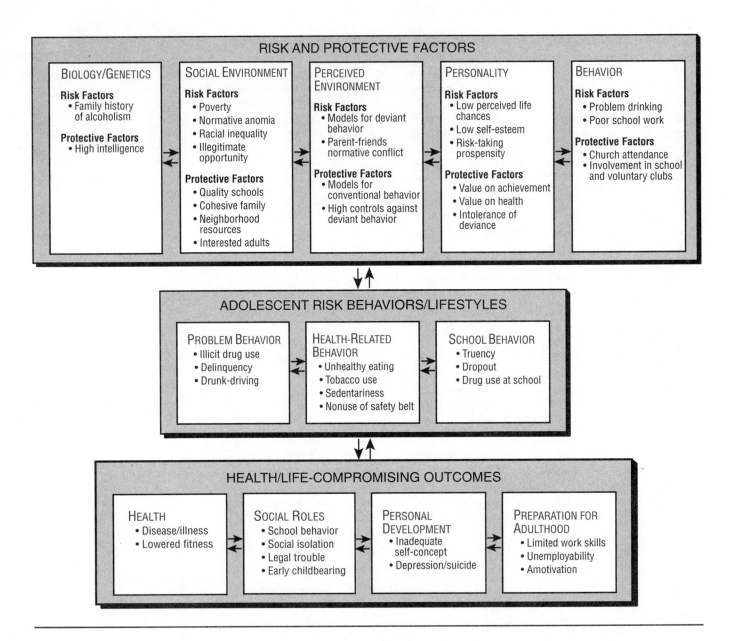

RISK AND PROTECTIVE FACTORS

BIOLOGY/GENETICS

Risk Factors
• Family history of alcoholism

Protective Factors
• High intelligence

SOCIAL ENVIRONMENT

Risk Factors
• Poverty
• Normative anomia
• Racial inequality
• Illegitimate opportunity

Protective Factors
• Quality schools
• Cohesive family
• Neighborhood resources
• Interested adults

PERCEIVED ENVIRONMENT

Risk Factors
• Models for deviant behavior
• Parent-friends normative conflict

Protective Factors
• Models for conventional behavior
• High controls against deviant behavior

PERSONALITY

Risk Factors
• Low perceived life chances
• Low self-esteem
• Risk-taking prospensity

Protective Factors
• Value on achievement
• Value on health
• Intolerance of deviance

BEHAVIOR

Risk Factors
• Problem drinking
• Poor school work

Protective Factors
• Church attendance
• Involvement in school and voluntary clubs

ADOLESCENT RISK BEHAVIORS/LIFESTYLES

PROBLEM BEHAVIOR
• Illicit drug use
• Delinquency
• Drunk-driving

HEALTH-RELATED BEHAVIOR
• Unhealthy eating
• Tobacco use
• Sedentariness
• Nonuse of safety belt

SCHOOL BEHAVIOR
• Truency
• Dropout
• Drug use at school

HEALTH/LIFE-COMPROMISING OUTCOMES

HEALTH
• Disease/illness
• Lowered fitness

SOCIAL ROLES
• School behavior
• Social isolation
• Legal trouble
• Early childbearing

PERSONAL DEVELOPMENT
• Inadequate self-concept
• Depression/suicide

PREPARATION FOR ADULTHOOD
• Limited work skills
• Unemployability
• Amotivation

■ ■ FIGURE 3.7

A conceptual framework for adolescent risk behavior: Risk and protective factors, risk behaviors, and risk outcomes

Source: From "Risk Behavior in Adolescence: A Psychosocial Framework for Understanding and Action" (p. 27) by Richard Jessor, 1992, in *Adolescents at Risk: Medical and Social Perspectives*, edited by D. E. Rogers and E. Ginzburg, Boulder, CO: Westview Press. Copyright 1992 by Westview Press. Reprinted by permission.

they are stubborn, lie to teachers and parents, are bullies, and commit petty thefts; these adolescents are the ones most likely to become persistent offenders.

The Loeber research is important because it shows that delinquency does in fact escalate as children move along the life course. It also indicates that antisocial behaviors may take more than one path as the offender moves from delinquent to criminal.

Problem Behavior Syndrome

Evidence is mounting that persistent delinquency is part of a general **problem behavior syndrome** in adolescence.[71] Unconventional adolescent behavior

patterns that are thought to cluster together include substance abuse, smoking, precocious sexual experimentation, pregnancy, school failure, suicide attempts, risk taking and thrill seeking, theft, and violence. A number of research efforts have found that kids who are involved in crime also are likely to engage in a variety of other antisocial behaviors.[72]

In one important analysis, Helene Raskin White studied antisocial behavior clusters in a cohort of more than four hundred male and female adolescents measured repeatedly over six years. Problem behaviors that clustered together included delinquency, substance abuse, school misconduct and underachievement, precocious sexual behavior, violence (for males only), and suicide and mental health problems (for females only).[73] White found that general problem behaviors were stable over the six years: kids who were having multiple problems at age 15 were also having problems at age 21.

Table 3.3 lists some of the problem behaviors found by David Farrington to be significantly associated with both self-reported and official delinquency in a cohort of English youth. The breadth of these behaviors supports the existence of a problem behavior syndrome.

The correlation of these factors is important because they suggest that delinquency may be one of a cluster of antisocial behaviors that may have a common cause. Research efforts are going on to evaluate the possibility of a single, general explanation of all deviant behavior patterns.

Offense Specialization

Most persistent offenders do not seem to specialize in any one type of behavior but, with few exceptions, engage in a variety of delinquent acts and antisocial behaviors as they mature. For example, they cheat on tests, bully kids in the schoolyard, take drugs, commit a burglary, go on to steal a car, and then shoplift from a store.

■ ■ TABLE 3.3   Risk Factors for Delinquency and Age at Which They Occur

(a) *Child problem behavior*
Troublesome 8-10
Dishonest 10
Lies frequently 12-14
Aggressive 12-14
Bullies 14

(b) *Teenage antisocial behavior*
Heavy drinker 18
Heavy smoker 18
Drug user 18
Heavy gambler 18
High sexual activity 18

(c) *Physical measures*
Small 8-10
Small 18
Tattooed 18

(d) *Impulsivity*
Lacks concentration/restless 8-10
High daring 8-10
Lacks concentration/restless 12-14
High daring 12-14
High impulsivity 18

(e) *School problems*
Low intelligence 8-10

Low attainment 11
High delinquency school 11
Frequently truants 12-14
Left school 15
No exams taken by 18

(f) *Family influences*
Poor parental child-rearing 8
Poor parental supervision 8
Low parent interest in education 8
Separated from parents 10
Poor relation with parents 18

(g) *Antisocial influences*
Convicted parent 10
Delinquent sibling 10
Sibling behavior problems 8
Delinquent friends 14

(h) *Socioeconomic factors*
Low family income 8
Low socioeconomic status family 8-10
Poor housing 8-10
Large family size 10
Unstable job record 18
Unskilled manual job 18

Source: David Farrington, "**Juvenile Delinquency**", in J. Coleman, ed. *The School Years* (London: Routledge, 1992), p. 129.

Recent evidence indicates that over their lifetime, however, some chronic offenders may begin to specialize in particular forms of delinquency.[74] For example, Randall Shelden found that some chronic offenders specialized in serious crimes, while others could be categorized as "chronic nuisance offenders" who were repeatedly referred to court on status- and neglect-type petitions; this latter group "specialized" in running away and truancy.[75]

In another study using a very large sample of about seventy thousand court-adjudicated youths in Arizona and Utah, David Farrington, Howard Snyder, and Terrence Finnegan found that about 20 percent of the youths could be considered offense "specialists" who persistently committed one type of offense.[76] The delinquent acts most likely to be the domain of "specialists" included running away from home, liquor violations, incorrigibility, burglary, motor vehicle theft, and drug abuse. Not surprisingly, two of these are status offenses (to which a desperate youth might repeatedly turn for survival), two are criminal offenses that require some degree of skill (burglary and auto theft), and two involve substance abuse (and therefore might require habitual behavior).[77]

From Delinquent to Criminal

Because the life course concept is considered so important, a number of longitudinal studies are being conducted to track delinquents as they mature.[78]

The early data seems to support what is already known about delinquent-criminal career patterns: that early onset predicts later offending; that there is continuity in crime (juvenile offenders are the ones most likely to become adult criminals); and that chronic offenders commit a significant portion of all crimes.[79]

One of the most important of these longitudinal studies, the *Cambridge study in delinquent development,* followed the offending careers of 411 London boys born in 1953.[80] This longitudinal cohort study, directed since 1982 by David Farrington, is one of the most serious attempts to isolate the factors that predict the continuity of criminal behavior through the life course. The study used self-report data, as well as in-depth interviews and psychological testing. The boys were interviewed eight times over a period of twenty-four years, beginning at age 8 and continuing to age 32.

The results of the Cambridge study are quite important because they showed that many of the same patterns found in the United States were repeated in a cross-national sample: the existence of chronic offenders; continuity of offending; early onset leading to persistent delinquency.

The Cambridge study also suggested that life events can influence the direction of a delinquent career. Farrington reported that a brush with the law can escalate delinquent involvement because it actually reduces fear of the justice system. The study showed that unemployment was related to the escalation of theft offenses; violence and substance abuse were unaffected by unemployment. Getting married also helped reduce criminal activity. However, marriage to a woman convicted of earlier crime actually increased criminal involvement. Finally, moving out of the city to more rural or suburban areas helped offenders desist; perhaps moving to the country forced them to sever ties with co-offenders.

Data from the Cambridge study can be used to build a composite picture of the male delinquent offender and the factors that influence his behavior over the life course; these are discussed in the following Focus on Delinquency.

Turning Points in Crime

If there are various pathways to crime and delinquency, are there trails back to conformity? In an important new work, *Crime in the Making,* Robert Sampson and John Laub identify the "turning points" in a criminal career.[81] As devotees of the life course perspective, Sampson and Laub find that the stability of delinquent behavior can be effected by events that occur later in life, even after a chronic delinquent career has been undertaken. Two critical "turning points" are marriage and career. Kids who had significant problems with the law are able to desist from crime as adults if they can become attached to a spouse who supports and sustains them, even when the partner knows they had been in trouble when they were kids. They may encounter employers who are willing to give them a chance despite their record. People who cannot sustain secure marital relations or are failures in the labor market are less likely to desist from crime.

According to Sampson and Laub, these life events help people build relations with individuals and institutions that are life sustaining. Building this social capital supports conventional behavior and inhibits deviant behavior. For example, a successful marriage creates social capital when it improves a person's stature and feelings of self-worth and encourages others to "take a chance" on

FOCUS ON DELINQUENCY

Portrait of a Delinquent

Who are delinquent offenders? What are their predominant personal, social, and developmental traits? What factors predict their behavior as they go through their life cycle from the onset of their antisocial activity into their adulthood? David Farrington's longitudinal analysis of London youth helps provide answers to these questions.

Farrington found that the traits present in persistent offenders can be observed as early as age 8. The typical chronic delinquent is a male property offender born into a low-income, large-sized family headed by parents who had criminal records and with delinquent older siblings. The future delinquent receives poor parental supervision, including harsh or erratic punishments; his parents are likely to be in conflict and to separate. He tends to associate with friends who are also delinquents. By age 8, he is already exhibiting antisocial behavior, including dishonesty and aggressiveness. At school, he tends to have low educational achievement and attainment and is restless, troublesome, hyperactive, impulsive and often truant.

After leaving school at age 18, the persistent delinquent tends to maintain a relatively well-paid but low-status job and is likely to have an erratic work history and periods of unemployment. Deviant behavior tends to be versatile, rather than specialized. That is, the typical offender not only commits property offenses, such as theft and burglary, but also engages in violence, vandalism, drug use, excessive drinking, drunk driving, smoking, reckless driving, and sexual promiscuity. He is more likely than nonoffenders to live away from home and have conflict with his parents. The persistent delinquent tends to get tattoos, go out most evenings, and enjoy "hanging out" with groups of friends. He is much more likely than nonoffenders to get involved in fights, to carry weapons, and to use them in violent encounters. The frequency of his offending reaches a peak in his teenage years (about 17 or 18), then declines in his twenties, when he marries or lives with a woman.

By the time he reaches his thirties, the former delinquent is likely to be separated or divorced from his wife and be an absent parent. His employment record remains spotty, and he moves often to rental units, rather than owning his housing. His life is still characterized by evenings out, heavy drinking and substance abuse, and more violent behavior than that of his contemporaries. Because the typical offender provides the same kind of deprived and disrupted family life for his own children that he himself experienced, the social experiences and conditions that produce delinquency are carried on from one generation to the next.

Interestingly, Farrington's research also identified the factors that predict the discontinuity of delinquent offenses: boys whose background make them vulnerable to delinquency but are able to remain nonoffenders tend to be somewhat shy, have few friends (at age 8), have nondeviant parents and siblings, and are rated highly by their mother (at age 10). Unfortunately, at-risk youths who manage to attain age 32 without a criminal conviction are not necessarily leading a successful life. They are unlikely to be home owners and tend to live in dirty home conditions, have large debts and low paid jobs. They are the youth most likely to never marry and to be living alone. Youths who experience social isolation at age 8 also experience it at age 32.

While not all experts agree with Farrington that these personal and social factors are associated with delinquency, the majority do view delinquent youth as needing society's help to overcome overwhelming social, economic, and personal problems that they are ill equipped to handle. ■

Source: David Farrington, "The Development of Offending and Antisocial Behavior from Childhood to Adulthood," paper presented at the Congress on Rethinking Delinquency, University of Minho, Braga, Portugal, July 1992; idem., "Psychobiological Factors in the Explanation and Reduction of Delinquency," *Today's Delinquent* 7:44-46 (1988).

the individual. In the same way, having a good career can inhibit crime by creating a stake in conformity; why commit crime when you are doing well at your job? These relationships are reciprocal: if a person is chosen as an employee, he or she returns the "favor" by doing the best job possible; if the person is chosen as a spouse, he or she blossoms into a devoted partner. Building social capital reduces the likelihood of deviance.

Sampson and Laub's research indicates that events that occur in later adolescence and adulthood do influence the direction of delinquent and criminal careers. Life events can either help terminate or sustain deviant careers. Having established that change is possible, some important questions still need answering: Why do some kids change while others resist? Why do some people enter strong marriages while others fail? Why are some troubled youths able to conform to the requirements or a job or career while others cannot?

Policy Implications

The ongoing research efforts to chart the life cycle of crime and delinquency will have a major influence on both theory and policy. Delinquency theories are beginning to incorporate life course concepts. Rather than simply asking why kids become delinquent or commit antisocial acts, theorists are charting the onset, escalation, frequency, and cessation of delinquent behavior. Some of the theories that rely on a life course model will be reviewed in Chapters 4 through 8.

Life course concepts also influence delinquency control policy. If a relatively few persistent offenders commit a great portion of all delinquent acts and then persist as adult criminals, it follows that steps should be taken to limit their criminal opportunities.[82] One approach is to identify persistent offenders at an early stage of their offending career; a significant share of juvenile justice resources might then be devoted to their treatment and control.[83] Life course advocates suggest that persistent offenders bear particular traits (impulsive personalities) and engage in easily identifiable behaviors (early onset of crime) that can be used to classify high-risk offenders.[84] Special legal provisions for persistent offenders might then include mandatory incarceration or waiver to adult court.

These solutions are troubling to civil libertarians since they involve the prediction of future behavior. Is it not possible that some people will be unfairly punished because their background characteristics mistakenly indicate they are potential chronic offenders? Conversely, might not some serious offenders be overlooked because they have a conventional background? No prediction method is totally accurate, and a mistake can involve a significant infringement on a person's civil rights. For example, even the most sophisticated attempts at predicting chronic offending are erroneous more than half the time.[85] Efforts to predict individual cases of chronic offending have proven unreliable.[86]

The danger also exists that early identification, arrest, and custody of youth will promote, rather than inhibit, their delinquent careers. For example, Pamela Tontodonato found that youths who have three arrests by age 15 have a greater likelihood of accumulating additional more serious arrests than those juveniles who accumulate arrests more slowly.[87] While an intensive law enforcement policy aimed at multiple offenders may have political appeal, it might actually produce a higher overall delinquency rate.

Despite reservations civil libertarians may have about the concept of the chronic career offender, it already has profoundly influenced the daily operations of the juvenile justice system. Few concepts have shaken the study of crime and delinquency as much as the "discovery" of the chronic or persistent delinquent offender. The belief that a few persistent offenders are responsible for a significant portion of the serious crime in a community has been translated into a number of policy initiatives within the juvenile justice system. First, it has strengthened the position of conservative policymakers who call for a "get tough" approach to juvenile delinquency." while it might seem futile, cruel, and expensive to lock up all juvenile offenders, it makes both economic and practical sense to incarcerate the few chronic offenders who are responsible for most of the crime problem. This view has resulted in the development of tough juvenile sentencing codes, as well as the transfer of serious delinquency cases to the adult court.

The discovery of the chronic offender has significantly shifted juvenile justice philosophy away from a liberal treatment orientation toward a more conservative crime-control model. It may also produce a review of the *parens patriae* doctrine and the jurisdiction of the juvenile court. As Kimberly Kempf suggests, it may make sense to reconstruct the criminal court system so that both petty adult and juvenile cases are handled in one court, chronic adult and juvenile felony offenders in another, and status offenders in a third. The problems of juvenile and adult chronic offenders may be similar enough to warrant the attention of the same judicial authority.[88] The following Case in Point explores some of these issues.

■■■■■■■■■■■■■■■■

CASE IN POINT

You are a newly appointed judge in the county juvenile court.

A 12-year-old boy, Joseph L., is petitioned to court on a robbery charge. It seems that Joseph, a five-foot-four, 110-pound youngster, used a knife in a schoolyard robbery. You note that this is already his fifth offense. He was arrested at age 9 on a petty larceny, and six months later, he was picked up for breaking into a home. At age 10, he was again arrested for a break-in, and at 11, he assaulted and badly beat a younger boy after school. Despite his youth, the boy seems defiant and unafraid when he is found to be a delinquent.

At the sentencing hearing, the prosecutor presents evidence that Joseph has all the character traits of a chronic offender: early onset of delinquency, multiple arrests, increased seriousness of offenses, a history of school failure, low intelligence, siblings who are law violators. The prosecution demands a three-year placement in the state correctional facility for dangerous youth. Defense counsel asks for community supervision. She claims that the state's high-security juvenile facility usually houses much older offenders, many of whom are over 16. Placement will only exacerbate an already serious situation. Considering the boy's tender age, she argues, the case can better be handled by community treatment agencies.

The prosecution counters that chronic offenders will not be impressed with leniency and that community treatment is therefore a waste of time. Though the prosecutor agrees with defense counsel's claim that placement with older delinquents will certainly diminish any chance of future rehabilitation, he believes that this youth has already proven himself beyond control. Society's need for safety outweighs the remote likelihood of rehabilitation, he contends. A period of incarceration is needed in this case to protect the public from a dangerous chronic offender.

Is it fair to place this child with older youth in a high-security treatment center?

Should the needs of society outweigh a child's right to treatment?

Should predictions of future behavior patterns influence the treatment of children?

SUMMARY

This chapter reviewed personal and social factors correlated with delinquent behavior. Delinquents are disproportionately male. The overall gender ratio in the arrest rate is about four to one; for violent crime, it is about eight to one. Minority youth are overrepresented in the delinquency rate, especially for violent crime arrests. Experts are split on the cause of racial differences: some believe they are a function of system bias; others see them as representing actual differences in the delinquency rate. Disagreement also exists over the relationship between class position and delinquency. Some hold that adolescent crime is a lower-class phenomenon, while others see it spread throughout the social structure. Problems in methodology and data collection have obscured the true class-crime relationship. However, official statistics indicate that lower-class youth are responsible for the most serious criminal acts.

Quite a bit of attention has been paid to the age-crime relationship. There is general agreement that delinquency rates decline with age. Some experts believe this phenomenon is universal, while others believe that a small group of offenders persists in crime at a high rate.

The age-crime relationship has spurred research on the nature of delinquency over the life course. One discovery is the chronic persistent offender, who begins his offending career early in life and persists as an adult. The Gluecks first identified the traits of persistent offenders. Wolfgang and his colleagues identified chronic offenders in a series of cohort studies conducted in Philadelphia. Ongoing research has identified the characteristics of persistent offenders as they mature. There seem to be both personality and social factors that predict long-term offending patterns.

KEY TERMS

chronic
life course
aggregate
aging out
desistance
spontaneous remission
age of onset

longitudinal studies
life history
chronic delinquent offender
serious career offender type
life cycle of crime
pathways
problem behavior syndrome

QUESTIONS FOR DISCUSSION

1. What factors contribute to the aging-out process?
2. Why are males more delinquent than females? Is it a matter of life-style, culture, or physical properties?
3. Discuss the racial differences found in the crime rate. What factors account for the differences in the black and white crime rates?
4. Discuss the controversy surrounding the role social class plays in delinquency. Do you believe that middle-class youth are as delinquent as lower-class boys?
5. What can be done to control the chronic delinquent? Is it fair to punish someone because he or she fits the profile of a potential repeat offender?

NOTES

1. Cesare Lombroso, *The Female Offender* (New York: Appleton, 1920); W. I. Thomas, *The Unadjusted Girl* (New York: Harper & Row, 1923).

2. Chapter 5 will discuss the work of Albert Cohen and Richard Cloward and Lloyd Ohlin, who stress delinquent behavior as a product of youth sub-culture.

3. Cited in David Farrington, "Juvenile Delinquency," in John Coleman, *The School Years* (London: Routledge, 1992), p. 132.

4. For a discussion of sex bias, see Meda Chesney-Lind, "Guilty by Reason of Sex: Young Women and the Criminal Justice System" (Paper presented before the American Society of Criminology, Toronto, 1980).

5. Michael Hindelang, Travis Hirschi, and Joseph Weis, *Measuring Delinquency* (Beverly Hills, Calif.: Sage, 1981); Gary Jensen and Raymond Eve, "Sex Differences in Delinquency: An Examination of Popular Sociological Explanation," *Criminology* 13:427-48 (1976); Michael Hindelang, "Age, Sex, and the Versatility of Delinquent Involvements," *Social Problems* 18:522-35 (1979); James Short and F. Ivan Nye, "Extent of Unrecorded Juvenile Delinquency, Tentative Conclusions," *Journal of Criminal Law, Criminology, and Police Science* 49:296-302 (1958).

6. Rosemary Sarri, "Gender Issues in Juvenile Justice," *Crime and Delinquency* 29:381-97 (1983).

7. For a review, see Meda Chesney-Lind and Randall Shelden, *Girls Delinquency and Juvenile Justice* (Pacific Grove, Calif.: Brooks/Cole, 1992), pp. 7-14.

8. Leroy Gould, "Who Defines Delinquency? A Comparison of Self-Report and Officially-Reported Indices of Delinquency for Three Racial Groups," *Social Problems* 16:325-36 (1969); Harwin Voss, "Ethnic Differentials in Delinquency in Honolulu," *Journal of Criminal Law, Criminology, and Police Science* 54:322-27 (1963); Ronald Akers, Marvin Krohn, Marcia Radosevich, and Lonn Lanza-Kaduce, "Social Characteristics and Self-Reported Delinquency," in Gary Jensen, ed., *Sociology of Delinquency* (Beverly Hills, Calif.: Sage, 1981), pp. 48-62.

9. Jerald Bachman, Lloyd Johnston, and Patrick O'Malley, *Monitoring the Future: Questionnaire Responses from the Nation's High School Seniors, 1986* (Ann Arbor, Mich.: Institute for Social Research, 1988), pp. 102-4.

10. David Huizinga and Delbert Elliott, "Juvenile Offenders: Prevalence, Offender Incidence, and Arrest Rates by Race," *Crime and Delinquency* 33:206-23 (1987). See also Dale Dannefer and Russell Schutt, "Race and Juvenile Justice Processing in Court and Police Agencies," *American Journal of Sociology* 87:1113-32 (1982).

11. Paul Tracy, "Race and Class Differences in Official and Self-Reported Delinquency," in Marvin Wolfgang, Terrence Thornberry, and Robert Figlio, eds., *From Boy to Man, from Delinquency to Crime* (Chicago: University of Chicago Press, 1987), p. 120.

12. For a general review, see Carl Pope and William Feyerherm, "Minority Status and Juvenile Justice Processing (Part I)," *Criminal Justice Abstracts* 22:327-35 (1990); see also Douglas Smith and Jody Klein, "Police Control of Interpersonal Disputes," *Social Problems* 31:468-81 (1984); Dannefer and Schutt, "Race and Juvenile Justice Processing in Court and Police Agencies."

13. Donna Bishop and Charles Frazier, "The Influence of Race in Juvenile Justice Processing," *Journal of Research in Crime and Delinquency* 25:242-63 (1989).

14. For a general review, see William Wilbanks, *The Myth of a Racist Criminal Justice System* (Monterey, Calif.: Brooks Cole, 1987).

15. Daniel Georges-Abeyie, cited in James Byrne and Robert Sampson, *The Social Ecology of Crime* (New York: Springer-Verlag, 1986), p. 99.

16. Tom Joe, "Economic Inequality: The Picture in Black and White," *Crime and Delinquency* 33:287-99 (1987).

17. Troy Duster, "Crime, Youth Unemployment, and the Black Urban Underclass," *Crime and Delinquency* 33:300-16 (1987); Joe, "Economic Inequality."

18. Duster, "Crime, Youth Unemployment, and the Black Urban Underclass" pp. 301-3.

19. Carl Pope and William Feyerherm, "Minority Status and Juvenile Processing: An Assessment of the Research Literature" (Paper presented at the American Society of Criminology, Reno, Nevada, November 1989).

20. Jefferey Fagan, Elizabeth Piper, and Melinda Moore, "Violent Delinquents and Urban Youths," *Criminology* 24:439-71 (1986).

21. Robert Nash Parker and Allan Horwitz, "Unemployment, Crime, and Imprisonment: A Panel Approach," *Criminology* 24:751-73 (1986).

22. For a general review of these issues, see James Byrne and Robert Sampson, *The Social Ecology of Crime* (New York: Springer-Verlag, 1986).

23. John Braithwaite, "The Myth of Social Class and Criminality Reconsidered," *American Sociological Review* 46:36-57 (1981).

24. James Short and Ivan Nye, "Reported Behavior as a Criterion of Deviant Behavior," *Social Problems* 5:207-13 (1958).

25. Ivan Nye, James Short, and Virgil Olsen, "Socioeconomic Status and Delinquent Behavior," *American Journal of Sociology* 63:381-89 (1958); Robert Dentler and Lawrence Monroe, "Social Correlates of Early Adolescent Theft," *American Sociological Review* 26:733-43 (1961); John Clark and Eugene Wenninger, "Socioeconomic Class and Areas as Correlates of Illegal Behavior among Juveniles," *American Sociological Review* 27:826-34 (1962); William Arnold, "Continuities in Research: Scaling Delinquent Behavior," *Social Problems* 13:59-66 (1965); LaMar Empey and Maynard Erickson, "Hidden Delinquency and Social Status," *Social Forces* 44:1546-54 (1966); Ronald Akers, "Socioeconomic Status and Delinquent Behavior: A Retest," *Journal of Research in Crime and Delinquency* 1:38-46 (1964); Voss, "Ethnic Differentials in Delinquency in Honolulu."

26. Gold, "Undetected Delinquent Behavior", *Journal of Research in Crime and Delinquency* 3:35-41 (1966); Jay Williams and Martin Gold, "From Delinquent Behavior

to Official Delinquency," *Social Problems* 20:209‑29 (1972).

27. Douglas Smith and G. Roger Jarjoura, "Social Structure and Criminal Victimization," *Journal of Research in Crime and Delinquency* 25:25‑72 (1988).

28. Charles Tittle, Wayne Villemez, and Douglas Smith, "The Myth of Social Class and Criminality: An Empirical Assessment of the Empirical Evidence," *American Sociological Review* 43:643‑56 (1978).

29. Charles Tittle and Robert Meier, "Specifying the SES/Delinquency Relationship by Social Characteristics of Contexts," *Journal of Research in Crime and Delinquency* 28:430‑55 (1991); idem, "Specifying the SES/Delinquency Relationship," *Criminology* 28:271‑99 (1990).

30. For supporting research, see Gary Jensen and Kevin Thompson, "What's Class Got to Do with It? A Further Examination of Power‑Control Theory," *American Journal of Sociology* 95:1009‑23 (1990); Paul Tracy, "Race and Class Differences in Official and Self‑Reported Delinquency," in Marvin Wolfgang, Terrence Thornberry, and Robert Figlio eds., *From Boy to Man, from Delinquency to Crime* (Chicago: University of Chicago Press, 1987), p. 118.

31. Delbert Eliott and Suzanne Ageton, "Reconciling Race and Class Differences in Self‑Reported and Official Estimates of Delinquency," *American Sociological Review* 45:95‑110 (1980). For a similar view, see John Braithwaite, "The Myth of Social Class and Criminality Reconsidered," *American Sociological Review* 46:35‑58 (1981).

32. Margaret Farnworth, Terence Thornberry, Marvin Krohn, and Alan Lizotte, *Measurement in the Study of Class and Delinquency: Integrating Theory and Research*, working paper no. 4, rev. (Albany, N.Y.: Rochester Youth Development Survey, 1992), p. 19.

33. David Brownfield, "Social Class and Violent Behavior," *Criminology* 24:421‑38 (1986).

34. Simon Singer and Susyan Jou, "Specifying the SES/Delinquency Relationship by Subjective and Objective Indicators of Parental and Youth Social Status" (Paper presented at the annual meeting of the American Society of Criminology, New Orleans, Louisiana, November 1992).

35. See, generally, David Farrington, "Age and Crime," in Michael Tonry and Norval Morris, eds., *Crime and Justice, An Annual Review*, vol. 7 (Chicago: University of Chicago Press, 1986), pp. 189‑250.

36. Census data is from U.S. Department of Commerce, *Estimates of the Population of the United States by Age, Sex, Race: 1990* (Washington, D.C.: Government Printing Office, 1991).

37. Patrick O'Malley, Jerald Bachman, and Lloyd Johnston, "Period, Age and Cohort Effects on Substance Abuse among Young Americans: A Decade of Change, 1976‑1986," *American Journal of Public Health* 78:1315‑21 (1989); Darrell Steffensmeier, Emilie Allan, Miles Harer,

and Cathy Streifel, "Age and the Distribution of Crime," *American Journal of Sociology* 94:803‑31 (1989); Alfred Blumstein and Jacqueline Cohen, "Characterizing Criminal Careers," *Science* 237:985‑91 (1987).

38. John Laub, David Clark, Leslie Siegel, and James Garofalo, *Trends in Juvenile Crime in the United States: 1973‑1983* (Albany, N.Y.: Hindelang Criminal Justice Research Center, preliminary draft, 1987).

39. Travis Hirschi and Michael Gottfredson, "Age and the Explanation of Crime," *American Journal of Sociology* 89:552‑84 (1983).

40. Michael Gottfredson and Travis Hirschi, "The True Value of Lambda Would Appear to Be Zero: An Essay on Career Criminals, Criminal Careers, Selective Incapacitation, Cohort Studies, and Related Topics," *Criminology* 24:213‑34 (1986); further support for their position can be found in Lawrence Cohen and Kenneth Land," Age Structure and Crime," *American Sociological Review* 52:170‑83 (1987).

41. David Greenberg, "Age, Crime and Social Explanation," *American Journal of Sociology* 91:1‑21 (1985).

42. Robert Sampson and John Laub, *Crime in the Making: Pathways and Turning Points Through Life* (Cambridge: Harvard University Press, 1993).

43. Farrington, "Age and Crime," pp. 236‑37.

44. Marvin Wolfgang, Robert Figlio, and Thorsten Sellin, *Delinquency in a Birth Cohort* (Chicago: University of Chicago Press, 1972); Lyle Shannon, *Assessing the Relationship of Adult Criminal Careers to Juvenile Careers: A Summary* (Washington, D.C.: U.S. Department of Justice, 1982); D.J. West and David P. Farrington, *The Delinquent Way of Life* (London: Hienemann, 1977); Donna Hamparian, Richard Schuster, Simon Dinitz, and John Conrad, *The Violent Few* (Lexington, Mass.: Lexington Books, 1978).

45. Rolf Loeber and Howard Snyder, "Rate of Offending in Juvenile Careers: Findings of Constancy and Change in Lambda," *Criminology* 28:97‑109 (1990).

46. Travis Hirschi and Michael Gottfredson, "Age and Crime, Logic and Scholarship: Comment on Greenberg," *American Journal of Sociology* 91:22‑27 (1985); idem, "All Wise after the Fact Learning Theory, Again: Reply to Baldwin," *American Journal of Sociology* 90:1330‑33 (1985); John Baldwin, "Thrill and Adventure Seeking and the Age Distribution of Crime: Comment on Hirschi and Gottfredson," *American Journal of Sociology* 90:1326‑29 (1985).

47. O'Malley, Bachman, and Johnston, "Period, Age, and Cohort Effects on Substance Use among Young Americans."

48. D. Wayne Osgood, "The Covariation Among Adolescent Problem Behaviors" (Paper presented at the annual meetings of the American Society of Criminology, Baltimore, November 1990).

49. See, for example, Sheldon Glueck and Eleanor Glueck, *500 Criminal Careers* (New York: Knopf, 1930); idem,

One Thousand Juvenile Delinquents (Cambridge: Harvard University Press, 1934); idem, *Unraveling Juvenile Delinquency* (Cambridge: Harvard University Press, 1950).

50. Sheldon Glueck and Eleanor Glueck, *Predicting Delinquency and Crime* (Cambridge): Harvard University Press, 1967), pp. 82-83.

51. For a review of the Gluecks' careers, see John Laub and Robert Sampson, "The Sutherland-Glueck Debate: On the Sociology of Criminological Knowledge," *American Journal of Sociology* 96:1402-40 (1991).

52. John Laub and Robert Sampson, "Unraveling Families and Delinquency: A Reanalysis of the Gluecks' Data," *Criminology* 26:355-80 (1988).

53. Arnold Barnett, Alfred Blumstein, and David Farrington, "A Prospective Test of a Criminal Career Model," *Criminology* 27:373-88 (1989).

54. Marvin Wolfgang, Robert Figlio, and Thorsten Sellin, *Delinquency in a Birth Cohort* (Chicago: University of Chicago Press, 1972).

55. Marvin Wolfgang, Terence Thornberry and Robert Figlio, eds., *From Boy to Man, from Delinquency to Crime* (Chicago: University of Chicago Press, 1987); see also Paul Tracy and Robert Figlio, "Chronic Recidivism in the 1958 Birth Cohort" (Paper presented at the American Society of Criminology meeting, Toronto, October 1982), p. 3. This and the next sections lean heavily on this work.

56. Ibid., p. 34.

57. Paul Tracy, Marvin Wolfgang, and Robert Figlio, *Delinquency in Two Birth Cohorts, Executive Summary* (Washington, D.C.: U.S. Department of Justice, 1985).

58. See also D.J. West and David P. Farrington, *The Delinquent Way of Life* (London: Hienemann, 1977), p. 15; and Donna Hamparian, Richard Schuster, Simon Dinitz, and John Conrad, *The Violent Few* (Lexington, Mass.: Lexington Books, 1978).

59. Shannon, *Assessing the Relationship of Adult Criminal Careers to Juvenile Careers.*

60. Franklyn Dunford and Delbert Eliott, "Identifying Career Offenders Using Self-Reported Data," *Journal of Research in Crime and Delinquency* 21:57-86 (1984).

61. Howard Snyder, *Court Careers of Juvenile Offenders* (Washington, D.C.: Office of Juvenile Justice and Delinquency Prevention, 1988).

62. Ibid., p. 66.

63. Robert Sampson and John Laub, "Crime and Deviance in the Life Course", *American Review of Sociology* 18:63-84 (1992).

64. Farnworth, Thornberry, Krohn, and Lizotte, "Measurement in the Study of Class and Delinquency."

65. Joan McCord, "Family Relationships, Juvenile Delinquency, and Adult Criminality," *Criminology* 29:397-417 (1991).

66. Daniel Nagin and David Farrington, "The Onset and Persistence of Offending," *Criminology* 30:501-23 (1992).

67. David Rowe and Chester Britt, III, "Developmental Explanations of Delinquent Behavior among Siblings: Common Factor vs. Transmission Mechanisms," *Journal of Quantitative Criminology* 7:315-31 (1991).

68. Michael Gottfredson and Travis Hirschi, *A General Theory of Crime* (Stanford, Calif.: Stanford University Press, 1990).

69. Richard Jessor, "Risk Behavior in Adolescence: A Psychosocial Framework for Understanding and Action," in D. E. Rogers and E. Ginzburg, eds., *Adolescents at Risk: Medical and Social Perspectives* (Boulder, Colo.: Westview, 1992).

70. Rolf Loeber, Phen Wung, Kate Keenan, Bruce Giroux, Magda Stouthamer-Loeber, Wemoet Van Kammen, and Barbara Maughan, "Developmental Pathways in Disruptive Behavior," *Development and Psychopathology* (In Press, 1993).

71. Richard Jessor, John Donovan, and Francis Costa, *Beyond Adolescence: Problem Behavior and Young Adult Development* (New York : Cambridge University Press, 1991).

72. D. Wayne Osgood, "The Covariation among Adolescent Problem Behaviors" (Paper presented at the annual meeting of the American Society of Criminology, Baltimore, November 1990).

73. Helene Raskin White, "Early Problem Behavior and Later Drug Problems," *Journal of Research in Crime and Delinquency* 29:412-29 (1992).

74. Robert Bursik, "The Dynamics of Specialization in Juvenile Offenses," *Social Forces* 58:851-64 (1980).

75. Randall Shelden, "The Chronic Delinquent: Some Clarifications of a Vague Concept," *Juvenile and Family Court Journal* 40:37-44 (1989).

76. David Farrington, Howard Snyder, and Terrence Finnegan, "Specialization in Juvenile Court Careers," *Criminology* 26:461-85 (1988).

77. Ibid.

78. See, for example, the Rochester Youth Development Study, Hindelang Criminal Justice Research Center, 135 Western Avenue, Albany, New York 12222.

79. David Farrington, "The Development of Offending and Antisocial Behavior from Childhood to Adulthood" (Paper presented at the Congress on Rethinking Delinquency, University of Minho, Braga, Portugal, July 1992).

80. See, generally, D. J. West and David P. Farrington, *The Delinquent Way of Life* (London: Hienemann, 1977); the findings here are reported in David Farrington, "The Development of Offending and Antisocial Behavior from Childhood to Adulthood."

81. Sampson and Laub, *Crime in the Making: Pathways and Turning Points through Life;* John Laub and Robert Sampson, "Turning Points in the Life Course: Why Change Matters to the Study of Crime" (Paper presented at the annual meeting of the American Society of Criminology, New Orleans, Louisiana, November 1992).

82. Kimberly Kempf, "Crime Severity and Criminal Career Progression," *Journal of Criminal Law and Criminology* 79:524-40 (1988).

83. Jeffrey Fagan, "Social and Legal Policy Dimensions of Violent Juvenile Crime," *Criminal Justice and Behavior* 17:93-133 (1990).

84. Peter Greenwood, *Selective Incapacitation* (Santa Monica, Calif.: Rand Corp., 1982).

85. Andrew Von Hirsch and Donald Gottfredson, "Selective Incapacitation: Some Queries about Research Design and Equity," *New York University Review of Law and Social Change* 12:11-19 (1984).

86. Scott Decker and Barbara Salert, "Predicting the Career Criminal: An Empirical Test of the Greenwood Scale," *Journal of Criminal Law and Criminology* 77:215-36 (1986).

87. Pamela Tontodonato, "Explaining Rate Changes in Delinquent Arrest Transitions Using Event History Analysis," *Criminology* 26:439-59 (1988).

88. Kimberly Kempf, "Career Criminals in the 1958 Philadelphia Birth Cohort," *Criminal Justice Review* 15:212-35 (1990).

II THEORIES OF DELINQUENCY

■■■

What causes delinquent behavior? Why do some youths enter a life of crime that persists into their adulthood? Are people products of their environment, or is their life course determined at birth?

Social scientists have speculated on the cause of delinquency for two hundred years. They have organized observed facts about delinquent behavior into complex theoretical models. A theory is a statement that explains the relationship between abstract concepts in a meaningful way. For example, if scientists observe that delinquency rates are usually higher in neighborhoods with high unemployment rates, poor housing, and inadequate schools, they might theorize that environmental conditions influence delinquent behavior. This theory suggests that social conditions can exert a powerful influence on human behavior.

Since the study of delinquency is essentially interdisciplinary, it is not surprising that a variety of theoretical models have been formulated to explain juvenile misbehavior. Each reflects the training and orientation of its creator. Consequently, theories of delinquency reflect many different avenues of inquiry, including biology, psychology, sociology, political science, and economics. Chapter 4 reviews theories that hold that delinquency is essentially an individual factor, caused either by personal choices and decision making or by psychological and biological aspects of human development. Chapters 5, 6, and 7 review sociological theories of delinquency. Chapter 5 reviews those theories that hold that youthful misbehavior is caused by a child's place in the social structure; Chapter 6 covers theories that regard the child's relationships with social institutions and processes as the key to understanding delinquency. Chapter 7 views how delinquents may be the victim of class conflict and struggle. Finally, Chapter 8 reviews theories devoted specifically to the female delinquent.

To the student, the variety of delinquency theories is often confusing. Logic dictates that the competing and contradictory theoretical models presented here cannot all be correct. Yet every branch of social science—sociology, psychology, political science, economics—contains competing theoretical models. Why people behave the way they do and how society functions are issues that are far from being settled. So do not lose patience! Recognize that theories of delinquency are attempts to bring together existing knowledge in an attempt to explain the onset and patterns of delinquent behavior. These explanations take on different perspectives because it is possible to view the world and to explain similar facts and data differently. The variation in delinquency theories reflects their creators' interpretations of the world and of events. ■

FOCUS ON THE INDIVIDUAL

CHOICE, BIOSOCIAL AND PSYCHOLOGICAL
THEORIES

The dynamic center of the whole problem of delinquency and crime will never be the individual offender.
WILLIAM HEALY,
The Individual Delinquent (1915)

If delinquents were a "product of their environment," as some experts suggest, how is it possible that many at-risk youths residing in the most criminogenic neighborhoods live conventional, law-abiding lives? Conversely, why are so many middle-class youth involved in delinquency and substance abuse? Research on persistent offending indicates that relatively few youths in any population become hard-core delinquents.[1] The quality of neighborhood and family life may actually have little impact on individual behavior through the life cycle.[2] To some theorists, the factors that promote the onset of delinquency and sustain it through the life course are rooted in the individual: how each person makes decisions, his or her biological makeup, his or her personality and psychological profile. Research on delinquency shows that persistent offenders maintain a unique set of individual physical and personality traits that may cause or amplify their delinquency and prevent them from desisting.

More than one view exists on the relationship between individual traits and delinquent offending. One position, referred to as *choice theory,* suggests that young offenders engage in antisocial activity because they believe their actions will be beneficial and profitable. Whether they join a gang, steal cars, or sell drugs, their delinquent acts are motivated by the reasoned belief that crime can be a relatively risk-free way to better their personal situation. They have little fear of getting caught or of the consequences of punishment. Fantasies of riches produced by criminal acts fuel their antisocial activities.

All youthful misbehavior, however, cannot be traced to choice, the profit motive, and criminal entrepreneurship. Some delinquent acts, especially violent ones, seem irrational, selfish, and/or hedonistic. Many forms of delinquency, such as substance abuse and vandalism, appear more impulsive than rational. It is believed that these antisocial behaviors may be inspired by aberrant physical or psychological traits that govern behavioral choices. While some youths may choose to commit crime simply because they desire conventional luxuries and power, others may be influenced by constitutional abnormalities, such as hyperactivity, low intelligence, biochemical imbalance, or genetic defects. This view of delinquency is referred to here generally as biosocial and psychological theory because it links delinquency to biological and psychological traits and environmental conditions that control human development.

Choice and biosocial and psychological theories share common ground because they focus on the individual's mental and behavioral processes. However, neither view is meant to explain all delinquent acts. Not even the most ardent biosocial and psychological theorist would argue that all delinquents are physically or mentally abnormal, nor would a choice advocate hold that all delinquents commit crime after carefully weighing the chance for profit. Rather, delinquency experts who focus on the individual argue that biological and psychological traits and decision-making capability should not be ignored when seeking valid explanations of delinquent behavior over the life course. While some delinquents may be purely a "product of their environment," others are motivated by forces ingrained in their personality and biological makeup.

Part II Theories of Delinquency

This chapter first covers those theoretical models that focus on individual choice. Then, it discusses the view that the biological and psychological development of some youngsters makes them violent, aggressive, and antisocial. Finally, it analyzes an attempt to integrate individual choice and trait factors into a singular view of delinquent behavior causation.

CHOICE THEORY AND DELINQUENCY

The first formal explanations of crime and delinquency held that human behavior was a matter of choice. Since it was assumed that people had *free will* to choose their behavior, those who violated the law were motivated by personal needs: greed, revenge, survival, hedonism. Over two hundred years ago, *utilitarian* philosophers *Cesare Beccaria* and *Jeremy Bentham* argued that people weigh the benefits and consequences of their future actions before deciding on a course of behavior.[3] Their writings formed the core of what is today referred to as *classical criminology.*

The classical view of crime and delinquency holds that the decision to violate the law comes after a careful weighing of the benefits and costs of criminal behaviors. Most potential law violators would cease their actions if the potential pain associated with a behavior outweighed its anticipated gain; conversely, law-violating behavior becomes attractive if the future rewards seem far greater than the potential punishment.[4]

According to the classical view, youths who decide to become a drug dealer weigh and compare the possible benefits, such as cash to buy cars, clothes and other luxury items, with the potential penalties, such as arrest followed by a long stay in a juvenile facility. If they believe that drug dealers are rarely caught and even then usually avoid severe punishments, the youths will more likely choose to become dealers than if they believe that dealers are almost always caught and punished by lengthy prison terms. Put simply, in order to deter or prevent crime, the pain of punishment must outweigh the benefit of illegal gain.[5]

The classical criminologists argued that punishment should be only severe enough to deter a particular offense and that punishments should be graded according to the seriousness of particular crimes: "Let the punishment fit the crime." For example, Beccaria argued that it would be foolish to punish pickpockets and murderers in a similar fashion because this would encourage thieves to kill the victims or witnesses to their crimes.[6] The popularity of the classical approach was in part responsible for the development of the prison as an alternative to physical punishment and the eventual creation of criminal sentences geared to the seriousness of crimes.[7] The choice approach dominated the policy of the U.S. justice system for about 150 years.

By the mid-twentieth century, the concept of the "rational criminal" was challenged by those who believed that crime and delinquency were products of social forces, such as environment and socialization. Breakthroughs in psychology and sociology showed that human behavior was often controlled by outside influences, such as family, school, and peer relations, and that the concept of free will was merely wishful thinking. Mental health professionals argued that delinquents should be treated and not punished for their misdeeds. Delinquents were viewed as troubled or "sick" individuals who needed *rehabilitation,* rather than punishment; this was known as the *medical model* of crime.[8] Rather than

According to rational choice theory, young criminals calculate the benefits and disadvantages of crime before deciding to attack a victim.

being punished in prisons for their crimes, youthful (and adult) criminals were offered rehabilitation in secure treatment facilities until they were deemed fit to return to society. Since this position was particularly amenable to the juvenile justice system's *parens patriae* philosophy, the concept of "punishing" delinquents all but disappeared during the twentieth century.[9]

THE RATIONAL DELINQUENT

In the past few years, the view that delinquents choose to violate the law has regained prominence as a theoretical approach to the study and control of delinquency. Its reemergence can be traced to a number of trends. Conservatives have viewed efforts to treat known delinquents by treatment, counseling, and other rehabilitation strategies as failures. To some experts, the failure of treatment-oriented programs is a signal that delinquency is not a function of social ills, such as a lack of economic opportunity or family dysfunction. If it were, then educational enrichment, family counseling, job training programs, and the like should be more effective alternatives to crime.

The reasoning goes that if youths are not amenable to treatment for their social ills (since they are not really social victims), then they may be more receptive to the threat of punishments that will "scare" them into choosing conventional over criminal behaviors (since their behavior choices are controlled by the perception of a negative outcome). Well-known social scientists James Q. Wilson and Richard Herrnstein conclude in their controversial book *Crime and Human Nature* that delinquent behavior is deterrable if offenders experience first-hand the consequences of their behavior:

That is, a person may become less likely to commit an offense either because he has learned (by experiencing punishment) that certain consequences of that offense are more likely than he had once supposed or because he has come to take more seriously the consequences (again, by having experienced them) that he knew were attached to that behavior.[10]

The rational choice approach has also been supported by the well-publicized resurgence of youth gang activity (see Chapter 10 for more on gangs). The emergence of gangs and their involvement in the drug trade strengthens the case for rational choice: these young, well-armed entrepreneurs are seeking to cash in on a lucrative, albeit illegal, "business enterprise." These delinquent youths are constantly processing information to make profitable trading decisions: Will this act turn a profit? Is it good for my career? What are the consequences? How will my competitors react? What do my clients want?[11]

The alleged failure of treatment and the prominence of drug-dealing gangs made it reasonable to view delinquents as individuals who are responsible for their actions and who might respond better to the fear of punish than to the preventive influence of rehabilitative treatment. Choice theory reemerged as a force both in the study of the causes of delinquency and as a guide for creating policies to control delinquent behavior.[12] In sum, those who embraced the utility of punishment as a delinquency control mechanism consider the delinquent to be a rational person who is willing and able to consider the consequences of his or her action before making a decision.

The Concept of Rational Choice

The concept that crime and delinquency is a function of the opportunities presented to motivated offenders has received widespread support from prominent social scientists.[13] Law-violating behavior is viewed as an event that occurs when an offender decides to take the chance of violating the law after considering his or her personal situation (need for money, learning experiences, opportunities for conventional success), values (conscience, moral values, need for peer approval), and situational factors (how well the target is protected, whether people are at home, how wealthy the neighborhood is, the likelihood of getting caught, the punishment if apprehended) (See Figure 4.1). Accordingly, the decision to commit a specific type of crime and the subsequent entry into a criminal life-style is a matter of personal decision making based on a weighing of available information; hence, the term *rational choice*. For example, Felix Padilla observed "rational" delinquency in his study of the activities of contemporary gang boys involved in drug trafficking. Padilla found that gangs are like "employers" who can provide their business associates with security and know-how to conduct "business deals." Gang membership helps kids achieve financial success

The decision to commit
delinquent acts

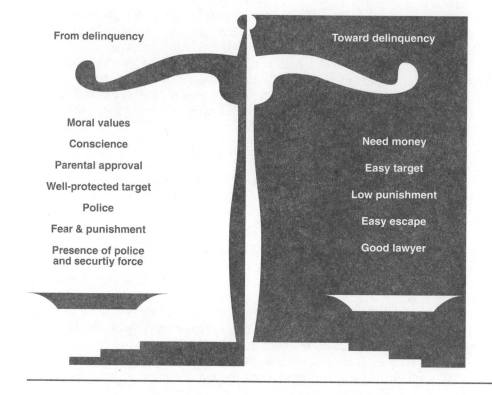

From delinquency

Moral values
Conscience
Parental approval
Well-protected target
Police
Fear & punishment
Presence of police
and securtiy force

Toward delinquency

Need money
Easy target
Low punishment
Easy escape
Good lawyer

that would otherwise be impossible. As do legitimate business enterprises, some gangs actively recruit new personnel and cut deals with rivals over products and territory.[14] Padilla's research is discussed further in Chapter 10.

Conversely, the decision to forgo law-violating behavior may be based on the person's perception that the economic benefits are no longer there or the probability of successfully completing a crime is less than the chances of being caught and punished. For example, the aging-out process may occur because old offenders desist after they realize that the risks of crime are greater than its potential profit. The solution to crime, therefore, may be the formulation of policies that will cause the potential criminal to choose conventional behaviors over criminal ones.

Choosing Delinquency

No matter how pathological or socially maladjusted youths may be, there are rational components to their personalities that allow them to choose one target or crime method over another. The focus, then, is on the crime and not the offender: for example, how can the commission of a burglary in a wealthy suburb be explained? How does it differ from one in an inner-city housing project? What can be done to prevent each type of burglary? Rational choice views the concept of crime and criminality as two separate issues. Criminality is the "relatively stable differences among individuals in their propensity to engage in criminal or equivalent acts."[15] Crimes are events that are in violation of the criminal law. The reasons why a person becomes a delinquent are quite distinct from the reasons a delinquent decides to break into a particular house one day or sell narcotics the next.

The "Seductions of Crime"

In a recent book, sociologist Jack Katz argues that there are **"seductions of crime"** that result from the thrills and benefits provided by delinquent acts.[16] These situational inducements directly precede the commission of a delinquent act and propel offenders into law violations: someone challenges their authority or moral position and they vanquish their opponent with a beating; they want to maximize their pleasure by doing something exciting so they break into and vandalize a school building.

According to Katz, choosing crime satisfies the need to relieve emotional upheavals brought about by moral challenges. Gang boys are rejecting society's expectations that they become conventional adults. They violently defend meaningless turf boundaries and get into brawls in an effort to show their indifference to social expectations. For many youngsters, shoplifting and vandalism are attractive because "getting away with it" is a thrilling demonstration of personal competence, especially when the crime is consummated under the eyes of an adult. Young killers are choosing to carry on like the avenging gods of mythology, electing to have life or death control over their victims.

Katz finds that the central theme in the choice to commit crime is one of situational inducements for emotional upheaval: humiliation, righteousness, arrogance, ridicule, cynicism, defilement, and vengeance. For example, the assailant interprets the victim's behavior as disrespectful and humiliating, and violence is a way of expressing her resulting rage. When the drunk at a party is told to "shut up and go home" because she is disturbing people, she responds, "So, I'm acting like a fool, am I?" Public embarrassment leads to action: she must "sacrifice" or injure the body of the victim to maintain her "honor."[17]

Katz's view that situational inducements play an important role in causing adolescents' misbehavior has been supported by recent research conducted with street kids in Toronto, Canada, by Bill McCarthy and John Hagan.[18] Among street kids, motives to commit crime are linked to survival rather than emotional issues: the need for food, shelter, employment. Kids steal for food and become prostitutes because they cannot get jobs. The problems of street life, then, are a function of the conditions on the street itself; crime has an immediate and rational cause.

ROUTINE ACTIVITIES

To some crime experts, the concept of the "motivated offender" is insufficient to explain the cause of crime and delinquency. They argue that illegal behavior is tied not only to the rational and cunning acts of an offender but also to the behavior of both potential victims and those who are charged with guarding them, for example, police officers. Crime may occur not only because a criminal decides to break the law but also because a victim is in "the wrong place at the wrong time" and the police are not around.[19]

One of the most prominent examples of this view is *routine activity theory,* developed by Lawrence Cohen and Marcus Felson.[20] Cohen and Felson assume that the motivation to commit crime and the supply of offenders is constant.[21] Consequently, the volume and distribution of *predatory crime* (violent crimes against the person and crimes in which an offender attempts to steal an object directly from its holder) are closely related to the interaction of three variables that reflect the routine activities found in everyday American life: the availability of *suitable targets* (such as homes containing easily salable goods); the absence of *capable guardians* (such as home owners and their neighbors, friends, and relatives); and the presence of *motivated offenders* (such as unemployed teenagers). If each of these components is present, the likelihood that a predatory crime will take place is greater. (see Figure 4.2).

Cohen and Felson have used the routine activities approach to explain the changes in the crime and delinquency rate since 1960. They argue that one reason the crime rate has increased is that the number of adult caretakers at home during the day (guardians) has been decreasing because of expanded female participation in the work force. Since mothers are at work and children are in day care, homes are left unguarded and become more "suitable targets." Similarly, with the growth of suburbia and the decline of the traditional neighborhood, the number of such familiar "guardians" as family, neighbors, and friends has diminished. Research conducted in the United States and other countries has confirmed this hypothesis.[22]

■■ **FIGURE 4.2**

Routine activities

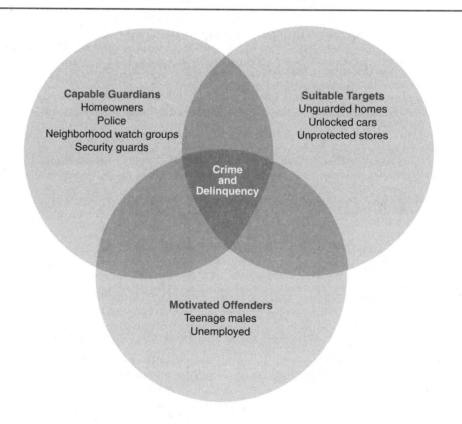

　　　　Part II   Theories of Delinquency

Another influence on the crime rate is the growth of easily transportable wealth, which has created a greater number of available targets. Research has generally supported the fact that the more wealth a home contains, the more likely it will be a crime target.[23] In one study, Cohen and his associates linked burglary rates to color television set purchases, reasoning that the more these high-priced and easily sold goods are available, the more offenders will be "motivated" to steal.[24]

Routine activity theory also links the delinquency rates to social changes that increase the number and motivation of offenders. Robert O'Brien found that delinquency rates will increase if there is a surplus of youths of the same age category all competing for a limited number of jobs and educational opportunities. For example, if during any given year there are too many 17-year-olds for the number of available part-time and after-school jobs, the supply of motivated offenders may be increased simply because many potential offenders are competing for a limited number of legitimate resources.[25]

A critical component of the routine activities approach is that it gives equal weight to the role of both the victim and the offender in the crime process. While Cohen and Felson hold that predatory crime is a matter of rational choice, they also maintain that criminal opportunity is significantly influenced by the victim's *life-style* and behavior. Other research efforts have substantiated this claim. For example, Steven Messner and Kenneth Tardiff studied patterns of urban homicide and found that a person's life-style significantly influenced his or her victimization: people who tended to stay at home were the ones most likely to be killed by family or friends, while those who went out more often were victimized by strangers.[26] In a recent study, Leslie Kennedy and David Forde found that lower-class young males who go to bars, work or go to class, or walk or drive at night are the most likely to become crime victims.[27] Put another way, the greater the opportunity there is for criminals and victims to interact, the greater the probability of crime; reduce the interaction, and the opportunity for crime will decline.[28]

DETERRENCE THEORY

The core of choice theory is that youths choose to commit crimes. The **deterrence** concept holds that their choice can be controlled or deterred by the threat of punishment. Put another way, only if kids come to fear the power of the law, to believe that their illegal behaviors will be met with certain and severe sanctions, will they forgo the benefits of outlawed activities, such as substance abuse and theft.[29]

One of the guiding principles of deterrence theory is that *the more severe, certain, and swift the punishment, the greater its deterrent effect will be.*[30] For example, there will be relatively little deterrent effect, even though a particular crime is punished quite severely, if most people do not believe they will be caught.[31] Conversely, even a mild sanction may be sufficient to deter crime if people believe that punishment is certain. And even the most severe sanctions will have little deterrent effect if they are slow, delayed, and easily put off.

Can a deterrence strategy work with juvenile offenders? The juvenile justice system has been reluctant to incorporate deterrence-based punishments on the grounds that they interfere with its stated *parens patriae* philosophy. Yet, in recent years, the increase in teenage violence, gang activity, and drug abuse has prompted a reevaluation of deterrence strategies. Consequently, police have been more willing to use aggressive tactics, such as gang busting units, to deter membership in drug trafficking gangs; juvenile court judges have been willing to waive youths to adult courts and place ever greater numbers of them in secure treatment programs; legislators seem willing to pass more restrictive juvenile codes; and the U.S. Supreme Court has upheld the use of the death penalty for youths over 16.[32]

Can deterrence strategies work? This issue generates considerable debate. A number of studies have contributed data supportive of deterrence concepts. Evidence indicates that the threat of police arrest can deter property crimes.[33] Areas of the country in which punishment is more certain seem to have lower delinquency rates; the more likely people are to perceive that they will be punished for a crime, the less likely they are to engage in that activity.[34] The deterrent effect of apprehension and punishment, however, is usually slight and certainly less than projected by deterrence theory.[35] Little reason exists to believe that crime and delinquency can be eliminated merely by the fear of legal punishment alone.[36] More evidence exists that fear of social disapproval and informal penalties, criticisms, and punishments from parents and friends may actually be a greater deterrent to crime than legal punishments.[37]

Deterring Delinquency

Deterring juvenile delinquency may present a greater problem than deterring adult criminality. Minors are subject to far more lenient sanctions than adults and by definition are less capable of making mature judgments about their behavior choices. It seems futile, therefore, to try to deter delinquency through fear of punishment. Research indicates that many offenders are under the influence of drugs and/or alcohol when they break the law, a condition that might impair their decision-making ability.[38] Similarly, juveniles often commit crimes in groups, and peer pressure can outweigh the deterrent effect of the law.

Research by Maynard Erickson and Jack Gibbs suggests that deterrence efforts may have little success with delinquent offenders.[39] First, they found that youths do not report being deterred by the threat of a one-year jail sentence any more than they would be by losing spending money or having a 7 P.M. curfew. Second, adults do not seem willing to support a policy of harsh punishments for juveniles, which would be needed to produce a deterrent effect. Finally, Erickson and Gibbs could not find a clear-cut relationship between perceived certainty of punishment and delinquency rates.

Thus, while on the surface deterrence appears to have benefit as a delinquency control device, there is also reason to believe that it has limited demonstrable effectiveness.

CHOICE THEORY IN REVIEW

Regardless of their form, choice theories have at their core a motivated offender who breaks the law because he or she perceives an abundance of benefits and an absence of threat. Increase the threat and reduce the benefits, and the crime rate should move ever downward.

This logic is hard to refute. After all, by definition, a person who commits an illegal act but is not rational cannot be considered a criminal or delinquent but instead is "not guilty by reason of insanity." To say that delinquents choose their crimes is for the most part entirely logical. Yet several questions remain unanswered by choice theorists. First, why do some people continually choose to break the law even after suffering its consequences, while others are content with living law-abiding yet indigent lives; that is, how can "the good boy in the high crime area" be explained?[40] Conversely, why do millionaires, such as Ivan Boesky and Leona Helmsley, break the law when they have everything to lose and little more to gain?

Choice theorists also have problems explaining seemingly irrational crimes, such as vandalism, arson, and even drug abuse. To say a teenager painted swatiskas on a synagogue after making a "rational choice" seems inadequate to explain such a destructive, unbeneficial act.

The relationships observed by rational choice theorists can be explained in other ways. For example, while the high victimization rates in lower-class neighborhoods can be explained by an oversupply of "motivated offenders," they may also be due to other factors, such as social conflict and disorganization.[41]

In sum, choice theories have utility as a way to understand criminal events and victim patterns. However, the question remains, why are some people "motivated" to commit crime and delinquency while others in similar circumstances remain law-abiding? Why do some people choose crime over legal activities?

BIOSOCIAL AND PSYCHOLOGICAL THEORY

Why, then, do delinquents *choose* crime over law-abiding behavior? A faithful and loyal choice theorist would answer that selecting crime is a function of carefully weighing the benefits of criminal over legal behavior. For example, youths decide to commit a robbery if they believe they will make a good profit, have a good chance of getting away, and, even if caught, stand little chance of being severely punished.

A number of delinquency experts believe that this model is incomplete. They believe it is wrong to infer that all youths choose crime simply because they believe its advantages outweigh its risks. These experts argue that human behavioral choices are a function of an individual's mental and/or physical makeup. Most law-abiding youths have personal traits that keep them within the mainstream of conventional society. In contrast, youths who choose to engage in repeated aggressive, antisocial, or conflict-oriented behavior manifest abnormal traits that influence their behavior choices.[42] Uncontrollable, impulsive behavior patterns place some youths at odds with society, and they soon find themselves in trouble with the law. In sum, while delinquents may choose their actions, the decision is a product of all but uncontrollable mental and physical properties and traits.

The view that delinquents are somehow "abnormal" is not a new one. Some of the earliest theories of criminal and delinquent behavior stressed that crime was a product of personal traits and that measurable physical and mental conditions, such as IQ and body build, determined behavior. This view is generally referred to today as *positivism*. Positivists believe that the scientific method can be used to measure the causes of human behavior and that behavior is a function of often uncontrollable factors, such as mental illness.

The issue of behavioral control is one significant difference between trait and choice theories: while the former reasons that behavior is controlled by personal traits, the latter views behavior as purely a product of human reasoning. To a choice theorist, reducing the benefits of crime by increasing the likelihood and severity of punishment will eventually lower the crime rate; biosocial and psychological theory focuses less on the effects of punishment and more on the treatment of abnormal mental and physical conditions as a crime-reduction method.

In the following sections, the primary components of trait theory are reviewed.

The Origins of Biosocial and Psychological Theory

The first attempts to discover why criminal tendencies develop focused on the physical makeup of offenders. Biological traits present at birth were thought to predetermine whether people would live a life of crime.

The origin of this school of thought is generally credited to the Italian physician Cesare Lombroso (1835–1909).[43] Known as the father of criminology, Lombroso put his many years of medical research to use in his theory of *criminal atavism*.[44] Lombroso found that delinquents manifest physical anomalies that make them biologically and physiologically similar to our primitive ancestors. These atavistic individuals are savage throwbacks to an earlier stage of human evolution. Because of this link, the "born criminal" has such physical traits as enormous jaws, strong canines, a flattened nose, and supernumerary teeth (double rows, as in snakes). Lombroso made such statements as "it was easy to understand why the span of the arms in criminals so often exceeds the height, for this is a characteristic of apes, whose forelimbs are used in walking and climbing."[45]

Contemporaries of Lombroso refined the notion of a physical basis of crime. Raffaele Garofalo (1851–1934) shared Lombroso's belief that certain physical characteristics indicate a criminal or delinquent nature.[46] Enrico Ferri (1856–1929), a student of Lombroso, believed that a number of biological, social, and organic factors caused delinquency and crime. While Ferri accepted the validity of the biological approach to explaining criminal activity, he attempted to interweave physical, anthropological, and social factors into his explanation of the causes of illegal behavior.[47] The English criminologist Charles Goring (1870–1919) challenged the validity of Lombroso's research and claimed instead that delinquent behaviors bore a significant relationship to a condition he referred to as "defective intelligence."[48] Consequently, Goring believed that delinquent behavior was inherited and could therefore best be controlled by regulating the reproduction of families exhibiting such traits as "feeble-mindedness, epilepsy, insanity, and defective social instinct."[49]

Advocates of the inheritance school studied the family trees of criminal and delinquent offenders. They traced the activities of several generations of families believed to have an especially large number of criminal members. The most famous of these studies involved the Jukes and the Kallikaks. Richard Dugdale's *The Jukes: A Study in Crime, Pauperism, Disease, and Heredity* (1875) and Arthur Estabrook's later work *The Jukes in 1915* traced the history of the Jukes, a family responsible for a disproportionate amount of crime.[50]

Advocates of the body-build, or **somatotype,** school argued that delinquents and criminals manifest distinct physiques that make them susceptible to particular types of delinquent behavior.[51] William H. Sheldon linked body type to delinquency.[52] *Mesomorphs* have well-developed muscles and an athletic appearance. They are active, aggressive, sometimes violent, and the most likely to become delinquents. *Endomorphs* have heavy builds and are slow-moving and lethargic. *Ectomorphs* are tall and thin and less social and more intellectual than the other types.[53]

These early views portrayed delinquent behavior as a function of a single factor or trait, such as body build or defective intelligence. They had a significant impact on early American criminology, which relied heavily on developing a science of "criminal anthropology."[54] Eventually, these views evoked criticism for their unsound methodology and lack of proper scientific controls. Many used captive offender populations and failed to compare experimental subjects with nondelinquents or undetected delinquents.[55] These omissions make it impossible to determine if biological traits produce delinquency. It is equally plausible that police are more likely to arrest, and courts convict, the mentally and physically abnormal. By the middle of the twentieth century, biological theories had fallen out of favor as an explanation of delinquency.

Contemporary Biosocial and Psychological Theory

For most of the twentieth century, delinquency experts scoffed at the notion that a youth's behavior was controlled by physical conditions present at birth. During this period, the majority of delinquency research focused on the social factors, such as poverty and family life, that were believed to be responsible for law-violating behavior. However, a small group of criminologists and penologists kept alive the biological approach. With the publication of Edmond O. Wilson's *Sociobiology: The New Synthesis*, the biological perspective was given a new impetus in the 1980s.[56]

Sociobiology suggests that behavior will adapt to the environment in which it evolved.[57] Most important, creatures of all species are influenced by the innate need to have their genetic material survive and dominate others. Consequently, they do everything in their power to ensure their own survival and that of others who share their gene pool (relatives, ethnic group, etc.). Even when they come to the aid of others *(reciprocal altruism)*, people are motivated by the belief that their actions will be reciprocated and that their gene survival capability will be enhanced. For the aid to occur, the benefit to the recipient must be high, the cost to the helper relatively low, and the chances of their positions being reversed in the future high.

Although sociobiology has been criticized as methodologically unsound and socially dangerous, it has had a tremendous effect on reviving interest in finding a biological basis for crime and delinquency, because if biological (genetic) makeup controls all human behavior, it follows that it should also be responsible for determining whether a person chooses law-violating or conventional behavior.[58]

Two schools of thought have emerged. *Biosocial theory* maintains that the development of delinquency is an effect of the interaction of biological traits and social conditions. The second, **psychological theory,** leans more heavily on such factors as personality, mental illness, and intelligence. These two views are discussed in detail below.

BIOSOCIAL THEORY AND DELINQUENCY

Biosocial theorists seek to explain the onset of delinquent behaviors, such as aggression and violence, from the standpoint of the physical qualities of the offenders.[59] Though many of these criminologists have medical or natural science backgrounds, a number are converts from the social science tradition.

Biosocial theorists charge that traditional criminologists ignore the biological basis for human behavior.[60] Sociologically trained criminologists disregard all the advances made in the sciences of biology and experimental psychology. Furthermore, traditional criminologists seem content to study reports of behavior, either through surveys or self-reports, rather than to observe the actual behaviors.

Biosocial theory rejects the traditional assumptions that all humans are born with equal potential to learn and achieve **(equipotentiality)** and that thereafter their behavior is controlled by social forces. While traditional criminologists suggest (either explicitly or implicitly) that all people are born equal and that parents, schools, neighborhoods, and friends control subsequent development, biosocial theorists argue that no two people (with rare exceptions, such as identical twins) are alike and that the combination of human genetic traits and the environment produces individual behavior patterns. In other words, while the influences of the social environment cannot be ignored, it is likewise foolish to ignore the effect of biological traits on behavior.

Although biosocial criminology has advanced in many directions, its major research efforts are in three distinct areas of study: biochemical reactions, neurological dysfunction, and genetic influences.

Biochemical Factors

One area of biosocial research concerns the suspected relationship between antisocial behavior and biochemical makeup.[61] It is alleged that the body chemistry, influenced and/or controlled by diet, can govern behavior and personality; traits affected by diet are thought to include aggression and depression.[62]

Of particular concern is an unusually high intake of such items as artificial food coloring, milk, and sweets. Some scientists believe that chronic under- or oversupply of vitamins, such as C and B_3 and B_6, may be related to restlessness and antisocial behavior in youths. Minerals linked to aggression include magnesium, copper, and zinc. Evidence also exists that allergies to foods can influence mood and behavior, resulting in personality swings between hyperactivity and depression.[63]

Hormonal levels are another area of biosocial research. Antisocial behavior allegedly peaks in the teenage years because hormonal activity is at its greatest level during this period. It is argued that increased levels of the male androgen testosterone are responsible for excessive levels of violence among teenage boys. In an impressive review of the literature, Christy Miller Buchanan, Jacquelynne Eccles, and Jill Becker found evidence that hormonal changes are related to mood and behavior, that adolescents may experience more intense moods, mood swings, anxiety, and restlessness than people at other points in development.[64] These mood and behavior changes have been associated with family conflict and antisocial behavior. Hormonal activity as an explanation of gender differences in the delinquency crime rate will be discussed further in Chapter 8.

Experimental Evidence. Experimental evidence exists that institutionalized youths have had a long history of poor nutrition, involving diets that were low in protein and high in sugar and other carbohydrates. This evidence suggests a link between food intake, body chemistry, and behavior.[65] Some highly sophisticated experiments show that antisocial youths who are given a diet balanced in nutrients have significantly reduced episodes of antisocial behavior and improved scores on psychological inventories.[66]

In one study, Alexander Schauss compared a sample of incarcerated youths with a nondelinquent control group and found that the most significant factor separating the youths was the extremely high milk intake among the delinquents.[67]

In another study on the influence of diet on such crime-related acts as aggression and hostility, J. Kershner and W. Hawke evaluated the effect that a high-protein, low-carbohydrate, sugarless diet, supplemented by megavitamins, had on children labeled as behavior problems.[68] Kershner and Hawke asked the subjects' parents to evaluate their children on thirteen behavior qualities, including hyperactivity, aggression, and attention span. The researchers discovered that the children had significantly improved behavior patterns and that the diet was the most important factor in producing positive change.

In the most oft-cited research on the subject, Stephen Schoenthaler tested 276 incarcerated youths to determine whether a change in the amount of sugar in their diet would have a corresponding influence on their behavior within the institution.[69] Schoenthaler instituted a number of dietary changes: sweet drinks were replaced with fruit juices; table sugar was replaced with honey; breakfast cereals with high sugar content were eliminated; molasses was substituted for sugar in cooking. Schoenthaler found that these changes produced a significant reduction in disciplinary actions within the institution: the number of assaults, thefts, fighting, and acts of disobedience declined about 45 percent. It is important to note that these results were consistent when such factors as age, previous offense record, and race of the offender were considered.

In another experiment, Schoenthaler and his colleagues found that enriching students' diets in New York City schools was correlated with improved school performance. Gradually eliminating synthetic (artificial) flavors and preservatives (BHA and BHT) and reducing sucrose intake (by limiting ice cream and sweetened cereals) preceded improved scores on national achievement tests. Since school achievement has been consistently linked to delinquent behavior, any improvement in academic performance resulting from dietary changes may help reduce the rate of antisocial activities among the student population.[70]

Dissenting Views. While this evidence seems persuasive, the relationship between biochemical intake and abnormal behavior is far from settled. Research has been criticized as being both methodologically unsound and also impractical because of the cost of providing dietary supplements for actual and potential delinquents. In addition, a number of controlled experiments have failed to substantiate any real link between the two variables.[71] Nutritionist Dian Gans reviewed the available evidence and found reason to doubt a diet-delinquency link. She cites the fact that the United States, with one of the highest crime and delinquency rates in the world, has a far lower per capita consumption of sugar than other Western nations. Furthermore, adolescents, who usually have the highest crime rate, actually have sugar intakes about one half that of the general population. Gans concludes that

recommendations to lower the amount of sucrose in children's diets in hope of preventing or treating behavioral problems is, at best, premature.[72]

Despite these criticisms, the relationship remains unresolved. As Schoenthaler argues:

Diet appears to be a significant factor in the presence or absence of juvenile antisocial behavior. Replication and subsequent interdisciplinary research to isolate the causes is certainly warranted.[73]

Neurological Dysfunction

Another focus of biocriminological research on delinquency is the **neurological,** or brain and nervous system, structure of offenders. One view is that the neuroendocrine system that controls brain chemistry is the key to understanding violence and aggression. Imbalance in the central nervous system's chemical and hormonal activity has been linked to antisocial behavior and drug abuse.[74]

Another view is that neurological functions, commonly measured with an electroencephalogram (EEG), a CAT scan, or performance indicators (gross motor functions, visual processing, auditory-language functioning) are the key factor in causing aggression and violence. Research indicates that children exhibiting an abnormal EEG at birth may also have developmental problems, such as low IQ scores, later in life.[75] Children who manifest behavior disturbances may have identifiable neurological deficits, such as damage to the hemispheres of the brain.[76] This is sometimes referred to as *minimal brain dysfunction (MBD).* MBD is defined as an abnormality in the cerebral or brain structure that causes behavior injurious to a person's life-style and social adjustment.

A few research efforts have tried to substantiate the link between neurological impairment and crime. Clinical analysis of death row inmates found that a significant number had suffered head injuries as children, resulting in damage to their central nervous system and neurological impairment.[77] Measurement of the brain activity of antisocial youths has revealed impairments that might cause them to experience otherwise unexplainable outbursts of anger, hostility, and aggression.[78] Evidence has been found linking the ability of the brain to process information with schizophrenia, depression, and other mental illnesses.[79]

A number of research studies have used an electroencephalogram to measure the brain waves and activity of delinquents and then compare them with those of law-abiding adolescents. In what is considered the most significant investigation of EEG abnormality and delinquency, 335 violent delinquents were classified on the basis of their antisocial activities and measured on an EEG.[80] While youths who committed a single violent act had a 12 percent abnormality rate, the same as the general population, the habitually aggressive youths tested at a 57 percent abnormality rate, almost five times normal. Behaviors believed to be highly correlated with abnormal EEG functions include poor impulse control, inadequate social ability, hostility, temper tantrums, destructiveness, and hyperactivity.[81]

The Learning Disability-Juvenile Delinquency Link. One specific type of MBD that has generated considerable interest is *learning disability (LD),* a term that has been defined by the National Advisory Committee on Handicapped Children:

Children with special learning disabilities exhibit a disorder in one or more of the basic psychological processes involved in understanding or using spoken or written languages. They may be manifested in disorders of listening, thinking, talking, reading, writing or arithmetic. They include conditions which have been referred to as perceptual handicaps, brain injury, minimal brain dysfunction, dyslexia, developmental aphasia, etc. They do not include learning problems which are due to visual, hearing or motor handicaps, to mental retardation, emotional disturbance, or to environmental disadvantages.[82]

Learning disabled kids usually exhibit poor motor coordination (poor hand-eye coordination, trouble climbing stairs; they are clumsy, cannot catch a ball, cannot stay neat), have behavior problems (lack emotional control, appear hostile, daydream a lot), and improper auditory and vocal responses (do not seem to hear, cannot differentiate sounds and noises).

The relationship between learning disabilities and delinquency has been highlighted by studies showing that arrested and incarcerated children have a far higher LD rate than do children in the general population.[83] While it is estimated that approximately 10 percent of all youths have learning disorders, estimates of LD among adjudicated delinquents range from 26 percent to 73 percent.[84]

Charles Murray, writing in a widely read 1976 federally sponsored study, offered two possible explanations of the link between learning disabilities and delinquency.[85] One view, known as the *susceptibility rationale,* argues that the link is caused by certain side effects of learning disabilities, such as impulsiveness, poor ability to learn from experience, and inability to take social cues. In contrast, the *school failure rationale* assumes that the frustration caused by the LD child's poor school performance will lead to a negative self-image and acting-out behavior.

A number of recent research efforts have found that the LD child may not be any more susceptible to delinquent behavior than the non-LD child. Studies by Robert Pasternack and Reid Lyon, as well as by Joel Zimmerman and his associates, indicate that the proposed link between learning disabilities and delinquency may be an artifact of bias in the way the juvenile justice system treats LD youths.[86] For example, when Zimmerman and his colleagues evaluated the self-reported delinquent behavior of LD and non-LD youth, they found that it was actually quite similar.[87] Similarly, Lynn Meltzer and her associates found that while a small number of delinquents had learning disabilities, the majority could not be classified as learning disabled.[88]

These findings can be interpreted as meaning that when LD children get in trouble with the law, they bring with them a record of school problems and low grades and a history of frustrating efforts by agents of the educational system to help them. When information is gleaned from the school personnel at juvenile trials, LD children's poor performance may work against them in the court. Consequently, the view that learning disabilities cause delinquency has been questioned, and the view that LD children are more likely to be arrested and officially labeled delinquent demands further inquiry.

Terrie Moffitt has recently evaluated the relevant literature on the link between LD and other neurological dysfunctions and delinquency and concludes that they are a significant correlate of persistent antisocial behavior *(conduct disorders).*[89] She finds that neurological symptoms, such as LD and MBD, correlate highly with factors pointing to a high risk for persistent antisocial behavior: early onset of deviance, hyperactivity, and aggressiveness. Moffitt's review indicates further research is needed on the cause and impact of neurological dysfunction: When do such problems begin? Are they the result of injury during birth? Or of child abuse and neglect?[90] Is there a continuum of learning disabilities, and are the most severely disabled also the most prone to delinquency?[91] Efforts are being made to introduce new technologies in the measurement of brain function and behavior to investigate early detection, prevention, and control of mal-adapted behaviors.[92]

In the following Focus on Delinquency, attention deficit disorder, a neurological condition associated with antisocial behavior, is discussed in some detail.

Genetic Influences

Another area of concern for biosocial theorists is the genetic makeup of delinquents.[93] It has been hypothesized that some youths inherit a genetic configuration that predisposes them to violence and aggression over the life course.[94] Biosocial theorists believe that in the same way that people inherit genes that control height and eye color, antisocial behavior characteristics and mental disorders may be passed down.[95]

FOCUS ON DELINQUENCY

Attention Deficit Disorder

Many parents have noticed that their children do not pay attention to them—they run around and do things in their own way. Sometimes this inattention is a function of age; in other instances, it is a symptom of attention-deficit disorder (ADD), a condition in which a child shows a developmentally inappropriate lack of attention, impulsivity, and hyperactivity. The various symptoms of ADD are described in Table A.

About 3 percent of American children, most often boys, are believed to suffer from this disorder, and it is the most common reason children are referred to mental health clinics. The condition usually results in poor school performance, bullying, stubbornness, and a lack of response to discipline. While the origin of ADD is still unknown, suspected causes include neurological damage, prenatal stress, and even food additives and chemical allergies. ADD children are most often treated by giving them doses of stimulants, such as Ritalin and Dexedrine, which ironically help these children to control their emotional and behavioral outbursts.

A series of research studies now link ADD, minimum brain dysfunctions, such as poor motor function and below average written and verbal cognitive ability, to the onset and sustenance of a delinquent career. Research by Terrie Moffitt and Phil Silva seems to suggest that youths who suffer both ADD and MBD and who grow up in a dysfunctional family are the most vulnerable to chronic delinquency that continues into their adulthood. However, Moffitt and Silva found that ADD kids who did not suffer from other forms of impairment were at no more risk for delinquency than non-ADD kids. By implication, early diagnosis and treatment of ADD and MBD may enhance the life chances of at-risk youth. ■

Source: Terrie Moffitt and Phil Silva, "Self-Reported Delinquency, Neuropsychological Deficit, and History of Attention Deficit Disorder," *Journal of Abnormal Child Psychology* 16:553–69 (1988).

■ ■ TABLE A   Symptoms of Attention Deficit Disorder

LACK OF ATTENTION

Frequently fails to finish projects
Does not seem to pay attention
Does not sustain interest in play activities
Cannot sustain concentration on schoolwork or related tasks
Is easily distracted

IMPULSIVITY

Frequently acts without thinking
Often "calls out" in class
Does not want to wait his or her turn in line or games
Shifts from activity to activity
Cannot organize tasks or work
Requires constant supervision

HYPERACTIVITY

Constantly runs around and climbs on things
Shows excessive motor activity while asleep
Cannot sit still; is constantly fidgeting
Does not remain in his or her seat in class
Is constantly on the go like a "motor"

Source: Adapted from American Psychiatric Association, *Diagnostic and Statistical Manual of the Mental Disorders,* 3rd ed. (Washington, D.C.: American Psychiatric Press, 1987), pp. 50–53.

Early theories of heredity suggested that delinquency-proneness ran in families. However, most families share a similar life-style as well as a similar gene pool, making it difficult to determine whether behavior is a function of heredity or the environment. Interest in a genetic basis of crime was given new license because of the highly publicized killing of eight Chicago nurses in 1966 by Richard Speck. It was soon reported that Speck possessed an extra male chromosome; instead of the normal 46XY chromosomal structure, his was

47XYY. Though numerous research studies failed to find conclusive proof that males with an extra Y chromosome were disproportionately violent and criminal, interest brought about by the Speck case boosted research on genetic influences on delinquency (it was later revealed that Speck's genetic structure was misidentified).[96]

Biosocial theorists have once again taken up the study of family transmission of delinquent traits. Some recent research shows a significant association in sibling behavior: brothers and sisters seem to share antisocial life-styles.[97] Siblings share the same environment, so it is not surprising that their behavior co-varies. To establish the influence of environment and genetics independently, criminologists have employed samples of twins and adopted children.

Twin Studies. One method of studying the genetic basis of delinquency is to compare the behavior of twins to non-twin siblings. If a crime is an inherited trait, identical twins should be quite similar in their behavior because they share a common genetic makeup.

Because twins are usually brought up in the same household and share common life experiences, however, any similarity in their delinquent behavior might be a function of comparable environmental influences and not genetics at all. To guard against this, biosocial theorists have compared the behavior of identical monozygotic (MZ) twins with fraternal dizygotic (DZ) twins; while the former have an identical genetic makeup, the latter share only about 50 percent of their genetic combinations. Research has shown that MZ twins are significantly closer in their personal characteristics, such as intelligence, than are DZ twins.[98] Reviews of twin studies found that in almost all cases, MZ twins have delinquent and antisocial behavior patterns more similar than that of DZ twins.[99]

■ ■ ■ ■ ■ ■ ■ ■ ■ ■ ■ ■ ■ ■

Those who believe that delinquent behavior has a genetic basis study the behavior of identical twins in order to determine whether their behavior is more similar than other sibling pairs.

Of particular importance is the work of Karl Christiansen in Denmark, who studied thousands of twin pairs and found MZ pairs more than twice as likely to be similar as DZ pairs.[100]

While this seems to support a connection between genetic makeup and delinquency, little conclusive evidence exists of such an actual link. MZ twins are more likely to look alike and to share physical traits than DZ twins, and they are more likely to be treated similarly. Shared behavior patterns may therefore be a function of socialization and not heredity. Critics have also challenged the methodology of these studies and suggest that those that show a conclusive genetic link to behavior use faulty data.[101]

Against this interpretation is research evidence that identical twins reared apart are quite as similar in many traits, including personality, intelligence, and attitudes, as twins who live in the same household.[102] The Minnesota study of twins reared apart is an ongoing effort to evaluate the behavioral characteristics of MZ twins who were separated at birth. During the past twelve years, researchers have been struck by the many similarities in personal style and behavior of the two hundred individual MZ twins reared apart; in contrast, the DZ twins reared apart seldom produce similar behavior patterns.[103] Such findings support a genetic basis of behavior.

Adoption Studies. Another way to determine whether delinquency is an inherited trait is to compare the behavior of adopted children with that of their biological parents. If the criminal behavior of children is more like that of their biological parents, whom they have never met, than that of their adopted parents, who brought them up, it would indicate that the tendency toward delinquency is inherited, rather than shaped by the environment.

Studies of this kind have generally supported the hypothesis that there is a link between genetics and delinquency.[104] Some of the most influential research in this area has been conducted by Sarnoff Mednick. In one study, Mednick and Bernard Hutchings found that while only 13 percent of the adopted fathers of a sample of adjudicated delinquent youths had criminal records, 31 percent of their biological fathers had criminal records.[105] Analysis of a control group's background indicated that about 11 percent of all fathers will have criminal records. Hutchings and Mednick were forced to conclude that genetics played at least some role in creating delinquent tendencies, because the biological fathers of delinquents were much more likely than the fathers of noncriminal youths to be criminals. Mednick reported similar results in another effort conducted with William Gabrielli.[106]

In addition to a direct link between heredity and delinquency, the literature also shows that behavior traits linked closely to delinquency may be at least in part inherited. For example, recent research by Jody Alberts-Corush and her associates shows that the biological parents of adopted hyperactive children are more likely to show symptoms of hyperactivity than are the adoptive parents.[107] And several studies have reported a higher incidence of psychological problems in parents of hyperactive children when compared to control groups. While all hyperactive children do not become delinquent, the link between this neurological condition and delinquency has been long suspected.

Similarly, there is evidence (disputed) that intelligence is related to heredity and that low intelligence is a cause of impulsive delinquent acts that are easier to detect and more likely to result in arrest.[108] This connection can create the appearance of a relationship between heredity and delinquency.

Connecting delinquent behavior to heredity is quite controversial since it implies that the cause of delinquency is (a) present at birth, (b) "transmitted" from one generation to the next, and (c) immune to treatment efforts (since genes cannot be altered). Recent evaluations of the gene-crime relationship find that though a relationship can be detected, the better designed research efforts provide less support than earlier and weaker studies.[109] If there is a genetic basis of delinquency, it is likely that genetic factors contribute to certain individual differences that interact with specific social and environmental conditions to bring about antisocial behavior.[110]

PSYCHOLOGICAL THEORIES

Some experts view the cause of delinquency as essentially psychological.[111] After all, most behaviors labeled delinquent—for example, violence, theft, sexual misconduct—seem to be symptomatic of some underlying psychological problem. Psychologists point out that many delinquent youths have poor home lives, destructive relationships with neighbors, friends, and teachers, and conflicts with authority figures in general. These relationships seem to indicate a disturbed personality structure. Furthermore, numerous studies of incarcerated youths indicate that the youths' personalities are marked by negative, antisocial behavior characteristics. And since delinquent behavior occurs among youths in every racial, ethnic, and socioeconomic group, psychologists view it as a function of emotional and mental disturbance, rather than purely a result of social factors, such as racism, poverty, and class conflict.

Considering the presumed relationship between personality disturbance and antisocial behavior, it is not surprising that psychologists have played a prominent role in the study of delinquency. While many delinquents do not manifest significant psychological problems, enough do to give clinicians a powerful influence on delinquency theory.

Because psychology is a complex and diversified discipline, more than one psychological perspective on crime exists. Three prominent psychological perspectives on delinquency are: the psychodynamic, the behavioral, and the cognitive.[112] (See Figure 4.3.)

Psychodynamic Theory

One long-held psychological view of delinquency is based on the pioneering work of the Austrian physician *Sigmund Freud* (1856–1939).[113] Freud's views are referred to as **psychodynamic or psychoanalytic theory,** and his method of treatment is called **psychoanalysis.**

Psychodynamic theory argues that the human personality contains three major components. The *id* is the unrestrained, primitive, pleasure-seeking component with which each child is born. The *ego* develops through the reality of living in the world and helps manage and restrain the id's need for immediate gratification. The *superego* develops through interactions with parents and other significant people and represents the development of conscience and the moral rules that are shared by most adults.

Part II Theories of Delinquency

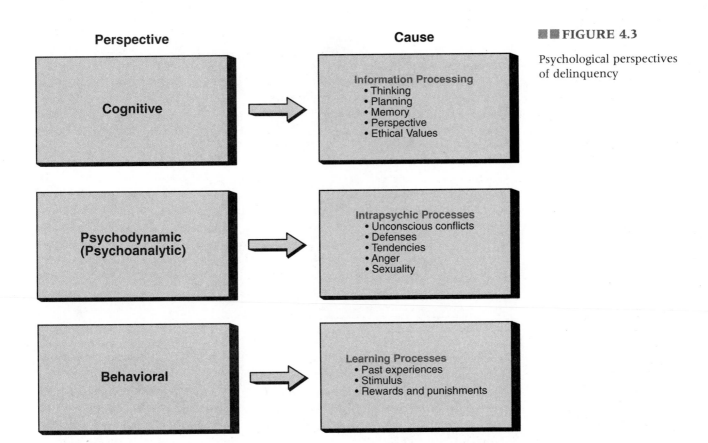

FIGURE 4.3

Psychological perspectives
of delinquency

Perspective		Cause
Cognitive	⟹	**Information Processing** • Thinking • Planning • Memory • Perspective • Ethical Values
Psychodynamic (Psychoanalytic)	⟹	**Intrapsychic Processes** • Unconscious conflicts • Defenses • Tendencies • Anger • Sexuality
Behavioral	⟹	**Learning Processes** • Past experiences • Stimulus • Rewards and punishments

Psychodynamic theory suggests that unconscious motivations for behavior come from the id's action to account for two primal needs—sex and aggression. Human behavior is often marked by symbolic actions that reflect hidden feelings about these needs. For example, stealing a car may reflect a person's unconscious need for shelter and mobility to escape from hostile enemies (aggression) or perhaps an urge to enter a closed, dark, womb-like structure that reflects the earliest memories (sex).

All three segments of the personality operate simultaneously. The id dictates needs and desires, the superego counteracts the id by fostering feelings of morality and righteousness, and the ego evaluates the reality of a position between these two extremes. If these components are properly balanced, the individual can lead a normal life. If one aspect of the personality becomes dominant at the expense of the others, however, the individual exhibits neurotic or even psychotic personality traits (see Figure 4.4).

Psychodynamic theory also suggests that every person goes through a series of life stages that shape the personality. The first, experienced by the newborn infant, is the *oral stage.* This period is marked by receiving pleasure through eating, sucking, and chewing. In the second, the *anal stage,* occurring between 1 and 3 years of age, urinary and bowel movements replace sucking as a major source of pleasure. During this period, toilet training occurs, and for the first time, pressure is put on the child to conform to social rules.

FIGURE 4.4

Segments of the personality

Source: Adapted from Ronald Smith, *Psychology* (St. Paul: West, 1993), p. 442.

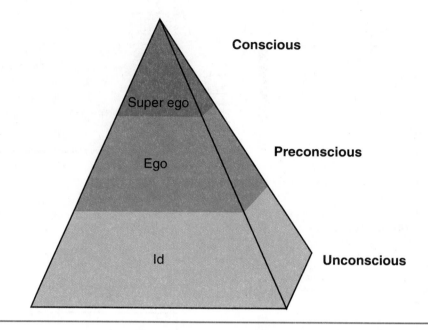

The third influential stage is the *phallic stage,* in which children from ages 3 to 6 receive pleasure from fondling their genitals. During this period, the male child develops great unconscious feelings for his mother (Oedipus complex) and the female child for her father (Electra complex). There are two later stages, genital and latency, but these are considered less important for human development because for all intents and purposes, the personality is formed by age 5.

Any trauma that occurs during any of these early life stages may have a lasting effect on the child's personality. For example, premature weaning during the oral stage may cause an individual to be fixated on oral satisfaction, such as through smoking cigarettes and drinking alcohol. If toilet training is a frightening or frustrating experience, the child's superego may be damaged, and sometimes a sadistic and cruel anal personality will develop.

Furthermore, the theory suggests that an imbalance in personality traits caused by a traumatic early childhood can produce a damaged adolescent personality. That is, deep-rooted problems developed early in childhood will cause long-term psychological difficulties. For example, if neglectful parents fail to develop a child's superego adequately, the child's id may become the predominant personality force. Later, the youth may demand immediate gratification, lack compassion and sensitivity for the needs of others, disassociate feelings, act aggressively and impulsively, and demonstrate other psychotic symptoms. As a result, delinquent activity may become an outlet for violent and antisocial feelings. Thus, to explain antisocial behavior, Freudian thought focuses on traumas during early developmental stages and the resulting personality imbalances.

According to psychodynamic theory, people who experience feelings of mental anguish and are afraid that they are losing control of their personalities are said to be suffering from a form of *neuroses* and are referred to as *neurotics.* People who have lost total control and who are dominated by their primitive id are known as *psychotics.* Their behavior may be marked by bizarre episodes, hallucinations, and inappropriate responses. *Psychosis* takes many forms, the most common being labeled *schizophrenia,* a condition marked by illogical thought processes and a lack of insight into behavior. According to the psychoanalytic view, the most serious types of youthful antisocial behavior, such as murder, might be motivated by psychosis, while neurotic feelings would be responsible for less serious delinquent acts and status offenses, such as petty theft and truancy.[114]

The Psychodynamic Tradition and Delinquency

A number of psychoanalysts have expanded upon Freud's original model to explain the onset of antisocial behaviors. Erik Erickson speculated that many adolescents experience a life crisis in which they feel emotional, impulsive, and uncertain of their role and purpose.[115] To resolve this crisis, most youths achieve a sense of *ego identity,* a firm sense of who they are and what they stand for. However, some youths cannot adequately deal with their feelings of role conflict and experience a sense of *role diffusion,* feelings of uncertainty that make them susceptible to suggestion and at the mercy of others who might lead them astray. The clash between ego identity and role diffusion is precipitated by an **identity crisis**—a period of inner turmoil during which they examine inner values and make decisions about life roles. Using Erickson's approach, the behavior of youthful drug abusers might be viewed as an expression of confusion over their place in society, their inability to direct behavior toward useful outlets, and perhaps their dependency on others to offer them solutions to their problems.

Another psychoanalyst long associated with understanding delinquency, David Abrahamsen, views youth crime as a result of unresolved conflict between the ego and superego aspects of the personality:

In the child between four and six years of age, incestuous unconscious feelings associated with resentment, fear and hatred are present. If [this] merging of Ego and Superego is unsuccessful, a regression to these earlier drives more or less takes place. This regression may be considered responsible for a great number of mental diseases, from neuroses to psychoses, and in many cases it may be related to criminal behavior.[116]

Psychoanalysts such as Abrahamsen view delinquents as id-dominated people who suffer from the inability to control impulsive, pleasure-seeking drives. Perhaps because they suffered unhappy experiences in childhood or had families who could not provide proper love and care, delinquents suffer from weak or damaged egos that make them unable to cope with conventional society.[117] In its most extreme form, delinquency may be viewed as a form of psychosis that prevents delinquent youths from appreciating the feelings of their victims or controlling their own impulsive needs for gratification. For example, psychoanalyst August Aichorn claims that social stress alone could not produce such an emotional state. He identifies **latent delinquents**—youths whose troubled family life lead them to seek immediate gratification without consideration of right and wrong or the feelings of others.[118]

Psychiatrist Seymour Halleck views delinquency as a manifestation of feelings of oppression and the inability of youths to do much about it. Criminality actually allows youths to strive by producing positive psychic results: helping them to feel free and independent; giving them the possibility of excitement and the chance to use their skills and imagination; providing the promise of positive gain; allowing them to blame others for their predicament (for example, the police); and giving them a chance to rationalize their own sense of failure ("If I hadn't gotten into the trouble, I could have been a success").[119]

The views of psychoanalysts such as Abrahamsen and Halleck are supported by research that shows that a number of serious, violent juvenile offenders suffer from some sort of personality disturbance. James Sorrells's well-known study of juvenile murderers, "Kids Who Kill," found that many homicidal youths could be described as "overtly hostile," "explosive or volatile," "anxious," and "depressed."[120] Likewise, Richard Rosner and his associates found that 75 percent of male adolescents accused of murder could be classified as having some mental illness, including schizophrenia.[121] Abused, depressed, and suicidal children may grow up to vent their feelings in a homicidal rage.[122]

The psychoanalytic approach places heavy emphasis on the family's role in producing a delinquent child. When parents fail to maintain a stable, balanced home life, a child may adapt by turning inward and revamping his or her internal personality components. Antisocial youths frequently come from families in which parents are unable to give love, set consistent limits, and provide the controls that allow children to develop the necessary personal tools to cope with the world within which they live.[123] The exploitive, destructive behavior of a youth may actually be a symbolic call for help. In fact, some psychoanalysts view delinquents' behavior as being motivated by an unconscious urge to be punished. Since these children believe that they are unloved at home, the reason must be their own inadequacy—hence, they deserve punishment.

BEHAVIORAL THEORY

Not all psychologists agree that behavior is controlled by unconscious mental processes determined by parental relationships developed early in childhood. Behavioral psychologists argue that a person's personality is learned throughout life during interaction with others. Based primarily on the works of the American psychologist John B. Watson (1878–1958) and popularized by Harvard professor B. F. Skinner, (1904–1990), **behaviorism** concerns itself solely with measurable events and not the unobservable psychic phenomenon described by psychoanalysts.

Behaviorists suggest that individuals learn by observing how people react to their behavior. Behavior is triggered initially by a stimulus or change in the environment. If a particular behavior is reinforced by some positive reaction or event, that behavior will be continued and eventually learned. However, behaviors that are not reinforced or are punished will be extinguished or become extinct. For example, if children are given a reward (ice cream for dessert) for eating their entire dinner, eventually they will learn to eat properly as a matter of habit. Conversely, if children are punished for some misbehavior, they will eventually learn to associate disapproval with that act and avoid it.

Social Learning Theory

Not all behaviorists follow the teachings of Watson and Skinner strictly. Some hold that a person's learning and social experiences, coupled with his or her values and expectations, determine behavior. This is known as the **social learning** approach. The most widely read social learning theorists are Albert

Bandura, Walter Mischel, and Richard Walters.[124] In general, they hold that children will model their behavior according to the reactions they receive from others, either positive or negative; the behavior of those adults they are in close contact with, especially parents; and the behavior they view on television and in movies. If children observe aggression, such as an adult slapping or punching someone during an argument, and see that the aggressive behavior is approved or rewarded, they will likely react violently during a similar incident. Eventually, the children will master the techniques of aggression and become more confident that their behavior will bring tangible rewards.[125]

By implication, social learning suggests that children who grow up in a home where violence is a way of life may learn to believe that such behavior is acceptable and rewarding. Even if parents tell children not to be violent and punish them if they are, the children will still model their behavior on the observed parental violence. Thus, children are more likely to heed what parents *do* than what they *say*. Bonnie Carlson found that by middle childhood, some children have already acquired an association between their use of aggression against others and the physical punishment they receive at home. Often their aggressive responses are directed at other family members and siblings. Carlson's conclusion: the family serves as a training ground for violence, with physical punishment playing a prominent role in normalizing the child's use of violence during conflict situations with others.[126]

Bandura has also suggested that adolescent aggression is a result of disrupted dependency relations with parents. This refers to the frustration and anger a child feels when parents provide poor role models and hold back affection and nurturing. He states:

A child who lacks close dependent ties to his parents can have little opportunity or desire to model himself after them and to internalize their standards of behavior. In the absence of such internalized controls, the child's aggression is likely to be expressed in an immediate, direct and socially unacceptable fashion.[127]

The Media and Delinquency

One aspect of social learning theory that has received a great deal of attention is the view that children will model their behavior after characters they observe on TV or see in movies. This is of special concern since the content of both media has been considerably violent for quite some time. Often the violence is of a sexual nature, and some experts fear that there is a link between sexual violence and the viewing of pornography.[128]

Children are particularly susceptible to TV imagery. It is believed that many children consider television images to be real, especially if they are authoritatively presented by an adult (as in a commercial). Of concern is the fact that some children, especially those who are considered "emotionally disturbed," may be unable to distinguish between fantasy and reality when watching TV shows.[129] This is especially important when we consider that systematic viewing of TV begins at 2.5 years of age and continues at a high level during the preschool and early school years; it has been estimated that children ages 2 to 5 watch TV 27.8 hours each week; children 6 to 11, 24.3 hours per week; and teens, 23 hours per week.[130]

A number of research methods have been used to measure the effect of TV viewing on behavior. One method is to expose groups of subjects to violent TV shows in a laboratory setting and then compare their behavior to control groups who viewed nonviolent programming; observations have also been made in playgrounds, athletic fields, and residences. Other experiments require subjects to answer attitude surveys after watching violent TV shows. Still another approach is to use aggregate measures of TV viewing; for example, the number of violent TV shows on the air during a given time period is compared to crime rates during the same period.

Most evaluations of experimental data indicate that watching violence on TV is correlated to aggressive behaviors.[131] Such august bodies as the American Psychological Association and the National Institute of Mental Health support the TV-violence link.[132] In an important review of the literature, Wendy Wood, Frank Wong, and J. Gregory Chachere conclude that violent media has at least a short-term impact on behavior.[133] Subjects who view violent TV shows are likely to commence aggressive behavior almost immediately.

Though this evidence is persuasive, the relationship between TV viewing and violence is still uncertain. A number of critics claim that the evidence simply does not support the claim that TV viewing is related to antisocial behavior.[134] Some critics assert that experimental results are inconclusive and short-lived. Kids may have an immediate reaction to viewing violence on TV, but aggression is quickly extinguished once the viewing ends.[135] Experiments that show that kids act aggressively after watching violent TV shows fail to link aggression to actual criminal behaviors, such as rape or assault.

Aggregate data is also inconclusive. Little evidence exists that areas that have the highest levels of violent TV viewing also have rates of violent crime that are above the norm.[136] Millions of children watch violence every night yet fail to become violent criminals. And even if a violent behavior-TV link could be established, it would be difficult to show that antisocial people develop aggressive traits merely from watching TV. It is also possible that already aggressive youths enjoy watching TV shows that conform to and support their behavioral orientation.

COGNITIVE THEORY

One area of psychology that has received increasing recognition in recent years has been the *cognitive school.* Psychologists with a cognitive perspective focus on mental processes, the way people perceive and mentally represent the world around them, and how they solve problems. The pioneers of this school were Wilhelm Wundt (1832–1920), Edward Titchener (1867–1927), and William James (1842–1920). The cognitive perspective contains several subgroups. *Gestalt psychology* is concerned with perception of the world in whole units, rather than individual pieces. The *moral and intellectual development* branch is concerned with how adults morally represent and reason about the world. *Humanistic psychology* stresses self-awareness and "getting in touch with feelings."

Moral and Intellectual Development Theory

The moral and intellectual development branch of cognitive psychology is perhaps the most important for criminological theory. Jean Piaget (1896–1980), the founder of this approach, hypothesized that people's reasoning processes develop in an orderly fashion, beginning at birth and continuing until they are 12 and older.[137] At first, during the *sensormotor stage,* children respond to the environment in a simple manner, seeking interesting objects and developing their reflexes. By the fourth and final stage, the *formal operations* stage, they have developed into mature adults who can use logic and abstract thought.

Lawrence Kohlberg applied the concept of moral development to issues in criminology.[138] He suggests that people travel through stages of moral development, during which their decisions and judgments on issues of right and wrong are made for different reasons. It is possible that serious offenders have a moral orientation that differs from that of law-abiding citizens. Kohlberg's stages of development are:

- STAGE 1—Right is obedience to power and avoidance of punishment.
- STAGE 2—Right is taking responsibility for oneself, meeting one's own needs, and leaving to others the responsibility for themselves.
- STAGE 3   Right is being good in the sense of having good motives, having concern for others, and "putting yourself in the other person's shoes."
- STAGE 4—Right is maintaining the rules of a society and serving the welfare of the group or society.
- STAGE 5—Right is based on recognized individual rights within a society with agreed-upon rules—a social contract.
- STAGE 6—Right is an assumed obligation to principles applying to all humankind—principles of justice, equality, and respect for human personality.

Kohlberg classified people according to the stage on this continuum at which their moral development has ceased to grow. In studies conducted by Kohlberg and his associates, criminals were found to be significantly lower in their moral judgment development than noncriminals of the same social background.[139] The majority of noncriminals were classified in stages three and four, while a majority of criminals were in stages one and two. Moral development theory, then, suggests that people who obey the law simply to avoid punishment or who have outlooks mainly characterized by self-interest are more likely to commit crimes than those who view the law as something that benefits all of society and who honor the rights of others. Research efforts using delinquent youth have found that a significant number were in the first two moral development categories, while nondelinquents were ranked higher.[140] In addition, higher stages of moral reasoning are associated with such behaviors as honesty, generosity, and nonviolence, which are considered incompatible with delinquency.[141]

PSYCHOLOGICAL TRAITS AND DELINQUENCY

Each of the various perspectives and theories of psychology has its own view of how important psychological traits, such as sensation, perception, thought, memory, emotion, and motivation, develop. A number of these traits have been linked to the onset of delinquency. Of these, the two most prominent are personality and intelligence.

Personality and Delinquency

Personality can be defined as the reasonably stable patterns of behavior, including thoughts and emotions, that distinguish one person from another.[142] An individual's personality reflects characteristic ways of adapting to life's demands and problems. The way we behave is a function of how our personality enables us to interpret life events and make appropriate behavioral choices.

Can the cause of delinquency be linked to personality? There has been a great deal of research on this subject and an equal amount of controversy and debate over the findings.[143] In their early work, Sheldon Glueck and Eleanor Glueck identified a number of personality traits that characterize delinquents:

- self-assertiveness
- defiance
- impulsiveness
- narcissism
- suspicion
- destructiveness
- sadism
- lack of concern for others
- extroversion
- ambivalence
- feeling unappreciated
- distrust of authority
- poor personal skills
- mental instability
- hostility
- resentment[144]

The Gluecks' research is representative of the view that delinquents maintain a distinct personality whose characteristics increase the probability that (a) they will be aggressive and antisocial and (b) their actions will involve them with agents of social control, ranging from teachers to police. Since the Gluecks' findings were published, other research efforts have attempted to identify personality traits that would increase the chances for a delinquent career.[145] For example, the well-known psychologist Hans Eysenck identified two important personality traits that he associated with antisocial behavior: extraversion and neuroticism. Extraverts are impulsive individuals who lack the ability to examine their own motives and behaviors; neuroticism is a trait in which a person is given to anxiety, tension, and emotional instability.[146] Youths who lack self-insight and are impulsive and emotionally unstable are likely to interpret events differently than youths who are able to give reasoned judgments to life events. While the former may act destructively, for example, by taking drugs, the latter will be able to reason that such behavior is ultimately destructive and life-threatening.

A number of personality deficits have been identified in the delinquent population. A common theme is that delinquents are hyperactive, impulsive individuals with short attention spans (attention deficit disorder), conduct disorders, anxiety disorders, and depression.[147] These traits make them prone to problems ranging from psychopathology to drug abuse, sexual promiscuity, and violence.[148]

The Antisocial Personality

It has also been suggested the delinquency may result from a personality pattern or syndrome commonly referred to as the *psychopathic* or *sociopathic* personality (the terms are used interchangeably).

Psychopathic (sociopathic) youths exhibit a low level of guilt and anxiety and persistently violate the rights of others. Although they may exhibit superficial charm and above-average intelligence, these often mask a disturbed personality that makes them incapable of forming enduring relationships with others and continually involves them in such deviant behaviors as truancy, running away, lying, substance abuse, and impulsivity. David Abrahamsen describes the genuine psychopath as someone who has never been able to identify with anyone. From an early age, the psychopath's home life was filled with frustrations, bitterness, and quarreling. Consequently, throughout life, he or she is unreliable, unstable, demanding, and egocentric. Hervey Cleckley, a leading authority on psychopathy, uses this definition:

[Psychopaths are] chronically antisocial individuals who are always in trouble, profiting neither from experience nor punishment, and maintaining no real loyalties to any person, group, or code. They are frequently callous and hedonistic, showing marked emotional immaturity, with lack of responsibility, lack of judgment and an ability to rationalize their behavior so that it appears warranted, reasonable and justified.[149]

A number of factors have been found to contribute to the development of psychopathic/sociopathic personalities. They include have a psychopathic parent, a lack of love, parental rejection during childhood, and inconsistent discipline.[150] However, according to some psychologists, psychopathy has its basis in a measurable physical condition—psychopaths suffer from levels of arousal that are lower than those of the general population. Consequently, psychopathic youths may need greater-than-average stimulation to bring them up to comfortable levels. Youths diagnosed as psychopaths are believed to be thrill seekers who engage in violent, destructive behavior. For example, Lewis Yablonsky has described the psychopathic/sociopathic gang boy who engages in violent and destructive sexual escapades to compensate for a fear of responsibility and an inability to maintain interpersonal relationships.[151] And while the research of Helene Raskin White, Erich Labouvie, and Marsha Bates did not directly link delinquency to psychopathy, they did find that delinquents were more likely than nondelinquents to be sensation seekers who desired a hedonistic pursuit of pleasure, an extraverted life-style, partying, drinking, and a variety of sexual partners.[152] Psychologists have attempted to treat patients diagnosed as psychopaths by giving them adrenaline, which increases their arousal levels.

Personality Testing

Numerous attempts have been made to correlate measures of personality with deviant behavior. If personality traits control behavior, it stands to reason that delinquent behavior can be predicted by scores on widely used psychological tests. The most common of these is the Minnesota Multiphasic Personality Inventory, commonly called the MMPI. Developed by R. Starke Hathaway and J. Charnley McKinley, the MMPI has subscales that purport to measure many different personality traits, including psychopathic deviation (Pd scale), schizophrenia (Sc), and hypomania (overactivity, Ma).[153]

Elio Monachesi and R. Starke Hathaway pioneered the use of the MMPI to predict delinquent behavior.[154] They concluded that scores on some of the MMPI subscales, especially the Pd scale, predicted delinquency. In one major effort, they administered the MMPI to a sample of ninth-grade boys and girls in Minneapolis and found that Pd scores had a significant relationship to later delinquent involvement.[155] Similar studies have been conducted to classify both criminal and juvenile offenders, as well as substance abusers.[156]

Despite the time and energy put into using MMPI scales to predict delinquency, the results have proved inconclusive. Three surveys of the literature of personality testing, one by Karl Schuessler and Donald Cressey (covering the pre-1950 period), another by Gordon Waldo and Simon Dinitz (covering 1950 to 1965), and a more recent one by David Tennenbaum, found inconclusive evidence that personality traits could indeed predict delinquent involvement.[157] The personality tests reviewed in these surveys, however, often had methodological flaws, so any negative conclusions must be interpreted with caution. Some recent research efforts have successfully classified offenders and predicted their behavioral traits on the basis of personality inventory scores.[158] Sufficient evidence exists of an association between some delinquency and personality disturbance to warrant further research on this important yet sensitive issue.

Mental Ability and Delinquency

Psychologists are concerned with the development of intelligence and its subsequent relationship to behavior (See Figure 4.5). Of particular importance to the study of delinquency is the allegation that there is an inverse relationship between IQ and youthful law violations. It has been charged that children with low IQs are responsible for a disproportionate share of delinquency.

Early criminologists believed that low intelligence was a major cause of delinquency. They thought that if one could determine which individuals had low IQs, one might be able to identify potential delinquents before they committed socially harmful acts.[159] Since social scientists had a captive group of subjects in training schools and penal institutions, studies began to appear that measured the correlation between IQ and crime by testing adjudicated juvenile delinquents. Delinquent juveniles were believed to be inherently substandard in

■■**FIGURE 4.5**

The Distribution of Intelligence. Intelligence tests yield a normal, or bell-shaped, distribution of IQ scores. The mean of the distribution is set at 100, and each 16 points equal one standard deviation above and below that mean. Common descriptive labels are shown relative to the bell-shaped distribution. The range of scores from 90 to 110 is labeled average and includes nearly half of the population.

Source: Ronald Smith, *Psychology* (St. Paul, Minn. West, 1993), p. 347.

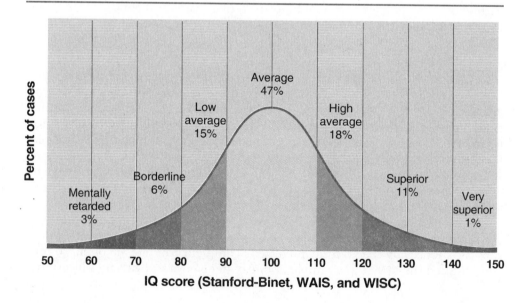

Part II Theories of Delinquency

intelligence and thus naturally inclined to commit more crimes than more intelligent persons. Thus, juvenile delinquents were used as a test group around which numerous theories about intelligence were built.

When the newly developed IQ tests were administered to inmates of prisons and juvenile training schools in the first decades of the twentieth century, the nature position gained support because a large proportion of the inmates scored low on the tests. Henry Goddard found in his studies in 1920 that many institutionalized persons were what he considered "feeble-minded" and thus concluded that at least half of all juvenile delinquents were mental defectives.[160]

In 1926, William Healy and Augusta Bronner tested a group of delinquents in Chicago and Boston and found that 37 percent were subnormal in intelligence.[161] They concluded that delinquents were five to ten times more likely to be mentally deficient than nondelinquent boys.

These and other early studies were embraced as proof that low IQ scores indicated potentially delinquent children and that a correlation existed between innate low intelligence and deviant behavior. IQ tests were believed to measure the inborn genetic makeup of individuals, and many criminologists accepted the predisposition of substandard individuals toward delinquency.

Nurture Theory

The rise of culturally sensitive explanations of human behavior in the 1930s led to the *nurture school* of intelligence. This view holds that intelligence must be viewed as partly biological but primarily sociological. Nurture theorists discredit the notion that people commit crimes because they have low IQ scores. Instead, they postulate that environmental stimulation from parents, relatives, social contacts, schools, peer groups, and innumerable others create a child's IQ level and that low IQs result from an environment that also encourages delinquent and criminal behavior.[162] For example, if educational environments could be improved, the result might be both an elevation in IQ scores and a decrease in delinquency.[163]

Studies challenging the assumption that people automatically committed delinquent acts because they had below-average IQs began to appear as early as the 1920s. John Slawson studied 1,543 delinquent boys in New York institutions and compared them with a control group of New York City boys in 1926.[164] He found that although 80 percent of the delinquents achieved lower scores in abstract verbal intelligence, delinquents were about normal in mechanical aptitude and nonverbal intelligence. These results indicated the possibility of cultural bias in portions of the IQ tests. He also found no relationship between the number of arrests, the types of offenses, and IQ. In 1931, Edwin Sutherland evaluated IQ studies of criminals and delinquents and noted significant variations in their findings.[165] The discrepancies were believed to reflect refinements in testing methods and scoring, rather than differences in the mental ability of criminals.

These findings did much to discredit the notion that a strong relationship existed between IQ and criminality.

IQ and Delinquency Today

An oft-cited 1977 study by Travis Hirschi and Michael Hindelang revived interest in the association between IQ and delinquency.[166] After conducting a statistical analysis of a number of data sets, Hirschi and Hindelang concluded both that IQ tests are a valid predictor of intelligence and that "the weight of evidence is that IQ is more important than race and social class" for predicting delinquent involvement. They argued that a low IQ increases the likelihood of delinquent behavior through its effect on school performance: youths with low IQs do poorly in school, and school failure and academic incompetence are highly related to delinquency.

The Hirschi-Hindelang findings have been supported by a number of research efforts.[167] In their widely read *Crime and Human Nature,* James Q. Wilson and Richard Herrnstein concluded:

> . . . there appears to be a clear and consistent link between criminality and low intelligence. That is, taking all offenders as a group, and ignoring differences among kinds of crime, criminals seem, on the average, to be a bit less bright and to have a different set of intellectual strengths and weaknesses than do noncriminals as a group.[168]

Those social scientists who conclude that IQ influences delinquent behavior are split on the structure of the associations. Some believe that IQ has an indirect influence on delinquency. For example, when Terrie Moffitt and her associates found a significant relationship between low IQ and delinquency in a Danish cohort, they concluded that children with a low IQ are more likely to engage in delinquent behavior because their poor verbal ability is a handicap in school: low IQ leads to school failure, and educational underachievement has consistently been associated with delinquency.[169] In a later study, Moffitt, writing with Jennifer White and Phil Silva, found that "high risk" youths were less likely to become persistent delinquents if they had a relatively high IQ; low IQ increased the probability of a stable delinquent career.[170] The relationship between IQ and delinquency has been found to be consistent after controlling for class, race, and personality traits.[171]

Some experts believe that IQ may have a direct influence on the onset of delinquent involvement. David Farrington's research on the delinquent life cycle (discussed in Chapter 3) suggests that the key linkage between IQ and delinquency is the ability to manipulate abstract concepts. Low intelligence limits adolescents' ability to "foresee the consequences of their offending and to appreciate the feelings of victims."[172]

IQ and Delinquency Reconsidered

The relationship between IQ and delinquency is an extremely controversial issue since it implies there is a condition present at birth that accounts for a child's delinquent behavior throughout the life cycle and that this condition is not easily changed or improved; research shows that measurements of intelligence taken in infancy are a good predictor of later IQ.[173] By implication, if delinquency is not spread evenly through the social structure, neither is intelligence. There is also research, such as that conducted by Scott Menard and Barbara Morse, that finds that IQ level has negligible influence on delinquent behavior.[174] IQ research involving charges that tests are culturally biased and invalid makes any existing evidence at best inconclusive.[175]

Thus, there is some, albeit inconclusive, evidence that some youths with limited intellectual ability may be more likely to engage in delinquent behaviors.

Even those who believe IQ and crime are associated recognize that the linkage is indirect: intelligence is associated with poor school performance, which leads to delinquency.[176] As Wilson and Herrnstein put it, "A child who chronically loses standing in the competition of the classroom may feel justified in settling the score outside, by violence, theft, and other forms of defiant illegality."[177] Since the relationship runs from low IQ to poor school performance to frustration to delinquency, it is important for school officials to recognize the problem and plan programs to help underachievers perform better in school. Since the hypothesized relationship between IQ and delinquency, even if proved to be valid, is an indirect one, educational enrichment programs can help counteract any influence intellectual impairment has on the predilection of young people to commit crime.

CRIME AND HUMAN NATURE

In 1985, James Q. Wilson and Richard Herrnstein published *Crime and Human Nature,* which soon became one of the most talked-about works in criminological literature.[178] This work integrates biosocial factors, such as genetic makeup, IQ, and body build, with the concept of criminal choice theory into a theory of delinquency through the life course that the authors refer to as *crime as choice.*

According to Wilson and Herrnstein, throughout the life course, human behavior is determined by its perceived consequences. Choosing between committing a crime and not committing it (referred to as "noncrime") will depend on perception of gains and losses:

the larger the ratio of net rewards of crime to the net rewards of noncrime, the greater the tendency to commit the crime.[179]

The rewards for crime come in the form of material gain, sexual gratification, gaining revenge against an enemy, peer approval, and so on; the consequences can include pangs of conscience, revenge of the victim, disapproval of friends and associates, and the possibility of punishment. Noncrime rewards are usually gained in the future: they involve the maintenance of one's self-image, reputation, potential for a happier life, freedom, and so on.

The crime-noncrime choice is influenced by a number of factors. Decisions are reinforced by the desire to obtain basic rewards—food, clothing, shelter, sex—or learned goals—wealth, power, status. The choice of crime may be influenced by a person's perceived sense of inequity; those who feel cheated by society may turn to crime in order to "catch up."

The crime-noncrime choice is influenced by biosocial factors present at birth or soon after. These include: low intelligence; mesomorphic body type; a criminal father; an impulsive or extraverted personality; an autonomic nervous system that responds less slowly to stimuli.[180] Wilson and Herrnstein recognize that social factors that develop during the life cycle can also influence behavior. These factors include a turbulent family life, educational underachievement, and membership within a deviant teenage subculture.

According to Wilson and Herrnstein, biological, psychological and social conditions working in concert can influence thought patterns and eventually individual behavior patterns. The persistence of antisocial behavior through the life course, then, is a function of traits existing at birth and social factors that develop over the life span.

CRITIQUING INDIVIDUAL VIEWS

Individual views have been criticized on a number of grounds. One view is that the research methodology they employ is weak and invalid. Most research efforts use adjudicated or incarcerated offenders. It is often difficult to determine whether findings represent the delinquent population or merely those most likely to be arrested and adjudicated by officials of the justice system. For example, in a recent review of heredity studies, Glenn Walters and Thomas White concluded:

Our review leads us to the inevitable conclusion that current genetic research on crime has been poorly designed, ambiguously reported and exceedingly inadequate in addressing the relevant issues.[181]

Some critics also fear that individual-level research can be socially and politically damaging. If a significant number of known delinquents come from particular economic, racial, and ethnic groups, is it possible that a corresponding percentage of people in these groups share physical, personality, and mental traits that differ from the norm? If an above-average number of indigent youth become delinquent offenders, can it be assumed that the less affluent are impulsive, greedy, have low IQs, or are genetically inferior? To many social scientists, the implications of this conclusion are unacceptable in light of what is known about race, gender, and class bias.

Critics also suggest that individual-level theory is limited as a generalized explanation of delinquent behavior because it fails to account for the known patterns of criminal behavior. Delinquent behavior trends seem to conform to certain patterns linked to social-ecological rather than individual factors—social class, seasonality, population density, and gender roles. Social forces that appear to be influencing the onset and maintenance of delinquent behavior are not accounted for by explanations of delinquency that focus on the individual. If, as is often the case, the delinquent rate is higher in one neighborhood than another, are we to conclude that youths in the high-crime area are more likely to be watching violent TV shows or eating more sugar-coated cereals than those in low-crime neighborhoods? How can individual traits explain the fact that crime rates vary between cities and between regions?

Theorists who focus on individual behavior contend that critics overlook the fact that their research gives equal weight to environmental and social as well as mental and physical factors.[182] According to this view, some people have particular developmental problems that place them at a disadvantage in society, limit their chances of conventional success, and heighten their feelings of anger, frustration, and rage. Though the incidence of these personal traits may be spread evenly across the social structure, families in one segment of the population have the financial wherewithal to help ameliorate the problem, while families in another segment lack the economic means and the institutional support needed to help their children. If individual-level theorists are correct, crime rate differences are a result of differential access to opportunities to either commit crime or receive the care and treatment needed to correct and compensate for developmental problems.

In addition, individual-level theorists believe that, like it or not, people are in fact different and may have differing potentials for antisocial acts. For example, gender differences in the violence rate may be explained by the fact that after centuries of aggressive mating behavior, males have become naturally more violent than females.[183] Male aggression may be more a matter of genetic transfer than socialization or cultural patterns.

BIOLOGICAL/PSYCHOLOGICAL APPROACHES TO DELINQUENCY PREVENTION

Since many individual-oriented theorists are also practitioners and clinicians, it is not surprising that a great deal of delinquency prevention efforts are based in psychological and biosocial theory.

As a group, individual perspectives on delinquency suggest that prevention efforts should be directed at strengthening a youth's home life and personal relationships. Almost all of these theoretical efforts point to the child's home life as a key factor in delinquent behavior. If parents cannot supply proper nurturing, love, care, discipline, nutrition, and so on, the child cannot develop properly. Whether one believes that delinquency has a biosocial basis, a psychological basis, or a combination of both, it is evident that delinquency prevention efforts should be oriented to reach children early in their development.

It is, therefore, not surprising that county welfare agencies and privately funded treatment centers have offered counseling and other mental health

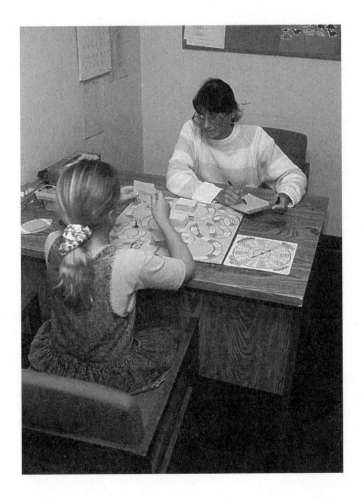

If delinquency has a psychological basis as some experts believe, then treatment efforts should include counseling. Here a child psychologist uses an assessment tool with a young client.

services to families referred by schools, welfare agents, and juvenile court authorities. In some instances, intervention is focused on a particular family problem that has the potential for producing delinquent behavior, for example, alcohol and drug problems, child abuse, and sexual abuse. In other situations, intervention is more generalized and oriented toward developing the self-image of parents and children or improving discipline in the family.

In addition, individual approaches have been used to prevent court-adjudicated youth from engaging in further criminal activities. This is sometimes referred to as *secondary* or *special prevention*. It has become almost universal for incarcerated and court-adjudicated youths to be given some sort of mental and physical evaluation before they begin their term of correctional treatment. Such rehabilitation methods as psychological counseling and psychotropic medication (involving such drugs as Valium or Ritalin) are often prescribed. In some instances, rehabilitation programs are provided through "drop-in" centers that service youths who are able to remain in their homes, while more intensive programs require residential care and treatment. At the least, this illustrates how agents of the juvenile justice system believe that many delinquent youths and status offenders have psychological or physical problems and that their successful "cure" can reduce repeat criminal behavior. Faith in this treatment approach suggests widespread agreement among juvenile justice system professionals that the cause of delinquency can be traced to individual pathology; if not, why else bother treating them?

While the influence of psychological theory on delinquency prevention has been extensive, programs based on biosocial theory have been dormant for some time. Institutions, however, are beginning to sponsor demonstration projects designed to study the influence of diet on crime and to determine whether regulating the metabolism can affect behavior. Such efforts are relatively new and untested. Similarly, schools are making an effort to help youths with learning disabilities and other developmental problems. Delinquency prevention efforts based on biocriminological theory are still in their infancy. The following Case in Point explores some questions arising out of the biosocial approach.

Some questions remain about the effectiveness of individual treatment as a delinquency prevention technique. Little hard evidence exists that clinical treatment alone can prevent delinquency or rehabilitate known delinquents. Critics still point to the failure of the famous Cambridge-Somerville Youth Study as evidence that clinical treatment has little value. In that effort, 325 high-risk predelinquents were given intense counseling and treatment, and their progress was compared with a control group that received no special attention. A well-known evaluation of the project by Joan McCord and William McCord found that the treated youths were more likely to become involved in law violation than the untreated controls.[184] By implication, the danger is that the efforts designed to help youths may actually stigmatize and label them, hindering their efforts to live conventional lives. Critics such as Edwin Schur argue that less is better, that the more we try to help youths, the more likely they will be to see themselves as different, outcasts, troublemakers, and so on.[185] Such questions have led to the development of prevention efforts designed to influence the social as well as the psychological world of delinquent and predelinquent youths (see Chapters 5 and 6).

Both choice and trait theories are usually considered conservative since they focus on the individual offender's personal characteristics and traits, rather than

You are a state legislator who is a member of the subcommittee on juvenile justice. Your committee has been asked to redesign the state's juvenile code because of public outrage over serious juvenile crime.

At an open hearing, a professor from the local university testifies that she has devised a sure-fire test to predict violence-prone delinquents. The procedure involves brain scans, DNA testing, and blood analysis. Used with samples of incarcerated adolescents, her procedure has been able to distinguish with 90 percent accuracy between youths with a history of violence and those who are exclusively property offenders. The professor testifies that if each juvenile offender were tested with her techniques, the violence-prone career offender could be easily identified and given special treatment, for example, separated from the general juvenile population or given a longer sentence.

Opponents argue that this type of testing is unconstitutional because it violates the youth's Fifth Amendment right against self-incrimination and can unjustly label nonviolent offenders. Any attempt to base policy on biosocial makeup seems inherently wrong and unfair. Those who favor the professor's approach maintain that it is not uncommon to single out the insane or mentally incompetent for special treatment and that these conditions often have a biological basis. It is better that a few delinquents be unfairly labeled than seriously violent offenders be ignored before it is too late.

Should special laws be created to deal with the "potentially" dangerous offender?

Should offenders be typed on the basis of their biological characteristics?

Is a 10 percent rate of inaccuracy too high to be considered for a basis of prediction? What would you do if the test were 100 percent reliable?

on the social environment in which they live. Both theoretical positions agree that delinquency can be prevented by dealing with the youths who engage in crime, not by transforming the social conditions associated with youth crime. In contrast, more liberal delinquency experts, whose work will be discussed in Chapters 5, 6, and 7, view the environment as the main source of delinquency-producing phenomena.

■ ■ ■ ■ ■ ■ ■ ■ ■ ■ ■ ■ ■ ■ ■ ■ ■

SUMMARY

Choice theory holds that people have free will to control their actions. Crime is a product of the weighing of the risks of crime against its benefits. If the risk is greater than the gain, people will choose not to commit crime. One way of creating a greater risk is to make sure that the punishments associated with crime are severe, certain, and fast.

Choice theorists argue that delinquent behavior can be prevented if youths can be deterred from illegal acts. Consequently, they agree that the punishment for delinquency should be increased. One method is to transfer youths to the criminal courts or to grant the adult justice system original jurisdiction over serious juvenile cases. Similarly, some delinquent ex-

THEORY	MAJOR PREMISE	STRENGTHS
CHOICE THEORIES		
rational choice	Law-violating behavior is an event that occurs after offenders weigh information on their personal needs and the situational factors involved in the difficulty and risk of committing a crime.	Explains why high-risk youth do not constantly engage in delinquent acts. Relates theory to delinquency control policy. It is not limited by class or other social variables.
routine activities	Crime and delinquency is a function of the presence of motivated offenders, the availability of suitable targets, and the absence of capable guardians.	Can explain fluctuations in crime and delinquency rates. Shows how victim behavior influences criminal choice.
deterrence	People will commit crime and delinquency if they perceive that the benefits outweigh the risks. Crime is a function of the severity, certainty, and speed of punishment.	Shows the relationship between crime and punishment. Suggests a real solution to crime.
BIOSOCIAL THEORIES		
biochemical	Crime, especially violence, is a function of diet, vitamin intake, hormonal imbalance, or food allergies.	Explains irrational violence. Shows how the environment interacts with personal traits to influence behavior.
neurological	Criminals and delinquents often suffer brain impairment, as measured by the EEG. Attention deficit disorder and minimum brain dysfunction are related to antisocial behavior.	Explains irrational violence. Shows how the environment interacts with personal traits to influence behavior.
genetic	Delinquent traits and predispositions are inherited. Criminality of parents can predict the delinquency of children.	Explains why only a small percentage of youth in a high-crime area become chronic offenders.
PSYCHOLOGICAL THEORIES		
psychodynamic	The development of the unconscious personality early in childhood influences behavior for the rest of a person's life. Delinquents have weak egos and damaged personalities.	Explains the onset of crime and delinquency. Shows why delinquency and drug abuse cut across class lines.
behavioral	People commit crime when they model their behavior after others they see being rewarded for the same acts. Behavior is enforced by rewards and extinguished by punishment.	Explains the role of others in the crime process. Shows how family life and media can influence delinquency.
cognitive	Individual reasoning processes influence behavior. Reasoning is influenced by the way people perceive their environment and by their moral and intellectual development.	Shows why delinquent behavior patterns change over time as people mature and develop their moral reasoning.
INTEGRATED THEORIES		
Wilson and Herrnstein's human nature theory	People choose to commit crime when they are biologically and psychologically impaired.	Shows how physical traits interact with social conditions to produce crime. Can account for noncriminal behavior in high-crime areas. Integrates choice and developmental theories.

perts advocate the use of incapacitation for serious juvenile offenders—for example, using mandatory, long-term sentences for chronic delinquents.

Classical theorists also advocate desert-based sentencing. Some states now punish offenders according to the crimes they commit and not their need for treatment.

Biosocial and psychological theories hold that personal and environmental factors dictate behavior choices, that delinquents do not choose to commit crimes freely but are influenced by forces beyond their control.

One of the earliest branches of biosocial theory focused on the biological bases of delinquency. Cesare Lombroso originated the concept of the "born criminal" and linked delinquency to inborn traits. Following his lead were theories based on genetic inheritance and body build. While biological theory was in disrepute for many years, it has recently reemerged in importance. Biochemical, neurological, and genetic factors have been linked to aggressiveness and violence in youth. However, because biosocial theory has not been subjected to methodologically sound tests, the results remain problematic.

Another type of individual-level theory has a psychological orientation. Some theorists rely on Freud's psychoanalytic theory and link delinquency to ego development and personality. Others use a behavioral perspective. Social-learning theorists hold that children imitate the adult behavior they observe live or on television. Physiological psychologists study the relationship between physical and mental properties. Table 4.1 summarizes these views.

Many delinquency prevention efforts are based on psychological theory. Judges commonly order delinquent youths to receive counseling and other mental health care. Recently, some adjudicated delinquent offenders have been given biochemical therapy.

KEY TERMS

choice theory
free will
utilitarian
classical criminology
rehabilitation
medical model
rational choice
"seductions of crime"
routine activity theory
life-style
deterrence
criminal atavism
somatotype
reciprocal altruism
biosocial theory

psychological theory
equipotentiality
neurological
minimal brain dysfunction (MBD)
learning disability (LD)
psychoanalytic theory
psychoanalysis
identity crisis
latent delinquents
behaviorism
social learning
cognitive school
psychopathic
sociopathic
nuture school

QUESTIONS FOR DISCUSSION

1. Is there such a thing as the "criminal man"?
2. Is crime psychologically abnormal? Can there be "normal" crimes?
3. Apply psychodynamic theory to such delinquent acts as shoplifting and breaking and entering a house.
4. Can delinquent behavior be deterred by the threat of punishment? If not, how can it be controlled?
5. Should we incapacitate violent juvenile offenders for long periods of time—ten years or more?
6. Does watching violent TV and films encourage youth to be aggressive and antisocial? Do advertisements for beer featuring attractive, scantily dressed young men and women encourage drinking and precocious sex? If not, why bother advertising?
7. Discuss the characteristics of psychopaths. Do you know anyone who fits the description?

NOTES

1. Marvin Wolfgang, Robert Figlio and Thorsten Sellin, Delinquency in a Birth Cohort (Chicago: University of Chicago Press, 1972).
2. Alan Lizotte, Terence Thornberry, Marvin Krohn, Deborah Chard-Wierschem, and David McDowall, "Neighborhood Context and Delinquency: A Longitudinal Analysis," In H. J. Kerner and E. Weitekamp, eds., Cross-National Longitudinal Research on Human Development and Criminal Behavior (Dordrecht, The Netherlands: Kluwer Academic Publishers, 1993), pp. 11–15.
3. Jeremy Bentham, A Fragment on Government and an Introduction to the Principles of Morals and Legislation, ed. Wilfred Harrison (Oxford: Basic Blackwell, 1967).
4. See, generally, Ernest Van den Haag, Punishing Criminals (New York: Basic Books, 1975).
5. See, generally, James Q. Wilson, Thinking about Crime (New York: Basic Books, 1975).
6. Cesare Beccaria, On Crimes and Punishments, 6th ed., trans. Henry Paolucci (Indianapolis: Bobbs-Merrill, 1977), p. 43.
7. F. E. Devine, "Cesare Beccaria and the Theoretical Foundations of Modern Penal Jurisprudence," New England Journal on Prison Law 7:8–21 (1982).
8. For an analysis of the rehabilitation philosophy, see Ted Palmer, Correctional Intervention and Research (Lexington, Mass.: Lexington Books, 1978).
9. Sanford Fox, "The Reform of Juvenile Justice: The Child's Right to Punishment," Juvenile Justice 25:2–9 (1974).
10. James Q. Wilson and Richard Herrnstein, Crime and Human Nature (New York: Simon and Schuster, 1985), p. 396.
11. Mary Tuck and David Riley, "The Theory of Reasoned Action: A Decision Theory of Crime," in D. Cornish and R. Clarke, eds., The Reasoning Criminal (New York: Springer-Verlag, 1986), p. 156–69.
12. Wilson, Thinking about Crime; Van den Haag, Punishing Criminals; Andrew von Hirsch, Doing Justice: The Choice of Punishments (New York: Hill & Wang, 1976); Graeme Newman, Just and Painful (New York: Macmillan, 1983).
13. See, generally, Derek Cornish and Ronald Clarke, eds. The Reasoning Criminal (New York: Springer-Verlag, 1986); see also Philip Cook, "The Demand and Supply of Criminal Opportunities," in Michael Tonry and Norval Morris, eds., Crime and Justice, vol. 7 (Chicago: University of Chicago Press, 1986), pp. 1–28; Ronald Clarke and Derek Cornish, "Modeling Offender's Decisions: A Framework for Research and Policy," in Michael Tonry and Norval Morris, eds., Crime and Justice, vol. 6 (Chicago: University of Chicago Press, 1985), pp. 147–87; Morgan Reynolds, Crime by Choice: An Economic Analysis (Dallas: Fisher Institute, 1985).
14. Felix Padilla, The Gang as an American Enterprise (New Brunswick, N.J.: Rutgers University Press, 1992); see also Martin Sanchez-Jankowski, Islands in the Stream: Gangs and American Urban Society (Berkeley: University of California Press, 1991).
15. Travis Hirschi, "Rational Choice and Social Control Theories of Crime," in D. Cornish and R. Clarke, eds., The Reasoning Criminal (New York: Springer-Verlag, 1986), p. 114.
16. Jack Katz, Seductions of Crime (New York: Basic Books, 1988).
17. Ibid., pp. 12–52.
18. Bill McCarthy and John Hagan, "Mean Streets: The Theoretical Significance of Situational Delinquency among Homeless Youths," American Journal of Sociology 3:597–627 (1992).
19. James Massey, Marvin Krohn, and Lisa Bonati, "Property Crime and the Routine Activities of Individuals," Journal of Research in Crime and Delinquency 26:378–400 (1989).
20. Lawrence Cohen and Marcus Felson, "Social Change and Crime Rate Trends: A Routine Activities Approach," American Sociological Review 44:588–608 (1979).
21. For a review, see James LeBeau and Thomas Castellano, "The Routine Activities Approach: An Inventory and Critique" (Unpublished, Center for the Studies of Crime, Delinquency and Corrections, Southern Illinois University-Carbondale, 1987).
22. Denise Osborn, Alan Trickett, and Rob Elder, "Area Characteristics and Regional Variates as Determinants of Area Property Crime Levels," Journal of Quantitative Criminology 8:265–82 (1992).
23. Massey, Krohn, and Bonati, "Property Crime and Routine Activities of Individuals," p. 397.
24. Lawrence Cohen, Marcus Felson, and Kenneth Land, "Property Crime Rates in the United States: A Macrodynamic Analysis, 1947–1977, with Ex-Ante Forecasts for the Mid-1980's," American Journal of Sociology 86:90–118 (1980).
25. Robert O'Brien, "Relative Cohort Sex and Age-Specific Crime Rates: An Age-Period-Relative-Cohort-Size Model," Criminology 27:57–78 (1989).
26. Steven Messner and Kenneth Tardiff, "The Social Ecology of Urban Homicide: An Application of the 'Routine Activities' Approach," Criminology 23:241–67 (1985).
27. Leslie Kennedy and David Forde, "Routine Activities and Crime: An Analysis of Victimization in Canada," Criminology 28:137–52 (1990).
28. David Maume, "Inequality and Metropolitan Rape Rates: A Routine Activity Approach," Justice Quarterly 6:513–27 (1989).

29. Ernest Van den Haag, "The Criminal Law as a Threat System," *Journal of Criminal Law and Criminology* 73:709–85 (1982).

30. Beccaria, *On Crimes and Punishments*.

31. For the classic analysis on the subject, see Johannes Andenaes, *Punishment and Deterrence* (Ann Arbor: University of Michigan Press, 1974).

32. *Wilkins v. Missouri; Stanford v. Kentucky*, 109 S.Ct. 2969 (1989).

33. Carol Kohfeld and John Sprague, "Demography, Police Behavior, and Deterrence," *Criminology* 28:111–36 (1990).

34. Steven Klepper and Daniel Nagin, "The Deterrent Effect of Perceived Certainty and Severity of Punishment Revisited," *Criminology* 27:721–46 (1989).

35. See, generally, Raymond Paternoster, "The Deterrent Effect of Perceived and Severity of Punishment: A Review of the Evidence and Issues," *Justice Quarterly* 42:173–217 (1987).

36. Raymond Paternoster, "Absolute and Restrictive Deterrence in a Panel of Youth: Explaining the Onset, Persistence/Desistance, and Frequency of Delinquent Offending," *Social Problems* 36:289–307 (1989).

37. Donald Green, "Measures of Illegal Behavior in Individual-Level Deterrence Research," *Journal of Research in Crime and Delinquency* 26:253–75 (1989); Charles Tittle, *Sanctions and Social Deviance: The Question of Deterrence* (New York: Praeger, 1980).

38. Bureau of Justice Statistics, *Prisoners and Drugs* (Washington, D.C.: Government Printing Office, 1983); idem, *Prisoners and Alcohol* (Washington, D.C.: Government Printing Office, 1983).

39. Maynard Erickson and Jack Gibbs, "Punishment, Deterrence, and Juvenile Justice," in D. Shichor and D. Kelly, eds., *Critical Issues in Juvenile Justice* (Lexington, Mass.: Lexington Books, 1980), pp. 183–202.

40. Taken from the famous title of an article by Walter Reckless, Simon Dinitz, and Ellen Murray: "The Good Boy in a High Delinquency Area," *Journal of Criminal Law, Criminology, and Police Science* 48:18–26 (1957).

41. Massey, Krohn, and Bonati, "Property Crime and the Routine Activities of Individuals."

42. David Shantz, "Conflict, Aggression, and Peer Status: An Observational Study," *Child Development* 57:1322–32 (1986).

43. For an excellent review of Lombroso's work, as well as that of other well-known theorists, see Randy Martin, Robert Mutchnick, and W. Timothy Austin, *Criminological Thought, Pioneers Past and Present* (New York: Macmillan, 1990).

44. Marvin Wolfgang, "Cesare Lombroso," in Herman Mannheim, ed., *Pioneers in Criminology* (Montclair, N.J.: Patterson Smith, 1970), pp. 232–71.

45. Gina Lombroso-Ferrero, *Criminal Man According to the Classification of Cesare Lombroso* (1911; reprint, Montclair, N.J.: Patterson Smith, 1972), p. 7.

46. Edwin Driver, "Charles Buckman Goring," in Herman Mannheim, ed., *Pioneers in Criminology* (Montclair, N.J.: Patterson Smith, 1970), pp. 429–42.

47. See, generally, Thorsten Sellin, "Enrico Ferri," in Herman Mannheim, ed., *Pioneers in Criminology* (Montclair, N.J.: Patterson Smith, 1970), pp. 361–84.

48. Driver, "Charles Buckman Goring," pp. 434–435.

49. Ibid., p. 440.

50. See Richard Dugdale, *The Jukes* (New York: Putnam, 1910); Arthur Estabrook, *The Jukes in 1915* (Washington, D.C.: Carnegie Institute of Washington, 1916).

51. Ernst Kretschmer, *Physique and Character,* trans. W.J.H. Spratt (London: Kegan Paul, 1925).

52. William Sheldon, *Varieties of Delinquent Youth* (New York: Harper Bros., 1949).

53. For a review of Sheldon's legacy, see C. Peter Herman, "The Shape of Man," *Contemporary Psychology* 37:525–30 (1992).

54. Nicole Hahn Rafter, "Criminal Anthropology in the United States," *Criminology* 30:525–47 (1992).

55. B. R. McCandless, W. S. Persons, and A. Roberts, "Perceived Opportunity, Delinquency, Race, and Body Build among Delinquent Youth," *Journal of Consulting and Clinical Psychology* 38:281–83 (1972).

56. Edmond O. Wilson, *Sociobiology: The New Synthesis* (Cambridge: Harvard University Press, 1975).

57. For a general review, see John Archer, "Human Sociobiology: Basic Concepts and Limitations," *Journal of Social Issues* 47:11–26 (1991).

58. Arthur Caplan, *The Sociobiology Debate: Readings on Ethical and Scientific Issues* (New York: Harper & Row, 1978).

59. For a thorough review of the biosocial perspective, see Diana Fishbein, "Biological Perspectives in Criminology," *Criminology* 28:27–72 (1990).

60. See C. Ray Jeffrey, "Criminology as an Interdisciplinary Behavioral Science," *Criminology* 16:149–67 (1978).

61. See, generally, Leonard Hippchen, *The Ecologic-Biochemical Approaches to Treatment of Delinquents and Criminals* (New York: Van Nostrand Reinhold, 1978).

62. Paul Marshall, "Allergy and Depression: A Neurochemical Threshold Model of the Relation between the Illnesses," *Psychological Bulletin* 113:23–43 (1993); Elizabeth McNeal and Peter Cimbolic, "Antidepressants and Biochemical Theories of Depression," *Psychological Bulletin* 99:361–74 (1986); for an opposing view, see "Adverse Reactions to Food in Young Children," *Nutrition Reviews* 46:120–21 (1988).

63. Marshall, "Allergy and Depression: A Neurochemical Threshold Model of the Relation between the Illnesses."

64. Christy Miller Buchanan, Jacquelynne Eccles, and Jill Becker, "Are Adolescents the Victims of Raging Hormones? Evidence for Activational Effects of Hormones on Moods and Behavior at Adolescence," *Psychological Bulletin* 111:62–107 (1992).

65. Leonard Hippchen, "Some Possible Biochemical Aspects of Criminal Behavior," *Journal of Behavioral Ecology* 2:1–6 (1981); Sarnoff Mednick and Jan Volavka, "Biology and Crime," in N. Morris and M. Tonry, eds., *Crime and Justice*, vol. 2 (Chicago: University of Chicago Press, 1980), pp. 85–159.

66. Stephen Schoenthaler, "Malnutrition and Maladaptive Behavior: Two Correlational Analyses and a Double-Blind Placebo-Controlled Challenge in Five States," in W. B. Essman, ed., *Nutrients and Brain Function* (New York: Karger, 1987).

67. Alexander Schauss and C. Simonsen, "A Critical Analysis of the Diets of Chronic Juvenile Offenders, Part I," *Journal of Orthomolecular Psychiatry* 8:149–57 (1979).

68. J. Kershner and W. Hawke, "Megavitamins and Learning Disorders: A Controlled Double-Blind Experiment," *Journal of Nutrition* 109:819–26 (1979).

69. Stephen Schoenthaler and Walter Doraz, "Types of Offenses Which Can Be Reduced in an Institutional Setting Using Nutritional Intervention," *International Journal of Biosocial Research* 4:74–84 (1983); and idem, "Diet and Crime," *International Journal of Biosocial Research* 4:29–39 (1983).

70. Stephen Schoenthaler, Walter Doraz, and James Wakefield, "The Impact of a Low Food Additive and Sucrose Diet on Academic Performance in 803 New York City Public Schools," *International Journal of Biosocial Research* 8:185–95 (1986).

71. Richard Milich and William Pelham, "Effects of Sugar Ingestion on the Classroom and Playgroup Behavior of Attention Deficit Disordered Boys," *Journal of Counseling and Clinical Psychology* 54:714–18 (1986).

72. Dian Gans, "Sucrose and Unusual Childhood Behavior," *Nutrition Today* 26:8–14 (1991).

73. Stephen Schoenthaler, "Institutional Nutritional Policies and Criminal Behavior," *Nutrition Today* 24:16–24 (1985), at 24.

74. Diana Fishbein, David Lozovsky, and Jerome Jaffe, "Impulsivity, Aggression and Neuroendocrine Responses to Serotonergic Stimulation in Substance Abusers," (Paper presented at the American Society of Criminology, Reno, Nevada, November 1989).

75. Leila Beckwith and Arthur Parmelee, "EEG Patterns of Preterm Infants, Home Environment, and Later IQ," *Child Development* 57:777–89 (1986).

76. Kytja Voeller, "Right-Hemisphere Deficit Syndrome in Children," *American Journal of Psychiatry* 143:1004–9 (1986).

77. Dorothy Otnow Lewis, Johnathan Pincus, Marilyn Feldman, Lori Jackson, and Barbara Bard, "Psychiatric, Neurological, and Psychoeducational Characteristics of 15 Death Row Inmates in the United States," *American Journal of Psychiatry* 143:838–45 (1986).

78. See, generally, R. R. Monroe, *Brain Dysfunction in Aggressive Criminals* (Lexington, Mass.: D. C. Heath, 1978).

79. Adrian Raine, et al., "Interhemispheric Transfer in Schizophrenics, Depressives and Normals with Schizoid Tendencies," *Journal of Abnormal Psychology* 98:35–41 (1989).

80. D. Williams, "Neural Factors Related to Habitual Aggression—Consideration of Differences between Habitual Aggressives and Others Who Have Committed Crimes of Violence," *Brain* 92:503–20 (1969).

81. Charlotte Johnson and William Pelham, "Teacher Ratings Predict Peer Ratings of Aggression at 3-Year Follow-Up in Boys with Attention Deficit Disorder with Hyperactivity," *Journal of Consulting and Clinical Psychology* 54:571–72 (1987).

82. Cited in Charles Post, "The Link between Learning Disabilities and Juvenile Delinquency: Cause, Effect, and 'Present Solutions,'" *Juvenile and Family Court Journal* 31:59 (1981).

83. For a general review, see Concetta Culliver, "Juvenile Delinquency and Learning Disability: Any Link?" (Paper presented at the Academy of Criminal Justice Sciences, San Francisco, April 1988).

84. Joel Zimmerman, William Rich, Ingo Keilitz, and Paul Broder, "Some Observations on the Link between Learning Disabilities and Juvenile Delinquency," *Journal of Criminal Justice* 9:9–17 (1981); J. W. Podboy and W. A. Mallory, "The Diagnosis of Specific Learning Disabilities in a Juvenile Delinquent Population," *Juvenile and Family Court Journal* 30:11–13 (1978).

85. Charles Murray, *The Link between Learning Disabilities and Juvenile Delinquency: A Current Theory and Knowledge* (Washington, D.C.: Government Printing Office, 1976).

86. Robert Pasternak and Reid Lyon, "Clinical and Empirical Identification of Learning Disabled Juvenile Delinquents," *Journal of Correctional Education* 33:7–13 (1982).

87. Zimmerman, et al., "Some Observations on the Link between Learning Disabilities and Juvenile Delinquency."

88. Lynn Meltzer, Bethany Roditi, and Terence Fenton, "Cognitive and Learning Profiles of Delinquent and Learning-Disabled Adolescents," *Adolescence* 21:581–91 (1986).

89. Terrie Moffitt, "The Neuropsychology of Conduct Disorder" (University of Wisconsin-Madison, mimeo, 1992).

90. Elizabeth Kandel and Sarnoff Mednick, "Perinatal Complications Predict Violent Offending," *Criminology* 29:519–30 (1991).

91. James Creechan, "The Masking of Learning Disabilities and Juvenile Delinquency: The Learning Disabilities–Juvenile Delinquency Amplification Model" (Paper presented at the annual meeting of the American Society of Criminology, New Orleans, November 1992).

92. Diana Fishbein and Robert Thatcher, "New Diagnostic Methods in Criminology: Assessing Organic Sources of Behavioral Disorder," *Journal of Research in Crime and Delinquency* 23:240–67 (1986).

93. For a review, see Lisabeth Fisher DiLalla and Irving Gottesman, "Biological and Genetic Contributors to Violence—Widom's Untold Tale," *Psychological Bulletin* 109:125–29 (1991).

94. Ibid.

95. L. Erlenmeyer-Kimling, Robert Golden, and Barbara Cornblatt, "A Taxometric Analysis of Cognitive and Neuromotor Variables in Children in Risk for Schizophrenia," *Journal of Abnormal Psychology* 98:203–8 (1989).

96. A. A. Sandberg, G. F. Koeph, T. Ishiara, and T. S. Hauschka, "An XYY Human Male," *Lancet* 262:448–49 (1961); T. R. Sarbin and L. E. Miller, " "Demonism Revisited: The XYY Chromosome Anomaly," *Issues in Criminology* 5:195–207 (1970).

97. David Rowe, Joseph Rogers, and Sylvia Meseck-Bushey, "Sibling Delinquency and the Family Environment: Shared and Unshared Influences," *Child Development* 63:59–67 (1992).

98. David Rowe, "Sibling Interaction and Self-Reported Delinquent Behavior: A Study of 265 Twin Pairs," *Criminology* 23:223–40 (1985); Nancy Segal, "Monozygotic and Dizygotic Twins: A Comparative Analysis of Mental Ability Profiles," *Child Development* 56:1051–58 (1985).

99. Mednick and Volavka, "Biology and Crime"; in Noval Morris and Michael Tonry, eds. *Crime and Justice* vol. 1 (Chicago; University of Chicago Press, 1980), pp. 85–159: Lee Ellis, "Genetics and Criminal Behavior," *Criminology* 10:43–66 (1982).

100. Karl O. Christiansen, "A Preliminary Study of Criminality among Twins," in S. A. Mednick and Karl O. Christiansen, eds., *The Biosocial Bases of Criminal Behavior* (New York: Gardner Press, 1977).

101. Glenn Walters, "A Meta-Analysis of the Gene-Crime Relationship," *Criminology 30:595–613 (1992)*.

102. T. J. Bouchard, D. T. Lykken, D. T. McGue, N. L. Segal, and A. Tellegen, "Sources of Human Psychological Differences: The Minnesota Study of Twins Reared Apart," *Science* 250:223–28 (1990).

103. D. T. Lykken, M. McGue, A. Tellegen, and T. J. Bouchard, Jr., "Emergenesis, Genetic Traits That May Not Run in Families," *American Psychologist* 47:1565–77 (1992).

104. Remi Cadoret, Colleen Cain, and Raymond Crowe, "Evidence for a Gene-Environment Interaction in the Development of Adolescent Antisocial Behavior," *Behavior Genetics* 13:301–10 (1983).

105. Bernard Hutchings and Sarnoff Mednick, "Criminality in Adoptees and Their Adoptive and Biological Parents: A Pilot Study," in S. A. Mednick and Karl O. Christiansen, eds., *Biosocial Bases of Criminal Behavior* (New York: Gardner Press, 1977).

106. William Gabrielli and Sarnoff Mednick, "Urban Environment, Genetics, and Crime," *Criminology* 22:645–53 (1984).

107. Jody Alberts-Corush, Philip Firestone, and John Goodman, "Attention and Impulsivity Characteristics of the Biological and Adoptive Parents of Hyperactive and Normal Control Children," *American Journal of Orthopsychiatry* 56:413–23 (1986).

108. Wilson and Herrnstein, *Crime and Human Nature,* p. 131.

109. Walters, "A Meta-Analysis of the Gene-Crime Relationship."

110. Ibid., p. 108.

111. For a thorough review of this issue, see David Brandt and S. Jack Zlotnick, "The Psychology and Treatment of the Youthful Offender (Springfield, Ill.: Charles C. Thomas, 1988).

112. Spencer Rathus, *Psychology* (New York: Holt, Rinehart & Winston, 1984).

113. See, generally, Sigmund Freud, *An Outline of Psychoanalysis,* trans. James Strachey (New York: Norton, 1963).

114. Seymour Halleck, *Psychiatry and the Dilemmas of Crime* (Berkeley: University of California Press, 1971).

115. See, generally, Erik Erickson, *Identity, Youth, and Crisis* (New York: Norton, 1968).

116. David Abrahamsen, *Crime and Human Mind* (New York: Columbia University Press, 1944), p. 137.

117. See, generally, Fritz Redl and Hans Toch, "The Psychoanalytic Perspective," in Hans Toch, ed., *Psychology of Crime and Criminal Justice* (New York: Holt, Rinehart & Winston, 1979), pp. 193–95.

118. August Aichorn, *Wayward Youth* (New York: Viking Press, 1935).

119. Halleck, *Psychiatry and the Dilemmas of Crime.*

120. James Sorrells, "Kids Who Kill," *Crime and Delinquency* 23:312–20 (1977).

121. Richard Rosner, et al., "Adolescents Accused of Murder and Manslaughter: A Five-Year Descriptive Study," *Bulletin of the American Academy of Psychiatry and the Law* 7:342–51 (1979).

122. Milton Rosenbaum and Binni Bennet, "Homicide and Depression," *American Journal of Psychiatry* 143:367–70 (1986).

123. Brandt and Zlotnick, *The Psychology and Treatment of the Youthful Offender,* pp. 72–73.

124. See Albert Bandura and Frances Menlove, "Factors Determining Vicarious Extinction of Avoidance Behavior through Symbolic Modeling," *Journal of Personality and Social Psychology* 8:99–108 (1965); and Albert Bandura and Richard Walters, *Social Learning and Personality Development* (New York: Holt, Rinehart & Winston, 1963).

125. David Perry, Louise Perry, and Paul Rasmussen, "Cognitive Social Learning Mediators of Aggression," *Child Development* 57:700–11 (1986).

126. Bonnie Carlson, "Children's Beliefs about Punishment," *American Journal of Orthopsychiatry* 56:308–12 (1986).

127. Albert Bandura and Richard Walters, *Adolescent Aggression* (New York: Ronald Press, 1959), p. 32.

128. Edward Donnerstein and Daniel Linz, "The Question of Pornography," *Psychology Today* 20:56–59 (1986).

129. Joyce Sprafkin, Kenneth Gadow, and Monique Dussault, "Reality Perceptions of Television: A Preliminary Comparison of Emotionally Disturbed and Nonhandicapped Children," *American Journal of Orthopsychiatry* 56:147–52 (1986).

130. Daniel Anderson, Elizabeth Pugzles Lorch, Diane Field, Patricia Collins, and John Nathan, "Television Viewing at Home: Age Trends in Visual Attention Time with TV," *Child Development* 57:1024–33 (1986).

131. Lynette Friedrich-Cofer and Aletha Huston, "Television Violence and Aggression: The Debate Continues," *Psychological Bulletin* 100:364–71 (1986).

132. American Psychological Association, *Violence on TV. A Social Issue Release from the Board of Social and Ethical Responsibility for Psychology* (Washington, D.C.: APA, 1985).

133. Wendy Wood, Frank Wong, and J. Gregory Chachere, "Effects of Media Violence on Viewers' Aggression in Unconstrained Social Interaction," *Psychological Bulletin* 109:371–83 (1991).

134. Johnathon Freedman, "Television Violence and Aggression: What the Evidence Shows," in S. Oskamp, ed., *Applied Social Psychology Annual: Television as a Social Issue* (Newbury Park, Calif.: Sage, 1988), pp. 144–62.

135. Johnathon Freedman, "Effect of Television Violence on Aggressiveness," *Psychological Bulletin* 96:227–46 (1984); idem, "Television Violence and Aggression: A Rejoinder," *Psychological Bulletin* 100:372–78 (1986).

136. Steven Messner, "Television Violence and Violent Crime: An Aggregate Analysis," *Social Problems* 33:218–35 (1986).

137. See, generally, Jean Piaget, *The Moral Judgement of the Child* (London: Keagan Paul, 1932).

138. Lawrence Kohlberg, *Stages in the Development of Moral Thought and Action* (New York: Holt, Rinehart and Winston, 1969).

139. L. Kohlberg, K. Kauffman, P. Scharf, and J. Hickey, *The Just Community Approach in Corrections: A Manual* (Niantic, Conn.: Connecticut Department of Corrections, 1973).

140. Scott Henggeler, *Delinquency in Adolescence* (Newbury Park, Calif.: Sage, 1989), p. 26.

141. Ibid.

142. See, generally, Walter Mischel, *Introduction to Personality*, 4th ed. (New York: Holt, Rinehart and Winston, 1986).

143. D. A. Andrews and J. Stephen Wormith, "Personality and Crime: Knowledge and Construction in Criminology," *Justice Quarterly* 6:289–310 (1989); Donald Gibbons, "Comment—Personality and Crime: Non-Issues, Real Issues, and a Theory and Research Agenda," *Justice Quarterly* 6:311–24 (1989).

144. Sheldon Glueck and Eleanor Glueck, *Unraveling Juvenile Delinquency* (Cambridge: Harvard University Press, 1950).

145. See, generally, Hans Eysenck, *Personality and Crime* (London: Routledge and Kegan Paul, 1977).

146. Hans Eysenck and M. W. Eysenck, *Personality and Individual Differences* (New York: Plenum, 1985).

147. David Farrington, "Psychobiological Factors in the Explanation and Reduction of Delinquency," *Today's Delinquent* 7:37–51 (1988).

148. Laurie Frost, Terrie Moffitt, and Rob McGee, "Neuropsychological Correlates of Psychopathology in an Unselected Cohort of Young Adolescents," *Journal of Abnormal Psychology* 98:307–13 (1989).

149. Harvey Cleckley, "Psychopathic States," in S. Aneti, ed., *American Handbook of Psychiatry* (New York: Basic Books, 1959), pp. 567–69.

150. Rathus, *Psychology*, p. 452.

151. Lewis Yablonsky, *The Violent Gang* (Baltimore: Penguin, 1971), pp. 195–205.

152. Helen Raskin White, Erich Labouvie, and Marsha Bates, "The Relationship between Sensation Seeking and Delinquency: A Longitudinal Analysis," *Journal of Research in Crime and Delinquency* 22:197–211 (1985).

153. See, for example, R. Starke Hathaway and Elio Monachesi, "The M.M.P.I. in the Study of Juvenile Delinquents," in A. M. Rose, ed., *Mental Health and Mental Disorder* (London: Routledge, 1956).

154. R. Starke Hathaway and Elio Monachesi, *Analyzing and Predicting Juvenile Delinquency with the M.M.P.I.* (Minneapolis: University of Minnesota Press, 1953).

155. Ibid.

156. Deborah Decker Roman and David Gerbing, "The Mentally Disordered Criminal Offender: A Description Based on Demographic, Clinical and MMPI D," *Journal of Clinical Psychology* 45:983–90 (1989).

157. Karl Schuessler and Donald Cressey, "Personality Characteristics of Criminals," *American Journal of Sociology* 55:476–84 (1950); Gordon Waldo and Simon Dinitz, "Personality Attributes of the Criminal: An Analysis of Research Studies, 1950–1965," *Journal of Research in Crime and Delinquency* 4:185–201 (1967); David Tennenbaum, "Research Studies of Personality and Criminality," *Journal of Criminal Justice* 5:1–19 (1977).

158. Donald Calsyn, Douglass Roszell, and Edmund Chaney, "Validation of MMPI Profile Subtypes among Opioid Addicts Who Are Beginning Methadone Maintenance Treatment," *Journal of Clinical Psychology* 45:991–99 (1989).

159. L. M. Terman, "Research on the Diagnosis of Predelinquent Tendencies," *Journal of Delinquency* 9:124–30 (1925); L. M. Terman, *Measurement of Intelligence* (Boston: Houghton-Mifflin, 1916). For example, see M. G. Caldwell, "The Intelligence of Delinquent Boys Committed to Wisconsin Industrial School," *Journal of Criminal Law and Criminology* 20:421–28 (1929); and C. Murcheson, *Criminal Intelligence* (Worcester, Mass.: Clark University, 1926), pp. 41–44.

160. Henry Goddard, *Efficiency and Levels of Intelligence* (Princeton, N.J.: Princeton University Press, 1920).

161. William Healy and Augusta Bronner, *Delinquency and Criminals: Their Making and Unmaking* (New York: Macmillan, 1926).

162. Kenneth Eels, *Intelligence and Cultural Differences* (Chicago: University of Chicago Press, 1951), p. 181.

163. Sorel Cahahn and Nora Cohen, "Age versus Schooling Effects on Intelligence Development," *Child Development* 60:1239–49 (1989).

164. John Slawson, *The Delinquent Boys* (Boston: Budget Press, 1926).

165. Edwin Sutherland, "Mental Deficiency and Crime," in Kimball Young, ed., *Social Attitudes* (New York: Henry Holt, 1973), chap. 15.

166. Travis Hirschi and Michael Hindelang, "Intelligence and Delinquency: A Revisionist Review," *American Sociological Review* 42:471–586 (1977).

167. Terrie Moffitt and Phil Silva, "IQ and Delinquency: A Direct Test of the Differential Detection Hypothesis," *Journal of Abnormal Psychology* 97:1–4 (1988); E. Kandel, S. Mednick, L. Sorenson-Kirkegaard, B. Hutchings, J. Knop, R. Rosenberg, and F. Schulsinger, "IQ as a Protective Factor for Subjects at a High Risk for Antisocial Behavior," *Journal of Consulting and Clinical Psychology* 56:224–26 (1988); Christine Ward and Richard McFall, "Further Validation of the Problem Inventory for Adolescent Girls: Comparing Caucasian and Black Delinquents and Nondelinquents," *Journal of Consulting and Clinical Psychology* 54:732–33 (1986).

168. Wilson and Herrnstein, *Crime and Human Nature* p. 148.

169. Terri Moffitt, William Gabrielli, Sarnoff Mednick, and Fini Schulsinger, "Socioeconomic Status, IQ, and Delinquency," *Journal of Abnormal Psychology* 90:152–56 (1981); for a similar finding, see L. Hubble and M. Groff, "Magnitude and Direction of WISC-R Verbal Performance IQ Discrepancies among Adjudicated Male Delinquents," *Journal of Youth and Adolescence* 10:179–83 (1981).

170. Jennifer White, Terrie Moffitt, and Phil Silva, "A Prospective Replication of the Protective Effects of IQ in Subjects at High Risk for Juvenile Delinquency," *Journal of Consulting and Clinical Psychology* 37:719–24 (1989).

171. Donald Lynam, Terrie Moffitt, and Magda Stouthamer-Loeber, "Explaining the Relations between IQ and Delinquency: Class, Race, Test Motivation, School Failure or Self-Control," *Journal of Abnormal Psychology* (in press, 1993).

172. David Farrington, "Juvenile Delinquency," in John C. Coleman, ed., *The School Years* (London: Routledge: 1992), p. 137.

173. Robert McCall and Michael Carriger, "A Meta-Analysis of Infant Habituation and Recognition Memory Performance as Predictors of Later IQ," *Child Development* 64:57–79 (1993).

174. Scott Menard and Barbara Morse, "A Structuralist Critique of the IQ-Delinquency Hypothesis: Theory and Evidence," *American Journal of Sociology* 89:1347–78 (1984).

175. Ibid.

176. Deborah Denno, "Sociological and Human Developmental Explanations of Crime: Conflict or Consensus," *Criminology* 23:711–41 (1985).

177. Ibid., p. 171.

178. Wilson and Herrnstein, *Crime and Human Nature*.

179. Ibid., p. 44.

180. Ibid., p. 171.

181. Glenn Walters and Thomas White, "Heredity and Crime: Bad Genes or Bad Research," *Justice Quarterly* 27:455–85 (1989), at 478.

182. Ellis, "Genetics and Criminal Behavior," *Criminology* 10:43–66 (1982) at 58.

183. Lee Ellis, "The Evolution of the Nonlegal Equivalent of Aggressive Criminal Behavior," *Aggressive Behavior* 12:57–71 (1986).

184. Joan McCord and William McCord, "A Follow-Up Report on the Cambridge-Somerville Youth Study," *Annals* 322:89–98 (1959).

185. Edwin Schur, *Radical Nonintervention: Rethinking the Delinquency Problem* (Englewood Cliffs, N.J.: Prentice-Hall, 1973).

SOCIAL
STRUCTURE
THEORIES

DISORGANIZATION, STRAIN, AND
CULTURAL DEVIANCE

In 1966, sociologist Oscar Lewis coined the phrase the **culture of poverty** to describe the crushing burden faced daily by the large mass of urban poor.[1] The culture of poverty is marked by apathy, cynicism, helplessness, and mistrust of such institutions as police, courts, schools, and government. Mistrust of authority prevents slum dwellers from taking advantage of the few conventional opportunities that are available to them. The result is a permanent American **underclass** whose members have little chance of upward mobility or improvement.[2]

This underclass is forced to live in deteriorated inner-city areas. These neighborhoods experience constant population turnover as their more affluent residents move out to stable suburbs. As cities become "hollowed out"—with a deteriorated inner-core surrounded by less devastated but declining suburban communities—delinquency rates spiral upward.[3] Those remaining are forced to live in areas with poorly organized social networks, heterogeneous and alienated populations, and high crime.

SOCIAL STRATIFICATION

Data gathered by a number of sources support this vision of a racially, socially, and economically **stratified** society. Stratification refers to the unequal distribution of scarce resources. It can involve different dimensions of human behavior. For example, economic stratification refers to the unequal distribution of wealth and income; political stratification refers to the unequal ability to gain power or hold office; prestige stratification involves the ability to be well regarded in the community. Family, education, group or religious affiliation, and race all influence the individual's ability to gain a disproportionate share of wealth, power, and prestige.

The United States has an economically structured society. At the bottom rung are the "truly disadvantaged" who may be both unemployed and homeless.

The United States maintains a stratified society. While most of us have the financial means to enjoy the fruits of U.S. technology and achievement, about 50 million people live below the poverty line (estimated to be an annual income of about fifteen thousand dollars for a family of four in 1992). Stratification effects are today becoming sharper. The wealthiest Americans now enjoy a greater share of the economy than ever before: the top 5 percent earn more than half of all income; the poorest Americans, the bottom 20 percent, get less than 5 percent. Children are especially hard hit by poverty; an estimated 12-14 million youth live below the poverty line.[4]

The poor in the United States often reside in deteriorated sections of the nation's largest cities, deprived of a standard of living enjoyed by most other citizens. Many, supported by public welfare and private charity throughout their entire lives, have no hope of achieving higher status within conventional society. They attend poor schools, live in substandard housing, and lack good health care. More than half the families are fatherless and husbandless, headed by a female who is the sole breadwinner; many are supported entirely by county welfare and Aid to Families with Dependent Children (AFDC). The Census Bureau estimates that about 20 percent of white children and 75 percent of black children are born out of wedlock; about 26 percent of all American families are single-parent households, and 88 percent of these are headed by a woman.[5]

The problems of providing adequate care and discipline to children under these circumstances can be immense. Over 2 million **latchkey children,** about 7 percent of all U.S. youth under 13, are left unattended after school every day. About 10 million children under age 5 are being cared for by someone other than a parent (see Figure 5.1).

Although little empirical evidence exists that living in a single-parent household alone is sufficient to produce delinquent behavior trends, it seems logical that the problems presented by raising a family in a deteriorated neighborhood are better met by two parents than one.[6]

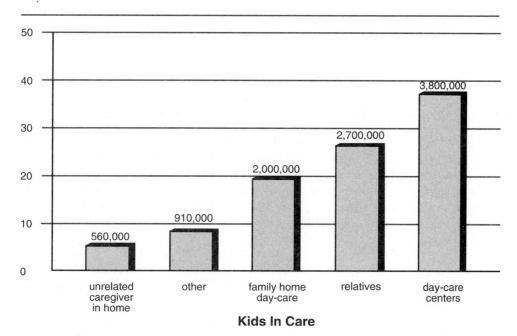

Kids In Care

■■**FIGURE 5.1**

Child care in the United States: 10 million kids are cared for by someone other than their parents

Source: Children's Defense Fund, *The State of America's Children, 1992* (Washington, D.C.: Children's Defense Fund, 1992), p. 17.

The effects of poverty are most often felt by minority-group members. It is estimated that 31 percent of black families and 26 percent of Hispanic families, as compared to 10 percent of white families, live in poverty; in all, these families contain about 20 percent of all children under 18.[7] A report by the National Research Council, a private, nonprofit group, found that African-Americans are either losing ground or maintaining a second-class rank in such critical areas as economic and educational status.[8]

While this picture is bleak, indications are that conditions are actually deteriorating: there is increasing inequality in socioeconomic position, greater dependence on social assistance and welfare, and growing numbers of single-parent families.[9]

SOCIAL STRUCTURE AND DELINQUENCY

The picture that emerges is one of destructive social forces impacting all too many adolescents and their families. To some delinquency experts, these unfair and destructive economic and social conditions within the nation's slum areas are the root cause of delinquency. While middle- and upper-class children may engage in minor and occasional delinquent acts—vandalism, use of nonaddictive drugs such as marijuana, petty theft, motor vehicle violations—they refrain from the more serious acts of violence, theft, and gang membership. Middle-class youths are better able to organize their resources in education and in the marketplace. Even those who do engage in delinquent acts are eventually able to age out of criminality and become responsible citizens.[10]

Considering their social and economic decay, it comes as no surprise that deteriorated inner-city areas in such cities as New York, Miami, and Los Angeles are the spawning ground of youth gangs and groups whose members graduate into adult criminal careers. Is it any wonder that without hope of earning money and achieving success through legitimate means, many inner-city youth turn to crime as a means of survival, self-esteem, and revenge on a society that has turned its back on them?

Lower-class slum areas are also the scene of the highest crime and victimization rates. Official delinquency rates for such crimes as robbery and larceny are much higher in urban than in suburban and rural areas. Likewise, self-report and official record studies seem to indicate that lower-class youths are the most likely to commit serious delinquent and criminal acts.

This view of delinquency then is essentially **structural** and cultural. It holds that delinquency is a consequence of the social and economic inequalities built into the U.S. social structure. Even those youths who receive the loving support of parents and family members are at risk of crime, delinquency, and arrest over the life course if they suffer from social disadvantage.[11]

Social structure theories tie delinquency rates to socioeconomic conditions and cultural values. Areas that experience high levels of poverty and social disorganization will also have high delinquency rates. Residents view prevailing social values skeptically; they are frustrated by their class position and inability to be part of the "American dream." Structural theories are less concerned with why an individual youth becomes delinquent than why certain ecological areas experience high delinquency rates. The following Case in Point explores the question of how to reverse social disorganization.

CASE IN POINT

You have been appointed as a presidential advisor on urban problems.

The president informs you that he wants to create a major urban restructuring program in a large city that is aimed at reducing poverty, crime, and drug abuse. The area he has chosen for development is a large inner-city neighborhood with more than 100,000 residents. It suffers from disorganized community structure, poverty, and hopelessness. Predatory delinquent gangs run free and terrorize local merchants and citizens. The school system has failed to provide opportunities and educational experiences sufficient to dampen enthusiasm for gang recruitment. Stores, homes, and public buildings are deteriorated and decayed. Commercial enterprise has fled the area, and civil servants are reluctant to enter the neighborhood. There is an uneasy truce between the varied ethnic and racial groups that populate the area. Residents feel little can be done to bring the neighborhood back to life.

You are faced with suggesting an urban redevelopment program that can revitalize the area and eventually bring down the crime rate. You can bring any element of the public and private sector to bear on this rather overwhelming problem. Your budget is $500 million.

What programs do you feel could break the cycle of urban poverty?

Would reducing the poverty rate produce a lowered delinquency rate?

How might such conditions as cultural transmission and cultural deviance thwart your plans?

Is there a place for private industry in social reorganization?

THE BRANCHES OF SOCIAL STRUCTURE THEORY

The social structure approach has had a long tradition in the study of juvenile delinquency. As Figure 5.2 shows, social structure theories can be classified into three independent yet interrelated subgroups: **social disorganization, strain,** and **cultural deviance** (also called **subcultural theory**).

Social disorganization theory views delinquency as a product of the social forces existing in inner-city slum areas. Neighborhoods that lack or have lost the means to control deviance, protect residents, and regulate social conduct are at risk. Within these areas, the unsupervised behavior of juvenile gangs and groups overwhelms the ability of social institutions, such as the family and the school, to maintain order. The result is stable pockets of crime and deviance. Predictive of a high incidence of delinquency are such environmental and ecological factors as substandard housing, low income, unemployment levels, deteriorated housing, substandard schools, broken families, urban density, and overcrowding.

Strain theorists also view delinquency as being caused by poverty and economic inequality.[12] But rather than focusing on social disorganization, strain theorists link crime and delinquency to the frustration and anger members of the lower class feel when they are locked out of the mainstream of U.S. society. Strain results when the desire for middle-class benefits and luxuries cannot be met by the legitimate means available. Anger and frustration creates pressure for corrective action, including attacking the sources of frustration or escaping with drugs and alcohol.

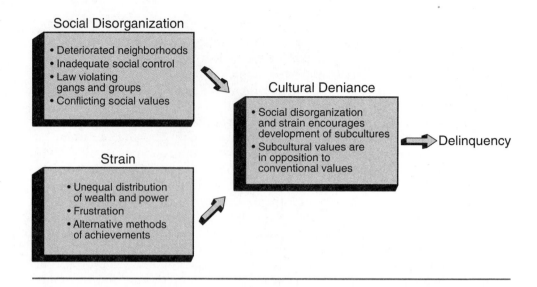

Cultural deviance theory, also referred to as subcultural theory, combines elements and concepts of both strain and social disorganization. According to this view, adolescent residents of disorganized slum areas are quickly alienated from the values of the dominant culture. The resulting strain and frustration prompts the formation of independent **subcultures** that maintain rules and values in opposition to existing law and custom. Conflict arises when subcultural values and beliefs clash with those of the general culture. Delinquency is not caused then by rebellion against the dominant society but by conformity to the rules of a deviant subculture.

The three branches of structural theory are linked together here because each maintains that a person's place in the social structure controls the direction of his or her behavior. Because each theoretical branch is an important concept of delinquency, they are set out in detail below.

SOCIAL DISORGANIZATION

The roots of the social disorganization tradition can be traced to the pioneering research conducted in the famed sociology department at the University of Chicago early in the twentieth century. Chicago's evolution as a city was typical of the transition occurring in many other urban areas as industrialization expanded. Large populations of workers were needed to staff factories and commercial establishments. Waves of Europeans settled in the city to work in the factories and stockyards. The city's wealthy, established citizens were concerned about the moral fabric of society. The belief was widespread that foreign immigrants were crime-prone and morally dissolute. In fact, local groups were created for the very purpose of "saving" the children of poor families from moral decadence. Delinquency was popularly viewed as the property of inferior racial and ethnic groups. (See Chapter 13 for a discussion of the child savers.)

Robert Ezra Park (1864-1944), Ernest W. Burgess (1886-1966), Louis Wirth (1897-1952), and their colleagues pioneered research work on the **social**

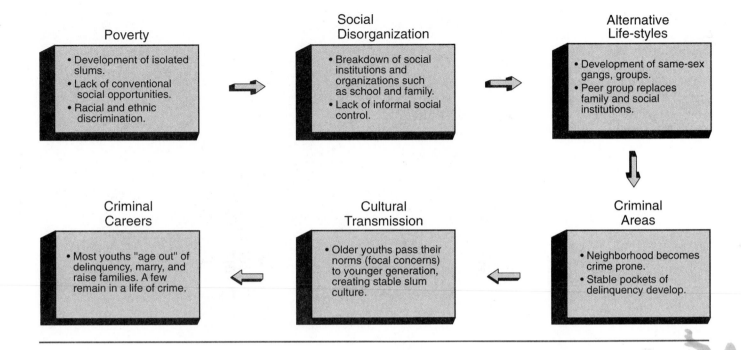

Poverty
- Development of isolated slums.
- Lack of conventional social opportunities.
- Racial and ethnic discrimination.

Social Disorganization
- Breakdown of social institutions and organizations such as school and family.
- Lack of informal social control.

Alternative Life-styles
- Development of same-sex gangs, groups.
- Peer group replaces family and social institutions.

Criminal Careers
- Most youths "age out" of delinquency, marry, and raise families. A few remain in a life of crime.

Cultural Transmission
- Older youths pass their norms (focal concerns) to younger generation, creating stable slum culture.

Criminal Areas
- Neighborhood becomes crime prone.
- Stable pockets of delinquency develop.

■■ **FIGURE 5.3**

Social disorganization theory

ecology of urban areas. These sociologists focused attention on the influence social institutions have on human behavior. They pioneered the **ecological study** of crime: law-violating behavior is a function of social-level (and not individual-level) forces operating in an urban environment. They found that key element of a community is its ability to regulate itself so that common goals (such as living in a crime-free area) can be achieved; this is referred to as **social control**.[13] Those neighborhoods that are incapable of social control are the ones most at risk for criminal interactions.

These **Chicago School** researchers found that deteriorated inner-city neighborhoods become **natural areas** for crime. The extraordinarily high level of poverty in these urban neighborhoods causes a breakdown of critical social control institutions, such as the school and the family. According to Wirth, urban areas undergoing rapid growth in population density and diversity experience "segmentalization" of life. People look inward for achievement and shun interpersonal relationships. Interactions among residents in large cities are superficial, fleeting, and exploitive.[14] The resulting *social disorganization* reduces the ability of social institutions to control behavior, thus causing a high crime rate (see Figure 5.3).

THE AREA STUDIES OF SHAW AND MCKAY

Social disorganization theory is today most closely associated with the pioneering research conducted in Chicago by sociologists Clifford Shaw and Henry McKay.[15] Shaw and McKay sought to explain delinquency within the context of the changing urban ecology. They collected extensive crime data, including the records of almost 25,000 alleged delinquents brought before the Juvenile Court of Cook County from 1900 to 1933.

According to the social disorganization view, decayed
urban areas lack the means
to provide social control
and protect their residents.
Deteriorated neighborhoods
are the spawning ground of
delinquent gangs and
groups.

Analysis of this data indicated that the then-popular individual-level explanations of delinquency, which rested on such factors as IQ or body build, were
fallacious. It was the ecological conditions of the city itself that caused delinquency. They saw that Chicago had developed into distinct neighborhoods, some
marked by wealth and luxury, others by overcrowding, poor health and sanitary
conditions, and extreme poverty. These slum areas were believed to be the
spawning grounds of delinquency.

Shaw and McKay viewed delinquency as a product of the decaying **transitional neighborhood,** which was changing from affluence to decay. Factories
and commercial establishments were interspersed with residences. In this environment, teenage gangs developed as a means of survival, economic gain,
defense, and friendship. Gang youths developed a unique set of cultural values
that conflicted with generally accepted social norms and traditions. Gang leaders
recruited younger members, passing on delinquent traditions and ensuring
survival of the gang from one generation to the next—a process referred to as
cultural transmission.

While mapping crime and delinquency rates in Chicago, Shaw and McKay
noted that distinct ecological areas had developed in the city. These comprised a
series of concentric circles, or zones, each with stable delinquency rates (see
Figure 5.4).[16] The areas of heaviest delinquency concentration appeared to be the
transitional, inner-city zones, where large portions of foreign-born citizens had
recently immigrated. The zones farthest from the city's center were the least
prone to delinquency. Analysis of these data indicated a surprisingly stable
pattern of delinquent activity in the ecological zones over a sixty-five-year
period. Shaw and McKay noted that delinquency rates in these areas were
unaffected by population makeup and transition. It seemed that high-risk areas
and not high-risk people were associated with delinquency rates.

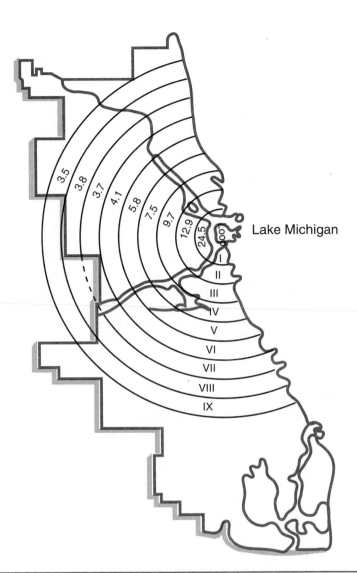

■■ FIGURE 5.4

Shaw and McKay's concentric zones map of Chicago

Note: Arabic numerals represent the rate of male delinquency.
Source: Clifford R. Shaw et al., *Delinquency Areas* (Chicago: University of Chicago Press, 1929), p. 99. Reprinted with permission. Copyright 1929 by the University of Chicago. All rights reserved.

The Culture of the Slum

Shaw and McKay did not restrict their analysis to ecological factors alone. They found a significant correlation between social values and crime rates. Areas with low delinquency rates were marked by "uniformity, consistency, and universality of conventional values and attitudes."[17] In these low-crime areas, middle-class child-rearing practices prevailed, and residents conformed to the legal code. In contrast, conflicting moral values and powerful attractions to deviant modes of behavior existed in high-crime areas. In disorganized neighborhoods, delinquency provides a means for financially deprived youths to gain prestige, economic achievement, and other satisfactions.

Parent-child relationships were seen by Shaw and McKay as having an important influence on the development of social values. In zones with low delinquency rates, parents stressed such values as attending school and church and being involved in community organizations. In high-rate, transitional areas, a diversity of values existed. Some youths were taught to strive for basic middle-class goals; others were exposed to the rackets and illegal activities, such as theft.

Shaw and McKay concluded that in transitional neighborhoods, deviant and conventional values compete with one another. Adolescents exposed to both value systems are often forced to choose between them and, consequently, may seek out groups that share similar ideas and behavior. Those who choose illegitimate values may find membership in law-violating groups and gangs an essential element of life in slum areas. (See Chapter 10 on gang behavior.)

Because of their deviant values, slum youths often come into conflict with existing middle-class norms, which demand strict obedience to the legal code. Such value conflicts set delinquents and their peer group even farther from conventional society. The result is a fuller acceptance of deviant goals and behavior. Shunned by the mainstream, neighborhood street gangs become fixed institutions, recruiting new members and passing on delinquent traditions from one generation to the next.

The quality of social organizations and institutions also varies considerably between high- and low-crime areas. In high-crime sections, conflicting social values neutralize the influence of social control organizations. A close-knit family, which should serve as a buffer against delinquency, exercises little social control in disorganized areas. Families in transitional areas often contain adult members who are themselves profiting from theft, violence, and drug dealing. In these circumstances, family ties can actually encourage delinquency. Even those social control agents with an expressed agenda of crime control and prevention, such as schools and community centers, have only limited utility because they are staffed and funded by outsiders who are not trusted by neighborhood residents.

Legacy of Shaw and McKay

Most prominent among the many achievements of Shaw and McKay was locating the cause of delinquency within the domain of social ecology. The Shaw-McKay model replaced the view that delinquents were either biological throwbacks, intellectually impaired, or psychologically damaged. Their research refuted the assumption that delinquency is a property of any one minority or ethnic group.

Since the basis of their theory was that neighborhood disintegration and slum conditions are the primary cause of delinquent behavior, Shaw and McKay paved the way for the many community action and treatment programs developed in the last half-century. Shaw himself was the founder of one very influential community-based treatment program, the Chicago Area Project, which will be discussed later in this chapter.[18]

Another important feature of Shaw and McKay's work was its depiction of delinquent gang membership as a "normal" response to the adverse social conditions in urban slum areas. Gangs provide social and economic advantages that would otherwise be denied youths in these areas. Shaw, McKay, and other Chicago-based theorists, such as Frederick Thrasher, viewed gang members as neither troubled nor depressed.[19] Their illegal behavior was merely a way of achieving excitement, social success, and financial gain when all other avenues seemed to be closed.

Shaw and McKay's work has been subject to criticism. Dependence on official statistics is always suspect. The stable patterns of inner-city delinquency depicted by Shaw and McKay may not actually exist. Social mobility and change in neighborhood composition may in fact influence crime rates.[20]

These criticisms aside, by introducing a new variable—the ecology of the city—into the study of delinquency, the Shaw and McKay paved the way for a whole generation of criminologists to focus on the social influences on delinquent behavior.

THE SOCIAL ECOLOGY OF DELINQUENCY

Shaw and McKay's legacy was advanced by area studies conducted by Bernard Lander in Baltimore, David Bordua in Detroit, and Roland Chilton in Indianapolis. As a group, they showed that such ecological conditions as substandard housing, low income, and unrelated people living together predicted a high incidence of delinquency.[21]

A great deal of recent scholarship uses complex statistical models to determine the effects ecological and social conditions have on delinquent crime patterns.[22] A growing body of important studies indicate that the social context of urban areas has significant influence on delinquency rates.[23] The sections below describe some of the most significant areas of research.

Relative Deprivation

According to Judith Blau and Peter Blau, a sense of social injustice occurs in communities in which the poor and the wealthy live close to one another. Income inequality causes feelings of **relative deprivation.** The relatively deprived are prone to have feelings of anger and hostility, which precede criminal behavior.

The Blaus believe that adolescents residing in a poor inner-city area will experience delinquency-producing status frustration because their neighborhoods are contiguous to some of the most affluent areas in the United States. So while deprived teenagers can observe wealth and luxury close up, they have no hope of actually achieving riches themselves. This condition is felt most acutely by racial and ethnic minorities because they tend to live in low-status areas and in substandard housing.[24]

Research supportive of the Blaus' relative deprivation model has been conducted by a number of criminologists. Richard Block found that the variable best able to predict crime rates was the proximity in which poor and wealthy people lived to one another.[25] Robert Sampson found that income inequality, along with peer relations, predicts crime rates.[26] Richard Rosenfeld's analysis of national census and crime patterns found that inequality was strongly related to crime rates, especially in areas where residents have high achievement aspirations but few economic opportunities.[27]

In sum, these studies indicate that youths living in deteriorated areas of the city that are close to more affluent neighborhoods will be the most likely to resort to such crimes as homicide, robbery, and aggravated assault to express their frustration or achieve monetary gain.

Community Change

Some social ecologists contend that, like people, urban areas and neighborhoods have a life cycle in which they undergo significant change: from affluent to impoverished; from impoverished to rehabilitated or **gentrified;** from residential to commercial; from stable to transient. It has been observed that as communities go through these structural changes, levels of social disorder and criminality likewise change.[28]

An example of this view can be found in Leo Scheurman and Solomon Kobrin's examination of the factors that relate to crime-rate change in urban settings. Scheurman and Kobrin found that communities go through cycles in which neighborhood deterioration precedes increasing rates of crime and delinquency.[29] Communities that are suffering a rapid increase in antisocial behavior are also the ones most likely to be experiencing rapid increases in the number of single-parent families and unrelated people living together; a change in housing from owner- to renter-occupied units; a loss of semi-skilled and unskilled jobs; and a growth in discouraged unemployed workers who are no longer seeking jobs.[30]

The changing racial makeup of communities may also influence crime and delinquency rates. Janet Heitgerd and Robert Bursik have found that areas undergoing change in their racial composition will experience corresponding increases in their delinquency rates.[31] The authors speculate that this phenomenon may reflect community fear of racial conflict: adults support the law-violating behavior of neighborhoods youths in order to protect their property and way of life. The result is conflict, violence, and disorder.

Wealth and Opportunity

While Shaw and Mckay did not assume a direct relationship between economic status and criminality, they did imply that areas wracked by poverty would also experience social disorganization.

Research has shown that neighborhoods that provide a few employment opportunities for youth and adults are the most vulnerable to predatory crime. Unemployment helps destabilize households, and unstable families are the ones most likely to contain children who choose violence and aggression as a means of dealing with limited opportunity.[32] A lack of employment opportunities reduces the influence of parents and neighborhood adults, resulting in the domination of street life by youth gangs. Predatory crime increases to levels that cannot easily be controlled by police. Although even the most deteriorated neighborhoods have a surprising degree of familial and kinship strength, the consistent pattern of crime and neighborhood disorganization that follows periods of high unemployment can neutralize social control capability.

Fear

In socially disorganized neighborhoods, residents fear crime and delinquency.[33] Juvenile gangs and groups terrorize the neighborhood. People who live in gang-infested, disorganized areas believe they have a considerable chance of becoming crime victims; perceptions of crime and victimization produce neighborhood fear. People tell others of their personal experiences of being victimized, spreading the word that the neighborhood is getting dangerous and that the chances of future victimization are high.

When fear grips a neighborhood, people do not want to leave their homes at night, so they withdraw from community life. High levels of fear are related to deteriorating business conditions, increased population mobility, and the importation of a criminal element. These factors in turn produce more crime, greater chances of victimization, and more fear in a never-ending loop.

Social Controls

Most neighborhood residents share the common goal of living in a crime-free area. Some communities have the power to regulate the behavior of their residents through the influence of such institutions as the family and the school. Other neighborhoods, experiencing social disorganization, find that efforts at social control are weak and attenuated. When community social control efforts are blunted, crime rates increase, further weakening neighborhood cohesiveness in an endless cycle.

Neighborhoods maintain a variety of agencies and institutions of social control. Some operate on the primary or private level and involve peers, families, and relatives. These sources exert informal control over behavior by either awarding or withholding approval, respect, and admiration. Informal control mechanisms include direct criticism, ridicule, ostracism, desertion, and physical punishment.[34]

Communities also use internal networks and local institutions to control crime. These include stores, schools, churches, and voluntary organizations.[35] Stable neighborhoods are able to marshal external sources of social control; for example, they can use their political clout to get state funding to increase levels of police services. The presence of police sends a message that the area will not tolerate deviant behavior. Current and potential delinquents may avoid such areas for easier and more appealing "targets."[36]

Neighborhoods that are disorganized cannot mount an effective social control effort. Since the population is transient, interpersonal relationships remain superficial and cannot help reduce deviant behavior. Wesley Skogan has shown how residents of crime-ridden neighborhoods withdraw from local activities because they fear their physical environment, mistrust other residents, and worry about becoming crime victims.[37] Social institutions, such as schools and churches, cannot work effectively in a climate of alienation and mistrust. In these areas, the absence of political power brokers limits access to external funding and police protection.

Social control is also weakened because unsupervised peer groups and gangs, which flourish in disorganized areas, disrupt the influence of neighborhood control agents.[38] Children surveyed in disorganized areas report that they are unable to become involved with conventional social institutions and are therefore vulnerable to interpersonal aggression and delinquency.[39]

In sum, recent ecological research supports the original social disorganization model: areas that are deteriorated and disorganized are unable to assemble social forces sufficient to control the behavior of their residents. Social forces in these areas encourage, rather than contain, antisocial behavior.

STRAIN THEORY

Strain theory is the second branch of the social structure perspective. According to this view, crime and delinquency is a result of the frustration and anger people experience when they are unable to achieve social and financial success through conventional means. Strain theorists believe that most people share similar values and goals but that the ability to achieve them is stratified by socioeconomic class. In middle- and upper-class communities, strain does not exist, since education and prestigious occupations are readily obtainable. In lower-class areas, strain occurs because legitimate avenues for success are all but closed to young people. When acceptable means for obtaining success do not exist, individuals may either use deviant methods to achieve their goals or reject socially accepted goals and substitute deviant ones.

Strain theories seem to have an internal logic. (See Figure 5.5.) They propose that youths begin a delinquent career when they realize that desirable goods and services, readily available to other members of society, will always be beyond their grasp. The goals and values in U.S. society are common to all people. Billions of dollars are spent each year on media advertising to convince people to drive the right car, wear the right clothes, and live in the right neighborhood. It is certainly not surprising to conclude that lower-class youths, frustrated because they are shut out of the legitimate marketplace, will seek alternative means to get ahead.

Strain theory is consistent with social disorganization models because the likelihood of strain is greatest in deteriorated inner-city areas. However, strain theory goes a step further because it explains how adverse ecological factors create a sense of rage and frustration, which result in antisocial behaviors.

We now turn to the most well-known formulation of strain theory, Robert Merton's theory of anomie.

■■ FIGURE 5.5

Strain theory

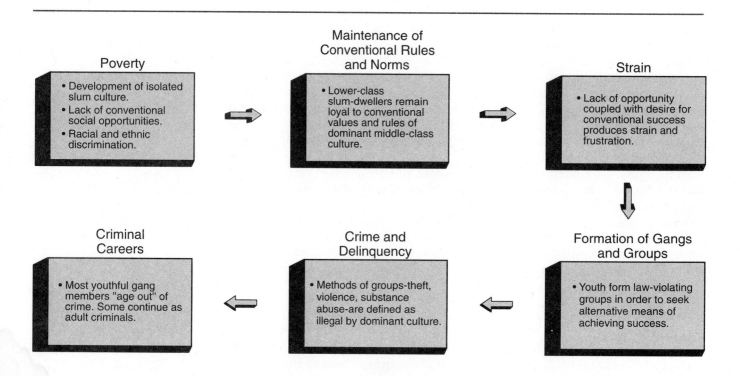

MERTON'S THEORY OF ANOMIE

Strain theories probably owe their popularity to the distinguished U.S. sociologist *Robert Merton*.[40] In 1938, Merton proposed a revised version of the concept of **anomie** that has proved to be one of the most durable theoretical concepts in twentieth-century social thought.[41] In his theory, Merton attempted to adapt the abstract concept of anomie to conditions in U.S. society. French sociologist Emile Durkheim had employed the concept of anomie to describe the "normlessness" and social malaise that occur during a breakdown of existing social rules, laws, and values.[42] Durkheim believed that an anomic condition results when the existing social structure can no longer establish and maintain controls over an individual's wants and desires. It is a breakdown of the rule of law. Under these conditions, crime can be considered a "normal" response to existing social conditions.

Merton adapted Durkheim's abstract concept to fit the conditions of modern U.S. society. He argued that two elements of modern culture interact to produce potentially anomic conditions: culturally defined *goals* of acquiring wealth, success, and power; and socially permissible *means*, such as hard work, education, and thrift. According to Merton, U.S. society is goal-oriented, and wealth and material goods are coveted most of all. Merton held that the legitimate means to acquiring wealth are stratified across class and status lines. Those with little formal education and few economic resources soon find that they are denied the ability to acquire money and other success symbols legally.[43] Since socially mandated success goals are uniform throughout any society and access to legitimate means is bound by class and status, the resulting strain produces an anomic condition among those who are locked out of the legitimate opportunity structure. Consequently, they develop criminal or delinquent solutions to the problem of attaining goals.[44] Merton also recognized that some people reject social goals, thereby becoming classified as rebels who are opposed to the mainstream of society.

Social Adaptations

Merton identified five possible modes of adaptation or adjustment an individual can adopt when presented with the various combinations of culturally defined goals and means: conformity, innovation, ritualism, retreatism, and rebellion. Each represents a way of coping with a balance or imbalance of goals and means.

Conformity.   Conformity occurs when an individual adheres to social goals and can attain them legitimately through conventional means. For example, middle-class, college-bound students will obey the law because they recognize that their future education and social position will land them a good job so they do not need to steal or commit other crimes to get what they want in life. This most common form of adaptation signals the absence of an anomic condition (and deviant behavior as well).

Innovation.   Innovation occurs when an individual accepts the goals of society but rejects or is incapable of following legitimate means of attaining them. For

Kids may feel strain when they become convinced that legitimate success goals can never be achieved. When they use "innovative" methods such as theft and violence, they run afoul of the law.

example, when youths desire automobiles but lack money, the resulting conflict forces them to adopt an innovative solution to the problem: they steal cars.

Of the five adaptations, innovation is most closely associated with delinquent behavior. The inescapable demand to succeed that pervades U.S. culture places such an enormous burden on those lacking economic opportunity that delinquent modes of adaptation are not a surprising result. This condition accounts for the high rate of delinquency in poverty areas, where access to legitimate means is severely limited. However, innovative adaptations can occur in any social class when members perceive the lack of appropriate means to gain social success they aspire to. Witness, for example, the insider trading scandal involving people who were already millionaires that rocked Wall Street in the late 1980s.

Ritualism.   Ritualism results from the diminution of goals and a rigid adherence to means. The maintenance of a strict set of manners and customs that serve no particular purpose is an example of ritualism. Such practices often exist in religious groups, feudal societies, clubs, college fraternities, and social organizations. Ritualists gain pleasure from traditional ceremonies that have neither a real purpose nor a goal.

Retreatism.   Retreatism entails a rejection of both the goals and the means of society. Merton suggested that people who adjust in this fashion are "in society but not of it."[45] Included in this category are "psychotics, psychoneurotics, chronic autists, pariahs, outcasts, vagrants, tramps, chronic drunkards, and drug addicts."[46] This posture often results when an individual accepts socially acceptable goals but is denied the means to attain them. Because such people are also morally or otherwise incapable of using illegitimate means, they attempt to escape their lack of success by withdrawing, either mentally or physically.

Rebellion. A rebellious adaptation involves the substitution of alternative sets of goals and means for the accepted ones of society. This adaptation is typical of revolutionaries, who promote radical change in the existing social structure and advocate alternative life-styles, goals, and beliefs. Revolutionary groups and cults have abounded in the United States, some espousing the violent overthrow of the existing social order and others advocating the use of nonviolent, passive resistance to change society. The revolutionary orientation can be used as a reaction against a corrupt and hated regime or as an effort to create alternate opportunities and life-styles within the existing system.

Analyzing Anomie

Merton's adaptations apply to both deviant and nondeviant behavior. In our culture, innovation, retreatism, and rebellion seem most relevant to the understanding of delinquent behavior. Considering the apparent inequality in the social distribution of legitimate means, it is not surprising that large segments of our population react to the resulting anomic condition with innovations such as theft or extortion, with retreat into drugs or alcohol, or with rebellion by joining revolutionary or cultist groups.

A number of questions are left unanswered by anomie theory. Merton did not explain why people choose different adaptations to anomie: Why does one adolescent choose innovation and become a thief, while another becomes a "retreatist" and takes drugs? Anomie does not address life course concepts: does a sense of anomie decline with age? If not, how can the aging-out phenomenon be explained? If anomie erodes as people go through the life cycle, why and how does this happen? Critics have suggested that people actually pursue a number of different life goals and that the economic success goal is merely one among many. Other goals include educational, athletic, and social success and prominence. Achieving these goals is not a matter of social class alone; other factors, including physical ability, intelligence, personality, and family life, can either hinder or assist their attainment.[47]

GENERAL STRAIN THEORY

Robert Agnew has formulated a general strain theory that further amplifies the strain concept so that it might explain all forms of delinquent behavior.[48] Agnew found that, as a general principle, adolescents engage in delinquency as a result of **negative affective states**—the anger, frustration, and other adverse emotions that derive from the pressure placed on people by negative and destructive social relationships.

According to Agnew, there are actually three sources of strain:

1. *Strain caused by the failure to achieve positively valued goals.* This category of strain includes the disjunction between aspirations and expectations; this is what Merton spoke of in his theory of anomie. Such strain will occur when youths aspire for wealth and fame but, because they are poor and undereducated, assume that such goals are impossible to achieve.

   Also falling within this general category is the strain induced by the disjunction between expectations and actual achievements; for example, when a person compares him- or herself to peers who seem to be doing a lot better financially or socially. A similar form of strain occurs when youths perceive that they are not being treated fairly or that the "playing field" is being tilted against them. Perceptions of inequity may result in many adverse reactions ranging from running away from its source to lowering the benefits of others through physical attacks or vandalism of their property.

2. *Strain as the removal of positively valued stimuli from the individual.* Strain may occur because of the actual or anticipated removal or loss of a positively valued stimuli from the individual.[49] For example, the loss of a girl- or boyfriend can produce strain, as can the death of a loved one, moving to a new neighborhood or school, and the divorce or separation of parents. The loss of positive stimuli may lead to delinquency as the adolescent tries to prevent the loss, retrieve what has been lost, obtain substitutes, or seek revenge against those responsible for the loss.

3. *Strain as the presentation of negative stimuli.* Strain may also be caused by negative or noxious stimuli. Included within this category are such pain-inducing social interactions as child abuse and neglect, criminal victimization, physical punishment, family and peer conflict, school failure, and interaction with stressful life events ranging from verbal threats to air pollution.

While these three main sources of strain are independent from one another, they may overlap and be cumulative. For example, insults from a teacher may be viewed as an unfair application of negative stimuli that interferes with academic aspirations. The greater the intensity and frequency of strain experiences, the greater their impact and the more likely they are to cause delinquency.

According to Agnew, each type of strain will increase the likelihood that people will experience such negative emotions as disappointment, depression, fear, and, most important, anger. Anger increases perceptions of injury and of being wronged. It produces a desire for revenge, energizes individuals to take action, and lowers inhibitions; violence and aggression seem justified if you have been wronged and are righteously angry.

Because it produces these emotions, strain can be considered a predisposing factor for delinquency when it is chronic and repetitive and creates a hostile, suspicious, and aggressive attitude. An individual strain episode may be a situational event or "trigger" that produces delinquency; for example, by igniting a violent reaction.

Coping with Strain

Agnew recognizes that not all youths who experience strain become delinquents. Some are able to marshal their emotional, mental, and behavioral resources to cope with the anger and frustration produced by strain. Some defenses are cognitive; individuals may be able to rationalize frustrating circumstances. They may believe that not getting the career they desire is "just not that important"; they may be poor but the "next guy is worse off"; and if things didn't work out, then they got what they deserved. Others seek behavioral solutions: they run away from adverse conditions or seek revenge against those who caused the strain. Still others will try to regain emotional equilibrium with techniques ranging from physical exercise to drug abuse.

The general strain theory acknowledges that the ability to cope with strain varies with personal experiences over the life course. Kids who lack economic

According to cultural deviance theory, delinquent kids are not rebelling against society but obeying the norms of their own deviant subculture.

means are less likely to cope than those who have financial resources sufficient to combat strain. Personal temperament, prior learning of delinquent attitudes and behaviors, and association with delinquent peers who reinforce anger are among other factors affecting the ability to cope with strain.

Agnew's work is quite important because it both clarifies the concept of strain and directs future research agendas. It also adds to the body of literature describing how events over the life cycle influence delinquency patterns. Because sources of strain vary over time, so too should crime rates. In a recent empirical analysis of his theory using longitudinal survey data, Agnew, with Helene Raskin White, found that adolescents who score high on scales measuring perceptions of strain labeled "life hassles" (for example, "my classmates do not like me," adults and friends "don't respect my opinions") and "negative life events" (being a victim of crime, the death of a close friend, serious illness) are also the ones most likely to engage in delinquency.[50] This research indicates that as adolescents travel through the life course, events and relationships which produce strain shape the direction and frequency of their behavior.

CULTURAL DEVIANCE THEORY

Cultural deviance theories (also called subcultural theory) hold that youth crime is a result of individuals' desire to conform to the cultural values of their immediate environment that are in conflict with those of the greater society. Conformity to the rules, values, and norms of unconventional groups and individuals with whom a youth is in close contact is interpreted as disobedience to the rules of conventional society. As Joseph Weis and John Sederstrom

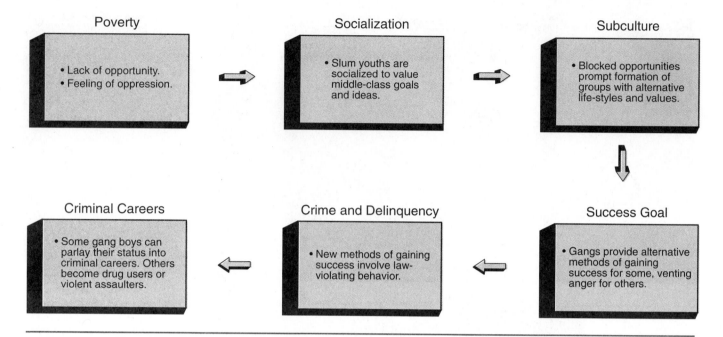

FIGURE 5.6

Cultural deviance theory

interpret cultural deviance, "[d]elinquent behavior is caused by proper socialization within a 'deviant' social group or culture. Juvenile delinquency is merely 'marching to a different drummer.'"[51]

Cultural deviance theories suggest that slum youths violate the law because they adhere to the unique, independent value system existing within lower-class areas. Lower-class values include using any means to get what is desired being tough, never showing fear, living for today, and never respecting authority. These new values exist because in socially disorganized slums, such conventional values as honesty, obedience, and hard work make little sense to youths whose only successful adult role models—the neighborhood gun runner, drug dealer or pimp—earn their living though crime and deviant behaviors (see Figure 5.6).

Cultural deviance/subcultural theory is a link between the concepts of social disorganization and strain theory. As advocated in the strain approach, subcultural theorists argue that youths who live in poverty areas lack the means to acquire conventional success goals. Because they develop feelings of anomie and strain, slum youth create a unique set of cultural values and standards of their own. Instead of aspiring to be "preppies" or "yuppies," lower-class citizens want to be considered tough, street-smart, and have a bad "rep." In other words, the strain between middle-class goals and lower-class means produces an independent lower-class subculture that provides ghetto youths with avenues for obtaining alternate forms of success and self-esteem.

Development of Subcultures

Because subcultural values can be anti-social and dysfunctional, members of the middle-class often have trouble understanding their attraction, especially when they sanction violence and vengeance. In 1938, sociologist Thorsten Sellin identified the social factors that promote and sustain independent subcultures.[52] He found that newly arrived immigrant groups brought with them views and beliefs that clashed with the dominant values of U.S. society. For example, some European and Latin cultures demand that males seek violent revenge for perceived slights or insults to female family members. The resulting **culture conflict** makes it difficult to maintain a uniform U.S. culture with agreed-upon values and attitudes. The result is that small pockets or subcultures develop that maintain a unique value structure.

Similarly, Marvin Wolfgang and Franco Ferracuti identified a **subculture of violence** in certain areas of the nation that has norms separate from those of the dominant, parent culture.[53] In the subculture, a potent theme of violence influences the life-styles of younger males.

A number of significant theoretical models articulate the cultural deviance approach. Some of the most prominent are discussed below in detail.

WALTER MILLER'S THEORY OF LOWER-CLASS CULTURE CONFLICT

Sociologist Walter Miller's theory of lower-class culture conflict is another well-known attempt to explain the gang activity found in lower-class environments.[54]

Miller studied the daily activities of working-class citizens while conducting a delinquent gang control program in Boston.[55] He found that slum areas manifest a distinct cultural climate that remains stable over long periods of time. Because citizens in these areas are on the fringe of the established economic system with little chance for success within the legitimate social order, they seek to achieve personal satisfaction in their own neighborhoods and culture.

Miller describes the lower-class culture as initially female-dominated (since so many families have absent fathers) but eventually controlled by same-sex groups and gangs that provide a family substitute and define the male role for adolescent boys.

Lower-Class Focal Concerns

According to Miller, a unique group of value-like **focal concerns** dominate life among the lower class. These concerns do not necessarily represent a rebellion against middle-class values; rather, they have evolved specifically to fit conditions in slum areas. The major focal concerns that Miller identifies are trouble, toughness, smartness, excitement, fate, and autonomy.

Trouble. Getting into and staying out of trouble are major concerns of lower-class citizens. Trouble includes such behavior as fighting, drinking, and sexual misconduct. In lower-class communities, people are evaluated in terms of their actual, or potential, involvement in trouble-making activity. The attitude toward trouble is not always clear-cut. Sometimes it confers prestige, for example, when a man gets a reputation for being able to handle himself well in a fight. However, getting into trouble and having to pay the consequences can make a person look foolish and incompetent. In most instances, trouble-making escapades are designed with a goal in mind, such as stealing an automobile when the money to buy one is unattainable.

Toughness. Lower-class males want local recognition of their physical and spiritual toughness. They refuse to be sentimental or soft and instead value physical strength, fighting ability, and athletic skill. Miller attributes the concern about toughness to a reaction to the female-dominated household. Fearing an accusation of homosexuality, lower-class men react strongly to any indication that they are female-dominated and therefore strive for a macho identity. Toughness involves a high tolerance of pain, disdain of fear, fighting skill, and the willingness to accept all manner of hardships without complaint. Lower-class males who cannot meet these standards risk getting a reputation for being weak, inept, and effeminate.

Smartness. Another critical concern of lower-class citizens is maintenance of an image of streetwise savvy, which carries with it the ability to outfox and outcon the opponent. This does not mean that intellectual brilliance is admired; in fact, ivory-tower types are disdained. Smartness to the lower-class citizen means knowing essential survival techniques, such as gambling, conning, and outsmarting the law. One unique example of smartness especially prevalent among teenage boys is a verbal repartee sometimes called "sounding" or "dissing." During these exchanges, boys try to outdo each other in producing half-serious put-downs and insults to prove their quick wit and ingenuity. Youths who fail to attain a reputation for smartness may find themselves with the odious reputation of being a dupe or a sucker.

Excitement. Another important feature of the lower-class life-style is the search for fun and excitement to enliven an otherwise drab existence. The search for excitement may mean involvement in gambling, fighting, getting drunk, sexual adventures, and so on. Going out on the town looking for excitement may eventually lead to that other focal concern, trouble. Excitement is not sought all the time. In between, the lower-class citizen may simply "hang out" and "be cool." Those who do not seek excitement are considered "deadheads." They are safe and passive.

Fate. Lower-class citizens believe that their lives are in the hands of strong spiritual forces that guide their destinies. Getting lucky, finding good fortune, and hitting the jackpot are all dreams that are present daily in each slum dweller's life. Getting lucky can mean a trip out of the ghetto and into the world of luxury and excitement. The belief in fate is behind the interest in playing the numbers, the horses, and the other forms of gambling that are so prevalent in the lower-class world.

Autonomy. In lower-class cultures, there is a general concern about personal freedom and autonomy. Being in the control of authority figures, such as the police, teachers, and parents, is an unacceptable weakness, incompatible with toughness. Conflicts arise when the lower-class citizen is confronted with rigidly controlled environments, such as schools, hospitals, the military, courts, and prisons. The usual manner of dealing with these authoritarian regimes is to actively disdain them, a response that frequently results in a continuing relationship with them. For example, the behavior of youths can result in their getting held back in school.

In addition to the focal concerns listed above, Miller finds two concerns unique to gang youths—belonging and status.

Belonging. Lower-class youths find it essential to belong to a structured group and to be a well-thought-of member of that group. This coveted membership is achieved by excelling at the general focal concerns, for example, toughness and smartness.

Status. Status is achieved and maintained by demonstrating excellence in the five generalized focal concerns. By achieving status, lower-class adolescents are able to feel grown up. Therefore, they can participate in adult activities, such as gambling and drinking. Furthermore, when some members of a peer group or a gang achieve status, the group as a whole develops a significant reputation in the community.

Focal Concerns and Delinquency

Miller argues that by strictly satisfying the behavioral demands imposed by lower-class focal concerns, an adolescent is drawn into an ever-expanding pattern of delinquent behavior. By adhering to the cultural values, rules, and norms around them, lower-class youths often find that they are in conflict with representatives of the larger society's legal system. For example, proving their toughness may demand that lower-class youths engage in constant fighting, both individually and in groups. Smartness may lead them into theft schemes and con games. Excitement causes them to gamble, drink, and engage in premarital sex. Thus, obedience to unavoidable cultural demands, not a sense of alienation or anger, precipitates lower-class delinquent behavior.

Albert Cohen's Theory of Delinquent Subculture

Albert K. Cohen first articulated the theory of delinquent subculture in his 1955 book, *Delinquent Boys.*[56] Cohen's main purpose was to explain the disproportionate amount of official delinquent behavior found in slum neighborhoods. His central position is that delinquent behavior of lower-class youths is actually a protest against the norms and values of the middle-class U.S. culture. Because social conditions make them incapable of achieving success in a legitimate fashion, lower-class youths experience a form of culture conflict that Cohen labels "status frustration." As a result, many of them join together in teenage gangs and engage in behavior that is nonutilitarian, malicious, and negativistic.[57] Cohen views delinquents as forming a separate subculture and possessing a value system directly in opposition to that of the larger society. He describes the subculture as one that takes "its norms from the larger culture but turns them upside down. The delinquent's conduct is right, by the standards of his subculture, precisely because it is wrong by the norms of the larger cultures."[58]

Causes of Delinquency

According to Cohen, the development of the delinquent subculture is a function of the social and familial conditions children experience as they mature in the ghetto or slum environment. Delinquency is not a product of inherent class inferiority but rather a function of the social and economic limitations suffered by members of the less fortunate groups in U.S. society. The numbing burden of poverty is the real villain in the creation of delinquent careers.[59]

A critical element of lower-class life, one that directly influences later delinquent behavior, is the nature of the child's family structure. Cohen argues that the relative position of a child's family in the social structure determines the quality of experiences and problems that the child will encounter later in life.[60] By implication, Cohen suggests that lower-class families are incapable of teaching their offspring proper socialization techniques for entry into the dominant middle-class culture. Lower-class families, permanently cut off from the middle-class way of life, produce children who lack the basic skills necessary to achieve social and economic success in our demanding society. Developmental handicaps produced by a lower-class upbringing include a lack of educational training, poor speech and communication skills, and an inability to delay gratification.[61]

Middle-Class Measuring Rods

One of the more significant handicaps that lower-class children face is the inability to positively impress such authority figures as teachers, employers, or supervisors. In U.S. society, these positions tend to be held by members of the middle- or upper-class who have difficulty relating to the lower-class youngster. Cohen calls the standards these authority figures set **middle-class measuring rods** and maintains that the conflict lower-class youths feel when they fail to meet these standards is a primary cause of delinquency.

Middle-class measuring rods develop because the most important institutions in society—schools, churches, businesses, the military, the justice system, and so on—are dominated by agents of the middle class. Clients of these institutions (for example, students, workers, soldiers) are expected to display middle-class values and behaviors, such as verbal skills, ambition, neatness, cleanliness, good manners, and the ability to delay gratification. When lower-class youths cannot meet these criteria, their failures become part of an enduring public record that is consulted whenever they apply for a job, seek educational advancement, or wish to join a social organization. Failure to meet middle-class measuring rods is therefore not an isolated incident that, if not repeated, will be forgotten. It becomes an enduring part of lower-class youths' permanent records that follows them throughout life and helps thwart personal ambitions.

Reactions to Middle-Class Measuring Rods

Cohen's position is that lower-class boys who suffer the rejection of middle-class decision makers are deeply affected by their lack of social recognition.[62] Typically, they may elect to adopt one of three alternative behaviors: the "corner boy" role, the "college boy" role, or the "delinquent boy" role.

The stable corner-boy role is the most common response to middle-class rejection. The corner boy is not overtly delinquent but behaves in a way that is sometimes defined as delinquent. For example, he is a truant.[63] He hangs out in the neighborhood; engages in gambling, athletics, and other group activities; and eventually obtains a menial job. His main loyalty is to his peer group, on which he depends for support, motivation, and interest. His values, therefore, are those of this group. The corner boy, well aware of his failure to achieve the standards of the American dream, retreats into the comforting world of his lower-class peers and eventually becomes a stable member of his society.

The college boy embraces the cultural and social values of the middle class. Rather than scorning middle-class measuring rods, he actively strives to meet them. Cohen views this type of youth as one who is embarking on an almost hopeless path, since he is ill-equipped academically, socially, and linguistically to achieve the rewards of middle-class life.

The delinquent boy adopts a set of norms and principles in direct opposition to middle-class society. Cohen describes a number of general properties of the delinquent subculture. For one thing, its members often manifest "short-run hedonism."[64] Delinquents are believed to live for today and to let tomorrow take care of itself. Although Cohen believes short-run hedonism is a characteristic of lower-class culture as a whole, he finds it especially applicable to delinquent groups.

Members of the delinquent subculture are also careful to maintain **group autonomy.** They resist efforts by family, schools, or other sources of authority to control their behavior. Although some individual delinquents may respond to direction from others, the gang itself is autonomous, independent, and the focus of "attraction, loyalty, and solidarity."[65]

While members of the delinquent subculture often manifest negativistic and malicious behavior, Cohen believes they are still controlled to some degree by the norms and values of the larger culture. They really want to be successful at school, jobs, and so on. To deal with the conflict inherent in this frustrating dilemma, they resort to a process Cohen calls "reaction formation."[66] Symptoms of reaction formation include a response that seems to be disproportionate to the stimulus by which it is triggered. For the delinquent boy, this takes the form of "irrational," "malicious," "unaccountable" hostility to the enemy within the gates as well as without—the norms of respectable middle-class society.[67]

In a later work, Cohen, writing with James Short, presented a refined version of his original theory in which he recognized that the original formulation of the delinquent subculture may have been too simplistic and that a more complex model is called for. He and Short therefore describe the following five delinquent orientations:[68]

1. *Parent male subculture:* the negativistic subculture originally identified in *Delinquent Boys.*
2. *The conflict-oriented subculture:* the culture of a large gang that engages in collective violence.
3. *The drug addict subculture:* groups of youths whose lives revolve around the purchase, sale, and use of narcotics.
4. *Semiprofessional theft subculture:* youths who engage in the theft or robbery of merchandise for the purpose of later sale and monetary gain.
5. *Middle-class subculture:* delinquent groups that arise because of the pressures of living in middle-class environments.[69]

Thus, Cohen has attempted to broaden the behavior that can be explained by his original subcultural strain model.

RICHARD CLOWARD AND LLOYD OHLIN'S OPPORTUNITY THEORY

In their well-known 1960 work, *Delinquency and Opportunity,* Richard Cloward and Lloyd Ohlin added significantly to the knowledge of delinquent subcultures.[70] Cloward and Ohlin agree with Robert Merton that socioeconomic class membership controls access to the legitimate means of achieving social goals.[71] However, they maintain that Merton's theory pays scant attention to the fact that even *illegitimate* means are unevenly distributed in the class structure. Cloward and Ohlin argue that some lower-class neighborhoods actually provide more opportunity for illegal gain than others do. These opportunities come in the form of access to rackets, organized crime, theft, and other high-payoff illegal activities. Cloward and Ohlin's view, therefore, is that in a particular urban area or neighborhood, both legitimate and illegitimate opportunities are deferentially available.

Gang Subcultures

A key element in opportunity theory is the assumption that a strong relationship exists between the environment youths live in, its economic structure, and their subsequent behavior choices. For example, in wealthy or middle-class areas, educational and vocational opportunities abound, and youths can avail themselves of conventional means of getting ahead, such as going to college. However, in low-income areas, legitimate means are more difficult to come by, and therefore, youths must seek illegitimate avenues of success.

Cloward and Ohlin propose that even illegitimate avenues of success are blocked for some youths. In fact, they are available only to children growing up in areas where "stable patterns of accommodation" exist between the criminal world and conventional society.[72] In these areas, adult criminals have worked out relationships with businesses, police, and court officials through bribery and corruption so that they are almost immune from prosecution. Their criminal activity—organized crime, drug trafficking, gambling—provides a stable income and an alternative avenue to legitimate success. Under adult tutelage, youths fit right into this model and form a *criminal subculture.* To prepare for adult crime, they join gangs specializing in theft, extortion, and other profitable criminal activities. Later, they become part of the even more profitable adult crime organizations.

Not all youths join criminal gangs. Some lower-class youths remain loyal to the values and rules of conventional society. Furthermore, some youths are temperamentally incapable of following either criminal or conventional rules. They take drugs and alcohol and stress playing it cool and being high and strung out. Cloward and Ohlin call their world the *retreatist subculture.*

Finally, opportunity theory recognizes that some poverty areas are so unstable and disorganized that even illegitimate means to success are blocked. Youths in these areas become members of the *conflict subculture.*[73] They form fighting gangs that provide the opportunity for success and ego gratification by enabling their members to show their bravery, strength, and fighting prowess.[74]

In sum, Cloward and Ohlin view urban delinquency as a function of the different opportunities youths have to gain both *legitimate* and *illegitimate* goals. Where opportunities for legal gain are blocked, criminal activity is attempted. When even criminal gain is unattainable, then drug use (retreatist gangs) or violence (conflict gangs) will ensue. Cloward and Ohlin's theory integrates the three main streams of delinquency theory: anomie, subculture, and social learning.

Empirical Verification

Research support on opportunity theory has been inconclusive. One criticism is that marked differences exist in both the values of the middle and lower classes and those of delinquent and nondelinquent youths, a finding that contradicts Cloward and Ohlin. Research comparing the values of lower- and middle-class adolescents has found that the former consider themselves to be tougher, more powerful, fierce, fearless, and dangerous, while the latter describe themselves as being more loyal, clever, and smart.[75] Class differences have been recorded in the commitment to deviant peers and other attitudes, behaviors, and values.[76]

Recent surveys of gang delinquency have shown that gangs are more pervasive than Cloward and Ohlin imagined, that more than one type of gang (conflict, violent, drug dealing, social) exists in a particular area and that the commitment of gang boys to one another is less intense than opportunity theory would suggest.[77]

While these results are discouraging, several other studies appear to support opportunity theory. In one classic work, Judson Landis and Frank Scarpitti used self-report scales with 1,030 youths in Columbus, Ohio, and 515 boys at an industrial school in Lancaster, Ohio. The industrial school boys exhibited greater perception of limited opportunity than did the public school boys; public school youths who admitted delinquency also perceived less opportunity than nonde-linquents.[78] Other research efforts have found that lower-class delinquents report less perception of opportunity than middle-class youth who engage in conventional behavior patterns.[79]

Some recent evidence from gang research projects is also supportive of opportunity theory. Studies of gang boys in Detroit by Carl Taylor and Chicago by Felix Padilla suggest that gangs are formed as business enterprises to provide economic opportunity via drug dealing to youths who otherwise would be left out of the economic mainstream.[80] They found evidence that gang boys do in fact share the economic values of the American middle class but lack the opportunity to achieve them through conventional means. Padilla, for example, found that the gang boys he studied certainly know what they are doing violates social norms and laws; they believe that it is really the only course of action readily open.[81]

SOCIAL STRUCTURE THEORY AND DELINQUENCY PREVENTION

Social structure theories suggest that the best method of primary delinquency prevention is local community organization. The effort should be two-pronged. First, deteriorated neighborhoods must be refurbished in order to provide an environment that meets the basic needs of the residents. Second, educational and job opportunities must be created to provide legitimate alternatives to delinquent gangs. In order to achieve these goals, financial support must be made available to needy families to sustain their ability to survive.

Delinquency prevention through community organizations was pioneered in Chicago by Clifford Shaw in the 1930s. In 1933, Shaw initiated the *Chicago Area Project,* which was designed to produce social change in communities that suffered from high delinquency rates and gang activity. As part of the project, qualified local leaders coordinated social service centers that promoted community solidarity and counteracted social disorganization. More than twenty different projects were developed, featuring discussion groups, counseling services, hobby groups, school-related activities, and recreation. There is still some question of whether these programs had a positive influence on the delinquency rate. While some evaluations indicated positive results, others showed that the Chicago Area Project efforts did little to reduce juvenile criminality.[82]

In the 1950s, delinquency prevention programs sought to reach out to youths who were unlikely to use settlement houses or community centers. Instead of having troubled youths come to them, **detached street workers** went out into urban slums and created close relationships with juvenile gangs and groups in their own milieu.[83] The most well-known detached street worker program was Boston's *Mid-City Project.* There, trained social workers sought out and met with youth gangs three to four times a week on the gangs' own turf. Their goal was to modify the organization of the gang and allow gang members a chance to engage in more conventional behaviors. The detached street workers tried to help gang members get jobs and educational opportunities. They acted as go-betweens for gang members with agents of the power structure—lawyers, judges, parole officers, and the like. Despite these efforts, an evaluation of the program by Walter Miller failed to show that it resulted in significant reduction in criminal activity.[84]

The heyday of delinquency prevention programs based on social structure theory was in the 1960s. The approach seemed to jibe politically with the New Frontier policies of the Kennedy administration and the Great Society/War on Poverty approach of the Johnson administration. A great deal of federal money was pumped into delinquency prevention programs using community organization and redevelopment techniques. The most ambitious of these was the New York City-based *Mobilization for Youth (MOBY).* Funded by more than $50 million, MOBY attempted an integrated approach to community development. Based securely on Cloward and Ohlin's concept of providing opportunities for legitimate success, MOBY organizers attempted to create new employment opportunities in the community, coordinated social services, and sponsored social action groups, such as, tenant's committees, legal action services, and voter registration and political action committees. But MOBY died for lack of funding amid serious questions about its utility and use of funds.

The concept of community organization and change to combat delinquency fell into disfavor in the 1970s and 1980s. However, attempts to improve the lives of families to prevent and control delinquency have not ended. Today's efforts seem to be directed at helping families in need, giving them the resources needed to sustain and improve their lives. If opportunities are available, then families will be better able to control children and remain a primary source of social control. In the following Focus on Delinquency, one such program begun in New York state is discussed in some detail.

Beyond Welfare Reform: New York's Child Assistance Program

New York's Child Assistance Program (CAP) is designed to provide a rational, efficient, and dignified alternative to the current system of support for the thousands of poor children in single-parent families who now are forced to depend on welfare. CAP's premise is that the support of children is the responsibility of custodial and noncustodial parents alike, with supplementary assistance to be provided by the state only when the parents' contributions are insufficient.

CAP provides single parents with real financial incentives to work and underscores the responsibility of absent parents to support their children. It is not just an enhancement or modification of Aid For Dependent Children (AFDC) but a real alternative to the welfare system.

■ CAP helps children escape poverty by providing incentives for increasing the contributions made by the absent parent (through child support) and the custodial parent (through earnings) and supplementing income as necessary. Unlike AFDC, under which modest earnings generally mean the loss of aid at a point that leaves the family little or no better off than if the adult were not working at all, CAP supplementation can continue until the family is out of poverty.

■ CAP encourages single mothers to work by ensuring that their increased earnings will mean greater household income. Unlike AFDC, which generally reduces benefits by a dollar for each dollar of earnings, CAP's benefit reduction rate is much lower, only 10 percent for earnings below the poverty level.

■ CAP encourages custodial parents to obtain child support orders. The government collects the payments owed and guarantees at least a minimum level of income for the children.

CAP gives and AFDC parent (most often the mother) the choice of leaving welfare to participate in an alternative program under which she can combine her own earnings and child support payments from the absent father with state supplementation to improve her family's economic well-being. CAP offers a carefully designed program built on:

■ Intensive case management to coordinate the family's needs with the provision of benefits and services.

■ Simplified reporting requirements and procedures to minimize inconvenience in establishing and maintaining eligibility for assistance.

■ Respect for the participant by providing greater autonomy (for example, furnishing food stamp benefits in cash rather than coupons) and a dignified office setting.

CAP enrolled its first participants at the beginning of October 1988 and now has about 1,910 families.

Current program data indicate that CAP is succeeding in bringing single mothers and their children out of poverty. The average CAP participant relies primarily on her own earnings of $690 a month, supplemented by approximately $280 in CAP benefits and about $120 in cash benefits under the food stamp program; about 60 percent of all participants receive child care subsidies averaging $195 a month. Child support collections further reduce the net public outlay (including child care) to about $420 per month, or about 35 percent of total household income.

The long-range impact of CAP is being examined. A 1991 study of participants found that a third of CAP participants had obtained employment or increased their earnings and a quarter had assisted in efforts to secure support orders for their children to take advantage of CAP's benefits. An interim impact report found that during the first twelve months after they were exposed to CAP, AFDC recipients had 25 percent more work hours and earnings than recipients who were not in the program. CAP families are able to enjoy higher total income without government having to spend additional money for benefits.

CAP's success in bringing single-parent families out of poverty has captured the attention of social policymakers nationwide. In 1991, CAP was a finalist for the American Public Welfare Association's Successful Projects Initiative Awards Program, and in 1992, it was one of ten programs selected for the Ford Foundation/Harvard University's Innovations in State and Local Government Award. ■

Source: Child Assistance Program, New York State Department of Social Service, February 1993.

■■■■■■■■■■■■■■■■

Summary

Social structure theories hold that delinquent behavior is an adaptation to conditions that predominate in lower-class environments. Social structure theory has three main branches (see Table 5.1). The first, social disorganization, suggests that economically deprived areas lose their ability to control and direct the behavior of their residents. Gangs and groups flourish in these disorganized areas. Deviant values are transmitted from one generation to the next. Shaw and McKay viewed this development principally as a

■■ TABLE 5.1   Social Structure Theories

THEORY	MAJOR PREMISE	STRENGTHS
SOCIAL DISORGANIZATION THEORY		
	The conflicts and problems of urban social life and communities control the crime rate.	Accounts for urban crime rates and trends.
relative deprivation	Crime occurs when the wealthy and poor live in close proximity to one another.	Explains high crime rates in deteriorated inner-city areas located near more affluent neighborhoods.
STRAIN THEORY		
	People who adopt the goals of society but lack the means to attain them seek alternatives, such as crime.	Points out how competition for success creates conflict and crime. Suggests that social conditions and not personality can account for crime. Can explain middle- and upper-class crime.
general strain theory	Strain has a variety of sources. Strain causes crime in the absence of adequate coping mechanisms.	Identifies the complexities of strain in modern society. Expands on anomie theory. Shows the influences of social events on behavior over the life course.
CULTURAL DEVIANCE THEORY		
	Citizens who obey the street rules of lower-class life (focal concerns) find themselves in conflict with the dominant culture.	Identifies more coherently the elements of lower-class culture that push people into committing street crimes.
Cohen's theory of delinquent gangs	Status frustration of lower-class boys, created by their failure to achieve middle-class success, causes them to join gangs.	Shows how the conditions of lower-class life produce crime. Explains violence and destructive acts. Identifies conflict of lower class with middle class.
Cloward and Ohlin's theory of opportunity	Blockage of conventional opportunities causes lower-class youths to join criminal, conflict, or retreatist gangs.	Shows that even illegal opportunities are structured in society. Indicates why people become involved in a particular type of criminal activity. Presents a way of preventing crime.

property of youthful street gangs. They found in their study of Chicago that delinquency rates vary widely throughout the city. The probability of adolescents becoming delinquent and getting arrested and later incarcerated depends on whether they live in one of these high-rate areas. Delinquency is a product of the socialization mechanisms within a neighborhood. Unstable neighborhoods have the greatest chance of producing delinquents. Delinquency is not the property of any one ethnic or racial group. Members of any racial or ethnic group will be delinquent if they live in the high-crime areas. Their rate of criminal activity will be reduced once they leave these areas.

The second branch of social structure theory is made up of strain theories. These hold that lower-class youths may actually desire legitimate goals but their unavailability causes rage, frustration, and substitution of deviant behavior. Robert Merton linked strain to anomie, a condition caused when there is a conflict of disjunction between goals and means. In his general strain theory, Robert Agnew identifies the sources of strain, the way strain causes delinquent behavior, and the means adolescents employ to cope with strain.

The third branch of structural theory is referred to as cultural deviance or subcultural theory. This maintains that the result of social disorganization and strain is the development of independent subcultures that hold values in opposition to mainstream society. Walter Miller argues that almost all lower-class citizens maintain separate value systems, which he calls focal concerns. Albert Cohen identifies a delinquent subculture that was negativistic and destructive. Sociologists Richard Cloward and Lloyd Ohlin take this idea one step further by suggesting that some neighborhoods deny their residents the opportunity for even illegal gain, thereby creating the rise of violence and drug-related subcultures.

The social structure view is still influential today. Modern theorists consider the high level of crime in certain areas to be a function of social disorganization, relative deprivation, and neighborhood transition.

Over the years, a number of delinquency prevention efforts have been based on a social structure approach.

KEY TERMS

culture of poverty
underclass
stratified
latchkey children
structural
social disorganization
strain
cultural deviance
subcultural theory
subcultures social ecology
ecological study
social control
Chicago School
natural areas

transitional neighborhood
cultural transmission
relative deprivation
gentrified
anomie
negative affective states
culture conflict
subculture of violence
focal concerns
Albert K. Cohen
   middle-class measuring rods
group autonomy
detached street workers

QUESTIONS FOR DISCUSSION

1. Is there a "transitional" area in your town or city?
2. Is it possible that a distinct lower-class culture exists? Do you know anyone who has the focal concerns Miller talks about?
3. Have you ever perceived anomie? What causes anomie? Is there more than one cause of strain?

4. How does poverty cause delinquency?
5. Do middle-class youths become delinquent for the same reasons as lower-class youths?
6. Does "relative deprivation" produce delinquency?

NOTES

1. Oscar Lewis, "The Culture of Poverty," *Scientific American* 215:19–25 (1966).
2. Ken Auletta, *The Under Class* (New York: Random House, 1982); William Julius Wilson, *The Truly Disadvantaged* (Chicago: University of Chicago Press, 1987).
3. Rodrick Wallace, "Expanding Coupled Shock Fronts of Urban Decay and Criminal Behavior: How U.S. Cities Are Becoming 'Hollowed Out'," *Journal of Quantitative Criminology* 7:333–55 (1991).
4. Children's Defense Fund, *The State of America's Children 1991* (Washington, D.C.: Children's Defense Fund, 1992), pp. 22–23.
5. Ibid. p. 28.
6. James Q. Wilson and Richard Herrnstein, *Crime and Human Nature* (New York: Simon and Schuster, 1985).
7. National Research Council, *Common Destiny: Blacks and American Society* (Washington, D.C.: National Research Council, 1989).
8. Ibid.
9. Greg Duncan and Willard Rogers, "Has Children's Poverty Become More Persistent?" *American Sociological Review* 56:538–50 (1991).
10. Herman Schwendinger and Julia Siegel Schwendinger, *Adolescent Subcultures and Delinquency* (New York: Prager, 1985).
11. G. R. Patterson, L. Crosby, and S. Vuchnich, "Predicting Risk for Early Police Arrest," *Journal of Quantitative Criminology* 8:335–53 (1992).
12. Robert Agnew, "Foundation for a General Strain Theory of Crime and Delinquency," *Criminology* 30:47–87 (1992), at 48.
13. Robert Bursik and Harold Grasmick, "The Multiple Layers of Social Disorganization" (Paper presented at the annual meeting of the American Society of Criminology, New Orleans, November 1992); Robert Bursik and Harold Grasmick, "Longitudinal Neighborhood Profiles in Delinquency: The Decomposition of Change," *Journal of Quantitative Criminology* 8:247–56 (1992).
14. Louis Wirth, "Urbanism as a Way of Life," *American Journal of Sociology* 44:1–24 (1938).
15. Clifford R. Shaw and Henry D. McKay, *Juvenile Delinquency and Urban Areas*, rev. ed. (Chicago: University of Chicago Press, 1972).
16. Ibid., p. 52.
17. Ibid., p. 170.
18. Solomon Kobrin, "Chicago Area Project—A Twenty-Five Year Assessment," *Annals of the American Academy of Political and Social Science* 322:20–29 (1950).
19. Frederick Thrasher, *The Gang* (Chicago: University of Chicago Press, 1927).
20. Robert Bursik and James Webb, "Community Change and Patterns of Delinquency," *American Journal of Sociology* 88:24–42 (1982).
21. Bernard Lander, *Towards an Understanding of Juvenile Delinquency* (New York: Columbia University Press, 1954); David Bordua, "Juvenile Delinquency and 'Anomie': An Attempt at Replication," *Social Problems* 6:230–38 (1958); Roland Chilton, "Continuities in Delinquency Area Research: A Comparison of Studies in Baltimore, Detroit, and Indianapolis," *American Sociological Review* 29:71–73 (1964).
22. For a general review, see James Byrne and Robert Sampson, eds., *The Social Ecology of Crime* (New York: Springer-Verlag, 1985).
23. Leo Carroll and Pamela Irving Jackson, "Inequality, Opportunity, and Crime Rates in Central Cities," *Criminology* 21:178–94 (1983).
24. Judith Blau and Peter Blau, "The Cost of Inequality: Metropolitan Structure and Violent Crime," *American Sociological Review* 147:114–29 (1982).
25. Richard Block, "Community Environment and Violent Crime," *Criminology* 17:46–57 (1979).
26. Robert Sampson, "Structural Sources of Variation in Race-Age-Specific Rates of Offending across Major U.S. Cities," *Criminology* 23:647–73 (1985).
27. Richard Rosenfeld, "Urban Crime Rates: Effects of Inequality, Welfare Dependency, Region and Race," in James Byrne and Robert Sampson, eds., *The Social Ecology of Crime,* (New York: Springer-Verlag, 1985), pp. 116–30.
28. Ora Simcha-Fagan and Joseph Schwartz, "Neighborhood and Delinquency: An Assessment of Contextual Effects," *Criminology* 24:667–703 (1986).
29. Leo Scheurman and Solomon Kobrin, "Community Careers in Crime," in Albert Reiss and Michael Tonry, eds., *Communities and Crime* (Chicago: University of Chicago Press, 1986), pp. 67–100.
30. Ibid., p. 96.
31. Janet Heitgerd and Robert Bursik, Jr. "Extracommunity Dynamics and the Ecology of Delinquency," *American Journal of Sociology* 92:775–87 (1987).
32. Richard McGahey, "Economic Conditions, Organization, and Urban Crime," in Albert Reiss and Michael Tonry, eds., *Communities and Crime* (Chicago: University of Chicago Press, 1986), pp. 231–70.
33. See, generally, Wesley Skogan, "Fear of Crime and Neighborhood Change," in Albert Reiss and Michael Tonry, eds., *Communities and Crime* (Chicago: University of Chicago Press, 1986), pp. 191–232; Stephanie Greenberg, "Fear and Its Relationship to Crime, Neighborhood Deterioration and Informal Social Control," in James Byrne and Robert Sampson, eds. *The Social Ecology of Crime* (New York: Springer-Verlag, 1985), pp. 47–62.
34. Donald Black, "Social Control as a Dependent Variable," in D. Black, ed., *Toward a General Theory of Social Control* (Orlando: Academic Press, 1990).

35. Bursik and Grasmick, "The Multiple Layers of Social Disorganization", pp. 8–10.
36. Rodney Stark, "Deviant Places: A Theory of the Ecology of Crime," *Criminology* 25:893–911 (1987).
37. Wesley Skogan, *Disorder and Decline: Crime and the Spiral of Decay in American Neighborhoods* (New York: Free Press, 1990).
38. Robert Sampson and W. Byron Groves, "Community Structure and Crime: Testing Social Disorganization Theory," *American Journal of Sociology* 94:774–802 (1989).
39. Denise Gottfredson, Richard McNeill, and Gary Gottfredson, "Social Area Influences on Delinquency: A Multilevel Analysis," *Journal of Research in Crime and Delinquency* 28:197–206 (1991).
40. See, for example, Robert Merton, *Social Theory and Social Structure* (Glencoe, Ill.: Free Press, 1957).
41. Robert Merton, "Social Structure and Anomie," *American Sociological Review* 3:672–82 (1938).
42. For samples of his work, see Emile Durkheim, *The Rules of Sociological Method,* 8th ed. (Glencoe, Ill.: Free Press, 1950); idem, *Suicide* (Glencoe, Ill.: Free Press, 1951).
43. Ibid., p. 680.
44. Ibid.
45. Robert Merton, "Social Structure and Anomie," in Marvin Wolfgang, Lenoard Savitz, and Norman Johnston, eds., *The Sociology of Crime and Delinquency* (New York: Wiley, 1970), p. 242.
46. Ibid.
47. Robert Agnew, "Goal Achievement and Delinquency," *Sociology and Social Research* 68:435–51 (1984). See also Margaret Farnworth and Michael Leiber, "Strain Theory Revisited: Economic Goals, Educational Means and Delinquency," *American Sociological Review* 54:263–74 (1989).
48. Agnew, "Foundation for a General Strain Theory of Crime and Delinquency."
49. Ibid., p. 57.
50. Robert Agnew and Helene Raskin White, "An Empirical Test of General Strain Theory," *Criminology* 30:475–99 (1992).
51. Joseph Weis and John Sederstrom, *The Prevention of Serious Delinquency: What to Do?* (Washington, D.C.: Government Printing Office, 1981), p. 30.
52. Thorsten Sellin, *Culture Conflict and Crime,* bulletin no. 41 (New York: Social Science Research Council, 1938).
53. Marvin Wolfgang and Franco Ferracuti, *The Subculture of Violence* (London: Tavistock, 1967).
54. Walter Miller, "Lower Class Culture as a Generating Milieu of Gang Delinquency," *Journal of Social Issues* 14:5–19 (1958).
55. Ibid., p. 6.
56. Albert Cohen, *Delinquent Boys* (New York: Free Press, 1955).
57. Ibid., p. 25.
58. Ibid., p. 28.
59. Ibid., pp. 73–74.
60. Ibid.
61. Ibid., p. 86.
62. Ibid., p. 128.
63. Ibid., p. 129.
64. Ibid., p. 30.
65. Ibid., p. 31
66. Ibid., p. 133.
67. Albert Cohen and James Short, "Research on Delinquent Subcultures," *Journal of Social Issues* 14:20 (1958).
68. Ibid., p. 22.
69. Ibid., pp. 25–31.
70. Richard Cloward and Lloyd Ohlin, *Delinquency and Opportunity* (New York: Free Press, 1960).
71. See Edwin Sutherland, *Principles of Criminology,* 4th ed. (Philadelphia: J.B. Lippincott, 1947).
72. Cloward and Ohlin, *Delinquency and Opportunity,* p. 159.
73. Clarence Schrag, *Crime and Justice, American Style* (Washington, D.C.: Government Printing Office, 1971), p. 67.
74. See, for example, Irving Spergel, *Racketville, Slumtown, and Haulburg* (Chicago: University of Chicago Press, 1964).
75. Leon Fannin and Marshall Clinard, "Differences in the Conception of Self as a Male among Lower- and Middle-Class Delinquents," *Social Problems* 13:205–15 (1965).
76. LaMar Empey and Maynard Erickson, "Class Position, Peers, and Delinquency," *Sociology and Social Research* 49:268–82 (1965).
77. Jeffery Fagan, "The Social Organization of Drug Use and Drug Dealing among Urban Gangs," *Criminology* 27:633–69 (1989).
78. Judson Landis and Frank Scarpitti, "Perceptions Regarding Value Orientation and Legitimate Opportunity: Delinquents and Non-Delinquents," *Social Forces* 84:57–61 (1965).
79. James Short, Ramon Rivera, and Ray Tennyson, "Perceived Opportunities, Gang Membership, and Delinquency," *American Sociological Review* 30:56–57 (1965).
80. Carl Taylor, *Dangerous Society* (East Lansing: Michigan State University Press, 1990); Felix Padilla, *The Gang as American Enterprise* (New Brunswick, N.J.: Rutgers University Press, 1992).
81. Padilla, *The Gang as an American Enterprise,* p. 4.
82. For an intensive look at the Chicago Area Project, see Steven Schlossman and Michael Sedlak, "The Chicago Area Project Revisited," *Crime and Delinquency* 29:398–462 (1983).
83. See New York City Youth Board, *Reaching the Fighting Gang* (New York: New York City Youth Board, 1960).
84. Walter Miller, "The Impact of a 'Total Community' Delinquency Control Project," *Social Problems* 10:168–91 (1962).

SOCIAL PROCESS THEORIES

LEARNING AND CONTROL

Not all sociologists view poverty, cultural deviance, and social disorganization as the primary causes of delinquency. Most youths, even those in slum areas, do not become delinquents or adult criminals. A number of research efforts have concluded that residence in a disorganized neighborhood alone is insufficient to predict the onset of individual delinquency.[1] Self-report studies find that middle-class youths engage in delinquent acts, such as car theft, drug use, and vandalism; this finding suggests that delinquency is spread throughout the social structure and not restricted to lower-class areas. If the presence of social disorganization and culture conflict alone caused delinquency, then how can the presence of the "good boy" in a high-crime area be explained?[2]

Of equal importance to some experts is the fact that the crime rate declines with age. Most offenders desist, and only a few persist into adulthood. Since environmental conditions are constant, explaining why crime rates vary with age is difficult. Poverty and social disorganization should effect all area residents equally, regardless of their age.

If the culture of poverty alone does not cause delinquency, what does? One argument is that the onset of delinquency and its maintenance through the life course can be traced to the quality of a youth's *socialization.* Socialization is the process in which people learn through interaction with significant individuals and social institutions—the family, peer group, school, justice system—what they must know to survive and function in society. Socialization and its accompanying *social processes* can have a powerful influence on a child's self-image, beliefs, values, and, subsequently, behavior.

According to this view, such factors as learning delinquent attitudes from peers, feeling alienated or detached from school, and experiencing conflict in the home help produce antisocial activity. Conflict-ridden social relationships help create a youth alienated from conventional social institutions, who may have a poor self-image, and who feels little attachment to a law-abiding life-style.

Social process theorists believe little distinction exists in American society between the goal and value orientations of the various social classes. Even youths growing up in the most deteriorated urban areas learn the same values at home, school, and church as upper- and middle-class youths. Though lower-class kids face the burden of coping with economic hardships, family strain, delinquent peers, inadequate schools, low self-esteem, and racism, most are willing to obey legal and moral rules. Some are able to cope because they enjoy a good home life, supportive friends, and caring teachers. In contrast, many middle-class youths may experience the social and familial conflicts that are associated with the onset of delinquency.

According to this view then, delinquency can occur among any youths, the affluent as well as the poor, who learn to ignore social rules and/or whose bond to society is so weakened that they are free from constraining moral forces. Unlike social structure theories, which focus on the law violations of the lower class, socialization theories attempt to identify the factors within any social setting that cause a youth to become involved in criminal behavior or to remain stable and law-abiding.

SOCIAL PROCESSES AND DELINQUENCY

Social process theories are grounded in the extensive literature examining the relationship between socialization and delinquent behavior. Numerous research studies have found that as children mature, elements of society with which they have close and intimate contact influence their behavior patterns. The primary influence is the family. When parenting is inadequate, absent, or destructive, a child's normal maturation processes will be interrupted and damaged. And while much debate still occurs over which elements of the parent-child relationship are the most critical, there is little question that family relationships have a significant influence on antisocial behavior.[3] (Chapter 9 reviews the family's role in delinquency causation.)

The literature linking delinquency to poor school performance, educational disabilities, boredom, and inadequate educational facilities is extensive. A youth who feels that teachers do not care or who has been made to feel he or she is a hopeless academic failure is more likely to become involved in a delinquent way of life.[4] (Chapter 10 reviews the relationship between schools and delinquency.)

Still another suspected element of deviant socialization are peer-group relations that stress substance abuse, theft, and violence. Youths who form close relations with peers who engage in antisocial behavior may learn the techniques and attitudes that support delinquency and may also find themselves cut off from more conventional associates and institutions.[5] (Chapter 11 reviews peer relations and delinquency.)

In sum, social process theory portrays the delinquent youth as someone whose personality and behavior, formed in the crucible of social relationships and societal processes, is at odds with conventional society.

The social process perspective has two branches (see Figure 6.1). The first, **learning theory,** holds that delinquency is learned through close relationships with others. Both the techniques of crime and the attitudes necessary to support delinquency are learned.

The second branch, **control theory,** views delinquency as a result of youths' feeling cut off from the major institutions of society—family, peers, and school. Because the bond to these institutions is severed, the control that conventional society normally exerts on youths is absent, and they feel free to exercise antisocial behavior choices.

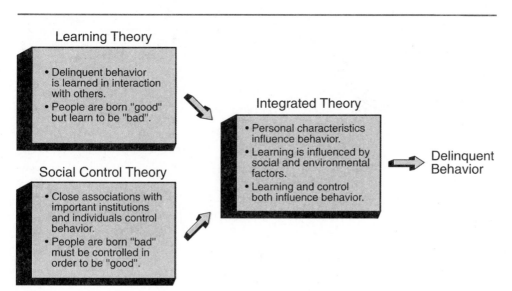

■■**FIGURE 6.1**

The branches of social process theory

The main distinction between these two theories lies in their concept of human development and change. Learning theories assume that people are born "good" and then learn from other to be "bad." In contrast, control theories assume that people are born "bad" ("out of control") and are then socialized by others to be "good." Learning theorists reflect the concerned mother's lament that her formerly well-behaved daughter is "being ruined by her friends"; control theorists sympathize with the irate father who says his rebellious son will not listen because he is "in his own world." This distinction is a key to understanding the differences between these two versions of the association between the socialization process and delinquency.

LEARNING THEORIES

Learning theory stresses the learning of the attitudes, morals, skills, and behaviors needed to sustain a delinquent career (see Figure 6.2). Borrowing heavily

■■ FIGURE 6.2

The learning theory perspective

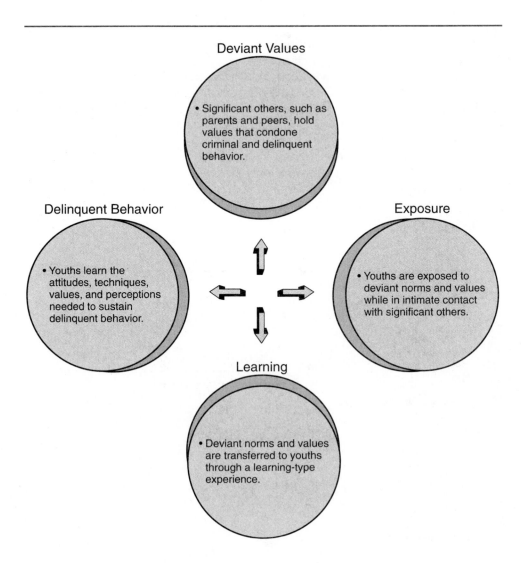

Deviant Values
• Significant others, such as parents and peers, hold values that condone criminal and delinquent behavior.

Delinquent Behavior
• Youths learn the attitudes, techniques, values, and perceptions needed to sustain delinquent behavior.

Exposure
• Youths are exposed to deviant norms and values while in intimate contact with significant others.

Learning
• Deviant norms and values are transferred to youths through a learning-type experience.

Part II   Theories of Delinquency

from psychological views of social learning (see Chapter 4), such sociologists as Edwin Sutherland, Daniel Glaser, and David Matza focus on the learning of delinquent values within the social context of family and peer groups. As a group, their theoretical position is that poverty or social class differences alone are not enough to explain delinquency. Youthful law violators must learn how to become delinquent and how to cope emotionally with the consequences of their behavior. We now turn to descriptions of the most important examples of learning theory.

DIFFERENTIAL ASSOCIATION THEORY

Edwin Sutherland, long considered the preeminent U.S. criminologist, first formulated the theory of ***differential association*** (DA) in 1939 in his text *Principles of Criminology*.[6] The theory appeared in its final form in 1947. At that time, DA was applied to all criminal and delinquent behavior patterns and has remained unchanged ever since. After Sutherland's death in 1950, his work was continued by his longtime associate Donald Cressey. Cressey was so successful in explaining and popularizing his mentor's efforts that DA remains one of the most enduring explanations of delinquent behavior.

Principles of Differential Association

The basic principles of differential association are contained in the following statements:[7]

First, *criminal behavior is learned*. This statement differentiates Sutherland's theory from prior attempts to classify delinquent behavior as an inherent characteristic of born criminals. By suggesting that delinquent and criminal behavior is actually learned, Sutherland implied that it can be classified like any other learned behavior, such as writing, painting, or reading. This statement reveals Sutherland's allegiance to the psychological learning theories discussed Chapter 4.

Second, *criminal behavior is learned in interaction with other persons in a process of communication*. Sutherland believed that delinquent behavior is learned actively. An individual does not become a delinquent simply by living in a criminogenic environment or by manifesting personal characteristics associated with delinquency, such as low IQ and family problems. Instead, criminal and other deviant behavior patterns are learned. Youths actively participate in the process with other individuals who serve as teachers and guides to delinquent behavior. Thus, delinquency cannot appear without the aid of others.

Third, *learning of criminal behavior occurs principally within intimate personal groups*. Children's contacts with their closest social companions—family, friends, and peers—have the greatest influence on their learning of deviant behavior and attitudes. Relationships with these individuals can color and control the interpretation of everyday events and thus help youths overcome social controls so that they can embrace delinquent values and behavior. The intimacy of these associations far outweighs the importance of any other form of communications, for example, movies or television. Even on those rare occasions when violent films seem to provoke mass delinquent episodes, the outbreaks can be more readily explained as a reaction to peer-group pressure than as a reaction to the films themselves.

According to Sutherland, adolescents learn deviant behaviors directly during personal interactions with family and peer group members.

Fourth, *the learning of criminal behavior includes techniques of committing the crime, which are sometimes very complicated and sometimes very simple, and the specific direction of motives, drives, rationalizations, and attitudes.* Because delinquent behavior is similar to other learned behavior, it follows that the actual techniques of criminality must also be acquired and learned. For example, young delinquents learn from their associates the proper way to pick a lock, shoplift, and obtain and use narcotics. In addition, delinquents must learn to use the proper terminology for their acts and then acquire the proper personal reactions to them. For example, as Howard Becker points out, getting high on marijuana and learning the proper way to "smoke a joint" are behavior patterns usually acquired from more experienced companions.[8] Moreover, delinquents must learn how to react properly to their criminal acts—when to defend them, rationalize them, show remorse for them.

Fifth, *the specific direction of motives and drives is learned from various favorable and unfavorable definitions of the legal codes.* Since the reaction to social rules and laws is not uniform across society, youths constantly come in contact with people who maintain different views on the utility of obeying the legal code. When definitions of right and wrong are extremely varied, people experience what Sutherland called ***culture conflict.*** The attitudes toward criminal behavior of the important people in young people's lives influence the attitudes that the youths themselves develop. The conflict of social attitudes is the basis for the concept of DA.

Sixth, *a person becomes delinquent if definitions favorable to violating the law exceed definitions favorable to it.* According to Sutherland's theory, individuals will become delinquent when they are in contact with persons, groups, or events that produce an excess of "definitions toward delinquency" and, concomitantly, when they are isolated from counteracting forces. A definition *toward* delinquency occurs, for example, when a youth is exposed to friends sneaking into a theater to avoid paying for a ticket or to friends talking about the virtues of getting high. A definition *against* delinquency occurs when friends or parents demonstrate their disapproval of crime (see Figure 6.3). Of course, neutral behavior, such as reading a book, exists. It is neither positive nor negative with respect to law violation. Cressey argues that it is important "especially as an occupier of the time of a child so that he is not in contact with criminal behaviors during the time he is so engaged in the neutral behavior."[9]

Seventh, *differential associations may vary in frequency, duration, priority, or intensity.* Whether a child learns to obey the law or to disregard it is influenced by the quality of social interactions. Those of lasting duration will have greater influence than those that are shorter. Similarly, frequent contacts have greater effect than rare and haphazard ones. Sutherland did not specify what he meant by *priority,* but Cressey and others have interpreted the term to mean the age of children when they first encounter definitions toward criminality.[10] Contacts made early in life will probably have a greater and more far-reaching influence than those developed later on. Finally, *intensity* is generally interpreted to mean

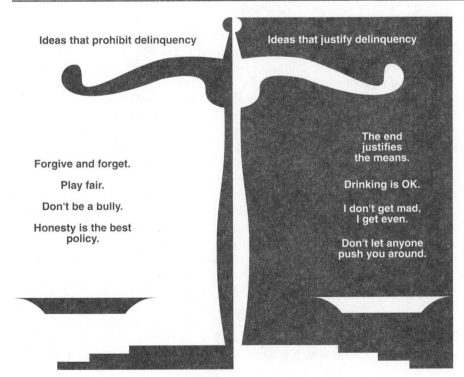

Ideas that prohibit delinquency

Ideas that justify delinquency

Forgive and forget.

Play fair.

Don't be a bully.

Honesty is the best policy.

The end justifies the means.

Drinking is OK.

I don't get mad, I get even.

Don't let anyone push you around.

Differential Associations

■■ FIGURE 6.3

Differential association theory
Differential association theory assumes that delinquent behavior will occur when the definitions against delinquency outweigh the definitions toward delinquency.

the importance and prestige attributed to the individual or groups from whom the definitions are learned. For example, the influence of a father, mother, or trusted friend will far outweigh that of more socially distant figures.

Eighth, *the process of learning criminal behavior by association with criminal and anticriminal patterns involves all the mechanisms involved in any other learning.* This statement suggests that the learning of criminal behavior patterns is similar to the learning of nearly all other patterns and is not a matter of mere imitation.

Finally, *while criminal behavior is an explanation of general needs and values, it is not explained by those needs and values, since noncriminal behavior is an explanation of the same needs and values.* By this principle, Sutherland suggested that the motives for delinquent behavior cannot logically be the same as those for conventional behavior. He ruled out such motives as a desire to accumulate money or social status, a sense of personal frustration, a low self-concept, or any other similar motive as causes of delinquency. They are just as likely to produce such noncriminal behavior as getting a better education or working harder on a job. It is only the learning of deviant norms through contact with an excess of definitions toward criminality that produces delinquent behavior.

Testing Differential Association

A number of important research efforts have been devoted to testing the validity of DA. Some find maintaining close relations with peers who hold delinquent values does in fact influence deviant behavior.[11] In one classic work, James Short tested a sample of 126 boys and 50 girls incarcerated in state training schools to measure the relationship between frequency, duration, priority, and intensity of interaction with delinquent peers and exposure to crime and delinquency.[12] Short used such measures as the number of friends a youth had who were delinquent, the degree to which a youth associated with criminals, and the intimacy of friendships with delinquents. He found that a consistent relationship existed between delinquent behavior and delinquent associations and that such associations were highly significant for both boys and girls. However, because the study was conducted with institutionalized youths regarded as seriously delinquent, it may not be applicable to the "average" law-violating child.

Some recent research efforts have provided empirical evidence that supports the core concepts of DA. For example, Ross Matsueda and Karen Heimer found evidence that youths who are exposed to deviant definitions are also the ones most likely to become delinquent and that this process holds true across racial, age, and class lines.[13] Law-violating behavior has been linked to exposure to deviant attitudes.[14] A number of research efforts have found that adolescent substance abusers maintain strong ties to drug-abusing peers and that shared interests in illegal activities brings drug users closer together.[15]

Other research has shown that people are deterred from criminality by the threat of peer and family disapproval.[16] By implication, youths who believe their friends and family hold attitudes in support of deviance will feel free to violate the law; those who believe that their friends and family will condemn their behavior will be deterred from criminal violations. These conclusions have been supported by research data acquired in the United States and other cultures.[17]

Is Differential Association Valid?

Despite these affirmations, efforts to verify DA principles have not all been successful.[18] Designing research to test the assumptions of DA has proven to be a formidable task. It is difficult to conceptualize the principles of the theory, such as a *definition toward delinquency,* in a way that lends itself to empirical measurement.[19] Causal ordering is also a problem: even if delinquent youths have many like-minded friends and report exposure to an excess of prodelinquent definitions, it is difficult to determine whether these associations and definitions caused law-violating behaviors or were their result. It is possible that the process is one in which youngsters who continually break the law develop a group of like-minded peers who support their behavior, rather than a process in which "innocent" youth are "seduced" into crime by exposure to the deviant attitudes of more delinquent peers. These problems have led such critics as Robert Burgess and Ronald Akers to state: "The attempts to subject the theory to empirical test are marked by inconsistent findings both within the same study and between studies, as well as by highly circumscribed and qualified findings and conclusions."[20]

To remedy this problem, future research may be directed at creating more accurate means with which to test the theory's basic principles.[21] A more valid approach may be to follow a cohort over time to assess the impact of delinquent friends and associations: does repeated exposure to excess definitions toward deviance escalate deviance through the life course? Some recent research by Mark Warr illustrates the utility of this approach. Warr found that adolescents who acquire delinquent friends are also the ones most likely to engage in delinquent behavior—a finding that supports DA. Warr notes that delinquent friends are "sticky"; once gotten, they are hard to shake. They help lock kids into antisocial behavior patterns through the life course. In fact, youths who maintain deviant friendships and close relationships with deviant peers are the ones most likely to continue their offending careers as they mature. Deviant friends counteract the aging-out process.[22]

Analysis of Differential Association Theory

Misconceptions about DA theory have tended to produce unwarranted criticism of its principles and meaning.[23] For example, some criminologists claim that the theory is concerned solely with the number of personal contacts and associations a delinquent has with other criminal or delinquent offenders.[24] If this assumption were true, those most likely to become criminals would be police, judges, and correctional authorities, since they are constantly associating with criminals. Sutherland stressed "excess definitions toward criminality," not mere association with criminals. Personnel of the juvenile justice system do have extensive associations with criminals, but these are more than counterbalanced by their associations with law-abiding citizens.

Another misconception is that definitions toward delinquency are acquired from learning the values of a deviant subculture.[25] Though DA stresses an excess of definitions toward delinquency, it does not specify that they must come solely from lower-class criminal sources. This distinguishes Sutherland's work from social structure theories. Outwardly law-abiding middle-class parents can encourage delinquent behavior by their own drinking, drug use, or family violence. And both middle- and lower-class youth are exposed to media images that express open admiration for violent heroes, such as those played by Arnold Schwarzenegger or Jean-Claude Van Damm, who take the law into their own hands. Research by Craig Reinerman and Jeffrey Fagan indicates that the influence of differential associations is not affected by social class, supporting Sutherland's belief that deviant learning can effect middle-class as well as lower-class youth.[26]

There are, however, a number of valid criticisms of Sutherland's work. It fails to explain why one youth who is exposed to delinquent definitions eventually succumbs to them, while another, living under the same conditions, avoids them.[27] It also fails to account for the origin of delinquent definitions. How did the first "teacher" learn delinquent attitudes and definitions in order to pass them on? Another apparently valid criticism of DA is that it assumes criminal and delinquent acts to be rational and systematic. This ignores spontaneous and wanton acts of violence and damage that appear to have little utility or purpose, such as the isolated psychopathic killing, which is virtually unsolvable because of the killer's anonymity and lack of delinquent associations.

The most serious criticism of DA theory concerns the vagueness of its terms, which makes it very difficult to test its assumptions. For example, what constitutes an "excess of definition toward criminality"? How can we determine whether an individual actually has a prodelinquent imbalance of these definitions? It is simplistic to assume that, by definition, all delinquents have experienced a majority of definitions toward delinquency and all nondelinquents, a minority of them. Unless the terms employed in the theory can be defined more precisely, its validity remains a matter of guesswork.

Despite these criticisms, DA theory maintains an important place in the study of delinquent behavior. For one thing, it provides a consistent explanation of *all* types of delinquent and criminal behavior. Unlike the social structure theories discussed previously, it is not limited to the explanation of a single facet of antisocial activity, for example, lower-class gang activity. The theory can also account for the extensive delinquent behavior found even in middle- and upper-class areas, where youths may be exposed to a variety of prodelinquent definitions from such sources as overly opportunistic parents and friends. And the recent Warr research (cited above) indicates that differential associations might be one of the keys to explaining deviance through the life course.

DIFFERENTIAL REINFORCEMENT THEORY

A number of attempts have been made to reformulate the concept of differential association, the most important being Robert Burgess and Ronald Akers's effort to frame Sutherland's model in a behavioral theory format. They suggest that delinquent behavior, like all behavior, is shaped by the stimuli or reactions of others to that behavior.[28] Social behavior is learned through direct conditioning, or modeling of others' behavior. Likewise, behavior is strengthened through reward or positive reinforcement and weakened by loss of reward (negative punishment) or actual punishment (positive punishment). Youths who receive more rewards than punishments for conforming behavior will be the most likely to remain nondelinquent—a process called *differential reinforcement.* Reinforcements, both positive and negative, are usually received in group settings. The most powerful influences are peers and family, but a youth may also be affected by school, social groups, clergy, and so on.

In an empirical analysis of the differential reinforcement theory, Ronald Akers and his associates surveyed a large group of high school students on their alcohol and substance abuse patterns.[29] They found that additional survey items measuring DA, differential reinforcement, and imitation of friends' behavior predicted significant amounts of marijuana use (39 percent) and alcohol abuse (32 percent). Similarly, a more recent study by Marvin Krohn and his associates found that Akers's social learning principles were effective for predicting the maintenance (or cessation) of a particular deviant behavior, cigarette smoking, in a sample of junior and senior high school boys measured over a three-year period.[30] Krohn found that reinforcement of smoking by parents and friends contributed to adolescent misbehavior and that differential associations by themselves were insufficient to predict deviance. Richard Lawrence also found that peer influence helps shape adolescent behavior.[31]

Akers's work has emerged as an important view of the cause of criminal activity. It is one of the few prominent theoretical models that successfully links sociological and psychological variables. In addition, as Akers himself argues, social learning ties in with rational choice theory because they both suggest that people learn the techniques and attitudes necessary to commit crime. Criminal knowledge is gained through experience. After considering the outcome of their past experiences, potential offenders decide which criminal acts will be profitable and which are dangerous and should be avoided.[32] Why do people make rational choices about crime? Because they have learned to balance risks against the potential for criminal gain.

NEUTRALIZATION THEORY

Neutralization theory, sometimes referred to as *drift theory*, is identified with the writings of David Matza and his associate Gresham Sykes.[33] In furthering Sutherland's views, Sykes and Matza suggest that delinquents hold attitudes and values similar to those of law-abiding citizens but that they learn techniques that enable them to neutralize those values and attitudes temporarily and drift back and forth between legitimate and delinquent behavior. The techniques used by delinquents to weaken the hold of social values are learned through interaction with others.

Elements of Neutralization Theory

In his major work, *Delinquency and Drift*, Matza explains neutralization, or drift, theory. He suggests that most individuals spend their lives behaving on a continuum somewhere between total freedom and total restraint. **Drift** is the process by which an individual moves from one extreme of behavior to another, behaving sometimes in an unconventional, free, or deviant manner and at other times with constraint and sobriety.

The subculture of delinquency, in which criminal behavior is regularly supported, encourages drift in young people. Matza views the subculture as relatively amorphous and without formal rules or values (except those that are bestowed on it by sociologists). He characterizes it as an informal, relatively inarticulate oral tradition. Members of the subculture infer the behavior they are to follow from behavior cues of their comrades, including slogans and actions.[34]

Writing with Gresham Sykes, Matza subsequently rejects the notion that the subculture of delinquency maintains an independent set of values and attitudes that place the delinquent in direct opposition to the values of the dominant culture. Rather, Matza and Sykes point to the complex pluralistic culture in our society that is both deviant and ethical. Though most youths actually appreciate goal-oriented middle-class values, they may feel that expressing conventional virtues and engaging in accepted behavior would be frowned upon by their peers. Therefore, these beliefs remain unconscious or subterranean because juveniles are afraid to express them to members of their own group. Juveniles are particularly susceptible to holding **subterranean values** because society does not provide them with specific goals or role orientation.

In a later paper, Matza further defines his concept of the teenage subculture as a conventional version of the delinquent's traditional behavior. That subculture emphasizes fun and adventure, and its members are persistently involved in status offenses, such as smoking, drinking, gambling, and making out. They disdain schoolwork and scholars and are overly concerned with proving masculinity or femininity.[35]

Techniques of Neutralization

Sykes and Matza suggest that juveniles develop a distinct set of justifications for their behavior when it violates accepted social norms. These neutralization techniques allow youths to temporarily drift away from the rules of the normative society and participate in subterranean behaviors. Sykes and Matza base their theoretical model on the following observations.[36]

First, delinquents sometimes voice a sense of guilt over their illegal acts. If a stable delinquent value system existed in opposition to generally held values and rules, delinquents likely would not exhibit any remorse for their acts, other than regret at being apprehended.

Second, juvenile offenders frequently respect and admire honest, law-abiding persons. "Really honest" persons are often revered, and if for some reason they are accused of misbehavior, the delinquent is quick to defend their integrity. Those admired may include sports figures, clergy, parents, teachers, and neighbors.

Third, delinquents draw a line between those whom they can victimize and those whom they cannot. Members of youths' ethnic groups, churches, or neighborhoods are off limits as far as crime goes. This practice implies that delinquents are aware of the wrongfulness of their acts. Why else would they limit them?

Finally, delinquents are not immune to the demands of conformity. Most delinquents frequently participate in many of the same social functions as law-abiding youths, for example, school, church, and family activities.

Sykes and Matza argue that these observations substantiate the fact that delinquents operate as part of the normative culture and adhere to its values and standards. How, then, do they account for delinquency? They suggest that delinquency is a result of the neutralization of accepted social values through employment of a standard set of rationalizations for illegal behavior. Thus, most youths generally adhere to the rules of society but learn certain techniques to temporarily release themselves from their moral constraints—the denial of responsibility, denial of injury, denial of a victim, condemnation of the condemners, and appeals to higher authorities.[37]

Denial of Responsibility. Delinquents sometimes claim that their unlawful acts were simply not their fault, that they were due to forces beyond their control or were an accident.

Denial of Injury. By denying the wrongfulness of an act, delinquents are able to rationalize their illegal behavior. For example, stealing is viewed as "borrowing," vandalism is considered mischief that got out of hand. Society often agrees with delinquents, labeling their illegal behavior "pranks" and thereby reaffirming that delinquency can be socially acceptable.

■ ■ ■ ■ ■ ■ ■ ■ ■ ■ ■ ■ ■ ■ ■

Some kids will neutralize delinquent activities by reasoning that they have to stick up for their buddies (appeal to higher loyalties).

Denial of Victim. Delinquents sometimes rationalize their behavior by maintaining that the victim of crime "had it coming." Thus, vandalism may be directed against a disliked teacher or neighbor, or homosexuals may be beaten up by a gang because the gang finds their behavior offensive.[38] Denying the victim may also take the form of ignoring the rights of an absent or unknown victim, for example, the unseen owner of a department store. It becomes morally acceptable for delinquents to commit crimes, such as vandalism, when the victims cannot be sympathized with or respected because of their absence.

Condemnation of the Condemnors. Delinquents view the world as a corrupt place with a dog-eat-dog moral code. Since police and judges are on the take, teachers show favoritism, and parents take out their frustrations on their children, it is ironic and unfair for these authorities to turn around and condemn youthful misconduct. By shifting the blame to others, delinquents are able to repress the feeling that their own acts are wrong.

Appeal to Higher Loyalties. Delinquents argue that they are caught in the dilemma of being loyal to their own peer group while at the same time attempting to abide by the rules of the larger society. The needs of the group take precedence over the rules of society because the demands of the former are immediate and localized.[39]

In sum, the theory of neutralization presupposes a condition in which such statements as "I didn't mean to do it," "I didn't really hurt anybody," "They had it coming to them," "Everybody's picking on me," and "I didn't do it for myself" are used by youths to rationalize violating accepted social norms and values so that they can enter, or drift, into delinquent modes of behavior (see Figure 6.4).

■■ **FIGURE 6.4**

Techniques of neutralization

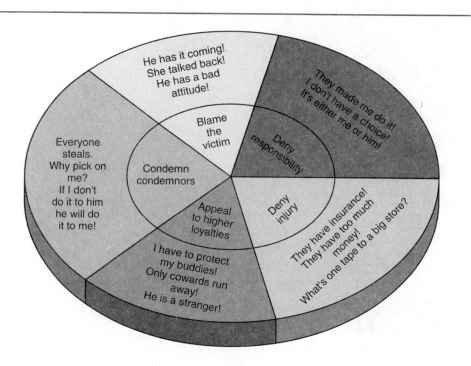

Part II   Theories of Delinquency

Analysis of Neutralization Theory

The theory of neutralization is a major contribution to the literature of crime and delinquency because it accounts for the fact that many teenage delinquents do not evolve into adult criminals. Neutralization theory implies that youths can forgo criminal behavior when they reach their majority because they never really rejected the morality of normative society. Once the needs and pressures of the post-teenage world exert themselves—marriage, family, job—delinquents are more likely than ever to drift into legitimate modes of behavior. This helps explain the behavior of the occasional or nonchronic delinquent, who is able to successfully age out of crime. Teenage recreational drug users employ such neutralizations as "Everybody's doing it" and "No one is really hurt"; as they mature, they simply drift back into conventional behavior patterns.

Neutralization theory leaves important questions unanswered, however. Do delinquents neutralize law-violating behavior *before* or *after* they commit crimes?[40] If they neutralize their guilt after engaging in illegal activity, then neutralization theory loses its power as an explanation of the *cause* of delinquency and becomes a theory describing the *reactions* of juveniles to their misdeeds. While this question seems critical, criminologist John Hamlin argues that neutralizations *should be considered* as post-delinquency rationalizations of behavior. He finds they are used only when deviant behavior is detected and condemned by others. It is only when the youth's behavior is viewed as a major threat that the need to neutralize its moral taint occurs. Justifications and excuses neutralize guilt and enable individuals to continue to feel good about themselves.[41]

Even if neutralization techniques are actually used before the commission of delinquent acts, the theory fails to distinguish why some youths consistently drift into delinquency and others do not. Unless we can understand why drift occurs, the theory will remain too abstract and vague to be of practical use.

Attempts have been made to verify the assumptions of neutralization theory empirically, but the results have been inconclusive.[42] Some studies indicate that delinquents generally approve of social values; others come to the opposite conclusion. Some studies show that delinquent youths approve of criminal behavior; still others find evidence that they oppose illegal behavior. If neutralization theory is to become a valid and practical explanation of delinquency, further research aimed at testing its assumptions is needed.

SOCIAL CONTROL THEORIES

Social control theories suggest that many forms of delinquent behavior—using drugs, engaging in sexual acts, skipping school, fighting, getting drunk, and so on—are attractive to almost every teenager. These acts represent the exciting, illicit, adventurous behavior that is glorified on television and in the movies and that serves as a theme for rock music.

Why, then, do most youths obey conventional rules and grow up to be law-abiding adults? For a social control theorist, the answer lies in the strength and direction of their ties with conventional groups, individuals, and institutions. Those who have close relationships with their parents, friends, and teachers and who maintain a positive self-image will be able to resist the lure of deviant behaviors. To not jeopardize their good standing in the community, they refuse to risk detection and punishment for delinquent offenses. On the other hand,

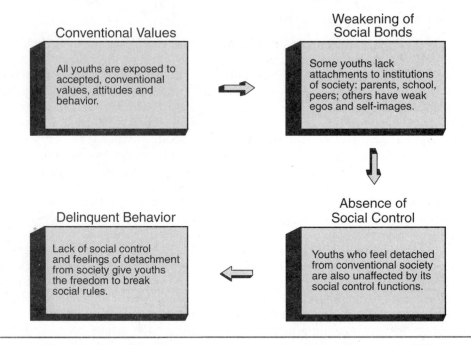

Conventional Values

All youths are exposed to accepted, conventional values, attitudes and behavior.

Weakening of Social Bonds

Some youths lack attachments to institutions of society: parents, school, peers; others have weak egos and self-images.

Delinquent Behavior

Lack of social control and feelings of detachment from society give youths the freedom to break social rules.

Absence of Social Control

Youths who feel detached from conventional society are also unaffected by its social control functions.

youths without these social supports feel free to violate the law; if caught, they have nothing to lose. (See Figure 6.5.)

Self-Concept and Delinquency

The first versions of control theory speculated that delinquency was a product of weak self-concept and poor self-esteem. Youths who felt good about themselves were able to resist the temptations of the streets; those with a poor self-image were more likely to succumb. As early as 1951, Albert Reiss described how delinquents had weak "ego ideals" and lacked the "personal controls" to produce conforming behavior.[43] In a similar vein, Scott Briar and Irving Piliavin described how delinquents have a weak *commitment to conformity.*[44] They concluded that youths who fear that apprehension for criminal activity will damage their self-image as well as their relationships with others will be most likely to conform to social roles.

CONTAINMENT THEORY

The best-known theoretical model linking the production of delinquent behavior with self-concept is Walter Reckless's *containment theory.*[45] Containment theory contends that society produces a series of pushes and pulls toward delinquency. Among these are:

1. *Internal Pushes.* Internal pushes involve such personal factors as restlessness, discontent, hostility, rebellion, mental conflict, anxieties, and the need for immediate gratification.

2. *External Pressures.* External pressures are adverse living conditions that influence deviant behavior. They include relative deprivation poverty, unemployment, insecurity, minority status, limited opportunities, and inequalities.
3. *External Pulls.* External pulls are deviant companions, membership in criminal subcultures or other deviant groups, and such influences as mass media and pornography.

These in turn are counteracted by internal and external containments, which help insulate the individual from delinquency. These include:

1. *Inner Containments.* Inner containments consist of the elements of the inner strength of an individual personality—for example, good self-concept, ego strength, high frustration tolerance, goal orientation, and tension-reducing capabilities.
2. *Outer Containments.* Outer containments are the normative constraints that societies and social groups ordinarily use to control their members—for example, a sense of belonging; a consistent moral front; reinforcement of norms, goals, and values; effective supervision; discipline; and a meaningful social role.

Simply put, containment theory suggests that the two containments act as a defense against a person's potential deviation from legal and social norms and work to insulate a youth from the pressures and pulls of criminogenic influences.

Reckless and his associates made an extensive effort to validate the principles of containment theory.[46] In a series of studies analyzing containment principles within the school setting, they concluded that the ability of nondelinquents to maintain their conventional "good boy" behavior depends on their holding a positive self-image in the face of environmental pressures toward delinquency.[47]

According to control type theories, attachment to significant others helps insulate a youth from delinquent behavior.

The work of Reckless and his associates has been criticized for a lack of methodological rigor.[48] A series of research studies found little relationship between self-esteem and delinquency, a finding in opposition to the key elements of containment theory. This has led to containment theory being superseded by other control theories, specifically Travis Hirschi's attempt to articulate the elements of social control.

CONTROL THEORY

Travis Hirschi's version of control theory, first articulated in his famous book *Causes of Delinquency*, links delinquent behavior to the bond an individual maintains with society. When that bond weakens or breaks, the constraints that society puts on its members are lifted, and an individual may violate the law. Unlike some of the other theoretical models discussed here, Hirschi's control theory assumes that all individuals are potential delinquents and criminals ("born bad") and that social controls, not moral values, maintain law and order. Without controls and in the absence of sensitivity to and interest in others, a youth is free to commit criminal acts.[49]

Hirschi speculates that a consistent value system exists and that all people in society are exposed to it. Delinquents defy this moral code because their attachment to society is weak. Hirschi views the youthful law violator as someone who rejects social norms and beliefs. The major elements of his argument are (1) there is a "variation in belief in the moral validity of social rules,"[50] (2) this variation is brought about by a weakening of the attachment of the individual to elements of society, and (3) this condition produces delinquent behavior.

Elements of the Social Bond

Hirschi argues that the *social bond* a person maintains with society is divided into four main elements: attachment, commitment, involvement, and belief (see Figure 6.6).

Attachment.   Attachment refers to a person's sensitivity to and interest in others. Psychologists believe that without a sense of attachment, a person becomes a psychopath and loses the ability to relate coherently to the world. The acceptance of social norms and the development of a social conscience depend on attachment to and caring for other human beings. Hirschi views parents, peers, and schools as the most important social institutions with which a person should maintain ties. Attachment to parents is the most important. Even if a family is shattered by divorce and separation, a child must retain a strong attachment to one or both parents. Without attachment to the family, a child is unlikely to develop feelings of respect for others in authority.

Commitment.   Commitment involves the time, energy, and effort expended in pursuit of conventional lines of action. It embraces such activities as getting an education and saving money for the future. Control theory holds that if people build up a strong involvement in life, property, and reputation, they will be less

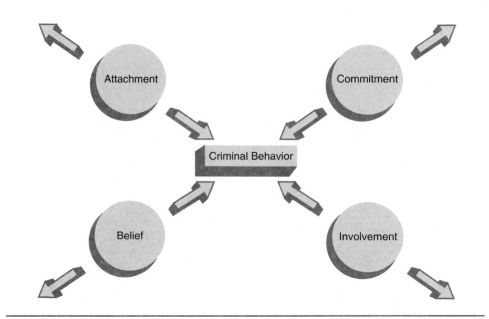

FIGURE 6.6

Elements of the social bond

likely to engage in acts that will jeopardize their position. Conversely, a lack of commitment to conventional values may foreshadow a condition in which risk-taking behavior, such as delinquency, becomes a reasonable behavior alternative.

Involvement. An individual's heavy involvement in conventional activities does not leave time for illegal behavior. Hirschi believes that involvement—in school, recreation, and family—insulates a youth from the potential lure of delinquent behavior that idleness encourages.

Belief. People who live in common social settings often share a similar moral doctrine and revere such human values as sharing, sensitivity to the rights of others, and admiration for the legal code. If these beliefs are absent or weakened, individuals are more likely to share in antisocial acts.

Hirschi further suggests that the interrelationship of elements of the social bond influences whether an individual pursues delinquent or conventional activities. For example, boys or girls who feel kinship with and sensitivity toward parents and friends should be more likely to desire and work toward legitimate goals. On the other hand, youths who reject social relationships will probably lack commitment to conventional goals and more likely will be involved in unconventional activities.

Empirical Research on Control Theory

The most powerful empirical support for social bond theory comes from the significant body of literature that indicates that poor familial, educational, and peer relationships are all related to delinquency. Numerous studies over twenty years have found that, as Hirschi predicted, delinquent youths have weak and strained relationships with their parents, experience school failure and lack interest in school activities, and exhibit inadequate peer-group relations.

This evidence alone, however, is not sufficient proof of the validity of control theory, because these strained relationships may be a result of delinquent behavior and not its cause. It would not be surprising that kids who engage in repeated criminal activity have poor relationships at home and at school. To confirm control theory, it must be shown that a weakened social bond preceded the delinquent behavior.

One of Hirschi's most significant contributions to delinquency research is his impartial verification of the principal hypothesis of control theory. He administered a complex self-report survey to a sample of more than four thousand junior and senior high school students in Contra Costa County, California.[51] In a detailed analysis of the data, Hirschi found considerable evidence to support the control theory model. We will now look at some of his more important findings in detail.

Hirschi measured attachment to society with such survey items as "Would you like to be the kind of person your father is?" and "When you come across things you don't understand, does your mother (father) help you with them?" He found that youths who were strongly attached to their parents were less likely to participate in delinquent behavior. This relationship also existed when race, social class, and the parents' own values were controlled.

With regard to this point, Hirschi found that lower-class parents, even those who themselves are committing criminal acts, express allegiance to the law and conventional society. Thus, attachment to the parents counteracts delinquent behavior even when the parents themselves are delinquent.

■ ■ ■ ■ ■ ■ ■ ■ ■ ■ ■ ■ ■ ■ ■

Hirschi portrays the delinquent as a loner, who lacks attachment to peers and family group members.

Hirschi also found that lack of attachment to the school and to education, measured by such items as "Do you care what teachers think of you?" and "It is none of the school's business if a student wants to smoke outside the classroom" is a strong predictor of delinquent behavior. Poor school performance and academic incompetence affect this relationship significantly. Youths with poor basic academic skills are likely to become detached from school and involved in delinquency. Hirschi traces this important relationship as follows: "The causal chain runs from academic incompetence to poor school performance to disliking of school to rejection of the school's authority to the commission of delinquent acts."[52]

Hirschi also examined the attachment of youths to their friends and other peers, using such questions as "Would you like to be the kind of person your best friends are?" He found that youths who maintain close associations with friends are less likely to commit delinquent acts. Delinquent youths, on the other hand, often maintain weak and distant relationships with their peers. Hirschi did find that boys with a high stake in conformity who maintain delinquent friends are more likely to commit delinquent acts than boys with a high stake in conformity without delinquent friends. However, this relationship does not immediately contradict the control approach. First, only 22 percent of the high-stake boys had delinquent friends. Second, the greater a youth's stake in conformity, the less likely he was to maintain delinquent companions.

Among Hirschi's most important discoveries are the following:

- Contrary to subcultural theories, the gang rarely recruits "good" boys or influences them to turn "bad."
- Boys who maintain middle-class values are relatively unaffected by the delinquent behavior of their friends, although having delinquent friends was generally related to criminality.
- The idea that delinquents have warm, intimate relationships with one another is a myth.
- "The child with little stake in conformity is susceptible to pro-delinquent influences in his environment; the child with a large stake in conformity is relatively immune to these influences."[53]

Hirschi examined commitment to both deviant and conventional activities with questionnaire items dealing with frequency of smoking, drinking, and dating behaviors, level of educational aspiration (desire for a college education, for example), and level of vocational expectation (blue-collar, white-collar, professional). Again Hirschi found evidence that commitment to conventional values is related to rejection of delinquent behavior. He states, "The picture of the delinquent as a striver, either in word or deed, simply does not fit the data."[54]

Involvement in conventional activities was defined as time spent on homework, and involvement in unconventional activities was defined as hours a week spent riding around in cars. Hirschi also found that involvement in school inhibits delinquency. Youths who smoke, drink, date, ride around in cars, and find adolescence "boring" are more prone to delinquency. However, this relationship is not as strong as Hirschi expected, and he found that boys who are involved in unconventional activities (smoking, drinking, and so on) are more likely to engage in delinquent acts regardless of their commitment to education and their involvement in school activities.

Hirschi measured a large variety of commonly held beliefs and values. It is not surprising that he found that youths who expressed respect for the police and the law were less likely to commit delinquent acts. In general, there was little difference in the beliefs of delinquents and nondelinquents. In fact, delinquents often respected middle-class attitudes. For example, Hirschi reports that children who do not personally care about good grades still believe that youths who do care about school and get good grades are taking a path preferable to their own.

Hirschi's data lend important support to the validity of control theory. While the statistical significance of his findings is sometimes less than he expected, his research data are extremely consistent. Only in very rare instances do his findings contradict the theory's most critical assumptions.

Corroborating Research

Many attempts have been made to corroborate Hirschi's findings. Support for the theory comes from research conducted on the quality of the relationships delinquent youth have with the rest of society.[55] In general, this body of knowledge has been supportive of Hirschi's work: delinquents tend to have the strained relationships within the family, peer group, and school, which are indicative of a weakened social bond.[56] Cross-national surveys also support the general finding of control theory.[57] For example, when Marvin Krohn and his associates surveyed a large sample of adolescents and their parents about aspects of their family life and relations, they found that the quality of the bonds that parents and children have for one another is the key determinant of delinquent behavior. Low attachment, perceived by either the parent or child, is the most consistent predictor of both self-report and official delinquency.[58]

Attempts also have been made to test control theory directly by replicating Hirschi's original survey techniques. In a classic study by Michael Hindelang, subjects in the sixth through twelfth grades in a rural New York state school system were asked many of the same questions used in Hirschi's original survey instrument.[59] With few exceptions, Hindelang's evidence supported Hirschi's control theory principles. The major difference between the two studies was in the area of attachment to delinquent peers. Hindelang found that close identification with delinquent peers was directly related to delinquent activity, while Hirschi's research produced the opposite result.

Do elements of the social bond and its influence on delinquency change over time?[60] Using samples of 12-, 15-, and 18-year-old boys, Randy LaGrange and Helene Raskin White found that there are indeed age differences in the way elements of the bond influence delinquency. Mid-teens are more likely to be influenced by their parents and teachers than boys in the other age groups, who are more deeply influenced by their deviant peers. LaGrange and White attribute this finding to the problems of mid-adolescence, when youths have a great need to develop "psychological anchors" to conformity.

Dissenting Opinions

While there has been significant empirical support for Hirschi's work, there are also those who question some or all of its elements. For example, Hirschi maintains that delinquents are detached loners whose bond to their family and friends has been broken. Some critics have questioned whether delinquents (1) do in fact have strained relations with family and peers and (2) whether they may in fact be influenced by close relationships with *deviant* peers and family members. Hindelang indicated that delinquent youths are attached to deviant peers and parents. Gary Jensen and David Brownfield also found that drug-abusing adolescents express attachment to parents who use drugs themselves.[61] A number of other research efforts show that delinquents are not lone wolves whose only personal relationships are exploitive and that their friendship patterns are quite close to those of conventional youth.[62] For example, Denise Kandel and Mark Davies found that young male drug abusers maintained even more intimate relations with their peers than nonabusers; illicit drug abuse can be used to predict strong social ties and high levels of intimacy.[63]

Criticism has also been directed at control theory's ability to explain all modes of delinquency. Some charge that its predictive power is restricted to particular groups of potential delinquents or forms of delinquent behavior. Marvin Krohn and James Massey surveyed a sample of 3,065 junior and senior high school students and found that control variables were better able to explain female delinquency than male delinquency and minor delinquency (such as alcohol and marijuana abuse) than more serious delinquent acts. Krohn and Massey conclude that Hirschi's model has utility as an explanation of the onset of delinquency, a period when youthful offenders are both engaging in petty offenses and questioning their commitment and attachment to social institutions.[64]

The most comprehensive criticism of control theory comes from sociologist Robert Agnew, who questions the power of control variables to explain delinquency and drug abuse.[65] Agnew charges that the importance of Hirschi's theory has been exaggerated because the influence of social relationships declines as an adolescent matures. In addition, Agnew questions the control theory assumption that a weak bond to society causes delinquency. He suggests that the chain of events may be opposite of that flow: chronic delinquents may find that their bonds to parents, schools and society are becoming weak and attenuated; in other words, delinquency causes the weakening of social bonds and not vice versa.[66]

In sum, some research has given unqualified support to control theory while other efforts have questioned its explanatory power. However, even its greatest detractors recognize that the theory has been the most influential model of delinquency for the past twenty-five years.

SELF-CONTROL THEORY

In an important recent work called *A General Theory of Crime,* Travis Hirschi with his colleague Michael Gottfredson have refined and extended control theory while integrating some of the concepts of choice (Chapter 4), life course (Chapter 3), and psychological theories (Chapter 4).[67]

In their *self-control theory* (also referred to as the general theory of crime), Gottfredson and Hirschi argue that to properly understand the nature of crime and delinquency, offenders and their acts must be dealt with as separate issues. *Crimes,* such as robberies or burglaries, are illegal events or deeds that people engage in when they perceive them to be advantageous. For example, burglaries are typically committed by male adolescents seeking cash, liquor, and entertainment; the delinquency provides "easy short term gratification."[68] In contrast, *criminals* are people who maintain a status that maximizes the possibility that they will engage in crimes. Adolescents with delinquent inclinations do not constantly commit crimes; their days are filled with nondelinquent behaviors, such as going to school, parties, concerts, and church. But, given the same set of life circumstances, they have a much higher probability of committing illegal acts than do nondelinquents.

What, then, causes youths to become excessively delinquency prone? To Gottfredson and Hirschi, the explanation for individual differences in the tendency to commit delinquent acts can be found in an adolescent's level of self-control. People with limited self-control have *impulsive* personalities. They tend to be insensitive, physical (rather than mental), risk-taking, short-sighted, and nonverbal.[69] They have a "here and now" orientation and refuse to work for distant goals; they lack diligence, tenacity, and persistence in a course of action. People lacking self-control tend to be adventuresome, active, physical, and self-centered. As they mature, they have unstable marriages, jobs, and friendships.[70] Criminal acts are attractive to them because they provide easy and immediate gratification or, as Gottfredson and Hirschi put it, "money without work, sex without courtship, revenge without court delays."[71] Since those with low self-control enjoy risky, exciting, or thrilling behaviors with immediate benefits, they are more likely to enjoy criminal acts, which require stealth, danger, agility, speed, and power, than conventional acts, which demand long-term study and require cognitive and verbal skills. Considering their desire for easy pleasures, it should come as no surprise that people lacking self-control will also engage in noncriminal behaviors that provide them with immediate and short-term gratification, for example, smoking, drinking, gambling, illicit sexuality, or having out-of-wedlock children.[72] (See Figure 6.7.)

Self-Control and Social Bonds

How does the concept of self-control relate to Hirschi's earlier social control theory? The relationship appears reciprocal and mutually supporting. Gottfredson and Hirschi trace the root cause of poor self-control to inadequate child-rearing practices. Parents who refuse or are unable to monitor a child's behavior, recognize deviant behavior when it occurs, and punish that behavior will produce children who lack self-control. Kids who lack self-control are unlikely to be attached to parents, committed to orthodox value and beliefs, and involved in conventional activities. It may be possible that an attenuated bond to society further weakens self-control, thereby sustaining and amplifying the deviant career throughout the life span.

Gottfredson and Hirschi conclude that the cause of persistent delinquency—the development of impulsivity—occurs during the early formative years and

■■ FIGURE 6.7

Self-control and delinquency

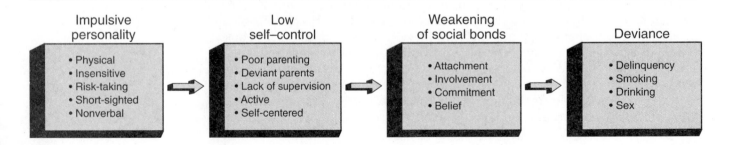

Part II   Theories of Delinquency

then controls behavior throughout the life course. Nonetheless, the effects of a weakened social bond are not disputed or discounted by the general theory of crime.

An Analysis of Self-Control Theory

Gottfredson and Hirschi's general theory of crime provides answers to many of the questions left open by the original control model. By separating the concepts of delinquency and delinquents, Gottfredson and Hirschi help explain why some kids who lack self-control can escape criminality: they lack criminal opportunity. Similarly, even those people who have a strong bond to social institutions and maintain self-control may on occasion engage in law-violating behavior: if the opportunity is strong enough, the incentives may overcome self-control. This explains why the so-called "good kid," who has a strong school record and positive parental relationships, can get involved in drugs or vandalism or why the corporate executive with a spotless record gets caught up in business fraud. Even successful executives may find their self-control inadequate if the potential for illegal gain runs into the tens of millions.

The general theory of crime may also be evaluated from the life-course perspective. Gottfredson and Hirschi argue vehemently that life events *do not* influence the propensity to commit crime; the tendency to commit crime is stable. However, they also recognize that criminal opportunities—the occasion to commit crime—vary significantly over the life course; individual crime rates fluctuate with criminal opportunities. Their views then are not entirely dissimilar from life-course theorists, who believe events that occur over a person's life cycle influence behavior. Though Gottfredson and Hirschi deny that an individual's propensity to commit crime changes over the life course, they strongly support the influence of environmental change on crime rates. Put another way, even Gottfredson and Hirschi recognize that events encountered over the life cycle influence the *likelihood* of crime and delinquency.

Though the self-control approach seems to have merit as a general theory of delinquency, several questions remain unanswered. Saying someone lacks self-control implies that the person suffers from a personality defect that makes him or her impulsive and rash. The view that criminals maintain a deviant personality is not new since, as you may recall, psychologists have long sought evidence of a "criminal personality."[73] Yet, the search for the criminal personality has proven elusive, and no conclusive proof has been found that criminals can be distinguished from noncriminals on the basis of personality alone.

The strength of Gottfredson and Hirschi's work is its ability to integrate the concepts of criminal choice, socialization, and personality. In so doing, these researchers join with other criminologists who embrace both social and individual variables in their effort to understand crime and criminality. Since self-control theory is relatively new, research is needed to test its major premises.

INTEGRATED THEORIES

In recent years, delinquency experts have attempted to integrate concepts and features of a number of existing theoretical models into a single theoretical model of delinquent career formation. To explain delinquency through the life course, integrated theories apply biological, psychological, choice, social structure, and social process theories. In the sections below, some of the more prominent integrated theories are discussed.

Social Development Theory

Joseph Weis and his associates have attempted to integrate some of the most important features of social control theory with aspects of the social structure approach discussed in Chapter 5.[74] Weis argues that control theory is useful when it describes how children become delinquent because of their inadequate socialization and alienation from important institutional forces, such as the family and the school. Social structure theory can also be useful because it accounts for the community context of delinquency. The two theoretical perspectives also complement one another in the area of the role of socialization. While control theory views delinquency as a result of inadequate relationships with such formal institutions as the school, the family, and the criminal justice system, social structure theories focus on the influence of informal peer groups and companions. Consequently, after reviewing the core premises of each type of theory, Weis found that both can contribute to an integrated model of delinquency.

According to Weis's **social development theory,** a positive relationship exists between community organization and social control, and both factors in turn exert influence on delinquent behavior. That is, in a low-income, disorganized community, social control is less effective because the frontline socializing institutions are weak: families are disorganized; educational facilities are inadequate; there are fewer material, social, and psychological resources; and respect for the law is inadequate. Because crime rates are traditionally higher in these areas, more opportunities exist to commit crime, putting even greater strain on the institutions of socialization. Within this context of weak social controls and community disorganization, legitimate social institutions are incapable of combating the lure of delinquent peer groups and gangs.

Weis's model of delinquency is illustrated in Figure 6.8, which shows the direction of delinquency-producing relationships. Socialization within the family is influenced by the youth's sex, race, and economic status: children of a particular race and sex living within a certain area will have familial experiences different from those of children with a different set of personal and economic characteristics. It is anticipated that males who are members of the lowest economic strata will have the highest potential for disrupted, unrewarding family lives and a lack of attachment to their parents.

Opportunities for involvement in the family, plus specific parental skills, lead to a close attachment with parents. This attachment influences subsequent school experiences and beliefs and values. For those with strong family relationships, school will be a meaningful experience marked by academic success and commitment to education. Youths in this category are more likely to develop conventional beliefs and values, become committed to conventional activities, and form attachments to conventional others. But if a youth does not find participation in conventional activities rewarding, he or she will be likely to seek associations with youths who are equally disillusioned and to engage in deviant activities that promise alternative rewards. Together, these alienated youths are likely to influence one another in the pursuit of illegal gain and illicit experiences.

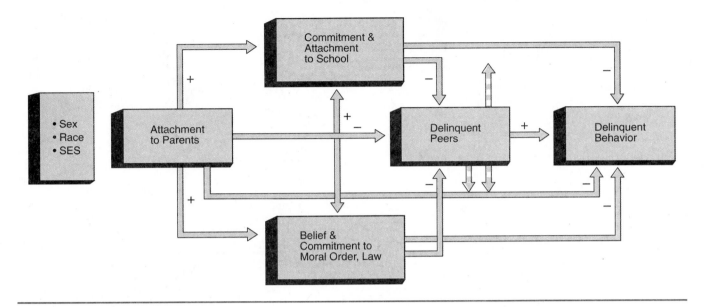

■■ FIGURE 6.8

Overview of the social
development theory of
delinquency

Source: Joseph Weis and John
Sederstrom, *Reports of the National
Juvenile Assessment Centers, The Prevention
of Serious Delinquency: What to Do*
(Washington, D.C.: U.S. Department of
Justice, 1981) p. 35.

Weis's social development model combines features of social structure and social control theories. Like the former, it suggests that youths living in disorganized neighborhoods are the most likely to succumb to the lure of youth gangs and groups. And like the latter, it holds that commitment and attachment to conventional institutions, activities, and beliefs work to insulate youths from the criminogenic influences of their environment. This approach seems to have great power as an explanation of delinquent behavior and deserves the serious attention of students of delinquency.

Elliott's Integrated Theory

Another attempt to integrate theories of delinquency has been proposed by Delbert Elliott and his colleagues David Huizinga and Suzanne Ageton of the Behavioral Research Institute.[75] Elliott and his associates discount some aspects of "pure" strain, control, and learning theory. They contend that strain theory can account for some initial delinquent acts but does not adequately explain why some youths enter into delinquent careers while others forgo them (since prolonged delinquency places the offender's valued conventional roles in jeopardy). Similarly, control theory cannot explain prolonged delinquent involvement because there is no group support or rewards for this behavior (since control theorists, such as Hirschi, portray the delinquent as a loner without close bonds to peers or society). And learning theories usually portray the delinquent as a passive actor who simply reacts when confronted with delinquency-producing reinforcements.

Elliott and his colleagues integrate the strongest features of strain, social learning, and control theories into a single theoretical model (see Figure 6.9). According to this view, perceptions of strain, inadequate socialization, and living in a socially disorganized areas lead youths to develop weak bonds with conventional groups, activities, and norms. Weak conventional bonds and high

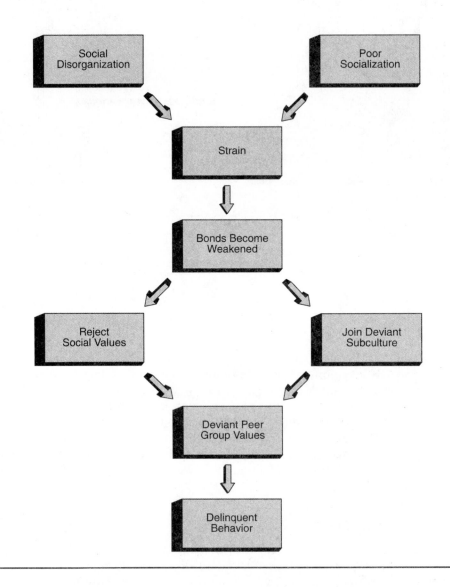

levels of perceived strain lead some youths to seek out and become bonded to peer groups. From these delinquent associations come positive reinforcements for delinquent behaviors; delinquent peers help provide role models for antisocial behavior. Bonding to delinquent groups when combined with weak bonding to conventional groups and norms lead to a high probability of involvement in delinquent behavior.

Elliott and his colleagues tested their theoretical model with data taken from a national survey of approximately eighteen hundred youths who were interviewed annually over a three-year period. With only a few minor exceptions, the results generally supported their integrated theory. One difference was that some subjects reported developing strong bonds to delinquent peers even if they did not reject the values of conventional society. Elliott and his associates interpret this finding as suggesting that youths living in disorganized areas may have little choice but to join with law-violating youth groups since conventional groups simply do not exist.[76] They also found that initial experimentation with drugs and delinquency predicted both joining a teenage law-violating peer group and becoming involved in additional delinquency.

The picture Elliott and his colleagues draw of the teenage delinquent is not dissimilar to the one drawn by Weis's social development model: Living in a disorganized neighborhood, feeling hopeless and unable to get ahead, and becoming involved in petty crimes eventually leads to a condition where conventional social values become weak and attenuated. Concern for education, family relations, and respect for the social order are weakened. A deviant peer group becomes an acceptable substitute, and consequently, the attitudes and skills that support delinquent tendencies are amplified. The result is early experimentation with drugs, and delinquency becomes a way of life.

Interactional Theory

Another addition to theory integration is Terence Thornberry's interactional theory.[77] (See Figure 6.10.)

Thornberry agrees (with both Weis and Elliott) that the onset of crime can be traced to a deterioration of the social bond during adolescence, marked by a weakened attachment to parents, commitment to school, and belief in conventional values. Thornberry's theory similarly recognizes the influence of social class position and other structural variables: youths growing up in socially disorganized areas are at the greatest risk of having a weakened social bond and subsequently becoming delinquent. The onset of a criminal career is supported by residence in a social setting in which deviant values and attitudes can be learned and reinforced by delinquent peers.

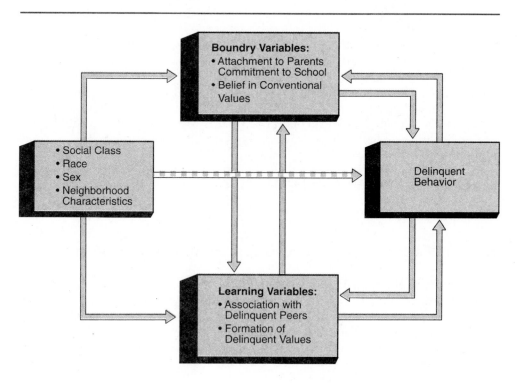

■■ **FIGURE 6.10**

Overview of the interactional theory of delinquency

Source: Terence Thornberry, Margaret Farnsworth, Alan Lizotte, and Susan Stern, "A Longitudinal Examination of the Causes and Correlates of Delinquency," working paper #1, Rochester Youth Development Study (Albany, N.Y.: Hindelang Criminal Justice Research Center, 1987) p. 11.

Interactional theory also holds that serious delinquent youths form belief systems that are consistent with their deviant life-style. They seek out the company of other kids who share their interests and who are likely to reinforce their beliefs about the world and support their delinquent behavior. According to interactional theory, then, delinquents seek out a criminal peer group in the same fashion that chess buffs look for others who share their passion for the game. Deviant peers do not turn "innocent" boys into delinquents. They support and amplify the behavior of kids who have already accepted a delinquent way of life.

Interactional theory is unique because it integrates life-course concepts when it suggests that adolescents pass through different stages of reasoning and sophistication as they mature. Thornberry applies this concept when he suggests that criminality is a developmental process that takes on different meaning and form as a person matures. The causal process is a dynamic one that develops over a person's life. During early adolescence, attachment to the family is the single most important determinant of whether a youth will adjust to conventional society and be shielded from delinquency. By mid-adolescence, the influence of the family is replaced by the world of friends, school and youth culture. In adulthood, people's behavioral choices are shaped by their place in conventional society and their own nuclear family. The process is reciprocal: people are shaped by the quality of their social world, and the quality of their social world is influenced by their behavior.

Testing Interactional Theory

Thornberry's model is in its early stages of development and is being tested with a panel of Rochester, New York, youth who will be followed through the cycle of their offending careers. Preliminary results seem to support interactional theory. In one analysis, Thornberry and his colleagues examined the influence of peer associations on delinquency and found that they conformed to interactional principles: associating with delinquent peers leads to increases in delinquency; increased delinquency leads to associations with delinquent peers. As this process unfolds over the life course, antisocial kids will become part of a deviant peer network that will reinforce their behavior; conventional youth will, in turn, be reinforced by their conventional friends.[78] In another analysis, Thornberry and his colleagues found similar relationships with family and school relations: delinquency is related to weakened attachments to family and the educational process; delinquent behavior further weakens the strength of the bonds to family and school.[79]

In sum, interactional theory rests on life-course assumptions: events and relationships that develop during a person's life-cycle influence his or her behavior.

SOCIAL PROCESS THEORY AND DELINQUENCY PREVENTION

Social process theory suggests that delinquency is a result of (1) improper socialization, leading to (2) conflict with important social institutions, which leads to (3) deviant forms of behavior. The learning theory branch holds that this process is triggered by values, attitudes, and behaviors learned in close contact with significant others. The control theory branch points to the youth's weakened relationship with the major deviance-controlling institutions—family, schools, and peers.

By implication, social process theories suggest that delinquency can be prevented by strengthening the relationship between youths and the institutions primarily responsible for their socialization. This objective can be reached either by strengthening the institutions themselves or by helping the youths better handle preexisting conditions. For example, the neighborhood school might be improved as a delinquency-controlling institution by getting teachers to realize that all students can and should be educated; by expanding preschool education programs; by developing curriculums and educational materials that are relevant to students' lives; by developing teaching methods appropriate to the students; by developing individualized curriculums; by stressing teacher development; and so on. At the same time, school-based delinquency prevention efforts must be available to help the youth who is manifesting problems in school, experiencing school failure, and finding that his or her bond to the educational system has eroded. This implies a need for individual counseling and remedial services for troubled youths. The following Case in Point raises some prevention issues.

■■■■■■■■■■■■■■■

CASE IN POINT

You have just been appointed the head of curriculum for the local school system.

The school board is interested in creating courses that will reduce the incidence of student delinquency and drug abuse. They fear that TV shows, popular music, and films that glorify the use of drugs teach kids that substance abuse and crime are exciting and socially desirable activities. They feel the school must present courses that can counteract the weight of these destructive influences.

You are faced with designing a program that can teach students to "say no" to drugs and crime. One of your advisors suggests that the best approach is to teach kids about the effects of drugs through media and live presentations in which former users discuss their experiences and problems. She believes that learning about the evils of drugs can counteract the pro-drug influence of commercial TV and rock and roll. In contrast, another advisor argues that the best approach is a series of workshops that help students develop a bond with their parents and community and learn the value of commitment to conventional behavior and actions. Such workshops would stress techniques of interfamily communications and life skills. While both of these approaches have merit, only one can be chosen to serve as the basis of the new course.

What type of information would you present to the students?

Can students learn not to commit crime and take drugs?

Who could best help students learn not to use drugs or engage in delinquency: other students? Parents? Teachers? Ex-offenders?

Prevention programs must also work to strengthen the internal structure of families in crisis. Because attachment to parents who can provide proper socialization is a cornerstone of all social process theories, it is an essential element of delinquency prevention. This should not mean, however, that all families are expected to conform to a particular life-style or pattern. Efforts should be directed at helping the family become a living unit that provides care and support for its members. What should be developed is a family structure that can encourage the positive self-image the child needs to resist the delinquency-promoting forces in his or her environment.

Agents of the juvenile justice system must also recognize that their actions have a bearing on the future behavior of youths. For example, if a youth feels that he or she is not being treated fairly by police or court officials, that youth will be likely to seek out peers who share similar views. Consequently, the youth will be likely to experience an excess of definitions toward delinquency as well as a weakening of belief in conventional social rules and values.

Over the years, many local prevention programs have had as their objective goals that coincide with the premise of the social process approach. These efforts replaced, for the most part, the large-scale community development programs based on the social structure theories discussed in Chapter 5. Many were demonstration programs that operated for a few years on federal funds; others are ongoing, with funding from state and local governments. Some efforts have been directed at primary prevention (before the onset of delinquency), while others have focused on secondary prevention (treating troubled youths) and tertiary prevention (helping ex-offenders "go straight").

Many primary prevention efforts have been aimed at improving the school experience. For example, the Alternative Learning Project (ALP) in Providence, Rhode Island, helps educationally disillusioned youths develop a learning experience that would create positive attachments with their school.[80] It uses such features as a low student-teacher ratio (sixteen to one), individualized programs, emphasis on basic skills, special projects, tutoring, and courses at local colleges. An evaluation of the program indicated that 55 percent of its students go on to college and that absenteeism and dropout rates are greatly reduced. It is unlikely that such results for these youths would have been achieved without the ALP.

Prevention programs have also focused on providing services for youngsters who have been identified as delinquents or predelinquents. Such services usually include counseling, job placement, legal assistance, and so on. The following Focus on Delinquency describes a number of recent efforts to restore and/or maintain youths' bonds to society.

In addition to these local efforts, the federal government has sponsored several national delinquency prevention efforts using the principles of social process theory. These include vocational training programs, such as the Job Corps and the Comprehensive Employment Training Act, as well as educational enrichment programs, such as Head Start for preschoolers and Upward Bound for high school students interested in going on to college. Federal budget cutbacks in the past decade have severely restricted these efforts, but local efforts keep these traditions alive.

Programs That Work for Teens and Young Adults

MULTI-SERVICE FAMILY LIFE AND SEX EDUCATION PROGRAM

While reducing teen pregnancy is a primary goal of the Multi-Service Family Life and Sex Education Program of the New York Children's Aid Society, the program tackles much more. Serving the young people of Harlem's mostly black and Latino central, east, and west communities, the program takes a holistic approach, offering parallel but separate services for teens and their parents in seven areas.

Counseling, academic help, sports activities, self-expression, employment experience, and health services, as well as family life and sex education, all are part of the five-day-a-week program, run almost entirely by professional staff. The sex education course, offered separately to teens and their parents, includes not only sexual anatomy and reproduction, AIDS education, and information about contraception, but discussions of gender and family roles, body image, and values. The program serves about 300 young people and 110 adults at three separate sites.

Co-director Michael Carrera says perseverance and long-term commitment are keys to success when working with vulnerable teens. The youths in his program participate for at least five years, constantly interacting with staff members who provide consistent nurturing and role modeling. Every participant is guaranteed admission to Hunter College upon completing high school; financial aid is available through a Children's Aid Society Scholarship Fund. In June 1992, a young woman who was one of the program's original participants in 1985 graduated from Hunter.

PARENT—CHILD SEXUALITY EDUCATION

"Parents usually want to discuss issues of sexuality with their children, but in most cases they are nervous or scared. That's where we help," says Jean Brown, vice-president of the Family Guidance Center in St. Joseph, Missouri. For the past sixteen years, the center has sponsored the Parent—Child Sexuality Education course, designed to strengthen the parent—child relationship and increase parent—child communication about sexuality.

Aimed at youths ages 9 to 17 and their parents, the course uses informal discussions in a relaxed atmosphere to explore the facts, feelings, and values related to human sexuality. The course also focuses on developing communication, decision-making, and friendship-building skills. Classes generally are cosponsored by community groups, such as the Parent-Teachers Association, Girl Scouts, and YWCA/YMCA.

The program was developed to respond to teens and their families in a predominantly rural area, and it appears to be contributing to a decrease in teen pregnancy rates for the nine-county area served by the program. Statewide, there was a 16 percent drop in teen birth rates between 1980 and 1990, while there was a 34 percent drop in the nine-county area.

Brown attributes the course's success to its family-centered approach. She says many parents have told her that the program permanently altered the way their family interacts and communicates.

YOUTHBUILD U.S.A.

In 1987, when James joined the Youth Action Program (YAP) in East Harlem, he was a shy high school dropout with few employment skills and little confidence. Eighteen months later, he had a GED, a driver's license, solid carpentry skills, and enough self-confidence to set up a carpentry company with fifteen other program graduates.

James is typical of the hundreds of young people between the ages of 16 and 24, mostly school dropouts, who have spent six to eighteen months in YAP, the model on which YouthBuild programs in at least nine other cities are based. The idea, says Dorothy Stoneman, founder of both YAP and YouthBuild, is to put young people to work rebuilding neighborhoods "while putting their own lives in order."

Participants spend half their time in closely supervised paid work, rehabilitating old and abandoned buildings, and the other half in classrooms working on their academic skills. The renovated buildings become apartments for homeless and other low-income families and community centers for poor neighborhoods. The youths, armed with new skills and aided by program staff, move on to apprenticeships or full-time jobs in the building trade or go on to school or vocational programs.

Because YouthBuild's goals include developing participants' life skills and leadership potential, the program makes a point of involving participants in decision-making at every level—from policy decisions to deciding what kind of bricks to use in a renovation. ■

Source: Children's Defense Fund, *The State of America's Children 1992* (Washington, D.C.: Children's Defense Fund, 1992), p. 57.

SUMMARY

Social process theories explain delinquency as a function of the human interactions that occur daily in society. (See Table 6.1.) As a group, they reject the view that delinquents are born criminals or that they are intellectually and psychologically impaired. In a similar vein, social process adherents take a dim view of theoretical models that blame delinquent behavior on the socioeconomic structure of society or on any of its class, racial, or social groupings.

Social process theories often stress the learning of delinquent or nondelinquent behavior. For example, Sutherland's theory of Differential Association (DA) suggests that delinquency is almost purely a learning process. Similarly, David Matza's neutralization approach describes how youngsters are able to learn techniques that can effectively neutralize the constraints of conventional values.

A second branch of social process theory is concerned with the forces of social control. Theorists such as Travis Hirschi view delinquency as a result of the inability of conventional institutions and relationships to restrain the behavior of youths.

While Hirschi's social control theory does not stress learning per se, it is evident that the weakening of the social bond is a long-term development that involves delinquent youths in an escalating process of antisocial behavior accompanied by a continuous diminution of their attachment to society. In Gottfredson and Hirschi's general theory of crime, impulsivity and lack of self-control are blamed for the onset and stability of delinquent behavior. Kids who lack self-control may find that their bond to society is weak and attenuated.

A new approach has been to integrate process concepts with elements taken from other theoretical models. Weis's social development theory and Elliott's integrated theory contain elements of both social process theory and social structure theory. In general, they hold that youths' place in the social structure, coupled with their interpersonal relationships, creates differential probabilities that they will engage in delinquency. Thornberry adds a life-course component to his interactional theory: the causes of delinquency change as an adolescent passes through the life cycle.

Prevention programs based on social process theories usually prescribe treatment designed to strengthen family ties, improve school performance, or develop a youth's bond to society.

KEY TERMS

socialization
social processes
learning theory
control theory
differential association
culture conflict
differential reinforcement
drift

subterranean values
social control theories
commitment to conformity
containment theory
social bond
self-control theory
impulsive
social development theory

QUESTIONS FOR DISCUSSION

1. Identify the "processes" that produce delinquent behaviors.
2. Have you ever rationalized your deviant acts? What neutralization techniques did you use?
3. Discuss your "inner" and "outer" containments. Does self-esteem really influence behavior?
4. Comment on the statement "Delinquents are made, not born."
5. Does the integration of social process and social structure theories make sense?

THEORY	MAJOR PREMISE	STRENGTHS
SOCIAL LEARNING THEORIES		
differential association theory	People learn to commit crime from exposure to antisocial definitions.	Explains onset of criminality. Explains the presence of crime in all elements of social structure. Explains why some people in high-crime areas refrain from criminality. Can apply to adults and juveniles.
differential reinforcement theory	Criminal behavior depends on the person's experiences with rewards for conventional behaviors and punishments for deviant ones. Being rewarded for deviance leads to crime.	Adds learning theory principles to differential association. Links sociological and psychological principles.
neutralization theory	Youths learn ways of neutralizing moral restraints and periodically drift in and out of criminal behavior patterns.	Explains why many delinquents do not become adult criminals. Explains why youthful law violators can participate in conventional behavior.
SOCIAL CONTROL THEORIES		
containment theory	Society produces pushes and pulls toward crime. In some people, they are counteracted by internal and external containments, such as a good self-concept and group cohesiveness.	Brings together psychological and sociological principles. Can explain why some people are able to resist the strongest social pressures to commit crime.
control theory	A person's bond to society prevents him or her from violating social rules. If the bond weakens, the person is free to commit crime.	Explains onset of crime; can apply to both middle- and lower-class crime. Explains its theoretical constructs adequately so they can be measured. Has been empirically tested.
general theory of crime	Kids with impulsive personalities are crime-prone. The likelihood of crime is a function of criminal propensity and criminal opportunity.	Explains the age-crime relationship. Can account for all criminal activities. Identifies criminal opportunity and propensity as independent concepts.
INTEGRATED THEORIES		
social development theory	Weak social controls produce crime. A person's place in the social structure influences his or her bond to society.	Combines elements of social structural and social process theories. Accounts for variations in the crime rate.
Elliott's integrated theory	Strained and weak social bonds lead youths to associate and learn from deviant peers.	Combines elements of learning, strain, and control theories.
Interactional theory	Delinquents go through lifestyle changes during their offending career.	Combines sociological and psychological theories.

NOTES

1. Alan Lizotte, Terence Thornberry, Marvin Krohn, Deborah Chard-Wierschem, and David McDowall, "Neighborhood Context and Delinquency: A Longitudinal Analysis," in H.J. Kerner and E. Weitekamp, eds., *Cross-National Longitudinal Research on Human Development and Criminal Behavior* (Dordrecht, The Netherlands: Kluwer Academic Publishers, 1993), pp. 1–11.
2. Walter Reckless, Simon Dinitz, and Ellen Murray, "The Good Boy in a High Delinquency Area," *Journal of Criminal Law, Criminology, and Police Science* 48:18–26 (1957).
3. Lawrence Rosen, "Family and Delinquency: Structure or Function," *Criminology* 23:553–73 (1985).
4. .Kenneth Polk and Walter Schafer, eds., *Schools and Delinquency* (Englewood Cliffs, N.J.: Prentice Hall, 1972).
5. Thomas Berndt, "The Features and Effects of Friendship in Early Adolescence," *Child Development* 53:1447–60 (1982).
6. Edwin Sutherland, *Principles of Criminology* (Philadelphia: J.B. Lippincott, 1939).
7. Edwin Sutherland and Donald Cressey, *Criminology*, 8th ed. (Philadelphia: J.B. Lippincott, 1970), pp. 75–77.
8. Howard Becker, *Outsiders* (New York: Free Press, 1963).
9. Sutherland and Cressey, *Criminology*, pp. 77–79.
10. Ibid.
11. Albert Reiss and A. Lewis Rhodes, "The Distribution of Delinquency in the Social Class Structure," *American Sociological Review* 26:732 (1961).
12. James Short, "Differential Association as a Hypothesis: Problems of Empirical Testing," *Social Problems* 8:14–25 (1960).
13. Ross Matsueda and Karen Heimer, "Race, Family Structure and Delinquency: A Test of Differential Association and Control Theories," *American Sociological Review* 52:826–40 (1987).
14. Elton Jackson, Charles Tittle, and Mary Jean Burke, "Offense-Specific Models of the Differential Association Process," *Social Problems* 33:335–56 (1986).
15. James Orcutt, "Differential Association and Substance Abuse: A Closer Look at Sutherland (With a Little Help from Becker)," *Criminology* 25:341–58 (1987); Denise Kandel, "Friendship Networks, Intimacy, and Illicit Drug Use in Young Adulthood: A Comparison of Two Competing Theories," *Criminology* 29:441–69 (1991); Marvin Krohn and Terence Thornberry, Rochester Youth Development Study *Network Theory: A Model for Understanding Drug Abuse among African-American and Hispanic Youth*, working paper no. 10, (Albany, N.Y.: Hindelang Research Center, 1991).
16. Donald Green, "Measures of Illegal Behavior in Individual-Level Deterrence Research," *Journal of Research in Crime and Delinquency* 26:253–75 (1989).
17. Gerben J.N. Bruinsma, "Differential Association Theory Reconsidered: An Extension and Its Empirical Test," *Journal of Quantitative Criminology* 8:29–46 (1992); Charles Tittle, *Sanctions and Social Deviance: The Question of Deterrence* (New York: Praeger, 1980).
18. Reed Adams, "The Adequacy of Differential Association Theory," *Journal of Research in Crime and Delinquency* 11:1–8 (1974).
19. Jack Gibbs, "The State of Criminological Theory," *Criminology* 25:821–40 (1987).
20. Robert Burgess and Ronald Akers, "A Differential Association-Reinforcement Theory of Criminal Behavior," *Social Problems* 14:128–47 (1966).
21. Ross Matsueda, "The Current State of Differential Association Theory," *Crime and Delinquency* 34:277–306 (1988).
22. Mark Warr, "Age, Peers and Delinquency," *Criminology* 31:17–40 (1993).
23. The most influential critique of differential association is contained in Ruth Kornhauser, *Social Sources of Delinquency* (Chicago: University of Chicago Press, 1978).
24. These misconceptions are derived from Donald Cressey, "Epidemiologies and Individual Conduct: A Case from Criminology," *Pacific Sociological Review* 3:47–58 (1960).
25. Kornhauser, *Social Sources of Delinquency;* in contrast, see Matsueda, "The Current State of Differential Association Theory."
26. Craig Reinerman and Jeffrey Fagan, "Social Organization and Differential Association: A Research Note from a Longitudinal Study of Violent Juvenile Offenders," *Crime and Delinquency* 34:307–27 (1988).
27. Sue Titus Reed, *Crime and Criminology*, 2d ed. (New York: Holt, Rinehart & Winston, 1979), p. 234.
28. Robert Burgess and Ronald Akers, "Differential Association—Reinforcement Theory of Criminal Behavior," *Social Problems* 14:128–47 (1968).
29. Ronald Akers, Marvin Krohn, Lonn Lonza-Kaduce, and Marcia Radosevich, "Social Learning and Deviant Behavior: A Specific Test of a General Theory," *American Sociological Review* 44:636–55 (1979).
30. Marvin Krohn, William Skinner, James Massey, and Ronald Akers, "Social Learning Theory and Adolescent Cigarette Smoking: A Longitudinal Study," *Social Problems* 32:455–71 (1985).
31. Richard Lawrence, "School Performance, Peers and Delinquency: Implications for Juvenile Justice," *Juvenile and Family Court Journal* 42:59–69 (1991).
32. John Hamlin, "Misplaced Role of Rational Choice in Neutralization Theory," *Criminology* 26:425–38 (1988).
33. Gresham Sykes and David Matza, "Techniques of Neutralization: A Theory of Delinquency," *American Sociological Review* 22:664–70 (1957); and David Matza, *Delinquency and Drift* (New York: Wiley, 1964).

34. Matza, *Delinquency and Drift,* p. 51.
35. David Matza, "Subterranean Traditions of Youth," *Annals* 378:116 (1961).
36. Sykes and Matza, "Techniques of Neutralization," pp. 664–70.
37. Ibid.
38. See, for example, John Kitsuse, "Societal Reaction to Deviant Behavior," *Social Problems* 9:247–56 (1962).
39. For a vivid example of these values, see William F. Whyte, *Street Corner Society* (Chicago: University of Chicago Press, 1955).
40. Travis Hirschi, *Causes of Delinquency* (Berkeley: University of California Press, 1969), p. 208.
41. John Hamlin, "Misplaced Role of Rational Choice in Neutralization Theory," *Criminology* 26:425–38 (1988).
42. Robert A. Ball, "An Empirical Exploration of Neutralization Theory," *Criminologica* 4:22–32 (1966). See also M. William Minor, "The Neutralization of Criminal Offense," *Criminology* 18:103–20 (1980); Michael Hindelang, "The Commitment of Delinquents to Their Misdeeds: Do Delinquents Drift?" *Social Problems* 17:500–9 (1970); Robert Regoli and Eric Poole, "The Commitment of Delinquents to Their Misdeeds: A Reexamination," *Journal of Criminal Justice* 6:261–69 (1978); Robert Gordon, James Short, Desmond Cartwright, and Fred Strodtbeck, "Values and Gang Delinquency: A Study of Street Corner Groups," *American Journal of Sociology* 69:109–28 (1963); Larry Siegel, Spencer Rathus, and Carol Ruppert, "Values and Delinquent Youth: An Empirical Reexamination of Theories of Delinquency," *British Journal of Criminology* 13:237–44 (1973).
43. Albert Reiss, "Delinquency as the Failure of Personal and Social Controls," *American Sociological Review* 16:196–207 (1951).
44. Scott Briar and Irving Piliavin, "Delinquency: Situational Inducements and Commitment to Conformity," *Social Problems* 13:35–45 (1965–66).
45. Walter Reckless, *The Crime Problem* (New York: Appleton-Century Crofts, 1967), pp. 469–83.
46. Among the many research reports by Reckless and his colleagues are Walter Reckless, Simon Dinitz, and Ellen Murray, "The Good Boy in a High Delinquency Area," *Journal of Criminal Law, Criminology, and Police Science* 48:12–26 (1957); idem, "Self-Concept as an Insulator against Delinquency," *American Sociological Review* 21:744–46 (1956); Walter Reckless and Simon Dinitz, "Pioneering with Self-Concept as a Vulnerability Factor in Delinquency," *Journal of Criminal Law, Criminology, and Police Science* 58:515–23 (1967); Walter Reckless, Simon Dinitz, and Barbara Kay, "The Self-Component in Potential Delinquency and Potential Non-Delinquency," *American Sociological Review* 22:566–70 (1957).
47. Reckless, Dinitz, and Kay, "The Self-Component in Potential Delinquency and Potential Non-Delinquency";

Frank Scarpitti, Ellen Murray, Simon Dinitz, and Walter Reckless, "The Good Boy in a High Delinquency Area: Four Years Later," *American Sociological Review* 23:555–58 (1960).
48. Michael Schwartz and Sandra Tangri, "A Note on Self-Concept as an Insulator against Delinquency," *American Sociological Review* 30:922–26 (1965); Clarence Schrag, *Crime and Justice, American Style* (Washington, D.C.: Government Printing Office, 1971), p. 84.
49. Ibid.
50. Ibid., p. 8.
51. Hirschi's data are examined in his *Causes of Delinquency.*
52. Ibid., p. 132.
53. Ibid., pp. 160–61.
54. Ibid., p. 185.
55. Michael Wiatroski, David Griswold, and Mary K. Roberts, "Social Control Theory and Delinquency," *American Sociological Review* 46:525–41 (1981).
56. Patricia Van Voorhis, Francis Cullen, Richard Mathers, and Connie Chenoweth Garner, "The Impact of Family Structure and Quality on Delinquency: A Comparative Assessment of Structural and Functional Factors," *Criminology* 26:235–61 (1988).
57. Josine Junger-Tas, "An Empirical Test of Social Control Theory," *Journal of Quantitative Criminology* 8:18–29 (1992).
58. Marvin Krohn, Susan Stern, Terence Thornberry, and Sung Joon Jang, "The Measurement of Family Process Variables: the Effect of Adolescent and Parent Perceptions of Family Life on Delinquent Behavior," *Journal of Quantitative Criminology* 3:287–315 (1992).
59. Michael Hindelang, "Causes of Delinquency: A Partial Replication and Extension," *Social Problems* 21:471–87 (1973).
60. Randy LaGrange and Helene Raskin White, "Age Differences in Delinquency: A Test of Theory," *Criminology* 23:19–45 (1985).
61. Gary Jensen and David Brownfield, "Parents and Drugs," *Criminology* 21:543–54 (1983). See also M. Wiatrowski, D. Griswold, and M. Roberts, "Social Control Theory and Delinquency," *American Sociological Review* 46:525–41 (1981).
62. Peggy Giordano, Stephen Cernkovich, and M.D. Pugh, "Friendships and Delinquency," *American Journal of Sociology* 91:1170–1202 (1986).
63. Denise Kandel and Mark Davies, "Friendship Networks, Intimacy, and Illicit Drug Use in Young Adulthood: A Comparison of Two Competing Theories," *Criminology* 29:441–67 (1991).
64. Marvin Krohn and James Massey, "Social Control and Delinquent Behavior: An Examination of the Elements of the Social Bond," *Sociological Quarterly* 21:529–43 (1980).
65. Robert Agnew, "Social Control Theory and Delinquency: A Longitudinal Test," *Criminology* 23:47–61 (1985).

66. For a similar result, see A.E. Liska and M.D. Reed, "Ties to Conventional Institutions and Delinquency: Estimating Reciprocal Effects," *American Sociological Review* 50:547–60 (1985).

67. Michael Gottfredson and Travis Hirschi, *A General Theory of Crime* (Stanford, Calif.: Stanford University Press, 1990).

68. Ibid., p. 27.

69. Ibid., p. 90.

70. Ibid., p. 89.

71. Ibid.

72. Ibid.

73. Donald Gibbons, "Personality and Crime: Non-Issues, Real Issues, and a Theory and Research Agenda," *Justice Quarterly,* 27:311–24 (1987).

74. Joseph Weis and J. David Hawkins, *Reports of the National Juvenile Justice Assessment Centers, Preventing Delinquency* (Washington, D.C.: U.S. Department of Justice, 1981); Joseph Weis and John Sederstrom, *Reports of the National Juvenile Justice Assessment Centers, The Prevention of Serious Delinquency: What to Do* (Washington, D.C.: U.S. Department of Justice, 1981).

75. Delbert Elliott, David Huizinga, and Suzanne Ageton, *Explaining Delinquency and Drug Use* (Beverly Hills, Calif.: Sage, 1985).

76. Ibid., p. 147.

77. Terence Thornberry, "Towards an Interactional Theory of Delinquency," *Criminology,* 25:863–81 (1997).

78. Terence Thornberry, Alan Lizotte, Marvin Krohn, Margaret Farnworth, and Sung Joon Jang, *Delinquent Peers, Beliefs, and Delinquent Behavior: A Longitudinal Test of Interactional Theory,* working paper no. 6, rev., Rochester Youth Development Study (Albany, N.Y.: Hindelang Criminal Justice Research Center, 1992).

79. Terence Thornberry, Alan Lizotte, Marvin Krohn, Margaret Farnworth, and Sung Joon Jang, "Testing Interactional Theory: An Examination of Reciprocal Causal Relationships among Family, School and Delinquency," *Journal of Criminal Law and Criminology* 82:3–35 (1991).

80. J. Wall, J. David Hawkins, D. Lishner, and M. Fraser, *Reports of the National Juvenile Justice Assessment Centers, Juvenile Delinquency Prevention: A Compendium of 36 Program Models* (Washington, D.C.: U.S. Department of Justice, 1981).

SOCIAL REACTION THEORIES

LABELING AND CONFLICT

The two theoretical models discussed in this chapter, although quite different from one another, share one important characteristic differentiating them from all other theories of delinquency. While other theories portray the youthful law violator as a rebel who for one reason or another cannot conform to the rules of society, labeling theory and conflict theory focus on the role that social and economic institutions play in *producing* delinquent behaviors and how the application of the rule of law in American society influences delinquent behavior. In a sense, the way society reacts to individuals and their behavior determines whether their actions will be considered criminal or conventional and whether they will become delinquents or not. These perspectives, therefore, may be considered theories of *social reaction*.

The influence of both of these perspectives on delinquency theory and policy was first felt in the late 1960s and early 1970s. In this period of social ferment, many traditional social institutions began to be questioned and criticized. The role of the government became suspect because of the generally unpopular war in Vietnam and the corruption uncovered in the Nixon administration. Likewise, legal and academic scholars voiced growing suspicions of the juvenile justice system because of its alleged inefficiency and discriminatory practices. Even the educational system was criticized for its failure to provide equal educational opportunities for all.[1]

Considering the climate of those times, it is not surprising that social scientists began to question the role that powerful social institutions played in shaping the direction of the society and influencing the behavior of people living within it. Scholars who were critical of big governmental, educational, corporate, and criminal justice organizations claimed that the efforts of these institutions actually helped produce crime and delinquency. Those holding power were accused of devoting their efforts to controlling the behavior of the lower class and protecting the interests of the wealthy and powerful.

Some scholars felt that those in power used their influence to control the criminal law for their own benefit.[2] While the illegal behaviors of the have-not members of society were heavily punished, the violations of the upper classes—tax evasion, stock market manipulation, price fixing, political corruption, and so on—were often immune from prosecution or considered civil violations and punished financially. Critics argued that those in power used their control over social institutions to stigmatize the powerless and brand them as outcasts from society. Even when sincere efforts were made to help the less fortunate, the outcome was to enmesh them further in a deviant or outcast status. For example, educational enrichment efforts, such as the *Head Start program*, were suspected of helping identify children as intellectually backward and in need of special attention; efforts to provide mental health services branded individuals as "sick" or "crazy." Out of this critical inquiry emerged two potent themes: (1) concepts of law and justice are differently applied in American society and (2) those who become involved with the justice system are soon branded deviants or outcasts and launched into a deviant "career."

This type of analysis was soon applied to the study of delinquent behavior. It was alleged that delinquency results from the reactions of politically powerful individuals and groups, especially government social control agencies, to society's less fortunate members. Delinquents are not inherently wrong or "evil" but kids who have had a deviant status conferred on them by those holding economic, political, and social power. A delinquent status results from interpersonal inter-actions in which youths are made to feel inferior or outcast because of socially unacceptable behavior. These reactions are stratified by class: while lower-class youngsters are arrested, tried, and punished, middle-class youths are sent on their way by a benign, understanding police officer or juvenile court judge.[3] Thus, it is not the quality of the delinquent act itself that is important, but the way society and its institutions react to the act. The purpose of social control is to maintain the status quo, ensuring that those in power will stay there.

In this chapter, we will first review labeling theory, which maintains that official reactions to delinquent acts help label youths as criminals, troublemakers, and outcasts and lock them in a cycle of escalating delinquent acts and social sanctions. Then, we will turn to conflict theory, which holds that the decision to confer a delinquent label is a product of the capitalist system of economic production and its destructive influence on human behavior.

LABELING THEORY

Labeling theory is concerned less with what causes the onset of an initial delinquent act and more with the effect that official handling by police, court, and correctional agencies has on the future of youths who fall into the arms of the law. It is more a theory of delinquent career formation than one that predicts the onset of individual delinquent behaviors.[4]

According to labeling theory, youths may violate the law for a variety of reasons, including but not limited to poor family relationships, neighborhood conflict, peer pressure, psychological and/or biological abnormality, and prode-linquent learning experiences. Regardless of the cause, if a youth's delinquent behavior is detected by law enforcement or school officials, the offender will be given a negative social label that can follow him or her throughout life. These labels include "troublemaker," "juvenile delinquent," "mentally ill," "retarded," "criminal," "junkie," and "thief."

Applying Labels

The way labels are applied and the nature of the labels themselves are likely to have important future consequences for the delinquent. The degree to which youngsters are perceived as criminals may affect their treatment at home, at work, and at school. Young offenders may find that their parents consider them a detrimental influence on younger brothers and sisters. Their teachers may place them in classes or tracks reserved especially for students with behavior problems, thus minimizing their chances of obtaining higher education. The delinquency label may also restrict eligibility for employment and negatively affect the attitudes of society in general. And depending on the severity of the label, youthful offenders will be subjected to official sanctions ranging from a mild reprimand to incarceration.

Beyond these immediate results, labeling theory argues that, depending on the visibility of the label and the manner and severity with which it is applied, youths will have an increasing commitment to delinquent careers. As the negative feedback of law enforcement agencies, parents, friends, teachers, and other figures strengthens the commitment, delinquents may begin to reevaluate

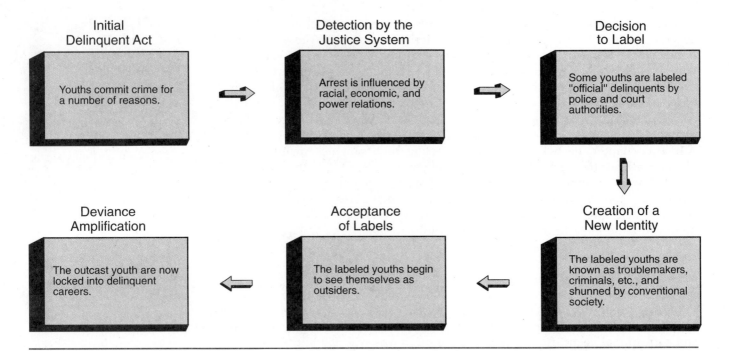

Initial Delinquent Act	Detection by the Justice System	Decision to Label
Youths commit crime for a number of reasons.	Arrest is influenced by racial, economic, and power relations.	Some youths are labeled "official" delinquents by police and court authorities.

Deviance Amplification	Acceptance of Labels	Creation of a New Identity
The outcast youth are now locked into delinquent careers.	The labeled youths begin to see themselves as outsiders.	The labeled youths are known as troublemakers, criminals, etc., and shunned by conventional society.

■■ **FIGURE 7.1**

Labeling theory

their identity and come to see themselves as criminals, troublemakers, or "screwups." Thus, through a process of identification and sanctioning, reidentification, and increased sanctioning, the identity of young offenders becomes transformed. They are no longer children in trouble; they are *delinquents*, and they accept that label as a personal identity—a process called *self-labeling*.[5] (See Figure 7.1.)

LABELING AND JUVENILE JUSTICE

The system of juvenile justice began to become sensitized to the problems of labeling and stigmatization in 1967, when the consequences of a negative label were identified by the President's Commission on Law Enforcement and the Administration of Justice. In its report on juvenile delinquency, the commission stated:

The affixing of that label [delinquency] can be a momentous occurrence in a youngster's life. Thereafter he may be watched; he may be suspect; his every misstep may be evidence of his delinquent nature. He may be excluded more and more from legitimate activities and opportunities. Soon he may be designed and dealt with as a delinquent and will find it very difficult to move into a law-abiding path even if he can overcome his own belligerent reaction and self-image and seeks to do so.[6]

These sentiments helped set the course for juvenile justice policy in the 1970s. National programs were created to insulate youths from the label-producing processes of the juvenile justice system. Policy initiatives included the ***diversion*** of offenders from juvenile court into alternative programs and the creation of nonsecure community-based treatment to replace traditional juvenile training schools and institutions (***deinstitutionalization***). Whenever possible, anything producing stigma was to be avoided, a philosophy of justice referred to as *nonintervention.*

The Nature of Crime and Delinquency

Another important principle of the labeling approach is that the concepts of crime and delinquency are relative. Acts become outlawed because people in power view them as harmful behaviors. A number of pioneering labeling theorists helped define the perspective by declaring that deviance is not an absolute concept but one that is relative in both place and time. "Deviance is not a property inherent in certain forms of behavior," argues sociologist Kai Erikson in a classic statement. "It is a property conferred upon those forms by the audiences which directly or indirectly witness them."[7] Erikson's definition was later amplified by Edwin Schur, who argued that human behavior is deviant to the extent that it comes to be viewed as involving a departure from a group's expected behavior patterns and it elicits interpersonal and collective reactions that serve to isolate, treat, correct, or punish individuals engaged in such behavior.[8]

In what is probably the most well-known statement by a labeling theorist, ***Howard Becker*** says:

Deviance is *not* a quality of the act the person commits, but rather a consequence of the application by others of rules and sanctions to an "offender." The deviant is one to whom that label has successfully been applied; deviant behavior is behavior that people so label.[9]

Becker argues that legal and social rules are created by "moral entrepreneurs," people who are concerned about social morality and work to control its definition and application. Consequently, who is to be labeled and the forms labeling takes depend on social forces that vary considerably within cultures. Who is in power and how they interpret right and wrong play an important role in defining crime and delinquency. For example, during our own lifetimes, some of us have witnessed the legalization of abortions, the banning of school prayer, and in some states the decriminalization of marijuana. Becker and other labeling theorists help us recognize that our concept of deviance evolves over time.

THE EFFECT OF LABELING

The labeling approach focuses primarily on the social audience's reaction to persons and their behavior and the subsequent effects of that reaction, rather than on the cause of the deviant behavior itself. Furthermore, labeling theorists allege that the treatment of offenders in the labeling process depends far less on their behavior than on the way others view their acts.

People form enduring opinions of others based on brief first impressions.[10] If interactions involve perceptions of deviance, individuals may be assigned negative labels, such as "troublemaker," "nerd," or "fag." People who are suspected of having these behavior "problems" are carefully scrutinized by those they interact with; people are cautious with them, search for signs of deviance, or shun them outright.[11]

Official labels may be applied when deviant behavior runs afoul of socially accepted rules, laws, or conventions. Official or formal labels may include "criminal," "mentally ill," or "dropout." Official labels are often bestowed during ceremonies designed to redefine the deviants' identity and place them apart from the normative social structure, for example, during trials or civil commitment or school disciplinary board hearings.[12] The net effect of this legal and social process is a *durable negative label and an accompanying loss of status.* The labeled deviant becomes a social outcast who is prevented from enjoying higher education, well-paying jobs, and other societal benefits.

We can see an example of this process in stigma-producing ceremonies, such as those that sometimes occur in juvenile courts. Here, young offenders find, perhaps for the first time, that people in authority, in the person of the juvenile court judge, consider them incorrigible outcasts who must be separated from the right-thinking members of society. To reach that decision, the judge relies on the testimony of a parade of witnesses—parents, teachers, police officers, social workers, psychologists—all of whom may testify that the offenders are unfit to be part of conventional society.[13] As the label "juvenile delinquent" is conferred on

■ ■ ■ ■ ■ ■ ■ ■ ■ ■ ■ ■ ■ ■ ■ ■

Negative labels define the targets entire being. Describe the personality and character of the adolescents in this photo. Are they more likely to attend college or go to prison.

the offenders, their identity may forever be transformed from boys or girls who have done something bad to "bad" girls or boys.[14]

Labeling theorists see these negative labels as creating a *self-fulfilling prophecy*.[15] If children are reacted to negatively by parents, teachers, and others, they will view these negative labels as an accurate portrayal of their personality. If the labels are consistently applied, they will join with their detractors and view themselves in a negative light. Eventually, their behavior will begin to conform to these negative expectations. It is expected that labeled delinquents will seek out others who are similarly stigmatized because members of conventional society shun and avoid them.[16]

The outcome of the labeling and stigmatization process is the development of a new, deviant identity. Individuals become what society says they are and then begin to behave predictably. Delinquent youths will seek out others who sympathize with their plight and can identify with their needs. Their peers may help the labeled youths "reject their rejector": If conventional society cannot accept them, it's not their fault; besides, teachers are stupid, cops dishonest, and parents just don't understand.

Primary and Secondary Deviance

The effect of the labeling process was refined by Edwin Lemert in his formulation of the *primary-secondary deviance* model.[17]

Lemert argues that deviant acts actually form two distinct classes, primary and secondary, each of which comprises a specific role orientation of the individual. Primary acts can be rationalized by the offender or considered a function of a socially acceptable role, such as a youngster's getting drunk at an older sibling's wedding party. Although primary acts may be considered serious, they do not materially affect self-concept. Primary deviants are not recognized by others as deviant, nor do they recognize themselves in these terms. Lemert attaches little importance to this category of offense, but he argues that deviations become significant (secondary) when they are organized into active roles that become the social criteria for assigning status. Lemert suggests that deviant role reorganization, although dependent to some extent on cultural and psychological factors, is controlled mostly by the labeling that results from a negative social interaction. When discussing secondary deviant identity, he states that if a person's behavior is repetitive, highly visible, and subject to severe social reaction, it is likely that the person will incorporate a deviant identity into his or her psyche. Thereafter, all life roles will be predicated on this new, deviant model.[18]

To further define and clarify the process of secondary deviance, Lemert suggests that stigmatization, punishment, segregation, and social control are all contributing factors in the transformation of personal roles and identity. That is, secondary deviance is a product of resocialization in which the deviant role becomes the central fact of existence and a person is transformed into one who "employs his behavior (deviant) or a role based upon it as a means of defense, attack, or adjustment to the overt and covert problems created by the consequent societal reaction to him."[19]

Thus, an important part of secondary deviance involves the labeled person's maintaining behavior and beliefs that society considers deviant. Yet this behavior enables offenders to cope with the subsequent negative social reactions to their label. Personal acceptance of this behavior and beliefs comprises label internalization, in other words, successful self-labeling.

Lemert's model highlights the deviance-producing properties of the labeling process. The model portrays immersion in a deviant identity as a cycle of events (Figure 7.2) in which a deviant act (A) leads to a social reaction (B), to self-conception as a "deviant" (C), to increased, more serious deviant acts (offense escalation) (D), and to greater and more severe social reactions, including legal reprisals (E), until identification with a deviant identity, which increases the probability of future deviant acts, is complete.[20]

A number of attempts have been made to verify Lemert's model. In one study, Melvin Ray and William Downs found evidence that boys who label themselves as deviants are more likely to later use drugs than boys who refrain from self-labeling; the relationship was not significant for girls.[21]

In sum, secondary deviance (or self-labeling) is a function of both prior deviant behavior and social labels and at the same time causes future misconduct. Lemert's conceptualization of the labeling process and his description of the primary-secondary deviance dichotomy are major theoretical underpinnings of the labeling approach.

██ ■ **FIGURE 7.2**

The cycle of secondary deviance

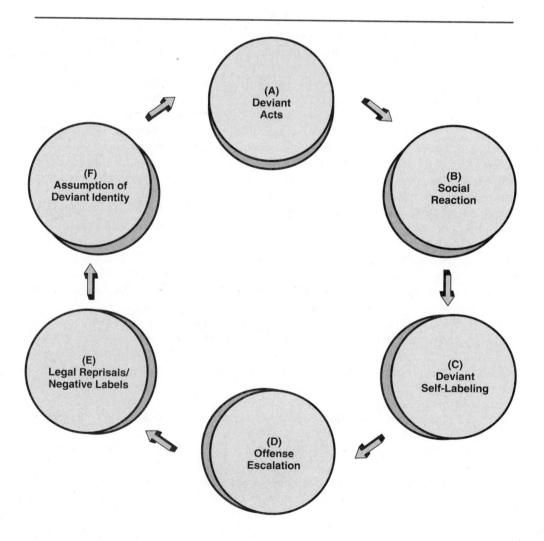

Part II   Theories of Delinquency

THE JUVENILE JUSTICE PROCESS AND LABELING

The labeling hypothesis has received strong support from the literature of crime and delinquency. Frank Tannenbaum first suggested that social typing, which he called "dramatization of evil," transforms the offender's identity from a doer of evil to an "evil person."[22] Tannenbaum emphasized the role of the juvenile justice system in this scheme: "The entire process of dealing with young delinquents is mischievous insofar as it identifies *him* to *himself* and to the environment as a delinquent person."[23]

Theorists have built upon the work of Tannenbaum, continuing to describe the impact of juvenile justice processing on delinquent labeling and consequent illegal behavior. For example, Aaron Cicourel contends that delinquents are in reality the finished products of the juvenile justice "assembly line."[24] Although they enter as children in trouble, they emerge as individuals transformed by decision makers into bearers of criminal histories, which are likely to reinvolve them in criminal activity. Arguing from a similar prospective, David Matza concludes that apprehension of delinquents will lead sanctioning bodies to anticipate further illegal actions by the individuals.[25] Apprehended offenders are invested with all the behavioral characteristics associated with the labels, and although they have not necessarily demonstrated these characteristics by their behavior, they become "perennial suspects."[26] As a result, labeled youthful offenders may begin to reconsider their own self-concepts. This reconsideration, Matza explains, relates directly to their interaction with the system and the treatment they receive from it.

These statements imply that labeling by the juvenile system turns the self-perception of a youthful suspect into that of a delinquent.[27] Processing by the juvenile authorities may cause a youth to enter into a delinquent career and be committed to criminal activity. Sociologist Harold Garfinkel has provided a concise analysis of this process in his description of the interactions that occur when the public identity of an offender is transformed via a successful degradation ceremony into "something looked on as lower in the social scheme of social types."[28] Garfinkel concludes that this process may be similar in form and function to what is currently practiced in juvenile court.

Labeling theory predicts two relationships with regard to juvenile justice processing: the delinquency label will be bestowed upon the powerless members of society in a discriminatory fashion, and the more frequent, prolonged, or decisive the contacts with the juvenile justice system, the more likely it is that an offender will ultimately accept the delinquency label as a personal identity and enter into a life of crime. These two relationships are discussed below.

Discrimination in the Labeling Process

One of the cornerstones of the labeling perspective is that the probability of being labeled falls heavily on the disadvantaged, the poor, and the powerless. Because of stereotypes that portray offenders as young, male, minority group members, and urban dwellers, individuals who belong to such groups are more likely than others to be labeled delinquent.[29]

Evidence in support of this hypothesis has been derived in studies that find that police are more likely to arrest and officially process males, minority group members, and those in the lower economic classes than youths who do not share these traits.[30] For example, Carl Pope and William Feyerherm recently reviewed more than thirty years of research on minorities in the juvenile justice system

Labeling theorists assume that the poor and minority group members are the most likely targets of negative labels. Failure to find descrimination within the juvenile justice system undermines the validity of labeling theory.

and found that race, to the disadvantage of minority youths, influences decision making.[31]

Evidence also exists that offenders whose families have economic or political power are likely merely to be given a warning by police officers rather than be processed to the juvenile court.[32] And the juvenile court is believed to respond more favorably to youths from middle-class homes than to those from the lower class. Living in a single-parent home has been related to discrimination in the juvenile justice system; under these circumstances, black youth were found to be more at risk than white youth.[33]

While this evidence is persuasive, some critics dispute the charge that the justice system operates in a distinctly discriminatory fashion.[34] Evidence exists that the factors related to official juvenile justice processing are influenced more by crime-related issues, such as offense seriousness and prior record, than by personal factors, such as racial or economic bias. For example, in one recent study, Merry Morash found that police action did not reflect race or economic status.[35] The factors most closely related to the decision of police to take formal action reflected legal and crime-related variables: prior offense record, association with known delinquents, involvement in gang violence, and drug involvement. Morash found that regardless of race or class, kids who commit a lot of crime with their friends, use drugs, and get into fights will also get arrested.

The Effects of Official Labeling

Equally disturbing to labeling theorists is the failure of empirical evidence to consistently confirm that experience with the juvenile justice system produces enduring negative labels. Studies attempting to measure the identity transformation of adolescents at the onset and conclusion of official contact have been contradictory and inconclusive.[36] Some indicate that youths actually feel relief after the conclusion of their juvenile justice experience, rather than shame, stigma, or a diminution of their self-image, as labeling theorists would predict.[37]

A few research efforts have found that while youths who have had experience with the juvenile justice system are the ones most likely to maintain a delinquent self-concept, the relationship between sanctions and labels is far from clear. For example, Gary Jensen found that youths who experience arrest are the ones most likely to have negative self-images beforehand.[38] Jensen did not find that delinquent self-concept increases after police contact. It is possible that youths who already maintain a delinquent self-concept are the ones most likely to be arrested and officially processed.[39]

Research, then, has not supported the labeling theory contention that juvenile justice processing will amplify self-labels. Studies that focus on the labeling impact of arrest, detention, trial, and incarceration have not found that sanctions and labels transform identity or amplify criminality.[40] In one such study, Charles Thomas and Donna Bishop surveyed 2,147 Virginia youths and found that formal sanctions by the juvenile justice system actually had very little impact on a child's self-image: the relationship between sanctions and escalation of delinquent self-image was very modest.[41]

How can these insignificant labeling effects be explained? Why does juvenile justice processing have little measurable influence on the self-image of court-processed youth? One possibility is that youths who suffer arrest and official processing already have such a long and active career as undetected "secret deviants" that their experience with the juvenile justice system has little effect on their self-concept and identity. Another explanation may be that the aggregate measurements used in most research studies mask individual differences among delinquents: while some delinquents are deeply influenced by punitive treatment, others who find themselves the target of rehabilitation efforts and encouragement by social service personnel may actually gain psychic benefits from their experience. Sociologist Stanley Cohen has written that the quality of treatment by the justice system helps categorize offenders into two distinct groups: one made up of unrepentant and antisocial offenders who are placed in programs that dish out harsh punishments (exclusionary programs) and another that contains more amenable offenders who are placed in programs that continually encourage them to join the mainstream of social life (inclusionary programs). The contrary experiences of members of these two groups may help cancel out the overall stigma generated by juvenile justice processing: while youths in the excluded group suffer deeply from their experiences, those in the included group benefit because people have taken a greater interest in them than they have ever experienced before in their lives.[42]

In sum, little hard evidence exists that juvenile justice processing has a deep or lasting effect on a youth's self-image. It may simply be that the effects of growing up in a troubled or abusive family and attending a deteriorated school in a socially disorganized neighborhood are so overwhelming that processing by the juvenile justice system can take away little from an already troubled youth.

EVALUATION OF LABELING THEORY

While quite influential in the 1970s, labeling theory has declined in importance as a primary theory of delinquency. Four important criticisms of the labeling approach have led to its decline:

1. Labeling theorists failed to explain the onset of the first or primary deviation. Why is it that some people engage in the initial deviant act that leads to their label, while others in the same circumstances stick to conventional behaviors?[43] As criminologist Ronald Akers puts it: "One sometimes gets the impression from reading the literature that people go about minding their own business and then—'wham'—bad society comes along and slaps them with a stigmatized label."[44]

2. According to labeling theory, the overrepresentation of males, minorities, and the poor in the crime rate is a function of discriminatory labeling by social control agents. However, empirical research has failed to consistently show that labels are bestowed in a discriminatory fashion.[45] For example, in a recent review of the literature, Charles Tittle and Deborah Curran found that about 40 percent of the research studies indicate a racial effect on juvenile justice decision making and 60 percent do not; about 33 percent of the research studies show a class effect, while 67 percent indicate that class does not influence the labeling process.[46] While some individual-level discrimination exists, such label-producing actions as arrest, prosecution, and sentencing seem more closely related to the seriousness of the criminal act and the youth's prior record than to personal characteristics. Discrimination in the labeling process is a cornerstone of the theory because it indicates that the manner in which labels are bestowed is the key issue in determining criminality. If people were labeled only because they deserved negative social reactions (that is, they committed serious crimes), then the theory would lose its power since the labeling process would be an effect of crime, rather than its cause.[47]

3. Studies that evaluated the aftermath of labeling failed to show it had a deviance amplification effect. Youngsters undergoing the labeling process were simply not as deeply affected by their experiences as labeling theory predicts.[48]

4. Criminologists found that the labeling concept that "no act is inherently evil or criminal" is naive. This point was driven home by sociologist Charles Wellford, who argues rather conclusively that some crimes, such as rape and homicide, are almost universally sanctioned.[49] He says, "Serious violations of the law are universally understood and *are*, therefore, *in that sense*, intrinsically criminal."[50]

The Future of Labeling Theory

Enthusiasm for the labeling approach diminished in the 1980s because empirical support was less than conclusive and noted criminologists were critical of its theoretical validity. Politically, labeling theory suffered because of the conservative trend in the United States: instead of worrying about how the self-image of young offenders was being damaged by the justice system, the general public and academic community seemed more concerned with crime control and the best method of curbing delinquent youth. Enthusiasm for the theory was also dampened because efforts to reduce labels and stigma in the juvenile justice system seemed to have no appreciable effects on delinquency. In one influential work, *Beyond Delinquency,* sociologists Charles Murray and Louis Cox found that youths assigned to a treatment program designed to reduce labels were more likely to later commit delinquent acts than a comparison group who were placed in a traditional and more punitive state training school. The implication was that the deterrent threat of punishment had a greater impact on youths than the feared influence of negative labels.[51]

Should labeling theory then be dropped from consideration as an important explanation of delinquency? Such a step is certainly premature, argue criminologists Raymond Paternoster and Leeann Iovanni, considering the important insights into the study of delinquent behavior that the labeling perspective has provided and the fact that the criticism directed against labeling theory has often been misdirected.[52] Among the features of labeling theory that make it an important part of the study of delinquency are:

1. It identifies the role played by social control agents in the process of delinquency causation. Delinquent behavior cannot be fully understood if the agencies and individuals empowered to control and treat it are ignored.
2. It recognizes that delinquency is not a disease or pathological behavior. It focuses attention on the social interactions and reactions that shape individuals and their behavior.
3. It distinguishes between delinquent acts (primary deviance) and delinquent careers (secondary deviance) and shows that these must be interpreted and treated differently.

This view is supported by some recent research by Ross Matsueda, which shows that offenders are indeed influenced by labeling: kids who are negatively labeled by their parents, teachers, and friends begin to appraise themselves in negative terms. Labeling is a function of past transgressions: parents who label their kids as "troublemakers" are reacting to prior behavior problems. Finally, Matsueda found evidence that supports one of labeling theories key concepts, *deviance amplification:* kids who are troublemakers become labeled as such by parents, which also causes parents to become alienated from their children; negative labels affect self-image and lead to increased delinquency.[53]

Labeling theory should also be reconsidered given what is known today about the life course of chronic offenders. As you may recall, chronic offenders begin their antisocial activity early in their lives and persist in their delinquent activities despite being apprehended by police and punished by the juvenile court. The evidence indicates that sanctions tend to amplify rather than extinguish their deviant careers. Until recently, scant attention has been paid to the parallels between these features of chronic offending and the theoretical concept of secondary deviance. That is, the negative labels some youths acquire and the subsequent onset of a secondary deviant identity may create and sustain chronic offending and criminal careers.[54] In fact, the very definition of a chronic offender is a person who has been arrested and therefore labeled multiple times in his or her offending career. Who are these youths and why do they begin to acquire a deviant identity are questions addressed by labeling theory. The ability of labeling theory to account for deviance amplification, the status factors that contribute to labeling choices, and secondary deviance may be of critical value in explaining the criminal career patterns of the chronic offender.

SOCIAL CONFLICT THEORY

Unlike traditional theoretical perspectives, which try to explain why an individual violates the law, *social conflict theory* focuses on why governments make and enforce rules of law and morality. Conflict criminologists, therefore, do not view delinquents as rebels who cannot conform to proper social norms, nor do they try to devise innovative ways of controlling youthful misbehavior. Their interests

You are planning director for the state department of juvenile justice correctional services.

One of your main concerns is the effect of stigma on the criminal offending patterns of delinquent youth. Some of your advisors suggest that processing youths through the juvenile correctional justice system produces deviant identities that lock them into a criminal way of life. Rather than rehabilitate, the system produces hard-core delinquents who are likely to recidivate. They point to studies that show that an experience with the juvenile justice system has relatively little impact on chronic offenders and, if anything, is associated with escalating the seriousness of their criminal behavior.

Some of the more conservative members of your staff are opposed to making the reduction of stigma and labeling a top correctional concern. They remind you that an experience with the juvenile justice system may actually help deter crime. They point to studies that suggest that youth who have been processed through the correctional system are less likely to recidivate than youths who receive lesser punishments, such as community corrections or probation. In addition, they believe that hard-core, violent offenders deserve to be punished; excessive concern for the offender and not their acts ignores the rights of victims and society in general.

These opposing views have left you in a quandary. On the one hand, the system must be sensitive to the adverse effects of stigma and labeling. On the other hand, the need for control and deterrence must not be ignored. Despite your dilemma, you must come up with a plan that satisfies both positions.

What types of correctional programs might avoid excessive stigma yet control juvenile offenders?

Should more concern be given to control or to labeling?

lie in other areas: identifying "real" crimes in the society, such as profiteering, sexism, and racism; evaluating how the criminal law is used as a mechanism of social control; and turning the attention of citizens to the inequities in our society. (See Figure 7.3.)

It is not accidental that the emergence of conflict theory as an explanation of deviant behavior had its roots in the widespread social and political upheavals of the 1960s.[55] These forces included the Vietnam War, the counterculture movement, and various forms of political protest. Conflict theory flourished within this framework, because it provided a theoretical basis to challenge the legitimacy of the government's creation and application of law.

Another influence that helped bring conflict theory to the forefront was the apparent failure of more traditional theories of deviance to explain the challenges to government authority.[56] Experts on the causes of deviant behavior were at a loss to explain such phenomena as the increase in illicit drug use among middle-class students; campus, prison, and urban riots; and civil rights demonstrations and other political protests against the government.

At the same time, critical thinkers hurled challenges at the academic world, the center of most theoretical thought in criminology. They claimed that it was

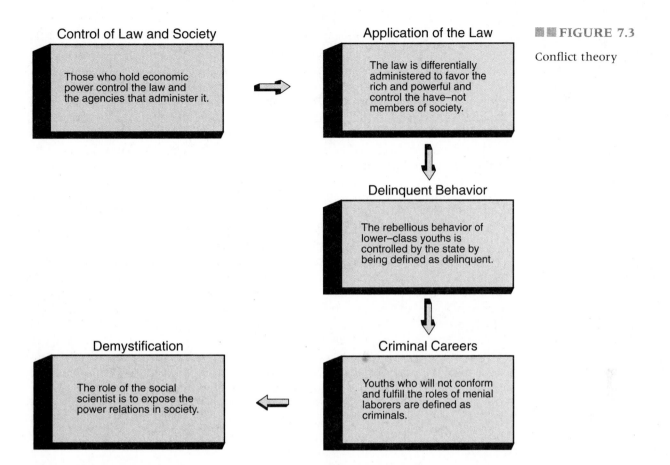

FIGURE 7.3

Conflict theory

Control of Law and Society

Those who hold economic power control the law and the agencies that administer it.

Application of the Law

The law is differentially administered to favor the rich and powerful and control the have–not members of society.

Delinquent Behavior

The rebellious behavior of lower–class youths is controlled by the state by being defined as delinquent.

Criminal Careers

Youths who will not conform and fulfill the roles of menial laborers are defined as criminals.

Demystification

The role of the social scientist is to expose the power relations in society.

archaic, conservative, and out of tune with recent changes in society.[57] Critical criminology, which represents one view of social conflict theory, began to challenge the fundamental role criminologists play in uncovering the causes of crime and delinquency. At a time of general turmoil in society, conflict theorists called for sweeping innovation in academic settings—including changes in the way courses were taught, grading, and tenure. Criminologists were asked to evaluate their own lives and activities to understand their personal role in the crime problem. Was it possible that they were acting as agents of the state, taking money from government agencies to achieve more effective repression of the poor and laboring classes?[58] These social conflict theorists called for a reprisal of the entire field of law and criminology.[59]

Several views exist about what produces social conflict. "Pure" conflict theorists believe that conflict between the haves and have-nots of society can occur in any social system. Other theorists view the American capitalist system as the primary cause of social and class conflict. The former view is usually referred to as *conflict criminology,* while the latter is called *Marxist* or *critical criminology.* Despite this significant dogmatic difference between them, social conflict theorists agree that those in power define the behavior of the poor as criminal and delinquent while shaping the law to define their own actions as acceptable and appropriate.

The social conflict approach can also be contrasted with the social reaction (labeling) perspective. Social conflict theorists charge that labeling advocates do not go far enough in exposing the crime-producing elements of American culture, that they seem content merely to analyze the behavior of strange and different people. In contrast, social conflict thinkers use historical research and political analysis to understand the social relationships, power relations, and institutional arrangements that produce delinquent and criminal behavior.

To understand the social conflict view better, it is helpful to know some of its philosophical underpinnings, more specifically the works of Karl Marx.

Marxist Thought

The foundation of social conflict theory can be traced to the political and economic philosophy of Karl Marx (1818–1883).[60]

Marx believed that the character of every civilization is determined by its mode of production—the way its people develop and produce material goods. This concept has two components: (1) productive forces, which include such things as technology, energy sources, and material resources; and (2) productive relations, which are the relationships between the people producing the goods and services. The most important relationship in industrial culture is between the owners of the means of production, the capitalist bourgeoisie, and those who do the actual labor, the *proletariat.* Throughout history, society has been organized this way—master and slave, lord and serf, and now capitalist and proletariat.

The political and economic philosophy of the dominant class influences all aspects of life. Consciously or unconsciously, artists, writers, and teachers bend their work to the whims of the capitalist system. Thus, the economic system

■ ■ ■ ■ ■ ■ ■ ■ ■ ■ ■ ■ ■ ■ ■

Conflict theory assumes that society is composed of competing groups vying for power, prestige and control. Social conflict can produce unrest and violence.

Part II   Theories of Delinquency

controls all facets of human life, and consequently, people's lives revolve around the means of production.

Marx held that the laboring class produces goods that exceed wages in value. The excess value then goes to the capitalists as profit. While some of this profit is spent on personal luxuries, most is spent on acquiring an ever-expanding capitalist base that relies on advanced technology for efficiency. Thus, capitalists constantly compete with one another to maintain market position. To compete, they must produce goods more efficiently and cheaply, a condition that requires them either to pay workers the lowest possible wages or to replace them with labor-saving machinery. Soon the supply of efficiently made goods outstrips the ability of the laboring classes to purchase them, a condition that precipitates an economic crisis. During this period, weaker enterprises go under and are consequently incorporated in ever-expanding, monopolistic megacorporations that are strong enough to further exploit the workers. Marx believed that in the ebb and flow of the business cycle, the capitalist system contains the seeds of its own destruction and that from its ashes would grow a socialist state in which the workers themselves own the means of production.

In his analysis, Marx used the dialectic method based on the analysis developed by philosopher George Hegel (1770–1831). Hegel argued that for every idea, or *thesis,* there exists an opposing argument, or *antithesis.* Since neither position can ever be truly accepted, the result is a merger of the two ideas, or *synthesis.* Marx adopted this analytic method for his study of class struggle. History, argued Marx, is replete with examples of two opposing forces whose conflict promotes social change. When conditions are bad enough, the oppressed will eventually rise up to fight the owners and replace them. Thus, in the end, the capitalist system will destroy itself.[61]

Although this brief discussion of Marxist thought is only the barest outline of a complex, highly technical topic, it does provide a glimpse of the thought patterns that are the basis of social conflict theory.

ELEMENTS OF SOCIAL CONFLICT THEORY

Based on Marx's theories of economic analysis, the primary goal of social conflict theory is to examine the relationship between the ruling class and the process by which deviance is defined and controlled in capitalist society. By broadening the search for an explanation of deviance to include its defining process, social conflict theorists depart from the narrower focus of earlier positivist models of deviant behavior (discussed in Chapters 4, 5, and 6).

The most important of these concerns are the nature and purpose of social control. Conflict theorists believe that the state creates laws and rules to maintain the power and position of the power elite. This new criminology centers around a view of society in which an elite class uses the criminal law as a means of meeting and controlling threats to its status. The ruling class, then, is a self-interested collective whose primary interest is self-gain.[62] In a classic statement, Richard Quinney argues, "Capitalist justice is by the capitalist class, for the capitalist class, and against the working class."[63]

Social conflict theory views the criminal law and the criminal justice system as vehicles for controlling the poor, have-not members of society. They help the powerful and rich to impose their particular morality and standards of good behavior on the entire society; protect their property and physical safety from the depredations of the have-nots, even though the cost may be high in terms of the legal rights of those it perceives as a threat; and extend the definition of illegal or criminal behavior to encompass those who might threaten the status quo.[64] The ruling elite draws the lower middle class into this pattern of control, leading it to believe that it also has a stake in maintaining the status quo.[65]

According to social conflict theory, the poor may or may not commit more crimes than the rich, but they certainly are arrested and punished more often. The poor are driven to crime because:

1. The middle- and upper-class rules and laws have little relationship to the life-style of the poor.
2. A natural frustration exists in a society where affluence is well-publicized but unattainable to the majority of citizens.
3. A deep-rooted hostility is generated among members of the lower class toward a social order that they are not allowed to shape or participate in.[66]

According to Herman Schwendinger and Julie Schwendinger, the conflict view of society, law, and deviant behavior can be summarized in this way:

1. Legal relations in the United States secure an economic infrastructure that centers around a capitalist mode of production. The legal system is designed to guard the position of the owners (bourgeoisie) at the expense of the workers (proletariat).
2. Legal relations maintain the family and school structure so as to secure the labor force. Sanctions against even common law crimes, such as murder and rape, are implemented to protect capitalism.
3. The capitalist state is made up of a civil society in which the dominance of the bourgeoisie is challenged by the antagonistic rural and urban proletariat.
4. The class interests that underlie the basic laws of the land (such as constitutional laws) are based on the conditions that reproduce the class system as a whole. Laws are aimed at securing the domination of the capitalist system.
5. Legal relations in the capitalist system may at times secure the interests of the working class, for example, laws protecting collective bargaining and personal income.
6. Because of the inherent antagonisms built into the capitalist system, all laws generally contradict their stated purpose of producing justice. Legal relations maintain patterns of individualism and selfishness and in so doing perpetuate a class system characterized by anarchy, oppression, and crime.[67]

Conflict theorists seriously contradict the long-held presumption that the American system of law and justice is humane and fair to all citizens. Conflict theory asks us to reevaluate many basic beliefs. For example, that laws protecting private property may actually be designed to preserve the dominance of a ruling elite seems to strike at the very heart of our moral beliefs. For this reason alone, conflict theory has had a profound effect on mid-twentieth-century criminological thought.

Demystification

Social conflict theorists consider it essential to demystify law and science. This complex concept entails a number of different actions. For one thing, radical criminologists charge that an inordinate amount of scientific effort is devoted to

The LA riots were set off when 4 white police officers were found not guilty of beating black motorist Rodney King. The King case typifies the way conflict theorists view the relations between agents of social control and the minority community.

unmasking the social conditions of lower-class citizens with the ostensible purpose of improving their lives. Such studies include examinations of lower-class family life, IQs, school performance, and so on. Conflict criminologists argue, however, that these efforts actually serve to keep the lower classes down by "proving" that they are more delinquent and less intelligent and that they have poorer school performance than the middle class. All the while, the tests and instruments used to conduct these studies are biased and inaccurate.[68] Thus, in one sense, *demystification* entails uncovering the real reasons behind scientific research.

Another aspect of demystification involves identifying the historical development of criminal law. By drawing attention to the "real" reasons such laws as tax codes and statutes prohibiting theft and drug use were created, people will understand the purpose and intent of these laws. If it is found that theft laws, for example, were originally created to maintain the wealth and capital of the rich, then those who violate the law should not perceive themselves as evil, immoral, or wrong but rather as victims of an unjust system.

Finally, the demystification of capitalist society reveals the controlling nature of the "professional mystique."[69] It is alleged that our society grants inordinate power to professionals to judge and control the population. When teachers, doctors, lawyers, and psychologists judge persons to be crazy, stupid, sick, unfit, delinquent, or criminal, that label becomes their social identity. Radical criminologists charge that professionals often suppress and distort the truth, "unmasking" powerless people so that their position of social inferiority is maintained. The system quickly condemns those who speak against it as "subversive," traitorous," or "mentally ill."

The Conflict Concept of Delinquency

Conflict theorists view delinquency as a normal response by youth to the social conditions created by capitalist society.[70] In fact, the very creation of a unique legal category, delinquency, is a function of the class consciousness that occurred around the turn of the century.[71] In his book *The Child Savers,* Anthony Platt documents the creation of the delinquency concept and the role played by wealthy child savers in forming the philosophy of the juvenile court. In a later work, Platt claims:

The child-saving movement tried to do for the criminal justice system what industrialists and corporate leaders were trying to do by the economy—that is, achieve order, stability and control while preserving the existing class system and distribution of wealth.[72]

Thus, the roots of the juvenile delinquency concept can be traced to nineteenth-century efforts of powerful and wealthy citizens to control the behavior of weak and disenfranchised youths.[73]

The Schwendingers describe today's delinquent behavior as a function of the capitalist system. They argue that capitalism accelerates the trend toward replacing human labor with machines so that youths are removed from a useful place in the labor force.[74] This process prolongs their dependency and forces them to be controlled by socialization agencies, such as the family and, most important, the school. These social control agencies prepare youths for placement in the capitalist system by presenting them with behavior models that will help them conform to later job expectations. For example, rewards for good schoolwork correspond to the rewards a factory supervisor uses with subordinate employees. In fact, most schools are set up to reward and nurture youths who show early promise in such areas as self-discipline, achievement, and motivation and who are therefore judged likely to perform well in the capitalist system. Youths who are judged inferior as potential job prospects (the Schwendingers refer to them as "prototypical marginals") become known to the school community as "greasers," "dudes," and "hoods" and eventually wind up in delinquent roles.[75]

The Schwendingers also view the juvenile justice system as creating and sustaining delinquency. They claim that the capitalist state fails to control delinquents because it is actually in the state's own best interest to maintain a large number of outcast deviant youths. These youths can then be employed as low-paid factory labor in jobs no one else wants. Thus, it behooves capitalist managers to maintain an underclass of cheap labor to be employed in its factories and to buy inferior goods.

The capitalist system affects youths in each element of the class structure differently. In the lowest classes, youths form delinquent gangs, which can be found in the most desolated ghetto areas of the nation. These violent gangs serve outcast youths as a means of survival in a system that offers no other reasonable alternative. Other lower-class youths, who live in more stable areas, are usually on the fringe of criminal activity because the economic system excludes them from meaningful opportunity. Conflict theory also acknowledges middle-class delinquency. The alienation of individuals from one another, the never-ending competitive struggle, and the absence of human interest and feeling—all inherent qualities of capitalism—contribute to middle-class delinquency. Since capitalism is such a dehumanizing system, it is not surprising that even middle-class youths turn to drugs, gambling, and illicit sex to find escape and excitement. Thus, conflict theory explains the various forms of delinquent behavior in our society. See the following Focus on Delinquency for more on this idea.

Children and the Age Structure of Society

In a well-respected article, sociologist David Greenberg has attempted to use conflict analysis to describe how children's place in the socioeconomic structure determines their law-violating behavior.

According to Greenberg, delinquency is a function of the goals associated with a person's place in the human life cycle. During adolescence, personal goals focus on peer group relations and receiving acceptance from friends. Since young people are excluded from adult associations, these relationships take on even greater importance. As long as parents can provide support and funds for these relationships, they can develop along legitimate lines. However, those youths whose parents' economic positions make this support impossible may turn to delinquent behavior to support their life-styles. The capitalist system hastens this process because it makes it difficult for teenagers to become part of the job market. As Greenberg states: "Adolescent theft then occurs as a response to the disjunction between the desire to participate in social activities with peers and the absence of legitimate sources of funds needed to finance this participation." Greenberg argues that this view helps explain the occurrence of middle-class delinquency. Even though the parents of middle-class youths are more likely to be able to provide them with funds than parents of lower-class youths, the cost of their leisure life-style is proportionately greater, so they will be unable to receive the economic support they need. The delinquency of females can be explained in a similar fashion.

As teenagers mature, their vulnerability to the expectations of peers is reduced because of involvements that provide an alternative source of self-esteem and gratification. Also, the opportunity for earning money legitimately increases. These two factors explain why the crime rate decreases with age.

Greenberg sees the school having a significant role in the delinquency equation. The educational experience deprives many adolescents of autonomy and freedom of movement. It demands a discipline and obedience that contradict the independent life-style teenagers crave. In addition, the educational system deprives low-achievement students of self-respect and holds them up for ridicule. Faced with this situation, some youngsters compensate by engaging in high-risk activities whose reward is a reputation for bravery and consequent increase in self-esteem. Of course, the risktaking activities include such illegal acts as vandalism, drinking, and fighting. These pressures are reduced when a student drops out or graduates:

When students drop out or graduate from high school, they enter a world that, while sometimes inhospitable, does not restrict their autonomy and assault their dignity in the same way the school does. The need to engage in crime to establish a sense of an autonomous self and to preserve moral character through risk taking is thus reduced.

Thus, leaving the educational environment reduces a major motivation for delinquency.

There are other class- and age-oriented motivations toward delinquency. Males may experience status anxiety when they perceive that their opportunities for economic success are limited and that they will not be able to fulfill the conventional male role of family breadwinner. Their anxiety is heightened when they observe that the adult males in their environment have high unemployment rates and cannot provide for their families.

Finally, the leniency afforded delinquents by the juvenile court—a function of the belief that they are not fully responsible for their actions—promotes their illegal activities. If for no other reason, youngsters engage in law violations because they know that this is their best opportunity to be treated leniently, that as adults they will be punished to the full extent of the law.

In sum, Greenberg views the removal of children from the labor force in twentieth-century America as a primary motive behind their law-violating behavior: "The high and increasing level of juvenile crime we are seeing in the present-day United States and in other Western countries originates in the structural position of juveniles in an advanced capitalist economy." ■

Source: David Greenberg, "Delinquency and the Age Structure of Crime," in *Crime and Capitalism* (Palo Alto, Calif.: Mayfield, 1981), pp. 118–39. Quotations from pp. 123, 130, 135.

INSTRUMENTAL THEORY

One of the few social conflict models directed at explaining delinquency is **instrumental theory,** developed by Herman Schwendinger and Julia Schwendinger.[76] The Schwendingers' work seeks to explain, in theoretical terms, the paradox caused by the seeming lack of relationship between social class and delinquency. As noted in Chapter 3, many self-report surveys find that middle-class youths commit as many delinquent acts as lower-class youths, despite the commonsense view that poor, underprivileged children commit more crime. Although official record surveys, such as Wolfgang's cohort study, support a lower-class status-delinquency relationship, this has not been the case in most self-report studies.

The Schwendingers believe that this puzzling situation can be explained by the nature of the delinquent experience itself. They find that delinquency is overwhelmingly concentrated within *stratified adolescent formations* that are relatively independent of social class; they refer to these as "stradom formations."

Stradom formations are adolescent social networks whose members have distinct dress, grooming, and linguistic behavior. Many of us remember these groups from our high school experience and recall referring to someone as a "greaser," "hood," "preppie," "socialite," or "jock," based on their friendship patterns, dress, attitudes, and concerns (in fact, we ourselves may have been part of such a group).

According to instrumental theory, economically diverse communities produce three distinct adolescent groupings that emerge as early as the sixth grade. The "socialites" (sometimes called "soshes," "frats," "elites," or "colleges") are predominantly middle-class youths who band together in cliques that remain intact throughout high school. These youths are the children of less affluent but still middle-class parents who wish to imitate the life-style of the rich and affluent.[77]

At the other end of the economic spectrum are street-corner groups known as "greasers," "homeboys," "hodads," or "hoods." Falling between these two extremes are groups characterized by an independent life-style or intermediate status, for example, "surfers," "hot rodders," or "gremmies." Some intermediate groups have mixed identities, such as "sosh-surfers." Each of the three stradom formations is marked by a relatively high delinquency rate.

Not all youths become members of a stradom group. Some are involved in organized, adult-controlled activities—the science club, church groups, 4-H. Others, because of school achievements, are known as "brains" or "intellectuals"; still others are "turkeys," "clods," or "nerds." In general, nonstradom youths have lower delinquency rates.

Stradom groups may display a class bias and contain members of predominantly one class, but this does not prevent crossovers. For example, some hoods and greasers may come from middle-class backgrounds, while lower-class youths can become members of the socialite stradom; intermediary groups can be even more economically heterogeneous.

Delinquency Modalities

According to the Schwendingers' theory, delinquency participation has a natural history or life cycle. As the stradoms change, as their members mature, so do the varieties of their delinquent behavior.

At first, the *generalized modality* of delinquency occurs. Arising early in adolescence, it is marked by an indifference to the needs of others and a cynical attitude toward outsiders in general. Delinquency during this period includes petty thievery, vandalism, truancy, fighting, and other "less serious" delinquent acts.

By the end of junior high school, *ethnocentric delinquency* emerges. This is characterized by stradom rivalries and includes group fights and vandalism motivated by group rivalries and the placing of graffiti that proclaims the superiority of one's stradom over another. Conflict may be intra- or interstradom.

In later adolescence, delinquency enters the *informal economic stage*. Now, for the first time, delinquent acts are instrumental—designed to being economic reward to the offender. They involve burglary, larceny, robbery, drug sales, and so on. Violence and other acting-out behaviors are supported by this modality. Generally, the development of the informal economic stage is dependent on the financial status of individuals and communities. Economically deprived youths are much more likely to be thrust into economic delinquency than middle-class stradom members. However, members of all groups help sustain delinquency because they are consumers of illegally gained materials, ranging from stolen auto parts to illegal drugs.

In sum, stradom members are more likely to become delinquent than nonstradom youths, and lower-class street-corner groups are more likely than socialite and intermediate groups to contain conventional delinquents. However, since middle-class stradom members are more often delinquent than nonstradom lower-class youths, the relationship between class and delinquency is confounded. This explains the apparent failure of self-report studies to detect an economic bias in delinquency.

The Schwendingers' work is important for the study of delinquency. It disputes theories that view delinquency as a function of perceived normlessness or blocked opportunities (Chapter 5) when it recognizes that delinquent groups form early in adolescence, before most youths are even aware of their limited social standing. Similarly, it accounts for middle-class delinquency, an issue left unexplained by the social structure view. While the theory does clash somewhat with social process theories, the differences are not pronounced. However, instrumental theory does not portray as an outcast the delinquent who has a weakened bond to social institutions, such as parents, school, peers, and society. In fact, the delinquent is viewed here as a socially entrenched member of a close peer-group association. Instead, according to the Schwendingers, delinquency is more a product of market relations and demands, societal relationships, and the changing life-style of adolescence.

Integrated Structural Marxist Theory

Mark Colvin and John Pauly have created an integrated conflict theory of delinquency that they call *integrated structural theory*.[78]

According to Colvin and Pauly, delinquency is a result of socialization within the family. However, family relations are actually controlled by the parents' location in economic marketplace. The quality of one's work experience is shaped by the historical competition among capitalists and the level of class struggle.[79] Wage earners who occupy a inferior position in the economic hierarchy will experience coercive relationships with their supervisors and employers. Negative experiences in the workplace create strain and alienation within the family setting, which in turn relate to inconsistent and overly punitive discipline at home. Juveniles who live in such an environment will become alienated from their parents and at the same time experience conflict with social institutions, especially the school. For example, youths growing up in a family headed by parents who are at the bottom of workplace control structures are also the ones most likely to go to underfunded schools, do poorly on standardized tests, and be placed in slow learning tracks; each of these factors has been correlated with delinquent behavior.

The subsequent feelings of alienation are reinforced by associations with groups of similarly alienated peers. In some cases, the peer groups will be oriented toward patterns of violent behavior, while in other instances, they will enable their members to benefit economically from criminal behavior.

According to integrated structural theory, it is naive to believe that a delinquency control policy can be formulated without regard for the basic root causes of delinquency. Coercive punishments or misguided treatments cannot be effective unless the core relationships with regard to material production are changed. Those who produce goods must be given a greater opportunity to control the forms of production and thus the power to shape their lives and the lives of their families.

EVALUATION OF SOCIAL CONFLICT THEORY

The major achievement of social conflict theory is its call to reevaluate the institutions and processes of society and government. Barry Krisberg and James Austin state that the social turmoil of the 1960s and 1970s—generated by such events as the war in Vietnam, Watergate, FBI and CIA plots, the fight for civil rights, and worldwide revolutionary struggles—led many Americans to question conventional values and social arrangements. Official wisdom is no longer simply accepted without question.[80]

Conflict theory does indeed question the many instances of misguided "official wisdom" that pervade our society, but despite its lofty goals and ideals, critics question its lack of empirical verification.[81] Most research has been by necessity historical and theoretical. Even when a specific Marxist theory of deviance has been attempted, such as Stephen Spitzer's in "Toward a Marxian Theory of Deviance,"[82] it lacks the specific propositions sociologists require to test theories properly.[83]

In a similar vein, Jackson Toby argues that conflict theory is a simple rehash of the old tradition of helping the underdog.[84] He likens the ideas behind Marxist criminology to those of such literary works as *Robin Hood* and Victor Hugo's *Les Miserables,* in which the poor steal from the rich to survive. In reality, Toby claims, most theft is for luxury, not survival. Moreover, he disputes the claim that the crimes of the rich are more reprehensible and less understandable than those of the poor. Criminality and immoral behavior occur on every social level, but Toby believes that the relatively disadvantaged contribute disproportionately to the crime and delinquency rates.

In general, criticism of Marxist theory is directed at its utopianism. To blame the state for all evil seems to ignore the great variety of human differences. Not all people react in the same way to social and economic conditions. Why is it that many people suffering the pains of capitalist existence refrain from committing crimes?

■ ■ ■ ■ ■ ■ ■ ■ ■ ■ ■ ■ ■ ■ ■ ■ ■
Is conflict unavoidable?
Can society do something
to reduce levels of interpersonal conflict?

LABELING, CONFLICT, AND DELINQUENCY PREVENTION

Labeling and social conflict theories have had an important influence on delinquency prevention policy during the past two decades. These theoretical models
have drawn attention to the biases in the juvenile justice system and how interacting with the system can actually produce rather than eliminate delinquent
behavior.

The philosophical underpinnings of these policies were described by Edwin
Schur in his widely read book, *Radical Nonintervention.* Schur captured the essence
of the social reaction and social conflict approach to delinquency by decrying
rehabilitation that stigmatized youth:

A great deal of the labeling of delinquents is socially unnecessary and
counterproductive. Policies should be adopted, therefore, that accept a greater
diversity in youth behavior; special delinquency laws should be exceedingly narrow
in scope or else abolished completely, along with preventive efforts that single out
specific individuals and programs that employ "compulsory treatment."[85]

Schur argued that the treatment orientation of the juvenile court, directed at
dealing with the problems of the "whole" person and not the delinquent
violations, helped enmesh many youths who were simply status offenders (for
example, runaways, truants) in what was essentially a criminal signifying
process. Thus, Schur called for delinquency prevention programs that treated the
individual and focused on community action and collective solutions.

The acceptance of this approach by policymakers had a dramatic influence on
juvenile justice operations. A massive effort has been made on the local, state,
and federal levels to limit the interface of youths with the juvenile justice system.
One approach has been to *divert* youths from official processing channels at the
time of their initial contact with police authorities. The usual practice is to have
police refer children to community treatment facilities and clinics, rather than to
the juvenile court.

In a similar vein, children who have been petitioned to juvenile court are eligible for an additional round of court-based diversion programs. For example, *restitution* allows children to pay back the victims of their crimes for the damage (or inconvenience) they have caused, instead of receiving an official delinquency label.

If a youth is found delinquent, efforts are continued to reduce stigma by using alternative sanction programs, such as boot camps and intensive probation monitoring. Alternative sanctions substitute for the more heavily intrusive state training schools. These programs will be discussed further in Chapter 18.

The federal government was a prime mover in the effort to divert as many children from the justice system as possible. The Office of Juvenile Justice and Delinquency Prevention sponsored numerous diversion and restitution programs around the nation. In addition, it made one of its most important priorities the removal of juveniles from adult jails and the discontinuance of housing status offenders and juvenile delinquents together. In sum, these programs were designed to limit, whenever possible, the juvenile's interaction with the formal justice system, to reduce stigma, and to make use of informal, nonpunitive treatment modalities.[86]

While diversion and restitution continue to be widely used, the impetus for the movement seems to have waned. Evaluation of existing programs has shown that they have little or no effect on the recidivism rate of clients.[87] Also, while numerous evaluations have been attempted, their findings have been mitigated by poor research designs and inconsistency of goals, procedures, and operations.

The philosophy of nonintervention has been criticized on several levels. First, it institutionalized a practice that had been carried out informally for years. Police officers and probation officers commonly released children they felt were deserving of a second chance, and only a small percentage of all offenders were continued through the juvenile justice process.[88] Second, many diversion program clients were young and first offenders who had been routinely released informally by the police; hard-core delinquents were not eligible for diversion programs. Finally, and perhaps most important, the diversion and restitution movement actually created new juvenile justice agencies whose need for clients developed a whole new stigmatizing mechanism; critics referred to this as *widening the net.*[89]

The variety of diversion, restitution, and deinstitutionalization programs will be discussed more fully in Chapters 16 and 18. Their influence has had a profound effect on the way we view delinquency and plan for its prevention.

■■■■■■■■■■■■■■■■

SUMMARY

Social reaction theories view delinquent behavior as a function of the influence that powerful members of society have on less fortunate youths. (See Table 7.1.) Two main branches of the theory are currently popular. Labeling theory views deviant behavior as a product of the deviant labels society imposes on its least powerful citizens. Deviant labels mark people as social outcasts and create barriers between them and the general social order. Eventually, deviant labels transform the offenders' personalities, so that they come to accept their new "criminal or delinquent" identities as personal ones.

Labeling theorists suggest that delinquent labels lock individuals out of the mainstream of society, thereby assuring that they will turn to additional illegal behavior for survival. Who is to be labeled and

■■ TABLE 7.1   Social Reaction Theories

THEORY	MAJOR PREMISE	STRENGTHS
LABELING	Youths are locked into a delinquent career when their behavior is labeled by agents of the justice system and they reorganize their identities around a deviant role.	Explains delinquent careers and the role of social control agents in sustaining deviance.
CONFLICT	Crime is a function of class conflict. The definition of the law is controlled by people who hold social and political power.	Accounts for class differences in the delinquency rate. Shows how class conflict influences behavior.
Instrumental	In early adolescence, delinquency cuts across class lines. However, lower-class youth are more likely to persist because of economic needs, while middle-class youths enter into conventional life-styles.	Can account for the aging-out process. Explains why it is often difficult to show class differences in self-reported delinquency.
Integrated structural	Delinquency is a function of family life, which is in turn controlled by the family's place in the economic system.	Explains the relationship between family problems and delinquency in terms of social and economic conditions.

the type of labeling depends on a youth's position in the social structure. The poor and powerless are much more likely to be labeled than the wealthy and powerful.

Edwin Lemert has defined the difference between primary and secondary deviants. The former are people who cling to a conventional self-image, the latter are people who have accepted the traits implied by deviant labels bestowed on them. Howard Becker has analyzed the different forms that labeling takes with respect to the individual audience's reactions to labeling.

Despite its popularity among criminologists, relatively few studies have empirically validated the labeling perspective. Research efforts aimed at the influence of juvenile justice processing on delinquent youths fail to find that labels produce their expected damaging results.

Social conflict theory holds that the class conflicts present in modern society produce crime and delin-quency. The law and legal systems are controlled by those in power, whose aim is to maintain their hold over society. Consequently, their activities are immune, while the deviant behaviors of the lower classes are severely punished. Delinquency occurs when lower-class youngsters rebel against the constraints placed on them by those in power. Middle-class crime is motivated more by rebellion than by economic need. David Greenberg links delinquency to the economic constraints placed on youths in a capitalist society. The Schwendingers hold that role and economic position in capitalist societies influence delinquency modalities.

Social reaction and social control theories had an important effect on delinquency prevention policy in the 1970s. Efforts were made to eliminate, whenever possible, the stigma of the juvenile justice system. This resulted in efforts aimed at diverting offenders before trial, limiting detention, and deinstitutionalization.

KEY TERMS

labeling theory
diversion
deinstitutionalization
Howard Becker
self-fulfilling prophecy
primary-secondary deviance
deviance amplification
social conflict theory

proletariat
thesis
antithesis
synthesis
demystification
instrumental theory
stradom formations
widening the net

QUESTIONS FOR DISCUSSION

1. What are some common labels used in the school setting? How can these hurt youths?
2. Can labels be beneficial to a person? What are some positive effects of labeling?
3. Is it possible to overcome labels? What methods could a person employ to counteract labels?
4. Are there laws that seem to be designed to protect the rich? Is it possible that laws are actually applied fairly?
5. Are there factors in our economy that make Marx's predictions about capitalism obsolete?
6. Discuss examples of the blind obedience we give to professionals, such as doctors, lawyers, and teachers.

NOTES

1. Charles Silberman, *Crises in the Classroom: The Remaking of American Education* (New York: Random House, 1971); idem, "Murder in the Classroom: How the Public Schools Kill Dreams and Mutilate Minds," *Atlantic* 255:82–94 (1970).
2. Richard Quinney, *The Social Reality of Crime* (Boston: Little, Brown, 1970); William Chambliss and Robert Seidman, *Law, Order, and Power* (Reading, Mass.: Addison-Wesley, 1971).
3. These sentiments are contained in some pioneering studies of police discretion, such as Nathan Goldman, *The Differential Selection of Juvenile Offenders for Court Appearance* (New York: National Council on Crime and Delinquency, 1963).
4. For a review of this position, see Anne R. Mahoney, "The Effect of Labeling upon Youths in the Juvenile Justice System: A Review of the Evidence," *Law and Society Review* 8:583–614 (1974). See also David Matza, *Becoming Deviant* (Englewood Cliffs, N.J.: Prentice-Hall, 1974).
5. The self-labeling concept originated in Edwin Lemert, *Social Pathology* (New York: McGraw-Hill, 1951). See also Frank Tannenbaum, *Crime and the Community* (Boston: Ginn, 1936).
6. President's Commission on Law Enforcement and the Administration of Justice, *Task Force Report: Juvenile Delinquency and Youth Crime* (Washington, D.C.: Government Printing Office, 1967), p. 43.
7. Kai Erikson, "Notes on the Sociology of Deviance," *Social Problems* 10:307–314 (1962).
8. Edwin Schur, *Labeling Deviant Behavior* (New York: Harper & Row, 1972), p. 21.
9. Howard Becker, *Outsiders: Studies in the Sociology of Deviance* (New York: Macmillan, 1963), p. 9.
10. Nalini Ambady and Robert Rosenthal, "Half a Minute: Predicting Teacher Evaluations from Thin Slices of Nonverbal Behavior and Physical Attractiveness," *Journal of Personality and Social Psychology* 64:431–41 (1993).
11. Monica Harris, Richard Milich, Elizabeth Corbitt, Daniel Hoover, and Marianne Brady, "Self-Fulfilling Effects of Stigmatizing Information on Children's Social Interactions," *Journal of Personality and Social Psychology* 33:41–50 (1992).
12. Harold Garfinkle, "Conditions of Successful Degradation Ceremonies," *American Journal of Sociology* 61:420–24 (1956).
13. M.A. Bortner, *Inside a Juvenile Court: The Tarnished Ideal of Individualized Justice* (New York: University Press, 1982).
14. Edwin Lemert, *Human Deviance, Social Problems, and Social Control* (Englewood Cliffs, N.J.: Prentice-Hall, 1967), p. 15.
15. Charles H. Cooley, *Human Nature and the Social Order* (New York: Scribner, 1902).
16. Harris et al., "Self-Fulfilling Effects of Stigmatizing Information on Children's Social Interactions," pp. 48–50.
17. Lemert, *Social Pathology.*
18. Ibid., p. 73.
19. Ibid., p. 75.
20. Ibid.
21. Melvin Ray and William Downs, "An Empirical Test of Labeling Theory Using Longitudinal Data," *Journal of Research in Crime and Delinquency* 23:169–74 (1986).
22. Tannenbaum, *Crime and the Community.*
23. Ibid., p. 27.
24. Aaron Cicourel, *The Social Organization of Juvenile Justice* (New York: Wiley, 1968).
25. Matza, *Becoming Deviant.*
26. Ibid., p. 78.
27. Stanton Wheeler and Leonard Cottrell, "Juvenile Delinquency: Its Prevention and Control," in Donald Cressey and David Ward, eds., *Delinquency, Crime, and Social Processes* (New York: Harper & Row, 1969), p. 609.
28. Garfinkel, "Conditions of Successful Degradation Ceremonies," p. 424.

29. Ross Matsueda, "Reflected Appraisals: Parental Labeling, and Delinquency: Specifying a Symbolic Interactionist Theory," *American Journal of Sociology* 97:1577–1611 (1992).

30. See, generally, Carl Pope, "Race and Crime Revisited," *Crime and Delinquency* 25:347–57 (1979).

31. Carl Pope and William Feyerherm, "Minority Status and Juvenile Justice Processing," *Criminal Justice Abstracts* 22:327–36 (1990).

32. Nathan Goldman, *The Differential Selection of Juvenile Offenders for Court Appearance* (New York: National Council on Crime and Delinquency, 1963).

33. Carl Pope, "Juvenile Crime and Justice," in Brian Forst, ed., *The Socioeconomics of Crime and Justice* (New York: M. E. Sharpe, in press).

34. See, for example, William Wilbanks, *The Myth of a Racist Criminal Justice System* (Monterey, Cal.; Brooks-Cole, 1987).

35. Merry Morash, "Establishment of a Juvenile Police Record," *Criminology* 22:97–111 (1984).

36. Paul Lipsett, "The Juvenile Offender's Perception," *Crime and Delinquency* 14:49 (1968).

37. Eloise Snyder, "The Impact of the Juvenile Court Hearing on the Child," *Crime and Delinquency* 17:180–82 (1971).

38. For an opposing view, see John Hepburn, "The Impact of Police Intervention upon Juvenile Delinquents," *Criminology* 15:235–62 (1977). See also Gary Jensen, "Labeling and Identity," *Criminology* 18:121–29 (1980).

39. For a similar view, see Suzanne Ageton and Delbert Elliot, "The Effect of Legal Processing on Self-Concept," (Institute of Behavioral Science, University of Colorado, 1973), cited in Anne R. Mahoney, "The Effect of Labeling upon Youths in the Juvenile Justice System,: A Review of the Evidence," *Law and Society Review* 8:583–614 (1974), at pp. 607–8.

40. Richard Anson and Carol Eason, "The Effects of Confinement on Delinquent Self-Image," *Juvenile and Family Court Journal* 37:39–47 (1986); Gerald O'Connor, "The Effect of Detention upon Male Delinquency," *Social Problems* 18:194–97 (1970); David Street, Robert Vintner, and Charles Perrow, *Organization for Treatment* (New York: Free Press, 1966); Jack Foster, Simon Dinitz, and Walter Reckless, "Perception of Stigma Following Public Intervention for Delinquent Behavior," *Social Problems* 20:202 (1972).

41. Charles Thomas and Donna Bishop, "The Effect of Formal and Informal Sanctions on Delinquency: A Longitudinal Comparison of Labeling and Deterrence Theory," *Journal of Criminal Law and Criminology* 75:1222–45 (1984).

42. Stanley Cohen, *Visions of Social Control* (Cambridge: Polity Press, 1985).

43. Schur, *Labeling Delinquent Behavior*, p. 14.

44. Ronald Akers, "Problems in the Sociology of Deviance," *Social Forces* 46:463 (1968).

45. Peter Manning, "On Deviance," *Contemporary Sociology* 2:697–99 (1973).

46. Charles Tittle and Debra Curran, "Contingencies for Dispostional Disparities in Juvenile Justice," *Social Forces* 67:23–58 (1988).

47. Charles Wellford, "Labeling Theory and Criminology: An Assessment," *Social Problems* 22:335–347 (1975), at p. 337.

48. David Bordua, "On Deviance," *Annals* 312:121–23 (1969).

49. Wellford, "Labeling Theory and Criminology."

50. Ibid.

51. Charles Murray and Lewis Cox, *Beyond Probation* (Beverly Hills, Cal.; Sage, 1979).

52. Raymond Paternoster and Leeann Iovanni, "The Labeling Perspective and Delinquency: An Elaboration of the Theory and an Assessment of the Evidence," *Justice Quarterly* 6:358–94 (1989).

53. Matsueda, "Reflected Appraisals, Parental Labeling and Delinquency."

54. Charles Tittle, "Two Empirical Regularities (Maybe) in Search of an Explanation: Commentary on the Age/Crime Debate," *Criminology* 26:75–85 (1988).

55. Gresham Sykes, "The Rise of Critical Criminology," *Journal of Criminal Law and Criminology* 65:211–17 (1974).

56. Robert Meier, "The New Criminology: Continuity in Criminological Theory," *Journal of Criminal Law and Criminology* 67:461–72 (1976).

57. See, for example, Dennis Sullivan, Larry Tifft, and Larry Siegel, "Criminology, Science and Politics," in Emilio Viano, ed., *Criminal Justice Research* (Lexington, Mass.: Lexington Books, 1978).

58. Ibid., p. 10.

59. Meier, "The New Criminology," p. 463.

60. The ideas in this section are taken in part from C. D. Kerning, ed., *Marxism, Communism, and Western Society*, vol. 5 (New York: Herden and Herden, 1972), pp. 342–60.

61. Stephen Spitzer, "Toward a Marxian Theory of Deviance," *Social Problems* 22:638–51 (1975).

62. Meier, "The New Criminology," p. 463.

63. Richard Quinney, *Class, State, and Crime* (New York: Longman, 1977), p. 3.

64. Sykes, "The Rise of Critical Criminology," pp. 211–13.

65. Ibid.

66. Ibid.

67. Herman Schwendinger and Julia Schwendinger, "Delinquency and Social Reform: A Radical Perspective," in LaMar Empey, ed., *Juvenile Justice* (Charlottesville: University of Virginia Press, 1979), pp. 246–90.

68. Sullivan, Tifft, and Siegel, "Criminology, Science, and Politics," p. 11.

69. Ibid.

70. Robert Gordon, "Capitalism, Class, and Crime in America," *Crime and Delinquency* 19:174 (1973).

71. Quinney, *Class, State, and Crime,* p. 52.
72. Anthony Platt, "The Triumph of Benevolence: The Origins of the Juvenile Justice System in the United States," in Richard Quinney, ed., *Criminal Justice in America: A Critical Understanding* (Boston: Little, Brown, 1974), p. 367. See also Anthony Platt, *The Child Savers* (Chicago: University of Chicago Press, 1969).
73. Barry Krisberg and James Austin, *Children of Ishmael* (Palo Alto, Calif.: Mayfield, 1978), p. 2.
74. Schwendinger and Schwendinger, "Delinquency and Social Reform," p. 250.
75. Ibid., p. 252.
76. Herman Schwendinger and Julia Schwendinger, *Adolescent Subcultures and Delinquency* (New York: Praeger, 1985). See also idem, "The Paradigmatic Crisis in Delinquency Theory," *Crime and Social Justice* 18:70–78 (1982); idem, "The Collective Varieties of Youth," *Crime and Social Justice* 5:7–25 (1976); and idem, "Marginal Youth and Social Policy," *Social Problems* 24:184–91 (1976).
77. Schwendinger and Schwendinger, *Adolescent Subcultures and Delinquency,* p. 55.
78. Mark Colvin and John Pauly, "A Critique of Criminology: Toward an Integrated Structural-Marxist Theory of Delinquency Production," *American Journal of Sociology* 89:513–51 (1983).
79. Ibid., p. 542.
80. Krisberg and Austin, *Children of Ishmael,* p. 4.
81. Carl Klockars, "The Contemporary Crises of Marxist Criminology," in James Inciardi, ed., *Radical Criminology: The Coming Crisis* (Beverly Hills, Calif.: Sage, 1980), pp. 92–123.
82. Spitzer, "Toward a Marxian Theory of Deviance."
83. Alan Horowitz, "Marxist Theory of Deviance and Teleology: A Critique of Spitzer," *Social Problems* 24:362 (1977).
84. Jackson Toby, "The New Criminology Is the Old Sentimentality," *Criminology* 16:516–26 (1979).
85. Edwin Schur, *Radical Nonintervention* (Englewood Cliffs, N.J.: Prentice-Hall, 1973), p. 88.
86. Malcolm Klein, "Deinstitutionalization and Diversion of Juvenile Offenders: A Litany of Impediments," in Norval Morris and Michael Tonry, eds., *Crime and Justice,* vol. 1 (Chicago: University of Chicago Press, 1979).
87. William Selke, "Diversion and Crime Prevention," *Criminology* 20:395–406 (1982).
88. LaMar Empey, "Revolution and Counter Revolution: Current Trends in Juvenile Justice," in David Shichor and Delos Kelly, eds., *Critical Issues in Juvenile Delinquency* (Lexington, Mass.: Lexington Books, 1980), pp. 157–82.
89. James Austin and Barry Krisberg, "The Unmet Promise of Alternatives to Incarceration," *Crime and Delinquency* 28:3–19 (1982).

THEORIES
OF FEMALE
DELINQUENCY

. . . male-oriented theories of delinquency are not necessarily applicable to females; the "just-add-girls-and-mix" approach to general theories of delinquency will no longer apply.[1]

With few exceptions, prevailing theories of delinquent behavior tend to be male-oriented. A few of the theoretical models discussed so far have relevance for female delinquency, but the majority are directed solely at explaining the behavior of male law violators. Empirical support for "general" theories of delinquency has typically employed samples of male subjects to test hypotheses.[2] Efforts to show that male-oriented theories have relevance for females have proven inconclusive at best.[3]

How can this theoretical bias be explained? For one thing, female delinquency was not taken seriously by early criminologists (the majority of whom were males). After all, official statistics show that girls are arrested far less often than boys and then for relatively minor offenses. Similarly, prison statistics indicate that about 96 percent of incarcerated inmates are males.

Early criminologists, such as Cesare Lombroso, viewed females as sexual delinquents who engaged in prostitution, had sexual relations while still in their minority, or were involved in acts that implied that sexual misconduct had occurred or would soon occur, such as running away from home, staying out late at night, and associating with older boys. Consequently, girls were considered neither violent nor responsible for major theft. Their delinquency was viewed as moral, emotional, or family-related, and such problems were not an important concern of traditional criminologists. In fact, the few "true" female delinquents were considered aberrations whose criminal or delinquent activity was a function of their abandoning accepted feminine roles and taking on masculine characteristics.[4]

With the women's movement, conceptions of female delinquency have been altered. First, interest in a feminist approach to crime has been growing. While the female delinquency rate is still much lower than the male rate, little gender difference exists in crime patterns. For example, larceny and burglary, the two most common forms of male criminality (as measured by the UCR), are also the most common types of female criminality. The stereotype of the female delinquent as a purely sexual deviant is no longer taken seriously.[5]

This chapter provides an overview of conceptions of female delinquency. It is divided into four sections: (1) biosocial theories, (2) socialization theories, (3) liberal feminist theories, and (4) radical feminist theories.

BIOSOCIAL THEORIES

As you may recall, biosocial theories view the cause of delinquency as stemming from the interaction of physical, psychological, and environmental conditions. There has been a long tradition of tracing the onset of female delinquency to traits that are uniquely feminine. The argument is that biological and psychological differences in males and females can explain differences in their crime rates. The sections below briefly trace the histroy of this concept and discuss some modern views.

The Female Offender

The earliest conceptualizations of female offenders viewed them as a bizarre aberration. Since the female crime rate was so low and most girls were not delinquents, girls whose behavior deviated from what was considered appropriate for females were believed to be inherently evil or physically maladapted. Early positivist criminologists believed that the interplay of the biological characteristics of women and girls, the psychology of the "female mind," and the social order produced female delinquency.

With the publication in 1895 of his book *The Female Offender*, Cesare Lombroso, writing with William Ferrero, extended his pioneering work on criminality to females.[6] Lombroso maintained that women were lower on the evolutionary scale than men, more childlike, less sensitive, and less intelligent.[7] Women who committed crimes (most often prostitution and other sex-related offenses) could be distinguished from "normal" women by physical characteristics—excessive body hair, wrinkles, crow's feet, and an abnormal cranium, for example.[8] In physical appearance, delinquent females appeared closer both to criminal and noncriminal men than to other women.

Lombroso's contention that women were lower on the evolutionary scale than men is puzzling because he viewed atavism or primitivism as the key element in producing criminal behavior, yet the crime rate of females is lower than that of males. Lombroso explained this apparent inconsistency by arguing that most girls are restrained from committing delinquent acts by such counterbalancing traits as "piety, maternity, want of passion, sexual coldness, weakness, and undeveloped intelligence."[9] The delinquent female lacks these traits and is therefore unrestrained in her childlike, unreasoned passions. Lombroso also believed that much female delinquency is masked and hidden.

Lombroso did recognize, however, that there were far fewer female than male delinquents. He suggested that this was a function of the relative homogeneity and uniformity among females; the female "born criminal" was indeed a rare creature. But he also believed that if a girl did become a delinquent, her behavior might become even more vicious than that of males.

What terrific criminals would children be if they had strong passions, muscular strength, and sufficient intelligence; and if, moreover, their evil tendencies were exasperated by a morbid physical activity! And women are big children; their evil tendencies are more numerous and more varied than men's, but generally remain latent. When they are awakened and excited they produce results proportionately greater.

Moreover, the born female criminal is, so to speak, doubly exceptional as a woman and as a criminal. For criminals are an exception among civilized people, and women are an exception among criminals, the natural form of retrogression in women being prostitution and not crime. The primitive woman was impure rather than criminal.

As a double exception, the criminal woman is consequently a monster. Her normal sister is kept in the paths of virtue by many causes, such as maternity, piety, weakness, and when these counter influences fail, and a woman commits a crime, we may conclude that her wickedness must have been enormous before it could triumph over so many obstacles.[10]

Lombroso's writing considerably influenced his contemporaries. A number of attempts were made in the early twentieth century to connect the cause of female delinquency with physical traits. For example, Cyril Burt in 1925 linked female delinquency to menstruation, a relationship later supported by Warren Middleton.[11] Similarly, William Healy and Augusta Bronner's research efforts found that about 70 percent of the delinquent girls they studied had abnormal weight and size characteristics.[12] This is sometimes referred to as the origin of the *masculinity hypothesis*—the belief that delinquent girls have excessive male characteristics.[13]

Female Sexuality and Crime

Lombroso's early work on the physical abnormalities of deviant girls portrayed female offenders as suffering from weak egos, abnormal or impulsive personalities, and other psychological problems. Another theme, begun by Lombroso, was that female delinquency was almost always linked to anatomy and sexuality.

In a 1928 work, *The Unadjusted Girl,* W. I. Thomas forged a link between sexuality and delinquency. He suggested that some impoverished girls who have not been socialized under middle-class family controls can become impulsive thrill seekers. Their delinquency is linked to their "wish" for luxury and

■ ■ ■ ■ ■ ■ ■ ■ ■ ■ ■ ■ ■ ■ ■

The chivalry hypothesis suggests that female criminality may be hidden because police and other state officials have been socialized to protect girls from the pains of criminal punishment. Do you think police are less becoming chivalrous?

excitement.[14] Inequities in the social class system condemned poor girls from demoralized families to use sex as a means to gain amusement, adventure, pretty clothes, and other luxuries. Precocious sexuality makes these disadvantaged girls vulnerable to older men who, taking advantage of their naïveté, lead them down the path to crime and decadence.[15]

In a later work (1950), *The Criminality of Women*, Otto Pollak reinforced the view that female delinquency is tied to sexuality. Pollak linked the onset of female criminality to the impact of biological conditions: ***menstruation, pregnancy,*** and ***menopause***:[16]

Thefts, particularly shoplifting, arson, homicide, and resistance against public officials seem to show a significant correlation between the menstruation of the offender and the time of the offense. The turmoil of the onset of menstruation and the puberty of girls appears to express itself in the relatively high frequency of false accusations and—where cultural opportunities permit—of incendiarism. Pregnancy in its turn is a crime-promoting influence with regard to attacks against the life of the fetus and the newborn. The menopause finally seems to bring about a distinct increase in crime, especially in offenses resulting from irritability such as arson, breaches of the peace, perjury, and insults.[17]

Like Lombroso before him, Pollak distrusted females and viewed them as "devious" and deceitful. He argued that most female delinquency goes unrecorded because the female is the instigator, rather than the perpetrator, of illegal behavior.[18] Females first use their sexuality to instigate crime and then beguile males in the justice system to obtain deferential treatment. This observation is referred to as the ***chivalry hypothesis:*** gender differences in the delinquency rate can be explained by the fact that female criminality is overlooked by agents of the criminal justice system. Police and judges are deceived into maintaining a chivalrous attitude partly because they are gullible and easily misled by seemingly "innocent" young girls and partly because they have been taught to respect and defer to females. Those who believe in the chivalry hypothesis point to data that show that while women make up about 20 percent of all arrestees, they account for less than 5 percent of all inmates.

Precocious Sexuality

Early theorists linked female sexuality and delinquency to the effects of early or ***precocious sexuality.*** According to this view, girls who experience an early onset of physical maturity are most likely to engage in antisocial behavior. Sheldon Glueck and Eleanor Glueck found that the five hundred delinquent girls in their sample engaged in sex relations at an early age.[19] In their 1968 work, *Delinquency in Girls,* Cowie, Cowie, and Slater also linked female delinquency to precocious sexuality. Female delinquents were typically promiscuous, a type of deviance that required a "more advanced degree of maturation than the (mainly nonsexual) delinquencies of the boys."[20]

Equating female delinquency with sexuality was responsible in part for the view that female delinquency is symptomatic of maladjustment and social isolation.[21] This conclusion had a profound influence on the judicial processing of delinquent girls during much of the twentieth century. The following Focus on Delinquency discusses one study that uncovered this "sexualization" of female delinquency.

Guardians of Virtue

The view that female delinquency is sexual in nature and that the great majority of female delinquents' troubles can be linked to their sexual precociousness influenced the treatment of young female offenders in the first juvenile courts. Mary Odem and Steven Schlossman explored this "sexualization" of female delinquency in their study of all girls (n=220) petitioned to the Los Angeles Juvenile Court in a single year, 1920.

Odem and Schlossman argue that in the first decades of the twentieth century, delinquency "experts" identified young female "sex delinquents" as a major social problem that required a forceful public response. There was concern about a rise in illicit sexual activity among young working-class females. This national concern was in part a product of new-found freedoms enjoyed by girls after the turn of the century. Young females were getting jobs in stores and offices where they were more likely to meet eligible young men. Recreation now included dance halls, movie theaters, beaches, and amusement parks—areas fraught with the danger of "sexual experimentation." Civic leaders concerned about immorality mounted a eugenics and social hygiene campaign that identified the "sex delinquent" as a moral and sexual threat to American society and advocated a policy of *eugenics*—sterilization to prevent these inferior individuals from having children.

The juvenile justice system also responded to this "epidemic" of sexuality effecting Los Angeles lower-class female population. At first, to prevent "moral ruin," female civic leaders and social workers campaigned for special attention to be given to female delinquency. Los Angeles responded by hiring the first female police officers in the nation to deal with girls under arrest and female judges to hear girls' cases in juvenile court. The city also developed a nationally recognized female detention center and a girl's reformatory.

The first female officer in the country was Alice Stebbins Wells, appointed on September 13, 1910. A social worker, Wells argued that she could better serve her clients if she had full police powers. She and her fellow female officers inspected dance halls, cafes, theaters, and other public amusement places to ferret out girls who were in danger of moral ruin, sending some home and bringing the incorrigible to the detention center.

Female "referees" were appointed to hear cases involving girls, and female probation officers were assigned to supervise them. The influx of new cases prompted the county to open custodial institutions for girls, including the El Retiro School, which was considered the latest in modern rehabilitative treatment.

When Odem and Schlossman evaluated the juvenile court records of delinquent girls who entered the Los Angeles Juvenile Court in 1920, they found that the majority were petitioned for either suspected sexual activity or behavior that placed them at risk of sexual relations. Despite the limited seriousness of these charges, the majority of girls were detained prior to their trials, and while in Juvenile Hall, all were given a compulsary pelvic exam. Girls adjudged sexually delinquent on the basis of the exam were segregated from the merely incorrigible girls to prevent moral corruption. Those testing positive for venereal disease were confined in Juvenile Hall Hospital, usually for one to three months.

After trial, *29 percent* of these female adolescents were committed to custodial institutions, a high price to pay for moral transgressions. While society was undergoing a sexual revolution, the juvenile court seemed wedded to a philosophy of controlling "immoral" young women, a policy that was to last more than thirty years. ■

Source: Mary Odem and Steven Schlossman, "Guardians of Virtue: The Juvenile Court and Female Delinquency in Early 20th-Century Los Angeles," *Crime and Delinquency* 37:186-203 (1991).

The Psychology of Sex

Sigmund Freud maintained that girls view their lack of a penis as a sign that they have been punished. Boys fear that they also can be punished by having their penis cut off and thus learn to fear women. Form this conflict comes **penis envy** and the girl's wish to become a boy. Penis envy often produces an inferiority complex in girls, forcing them to make an effort to compensate for their defect.

One way is to identify with their mother and accept a maternal role as wife and childbearer. Also, girls may become narcissistic and attempt to compensate for their lack of a penis by dressing well and beautifying themselves.[22]

Freud also claimed that if a young girl does not overcome her penis envy, neurotic episodes may follow: "If a little girl persists in her first wish—to grow into a boy—in extreme cases she will end as a manifest homosexual, and otherwise she will exhibit markedly masculine traits in the conduct of her later life, will choose a masculine vocation, and so on."[23]

Freud's concept of penis envy has been strongly questioned by more modern psychoanalysts who scoff at the notion that little girls feel inferior to little boys and charge that Freud's thinking was influenced by the sexist culture he lived in.[24]

Others using the psychoanalytic perspective have suggested that girls are socialized to be passive and need affection, which helps to explain their low crime rate. However, this personality condition also makes some females susceptible to being manipulated by men; hence, their participation in sex-related crimes, such as prostitution.

This theme has been amplified by a number of psychoanalysts who link feminine crime and delinquency to sexuality. Peter Blos states:

The girls' wayward behavior is restricted to stealing of the kleptomaniac type; to vagrancy; to provocative impudent behavior in public; and to frank sexual waywardness. In the girl it seems delinquency is a overt sexual act, or to be more correct, a sexual acting out.[25]

Similarly, psychiatrist Walter Bromberg suggests that the sexual conflict that produces prostitution may be found in "every woman" and may be attributed to "conflicts surrounding enjoyment of sexuality."[26]

According to the psychoanalytic approach, therefore, female delinquency is a product of young girl's psychosexual development. Female delinquency is viewed as a function of repressed sexuality, gender conflict, and abnormal socialization.

CONTEMPORARY BIOSOCIAL VIEWS

Contemporary biosocial and psychological theorists have continued the tradition of explaining female delinquency as a function of the interaction of physical, social, and psychological traits unique to women and girls.[27] One biological factor long suspected as a cause of female criminality is *premenstrual syndrome (PMS):*

For several days prior to and during menstruation, the stereotype has been that "raging hormones" doom women to irritability and poor judgment—two facets of premenstrual syndrome.[28]

The link between PMS and delinquency was popularized by Katharina Dalton, whose studies of English women led her to conclude that females are more likely to commit suicide and be aggressive and otherwise antisocial before or during menstruation.[29] While Dalton's research is often cited as evidence of the link between PMS and crime, methodological problems make it impossible to accept her findings at face value. Moreover, most other research efforts indicate that women do suffer anxiety and hostility prior to and during menstruation but that there is little evidence linking these conditions to crime or long-term psychological problems.[30] Criminologist Julie Horney impressively reviewed the literature on PMS and crime and found that existing evidence is inconclusive. Horney suggests there may be alternative explanations for a PMS-delinquency link; for example, it is possible that the psychological and physical stress of antisocial events and their aftermath produce early menstruation and not vice versa.[31]

Sexuality

While equating female delinquency with sex activity alone is no longer taken seriously, biosocial theorists are again looking at the relationship between early sexual activity and antisocial behavior. Empirical evidence suggests that girls who reach puberty at an early age are at the highest risk for delinquency.[32] Research by Avshalom Caspi and his associates show that early physical maturity accelerates the contact young girls have with older adolescent boys. After reaching sexual maturity, girls who had not before engaged in antisocial behavior will be brought through peer relations into contact with delinquent patterns of behavior after which they may begin to "sample" some of these activities.[33] In contrast, girls who had histories of childhood misbehavior were likely to become involved in delinquency regardless of the timing of their physical maturity. The Caspi research is important because it shows that factors that develop during the life course can have an important influence on accelerating (or restraining) delinquent activity.

Hormonal Differences

Some biosocial theorists link antisocial behavior to hormonal influences. The argument is that male sex hormones (**androgens**) account for their more aggressive behavior and that gender-related hormonal differences can also explain the gender gap in delinquency.[34]

Research indicates that levels of the male hormone **testosterone** are predictive of both juvenile delinquency and adult criminality.[35] Walter Gove found that testosterone levels are a key to understanding crime rate differences: the decline in this key hormone during the life cycle accounts for the aging-out process; below-average levels in females explain their lower delinquency rate.[36]

Lee Ellis also links gender differences to the influence of male androgens. These hormones cause areas of the brain to become less sensitive to environmental stimulii, making males more likely to seek high levels of stimulation and to tolerate more pain in the process. Androgens are also linked to brain seizures, which result in greater emotional volatility, especially when stresses are present. Ellis believes that androgens affect the brain structure itself (the left hemisphere of the neocortex), which effectively reduces sympathetic feelings toward others that help to inhibit the urge to victimize.[37]

A great deal of research has been done on the relationship of hormonal levels and aggression. In general, the research indicates that females who have naturally low androgen levels are more passive than males, while females who were exposed to male hormones, either before birth (in utero) or soon after, will take on characteristically male traits, including aggression. For example, research by Donald Baucom and his associates indicates that college women who tested higher on the male hormone testosterone were more likely to engage in stereotypically male behaviors.[38]

Are Females Less Aggressive?

Biosocial theory, then, relates gender differences in the delinquency rate to the fact that gender-based biological differences make females less aggressive than males.[39] Some psychologists have suggested that gender-based differences in aggression are present very early in life before socialization can influence behavior. Eleanor Maccoby and Carol Jacklin's influential research found that males were more aggressive in all human societies for which data was available and that gender differences could also be found in subhuman primates. Maccoby and Jacklin linked gender differences to hormonal variations (testosterone) that control behavior.[40]

Not all biosocial theorists view gender differences as merely a matter of hormonal variation. Lee Ellis suggests that gender-based differences in aggression reflect the essential physical dissimilarities in the male and female reproductive systems. Ellis links human behavior to the sociobiological urge to reproduce and maintain the gene pool. He finds that males are naturally more aggressive because they wish to possess and control as many sex partners as possible to increase their chances of producing offspring. Females have learned to control their aggressive impulses because multiple mates do not increase their chances of conception. They instead concentrate their efforts on acquiring things that will help them successfully rear their offspring, such as a reliable mate who will supply material resources.[41]

The weight of the evidence is that males are more aggressive than females. However, evidence also exists that females are more likely to act aggressively under some circumstances than others:

1. Males are more likely than females to report physical aggression in their behavior, intentions, and dreams.
2. Females are more likely to feel anxious or guilty about behaving aggressively, and these feelings tend to inhibit aggression.
3. Females behave as aggressively as males when they have the means to do so and believe that their behavior is justified.
4. Females are more likely to empathize with the victim—to put themselves in the victim's place.
5. Sex differences in aggression decrease when the victim is anonymous. Anonymity may prevent females from empathizing with the victim.[42]
6. Females may feel more freedom than males to express anger and aggression in the family setting.[43]

In sum, biosocial theorists find that qualities of male biological traits make males "naturally" more aggressive than females; it should come as no surprise, then, that male delinquency rates are higher. According to this view, though females can be aggressive under some circumstances, their delinquency will only equal males if they have been born with or somehow acquired male characteristics and traits.

SOCIALIZATION THEORIES

Socialization theories hold that the social development of a girl, influenced and controlled by her family, her peers, and society, may be the key to understanding delinquent behavior. If she experiences impairment, trauma, family disruption, and so on, a girl will eventually be forced to engage in delinquent associations and criminality.

The view that socialization influences antisocial behavior is not unique to female delinquency. Nonetheless, scholars concerned with gender differences in the crime rate attempt to distinguish between the life-styles of males and females. Girls may be supervised more closely than boys and are expected to stay at home more often. If girls behave in a socially disapproved fashion, their parents may be more likely to notice and take action. Adults may be more tolerant of deviant behavior in boys than in girls and expect the former to act tough and take risks.[44] Closer supervision restricts the opportunity for crime and the time available to mingle with delinquent peers. It follows, then, that the adolescent girl who is growing up in a troubled home or one marked by abuse, conflict, or neglect and who lacks concern and supervision may be the one most prone to delinquency.

Focus on Socialization

At mid-century, a number of writers began to focus on the socialization patterns of girls as a key determinant of their antisocial behavior. Most research relied on three assumptions about female socialization: families exerted a more powerful influence on girls than boys; girls did not form close same-sex friendships and generally competed with their peers; and females were primarily sexual offenders. The first assumption was that parents were stricter with girls, whom they perceived as vulnerable and in need of control. In some families, adolescent girls rebelled against strict controls, while in others, where parents were absent or unavailable, they turned to the streets for support and companionship. Girls rarely formed close relationships with female peers whom they viewed as rivals for the few males who would make eligible marriage partners.[45] Instead, girls

■ ■ ■ ■ ■ ■ ■ ■ ■ ■ ■ ■ ■ ■ ■ ■

Socialization views depict the female delinquent as a troubled adolescent who finds little support at home and may turn to the streets for love and affection. Teen-age pregnancy is the result of sexual experimentation at an early age.

Part II Theories of Delinquency

entered into sexual affairs with older men who would exploit them, involve them in sexual deviance, and father their illegitimate children.[46] The result was prostitution, petty theft, drug abuse, and marginal lives. Their daughters then would repeat this pattern in a never-ending cycle of despair and exploitation.

Perhaps the best-known work focusing on female socialization as a cause of delinquency is Gisela Konopka's *The Adolescent Girl in Conflict* (1966). Konopka incorporates many of the principles expounded by Freud but also emphasizes the influence of peers and socialization in causing deviant behavior.[47]

Konopka suggests that delinquency has its roots in a girl's feeling of uncertainty and loneliness. During her adolescence, a girl's major emotional need is to be accepted by members of the opposite sex. If normal channels for receiving such approval—family, friends, relatives—are impaired, she may fight isolation by joining a "crowd" or engaging in gratuitous sexual relationships. This behavior eventually leads to "rejection by the community, general experience of having no recognized success . . . and more behavior which increases the feeling of worthlessness."[48] Konopka identifies four major influences on the loneliness and consequent delinquent behavior of girls:[49]

- The onset of puberty in girls is traumatic because of the often cruel way in which it is received by parents and the fear it creates in girls.
- The social identification process can be dramatic and difficult because of a girl's competitiveness with her mother. In fatherless homes, girls have an especially hard time, since "the road to a healthy development toward womanhood through affection for the male and identification with the female simply does not exist."[50]
- Changing the pattern of females' cultural position can create problems. Delinquent girls are believed to suffer from a lack of training and education. This locks them into low-paying jobs with little hope for advancement. These conditions lead girls to relieve their thwarted ambition through aggressive or destructive behavior.
- The world presents a hostile environment to some girls. Adult authority figures tell them what to do, but no one is there to listen to their needs.

Konopka emphasizes the effect of the family and society on female emotions as a primary influence on a girl's delinquent behavior. A number of authorities have shared Konopka's views since the publication of her study. One significant work, by Clyde Vedder and Dora Somerville, *The Delinquent Girl* (1970), also suggests that the delinquent behavior of girls is usually a problem of adjustment to family and social pressure.[51] In fact, the authors estimate that 75 percent of institutionalized girls have family problems. They also suggest that girls have serious problems in a male-dominated culture with rigid and sometimes unfair social practices.

Research on Female Socialization

A great deal of research has been done that indicates that delinquent girls do in fact come from troubled, uncertain homes and are the victims of sexual and physical abuse. In their classic work *Five Hundred Delinquent Women*, Eleanor Glueck and Sheldon Glueck examined the life histories of institutionalized female offenders.[52] A significant majority of the subjects had been involved in sexual deviance that began early in their teens. The Gluecks concluded that sexual delinquency and general behavior maladjustment developed in girls simultaneously with unstable home lives.[53] Similarly, Ruth Morris described delinquent girls as unattractive, poorly groomed youths who reside in homes marked by family tensions of absent parents.[54]

Other early efforts linked "rebellious" or sexually precocious behavior to sexual conficts in the home and incestuous relationships.[55] Broken or disrupted homes were found to predict female delinquency.[56] Females petitioned to juvenile court were more likely than boys to be charged with ungovernable behavior, running away, and sex offenses and were more likely to reside in a single-parent home.[57] Studies of incarcerated juveniles found that most of the male delinquents were incarcerated for burglary, robbery, and other theft-related offenses, but girls tended to be involved in incorrigibility, sex offenses, and truancy. The conclusion: boys became delinquent in order to gain status and demonstrate their masculinity by adventurous behavior; girls were delinquent because of hostility toward parents and a consequent need to obtain gratification and attention from others.[58]

Contemporary Socialization Theory

The view that female delinquents are motivated by improper socialization has continued to receive research attention. Meda Chesney-Lind found that a significant amount of female delinquency, which most often involves such acts as truancy, running away, and petty theft, can be traced to physical and sexual abuse in the home.[59] She writes, "Young women on the run from homes characterized by sexual abuse and parental neglect are forced, by the very statutes designed to protect them, into the life of an escaped convict."[60]

Chesney-Lind's research is supported by some recent research on female gang members. Joan Moore's analysis of gang girls in east Los Angeles found that many came from troubled homes. Sixty-eight percent of the girls she interviewed were afraid of their fathers, and 55 percent reported fear of their mothers. One girl told Moore about the abuse she received from her mother:

She would hit me, pinch me, and pull my hair, and then she'd have my brother—the oldest one—get a whip, and whip me, and then I'd have stripes all over my body like a zebra, and I went to school like that.[61]

Many of the girls reported that parents were overly strict and controlling despite the fact that they engaged in drug abuse and criminality themselves. Moore also details accounts of incest and sexual abuse; about 30 percent of the gang girls reported that family members made sexual advances. Considering the restrictions placed on girls and the high incidence of incest, it comes as no surprise that three-quarters reported having run away at least once. Moore concludes:

. . . clearly more women than men came from troubled families. They were more likely to have been living with a chronically sick relative, one who died, one who was a heroin addict, or one who was arrested. . . . This seems on the face of it to imply that the gang represents [for girls] . . . a refuge from family problems. . . .[62]

In sum, the socialization approach to female delinquency posits that family interaction and child-parent relations are the keys to understanding the antisocial behavior of girls. If a girl grows up in an atmosphere of sexual tension, where hostility exists between her parents or where the parents are absent, she likely will turn to outside sources for affection and support. Unlike boys, girls must follow very narrowly defined behavioral patterns. It their reaction to loneliness, frustration, and parental hostility is sexual activity, running away, staying out late at night, and so on, they are likely to be defined as delinquent or wayward. The socialization approach holds that the psychological pressure of a poor home life is likely to have an even more damaging effect on females than males. Because girls are less likely than boys to have the support of close-knit peer associations, they are more likely to need close parental relationships to retain emotional stability. In fact, girls may become sexually involved with boys to receive support from them, a practice that tends only to magnify their problems.

LIBERAL FEMINIST THEORY

All of us, despite our differences, are constantly growing and trying to understand each other's oppression, be it as working class women, black or brown women, gay women or middle class women. We are, by struggling, finding new ways of caring about each other, and it is this that gives us hope of having a movement, finally, which will provide for all of our needs.[63]

This statement represents the sentiments of women who are active participants in the feminist movement. Feminist leaders have fought to help women break away from their traditional roles of homemaker and mother and secure for themselves economic, professional, educational, and social advancement. There is little question that the women's movement has revised the way women perceive their roles in society, and it has significantly altered the relationships of women to many important social institutions.

Liberal feminism also has influenced thinking about the nature and extent of female delinquency. A number of scholars, including Rita Simon and Freda Adler, have drawn national attention to the changing pattern of female criminality and offered new explanations for its cause.[64] Their position is that economic conditions and sex role differences influence female crime more than do dysfunctional family relationships. Females are less delinquent than males because their social roles provide them with fewer opportunities to commit crime. As the roles of girls and women become more similar to those of males, so too will their crime patterns. Female criminality is actually motivated by the same crime-producing influences as male criminality.

"Sisters in Crime"

Freda Adler's book *Sisters in Crime* has been an influential source of information on how changing roles have affected female crime and delinquency. Adler's major thesis is that by striving for social and economic independence, women have begun to alter social institutions, which until recently protected males in their position of power. "The phenomenon of female criminality," she claims, "is but one wave in this rising tide of female assertiveness."[65]

Adler argues that female delinquency is affected by the changing patterns of females' behavior. Girls are becoming increasingly involved in traditionally masculine crimes, such as stealing, gang activity, and fighting. Adler predicts that in the future, the women's liberation movement will produce even steeper increases in the rate of female delinquency because it creates an environment in which the social roles of girls and boys converge. Boys, she argues, have traditionally entered puberty ill-prepared for the world of aggression and competition they encounter in the activities of their peer groups. The consequent emotional strain leads them to engage in delinquent activities. Girls, on the other hand, have always maintained traditional, relatively static behavior patterns. These patterns have protected them from the pressures of transition into the adult world. However, Adler claims, "the modern girl . . . is passing from childhood to adulthood via a new and uncharted course. . . . She is partly pushed and partly impelled into fields previously closed to women. . . . Clearly, the developmental difficulties which encouraged male delinquency in the past are exerting a similar influence on girls."[66]

Adler proclaims that the changing female role will eventually produce female delinquents and criminals who are quite similar to their male counterparts:

Women are no longer behaving like subhuman primates with only one option. Medical, educational, political and technological advances have freed women from unwanted

■ ■ ■ ■ ■ ■ ■ ■ ■ ■ ■ ■ ■ ■ ■ ■

According to liberal feminist theory, as gender roles change so too will the nature and extent of female delinquency.

Part II   Theories of Delinquency

pregnancies, provided them with male occupational skills, and equalized their strengths with weapons. Is it any wonder that once women were armed with male opportunities, they should strive for status, criminal as well as civil, through established male hierarchial channels.

In the cities . . . young girls are now taking to the streets just as boys have traditionally done. It has now become quite common for adolescent girls to participate in muggings, burglaries, and extortion rings which prey on schoolmates.[67]

Research on Liberal Feminist Theory

A number of recent studies have supported the determinist view of female delinquency.[68] The most notable may be Rita Simon's 1975 effort, *The Contemporary Woman and Crime*. While not specifically devoted to youth crime, Simon's work points to the consistent increase in the crime rate of females in general. Her comparison of arrest rates for the years 1953, 1963, and 1972 indicates that women's crime rates have increased dramatically and that the type of female criminality has changed. Simon suggests that women commit significantly more larceny, fraud, forgery, and embezzlement—all business-related and economic crimes. Their violent crime rate has remained somewhat static. Simon explains that her findings are a function of the changing role of women:

The same factors and conditions that explain women's increased participation in property offenses also serve to explain the slight decline or lack of increase in violent offenses during the same time period. The fact that women have more economic opportunities and more legal rights (divorces and abortions are easier to obtain) and that in recent years they have been developing a rhetoric which legitimizes their newly established socio-legal-economic status seems to lessen the likelihood that they will feel victimized, dependent, and oppressed. The diminishment of such feelings means that they will be less likely to attack their traditional targets: their husbands, lovers, pimps (that is, men with whom they are emotionally involved and dependent upon), and their babies (those recently born and those not yet delivered).[69]

Simon's view has been supported in part by Roy Austin's analysis of the effect the women's liberation and economic emancipation movement has had on the female crime rate.[70] Using 1966 as a jumping-off point (because The National Organization for Women was founded in that year), Austin's research shows that patterns of serious female crime (robbery and auto theft) correlate with indicators of female emancipation (namely, the divorce rate and participation in the labor force). While, as Austin admits, this research does not conclusively prove that female crime is related to economic and social change, it certainly identifies behavior patterns that support that hypothesis.

In addition to these efforts, a number of self-report studies have supported the liberal feminism view by showing that gender differences in delinquency *patterns* are fading. That is, the delinquent acts committed most (petty larceny) and least often (heroin addiction, armed robbery) by girls are nearly identical to those reported most and least often by boys.[71] Evidence uncovered in numerous self-report studies seems to indicate that the pattern of female delinquency, if not the extent, is now similar to that of male delinquency.[72]

In addition, evidence is growing that social forces predictive of male delinquency, such as identification with a delinquent peer group, are also associated with female delinquency.[73] For example, Margaret Farnworth found that with some forms of youthful misconduct, such as status offenses and violent crimes, male and female delinquency is motivated by the same social relationships, for example, family structure and function.[74] A study of gang membership by Beth Bjerregaard and Carolyn Smith found that the factors that motivated both males and females to join gangs were quite similar: family dysfunction and precocious sexuality. One significant difference was that female membership in gangs was motivated by a lack of educational success.[75] Perceived closure of opportunity through educational advancement had a significant impact on females and helped them decide to join gangs as a vehicle for economic advancement.

These studies suggest that as the sex roles of males and females become more equivalent, their offending patterns also have become more similar. Girls may be joining gangs and committing crimes as a means of economic advancement. Both these patterns are predicted by liberal feminist theory.

Critiques of Liberal Feminism

Not all delinquency experts believe that changing sex roles actually influence female crime rates. Some argue that the delinquent behavior patterns of girls have remained static and have not been influenced by the women's movement. Others feel that there has been change but that the cause is something other than the feminist revolution. For example, Darrell Steffensmeier and Renee Hoffman Steffensmeier conclude that arrest data and juvenile gang studies show little increase in female violence or gang-related acts and that young female offenders do not seem to be catching up with males in terms of violent or serious crimes. They also find that increases in serious crimes by female offenders (as measured by the UCR) have leveled off. Female crime had reflected the general increase in the overall crime rate occurring in the 1970s. In addition, the Steffensmeiers note that self-report studies show that female participation in most crime patterns has remained stable for the past ten years, with increases in the area of drug use and alcohol abuse.[76]

Similarly, Joseph Weis discusses the "invention" of the new female criminal. In a self-report study, he found that girls still engage in traditional sex-role behaviors, such as shoplifting, and are least involved in typically masculine crimes, such as fighting. Weis sees this as evidence that female crime patterns are not related to female liberation and calls such an equation "absurd"; "after all, the women's movement is dedicated to stopping and preventing the kinds of explorations and victimization which comprise many criminal as well as non-criminal activities and relationships."[77]

These sentiments have been duplicated by other researchers, such as Carol Smart, who suggests that swings in the female crime rate have been recorded since the 1920s.[78] Smart maintains that the cause of female delinquency is so complex, as is the cause of all criminal behaviors, that it is meaningless to attribute it to a single cause, such as the women's movement.

In sum, the evidence indicates that gender differences in the crime rate have not changed as much as liberal feminist writers had predicted. Consequently, the argument that female crime and delinquency will be elevated by the women's movement has not been given unqualified support.

RADICAL FEMINIST VIEWS

A number of feminist writers take a more revolutionary view of female criminality. Some can be categorized as *Marxist feminists* who view gender inequality as stemming from the unequal power of men and women in a capitalist society and the exploitation of females by fathers and husbands; women are considered a "commodity" worth possessing, like land or money.[79] In contrast, *radical feminists* view the cause of female delinquency as originating with the onset of male supremacy (*patriarchy*), the subsequent subordination of women, male aggression, and the efforts of men to control females sexually.[80]

Radical feminists focus on the social forces that shape girls' lives and experiences to explain female criminality.[81] They attempt to show how the sexual victimization of girls is often a function of male socialization and that young males learn to be aggressive and exploitive of women. This view is supported by a recent (1993) national survey conducted by the Center for Research on Women at Wellesley College, which found that 90 percent of adolescent girls are sexually harassed in school, with almost 30 percent reporting having been psychologically pressured to "do something sexual" and 10 percent physically forced to do something sexual.[82]

According to the radical view, exploitation acts as a trigger for delinquent behavior and status offending. When female victims run away and abuse substances, they may be reacting to abuse at home and at school. Their attempts at survival are then labeled deviant or delinquent; victim blaming is not uncommon.[83] The Wellesley survey of sexual harassment found that teachers

■ ■ ■ ■ ■ ■ ■ ■ ■ ■ ■ ■ ■ ■ ■ ■

Radical feminists view the female delinquent as a victim. Running away from an abusive, male-dominated home, the female delinquent may commit crime to survive.

and school officials ignore about 45 percent of the complaints made by female students. Researchers found that some school officials responded to reports of sexual harassment by asking the young victim, "Do you like it?" and saying, "They must be doing it for a reason." Because agents of social control often choose to ignore reports of abuse and harassment, young girls may feel trapped and desperate. The following Case in Point explores attitudes about girls and sexuality.

A number of theoretical models have attempted to use a radical or Marxist feminist perspective to explain gender differences in the delinquency rate and the nature of female delinquency. For example, in *Capitalism, Patriarchy, and Crime,* Marxist James Messerschmidt argues that capitalist society is marked by both patriarchy and class conflict. Capitalists control the labor of workers, while men control women both economically and biologically.[84] This "double marginality" explains why females in a capitalist society commit fewer crimes than males: they are isolated in the family and have fewer opportunities to engage in elite deviance (white-collar and economic crimes); they are also denied access to male-dominated street crimes. Since capitalism renders women powerless, they are forced to commit less serious, nonviolent, and self-destructive crimes, such as abusing drugs. Supporting Messerschmidt's conclusions is the self-report data that shows girls report equal rates of substance abuse as males.

■ ■ ■ ■ ■ ■ ■ ■ ■ ■ ■ ■ ■ ■ ■

CASE IN POINT

As the principal of a Northeast junior high school, you are disturbed to hear from the faculty advisor to the student literary digest that the students plan to publish a story with a sexual theme. The work is written by a junior high school girl who became pregnant during the year and underwent an abortion. You ask for and receive a copy of the narrative.

The girl's theme is actually a cautionary tale of young love that results in an unwanted pregnancy. The author details her abusive home life that led her to engage in an intimate relationship with another student, her pregnancy, her conflict with her parents, her decision to abort, and the emotional turmoil that the incident created. She tells students to use contraception if they are sexually active and recommends appropriate types of birth control. There is nothing provocative or sexually explicit in the work.

Some teachers argue that girls should not be allowed to read this material because it has a sexual content that they must be protected from and that, in a sense, it advocates defiance of parents. Those who advocate publication believe that girls have a right to read about such important issues and decide on their own course of action. Censorship would also be a violation of the author's First Amendment rights.

Should you force the story's deletion because its theme is essentially sexual and controversial?

Should you allow publication because it deals with the subject matter in a mature fashion?

Power-Control Theory

In one prominent radical feminist work, John Hagan and his associates have speculated that gender differences in the delinquency rate are a function of class differences and economic conditions that in turn influence the structure of family life. Hagan calls his view *power-control theory*.[85]

According to this view, class position influences delinquency by controlling the quality of family life. In paternalistic families, fathers assume the traditional role of breadwinners, while mothers have menial jobs or remain at home. In these homes, mothers are expected to control the behavior of their daughters while granting greater freedom to sons. The parent-daughter relationship can be viewed as a preparation for the "cult of domesticity," which makes daughters' involvement in delinquency unlikely; hence, males exhibit a higher degree of delinquent behavior than their sisters.

On the other hand, in *egalitarian* families—those in which the husband and the wife share similar positions of power at home and in the workplace—daughters gain a kind of freedom that reflects reduced parental control. These families produce daughters whose law-violating behavior mirrors that of their brothers. Ironically, these kind of relationships also occur in female-headed households with absent fathers. Similarly, Hagan and his associates found that when both fathers and mothers hold equally valued managerial positions, the similarity between the rates of their daughters' and sons' delinquency is greatest. By implication, middle-class girls are the most likely to violate the law because they are less closely controlled than their lower-class sisters.

Some of the power-control theory's basic premises, such as the relationship between social class and delinquency, have been challenged. For example, the theory holds that upper-class youths may engage in more petty delinquency than lower-class youths because they are brought up to be "risk takers" who do not fear the consequences of their misdeeds. Some recent research indicates that such relationships may not exist.[86] However, ongoing research by Hagan and his colleagues has tended to support the core relationship between family structure and gender differences in the delinquency rate.[87]

Power-control theory is important because it encourages a new approach to the study of delinquency, one that includes gender differences, class position, and family structure. It also has value as an explanation of the relative increase in female delinquency because it incorporates the effects of the social changes occurring in the feminine role within its explanation of delinquency. With the shift toward single-parent homes brought about by the significant numbers of unwed teenage mothers and the high divorce rate, the patterns Hagan has identified may also undergo change. The decline of the patriarchal family may produce looser family ties on girls, changing sex roles, and increased delinquency.

GIRLS IN THE JUVENILE JUSTICE SYSTEM

Several feminist scholars argue that girls are not only the victims of injustice at home but also risk being victimized by agents of the juvenile justice system. In many respects, the treatment they receive today is not too dissimilar from the "sexualization" of female delinquency found by Odem and Schlossman in 1920

Los Angeles (see the Focus on Delinquency in this chapter). Paternalistic attitudes and the sexual "double standard" increase the likelihood that girls will be referred to juvenile court for status-type offenses and, after adjudication, receive a disposition involving incarceration.

Are girls the "victim" of the juvenile justice system? In her classic 1973 study, Meda Chesney-Lind found that police in Honolulu, Hawaii, were likely to arrest female adolescents for sexual activity and to ignore the same behavior among male delinquents.[88] Some 74 percent of the females in her sample were charged with sexual activity or incorrigibility; in comparison, only 27 percent of the boys were so charged. Similar to 1920 Los Angeles, the court ordered 70 percent of the females to undergo physical examinations, while requiring only 15 percent of the males to undergo this embarrassing procedure. Girls were also more likely to be sent to a detention facility before trial, and the length of their detention averaged three times that of the boys.

Chesney-Lind concluded that female adolescents have a much narrower range of acceptable behavior than male adolescents. Any sign of misbehavior in girls is seen as a substantial challenge to authority and to the viability of the sexual double standard.

Twenty years later, Donna Bishop and Charles Frazier also found that girls are more likely to be petitioned to court and punished for the status offense of incorrigibility than males; the differences, according to Bishop and Frazier, are "striking and dramatic."[89] Though boys are more likely to be petitioned to court and punished for criminal acts, girls are still disadvantaged if their behavior is viewed as morally incorrect by government officials.

■ ■ ■ ■ ■ ■ ■ ■ ■ ■ ■ ■ ■ ■ ■

SUMMARY

Female delinquency has become a topic of considerable interest to criminologists and other experts interested in youth crimes. The nature and extent of female delinquent activities have changed, and it appears that girls are now engaging in more frequent and serious illegal activity.

Attempts to discover the cause of female delinquency can be placed in a number of different categories. (See Table 8.1). Early efforts by Cesare Lombroso and W. I. Thomas and a later effort by Otto Pollak place the blame for female crime on the inherent biological nature of the female. Later, biosocial theorists viewed a girl's psychological makeup and family environment as important factors in her misbehavior. The adolescent female offender was portrayed as a troubled girl who lacked love at home and supportive peer relations. The female delinquent was viewed as a sexual offender whose criminal activities were linked to destructive relationships with men.

More recent views of female delinquency incorporate the changes brought about by the women's movement. It is argued by such experts as Freda Adler and Rita Simon that as the social and economic roles of women change, so will their crime patterns. While a number of research studies support this view, some theorists question its validity. Though the female crime rate has increased and female delinquency patterns now resemble those of male delinquency, the gender gap has not narrowed after more than a decade since the women's rights movement began. Hagan's power-control theory helps us understand why these differences exist and whether change may be forthcoming.

Debate also arises over the treatment girls receive at the hands of the juvenile justice system. Originally, it was thought that police treated girls with chivalry and protected them from the stigma of a delinquency label. Contemporary criminologists charge, however, that girls are actually discriminated against by agents of the justice system.

██ TABLE 8.1 Theories of Female Delinquency

THEORY	MAJOR PREMISE	STRENGTH
BIOSOCIAL	Physical and psychological differences between males and females may explain the differences in their delinquency rates. Most important are hormonal traits and genetic makeup.	Explains the significant differences between male and female violence rates, which exist even among at-risk youths.
SOCIALIZATION	Girls are socialized to be more dependent than boys. Girls who lack love and affection at home will seek substitutes in the streets.	Shows why females are likely to engage in status offenses, such as running away.
LIBERAL FEMINIST	Gender differences in the crime rate can be explained by the economic and social double standards that exist in American society. As educational, economic, and social differences between males and females evaporate, their delinquency rates should become similar.	Explains why female delinquency rates have risen faster than male delinquency rates.
RADICAL FEMINIST	Female delinquency is a result of oppressive conditions suffered by girls, including sex abuse, exploitation, and physical dominance by male authority figures. Capitalism favors male domination.	Shows how oppression and abuse lead to female delinquency.

KEY TERMS

masculinity hypothesis
menstruation
pregnancy
menopause
chivalry hypothesis
precocious sexuality
penis envy

premenstrual syndrome (PMS)
androgens
testosterone
Marxist feminists
radical feminists
power-control theory
egalitarian

QUESTIONS FOR DISCUSSION

1. Are girls delinquent for different reasons than boys? Do they have a unique set of problems?
2. Are girls the victims of unfairness at the hands of the justice system, or do they benefit from "chivalry"?
3. Do you believe that as sex roles become more homogenous, female delinquency will become identical to male delinquency in rate and type?
4. Does the sexual double standard still exist?
5. Are lower-class girls more strictly supervised than upper- and middle-class girls? Is control stratified across class lines?

NOTES

1. Roy Roberg, Foreword, in Meda Chesney-Lind and Randall Shelden, *Girls Delinquency and Juvenile Justice* (Belmont, Calif.: Wadsworth, 1992), p. x.

2. For a general review of this issue, see Kathleen Daly and Meda Chesney-Lind, "Feminism and Criminology," *Justice Quarterly* 5:497-538 (1988).

3. Douglas Smith and Raymond Paternoster, "The Gender Gap in Theories of Deviance: Issues and Evidence," *Journal of Research in Crime and Delinquency* 24:140-72 (1987).

4. Cesare Lombroso and William Ferrero, *The Female Offender* (New York: Philosophical Library, 1895).

5. Rita James Simon, *The Contemporary Woman and Crime* (Washington, D.C.: Government Printing Office, 1975).

6. Lombroso and Ferrero, *The Female Offender*.

7. Ibid., p. 122.

8. Ibid., pp. 51-52.

9. Ibid., p. 151.

10. Ibid., pp. 150-152.

11. Cyril Burt, *The Young Delinquent* (New York: Appleton, 1925); Warren Middleton, "Is There a Relation between Kleptomania and Female Periodicity in Neurotic Individuals?" *Psychology Clinic*, December 1933, pp. 232-47.

12. William Healy and Augusta Bronner, *Delinquents and Criminals, Their Making and Unmaking* (New York: Macmillan, 1926).

13. For a review, see Anne Campbell, *Girl Delinquents* (Oxford: Basic Blackwell, 1981), pp. 41-48.

14. William I. Thomas, *The Unadjusted Girl* (New York: Harper & Row, 1928).

15. Ibid., p. 109.

16. Otto Pollak, *The Criminality of Women* (Philadelphia: University of Pennsylvania Press, 1950).

17. Ibid., p. 158.

18. Ibid., p. 10.

19. Sheldon Glueck and Eleanor Glueck, *Five Hundred Delinquent Women* (New York: Knopf, 1934).

20. J. Cowie, V. Cowie, and E. Slater, *Delinquency in Girls* (London: Heinemann, 1968).

21. Anne Campbell, "On the Invisibility of the Female Delinquent Peer Group," *Women and Criminal Justice* 2:41-62 (1990).

22. Sigmund Freud, *An Outline of Psychoanalysis,* trans. James Strachey (New York: Norton, 1949), p. 278.

23. Dorie Klein, "The Etiology of Female Crime: A Review of the Literature," in Fred Adler and Rita Simon, eds., *The Criminology of Deviant Women* (Boston: Houghton Mifflin, 1979), pp. 69-71.

24. Phyliss Chesler, *Women and Madness* (Garden City, N.Y.: Doubleday, 1972); Karen Horney, *Feminine Psychology* (New York: Norton, 1967).

25. Peter Blos, "Preoedipal Factors in the Etiology of Female Delinquency," *Psychoanalytic Studies of the Child* 12:229-42 (1957).

26. Walter Bromberg, *Crime and the Mind* (New York: Macmillan, 1965), p. 350.

27. See, generally, Ralph Weisheit and Sue Mahan, *Women, Crime and Criminal Justice* (Cincinnati: Anderson Publishing, 1988).

28. Spencer Rathus, *Psychology, 3d ed.* (New York: Holt, Rinehart and Winston, 1987), p. 88.

29. See, generally, Katharina Dalton, *The Premenstrual Syndrome* (Springfield, Ill.: Charles C. Thomas, 1971).

30. Karen Paige, "Effects of Oral Contraceptives on Affective Fluctuations Associated with the Menstrual Cycle," *Psychosomatic Medicine* 33:515-37 (1971).

31. Julie Horney, "Menstrual Cycles and Criminal Responsibility," *Law and Human Nature* 2:25-36 (1978).

32. For a review, see Christy Miller Buchanan, Jacquelynne Eccles, and Jill Becker, "Are Adolescents the Victims of Raging Hormones? Evidence for Activational Effects of Hormones on Moods and Behavior at Adolescence," *Psychological Bulletin* 111:63-107 (1992). (Herein cited as "Raging Hormones".)

33. Avshalom Caspi, Donald Lyman, Terrie Moffitt, and Phil Silva, "Unraveling Girl's Delinquency: Biological, Dispositional, and Contextual Contributions to Adolescent Misbehavior," *Developmental Psychology* (in press, 1993).

34. Eleanor Maccoby and Carol Jacklin, *The Psychology of Sex Differences* (Palo Alto, Calif.: Stanford University Press, 1974).

35. Alan Booth and D. Wayne Osgood, "The Influence of Testosterone on Deviance in Adulthood : Assessing and Explaining the Relationship," *Criminology* 31:93-118 (1993).

36. Walter Gove, "The Effect of Age and Gender on Deviant Behavior: A Biopsychosocial Perspective," in A. S. Rossi, ed., *Gender and the Life Course* (New York: Aldine, 1985), pp. 115-44.

37. Lee Ellis, "Evolutionary and Neurochemical Causes of Sex Differences in Victimizing Behavior: Toward a Unified Theory of Criminal Behavior and Social stratification," *Social Science Information* 28:625-26 (1989).

38. D. H. Baucom, P. K. Besch, and S. Callahan, "Relationship between Testosterone Concentration, Sex Roles Identity, and Personality among Females," *Journal of Personality and Social Psychology* 48:1218-26 (1985).

39. Lee Ellis, "The Victimful-Victimless Crime Distinction and Seven Universal Demographic Correlates of Victimful Criminal Behavior," *Personality and Individual Differences* 9:525-48 (1988).

40. Eleanor Maccoby and Carol Jacklin, *The Psychology of Sex Differences* (Stanford, Calif.: Stanford University Press, 1974).

41. Ellis, "Evolutionary and Neurochemical Causes of Sex Differences in Victimizing Behavior," pp. 605-36.

42. Ann Frodi, J. Maccauley, and P. R. Thome, "Are Women Always Less Aggressive Than Men? A Review of the Experimental Literature," *Psychological Bulletin* 84:634-60 (1977).

43. Buchanan, Eccles, and Becker, "Raging Hormones," p. 94.

44. David Farrington, "Juvenile Delinquency," in John Coleman, ed., *The School Years* (London: Routledge, 1992), p. 133.

45. Ruth Morris, "Female Delinquents and Relational Problems," *Social Forces* 43 82-89: (1964).
46. Cowie, Cowie, and Slater, *Delinquency in Girls*, p, 27.
47. Gisela Konopka, *The Adolescent Girl in Conflict* (Englewood Cliffs, N.J.: Prentice-Hall, 1966).
48. Ibid., p. 40.
49. Peter Kratcoski and Lucille Kratcoski, *Juvenile Delinquency* (Englewood Cliffs, N.J.: Prentice-Hall, 1979), pp. 146-47.
50. Konopka, *The Adolescent Girl in Conflict*, p. 50.
51. Clyde Vedder and Dora Somerville, *The Delinquent Girl* (Springfield, Ill.: Charles C. Thomas, 1970).
52. Glueck and Glueck, *Five Hundred Delinquent Women*.
53. Ibid., p. 90.
54. Ruth Morris, "Female Delinquency and Relational Problems," *Social Forces* 43:82-89 (1964).
55. Ames Robey, Richard Rosenwal, John Small, and Ruth Lee, "The Runaway Girl: A Reaction to Family Stress," *American Journal of Orthopsychiatry* 34:763-67 (1964).
56. William Wattenberg and Frank Saunders, "Sex Differences among Juvenile Court Offenders," *Sociology and Social Research* 39:24-31 (1954).
57. Don Gibbons and Manzer Griswold, "Sex Differences among Juvenile Court Referrals," *Sociology and Social Research* 42:106-10 (1957).
58. Gordon Barker and William Adams, "Comparison of the Delinquencies of Boys and Girls," *Journal of Criminal Law, Criminology, and Police Science* 53:470-75 (1962).
59. Meda Chesney-Lind, "Girls' Crime and Women's Place: Toward a Feminist Model of Female Delinquency" (Paper presented at the American Society of Criminology meeting, Montreal, November 1987).
60. Ibid., p. 20.
61. Joan Moore, *Going Down to the Barrio: Homeboys and Homegirls in Change* (Philadelphia: Temple University Press, 1991), p. 93.
62. Ibid., p. 101.
63. Deborah Babcox and Madeline Belken, *Liberation: NOW* (New York: Dell, 1971).
64. Simon, *The Contemporary Woman and Crime;* Freda Adler, *Sisters in Crime* (New York: McGraw-Hill, 1975).
65. Adler, *Sisters in Crime*.
66. Ibid., p. 104.
67. Ibid., pp. 10-11.
68. Rita James Simon, "Women and Crime Revisited," *Social Science Quarterly* 56:658-63 (1976).
69. Ibid., pp. 660-61.
70. Roy Austin, "Women's Liberation and Increase in Minor, Major, and Occupational Offenses," *Criminology* 20:407-30 (1982).
71. Michael Hindelang, "Age, Sex, and the Versatility of Delinquency Involvements," *Social Forces* 14:525-34 (1971).
72. Martin Gold, *Delinquent Behavior in an American City* (Belmont, Calif.: Brooks/Cole, 1970), p. 118; John Clark and Edward Haurek, "Age and Sex Roles of Adolescents and Their Involvement in Misconduct: A Reappraisal," *Sociology and Social Research* 50:495-508 (1966); Nancy Wise, "Juvenile Delinquency in Middle-Class Girls," in E. Vaz, ed., *Middle Class Delinquency* (New York: Harper & Row, 1967), pp. 179-88; Gary Jensen and Raymond Eve, "Sex Differences in Delinquency: An Examination of Popular Sociological Explanations," *Criminology* 13:427-48 (1976).
73. Merry Morash, "Gender, Peer Group Experiences, and Seriousness of Delinquency," *Journal of Research in Crime and Delinquency* 23:43-67 (1986).
74. Margaret Farnworth, "Male-Female Differences in Delinquency in Minority-Group Sample," *Journal of Research in Crime and Delinquency* 21:191-212 (1986).
75. Beth Bjerregaard and Carolyn Smith, "Gender Differences in Gang Participation and Delinquency," *Journal of Quantitative Criminology* (in press, 1993).
76. Darrell Steffensmeier and Renee Hoffman Steffensmeier, "Trends in Female Delinquency," *Criminology* 18:62-85 (1980). See also idem, "Crime and the Contemporary Woman: An Analysis of Changing Levels of Female Property Crime, 1960-1975," *Social Forces* 57:566-84 (1978); Darrell Steffensmeier and Michael Cobb, "Sex Differences in Urban Arrest Patterns, 1934-1979," *Social Problems* 29:37-49 (1981).
77. Joseph Weis, "Liberation and Crime: The Invention of the New Female Criminal," *Crime and Social Justice* 1:17-27 (1976).
78. Carol Smart, "The New Female Offender: Reality or Myth?" *British Journal of Criminology* 19:50-59 (1979).
79. Julia Schwendinger and Herman Schwendinger, *Rape and Inequality* (Beverly Hills, Calif.: Sage, 1983).
80. For a review of feminist theory, see Sally Simpson, "Feminist Theory, Crime and Justice," *Criminology* 27:605-32 (1989).
81. Ibid., p. 611.
82. Center for Research on Women, *Secrets in Public: Sexual Harassment in Our Schools* (Wellesley, Mass.: Wellesley College, 1993).
83. Kathleen Daly and Meda Chesney-Lind, "Feminism and Criminology," *Justice Quarterly* 5:497-538 (1988).
84. James Messerschmidt, *Capitalism, Patriarchy and Crime* (Totowa, N.J.: Rowman and Littlefield, 1986); for a critique of this work, see Herman Schwendinger and Julia Schwendinger, "The World According to James Messerschmidt," *Social Justice* 15:123-45 (1988).
85. John Hagan, A. R. Gillis, and John Simpson, "The Class Structure and Delinquency: Toward a Power-Control Theory of Common Delinquent Behavior," *American Journal of Sociology* 90:1151-78 (1985); John Hagan, John Simpson, and A. R. Gillis, "Class in the Household: A Power-Control Theory of Gender and Delinquency," *American Journal of Sociology* 92:788-816 (1987).

86. Gary Jensen and Kevin Thompson, "What's Class Got to Do with It? A Further Examination of Power-Control Theory," *American Journal of Sociology* 95:1009-23 (1990); Kevin Thompson, "Gender and Adolescent Drinking Problems: The Effects of Occupational Structure," *Social Problems* 36:30-44 (1989). For some critical research, see Simon Singer and Murray Levine, "Power Control Theory, Gender and Delinquency: A Partial Replication with Additional Evidence on the Effects of Peers," *Criminology* 26:627-48 (1988).

87. John Hagan, A. R. Gillis, and John Simpson, "Clarifying and Extending Power Control Theory," *American Journal of Sociology* 95:1024-37 (1990).

88. Meda Chesney-Lind, "Judicial Enforcement of the Female Sex Role: The Family Court and the Female Delinquent," *Issues in Criminology* 8:51-59 (1973).

89. Donna Bishop and Charles Frazier, "Gender Bias in Juvenile Justice Processing: Implications of the JDDP Act," *Journal of Criminal Law and Criminology* 82:1162-86 (1992).

III

ENVIRONMENTAL INFLUENCES ON DELINQUENCY

■■■

C hildren's interactions with parents, peers, schools, and substance abuse are thought to exert a powerful influence on their involvement in delinquent activities. Kids who fail at home, at school, and in the neighborhood are considered prone to sustaining delinquent careers over the life course. Research indicates that chronic, persistent offenders are the ones most likely to experience educational failure, poor home life, and unsatisfactory peer relations.

These social relationships are certainly not simple ones and are subject to different interpretations. For example, there may be little question that educational underachievement is related to delinquency, but significant disagreement exists over the cause and direction of the relationship. A conflict theorist might view children's school failure as a consequence of class conflict and discrimination. A biosocial theorist may view it as a function of learning disabilities or some other neurological dysfunction. Although both experts conclude that children who do poorly in school are among the most likely to violate the law, their explanations of school failure and its relationship to delinquency are markedly different. Similarly, the influences of family life, substance abuse, and peer relations can also be viewed in a number of different ways, depending on the observer's orientation.

Beyond their theoretical importance, the family, the school, and the peer group occupy significant positions in daily social life. They can help insulate a child from delinquency or encourage illegal activities. Many delinquency prevention efforts focus on improving family relations, supporting educational achievement, and reducing substance abuse. If the family is believed to be a cause of delinquency, family counseling and therapy may be used to prevent delinquency. Similarly, gang control efforts have been made to counteract the influence of peer group pressure toward delinquency.

Part III contains four chapters devoted to the influences these critical social forces have on delinquency. Chapter 9 is devoted to the family; Chapter 10 focuses on the peer group and gang; Chapter 11 examines the relationship between education and delinquency; and Chapter 12 concerns substance abuse. Among the special topics considered are child abuse and neglect, school-based crime, gang control efforts, and the relationship between delinquency and drug abuse. ■

OUTLINE

THE FAMILY AND DELINQUENCY

■■■

*T*he family is the key social institution for providing the nurturant socialization of young children.[1]

There seems to be little disagreement that family relationships are a pivotal determinant of adolescent behavior through the life-course (see Table 9.1). Children growing up in a household characterized by abuse, conflict, and tension, whose parents are absent or separated, and who lack familial love and support will be the ones most likely to engage in violence and delinquency.[2] Conversely, the effects of a supportive family life can be very beneficial to children in any social environment or group. Even those children living in so-called high-crime areas are better able to resist the temptation of the streets if they receive fair discipline, care, and support from parents who provide them with strong, positive role models.[3] The relationship between family life and delinquency is not unique

■■ **TABLE 9.1**   Theoretical Views on the Family and Delinquency

CHOICE	Parents who do not teach children the consequences of rule-violating behavior will encourage them to be law violators. Parents may promote delinquent behavior choices by encouraging success at any cost; "greed is good."
BIOSOCIAL AND PSYCHOLOGICAL	The predisposition to commit crime may be inherited or encouraged by such elements as diet and living conditions. Some delinquency-promoting traits, such as low intelligence and impulsivity, may be inherited.[22] Family interaction influences personality traits that have been associated with delinquent behavior.[23]
SOCIAL STRUCTURE	The environment children grow up in is controlled by their family's socioeconomic position. The makeup of the family may be controlled by economic conditions. Strain may be produced when families are unable to provide children with the means to achieve socially defined goals.
SOCIAL PROCESS	The attachment of children to their family will negate delinquency-promoting inducements. Children who participate in family activities will be less likely to get involved with deviant peers and groups. Children may learn deviant values from parents.[24] Impulsivity is exacerbated by poor family relations and a lack of discipline.
SOCIAL REACTION	Some youths are actually labeled as deviants within their own family and made to feel like outcasts. Socioeconomic class position controls both the family's economic well-being and its child-rearing practices. Lower-class families are paternalistic and tend to control girls more than boys, freeing the latter to engage in delinquency.

to American culture; cross-national data supports a significant association between family variables and delinquency.[4]

The assumed relationship between delinquency and family life is critical today because the traditional American family is rapidly changing. Extended families, once common because of the economic necessity of sharing housing with many family members, are now for the most part an anachronism. In their place is the isolated *nuclear family*, described as a "dangerous hot-house of emotions" because of the intensely close contact between parents and children; in these families, problems are unrelieved by contact with other kin living nearby.[5]

The nuclear family is showing signs of breakdown. Much of the parental responsibility for child rearing is delegated to baby-sitters, television, and day-care providers. Despite such changes, some families are able to adapt and continue functioning as healthy and caring units, producing well-adjusted children. Others have crumbled under the burden of stress, with severely damaging effects on the present and future lives of their children.[6] This is particularly true when child abuse and neglect become part of family life.

Because these domestic issues are so critical for understanding juvenile delinquency, this chapter is devoted to an analysis of the family's role as a delinquency-producing or -inhibiting social institution. The chapter first covers the changing face of the American family. It then reviews how family structure and function influence delinquent behavior. The relationship between child abuse and neglect is then covered in some depth. Finally, programs designed to improve family functioning are briefly reviewed.

THE CHANGING AMERICAN FAMILY

The concept of the American family is changing. The traditional concept of the family in which there is a male breadwinner and a female who cares for the

■ ■ ■ ■ ■ ■ ■ ■ ■ ■ ■ ■ ■ ■ ■

The family is the key social institution for providing proper socialization of young children. Parents who provide children with positive role models can insulate them from delinquency.

home and the children is a thing of the past. No longer can the **paternalistic family** depicted in the 1960s television sitcoms "Father Knows Best" and "Ozzie and Harriet" be considered the norm; the TV character Murphy Brown, lambasted in the media by former Vice-President Dan Quayle during the 1992 presidential campaign because she chose to have a child as a single woman, is a better reflection of the modern American family.

The very structure and definition of the family are undergoing change. The divorce rate is now about one for every two new marriages.[7] Children of divorce often feel "caught" between their parents, especially in families marked by high levels of hostility and low levels of cooperation; feeling caught or trapped is related to adjustment problems and later deviant behavior.[8]

As Figure 9.1 shows, about 70 percent of all mothers of school-age children are now employed, up from 50 percent in 1970 and 40 percent in 1960.[9] Slightly more than half of all mothers with infants under 1 year old are employed outside the home; by 1995, there will be 14.6 million preschool children and 37.4 million school-age children whose mothers work outside the home.[10]

People are waiting longer to marry and are having fewer children. Single-parent households have become common. Today in the United States, every 32 seconds, a 15- to 19-year-old woman becomes pregnant; every 31 seconds, a child is born to an unmarried mother; the number of children born outside of marriage is steadily increasing.[11] In 1970, 12 percent of children lived with one parent; today, that number is about 25 percent. More single women than ever are deciding to keep and raise their children.

Charged with caring for children is a day-care system whose workers are often paid minimum wage. Of special concern are the hundreds of thousands of *family day-care homes* in which a single provider takes care of three to nine children. Several states do not license or monitor these small private providers. Even in

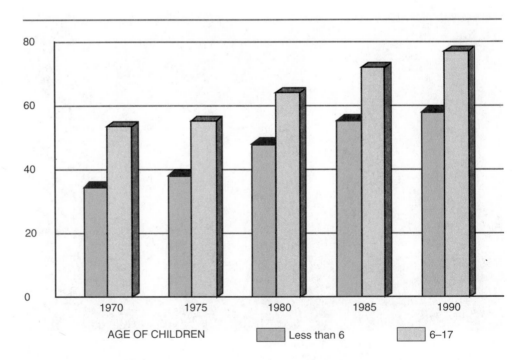

■■FIGURE 9.1

Mothers in the paid labor force, 1970–1990

Source: U.S. Department of Labor, Bureau of Labor Statistics, *Handbook of Labor Statistics,* bull. 2340 (Washington, DC: Government Printing Office, 1989), p. 244, tables 56 and 57; U.S. Department of Labor, Bureau of Labor Statistics, unpublished data from March 1990 Current Population Survey. *Beyond Rhetoric,* p. 7.

Part III Environmental Influences on Delinquency

those states that do mandate registration and inspection of day care providers, it is estimated that 90 percent or more of the facilities operate "underground." It is not uncommon for one adult to care for eight infants, an impossible task regardless of training or concern; the development of many children in day care is being compromised.[12]

Economic Stress

The American family is also undergoing economic hardships. The Census Bureau estimates that the child poverty rate is about 20 percent, effecting some 13 million children.[13] A number of national organizations suggest that these figures are too low. A study by the National Research Council indicates that close to 40 percent of black families and 20 percent of white families live below the poverty line.[14] The council also estimates that one out of six white children and one out of two black children live in poverty; 44 percent of black families and 13 percent of white families were headed by a single mother.[15] The plight of these single

■ ■ ■ ■ ■ ■ ■ ■ ■ ■ ■ ■ ■ ■ ■

The paternalistic two-parent family is no longer the norm. The number of children living with one parent has doubled since 1970. Children today are likely to be cared for by a grandparent, guardian, or non-related caretaker.

parents is extremely desperate: about one-fifth of all single mothers have incomes *50 percent less than the poverty line* (less than fifty-five hundred dollars annually for a family of three).[16]

How do families cope with these problems? According to the Children's Defense Fund, the vast majority are forced to live in hazardous housing, forgo regular health care, weigh paying utility bills against other necessities, cut down on the size of meals or skip some altogether, and place children in substandard child care. Those whose income places them above the poverty line are deprived of government assistance that might help children develop into productive adults.[17]

Will family stress be reduced in the coming years? As Figure 9.2 shows, the percentage of youth in the population is steadily declining while the number of senior citizens is increasing. As people retire, there will be fewer workers to pay the Social Security, medical, and nursing home bills. These costs will put greater economic stress on already burdened American families.

The Effects of Stress and Conflict

Stress and conflict in the family have been linked to delinquency. Family stress makes it likely that many parents will act destructively toward their children. Abuse and neglect of children have become widespread and serious problems in the United States. Each year, 1 million children or more are maltreated in a variety of ways, ranging from gross neglect and starvation to overt physical and mental cruelty.[18] Juvenile courts throughout the nation annually hear approximately half a million child neglect and abuse cases. As child abuse experts Richard Gelles and Murray Straus put it:

Parent-to-child violence is so common and so widely approved that one needs few case studies to make the point. In general, the large majority of Americans believes that

FIGURE 9.2

Children and the elderly as a proportion of the U.S. population

*Middle series projections
Source: U.S Department of Commerce, Bureau of the Census, *Current Population Reports,* ser. p-25, no. 1018, *Projections of the Population of the United States by Age, Sex, and Race: 1988–2080* (Washington, DC: Government Printing Office, 1989), p. 8, table G. In *Beyond Rhetoric,* p. 5.

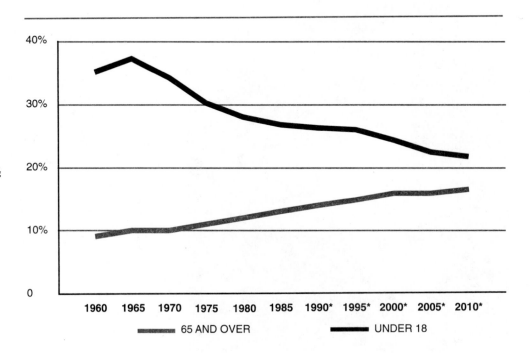

Part III   Environmental Influences on Delinquency

good parenting requires some physical punishment. . . . Among the thousands of people we have interviewed, it was the absence of physical punishment that was thought to be deviant, not the hitting of children.[19]

Children who are the victims of abuse suffer physical and psychological damage both when the abuse takes place and later in life. Evidence supports a link between the abuse of young children and their subsequent violent and aggressive behavior as juvenile delinquents and status offenders.

It is believed that a destructive and disturbed home environment can have such a significant impact on socialization because the family is the primary unit in which children learn the values, attitudes, and processes that guide their actions throughout their lives. Experts in the fields of juvenile delinquency, sociology, and psychology generally agree that "it is the social interaction between the child and those in its immediate environment that constitutes the vast majority of the steps contributing to the production of a healthy and normal young person. . . . The learning process is enhanced by environmental stimulation, . . . but the central developmental relationship occurs within the family."[20] Considering the significance of the family in the early development of children, it is not surprising that a national study group found:

Family life that is shattered by episodes of physical or emotional mistreatment may breed feelings of rejection among children and retard the youngsters' normal development. Thus, programs designed to insure that all children are raised in home situations beneficial to their healthy growth should be a major component of a community delinquency prevention plan.[21]

THE FAMILY'S INFLUENCE ON DELINQUENCY

Most delinquency experts agree that the family is a frontline defense against delinquency. A disrupted family life may encourage any preexisting criminogenic forces and sustain delinquency over the life course. The relationship is complex and varies between racial and ethnic groups. Research by Carolyn Smith and Marvin Krohn indicates that Hispanic youths are more deeply influenced by family processes than African-American or white youths; family hardship has a greater effect on the behavior of white than on African American youths.[25]

Four broad categories of family functioning seem to promote delinquent behavior: families disrupted by spousal conflict or breakup (broken homes); families involved in interpersonal conflict (quality of family life; family conflict); families that neglect their children's behavior and emotional problems (supervision and discipline, family size); and families that contain deviant parents who may transmit their behavior to children (parental criminality).[26] (See Figure 9.3). Each of these factors may interact to intensify individual effects; for example, family conflict may lead to child neglect and eventual marital breakup. We now turn to the specific types of family problems that have been linked to delinquent behavior.

Family Breakup: Broken Homes

One of the most enduring controversies in the study of juvenile delinquency is the relationship between a parent being absent from the home and the onset of delinquent behavior. Research indicates that parents whose marriage is secure,

Family influences on behavior Each of these four factors have been linked to anti-social behavior and delinquency. Interaction between these factors may escalate delinquent activity.

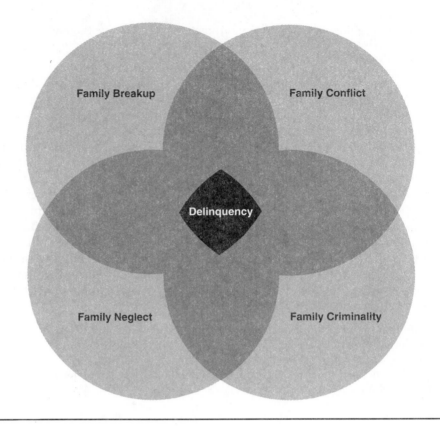

who maintain communications and avoid conflict also produce children who are secure and independent.[27] In contrast, children growing up in a home filled with conflict that leads to divorce and disruption may be prone to antisocial behavior. A number of prominent delinquency experts have contended that a **broken home** is a strong determinant of a child's law-violating behavior. The connection seems self-evident, since a child is first socialized at home and from the beginning learns behaviors, values, and beliefs from parents. Any disjunction in an orderly family structure should have a negative impact on the child's life. Family breakup is related to such delinquency-promoting factors as greater autonomy, lax supervision, weakened attachment, and greater susceptibility to peer pressure.[28] The broken home-delinquency relationship is acute because if current trends continue, less than half of all children born today will live continuously with their own mother and father throughout childhood. And because step-families are less stable than families consisting of two biological parents, an increasing number of children will experience family breakup two or even three times during childhood.[29]

A number of clinical studies of youth who have experienced family breakup indicate they are more likely to demonstrate behavior problems, inappropriate conduct, and hyperactivity when compared to children in intact families.[30] Family breakup is often associated with discord, conflict, hostility, and aggression—factors also associated with a delinquent orientation.

Broken Home Research

The relationship between broken homes and delinquency was established in early research conducted by Ashley Weeks and by Sheldon Glueck and Eleanor Glueck.[31] Parental absence seemed to affect girls and white youths more than males and minorities.[32] Children from affluent homes seemed more deeply affected by parental absence than lower-class children.[33]

Despite the strong hypothetical case linking broken homes to delinquency, the bulk of empirical research on the matter has been inconclusive. The early studies that established the link between broken homes and delinquency used the records of police, courts, and correctional institutions.[34] This research may be tainted by sampling bias: youths from broken homes may get arrested, petitioned to juvenile court, and institutionalized more often than youths from intact families, but this does not necessarily mean that they actually engage in more frequent and serious delinquent behavior. Official statistics may reflect the fact that agents of the justice system treat children from disrupted households more severely because they cannot call on parents for support. The juvenile courts' *parens patriae* philosophy calls for official intervention when parental supervision is considered inadequate.

This revisionist view was supported in early works of Clifford Shaw and Henry McKay, who were among the first to provide important evidence that broken homes were not necessarily related to delinquency. They found that the proportion of children living in broken homes in a sample taken from the general population (36 percent) was not significantly different from that found in samples of known delinquents (42 percent).[35]

Numerous subsequent studies, using both official and self-report data, have failed to establish any clear-cut relationship between broken homes and delinquent behavior.[36] Boys and girls from intact families seem as likely to *self-report* delinquency as those whose parents are divorced or separated. Children from broken homes are still more likely to show up in the official statistics. Researchers conclude that the absence of parents has a greater effect on agents of the justice system than it does on the behavior of children.

Broken Homes Reconsidered

In a well-known work, Lawrence Rosen and Kathleen Neilson reviewed the literature on the subject and concluded: "The concept of broken homes, no matter how it is defined or measured, has little explanatory power in terms of delinquency."[37] This statement represents the consensus of opinion today on the connection between broken homes and delinquency. As a result, the focus of recent research efforts has been on other aspects of the parent-child relationship.

Although researchers have not found a definite relationship between a broken home and delinquency, it may be premature to dismiss the relationship as spurious. A number of recent studies have found that family breakup may have at least an indirect influence on adolescent misbehavior. Among the recent findings are the following:

■ Family structure is linked to rebellious acts, such as running away and truancy. Reviewing fifty prior studies on family structure and delinquency, L. Edward Wells and Joseph Rankin found that (a) the prevalence of delinquency is 10 to

15 percent higher in broken homes than in intact homes and (b) the relationship between broken homes and delinquency is strongest for status-type offenses and weakest for serious delinquencies.[38] If broken homes are in fact related to status offenses and not delinquency, the relationship may be caused by weakened parental control and supervision.[39]

■ James Q. Wilson and Richard Herrnstein claim that even if single mothers (or fathers) can make up for the loss of a second parent, it is simply difficult to do so and the chances of failure are great.[40] Care givers in single-parent households who maintain high levels of supervision help reduce the likelihood that their children will have police contacts.[41] Single parents may find it difficult to provide adequate supervision.

■ Evidence exists that children who live with single parents receive less encouragement and less help with schoolwork. Children in two-parent households are more likely to want to go on to college than kids in single-parent homes.[42] Poor school achievement and limited educational aspirations have been associated with delinquent behavior. Single parents who become involved in their children's education may counteract this effect and help improve their children's school achievement.

The relationship between broken homes and delinquency then may be more complex than previously believed. It is also possible that both are related to some external factor that is responsible for the presence of *both* conditions. White single mothers find that their income declines about 30 percent, to an average of $13,500, after divorce; nonwhite single mothers average $9,000 annually. Many divorced mothers are forced to move to cheaper residences located in deteriorated, disorganized neighborhoods. Mary Pat Traxler found in a study of African-American boys that the social and economic conditions in slum areas—poverty, unemployment, alienation—may be the cause of *both* delinquent behaviors and marital breakup.[43]

Family Conflict

Not all unhappy marriages end in divorce. Some continue in an atmosphere of discord and conflict; *intrafamily conflict* is an all too common experience in many American families.[44] The link between parental conflict and delinquency was established almost forty years ago, when pioneering research by F. Ivan Nye found that a child's perception of his or her parents' marital happiness was a significant predictor of self-reported delinquency.[45]

Contemporary studies have also found that children who grow up in maladapted homes and who witness violence and conflict later exhibit patterns of emotional disturbance, behavior problems, and social conflict.[46] There seems to be little difference between the behavioral patterns of children who merely *witness* intrafamily violence and those who are its victims.[47]

Research efforts have consistently supported the relationship between family conflict, hostility, low warmth and affection, and delinquency.[48] Jill Leslie Rosenbaum found that the family background of incarcerated female delinquents was almost universally dysfunctional; some of the homes were described as "an animal-like environment."[49] Parents of **beyond control** youngsters have been found to be inconsistent rule-setters, to be less likely to praise, encourage, and show interest in their children, and to display high levels of hostile detachment.[50]

While negative parent-child relationships are generally associated with delinquency, it is difficult to assess the causal relationship. While it is often assumed that preexisting family problems cause delinquency, it may also be true that acting-out children put enormous stress on a family, causing even more problems to emerge.[51] Adolescent misbehavior may *cause* parental conflict, which produces increased family stress, leading to even greater misconduct, on and on in an endless loop.[52]

Family Conflict versus Broken Homes

Which is worse, growing up in a home marked by extreme conflict or growing up in a broken home? Should parents stay together "for the sake of the children"? Paul Amato and Bruce Keith reviewed the literature on divorce and family conflict and found that children in both "broken homes" and high-conflict intact families were, as might be expected, considerably worse off than children in low-conflict, intact families.[53] However, children in high-conflict families also exhibited lower levels of adjustment and well-being than did children in divorced families; family conflict, then, may have a *more damaging* effect on children than divorce. Amato and Keith's other findings include:

- Children growing up in families disrupted by parental death are better adjusted than children of divorce. Parental absence is not a per se cause of antisocial behavior.
- Remarriage did not mitigate the effects of divorce on youth: children living with a stepparent exhibit (a) as many problems as youths in divorce situations and (b) considerably more problems than do children living with both biological parents.

Family conflict, lack of communication and inconsistent discipline all have been linked to delinquent behavior.

■ Continued contact with the noncustodial parent has little effect on a child's well-being.

■ Evidence that children of divorce improve over time is inconclusive.

■ Post-divorce conflict between parents is related to child maladjustment.

Should parents stay together "for the sake of the children"? Amato and Keith suggest that divorce is harmful but family conflict may have a more negative impact on children than family separation.

The Quality of Parent-Child Relations

It is believed that children need a warm, close, supportive relationship with their parents. Researchers have found that youths who lack closeness with their parents or perceive a lack of family cohesiveness are the ones most likely to engage in delinquent acts and status offenses.[54] Some studies indicate that maternal relations regulate delinquent activity, while others point to the paternal relationship as the key factor.[55] Joan McCord has found that "competent" mothers who are self-confident, nonpunitive, affectionate, and leaders are able to insulate their children from delinquency in even the most deteriorated urban neighborhoods.[56] McCord found that paternal relationships take on greater importance later on in the life course. Adolescents best able to avoid delinquent involvement report having unaggressive, nonviolent fathers who hold their wives in high esteem.

A number of independent research studies support the link between the quality of family life and delinquency. Children who feel inhibited with their parents and therefore refuse to discuss important issues with them are more likely to engage in deviant activities (such as smoking marijuana). Poor child-parent communications have been related to the child running away and subsequently entering the ranks of homeless street kids who get involved in theft and prostitution to survive.[57]

Parent-child relations that are cold and distant have also been linked to the likelihood that the children will have police contacts.[58] Research of the factors distinguishing samples of incarcerated youths from the general population shows that they lack a warm, loving, supportive relationship with their fathers and have families characterized by minimal paternal involvement with children.[59] John Laub and Robert Sampson found that the quality of family life, including measures of supervision, attachment to parents, and discipline, are far more important predictors of delinquent or conforming behavior than measures of family structure (such as absent parents, large families, or family income).[60] And David Farrington's analysis of the data from his London-based longitudinal cohort study found that at-risk youths who were able to avoid criminality had supportive mothers who reinforced their sons' favorable self-concept.[61]

Discipline and Supervision

Studies using both self-report and official samples show that the parents of delinquent youth tend to be inconsistent disciplinarians or are overly harsh or extremely lenient in their disciplinary practices.[62]

The link between discipline and deviant behavior is still uncertain. Most Americans still support the use of corporal punishment to discipline children, and attitudes toward physical discipline have changed little during the past twenty-five years. The use of physical punishment cuts across racial, ethnic, and religious groups. In fact, corporal punishment is actually used more often in families with strong religious orientations because devout parents believe that (a) human nature is sinful and (b) sin deserves punishment.[63]

Good intentions notwithstanding, there is growing evidence of a "violence begetting violence" interaction. Children who are subject to even minimum amounts of physical punishment may be more likely to use violence themselves in personal interactions. Murray Straus reviewed the concept of discipline in a series of cross-sectional surveys and found a powerful relationship between exposure to physical punishment and later aggression throughout the life course.[64] Physical punishment weakens the bond between parent and child, lowers the child's self-esteem, labels him or her "bad," and undermines his or her faith in justice. It is not surprising, then, that Straus finds a high correlation between exposure to physical discipline and street crime.

Evidence also exists that uncertain and inconsistent supervision and discipline can promote delinquency. Youths who believe that their parents care little about their activities and companions are more likely to engage in criminal acts than those who believe that their actions will be closely supervised. In his early

---

■■

FOCUS ON DELINQUENCY

Disciplining Parents

Since parental control and discipline are assumed to be related to youthful misbehavior, it is not surprising that some jurisdictions have actually punished parents for their children's misconduct. The initial approach was to create laws disciplining parents for "contributing to the delinquency of a minor." The first of these statutes was enacted in Colorado in 1903, and today, forty-two states and the District of Columbia maintain similar laws. As a group, such "contributing" laws allow parents to be sanctioned in juvenile courts for behaviors associated with or suspected of encouraging their child's delinquency.

A second approach has been to make parents civilly liable for the actions of their minor children. This might include having parents pay for damage caused by their children who vandalized a school. All states except New Hampshire have incorporated parental liability laws within their statutes, though most recent legislation places limits on recovery somewhere between the $250 of Vermont and the $15,000 of Texas; the average is $2,500.

Some states now also make parents criminally liable for the actions of their children. Since 1990, there have been more than eighteen cases in which parents have been ordered to serve time in jail because their children have

been truant from school. In May 1992, a judge in Elgin, Illinois, sentenced a mother to thirty days in jail for failing to keep her second-grader in school. In California, a 1988 antigang law allows judges to sentence parents to up to a year in jail if they fail to exercise sufficient care to prevent their children from engaging in delinquent acts. A judge in Patterson, New Jersey, has ordered fifteen parents to serve time in classrooms with their chronically truant children.

Whether such measures are legal and effective remains to be seen. Civil libertarians charge that they violate the constitutional right to due process and seem to be used only against lower-class parents. The California law has been successfully challenged in the lower courts. Criminologists Gilbert Geis and Arnold Binder find little evidence that punishing parents can deter delinquency and conclude that laws sanctioning parents are not only misguided and inadequate but can be described as "nasty and vicious." ■

Source: Gilbert Geis and Arnold Binder, "Sins of Their Children: Parental Responsibility for Juvenile Delinquency," *Notre Dame Journal of Law, Ethics, and Public Policy* 5: 303–22 (1991); Christi Harlan and Arthur Hayes, "Jailing Parents," *Wall Street Journal,* 18 May 1992, p. B6.

research, F. Ivan Nye found that mothers who threatened discipline but failed to carry it out were more likely to have delinquent children than those who were consistent in their discipline.[65] Contemporary research efforts find that assaultive boys can be characterized as growing up in homes in which there are poor problem-solving skills and inconsistent discipline.[66] John Laub and Robert Sampson report that substance-abusing or criminal parents are the ones most likely to use harsh and inconsistent discipline.[67]

In sum, significant evidence exists that both inconsistent and overly harsh discipline are significant predictors of delinquent behavior.[68]

Family Size

Parents may find it hard to control and discipline their children because they have such large families that economic and time resources are spread too thin. Larger families are more likely to produce delinquents than smaller ones, and middle children are more likely to engage in delinquent acts than first- or last-born children. Criminologists attribute this phenomenon to the stretched resources of the large family and the relatively limited supervision parents can provide for each child. Research now shows that relatively affluent, two-wage earner families are having fewer children, while indigent, single-parent households are growing larger; children are at a greater risk today of being poor because indigent families are the ones most likely to have more children![69]

Middle children may suffer because they are the most likely to be home when large numbers of siblings are also at home and economic resources are the most stressed.[70] While family size has not been linked to deviant behavior per se, larger families may run a greater risk of disruption and conflict.[71]

Parental Criminality

A number of studies have found that parental criminality and deviance have a powerful influence on delinquent behavior.[72] As John Laub and Robert Sampson state:

Parental deviance of both mother and father strongly disrupts family processes of social control, which in turn increases delinquency.[73]

Some of the most important data was gathered by Donald J. West and David P. Farrington as part of the long-term Cambridge Youth Survey. Their longitudinal life course research (see Chapter 3) indicates that a significant number of delinquent youths have fathers who engage in criminal behavior themselves.[74] While *8.4 percent* of the sons of noncriminal fathers eventually became chronic offenders, about *37 percent* of youths with criminal fathers were multiple offenders.[75] In a more recent analysis, Farrington found that one type of parental deviance, "bullying," may be both inter- and intragenerational. Bullies have children who bully others, and these "second-generation bullies" grow up to become the fathers of children who are also bullies, in a never-ending cycle.[76]

The cause of intergenerational deviance is still uncertain. It is possible that environmental, genetic, psychological, or child-rearing factors are responsible for the linkage between generations. The quality of family life may be the key: criminal parents should be the ones *least* likely to have close, intimate relationships with their offspring. Perhaps the link is related to stigma: social control agents may be quick to fix a delinquent label on the children of known law violators; "the acorn," the reasoning goes, "does not fall far from the tree."[77]

So while there is some agreement that criminal parents produce delinquent offspring, there is by no means certainty about the nature and causal direction of the relationship.[78]

Siblings

Most research on the family's influence on delinquency is directed at parental effects. Some evidence exists that siblings may also have an important influence on behavior. In a recent paper, David Rowe and Bill Gulley found that sibling pairs who report warm, mutual relationships and share friends were the most likely to behave in a similar fashion. Sibling pairs who maintain a close relationship also had similar rates of drug abuse and delinquency.[79]

Though a number of interpretations of this data are possible (for example, deviant siblings grow closer because of shared interests), Rowe and Gulley believe that the relationship is due to interpersonal interactions: older siblings and their peers are admired and imitated by the younger siblings. What seems to be a genetic effect may actually be the result of warm and close sibling interaction.

In sum, what has developed from the research on delinquency and family relationships is a picture of family life that does little to support and much to hinder a growing child's development. The delinquent child grows up in a large family and has parents who may drink, participate in criminal acts, be harsh and inconsistent disciplinarians, be cold and unaffectionate, have marital conflicts, and be poor role models. The *quality* of a child's family life seems more important than its structure.

CHILD ABUSE AND NEGLECT

Family violence—particularly violence against children—is a critical priority for criminal justice officials, political leaders and the public we serve.[80]

Concern about the quality of family life has recently increased because of the disturbing reports that many children are physically abused and neglected by their parents and that this harsh treatment has serious consequences for their future behavior. Because of this topic's great importance, the remainder of this chapter is devoted to this issue of child abuse and neglect and its relationship to delinquent behavior.

Historical Foundation

Parental abuse and neglect is not a modern phenomenon. From infanticide to severe physical beatings for disciplinary purposes, maltreatment of children has occurred throughout history. Some concern for the negative effects of such maltreatment was voiced in the eighteenth century in the United States, but concerted efforts to deal with the problem of endangered children did not begin until 1874.

In that year, residents of a New York City apartment building reported to a public health nurse, Etta Wheeler, that a child in one of the apartments was

In 1874 Henry Bugh and Etta Angell Wheeler persuaded a New York court to take a child, Mary Ellen, away from her mother on the grounds of child abuse. This is the first recorded case in which a court was used to protect a child. Mary Ellen is shown at age 9 when she appeared in court showing bruises from a whipping and several gashes from a pair of scissors. The other photograph shows her a year later.

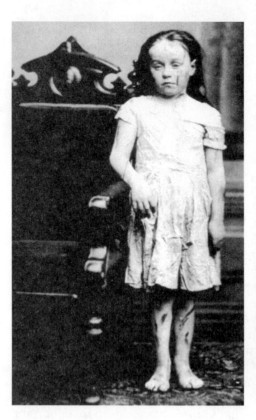

being abused by her stepmother. The nurse found a young child named Mary Ellen Wilson who was repeatedly beaten and chained to her bed and was malnourished from a continuous diet of bread and water. The child was obviously seriously ill, but the police agreed with her parents that the law entitled them to raise Mary Ellen as they saw fit; the New York City Department of Charities claimed it had no custody right over Mary Ellen.

According to legend, Mary Ellen's removal from her parents had to be arranged through the Society for Prevention of Cruelty to Animals (SPCA) on the ground that she was a member of the animal kingdom, which the SPCA was founded to protect. According to sociologists Richard Gelles and Claire Pedrick Cornell, the truth is less sensational: Mary Ellen's case was heard by a judge because the child needed protection; she eventually was placed in an orphanage.[81]

The case and subsequent jail sentence for Mary Ellen's stepmother received a great deal of press coverage. Not coincidentally, the Society for Prevention of Cruelty to Children was founded the following year, marking the extension of humane organizations from animals to humans.[82]

The Battered Child Syndrome

In the twentieth century, little legal or medical research into the problems of maltreated children occurred before the work of Dr. C. Henry Kempe of the University of Colorado. In 1962, Kempe reported the results of a survey of medical and law enforcement agencies that indicated that the child abuse rate was much higher than had been thought. He coined a new term, the **battered**

child syndrome, which he applied to cases of nonaccidental physical injury of children by their parents or guardians.[83] Kempe's work sparked a flurry of research into the problems of the battered child, and a network of law enforcement, medical, and social service agencies was formed to deal with battered children.[84]

Professionals dealing with such children soon discovered the limitations of Kempe's definition as they came face to face with a wide range of physical and emotional abuse inflicted on children by their parents. As Kempe himself recognized in 1976,

The term "battered child" has been dropped. . . . When coined 15 years ago, its purpose was to gain the attention of both physicians and the public. We feel, now, that enough progress has been made to move on to a more inclusive phrase—child abuse and neglect. The problem is clearly not just one of *physical* battering. Save for the children who are killed or endure permanent brain damage . . . the most devastating aspect of abuse and neglect is the permanent adverse effects on the developmental process and the child's emotional well-being.[85]

Kempe's pioneering efforts paved the way for a national consciousness on child abuse.

ABUSE AND NEGLECT

The definition of battered children has expanded, and the term **child abuse** is now a generic expression that includes neglect as well as overt physical beating. Specifically, it now describes any physical or emotional trauma to a child for which no reasonable explanation, such as an accident or ordinary disciplinary practices, can be found. Child abuse is generally seen as a pattern of behavior, rather than a single beating or act of neglect. The effects of a pattern of behavior are cumulative. That is, the longer the abuse continues, the more severe the effect on the child.[86]

Although the terms *child abuse* and **neglect** are sometimes used interchangeably, they represent different forms of maltreatment. *Neglect* is the more passive term, referring to deprivations that children suffer at the hands of their parents— lack of food, shelter, health care, and love. *Abuse,* on the other hand, is a more overt form of physical aggression against the child, one that often requires medical attention. Yet the distinction between the two terms is often unclear. In many cases, both occur simultaneously.

Legally, each state has its own definition of child abuse. Despite the variety of these definitions, they all contain a combination of two or more of the following components:

- Nonaccidental physical injury
- Physical neglect
- Emotional abuse or neglect
- Sexual abuse
- Abandonment[87]

Physically harmful action by parents includes throwing, shooting, stabbing, burning, drowning, suffocating, biting, and deliberately disfiguring their children. The greatest number of injuries result from beatings with various kinds of implements and instruments. Some children have been strangled or suffocated with pillows held over their mouths or plastic bags thrown over their heads; a number have been drowned in bathtubs.[88]

Physical neglect results from parents' failure to provide adequate food, shelter, or medical care for their children, as well as failure to protect them from physical danger. Emotional abuse or neglect frequently accompanies physical abuse; it is manifested by constant criticism and rejection of the child, who as a result loses self-esteem.[89] Sexual abuse refers to the exploitation of children through rape, incest, and molestation by parents, family members, friends, or legal guardians. Finally, abandonment refers to the situation in which parents physically leave their children with the intention of completely severing the parent-child relationship.[90]

SEXUAL ABUSE

One aspect of child abuse that has become an issue of growing national concern is sexual abuse. Sexual abuse can vary in content and style. It may range from rewarding a child for sexual behavior that is inappropriate for his or her level of development, to using force or the threat of force for the purposes of sex. Sexual abuse can involve children who are well aware of the sexual content of their actions and others too young to have any real idea of what their actions mean. It can involve a variety of acts from inappropriate touching and fondling to forcible sexual penetration.

The effect of sexual abuse can be devastating. Abused children suffer disrupted ego development and personality development.[91] Guilt and shame are commonly experienced by survivors, and psychological trauma sometimes continues into adulthood. The ego of the victim may be overwhelmed by rage and horror over the incident.[92] David Finkelhor and Angela Browne of the Family Violence Research Program at the University of New Hampshire have described the aftermath of sexual abuse as involving one of four dynamics:

- **traumatic sexualization**—the process in which a child's sexual identity is shaped in an inappropriate and dysfunctional way by the result of the abuse episode.
- **betrayal**—the discovery by abused children that someone whom they trusted and on whom they are dependent caused them harm.
- **powerlessness**—the process in which the child's will, desires, and sense of competence are negated.
- **stigmatization**—the negative connotations, such as shame and guilt, that are communicated to children around their experiences and that then become incorporated into their self-image.[93]

The victims of child sexual abuse and their families can experience a number of postabuse traumas. The mothers of abused children experience severe psychological symptoms, including depression and other forms of psychopathology.[94] Traumatic sexualization can lead young victims into such diverse behavior patterns as victimizing their peers, acting in a promiscuous and compulsive fashion, experiencing aversion to sex, or trading sex for affection.[95] Victims commonly suffer frightening hallucinations, nightmares, and periods of profound rage.[96] Some victims find themselves sexualizing their own children in ways that lead them to sexual or physical abuse. Several studies have found a close association of sexual abuse and adolescent prostitution.[97] (see the following Focus on Delinquency entitled "Juvenile Prostitution").

The effects of sexual abuse can be devastating. Victims suffer guilt and shame, disrupted development and personality disorders.

In an important review of forty-five studies of the impact of sexual abuse, Kathleen Kendall-Tackett and her associates found that sexually abused children demonstrate symptoms including posttraumatic stress syndrome, precocious sexuality, and poor self-esteem. Children who were frequently abused over long periods of time and who suffered actual penetration of sexual organs were most likely to experience long-term trauma. Kendall-Tackett also found that no single behavior syndrome could be used to identify sexual abuse victims, making diagnosis of the problem at best complex.[98]

The Aftermath of Abuse

Sexual abuse can lead to low self-esteem, drug abuse, alcoholism, and criminality. The resulting feelings of betrayal correspond to depression, disillusionment, hostility, and anger in some victims; others react with impaired judgment and insecurity, which makes them vulnerable to further abuse.[99] The powerlessness associated with abuse is manifested in fear, anxiety, nightmares, phobias, clinging behavior, hypersensitivity, and lack of coping skills. Research indicates a correlation between the severity of abuse and its long-term effects: the less serious the form of abuse, the more quickly the child can recover.[100] For many kids, the long-term consequence of sexual abuse is leaving home for the streets. All too often these abandoned, "throwaway" kids are further victimized as juvenile prostitutes. This phenomenon is discussed in the following Focus on Delinquency.

The Extent of Child Abuse: Unreported

How extensive is the incidence of child abuse? Some of the first and most explosive indications of the severity of the problem came from a widely

Juvenile Prostitution

One of the most devastating forms of child sexual exploitation is juvenile prostitution. The National Center on Child Abuse and Neglect defines juvenile prostitution as "the use of, or participation by, children under the age of majority in sexual acts with adults or other minors where no force is present." The lack of force may make the relationship between a juvenile prostitute and the customer appear to be an equal economic exchange; however, victims' advocates acknowledge that in reality, the juvenile is a victim, often of an abusive family life, low self-esteem, and a lack of economic alternatives.

HOW PREVALENT IS JUVENILE PROSTITUTION?

It is difficult to measure the number of children who are actually involved in prostitution. Estimates from law enforcement officials, social service providers, and researchers have ranged from tens of thousands to 2.4 million children annually. A reasonable estimate is that there are between one hundred thousand and three hundred thousand juvenile prostitutes per year.

Even this estimate indicates a consistent nationwide problem of child sexual exploitation through prostitution. The questions remain: Where do these children come from, and how do they get recruited into prostitution? Youth service professionals suggest several traits or characteristics shared by juvenile prostitutes. Often, these children come from dysfunctional families. Having suffered physical, sexual, or emotional abuse, a majority of child prostitutes are runaways trying to escape their home environment. About 75 percent of juvenile prostitutes are runaways or "throwaways," having been encouraged or forced to leave home by their families.

Research suggests that most of the children who become prostitutes seem to suffer from a negative self-image. Whether by parents, school officials, or peers, these youngsters have been convinced that they have little self-worth. Many of the children "want to be wanted," and the attention of customers and pimps can foster the illusion that these people really care.

A negative self-image and a lack of marketable skills may force children into prostitution as a means of economic survival. Pimps and other prostitutes may offer food and shelter in exchange for money raised through prostitution. Once the juveniles have entered this lifestyle, they may find it difficult to get out.

WHO ARE THE PIMPS?

Recognizing that runaway children are emotionally and financially desperate, pimps exploit these needs for their own personal gain. Almost always men, they will often wait in bus terminals and train stations, offering juveniles traveling alone some companionship and a place to stay. Initially, attention and affection are provided "with no strings attached." Once the juveniles become indebted to him, the pimp "turns them out" in prostitution as a form of repayment.

To increase his profits, a pimp may be a member of an organized ring, sending the juvenile on a circuit that could encompass numerous locations over several states. A booking agent often works as the middleman, organizing the circuit schedule and providing a facade of legitimacy between the pimp and the police.

WHAT ARE THE RISKS IN THE LIFE OF A JUVENILE PROSTITUTE?

Aside from any possible emotional traumas associated with life as a juvenile prostitute, numerous physical risks endanger the child as well. Sexually transmitted diseases, pregnancy, and AIDS are constant dangers. The biological effects of sex at such an early age are not clearly documented but include damage to the vaginal and anal areas. The juveniles rarely seek medical help, for fear they may be brought to the attention of authorities.

Along with risks of disease come the risks of violence, both from pimps and from customers. Although they claim to protect the juveniles, the pimps may allow customers to "rough up" the youths "to teach them a lesson." Some pimps may use cruel and bizarre punishments, such as forcing juveniles to sit on a hot stove, for prostitutes who don't meet their quotas or who cause problems. More commonly, a pimp controls the juveniles through battering or the threat of violence. Prostitutes are also easy targets for muggers and other criminals. These juveniles are often out late at night with large amounts of cash and are unlikely to report a victimization to the police. Prostitutes are also common targets of serial murderers. ■

Source: Adapted from Jennifer Williard, *Juvenile Prostitution* (Washington, D.C.: National Victim Resource Center, 1991).

publicized 1980 national survey conducted by sociologists Richard Gelles and Murray Straus.[101] Gelles and Straus estimated that between 1.4 million and 1.9 million children in the United States were annually subject to physical abuse from their parents.

Physical abuse was rarely a one-time act; the average number of assaults per year was 10.5, and the median was 4.5. Gelles and Straus also found that 16 percent of the couples in their sample reported spousal abuse; 50 percent of the multichild families reported attacks between siblings; 20 percent of the families reported incidents in which children attacked parents.[102]

Gelles and Strauss conducted a second national survey of family violence in 1985 and found, somewhat surprisingly, that the incidence of very severe violence toward children had declined. They estimate the decline between 1975 and 1985 may be as much as 47 percent.[103] Nonetheless, more than 1 million children were still being subjected to *severe violence* annually. And this second research effort focused exclusively on two-parent families; including children from single-parent households would have expanded their estimate.[104] And if the definition of "severe abuse" used in the survey had included hitting with objects, such as a stick or belt, the actual number of child victims would have been closer to *7 million per year.*

Attempts to determine the extent of sexual abuse indicate that perhaps one in ten boys and one in three girls have been the victims of some form of sexual exploitation. An oft-cited survey by Diana Russell found that 16 percent of women reported sexual abuse by a relative and an additional 4.5 percent reported abuse by a father or stepfather.[105] It has been estimated that 30 percent to 75 percent of women in treatment for substance abuse disorders had experienced childhood sexual abuse and rape.[106]

The Extent of Child Abuse: Reported

Not all child abuse and neglect cases are reported to authorities, but those that are take on added importance because they become the focus of state action. A number of national organizations have been collecting data on reported child abuse. Obtaining an accurate estimate of child maltreatment has proven difficult because (a) the methods used to collect data, (b) the data sources, and (c) the definition of child abuse and neglect all vary across reporting jurisdictions.

One important resource is the National Incidence and Prevalence of Child Abuse and Neglect Survey, commissioned by the National Center on Child Abuse and Neglect, a component of the U.S. Department of Health and Human Services. This National Incidence Survey polled protection service professionals around the nation and found that in a given year (1986), about 1.5 million children experienced harm from child abuse and neglect; this number represents an increase of 64 percent over estimates made in 1980. The survey found that an additional half a million youths were "endangered" but had not yet been harmed.[107]

The National Incidence Survey found that less than half (46 percent) of these cases were reported to child protection services (CPS); the rest were known to professionals outside of child protection services (doctors, teachers). These numbers represent 25.2 children per 1,000 in the United States who are endangered or already harmed as a result of abuse and neglect.

Another important source of reported child abuse and neglect data is the National Committee for Prevention of Child Abuse (NCPCA). The committee

Number of child abuse cases
reported in millions and rate
per 1000 children

Source: Deborah Daro and Karen
McCurdy, *Current Trends in Child Abuse
Reporting and Fatalities: The Results of the
1992 Annual Fifty-State Survey* (Chicago:
National Committee for the Prevention
of Child Abuse, Press Release, 1993).

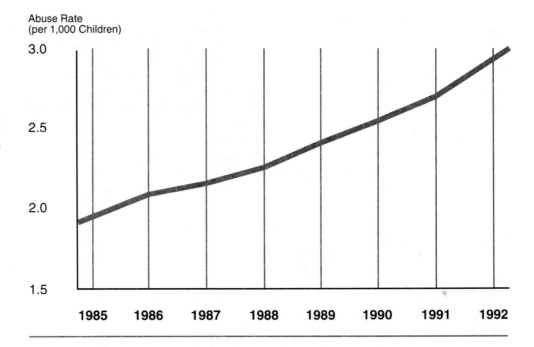

conducts an annual survey of all fifty states to determine the number and trends
of reported child abuse cases.[108] The NCPCA survey indicates that about 3 million
cases were reported in 1992 (the last data available), an increase of 8 percent
from the preceding year and up almost 50 percent from 1985. Of the total cases,
about 27 percent involved physical abuse, 17 percent sexual abuse, 45 percent
neglect, 7 percent emotional maltreatment, and the rest (8 percent) such "other"
situations as abandonment and chemical dependency (see Figure 9.4).

The NCPCA survey also found that about 40 percent of the cases reported
were considered substantiated, and received some form of child-care services;
the other 60 percent were still under investigation. If these unsubstantiated
cases are subtracted from the total, the NCPCA and National Incidence Survey
results are not dissimilar: on an annual basis, about 1.5 million to 1.8 million
children are reported as being neglected, abused, or otherwise endangered.

The greatest tragedy resulting from child maltreatment is the death of a child.
The NCPCA survey estimates that 1,261 children were killed in 1992 as a result
of child abuse, a rate of about 2 per 100,000 children. As was the case for general
child abuse, the number of mistreatment-related fatalities has increased notice-
ably since 1985, when the rate was 1.4 per 100,000 (878 deaths). Young children
remain at the highest risk for loss of life: 84 percent of victims were under 5;
sadly, 43 percent were 1 year old or younger.

THE CAUSES OF CHILD ABUSE AND NEGLECT

Parental maltreatment of children is a complex problem with neither a single
cause nor a single solution. It cuts across racial, ethnic, religious, and socioeconomic lines, affecting the entire spectrum of society. Abusive parents cannot be

categorized by sex, age, or educational level. They are persons from all walks of life, with varying cultural and economic backgrounds.

Of all factors associated with child abuse, two are discussed most often: (1) parents who themselves suffered abuse as children tend to abuse their own children, and (2) isolated and alienated families tend to become abusive. A cyclical pattern of family violence seems to be perpetuated from one generation to another within families. Evidence indicates that a large number of abused and neglected children grow into adolescence and adulthood with a tendency to engage in violent behavior. The behavior of abusive parents can often be traced to negative experiences in their own childhood—physical abuse, lack of love, emotional neglect, and incest. These parents become unable to separate their own childhood traumas from their relationships with their children.

Abusive parents often have unrealistic perceptions of the appropriate stages of childhood development. When their children are unable to act "appropriately"— when they cry, throw food, or strike their parents—the parents may react in an abusive manner.[109] For parents such as these, "the axiom about not being able to love when you have not known love yourself is painfully borne out in their case histories. . . . They spend their days going around the house, ticking away like unexploded bombs. A fussy baby can be the lighted match."[110]

Parents may also become abusive if they are isolated from friends, neighbors, or relatives who can provide a lifeline in times of crisis:

Potentially or actually abusing parents are those who live in states of alienation from society, couples who have carried the concept of the shrinking nuclear family to its most extreme form, cut off as they are from ties of kinship and contact with other people in the neighborhood.[111]

Many abusive and neglectful parents describe themselves as highly alienated from their families and lacking close relationships with persons who could provide help and support in stressful situations.[112] The relationship between alienation and abuse may be particularly acute in homes where there has been divorce or separation or in which parents have never actually married: abusive punishment in single-parent homes has been found to be twice that of two-parent families.[113] Parents who are unable to cope with stressful life-styles or events—divorce, alcoholism, financial stress, poor housing conditions, recurring mental illness, and drug addiction—are the most at risk.[114]

In sum, Richard Gelles and Murray Straus describe the abusive parent as follows:

. . . a single parent who was young (under thirty) had been married for less than ten years, had his or her first child before the age of eighteen, and was unemployed or employed part-time. If he or she worked, it would be at a manual labor job . . . women are slightly more likely to abuse their children than men. The reason is rather obvious: Women typically spend more time with children.[115]

It must be noted that no one of these factors provides a definitive explanation of why abuse and neglect occur.

Substance Abuse and Child Abuse

Abusive and neglectful families suffer from severe stress, and it is therefore not surprising that they frequently harbor members who turn to drugs and alcohol. The NCPCA survey found that substance abuse was the cause of child maltreatment most often cited by CPS professionals (63 percent).[116]

Research studies have found a strong association between child abuse and parental alcoholism.[117] In addition, evidence exists of a significant relationship between cocaine and heroin abuse and the neglect and physical abuse of children. In Massachusetts, almost 90 percent of the confirmed cases of abuse and neglect involving a victim under 1 year in age occurred in families in which one or more members were drug users; about 68 percent of the abused infants were diagnosed as suffering congenital drug addiction.[118]

States are just beginning to respond to women with substance abuse problems who also abuse their children. For example, Illinois employs Project SAFE (Substance Abuse Free Environment) to provide drug- and alcohol-involved women with intensive treatment and training in parenting skills.[119]

Social Class and Abuse

Surveys indicate a high rate of reported abuse and neglect cases among lower economic classes. The National Incidence Survey found that children from families earning less than fifteen thousand dollars per year experienced more abuse and suffered greater injury than children living in more affluent homes.[120] The NCPCA survey found that 43 percent of CPS workers indicated that most families in their caseload either lived in poverty or faced increased financial stress due to unemployment and economic recession.[121] These findings suggest that parental maltreatment of children is predominantly a lower-class problem. Is this conclusion valid?

One view is that the survey statistics are generally accurate and that lower-class parents are in fact more abusive of their children. Low-income families, especially those headed by a single parent, are often subject to greater levels of environmental stress and have fewer resources available to deal with such stress than families with higher incomes.[122] A relationship seems to exist between the burdens of raising a child without adequate economic and social resources and the use of excessive force and discipline.

Another view is that child abuse rates are so high among the lower class because poor families are more often dealt with by public agencies that automatically report suspected cases to CPS agencies. Higher-income families can afford private treatment, which shields their problems from public view.[123] CPS agents and judges may look differently on abuse cases that involve well-educated suburban-dwellers than they do on those involving members of the lower class. Attending physicians may label a child of middle-class parents "accident-prone" under circumstances in which they would judge a lower-class child "abused."[124] While this view seems plausible, research by Cecil Willis and Richard Wells indicates that police may be less likely to report child abuse by lower-class or minority families because they perceive that violence is more "normal" in these families and that minority children "need" harsher discipline than white children.[125]

Robert Burgess and Patricia Draper offer a third, biosocial explanation for the apparent class differences in child abuse.[126] They find that treatment of children is related to the actual "cost" to parents of perpetuating their genes through raising offspring. Higher rates of maltreatment in low-income families reflect the stress caused by the burdensome "investment" of resources lower-class parents make in raising their children. In contrast, middle-class parents devote a smaller percentage of their total resources to raising a family and therefore are less likely to perceive economic and social stress. According to this view, child abuse rates should be highest among lower-class families with large number of children: few resources must be spread among a large number of gene carriers, limiting the investment in each one's well-being. Burgess and Draper also note that higher abuse rates of emotionally and physically handicapped children may occur because these youngsters are "poor prospects for investment that will lead to their successful reproduction as adults."[127]

THE CHILD PROTECTION SYSTEM: PHILOSOPHY AND PRACTICE

For most of the nation's history, courts have operated on the assumption that parents have the right to bring up their children as they see fit. Though child protection agencies have been dealing with the problems of abuse and neglect since the late nineteenth century, recent awareness of child abuse and neglect has prompted judicial authorities to take increasingly bold steps to ensure the safety of children.[128] The age-old assumption that the parent-child relationship is inviolate has been breached. In 1974, Congress passed the **Child Abuse Prevention and Treatment Act,** which provides funds to states to bolster their services to maltreated children and their parents.[129] This act has been the impetus for all fifty states to improve the legal framework of their child protection systems. Abusive parents are subject to prosecution in criminal courts under the traditional statutes against assault, battery, and homicide. Many states have specific child abuse statutes that make it a felony to injure and abuse children.

State laws specifically prescribe procedures for investigation and prosecution of cases. The legal rights of both parents and children are constitutionally protected. In the cases of *Lassiter v. Department of Social Services* and *Santosky v. Kramer,* the U.S. Supreme Court recognized the child's right to be free from parental abuse and set down guidelines for a termination-of-custody hearing, including the right to legal representation.[130] States provide a *guardian ad litem* for the child (a lawyer appointed by the court to look after the interests of those who do not have the capacity to assert their own rights). States also ensure confidentiality of reporting and mandate professional training and public education programs.[131]

Investigating and Reporting Abuse

One major problem in enforcing abuse and neglect statutes is that maltreatment of children can easily be hidden from public view. Although state laws require doctors, teachers, and others who deal with children to report suspected cases to child protection agencies, many maltreated children are out of the law's reach because they are too young for school or because their parents do not take them to a doctor or a hospital. Parents abuse their children in private and, even when confronted, often accuse the child of lying or blame the child's medical problems on accidents of legitimate discipline. Legal and social service agencies must find more effective ways to locate abused and neglected children and to handle such cases once they are found.

All fifty states have statutes requiring that persons suspected of abuse and neglect be reported. Many have gone as far as making failure to report child abuse a criminal offense. Though such statutes are rarely enforced, teachers have been arrested for failing to report abuse or neglect cases.[132]

Once reported to a child protection service agency via a "hotline" or some other procedure, the case is first screened by an intake worker and then turned over to an investigative caseworker. While stories of children abruptly and erroneously taken from their home abound, it is more likely that these "gate-keepers" will consider cases "unfounded" and take no further action; more than 50 percent of all reported cases are so classified.[133] Among the most common reasons for screening out cases is that the reporting party is involved in a child custody case and the screener believes the accusation is a consequence of marital turmoil.[134]

THE PROCESS OF STATE INTERVENTION

Although procedures vary from state to state, most follow a similar legal process once a social service agency files a petition in juvenile or family court alleging abuse or neglect.[135] Parents have the right to counsel in all cases of abuse and neglect, and many states require the court to appoint an attorney for the child as well. The child's attorney, a guardian *ad litem,* often acts as an advocate for the child's welfare as well as provides legal assistance.

When an abuse or neglect petition is prosecuted, an ***advisement hearing*** is held to notify the parents of the nature of the charges against them. If the parents admit the allegations, the court enters a consent decree, and the case is continued for disposition. Approximately half of all cases are settled by admission at the advisement hearing. If the parents deny the petition, an attorney is appointed for the child, and the case is continued for a pretrial conference.

At the ***pretrial conference,*** the attorney for the social service agency presents an overview of the case and summarizes the evidence. Such matters as admissibility of photos and written reports are settled. The parents' attorney also reviews the facts of the case and reveals the evidence that will be used. At this point in the process, the attorneys can plea-bargain. As a result, about three-fourths of the cases that go to pretrial conference are settled by a consent decree. About eighty-five out of every one hundred petitions filed will be settled at either the advisement hearing or the pretrial conference.

Of the fifteen remaining cases, five will generally be settled before trial. Usually, no more than ten cases out of every one hundred will actually reach the ***trial stage*** of the process. These few cases are tried with the regular adversary process, and the allegation of abuse and neglect is almost always readily proved. However, in recent years, some well-publicized trials, including the McMartin Day Care Center case (the longest trial in U.S. history), have resulted in not guilty verdicts. In the McMartin case, as in others, some jurors believed that prosecutors were so anxious to get a conviction that they led young children to believe they were abused while the physical evidence told another story.

From the perspective of both the child and the parents, the most crucial part of an abuse or neglect proceeding is the ***disposition hearing,*** an entirely separate process held after the adjudication. The social service agency presents its case plan, which includes recommendations for returning the child to the parents, any conditions the parents must meet, a visitation plan if the child is to be taken from the parents, and so on. The plan is discussed with the parents, and an agreement is reached by which the parents commit themselves to following the state orders. Between half and two-thirds of all convicted offenders will be required to serve time in incarceration; almost half will be assigned to a form of counseling and treatment.

In making their decisions, juvenile or family courts are generally guided by three interests: the role of the parents, protection for the child, and the responsibility of the state. Frequently, these interests conflict. In fact, at times, even the interests of the two parents are not in harmony. Ideally, the state attempts to balance the parents' natural right to control their child's upbringing with the child's right to grow into adulthood free from severe physical or emotional harm. This is generally referred to as the *balancing-of-the-interest approach.*

Periodically, *review hearings* are held to determine if the conditions of the case plan are being met. Parents who fail to cooperate are warned that they may lose their parental rights. Most abuse and neglect cases are concluded within a year. Either the parents lose their rights and the child is given a permanent placement, or the child is returned to the parents and the court's jurisdiction ends. This process is summarized in Figure 9.5. The following case in point explores some questions about state intervention.

■■FIGURE 9.5

Process of state intervention in child abuse cases

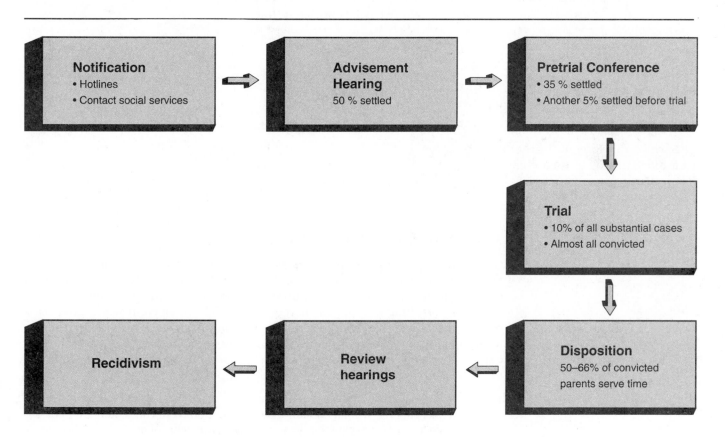

You are an investigator with the county Bureau of Social Services.

A case has been referred to you by the middle school's head guidance counselor. It seems that a young girl, Emily M., has been showing up to school in a dazed and listless condition. She has had a hard time concentrating in class and seems withdrawn and uncommunicative. The 13-year-old has missed more than a normal share of school days and has often been late to class. Last week, she seemed so lethargic that her homeroom teacher sent her to the school nurse. A physical examination revealed that she was malnourished and in poor physical health. She also had evidence of bruising that could only come from a beating. Emily told the nurse that she had been punished by her parents for doing poorly at school and for failing to do her chores at home.

When her parents were called in to school to meet with the principal and head guidance counselor, they claimed that they are members of a religious order that strongly believes that children should be punished severely for their misdeeds. Emily had been placed on a restricted diet as well as beaten with a belt to correct her misbehavior. When the guidance counselor asked them if they would be willing to go into family therapy, they were furious and told her to "mind her own business." It's a sad day, they said, when "God-fearing American citizens cannot bring up their children according to their religious beliefs." The girl is in no immediate danger insofar as her punishment has not been life-threatening.

The case is then referred to your office. When you go to see the parents at home, they refuse to make any change in their behavior and claim they are in the right and you are representative of all that is wrong with society. The lax discipline you want imposed leads to drugs, sex, and other teenage problems.

Should you get a court order removing Emily from her house and requiring the parents to go into counseling?

Should you report the case to the district attorney's office so it could proceed against her parents criminally under the state's Child Protection Act?

Should you take no further action, reasoning that Emily's parents have the right to discipline their child as they see fit?

Should you talk with Emily and see what she wants to happen?

The Abused Child in Court

One of the most significant problems associated with the prosecution of child abuse and sexual abuse cases is the trauma that a child must go through in a court hearing. Children get confused and frightened and may change their testimony, resulting in dropped charges or mistrial. Much controversy has arisen over the accuracy of children's reports of family violence and sexual abuse, resulting in hung juries in some well-known cases, including the McMartin Day Care case in California.[136] As one expert, Judge Lindsay Arthur of the National Council of Juvenile and Family Court Judges, put it:

The system may interview the child time and again, each time making her relive the experience, keeping the wound open. It may force her down to court waiting rooms where she sits uncomfortably without even the accoutrements of a dentist's office for hours and then often to be told that the case was continued and to come back next week. She may be put on a witness stand, in a big formal room, with what seems like a thousand eyes staring at her, and a bailiff in full uniform ready to lock her up, and a judge in a black robe towering above her. She may find that the newspapers and television are full of her name and pictures and stories about what happened to her which they obtained from the official records. And this may make her the focus of her classmates with all the brutal teasing that can involve.

The system may also suddenly arrest her father and just as suddenly release him. It may plea bargain away her future hope of rehabilitation without even talking to her, in the name of speedy justice.[137]

State jurisdictions have instituted a number of innovative procedures to minimize the trauma to the child. More than thirty-six have enacted legislation allowing videotaped statements or interviews with child witnesses, taken at a preliminary hearing or at a formal deposition, to be admissible in court. Videotaped testimony spares child witnesses the trauma of testifying in open court. States that allow videotaped testimony usually put some restrictions on its use: some prohibit the government from calling the child to testify at trial if the videotape is used; some require that the defendant be present during the videotaping; a few specify that the child not be able to see or hear the defendant; some states require a finding that the child is "medically unavailable" because of the trauma of the case before videotaping can be used.[138] An example of one state's provisions for videotaping children's statements is provided in Table 9.2.

■ ■ **TABLE 9.2**   Hawaii's Provisions for Videotaping Children's Statements

Rule 616. Videotaping the testimony of a child who is a victim of an abuse offense or a sexual offense. (a) This rule applies only to a proceeding in the prosecution of an abuse offense or sexual offense alleged to have been committed against a child less than sixteen years of age at the time of the offense, and applies only to the statements or testimony of that child. (b) The recording of an oral statement of the child made before the proceedings begins is admissible into evidence if:
1)   No attorney of either party was present when the statement was made;
2)   The recording is both visual and aural and recorded on film or videotape or by other electronic means;
3)   The recording equipment was capable of making an accurate recording, the operator of the equipment was competent, and the recording is accurate and unaltered;
4)   The statement was not made in response to questioning calculated to lead the child to make a particular statement;
5)   Every voice on the recording and every person present at the interview is identified;
6)   The person conducting the interview of the child in the recording is present at the proceeding and available to testify for or to be cross-examined by either party and every other person present at the interview is available to testify;
7)   The defendant or the attorney for the defendant is afforded discovery of the recording before it is offered into evidence; and
8)   The child is present to testify.
(c)If the electronic recording of the statement of a child is admitted into evidence under this section, either party may call the child to testify, and the opposing party may cross-examine the child.

Source: Haw. Rev. Stat, 626-1 Rule 616 (a) to (c) (1985).

About thirty-two states now allow a child's testimony to be given on closed-circuit television (CCTV). The child is able to view the judge and attorneys, and the courtroom participants are able to observe the child. The standards for CCTV testimony vary widely. Some states, such as New Hampshire, assume that any child witness under age 12 would benefit from not having to appear in court. Others require an independent examination by a mental health professional to determine whether there is a "compelling need" for CCTV testimony.

In addition to innovative methods of testimony, children in sexual abuse cases have been allowed to use anatomically correct dolls to demonstrate happenings that they cannot describe verbally. The Victims of Child Abuse Act of 1990 allows children to use these dolls when testifying in federal courts; at least eight states have passed similar legislation.[139] Similarly, states have relaxed their laws of evidence to allow out-of-court statements by the child to a social worker, teacher, or police officer to be used as evidence (such statements would be otherwise considered **hearsay**). Typically, corroboration is required to support these statements if the child does not also testify.

The prevalence of sexual abuse cases has created new problems for the justice system. All too often accusations are made in conjunction with marital disputes and separation. The fear is growing that children may become unwitting pawns in custody battles; the mere suggestion of sexual abuse is enough to galvanize social service workers and affect the outcome of a bitter divorce action. The juvenile justice system, therefore, must develop techniques that can get at the truth of the matter without creating a lifelong scar on the child's psyche.

LEGAL ISSUES

A number of cases have been brought before the Supreme Court testing the right of children to present evidence at trial using nontraditional methods and settings. Two issues stand out. One is the ability of physicians and mental health professionals to testify about statements made to them by victims of child abuse, especially when the children are incapable of testifying. The second concerns the way children testify in court and the leeway given prosecutors to make them feel at ease.

Out-of-Court Statements

The use of out-of-court statements has undergone a rapid legal transformation. In the 1990 case, *Idaho v. Wright*, the Court disallowed the use of statements made to a physician by a child considered incapable of communicating with a jury.[140] The Court ruled that Idaho law was not adequate to guarantee that the child's statements were sufficiently trustworthy and reliable to meet common evidentiary standards. In deciding whether out-of-court statements can be admitted, the Court suggested that judges will have to take into consideration such factors as the child's motives, his or her description of sexual practices, witnesses to the out-of-court statements, whether the statement was spontaneous, and other similar factors that might help determine the validity of the pretrial admissions.

Then in a 1992 case, *White v. Illinois*, the Court significantly eased the prosecution of child abuse cases by ruling that the state's attorney is required neither to produce young victims at trial nor to demonstrate the reason they were unavailable to serve as witnesses.[141] *White* involved the use as testimony of statements given by the child to the child's baby-sitter and mother, a doctor, a nurse, and a police officer concerning the facts and identity of the alleged assailant in a sexual assault case. The prosecutor twice tried to call the child to testify, but both times the 4-year-old experienced emotional difficulty and could not appear in court. The case outcome then hinged solely on the testimony of the five witnesses who repeated in court the statements made to them by the child.

By allowing the use of hearsay evidence in this case, *White* removes the requirement that prosecutors produce child victims in court. This facilitates the prosecution of child abusers in cases where a court appearance by a victim would prove too disturbing or where the victim is too young to understand the court process.[142] In its decision, the Court noted that statements made to doctors during medical exams or those made when a victim is upset or excited carry more weight than ones made after careful reflection. The Court ruled that such statements can be repeated during trial because the circumstances in which they were made (for example, during an examination in an emergency room) could not be duplicated simply by having the child testify to them in court.

In-Court Statements

Children who are victims of sexual or physical abuse often make poor witnesses because they are traumatized and overwhelmed by court processes. Yet their testimony may be crucial to convict child abusers. In an important 1988 case, *Coy v. Iowa,* the Court placed limitations on efforts to protect child witnesses in court. During testimony in a sexual assault case, a "one-way" glass screen was set up so that the child victims would not be able to view the defendant (the defendant, however, could view the witnesses as they testified).[143] The Iowa statute that allowed the protective screen assumed that children would be traumatized by their courtroom experience. The Court ruled that unless there was a finding that the child witness needs special protection, the Sixth Amendment of the Constitution grants defendants "face-to-face" confrontation with their accusers. *Coy* was viewed as a setback in the prosecution of child abuse cases. In her opinion, Justice Sandra Day O'Connor suggested that if courts found necessity, it would not be inappropriate to allow children to testify via CCTV or videotape.

Justice O'Connor's views became law in the landmark case of *Craig v. Maryland.*[144] In this case, a day care operator was convicted of sexually abusing a 6-year-old child; one-way CCTV testimony was used during the trial. The decision was overturned in the Maryland Court of Appeals on the grounds that the procedures used were insufficient to show that the child could only testify in this manner (via one-way CCTV) because a trial appearance would be too traumatic. On appeal, the Court ruled that the Maryland statute that allows CCTV testimony is sufficient because it requires a determination be made that the child will suffer emotional distress if forced to testify and would not therefore be able to communicate with a jury. The Court stated that before alternatives to in-trial testimony, such as CCTV, could be used, a determination must be made that the child would be traumatized by being forced to testify in the presence of the defendant and that the distress would be more than minimal. In its decision, the Court noted that CCTV could serve as the equivalent of in-court testimony and, properly applied, would not interfere with the defendant's right to confront witnesses.

Taken together, these cases significantly increase the legal tools prosecutors can employ in child abuse cases. They open the door for prosecutions in cases that would have been impossible to pursue before.

Disposition of Abuse and Neglect Cases

Just as disagreement is widespread about when state intervention into family life is appropriate, there is also considerable controversy over what forms of intervention are helpful in abuse and neglect cases. Today, social service agents avoid removing children from the home whenever possible and instead try to employ counseling and support techniques to control abusive relationships. In serious cases, the state may remove children from their parents and place them in shelter care or foster homes. Placement of these children in foster care is intended to be temporary, but it is not uncommon for children to remain in foster care for three years or more. Furthermore, children are likely to be shifted from one temporary home to another during this period, which severely deprives them of a stable home. While some recent research by Cathy Spatz Widom indicates that the effect of out-of-home placements may not be as traumatic as previously believed, those children who were moved around more than three times were twice as likely to get arrested as children who had more stable foster home placements.[145]

Ultimately, the court has the power to permanently terminate the rights of parents over their children, but because the effects of destroying the family unit are serious and far-reaching, the court does so only in the most severe cases. Judicial hesitancy is illustrated in a recent Virginia appellate case in which grandparents contested a father being awarded custody of his children, though he had a history of alcohol abuse, had already been found to be an unfit parent, and was awaiting appeal of his conviction *for killing the children's mother;* the trial court claimed that he had turned his life around.[146]

In the vast majority of abuse and neglect cases, courts are reluctant to demand the permanent removal of the child. Parents and children are required to participate in treatment programs that seek to rehabilitate the family and prevent a recurrence of the maltreatment. Such programs attempt to alter the psychological, social, and environmental factors that are at the root of the problem. Social casework, mental health services, day-care centers, homemaker services, parent effectiveness training, group therapy, and foster grandparent programs are among some of the most frequently used efforts to help children and parents avoid abuse or neglect situations.

Efforts have been ongoing to improve the child protection system and reduce the chance of repeat abuse. Jurisdictions have expedited case processing, instituted court procedures designed not to frighten child witnesses, coordinated investigations between various social service and law enforcement agencies, and assigned an advocate or guardian *ad litem* to support the child in need of protection.

ABUSE, NEGLECT, AND DELINQUENCY

The immediate effects of abuse and neglect are evident—physical injury, malnutrition, emotional depression, death. Less obvious are the suspected effects. Maltreatment of children encourages them to use aggression as a means of solving problems and prevents them from feeling empathy for others. It diminishes their ability to cope with stress and makes them vulnerable to the aggression and violence in the culture. Abused children have fewer positive interactions with peers, are less well liked, and are more likely to have disturbed social interactions.[147]

A significant literature has developed suggesting that abuse and neglect may have a profound effect on behavior in later years. Exposure to excessive physical aggression and emotional chaos in early life provides a foundation for several varieties of violent and antisocial behavior. In fact, sociologists Richard Gelles and Murray Straus state that "with the exception of the police and the military, the family is perhaps the most violent social group, and the home the most violent social setting, in our society."[148] Ray Helfer and C. Henry Kempe contend:

The effects of child abuse and neglect are cumulative. Once the developmental process of a child is insulted or arrested by bizarre child rearing patterns, the scars remain. One should not be surprised, then, to find that the large majority of delinquent adolescents indicate that they were abused as children.[149]

Aggressive, delinquent behavior is the means by which many abused or neglected children act out their hostility toward their parents. Some join gangs, which furnish a sense of belonging and allow pent-up anger to be expressed in group-approved delinquent acts.

A considerable body of research examines the clinical histories of known delinquents, typically employing samples of court-adjudicated or incarcerated youth. A 1975 Philadelphia study found that 82 percent of the juvenile offenders in the sample were abused as children; 43 percent remembered being knocked unconscious by a parent. A research project among two hundred juveniles in a detention center in Denver reported that 72 percent remembered being seriously injured by their parents. Statements of one hundred of these juveniles, confirmed by their parents or other reliable sources, revealed that 84 percent were significantly abused before the age of 6 and 92 percent were bruised, lacerated, or fractured within one and a half years before their apprehension for delinquency.[150] Likewise, studies of persons convicted of murder reveal "a demonstrable association between homicide and maltreatment in early childhood."[151] Among children who kill or who attempt murder, the most common factor is said to be "the child's tendency to identify himself with aggressive parents, and pattern after their behavior."[152] One study of several cases of murder and murderous assault by juveniles indicated that in all cases, "one or both parents had fostered and condoned murderous assault."[153] Adolescent boys who had committed homicide reported being beaten more often by their brothers and sisters.[154]

Cohort Studies

While these findings are persuasive, they use intact samples of delinquent youth. It is possible that child abuse is a reaction to misbehavior and is caused by delinquency and not vice versa. In other words, it is possible that angry parents attack their delinquent and drug-abusing children, and that child abuse is a result of delinquency, not its cause.

One way of solving this methodological dilemma is to follow a cohort of youths who had been reported as victims of child abuse and neglect early in their lives and compare them with a similar cohort of unabused youth. One study conducted by Jose Alfaro in New York found that about half of all children reported to area hospitals as abused children later acquired arrest records. A significant number of boys (21 percent) and girls (29 percent) petitioned to juvenile court had prior histories as abuse cases. Children treated for abuse or neglect were disproportionately involved in violent offenses, including homicide, rape, and assault.[155]

In an important cohort study, Cathy Spatz Widom followed the offending careers of 908 youths reported as abused from 1967 to 1971 and compared them with a control group of 667 unabused youth. Widom found that the abuse and neglect involved a variety of perpetrators, including parents, relatives, strangers, and even grandparents (see Figure 9.6). Twenty-six percent of the abused and neglected sample had juvenile arrests, compared to 17 percent of the comparison group; 29 percent of those who were abused and neglected had adult criminal records, compared to 21 percent of the control group. Widom further found that race, gender, and age also affected the probability that abuse would lead to delinquency: the highest risk group was older, black males who had suffered abuse; about 67 percent of this group went on to become adult criminals. In contrast, only 4 percent of young, white, unabused females became adult offenders.[156] Her conclusion: Being abused or neglected as a child increased the likelihood of arrest as a juvenile by 53 percent, as an adult by 38 percent, and for a violent crime by 38 percent.[157]

Widom also tested the hypothesis that victims of childhood violence resort to violence themselves as they mature. The children in her sample who suffered from physical abuse were the most likely to get arrested for a violent crime; their violent crime arrest rate was double that of the control group. While this relationship was not unexpected, more surprising was the discovery that neglected children maintained significantly higher rates of violence than children in the comparison group. Clearly, family trauma of all kinds may influence violence.

Widom also interviewed a sample of five hundred subjects twenty years after their childhood victimization. Preliminary analysis of this sample indicates that the long-term consequences of childhood victimization continues throughout the life cycle. Potential problems associated with abuse and neglect include mental health concerns, such as depression and suicide attempts; educational problems, including low IQ and poor reading ability; health and safety problems, including substance abuse; and occupational difficulties, including under- and unaggressive employment.

Dissenting Views

Such research findings do not necessarily mean that most abused or neglected children eventually become delinquent. Many do not, and many seriously delinquent youths come from what appear to be model homes. Though Widom found that more abused children in her cohort became involved in crime and delinquency than did the unabused, the majority of *both* groups were neither delinquent nor adult offenders. She concludes: "The strength of the cycle of violence may be of less magnitude than some might have expected."[158]

Similar research by Matthew Zingraff and his associates compared the offending experiences of randomly selected samples of maltreated youth, nonmaltreated poor youth, and general school-age youth taken from a populous county in North Carolina.[159] Controlling for race, age, gender, and family structure, Zingraff found few significant differences between the groups. Only 14 percent of the abused youth were arrested (compared to 5 percent and 9 percent of the

Perpetrators of abuse and neglect

Source: Cathy Spatz Widom, *The Cycle of Violence* (Washington, D.C.: National Institute of Justice, 1992), p. 3.

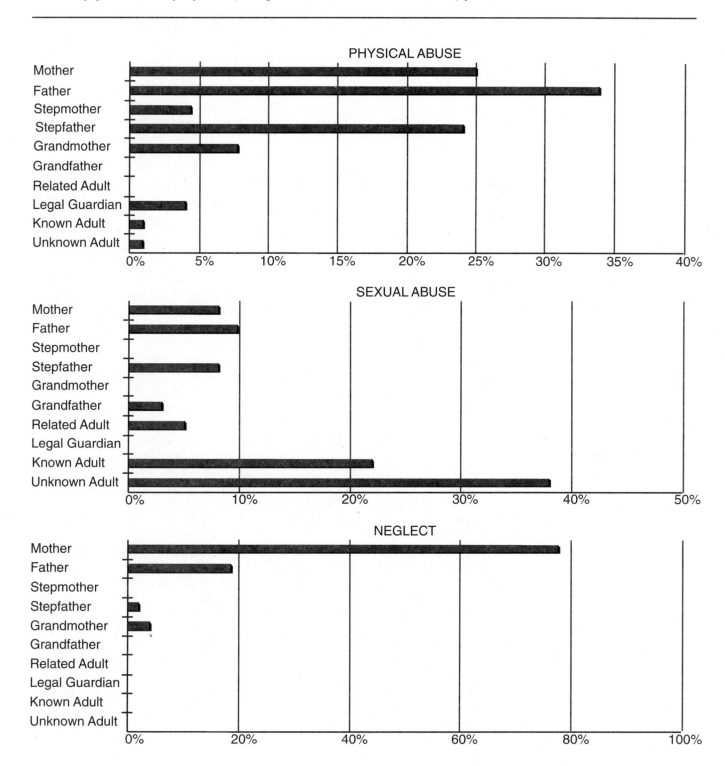

general school and poverty samples, respectively); clearly, a great majority of abused youth did not get into trouble with the law. Abused adolescents did get involved in significantly more status-type offenses, perhaps indicating that abused kids are more likely to "flee than fight." Their overall conclusion was: "Generally, our findings indicate that the risk of delinquency for maltreated children claimed by much of the previous research has been exaggerated."

While these cohort studies do not give overwhelming support to an abuse-delinquency link, the issue is certainly important enough to sustain further research. Even if abuse is not a direct cause, it may be a contributing factor in juvenile delinquency. Efforts to combat maltreatment are vital not only to prevent the immediate harms of abuse and neglect but also to reduce the possibility that the victims will settle into patterns of violent, aggressive criminal behavior throughout their life span.

THE FAMILY AND DELINQUENCY PREVENTION

Since the family is believed to play such an important role in the production of youth crime, it follows that improving family functioning can help prevent delinquency. Counselors commonly work with the families of antisocial youths as part of a court-ordered treatment strategy. Family counseling and therapy are almost mandatory when the child's acting out behavior is suspected to be the result of family-related problems, such as child abuse or neglect.[160] Some jurisdictions have integrated family counseling services into the juvenile court.[161]

Another approach to involving the family in delinquency prevention is to attack the problem before it occurs. Early childhood prevention programs have shown indications that they can relieve some of the symptoms associated with chronic delinquency.[162] Among the best known of these is the Syracuse University Family Development Research Program. This program identifies high-risk, indigent women during the latter stages of their pregnancy. After the women give birth, paraprofessionals are assigned to work with the mothers, encouraging sound parent-child relationships, providing nutrition information, and helping them to establish relationships with social service agencies. In addition to services for the mother, the program provides four-and-one-half years of quality child care at Syracuse University Children's Center. A similar program, the Houston Parent-Child Development Center, provides in-home services to parents, workshops on child rearing, and day care for children while parents attend family development classes.

The most widely cited program is the one created at the **Oregon Social Learning Center** (OSLC) by *Gerald R. Patterson* and his associates.[163] Patterson's long research into the life-styles of antisocial children convinced him that poor parenting skills were associated with antisocial behavior occurring in the home and at school. Family disruption and coercive exchanges between parent and children led to increased family tension, poor academic performance, and negative peer relations. The primary cause of the problem seemed to be that parents did not know how to deal effectively with their children. They sometimes ignored their children's behavior, while at other times, the same childish actions would trigger an explosive rage. Some parents would discipline their children for reasons that had little to do with the children's behavior but rather reflected their own frustrations and conflicts.

Children in turn would react to indifferent parenting in a regular progression from learning to be noncompliant at home to learning to be physically assaultive. Their "coercive behavior," which included whining, yelling, and temper tantrums, would sometimes be acquired by other family members, exacerbating the already explosive situation. Eventually, family conflict would escalate and flow out of the home into the school and social environment.

The OSLC program uses behavior modification techniques to help parents of antisocial children acquire proper care and disciplinary methods. Parents are asked to select several particular behaviors for change. Staff counselors first analyze family dynamics and then work with parents to construct a change program. Parents are asked to closely monitor the particular behaviors and to count the weekly frequency of their occurrence. OSLC personnel teach both social skills to reinforce positive behaviors and constructive disciplinary methods to discourage negative ones. Incentive programs are initiated in which a child can earn points or praise for such desirable behaviors as being cooperative and doing chores. Points can be exchanged for allowance, prizes, or privileges. Parents are also taught effective disciplinary techniques that stress firmness and consistency, rather than "nattering" (low intensity, nonverbal, or negative verbal behaviors, such as scowling or scolding) or explosive discipline, such as hitting, making humiliating remarks, or screaming. One important technique is the "time out" in which the child is removed for brief isolation in a quiet room. Parents are taught the importance of setting rules and sticking to them.

Ongoing research and evaluation is needed to formulate the best methods of intervening with the family in particular problem areas. What works for 10-year-old kids who steal may not be the best method for assaultive teens.

Evidence suggests that early intervention in these cases may be appropriate and that the later the intervention, the more difficult the change process. Most evaluations indicate that the OSLC methods can be highly successful.[164] In a recent review of the effect of early childhood intervention programs, psychologist Edward Zigler and his associates found that early and intensive interventions in family functioning can result in significant improvement in parent-child relations and a concomitant reduction in antisocial activities.[165]

■■■■■■■■■■■■■■■

SUMMARY

Family relationships have long been linked to the problem of juvenile delinquency. Early theories viewed the broken home as a cause of youthful misconduct, but research indicates that divorce, separation, or parental death plays a smaller role in influencing delinquent acts than previously thought. Other experts have suggested that broken homes may now have a greater effect than once believed. The quality of family life also has a great influence on a child's behavior. Studies have explored the effect of discipline, parental misconduct, and family harmony on youth crime.

Concern over the relationship between family life and delinquency has been heightened by reports of widespread child abuse and neglect. Cases of abuse and neglect have been found in every level of the economic strata, and it has been estimated that almost 2 million children are abused each year by their parents.

Two factors are seen as causing child abuse. First, parents who themselves suffered abuse as children tend to abuse their own children. Second, isolated and alienated families tend to become abusive.

Local, state, and federal governments have attempted to alleviate the problem of child abuse. The major issue has been state interference in the family structure. All fifty states have statutes requiring that suspected cases of abuse and neglect be reported.

A number of studies have linked abuse and neglect to juvenile delinquency. They show that a dispropor-tionate number of court-adjudicated youths had been abused or neglected. While the evidence so far is not conclusive, it suggests that a strong relationship exists between child abuse and neglect and subsequent delinquent behavior.

KEY TERMS

paternalistic family
broken home
beyond control
battered child syndrome
child abuse
neglect
traumatic sexualization
betrayal
powerlessness
stigmatization

Child Abuse Prevention and Treatment Act
advisement hearing
pretrial conference
trial stage
disposition hearing
balancing-of-the-interest approach
review hearings
hearsay
Oregon Social Learning Center

QUESTIONS FOR DISCUSSION

1. What is the meaning of the terms *child abuse* and *child neglect*?
2. Social agencies, police departments, and health groups all indicate that child abuse and neglect are increasing. What is the incidence of such action by parents against children? Are the definitions of *child abuse* and *child neglect* the key elements in determining the volume of child abuse cases in various jurisdictions?
3. What causes parents to abuse their children?

4. What is meant by the *child protection system*? Do courts act in the best interest of the child when they allow an abused child to remain with the family?
5. Should children be allowed to testify in court via closed-circuit TV? Does this approach prevent de-fendants in child abuse cases from confronting their accusers?
6. Is corporal punishment ever permissible as a disci-plinary method?

NOTES

1. Paul Amato and Bruce Keith, "Parental Divorce and the Well-Being of Children: A Meta-Analysis," *Psychological Bulletin* 110:26–46 (1991).
2. For general reviews of the relationship between fami-lies and delinquency, see Alan Jay Lincoln and Murray Straus, *Crime and the Family* (Springfield, Ill.: Charles C. Thomas, 1985); Rolf Loeber and Magda Stouthamer-Loeber, "Family Factors as Correlates and Predictors of Juvenile Conduct Problems and Delinquency," in Michael Tonry and Norval Morris, eds., *Crime and Justice* vol. 7 (Chicago: University of Chicago Press, 1986), pp. 29–151. (Herein cited as "Family Factors.")
3. Joan McCord, "Family Relationships, Juvenile Delin-quency and Adult Criminality," *Criminology* 29:397–417 (1991); Scott Henggeler, ed., *Delinquency and Ado-lescent Psychopathology: A Family Ecological Systems Approach* (Littleton, Mass.: Wright-PSG, 1982).
4. David Farrington, "Juvenile Delinquency," in John Coleman, ed., *The School Years* (London: Routledge, 1992), pp. 139–40.
5. Ruth Inglis, *Sins of the Fathers: A Study of the Physical and Emotional Abuse of Children* (New York: St. Martin's Press, 1978), p. 131.
6. See Joseph J. Costa and Gordon K. Nelson, *Child Abuse and Neglect: Legislation, Reporting, and Prevention* (Lex-ington, Mass.: D.C. Heath, 1978), p. xiii.
7. Ian Robertson, *Sociology* (New York: Worth, 1988), p. 363.
8. Christy Buchanan, Eleanor Maccoby, and Sanford Dornbusch, "Caught between Parents: Adolescents'

Experience in Divorced Homes," *Child Development* 62:1008–29 (1991).

9. S. E. Shank, "Women and the Labor Market: The Link Grows Stronger," *Monthly Labor Review* 111:3–8 (1988).

10. Edward Zigler, "Addressing the Nation's Child Care Crisis: The School of the Twenty-First Century," *American Journal of Orthopsychiatry* 59:484–91 (1989).

11. Children's Defense Fund, *The State of America's Children 1991* (Washington, D.C.: Children's Defense Fund, 1992), p. 5. (Herein cited as *The State of America's Children 1991*.)

12. Zigler, "Addressing the Nation's Child Care Crisis," p. 486.

13. Bureau of the Census, *Current Population Reports, 1966-1989* (Washington, D.C.: Government Printing Office, 1991).

14. National Research Council, *Common Destiny: Blacks and American Society* (Washington, D.C.: National Research Council, 1989).

15. Ibid.

16. Zigler, "Addressing the Nation's Child Care Crisis."

17. *The State of America's Children 1991*, p. 22.

18. Deborah Daro and Karen McCurdy, *Current Trends in Child Abuse Reporting Fatalities: The Results of the 1992 Annual Fifty-State Survey* (Chicago: National Committee for Prevention of Child Abuse, 1993). (Herein cited as NCPCA, *Current Trends in Child Abuse, 1992*.)

19. Richard Gelles and Murray Straus, *Intimate Violence* (New York: Simon and Schuster, 1988), p. 27.

20. National Advisory Commission on Criminal Justice Standards and Goals, *Juvenile Justice and Delinquency Prevention* (Washington, D.C.: Government Printing Office, 1976), p. 78.

21. Ibid., p. 92.

22. J. C. Schwartz, "Childhood Origins of Psychopathology," *American Psychologist* 34:573–80 (1979).

23. Michael Rutter, *Changing Youth in a Changing Society* (Cambridge: Harvard University Press, 1980).

24. D. J. West, *Who Becomes Delinquent?* (London: Heinemann, 1973).

25. Carolyn Smith and Marvin Krohn, *Delinquency and Family Life: The Role of Ethnicity* (Albany, N.Y.: Hindelang Criminal Justice Research Center, n.d.).

26. Loeber and Stouthamer-Loeber, "Family Factors," pp. 39–41.

27. Paul Howes and Howard Markman, "Marital Quality and Child Functioning: A Longitudinal Investigation," *Child Development* 60:1044–51 (1989).

28. Scott Hongeller, *Delinquency in Adolescence* (Newbury Park, Calif.: Sage, 1989), p. 48.

29. Barbara Dafoe Whitehead, "Dan Quayle Was Right," *Atlantic Monthly* 271:47–84 (1993).

30. C. Patrick Brady, James Bray, and Linda Zeeb, "Behavior Problems of Clinic Children: Relation to Parental Marital Status, Age, and Sex of Child," *American Journal of Orthopsychiatry* 56:399–412 (1986).

31. Sheldon Glueck and Eleanor Glueck, *Unraveling Juvenile Delinquency* (Cambridge: Harvard University Press, 1950); Ashley Weeks, "Predicting Juvenile Delinquency," *American Sociological Review* 8:40–46 (1943).

32. Jackson Toby, "The Differential Impact of Family Disorganization," *American Sociological Review* 22:505–12 (1957); Ruth Morris, "Female Delinquency and Relation Problems," *Social Forces* 43:82–89 (1964).

33. Roland Chilton and Gerald Markle, "Family Disruption, Delinquent Conduct, and the Effects of Subclassification," *American Sociological Review* 37:93–99 (1972).

34. For a review of these early studies, see Thomas Monahan, "Family Status and the Delinquent Child: A Reappraisal and Some New Findings," *Social Forces* 35:250–58 (1957).

35. Clifford Shaw and Henry McKay, *Report on the Causes of Crime, Social Factors in Juvenile Delinquency*, vol. 2 (Washington, D.C.: Government Printing Office, 1931), p. 392.

36. John Laub and Robert Sampson, "Unraveling Families and Delinquency: A Reanalysis of the Gluecks' Data," *Criminology* 26:355–80 (1988); Lawrence Rosen, "The Broken Home and Male Delinquency," in M. Wolfgang, L. Savitz, and N. Johnston, eds., *The Sociology of Crime and Delinquency* (New York: Wiley, 1970), pp. 489–95.

37. Lawrence Rosen and Kathleen Neilson, "Broken Homes," in Leonard Savitz and Norman Johnston, eds., *Contemporary Criminology* (New York: Wiley, 1982), pp. 126–35.

38. L. Edward Wells and Joseph Rankin, "Families and Delinquency: A Meta-Analysis of the Impact of Broken Homes," *Social Problems* 38:71–90 (1991).

39. Joseph Rankin, "The Family Context of Delinquency," *Social Problems* 30:466–79 (1983).

40. James Q. Wilson and Richard Herrnstein, *Crime and Human Nature* (New York: Simon and Schuster, 1985), p. 249.

41. Loeber and Stouthamer-Loeber, "Family Factors," p. 78.

42. Nan Marie Astone and Sara McLanahan, "Family Structure, Parental Practices and High School Completion," *American Sociological Review* 56:309–20 (1991).

43. Mary Pat Traxler, "The Influence of the Father and Alternative Male Role Models on African-American Boys' Involvement in Antisocial Behavior" (Paper presented at the annual meeting of the American Society of Criminology, New Orleans, November 1992).

44. Judith Smetena, "Adolescents' and Parents' Reasoning about Actual Family Conflict," *Child Development* 60:1052–67 (1989).

45. F. Ivan Nye, "Child Adjustment in Broken and Unhappy Unbroken Homes," *Marriage and Family* 19:356–61 (1957); idem, *Family Relationships and Delinquent Behavior* (New York: Wiley, 1958).

46. Michael Hershorn and Alan Rosenbaum, "Children of Marital Violence: A Closer Look at the Unintended Victims," *American Journal of Orthopsychiatry* 55:260–66 (1985).

47. Peter Jaffe, David Wolfe, Susan Wilson, and Lydia Zak, "Similarities in Behavior and Social Maladjustment among Child Victims and Witnesses to Family Violence," *American Journal of Orthopsychiatry* 56:142–46 (1986).

48. Hongeller, *Delinquency in Adolescence*, p. 39.

49. Jill Leslie Rosenbaum, "Family Dysfunction and Female Delinquency," *Crime and Delinquency* 35:31–44 (1989), at 41.

50. Paul Robinson, "Parents of 'Beyond Control' Adolescents," *Adolescence* 13:116–19 (1978).

51. Cindy Hanson, Scott Hennggeler, William Haefele, and J. Douglas Rodick, "Demographic, Individual, and Familial Relationship Correlates of Serious and Repeated Crime among Adolescents and Their Siblings," *Journal of Consulting and Clinical Psychology* 52:528–38 (1984).

52. Hongeller, *Delinquency in Adolescence*, p. 42.

53. Amato and Keith, "Parental Divorce and the Well-Being of Children."

54. Keith Warren and Ray Johnson, "Family Environment, Affect, Ambivalence and Decisions about Unplanned Adolescent Pregnancy," *Adolescence* 24:630–41 (1989).

55. Richard Smith and James Walters, "Delinquent and Non-delinquent Males' Perceptions of Their Fathers," *Adolescence* 13:21–28 (1978).

56. McCord, "Family Relationships, Juvenile Delinquency and Adult Criminality," p. 411.

57. Bill McCarthy and John Hagan, "Mean Streets: The Theoretical Significance of Situational Delinquency among Homeless Youth," *American Journal of Sociology* 98:597–627 (1992).

58. Hanson et al., "Demographic, Individual, and Familial Relationship Correlates of Serious and Repeated Crime among Adolescents and Their Siblings," p. 536.

59. Smith and Walters, "Delinquent and Non-delinquent Males' Perceptions of Their Fathers."

60. Laub and Sampson, "Unraveling Families and Delinquency," p. 375.

61. David Farrington, "The Development of Offending and Antisocial Behavior from Childhood to Adulthood" (Paper presented at the Congress on Rethinking Delinquency, University of Minho, Braga, Portugal, July 1992), p. 9.

62. Gerald Patterson and Magda Stouthamer-Loeber, "The Correlation of Family Management Practices and Delinquency," *Child Development* 55:1299–1307 (1984); Gerald R. Patterson, *A Social Learning Approach: Coercive Family Process*, vol. 3 (Eugene, Ore.: Castalia, 1982).

63. Christopher Ellison and Darren Sherkat, "Conservative Protestantism and Support for Corporal Punishment," *American Sociological Review* 58:131–44 (1993).

64. Murray Straus, "Discipline and Deviance: Physical Punishment of Children and Violence and Other Crime in Adulthood," *Social Problems* 38:101–23 (1991).

65. Nye, *Family Relationships and Delinquent Behavior*.

66. Rolf Loeber and Thomas Dishion, "Boys Who Fight at Home and School: Family Conditions Influencing Cross-Setting Consistency," *Journal of Consulting and Clinical Psychology* 52:759–68 (1984).

67. Laub and Sampson, "Unraveling Families and Delinquency," p. 370.

68. Stephen Cernkovich and Peggy Giordano, "Family Relationships and Delinquency," *Criminology* 25:295–321 (1987).

69. David Eggebeen and Daniel Lichter, "Race, Family Structure, and Changing Poverty among American Children," *American Sociological Review* 56:801–17 (1991).

70. G. Rahav, "Birth Order and Delinquency," *British Journal of Criminology* 20:385–95 (1980); D. Viles and D. Challinger, "Family Size and Birth Order of Young Offenders," *International Journal of Offender Therapy and Comparative Criminology* 25:60–66 (1981).

71. Linda Waite and Lee Lillard, "Children and Marital Disruption," *American Journal of Sociology* 96:930–53 (1991).

72. For a early review, see Barbara Wooton, *Social Science and Social Pathology* (London: Allen and Unwin, 1959).

73. Laub and Sampson, "Unraveling Families and Delinquency," p. 375.

74. D. J. West and D. P. Farrington, eds., "Who Becomes Delinquent?" in *The Delinquent Way of Life* (London: Heinemann, 1977); D. J. West, *Delinquency, Its Roots, Careers, and Prospects* (Cambridge: Harvard University Press, 1982).

75. West, *Delinquency*, p. 114.

76. David Farrington, "Understanding and Preventing Bullying," in Michael Tonry and Norval Morris, eds., *Crime and Justice*, vol. 17 (Chicago: University of Chicago Press, 1993).

77. D. P. Farrington, Gwen Gundry, and D. J. West, "The Familial Transmission of Criminality," in Alan Lincoln and Murray Straus, eds., *Crime and the Family*, (Springfield, Ill.: Charles C. Thomas, 1985) pp. 193–206.

78. See, generally, Wooton, *Social Science and Social Pathology*; H. Wilson, "Juvenile Delinquency, Parental Criminality, and Social Handicaps," *British Journal of Criminology* 15:241–50 (1975).

79. David Rowe and Bill Gulley, "Sibling Effects on Substance Use and Delinquency," *Criminology* 30:217–32

(1992); see also David Rowe, Joseph Rogers, and Sylvia Meseck-Bushey, "Sibling Delinquency and the Family Environment: Shared and Unshared Influences," *Child Development* 63:59–67 (1992).

80. Charles De Witt, director of the National Institute of Justice, quoted in National Institute of Justice, Research in Brief, *They Cycle of Violence* (Washington, D.C.: National Institute of Justice, 1992), p. 1.

81. Richard Gelles and Claire Pedrick Cornell, *Intimate Violence in Families*, 2d ed. (Newbury Park, Calif.: Sage, 1990), p. 33.

82. Lois Hochhauser, "Child Abuse and the Law: A Mandate for Change," *Harvard Law Journal* 18:200 (1973); see also Douglas J. Besharov, "The Legal Aspects of Reporting Known and Suspected Child Abuse and Neglect," *Villanova Law Review* 23:458 (1978).

83. C. Henry Kempe, C. H. Kempe, F. N. Silverman, B. F. Steele, W. Droegemueller, and H. K. Silver, "The Battered-Child Syndrome," *Journal of the American Medical Association* 181:17–24 (1962).

84. Vincent J. Fontana, "The Maltreated Children of Our Times," *Villanova Law Review* 23:448 (1978).

85. Ray E. Helfer and C. Henry Kempe, eds., *Child Abuse and Neglect: The Family and the Community* (Cambridge, Mass.: Ballinger, 1976), p. xix.

86. Brian G. Fraser, "A Glance at the Past, a Gaze at the Present, a Glimpse at the Future: A Critical Analysis of the Development of Child Abuse Reporting Statutes," *Chicago-Kent Law Review* 54:643 (1977-78).

87. Ibid.

88. Vincent J. Fontana, "To Prevent the Abuse of the Future," *Trial* 10:14 (1974).

89. See, especially, Inglis, *Sins of the Fathers,* chap. 8.

90. Ruth S. Kempe and C. Henry Kempe, *Child Abuse* (Cambridge: Harvard University Press, 1978), pp. 6–7.

91. Herman Daldin, "The Fate of the Sexually Abused Child," *Clinical Social Work Journal* 16:20–26 (1988).

92. Gerald Ellenson, "Horror, Rage and Defenses in the Symptoms of Female Sexual Abuse Survivors," *Social Casework: The Journal of Contemporary Social Work* 70:589–96 (1989).

93. David Finkelhor and Angela Browne, "The Traumatic Impact of Child Sexual Abuse: A Conceptualization," *American Journal of Orthopsychiatry* 55:530–41 (1985).

94. Carolyn Moore Newberger, Isabelle Gremy, Christine Waternaux, and Eli Newberger, "Mothers of Sexually Abused Children: Trauma and Repair in Longitudinal Perspective," *American Journal of Orthopsychiatry* 63:92–98 (1993).

95. David Goldston, Dawn Turnquist, and John Knutson, "Presenting Problems of Sexually Abused Girls Receiving Psychiatric Services," *Journal of Abnormal Psychology* 98:314–17 (1989).

96. Ellenson, "Horror, Rage and Defenses in the Symptoms of Female Sexual Abuse Survivors," pp. 589–91.

97. Magnus Seng, "Child Sexual Abuse and Adolescent Prostitution: A Comparative Analysis," *Adolescence* 24:665–75 (1989); Dorothy Bracey, *Baby Pros: Preliminary Profiles of Juvenile Prostitutes* (New York: John Jay Press, 1979).

98. Kathleen Kendall-Tackett, Linda Meyer Williams, and David Finkelhor, "Impact of Sexual Abuse on Children: A Review and Synthesis of Recent Empirical Studies," *Psychological Bulletin* 113:164–80 (1993).

99. Angela Browne and David Finkelhor, "Impact of Child Sexual Abuse: A Review of the Research," *Psychological Bulletin* 99:66–77 (1986).

100. Judith Herman, Diana Russell, and Karen Trocki, "Long-Term Effects of Incestuous Abuse in Childhood," *American Journal of Psychiatry* 143:1293–96 (1986).

101. Murray Straus, Richard Gelles, and Suzanne Steinmentz, *Behind Closed Doors: Violence in the American Family* (Garden City, N.Y.: Anchor Books, 1980); Richard Gelles and Murray Straus, "Violence in the American Family," *Journal of Social Issues* 35:15–39 (1979).

102. Gelles and Straus, "Violence in the American Family," p. 24.

103. Gelles and Straus, *Intimate Violence,* pp. 108–9.

104. Richard Gelles and Murray Staus, *Is Violence Toward Children Increasing? A Comparison of 1975 and 1985 National Survey Rates* (Durham, N.H.: Family Violence Research Program, 1985).

105. Diana Russell, *Sexual Exploitation: Rape, Child Sexual Abuse, and Workplace Harassment* (Beverly Hills, Calif.: Sage, 1984).

106. Maria Root, "Treatment Failures: The Role of Sexual Victimization in Women's Addictive Behavior," *American Journal of Orthopsychiatry* 59:543–49 (1989).

107. *Study Findings, National Incidence and Prevalence of Child Abuse and Neglect* (Washington, D.C.: Government Printing Office, 1988). (Herein cited as National Incidence Survey.)

108. Deborah Daro and Karen McCurdy, *Current Trends in Child Abuse Reporting and Fatalities: The Results of the 1992 Annual Fifty-State Survey* (Chicago: National Committee for the Prevention of Child Abuse, Press Release, 1993).

109. Carolyn Webster-Stratton, "Comparison of Abusive and Nonabusive Families with Conduct-Disordered Children," *American Journal of Orthopsychiatry* 55:59–69 (1985); Fontana, "To Prevent the Abuse of the Future," p. 16; Fontana, "The Maltreated Children of Our Times," p. 451; Brandt F. Steele and Carl B. Pollock, "A Psychiatric Study of Parents Who Abuse Infants and Small Children," in Ray Helfer and C. Henry Kempe, eds., *The Battered Child* (Chicago: University of Chicago Press, 1968), pp. 103–45.

110. Inglis, *Sins of the Fathers*, p. 68.

111. Ibid., p. 53.

112. Brandt F. Steele, "Violence within the Family," in Ray E. Helfer and C. Henry Kempe, eds., *Child Abuse and Neglect: The Family and the Community* (Cambridge, Mass.: Ballinger, 1976), p. 13.

113. William Sack, Robert Mason, and James Higgins, "The Single-Parent Family and Abusive Punishment," *American Journal of Orthopsychiatry* 55:252–59 (1985).

114. Fontana, "The Maltreated Children of Our Times," pp. 450–51. See also Blair Justice and Rita Justice, *The Abusing Family* (New York: Human Sciences Press, 1976); Steele, "Violence within the Family," p. 12; and Nanette Dembitz, "Preventing Youth Crime by Preventing Child Neglect," *American Bar Association Journal* 65:920–23 (1979).

115. Gelles and Straus, *Intimate Violence*, p. 85.

116. NCPCA, *Current Trends in Child Abuse, 1992*, p. 11.

117. Richard Famularo, Karen Stone, Richard Barnum, and Robert Wharton, "Alcoholism and Severe Child Maltreatment," *American Journal of Orthopsychiatry* 56:481–85 (1987).

118. Jordana Hart, "Child Abuse Found Tied to Drug Use," *Boston Globe*, 2 June 1989, p. 23.

119. NCPCA, *Current Trends in Child Abuse, 1991*, p. 18.

120. National Incidence Survey, p. 10.

121. NCPCA, *Current Trends in Child Abuse, 1991*, p. 11.

122. Richard Gelles, "Child Abuse and Violence in Single-Parent Families: Parent Absence and Economic Deprivation," *American Journal of Orthopsychiatry* 59:492–501 (1989).

123. Karla McPherson and Laura Garcia, "Effects of Social Class and Familiarity on Pediatricians' Responses to Child Abuse," *Child Welfare* 62:387–93 (1983).

124. S. Bittner and E. H. Newberger, "Pediatric Understanding of Child Abuse," *Pediatrics in Review* 7:197–207 (1981); see also E. H. Newberger and P. Bourne, "The Medicalization and Legalization of Child Abuse," *American Journal of Orthopsychiatry* 48:593–607 (1978).

125. Cecil Willis and Richard Wells, "The Police and Child Abuse: An Analysis of Police Decisions to Report Illegal Behavior," *Criminology* 26:695–716 (1988).

126. Robert Burgess and Patricia Draper, "The Explanation of Family Violence," in Ohlin and Tonry, eds. *Family Violence* (Chicago: University of Chicago Press, 1989), pp. 59–117.

127. Ibid., pp. 103–4.

128. Linda Gordon, "Incest and Resistance: Patterns of Father-Daughter Incest, 1880-1930," *Social Problems* 33:253–67 (1986).

129. P.L. 93–247 (1974).

130. 452 U.S. 18, 101 S.Ct. 2153 (1981), 455 U.S. 745, 102 S.Ct. 1388 (1982).

131. Besharov, "The Legal Aspects of Reporting Known and Suspected Child Abuse and Neglect," pp. 459–460; and Glaser, *Crime in Our Changing Society*, p. 246. For a survey of each state's reporting requirements, abuse and neglect legislation, and available programs and agencies, see Costa and Nelson, *Child Abuse and Neglect*.

132. Martha Brannigan, "Arrests Spark Furor over the Reporting of Suspected Abuse," *Wall Street Journal*, 7 June 1989, p. B8.

133. Debra Whitcomb, *When the Victim Is a Child* (Washington, D.C.: National Institute of Justice, 1992), p. 5.

134. "False Accusations of Abuse Devastating to Families," *Crime Victims Digest* 6 (2):4–5 (1989).

135. Michael S. Wald, "State Intervention on Behalf of 'Neglected Children': A Search for Standards for Placement of Children in Foster Care, and Termination of Parental Rights," *Stanford Law Review* 28:626–706 (1976).

136. For an analysis of the accuracy of children's recollections of abuse, see Candace Kruttschnitt and Maude Dornfeld, "Will They Tell? Assessing Preadolescents' Reports of Family Violence" *Journal of Research in Crime and Delinquency* 29:136–47 (1992).

137. Lindsay Arthur, "Child Sexual Abuse: Improving the System's Response," *Juvenile and Family Court Journal* 37:27–36 (1986).

138. Ibid.

139. Whitcomb, *When the Victim Is a Child*, p. 33.

140. *Idaho v. Wright*, 110 S.Ct. 3139 (1990).

141. *White v. Illinois*, 112 S.Ct. 736 (1992).

142. Myrna Raeder, "*White's* Effect on the Right to Confront One's Accuser," *Criminal Justice* Winter 1993, pp. 2–7.

143. *Coy v. Iowa*, 487 U.S. 1012 (1988).

144. *Maryland v. Craig*, 110 S.Ct. 3157 (1990).

145. Cathy Spatz Widom, *The Cycle of Violence* (Washington, D.C.: National Institute of Justice, 1992), p. 1.

146. *Walker v. Fagg*, 400 S.E. 2d 708 (Va. App. 1991).

147. Mary Haskett and Janet Kistner, "Social Interactions and Peer Perceptions of Young Physically Abused Children," *Child Development* 62:679–90 (1991).

148. Richard Gelles and Murray Straus, "Violence in the American Family," *Journal of Social Issues* 35:15 (1979).

149. Helfer and Kempe, *Child Abuse and Neglect*, pp. xvii–xviii.

150. National Center on Child Abuse and Neglect, Department of Health, Education, and Welfare, *1977 Analysis of Child Abuse and Neglect Research* (Washington, D.C.: Government Printing Office, 1978), p. 29.

151. Steele, "Violence within the Family," p. 22.

152. L. Bender and F. J. Curran, "Children and Adolescents Who Kill," *Journal of Criminal Psychopathology* 1:297 (1940), cited in Steele, "Violence within the Family," p. 21.

153. W. M. Easson and R. M. Steinhilber, "Murderous Aggression by Children and Adolescents," *Archives of General Psychiatry* 4:1–11 (1961), cited in Steele, "Violence within the Family," p. 22. See also J. Duncan and G. Duncan, "Murder in the Family: A Study of

Some Homicidal Adolescents," *American Journal of Psychiatry* 127:1498–1502 (1971); C. King, "The Ego and Integration of Violence in Homicidal Youth," *American Journal of Orthopsychiatry* 45:134–45 (1975); and James Sorrells, "Kids Who Kill," *Crime and Delinquency* 23:312–26 (1977).

154. C. H. King, "The Ego and the Integration of Violence in Homicidal Youth," *American Journal of Orthopsychiatry* 45:134–45 (1975).

155. Jose Alfaro, "Report of the Relationship between Child Abuse and Neglect and Later Socially Deviant Behavior," *Exploring the Relationship between Child Abuse and Delinquency,* pp. 175–219.

156. Cathy Spatz Widom, "Child Abuse, Neglect, and Violent Criminal Behavior," *Criminology* 27:251–71 (1989).

157. Widom, *The Cycle of Violence,* p. 1.

158. Widom, "Child Abuse, Neglect, and Violent Criminal Behavior," p. 267.

159. Matthew Zingraff, "Child Maltreatment and Youthful Problem Behavior," *Criminology* (in press, May 1993).

160. Leonard Edwards and Inger Sagatun, "Dealing with Parent and Child in Serious Abuse Cases," *Juvenile and Family Court Journal* 34:9–14 (1983).

161. Susan McPherson, Lance McDonald, and Charles Ryer, "Intensive Counseling with Families of Juvenile Offenders," *Juvenile and Family Court Journal* 34:27–34 (1983).

162. The programs in this section are described in Edward Zigler, Cara Taussig, and Kathryn Black, "Early Childhood Intervention, A Promising Preventative for Juvenile Delinquency," *American Psychologist* 47:997–1006 (1992).

163. See, generally, Gerald Patterson, "Performance Models for Antisocial Boys," *American Psychologist* 41:432–44 (1986); idem, *Coercive Family Process* (Eugene, Ore.: Castalia, 1982).

164. N. A. Wiltz and G. R. Patterson, "An Evaluation of Parent Training Procedures Designed to Alter Inappropriate Aggressive Behavior in Boys," *Behavior Therapy* 5:215–21 (1974).

165. Zigler, Taussig, and Black, "Early Childhood Intervention, A Promising Preventative for Juvenile Delinquency," pp. 1000–1004.

PEERS AND DELINQUENCY

JUVENILE GANGS AND GROUPS

N o issue confronting the study of delinquency is more important today than the problems presented by law-violating gangs and groups. While some gangs are made up of only a few loosely organized neighborhood youths, others have thousands of members who cooperate in highly complex illegal enterprise. A significant portion of all drug distribution in the nation's inner cities is believed to be gang-controlled; gang violence accounts for more than one thousand homicides each year.[1]

Social service and law enforcement groups have made a concerted effort to contain gangs and reduce their criminal activity. Approaches range from introducing treatment-oriented settlement houses to deploying tactical gang control units. The problem of gang control is a difficult one: gangs flourish in inner-city areas that offer lower-class youths few conventional opportunities. Members are resistant to the offers of help that cannot deliver legitimate economic hope. Though gang members may be subject to arrest, prosecution, and incarceration, a new crop of young recruits is always ready to take the place of their fallen comrades. Those sent to prison find that upon release, their former gangs are only too willing to have them return to action.

This chapter discusses the nature and extent of gang and group delinquency. It begins with a discussion of peer relations and shows how group relations influence delinquent behavior. It then explores the definition, nature, and structure of delinquent gangs. In addition, theories of gang formation, the extent of gang activity, and gang-control efforts are presented.

ADOLESCENT PEER RELATIONS

Psychologists have long recognized that as children mature, the nature of their friendship patterns also evolves. While parents are the primary source of influence and attention in children's early years, between ages 8 and 14, children seek out a stable peer group; both the number and the variety of friendships increase as children go through adolescence. Friends soon begin having a greater influence over decision making than parents.[2] By their early teens, children report that their friends give them emotional support when they are feeling bad and that they can confide intimate feelings to peers without worrying about their confidences being betrayed.[3]

As they go through adolescence, children form *cliques,* small groups of friends who share activities and confidences.[4] They also belong to *crowds,* loosely organized groups of children who share interests and activities. While clique members share intimate knowledge, crowds are brought together by mutually shared activities, sports, religion, hobbies. Popular youths can be members of a variety of same-sex cliques and crowds, while also joining with groups containing members of the opposite sex.

In later adolescence, acceptance by their peers has a major impact on socialization. Popular youths do well in school and are socially astute. In contrast, children who are rejected by their peers are more likely to display aggressive behavior and disrupt group activities by bickering or behaving antisocially.[5]

Peer relations, then, are a significant aspect of maturation. Peers exert a powerful influence on youths and pressure them to conform to group values.

Peers guide children and help them learn to share and cooperate, cope with aggressive impulses, and discuss feelings they would not dare bring up at home. With peers, youths can compare their own experiences and learn that others have similar concerns and problems; they realize that they are not alone.[6]

Peer Relations and Delinquency

Experts have long debated the relationship between peer group interaction and delinquency. Reviews of the research show that delinquent acts tend to be committed in small groups, rather than alone; a process called *co-offending*.[7] Theft-related offenses are particularly likely to be committed by groups of co-offenders of the same gender and age; brothers have been found to commit offenses with brothers of a similar age.[8]

Does having antisocial peers cause delinquency, or are delinquents antisocial youths who seek out like-minded companions? Three opposing viewpoints exist on this question. Control theorists, such as Travis Hirschi, argue that delinquents are as detached from their peers as they are from other elements of society. While delinquent youths may acknowledge that they have "friends," their actual personal relationships are cold and exploitative. In an oft-cited work, James Short and Fred Strodtbeck described the importance delinquent youths attach to their peer groups, while at the same time they observed how delinquents lack the social skills to make their peer relations rewarding or fulfilling.[9] According to this view, if delinquency is committed in groups, it is because "birds of a feather flock together," not because deviant peers cause otherwise law-abiding youths to commit crimes.

The second view is that peer relations contribute directly to delinquency. Structural theorists view the delinquency experience as one marked by close peer

As they go through adolescence, children form cliques, small groups of friends who share activities and confidences.

group support. They link delinquency to the rewards gained by associating with like-minded youth and their formation of *law-violating youth groups* and *gangs.* Lower-class youths who find it difficult to achieve success and a sense of pride through legitimate means are open to achieving status in a group.

Influential peer relations are also a central issue of social learning theory. Social learning involves modeling the behavior of others and acquiring deviant knowledge and attitudes through intimate contact with valued peers.

A third view is that peers and delinquency are mutually supporting. Antisocial kids join up with like-minded friends; deviant peers sustain and amplify delinquent careers. As children move through the life course, friends will influence their behavior, and their behavior will influence their friends.[10] Mark Warr has found that these antisocial friends help delinquent careers to withstand the aging-out process.[11]

Delinquent Peers

The weight of the empirical evidence indicates that youths who are loyal to delinquent friends, belong to a gang, have "bad companions," and are otherwise involved with deviant peers are the ones most likely to commit crime.[12] Nonetheless, having deviant peers does not necessarily mean that the relationships are close, intimate, and influential. Are delinquents actually close to their peers?

Exploring the quality of delinquent peer relations directly, Peggy Giordano, Stephen Cernkovich, and M. D. Pugh found that both delinquents and nondelinquents actually had similar types of friendship patterns.[13] Delinquent youths reported that their peer relations contained elements of caring and trust and that they could be open and intimate with their friends. Delinquent youths also reported getting more intrinsic rewards from their peers than did nondelinquents. However, there were some differences between the peer relations of delinquents and nondelinquents: the former reported more conflict than the latter with their friends, more feelings of jealousy and competition, and, not unexpectedly, more pronounced feelings of loyalty in the face of trouble. These findings support the view that delinquents' peer group relations play an important part in their life-style and stand in contrast to the viewpoint that youthful law violators are loners without peer group support.

Comparable relationships have been found in studies of peer relations among young drug-involved males.[14] Marvin Krohn and Terence Thornberry, employing data from the Rochester Youth Development cohort study, reached similar conclusions: alcohol and marijuana users have friendships that are more intimate and varied than those of nonusers.[15]

These findings seem to contradict Hirschi's control theory model, which holds that delinquents are loners who are detached from their peers, and support the cultural deviance view that delinquents form close-knit peer groups and cliques that sustain their behavior. These new data on the peer relations of delinquents seem to suggest that adolescents are influenced by social relationships as they go through their life cycle and that these relationships can influence behavior patterns.

TEENAGE GANGS

As youths move through adolescence, they gravitate toward cliques that provide them with support, assurance, protection, and direction. Peer group membership allows them to devalue enemies, achieve status, and develop self-assurance. In some instances, the peer group provides the social and emotional basis for antisocial activity. In this instance, the clique is transformed into a *gang*.

The delinquent gang is a topic of considerable interest to many Americans. Such a powerful mystique has grown up around gangs that mere mention of the word *gang* evokes images of black-jacketed youths roaming the streets at night in groups bearing such colorful names as the Mafia Crips, the Bounty Hunters, and the Savage Skulls. Films, television shows, novels, and even Broadway musicals, such as *Boyz N the Hood, New Jack City, Trespass, Outsiders, West Side Story,* and *Colors* have popularized the teenage gang.[16]

Considering the suspected role gangs play in violent crime and drug activity, it is not surprising that they have recently become the target of a great deal of research interest. The secretive, constantly changing nature of juvenile gangs make them a difficult focus of study. Nonetheless, important attempts have been made to gauge their size, location, makeup, and activities.

WHAT ARE GANGS?

What exactly are delinquent gangs? Gangs are groups of youth who collectively engage in delinquent behaviors. Yet there is a distinction between *group delinquency* and *gang delinquency.* The former consists of a short-lived alliance created to commit a particular crime or engage in a random violent act. In contrast, gang delinquency involves long-lived, complex institutions that have a distinct structure and organization, including identifiable leadership, division of labor (some members are fighters, others burglars, while some are known as deal makers), rules, rituals, and possessions (such as a headquarters and weapons).

Despite the familiarity of gangs to the American public, delinquency experts are often at odds over the precise definition of a gang. The term is sometimes used broadly to describe any congregation of youths who have joined together to engage in delinquent acts. Some police departments use narrower definitions, designating as gangs only cohesive groups that hold and defend territory, or turf.[17]

Academic experts have also created a variety of definitions to distinguish delinquent gangs from delinquent groups. Some of the core elements generally included in the concept of the gang is that it is an **interstitial** group (a phrase coined by pioneering gang expert Frederick Thrasher to refer to the cracks that form in the fabric of society) and it maintains standard group processes, such as recruiting new members, setting goals (such as controlling the neighborhood drug trade), assigning roles (appointing someone to negotiate with rivals), and developing status (grooming young members for leadership roles).[18] Table 10.1 provides definitions of teen gangs by leading experts on delinquency.

While a great deal of divergence over the definition of *gang* exists, there is enough overlap to make possible the rational study of gangs.

Near Groups and Youth Groups

The standard definition of a gang implies that it is a cohesive group that maintains rules and customs and develops ongoing traditions. Not all gang experts share this view. Sociologist Lewis Yablonsky believes that gangs can best be described as **near groups.** According to Yablonsky, human collectives tend to

■■ TABLE 10.1   Definitions of Teen Gangs

FREDERICK THRASHER

An interstitial group originally formed spontaneously and then integrated through conflict. It is characterized by the following types of behavior: meeting face to face, milling, movement through space as a unit, conflict, and planning. The result of this collective behavior is the development of tradition, unreflective internal structure, esprit de corps, solidarity, morale, group awareness, and attachment to local territory.

MALCOLM KLEIN

Any denotable adolescent group of youngsters who (a) are generally perceived as a distinct aggregation by others in their neighborhood; (b) recognize themselves as a denotable group (almost invariably with a group name); and (c) have been involved in a sufficient number of delinquent incidents to call forth a consistent negative response from neighborhood residents and/or law enforcement agencies.

DESMOND CARTWRIGHT

An interstitial and integrated group of persons who meet face to face more or less regularly and whose existence and activities are considered an actual or potential threat to the prevailing social order.

WALTER MILLER

A self-formed association of peers, bound together by mutual interests, with identifiable leadership, well-developed lines of authority, and other organizational features, who act in concert to achieve a specific purpose or purposes, which generally include the conduct of illegal activity and control over a particular territory, facility, or type of enterprise.

G. DAVID CURRY AND IRVING SPERGEL

Groups containing law-violating juveniles and adults that are complexly organized, although sometimes diffuse, and sometimes cohesive, with established leadership and membership rules. The gang also engages in a range of crime (but with significantly more violence) within a framework of norms and values in respect to mutual support, conflict relations with other gangs, and a tradition of turf, colors, signs, and symbols. Subgroups of the gang may be deferentially committed to various delinquent or criminal patterns, such as drug trafficking, gang fighting, or burglary.

Source: Frederick Thrasher, *The Gang* (Chicago: University of Chicago Press, 1927), p. 57; Malcolm Klein, *Street Gangs and Street Workers* (Englewood Cliffs, N.J.: Prentice-Hall, 1971), p. 13; Desmond Cartwright, Barbara Tomson, and Hersey Schwarts, eds., *Gang Delinquency* (Monterey, Calif.: Brooks/Cole, 1975), pp. 149–50; Walter Miller, "Gangs, Groups, and Serious Youth Crime," in David Schicor and Delos Kelly, eds., *Critical Issues in Juvenile Delinquency* (Lexington, Mass.: Lexington Books, 1980); G. David Curry and Irving Spergel, "Gang Homicide, Delinquency, and Community," *Criminology* 26:382 (1988).

range from highly cohesive, tight-knit organizations to mobs with anonymous members who are motivated by emotions and disturbed leadership. Because teenage gangs fall between the two extremes, they can be characterized as near groups. They usually have diffuse role definition, limited cohesion, impermanence, minimal consensus of norms, shifting membership, disturbed leadership, and limited definitions of membership expectations.[19]

In Yablonsky's view, the gang maintains only a small core of totally committed members, who need the gang for satisfaction and other personal reasons. These core members work constantly to keep the momentum of the gang going. On a second level are affiliated youths, who participate in gang activity only when the mood suits them. At a third level are peripheral members, who participate in a particular situation or fight but who usually do not identify with the gang.

The near group model has been supported by the research of James Diego Vigil.[20] Vigil found that boys in Latino **barrio** (neighborhood) gangs could be separated into "regular" (inner core), "peripheral" (strong identity but less frequent activity), "temporary" (short-term membership), and "situational" (those who party with the gang but avoid violent confrontations) members.

Sociologist Walter Miller suggests that *law-violating youth group* is a more appropriate term than *gang* to identify collective youth crime.[21] He says, "A law-violating youth group is an association of three or more youths whose members engage recurrently in illegal activities with the cooperation and/or moral support of their companions."[22] Miller recognizes the loose affiliations found in many youth groups. He employs such terms as *cooperation* and *moral support* to convey the idea that collective activities rarely include all group members. While Miller also acknowledges "formal" delinquent gangs, he recognizes that they represent only one element of collective youth crime, which also includes cliques, networks, bands, corner groups, and so on. In sum, Miller sees the gang problem as one in which the formal street gang plays only a small part.

THE STUDY OF JUVENILE GANGS AND GROUPS

The study of juvenile gangs and groups was prompted by the Chicago School sociologists in the 1920s. Researchers such as Clifford Shaw and Henry McKay were concerned about the nature of the urban environment and how it influenced young people. Delinquency was believed to be a product of unsupervised groups made up of children of the urban poor and immigrants.

Frederick Thrasher initiated the study of the modern gang in his analysis of more than thirteen hundred youth groups in Chicago. His report on this effort, *The Gang,* was published in 1927.[23] Thrasher found that the social, economic, and ecological processes that affect the structure of great metropolitan cities create *interstitial* areas, or cracks, in the normal fabric of society, characterized by weak family controls, poverty, and social disorganization. According to Thrasher, groups of youths develop spontaneously to meet such childhood needs as play, fun, and adventure—activities that sometimes lead to delinquent acts.

The slum area presents many opportunities for conflict between groups of youths and between the groups and adult authority. If this conflict continues, the groups become more solidified and their activities become primarily illegal. The groups thus develop into gangs, with a name and a structure oriented toward delinquent behavior.

To Thrasher, the gang provides the young, lower-class boy with an opportunity for success. Since adult society does not meet the needs of slum dwellers, the gang solves the problem by offering what society fails to provide—excitement, fun, and opportunity. The gang is not a haven for disturbed youths but rather an alternative life-style for normal boys.

Thrasher's work has had an important influence on the accepted view of the gang. Recent studies of delinquent gang behavior are similar to Thrasher's in their emphasis on the gang as a means for lower-class boys to achieve advancement and opportunity as well as to defend themselves and attack rivals.

Gangs in the 1950s and 1960s

In the 1950s and early 1960s, the threat of gangs and gang violence swept the public consciousness. Rarely did a week go by without a major city newspaper featuring a story on the violent behavior of fighting gangs and their colorful leaders and names—the Egyptian Kings, the Vice Lords, the Blackstone Rangers. Social service and law enforcement agencies directed major efforts to either rehabilitate or destroy the gangs. Movies, such as *The Wild Ones* and *Blackboard Jungle,* were made about gangs, and the Broadway musical *West Side Story* romanticized violent gangs.

In his 1967 work, *Juvenile Gangs in Context,* Malcolm Klein summarized existing knowledge about gangs.[24] He concluded that gang membership was a way for individual boys to satisfy certain personal needs that were related to the development of youths caught up in the emotional turmoil typical of the period between adolescence and adulthood. A natural inclination to form gangs is reinforced by the perception that the gang represents a substitute for unattainable middle-class rewards. The experience of being a member of a gang will dominate a youngster's perceptions, values, expectations, and behavior. Finally, the gang is self-reinforcing:

It is within the gang more than anywhere else that a youngster may find forms of acceptance for delinquent behavior—rewards instead of negative sanctions. And as the gang strives for internal cohesion, the negative sanctions of the "outside world" become interpreted as threats to cohesion, thus providing secondary reinforcement for the values central to the legitimization of gang behavior.[25]

By the mid-1960s, the gang menace seemed to have disappeared. Some experts attribute the decline of gang activity to successful gang-control programs.[26] Others believe that gangs were eliminated because police gang-control units infiltrated gangs, arrested leaders, and constantly harassed members.[27] Gang boys were more likely to be sanctioned by the juvenile justice system and receive more severe sentences than nongang youths.[28] Another explanation for the decline in gang activity is the increase in political awareness that developed during the 1960s. Many gang leaders became involved in the social or political activities of ethnic pride, civil rights, and antiwar groups. In addition, many gang members were drafted. Still another explanation is that gang activity diminished during the 1960s because many gang members became active users of heroin and other drugs, which curtailed their group-related criminal activity.[29]

Gangs Emerge

Interest in gang activity began anew in the early 1970s. Walter Miller comments on the New York scene:

All was quiet on the gang front for almost 10 years. Then, suddenly and without advance warning, the gangs reappeared. Bearing such names as Savage Skulls and Black Assassins, they began to form in the South Bronx in the spring of 1971, quickly spread to other parts of the city, and by 1975 comprised 275 police-verified gangs with 11,000 members. These new and mysteriously merging gangs were far more lethal than their predecessors—heavily armed, incited and directed by violence-hardened older men, and directing their lethal activities far more to the victimization of ordinary citizens than to one another.[30]

Gang activity also reemerged in other major cities, including Detroit, El Paso, Los Angeles, and Chicago. Today, the number of gang youths appears, at least in these major cities, to be at an all-time high.[31] In addition, such cities as Cleveland and Columbus, Ohio, and Milwaukee, Wisconsin, which had not experienced serious gang problems before, saw the development of local gangs.[32] Large urban gangs sent representatives to organize chapters in distant areas or take over existing gangs. For example, Chicago gangs moved into Dade County, Florida, and demanded cooperation and obedience from local gangs. Two major Chicago gangs, the Black Gangster Disciples and their rivals, the Vice Lords, established branches in Milwaukee.[33] Members of Los Angeles's two largest gangs, the Crips and the Bloods, began operations in Midwest cities with the result that local police departments with little experience in gang control were confronted with well-organized, established gang activities. Even medium-sized cities, such as Columbus, Ohio, saw gangs emerge from local dance and "rap" groups and neighborhood street-corner groups.[34]

The explosion of gang activities in the 1980s was reflected in the renewed media interest in gang activity. Joan Moore reports that the *Los Angeles Times* printed 36 gang-related stories in 1977 and 15 in 1978; by 1988, 69 articles appeared, and in 1989, the number of stories concerning police sweeps, revenge shootings, and murder trials had risen to 267.[35]

Why Did Gang Activity Increase?

Why has gang activity increased? One compelling reason may be the involvement of youth gangs in distribution and sales of illegal drugs.[36] While early gangs relied on group loyalty and protection of turf to encourage membership, modern gang boys are lured by the quest for drug profits. In some areas, gangs have replaced traditional organized crime families as the dominant suppliers of cocaine and crack. The traditional weapons of gangs—chains, knives and homemade guns—have been replaced by the "heavy artillery" drug money can buy: Uzi and AK-47 automatic weapons. Felix Padilla studied a Latino gang in Chicago and found that the gang represents

[a] viable and persistent business enterprise within the U.S. economy, with its own culture, logic, and systematic means of transmitting and reinforcing its fundamental business virtues.[37]

Ironically, efforts by the FBI and other federal agencies to crack down on traditional organized crime families in the 1980s have opened the door to a more violent youth gangs that control the drug trade on a local level and will not hesitate to use violence to maintain and expand their authority.

While drug trafficking may be an important reason for gang activity, it is by no means the only one. Gang activity may also be on the rise because of economic and social dislocation. In her analyses of gangs in post-industrial America, Pamela Irving Jackson found that gang formation is the natural consequence of the evolution from a manufacturing economy with a surplus of relatively high-paying jobs to a low-wage service economy.[38] The American city, which traditionally required a large population base for its manufacturing plants, now faces incredible economic stress as these plants shut down. In this uneasy economic climate, gangs form and flourish while the moderating influence of successful adult role models and stable families declines. From this perspective, youth gangs are a response to the glooming of the American economy and industrial base.

CONTEMPORARY GANGS

Thousands of gangs are operating around the country today with hundreds of thousands members. The gang, however, cannot be viewed as a uniform or homogenous social concept. Gangs vary by activity, makeup, location, leadership style, and age. The following sections attempt to describe some of the most salient features of this heterogeneous social phenomenon.

Extent

Estimating the extent of the gang problem today is exceedingly difficult. As noted previously, gang experts and police departments, sources generally relied on to tally gang populations, use a variety of definitions of gang membership. Definitional diversity means that youths who would be considered gang members in one jurisdiction are ignored in another. For example, some cities have no "gang" problems but are the locale of drug "crews" and "posses," groups with more than a resemblance to gangs. In addition, gang membership is constantly changing; a continual influx and outflow of members makes creating accurate population estimates extremely problematic.

Despite these difficulties, a number of attempts have been made to inventory gang populations. One of the most recent and thorough is a national assessment of gang activity, sponsored by the National Institute of Justice and conducted by G. David Curry, Robert Fox, Richard Ball, and Daryl Stone.[39] This study, referred to here as the National Assessment, surveyed police departments in the nation's seventy-nine largest cities. It found that 91 percent (seventy-two cities) report the presence of youth gangs involved in criminal activity; three other areas report the presence of posses and crews. Only Memphis, Tennessee; Newark, New Jersey; Richmond, Virginia; and Pittsburgh claim to have no gang problems.

Data from these cities indicate the existence of at least 3,876 gangs containing 202,981 members (1992). Additional data collected from twenty-nine smaller cities and eleven county jurisdictions increase these numbers (by 1,099 gangs and 49,589 members) to 4,975 gangs with 252,570 members.

Some of the reporting cities indicate that the number of gang members far exceeds the personnel on the local police force: Chicago estimates it has twenty-nine thousand gang members, while Los Angeles has an estimated fifty-five thousand! Other cities reporting large gang populations (in excess of five thousand members) include Santa Ana and Long Beach, Calif.; Minneapolis, Milwaukee, Denver, Las Vegas, and Albuquerque. The quarter of a million gang members did not include gangs located in New York City and Philadelphia, cities with potentially large numbers of gangs but from which data was unavailable.

Types

Gangs are categorized by their activity: some are devoted to violence and protecting their neighborhood boundaries, or turf; others are devoted to theft; some specialize in drug trafficking; others are primarily social groups concerned with recreation, rather than crime.[40]

In their early work, Richard Cloward and Lloyd Ohlin recognized that some gangs specialized in violent behavior, others were *retreatists* whose members actively engaged in substance abuse, while a third type were criminal gangs that devoted their energy to crime for profit.[41] Today, experts continue to find that gangs can be characterized according to behavioral activities. For example, Jeffrey Fagan analyzed gang behavior in Chicago, San Diego, and Los Angeles and found that most gangs fall into one of four categories:

1. **Social gang**—Involved in few delinquent activities and little drug use other than alcohol and marijuana. Membership is more interested in the social aspects of group behavior.
2. **Party gang**—Concentrates on drug use and sales, while forgoing most delinquent behavior except vandalism. Drug sales are designed to finance members' personal drug use.
3. **Serious delinquent gang**—Engages in serious delinquent behavior while eschewing most drug use. Drugs are used only on social occasions.
4. **Organized gang**—Heavily involved in criminality and drug use and sales. Drug use and sales reflect a systemic relationship with other criminal acts. For example, violent acts are used to establish control over drug sale territories. Highly cohesive and organized, this gang is on the verge of becoming a formal criminal organization.[42]

Fagan's findings have been duplicated by other gang observations around the United States. After observing gangs in the Columbus, Ohio, area, C. Ronald Huff found that they could be organized into "hedonistic gangs" (similar to the "party gangs"), "instrumental gangs" (similar to the "serious delinquent gang") and "predatory gangs," whose heavy crime and crack use make them similar to the "organized gang" found by Fagan in Chicago and on the West Coast.[43] Carl Taylor adds the *scavenger gang,* a group of impulsive kids who have no common bond beyond surviving in a tough urban environment. These kids are typically low achievers who prey on any target they encounter. Taylor contrasts the scavenger gang with the *organized/corporate gang,* whose structure and goal orientation make it similar to a Fortune 500 company in its relentless pursuit of profit and market share.[44]

These more recent observations seem to validate Cloward and Ohlin's research findings from thirty years ago and show that some but not all gangs are involved in drug activity and some but not all are violent.

Location

The gang problem was traditionally considered an urban, lower-class phenomenon. Two types of urban areas are gang-prone. The first is the transitional neighborhood, which is marked by rapid population change in which diverse ethnic and racial groups find themselves living side by side and in competition with one another.[45] Intergang conflict and homicide rates are high in these areas, which house the urban "underclass."[46]

The second gang area is the *stable slum,* a neighborhood where population shifts have slowed down, permitting patterns of behavior and traditions to develop over a number of years. Most typical of these areas are the slums in New York and Chicago and the Mexican-American barrios of the Southwest and California.[47] The stable slum more often contains the large, structured gang clusters that are the most resistant to attempts by law enforcement and social service agencies to modify or disband them.

Shifting Gang Locales

Transitional neighborhood and the stable slum are not the only environments that produce gangs. In recent years, there has been a massive movement of people out of the central city into outlying communities and suburbs. Many of these people have been from the upper or middle class, but lower-income residents have also been affected. In some cities, once-fashionable outlying neighborhoods have declined, and downtown, central city areas have undergone extensive urban renewal. Central, inner-city districts of major cities such as New York and Chicago have become devoted to finance, retail stores, restaurants, and entertainment.[48] Two aspects of this development inhibit gang formation—first, there are few residential areas and thus few adolescent recruits, and second, there is intensive police patrol. In some areas, such as Miami and Boston, slums or ghettos have shifted from the downtown areas to outer-city, ring-city, or suburban areas—that is, to formerly middle-class areas now in decay. Suburban housing projects are also gang-prone. Thus, while gangs are still located in areas of urban blight today, these neighborhoods are often at some distance from their traditional inner-city locations.[49]

Gangs are also appearing in smaller cities. These gangs were first believed to be offshoots of big-city gangs whose members set up shop in new territory; recent research suggests, however, that many of these gangs may be homegrown. For example, in an impressive study, Richard Zevitz and Susan Takata found that gangs of local youth formed in Kenosha, Wisconsin (population of about eighty thousand) during the mid-'80s. Because these groups copied clothing, insignia, and hand signs of Chicago gangs, authorities leaped to the conclusion that they were recent arrivals from the Chicago area. Zevitz and Takata found, to the contrary, that Kenosha gangs were formed and populated by local youths.[50] Even though gang areas have shifted their locale, the ecological patterns that produce them remain unchanged.[51]

Neighborhood Reactions

The presence of gangs in areas unaccustomed to delinquent group activity can have a devastating effect on community life. In his study of Milwaukee gangs, John Hagedorn found that a great deal of neighborhood hostility was evoked when gangs formed in this midwestern city.[52] Community resistance to gangs arose for a number of reasons. First, Milwaukee's gangs had little neighborhood turf affiliation and were formed solely to profit from illegal gain and criminal activity. Second, the gangs were formed at the same time minority students were being bused to implement desegregation. Gang recruitment took place on the buses and in schools and not on neighborhood streets. Gang membership, therefore, cut across neighborhoods, rendering local social control ineffective. Finally, the neighborhoods most likely to be plagued by gang violence were strained economically. Residential segregation and a lack of affordable housing prevented many working-class residents from leaving. The result was mixed neighborhoods of struggling working-class and poor families coexisting with drug houses, gangs, and routine violence. Frightened residents had little recourse but to call police when they heard gunshots; neighborhoods became uneasy and unstable.

Age

The ages of gang members range widely, perhaps from as young as 8 to as old as 55.[53] Gang experts believe that the average age has been increasing yearly, a phenomenon explained in part by the changing structure of the American economy.[54] Desirable unskilled factory jobs that would entice older boys to leave the gang have been lost. Replacing these legitimate jobs are low-level drug dealing opportunities that require a gang affiliation. William Julius Wilson found that the inability of inner-city males to obtain adequate employment prevents them from attaining adult roles, for example, they cannot afford to marry and raise families. Criminal records acquired at an early age quickly lock them out of the job market. Remaining in a gang into their adulthood has become an economic necessity.[55]

In his Milwaukee research, John Hagedorn also found that economic deterioration has had an important impact on the age structure of gang membership. In the past, gangs had a shifting membership because older members could easily slip into the economic mainstream. Good-paying manufacturing jobs that required little education and few skills were an attractive alternative to gang activity. These jobs are simply no longer available, with the result that the economic lure of gangs continues past adolescence into young adulthood. Less than one in five founding members of the youth gangs Hagedorn studied were able to find full-time employment by their mid-twenties; 86 percent had spent considerable time in prison. Some had become fully involved as drug traffickers (called "hitten' 'em hard"), others were part-time drug distributors ("makin' it"), and some worked sporadically in the drug trade ("day one"). These "old heads" with powerful street reputations were held in high esteem by young gang boys. In the past, ex-members served as a moderating influence, helping steer gang boys into conventional roles and jobs. Today, young adults continue relationships with their old gangs and promote values of hustling, drug use, and sexual promiscuity. As a result, gang affiliations can last indefinitely so that it is not unusual to see intergenerational membership with the children and even grandchildren of gang members affiliating with the same gang.[56]

The National Assessment of gang delinquency provides some indication of the age makeup of gangs.[57] In some cities, a majority of people involved in gang-related incidents are adults. For example, police in Santa Ana, California, estimate that 80 percent of those involved in gangs are adults. In contrast, only 10 percent of the gang activity in Mobile, Alabama, involves adults. It is possible that cities in which the development of gangs is a recent phenomenon have a more youthful gang population.

Gender

Of the more than one thousand groups included in Thrasher's original survey, only half a dozen were female gangs. Females were traditionally involved in gang activities in one of three ways: as auxiliaries, or branches, of male gangs; as part of sexually mixed gangs; and occasionally as autonomous gangs. The first form was the most common. Often, the auxiliaries took on a feminized version of the male gang name, such as the Lady Disciples of The Devil's Disciples.

This may have been an accurate portrayal of female gang membership in the 1920s, but a change has taken place. Some gang experts, including Joan Moore and Anne Campbell, believe that female gang members are no longer satisfied with being in an auxiliary. While initial female gang participation may be forged by links to male gang members, once in gangs, girls form close ties with other female members. Peer interactions form the basis for independent female gangs and group criminal activity.[58]

It is still difficult to determine the precise number of female gangs or the size of their membership. Irving Spergel's national survey of gang activity indicated that females committed 5 percent or less of all reported gang crimes.[59] Recent gang surveys, however, indicate that the number of female gang members may be on the rise.[60] Carl Taylor's analysis of Detroit gangs found that girls were very much involved in gang activity.[61]

The National Assessment of gang activity found that many police departments do not bother to record the presence of females in gangs. The 40 large-city police departments that did keep records reported about 7,025 female members. The ratio of male to female gang members is still quite high, however, usually ten to one or more.

Formation

It has long been suggested that gangs form in order to defend their turf from outsiders; thus, gang formation involves a sense of territoriality. Most gang members live in close proximity to one another, and their sense of belonging and loyalty extends only to their small area of the city. At first, a gang may form when members of an ethnic minority newly settled in the neighborhood join together for self-preservation. As the group gains numerical domination over an area, it may view the neighborhood as its territory or turf, which needs to be defended. Defending turf involves fighting rivals who want to make the territory their own.

Once formed, gangs grow when youths who admire the older gang boys and wish to imitate their life-style "apply" and are accepted for membership. Sometimes, the new members will be given a special, diminished identity within the gang that reflects their inexperience and apprenticeship status. Joan Moore and her associates found that once formed, youth cliques (**klikas**) in Hispanic gangs remain together as unique groups with separate names (for example, the Termites), separate identities, and distinct experiences; they also have more intimate relationships among themselves than among the general gang membership.[62] She likens *klikas* to a particular class in a university, such as the class of '94, not a separate organization but one that has its own unique experiences.

Moore also found that gangs can expand by including members' kin, even if they do not live in the immediate neighborhood, and rival gang members who wish to join because they admire the gang's way of doing things. Adding outsiders gives the gang the ability to take over new territory. However, it also brings with it new problems, since outsider membership and the grasp for new territory usually results in greater conflicts with rival gangs.

Leadership

Most experts describe gang leaders as cool characters who have earned their position by demonstrating a variety of abilities—fighting prowess, verbal quickness, athletic distinction, and so on.[63]

Experts emphasize that gang leadership is held by one person and varies with particular activities, such as fighting, sex, and negotiations. In fact, in some gangs, each age level of the gang has its own leaders. Older members may be looked up to, but they are not necessarily considered leaders by younger members. In his analysis of Los Angeles gangs, Malcolm Klein observed that many gang leaders shrink from taking a leadership role and actively deny leadership. Klein overheard one gang boy claim, "We got no leaders, man. Everybody's a leader, and nobody can talk for nobody else."[64] The most plausible explanation of this ambivalence is the boy's fear that during times of crisis, his decisions will conflict with those of other leaders and he will lose status and face.

Communications

Gangs today seek recognition both from their rivals and the community as a whole. Image and reputation depend on a gang's ability to communicate to the rest of the world. (See Figure 10.1.)

One major source of gang communication is **graffiti.** These wall writings are especially elaborate among Latino gangs, who call their inscriptions *placasos* or *placa,* meaning sign or plaque.[65] Latino gang graffiti will usually contain the writer's street name and the name of the gang. Strength or power is frequently asserted through the use of the term *rifa,* which means to rule, and *controllo,* indicating that the gang controls the area. Another common inscription is "p/v," meaning *por vida;* this refers to the fact that the gang expects to control the area "for life." If the numeral 13 is used, it signifies that the gang is *loco,* or "wild."

Crossed-out graffiti indicates that a territory is being contested by a rival gang, while undisturbed writing indicates that the gang's power has gone unchallenged.

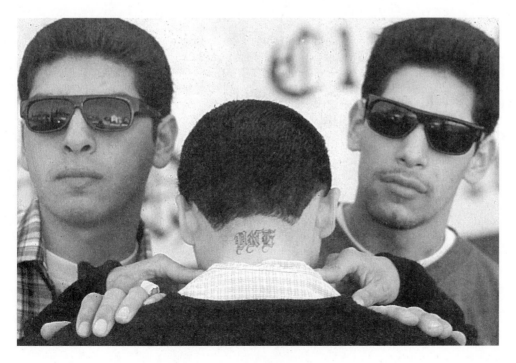

Hispanic gang members displaying gang identification symbols used as tattoos.

■■ FIGURE 10.1

Hand signs and logos of Los Angeles gangs

Source: Jerry Kaono, *Operation Safe Streets* (Los Angeles: Los Angeles County Sheriff's Department, n.d.).

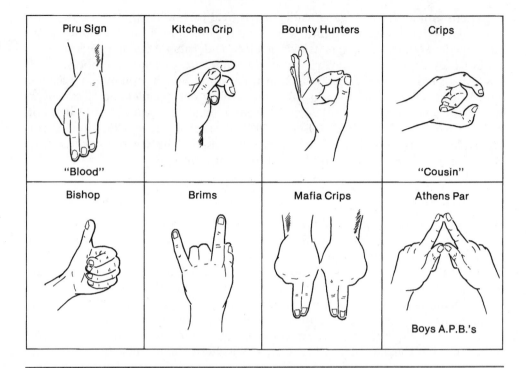

Logos of Chicago street gangs. Graffiti is used by one street gang to "put down" (ridicule) another. Placing the other gang's symbol upside down or marking their own over or through another is common practice.

Source: Illinois Gangs: Criminal Intelligence Bulletin #49, (Gang Control Unit, Illinois State Police) April, 1992.

AMBROSE putting down
PEOPLE and PARTY PEOPLE

COBRA STONES putting down
GANGSTER DISCIPLES

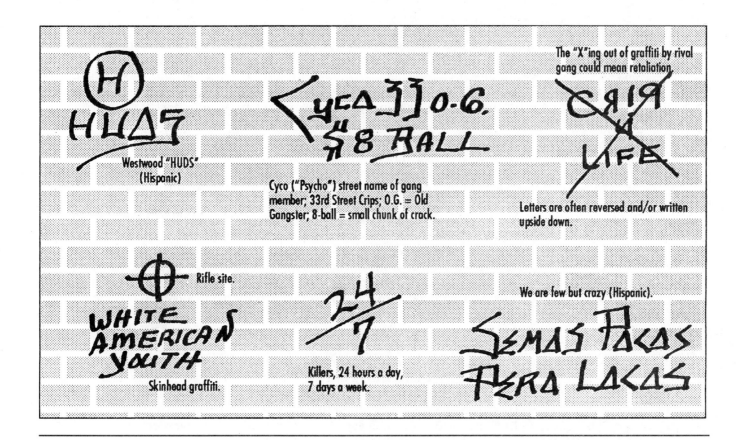

The "X"ing out of graffiti by rival gang could mean retaliation.

Westwood "HUDS" (Hispanic)

Cyco ("Psycho") street name of gang member; 33rd Street Crips; O.G. = Old Gangster; 8-ball = small chunk of crack.

Letters are often reversed and/or written upside down.

Rifle site.

Skinhead graffiti.

Killers, 24 hours a day, 7 days a week.

We are few but crazy (Hispanic).

■■ **FIGURE 10.1** *continued*

Graffiti of Colorado youth gangs.

Source: Sgt. Dallas Riedesel, *Street Gangs,* (Lakewood Police Department, Lakewood, CO) 1992.

Gangs also communicate by ritualistic argot (speech patterns) and hand signs. Flashing or tossing gang signs in the presence of rivals is often viewed as a direct challenge that can escalate into a verbal or physical confrontation. In Chicago, gangs call this **representing.** Gang boys will proclaim their affiliation ("Latin King Love!" "Stone Killers!") and ask victims "Who do you ride?" or "What do you be about?"; an incorrect response will provoke an attack.[66] False representing can be used to intentionally misinform witnesses and victims; it can be used to expose imposters or neutrals trying to make safe passage through gang-controlled territory.

Still another method of communication is clothing. In some areas, gang members communicate their membership by wearing jackets with the name of their gang embroidered on the back. In Boston neighborhoods, certain articles of clothing, for example, sneakers or jackets with a particular logo, are worn to identify gang membership. *Sneaker trees,* into which gang members throw dozens of pairs of sneakers whose laces have been tied together, designate gang turf; one gang area in Boston is called Adidas Park.[67] In Los Angeles, the two major black gangs are the Crips and the Bloods, each containing many thousands of members. Crips are identified with the color blue and will wear some article of blue clothing—hat, belt, or jacket—to communicate their allegiance; their rivals, the Bloods, identify with the color red.[68] In a 1988 incident, a Crips member waiting in line to see the gang film *Colors* was shot by a member of the Bloods who, after viewing the film, was apparently upset by the way his gang had been depicted; the victim's blue handkerchief gave away his gang affiliation to his assailant.[69]

Gang boys also commonly tattoo themselves with the name of their gang or a gang sign. This shows permanent loyalty to the gang and warns the community of their membership in a powerful and violent organization.

Criminality

Gang criminality has numerous patterns. As you may recall, each gang specializes in a different kind of criminal activity. Criminal gangs frequently engage in felony assaults, robberies, and other kinds of theft; drug-oriented gangs concentrate on the sale of marijuana, PCP, cocaine ("crack"), and amphetamines ("ice"); and organized gangs use violence to control a drug territory.

While it has become common to associate gangs with drug activity, not all experts agree that gangs are major players in drug trafficking. Research conducted in California by Malcolm Klein, Cheryl Maxson, and Lea Cunningham showed that neighborhoods that suffered a dramatic increase in crack distribution likewise reported an increase in street gang drug involvement. However, gang involvement in the drug trade usually consisted of the distribution of small amounts of drugs at the street level, not significant importation or trafficking. Gang members did not play a major role in drug dealing, nor were their violent episodes a function of drug dealing. The world of crack dealing in Los Angeles belonged to regular drug dealers and not street-gang youth.[70] Mel Wallace also concludes that gang violence in Illinois "has not been drug driven" but is related to many factors, including academic failure and economic decline.[71]

Gangs have also been the source of retaliatory violence directed toward rival gangs that are accused of insults, personal disputes, chance altercations, infringements on territory, or illegal enterprise. Once an insult is perceived or a challenge is offered, the gang's honor cannot be restored until the "debt" is repaid. Police efforts to cool down gang disputes only delay the inevitable revenge, a beating or a *drive-by shooting*. Though they are more common in movies than in reality, large street fights between rival gangs sometimes are planned and held to settle a turf dispute.

Retaliation is often directed against gang members who step out of line. If subordinates disobey orders, perhaps by using rather than selling drugs, they may be subject to harsh disciplinary action by other gang members. Violence is used to maintain the gang's internal discipline and security.

Another common gang crime is extortion, called "turf tax," which involves forcing people to pay the gang to be protected from dangerous neighborhood youths (presumably themselves). **Prestige crimes** occur when a gang boy steals or assaults someone, even a police officer, to gain prestige in the gang and neighborhood. These crimes may be part of an initiation right or an effort to establish a special reputation, a position of responsibility, or a leadership role; to prevail in an internal power struggle, or to respond to a challenge from a rival (proving the youth is not chicken).

Ethnic and Racial Composition

Most gangs seem to be racially exclusive. Although Lewis Yablonsky found racially mixed violent gangs, the majority of gang observers all view gangs as racially homogeneous groups: all white (English, Italian, Irish, and/or Slavic origin), all black (African origin), all Hispanic/Latino (Mexican, Puerto Rican, Panamanian, Colombian, and other Spanish-speaking people), or all Asian (Chinese, Japanese, Korean, Taiwanese, Samoan, and Vietnamese).[72] Most intergang conflict appears to be among groups of the same ethnic and racial background.[73]

The ethnic distribution of gangs corresponds to their geographic location. For example, in Philadelphia and Detroit, the overwhelming number of gang members are African-American. In New York and Los Angeles, Latino gangs predominate, and San Francisco's small gang population is mostly Asian.[74] Newly emerging immigrant groups are making their presence felt in gangs. Authorities in Buffalo, New York, estimate that 10 percent of their gang population are Jamaicans. Cambodian and Haitian youth are joining gangs in Boston. A significant portion of Honolulu's gangs are Samoans (19 percent) and Filipinos (46 percent).[75]

The National Assessment was able to acquire data on the ethnic distribution of gangs from twenty-six large cities. As Figure 10.2 shows, a significant majority of gang boys are African-American and Hispanic, followed by Asian and Anglo. While Anglos make up only a small percentage of all gang youth, those jurisdictions (eleven) that record year-to-year change in the ethnicity of gang populations indicate that their numbers are now growing at a faster rate than other groups. The following Focus on Delinquency examines barrio gangs.

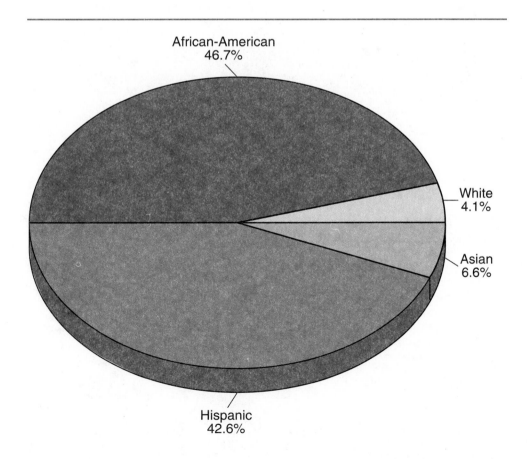

African-American
46.7%

White
4.1%

Asian
6.6%

Hispanic
42.6%

■■FIGURE 10.2

Distribution of major ethnic groups in 24 large cities, 1991. While Anglos and Asians have the smallest percentage of gang membership, their numbers are increasing at a faster pace than African-Americans and Latinos.

G. David Curry, Robert J. Fox, Richard Ball, and Daryl Stone, *National Assessment of Law Enforcement Anti-Gang Information Resources, Final Report* (Morgantown, W. Va., 1992), p. 56.

Barrio Gangs

According to experts such as Joan Moore and James Diego Vigil, Latino barrio gangs have evolved over time, sustained by continuous waves of poorly educated Mexican immigrants. Each new wave of immigrants settles in existing barrios or creates new ones. There, youngsters subscribe to the *cholo* (marginalized) subculture, with its own set of slang, clothing, style, and values. The *cholo* subculture places a high value on friendship, often imputing family and kinship relationships to peers (by calling them "brother" or "cousin"). Scholastic achievement is devalued and replaced with "partying." Employment is valued only if it requires little effort and brings in enough cash to party. An important aspect of the *cholo* culture is demonstrating *machismo*, or manliness. Barrio youths try to impress their peers and rivals with their ability to drink more than others, their fighting and sexual prowess, and their heart. The *cholo* culture helps these immigrants bridge the gap between the Mexican culture, which they left, and the U.S. culture, into which they have trouble assimilating.

Barrio gangs are not a recent development. Aggressive male youth groups have been a feature of the Mexican community as far back as the nineteenth century. The early barrio gangs were made up of young laborers whose behavior was more oriented around sports and socializing than criminality.

Then in the 1940s, the *pachuco* fad swept through the community; its advocates wore outlandish outfits (zoot suits) and spoke a unique Spanish-English slang. A well-publicized murder case and some urban disturbances helped brand the *pachucos* as vicious "rat packs." Though most zoot-suiters (who can be compared to members of the heavy metal music culture today) were not gang members or necessarily involved in crime, the press focused attention on them as a major social problem, and a popular stereotype was created. Mexican-American youths became suspect regardless of their actual interest in gangs.

In the 1950s, increasing stigmatization and isolation encouraged the development of deviance. Drug use, which had been quietly tolerated in an earlier generation, was now the target of police crackdowns, and many barrio residents went to prison. Mexican-Americans gained the stereotype of "evil dope dealers," and the early naïveté of *cholo* street life-style was ended.

In the 1960s, the Chicano political movement had an important influence on gangs. First, gangs were romanticized as social bandits in the tradition of earlier Mexican opposition to Anglo authority. Second, gangs (and their adult ex-offender members, the *pintos*) began to be viewed as the fighting branch of the movement that protected the community from the police. Protecting the community (*la raza*) was an extension of protecting their turf or neighborhood. Youth gangs and their extensions became enmeshed in community affairs, and their problems with the law came to be identified with the problems of the community as a whole.

In the last ten years, the nature of the Chicano gang has changed significantly. The image of the gang changed within the community, and its purpose was similarly reoriented. A number of reasons exist for this transformation. Publicity about violent Mexican-American prison gangs, such as La Familia, helped create the image that all Chicano gangs were criminally oriented. The *cholo* culture was viewed as a liability of the Chicano movement. When political activism cooled and street demonstrations ended, gang members were not needed as community protectors. The gangs became more closely identified with criminals than with social activists. A new wave of Mexican immigrants rejected the gang culture, and leaders of the existing community requested police protection from the gangs. As gang isolation increased, so too did gang violence and criminality. So from leaders in a sociopolitical movement, gang members became members of an ostracized underclass.

Los Angeles barrio gangs are now being influenced by economic restructuring. The kin-based job-finding networks that helped ease gang boys into conventional society broke down as employers hired the waves of immigrants who flooded into California. Without employment opportunities, young adults hang out with the gang cliques. Their presence empowers the gang and makes it seem more like a family with "older brothers" readily available to guide younger members. Because gang veterans get involved with the affairs of recruits, "street socialization" in the gang becomes more competitive with conventional socialization in the family and the school. ■

Source: Joan Moore, "Isolation and Stigmatization in the Development of an Underclass: The Case of Chicano Gangs in East Los Angeles," *Social Problems* 33:1–12 (1985); idem, *Homeboys: Gangs, Drugs and Prison in the Barrios of Los Angeles* (Philadelphia: Temple University Press, 1979); James Diego Vigil, *Barrio Gangs: Street Life and Identity in Southern California* (Austin: University of Texas Press, 1988); James Diego Vigil and John Long," Emic and Etic Perspectives on Gang Culture: The Chicano Case," in C. Ronald Huff, ed., *Gangs in America* (Newbury Park, Calif.: Sage, 1990), pp. 55–70; James Diego Vigil, "*Cholos* and Gangs: Culture Change and Street Youth in Los Angeles," in C. Ronald Huff, ed., *Gangs in America* (Newbury Park, Calif.: Sage, 1990), pp. 116–28.

African-American Gangs. The first black teenage gangs were organized in the early 1920s and specialized in common street crime activities.[76] Since they had few rival organizations in their inner-city locales, they were able to concentrate on criminal activity, rather than defending their turf. By the 1930s, the expanding number of rival gangs spawned competition, and inner-city gang warfare became commonplace.

In Los Angeles, which is today a hotspot of gang activity, the first black youth gang formed in the 1920s was the Boozies, named after a family that provided a significant portion of its membership. This gang virtually ran the inner city until the 1930s, when rivals began to challenge its criminal monopoly. In the next twenty years, a number of black gangs, including the Businessmen, Home Street, Slauson, and Neighborhood, emerged and met with varying degrees of criminal success.

In the 1970s, the dominant Crips gang was formed and began to spread over much of Los Angeles. Other neighborhood gangs merged into the Crips or affiliated with it by adding "Crips" to their name, so that the Main Street gang became the Main Street Crips. The Crips' dominance has since been challenged by its archrivals, the Bloods. Both of these groups, whose total membership exceeds twenty-five thousand youths, have an organization that resembles an organized crime family and are heavily involved in drug trafficking.

African-American gang members, especially those in Los Angeles, have some unique behavioral characteristics. They frequently use nicknames to identify themselves, often based on a behavioral trait: "Little .45" might be used by someone whose favorite weapon is a large handgun. While TV shows portray gangs as wearing distinctive attire and jackets, in reality, members usually favor nondescript attire in order to reduce police scrutiny; after all, a routine police search can turn up narcotics or weapons. However, gang boys do frequently use distinctive hairstyles, featuring shaving, corn rows, shaping, and/or braids, that are designed to look like their leaders'. Tattooing is popular, and members often wear colored scarves or "rags" to identify their gang affiliation. In Los Angeles, Crips use blue or black rags, while Bloods normally carry red.

It is also common for black gang members to mark their territory with distinctive graffiti. The messages are crude, rather than sophisticated: drawings of guns, dollar signs, proclamations of individual power, and profanity.

In the wake of the devastation caused by the April 1992 riots in Los Angeles, efforts have been made to call a truce among rival black gangs. Leaders have actually attended organized conferences designed to encourage gangs to work together to promote cooperation, rather than killing.[77] It remains to be seen whether such efforts can help reduce gang activity, considering that Los Angeles had about eight hundred gang-related killings in 1992, an all-time high.

Hispanic Gangs. Hispanic gangs are made up of boys whose ethnic ancestry can be traced to one of several Spanish-speaking cultures, such as Puerto Rico and Mexico. They are known for their fierce loyalty to their original or "home" gang; this affiliation is maintained, even if they move to a new neighborhood that contains a rival gang. Admission to the gang usually involves an initiation ritual in which boys are required to show their fearlessness and prove their *machismo,* or manliness. The most common test requires novices to fight several established members or commit some crime, such as a purse snatching or robbery. The code

A national gang summit was held in 1993 with the goal of creating cooperation between rival gangs and reducing the rate of inter-gang conflict. It remains to be seen whether mediation efforts can reduce gang violence.

of conduct associated with membership means never ratting on a brother or even a rival, facing death or prison without betraying their sense of honor.

In some areas, such as Miami, Hispanic gangs are rigidly organized with a fixed leadership hierarchy. However, in southern California, which has the largest concentration of Hispanic youth gangs, leadership is fluid. No youth is "elected" to a post such as president or warlord. During times of crisis, those with particular skills will assume command on a situational basis.[78] For example, one boy will lead in combat, while another will negotiate drug deals.

Hispanic gang boys are known for their distinctive dress codes. Some wear knit, dark-colored watch caps pulled down over the ears with a small roll at the bottom. Others wear a folded bandana over the forehead and tied in back. Another popular headpiece is the "stingy brim" fedora or a baseball cap with the wearer's nickname and gang affiliation written on the cap's turned up bill. Members favor tank-style T-shirts or an open Pendleton shirt, which gives them quick access to weapons.

Members also proclaim their affiliations by marking off territory with colorful and intricate graffiti. Hispanic gang graffiti has very stylized lettering, frequently uses three-dimensional designs, and proclaims members' organizational pride and power.

Hispanic gangs have a strong sense of territory or turf, and a great deal of gang violence is directed at warding off any threat to their control. Slights by rivals, including putdowns, staredowns ("mad-dogging"), defacing gang insignia, and territorial intrusions, can set off a violent and bloody gang confrontation. Newer gangs will carry out this violence with high-powered automatic weapons, a far cry from the zip guns and gravity knives of the past.

The Latino gang is discussed in the Focus on Delinquency in this chapter.

Asian Gangs. Asian gangs are prominent in such cities as New York, Los Angeles, San Francisco, Seattle, and Houston. The earliest gangs, *Wah Ching,* were formed in the nineteenth century by Chinese youth affiliated with adult crime groups (*tongs*). In the 1960s, two other gangs formed in San Francisco, the Joe Boys and Yu Li, now operate, along with the Wah Ching, in many major U.S. cities. National attention focused on the activities of these Chinese gangs in 1977, when a shootout in the Golden Dragon restaurant in San Francisco left five dead and eleven wounded. On the East Coast, prominent Asian gangs include Flying Dragon, Green Dragon, Ghost Shadows, Fu Ching, On Leong, Tong On, and Born to Kill (a Vietnamese gang).[79]

In an important work, Ko-Lin Chin has described the inner workings of Chinese youth gangs today.[80] Chin finds that these gangs have unique properties, such as their reliance on raising capital from the Chinese community through extortion and then investing this money in legitimate business enterprises. Chinese gangs recruit new members from the pool of dissaffected youth who have problems at school and consider themselves among the few educational failures in a culture that prizes academic achievement.

In addition to Chinese gangs, Samoan gangs, primarily the Sons of Samoa, have operated on the West Coast, as have Vietnamese gangs whose influence has been felt in Los Angeles, New York, and Boston. James Diego Vigil and Steve Chong Yun studied Vietnamese gangs and found that their formation can be tied to such external factors as racism, economic problems, and school failure and such internal problems as family stress and failure to achieve the level of success enjoyed by other Asians. Vietnamese gangs are formed when youths feel they need their *ahns,* or brothers, for protection and have unsatisfied needs for belonging.[81]

Asian gangs tend to victimize members of their own ethnic group. Because of group solidarity and distrust of outside authorities, little is known about their activities.

Anglo Gangs. The first American youth gangs were made up of white ethnic youths of European ancestry, especially Irish and Italian immigrants. During the 1950s such Ethnic youth gangs commonly competed with African-American and Hispanic gangs in the nation's largest cities.

Today, the number of organized white gangs is dwindling, though sporadic organized activity is not uncommon. The traditional white gangs have all but disappeared from the American scene. Taking their place are derivatives of the English punk and **skinhead** movement of the 1970s. In England, these youths, generally the daughters and sons of lower-class parents, sported wildly dyed hair, often shaved into "mohawks," military clothes, iron cross earrings, and high-topped military boots. Music was a big part of their lives, and the band that characterized their life-style was the punk band the Sex Pistols, led by Johnny Rotten and Sid Vicious. Their creed was antiestablishment, and their anger was directed toward foreigners, who they believed were taking their jobs.

The punker-skinhead style was brought over to the States by bands that replicated the Sex Pistols' antisocial music, stage presence, and dress; these included the Clash, the Dead Kennedys, and Human Sexual Response. The music, philosophy, and life-style of these rock bands inspired the formation of a variety of white youth gangs. However, unlike their British brothers, American

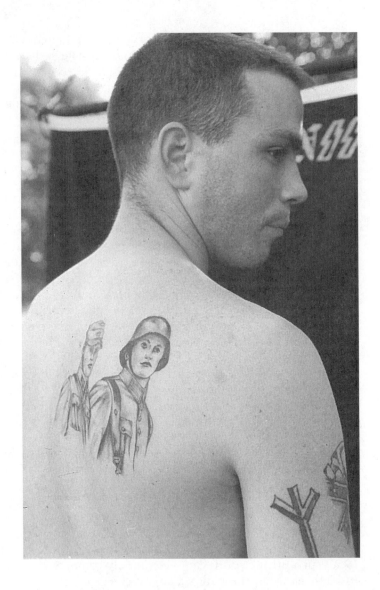

white gang members are often alienated middle-class youths, rather than poor, lower-class kids who are out of society's mainstream. These gang members include "punkers" or "stoners" who dress in the latest heavy metal rock fashions and engage in drug- and violence-related activities. There are also skinhead groups that are devoted to racist, white supremacist activities. Another variety of white youth gang engages in satanic rituals and becomes obsessed with occult themes, suicide, ritual killings, and animal mutilations. Members of these gangs get seriously involved in devil worship, tattoo themselves with occult symbols, and gouge their bodies to draw blood for satanic rituals.

Anglo gangs may be springing up in suburban areas. Members of one such gang, the Spurs Posse of suburban Lakewood, California, made national news when they were arrested in connection with a series of rapes committed to gain status in the group. The boys, aged 15 to 18, were accused of victimizing girls as young as 10; the group's members claimed the girls were willing participants.[82]

Spurs Posse boys were actually paid to appear on TV tabloid talk shows and brag about their "sexual exploits."

CAUSES OF GANG DELINQUENCY

What causes youths to join a gang? Though gangs flourish in lower-class, inner-city areas, gang membership cannot be assumed to be solely a function of lower-class subcultural identity: many lower-class youths do not join gangs, and middle-class kids are found in suburban skinhead and stoner groups. What are some of the suspected causes of gang delinquency?

Anthropoligical View

Writing about gangs in the 1950s, Herbert Block and Arthur Niederhoffer suggested that gangs appeal to adolescents' deep-seated longing for the tribal group process that sustained and nurtured their ancestors.[83] Block and Niederhoffer found that gang processes and functions do seem similar to the puberty rites of some tribal cultures; like their ancient counterparts, gang rituals help the child bridge the gap between childhood and adulthood. For example, uniforms, tattoos, and other identifying marks are an integral part of gang culture. Gang initiation ceremonies are similar to activities of young men in Pacific island cultures. Many gangs put new members through a hazing as an initiation to the gang to make sure they have "heart," a feature similar to tribal rites. In tribal societies, initiation into a cult is viewed as the death of childhood. By analogy, younger boys in lower-class urban areas yearn for the time when they can join the gang and really start to live. Membership in the adolescent gang "means the youth gives up his life as a child and assumes a new way of life.[84] Gang names are suggestive of "totemic ancestors" because they usually are symbolic (Cobras, Jaguars, and Kings, for example).

Evidence exists that contemporary gangs continue these traditions. James Diego Vigil has described the rituals of gang initiation, which include physical pummeling to show that the gang boy is brave and ready to leave his matricentric (mother-dominated) household; this process seems reminiscent of tribal initiation rights.[85] For gang members, these rituals become an important part of gang activities. Hand signs and graffiti have a tribal flavor. Gang members adopt nicknames and street identities that reflect personality or physical traits: the more volatile are called "Crazy," "Loco," or "Psycho," while those who wear glasses or read books are dubbed "Professor."[86]

Sociocultural View

Sociologists have commonly viewed the shattering, destructive sociocultural forces in inner-city slum areas as the major cause of gang formation. Thrasher introduced this concept in his pioneering work on gangs, and it is a theme found in the classic studies of Richard Cloward and Lloyd Ohlin and of Albert K. Cohen.[87] Irving Spergel's consummate study *Racketville, Slumtown, and Haulburg,* found that Slumtown, the area with the lowest income and the largest population, also had the highest number of violent gangs.[88] According to Spergel, the gang gives lower-class youths a means of attaining personal reputations and peer group status. Malcolm Klein's oft-cited research of the late '60s and '70s again found that typical gang members came from dysfunctional and destitute families, had family members with criminal histories, and lacked adequate educational and vocational role models.[89]

The sociocultural view retains its prominent position today. Vigil paints a vivid picture of the forces that drive kids into gangs in his well-respected work *Barrio Gangs*.[90] Vigil's gang kids are pushed into membership because of poverty and minority status. Those who join gangs are the most marginal youths in their neighborhoods and are outcasts in their own families. Vigil finds that all barrio dwellers experience some forms of psychological, economic, cultural, or social "stressors," which hinder their lives. Gang kids are usually afflicted with more than one of these problems, causing them to suffer from "multiple marginality." Barrio youths join gangs seeking a sense of belonging; gangs offer a set of peers with whom friendship and family-like relationships are expected.[91]

Overall, the sociocultural view assumes that gangs are a natural and normal response to the privations of lower-class life and that gangs are a status-generating medium for boys whose aspirations cannot be realized by legitimate means.

Psychological View

A minority position on the formation of gangs is that they serve as an outlet for psychologically diseased youths. One proponent of this view is Lewis Yablonsky, whose theory of violent-gang formation holds that violent gangs recruit their members among the more *sociopathic* youths living in disorganized slum communities.[92] Yablonsky views the sociopathic youth as one who lacks "social feelings." He "has not been trained to have human feelings or compassion or responsibility for another."[93] Yablonsky supports this contention by pointing to the eccentric, destructive, and hostile sexual attitudes and behavior of gang youths, who are often violent and sadistic. He sums up the sociopathic character traits of gang boys as (1) a defective social conscience marked by limited feelings of guilt for destructive acts against others; (2) limited compassion or empathy for others; (3) behavior dominated by egocentrism and self-seeking goals; and (4) the manipulation of others for immediate self-gratification (for example, sexually exploitative modes of behavior) without any moral concern or responsibility.

Sociopathic youth are most often drawn to violent gangs, which provide a vehicle for these violent, hostile youths to act out their aggressions and personal problems. Membership in violent gangs is fluid.

Rational Choice View

Some youths may join gangs after making the rational choice that gang membership may benefit their law-violating careers and be a source of income. Gang formation can be viewed as an "employment decision"; the gang can provide "partners" with the security of knowing they can call on the services of talented "associates" to successfully carry out business ventures. Research indicates that while gang membership increases the likelihood of delinquent acts, no conclusive evidence exists that gang membership is a necessary precondition for delinquency: antisocial kids may join gangs because (membership) facilitates their criminal careers.[94]

Felix Padilla found this when he studied the Diamonds, a Latino gang in Chicago.[95] Joining the gang was a decision made after a careful assessment of legitimate economic opportunities. The gang represented a means of achieving aspirations that were otherwise closed off. The Diamonds made collective business decisions; individuals who made their own deals were severely penalized. The gang maintained a distinct organizational structure and carried out other functions similar to those of legitimate enterprises, including personnel recruitment and financing business ventures with internal and external capital.

The rational choice view is also endorsed by Martin Sanchez-Jankowski in his important book *Islands in the Stream*.[96] Sanchez-Jankowski found gangs to be organizations made up of adolescents who maintain a "defiant individualist character." These individuals maintain distinct personality traits: wariness or mistrust of the outside world; self-reliance; isolation from society; good survival instincts; defiance against authority; and a strong belief in the survival of the fittest, that only the strong survive. Kids holding these views and possessing these character traits make a rational decision to join a gang because the gang presents an opportunity to improve the quality of their lives. The gang offers otherwise unobtainable economic and social opportunities, including both support for crime and access to parties, social events, and sexual outlets. Gangs that last the longest and are the most successful are the ones that can offer incentives to these ambitious but destitute youths and can control their behaviors.

The rational choice view holds that gangs provide support for criminal opportunities that might not otherwise be available. Some recent research by Terence Thornberry and his colleagues at the Rochester Youth Development Study support this model. They found that before kids become gang members, their substance abuse and delinquency rates are no higher than nongang members. When they are in the gang, their crime and drug abuse rates increase significantly, only to decrease when they leave the gang. Thornberry concludes that gangs facilitate criminality, rather than provide a haven for youth who are disturbed or already highly delinquent. This research is also important because it lends support to the life course model: events that take place during the life cycle, such as joining a gang, have significant impact on criminal behavior and drug abuse.[97] Criminal behavior is not determined solely by factors that are present at birth or soon after.

CONTROLLING GANG ACTIVITY

In recent years, gang control has often been left to local police departments. Gang control takes three basic forms:

1. *The youth service program,* in which traditional police personnel, usually from the youth unit, are given responsibility for gang control. No personnel are assigned exclusively or mainly to gang-control work.
2. The *gang detail,* in which one or more police officers, usually from youth or detective units, are assigned exclusively to gang-control work.
3. The *gang unit,* established solely to deal with gang problems, to which one or more officers are assigned exclusively to gang-control work.[98]

The National Assessment found that fifty-three of the seventy-two police departments surveyed maintained separate gang-control units. They are involved in such activities as processing information on youth gangs and gang leaders;

prevention efforts, such as mediation programs; enforcement efforts to suppress criminal activity and apprehend those who are believed to have committed crimes; and follow-up investigations directed at apprehending gang members alleged to have committed crimes. About 85 percent of these units have special training in gang control for their personnel, 73 percent have specific policies directed at dealing with gang boys, and 62 percent enforce special laws designed to control gang activity.[99]

A good example of these units is the Chicago Police Department's 462-officer gang crime section. This section maintains intelligence on gang problems and trains officers in dealing with gang problems. Through its gang target program, it identifies street gang members and enters their names in a computer bank that is programmed to alert the unit if the youths are picked up or arrested. Some departments also sponsor general prevention programs that can help control gang activities, including school-based lectures, police-school liaisons, information dissemination, recreation programs, and street worker programs that offer counseling, assistance to parents, and community organization, among other services.

Some police departments engage in *gang-breaking* activities, in which police will focus on the gang leaders and make special efforts to arrest, prosecute, convict, and incarcerate them whenever possible. For example, Los Angeles police conduct intensive antigang "sweeps" in which more than a thousand officers are put on the street to round up and intimidate gang boys. Police say that the sweeps let the gangs know "who the streets belong to" and show neighborhood residents that someone cares.[100] Despite such efforts, the police response to the gang and youth group problem seems fragmented at best; even in Los Angeles, gang membership and violence remain at all-time highs. Few departments have written policies or procedures on how to deal with youths, and many do not provide gang-control training.

Criminologists Mark Moore and Mark A. R. Kleiman suggest that gang sweeps and other traditional police tactics will not work on today's drug gangs. Instead, they argue, gangs should be viewed as organized criminal enterprises and dealt with as traditional organized crime families. They suggest (1) developing informants through criminal prosecutions, payments, and witness protection programs; (2) relying heavily on electronic surveillance and long-term undercover investigations; and (3) using special statutes that create criminal liabilities for conspiracy, extortion, or engaging in criminal enterprises.[101] Of course, such policies are expensive and difficult to implement because they may be needed only against the most sophisticated gangs. However, the gangs that present the greatest threat to urban life may be suitable targets for more intensive police efforts.

Community Control Efforts

In addition to law enforcement activities, there have been a number of community-based gang-control efforts. During the late nineteenth century, social workers of the YMCA worked with youths in Chicago gangs.[102] During the 1950s, at the height of perceived gang activity, the **detached street worker** program was developed in major centers of gang activity.[103] This unique approach sent social workers into the community to work with gangs on their own turf. The worker attached him- or herself to a gang, participated in its activities, and tried to get to know its members. The purpose was to act as an advocate of the youths, to provide them with a positive role model, to help orient their activities in a positive direction, and to treat individual problems. Gang-control efforts were common features of such community programs as the Chicago Area Project and the Mobilization for Youth in New York City. Detached street worker programs are sometimes credited with curbing gang activities in the 1950s and 1960s, although their effectiveness has been challenged on the ground that they helped legitimize delinquent groups by turning them into neighborhood organizations.[104]

In some areas, citywide coordinating groups help orient gang-control efforts. For example, the Chicago Intervention Network operates field offices around the city in low-income, high-crime areas that provide a variety of services, including neighborhood watches, parent patrols, alternative youth programming, and family support efforts.

Experts such as John Hagedorn have charged that the lack of legitimate economic opportunity for unskilled adolescents creates a powerful incentive for them to become involved in the illegal economy. To reduce the gang problem, hundreds of thousands of high-paying jobs are needed. This solution does not seem practical or probable. Increased use of deterrence and gang-breaking strategies by police can have only limited effect. A more reasonable and effective alternative would be to devote a greater degree of available resources to the most deteriorated urban areas, even if it requires pulling funds from groups that have traditionally been recipients of government aid, such as the elderly.[105]

While social solutions to the gang problem seem elusive, the evidence shows that gang involvement is a socioecological phenomenon and must therefore be treated as such. Kids join gangs when they live in deteriorated areas, where their need for economic growth and self-fulfillment cannot be met by existing social institutions, and when gang members are there to recruit them at home or at school.[106] Social causes demand social solutions. Programs that enhance the lives of adolescents at school or in the family are the key to reducing gang delinquency.

■ ■ ■ ■ ■ ■ ■ ■ ■ ■ ■ ■ ■ ■ ■ ■

SUMMARY

Gangs are a serious problem in many cities, yet little is known about them. Most gang members are males, aged 14 to 21, who live in urban ghetto areas. Ethnic minorities make up the majority of gang members. Gangs can be classified by their structure, behavior, or status. Some are believed to be social groups, others are criminally oriented, and still others are violent.

Gangs developed early in the nation's history and reached their heyday in the 1950s and early 1960s. After a lull of ten years, gang operations seem to be on the rise. Millions of crimes, including hundreds of murders, are believed to be committed annually by gangs. Gang and delinquent group membership may be in the millions.

We are still not sure what causes gangs. One view is that they serve as a bridge between adolescence and adulthood in communities where adult control is lacking. Another view suggests that gangs are a product of lower-class social disorganization and serve as an alternative means of advancement for disadvantaged boys. Still another view is that some gangs are havens for psychotic and disturbed youths.

Police departments have tried a number of gang-control techniques, but the efforts have not been well organized. A recent national survey found relatively few training efforts designed to help police officers deal with the gang problem.

KEY TERMS

cliques
crowds
co-offending
law violating youth groups
gangs
interstitial group
near groups
barrio
retreatists
social gang
party gang
serious delinquent gang

organized gang
scavenger gang
organized/corporate gang
stable slum
klikas
graffiti
representing
prestige crimes
cholo
skinhead
detached street worker

QUESTIONS FOR DISCUSSION

1. Do gangs serve a purpose? Differentiate between a gang and a fraternity.
2. Discuss the differences between violent, criminal, and drug-oriented gangs.
3. How do gangs in suburban areas differ from inner-city gangs?
4. Do delinquents have cold and distant relationships with their peers?

5. Can gangs be controlled without changing the economic opportunity structure of society? Are there any truly meaningful alternatives to gangs today for lower-class youths?
6. Can you think of other rituals in society that reflect an affinity or longing for more tribal times? Hint: Have you ever pledged a fraternity or sorority, gone to a wedding, or attended a football game?

NOTES

1. G. David Curry, Robert J. Fox, Richard Ball, and Daryl Stone, *National Assessment of Law Enforcement Anti-Gang Information Resources, Final Report* (Morgantown, W.V.: National Assessment Survey, 1992), Table 6, pp. 36–37. (Hereinafter cited as *National Assessment*.)
2. Thomas Berndt, "The Features and Effects of Friendships in Early Adolescence," *Child Development* 53:1447–69 (1982).
3. Thomas Berndt and T. B. Perry, "Children's Perceptions of Friendships as Supportive Relationships," *Developmental Psychology* 22:640–48 (1986).
4. Spencer Rathus, *Understanding Child Development* (New York: Holt, Rinehart and Winston, 1988), p. 462.
5. Ibid, p. 463.
6. Ibid., p. 463.
7. Albert Reiss, "Co-offending and Criminal Careers," in Michael Tonry and Norval Morris, eds., *Crime and Justice*, vol. 10 (Chicago: University of Chicago Press, 1988).
8. David Farrington and Donald West, "The Cambridge Study in Delinquent Development: A Long-term Follow-up of 411 London Males," in H.J. Kerner and

G. Kaiser, eds., *Criminality: Personality, Behavior, and Life History* (Berlin: Springer-Verlag, 1990).
9. James Short and Fred Strodtbeck, *Group Process and Gang Delinquency* (Chicago: Aldine, 1965).
10. Terence Thornberry, Alan Lizotte, Marvin Krohn, Margaret Farnworth, and Sung Joon Jang, "Delinquent Peers, Beliefs, and Delinquent Behavior: A Longitudinal Test of Interactional Theory" (Working Paper no. 6, rev.; Albany, N.Y.: Rochester Youth Development Study, Hindelang Criminal Justice Research Center, 1992), pp. 8–30.
11. Mark Warr, "Age, Peers and Delinquency," *Criminology* 31:17–40 (1993).
12. Cindy Hanson, Scott Henggeler, William Haefele, and J. Douglas Rodick, "Demographic, Individual, and Family Relationship Correlates of Serious Repeated Crime among Adolescents and Their Siblings," *Journal of Consulting and Clinical Psychology* 52:528–38 (1984).
13. Peggy Giordano, Stephen Cernkovich, and M. D. Pugh, "Friendships and Delinquency," *American Journal of Sociology* 91:1170–1202 (1986).

14. Denise Kandel, "Friendship Networks, Intimacy and Illicit Drug Use in Young Adulthood: A Comparison of Two Competing Theories," *Criminology* 29:441–69 (1991).

15. Marvin Krohn and Terence Thornberry, "Network Theory: A Model for Understanding Drug Abuse among African-American and Hispanic Youth" (Working Paper no. 10; Albany, N.Y.: Rochester Youth Development Study, Hindelang Criminal Justice Research Center, 1991).

16. Other well-known movie representations of gangs include *The Wild Ones* and *Hell's Angels on Wheels,* which depicted motorcycle gangs, and *Saturday Night Fever,* which focused on neighborhood street toughs. See also David Dawley, *A Nation of Lords* (Garden City, N.Y.: Anchor, 1973).

17. Walter Miller, *Violence by Youth Gangs and Youth Groups as a Crime Problem in Major American Cities* (Washington, D.C.: Government Printing Office, 1975).

18. Ibid., p. 20.

19. Lewis Yablonsky, *The Violent Gang* (Baltimore: Penguin, 1966), p. 109.

20. James Diego Vigil, *Barrio Gangs* (Austin: Texas University Press, 1988), pp. 11–19.

21. Walter Miller, "Gangs, Groups, and Serious Youth Crime," in David Schicor and Delos Kelly, eds., *Critical Issues in Juvenile Delinquency* (Lexington, Mass.: Lexington Books, 1980).

22. Ibid.

23. Thrasher, *The Gang* (Chicago: University of Chicago Press, 1927).

24. Malcolm Klein, ed., *Juvenile Gangs in Context* (Englewood Cliffs, N.J.: Prentice-Hall, 1967), pp. 1–12.

25. Ibid., p. 6.

26. Irving Spergel, *Street Gang Work: Theory and Practice* (Reading, Mass.: Addison-Wesley, 1966).

27. Miller, *Violence by Youth Gangs,* p. 2.

28. Marjorie Zatz, "*Los Cholos:* Legal Processing of Chicago Gang Members," *Social Problems* 33:13–30 (1985).

29. Miller, *Violence by Youth Gangs and Youth Groups as a Crime Problem in Major American Cities,* pp. 1–2.

30. Ibid., pp. 1–2.

31. "LA Gang Warfare Called Bloodiest in 5 Years,"*Boston Glove,* 18 December 1986, p. A4.

32. John Hagedorn, *People and Folks: Gangs, Crime and the Underclass in a Rustbelt City* (Chicago: Lake View Press, 1988).

33. National School Safety Center, *Gangs in Schools, Breaking Up Is Hard to Do* (Malibu, Calif.: Pepperdine University, 1988), p. 8. (Hereinafter cited as *Gangs in Schools.*)

34. C. Ronald Huff, "Youth Gangs and Public Policy," *Crime and Delinquency* 35:524–37 (1989).

35. Joan Moore, *Going Down to the Barrio: Homeboys and Homegirls in Change* (Philadelphia: Temple University Press, 1991), p. 3.

36. Irving Spergel, *Youth Gangs: Problem and Response* (Chicago: University of Chicago, School of Social Service Administration, 1989).

37. Felix Padilla, *The Gang as an American Enterprise* (New Brunswick, N.J.: Rutgers University Press, 1992), p. 3.

38. Pamela Irving Jackson, "Crime, Youth Gangs, and Urban Transition: The Social Dislocations of Postindustrial Economic Development," *Justice Quarterly* 8:379–97 (1991).

39. *National Assessment.*

40. Jeffery Fagan, "The Social Organization of Drug Use and Drug Dealing among Urban Gangs," *Criminology* 27: 633–69 (1989).

41. Richard Cloward and Lloyd Ohlin, *Delinquency and Opportunity* (New York: Free Press) p. 1–12.

42. Fagan, "The Social Organization of Drug Use and Drug Dealing among Urban Gangs."

43. Huff, "Youth Gangs and Public Policy," pp. 528–29.

44. Carl Taylor, *Dangerous Society* (East Lansing: Michigan State University Press, 1990).

45. Saul Bernstein, *Youth in the Streets: Work with Alienated Youth Gangs* (New York: Associated Press, 1964).

46. William Julius Wilson, *The Truly Disadvantaged* (Chicago: University of Chicago Press, 1987).

47. Vigil, *Barrio Gangs.*

48. Miller, *Violence by Youth Gangs,* pp. 17–20.

49. Jerome Needle and W. Vaughan Stapleton, *Reports of the National Juvenile Justice Assessment Centers, Police Handling of Youth Gangs* (Washington, D.C.: Office of Juvenile Justice and Delinquency Prevention, 1983), p. 12.

50. Richard Zevitz and Susan Takata, "Metropolitan Gang Influence and the Emergence of Group Delinquency in a Regional Community," *Journal of Criminal Justice* 20:93–106 (1992).

51. Ibid.

52. John Hagedorn, "Gangs, Neighborhoods and Public Policy" *Social Problems* 20:529–41 (1991).

53. *Gangs in Schools,* p. 7.

54. Spergel, *Youth Gangs,* p. 7; Hagedorn, *People and Folks.*

55. Wilson, *The Truly Disadvantaged.*

56. *Gangs in Schools,* p. 7.

57. *National Assessment,* p. 49.

58. Moore, *Going Down to the Barrio;* Anne Campbell, *The Girls in the Gang* (Cambridge, Mass.: Basil Blackwood, 1984).

59. Irving Spergel, "Youth Gangs: Continuity and Change," in Michael Tonry and Norval Morris, eds., *Crime and Justice,* vol. 12 (Chicago: University of Chicago Press, 1990), pp. 171–275.

60. Finn Esbensen, Terence Thornberry, and David Huizinga, "Gangs," in David Huizinga, Rolf Loeber, and Terence Thornberry, eds., *Urban Delinquency and Substance Abuse: Technical Report* (Washington, D.C.: Office of Juvenile Justice and Delinquency Prevention, 1991).

61. Taylor, *Dangerous Society,* p. 109.

62. Joan Moore, James Diego Vigil, and Robert Garcia, "Residence and Territoriality in Chicano Gangs," *Social Problems* 31:182–94 (1983).

63. William F. Whyte, *Street Corner Society* (Chicago: University of Chicago Press, 1955).

64. Malcolm Klein, "Impressions of Juvenile Gang Members," *Adolescence* 3:59 (1968).

65. Los Angeles County Sheriff's Department, *Street Gangs of Los Angeles County, White Paper* (Los Angeles: LACSD, n.d.), p. 14.

66. LeRoy Martin, *Collecting, Organizing and Reporting Street Gang Crime* (Chicago: Chicago Police Department, 1988).

67. Patricia Wen, "Boston Gangs: A Hard World," *Boston Globe* 10 May 1988, p. 1.

68. Rick Graves and Ed Allen, *Black Gangs and Narcotics and Black Gangs* (Los Angeles: Los Angeles County Sheriff's Department, n.d.).

69. Associated Press, "California Youth Slain outside Theater Showing *Colors*" *Boston Globe,* 26 April 1988, p. 6.

70. Malcolm Klein, Cheryl Maxson, and Lea Cunningham, "Crack, Street Gangs and Violence," *Criminology* 4:623–50 (1991).

71. Mel Wallace, "The Gang-Drug Debate Revisited" (Paper presented at the annual meeting of the American Society of Criminology, New Orleans, November 1992).

72. Miller, *Violence by Youth Gangs*, pp. 2–26.

73. Malcolm Klein, "Violence in American Juvenile Gangs," in *Crimes of Violence,* ed. Donald Muvihill, Melvin Tumin, and Lynn Curtis, *National Commission on the Causes and Prevention of Violence,* vol. 13 (Washington, D.C.: U.S. Government Printing Office, 1969), p. 1429.

74. Kevin Cullen, "Gangs Are Seen as Carefully Organized," *Boston Globe,* 7 January 1987, p. 17.

75. *National Assessment,* pp. 60–61.

76. The following description of ethnic gangs leans heavily on the material developed in *Gangs in Schools,* pp. 11–23.

77. John Mashek, "Gang Members Vow to Fight Urban Ills," *Boston Globe,* 5 February 1993, p. 3.

78. Los Angeles County Sheriff's Department, *Street Gangs of Los Angeles County.*

79. Zheng Wang, Indiana University of Pennsylvania, personnel communication, 3 February 1993.

80. Ko-Lin Chin, *Chinese Subculture and Criminality: Nontraditional Crime Groups in America* (Westport, Conn.: Greenwood Press, 1990).

81. James Diego Vigil and Steve Chong Yun, "Vietnamese Youth Gangs in Southern California," in C. Ronald Huff, ed., *Gangs in America* (Newbury Park, Calif.: Sage, 1990), pp. 146–63.

82. Associated Press, "California Youths Arrested for Gang-Related Rape Game," *Boston Globe,* 20 March 1993, p. 9.

83. Herbert Block and Arthur Niederhoffer, *The Gang: A Study in Adolescent Behavior* (New York: Philosophical Library, 1958).

84. Ibid., p. 113.

85. James Diego Vigil, "Group Processes and Street Identity: Adolescent Chicano Gang Members," *Ethos* 16:421–45 (1988).

86. James Diego Vigil and John Long, "Emic and Etic Perspectives on Gang Culture: The Chicano Case," in C. Ronald Huff, ed., *Gangs in America* (Newbury Park, Calif.: Sage, 1990), p. 66.

87. Albert Cohen, *Delinquent Boys* (New York: Free Press, 1955), p. 1–19.

88. Irving Spergel, *Racketville, Slumtown, and Haulburg: An Exploratory Study of Delinquent Subcultures* (Chicago: University of Chicago Press, 1964).

89. Malcolm Klein, *Street Gangs and Street Workers* (Englewood Cliffs, N.J.: Prentice-Hall, 1971) pp. 12–15.

90. Vigil, *Barrio Gangs.*

91. Vigil and Long, "Emic and Etic Perspectives on Gang Culture," p. 61.

92. Yablonsky, *The Violent Gang,* p. 237.

93. Ibid., pp. 239–41.

94. G. David Curry and Irving Spergel, "Gang Involvement and Delinquency among Hispanic and African-American Adolescent Males," *Journal of Research in Crime and Delinquency* 29:273–91 (1992).

95. Padilla, *The Gang as an American Enterprise,* p. 103.

96. Martin Sanchez-Jankowski, *Islands in the Stream: Gangs and American Urban Society* (Berkeley: University of California Press, 1991).

97. Terence Thornberry, Marvin Krohn, Alan Lizotte, and Deborah Chard-Wierschem, "The Role of Juvenile Gangs in Facilitating Delinquent Behavior," *Journal of Research in Crime and Delinquency* 30:55–87 (1993).

98. Needle and Stapleton, *Police Handling of Youth Gangs,* p. 19.

99. *National Assessment,* p. 65.

100. Scott Armstrong, "Los Angeles Seeks New Ways to Handle Gangs," *Christian Science Monitor,* 23 April 1988, p. 3.

101. Mark Moore and Mark A. R. Kleiman, *The Police and Drugs* (Washington, D.C.: National Institute of Justice, 1989), p. 8.

102. Barry Krisberg, "Preventing and Controlling Violent Youth Crime: The State of the Art," in Ira Schwartz, ed., *Violent Juvenile Crime* (Minneapolis: University of Minnesota, Hubert Humphrey Institute of Public Affairs, n.d.).

103. See, generally, Spergel, *Street Gang Work.*

104. For a revisionist view of gang delinquency, see Hedy Bookin-Weiner and Ruth Horowitz, "The End of the Youth Gang," *Criminology* 21:585–602 (1983).

105. Hagedorn, "Gangs, Neighborhoods and Public Policy."

106. Curry and Spergel, "Gang Involvement and Delinquency among Hispanic and African-American Adolescent Males."

SCHOOLS AND DELINQUENCY

Many of the underlying problems of delinquency, as well as their prevention and control, are intimately connected with the nature and quality of the school experience.[1]

Because the schools are responsible for educating virtually everyone during most of their formative years and because so much of an adolescent's time is spent in school, some relationship would seem logical between delinquent behavior and what is happening—or not happening—in classrooms throughout the United States. This relationship was pointed out as early as 1939, when a study by the New Jersey Delinquency Commission found that of 2,021 inmates of prisons and correctional institutions in that state, two out of every five had first been committed for *truancy.*[2]

Numerous studies have confirmed that delinquency is related to *academic achievement.* Some find that school-related variables are more important contributing factors to delinquent behavior than the effects of either family or friends.[3] Although there are differences of opinion, most theorists agree that the educational system bears some responsibility for the high rate of juvenile crime (see Table 11.1).

This chapter examines the relationship between the school and delinquency. We first explore how educational achievement and delinquency are related and what factors in the school experience appear to contribute to delinquent behavior. Next, we turn to delinquency within the school setting itself—vandalism, theft, violence, and so on. Finally, we look at the educational system's attempts to prevent and control delinquency.

THE SCHOOL IN MODERN AMERICAN SOCIETY

The school plays a significant role in shaping the values and norms of American children. In contrast to earlier periods, when formal education was a privilege of the upper classes, the American system of compulsory public education has made schooling a legal obligation. One study found that today, 94 percent of the school-age population attends school, compared with only 7 percent in 1890.[4] In contrast to the earlier, agrarian days of U.S. history, when most adolescents shared in the work of the family and became *socialized* into adulthood as part of the work force, today's young people, beginning as early as age 3 or 4, spend most of their time in school. The school has become the primary instrument of socialization, the "basic conduit through which the community and adult influences enter into the lives of adolescents."[5]

Because young people spend a longer time in school, the period of their adolescence is prolonged. As long as students are still economically dependent on their families and have not entered the work world, they are not considered adults, either in their own minds or in the estimation of the rest of society. The responsibilities of adulthood come later to modern-day youths than those in earlier generations, and some experts see this prolonged childhood as a factor that contributes to the irresponsible, childish, often irrational behavior of many juveniles who commit delinquent acts.

Socialization and Status

Another significant aspect of the educational experience of American youths is that it is overwhelmingly a peer encounter. Children spend their school hours

VIEW	EDUCATIONAL IMPACT
CHOICE	People commit crime because of poor social control. The school can educate youths about the pains of punishment and through disciplinary procedures teach youths that behavior transgressions lead to sanctions. Education can stress moral development.
BIOSOCIAL AND PSYCHOLOGICAL	The school can compensate for psychological and biological problems. For example, youths with low IQs or learning disabilities can be put in special classes to ease their frustration and reduce their delinquency-proneness.
SOCIAL STRUCTURE	The school is a primary cause of delinquency. Middle-class school officials penalize lower-class youths, intensifying their rage, frustration, and anomie.
SOCIAL PROCESS	A lack of bond to the school and nonparticipation in educational activities can intensify delinquency-proneness. The school fails to provide sufficient definitions toward conventional behavior to thwart delinquency.
LABELING	Labeling by school officials solidifies negative self-images. The stigma associated with school failure locks youths into a delinquent career pattern.
CONFLICT	Schools are designed to train lower-class youngsters for menial careers and upper-class youths to be part of the privileged society. Rebellion against these roles promotes delinquency.
LIFE COURSE	School failure can amplify preexisting crimogenic tendencies and elevate delinquency rates. School achievement can reduce preexisting antisocial pressures.

with their peers, and most of their activities after school take place with school friends. Young people rely increasingly on school friends and consequently become less and less interested in adult role models. The norms and values of the peer culture are often at odds with those of adult society, and a pseudoculture with a distinct social system develops, offering a united front to the adult world. Law-abiding behavior or conventional norms may not be among the values promoted in such an atmosphere. Youth culture may instead admire bravery, defiance, and having fun much more.

In addition to its role as an instrument of socialization, the school has become a primary determinant of economic and social status in American society. In this highly technological age, education is the key to a job that will mark its holder as "successful." No longer can parents ensure the status of their children through social-class origin alone. Educational achievement has become of equal, if not greater, importance as a determinant of economic success.

Schools, then, are geared toward success defined in terms of academic achievement, which provides the key to profit and position in society. Adolescents derive much of their identity out of what happens to them in school. Virtually all adolescents must participate in the educational system, not only because it is required by law but also because the notion of success is defined in terms of the possession of a technical or professional skill that can be acquired only through formal education.

This emphasis on the value of education is fostered by parents, the media, and the schools themselves. Regardless of their social or economic background, most children grow up believing that education is the key to success. Despite their apparent acceptance of the value of education, many youths do not meet acceptable standards of school achievement. Whether failure is measured by test scores, not being promoted, or dropping out, its incidence continues to be a major social problem of American society. A single school failure often leads to patterns of chronic academic failure. The links between school failure, academic and social aspirations, and delinquency will be explored more fully in the following sections.

Education in Crisis

The critical role schools play in adolescent development is underscored by the problems faced by the American education system. Budget cutting has severely reduced educational resources in many communities and curtailed state support for *local school systems.* Spending in the United States on elementary and secondary education (as a percent of the gross national product) trails that of other nations. While Sweden spends 7 percent of its gross national product on education, Austria 6 percent, and Japan 4.8 percent, the United States spends 4.1 percent.[6] As a consequence, the United States cannot provide the classroom services routinely available to children in other nations: Libya, Cuba, Israel, Norway, Finland, Portugal, and many other nations maintain lower student-teacher ratios than those generally found in the far wealthier United states.[7]

National evaluations indicate specific problem areas in the nation's educational system. Science education is a particular trouble spot. Fewer than one-half of high school seniors demonstrate in-depth knowledge of scientific information or the reasoning ability needed to interpret data in tables and graphs and evaluate and design scientific experiments.[8] By fourth grade, large disparities begin to appear between white and Asian-Pacific Islander children and their African-American and Hispanic peers, with the latter falling rapidly behind; children attending affluent school districts perform better than students in disadvantaged neighborhoods.

One reason American students seem to be lagging in educational achievement is that so many do not read in or out of school. In 1990, a government survey found that 45 percent of fourth graders, 63 percent of eighth graders, and 59 percent of twelfth graders read a total of ten or less pages each day; fewer than half of all students read outside of school; about 30 percent report never reading for fun; and about 22 percent said they either did not have homework assigned or simply did not do it.

Indications are that kids who read a lot outside of school are the ones most likely to do well on achievement tests.[9] Why don't kids read outside school? Some have nothing to read. About 5 percent of the students surveyed report having fewer than twenty-five books in their home, and 15 to 25 percent said

The threat of school crime
has prompted some juris-
dictions to create special
police forces to deal with
school-based delinquency.

they do not get magazines or newspapers. Another suspected culprit is excessive
TV viewing: 62 percent of fourth graders, 64 percent of eighth graders, and 40
percent of twelfth graders report watching at least three hours of TV each day;
about 25 percent of the fourth graders watch six hours or more per day.

As Figure 11.1 shows, with a few exceptions, achievement in science, math,
reading and writing has generally remained stable since 1970. Some improvement
was made in science and math in the 1980s, but this was offset by losses in reading
and writing. While encouraging overall, these test scores indicate that the national
commitment to excellence in education has not produced dramatic improvement
in key areas of scholastic competence.[10] The level of academic performance seems
critical considering its assumed association with delinquent forms of behavior.

ACADEMIC PERFORMANCE AND DELINQUENCY

The general path towards occupational prestige is education, and when youth are
deprived of this avenue of success through poor school performance there is a greater
likelihood of delinquent behavior.[11]

Poor academic performance has been directly linked to delinquent behavior:
there is general consensus that students who are chronic underachievers in
school are also among the most likely to be delinquent.[12] In fact, researchers
commonly find that school failure is a stronger predictor of delinquency than
such personal variables as economic class membership, racial or ethnic background, or peer group relations. Studies that compare the academic records of
delinquents and nondelinquents, including their scores on standardized tests of
basic skills, failure rate, teacher ratings, and other academic measures, have found
that delinquents are often academically deficient, a condition that may lead

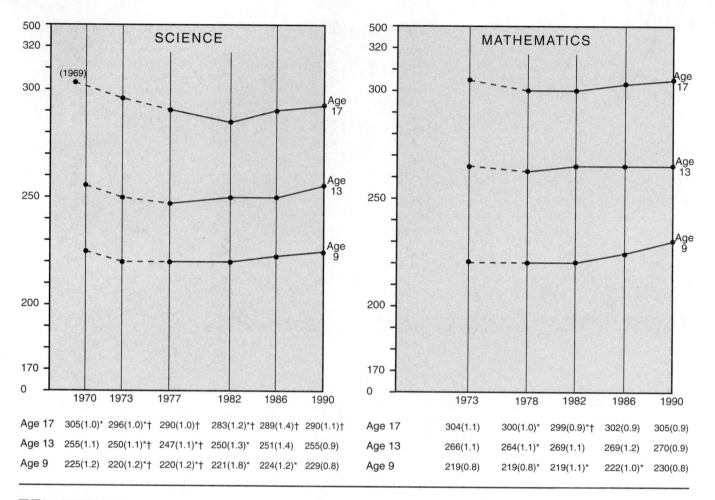

		SCIENCE			
	1970	1973	1977	1982	1986	1990
Age 17	305(1.0)*	296(1.0)*†	290(1.0)†	283(1.2)*†	289(1.4)†	290(1.1)†
Age 13	255(1.1)	250(1.1)*†	247(1.1)*†	250(1.3)*	251(1.4)	255(0.9)
Age 9	225(1.2)	220(1.2)*†	220(1.2)*†	221(1.8)*	224(1.2)*	229(0.8)

		MATHEMATICS			
	1973	1978	1982	1986	1990
Age 17	304(1.1)	300(1.0)*	299(0.9)*†	302(0.9)	305(0.9)
Age 13	266(1.1)	264(1.1)*	269(1.1)	269(1.2)	270(0.9)
Age 9	219(0.8)	219(0.8)*	219(1.1)*	222(1.0)*	230(0.8)

▪▪▪FIGURE 11.1

National trends in average achievement in science, mathematics, reading, and writing

• 95 percent confidence interval.

[- - -] Extrapolated from previous NAEP analyses.

* Statistically significant difference from 1990 and † statistically significant difference from 1969—70 for science, 1973 for mathematics, and 1971 for reading, as determined by an application of the Bonferroni procedure, where alpha equals .05 per set of comparisons. The standard errors of the estimated proficiencies appear in parentheses. It can be said with 95 percent certainty that for each population of interest, the value for the whole population is within plus or minus two standard errors of the estimate for the sample.

Source: Ina Mullis, John Dossey, Mary Foretsch, Lee Jones, and Claudia Gentile, *Trends in Academic Progress* (Washington, D.C.: Government Printing Office, 1991), p. 2.

to their leaving school and becoming involved in antisocial activities.[13] Kids who report that they do not like school, do not do well in school, and do not concentrate on their homework are also the ones most likely to self-report delinquent acts.[14]

Chronic Offenders

The academic failure-delinquency association is commonly found among chronic offenders. Lyle Shannon found that youths leaving school without a diploma

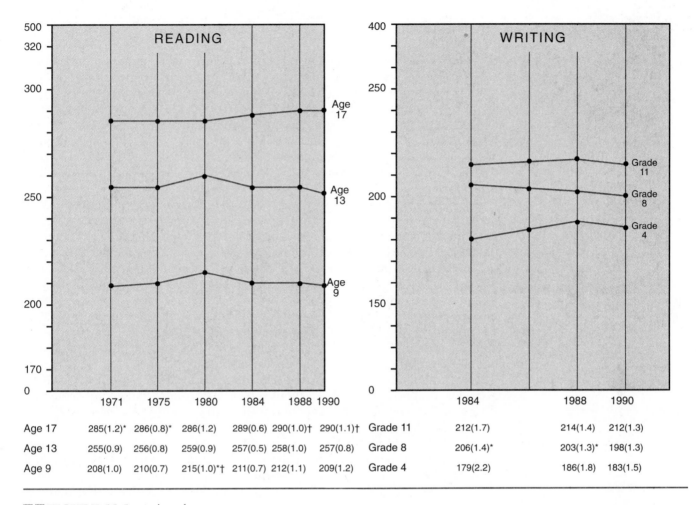

Age 17	285(1.2)*	286(0.8)*	286(1.2)	289(0.6)	290(1.0)†	290(1.1)†	Grade 11	212(1.7)		214(1.4)	212(1.3)
Age 13	255(0.9)	256(0.8)	259(0.9)	257(0.5)	258(1.0)	257(0.8)	Grade 8	206(1.4)*		203(1.3)*	198(1.3)
Age 9	208(1.0)	210(0.7)	215(1.0)*†	211(0.7)	212(1.1)	209(1.2)	Grade 4	179(2.2)		186(1.8)	183(1.5)

■■■ **FIGURE 11.1** *continued*

National trends in average achievement in science, mathematics, reading, and writing

were significantly more likely to become involved in chronic delinquency than graduates.[15] David Farrington and Donald J. West also found that chronic delinquents were school failures: 33 percent of youths in their sample who felt school was "of little use to them" were recidivists; only 7 percent of those saw benefit in school were repeat offenders.[16] Only 9 percent of the chronic offenders in Wolfgang's Philadelphia cohort graduated from high school, compared with 74 percent of nonoffenders.[17] Chronic offenders also had significantly more disciplinary actions and remedial/disciplinary placements than nonoffenders.[18]

The relationship between school achievement and crime is supported by surveys of prison inmates that indicate that only 40 percent of incarcerated felons had twelve or more years of education, compared with about 80 percent of the general population.[19]

School Failure

While there is general agreement that *school failure* and delinquency are related, some conflict exists over the nature and direction the relationship takes.

One view is that school failure and delinquency share a common cause, and it is therefore erroneous to conclude that school failure precedes and causes antisocial behavior. For example, some experts maintain that delinquents have lower IQs than nondelinquents, a factor that might also explain their poor academic achievement.[20] Delinquent behavior has also been associated with a turbulent family life, a condition that most likely leads to academic under-achievement.

The school-delinquency association may be influenced by self-esteem. Academic failure helps reduce self-esteem; studies using a variety of measures of academic competence and self-esteem clearly demonstrate that good students have a better attitude about themselves than do poor students.[21] Reduced self-esteem has also been found to contribute to delinquent behavior.[22] The association then runs from school failure to reduced self-concept to delinquency.

Gottfredson and Hirschi's general theory of crime associates delinquency with low self-control and impulsivity, traits that also may produce school failure.[23] The adolescent who both fails at school and engages in delinquency may be experiencing a variety of problems, including drug use, depression, malnutrition, abuse, and disease, all symptoms of a generally troubled life-style.[24]

A second view is that the school experience is a direct cause of delinquent behavior. Children who fail at school soon feel frustrated, angry, and rejected. Believing they will never achieve success through conventional means, they seek out like-minded companions and together engage in antisocial behaviors. Educational failure, beginning early in the life course, evokes negative responses from important people in the child's life, including teachers, parents, and perspective employers. These reactions help solidify feelings of social inadequacy and, in some cases, lead the under-achieving student into a pattern of chronic delinquency.

The Causes of School Failure

While disagreement still exists over the direction the relationship takes, there is little argument that delinquent behavior is closely related to a child's educational experiences. A number of factors have been linked to the onset of school failure; the most prominent are discussed in some detail below.

Social Class and School Failure

During the 1950s, research by Albert Cohen indicated that delinquency was fundamentally a phenomenon of working-class students who were poorly equipped to function in middle-class schools. Cohen referred to this phenomenon as a failure to live up to "middle-class measuring rods."[25] Jackson Toby reinforced this concept of class-based delinquency, contending that the disadvantages lower-class children have in school (for example, lack of verbal skills, parental education, and motivation) are a direct result of their position in the social structure and implicitly foster their delinquency.[26]

Some theorists contend that the high incidence of failure among lower-class youths is actually fostered by the schools themselves.[27] Kids from an impoverished background often find that the school experience can be a frightening one in which constant testing and the threat of failure are clear and ever-present dangers.[28] Research data confirm not only that such children begin school at lower levels of achievement but also that without help, their performance progressively deteriorates the longer they are in school. If this is true, the school itself becomes an active force in the generation of delinquency insofar as it is linked to failure.[29]

Does Class Really Matter?   Not all experts, however, agree with the social class-school failure-delinquency hypothesis. A number of early research studies found that boys who do poorly in school, regardless of their socioeconomic background, are more likely to be delinquent than those who perform well.[30] Arthur Stinchcombe's classic research on rebellion in a high school indicated that upper-class school failures were in fact more prone to be delinquent than lower-class **underachievers.** Stinchcombe concluded that a lack of consistency between school achievement and occupational goals was a more important contributor to delinquent behavior than social-class position: kids who wanted to get ahead but lacked the necessary grades were the most prone to rebel. According to Stinchcombe's *articulation hypothesis,* "[t]he key fact is the future of students, not their origins. Since we know that origins partly determine futures, social class will be an important variable, but in an unusual way."[31]

Other evidence has shown that affluent students are equally or even more deeply effected by school failure than lower-class kids. For example, Delos Kelly and Robert Balch found that middle-class youths who did poorly in school were actually more likely to become delinquent than their lower-class peers.[32]

Why might some affluent youth who fail at school be more vulnerable to delinquency than lower-class underachievers? Some research efforts have found that although the pressure to succeed cuts across class lines, there is a significant difference between the degree to which youth think its important to do well based on parental occupation: lower-class youth are significantly less likely to indicate that getting good grades or going to college is important.[33] Affluent children, the majority of whom live in intact homes, are generally given more encouragement at home to do well in school and are more likely to be high achievers.[34] School failure may cause more damage to their overinflated expectations while having a lesser effect on lower-class kids who maintain limited educational goals.

Tracking

Placement in non-college tracks of the contemporary high school means consignment to an educational oblivion without apparent purpose or meaning.[35]

Most researchers have looked at academic *tracking*—that is, dividing the students into groups according to ability and achievement level—as a contributor to student delinquency.[36] Studies overwhelmingly indicate that, compared with those in college tracks, noncollege preparatory students experience greater academic failure and progressive deterioration of achievement, participate less frequently in extracurricular activities, have an increased tendency to drop out, engage in more frequent misbehavior in school, and commit more delinquent acts. These differences are at least partially caused by assignment to a low academic track, whereby the student is effectively locked out of a chance to achieve educational success.

Some effects of tracking as it relates to delinquency are:[37]

- *Self-fulfilling prophecy.* Low-track students, from whom little achievement and more misbehavior are expected, tend to live up to these often unspoken assumptions about their behavior.
- *Stigma.* The labeling effect of placement in a low track leads to loss of self-esteem, which increases the potential for academic failure and trouble-making both in and out of school.
- *Student subculture.* Students segregated in lower tracks develop a value system that often rewards misbehavior, rather than the academic success they feel they can never achieve.
- *Future rewards.* Low-track students are less inclined to conform. Because they see no future rewards for their schooling, their futures are not threatened by a record of deviance or low academic achievement.
- *Grading policies.* Low-track students tend to receive lower grades than other students, even for work of equal quality, based on the rationale that students who are not college-bound are "obviously" less bright and do not need good grades to get into college.
- *Teacher effectiveness.* Teachers of high-ability students make more of an effort to teach in an interesting and challenging manner than those who instruct lower-level students.

Some school officials begin stereotyping and tracking students in the lowest grade levels.[38] Educators separate youths into special groups that have innocuous names ("Bluebirds" versus "Blackbirds") but may carry with them the taint of failure and academic incompetence. Junior and senior high school students may be tracked within individual subjects based on their perceived ability. Classes may be labeled in descending order as: advanced placement, academically enriched, average, basic, and remedial. And as Jeannie Oakes found in her national study of tracking, it is common for students to have all their courses in only one or two tracks.[39]

The effects of negative school labels (for example, "failure," or "slow" or "special needs") accumulate over time. Thus, if a student fails academically, this often means that he or she is probably destined to fail again, and over time, the repeated instances of failure can help to produce the career of the "misfit," "delinquent," or "dropout."[40] Consequently, a tracking system keeps certain students from having any hope of achieving academic success, thereby causing a lack of motivation, failure, and rebellion, all of which may foster delinquent behavior.[41]

Another disturbing outcome of tracking is that students are often stigmatized as academically backward if they voluntarily attend a program or institution designed to help underachievers.[42] Teachers consider remedial reading programs to be dumping grounds for youths with a "bad attitude" consequently, they expect youths who attended special-education programs to be disruptive in the classroom.[43]

Even more serious charges against tracking have been leveled by Jeannie Oakes, whose landmark study, *Keeping Track*, has helped expose the problems associated with the practice. Dr. Oakes found that

[t]racking seems to retard the academic progress of many students—those in average and low groups. Tracking seems to foster low self-esteem among these same students and promote school misbehavior and dropping out. Tracking also appears to lower the aspirations of students who are not in the top groups. And perhaps most important, in view of all the above, is that tracking separates students along socioeconomic lines, separating rich from poor, whites from minorities. The end result is that poor and minority children are found far more often than others in the bottom tracks. And once there they are likely to suffer far more negative consequences of schooling than are their more fortunate peers.[44]

There is general agreement that poor school performance is linked to delinquent behavior. Lower-class and minority youths may be overrepresented as school failures because teachers tend to stereotype them and expect disruptive behavior from them, strengthening the relationship between race, class, and official delinquency. School officials who feel tracking is necessary should be cautioned to create tracks that are flexible, encourage achievement, and allow student mobility in and between them.[45]

Alienation

Alienation of students from the educational experience has also been identified as a link between school failure and delinquency. Control theory (Chapter 6) assumes that a lack of attachment to school precedes delinquent behavior. Students who report they neither like school nor care about their teachers' opinions are the ones most likely to exhibit delinquent behaviors.[46]

Alienation has been linked to the isolation and impersonality that result from the large size of many modern public schools. Although larger schools are more economical to construct, their climate is often impersonal, and relatively few

■ ■ ■ ■ ■ ■ ■ ■ ■ ■ ■ ■ ■ ■ ■
Alienated youth who go to impersonal schools may be susceptible to delinquent behaviors.

students can find avenues for meaningful participation. The resulting resentment can breed an environment in which violence and vandalism are likely to occur. Smaller schools offer a more personal environment, in which students can experience more meaningful interaction with the rest of the educational community. Furthermore, teachers and other school personnel have the opportunity in a smaller school to deal with early indications of academic or behavior problems and thus act to prevent delinquency.

Students can also be alienated from the traditional student role that continues to operate in the schools. Students are expected to be passive, docile receivers of knowledge and are seldom encouraged to take responsibility for their own learning. In many schools, students have little voice in decision making. Some of them, therefore, feel excluded from the educational process, and such alienation may at times result in withdrawal from or overt hostility toward the school and all that it represents. Recent research by Patricia Harris Jenkins shows that students who believe that school rules are unfair and unevenly applied will be the ones most likely to engage in school misconduct and commit delinquent acts.[47]

Irrelevant Curriculum

Still another suspected cause of school failure is students' inability to see the relevance or significance of what they are taught in school. The gap between their education and the real world leads them to feel that the school experience is little more than a waste of time.[48]

Many students, particularly those from low-income families, believe that school has no payoff in terms of their future. Because the legitimate channel appears to be meaningless, "the illegitimate alternative becomes increasingly more attractive and delinquency sometimes results."[49] In his pioneering research, Stinchcombe found that rebelliousness in school was closely linked to the perception that school was irrelevant to future job prospects. He found that students who did not plan to attend college or to use their high school educations directly in their careers were particularly rebellious.[50] Along the same lines, Hirschi concluded that expectations of a college education and commitment to long-term goals are associated with low rates of delinquency.[51]

Irrelevant curriculum is a problem particularly among low-income and minority students because American schools are predominantly white, middle-class institutions. Although all states have had compulsory education statutes for several decades, today's schools are oriented toward middle-class youths who plan to go to college and ignore the needs and values of lower-class youths.

This middle- and upper-class bias is clearly evident in the preeminent role of the college preparatory curriculum and the second-class position of vocational and technical programs in many school systems. Furthermore, methods of instruction as well as curriculum materials reflect middle-class mores, language, and customs and have little meaning for the disadvantaged child. Middle-class bias in schools relates not only to class and ethnic background but to intellectual style as well.[52]

For some students, then, school is alien territory—a place where they feel unwelcome either because they lack academic skills or because they are different from the role models that the school holds out to them. Disruption of classes, vandalism, and violence in schools may in part be attempts to obtain enjoyment in otherwise lifeless institutions.[53] For the alienated student, delinquency often appears to be an attractive alternative to the hostile, or at best boring, atmosphere of the school.

Student Subculture

Alienated students attending isolated, impersonal schools that have curriculums irrelevant to their needs will develop support groups that encourage unconventional values. In fact, evidence exists that in many schools, alienated youths form a subculture and work in concert to subvert the educational system. Members of this subculture participate in a higher-than-normal amount of delinquent activity.

The problem, therefore, is not that individual students feel isolated from the educational process but that a loosely structured subculture of youths supporting each other's deviance exists. Individualized treatment efforts will have little effect if they do not take these subcultural influences into account.

Cheating

The student subculture may promote organized cheating rings. About 75 percent of high school students are estimated to cheat, up from 20 percent in the 1940s. Cheating has been alleged during college admissions exams, for example, by students secretly bringing dictionaries to the test site. Students pay to have homework done, steal tests, and use programmable calculators as electronic cheat sheets in math and science.

Cheating scandals routinely involve good students who are under pressure to get the A-level grades needed for acceptance at highly competitive colleges. Eleven students were suspended for cheating at a prestigious school in Winnetka, Illinois, in 1992; they had stolen a political science test. Another scandal made it to the front pages of the nation's newspapers because it involved students at the top-rated public high school in Pittsburgh. Numerous students, including the school's valedictorian, were accused of organized cheating and exam theft in order to maintain their class standing.[54]

Dropping out

The end result of school-related problems for all too many students is dropping out. Despite efforts to encourage students to remain in school, most large cities report a dropout rate ranging from about 8 to more than 20 percent of all students. (See Figure 11.2.) It is not unusual to later find dropouts in police files. As Table 11.2 shows, more than half of all adult arrestees had less than a twelfth-grade education.

While it is generally recognized that dropping out of school is fraught with negative social consequences, the impact of dropping out on delinquent behavior has generated much debate. Surprisingly, the bulk of research efforts point to a decline in delinquent behavior once a child leaves the school environment. Strain theory holds that once the pressure and conflict of the school experience end, the probability of continued delinquency among disaffected students should be reduced. This hypothesis was tested by Delbert Elliott and Harwin Voss in an oft-cited study of twenty-six hundred male and female students during their four years in high school. Elliott and Voss found that:

Dropout rates: In Baltimore, Dallas and Los Angeles, between 20 and 25 percent of all students drop out before completing high school.

Source: Children's Defense Fund, *The State of America's Children.* 1992 (Washington, D.C.: Children's Defense Fund, 1992).

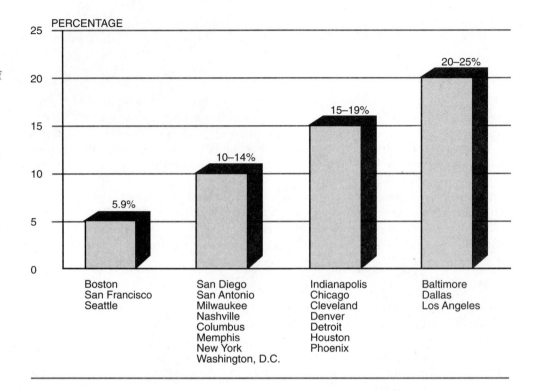

The rate of delinquency is significantly higher among those who drop out of school than among those who do not.

Dropouts' reasons for being delinquent while still in school are often rooted in the school experience itself (for example, limited academic achievement, feelings of alienation from school, or association with delinquent classmates).

The rate of delinquency for dropouts increases during the period immediately preceding their leaving school, but once they drop out, both police-recorded and self-admitted delinquency decline rapidly.[55]

Sociologist Daniel Glaser also notes that this phenomenon seems to cut across socioeconomic lines: "In *every* neighborhood and *every* socioeconomic class, most of those who are first arrested *while still in school* are less frequently arrested after they drop out."[56]

Several other research efforts are consistent with the results of the Elliott and Voss study.[57] However, in an important work, Terence Thornberry, Melanie Moore, and R.L. Christenson reexamined the Philadelphia cohort data to determine the effect of dropping out on the delinquency rate.[58] Their results were in sharp contrast to earlier research efforts. Thornberry and his associates found that dropouts were more likely to engage in antisocial behavior immediately after dropping out and then repeat their criminal behavior throughout their early twenties. Moreover, this finding is consistent for youths of various social backgrounds and races and held up when marital status and employment record were controlled. Thornberry and his associates conclude that these findings are in synch with the control theory hypothesis that severing ties with conventional society helps establish a youth in a delinquent way of life.

	MALES				FEMALES		
CITY	BLACK	WHITE	HISPANIC	CITY	BLACK	WHITE	HISPANIC
San Antonio	55	50	81	San Antonio	**	42	74
Kansas City	58	70	**	Kansas City	51	**	**
St. Louis	64	70	**	St. Louis	52	38	**
Philadelphia	55	54	69	Philadelphia	56	42	**
Dallas	56	69	86	Dallas	46	49	**
Cleveland	55	52	**	New Orleans	48	44	**
New Orleans	60	34	**	New York	57	54	64
New York	55	36	65	Indianapolis	36	64	**
Indianapolis	60	68	**	Chicago	48	**	**
Miami	46	57	68	Detroit	54	67	**
Chicago	56	50	65	Portland	51	65	**
Detroit	62	47	**	Birmingham	52	55	**
Portland	46	54	71	Los Angeles	29	42	72
Birmingham	49	57	**	Phoenix	47	50	74
Los Angeles	34	38	72	San Diego	31	46	71
Houston	52	34	75				
Omaha	36	54	**				
Phoenix	36	37	74				
San Diego	34	37	61				
Ft. Lauderdale	45	28	**				

*Data based on voluntary self-reports, 1988. Sample sizes for males are: African-American–5,622, white–2,936, Hispanic–1,794. Sample sizes for females are: African-American–1,533, white–1,169, Hispanic–438.

**Fewer than twenty cases.

Source: National Institute of Justice *Drug Use Forecasting Program* (Washington, D.C.: Government Printing Office, 1989).

In a recent paper criminologist G. Roger Jarjoura shows why research findings on the association between delinquency and dropping out may be confusing. Jarjoura examined longitudinal survey data and found that the reason a student dropped out of school had a significant impact on his future law violations. Those who left school because of problems at home, financial reasons or poor grades were unlikely to increase their delinquent activity after leaving school. In contrast, those who dropped out in order to get married or because of pregnancy were more likely to increase their violent activities. Those who left school early because they were expelled did not increase their violent activity but were more likely to engage in theft and drug abuse. Leaving school then was not a per se cause of future misconduct. In general kids who had long histories of misconduct while in school continued their antisocial behavior after dropping out; while dropouts engaged in more antisocial activity than graduates, it was not merely because they had dropped out.[59]

The focus of this debate has serious implications for educational policy in the United States. Evidence that delinquency rates decline after some students leave school has caused some educators and juvenile justice personnel to question the wisdom of compulsory education statutes. Some experts, such as Jackson Toby, argue that the effort to force unwilling teenagers to stay in school is counterproductive and that truancy and delinquency might be lessened by allowing them instead to assume a productive position in the work force.[60] For many youths, leaving school can actually have the beneficial effect of escape from a stressful, humiliating situation that has little promise of offering them any future benefits. However, if the recent literature proves accurate, dropping out may offer few short- or long-term benefits and therefore must be avoided at all costs.

DELINQUENCY WITHIN THE SCHOOL

It has become common to view school as a highly dangerous place in which intruders or students victimize teachers and other pupils, vandalize property, and disrupt the educational process. The federal government's pioneering 1977 study of the school system, *Violent Schools—Safe Schools,* alerted the public to the problem of school-based crime.[61] This survey found that although teenagers spend only 25 percent of their time in school, 40 percent of the robberies and 36 percent of the physical attacks involving this age group occur there. The survey recorded more than one hundred homicides, nine thousand rapes, twelve thousand armed robberies, and $600 million in destroyed property. Youths between the ages of 12 and 15 incur the highest risk, for children in this group are the victims of 68 percent of the robberies and 50 percent of the assaults on school grounds. The risk of being victimized is highest for minority students in largely white schools and for white students in minority-dominated schools.

Since this study was conducted, the level of school crime shows little evidence of waning. A 1991 Bureau of Justice Statistics report on school crime found that in a single year, about 9 percent of all students were crime victims, including 2 percent who were the victims of violent crimes (four hundred thousand violent victimizations).[62] Findings from a 1991 survey of five hundred Chicago students conducted by George Know and Edward Tromanhauser found that one-third reported something had been stolen from them at school or on the way to school during the two preceding months, about 10 percent had been physically assaulted, and 12 percent, threatened. More than half the students knew gang members, and 9 percent had been recruited for gangs.[63]

School-based delinquency and other antisocial acts are not ignored by administrators. A 1991 national survey of school principals found that many report experiencing a variety of problems on school grounds. As might be expected, secondary schools experienced more problems than elementary schools and urban schools more than those in rural areas. But schools in towns and rural areas are not immune from delinquency: principals in these areas report more student alcohol and tobacco use than those in city-based schools; the robbery and theft rate is as high in rural schools as in city schools.[64]

Weapons in Schools

On January 21, 1993, a .357 magnum handgun accidentally went off in a classroom at Los Angeles's Fairfax High School. The bullet passed through the chest of one student and struck and killed another. The gun's 15-year-old owner had brought the weapon to school for protection; after the discharge, he apologized to his classmates and waited for police to arrive.[65]

The school-based crime problem is fueled by students bringing weapons onto school grounds. The national survey of school principals showed that 3 percent considered student possession of weapons a problem; 7 percent of city school principals were concerned about weapon-carrying students. These national data are supported by local findings: California officials reported that during a single

school year (1988), teachers and administrators confiscated 8,539 weapons, including 789 guns, 4,408 knives, 2,216 explosives, and 1,126 "other weapons."[66] A self-report study of eleven thousand eighth- to tenth-grade boys in twenty states found that 3 percent had brought a concealed handgun with them to school.[67] A 1991 survey of 1,653 high school students in California, Louisiana, New Jersey, and Illinois found that 9 percent of males and 3 percent of females reported carrying a gun "at least now and then" to school.[68] Thirty-eight percent of the students agreed that there was a lot of violence in their schools, and 15 percent said they were "scared at school almost all the time"; 46 percent of the students said they knew someone who had carried guns to school during the past year.

Who Commits School Crime?

Who commits school crime, and what are the factors associated with high crime rates in schools? Gary Gottfredson and Denise Gottfredson reexamined the *Safe School* study data and found that the most important predictor of school crime is a condition they refer to as *social disorganization,* which is characterized by:

a high proportion of students behind grade level in reading, many students from families on welfare, a high proportion of minority students; and such community characteristics as high unemployment, high crime, much poverty and unemployment, and many female-headed households.[69]

Schools whose administrators cooperate with teachers, have highly regarded principals, are perceived to be fair and have well defined rules, and allow students a say in the way the school is run will have lower crime rates.

A number of researchers have observed that school crime and disruption are functions of the community in which the school is located. In other words, crime in schools does not occur in isolation from crime in the community.[70] In one important analysis, Joan McDermott found that the perpetrators and the victims of school crime cannot be divided into two separate groups.[71] Many young offenders have been victims of delinquency themselves and fear being victimized again. McDermott concludes that school-based violent and theft-related crimes have "survival value"; striking back against another, weaker victim is emotionally satisfying or simply a method of regaining lost possessions or self-respect.

McDermott also found that crime and fear in schools reflect the patterns of antisocial behavior that exist in the surrounding neighborhood. Schools in high-crime areas experience more crime than schools in safer areas; there is less fear in schools in safer neighborhoods than in high-crime ones. Students who report being afraid in school are actually *more* afraid of being in city parks, streets, or subways.

A number of other research efforts confirm the community influences on school crime. Using data collected from the Boston school system, Daryl Hellman and Susan Beaton found that measures of school disruption, such as suspension rates, are significantly related to community variables, such as family structure: communities with a high percentage of two-parent families experience fewer school problems. School problems were not related to income level, employment, or the racial composition of the community but were associated with housing quality, population density, and stability.[72]

McDermott's analysis suggests that it may be futile to attempt to eliminate school crime without considering the impact that prevention efforts will have on the community:

The school-community link suggests additional problems with some in-school crime prevention strategies. Law and order approaches such as tighter security, stricter rule enforcement, and fortress-like alterations in a school's physical plant may reduce acts of crime and violence in school, only to displace them to the community. Similarly, expelling or suspending troublemakers puts them on the street with nothing to do. Lowering the level of crime in schools may have no real impact on reducing the total amount of crime committed by young people.[73]

When communities undergo such changes as increases in unemployment and the number of single-parent households, both school disruption and community crime rates may rise.[74] Consequently, some experts contend that the school environment can be made safer only if community issues are addressed: for example, by taking steps to keep intruders out of school buildings, putting pressure on local police to develop community safety programs, increasing correctional services, strengthening laws on school safety, and making parents bear greater responsibility for their children's behavior.[75]

THE ROLE OF THE SCHOOL IN DELINQUENCY PREVENTION

For the past two decades, numerous national organizations and political groups have called for reforming the educational system to make it more responsive to the needs of students. Educational leaders now recognize that children undergo enormous pressures while in school that can lead to physical, emotional, and social problems. At one extreme are the pressures to succeed academically and earn admission to a top college; at the other are the crime and substance abuse students face on school grounds. It is difficult to talk of achieving academic excellence in a deteriorated school dominated by violence-prone gang members.

A report by the Carnegie Corporation, a leading educational foundation, found that the United States is indeed facing an educational crisis. Student dissatisfaction with school, which begins to increase after elementary school, is accompanied by a growing aversion for teachers and many academic subjects. The rate of student alienation and the social problems that accompany it—absenteeism, dropping out, and substance abuse—all increase as students enter junior high.

Educators have attempted to play a role in delinquency prevention in two areas: (1) controlling vandalism and crime within the school itself and (2) creating programs that will benefit youths and provide them with opportunities for conventional success in the outside world. Yet change has been slow in coming, and it has only been since the mid-1980s that concern about the educational system, prompted by the findings of the National Commission on Excellence in Education (in *A Nation at Risk*), focused efforts toward change.[76]

Skepticism exists over whether the American school system, viewed by critics as overly conservative and archaic, can play a significant role in delinquency prevention.

Some experts contend that no significant change in the lives of youths is possible by merely changing the schools. The entire social and economic structure of society must be altered if schools are to help students realize their full potential.[77]

■ ■ ■ ■ ■ ■ ■ ■ ■ ■ ■ ■ ■ ■

CASE IN POINT

As principal of the suburban regional high school, you are faced with a growing drug-use problem among the student body. There is evidence of dealing on campus, and parents have complained that their kids are bringing home drugs they bought at school. Last week, a 15-year-old overdosed and almost lost her life. At a school board meeting, angry parents charge that this kind of behavior may be okay in the city but this is a suburban community to which people come to get away from drugs and delinquency. There is some angry talk that if you can't handle the situation, then a new school chief should be found who can.

The local police offer a solution for the drug problem: institute a tough security policy that makes use of hidden cameras in public areas, such as the parking lot and cafeteria; allow random searches of student lockers and desks; hire a security director who will search students suspected of selling or possessing drugs; turn over to the police all evidence for prosecution; and suspend students possessing drugs on campus for the school year. Some teachers feel these draconian policies are misplaced in a suburban school. The relatively few offenders should be placed in counseling programs. Instead of security guards, the school should hire a drug awareness education teacher and teach kids about the dangers of taking drugs.

Should a school drug-prevention program stress law enforcement or education?

Is it fair to search student lockers at random?

Are hidden cameras an intrusion of student privacy or a needed security measure?

A danger also exists that the pressure being placed on schools to improve the educational experience of students can produce unforeseen problems for staff members. For example, there have been recent reports of teachers being prosecuted for encouraging students to cheat on tests and providing them with answer sheets. The pressure to improve student performance on standardized tests was the motive for the faculty cheating.[78]

Preventing School Crime

A number of school-based delinquency prevention efforts have been carried out around the nation. One approach has been to ensure the physical safety of students and school staff by using mechanical security devices such as surveillance cameras, electronic barriers to keep out intruders, and roving security guards. Critics claim that even though these methods are effective, they reduce staff and student morale.

Another approach used successfully by some school administrators is to set up and enforce strict disciplinary codes. Rather than suspending violators, some school districts now send them to a separate center for evaluation and counseling so they are kept separate from the law-abiding students.[79]

Other programs have been designed to improve the standards of the teaching staff and administrators and the educational climate in the school, increase the relevance of the curriculum, and provide law-related education classes.[80]

Most school districts refer problem students to social services outside the school. About 70 percent of public schools provide outside referrals for students with substance abuse problems, while 90 percent offer drug education within the school.[81]

While these efforts have been local in scope, there are some indications that they can be successful strategies to reduce school crime. The national survey of

■ ■ ■ ■ ■ ■ ■ ■ ■ ■ ■ ■ ■ ■

School administrators have made special efforts to control delinquent acts on school grounds. Violators may be suspended or transferred into special programs geared for behavior problems.

school principals found that a majority considered general discipline programs and policies to be effective in reducing disruptive behavior; drug and alcohol programs were viewed as being somewhat less effective.[82]

Preventing Delinquency

Education officials have instituted numerous programs to make schools more effective instruments of delinquency prevention.[83] Among the most prevalent strategies are:

- Cognitive—Increase students' awareness about the dangers of drug abuse and delinquency.
- Affective—Improve students' psychological assets and self-image, giving them the resources to resist antisocial behavior.
- Behavioral—Train students in techniques to resist peer pressure.
- Environmental—Establish school management and disciplinary programs that deter crime, such as locker searches.
- Therapeutic—Treat youths who have already manifested problems.[84]

More specific suggestions include creating special classes or schools with individualized educational programs that foster success, rather than failure, for nonadjusting students.[85] Efforts can be made to help students learn to deal constructively with academic failure when it does occur.

More personalized student-teacher relationships have been recommended. This effort to provide young persons with a caring, accepting adult role model will, it is hoped, strengthen the controls against delinquency.

Home-school counselors acting as liaisons between the family and the school might be effective in preventing delinquency. These counselors try to ensure cooperation between the parents and the school and to secure needed services—academic, social, and psychological—for troubled students before serious delinquency becomes a problem.

It has been proposed that experiments be undertaken to integrate job training and experience with the usual classroom instruction so that students may see education as a meaningful and relevant prelude to their future careers. Job training programs could emphasize public service, so that students could gain a sense of attachment to their communities while they are acquiring useful vocational training.

Table 11.3 illustrates some strategies for increasing the school's ability to prevent delinquency.

Demonstration Projects

A number of experimental programs have attempted to prevent or reduce delinquency by manipulating factors in the learning environment. One such project, known as Project PATHE (Positive Action through Holistic Education) was operated experimentally in four middle and three high schools in South Carolina for three years as part of the federal Office of Juvenile Justice and Delinquency Prevention's "Alternative Education Initiative."[86] Based on control theory, Project PATHE sought to reduce delinquency by raising students' stake in conformity through strengthening their commitment to school, successful experiences in school, attachment to conforming members of the educational com-

TABLE 11.3   School-Based Delinquency Prevention Concepts

1. Teacher training programs for parents
2. Policies and practices to ensure that schools and classrooms reflect the best examples of justice and democracy in their organization and operation and in the rules and regulations governing student conduct
3. A guarantee of literacy for elementary school students
4. Special language services for bicultural students
5. Career preparation in schools
6. Effective supportive services in schools
7. Alternative education programs for deviant students
8. Opening schools for community activities
9. Alternative education programs for students who require them
10. Community education programs
11. Alternatives to the suspension of troublesome students
12. Codes of rights and responsibilities drawn up by all elements of the school community (students, teachers, parents, and administrators)
13. Curriculum reform, especially the use of apprenticeship programs and law-related education
14. Police, school, and community liaison programs
15. Teacher education in appropriate disciplinary techniques and sensitivity to special students
16. Proper training of school security personnel
17. Improved counseling and guidance programs
18. Creation of a more personal atmosphere in schools through architectural design and use of smaller buildings
19. Student and parental involvement in programs to combat violence and vandalism in schools

munity, and participation in school activities. By increasing their sense of social competence, belonging, and usefulness, the project sought to promote the development of students in a positive direction.

To achieve these goals, teams were created in each school made up of staff members, students, parents, and community members and trained to implement change and revise policies; this involved diverse segments of the community in school improvement programs. A curriculum review and revision intervention was directed to improve teacher competence and curriculum development and delivery. Training in innovative teaching techniques and classroom management skills was ongoing. Schoolwide disciplinary practices were changed with the help of student input.

The overall academic quality of the schools was improved with mini-courses on such study skills as note taking and listening, practice in taking of standardized tests, and a reading hour. Student team learning was set up involving groups of youths working together to improve their educational ability and earn rewards for their improvement.

To improve school climate, a school pride campaign was launched, extracurricular activities were expanded, and peer counseling and rap sessions were introduced. In addition, a career exploration program, developed with the aid of a local technical school, introduced students to the possibility of a technical career in such areas as computer science and engineering; a job seeking program provided students with the skills needed to find and keep a job.

A final component of Project PATHE was to identify and give academic and counseling attention to children with special needs. Approximately 10 percent of the school population who had academic or behavioral problems received services designed to increase self-concept, improve academic success, and strengthen their ties to society.

The PATHE program has undergone extensive evaluation by sociologist Denise Gottfredson, who found that the schools in which it was used experienced a moderate reduction in delinquency and school misconduct; the services for high-risk students, however, did not reduce their delinquency levels. While crime reduction was somewhat less than desired, Project PATHE did produce a markedly improved school climate: teacher perceptions of school management and staff morale got better; student disciplinary problems declined; students' sense of belonging increased; and the dropout rate of problem students dropped and their test scores rose.

In a later analysis, Gottfredson compared Project PATHE with two other programs with similar goals: The Student Training through Urban Strategies (STATUS) program in Pasadena, California, and the Academy for Community Education (ACE) in Miami. The former was deemed a success, while the latter, like Project PATHE, failed to reduce delinquency among high-risk youth. Gottfredson found that the STATUS project's success was a function of its use of a special alternative class that involved experience-based learning programs over the course of the school year. STATUS was able to alter students' attitudes by increasing attachment to positive adult role models (teachers and counselors) and weakening the influence of negative forces (deviant peers).[87]

Schools may not be able to reduce delinquency single-handedly, but a number of viable alternatives to their present operations could aid a communitywide effort to lessen the problem of juvenile crime. The following Focus on Delinquency describes another school-based delinquency control program.

LEGAL RIGHTS WITHIN THE SCHOOL

As educational officials have attempted to restore order within the school, their actions often have run into opposition from the courts, which are concerned with maintaining the legal rights of minors. The U.S. Supreme Court has sought to balance the civil liberties of students with the school's mandate to provide a reasonable and safe educational environment. In some instances, the Court has sided with students, while in others, the balance has shifted toward the educational establishment. The main issues concerning the rights of children and the schools include compulsory attendance, free speech in school, and school discipline.

Compulsory School Attendance

In the United States, compulsory school attendance statutes have been in effect for more than half a century.[88] Children are required by law to attend school until a given age, normally 16 or 17.[89] Violations of compulsory attendance laws generally result in complaints that can lead to court action. Often, however, children are truant because of emotional problems or learning disabilities. They are then brought into the court system for problems beyond their control. Many

FOCUS ON DELINQUENCY

A School-Based Delinquency Prevention Program: Newsome Park Middle School, Newport News, Virginia

Newsome Park Middle School in Newport News, Virginia, is located in the city's second highest zone for drug-related arrests, and many of its students fit the definition of children at risk. Eight years ago, liquor bottles littered the school grounds, and students walked to school along streets on which drug paraphernalia had been discarded.

Today, school premises are immaculate, students and faculty show great pride in their school, and there have been no recorded incidents of drug use by students since 1985.

At the heart of this turnaround is a tough antidrug policy that is strongly endorsed by students, parents, teachers, and administrators. The policy forbids the possession, use, or sale of tobacco, alcohol, and other drugs. Parents are notified of violations of the school's antidrug policy, and law enforcement authorities are notified, consistent with confidentiality requirements, of violations of laws regarding drugs or alcohol.

Suspensions for use or possession range from four to ten days, at the discretion of the principal. In addition, to be readmitted to school following a drug-related suspension, student violators must complete an education or intervention program designated by the city's school board. Students are expelled after a third violation.

The antidrug program is integrated into the school's curriculum through the Advisory Program for Students and through health and social studies classes. Parents are asked to participate in workshops, and community agencies are involved as resources in the school.

Factors contributing to the success of Newsome Park Middle School's program are the leadership of an excellent principal, the commitment of concerned faculty and staff, and the active participation of parents and community groups in the school's efforts.

Newsome Park has won state and local clean community awards and a national award for a program sponsored by employees of Newport News Shipbuilding for special education students.

In addition, strong developmental and remedial programs have resulted in substantial gains in the number of students at grade level in reading and math. The school's programs to aid at-risk youth were recognized recently by the Commonwealth of Virginia. ■

Source: U.S. Department of Education, What Works, Schools without Drugs (Washington, D.C.: Department of Education, 1989), p. 22.

of them might be better off leaving school at an earlier age than the compulsory education law allows. On the other hand, emotionally disturbed and nonconforming children are pushed out of many school systems and thereby deprived of an education. Whether these children have a right to attend school is unclear. Many school systems ignore the difficult student, who may be classified as "bad" or "delinquent."

In 1925, the Supreme Court determined that compulsory education did not necessarily have to be provided by a public school system and that parochial schools could be a reasonable substitute.[90] From that time through the 1970s, the courts upheld the right of the state to make education compulsory. Then, in 1972, in the case of *Wisconsin v. Yoder,* the Supreme Court made an exception to the general compulsory education law by holding that traditional Amish culture was able to give its children the skills that would prepare them for adulthood within Amish society. Thus, the removal of Amish children from school after the completion of the eighth grade was justified.[91] It is not clear, however, whether this decision speaks directly to the issue of compulsory education or whether it is simply another instance of freedom of religion. Therefore, the state's role in requiring school attendance is still unsettled.

Free Speech

Freedom of speech is granted and guaranteed in the First Amendment to the U.S. Constitution. The right has been divided into two major categories as it affects children in schools. The first category involves what is known as *passive speech*, a form of expression not associated with the actual speaking of words. Examples include wearing arm bands or political protest buttons. The most important U.S. Supreme Court decision concerning a student's right to passive speech was in 1969 in the case of *Tinker v. Des Moines Independent Community School District.*[92] This case involved the right to wear black arm bands to protest the war in Vietnam. Two high school students, aged 16 and 17, were told they would be suspended if they demonstrated their objections to the Vietnam War by wearing black arm bands. They attended school wearing the arm bands and were suspended. According to the Court, in order for the state (in the person of a school official) to justify prohibiting an expression of opinion, it must be able to show that its action was caused by something more than a mere desire to avoid the discomfort and unpleasantness that accompany the expression of an unpopular view. Unless it can be shown that the forbidden conduct will interfere with the discipline required to operate the school, the prohibition cannot be sustained. In the *Tinker* case, the Court said there was no evidence that the school authorities had reason to believe that the wearing of arm bands would substantially interfere with the work of the school or infringe on the rights of the students.[93]

This decision is significant because it recognizes the child's right to free speech in a public school system. Justice Abe Fortas stated in his majority opinion, "Young people do not shed their constitutional rights at the schoolhouse door."[94] *Tinker* established two things: (1) a child is entitled to free speech in school under the First Amendment of the U.S. Constitution and (2) the test used to determine whether the child has gone beyond proper speech is whether he or she materially and substantially interferes with the requirements of appropriate discipline in the operation of the school.

The concept of free speech articulated in *Tinker* was used again in the 1986 case *Bethel School District No. 403 v. Fraser.*[95] This case upheld a school system's right to suspend or otherwise discipline a student who uses obscene or profane language and gestures. Matthew Fraser, a Bethel high school student, used sexual metaphors in making a speech nominating a friend for student office. His statement included these remarks:

I know a man who is firm—he's firm in his pants, he's firm in his shirt, his character is firm—but most . . . of all, his belief in you, the students of Bethel, is firm.

Jeff Kuhlman is a man who takes his point and pounds it in. If necessary, he'll take an issue and nail it to the wall. He doesn't attack things in spurts—he drives hard, pushing and pushing until finally—he succeeds.

Mary Beth Tinker and her brother, John Tinker, display the black armbands they wore to school to protest U.S. involvement in Vietnam in 1965 despite a school rule that prohibited armbands. When the Tinkers were suspended, they appealed to the Supreme Court, which ruled that under the First Amendment schools cannot punish students for expressing an opinion.

Jeff is a man who will go to the very end—even the climax, for each and every one of you.

So vote for Jeff for A.S.B. vice-president—he'll never come between you and the best our high school can be.

The Court found that a school has the right to control lewd and offensive speech that undermines the educational mission. The Court drew a distinction between the sexual content of Fraser's remarks and the political nature of Tinker's armband. It ruled that the pervasive sexual innuendo of the speech interfered with the school's mission to implant "the shared values of a civilized social order" in the student body.

In a 1988 case, *Hazelwood School District v. Kuhlmeier,* the Court extended the right of school officials to censor "active speech" when it ruled that the principal could censor articles in a student publication.[96] In this case, students had written about their personal experiences with pregnancy and parental divorce. The majority ruled that censorship was justified in this case because school-sponsored publications, activities, and productions were part of the curriculum and therefore designed to impart knowledge. Control over such school-supported activities could be differentiated from the action the Tinkers initiated on their own accord. In a dissent, Justice William J. Brennan accused school officials of favoring "thought control."

School Discipline

Most states have statutes permitting teachers to use corporal punishment to discipline students in public school systems. Under the concept of *in loco parentis* discipline is one of the assumed parental duties given to the school system. I two decisions, the Supreme Court upheld the school's right to use corporal punishment. In the case of *Baker v. Owen*, the Court stated:

We hold that the Fourteenth Amendment embraces the right of parents generally to control the means and discipline of their children, but that the state has a countervailing interest in the maintenance of order in the schools . . . sufficient to sustain the right of teachers and school officials must accord to students minimal due process in the course of inflicting such punishment.[97]

In 1977, the Supreme Court again spoke on the issue of corporal punishment in school systems in the case of *Ingraham v. Wright*, which upheld the right of teachers to use corporal punishment.[98] In this case, students James Ingraham and Roosevelt Andrews sustained injuries as a result of paddling in the Charles Drew Junior High School in Dade County, Florida. The legal problems raised in the case were (1) whether corporal punishment by teachers was a violation in this case of the Eighth Amendment against cruel and unusual punishment and (2) whether the due process clause of the Fourteenth Amendment required that the students receive proper notice and a hearing prior to receiving corporal punishment. The Court held that neither the Eighth Amendment nor the Fourteenth Amendment was violated in this case. Even though Ingraham suffered hematomas on his buttocks as a result of twenty blows with a wooden paddle and Andrews was hurt in the arm, the Supreme Court ruled that such punishment was not a constitutional violation. The Court established the standard that only reasonable discipline is allowed in school systems, but it excepted the degree of punishment administered in this case. The key principle in *Ingraham* is that the reasonableness standard that the Court articulated represents the judicial attitude that the scope of the school's right to discipline a child is by no means more restrictive than the rights of the child's own parents to impose corporal punishment.

Other issues involving the legal rights of students include their due process rights when interrogated, if corporal punishment is to be imposed, and when suspension and expulsion are threatened. When students are questioned by school personnel, no warning as to their legal rights to remain silent or right to counsel need be given. However, when school security guards, on-campus police officials, and public police officers question students, such constitutional warnings are required. In the area of corporal punishment, procedural due process established with the case of *Baker v. Owen* requires that students at least be forewarned about the possibility of corporal punishment as a discipline. In addition, the *Baker* case requires that there be a witness to the administration of corporal punishment and allows the student and the parent to elicit reasons for the punishment.

With regard to suspension and expulsion, the Supreme Court ruled in 1976 in the case of *Goss v. Lopez* that any time a student is to be suspended for up to a period of ten days, he or she is entitled to a hearing.[99] The hearing would not include a right to counsel or a right to confront or cross-examine witnesses. The Court went on to state in *Goss* that the extent of the procedural due process requirements would be established on a case-by-case basis. That is, each case would represent its own facts and have its own procedural due process elements.

In sum, schools have the right to discipline students, but students are protected from unreasonable, excessive, and arbitrary discipline.

SUMMARY

For several decades, criminologists have attempted to explain the relationship between schools and delinquency. Although no clear causal relationship has been established, research points to many definite links between the delinquent behavior of juveniles and their experiences within the educational system.

Contemporary youths spend much of their time in school because education has become increasingly important as a determinant of social and economic success. Educational institutions are one of the primary instruments of socialization, and it is believed that this role is bound to affect the amount of delinquent behavior by school-age children.

Those who claim a causal link between schools and delinquency cite two major factors in the relationship. The first is academic failure, which arises from a lack of aptitude, labeling, or class conflict and which results in tracking. The second factor is alienation from the educational experience, which is the result of the impersonal nature of schools, the traditionally passive role assigned to students, and students' perception of their education as irrelevant to their future lives.

Student misbehavior, which may have its roots in the school experience itself, ranges from minor infractions of school rules (for example, smoking and loitering in halls) to serious crimes, such as assault, burglary, arson, drug abuse, and vandalism of school property.

Dissatisfaction with the educational experience frequently sets the stage for more serious forms of delinquency both in and out of school. Some dissatisfied students choose to drop out of school as soon as they reach the legal age, and research has shown a rapid decline in delinquency among those who do drop out.

School administrators have attempted to eliminate school crime and prevent delinquency. Among the measures taken are security squads, electronic surveillance, and teacher training. Curriculums are being significantly revised to make the school experience more meaningful.

KEY TERMS

truancy
academic achievement
socialized
local school systems
school failure
underachievers
articulation hypothesis

tracking
self-fulfilling prophecy
stigma
student subculture
alienation
dropout
social disorganization

QUESTIONS FOR DISCUSSION

1. Was there a delinquency problem in your high school? If so, how was it dealt with?
2. Should disobedient youths be suspended from school? Does this solution hurt or help?
3. What can be done to improve the delinquency prevention capabilities of schools?
4. Is school failure responsible for delinquency, or are delinquents simply school failures?

NOTES

1. U.S. Senate Subcommittee on Delinquency, *Challenge for the Third Century: Education in a Safe Environment* (Washington, D.C.: Government Printing Office, 1977), p. 1.

2. *Justice and the Child in New Jersey*, report of the New Jersey Juvenile Delinquency Commission (1939), p. 110, cited in Paul H. Hahn, *The Juvenile Offender and the Law* (Cincinnati: Anderson, 1978).

3. Delbert S. Eliott and Harwin L. Voss, *Delinquency and the Dropout* (Lexington, Mass.: Lexington Books, 1974), p. 204.

4. U.S. Office of Education, *Digest of Educational Statistics* (Washington, D.C.: Government Printing Office, 1969), p. 25.

5. Kenneth Polk and Walter E. Schafer, eds., *Schools and Delinquency* (Englewood Cliffs, N.J.: Prentice-Hall, 1972), p. 13.

6. M. Edith Rasell and Laurence Mitchell, *Shortchanging Education: How the U.S. Spends on Grades K–12* (Washington, D.C.: Economic Policy Institute, 1990).

7. Ruth Leger Sivard, *World Military and Social Expenditures 1989* (Washington, D.C.: World Priorities, 1989).

8. Lee Jones, Ina Mullis, Senta Raizen, Iris Weiss, and Elizabeth Weston, *The 1990 Science Report Card* (Washington, D.C.: Government Printing Office, 1992), p. 3.

9. Mary Foretsch, *Reading in and out of School* (Washington, D.C.: Government Printing Office, 1992), pp. 4–5.

10. Eugene Owen, *Trends in Academic Progress: Achievement of American Students in Science, 1970–1990, Mathematics, 1973–1990, Reading, 1971–1990, and Writing, 1984–1990* (Washington, D.C.: National Center for Education Statistics, 1991), p. 19.

11. Simon Singer and Susyan Jou, "Specifying the SES/Delinquency Relationship by Subjective and Objective Indicators of Parental and Youth Social Status" (Paper presented at the annual meeting of the American Society of Criminology, New Orleans, November 1992).

12. Task Force on Juvenile Delinquency, *Juvenile Delinquency and Youth Crime* (Washington, D.C.: Government Printing Office, 1967), p. 51. See also Alexander Liazos, "Schools, Alienation, and Delinquency," *Crime and Delinquency* 24:355–61 (1978); Sheldon Glueck and Eleanor Glueck, *Unraveling Juvenile Delinquency* (New York: Commonwealth Fund, 1950); Kenneth Polk and David S. Halferty, "Adolescence, Commitment, and Delinquency," *Journal of Research in Crime and Delinquency* 4:82–86 (1966); Travis Hirschi, *Cause of Delinquency* (Berkeley: University of California Press, 1969); LaMar T. Empey and Steven G. Lubeck, *Explaining Delinquency* (Lexington, Mass.: D.C. Heath, 1971); and Polk and Schafer, *Schools and Delinquency.*

13. Frank W. Jerse and M. Ebrahim Fakouri, "Juvenile Delinquency and Academic Deficiency," *Contemporary Education* 49:108–9 (1978).

14. Terence Thornberry, Alan Lizotte, Marvin Krohn, Margaret Farnworth, and Sung Joon Jang, "Testing Interactional Theory: An Examination of Reciprocal Causal Relationships among Family, School and Delinquency," *Journal of Criminal Law and Criminology* 82:3–35 (1991).

15. Lyle Shannon, *Assessing the Relationship of Adult Criminal Careers to Juvenile Careers: A Summary* (Washington, D.C.: Government Printing Office, 1982).

16. D.J. West and David P. Farrington, *The Delinquent Way of Life* (London: Heineman, 1977), p. 76.

17. Marvin Wolfgang, Robert Figlio, and Thorsten Sellin, *Delinquency in a Birth Cohort* (Chicago: University of Chicago Press, 1972).

18. Ibid., p. 94.

19. Bureau of Justice Statistics, *Prisons and Prisoners* (Washington, D.C.: Government Printing Office, 1982), p. 2.

20. See generally, James Q. Wilson and Richard Herrnstein, *Crime and Human Nature* (New York: Simon and Schuster, 1985).

21. Martin Gold, "School Experiences, Self-Esteem, and Delinquent Behavior: A Theory for Alternative Schools," *Crime and Delinquency* 24:294–95 (1978).

22. Ibid.

23. Michael Gottfredson and Travis Hirschi, *A General Theory of Crime* (Stanford, Calif.: Stanford University Press, 1990); J.D. McKinney, "Longitudinal Research on the Behavioral Characteristics of Children with Learning Disabilities," *Journal of Learning Disabilities* 22:141–50.

24. David Farrington, "The Development of Offending and Antisocial Behavior from Childhood to Adulthood" (Paper presented at the Congress on Rethinking Delinquency, University of Minho, Braga, Portugal, July 1992).

25. Albert K. Cohen, *Delinquent Boys* (New York: Free Press, 1955). See also Kenneth Polk, Dean Frease, and F. Lynn Richmond, "Social Class, School Experience, and Delinquency," *Criminology* 12:84–85 (1974).

26. Jackson Toby, "Orientation to Education as a Factor in the School Maladjustment of Lower-Class Children," *Social Forces* 35:259–66 (1957).

27. William Glaser, *Schools without Failure* (New York: Harper & Row, 1969).

28. Gold, "School Experiences, Self Esteem, and Delinquent Behavior," p. 292.

29. Ibid., p. 283–85.

30. Polk, Frease, and Richmond, "Social Class, School Experience, and Delinquency," p. 92.

31. Arthur L. Stinchcombe, *Rebellion in a High School* (Chicago: Quadrangle Press, 1964), p. 70.

32. Delos Kelly and Robert Balch, "Social Origins and School Failure," *Pacific Sociological Review* 14:413–30 (1971).

33. Singer and Jou, "Specifying the SES/Delinquency Relationship by Subjective and Objective Indicators of Parental and Youth Social Status," p. 11.

34. Nan Marie Astone and Sara McLanahan, "Family Structure, Parental Practices and High School Completion," *American Sociological Review* 56:309–20 (1991).

35. Kenneth Polk, "Class, Strain, and Rebellion among Adolescents," in Kenneth Polk and Walter E. Schafer, eds., *Schools and Delinquency* (Englewood Cliffs, N.J.: Prentice-Hall, 1972), pp. 34–54.

36. For an opposing view, see Michael Waitrowski, Stephen Hansell, Charles Massey, and David Wilson, "Curricu-

lum Tracking and Delinquency," *American Sociological Review* 47:151–60 (1982).

37. Based on Walter E. Schafer, Carol Olexa, and Kenneth Polk, "Programmed for Social Class: Tracking in High School," in Kenneth Polk and Walter E. Schafer, eds., *Schools and Delinquency* (Englewood Cliffs, N.J.: Prentice-Hall, 1972), pp. 34–54.

38. Delos Kelly and William Pink, "School Crime and Individual Responsibility: The Perpetuation of a Myth," *Urban Review* 14:47–63 (1982).

39. Jeannie Oakes, *Keeping Track, How Schools Structure Inequality* (New Haven, Conn.: Yale University Press, 1985), p. 48.

40. Ibid., p. 57.

41. Delos Kelly, *Creating School Failure, Youth Crime, and Deviance* (Los Angeles: Trident Shop, 1982), p. 11.

42. Delos Kelly and W. Grove, "Teachers' Nominations and the Production of Academic Misfits," *Education* 101:246–63 (1981).

43. Delos Kelly, "The Role of Teacher's Nominations in the Perpetuation of Deviant Adolescent Careers," *Education* 96:209–17 (1976).

44. Oakes, *Keeping Track*, p. 48.

45. Adam Gamoran, "The Variable Effects of High School Tracking", *American Sociological Review* 57:812–28 (1992).

46. Hirschi, *Causes of Delinquency*, pp. 113–24, 132.

47. Patricia Harris Jenkins, "School Delinquency and Belief in School Rules" (Paper presented at the annual meeting of the American Society of Criminology, New Orleans, November 1992).

48. *Learning into the 21st Century, Report of Forum 5* (Washington, D.C.: White House Conference on Children, 1970).

49. Polk and Schafer, *Schools and Delinquency*, p. 72.

50. Stinchcombe, *Rebellion in a High School*, p. 70; and Daniel Glaser, *Crime in Our Changing Society* (New York: Holt, Rinehart & Winston, 1978), pp. 162–63.

51. Hirschi, *Causes of Delinquency*, pp. 170–83.

52. Polk and Schafer, *Schools and Delinquency*, p. 23.

53. Mihaly Czikszentmihalyi and Reed Larson, "Intrinsic Rewards in School Crime," *Crime and Delinquency* 24:322 (1978).

54. Gary Putka, "A Cheating Epidemic at a Top High School Teaches Sad Lessons," *Wall Street Journal*, 29 June 1992, p. 1.

55. Eliott and Voss, *Delinquency and the Dropout*.

56. Glaser, *Crime in Our Changing Society*, p. 164.

57. Daniel Glaser, *Strategic Criminal Justice Planning* (Washington, D.C.: Government Printing Office, 1975), Tables 3-2, 3-3, and 3-4, cited in Daniel Glaser, *Crime in Our Changing Society* (New York: Holt, Rinehart & Winston, 1978), p. 163.

58. Terence Thornberry, Melanie Moore, and R.L. Christenson, "The Effect of Dropping out of High School on Subsequent Criminal Behavior," *Criminology* 23:3–18 (1985).

59. G. Roger Jarjoura, "Does Dropping Out of School Enhance Delinquent Involvement? Results from a Large-Scale National Probability Sample", *Criminology* 31:149–72 (1993).

60. Jackson Toby, *Violence in Schools* (Washington, D.C.: National Institute of Justice, 1983), p. 2.

61. National Institute of Education, U.S. Department of Health, Education and Welfare, *Violent Schools—Safe Schools: The Safe Schools Study Report to the Congress*, vol. 1 (Washington, D.C.: Government Printing Office, 1977).

62. Linda Bastian and Bruce Taylor, *School Crime* (Washington, D.C.: Bureau of Justice Statistics, 1991).

63. George Know and Edward Tromanhauser, "Findings from the 1991 Safe School Survey" (Chicago: Chicago State University, 1991, mimeographed).

64. Wendy Mansfield and Elizabeth Farris, *Public School Principal Survey on Safe, Disciplined and Drug-Free Schools* (Washington, D.C.: Government Printing Office, 1992), p. 5.

65. Heidi Ericksen, "LA Pupil Is Killed in Accidental Shooting," *Boston Globe*, 22 January 1993, p. 3.

66. Terrance Donahue, *Weapons in Schools* (Washington, D.C.: Office of Juvenile Justice and Delinquency Prevention, 1989), p. 1.

67. National School Safety Center, *Weapons in Schools* (Malibu, Calif.: National School Safety Center, 1989).

68. Joseph Sheley, Zina McGee, and James Wright, "Gun-Related Violence in and around Inner-City Schools," *American Journal of Diseases of Children* 146:677–82 (1992).

69. Gary Gottfredson and Denise Gottfredson, *Victimization in Schools* (New York: Plenum Press, 1985), p. 18.

70. James Q. Wilson, "Crime in Society and Schools," in J. M. McPartland and E. L. McDill, eds., *Violence in Schools: Perspective, Programs and Positions* (Lexington, Mass.: D.C. Heath, 1977), p. 48.

71. Joan McDermott, "Crime in the School and in the Community: Offenders, Victims, and Fearful Youth," *Crime and Delinquency* 29:270–83 (1983).

72. Daryl Hellman and Susan Beaton, "The Pattern of Violence in Urban Public Schools: The Influence of School and Community," *Journal of Research in Crime and Delinquency* 23:102–27 (1986).

73. McDermott, "Crime in the School and in the Community," p. 281.

74. Hellman and Beaton, "The Pattern of Violence in Public Schools," pp. 122–23.

75. Julius Menacker, Ward Weldon, and Emanuel Hurwitz, "Community Influences on School Crime and Violence," *Urban Education* 25:68–80 (1990).

76. National Commission on Excellence in Education, *A Nation at Risk* (Washington, D.C.: Government Printing Office, 1983).

77. Alexander Liazos, "Schools, Alienation, and Delinquency," *Crime and Delinquency* 24:355–61 (1978).
78. Gary Putka, "Cheaters in Schools May Not Be Students but Their Teachers," *Wall Street Journal,* 2 November 1989, p. 1.
79. Bella English, "Hub Program to Counsel Violent Pupils," *Boston Globe,* 24 February 1987, p. 1.
80. Jackie Kimbrough, "School-Based Strategies for Delinquency Prevention," in Peter Greenwood, ed., *The Juvenile Rehabilitation Reader* (Santa Monica, Calif: Rand Corp., 1985), pp. IX.1–22.
81. Mansfield and Farris, *Public School Principal Survey,* p. iii.
82. Ibid., p. 12.
83. U.S. Senate Subcommittee on Delinquency, *Challenge for the Third Century,* p. 95.
84. William Bukoski, "School-Based Substance Abuse Prevention: A Review of Program Research," *Journal of Children in Contemporary Society* 18:95–116 (1985).
85. See, generally, J. David Hawkins and Denise Lishner, "Schooling and Delinquency," in E. H. Johnson, ed., *Handbook on Crime and Delinquency* (Westport, Conn.: Greenwood Press, 1987).
86. Denise Gottfredson, "An Empirical Test of School-Based Environmental and Individual Interventions to Reduce the Risk of Delinquent Behavior," *Criminology* 24:705–31 (1986).
87. Denise Gottfredson, "Changing School Structures to Benefit High Risk Youth," in Peter Leone, ed., *Understanding Troubled and Troubling Youth* (Newbury Park, Calif.: Sage, 1990), pp. 246–71.
88. S. Arons, "Compulsory Education: The Plain People Resist," *Saturday Review* 15:63–69 (1972).
89. Ibid.
90. See *Pierce v. Society of Sisters,* 268 U.S. 610, 45 S.Ct. 571, 69 L.Ed. 1070 (1925).
91. 406 U.S. 205, 92 S.Ct. 1526, 32 L.Ed.2d 15 (1972).
92. 393 U.S. 503, 89 S.Ct. 733 (1969).
93. Ibid.
94. Ibid., p. 741.
95. *Bethel School District No. 403 v. Fraser,* 478 U.S. 675, 106 S.Ct. 3159, 92 L.Ed.2d 549 (1986).
96. *Hazelwood School District v. Kuhlmeier,* 484 U.S. 260, 108 S.Ct. 562, 98 L.Ed.2d 592 (1988).
97. 423 U.S. 907, 96 S.Ct. 210, 46 L.Ed.2d 137 (1975).
98. 430 U.S. 651, 97 S.Ct. 1401 (1977).
99. 419 U.S. 565, 95 S.Ct. 729 (1976).

CHAPTER

12

OUTLINE

DRUGS AND DELINQUENCY

375

Adolescent *substance abuse* and its association with youth crime and delinquency continue to be vexing problems. Along with major metropolitan areas, such as Los Angeles, New York, and Washington, D.C., almost every town, village, and city in the United States has confronted some type of teenage substance abuse problem. Though drug abuse continues to be a significant topic of concern, national surveys of school-age children consistently show that the general usage of illegal drugs has been in a decade-long decline.

Despite such encouraging trends, far too many adolescents are involved with drugs and alcohol. Self-report surveys indicate that more than half of high school seniors have tried drugs and more than 90 percent use alcohol.[1] Those adolescents who remain at a high risk for drug abuse come from the most impoverished communities and experience a multitude of problems, including school failure and family conflict.[2] Equally troubling is the association between drug use and crime: drug users commit a significant amount of all crimes, and a significant portion of known criminals are drug abusers.[3] The consistent drug-crime pattern makes teenage substance abuse a key national concern.

This chapter addresses some of the most important issues involving teenage substance abuse. It first reviews the kinds of drugs kids are using and how often they are using them. It then goes into the why of drug abuse: who uses drugs and what are the suspected causes of substance abuse. After describing the association between drug abuse and criminal and delinquent behavior, the chapter concludes with a review of the efforts being made to control the use of drugs in the United States.

SUBSTANCES OF ABUSE

A wide variety of substances generically referred to as "drugs" are sold and used by teenagers. Many commonly abused drugs are identified in the following Focus on Delinquency. Some are addicting, others not. Some create hallucinations; others cause a depressing, relaxing stupor; and a few give an immediate, exhilarating uplift. This section will discuss some of the most widely used substances that, because of the danger they present for the user and their association with illegal activity, have been banned from private use.

Marijuana and Hashish

Commonly called "pot," "grass," and a variety of other names, marijuana is produced from the leaves of *cannabis sativa*, a plant grown throughout the world. Hashish (hash) is a concentrated form of cannabis made from unadulterated resin from the female plant. The main active ingredient in marijuana and hashish is tetrahydrocannabinol, or THC for short. THC is a mild hallucinogen that alters sensory impressions.

Marijuana is the drug most commonly used by teenagers. Smoking large amounts of pot or hash can cause drastic distortions in auditory and visual perception, even producing hallucinatory effects. Small doses produce an early excitement ("high") that gives way to a sedated effect and drowsiness. Pot use is also related to decreased physical activity, overestimation of time and space, and increased food consumption. When the user is alone, marijuana produces a quiet, dreamy state. In a group, users commonly become giddy and lose perspective.

Commonly Abused Drugs

Below are the proper name, street names, descriptions, and methods of use of commonly abused drugs.

TYPE	WHAT IS IT CALLED?	WHAT DOES IT LOOK LIKE?	HOW IS IT USED?
NARCOTICS			
Heroin	Smack Horse Brown sugar Junk Mud Big H Black Tar	Powder, white to dark brown Tarlike substance	Injected Inhaled through nasal passages Smoked
Methadone	Dolophine Methadose Amidone	Solution	Taken orally Injected
Codeine	Empirin compound with codeine Tylenol with codeine Codeine Codeine in cough medicines	Dark liquid varying in thickness Capsules Tablets	Taken orally Injected
Morphine	Pectoral syrup	White crystals Hypodermic tablets Injectable solutions	Injected Taken orally Smoked
Meperidine	Pethidine Demerol Mepergan	White Powder Solution Tablets	Taken orally Injected
Opium	Paregoric Dover's powder Parepectolin	Dark-brown chunks Powder	Smoked Eaten
Other narcotics	Percocet Percodan Tussionex Fentanyl Darvon Talwin Lomotil	Tablets Capsules Liquid	Taken orally Injected

TYPE	WHAT IS IT CALLED?	WHAT DOES IT LOOK LIKE?	HOW IS IT USED?
HALLUCINOGENS			
Phencyclidine	PCP Angel dust Loveboat Lovely Hog Killer weed	Liquid Capsules White crystalline powder Pills	Taken orally Injected Smoked-can be sprayed on cigarettes, parsley, and marijuana
Lysergic acid diethylamide	LSD Acid Green or red dragon White lightning Blue heaven Sugar cubes Microdot	Brightly colored tablets Impregnated blotter paper Thin squares of gelatin Clear liquid	Taken orally Licked off paper Gelatin and liquid can be put in the eyes
Mescaline and Peyote	Mesc Buttons Cactus	Hard, brown discs Tablets Capsules	Discs—chewed, swallowed, or smoked Tablets and capsules-taken orally
Psilocybin	Magic mushrooms 'Shrooms	Fresh or dried mushrooms	Chewed and swallowed
COCAINE			
Cocaine	Coke Snow Flake White Blow Nose candy Big C Snowbirds Lady	White crystalline powder, often diluted with other ingredients	Inhaled through nasal passages
Crack	Freebase rocks Rock	Light brown or beige pellets-or crystalline rocks that resemble coagulated soap; often packaged in small vials	Smoked
INHALANTS			
Nitrous Oxide	Laughing gas Whippets	Propellant for whipped cream in aerosol spray can Small 8-gram metal cylinder sold with a balloon or pipe (buzz bomb)	Vapors inhaled

TYPE	WHAT IS IT CALLED?	WHAT DOES IT LOOK LIKE?	HOW IS IT USED?
INHALANTS			
Amyl Nitrite	Poppers Snappers	Clear yellowish liquid in ampules	Vapors inhaled
Butyl Nitrite	Rush Bolt Locker room Bullet Climax	Packaged in small bottles	Vapors inhaled
Chlorohydrocarbons	Aerosol sprays	Aerosol paint cans Containers of cleaning fluid	Vapors inhaled
Hydrocarbons	Solvents	Cans of aerosol propellants gasoline, glue, paint thinner	Vapors inhaled
MARIJUANA-HASHISH			
Marijuana	Pot Grass Weed Reefer Dope Mary Jane Sinsemilla Acapulco gold Thai sticks	Dried parsley mixed with stems that may include seeds	Eaten Smoked
Tetrahydrocannabinol	THC	Soft gelatin capsules	Taken orally
Hashish	Hash	Brown or black cakes or balls	Eaten Smoked
Hashish oil	Hash oil	Concentrated syrupy liquid varying in color from clear to black	Smoked-mixed with tobacco
BARBITURATES			
Sedatives	Downers Barbs Blue devils Red devils Yellow jacket Yellows Nembutal Seconal Amytal Tuinals	Red, yellow, blue, or red and blue capsules	Taken orally
Methaqualone	Quaaludes Ludes Sopors	Tablets	Taken orally

TYPE	WHAT IS IT CALLED?	WHAT DOES IT LOOK LIKE?	HOW IS IT USED?
BARBITURATES			
Tranquilizers	Valium Librium Equanil Miltown Serax Tranxene	Tablets Capsules	Taken orally
STIMULANTS			
Amphetamines	Speed Uppers Ups Black beauties Pep pills Copilots Bumblebees Hearts Benzedrine Dexedrine Footballs Biphetamine	Capsules Pills Tablets	Taken orally Injected Inhaled through nasal passages
Methamphetamines	Crank Crystal meth Crystal methedrine Speed	White power pills A rock that resembles a block of paraffin	Taken orally Injected Inhaled through nasal passages
Additional stimulants	Ritalin Cylert Preludin Didrex Pre-State Voranil Tenuate Tepanil Pondimin Sandrex Plegine Ionamin	Pills Capsules Tablets	Taken orally Injected

Source: U.S. Department of Education, *What Works: Schools without Drugs, 1989* (Washington D.C.: Department of Education, 1989), pp. 63-70.

Though marijuana is not physically addicting, its long-term effects have been the subject of much debate. During the 1970s, it was reported that smoking pot caused a variety of serious physical and mental problems, including brain damage and mental illness. Though the dangers of pot and hash may have been significantly overstated, use of these drugs does present some health risks, including an increased risk of lung cancer, chronic bronchitis, and other diseases.

Marijuana smoking should be avoided by prospective parents: it lowers sperm counts in male users, and females experience disrupted ovulation and a greater chance of miscarriage.[4]

Cocaine

Cocaine is a alkaloid derivative of the coca plant first isolated in 1860. When discovered, it was considered a medicinal breakthrough that could relieve fatigue, depression, and various other symptoms, and it quickly became a staple of popular patent medicines. When its addictive qualities and dangerous side effects became apparent, its use was controlled by the Pure Food and Drug Act of 1906.

Cocaine is the most powerful natural stimulant. Its use produces euphoria, laughter, restlessness, and excitement. Overdoses can cause delirium, increased reflexes, violent manic behavior, and possible respiratory failure.

Cocaine can be sniffed, or "snorted," into the nostrils or injected. The immediate feeling of euphoria or rush is short-lived, and heavy users may snort coke as often as every ten minutes.

A number of deadly derivatives of cocaine have become popular on the street in recent years. Mixing cocaine and heroin is a highly dangerous practice called "speedballing." *Freebase* is a chemical produced by treating street cocaine with a liquid to remove the hydrochloric acid with which pure cocaine is bonded during manufacture. The freebase is then dissolved in a solvent, usually ether, that crystallizes the purified cocaine. The resulting crystals are crushed and then

Crack, a street-refined, smokable form of cocaine can be easily bought in many inner-city urban areas.

smoked in a special glass pipe, which provides a high more immediate and powerful than snorting street-strength coke. *Crack,* like freebase, is processed street cocaine. Its manufacture involves using ammonia or baking soda to remove the hydrochlorides and create a crystalline form of cocaine base that can then be smoked. However, unlike freebase, crack is not a pure form of cocaine and contains both remnants of hydrochloride along with additional residue from the baking soda (sodium bicarbonate). In fact, crack gets its name from the fact that the sodium bicarbonate often emits a crackling sound when the substance is smoked.

Also referred to as "rock," "gravel," and "roxanne," crack was introduced and gained popularity on both coasts simultaneously in the mid-1980s. It is relatively inexpensive, can provide a powerful high, and is considered to be highly psychologically addictive.

Cocaine and its derivitives continue to be the fastest-growing drug problem. In recent years, cocaine supplies have expanded, while costs have dramatically declined; it should not be surprising that the popularity of cocaine, crack, and freebase has concomitantly increased.

Heroin

Narcotic drugs have the ability to produce insensibility to pain and to free the mind of anxiety and emotion. Users experience a rush of euphoria, relief from fear and apprehension, release of tension, and elevation of spirits. After experiencing this uplifting mood for a short period, users become apathetic and drowsy and nod off. Heroin, the most commonly used narcotic in the United States, is produced from opium, a drug derived from the opium poppy flower. Dealers further cut the drug with neutral substances, such as sugar (lactose), so that street heroin is often only 1 to 4 percent pure.

Heroin is probably the most dangerous commonly used drug. Users rapidly build up a tolerance for it, fueling the need for increased doses to feel the desired effect. Some users will change their method of ingestion to get the required "kick." At first, heroin is usually sniffed or snorted; as tolerance builds, it is "skin popped" (shot into skin, but not into a vein) and then finally injected into a vein or "mainlined."

Through the progressive use of heroin, the user becomes an *addict*—a person with an overpowering physical and psychological need to continue taking a particular substance or drug by any means possible. If addicts cannot get enough heroin to satisfy their habit, they will suffer withdrawal symptoms. These include irritability, emotional depression, extreme nervousness, pain in the abdomen, and nausea.

Alcohol

Alcohol remains the drug of choice for most teenagers. More than 80 percent of high school seniors report using alcohol in the past year, and more than 90 percent say they have tried it sometime during their lifetime.[5] More than 20 million Americans are estimated to be problem drinkers, and at least half of these are alcoholics.

The cost of alcohol abuse is quite high. Alcohol may be a factor in nearly half of America's murders, suicides, and accidental deaths.[6] Alcohol-related deaths number one hundred thousand a year, far more than that of all other illegal drugs combined. About 1.7 million drivers are arrested each year for driving under the influence (DUI); DUI arrests increased 22 percent between 1980 and 1990.[7] The economic cost of America's drinking problem is equally staggering. An estimated $117 billion is lost each year, including $18 billion from premature deaths, $66 billion in reduced work effort, and $13 billion for treatment.[8]

Considering these problems, why do so many youths drink alcohol to excess? Youths who use alcohol report that it reduces tension, diverts worries, enhances pleasure, improves social skills, and transforms experiences for the better.[9] While these reactions may follow the limited use of alcohol, alcohol in higher doses acts as a sedative and depressant. Long-term use has been linked with depression and numerous physical ailments ranging from heart disease to cirrhosis of the liver (though there is research linking moderate drinking to a reduction in the probability of heart attack).[10] And while many teens think that drinking stirs their romantic urges, the weight of the scientific evidence indicates that alcohol decreases sexual response.[11]

Anesthetics

Anesthetic drugs are used as nervous system depressants. Local anesthetics block nervous system transmissions; general anesthetics act on the brain to produce a generalized loss of sensation, stupor, or unconsciousness.

The most widely abused anesthetic drug is *phencyclidine (PCP)*, known on the street as "angel dust." PCP can be sprayed on marijuana or other plant leaves and smoked, drunk, or injected. Originally developed as an animal tranquilizer, PCP creates hallucinations and a spaced-out feeling that causes heavy users to engage in extremely violent acts. The effects of PCP can last up to two days; the danger of overdose is extremely high.

Inhalants

Some substance-abusing youths inhale vapors from lighter fluid, paint thinner, cleaning fluid, and model airplane glue to reach a drowsy, dizzy state sometimes accompanied by hallucinations. Inhaling these substances produces a short-term sense of excitement and euphoria followed by a period of disorientation, slurred speech, and drowsiness. Amyl nitrate ("poppers") is a commonly used volatile liquid that is inhaled from capsules that are broken.

Sedatives/Barbiturates

Sedative, the most commonly used drugs of the barbiturate family, depress the central nervous system into a sleep-like condition. On the illegal market, sedatives are called "goofballs" or "downers" or are known by the color of the capsules—"reds" (Seconal), "blue devils" (Amytal), and "rainbows" (Tuinal). Methaqualone (quaaludes, ludes) is a commonly abused sedative.

Sedatives can be prescribed by doctors as sleeping pills. Illegal users employ them to create relaxed, sociable, and good-humored feelings; overdoses can cause irritability, repellent behavior, and eventual unconsciousness. Barbiturates are probably the major cause of drug-overdose deaths.

Tranquilizers

Tranquilizers relieve uncomfortable emotional feelings by reducing levels of anxiety and promoting relaxation. Legally prescribed tranquilizers, such as Ampazine, Thorazine, Pacatal, and Sparine, were originally designed to control the behavior of people suffering from psychoses, aggressiveness, and agitation. Less powerful tranquilizers, such as Valium, Librium, Miltown, and Equanil, are used to combat anxiety, tension, fast heart rate, and headaches. The use of increased dosages of illegally obtained tranquilizers can lead to addiction, and withdrawal can be painful and hazardous.

Hallucinogens

Hallucinogens, either natural or synthetic, produce vivid distortions of the senses without greatly disturbing the viewer's consciousness. Some produce hallucinations, and others cause psychotic behavior in otherwise normal people.

One common hallucinogen is mescaline, named after the Mescalero Apaches, who first discovered its potent effect. Mescaline occurs naturally in the peyote, a small cactus that grows in Mexico and the southwestern United States. After initial discomfort, mescaline produces vivid hallucinations in all ranges of colors and geometric patterns, a feeling of depersonalization, and out-of-body sensations.

A second group of hallucinogens are synthetic alkaloid compounds, such as psilocybin. These compounds can be transformed into lysergic acid diethylamide, commonly called LSD. This powerful substance (eight hundred times more potent than mescaline) stimulates cerebral sensory centers to produce visual hallucinations in all ranges of colors, to intensify hearing, and to increase sensitivity. Users often report a scrambling of sensations; they may "hear colors" and "smell music." Users also report feeling euphoric and mentally superior, though to an observer they appear disoriented and confused. Unfortunately, anxiety and panic may occur during the LSD experience, and overdoses can produce psychotic episodes, flashbacks, and even death.

Stimulants

Stimulants ("uppers," "speed," "pep pills," "ice") are synthetic drugs that stimulate action in the central nervous system. They produce an intense physical reaction: increased blood pressure, breathing rate, and bodily activity and elevation of mood. One widely used stimulant, amphetamine, produces psychological effects, such as increased confidence, euphoria, fearlessness, talkativeness, impulsive behavior, and loss of appetite.

The commonly used stimulants are Benzedrine ("bennies"), Dexedrine ("dex"), Dexamyl, Bephetamine ("whites"), and Methedrine ("math," "speed," "crystal meth").

Methedrine is probably the most widely used and most dangerous amphetamine. Some people swallow it; heavy users inject it for a quick rush. Long-term heavy use can result in exhaustion, anxiety, prolonged depression, and hallucinations. A new form of methamphetamine is a crystallized substance with the street name of "ice." Popular on the West Coast and Hawaii, it originated in Asian labs; it is called "batu" by Filipinos, "shaba" by the Japanese, and "hirropon" by

Koreans. Smoking this crystal causes weight loss, kidney damage, heart and respiratory problems, and paranoia, symptoms of its better-known competitor, crack.[12]

Steroids

Teenagers use highly dangerous anabolic steroids to gain muscle bulk and strength for athletics and body building.[13] Black-market sales of these drugs approach $1 billion annually. While not physically addicting, steroids can almost become an "obsession" among teens who desire athletic success. Long-term users may spend up to four hundred dollars a week on steroids and may support their habit by dealing the drug.

Steroids are dangerous because of the significant health problems associated with their long-term use: liver ailments, tumors, hepatitis, kidney problems, sexual dysfunction, hypertension, and mental problems, such as depression. Steroid use runs in cycles, and other drugs such as Clomid, Teslac, and Halotestin, which carry their own dangerous side effects, are used to curb the need for high dosages. Finally, steroid users often share needles, which puts them at high risk for contracting HIV, the virus that causes AIDS.

Drug Use Today

Drug abuse has become an alarming social problem in the United States. Each type of illegal substance, however, presents a different problem to legal authorities.[14] Indicators of cocaine use, such as drug-related deaths, arrests, emergency room overdose admissions, and possession arrests, have all increased faster than for any other drug. While "crack" or "rock" use is not widespread, its concentration in large urban areas has contributed to a growing urban crime rate.

Surveys also show that marijuana continues to be the most widely used drug but its popularity has peaked. Distributors have felt the heat of increased law enforcement efforts and attempts to eradicate crops; higher prices have hurt business.

As marijuana's popularity declines, synthetic (laboratory-made drugs) have become more popular. Some western states report that methamphetamine ("speed," "crank") use is increasing and that its low cost and high potency has encouraged manufacturers ("cookers") to increase production and distribution efforts. Other synthetics include PCP and LSD, the use of which is not widespread nationally but focused in particular areas of the country. For example, California leads the nation in the manufacture of PCP; about two-thirds of all drug labs seized are in California.[15]

Synthetics are popular because labs can be easily hidden in rural areas and traffickers do not have to worry about boarder searches or payoffs to foreign growers and middlemen. Users like synthetics because they are cheap and produce a powerful, long-lasting high that can be greater than provided by more expensive products, such as cocaine. Their manufacture is extremely profitable: the estimated street value of one gallon of PCP is $153,600, or $1,200 an ounce.[16]

While heroin use has stabilized in most of the country, the United States has an estimated half a million addicts. Heroin abuse seems to be concentrated in only a few areas of the country; about one half of all addicts reportedly reside in New York City.[17]

Though drug use has declined, more than 80 percent of high school seniors report using alcohol.

Despite the concern over these "hard drugs," the most persistent teenage substance abuse problem today is alcohol. While sometimes teenage alcoholism is considered less of a social problem than other types of substance abuse, it actually produces far more deaths and problems. Teenage alcohol abusers suffer depression, anxiety, and other symptoms of mental distress. It is well-established that alcoholism runs in families, so that it is possible today's teenage abusers will be the parents of the next generation of teenage alcoholics.[18]

Trends in Teenage Drug Use

While the national concern over teenage drug use doubtlessly is well placed, there are some indications that the overall teenage substance abuse rates have *declined* over the past decade. This rather surprising trend can be observed from a variety of data sources developed by a diverse group of government and private agencies. One national survey of high school seniors sponsored by the National Institute of Drug Abuse (NIDA) found that the percentage who drank frequently and heavily declined between 1980 and 1990. As Table 12.1 shows, the numbers

Percentage Distributions of Licensed Drivers and Arrests for Driving under the Influence (DUI), by Age, 1980 and 1989

| | 1980 | | | 1989 | | | PERCENT CHANGE IN RATE, 1980-89 |
| | PERCENT OF: | | ARRESTS PER 100,000 DRIVERS | PERCENT OF: | | ARRESTS PER 100,000 DRIVERS | |
AGE	DRIVERS	ARRESTS		DRIVERS	ARRESTS		
Total	100.0%	100.0%	981	100.0%	100.0%	1,048	6.8%
16-17	3.2%	2.2%	668	2.3%	1.1%	503	−24.7%
18-20	7.2	12.9	1,757	5.4	8.3	1,607	−8.5
21-24	10.6	19.3	1,784	8.3	17.3	2,183	22.4
25-29	13.0	17.9	1,347	12.4	22.2	1,869	38.8
30-34	12.0	13.1	1,076	12.4	17.6	1,486	38.1
35-39	9.4	9.6	996	11.2	12.0	1,123	12.8
40-44	7.7	7.4	944	9.7	8.1	872	−7.6
45-49	6.9	5.9	837	7.6	5.3	725	−13.4
50-54	6.9	4.9	686	6.2	3.3	558	−18.7
55-59	6.7	3.5	509	5.7	2.2	400	−21.4
60-64	5.7	1.9	335	5.6	1.4	262	−21.8
65 or older	10.7	1.5	140	13.0	1.2	100	−28.6

Robyn Cohen, *Drunk Driving* (Washington, D.C.: Bureau of Justice Statistics, 1992), p.

reporting drinking daily and binging on alcohol have steadily decreased.[19] It is not surprising, then, that the number of drunk driving arrests among youths 16 to 17 declined almost 25 percent during the same period.[20]

Drug Use Surveys

A number of attempts have been made to survey teenage drug abuse. The three primary sources of data on trends are:

1. The National Household Survey, conducted by the U.S. Department of Health and Human Services, involves interviews of approximately ten thousand people in their homes.[21] Data on drug abuse is disaggregated by age so that trends in adolescent substance abuse can be charted.

2. NIDA sponsors an annual survey conducted by social scientists at University of Michigan's Institute for Social Research. Since 1975, the Michigan research team has annually surveyed about 16,000 students on more than 125 high school campuses around the country. Participants (and the research team reports that students are enthusiastic participants) are queried about their lifetime, monthly, and annual use of sixteen commonly abused drugs and substances (including cigarettes and alcohol). In addition to the annual survey, about twenty-four hundred members of each class surveyed are followed up for ten years after high school to determine the lifetime incidence of their drug usage.

3. The Parents Resource Institute for Drug Abuse (PRIDE) is an Atlanta-based nonprofit group that for over the past four years has conducted annual surveys of more than two hundred thousand junior and senior high school students in thirty four states.

All three surveys show that teenage substance abuse is in decline.

Household Survey.   The most recent Household Survey indicates that drug use among teenagers 12 to 17 declined by more than one half between 1985 and 1991; the consumption trend in most drug and tobacco products is downward. But as Table 12.2 shows, millions of adolescents have tried drugs and hundreds of thousands are current users. Equally disturbing is the fact that more than 4 million are alcohol abusers (about 20 percent of the teenage population), another 11 percent are smokers, and 3 percent, about six hundred thousand kids, use smokeless tobacco.

The Household Survey shows that 20 percent of American youths 12 to 17 use alcohol. About one quarter million young Americans (12 to 25) have tired heroin and 5.5 million have used cocaine; of these, six hundred thousand are current users.

ISR Survey.   The most recent ISR survey available (1992) also indicates that fewer adolescents are taking drugs today than at any time since the survey began seventeen years ago. (See Figure 12.1.) The decreases applied to the number of seniors who report "ever using" any of the survey drugs and also to current use of drugs (past thirty days). Among the most encouraging trends is that lifetime crack use has declined from a high of 5.4 percent in 1987 to 2.6 percent in 1992; the number of seniors reporting using crack in the last thirty days has similarly declined from 1.3 percent to 0.6 percent. Probably the most encouraging trend is a reported decrease in drinking. While a large percentage of American teens still drink, the portion of high school seniors indicating that they had consumed any alcoholic beverage during the prior thirty days fell from 72 percent in 1980 to 51 percent in 1992.

▨▨ **TABLE 12.2**   Current and Lifetime Drug Usage of American Youth

	\%	EVER USED	\%	CURRENT USER	\%	EVER USED	\%	CURRENT USER
	12-17 YRS. (POP. 20,145,033)				18-25 YRS. (POP. 28,496,148)			
Marijuana and Hashish	13	2,625,000	4	874,000	51	14,395,000	13	3,714,000
Cocaine	2	491,000	*	83,000	18	5,099,000	2	582,000
Crack	1	179,000	*	22,000	4	1,068,000	*	114,000
Heroin	*	66,000	*	*	1	226,000	*	*
Hallucinogens	3	679,000	1	155,000	13	3,751,000	1	328,000
Inhalants	7	1,414,000	2	359,000	11	3,108,000	2	431,000
Stimulants	3	597,000	1	106,000	9	2,667,000	1	217,000
Sedatives	2	492,000	1	102,000	4	1,227,000	1	175,000
Tranquilizers	2	423,000	*	69,000	8	2,126,000	1	179,000
Analgesics	4	895,000	1	217,000	10	2,904,000	2	428,000
Alcohol	46	9,339,000	20	4,092,000	90	25,689,000	64	18,130,000
Cigarettes	38	7,632,000	11	2,180,000	71	20,299,000	32	9,167,000
Smokeless tobacco	12	2,367,000	3	599,000	22	6,222,000	6	1,666,000

* Low precision, no estimate shown

Terms: Ever Used: used at least once in a person's lifetime. Current User: used at least once in the 30 days prior to the survey.

Source: National Institute on Drug Abuse, *NIDA Capsules* December 1991.

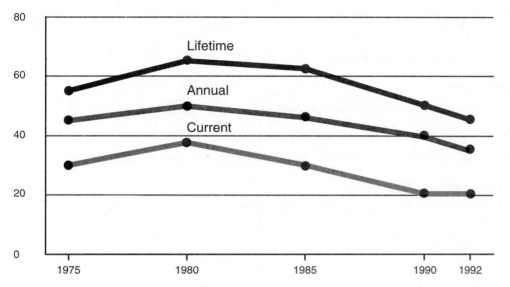

FIGURE 12.1

Any illicit drug use by high school seniors

Source: Institute of Social Research, Monitoring the Future, 1992 (Ann Arbor, MI: Institute of Social Research, 1993)

While the survey findings are generally positive, there are a few trouble spots. The ISR survey has included data on eighth and tenth graders since 1991. The most recent survey results indicate that the eighth graders actually increased their use of most drugs between 1991 and 1992. Though the increases were slight, the ISR researchers caution that they may be an early warning sign that drug use will be on the rise.

Despite the overall decline among the tenth and twelfth graders, the ISR survey shows that substance abuse is still widespread among teenagers. As Figure 12.2 shows, by the time they are seniors in high school, about one third of all adolescents have tried marijuana, almost 9 percent have used LSD, and 6 percent have experienced cocaine. Alcohol abuse is a major youth problem: more than 97 percent of all high school seniors have tried alcohol and 28 percent said they had five or more drinks in a row during the prior two weeks; 13 percent of the eighth graders reported similar heavy drinking bouts. If we assume that there are almost 20 million high school-age youths, then the ISR survey indicates that 5 million have tried illegal drugs sometime during their life.

Pride Survey. The most recent PRIDE survey indicates some increase in drug activity, specifically hallucinogens and inhalants, but as in the other surveys, students reported using less marijuana and cocaine. While the PRIDE survey indicates that drug use is stable, it does show that during the 1991-1992 year, a significant portion of American youths engaged in drug and alcohol abuse.

The survey shows that, as might be expected, substance abuse patterns increased between the sixth and twelfth grades. Yet, as Figure 12.3 indicates, even younger adolescents report significant experimentation with "gateway" drugs, such as liquor, alcohol, and cigarettes, and some involvement with illicit drugs, such as cocaine, uppers, and downers.

Figure 12.2 Use of drugs by high school students

Source: Institute of Social Research, Information Press Release, Ann Arbor, Michigan April 13, 1993.

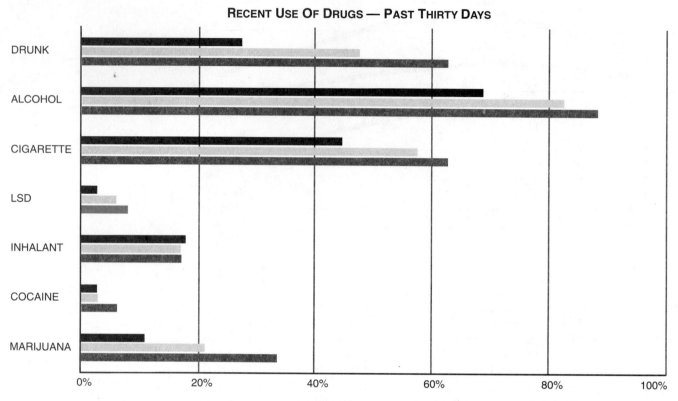

RECENT USE OF DRUGS — PAST THIRTY DAYS

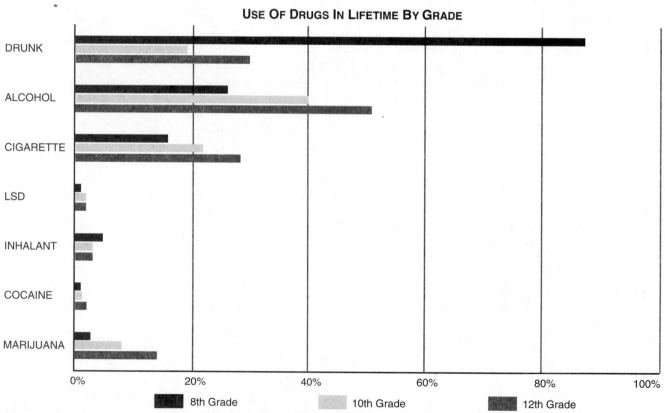

USE OF DRUGS IN LIFETIME BY GRADE

■ 8th Grade   ▨ 10th Grade   ▦ 12th Grade

Early Onset

While these national surveys show that drug abuse has been declining, there are also indications that drug use is now beginning at a very early age. While the ISR's most recent survey indicates that seniors are using drugs less frequently, adolescents in the eighth grade may be increasing their drug abuse. The PRIDE survey indicates that 20 percent of sixth graders are drinking beer and wine coolers and 10 percent are drinking hard liquor. Evidence exists that early involvement with alcohol is significantly related to involvement with illicit drugs over the life course.[22]

A recent survey in New Jersey shows that almost three fourths (71 percent) of the marijuana users reported having first used the drug prior to the tenth grade, as did a majority of youths using hallucinogens, amphetamines, barbiturates, and tranquilizers.[23] Considering the severity of this problem, it should come as no surprise that the National Association of State Alcohol and Drug Abuse Directors found that each year, more than 1.3 million youths are admitted to alcohol treatment programs and more than four hundred thousand receive drug treatment.[24]

Why Has Teenage Drug Use Declined?

If the national survey results are valid, teenage drug use has undergone a period of significant decline. How can this social change be explained? One reason may be changing perceptions about the harmfulness of drugs, such as cocaine and marijuana; as students come to view these drugs as harmful, they tend to use them less. In 1980, 31 percent of the youth surveyed believed cocaine was harmful, while by 1989, that number had increased to 55 percent. Considering the widespread publicity linking drug use, needle sharing, and the AIDS virus, it comes as no surprise that kids today see drug taking as more dangerous and risky than in the 1970s.

In addition, youths report greater disapproval of drug use among their friends, and peer pressure may help account for lower use rates. National ad campaigns to "just say no to drugs" and to stop friends from drinking and driving may be helping reduce peer approval of substance abuse.

While perceptions of harmfulness and peer disapproval are correlated with declines in drug use, kids actually report that it is easier to obtain drugs today than ever before. Though the availability of cocaine is at an all-time high, so too is its perceived risk. If use rates have declined, the change has come about because of a decline in demand and not in supply.

Are the Survey Results Accurate?

While these trends are encouraging, student drug surveys must be interpreted with caution. First, it may be overly optimistic to expect that heavy crack, "ice," and PCP users are going to cooperate with a drug use survey. Even if willing, they are the ones who are more than likely to be absent from school during testing periods.

Since the dropout rate among drug users is so high, it is also likely that the most deviant and drug-dependent portion of the adolescent population is omitted from the sample. Research indicates that more than half of all people arrested dropped out of school before the twelfth grade (when the ISR survey is

Figure 12.3

Student drug use: 1992–92 National Survey of Students

Source: PRIDE, Inc., 1991-1992 National Summary Grades 6-12 (Atlanta: PRIDE, Inc., 1993).

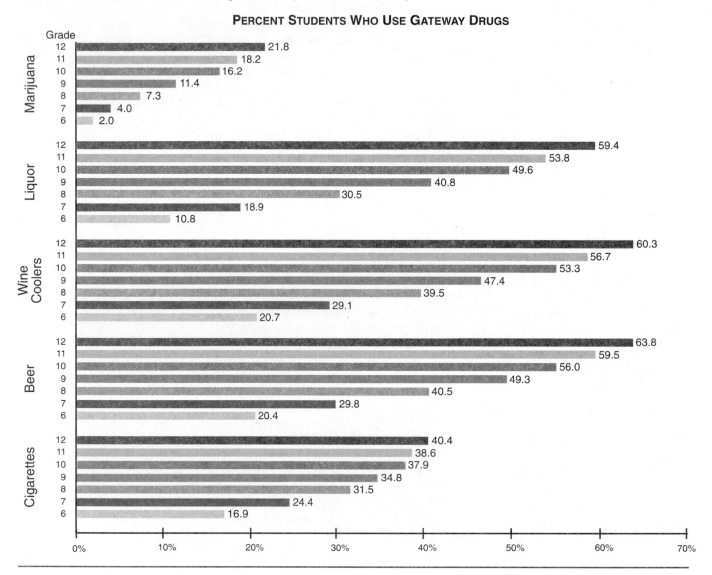

PERCENT STUDENTS WHO USE GATEWAY DRUGS

conducted) and more than two-thirds of these arrestees are drug users.[25] Eric Wish has found that the number of juvenile detainees (those arrested and held in a lock-up) who test positively for cocaine is many times higher than those reporting recent use in the ISR survey. For example, while about 3.4 percent of the seniors report using cocaine in the prior thirty days, about 22 percent of young detainees in Washington, D.C., and 18 percent in Phoenix tested positively for cocaine.[26] High school drug surveys are clearly excluding some of the most drug-prone kids.

Student drug use: 1992–92 National Survey of Students

Source: PRIDE, Inc., 1991-1992 National Summary Grades 6-12 (Atlanta: PRIDE, Inc., 1993).

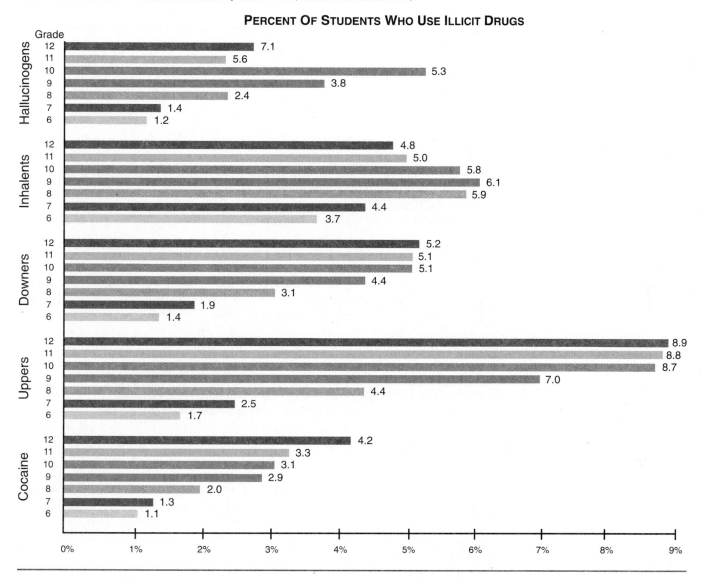

PERCENT OF STUDENTS WHO USE ILLICIT DRUGS

To account for these presumably absent heavy users, the ISR researchers compared the general high school population with kids who are frequently truant and have poor grades. They reasoned that these poor performers are the most like the dropouts. While the poor students did use drugs more than the general high school population, they too have reduced their substance abuse. This suggests that improvements cut across all segments of the teenage population.

At the least, national surveys show promising trends in teenage drug use. Though the surveys do not include dropouts and may be overlooking a large portion of the general adolescent drug problem, these methodological and measurement problems are consistent over time. That is, prior surveys may also have omitted dropouts and other high-risk youth and been otherwise tainted by over- and underreporting subjects. So while the *validity* of these surveys may be in doubt, they are more likely *reliable* indicators of trends in substance abuse. Nonetheless, while evidence exists that drug use is declining, even in the at-risk population, arrest data present a disturbing pattern of continued drug use among delinquent youth.

WHY DO KIDS TAKE DRUGS?

To most people, the "why" of teenage drug abuse remains a puzzle: Why do youths engage in an activity that is sure to bring them overwhelming personal problems? It is hard to imagine that even the youngest drug users are unaware of the social, physical, and legal problems associated with substance abuse. While it is easy to understand the dealers' desire for quick profits, how can we explain the users' casual disregard for long- and short-term consequences?

Social Disorganization

One explanation ties drug abuse to poverty, social disorganization, and a feeling of hopelessness. The involvement in drug use by young minority group members has been tied to such factors as racial prejudice, "devalued identities," low self-esteem, poor socioeconomic status, and the stress of living in the harsh urban environment.[27] The association between drug use, race, and poverty has been linked to the high level of mistrust, negativism, and defiance found in lower socioeconomic areas.[28]

While social disorganization has long been associated with drug use, the empirical data on the relationship between class and crime has so far been inconclusive. For example, the *National Youth Survey (NYS)*, a well-respected longitudinal study of delinquent behavior conducted by Delbert Elliott and his associates, found little if any association between drug use and social class. While the NYS found that drug use is higher among urban youth, little evidence existed that minority youth or members of the lower class were more likely to abuse drugs than white youth and the more affluent.[29] Research by the Rand Corporation indicates that many drug-dealing youths (about two-thirds) had legitimate jobs at the time they were arrested for drug trafficking.[30]

Peer Pressure

Drug use is typically a peer experience. Youths living in a deteriorated inner-city slum area, where feelings of alienation and hopelessness run high, often come in contact with established drug users who teach them that drugs provide an answer to their feelings of personal inadequacy and stress.[31] Perhaps they join with peers to learn the techniques of drug use; their friendships with other drug-dependent youths give them social support for their habit. Data acquired by Terence Thornberry and his associates as part of the Rochester Youth Development study do in fact show that a youth's association with friends who are committed to deviant values increases the probability of drug use.[32] Helene Raskin White's analysis of longitudinal data from a New Jersey cohort of 892 adolescents indicated that adolescent drug use was best predicted by friendships with other drug users.[33]

Peer networks that support drug use may be the most significant influence on long-term substance abuse. Shared feelings and a sense of intimacy lead youths to become fully enmeshed in what has been described as the "drug-use subculture."[34] Research now indicates that drug users do in fact have intimate and warm relationships with substance-abusing peers, which help support their habits and behaviors.[35] The street identity and life-style provide users with a clear identity, a role they can fulfill, activities and behaviors they enjoy, and an opportunity for attaining social status among their peers.[36] One of the reasons that it is so difficult to treat hard-core users is that quitting drugs means leaving the "fast life" of the streets.

Family Factors

Another explanation is that drug users have a poor family life and a troubled adolescence. Studies have found that the majority of drug users have had an unhappy childhood, which included harsh physical punishment and parental neglect and rejection.[37] It is also common to find substance abusers within large families and with parents who are divorced, separated, or absent.[38]

Social psychologists suggest that drug-abuse patterns may also result from the observation of parental drug use.[39] Youths who learn that drugs provide pleasurable sensations may be the most likely to experiment with illegal substances; a habit may develop if the user experiences lower anxiety, fear, and tension levels.[40]

James Inciardi, Ruth Horowitz, and Anne Pottieger found a clear pattern of adult involvement in early substance abuse when they studied serious adolescent drug users in Miami. Kids whose drug problems escalated to crack use began their substance abuse careers by experimenting with alcohol at age 7, getting drunk at age 8, having alcohol with an adult present by age 9, and becoming regular drinkers by the time they were 11 years old.[41] Inciardi and his associates found that drinking with an adult present, presumably a parent, was a significant precursor of future substance abuse and delinquency. "Adults," they argue, "who gave children alcohol were also giving them a head start in a delinquent career."[42] Crack-abusing kids do not necessarily come from socially disadvantaged families as much as from families wracked by conflict.

Genetic Factors

The association between parental drug abuse and adolescent behavior may have a genetic basis. Research has shown that the biological children of alcoholics reared by nonalcoholic adoptive parents more often develop alcohol problems than the natural children of the adoptive parents.[43] A number of studies comparing alcoholism among identical (MZ) and fraternal (DZ) twins have found that the degree of concordance (both siblings behaving identically) is twice as high among the MZ groups.[44]

Addiction-Prone Personalities

Not all drug-abusing youths reside in lower-class slum areas; the problem of middle-class substance abuse is very real. To explain drug abuse across the social

Some kids may have addiction prone personalities which compel them to take drugs.

structure, some experts have linked it to personality disturbance and emotional problems that can strike kids in any economic class. Psychodynamic explanations of substance abuse suggest that drugs help youths control or express unconscious needs and impulses. Addicts exhibit psychopathic or sociopathic behavior characteristics, forming what is called an ***addiction-prone personality.***[45] Drinking alcohol may reflect a teen's need to remain dependent on an overprotective mother or an effort to reduce the emotional turmoil of adolescence.[46]

Research on the psychological characteristics of narcotics abusers does in fact reveal the presence of a significant degree of personal pathology. Personality testing of known users suggests that a significant percentage suffer from psychotic disorders, including various levels of schizophrenia. Studies have found that addicts suffer personality disorders characterized by a weak ego, a low frustration tolerance, anxiety, and fantasies of omnipotence.

Problem Behavior Syndrome

For many adolescents, substance abuse is just one of many problem behaviors. Longitudinal studies show that kids who abuse drugs are maladjusted, alienated, and emotionally distressed and have many social problems.[47] Having a deviant life-style means associating with delinquent peers, living in a family in which parents and siblings abuse drugs, having a low commitment to education, being alienated from the dominant values of society, and engaging in delinquent behaviors at an early age.[48] Research shows that kids who abuse drugs lack commitment to religious values, disdain education, and spend most of their time in peer activities.[49]

Rational Choice

Kids may choose to use drugs and alcohol because they want to enjoy their anticipated effects: They want to get high, relax, improve their creativity, escape reality, and increase sexual responsiveness. Research indicates that adolescent alcohol abusers believe that getting high will make them powerful, increase their sexual performance, and facilitate their social behavior; they care little about negative future consequences.[50] Substance abuse, then, may be a function of the rational, albeit mistaken, belief that substance abuse benefits the user.

KIDS WHO USE DRUGS

What are the patterns of teenage drug use? Are all abusers similar, or are there different types of drug involvement? Research by Bruce Johnson and Marcia Chaiken indicates that drug-involved youth do take on different roles, life-styles, and behavior patterns, which are described below.[51]

Adolescents Who Distribute Small Amounts of Drugs

Many adolescents who are involved with the use and distribution of small amounts of drugs do not commit any other serious delinquent acts. Most of these petty dealers occasionally sell marijuana, "ice," and PCP to support their own drug use. Their customers are almost always known to them and include friends, relatives, and acquaintances. Deals are arranged over the phone, in school, or at public hangouts and meeting places; however, the actual distribution takes place in more private arenas, such as at home or in cars.

Petty dealers do not consider themselves "seriously" involved in drugs. One girl commented:

. . . I don't consider it dealing, I'll sell hits of speed to my friends and joints and nickel bags [of marijuana] to my friends, but that's not dealing.

Included in Inciardi, Horowitz, and Pottieger's sample of crack-using adolescents in Miami was Erica, a 16-year-old who modeled, played field hockey, and was a cheerleader. "I'm not really *in* the crack business," she told the investigators. "I just know someone who is and help him out once in a while." When Erica is paid for her services with crack, she may sell it to her friends.[52]

Petty dealers are insulated from the juvenile justice system because their activities rarely result in apprehension and sanction. In fact, few adults notice their activities because these adolescents are able to maintain a relatively conventional life-style. In several jurisdictions, however, agents of the justice system are cooperating in the development of educational programs to provide nonusers with the skills to resist the "sales pitch" of the petty dealers they meet at school or in the neighborhood.

Adolescents Who Frequently Sell Drugs

A small number of adolescents, most often multiple-drug users or heroin or cocaine users, are high-rate dealers who bridge the gap between adult drug distributors and the adolescent user. Though many are daily users, they are not strung-out junkies, and they take part in many normal adolescent activities, such as going to school and socializing with friends.

Frequent dealers often have adults who "front" for them, that is, sell them drugs for cash. The teenagers then distribute the drugs to friends and acquaintances. They return most of the proceeds to the supplier while keeping a commission for themselves. They may also keep drugs for their personal use, and in fact, some consider their drug dealing as a way of "getting high for free." Winston, aged 17, told Inciardi and his associates:

I sell the cracks for money and for cracks. The man, he give me this *much*. I sell most of it and I get the rest for me. I like this much. Every day I do this. . . .[53]

Inciardi and his associates found that frequent dealers were also likely to be regular users of crack. About 80 percent of kids who dealt crack regularly were daily users.[54]

Frequent dealers are more likely to sell drugs in public and can be seen in known drug hangouts in parks, schools, or other public places. Deals occur irregularly, so the chance of apprehension is not significant, nor is the payoff substantial. A recent survey by Robert MacCoun and Peter Reuter found that drug dealers make about thirty dollars per hour when they are working and clear on average about two thousand dollars per month. Though these amounts are certainly greater than most dealers could have hoped to have earned in legitimate jobs, they are certainly not enough to afford a steady stream of luxuries; most small-time dealers also hold conventional jobs.[55]

Teenage Drug Dealers Who Commit Other Delinquent Acts

A more serious type of drug-involved youth is the one who uses and distributes multiple substances and commits both property and violent crimes. Though these youngsters make up about 2 percent of the teenage population, they may commit up to 40 percent of the robberies and assaults and about 60 percent of all teenage felony thefts and drug sales. Few gender or racial differences exist among these youths: girls are as likely as boys to become high-rate, persistent drug-involved offenders, white youths as likely as black youths, middle-class adolescents raised outside cities as likely as lower-class city children.[56]

In cities, these youths are frequently hired by older dealers to act as street-level drug runners. Each member of a crew of three to twelve boys will handle small quantities of drugs, perhaps three bags of heroin, which are received on consignment and sold on the street; the supplier receives 50 percent to 70 percent of the drug's street value. The crew members also act as lookouts, recruiters, and guards. While they may be recreational drug users themselves, crew members refrain from using addictive drugs, such as heroin; some major suppliers will only hire "drug-free kids" to make street deals. Between drug sales, the young dealers commit robberies, burglaries, and other thefts.

Most youngsters in the street drug trade have few success skills and either terminate their dealing or become drug-dependent. A few, however, develop excellent entrepreneurial skills. Those that are rarely apprehended by police earn the trust of their older contacts and advance in the drug business. They develop their own crews and handle more than a half million dollars a year in drug business. Some are able to afford the BMW or Mercedes, jewelry, and expensive clothes that signify success in the drug trade.

Drug-Involved Gangs

Youths involved in teenage gangs commonly become serious suppliers of narcotics. At one time, primacy in the U.S. drug trade was maintained by traditional organized crime families, which used their control of the Asian heroin market as a principle source of mob income. The monopoly of these families, however, has been broken. Efforts to jail crime bosses coupled with the popularity and growth of cocaine and synthetic drugs (which are less easily controlled by a single source) have shattered this distribution monopoly. Stepping into the void have been local gangs that have used their drug income to expand their base and power. Prominent among these are biker gangs, such as the Hell's Angels, Outlaws, and Bandidos, which have become active in the manufacture and distribution of synthetics. The Jamaican Posse and Latino gangs control a large part of the East Coast cocaine business, while Chinese groups now import much of the nation's heroin supply.

Teenage gangs have also emerged as major players in the drug trade. Most prominent are the two largest Los Angeles youth gangs, the Bloods and the Crips, whose total membership is estimated to be more than twenty thousand (though actual membership is probably impossible to determine).

In Los Angeles itself, these drug-dealing gangs maintain "rock houses" or "stash houses." The houses receive drug shipments arranged by gang members who have the overseas connections and financial backing needed to wholesale drugs. The wholesalers pay the gang for permission to deal in their territory and hire members as a security force. Lower-echelon gang members help transport the drugs and work the houses, retailing cocaine and other drugs to neighborhood youths. Each member makes a profit for every ounce of "rock" sold. Police estimate that youths who work in "rock houses" will earn seven hundred dollars and up for a twelve-hour shift.[57]

Gangs cooperate in the purchase of legitimate businesses, such as car washes and liquor stores, to launder drug money. The "war on drugs" may produce the same atmosphere that prompted the growth of organized crime during Prohibition in the 1920s. Los Angeles street gangs may follow the path of New York's "Five Families" and Al Capone and the Chicago mob and become the leaders of a new version of organized crime.

Adolescents Who Cycle in and out of the Justice System

Some drug-involved youths are failures at both dealing and crime. They do not have the savvy to join gangs or groups and instead begin committing unplanned,

Some adolescents are petty thieves and drug users. They filter continually in and out of the justice system.

opportunistic crimes that increase their chances of arrest. Their heavy drug use both increases their risk of apprehension and decreases their value for organized drug-distribution networks.

Drug-involved "losers" can earn a living by steering customers to a seller in a "copping" area, touting drug availability for a dealer, or acting as a lookout. However, they are not considered trustworthy or deft enough to handle drugs or money. They may bungle other criminal acts, which solidifies their reputation as undesirable:

Buster is almost always stoned on ludes and beer. He is continually getting caught robbing and is in and out of treatment centers. Once he and another boy robbed [sic] a jewelry store. They smashed the window with a brick and the window fell on them, knocking them both out. The store owner called the cops and an ambulance.[60]

Though these persistent offenders get involved in drugs at a very early age, they receive little attention from the justice system until they have developed an extensive arrest record. By then, they are approaching the end of their minority and will either spontaneously desist or become so deeply entrapped in the drug-crime subculture that little can be done to treat or deter their illegal activities.

Drug-Involved Youth Who Continue to Commit Crimes as Adults

Though about two-thirds of substance-abusing youths continue to use drugs after they reach adulthood, about half desist from other criminal activities. Those who persist in both substance abuse and crime as adults maintain the following characteristics:

- they come from poor families
- other criminals are members of their families
- they do poorly in school
- they started using drugs and committing other delinquent acts at a relatively early age
- they use multiple types of drugs and commit crimes frequently
- they have few opportunities in late adolescence to participate in legitimate and rewarding adult activities.[61]

Some evidence exists that these drug-using persisters have low nonverbal IQs and poor physical coordination. Nonetheless, little scientific evidence exists to explain why some drug-abusing kids drop out of crime while others remain active into their adulthood.

DRUG USE AND DELINQUENCY

An association between drug use and delinquency is clearly established. It can be realized on a number of different levels. Violence erupts when rival drug gangs use their automatic weapons to settle differences and establish territorial monopolies. In New York City, authorities report that crack gangs will burn down their rival's headquarters, even if people living on the premises are not connected to the drug trade; it is estimated that between 35 percent and 40 percent of New York's homicides are drug-related.[62]

Drug use is also associated with the crimes addicts commit to pay for their habits. One study conducted in Miami found that to purchase drugs, 573 narcotics users *annually* committed more than 200,000 crimes, including 6,000 robberies, 6,700 burglaries, and 70,000 larceny offenses; similar research with a sample of 356 addicts accounted for 118,00 crimes annually.[63] If such proportions hold true, the nation's estimated half a million heroin addicts may alone be committing more than 100 million crimes each year, and this estimate ignores the criminal activity of cocaine and crack abusers.

The relationship between drugs and crime is dramatically illustrated by the extent of substance abuse among criminal suspects and those already convicted of crimes.

A number of efforts have been made to measure drug use by people immediately arrested for crime. The federal government's *Drug Use Forecasting (DUF)* program tests arrestees in major cities to determine their drug involvement. The results have been startling. In some cities, such as San Diego, New York, and Philadelphia, more than *70 percent* of all arrestees, both male and female, test positively for some drug, and this association crosses both gender and racial boundaries.[64]

The DUF survey tests male juvenile arrestees and detainees in twelve major U.S. cities. As Figure 12.4 shows, adolescent drug use in these sites ranges from

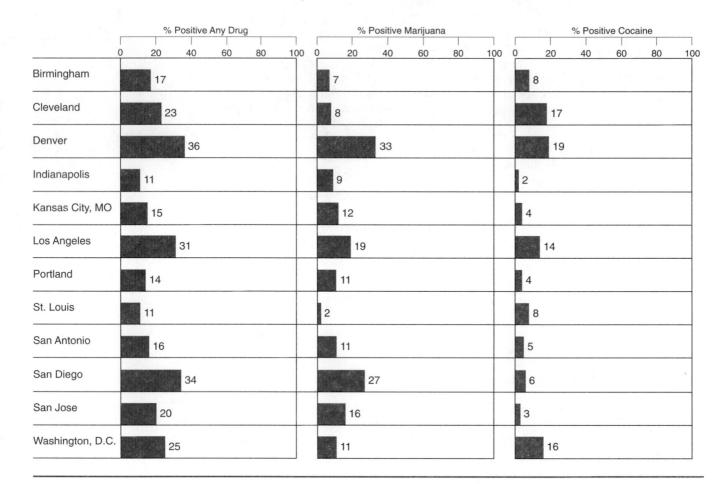

% Positive Any Drug | % Positive Marijuana | % Positive Cocaine

	% Positive Any Drug	% Positive Marijuana	% Positive Cocaine
Birmingham	17	7	8
Cleveland	23	8	17
Denver	36	33	19
Indianapolis	11	9	2
Kansas City, MO	15	12	4
Los Angeles	31	19	14
Portland	14	11	4
St. Louis	11	2	8
San Antonio	16	11	5
San Diego	34	27	6
San Jose	20	16	3
Washington, D.C.	25	11	16

▓▪FIGURE 12.4

Drug use by male juvenile
arrestees/detainees

Source: National Institute of
Justice/Drug Use Forecasting Program,
1991 Annual Report (Washington, D.C.:
NIJ, 1992). Note: Positive by urinalysis,
January through December 1991.
Drugs tested for include cocaine,
opiates, PCP, marijuana, amphetamines,
methadone, methaqualone,
benzodiazepines, barbiturates, and
propoxyphene.

11 percent in Indianapolis and St. Louis to 34 percent in San Diego and Denver. In Washington, D.C., Cleveland, and St. Louis, more kids tested positively for cocaine use than for marijuana. Though marijuana and cocaine were the most commonly used drugs, about 7 percent of the kids arrested in San Diego were on amphetamines and 5 percent in Los Angeles were on PCP (fewer than 1 percent of the juvenile arrestees tested positively for heroin).

The DUF data indicates that young offenders are quite likely to be substance abusers and that the drug-crime connection peaks between ages 25 to 35, then begins to decline after age 36.[65]

Drugs and Chronic Offending

It is possible that most delinquents are not actually drug users but that police are just more likely to apprehend muddled-headed substance abusers than clear-thinking "abstainers." A second and probably more plausible interpretation of the existing data is that the drug abuse-crime connection is so powerful because that many delinquents and criminals are in fact substance abusers. Some recent research by Bruce Johnson and his associates confirms this suspicion. Using data from a nationally drawn self-report survey, these researchers found that less than

Part III   Environmental Influences on Delinquency

2 percent of the youths who responded to the survey (a) report using cocaine or heroin and (b) commit two or more index crimes each year. However, these drug-abusing adolescents accounted for *40 percent to 60 percent* of all the index crimes (robbery, theft, drug sales) reported in the sample. Less than one-quarter of these hard-core delinquents committed crime solely to support a drug habit. This data suggests that a small core of substance-abusing adolescents commits a significant proportion of all serious crimes. It is also evident that a behavior, drug abuse, that develops later in adolescence influences the frequency and extent of delinquent activity through the life course.[66]

The relationship between drug abuse and chronic offending is aptly illustrated by Inciardi, Horowitz, and Pottienger's interviews with crack-involved youth in Miami. The 254 kids in their sample reported committing an astounding *223,439* criminal offenses during the twelve months prior to their interview. It is not surprising, considering that they averaged 879 offenses each, that 87 percent of the sample had been arrested. The greater the involvement in the crack business, the greater the likelihood of committing violent crime. About 74 percent of the hard-core dealers committed robbery and 17 percent engaged in assault; only 12 percent of the nondealers committed robbery and 4 percent engaged in assault.

Explaining Drug Use and Delinquency

The general association between delinquency and drug use has been well established in a variety of cultures.[67] It is still far from certain, however, whether (a) drug use *causes* delinquency, (b) delinquent behavior patterns *lead* youths to engage in substance abuse, or (c) both drug abuse and delinquency are *functions* of some other factor that is responsible for both behaviors.[68]

Some of the most sophisticated research on this topic has been conducted by Delbert Elliott and his associates at the Institute of Behavioral Science at the University of Colorado.[69] Using data from the National Youth Survey, a longitudinal study of self-reported delinquency and drug use, Elliott and his colleagues David Huizinga and Scott Menard found a strong association between delinquency and drug use.[70] However, they too found that the direction of the relationship is unclear. As a general rule, drug abuse appears to be a *type* of delinquent behavior and not a *cause* of delinquency. Most youths become involved in delinquent acts before they are initiated into drugs later in their adolescence; it is difficult, therefore, to conclude that drugs cause crime.

According to the Elliott research, both drug use and delinquency seem to reflect a developmental problem. Rather than causing one another, drug use and delinquency seem to be part of a disturbed socialization and life-style. This research does reveal some important associations between substance abuse and delinquency:

1. Alcohol abuse seems to be a cause of marijuana and drug abuse since (a) most drug users started with alcohol and (b) youths who abstain from alcohol almost never take drugs.
2. Marijuana use is a cause of multiple-drug use: about 95 percent of kids who use more serious drugs, such as crack, started on pot; only 5 percent of serious drug users never smoked pot.
3. Kids who commit felonies started off with minor delinquent acts. Few (1 percent) delinquents report committing felonies only.

The Elliott research has been supported by a number of other studies that also indicate that delinquency and substance abuse are actually part of a general pattern of deviance or problem behavior syndrome. Helene Raskin White, Robert Padina, and Randy LaGrange found that both forms of deviance are related to symptoms of social disturbance, such as association with a antisocial peer group and educational failure.[71] Similar research by Eric Wish also shows a pattern of deviance escalation in which troubled youth start by committing petty crimes and drinking alcohol and then proceed to both harder drugs and more serious crimes. Both their drug abuse and delinquency are part of an urban underclass life-style involving limited education, few job skills, unstable families, few social skills, and patterns of law violations.[72]

It is also possible that drug abuse and delinquency have independent causes. White has also found that the onset of both delinquency and drug abuse can be traced to the "preferred" deviant behavior of peers: kids whose friends are substance abusers are more likely to abuse substances themselves; adolescents whose peers engage in delinquent behavior are more likely to become delinquents.[73]

By implication, these studies indicate that restricting or reducing substance abuse may have *little* effect on delinquency rates because drugs are a *symptom* and not a *cause* of youthful misbehavior.

DRUG CONTROL STRATEGIES

The United States is in the midst of a well-publicized "war on drugs." Billions are being spent each year to reduce the importation of drugs, deter would-be drug dealers, and treat users. Yet, as most of us know, drug control efforts have been less than successful. Though the overall incidence of drug use has declined, drug use has concentrated in the nation's poorest neighborhoods, with a consequent association between substance abuse and crime.

A number of different drug control strategies have been tried with varying degrees of success. Some are designed to deter drug use by stopping the flow of drugs into the country, apprehending and punishing dealers, and cracking down on street-level drug deals. Another approach is to prevent drug use by educating would-be users and convincing them to "say no to drugs." A third approach is to treat users so they can terminate their addictions. Some of the more important of these efforts are discussed below.

Deterrence Strategies

One approach to drug control is to deter the sale and importation of drugs through the systematic apprehension of large-volume drug dealers, coupled with the enforcement of strict drug laws that carry heavy penalties. This approach is designed to punish known drug dealers and users and deter those who are considering entering into the drug trade.

A major effort has been made to cut off supplies of drugs by destroying overseas crops and arresting members of drug cartels; this approach is known as *source control*. The federal government has been encouraging exporting nations to step up efforts to destroy drug crops and prosecute dealers. Three South American nations, Peru, Bolivia, and Colombia, have agreed to coordinate control efforts with the United States.

However, translating words into deeds is a formidable task. Drug lords are willing and able to fight back through intimidation, violence, and corruption. The United States was forced to invade Panama with twenty thousand troops in 1989 to stop its leader, General Manuel Noriega, from trafficking in cocaine.

Adding to control problems is the fact that the drug trade is an important source of revenue for drug-producing countries and destroying it undermines their economy. For example, about 60 percent of the raw coca leaves used to make cocaine for the United States are grown in Peru. The drug trade supports two hundred thousand Peruvians and brings in over $3 billion annually. In Bolivia, which supplies 30 percent of the raw cocaine for the U.S. market, three hundred thousand people are supported with profits from the drug trade; coca is the country's single leading export. About 20 percent of Colombia's overseas exports are made by the Medellin and Cali drug cartels, which refine the coca leaves into cocaine before shipping it to the United States.[74] And even if the government of one nation is willing to cooperate in vigorous drug suppression efforts, suppliers in other nations, eager to cash in on the seller's market, would be encouraged to turn more acreage over to coca, poppy, or marijuana production.

Law enforcement efforts have also been directed at interdicting drug supplies as they enter the country. Border patrols and military personnel using sophisticated hardware have been involved in massive interdiction efforts; many impressive billion-dollar seizures have been made. Yet the United States's borders are so vast and unprotected that meaningful interdiction is impossible. And even if all importation were ended, homegrown marijuana and lab-made drugs, such as "ice," LSD, and PCP, could become the drugs of choice. Even now, their easy availability and relatively low cost are increasing their popularity among teenagers.

Efforts have also been made to bust large-scale drug rings. The long-term consequence has been to decentralize drug dealing and encourage teenage gangs to become major suppliers. Ironically, it has proven easier for federal agents to infiltrate and prosecute traditional organized crime groups than to take on drug-dealing youth gangs.

Police can also target, intimidate, and arrest street-level dealers and users in an effort to make drug use so much of a hassle that consumption is cut back and the crime rate reduced. While some street-level enforcement efforts have had success, others are considered failures. "Drug sweeps" have clogged courts and correctional facilities with petty offenders while proving a costly drain on police resources. These are also suspected of creating a displacement effect: stepped-up efforts to curb drug dealing in one area or city may simply encourage dealers to seek our friendlier "business" territory.[75]

Even if police are successful in eliminating existing drug networks, a new set of dealers may emerge. In Chicago, a police undercover program, Operation SKID (School Kids in Danger), turned up a new variety of drug dealer: school bus drivers who deal drugs on their bus routes![76]

Punishment Strategies

If law enforcement agents cannot deter drug abuse, how successful are the courts in trying and punishing drug dealers and traffickers? Despite the government's stated get-tough policy, adult drug traffickers are punished less severely than the public may be led to believe. The typical sentence is about three years, and the average prison stay before parole or early release averages out to slightly more than one year. Of all convicted criminals, those sentenced on drug charges spend the smallest percentage of their sentence behind bars.[77]

How have teenage drug abusers fared in court? Despite the leveling off of teen-age drug use, drug and alcohol offenses make up a significant portion of the juvenile court's docket. One study by the National Center for Juvenile Justice analyzed nearly 393,000 court records from 696 courts in 15 states to develop a picture of youthful substance abusers.[78] The records show that drug and alcohol cases accounted for about 14 percent of the delinquency cases handled by the courts, about six per one thousand youths aged 10 to 17 living in the courts' jurisdictions.

The study found that court handling of substance-abusing youth varied considerably depending on offense and jurisdiction variables. For example, repeat offenders were handled more formally than first offenders. Similarly, youths charged with driving while intoxicated were subject to out-of-home placement at a far higher rate than youths charged with merely being in possession of or drinking alcohol. Some courts formally handled over 80 percent of their drug cases, while others petitioned only 12 percent for formal trials.

A more recent (1989) survey on juvenile court case processing by the National Center for Juvenile Justice indicates that the number of cases involving drugs has stabilized at about 7 percent of all cases.[79] This national survey found that drug-involved offenders are more likely to be adjudicated, waived to adult court, and receive out-of-home placements than other categories of delinquent offenders, including those who commit violent crimes. The number of drug-involved youths waived to the jurisdiction of the adult court increased 469 percent between 1985 and 1989 (from four hundred to twenty-five hundred); in comparison, overall waivers increased 78 percent. These data indicate that courts are tougher on youths charged with drug violations than on youths involved in other crimes and that the level of punishment seems to be increasing.

Education Strategies

A third approach to reducing teenage substance abuse relies on school-based educational programs. One of the most familiar is the "McGruff, the Crime Dog" advertisements sponsored by the federal government's National Citizen's Crime Prevention Campaign. This friendly symbol, which is familiar to 99 percent of children between the ages of 6 and 12, has been used extensively in the media to warn kids about the dangers of drug use and crime. A multimedia drug prevention kit containing antidrug materials and videos has been distributed to almost every school district in the nation. A McGruff drug prevention curriculum featuring a McGruff puppet and accompanying audiocassette has been distributed to more than seventy-five thousand elementary classroom teachers. And more than 1.5 million McGruff antidrug comic books are being given away to students. There is some indication that students in the program learn and improve their antidrug attitudes, teachers like the program, and parents endorse the content and need for the program.[80]

Another familiar program is **Drug Abuse Resistance Education (DARE.)** This program is an elementary school course designed to give students the skills for resisting peer pressure to experiment with tobacco, drugs, and alcohol. It is unique because it employs uniformed police officers to carry the antidrug message to the students before they enter junior high school. The program focuses on five major areas:

1. Providing accurate information about tobacco, alcohol and drugs
2. Teaching students techniques to resist peer pressure
3. Teaching students respect for the law and law enforcers
4. Giving students ideas for alternative for drug use
5. Building the self-esteem of students

DARE is based on the concept that the young students need specific analytical and social skills to resist peer pressure and say no to drugs. Instructors work with children to raise their self-esteem, provide them with decision-making tools, and help them identify positive alternatives to substance abuse. More than 3 million students have taken the DARE program.[81] More than 40 percent of all school districts incorporate assistance from local law enforcement agencies in their drug-prevention programming.[82]

Schools districts have included drug education programs as a standard part of their curriculum. Drug education now begins in kindergarten and extends through the twelfth grade. More than 80 percent of public school districts include the following within all of their schools: teaching students about the causes and effects of alcohol, drug, and tobacco use; teaching students to resist peer pressure; and referring students for counseling and treatment outside the educational system.[83] Such education programs as Project ALERT, based in middle schools in California and Oregon, appear to be successful in training kids to not use recreational drugs and to resist peer pressure to use cigarettes and alcohol.[84]

Community Strategies

Another type of drug-control effort relies on the involvement of local community groups. Representatives of various local government agencies, churches, civic organizations, and similar institutions are being brought together to create drug-prevention awareness programs. Their activities often include the creation of drug-free school zones (which encourage police to keep drug dealers away from the areas near schools); Neighborhood Watch Programs, which are geared to spotting and reporting drug dealers; citizen patrols, which frighten dealers away from children in public housing projects; and community centers, which provide an alternative to the street culture.

Community-based programs reach out to high-risk youths, getting them involved in after-school programs; offering family and individual counseling sessions; delivering clothing, food, and medical care when needed; and encouraging school achievement through tutoring and other services. Community programs also sponsor drug-free activities involving the arts, clubs, and athletics. Evaluations of community programs have shown that they may encourage antidrug attitudes and help insulate participating youth from an environment that encourages drugs.[85]

Treatment Strategies

Several approaches are used to treat known users. Some efforts stem from the perspective that users have low self-esteem; these use various techniques to build up the user's sense of himself or herself. Another approach has been to involve users in outdoor activities, wilderness training, and after-school community programs.[86]

More intensive efforts use group therapy approaches in which leaders, many of whom have been substance abusers, try to give users the skills and support that can help them reject the social pressure to use drugs. These programs are based on the Alcoholics Anonymous philosophy that users must find within themselves the strength to stay clean and that peer support from those who understand their experiences can be a successful means of achieving a drug-free life.

Residential programs are used with the more heavily involved, and a large network of drug treatment units geared to juveniles has developed. Some are detoxification units that use medical procedures to wean patients from the more addicting drugs. Others are therapeutic communities that attempt to deal with the psychological causes of drug use. Hypnosis, aversion therapy (getting users to associate drugs with unpleasant sensations, such as nausea), counseling, biofeedback, and other techniques are often used.

Little evidence exists that these residential programs, despite their good intentions, can efficiently terminate teenage substance abuse. Many are restricted to families whose health insurance will pay for short-term residential care; when the insurance coverage ends, children are released, even though their treatment program is not completed. Adolescents do not often enter these programs voluntarily and have little motivation to change.[87] A stay can help stigmatize residents as addicts, even though they never used hard drugs; while in treatment, they may be introduced to hard-core users with whom they will associate upon release.

WHAT DOES THE FUTURE HOLD?

The United States appears willing to go to great lengths to fight the drug war. Law enforcement efforts, along with the institution of prevention programs and drug treatment projects, have been stepped up. Yet, all drug control strategies are doomed to fail as long as youth want to take drugs and dealers find that their sales efforts are a lucrative source of income. Prevention, deterrence, and treatment strategies ignore the core reasons for the drug problem: poverty, hopelessness, boredom, alienation, and family disruption. As the gap between rich and poor widens and the opportunities for legitimate advancement decrease, it should come as no surprise that adolescent drug use continues. It is a sad fact that a smaller percentage of the poor and minority-group members are attending college today than were ten years ago. The social failures of American society are being translated into teenage substance abuse.

Some commentators have called for the **legalization** of drugs. While this approach can have the short-term effect of reducing the association between drug use and crime (since, presumably, the cost of drugs would decrease), it may also have grave social consequences. Drug use would most certainly increase, creating an overflow of unproductive, drug-dependent people who must be cared for by the rest of society. The problems of teenage alcoholism should serve as a warning of what can happen when controlled substances are made readily available. However, as Kathryn Ann Farr has suggested, the implications of drug decriminalization should be further studied: what effect would a policy of partial decriminalization (for example, legalizing small amounts of marijuana) have on drug use rates? Does a get-tough policy on drugs help to "widen the net"? Are there alternatives to the criminalization of drugs that could help reduce their use?[88] The Rand Corporation study of drug dealing in Washington, D.C., suggests that law enforcement efforts can have little influence on drug abuse rates. Only by improving job prospects and giving kids legitimate future alternatives can hard-core users be made to desist and willingly forgo drug use.[89]

Part III Environmental Influences on Delinquency

The president has appointed you as the new "Drug Czar" to lead the fight against drugs.

You have $10 billion under your control with which to wage a campaign against drugs. You know that drug use is unacceptably high, especially among poor, inner-city kids, that a great deal of all criminal behavior is drug-related, and that drug-dealing gangs are expanding around the United States.

At an open hearing, drug-control experts express their policy strategies. One group favors putting the money into hiring new law enforcement agents who will patrol borders, target large dealers, and make drug raids here and abroad. They also call for such get-tough measures as the creation of strict drug laws, the mandatory waiver of young drug dealers to the adult court system, and the death penalty for drug-related gang killings.

A second group believes that the best way to deal with drugs is to spend the money on community treatment programs, expanding the number of beds in drug detoxification units, and funding research on how to clinically reduce drug dependency.

A third group argues that neither punishment nor treatment can restrict teenage drug use and that the best course is to educate at-risk kids about the dangers of substance abuse and then legalize all drugs but control their distribution. This course of action will help both to reduce crime and violence among drug users and to balance the national debt, since drugs could be heavily taxed.

Should drugs be legalized?

Can law enforcement strategies reduce drug consumption?

Is treatment an effective drug-control technique?

■■■■■■■■■■■■■■■■

SUMMARY

Drug abuse has been closely linked to juvenile delinquency. Among the most popular drugs are marijuana, cocaine and its derivative, crack, "ice," LSD, and PCP. However, the most commonly used drug is alcohol, which contributes to almost one hundred thousand deaths per year.

There is some question about the trends in teenage substance abuse. Self-report surveys indicate that fewer teenagers are using drugs today than ever before. However, surveys of arrestees indicate that a significant proportion are current drug users and that many are high school dropouts. This indicates that surveys of current high school students may be missing the most delinquent and drug-abusing students.

A variety of kids use drugs. Some are occasional users who might sell to friends. Others are seriously involved in both drug abuse and delinquency; many of these are gang members. There are also "losers" who filter in and out of the juvenile justice system. A small percentage of teenage users remain involved with drugs into their adulthood.

Despite years of research, it is not certain whether drug abuse causes delinquency. Many kids who break the law later abuse drugs. Some experts believe that there is a "common cause" for both delinquency and drug abuse, such as alienation, anger, and rage.

Many attempts have been made to control the drug trade. Some have attempted to inhibit the importation of drugs from overseas, others are aimed at closing down major drug rings, and a few have tried to stop street-level dealing. There have also been attempts to treat known users through rehabilitation programs and to reduce juvenile use by education efforts. Communities beset by drug problems have mounted grassroots drives to reduce the incidence of drug abuse. So far, these efforts have not been totally successful, though the overall use of drugs may have, in fact, declined.

KEY TERMS

substance abuse
marijuana
cocaine
freebase
crack
hashish
heroin
alcohol
anesthetics

inhalants
sedatives
tranquilizers
hallucinogens
stimulants
steroids
addiction-prone personality
Drug Abuse Resistance Education (DARE)
legalization

QUESTIONS FOR DISCUSSION

1. Discuss the differences between the various categories and types of substances of abuse. Is the term *drugs* too broad to have real meaning?
2. Why do you think kids take drugs? Do you know anyone with an addiction-prone personality?
3. What policy might be the best strategy to reduce teenage drug use: source control? reliance on treatment? national education efforts? community-level enforcement?
4. Under what circumstances, if any, might the legalization or decriminalization of drugs be beneficial to society?

5. Do you consider alcohol a drug? Should greater control be placed on the sale of alcohol?
6. Do TV shows and films glorify drug usage and encourage kids to enter the drug trade? Should all images of drinking and smoking be banned from TV? What about advertisements that try to convince kids how much fun it is to drink beer or smoke cigarettes?

NOTES

1. University of Michigan, Institute for Social Research News Release, April 1993. (Herein cited as ISR.)
2. Peter Greenwood, "Substance Abuse Problems among High-Risk Youth and Potential Interventions," *Crime and Delinquency* 38:444-58 (1992).
3. U.S. Department of Justice, *Drugs and Crime Facts, 1988* (Washington, D.C.: Bureau of Justice Statistics, 1989), pp. 3-4.
4. Dennis Coon, *Introduction to Psychology* (St. Paul: West, 1992), p. 178.
5. ISR, p. 1-3.
6. Special Issue, "Drugs—The American Family in Crisis," *Juvenile and Family Court* 39:45-46 (1988).
7. Robyn Cohen, *Drunk Driving* (Washington, D.C.: Bureau of Justice Statistics, 1992), p. 2.
8. Ibid.
9. D. J. Rohsenow, "Drinking Habits and Expectancies about Alcohol's Effects for Self versus Others," *Journal of Consulting and Clinical Psychology* 51:752-56 (1983).
10. William Castelli, cited in G. Kolata, "Study Backs Heart Benefits in Light Drinking," *New York Times*, 3 August 1988, p. A24.

11. Spencer Rathus, *Psychology,* (New York: Holt Rinehart & Winston, 1990) 4th ed., p. 161.
12. Mary Tabor, "'Ice' in an Island Paradise," *Boston Globe*, 8 December 1989, p. 3.
13. Paul Goldstein, "Anabolic Steroids: An Ethnographic Approach" (Unpublished, Narcotics and Drug Research, Inc., March 1989).
14. Bureau of Justice Assistance, *FY 1988 Report on Drug Control* (Washington, D.C.: Government Printing Office, 1989). (Herein cited as *FY 1988 Report.*)
15. Matt Lait, "California's New Role: Leading PCP Supplier," *Washington Post*, 17 April 1989, p. 1.
16. Ibid.
17. Ibid., p. 10.
18. Robert Brooner, Donald Templer, Dace Svikis, Chester Schmidt, and Spyros Monopolis, "Dimensions of Alcoholism: A Multivariate Analysis," *Journal of Studies on Alcohol* 51:77-81 (1990).
19. National Institute on Drug Abuse, *Drug Use among American High School Seniors, College Students and Young Adults, 1975-1990, Vol. 1: High School Seniors* (Rockville, Md.: National Institute on Drug Abuse, 1991).

20. Cohen, *Drunk Driving*, p. 3.

21. Data in this section comes from Department of Health and Human Services, *The Household Survey on Drug Abuse, 1991* (Washington, D.C.: Department of Health and Human Services, 1992).

22. James Inciardi, Ruth Horowitz, and Anne Pottieger, *Street Kids, Street Drugs, Street Crime: An Examination of Drug Use and Serious Delinquency in Miami* (Belmont, Calif: Wadsworth, 1993), pp. 136-37.

23. *FY 1988 Report*, p. 23.

24. Ibid.

25. Joyce Ann O'Neil and Eric Wish, *Drug Use Forecasting, Cocaine Use* (Washington, D.C.: Government Printing Office, 1989), p. 7.

26. Eric Wish, "U.S. Drug Policy in the 1990's: Insights from New Data from Arrestees," *International Journal of the Addictions* 25:1-15 (1990).

27. G. E. Vallant, "Parent-Child Disparity and Drug Addiction," *Journal of Nervous and Mental Disease* 142:534-39 (1966).

28. Charles Winick, "Epidemiology of Narcotics Use," in D. Wilner and G. Kassenbaum, eds., *Narcotics* (New York: McGraw-Hill, 1965), pp. 3-18.

29. Delbert Elliott, David Huizinga, and Scott Menard, *Multiple Problem Youth: Delinquency, Substance Abuse and Mental Health Problems* (New York: Springer-Verlag, 1989).

30. Peter Reuter, Robert MacCoun, and Patrick Murphy, *Money from Crime: A Study of the Economics of Drug Dealing in Washington, D.C.* (Santa Monica, Calif.: Rand, 1990).

31. C. Bowden, "Determinants of Initial Use of Opioids," *Comprehensive Psychiatry* 12:136-40 (1971).

32. Terence Thornberry, Margaret Farnworth, Marvin Krohn, and Alan Lizotte, *Peer Influence and the Initiation to Drug Use* (Albany, N.Y.: Hindelang Criminal Justice Research Center, n.d.).

33. Helene Raskin White, "Marijuana Use and Delinquency: A Test of the 'Independent Cause' Hypothesis," *Journal of Drug Issues* 21:231-56 (1991).

34. R. Cloward and L. Ohlin, *Delinquency and Opportunity: A Theory of Delinquent Gangs* (Glencoe, Ill.: Free Press, 1960).

35. Denise Kandel and Mark Davies, "Friendship Networks, Intimacy and Illicit Drug Use in Young Adulthood: A Comparison of Two Competing Theories," *Criminology* 29:441-71 (1991).

36. Inciardi, Horowitz, and Pottieger, *Street Kids, Street Drugs, Street Crime*, p. 43.

37. D. Baer and J. Corrado, "Heroin Addict Relationships with Parents during Childhood and Early Adolescent Years," *Journal of Genetic Psychology* 124:99-103 (1974).

38. See S. F. Bucky, "The Relationship between Background and Extent of Heroin Use," *American Journal of Psychiatry* 130:709-10 (1973); I. Chien, D. L. Gerard, R. Lee, and E. Rosenfield, *The Road to H: Narcotics Delinquency and Social Policy* (New York: Basic Books, 1964).

39. J. S. Mio, G. Nanjundappa, D. E. Verlur, and M. D. De-Rios, "Drug Abuse and the Adolescent Sex Offender: A Preliminary Analysis," *Journal of Psychoactive Drugs* 18:65-72 (1986).

40. G. T. Wilson, "Cognitive Studies in Alcoholism," *Journal of Consulting and Clinical Psychology* 55:325-31 (1987).

41. Inciardi, Horowitz, and Pottieger, *Street Kids, Street Drugs, Street Crime*, p. 135.

42. Ibid., p. 136.

43. D. W. Goodwin, "Alcoholism and Genetics," *Archives of General Psychiatry* 42:171-74 (1985).

44. Ibid.

45. Jerome Platt and Christina Platt, *Heroin Addiction* (New York: Wiley, 1976), p. 127.

46. Rathus, *Psychology*, p. 158.

47. J. Shedler and J. Block, "Adolescent Drug Use and Psychological Health: A Longitudinal Inquiry," *American Psychologist* 45:612-30 (1990).

48. Greenwood, "Substance Abuse Problems among High-Risk Youth and Potential Interventions," p. 448.

49. John Wallace and Jerald Bachman, "Explaining Racial/Ethnic Differences in Adolescent Drug Use: The Impact of Background and Lifestyle," *Social Problems* 38:333-57 (1991).

50. B. A. Christiansen, G. T. Smith, P. V. Roehling, and M. S. Goldman, "Using Alcohol Expectancies to Predict Adolescent Drinking Behavior after One Year," *Journal of Counseling and Clinical Psychology* 57:93-99 (1989).

51. The following sections lean heavily on Marcia Chaiken and Bruce Johnson, *Characteristics of Different Types of Drug-Involved Youth* (Washington, D.C.: National Institute of Justice, 1988). (Herein cited as *Characteristics*.)

52. Inciardi, Horowitz, and Pottieger, *Street Kids, Street Drugs and Street Crime*, p. 100.

53. Ibid., p. 100.

54. Ibid., p. 101.

55. Robert MacCoun and Peter Reuter, "Are the Wages of Sin $30 an Hour? Economic Aspects of Street-Level Drug Dealing," *Crime and Delinquency* 38:477-91 (1992).

56. Chaiken & Johnson, *Characteristics*, p. 12.

57. Rick Graves and Ed Allen, *Narcotics and Black Gangs* (Los Angeles: Los Angeles County Sheriff's Department, n.d.)

58. Scott Armstrong, "Los Angeles Gangs Go National," *Christian Science Monitor*, 19 July 1988, p. 3.

59. Ibid.

60. Ibid., p. 13.

61. *Characteristics*, p. 14.

62. *FY 1988 Report*, p. 19.

63. James Inciardi, "Heroin Use and Street Crime," *Crime and Delinquency* 25:335-46 (1979); idem, *The War on Drugs* (Palo Alto, Calif.: Mayfield, 1986). See also W. McGlothlin, M. Anglin, and B. Wilson, "Narcotic Addiction and Crime," *Criminology* 16:293-311 (1978); George Speckart and M. Douglas Anglin, "Narcotics Use and Crime: An Overview of Recent Research Advances," *Contemporary Drug Problems* 13:741-69 (1986); Charles Faupel and

Carl Klockars, "Drugs-Crime Connections: Elaborations from the Life Histories of Hard-core Heroin Addicts," *Social Problems* 34:54-68 (1987).

64. National Institute of Justice, *Drug Use Forecasting, 1991 Annual Report* (Washington, D.C.: National Institute of Justice, 1992).

65. National Institute of Justice, *Drug Use Forecasting Annual Report, 1989* (Washington, D.C.: National Institute of Justice, 1990); see also Eric Wish, Mary Toborg, and John Bellassai, *Identifying Drug Users and Monitoring Them during Conditional Release* (Washington, D.C.: National Institute of Justice, 1988), p. 11.

66. B. D. Hohnson, E. Wish, J. Schmeidler, and D. Huizinga, "Concentration of Delinquent Offending: Serious Drug Involvement and High Delinquency Rates," *Journal of Drug Issues* 21:205-29 (1991).

67. W. David Watts and Lloyd Wright, "The Relationship of Alcohol, Tobacco, Marijuana, and Other Illegal Drug Use to Delinquency among Mexican-American, Black, and White Adolescent Males," *Adolescence* 25:38-54 (1990).

68. For a general review of this issue, see Helene Raskin White, "The Drug Use-Delinquency Connection in Adolescence," in Ralph Weisheit, ed., *Drugs, Crime and Criminal Justice* (Cincinnati: Anderson, 1990), pp. 215-56.; Speckart and Anglin, "Narcotics Use and Crime;" Faupel and Klockars, "Drugs-Crime Connections."

69. Delbert Elliott, David Huizinga, and Susan Ageton, *Explaining Delinquency and Drug Abuse* (Beverly Hills, Calif.: Sage, 1985).

70. David Huizinga, Scott Menard, and Delbert Elliott, "Delinquency and Drug Use: Temporal and Developmental Patterns," *Justice Quarterly* 6:419-55 (1989).

71. Helene Raskin White, Robert Padina, and Randy LaGrange, "Longitudinal Predictors of Serious Substance Use and Delinquency," *Criminology* 25:715-40 (1987).

72. Wish, "U.S. Drug Policy in the 1990's."

73. White, "Marijuana Use and Delinquency."

74. Drug Enforcement Administration, *National Drug Control Strategy* (Washington, D.C.: Government Printing Office, 1989).

75. Mark Moore, *Drug Trafficking* (Washington, D.C: National Institute of Justice, 1988).

76. "Bus Drivers: Dealing While Working," *Newsweek*, 11 December 1989.

77. *Time Served in Prison and on Parole* (Washington, D.C.: Bureau of Justice Statistics, 1988).

78. Office of Juvenile Justice and Delinquency Prevention, *Juvenile Courts Vary Greatly in How They Handle Drug and Alcohol Cases* (Washington, D.C.: Office of Juvenile Justice and Delinquency Prevention, 1989).

79. Jeffrey Butts and Melissa Sickmund, *Offenders in Juvenile Court, 1989* (Washington, D.C.: Office of Juvenile Justice and Delinquency Prevention, 1992), p. 1.

80. *FY 1988 Report*, p. 50.

81. Ibid.

82. Judi Carpenter, *Public School District Survey on Safe, Disciplined and Drug-Free Schools* (Washington, D.C.: Government Printing Office, 1992), p. 111.

83. Ibid.

84. Phyllis Ellickson and Robert Bell, *Prospects for Preventing Drug Use among Young Adolescents* (Santa Monica, Calif.: Rand Corp., 1990).

85. Wayne Lucan and Steven Gilham, "Impact of a Drug Use Prevention Program: An Empirical Assessment" (Paper presented at the annual meeting of the American Society of Criminology, New Orleans, November, 1992).

86. Eli Ginzberg, Howard Berliner, and Miriam Ostrow, *Young People at Risk: Is Prevention Possible?* (Boulder, Colo.: Westview Press, 1988), p. 99.

87. Ibid.

88. Kathryn Ann Farr, "Revitalizing the Drug Decriminalization Debate," *Crime and Delinquency* 36:223-37 (1990).

89. Reuter, MacCoun, and Murphy, *Money from Crime*, pp. 165-68.

IV JUVENILE JUSTICE ADVOCACY

▪▪

Part IV provides a general overview of the juvenile justice system, including its process, history, and legal rules.

Since 1900, juveniles who violate the law have been treated differently from adults. A separate juvenile justice system has been developed that features its own judiciary, rules, and processes.

The separation of juvenile and adult offenders reflects society's concern for the plight of children. Since many experts believe children can be reformed or rehabilitated, it makes sense to treat their law violations more leniently than those of adults. Care, protection, and treatment are the bywords of the juvenile justice system. Of course, to some influential critics, the serious juvenile offender is not deserving of this approach. Consequently, efforts have been made recently to "toughen up" the juvenile justice system and treat some delinquents much more like adult offenders.

Chapter 13 reviews the history and development of juvenile justice. Chapter 14 provides an overview of the juvenile justice system and describes its major components, processes, goals, and institutions. Chapter 14 also describes the organization of juvenile court and the legal rights of minors. Throughout this part, it is stressed that while juveniles are supposed to be treated separately from adults, this division is often blurred by the need to both maintain public order and protect juveniles from the people allegedly trying to help them. The rhetoric of juvenile justice and its reality are often at odds. ▪

THE HISTORY AND PHILOSOPHY OF JUVENILE JUSTICE

OUTLINE

H ow has the role of children changed from the Middle Ages to the present time? Where did the term *delinquency* originate?[1] What historical developments led to the first modern juvenile court in Chicago in 1899? What were the origins of the social welfare movement, the state's role in the care and custody of children, and the segregation of delinquent children from adult criminal offenders?

This chapter reviews the history of childhood beginning with the development of the concept in the middle ages and ending with its status from the late 1800s to the mid-1960s. It explores the social and political factors that resulted in the creation of the contemporary juvenile court system. It also discusses efforts to reevaluate the motives of the child savers and other reformists who desired to control the lives of needy adolescents.

THE CARE OF CHILDREN IN THE MIDDLE AGES

Little is known about family during the Middle Ages (700 A.D. to 1500 A.D.). During this period, the concept of childhood as we know it today did not exist. Children were not seen as a distinct social group with unique needs and behaviors.

From diaries and writings, it is known that during the early Middle Ages, family life was essentially **paternalistic.**[2] The father was the final authority on all family matters and exercised complete control over the social, economic, and physical well-being of his wife and children. Ordinarily, if the father's will was not obeyed, his children and wife were subject to severe physical punishment, even death. The concept of the father's dominance had its roots in Roman law, which gave him unlimited authority over his family, including the right of life and death over all family members, the power to sell members of the family, and the right to order marriages or veto marital choices.

Family Life

Peasants lived a life tied to the soil and their feudal obligation to serve the lord of the manor.[3] Households were based on the nuclear rather than the extended family and typically consisted of husband, wife, and two or three children. Life revolved around the agricultural duties that came with the seasons. Most families slept and lived together in a single room, though the more affluent maintained a separate room for sleeping. As soon as they were physically capable, children would begin the life of the serf: the males farming and/or learning a skilled trade, such as masonry or metal working; the females preparing food and maintaining the household. Peasant youth went into domestic or agricultural service on the great estates or were apprenticed in trades or crafts. To some degree, this system of control over children lifted the burden from parents and placed the children in the care of wealthy families.

More is known about the family life of upper-class landholders during this period. Among these people, the nuclear family—father, mother, and children— was viewed as a small segment of a larger clan. This larger group, or extended family, was made up of many loosely related families sharing a common heritage and tradition. In England, for example, the de Montfort, York, and Lancaster clans were powerful congregate family groups. These families sought to expand their power and influence over rivals by intermarriage. The importance of improving and expanding the family influenced marriage, inheritance, and child-rearing practices. Marriages were not based on romantic love or affection, for example, but were political alliances made for family interest, to strengthen ties with potential allies, and to increase control over lands and wealth. Personal needs were subjugated to duty to family and relatives.

Girls born into aristocratic families were educated at home and trained at an early age to manage castles and estates. Since girls married in their early teens, they were expected to assume the duties of women—supervising servants and ensuring the food supply of the manor—at an early age. Some may have been taught to read, write, and do sufficient mathematics to handle household accounts.

At age 7 or 8, boys born to the nobility were either sent to a monastery or cathedral school to be trained for a life in the church or selected to be a member of the warrior class and apprenticed as a squire in the service of a relative or friend. After apprenticeship ended at age 21, the young nobles entered into the knighthood and returned home to live with their parents. Most remained single because it was widely believed there should only be one married couple residing in a castle. To pass the time and maintain their fighting edge, many entered the tournament circuit, engaging in melees and jousts to win fame and fortune. Upon the death of their fathers, young nobles assumed their inherited titles, married, and began their own families.

Custom and Practice

Custom and practice greatly influenced the daily life of children during the Middle Ages. *Primogeniture* required that the oldest surviving male child inherit family lands and titles. He could then distribute them as he saw fit to younger siblings. There was no absolute requirement, however, that portions of the estate be distributed equally, so many youths who received no lands were forced to enter religious orders, become soldiers, or seek wealthy patrons. Primogeniture often caused intense family rivalry that led to blood feuds and tragedy. For example, a mother would die in childbirth, leaving behind an infant who was the sole heir to a family estate and title. If the child's father remarried and produced offspring who had no hope of substantial inheritance, conflicts would arise over the inheritance rights of the first-born infant and subsequent siblings. Jealousy would create feuds between family members.

The *dower system* mandated that a woman's family bestow money, land, or other wealth on a potential husband or his family in exchange for his marriage to her. In return, the young woman received a promise of financial assistance, called a *jointure*, from the groom's family. Jointure provided a lifetime income if a wife outlived her mate. The dower system had a significant impact on the role of the women in medieval society and consequently on the role of children. It ensured that marriages would be contracted only within and not across social classes. It gave the woman's father control over whom she married because he could threaten to withhold funds. Females were viewed as economic drains on the family. A father with many daughters and few sons might find himself financially unable to obtain suitable marriages. The youngest girls in many families were forced to enter convents, abandoned, or left at home.

CHILD CARE IN THE FIFTEENTH AND SIXTEENTH CENTURIES

The harshness of medieval life influenced child-rearing practices during the fifteenth and sixteenth centuries. For instance, newborns were almost immediately handed over to **wet nurses,** who fed and cared for them during the first two years of their life. These women often lived away from the family so that parents had little contact with their children. Even the wealthiest families employed wet nurses, because it was considered demeaning for a noblewoman to nurse. *Swaddling,* a common practice, entailed wrapping a newborn entirely in bandages. The bandages prevented any movement and enabled the wet nurse to manage the child easily. This practice was thought to protect the child, but it most likely contributed to high infant mortality rates because the child could not be kept clean.

Discipline was severe during this period. Young children of all classes, both peasant and wealthy, were subjected to stringent rules and regulations. They were beaten severely for any sign of disobedience or ill-temper. Many children of this time would be considered abused if they lived in today's world. The relationship between parent and child was remote. Children were expected to enter the world of adults and to undertake responsibilities early in their lives, sharing in the work of siblings and parents.

The roots of the impersonal relationship between parent and child can be traced to high mortality rates, which made sentimental and affectionate relationships risky. It would have been foolish for parents to invest emotional effort in relationships that could so easily be terminated by violence, accidents, or disease. Parents often thought that children must be toughened to ensure their survival in a hostile world. Close family relationships were viewed as detrimental to this process. Also, since the oldest male child was viewed as the essential and important element in a family's well-being, younger male and female siblings were considered economic and social liabilities. Children thought to be suffering from disease or retardation were often abandoned to churches, orphanages, or foundling homes.[4]

In sum, lack of parental affection, physical and emotional remoteness, severe physical punishments and other discipline, rigid social class structure, and conflict, suspicion, hostility, and alienation among family groups characterized child care in the Middle Ages. These conditions precipitated the children's court movement in Great Britain in the seventeenth and eighteenth centuries.

THE DEVELOPMENT OF CONCERN FOR CHILDREN

Throughout the seventeenth and eighteenth centuries, a number of developments in England heralded the march toward the recognition of the rights of children. In many instances, these events eventually affected the juvenile legal system as it emerged in America. They include: (1) changes in family style and child care, (2) the English Poor Laws, (3) the apprenticeship movement, and (4) the role of the chancery court.[5]

Changes in Family Structure

Family structure and the role of children began to change after the Middle Ages as the influence of the great families began to wane. Extended families, which were created over centuries, gave way to the nuclear family structure with which we are familiar today. It became more common for marriage to be based on love and mutual attraction between men and women than on parental consent and paternal dominance. But parents still rigidly disciplined their children. Control of a child's actions was considered essential for proper maintenance of the family structure. At this time, the concept of childhood as an independent status was developing, and the needs of children were beginning to be understood.

To provide more controls over children, grammar and boarding schools were established and began to flourish in many large cities during this time.[6] Their structure and subject matter were quite different from those of today. Children studied grammar, Latin, law, and logic, often beginning at a young age. The growth of this scholastic movement was directly related to the emphasis such philosophers as John Locke and Jean Jacques Rousseau put on the learning process. Teachers in these institutions often ruled by fear, and flogging was their main method of discipline. Students were beaten for academic mistakes as well as moral lapses. Such brutal treatment fell on both the rich and the poor throughout all levels of educational life, including boarding schools and universities. This treatment abated in Europe with the rise of the Enlightenment, but it remained in full force in Great Britain. Although this brutal approach to children may be difficult to understand now, the child in that society was a second-class citizen.

Toward the close of the eighteenth century, the work of such philosophers as Voltaire, Rousseau, and Locke began to herald a new age for childhood and the family.[7] The Enlightenment stressed a humanistic view of life, freedom, family, reason, and law. The philosophers suggested that the ideal person was sympathetic to others and receptive to new ideas. These new beliefs influenced the life-style of the family. The father's authority was tempered, discipline in the home became more relaxed, and the expression of love and affection came to be of deep concern to family members. Upper- and middle-class families began to devote attention to child rearing.

As a result, toward the end of the eighteenth and beginning of the nineteenth centuries, children began to emerge as a readily distinguishable group with independent needs and interests, at least in the wealthier classes. Parents often took greater interest in their upbringing. In addition, serious questions arose over the treatment of children in school. Public outcries led to a decrease in excessive physical discipline. Restrictions were placed on the use of the whip, and in some schools, the imposition of academic assignments or the loss of privileges replaced corporal punishment. Nonetheless, not all customs changed for the better. Girls were still undereducated, parents were still excessively concerned with the moral and religious development of their children, punishment was still primarily physical, and schools continued to mistreat children. Yet the changes in England in this period paved the way for today's family structure of child care.

Poor Laws

While children of the upper classes were sent to school, poor children had different experiences. As early as 1535, the English passed statutes known as *Poor Laws.*[8] These laws allowed for the appointment of overseers to bind out destitute or neglected children as servants. The Poor Laws forced children to serve during their minority in the care of families who trained them in agricultural, trade, or domestic services. The Elizabethan Poor Laws of 1601 were a model for dealing with poor children for more than two hundred years. These laws created a system of church wardens and overseers who, with the consent of justices of the peace, identified vagrant, delinquent, and neglected children and took measures to put them to work. Often this meant placing them in poorhouses or work-houses or apprenticing them to masters.

The Apprenticeship Movement

Apprenticeship in Great Britain existed through almost the entire history of the country.[9] Under this practice, children were placed in the care of adults who trained them to discharge various duties and obtain different skills. Voluntary apprentices were bound out by parents or guardians who wished to secure training for their children. Involuntary apprentices were compelled by the authorities to serve until they were 21 or older. The master-apprentice relationship was similar to the parent-child relationship in that the master had complete responsibility for and authority over the apprentice. If an apprentice was unruly, a complaint could be made and the apprentice could be punished. Incarcerated apprentices were often placed in rooms or workshops apart from other prisoners and were generally treated differently from those charged with a criminal offense. Even at this early stage, the conviction was growing that the criminal law and its enforcement should be applied differently to children.

Chancery Court

The concept of *parens patriae* and the chancery court system played significant roles in shaping juvenile justice in Great Britain. *Chancery courts* existed throughout the Middle Ages. They were established primarily to protect property rights, although their authority extended to the welfare of children generally. The major issues in medieval cases that came before the chancery courts concerned guardianship, the uses and control of property, and the arrangement of people and power in relation to the monarchy. Agents of the chancery courts were responsible for controlling and settling problems involving rights to estates and guardianship interests with regard to the hierarchy of families and the state.

Chancery courts were founded on the proposition that children and other incompetents were under the protective control of the king; thus, the Latin phrase *parens patriae,* was used referring to the role of the king as the father of his country. As Douglas Besharov states, "The concept apparently was first used by English kings to justify their intervention in the lives of the children of their vassals—children whose position and property were of direct concern to the monarch."[10] In the famous 1827 English case *Wellesley v. Wellesley,* a duke's children were taken away from him in the name and interest of *parens patriae* because of his scandalous behavior.[11] Thus, the concept of *parens patriae* became the theoretical basis for the protective jurisdiction of the chancery courts acting as part of the crown's power.

As time passed, the monarchy used *parens patriae* more and more to justify its intervention in the lives of families and children by its interest in their general welfare. However, as Douglas Rendleman points out, "The idea of parens patriae was actually used to maintain the power of the crown and the structure of control over families known as feudalism."[12]

The chancery courts dealt with the property and custody problems of the wealthier classes. They did not have jurisdiction over children charged with criminal conduct. Juveniles who violated the law were handled within the framework of the regular criminal court system. Nonetheless, the concept of *parens patriae,* which was established with the English chancery court system, grew to refer primarily to the responsibility of the courts and the state to act in the best interests of the child. The idea that the state—and particularly the juvenile court—in the twentieth century should act to protect the young, the incompetent, the neglected, and the delinquent subsequently became a major influence on the development of the U.S. juvenile justice system.

CHILDREN IN COLONIAL AMERICA

While England was using its chancery courts and Poor Laws to deal with unfortunate children, the American colonies were struggling with similar concepts. Initially, the colonies were a haven for poor and unfortunate people looking for religious and economic opportunities denied them in England and Europe. Along with early settlers, many children came not as citizens but as indentured servants, apprentices, or agricultural workers. They were recruited from the various English workhouses, orphanages, prisons, and asylums that housed vagrant and delinquent youths during the sixteenth and seventeenth centuries.[13]

At the same time, the colonies themselves produced illegitimate, neglected, abandoned, and delinquent children. The colonies' initial response to caring for such unfortunate children was to adopt court and Poor Laws systems similar to the English ones. Involuntary apprenticeship and the indentury and binding out of children became integral parts of colonization in America. For example, Poor Law legislation was passed in Virginia in 1646 and in Massachusetts and Connecticut in 1673.[14] Poor and dependent children were required to serve apprenticeships.

The master in colonial America acted as a natural parent, and in certain instances, apprentices would actually become part of the nuclear family structure. If they disobeyed their masters, apprentices were punished by local tribunals. If masters abused apprentices, courts would make them pay damages, return the children to the parents, or find new guardians. Maryland and Virginia developed an orphan's court that supervised the treatment of youth placed with guardians and ensured that they were not mistreated or taken advantage of by their masters. These courts did not supervise children living with their natural parents, leaving intact the parents' right to care for their children.[15]

The apprenticeship system eventually eroded under the pressure of national growth prompted by the War of Independence, the industrial revolution, and the ever-increasing European immigration. The concepts of *parens patriae* and the chancery court system came to be unacceptable in America because they represented the ideas of monarchy and feudalism that were being rejected in the establishment of the new nation. This gave rise, after the American Revolution, to the factory system in which many poor youths sought jobs in mills and factories and lived in boarding homes and settlements provided by mill owners.

By the beginning of the nineteenth century, the apprenticeship system could no longer compete with the factory system. Yet the problems of how to deal effectively with growing numbers of dependent youths increased. Early American settlers were firm believers in hard work, strict discipline, and education. These principles were viewed as the only reliable method for salvation. A child's life was marked by work alongside parents, some schooling, prayer, more work, and further study. In keeping with the family interest in hard work and discipline, the Factory Act of the early nineteenth century limited the hours children were permitted to work and the age at which they could begin to work. It also prescribed a minimum amount of schooling to be provided by factory owners.[16] This and related statutes were often violated, and conditions of work and school remained troublesome issues well into the twentieth century. Nevertheless, the statutes were a step in the direction of reform.

Controlling Children

In America, as in England, moral discipline was rigidly enforced. Stubborn child laws were passed that required children to obey their parents.[17] It was not uncommon in the colonies for children who were disobedient or disrespectful to their families to be whipped or otherwise physically chastised. Children were often required to attend public whippings and executions because these events served as important forms of moral instruction. Parents often referred their children to published works and writings on behavior and discipline and expected them to follow their precepts carefully. The early colonists, however, viewed family violence as a sin, and child protection laws were passed as early as 1639 (in New Haven, Connecticut). These laws were generally symbolic and rarely enforced. They expressed the community's commitment to God to oppose sin; offenders usually received lenient sentences.[18]

While most colonies adopted a protectionist stance, few cases of child abuse were actually brought before the courts. The absence of child abuse cases may reflect the nature of life in what were essentially extremely religious households. Children were productive laborers and respected by their parents. In addition, large families provided many siblings and kinfolk who could care for children and relieve stress-producing burdens on parents.[19]

Another view is that children were harshly punished in Early American families but that the "acceptable" limits of discipline were so high that few parents were charged with assault. Any punishment that fell short of maiming or permanently harming a child was considered within the sphere of parental rights.[20]

THE NINETEENTH CENTURY

As the nineteenth century began, delinquent, neglected, dependent, and runaway children were not treated as separate groups.[21] Children were often charged and convicted of crimes, including capital offenses and received harsh sentences similar to those imposed on adults. The adult criminal code applied to children, and no juvenile court existed before the end of the nineteenth century.

Throughout the early nineteenth century, various pieces of legislation were introduced to humanize criminal procedures for children. The concept of probation, introduced in Massachusetts in 1841, was geared toward helping young people avoid the trauma of imprisonment.[22] The many books and reports written during this time made the subject of juvenile child care one of intense public interest.

Despite this interest, there were no special facilities for the care of youths in trouble with the law, nor were there separate laws or courts to control their

behavior. As in England, children in colonial America were subject to adult criminal procedures and punishments. Youths who committed petty crimes, such as stealing, gambling, or minor damage to property, were viewed as wayward or victims of neglect and were placed in community asylums or homes. Youths who were involved in serious crimes were subject to the same punishments as adults—imprisonment, whipping, or death. The criminal laws of the eighteenth and the nineteenth centuries in both England and the United States provided severe and often brutal punishments for convicted offenders. Children were even subject to the death penalty.

As America entered the nineteenth century, several events led to reform in the field of child care and nourished the eventual development of the U.S. juvenile justice system: urbanization, the child-saving movement, the concept of *parens patriae*, the reform school movement, and the development of Society for the Prevention of Cruelty to Children.

Urbanization

Especially during the first half of the nineteenth century, the United States experienced rapid population growth, primarily because of an increase in the birthrate and expanding European immigration. Members of the rural poor and immigrant groups settled in developing urban commercial centers that promised the opportunity for manufacturing jobs. In 1790, 5 percent of the population lived in cities, while 95 percent was in rural areas. By 1850, the share of the urban population had increased to 15 percent; it jumped to 40 percent in 1900 and 51 percent in 1920.[23] New York almost quadrupled its population in the thirty year stretch between 1825 to 1855: from 166,000 in 1825 to 630,000 in 1855.[24]

Growing urbanization marked the nation's development. The numbers of young people at risk who flooded the cities overwhelmed the existing system of work and training. To accommodate groups of dependent and destitute youths, local jurisdictions developed poorhouses (or almshouses) and workhouses. In these crowded, unhealthy conditions were housed the poor, the insane, the diseased, and vagrant and destitute children. Many children were placed in such institutions.

By the late eighteenth century, the family's ability to exert social control began to be doubted as villages developed into urban commercials centers and as work centered around factories and not the home. The children of destitute families left home or were cast loose to make out as best they could; families could no longer absorb vagrant youth as apprentices or servants.[25] Chronic poverty became an American dilemma, spurring the federal census department to create a new category of underclass citizens labeled "paupers." The affluent began to voice concern over the increase in the number of people in what they considered to be the *dangerous classes.*

Increased urbanization and industrialization also generated the belief that certain segments of the population, namely youths in urban areas and immigrants, were susceptible to the influences of their decayed environment. Environment and not innate immorality or physical degeneracy influenced criminal deviance and immorality. The children of these classes were considered a group that might be "saved" by state intervention.[26] Intervention into the lives of these potentially "dangerous classes" to help alleviate their burdens became acceptable for wealthy, civic-minded citizens. Such efforts included shelter care for youths, educational and social activities, and settlement houses.

THE CHILD-SAVING MOVEMENT

The problems generated by large-scale urban growth sparked tremendous interest in the situations of the "new" Americans whose arrival fueled this expansion. In 1817, prominent New Yorkers formed the Society for the Prevention of Pauperism, perhaps the first organized group to focus on the needs of the underclass. While they concerned themselves with attacking taverns, brothels, and gambling parlors, they also were concerned that the moral training of children of the dangerous classes was falling short of conventional standards. Soon other groups concerned with the general welfare began to form in major urban areas. Their main focus was on extending government control over a whole range of youthful activities that had previously been left to private or family control, including idleness, drinking, vagrancy, and delinquency.

These activists became known as *child savers.* Prominent among them were penologist Enoch Wines, Judge Richard Tuthill, Lucy Flowers of the Chicago Women's Association, Sara Cooper of the National Conference of Charities and Corrections, and Sophia Minton of the New York Committee on Children.[27] They believed that poor children presented a threat to the moral fabric of American society and should be controlled because their behavior could lead to the destruction of the nation's economic system.

Child-saving organizations influenced state legislatures to enact laws giving courts the power to commit children who were runaways, committed criminal acts, or were out of the control of parents to specialized institutions. The most

prominent of the care facilities developed by child savers was the *House of Refuge* in New York, opened in 1825.[28] It was founded on the concept of protecting youths by taking potential criminals off the streets and reforming them in a family-like environment.

When the House of Refuge opened, the majority of children admitted were status offenders placed there because of vagrancy or neglect. However, the institution was run more like a prison, with work and study schedules, strict discipline, and absolute separation of the sexes. Such a harsh program drove many children to run away, with the result that the House of Refuge was forced to take a more lenient approach. Children entered the institution by court order, sometimes over parents' objections, for vagrancy or delinquency. Their stay depended on need, age, and skill. Once there, youths were required to do piecework provided by local manufacturers or to work part of the day in the community.

Despite criticism of the program, the concept enjoyed expanding popularity. In 1826, the Boston City Council founded the House of Reformation for juvenile offenders. Similar institutions were opened in Massachusetts and New York in 1847.[29] To these schools, which were both privately and publicly supported, the courts committed children found guilty of criminal violations, as well as those beyond the control of their parents. Because the child savers held both convicted offenders and parents of delinquent children to be in the same category, they sought to have the reform schools establish control over the children. As Robert Mennel states, "By training destitute and delinquent children, and by separating them from their natural parents and adult criminals, refuge managers believed they were preventing poverty and crime."[30]

Parens Patriae and Its Legal Challenges

The philosophy of *parens patriae* was extended to refuge programs, which were given parental control over a committed child. Robert Mennel summarizes this attitude:

> The doctrine of parens patriae gave refuge managers the best of two worlds, familial and legal: it separated delinquent children from their natural parents and it circumvented the rigor of criminal law by allowing courts to commit children, under loosely worded statutes, to specially created schools instead of jails.[31]

Once a refuge received a child, procedures of criminal law no longer applied.

But this process of institutional control over children in the name of the state and family did not proceed without some significant legal challenges (see Table 13.1). Two of the more critical cases are described below.

Ex Parte Crouse

In 1838, a child's father attempted to free her from the Philadelphia House of Refuge, which claimed the right of parental control over her because of unmanageable behavior. The father argued that her commitment without a trial

■ ■ **TABLE 13.1**   Notable Legal Decisions in Juvenile Justice

CASE	HOLDING
WELLESLEY V. WELLESLEY (1827)	In this English case, the children of a duke were removed from his custody by the chancery court in the name of *parens patriae* because of his poor behavior.
EX PARTE CROUSE (1838)	In a case involving the commitment of a girl to an institution without a trial, the Pennsylvania Supreme Court held that a child did not require the protections of due process of law and that the House of Refuge could supersede the authority of the parent.
O'CONNELL V. TURNER (1870)	The Illinois Supreme Court declared that a child's vagrancy sentence to a reform school was unconstitutional—*the* opposite result achieved in *Ex Parte Crouse:* The State did not have the authority under *parens patriae* to remove poor children from their parents.
COMMONWEALTH V. FISHER (1905)	The Pennsylvania Supreme Court upheld the constitutionality of the newly enacted Juvenile Court Act to commit a child to the House of Refuge until his or her twenty-first birthday.
EX PARTE SHARPE (1908)	The Idaho Supreme Court upheld the right of the state juvenile court to act in a protective way, by applying the *parens patriae* doctrine concerning the role of juveniles. This decision gave further impetus to the development of the juvenile court movement in the United States.

by jury was unconstitutional. In its decision in the case, *Ex Parte Crouse*, the Pennsylvania Supreme Court held that the House of Refuge was specifically planned to reform, restrain, and protect children from depraved parents or their environment.[32]

Crouse, the 12-year-old girl, was classified as a pauper for the purpose of court jurisdiction. The petition, brought by her mother, alleged that she was a poor person and therefore subject to the court. She was then committed to the Philadelphia House of Refuge, even though delinquency laws did not exist and she had committed no violation of the criminal law. Crouse's father objected to the court action and filed a writ of habeus corpus seeking an explanation for her commitment.

The problem in this case was whether the state of Pennsylvania had the right to take custody of Crouse under the guise of helping her, even though she had committed no crime. The Superior Court decided that placing the child in the House of Refuge did not violate her constitutional rights.

According to the judge:

The object of the charity is reformation, by training its inmates to industry; by imbuing their minds with principles of morality and religion; by furnishing them with means to earn a living; and above all, by separating them from the corrupting influence of improper associates. To this end, may not the natural parents, when unequal to the task of education, or unworthy of it, be superseded by the parens patriae, or common guardian of the community?

The Court concluded that Crouse was being cared for and not punished and therefore could be placed in an institution even without due process of law.

The *Crouse* decision established the key legal concept of *parens patriae,* which became the basis of the juvenile court movement. *Crouse* was the first legal challenge to the practice of institutionalizing children who had not committed a

■ ■ ■ ■ ■ ■ ■ ■ ■ ■ ■ ■ ■ ■ ■ ■

The House of Refuge was one of the earliest juvenile institutions in the United States to offer residents vocational training.

crime. It gave the state almost complete authority to intervene in the parent-child relationship because of the state's role as *parens patriae*. The court stated:

The right of parental control is a natural, but not an inalienable one. It is not accepted by the Declaration of Rights out of the subjects of ordinary legislation; and it consequently remains subject to the ordinary legislative power which, if wantonly or inconveniently used, would soon be constitutionally restricted, but the competency of which, as the government is constituted, cannot be doubted.[33]

The *Crouse* decision demonstrated that children could be deprived of the constitutional liberties guaranteed to adults.

O'Connell v. Turner

Another, more significant case was later decided in favor of the parent and child against the state: *O'Connell v. Turner*.[34] In 1870, Daniel O'Connell was committed to the Chicago Reform School on the ground that he was a vagrant or destitute youth without proper parental care. The parents attacked the child's commitment because he was not convicted of a crime and had been apprehended and confined under a general grant of power to arrest for simple misfortune. The basic legal problem was whether children could be committed to reform schools in the absence of criminal conduct or because of gross misconduct on the part of their parents.

The law was held to be unconstitutional, and on subsequent appeal, the court ordered Daniel O'Connell discharged. As Justice Thornton noted in the case: "The warrant of commitment does not indicate that the arrest was made for a criminal offense. Hence, we conclude that it was made under the general grant of power to arrest and confine for misfortune."[35] The fact that the court distinguished between criminal acts and those arising from misfortune was significant, for all legislation dealing with misfortune cases was subsequently appealed as a direct result of the *O'Connell* decision. Also, as Sanford Fox indicates, the *O'Connell* case changed the course of events in Illinois. The Chicago Reform School was closed in 1872, and the case encouraged procedural due process reform for committed youths.[36]

The Development of Juvenile Institutions

Despite the *O'Connell* decision, state intervention in the lives of children continued throughout the latter portion of the nineteenth century and well into the twentieth century. The child savers influenced state and local governments to create institutions, called reform schools, exclusively devoted to the care of vagrant and delinquent youths. State institutions opened in Westboro, Massachusetts, in 1848 and in Rochester, New York, in 1849.[37] Institutional programs began in Ohio in 1850 and in Maine, Rhode Island, and Michigan in 1906.[38] Children lived in congregate conditions and spent their days working in the institution, learning a trade where possible and receiving some basic education. They were racially and sexually segregated, discipline was harsh and often involved whipping and isolation, and their physical care was poor. Beverly Smith found that girls admitted to the Western House of Refuge in Rochester, New York, during the 1880's were often labeled as deviant or criminal but were in reality abused, orphaned, and neglected. They too were subject to harsh working conditions, strict discipline, and intensive labor.[39]

This engraving depicts the work of the Children's Aid Society.

While some viewed houses of refuge and reform schools as humanitarian answers to poorhouses and prisons for vagrant, neglected, and delinquent youths, many were opposed to such programs. As an alternative, New York philanthropist Charles Brace helped develop the **Children's Aid Society** in 1853.[40] Brace's formula for dealing with neglected and delinquent youths was to rescue them from the harsh environment of the city and provide them with temporary shelter care. He then sought to place them in private homes throughout the nation. This program was very similar to today's foster home programs. As Fox points out, "The great value to be placed on family life for deviant and crime-prone children was later explicitly set forth in the juvenile court act."[41]

Although the child reformers provided services for children, they were unable to stop juvenile delinquency. Most reform schools were unable to hold youthful law violators and reform them. Institutional life was hard. Large numbers of children needing placement burdened the public coffers supporting such programs. So while state control over vagrant, delinquent, and neglected children became more widespread after the Civil War, it also became more controversial.

As the nation grew, it became evident that private charities and public organizations were not caring adequately for the growing number of troubled youths.

The SPCC Movement

In 1874, the first **Society for the Prevention of Cruelty to Children** (SPCC) was established in New York; by 1900, there were three hundred such societies in the United States.[42] Leaders of the SPCCs were concerned that neglected and abused boys would grow up to join the ranks of the "dangerous classes," becoming lower-class criminals, and mistreated young girls might become sexually promiscuous women. SPCC membership was swelled by the growing post-Civil War crime rate and concern about a rapidly shifting and changing population. There was also true concern for the welfare of children who were subject to cruelty and neglect at home and at school.

SPCC groups influenced state legislatures to pass statutes protecting children from exploitive or neglectful parents, including those who did not provide them with adequate food and clothing or made them beg or work in places where liquor was sold.[43] Criminal penalties were created, and provisions were established for removing children from the home. In some states, such as New York, agents of the SPCC could actually arrest abusive parents; in others, they would inform the police about suspected abuse cases and accompany officers when they made an arrest.[44]

The organization and control of SPCCs varied widely. For example, the New York City SPCC was a city agency supported by municipal funds. It conducted investigations of delinquent and neglected children for the court and had little to do with the city's other social welfare agencies. In contrast, the Boston SPCC emphasized delinquency prevention and worked closely with social welfare groups. The SPCCs in Cleveland and Chicago also handled cruelty to animal cases; the Philadelphia SPCC emphasized family unity and was involved with other charities.[45]

ESTABLISHMENT OF THE ILLINOIS JUVENILE COURT

Reform groups continued to lobby for government control over children. The commitment of children under the doctrine of *parens patriae* without due process of law began to be questioned. What care was in the best interest of a child? Could the state incarcerate children who had not violated the criminal law? Should children be held in the same facilities that housed adults? These and other questions began to plague reformers and those interested in the plight of children. Institutional deficiencies; the detention of delinquent children in adult jails and prisons; the handling of poor, dependent, ignorant, and noncriminal delinquents without due process by inadequate private child welfare organizations; and the religious segregation of children all spurred the argument that a juvenile court should be established.

Increasing delinquency rates also hastened development of a juvenile court. Theodore Ferdinand's analysis of the Boston juvenile court found that in the 1820s and 1830s, very few juvenile were charged with serious offenses. By 1850, juvenile delinquency was the fastest growing component of the local crime problem.[46] Ferdinand concluded that the sizable flow of juvenile cases strengthened the argument that juveniles needed their own special court attuned to their needs.[47]

The culmination of the child-saving movement was the ***Illinois Juvenile Court Act*** of 1899 (see Table 13.2). This was a major event in the history of the juvenile justice movement in the United States. Its significance was such that by 1917, juvenile courts had been established in all but three states.

What exactly did the passage of the Illinois Juvenile Court Act mean? The traditional interpretation is that the reformers had the highest motives and passed legislation that would serve the best interests of the child. U.S. Supreme Court Justice Abe Fortas took his position in the 1967 *In re Gault* case:

> The early reformers were appalled by adult procedures and penalties and by the fact that children could be given long prison sentences and mixed in jails with hardened criminals. They were profoundly convinced that society's duty to the child could not be confined by the concept of justice alone. . . . The child—essentially good, as they saw it—was to be made to feel that he was the object of the state's care and solicitude, not that he was under arrest or on trial. . . . The idea of crime and punishment was to be abandoned. The child was to be treated and rehabilitated and the procedures from apprehension through institutionalized were to be clinical rather than punitive.[48]

The child savers were imbued with a positivistic philosophy and emphasized individual values and judgments about children and their care. Society was to be concerned with where children came from, what their problems were, and how these problems could be handled in the interests of the children and the state.

Interpretations of its intentions and effects differ, but unquestionably, the Illinois Juvenile Court Act established juvenile delinquency as a legal concept and the juvenile court as a judicial forum.

The act for the first time distinguished between children who were dependent and neglected and those who were delinquent. Delinquent children were those under the age of 16 who violated the laws. The act also established a court specifically for children and an extensive probation program whereby children were to be the responsibility of probation officers. In addition, the legislation allowed children to be committed to institutions and reform programs under the laws and control of the state.

Among the most important provisions of the act were:

- A separate court was established for delinquent, dependent, and neglected children.
- Special legal procedures were to govern the adjudication and disposition of juvenile matters.
- Children were to be separated from adults in courts and in institutional programs.
- Probation programs were to be developed to assist the court in making decisions in the best interests of the state and the child.

Were They Really Child Savers?

Great debate continues over the true aims and objectives of the early child savers. Some historians conclude that they were what they seemed: concerned citizens motivated by humanitarian ideals.[49] Modern scholars, however, have reappraised the child saving movement. In his ground-breaking book *The Child Savers*, critical thinker Anthony Platt painted a picture of the child savers as representative of

Section 1. Definitions. This act shall apply only to children under the age of sixteen (16) years not now or hereafter inmates of a State institution, or any training school for boys or industrial school for girls or some institution incorporated under the laws of this State, except as provided in sections twelve (12) and eighteen (18). For the purposes of this act the words *dependent child* and *neglected child* shall mean any child who for any reason is destitute or homeless or abandoned; or dependent upon the public for support; or has not proper parental care or guardianship; or who habitually begs or receives alms; or who is found living in any house of ill fame or with any vicious or disreputable person; or whose home, by reason of neglect, cruelty or depravity on the part of its parents, guardian or other person in whose care it may be, is an unfit place for such a child; and any child under the age of eight (8) years who is found peddling or selling any article or singing or playing any musical instrument upon the streets or giving any public entertainment. The words *delinquent child* shall include any child under the age of 16 years who violates any law of this State or any city or village ordinance. The word *child or children* may mean one or more children, and the word *parent or parents* may be held to mean one or both parents, when consistent with the intent of this act. The word *association* shall include any corporation which includes in its purposes the care or disposition of children coming within the meaning of this act. . . .

§ 3. Juvenile Court. In counties having over 500,000 population the judges of the circuit court shall, at such times as they shall determine, designate one or more of their number whose duty it shall be to hear all cases coming under this act. A special courtroom, to be designated as the juvenile courtroom, shall be provided for the hearing of such cases, and the findings of the court shall be entered in a book or books to be kept for that purpose and known as the "Juvenile Record," and the court may, for convenience, be called the "Juvenile Court."

§ 4. Petition to the Court. Any reputable person, being resident in the county, having knowledge of a child in his county who appears to be either neglected, dependent or delinquent, may file with the clerk of court having jurisdiction in the matter a petition in writing, setting forth the facts, verified by affidavit. It shall be sufficient that the affidavit is upon information and belief. . . .

§ 6. Probation Officers. The court shall have authority to appoint or designate one or more discreet persons of good character to serve as probation officers during the pleasure of the court; said probation officers to receive no compensation from the public treasury. In case a probation officer shall be appointed by any court, it shall be the duty of the clerk of the court, if practicable, to notify the said probation officer in advance when any child is to be brought before the said court; it shall be the duty of the said probation officer to make such investigation as may be required by the court; to be present in court in order to represent the interests of the child when the case is heard; to furnish the court such information and assistance as the judge may require; and to take such charge of any child before and after trial as may be directed by the court.

Source: Illinois Statutes 1899, Section 131.

the ruling class who were galvanized by the threat of newly arriving immigrants and the urban poor to take action to preserve their way of life.[50] He claims:

> The child savers should not be considered humanists: (1) their reforms did not herald a new system of justice but rather expedited traditional policies which had been informally developed during the nineteenth century; (2) they implicitly assumed that natural dependence of adolescents and created a special court to impose sanctions on premature independents and behavior unbecoming to youth; (3) their attitudes toward delinquent youth were largely paternalistic and romantic but their commands were backed up by force; (4) they promoted correctional programs requiring longer terms of imprisonment, longer hours of labor, and militaristic discipline, and the inculcation of middle class values and lower class skills.[51]

Other critical thinkers followed Platt in finding that child saving was motivated more by self-interest than benevolence.[52] For example, in a recent paper, Randall Shelden and Lynn Osborne have traced the early child-saving movement in Memphis, Tennessee, and found that its leaders were a small group of upper-class citizens who desired to control the behavior and life-styles of another class of citizens: lower-class youth. The outcome was ominous: most cases petitioned to

§ 7. Dependent and Neglected Children. When any child under the age of sixteen (16) years shall be found to be dependent or neglected within the meaning of this act, the court may make an order committing the child to the care of some suitable State institution, or to the care of some reputable citizen of good moral character, or to the care of some training school or an industrial school, as provided by law, or to the care of some association willing to receive it embracing in its objects the purpose of caring or obtaining homes for dependent or neglected children, which association shall have been accredited as hereinafter provided. . . .

§ 9. Disposition of Delinquent Children. In the case of a delinquent child the court may continue the hearing from time to time and may commit the child to the care and guardianship of a probation officer duly appointed by the court and may allow said child to remain in its own home, subject to the visitation of the probation officer; such child to report to the probation officer as often as may be required and subject to be returned to the court for further proceedings, whenever such action may appear to be necessary, or the court may commit the child to the care and guardianship of the probation officer, to be placed in a suitable family home, subject to the friendly supervision of such probation officer; or it may authorize the said probation officer to board out the said child in some suitable family home, in case provision is made by voluntary contribution or otherwise for the payment of the board of such child, until a suitable provision may be made for the child in a home without such payment; or the court may commit the child, if a boy, to a training school for boys, or if a girl, to an industrial school for girls. Or, if the child is found guilty of any criminal offense, and the judge is of the opinion that the best interest requires it, the court may commit the child to any institution within said county incorporated under the laws of this State for the care of delinquent children, or provided by a city for the care of such offenders, or may commit the child, if a boy over the age of ten (10) years, to the State reformatory, or if a girl over the age of ten (10) years, to the State Home for Juvenile Female Offenders. In no case shall a child be committed beyond his or her minority. A child committed to such institution shall be subject to the control of the board of managers thereof, and the said board shall have power to parole such child on such conditions as it may prescribe, and the court shall, on the recommendation of the board, have power to discharge such child from custody whenever in the judgment of the court his or her reformation shall be complete; or the court may commit the child to the care and custody of some association that will receive it, embracing in its objects the care of neglected and dependent children and that has been duly accredited as hereinafter provided. . . .

§ 11. Children under Twelve Years Not to Be Committed to Jail. No court or magistrate shall commit a child under twelve (12) years of age to a jail or police station, but if such child is unable to give bail it may be committed to the care of the sheriff, police officer or probation officer. . . .

---

the juvenile court (which opened in 1910) were for petty crimes, truancy, and other status-type offenses, yet 25 percent of the youths were committed to some form of incarceration. More than 96 percent of the actions with which females were charged were status offenses.[53]

Sanford Fox, a respected legal scholar, has also been critical of the early child-saving reforms. According to Fox, the Illinois Juvenile Court Act restated the belief in the value of coercive prediction; continued nineteenth-century summary trials for children about whom the predictions were to be made; made no improvements in the long-condemned institutional care furnished these same children; codified the view that institutions should, even without badly needed financial help from the legislature, replicate family life; and reinforced the private sectarian interest whose role had long been decried by leading child welfare reformers in the area of juvenile care.[54]

Thus, according to the revisionist approach, the reformers applied the concept of *parens patriae* for their own purposes, including the continuance of middle- and upper-class values, the control of political systems, and the furtherance of a child labor system consisting of marginal and lower-class skilled workers. The following Focus on Delinquency further explores this issue.

Conscience and Convenience: The Progressive Era

David Rothman's important work, *Conscience and Convenience*, is an analysis of the social policies developed during what is referred to as the **Progressive Era** (1900–1920) of U.S. history.

According to Rothman, the Progressive Era was marked by a great deal of social change prompted by appeals to the conscience of the nation. Reformers were shocked by exposés of how society treated its less fortunate members. They were particularly concerned about what was going on in prisons and mental institutions. The poor, ill, and unfortunate were living in squalor, beaten and mistreated by their "keepers." Progressive reformers lobbied legislators and appealed to public opinion in order to force better conditions. Their efforts helped establish the probation and parole system and other liberal correctional reforms.

The question Rothman poses is whether reformers acted out of conscience or convenience. Did beneficial change really occur, or was it simply a matter of making control over minorities, immigrants, and the lower class in general easier and more "convenient"?

The development of the juvenile court is a case in point. Its operational philosophy reflected the core value of the Progressive Era reformers: individualized treatment. Because each child was considered unique, the cause of his or her delinquency, whether it was a poor home life, destructive peer relations, physical or emotional problems, for example, must be individually treated. The rule was "treat the child, not the crime."

The progressives used the findings of the emerging social sciences of psychology and sociology to guide the juvenile court's activities. As Rothman states: "The juvenile court was to concern itself first not with the specific charge facing the delinquent, but with his character and life-style, his psychological strengths and weaknesses, the advantages and disadvantages of his home life. It was not his act, but . . . his soul that was at issue."

However, such reform efforts were not without their pitfalls. The relaxed atmosphere and promise of rehabilitation espoused by the first juvenile courts prompted police and district attorneys to make extensive use of their services. Children who in the past might have been given their release by police officers after a stern warning were now placed in the hands of juvenile court judges who used their own discretion in deciding their fate. District attorneys were happy to have children sent to the new court because it freed up their crowded court schedules for more important matters and because the informal nature of the juvenile court demanded little of their time or effort. Likewise, reformatory directors applauded the juvenile court, whose rehabilitation philosophy gave them greater credibility in the community. Now if a child were sent to a reformatory, the purpose was treatment and kindness rather than punishment. Reformatory directors were no longer "ogres."

Was the juvenile court an early success? One indication may be the incarceration rate. Though it was originally expected that the number of youths who would have to be incarcerated would decline after a separate juvenile court was created, admission rates to juvenile reformatories actually rose rapidly between 1923 and 1933 (from 15.5 per 100,000 to 20.2 per 100,000). In 1923, there were about 25,000 youths in juvenile reformatories, while in 1933, the number rose to over 30,000. The juvenile court was not a panacea for all juvenile offenders.

According to Rothman, it was the juvenile reformatories themselves that really exposed the false promises of progressive reform. Although they were dedicated to rehabilitation and treatment, many were merely warehouses that provided little or no education or training and invoked harsh disciplinary codes. Children were subjected to solitary confinement and fierce physical punishment. There was actually scant difference between the reformatory and the adult prison. What started as a movement to ease the conscience of liberal reformers had become a mechanism for conveniently dealing with troublesome youths. ■

Source: David Rothman, *Conscience and Convenience* (Boston: Little Brown, 1980), quotation from p. 215.

DEVELOPING THE JUVENILE JUSTICE SYSTEM

Following the passage of the Illinois Juvenile Court Act, similar legislation was enacted throughout the nation. The special courts these laws created maintained jurisdiction over predelinquent (neglected and dependent) and delinquent children. Juvenile court jurisdiction was based primarily on a child's actions and status, not strictly on the violation of criminal law. The *parens patriae* philosophy predominated, ushering in a form of personalized justice characterized by a procedural laxity and informality that did not provide juvenile offenders with the full panoply of constitutional protections. The court's process was paternalistic rather than adversarial. Attorneys were not required, and hearsay evidence, inadmissible in criminal trials, was admissible in the adjudication of juvenile offenders. Verdicts were based on a "preponderance of the evidence," instead of "beyond a reasonable doubt," and children were often not granted any right to appeal their convictions. These characteristics allowed the juvenile court to function in a nonlegal manner and to provide various social services to children in need.

The major functions of the juvenile justice system were to prevent juvenile crime and to rehabilitate juvenile offenders. The roles of the two most important actors, the juvenile court judge and the probation staff, were to diagnose the child's condition and prescribe programs to alleviate it. Until 1967, judgments about children's actions and consideration for their constitutional rights were secondary.

By the 1920s, noncriminal behavior in the form of incorrigibility and truancy from school was added to the jurisdiction of many juvenile court systems. Of particular interest was the sexual behavior of young girls, which fell under the jurisdiction of the new courts. Mary Odem and Steven Schlossman have shown how the juvenile court articulated and enforced a strict moral code on working-class girls, not hesitating to incarcerate those who were sexually active.[55] Programs of all kinds—including individualized counseling and institutional care—were used to "cure" juvenile criminality. An entire group of new "experts"—criminologists, sociologists, social workers, probation officers, and psychologists—emerged to deal with delinquency and noncriminal behavior. Much of their effort involved seeking to rehabilitate children brought before the court.

By 1925, juvenile courts existed in virtually every jurisdiction in every state. Although the juvenile court concept expanded rapidly, it cannot be said that each state implemented the philosophy of the court thoroughly. Some jurisdictions established elaborate juvenile court systems, while others passed legislation but provided no services. Some courts had trained juvenile court judges; others had nonlawyers sitting in juvenile cases. Some courts had extensive probation departments; others had untrained probation personnel.[56]

Great diversity also marked juvenile institutions. While some maintained a lenient treatment orientation, others relied on harsh physical punishments, including beatings, restraining in straight jackets, immersion in cold water, and solitary confinement in dark cells with a diet of bread and water.

These conditions were exacerbated by the rapid growth in the juvenile institutional population. Between 1890 and 1920, the number of institutionalized kids jumped 112 percent, a rise that far exceeded the increase in the total number of adolescents in the United States.[57] Despite the juvenile court movement, private institutions were not driven to the margin by public institutions and in fact grew much faster and larger. John Sutton has carefully reviewed the growth of juvenile institutions during this period. He finds that after 1890, public institutions predominated in areas where people relied on government to solve social problems; private institutions persisted where government authority was weakest. Although professionals deplored the increased institutionalization of youth, the growth of juvenile institutions was due in part to the successful efforts by reformers to close poorhouses, thereby creating a need for more juvenile institutions to house their displaced populations. In addition, the lack of a coherent national policy on needy children allowed private entrepreneurs to open institutions and fill the void.[58] The following Case in Point explores the issues surrounding the design of a juvenile justice system.

CASE IN POINT

It is the year 1898, and you have just become a member of the local child-saving organization.

The state is now willing to create a separate juvenile justice system. The governor has become sensitive to newspaper articles in which members of your organization have taken him to task for the maltreatment of youth. The state has been trying young criminals in adult courts and sending them, if they are convicted, to state prisons to be housed with hardened adult criminals.

Concern also exists about the fate of neglected and wayward youth who have been maintained in orphanages, workhouses, and county jails. Rumors have arisen that these kids are being exploited by masters who sell their services to sweatshop owners and keep their earnings. There have also been charges that the county-run youth institutions use harsh physical punishments.

The child savers appoint you to head a committee charged with developing a plan for a new juvenile justice system. It is up to you to describe its goals, component parts, and jurisdiction. The state seems willing to go along with whatever you suggest, though you are suspicious that radical reform might cause a backlash from conservatives who cannot see why young criminals should be spared the "pains of imprisonment."

What agencies should control the juvenile justice system?

Would you make the system police-oriented or treatment-oriented?

Would you maintain control over all cases involving at-risk youth, including custody, paternity, and family problems?

Reforming the System

Concern and reform of this system was slow in forthcoming: After all, why criticize a reform movement designed to treat and not punish? In 1912, the U.S. Children's Bureau was formed as the first federal child welfare agency. By the 1930s, the Bureau began to investigate the state of juvenile institutions and tried to expose some of the more repressive aspects of these programs through a series of books and research reports.[59] After World War II, critics, such as Paul Tappan and Francis Allen, began to identify problems in the juvenile justice system, among which were the neglect of procedural rights and the warehousing of youth in dangerous and ineffective institutions. Status offenders commonly were housed with delinquents and received sentences that were more punitive than those given to delinquents.[60]

Reform efforts, began in earnest in the 1960s, changed the face of the juvenile justice system. In 1962, New York passed legislation creating a family court system.[61] The new family court was to assume responsibility for all matters involving family life. Its particular emphasis was to be on delinquent, dependent, and neglected children and paternity, adoption, and support proceedings involving parents. In addition, the legislation established a separate classification— person in need of supervision (PINS). This category, covering noncriminal behavior, was the forerunner of such legislative categories as children in need of supervision (CHINS), minors in need of supervision (MINS), and families in need of supervision (FINS). These labels covered individuals involved in such actions as truancy, running away, and incorrigibility. In using them to establish jurisdiction over children and their families, juvenile courts expanded their role as social agencies. Because noncriminal children were now involved in the juvenile court system to a greater degree, many juvenile courts had to improve their services as social agencies, and efforts were made to play down the authority of the court as a court of law and to personalize the system of justice for children. These reforms were soon followed by a "due process revolution," which ushered in an era of procedural rights for court-adjudicated youth.

History, philosophical ideals, legal decisions, and scientific theories all have influenced the shape of the contemporary juvenile justice system. The problem characteristics of this system—informal legal process, unclear goals and objectives, abuses of discretion by police and judges, ineffective programs, and unqualified personnel—will be examined in future chapters.

■ ■ ■ ■ ■ ■ ■ ■ ■ ■ ■ ■ ■ ■ ■ ■

SUMMARY

This chapter focused on the historical development of juvenile justice from the Middle Ages to the beginning of the twentieth century and the creation of the modern juvenile court system in the United States. The chapter described the care of children and the early concepts of family life in the fifteenth and sixteenth centuries. It also explored some of the early concepts of family living, such as dower, primogeniture, and punishment, in an attempt to understand how children and families lived during that period.

With the start of the seventeenth century came greater recognition of the needs of children. In Great Britain, the chancery court movement, the Poor Laws, and the apprenticeship programs greatly affected the lives of children. In colonial America, many of the characteristics of English family living were adopted.

In the nineteenth century, neglected, delinquent, and dependent or runaway children were treated no differently than criminal defendants. Children were often charged and convicted of crimes through procedures used with adults. During this time, however, because of philosophical shifts in the areas of crime and delinquency as well as a change in the emphasis of the concept of *parens patriae*, steps were taken to reduce the responsibility of children under the criminal law in both Great Britain and the United States. The child-saving movement, the development of reform schools, and the problems of urbanization in America all had a strong effect on the development of the juvenile court.

Finally, the chapter summarized the original Illinois Juvenile Court Act and its specific characteristics and goals.

KEY TERMS

paternalistic
primogeniture
wet nurses
swaddling
Poor Laws
apprenticeship
parens patriae
chancery courts
dangerous classes

child savers
House of Refuge
Ex Parte Crouse
Children's Aid Society
Society for the Prevention of Cruelty to Children
 (SPCC)
Illinois Juvenile Court Act
Progressive Era

QUESTIONS FOR DISCUSSION

1. What is the relationship between the historical and philosophical approaches to caring for children in the fifteenth, sixteenth, and seventeenth centuries and the basis of our present juvenile justice system?

2. What factors precipitated the development of the Illinois Juvenile Court Act of 1899? In Great Britain? In the United States?

3. Such terms as *apprenticeship, Poor Laws, chancery court,* and *parens patriae* exist in the early history of the juvenile court movement. What do these terms mean?

4. Throughout history, children have often been treated under the criminal law differently from adults. Before the twentieth century, were children held responsible for criminal actions? Are children responsible for crimes they commit today? Are they liable for civil wrong?

5. One of the most significant reforms in dealing with the juvenile offenders was the opening of the New York House of Refuge in 1825. What were the social and judicial impacts of this reform on the juvenile justice system?

NOTES

1. See Sanford J. Fox, "Juvenile Justice Reform: A Historical Perspective," *Sanford Law Review* 22:1187 (1970).

2. See Lawrence Stone, *The Family, Sex, and Marriage in England: 1500–1800* (New York: Harper & Row, 1977).

3. This section relies on Jackson Spielvogel, *Western Civilization* (St. Paul: West, 1991), pp. 279–86.

4. See Philipe Aries, *Century of Childhood: A Social History of Family Life* (New York: Vintage, 1962).

5. See Douglas R. Rendleman, "Parens Patriae: From Chancery to the Juvenile Court," *South Carolina Law Review* 23:205 (1971).

6. See Stone, *The Family, Sex, and Marriage in England,* and Lawrence Stone, ed., *Schooling and Society: Studies in the History of Education* (Baltimore: John Hopkins University Press, 1970).

7. Ibid.

8. See Wiley B. Sanders, *Some Early Beginnings of the Children's Court Movement in England,* National Probation Association Yearbook (New York: National Council on Crime and Delinquency, 1945).

9. Rendleman, "Parens Patriae," p. 205.

10. Douglas Besharov, *Juvenile Justice Advocacy—Practice in a Unique Court* (New York: Practicing Law Institute, 1974), p. 2.

11. *Wellesley v. Wellesley,* 4 Eng. Rep. 1078 (1827).

12. Rendleman, "Parens Patriae," p. 209.

13. See Anthony Platt, "The Rise of the Child Saving Movement: A Study in Social Policy and Correctional Reform," *Annals of the American Academy of Political and Social Science* 381:21–38 (1969).

14. Robert Bremmer, ed., and John Barnard, Hareven Tamara, and Robert Mennel, asst. eds., *Children and Youth in America* (Cambridge: Harvard University Press, 1970), p. 64.

15. Elizabeth Pleck, "Criminal Approaches to Family Violence, 1640–1980," in Lloyd Ohlin and Michael Tonry eds., *Family Violence* (Chicago: University of Chicago Press, 1989), pp. 19–58.

16. Ibid.

17. John R. Sutton, *Stubborn Children: Controlling Delinquency in the United States, 1640–1981* (Berkeley: University of California Press, 1988).

18. Pleck, "Criminal Approaches to Family Violence," p. 29.
19. John Demos, *Past, Present and Personal* (New York: Oxford University Press, 1986), pp. 80–88.
20. Elizabeth Pleck, *Domestic Tyranny: The Making of Social Policy against Family Violence from Colonial Times to the Present* (New York: Oxford University Press, 1987), p. 28–30.
21. Robert M. Mennel, "Origins of the Juvenile Court: Changing Perspectives on the Legal Rights of Juvenile Delinquents," *Crime and Delinquency* 18:68–78 (1972).
22. See, generally, Daniel Glaser, *The Effectiveness of a Prison and Parole System* (Indianapolis: Bobbs-Merrill, 1964); and Charles Newman, ed., *Sourcebook on Probation, Parole, and Pardons,* 2d ed. (Springfield, Ill.: Charles C. Thomas, 1964).
23. Anthony Salerno, "The Child Saving Movement: Altruism or Conspiracy," *Juvenile and Family Court Journal* 42:37 (1991).
24. Ronald Bayer, "The Darker Side of Urban Life: Slums in the City," in Frank Copp and P. C. Dolce, eds., *Cities in Transition: From the Ancient World to Urban America* (Chicago: Nelson Hall, 1974), p. 220.
25. Robert Mennel, "Attitudes and Policies towards Juvenile Delinquency," in Michael Tonry and Norval Morris, eds., *Crime and Justice,* vol. 5, (Chicago: University of Chicago Press, 1983), p. 198.
26. Anthony M. Platt, *The Child Savers: The Invention of Delinquency* (Chicago: University of Chicago Press, 1969).
27. Ibid.
28. Fox, "Juvenile Justice Reform," p. 1188.
29. See Robert S. Pickett, *House of Refuge—Origins of Juvenile Reform in New York State, 1815–1857* (Syracuse, N.Y.: Syracuse University Press, 1969).
30. Mennel, "Origins of the Juvenile Court," pp. 69–70.
31. Ibid., pp. 70–71.
32. 4 Whart. 9 (1839).
33. Ibid., p. 11.
34. 55 Ill. 280 (1870).
35. Ibid., p. 283.
36. Fox, "Juvenile Justice Reform," p. 1217.
37. See U.S. Department of Justice, Juvenile Justice and Delinquency Prevention, *Two Hundred Years of American Criminal Justice: An LEAA Bicentennial Study* (Washington, D.C.: Law Enforcement Assistance Administration, 1976).
38. Ibid., pp. 62–74.
39. Beverly Smith, "Female Admissions and Paroles of the Western House of Refuge in the 1880s," An Historical Example of Community Corrections," *Journal of Research in Crime and Delinquency* 26:36–66 (1989).
40. Fox, "Juvenile Justice Reform," p. 1229.
41. Ibid., p. 1211.
42. Pleck, "Criminal Approaches to Family Violence," p. 35.
43. Pleck, *Domestic Tyranny,* p. 82.
44. Linda Gordon, *Family Violence and Social Control* (New York: Viking Press, 1988).
45. Kathleen Block and Donna Hale, "Turf Wars in the Progressive Era Juvenile Justice: The Relationship of Private and Public Child Care Agencies," *Crime and Delinquency* 37:225–41 (1991).
46. Theodore Ferdinand, "Juvenile Delinquency or Juvenile Justice: Which Came First?" *Criminology* 27:79–106 (1989).
47. Ibid., p. 100.
48. *In re Gault,* 387 U.S. 1, 87 S.Ct. 1428, 18 L.Ed. 2d 527 (1967).
49. Salerno, "The Child Saving Movement," p. 47.
50. Anthony Platt, *The Child Savers: The Invention of Delinquency* (Chicago: University of Chicago Press, 1977).
51. Ibid., p. 116.
52. Herman Schwendinger and Julia Schwendinger, "Delinquency and the Collective Varieties of Youth," *Crime and Social Justice* 5:7–25 (1976).
53. Randall Shelden and Lynn Osborne, " 'For Their Own Good': Class Interests and the Child Saving Movement in Memphis, Tennessee, 1900–1917," *Criminology* 27:747–67 (1989).
54. Fox, "Juvenile Justice Reform," p. 1229.
55. Mary Odem and Steve Schlossman, "Guardians of Virtue: The Juvenile Court and Female Delinquency in Early 20th-Century Los Angeles," *Crime and Delinquency* 37:186–203 (1991).
56. Katherine Lenroot and Emma Lundberg, *Juvenile Courts at Work,* U.S. Children's Bureau Publication No. 141 (Washington, D.C.: Government Printing Office, 1925).
57. John Sutton, "Bureaucrats and Entrepreneurs: Institutional Responses to Deviant Children in the United States, 1890–1920," *American Journal of Sociology* 95:1367–1400 (1990).
58 Ibid., p. 1383.
59. Margueritte Rosenthal, "Reforming the Juvenile Correctional Institution: Efforts of the U.S. Children's Bureau in the 1930's," *Journal of Sociology and Social Welfare* 14:47–74 (1987).
60. For an overview of these developments, see Theodore Ferdinand, "History Overtakes the Juvenile Justice System," *Crime and Delinquency* 37:204–24 (1991).
61. See N.Y. Fam. Ct. Act, Art. 7, Sec. 712 (Consol.1962).

AN OVERVIEW OF THE JUVENILE JUSTICE SYSTEM AND ITS GOALS

This chapter is an overview of what juvenile justice means, how it is implemented, and the various philosophies, processes, organizations, and legal constraints that dominate its operations. A distinction is made between the terms *system,* which refers to the interrelationship among juvenile justice agencies, and *process,* which takes a youthful offender through a series of steps beginning with arrest and concluding with reentry into society. What happens to young people who violate the law? Do they have legal rights? How are they helped? How are they punished? What is the jurisdiction of a juvenile court? The answers to these questions explain why the juvenile system exists in its present form.

Included in this chapter is a discussion of the similarities and differences between the adult and juvenile justice systems. This helps the student recognize the important principle that children are treated separately in our society. By establishing legislation to segregate delinquent children from adult offenders, society has placed greater importance on the delinquent as a "child" than as a "criminal." Consequently, rehabilitation rather than punishment has traditionally been the goal. Today, with children committing more serious and violent crimes, the juvenile justice system is having greater difficulties finding solutions to handling these offenders.

What goals and strategies are now being used as a blueprint for juvenile justice reform—from crime prevention programs to innovative sentencing approaches?[1] Today, no single ideology or program dominates the system. New and traditional philosophies and models of juvenile justice are discussed in this chapter. Are the time-honored goals of *parens patriae* and "the best interest of the child" still in place? What is the "justice" model? Are we criminalizing the juvenile justice system?[2] This chapter also analyzes the role of the federal government in juvenile delinquency prevention and discusses the impact of the landmark Juvenile Justice and Delinquency Prevention Act of 1974.

The chapter's final section reviews the organization and jurisdiction of the juvenile court. The juvenile court plays a pivotal role in the juvenile justice system. It does much more than merely find facts and try cases. It provides social services, evaluates family dynamics, prevents delinquency, and champions the *parens patriae* philosophy. For the first sixty years of the juvenile court's existence, legal rules and procedures were usually absent from it, and its operations stressed social service functions. Hearings were informal, there were no attorneys, and the proceedings resembled activities of a social agency as much as a court of law. In the 1960s and 1970s, these procedures changed radically, however, when a series of U.S. Supreme Court decisions brought the juvenile justice system within the scope of the Constitution and fundamentally and permanently changed the face of the nation's juvenile courts.[3] This chapter explains how these decisions have influenced the day-to-day operations of the juvenile justice system.

THE DEVELOPMENT OF JUVENILE JUSTICE

The term **juvenile justice** refers to society's efforts to control juvenile crime through public and private crime prevention and social control agencies.[4] The term encompasses many areas of study, including the etiology of crime, institutional and agency controls, methods of prevention and community services, and the legal methods for dealing with young people who violate the law.

The contemporary American system of dealing with children in trouble began in 1899, with the establishment of the first juvenile court in the state of Illinois.[5] The principles motivating the Illinois reformers at that time were:

1. Children, because of their minority status, should not be held as accountable as adult transgressors;
2. The objective of juvenile justice is to help the youngster, to treat and rehabilitate rather than punish;
3. Disposition should be predicated on analysis of the youth's special circumstances and needs; and
4. The system should avoid the punitive, adversary, and formalized trappings of the adult criminal process, with all its confusing rules of evidence and tightly controlled procedures.[6]

The intention of the **Illinois Juvenile Court Act of 1899** was to create a special statewide court for predelinquent and delinquent youths. In such a setting, children were to be segregated from adults, and individual treatment programs to prevent future delinquency were to be adopted. Programs were to be administered by a juvenile court judge and other staff, such as probation and social service personnel, using individual and group rehabilitation techniques. This juvenile court was supposed to be a nonlegalistic social service agency providing care for delinquent and neglected children. In addition, the court and its personnel were to act under the concept of *parens patriae,* that is, in the child's best interest. The court's approach was to be paternalistic rather than adversarial in nature.

These concepts about juvenile justice spread rapidly across the nation during the early decades of the twentieth century. Statutes similar to the Illinois Juvenile Court Act were enacted in almost every state. In addition, juvenile courts came to be staffed by groups of probation officers, social workers, and treatment specialists. Thus, the goal of the early reform movement was to create a juvenile justice system geared to treatment, not punishment. The purpose of the court was to keep children from criminal behavior by rehabilitating instead of punishing them.

From its origin, the juvenile court system denied children procedural rights normally available to adult offenders. Due process rights such as representation by counsel, a jury trial, freedom from self-incrimination, and freedom from unreasonable search and seizure were not considered essential for the juvenile court system because the primary purpose of the system was not punishment but rehabilitation.[7] However, the dream of trying to rehabilitate children from a benign court setting was not achieved. Individual treatment approaches failed, and delinquency rates soared. In many instances, the courts deprived children of their liberty and treated them unfairly.

Conditions became so oppressive that in the early 1960s, the U.S. Supreme Court itself expressed a new and deep concern over the rights of minors and encouraged litigation to extend due process to juvenile offenders. As a result, the "due process revolution" of that era mandated procedural guarantees at virtually every level of the juvenile justice system.

Today, the juvenile system is very much a legal system. The Supreme Court has played a significant, if not monumental, role in the formulation of juvenile law

FOCUS ON DELINQUENCY

The Juvenile Justice System—
The Key Players, Programs, and Costs

PREVENTING DELINQUENCY

Under the Juvenile Justice and Delinquency Prevention Act of 1974 (PL 93-45) the appropriation amendment for 1992–93 grants approximately 60 million dollars for state juvenile justice programs. A portion of these funds are used for exemplary juvenile delinquency prevention programs.

Hundreds of thousands of children and families are serviced in primary prevention programs targeted at families, schools and the community. Since over 400,000 children live in foster care, programs such as Permanent Families for Abused and Neglected Children help to prevent delinquency in such children. Court Appointed Special Advocates (CASA) insures that the courts are familiar with the needs of these children. Schools provide Cities in Schools, law-related education, and peer leadership programs to reduce school violence and prevent students from dropping out. Youth gangs are often served by youth service bureaus, Jobs for Youth and detached worker programs. Drug prevention programs, such as Drug Abuse Resistance Education (DARE), help kids say no to drugs. Drug-free school zones and citizen's patrols help link youth-prevention agencies and organizations.

JUVENILE LAW ENFORCEMENT

Of the 13,000 municipal police agencies, approximately 75 percent provide special programs and services for juvenile offenders. Often police officers concerned with juveniles have a multiplicity of roles and duties. Cost of police services for children is undetermined, but more time is being spent dealing with troubled and violent youths committing serious crimes. Police officers make over 1.5 million juvenile arrests, of which 600,000 are for serious crimes. The community policing concept is being utilized to decentralize policing and make its services more amenable to juvenile delinquency prevention.

DETENTION AND PRETRIAL SERVICES

In the United States, there are over 3,300 jails and about 830 juvenile detention facilities. Many juveniles, upwards of 1,500 are housed in jails on any given day. From 200,000 to 300,000 are being jailed with adults each year. Upwards of 500,000 youths are held in detention facilities each year. Thousands of juveniles receive diversion as an alternative to official procedures. Over 16,000 are tried as adults. The amount of plea bargaining is uncertain because a significant number of juveniles enter guilty pleas admissions in the juvenile court. Forty-eight states and the District of Columbia have waiver proceedings to the criminal court.

continued on next page

and procedure over the past twenty years. Nevertheless, the courts have neither repudiated the goal of rehabilitating children nor subjected children totally to the procedures and philosophy of the adult criminal justice system.

THE JUVENILE JUSTICE SYSTEM

Today, the **juvenile justice system** exists in all states by statute. Each jurisdiction has a juvenile code and a special court structure to deal with children in trouble.

Nationwide, the juvenile justice system consists of thousands of public and private agencies, with a total budget amounting to hundreds of millions of dollars. Most of the nation's twenty thousand police agencies have a juvenile

PROSECUTORS AND PUBLIC DEFENDERS

Of the 30,000 lawyers in the justice system, including prosecutors and public defenders, only a small percentage work in the juvenile courts. They handle from 500,000 to 600,000 delinquency and status offense cases annually, in addition to thousands of informally handled cases. The public defense system provides the bulk of legal representation to children in the juvenile courts. In some areas, only 50 percent of the children in court receive the assistance of counsel. Cost ranges from 35 to 75 dollars per hour for legal services.

JUVENILE COURTS

Jurisdiction ordinarily is defined by state statute. There are independent juvenile court systems, family court structures and juvenile sessions of adult courts. Two factors, age and status, bring children under juvenile court jurisdiction. Judges, juvenile probation officers, court clerks and juvenile prosecutors control and influence court cases.

In a noted 1967 case, *In re Gault,* the Supreme Court declared that youths have a right to a lawyer and other legal protections. The juvenile courts handle about 1.2 million delinquency cases each year, in addition to about 80,000 status offense cases.

COMMUNITY TREATMENT

The most common community disposition employed by the juvenile court is probation. Over 400,000 youths are supervised on juvenile probation. Caseloads range from 60 to 80 per officer. Intensive probation services utilize very small caseloads and intense scrutiny. Statutory restitution programs exist in all 50 states. Residential programs include group homes, boarding schools, foster programs and rural residences such as farms and camps.

Community programs often cost half as much per child as a secure training school. Recidivism rates tend to be lower generally in the community treatment programs than in large-scale institutional settings.

JUVENILE CORRECTIONS (INSTITUTIONAL CARE)

There are about 1,100 public and 2,000 private juvenile facilities; 94,500 children are held in all types of facilities during a year. Public facilities have a one day count of 57,000 while 37,000 are confined in private juvenile facilities. Average length of stay is about eight months. The budget for juvenile corrections in the states is approximately 2.4 billion dollars for 1991–92.

Staff include custody, administrative, and treatment personnel. Institutional placement costs currently are about 25,000 to 40,000 dollars annually per child. Thirty-eight states are spending over 380 million dollars on contracts with private facilities for such specialized services such as marine programs and wilderness camps.

Twenty-three states indicate a problem with overcrowding. Juveniles in state custody range in age from 11 to 18 years of age. ■

component, and more than three thousand juvenile courts and about an equal number of juvenile correctional facilities exist throughout the nation. There are thousands of juvenile police officers, more than three thousand juvenile court judges, more than sixty-five hundred juvenile probation officers, and thousands of juvenile correctional employees.[8]

Annually, about 1.8 million juveniles are arrested, more than 1.3 million delinquency cases petitioned to the courts by police and others, and half a million children placed on formal or informal probation; approximately ninety thousand youths are held in secure and nonsecure treatment centers.[9]

These figures do not take into account the great number of children who are referred to community diversion and mental health programs. There are thousands of these programs throughout the nation, and thousands of youth are being held in these community-based institutions. This multitude of agencies and people dealing with juvenile delinquency and status offenses has led to the development of what professionals in the field view as an incredibly expanded and complex juvenile justice system. See the Focus on Delinquency on page 444.

The Systems Approach

It is important to clarify the meaning of the term *system*. It refers to groups or organizations with a formal structure and clearly stated goals. Often a system is considered the ideal kind of formal organization. The idea that all these agencies of juvenile justice are actually a coordinated system is popular among practitioners, academicians, and other professionals who deal with juvenile crime. It implies that interrelationships exist among the agencies concerned with juvenile delinquency prevention and control. The **systems approach,** as it is often called, sees a change in one part of the system effecting changes in other parts. It implies that a close-knit, coordinated structure of organizations exists among various agencies of juvenile justice.[10] For example, broadening the power of the police officer to arrest juvenile offenders adds to the burdens of the juvenile courts; changing dispositional procedures affects the juvenile correctional agencies; revising the juvenile code by eliminating status offenses decreases the number of children entering the system.

The systems approach exists more in theory than in practice. The various elements of the juvenile system are all related but only to the degree that they influence each other's policies and practices. They are not so coordinated that they operate in unison. In fact, many juvenile justice agencies compete for budgetary support, espouse different philosophies, and have personnel standards that differ significantly. It would be useful for all the agencies concerned with juvenile justice to be in an integrated system. As one national commission pointed out, "Even in the most disjointed system, police, prosecution, courts, and corrections function in a roughly interdependent fashion, linked, as if they are parts of a single system."[11] However, most program decisions are made without proper planning information or objective data, and effective evaluation is rare. Consequently, the vast majority of states operate fragmented and generally uncoordinated juvenile justice systems.

Police, courts, and juvenile correctional agencies comprise the major components of juvenile justice. This is the official government system that exists in each community. It is also the primary system for handling delinquent and noncriminal behavior. In most jurisdictions, however, other institutions also handle juvenile antisocial behavior—the mental health system, the schools, and extensive networks of private social service programs. Furthermore, the workload of the juvenile justice system is directly related to the ability of the family and the community to resolve and contain juvenile problems.[12] Which of the various institutional systems children are sent to depends on the community's ability to prevent juvenile misbehavior. Thus, a typical flowchart of a juvenile justice system often begins with the concept of prevention, followed by police, judicial, and correctional intervention. Figure 14.1 illustrates the system of juvenile justice.

THE JUVENILE JUSTICE PROCESS

How are children processed by the agencies and organizations of the juvenile justice system?[13] What are the sequential stages that juvenile offenders pass

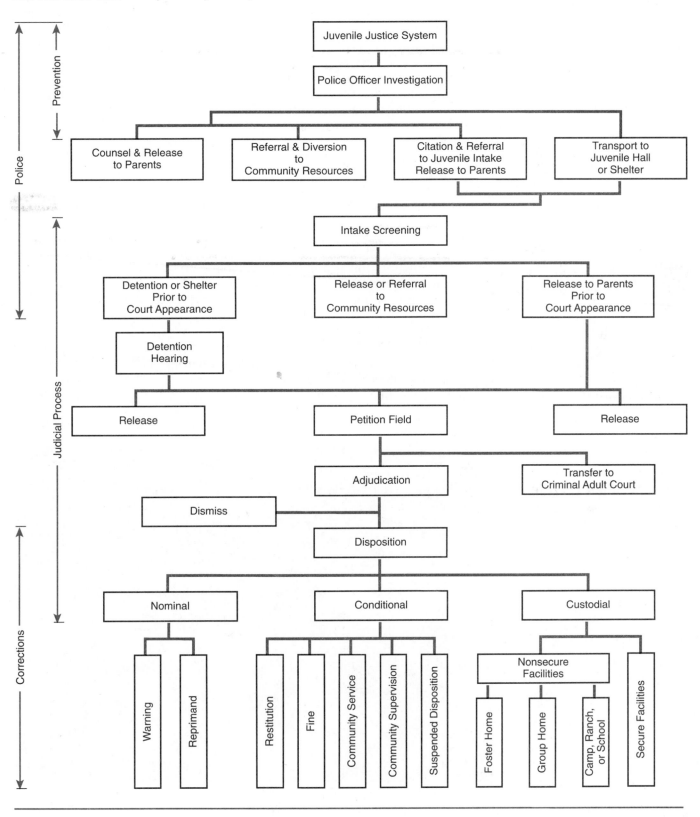

through? Most children initially come in contact with the police officer. When a juvenile commits a serious crime, the police are empowered to make an arrest. Less serious offenses may also require police action, but instead of being arrested, the child may be warned, the parents may be called, or a referral may be made to a juvenile social service program. Only about half of all children arrested by the police are actually referred to the juvenile court.

When a police officer takes a child into custody, the child may be brought to the station house lockup and then to a county detention program or intake program prior to a court appearance. At this point, further referral to a social service agency may occur. If the crime is a serious one, the juvenile court prosecutor may initiate a petition against the child. This begins the trial process. After a petition is filed, the child can be released to the custody of his or her parents until the court appearance, but sometimes the child may be detained. When the child appears before the court, the court can decide whether to **waive** the case (transfer it to an adult court) or to adjudicate it in juvenile court. If the adjudication or trial declares the child delinquent or in need of supervision, the court initiates a social study of the child's background. After this study, which is called a **predisposition report,** an appropriate disposition leading to a correctional and rehabilitation program is provided. A more detailed analysis of the stages in the process follows.

Police Investigation

When a juvenile commits a crime, police agencies have the authority to investigate the incident and then to decide whether to release the child or to detain and refer him or her to the juvenile court. This is often a discretionary

Police investigation of juvenile cases may begin with the questioning of suspects and search for evidence.

decision based not only on the nature of the offense committed but also on the conditions existing at the time of the arrest. Such factors as the type and seriousness of the offense, the child's past contacts with the police, and whether or not the child denies committing the crime determine whether a petition is filed. While juveniles are in the custody of the police, they have basic constitutional rights similar to those of adult offenders. Children are protected against unreasonable search and seizure under the Fourth and Fourteenth Amendments. Constitutional limitations are also placed on police interrogation procedures under the Fifth Amendment.

Intake Screening at the Court

If the police decide to file a petition, the child is referred to juvenile court. The primary issue at this point is whether the child should remain in the community or be placed in a detention facility or shelter home. Also, it is essential to determine whether referral services should be obtained before any further court action. In the past, too many children were routinely taken to court and held in detention facilities to await court appearances. Normally, a **detention hearing** is held to determine whether to remand the child to a shelter or to release the child. At this point, the child has a right to counsel and other procedural safeguards. A child who is not detained is usually released to his or her parent or guardian. Most state juvenile court acts provide for a child to return home to await further court action, except when it is necessary to protect the child, when the child presents a serious danger to the public, or when it is not certain that the child will return to court for further adjudication. In many cases, the police will refer the child to a community service program at intake instead of filing a formal charge.

Pretrial Procedures

In most juvenile court jurisdictions, the adjudication process begins with some sort of initial hearing. At this hearing, juvenile court rules of procedure normally require that the children be informed of their right to a trial, that the plea or admission be voluntary, and that they understand the charges and consequences of the plea. The case will often not be further adjudicated if a child admits to the crime at the initial hearing.

In some cases, youths may be detained pending a trial. Many states permit detention or the removal of children from their home where there is a likelihood of danger to themselves or others. Juveniles who are detained are eligible for bail in a handful of jurisdictions. Plea bargaining may also occur in the juvenile process, particularly involving a reduction in the charges or the severity of the disposition. Such negotiations may be pursued at any stage of the proceedings.

If the child denies the allegation of delinquency, an **adjudicatory hearing** or trial is scheduled. Under extraordinary circumstances, a juvenile who commits a serious crime may be transferred to an adult court instead of being adjudicated. Today, most jurisdictions have laws providing for such transfers. Whether they occur depends on the type of offense, the child's prior record, the nature of past treatment efforts, the availability of treatment services, and the likelihood that the child will be rehabilitated in the juvenile court.

Adjudication

The adjudication is the trial stage of the juvenile court process. If the child does not admit to the charges at the initial hearing and is not transferred to an adult court, an adjudication hearing is held to determine the facts of the case. The court hears evidence on the allegations in the delinquency petition. This is a trial on the merits, and rules of evidence similar to criminal proceedings generally apply. At this stage of the proceeding, the juvenile offender is entitled to many of the procedural guarantees given adult offenders. These rights include the right to representation by counsel, freedom from self-incrimination, the right to confront and cross-examine witnesses, and, in certain instances, the right to a jury trial. In addition, many states have their own procedures concerning rules of evidence, competence of witnesses, pleadings, and pretrial motions. At the end of the adjudicatory hearing, the court enters a judgment against the child.

Disposition

If the adjudication process finds the child delinquent, the court must then decide what should be done to treat the child. Most juvenile court acts require a dispositional hearing separate from the adjudication. This is often referred to as a *bifurcated process*. The dispositional hearing is less formal than adjudication. Here, the judge imposes a **disposition** on the juvenile offender in light of the offense, prior record, and family background. The judge has broad discretion and can prescribe a wide range of dispositions—from a simple warning or reprimand to community service or probation to more intense social control measures, such as institutional commitment, including group home, foster care, or secure facility care. In theory, the judge's decision serves the best interests of the child, the family, and the community. Many juvenile statutes require that the judge consider the least restrictive dispositional alternative before imposing any sentence. The disposition is one of the most important stages in the juvenile process because it may be the court's last opportunity to influence the child's behavior. Disposition is concerned primarily with treating the child and controlling antisocial behavior.

Postdisposition

Some jurisdictions allow for a program of juvenile aftercare or parole. A child can be paroled from an institution and placed under the supervision of a parole officer. This means that the child will complete the period of confinement in the community and receive assistance from the parole officer in the form of counseling, school referral, and vocational training.

In some jurisdictions, adjudication of a delinquency petition can be appealed to a higher court. Such an appeal may involve a review of the statutory basis under which the child is to receive treatment from the state. Provisions for such appeals vary greatly with each jurisdiction.

Juveniles who are committed to programs of treatment and control have a legal right to treatment. The right to treatment requires that states provide suitable rehabilitation programs for children that include counseling, education, and vocational services. Appellate courts have ruled that if such treatment is not provided, individuals must be released from confinement.

A child may find himself handcuffed and placed in secure detention after being taken into custody by police.

CRIMINAL JUSTICE VERSUS JUVENILE JUSTICE

The components of the adult and juvenile criminal processes are similar. Both include police investigation, arrest, administrative booking, preliminary hearings, bail, plea bargaining and admission of a plea, grand jury indictment, formal arraignment, trial, verdict, sentence, and appeal. However, the juvenile system has a separate, complementary (almost parallel) organizational structure. In many communities, juvenile justice is administered by people who bring special skills to the task. Also, more kinds of facilities and services are available to juveniles than to adults.

The juvenile court, emphasizing individualized treatment, was originally conceived of as a social court, not a formalized court of law. This view met with much criticism over the first sixty years of the twentieth century, resulting in the development of procedures and laws similar to those that protect adult offenders.

However, the purpose of the juvenile court is to treat and rehabilitate children, not to punish them. The juvenile justice system was designed not only to prevent juvenile crime and to rehabilitate juvenile offenders but also to provide for abused, neglected, and incorrigible children. In essence, it was to provide services to promote the normal growth and development of all adjudicated children.

One major concern of the juvenile court reform movement was to make certain that the stigma attached to a person who became a convicted criminal offender would not be affixed to children in juvenile proceedings. Thus, even the language used in the juvenile court differs from that used in the adult criminal court (see Table 14.1). Children are not formally indicted for a crime; they have a **petition** filed against them. Secure pretrial holding facilities are called detention centers rather than jails. Similarly, the criminal court trial is called a **hearing** in the juvenile justice system. The following Focus on Delinquency compares the two systems.

Legal expert Barry Feld, one of the leading scholars of the juvenile court, believes that the juvenile justice system has taken on more of the characteristics of the adult courts. He refers to this as the "criminalizing" of the juvenile court.[14] Robert Dawson suggests that since the legal differences between the juvenile and criminal systems are narrower than they have ever been, it may be time to abolish the juvenile court and merge it into the larger criminal justice system.[15] During the last fifteen years, the juvenile system has obviously become more consistent with current adult procedures.

██ ██ **TABLE 14.1**   Comparison of Terms Used in Adult and Juvenile Justice Systems

	JUVENILE TERMS	ADULT TERMS
THE PERSON AND THE ACT	Delinquent child	Criminal
	Delinquent act	Crime
PREADJUDICATORY STAGE	Take into custody	Arrest
	Petition	Indictment
	Agree to a finding	Plead guilty
	Deny the petition	Plead not guilty
	Adjustment	Plea bargain
	Detention facility; child-care shelter	Jail
ADJUDICATORY STAGE	Substitution	Reduction of charges
	Adjudicatory or fact-finding hearing	Trial
	Adjudication	Conviction
POSTADJUDICATORY STAGE	Dispositional hearing	Sentencing hearing
	Disposition	Sentence
	Commitment	Incarceration
	Youth development center; treatment center, training school	Prison
	Residential child-care facility	Halfway house
	Aftercare	Parole

Similarities and Differences between Adult and Juvenile Justice

Since its creation, the juvenile justice system has sought to maintain its independence from the adult justice system. Yet there are a number of similarities that characterize the institutions, processes, and law of the two systems.

SIMILARITIES BETWEEN JUVENILE AND ADULT JUSTICE SYSTEMS

- Police officers, judges, and correctional personnel use discretion in decision making in both the adult and the juvenile systems.
- The right to receive *Miranda* warnings applies to juveniles as well as to adults.
- Juveniles and adults are protected from prejudicial lineups or other identification procedures.
- Similar procedural safeguards protect juveniles and adults when they make an admission of guilt.
- Prosecutors and defense attorneys play equally critical roles in juvenile and adult advocacy.
- Juveniles and adults have the right to counsel at most key stages of the court process.
- Pretrial motions are available in juvenile and criminal court proceedings.
- Negotiations and plea bargain exist for children and adult offenders.
- Children and adults have a right to a hearing and an appeal.
- The standard of evidence in juvenile delinquency adjudications, as in adult criminal trials, is proof beyond a reasonable doubt.
- Juveniles and adults can be placed on probation by the court.
- Both juveniles and adults can be placed in pretrial detention facilities.
- Juveniles and adults can be kept in detention without bail if they are considered dangerous.
- After trial, both can be placed in community treatment programs.

DIFFERENCES BETWEEN JUVENILE AND ADULT JUSTICE SYSTEMS

- The primary purpose of juvenile procedures is protection and treatment. With adults, the aim is to punish the guilty.
- Age determines the jurisdiction of the juvenile court. The nature of the offense determines jurisdiction in the adult system.
- Juveniles can be apprehended for acts that would not be criminal if they were committed by an adult (status offenses).
- Juvenile proceedings are not considered criminal; adult proceedings are.
- Juvenile court procedures are generally informal and private. Those of adult courts are more formal and are open to the public.
- Courts cannot release identifying information about a juvenile to the press, but they must release information about an adult.
- Parents are highly involved in the juvenile process but not in the adult process.
- The standard of arrest is more stringent for adults than for juveniles.
- Juveniles are released into parental custody. Adults are generally given the opportunity for bail.
- Juveniles have no constitutional right to a jury trial. Adults have this right.
- Juveniles can be searched in school without probable cause or a warrant.
- A juvenile's record is sealed when the age of majority is reached. The record of an adult is permanent.
- A juvenile court cannot sentence juveniles to county jails or state prisons; these are reserved for adults.
- There is no death penalty in the juvenile justice system. The U.S. Supreme Court has declared that the Eighth Amendment does not prohibit the death penalty for crimes committed by juveniles ages 16 and 17. ■

GOALS AND STANDARDS OF JUVENILE JUSTICE

As we have seen, the juvenile justice system is entrusted with a variety of often conflicting tasks: upholding the law, protecting the victim, meting out justice, evaluating the best interests of the child, rehabilitating wayward youths, acting as a conduit to social agencies, and so on. The multiplicity of goals and priorities and the interrelationship between the juvenile justice system and other institutions make it difficult to assess whether the system is meeting the needs of children in trouble.

What exactly are the goals of juvenile justice today? Experts continue to debate which goals should be given priority. Some claim that the most important goal is to protect potential and actual victims and deter children from committing antisocial acts. Others argue that social reform, legislative progress, and programs leading to education, recreation, and employment are the most practical methods of reducing youth crime. To some experts, the threat of stigma and labeling by

■■■■■■■■■■■■■■■

While clear distinctions can be made between the adult and juvenile justice systems, there is also overlap in law, procedure and process.

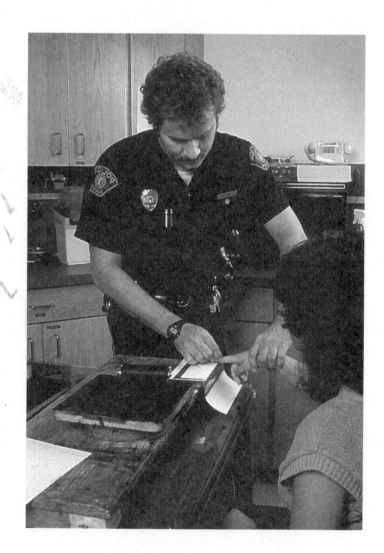

the justice system is an overriding problem; these experts emphasize diverting children before the formal trial. Still others spend considerable time talking about how to respond to children with special needs—the uneducated, the mentally ill, and the mentally retarded.

Government Goal Setting

Since the 1960s, four major efforts have been funded by the government and private sources to identify the goals of juvenile justice and delinquency reform. First, in 1967, the **President's Commission on Law Enforcement and the Administration of Justice,** a product of the Johnson administration's concern for social welfare, issued its well thought-out and documented report on juvenile delinquency and its control. Influenced by Cloward and Ohlin's then-popular opportunity theory, the commission suggested that the juvenile justice system must provide underprivileged youths with opportunities for success, including jobs and education. The commission also recognized the need to develop effective law enforcement procedures to control hard-core youthful offenders and at the same time grant them due process of law when they came before the courts. But the main thrust of the commission's report was that the juvenile justice system must become sensitive to the needs of young offenders:

there should be a response to the special needs of youths with special problems. They may be delinquent, they may be law abiding but alienated and uncooperative, they may be behavior or academic problems in school or misfits among their peers or disruptive in recreation groups. For such youths, it is imperative to furnish help that is particularized enough to deal with their individual needs but not separate them from their peers and label them for life.[16]

During the 1960s, the concern was primarily for individual treatment and the rights of juvenile offenders. Child advocates and federal lawmakers were interested in merging the rehabilitation model with due process of law.

The presidential commission report of 1967 acted as a catalyst for the passage of federal legislation, the *Juvenile Delinquency Prevention and Control (JDP) Act of 1968*.[17] This law created a Youth Development and Delinquency Prevention Administration, which concentrated on helping states develop new juvenile justice programs, particularly involving diversion of youth, decriminalization, and "decarceration." In 1968, Congress also passed the *Omnibus Safe Streets and Crime Control Act*.[18] Title I of this law established the *Law Enforcement Assistance Administration* (LEAA) to provide federal funds to improve the adult and juvenile justice systems. In 1972, Congress amended the JDP Act of 1968 to allow the LEAA to focus its funding on juvenile justice and delinquency prevention programs. State and local governments were required to develop and adopt comprehensive plans to obtain federal assistance.

Because crime continued to receive much publicity, a second effort called the **National Advisory Commission on Criminal Justice Standards and Goals** was established in 1973 by the more conservative Nixon administration.[19] Its report on juvenile justice and delinquency prevention identified such major goals as:

1. Develop programs for young people to prevent delinquent behavior before it occurs.
2. Develop diversion activities whereby youths are processed out of the juvenile justice system.

3. Establish dispositional alternatives so that institutionalization can be used only as a last resort.
4. Provide due process for all juveniles.
5. Control the violent and the chronic delinquent.[20]

This commission's recommendations formed the basis for additional legislation, the *Juvenile Justice and Delinquency Prevention Act of 1974*.[21] This important act eliminated the old Youth Development and Delinquency Prevention Administration and replaced it with the *Office of Juvenile Justice and Delinquency Prevention (OJJDP)* within the LEAA. In 1980, the LEAA was phased out, and the OJJDP became an independent agency in the Department of Justice, Attorney General's Office. The role of the OJJDP was to develop and implement worthwhile programs that prevent and reduce juvenile crimes.

Throughout the 1970s, its two most important goals were (1) removing juveniles from detention in adult jails and (2) eliminating the incarceration together of juvenile and status offenders. During this period, the OJJDP stressed the creation of formal diversion and restitution programs around the United States. These goals reflected the influence of labeling theory during this period, a movement that sparked the federal agency's effort to reduce stigma whenever possible.

In the 1980s, the OJJDP shifted its priorities from stigma reduction to the identification and control of chronic, violent juvenile offenders.[22] This goal was in line with the Reagan and Bush administrations' more conservative views of justice. The federal government poured millions of dollars into research projects designed to study chronic offenders, predict their behavior, and evaluate programs created to control their activities.

Since 1974, the Juvenile Justice and Delinquency Prevention Act has had a significant impact on juvenile justice policy. It has been an important instrument for removing status offenders from jails and detention centers, as well as providing funds for innovative and effective programs. Congress approved the OJJDP reauthorization in 1992 for another four years, while establishing many new programs, including challenge grants that could double states' federal funding for juvenile justice activities.[23] Challenge grants are awarded for efforts in the following areas:

(1) education and mental health for youth in the juvenile justice system; (2) juveniles' access to lawyers; (3) alternatives to incarceration; and (4) removing status offenders from juvenile court jurisdiction. This reauthorization allows up to $60 million for local and state incentives to deter and prevent delinquency. In passing the JJDPA in 1974, Congress responded to what it described as a "bankrupt" juvenile justice system, which neither provides individualized justice nor effective help to juveniles or protection for communities.[24]

Over the years, most experts believe that the act has been a meaningful federal response to the juvenile delinquency problem.[25]

American Bar Association Standards

While the federal effort was proceeding, the **Institute of Judicial Administration (IJA)** and the **American Bar Association (ABA)** created a widely read set of standards (the *Juvenile Justice Standards Project*) designed to promote proportionality and rational decision making in the juvenile justice system and to restrict the often unfair discretion that had marked its early existence.[26] The standards consist of twenty-three volumes covering every aspect of juvenile justice administration from police handling of juveniles to dispositional procedures and the rights of minors. The IJA/ABA recommended standards reflect the ideas of equal and "just deserts"-based sentencing reforms that were also popular in the adult system at that time.[27] "Just deserts" means that the application of penalties to convicted juveniles should be decided primarily by the seriousness of the offense, not by the number of prior convictions. Some of the major principles on which the IJA/ABA recommendations for changes are based are:

1. Sanctions for juvenile offenders should be proportional.
2. Sentences or dispositions should be determinate.
3. Decision makers should choose the least restrictive alternative when intervening in the lives of juveniles and their families.
4. Noncriminal misbehavior (status offenses, private offenses, victimless crimes) should be removed from juvenile court jurisdiction.
5. Open proceedings and accountability should replace closed proceedings and unrestrained official discretion.
6. All affected persons should have the right to counsel at all stages of the proceedings.[28]

Not surprisingly, some of the goals suggested by the IJA/ABA standards are controversial. For example, the first three eliminate indeterminate commitments and discretion and recommend the criminal law approach of definiteness in sentencing. The fourth principle limits the jurisdiction of the court and eliminates status offenses from the court's responsibility. The sixth principle views hearings as adversarial rather than informal and requires representation by counsel at all critical points in the proceedings.

Nonetheless, these standards are a comprehensive, well-researched set of guidelines for governing the juvenile justice system. They are considered by experts today to be the most universally accepted standards in the field, and many jurisdictions have adopted their key provisions.

A New Agenda

Examples of new approaches in juvenile justice abound. Ira Schwartz, a noted juvenile justice professional, has suggested that the juvenile justice system must adopt a different goal orientation. Some of his most significant recommendations deal with changes in juvenile corrections, such as closing training schools, prohibiting the confinement of juveniles in jails, and restructuring detention services. Others are grouped around reforming the juvenile court and include raising the age of juvenile court jurisdiction to 18 and eliminating minor juvenile crime and status offenses from the court's responsibility. Guaranteeing due process rights to children, upgrading the judiciary and probation services, and replacing the *parens patriae* model with a "justice" model are also part of Schwartz's 1990s action agenda.[29]

In reviewing proposed goals for the juvenile justice system—from both government and private sources—the ebb and flow of justice policy can be easily observed. Thirty years ago, the focus was on the treatment of unfortunate youths who had fallen into criminal behavior patterns through no fault of their own. Fifteen years ago, the main concern was avoiding criminal labels. Today, many experts are concerned with the control of serious juvenile offenders, the creation of firm but fair sentencing options in the juvenile court system, and the reform of juvenile correctional institutions. These cycles represent the shifting philosophies of juvenile justice and the theoretical **models of juvenile justice** upon which the goals are based.[30] (See Tables 14.2 and 14.3.) Whether the Clinton administration, with its concern for the well-being of children, will develop a priority agenda for juvenile reform remains uncertain at this writing.

IMPROVING THE JUVENILE JUSTICE SYSTEM

A review of the literature on juvenile justice and delinquency reveals a number of major themes on what the juvenile justice system should be doing to help youths in trouble and protect society as a whole. Today's experts seem to be saying that the system can be improved by concerted efforts directed at (1) the prevention of juvenile delinquency, (2) the diversion and removal of problem youths from the juvenile justice system, (3) the incapacitation of serious offenders, (4) fair and just treatment of all youthful offenders, and (5) making the juvenile justice system efficient and effective, particularly the juvenile court.

■■ TABLE 14..2   Shifting Philosophies of Juvenile Justice

TIME FRAME	ACTIVITY
PRIOR TO 1900S	Juveniles treated similar to adult offenders. No distinction by age or capacity to commit criminal acts.
FROM 1899 TO 1950S	Children treated differently, beginning with Illinois Juvenile Court Act of 1899. By 1925, juvenile court acts are established in virtually every state.
1950S TO 1970S	Recognition by experts that rehabilitation model and the protective nature of *parens patriae* have failed to prevent delinquency.
1960S TO 1970S	Introduction of constitutional due process into the juvenile justice system. Punishing children or protecting them under *parens patriae* requires due process of law.
1970S TO 1980S	Failure of rehabilitation and due process protections to control delinquency leads to a shift to a crime control and punishment philosophy similar to adult criminal justice system.
1990S	Mixed constitutional protections with some treatment. Uncertain goals and programs; the juvenile justice system relies on punishment and deterrence.

MODEL	DESCRIPTION	STAGE
REHABILITATION	Emphasis on treatment and individual needs of the juvenile; *parens patriae* philosophy; best interest of child is paramount.	
	Referral to social service; discretion in decision making; police-community prevention programs; arrest and prosecution in most serious cases.	Police
	Use of intake procedures, discretion and referral; limited use of detention, waiver, and plea bargaining.	Pretrial
	Procedural due process and fairness in a "helping court"; concern about diversion and community treatment.	Adjudication
	Use of indeterminate sentencing; institutional care only as last resort; bifurcated hearing with focus on community alternatives.	Disposition
JUSTICE	Goal is public protection, accountability and "just deserts"; actions similar to adult criminal justice system; decisions based on nature of offense.	
	Concern about delinquency and serious crimes (as opposed to status offenses); limited discretion; strict application of *Miranda* and search and seizure rules.	Police
	Increased role of prosecutor; full procedural safeguards; fact-finding is important. Plea bargaining acceptable; use of detention and waiver procedure.	Pretrial
	Juvenile guaranteed full procedural due process; admission of guilt allowed with proper rules of procedure; fairness and efficiency is goal of court; use of rules of evidence; procedure similar to adult court.	Adjudication
	Decisions based primarily on offense, as opposed to individual's needs; punishment is goal of the juvenile code; determinate sentencing to insure accountability for behavior.	Disposition
HYBRID	Combines treatment and punishment; goals often in conflict with each other. No consensus on purpose and nature of juvenile justice.	
	Juveniles codes recognize discretion and need for public protection. Arrest, search and seizure, and *Miranda* rules apply in all cases.	Police
	High priority given to crime-control policy; detention used with required hearing and due process; effort to retain the traditional goal of rehabilitation through diversion and discretion.	Pretrial
	Formal trial; focus on fact-finding and due process; concern for rules of law and procedure at expense of individual interests.	Adjudication
	Stress on sanctions proportionate to seriousness of child's crime; effort to balance community treatment and public protection; use of wide range of dispositional alternatives.	Disposition

Preventing Juvenile Crime

Prevention seeks to divert individual children from antisocial behavior during the early stages of their lives. Building stronger family units, providing counseling in schools, and improving living conditions are all examples of prevention efforts. Prevention also involves developing a comprehensive delinquency plan, collecting data about delinquency in local communities, clarifying delinquency goals, and providing an inventory of community resources and programs. Once these are accomplished, programs of prevention involving health, family, education, employment, recreation, housing, religion, and even the media can play an important role in thwarting juvenile delinquency.

Diversion and Delinquency

Even the most conservative critic sees the value of diverting minor offenders from the formal justice process and handling them in a nonpunitive, treatment-oriented fashion. A child can be diverted at any stage of the process. Basically, diversion has focused on certain groups—youths committing minor, noncriminal acts; first offenders; and youths committing minor criminal acts who might be more appropriately handled by social agencies. Diversion programs can be employed by the police, during the intake process or petition filing, and even at adjudication.

The goal of removing noncriminal misbehavior, such as status offenses, from juvenile court jurisdiction also should be seriously considered. In addition, whenever possible, delinquent offenders should be kept separate from adult criminals. School programs, counseling centers, and other activities within the mental health and educational systems might be more appropriate for children

■ ■ ■ ■ ■ ■ ■ ■ ■ ■ ■ ■ ■ ■

One of the goals of the juvenile justice system is to provide alternatives to traditional social control methods. Diverting youth and providing counseling as well as other non-punitive methods have been used in various jurisdictions around the nation.

with truancy problems. Children who are incorrigible can be handled in mental health settings.

Controlling Chronic Offenders

Research has shown that a small group of youthful offenders may be responsible for a significant amount of serious delinquency and may grow up to be adult offenders. A major national effort is being undertaken to study chronic offenders and develop mechanisms to identify them early in their careers. The juvenile justice system must also develop treatment facilities to deal effectively with the needs of these offenders, including serious drug offenders, while protecting the community from their activities. At first glance, incarceration in secure juvenile facilities may seem to be an inappropriate goal for juvenile justice, but it is actually more humane than the current practice of transferring these youths to the adult system so that they can be held in state prisons.

Fairness and Justice

All children processed through the juvenile justice system should be treated fairly and humanely. No distinction should be made between white and minority juvenile offenders or between those in the lower classes and those in the middle and upper strata of society. Nonetheless, research indicates that these distinctions are still being made.[31]

Procedures to ensure due process should be present in all areas of the juvenile justice system. Investigation, arrest, diversion, detention, arraignment, adjudication, sentencing, and institutionalization must be consistent with our democratic system. Recent U.S. Supreme Court decisions have made it clear that youths charged with delinquent acts and others brought into the juvenile justice system are entitled to virtually all of the due process rights accorded adults.

Increasing Effectiveness

Juvenile justice agencies should be well organized and managed. The efficient operation of juvenile services requires qualified personnel, adequate organizational structure, sound fiscal management and the development of successful programs. The general public has for the most part been unenthusiastic about providing money for the care and protection of children in the juvenile justice system. Often, facilities for juveniles are crowded, courts lack personnel, probation services are not sufficiently extensive, and educational and recreational programs are underfinanced and inadequate. Thus, resources must be developed to provide efficient, effective juvenile justice programs. The federal government needs to provide national leadership to encourage the adoption of such programs on the state level.

THE JUVENILE COURT AND ITS OPERATION

Whatever goals, models, or strategies for reform are adopted, the juvenile court is the centerpiece of the juvenile justice system. It plays a major role in controlling juvenile behavior and delivering social services to children in need. How it is organized and what laws apply to those who appear before it is critical to any meaningful reform effort. (See Fig. 14.2.)

Today's juvenile court is a specialized court for children. Its organizational structure varies in each state. A juvenile court can be (1) part of a high court of general trial jurisdiction, (2) a special session of a lower court of trial jurisdiction, (3) an independent statewide court, or even (4) part of a broader family court. The juvenile court includes a judge, probation staff, government prosecutors and defense attorneys, and a variety of social service programs. It functions in a sociolegal manner and seeks to promote rehabilitation within a framework of procedural due process. It is concerned with acting "in the best interest of the child" and public protection, often incompatible goals.

Most juvenile courts in the United States are established as *lower courts of limited jurisdiction,* where they are part of a district court, city court, or recorder's court and are limited solely to juvenile delinquency matters. Salaries, physical facilities, and even the prestige of the court can all be directly affected by its jurisdictional location. These factors tend to limit the ability of the court to attract competent personnel, including judges, and to obtain necessary resources from the state legislature. It is unclear why juvenile courts have been structured in lower trial courts in many states. Quite possibly it was to provide local attention to juvenile matters, since some experts believe that a lower court relates more efficiently and effectively to the concerns of parents and young people in the local community. In addition, legislators may have seen the juvenile court as an inferior court, relegated to the lowest level because of its jurisdiction over children. Massachusetts is an example of a state whose juvenile courts are placed in a special session of lower court of limited trial jurisdiction. The state allows juvenile sessions to be heard in its district courts, and it has established special juvenile courts in major urban areas.

■■ FIGURE 14.2

Juvenile judicial system

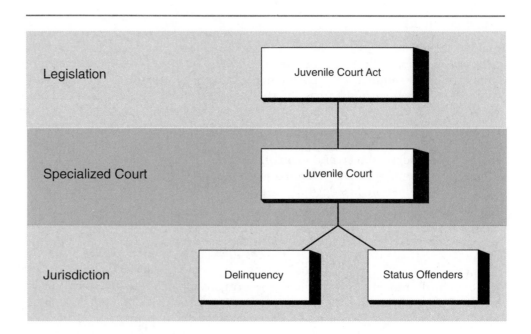

On the other hand, an increasing number of states—including Alaska, California, Colorado, Florida, Illinois, and Wisconsin—place juvenile matters at the *highest court of general trial jurisdiction.*.[32] Here, juvenile cases are tried in the more prestigious courts of general jurisdiction. States that deal with juvenile matters at the highest trial court level have an integrated organizational structure that results in more efficient and effective court administration. Such courts are better able to secure the funding they need to improve physical facilities and hire competent judicial and probation personnel.

Some states have *independent juvenile court systems.* Such systems may be referred to as statewide juvenile courts. Separately organized and independent juvenile courts exist in such states as Connecticut and Utah and in parts of other states, such as Georgia and Kansas. New York and Hawaii have also organized their juvenile courts on a statewide basis, although the New York system is called a family court system.[33] The major advantages to the statewide independent system are that it can serve sparsely populated areas within a given jurisdiction, it permits judicial personnel and others to deal exclusively with children's matters, and it can obtain legislative funding better than other court systems. On the other hand, the very reason for its form—obtaining legislative funding—can also act to its detriment. Separately organized juvenile courts encounter resistance from legislators concerned with duplication of effort and unwilling to provide resources for the control and prevention of juvenile delinquency.

The major disadvantage of implementing a *family court* structure is that it requires major reorganization of the existing court system by the legislature. The costs are substantial, especially in the first few years of the court's existence. Where family court structures do exist, there is little statistical data to indicate that they have reduced delinquency or improved family programs.

However, it has become apparent to some experts that to treat the related problems of intrafamily crime, divorce, and child neglect in separate courts is to encourage inconsistency in court administration and decision making and to foster ineffective case-flow management. Thus, it would be preferable to deal with juvenile matters in a family court system.

JUVENILE COURT JURISDICTION

Juvenile court jurisdiction is defined by state statutes, constitutional amendments, or state legislation. The New York family court, for example, is part of the New York constitution. Legislation is passed to implement the constitutional mandate and to specify the details of the court. More often, however, the juvenile courts are created by the authority of the legislature. Thus, the jurisdiction itself is generally controlled by legislative enactment.

Age

The states differ over the age that brings children under the jurisdiction of the juvenile court.[34] Most (such as Alaska, California, Minnesota, and Wyoming) include all children under 18. Others, including Louisiana, Massachusetts, and Michigan, set the upper limit at under 17. Still other jurisdictions (for example, North Carolina and Connecticut) have established the juvenile age as 16 or under (see Table 14.4).

■■ TABLE 14.4   Age at Which Criminal Courts Gain Jurisdiction of Young Offenders—Ranges from 16 to 19

AGE OF OFFENDER WHEN UNDER CRIMINAL COURT JURISDICTION	STATES
16 years	Connecticut, New York, North Carolina
17	Georgia, Illinois, Louisiana, Massachusetts, Missouri, South Carolina, Texas
18	Alabama, Alaska, Arizona, Arkansas, California, Colorado, Delaware, District of Columbia, Florida, Hawaii, Idaho, Indiana, Iowa, Kansas, Kentucky, Maine, Maryland, Michigan, Minnesota, Mississippi, Montana, Nebraska, Nevada, New Hampshire, New Jersey, New Mexico, North Dakota, Ohio, Oklahoma, Oregon, Pennsylvania, Rhode Island, South Dakota, Tennessee, Utah, Vermont, Virginia, Washington, West Virginia, Wisconsin, federal districts
19	Wyoming

Source: Linda A. Szymanski, *Upper Age of Juvenile Court Jurisdiction Statutes Analysis* (Pittsburgh: National Center for Juvenile Justice, March 1987).

At one time, some jurisdictions established age ranges that varied according to the sex or geographic location of the juvenile, but statutes employing these distinctions have been held to be in violation of the equal protection clause or due process clause of the Constitution. For example, in the case of *Lamb v. Brown,* an Oklahoma statute that allowed females under the age of 18 the benefits of juvenile court proceedings while limiting the same benefits to males under 16 was held to be unconstitutional.[35]

A few state statutes describe juvenile court jurisdiction in terms of minimum age. Massachusetts, for example, defines a child as a person who is under 17 but over 7 years of age.[36] Normally, what operates is the common law understanding of the responsibility of children. Under the age of 7, children are deemed incapable of committing crimes. There is a rebuttable presumption that children between 7 and 14 do not have the capacity for criminal behavior. Over the age of 14, children are believed to be responsible for their actions.

The Nature of the Offense—Delinquency

Juvenile court jurisdiction is also based on the nature of the child's actions. If a child commits a crime, this conduct normally falls in the category of juvenile delinquency. Definitions of delinquency vary from state to state, but most are based on the common element of a maximum age as well as on the fact that delinquency is an intentional violation of the criminal law.

In recent years, state legislatures concerned about serious juvenile crime have passed laws automatically excluding serious offenses from the jurisdiction of the juvenile court. For example, Maryland excludes crimes punishable by death or life in prison allegedly committed by children over 14 years of age and robbery committed with a dangerous weapon if the accused is over 16 (however, the case can be transferred back to juvenile court from the adult court).[37]

Another approach has been to give prosecutors the choice of bringing the case to either juvenile court or adult court. For example, Florida gives the prosecutor the right to decide where to bring a case if a child is accused of committing a crime punishable by death or life in prison or if the child is 16 or over and has committed two prior delinquent offenses.[38] These issues will be discussed more fully in Chapter 16 dealing with waiver procedures.

Such trends reflect a "toughening up" of juvenile justice policy—removing young offenders from the jurisdiction of the juvenile court so that they can be tried and punished as adults and eventually sentenced to adult prisons. However, this does not mean that the juvenile court has totally abandoned its rehabilitative ideals. Some states still require that juveniles manifest a "need for treatment" or supervision before they can be declared delinquents or status offenders; committing an illegal act is not enough for the state to take control of a child.[39] So there is still recognition that the juvenile court's mandate is something other than control and punishment.

The Nature of the Offense—Status Offenders

Juvenile courts also have jurisdiction over **status offenders,** children whose offenses are not the type of activities for which adults are normally prosecuted. Some juvenile delinquency statutes still include status offenses within their definition, but most states now have separate PINS and CHINS (persons or children in need of supervision) statutes so that separate proceedings can be held for children who are runaways, unmanageable, truant, and incorrigible.

The position of status offenders within the juvenile justice system remains controversial today. One of the most difficult problems with such jurisdiction is the statutes themselves. The behaviors commonly included in these statutes—for example, "unmanageable," "unruly," and "in danger of leading an idle, dissolute, lewd, or immoral life"—have been challenged in court for being unconstitutionally vague and indefinite. However, the courts that have addressed this issue have upheld the breadth of the statutes in view of their overall concern for the welfare of the child.[40]

The removal of status offenders from secure lockups with delinquent youths has been one of the more successful justice-related policy initiatives. Almost all states have legally prohibited incarcerating status offenders with delinquents. For example, a West Virginia court prohibited the housing of status offenders in "secure, prison-like facilities which also house children guilty of criminal conduct or needlessly subject status offenders to the degradation and physical abuse of incarceration."[41] However, it is not uncommon for judges to get around these prohibitions by holding status offenders in contempt of court if they refuse to honor judicial decrees; a number of states have permitted these youths to then be held in secure detention facilities.[42]

The status offense category often becomes a catchall for offenders who do not fit anywhere else. If there is not enough evidence to support a finding of delinquency, prosecutors sometimes charge youths with being status offenders on the grounds that their behavior endangered their morals, health, or general welfare.[43] Defense attorneys may welcome the substitution since it means that their clients will not be subject to the same degree of confinement and control as they would be if they had been found delinquent. Because youths originally charged as delinquents can wind up as status offenders, the line between status offenders and delinquency is often vague and ill-defined. In light of such overlap, the primary role of the juvenile court is to clarify the needs of the child, as is illustrated in the following Case in Point.

You are an experienced juvenile court social worker responsible for making decisions about screening children from the stigma of juvenile court jurisdiction.

Joann, 15, is charged with assault with a dangerous weapon, her first offense. She lives with two siblings and her 50-year-old mother, who is on welfare. Joann has had serious learning problems in school and views herself as intellectually limited. She began having problems when she entered junior high school and started using drugs and "fooling around with boys." In the last year, she has been absent from school for weeks at a time, and school counselors were preparing a petition for truancy to the juvenile court at the time of this offense.

In addition to school problems, Joann's behavior has become aggressive at home. She has taken to running away from home, staying out nights, and adopting what amounts to an incorrigible life-style.

As a multiple-problem youngster on the verge of delinquency (the assault case involved a fight with another juvenile), Joann exhibits behavioral characteristics indicating delinquency and a person in need of supervision (PINS). She has educational, family, and personal needs.

What role should the juvenile court play in this case? Develop a set of criteria that would guide you in deciding Joann's case.

LEGAL RIGHTS FOR THE JUVENILE OFFENDER

No overview of the juvenile court and its control over juvenile justice is complete without discussing the legal rights of juvenile offenders and the role of the U.S. Supreme Court in recognizing these rights. Throughout the 1960s and 1970s, the Court significantly increased procedural safeguards for the adult criminal offender. Nearly all the provisions of the Bill of Rights dealing with the criminal process were made applicable to the states through the due process clause of the Fourteenth Amendment. Some of the most significant of these decisions include the following:

- *Mapp v. Ohio,* which extended the exclusionary rule (preventing admission of illegally obtained evidence at trial) to state court proceedings.[44]
- *Escobedo v. Illinois,* which held that a state must afford the accused the right to counsel in a police station.[45]
- *Terry v. Ohio,* which upheld the right of the police to conduct threshold inquiries of suspicious persons when there is reason to believe that such persons may be armed and dangerous to the police or others.[46]
- *Miranda v. Arizona,* which defined the defendant's Fifth Amendment privilege against self-incrimination when taken into custody.[47]

- *Gideon v. Wainwright,* which established the right of the defendant in a felony trial to have counsel in a state prosecution.[48]
- *Argersinger v. Hamlin,* which extended the indigent defendant's right to counsel to all criminal cases where prison sentence could be imposed.[49]

As a result of these decisions and others affecting the adult process, children have been granted similar protections throughout the juvenile justice process.

Significant Supreme Court Decisions in Juvenile Law

The constitutional due process revolution in the adult system described above had a significant impact on the development of rights in the juvenile justice system. Within one decade—1966 to 1975—the Supreme Court handed down five major decisions affecting the equal rights of children within the jurisdiction of the juvenile court. A brief statement regarding each of these cases follows:

- *Kent v. United States (1966)* established that procedures concerning waiver (whether the juvenile court would hear a case or waive it to an adult court for trial) must measure up to the essentials of due process of law. A hearing, a right to counsel, and access to social records were required. This case was an important forerunner to the most significant juvenile decision by the Supreme Court, *In re Gault.*[50]
- *In re Gault (1967)* held that juveniles at trial, and faced with incarceration were entitled to many of the rights granted adult offenders. These included counsel, notice of the charges, cross-examination of witnesses, and protection against self-incrimination. *Gault* mandated a more formalized juvenile court system.[51]
- *In re Winship (1970)* ruled that the standard of proof in a delinquency proceeding that could result in a child's commitment must be "proof beyond a reasonable doubt" and not a "preponderance of the evidence." According to the Court, civil labels and good intentions do not obviate the need for criminal due process safeguards in juvenile courts.[52]
- *McKeiver v. Pennsylvania (1971)* held that juveniles were not to be afforded the constitutional right to a jury in a delinquency proceeding. The Court felt that this aspect of the adversarial process was not appropriate for the juvenile justice system.[53]
- *Breed v. Jones (1975)* established that the double jeopardy clause of the Fifth Amendment of the Constitution extends to juvenile offenders through the Fourteenth Amendment due process clause. Juveniles, henceforth, could not be tried in a juvenile court and transferred to an adult court for a similar action.[54]

Since 1975, the Supreme Court has decided a number of other important cases dealing with juvenile offenders:

- *Fare v. Michael C. (1979)* held that a child's request to see his probation officer at the time of interrogation did not operate to invoke his Fifth Amendment right to remain silent. According to the Court, the probation officer cannot be expected to offer the type of advice that an accused would expect from an attorney.[55]
- *Schall v. Martin (1984)* upheld a statute allowing for the placement of children in preventive detention before their trial. The Court concluded that it was not unreasonable to detain juveniles for their own protection.[56]

■ *New Jersey v. T.L.O. (1985)* determined that the Fourth Amendment applies to school searches. The Court adopted a "reasonable suspicion" standard, as opposed to "probable cause," to evaluate the legality of searches and seizures in a school setting.[57]

■ *Stanford v. Kentucky* and *Wilkins v. Missouri (1989)* concluded that the imposition of the death penalty on a juvenile who committed a crime between the ages of 16 and 18 was not unconstitutional and that the Eighth Amendment's cruel and unusual punishment clause did not prohibit capital punishment.[58]

In the hundred or so years that the juvenile court system has been in operation, the Supreme Court has heard very few cases dealing with juvenile delinquency proceedings. The most far-reaching was the *In re Gault* case of 1967, which extended the essentials of due process and fair treatment throughout the juvenile justice system.

Each of the above decisions is discussed in detail in subsequent chapters and is outlined in Figure 14.3.

The Due Process Revolution in Review

Although the *Gault* decision heralded the due process revolution, the movement toward broader procedural protections for juveniles was slowed by a more conservative Supreme Court in the 1970s. Chief Justice Warren Burger believed that the answer to the problems of the juvenile justice system was a return to the informality of the past. This view was operationalized in 1971, for example, in the case of *McKeiver v. Pennsylvania*.[59] The Court expressed its concern that juries in juvenile courts would impinge on the interests of the state and the public in

■■ **FIGURE 14.3**

Timeline of major constitutional decisions in juvenile justice

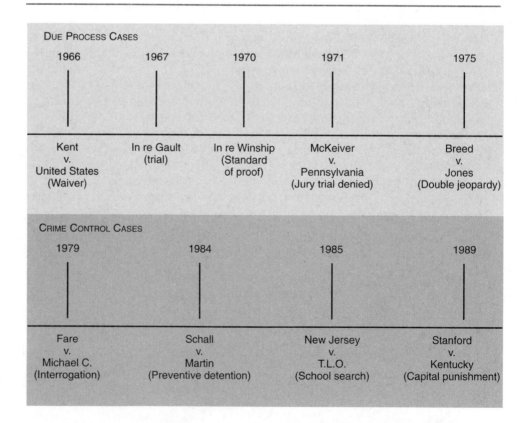

conducting juvenile court proceedings in an efficient, reasonably informal, and flexible manner. What the Court was saying was that a jury trial for juveniles was not essential to a fair and accurate fact-finding process in the juvenile court system.

In the 1980s, the Court continued to limit the expansion of juvenile rights with rulings that recognized the special needs of children. In the *Schall* case, the Court distinguished between adults and juveniles with respect to detaining them before trial, holding that juveniles could be denied bail and held for their own protection and the protection of society.[60] *Schall* played an important role because it dealt with the issue of preventive detention before trial, a process that affects all juvenile court systems. Similarly, in the *New Jersey v. T.L.O.* case, the Court limited the right of juveniles to be secure from search and seizures. In this case, the Court held that teachers had the right to search students if they violated school rules, even though the students were not suspected of a criminal law violation; adults would be legally immune from this type of search. The *T.L.O.* case concluded that school officials as representatives of the state may lawfully conduct searches without a warrant or probable cause.[61]

The future course of constitutional decisions affecting the rights of juveniles while William Rhenquist is chief justice and other conservatives, such as Antonin Scalia, Anthony Kennedy, and Clarence Thomas, are on the bench is difficult to ascertain. Another unknown is what role Justice Ruth Bader Ginsburg, the newest member of the Supreme Court, appointed by President Clinton in 1993, will play in children's rights issues. Certainly, the thrust of the Supreme Court has been clear over the past decade. Due process and fair treatment must be accorded juveniles throughout the entire juvenile justice process. However, the Court seems to be saying that the special status of minors gives the state the right to exercise legal controls from which an adult would be exempted. The *McKeiver*, *Schall*, and *T.L.O.* decisions appear to reflect a shift back to the informality and paternal protection of the juvenile court in preference to further formalizing court proceedings. Whether this trend will continue remains to be seen. However, as Justice Harry A. Blackmun stated in the *McKeiver* case, "If the formalities of the criminal adjudicative process are to be superimposed upon the juvenile court system, there is little need for its separate existence. Perhaps that ultimate disillusionment will come one day, but for the moment we are disinclined to give impetus to it."[62] Considering the makeup and direction of today's Court, we would expect to see Justice Blackmun's views taken quite seriously.[63]

The death penalty cases, on the other hand, seem to be a strong conservative reaction to liberal and ineffective crime-control programs.[64]

Given the more conservative mood of the nation and its legal system, it is unlikely that any liberalization of the legal rights of juveniles will take place in the near future. If anything, the Supreme Court will give states more opportunities to control minors. According to Samuel Davis, a leading expert on juvenile law, the court will most likely decide juvenile cases individually and apply the theory of due process under the Fourteenth Amendment to establish the child's constitutional rights in the future.[65]

For the time being, these cases affirm the Supreme Court's interest in applying constitutional principles of due process to juvenile justice while maintaining the *parens patriae* philosophy. In so doing, all the states are required to create juvenile court statutes that conform to the dictates of the Court.

In sum, the early cases from *Kent* to *Breed* provided due process protections for children; the latter cases, such as *Schall*, *T.L.O.*, and *Stanford*, rejected the rehabilitation ideal in favor of a punishment philosophy.[66]

Summary

The study of juvenile justice is concerned with juvenile delinquency and antisocial behavior and the agencies involved in their prevention, control, and treatment. The juvenile justice system is also a process consisting of the steps that a child takes from the initial investigation of a crime through the appeal of a case. These steps are the police investigation, the intake procedure in the juvenile court, the pretrial procedures used for juvenile offenders, adjudication, disposition, and the postdispositional procedures.

The juvenile system can be compared with the adult criminal justice system to show their similarities and differences in processing and terminology. The juvenile court is the heart of the juvenile process. Each jurisdiction organizes its court differently and has varying criteria. The most important factors determining jurisdiction are the age of the offender and the nature of his or her offense.

Over the past three decades, the courts have moved to eliminate the traditional view that a child brought into the juvenile justice system has no rights. Both the U.S. Supreme Court and the lower courts have granted children procedural safeguards and the protection of due process in the juvenile courts. Major Supreme Court and lower court decisions pertaining to the entire juvenile process have laid down the constitutional requirements for juvenile proceedings.[67] It is important to recognize that in years past, the protections currently afforded to both adults and children were not available to children.

How the juvenile justice system deals with the child is also determined by the multiple goals of the system and its individual agencies. There are a number of goals of juvenile justice, as stated by the National Advisory Commission on Criminal Justice Standards and Goals and the American Bar Association. The following are considered realistic strategies for juvenile justice: (1) delinquency prevention, (2) diversion, (3) incapacitation, (4) fairness and justice for children, and (5) efficiency and effectiveness. Depending upon the goals of juvenile justice, certain models or philosophies exist.

Juvenile justice is a very complex system and process whose many goals and strategies are often translated into day-to-day operations and programs. If professionals responsible for the administration of juvenile justice are to make progress against delinquency, the quest for knowledge and success must be based on clearly defined goals for the system. In addition, certain key agencies, such as the juvenile court and correctional institutions, must explore how they can deal with youths more comprehensively and effectively.

Key Terms

juvenile justice
Illinois Juvenile Court Act of 1989
parens patriae
juvenile justice system
systems approach
waive
predisposition report
detention hearing
adjudicatory hearing
disposition
petition
hearing
President's Commission on Law Enforcement and the Administration of Justice
National Advisory Commission on Criminal Justice Standards and Goals

Institute of Judicial Administration (IJA)
American Bar Association (ABA)
models of juvenile justice
status offenders
Kent v. United States (1966)
In re Gault (1967)
In re Winship (1971)
McKeiver v. Pennsylvania (1971)
Breed v. Jones (1975)
Fare v. Michael C. (1979)
Schall v. Martin (1984)
New Jersey v. T.L.O. (1985)
Stanford v. Kentucky and Wilkens v. Missouri (1989)

QUESTIONS FOR DISCUSSION

1. The terms *juvenile justice system* and *juvenile justice process* are often used synonymously. What is meant by each term, and how do they differ from each other?
2. The formal components of the criminal justice system are often considered to be the police, the court, and the correctional agency. How do these components compare with the major areas of the juvenile justice system? Is the operation of justice similar in the juvenile and adult systems?
3. Which philosophy of juvenile justice do you hold? What do you believe is wrong with the other philosophies?
4. Should there be a juvenile justice system, or should juveniles who commit serious crimes be treated as adults and the others be handled by social welfare agencies?
5. The Supreme Court has made a number of major decisions in the area of juvenile justice. What are these decisions? What is their impact on the juvenile justice system?
6. What is the meaning of the term *procedural due process of law*? Explain why and how procedural due process has had an impact on juvenile justice.
7. The juvenile court is considered a specialized court for children. How is it organized and why?
8. What are the differences between the justice and the rehabilitation models of juvenile justice?

NOTES

1. See *Report of the Task Force on Juvenile Justice and Delinquency Prevention, Juvenile Justice and Delinquency Prevention* (Washington, D.C.: Government Printing Office, 1976); and for a more current blueprint on reform, see Ira M. Schwartz, ed., *Juvenile Justice and Public Policy—Toward a National Agenda* (New York: Lexington Books, 1992).
2. Martin Forst and Martha Elin Blomquist, "Punishment, Accountability, and the Juvenile Justice System," *Juvenile and Family Court Journal* 43:1 (1992).
3. See, generally, Paul Kfoury, *Children before the Court: Reflections on Legal Issues Affecting Minors* (Boston: Butterworth's Legal Group, 1987); also see Francis Allen, *The Decline of the Rehabilitative Ideal* (New Haven: Yale University Press, 1981).
4. See, generally, President's Commission on Law Enforcement and the Administration of Justice, *The Challenge of Crime in a Free Society* (Washington, D.C.: Government Printing Office, 1967); National Advisory Commission on Criminal Justice Standards and Goals, *Report of the Task Force on Juvenile Justice and Delinquency Prevention* (Washington, D.C.: Law Enforcement Assistance Administration, 1976); American Bar Association and Institute of Judicial Administration, *Standards for Juvenile Justice: A Summary and Analysis* (Cambridge, Mass.: Ballinger, 1980); the OJJDP's Juvenile Justice Clearinghouse offers all twenty-four volumes of *Juvenile Justice Standards*, reprinted 1992.
5. See Herbert Lou, *Juvenile Courts in the United States* (Charlotte: University of North Carolina Press, 1927); also *Commonwealth v. Fisher*, 213 Pa. 48 (1905).
6. National Advisory Commission on Criminal Justice Standards and Goals, *Report of the Task Force on Juvenile*

Justice and Delinquency Prevention, p. 6. See how the principles of the Illinois Court have changed in Barry Feld, "The Punitive Juvenile Court and Quality of Procedural Justice: Disjunctions between Rhetoric and Reality," *Crime and Delinquency* 36:443–61 (1990).
7. See, for example, *Ex Parte Sharp*, Idaho 126, 96 P. 563 (1908). The Idaho Supreme Court upheld the right of the juvenile court to apply the *parens patriae* doctrine.
8. Timothy J. Flanagan, ed., *Sourcebook of Criminal Justice Statistics, 1991* (Washington, D.C.: Government Printing Office, 1992); National Institute of Juvenile Justice and Delinquency Prevention, *Annual Report 1990* (Washington, D.C.: U.S. Department of Justice, 1991).
9. Information in this section comes from a variety of sources, including Flanigan, *Sourcebook of Criminal Justice Statistics, 1991;* (Washington, D.C.: Government Printing Office, 1992) FBI, *Uniform Crime Reports, 1991;* National Institute of Juvenile Justice and Delinquency Prevention, *Annual Report 1990.*
10. See, generally, Herbert Packer, *The Limits of the Criminal Sanction* (Palo Alto, Calif.: Stanford University Press, 1968); see also Joseph Senna, "Models of Justice: Building Blocks for Change," *Judicature* 59:34–41 (1975).
11. National Advisory Commission on Criminal Justice Standards and Goals, *Report of the Task Force on Juvenile Justice and Delinquency Prevention*, p. 730.
12. Ibid., p. 720.
13. For an excellent review of the juvenile process, see Adrienne Volenik, *Checklists for Use in Juvenile Delinquency Proceedings* (Washington, D.C.: American Bar Association, 1985).

14. Barry Feld, "Criminology the Juvenile Court: A Research Agenda for the 1990s." In Ira M. Schwartz, *Juvenile Justice and Public Policy—Toward a National Agenda* (New York: Lexington Books, 1992), p. 59.

15. Robert O. Dawson, "The Future of Juvenile Justice: Is It Time to Abolish the System?" *Journal of Criminal Law and Criminology* 81:136–55 (1990).

16. President's Commission on Law Enforcement and the Administration of Justice, *The Challenge of Crime in a Free Society*, p. 88.

17. Juvenile Delinquency Prevention and Control Act of 1968.

18. Public Law 90–351, Title I—Omnibus Safe Streets and Crime Control Act of 1968, 90th Congress, 19 June 1968.

19. National Advisory Commission on Criminal Justice Standards and Goals, *A National Strategy to Reduce Crime* (Washington, D.C.: Government Printing Office, 1973).

20. Idem, *Report of the Task Force on Juvenile Justice and Delinquency Prevention*, pp. 11–14.

21. Juvenile Justice and Delinquency Prevention Act of 1974, Public Law 93–415 (1974). Funding under this act has declined from $100 million in 1979 to $70 million in 1981, $66 million in 1989, and about $60 million for 1993.

22. See *The Juvenile Courts' Response to Violent Crime*, UJJDP (1989).

23. "Congress Makes Changes in Juvenile Justice Law," *Criminal Justice Newsletter* 23:1 (1992).

24. U.S. Congress, Senate. The Juvenile Justice and Delinquency Prevention Act Report No. 95–165, 95th Cong., 1977.

25. See American Bar Association, Testimony of Robert Schwartz before Committee on the Judiciary, U.S. Senate, re: Juvenile Justice and Delinquency Act, March 1992.

26. See American Bar Association and Institute of Justice Administration, *Standards for Juvenile Justice*.

27. Andrew von Hirsch, *Doing Justice* (New York: Hill and Wang, 1976).

28. David Gilman, "IJA-ABA Juvenile Justice Standards Project: An Introduction," *Boston University Law Review* 57:622–23 (1977).

29. Ira M. Schwartz, *In Justice for Juveniles—Rethinking the Best Interests of the Child* (Lexington, Mass.: D.C. Heath & Co., 1989), p. 164.

30. Forst and Blomquist, "Punishment, Accountability, and the New Juvenile Justice"; also Thomas Bernard, *The Cycle of Juvenile Justice* (New York: Oxford University Press, 1992).

31. Robert Smith, "The Elephant in My Living Room," *Crime and Delinquency* 33: 317–24 (1987); also "Racial Disparity in California Juvenile Justice System," *Youth Law News: Journal of National Center for Youth Law* 5:10–11 (1992).

32. National Advisory Commission on Criminal Justice Standards and Goals, *Report of the Task Force on Juvenile Justice and Delinquency Prevention*, p. 277.

33. See N.Y. Fam. Ct. Act 712 (1982).

34. See Samuel Davis, *The Rights of Juveniles*, 2d. ed. (update 1992; New York: Clark Boardman, 1984); also Mark Soler, James Bell, Elizabeth Jameson, Carole Shauffer, Alice Shotton, and Loren Warboys, *Representing the Child Client* (New York: Matthew Bender, 1992).

35. *Lamb v. Brown*, 456 F.2d 18 (1972).

36. Mass. Gen. Laws Ann. Ch. 119, 53 (1979).

37. Md.Cts. & Jud.Proc. Code Ann. 3–804(d)(1)(4) (1980).

38. Fla. Stat. Ann. 39.025(5)(c)(Supp. 1982); Fla. Stat.Ann. 39.04 (2)(E)(4) (Supp. 1981).

39. N.Y. Fam.Ct.Act 73(1)(C) and 732(c) (McKinney Supp. 1979).

40. 359 Mass. 550 (1971); 322 A.2d 58(1975).

41. State ex rel. *Harris v. Calendine*, 33 S.E.2d 318 (1977).

42. *O. W. v. Bird*, 461 So.2d 967 (Fla.Dist.Ct.App. 1984); *In re Michael G.*, 214 Cal.Rptr. 755 App. Ct. 1(1985).

43. *In re A*, 130 N.J.Super.Ct. 138, 325 A.2d 837 (1974).

44. 367 U.S. 643, 81 S.Ct. 1684 (1961).

45. 378 U.S. 478, 84 S.Ct. 1758 (1964).

46. 392 U.S. 1, 88 S.Ct. 1868 (1968).

47. 384 U.S. 436, 86 S.Ct. 1602 (1966).

48. 372 U.S. 355, 83 S.Ct. 792 (1963).

49. 407 U.S. 25, 92 S.Ct. 2006 (1972).

50. 383 U.S. 541 (1966).

51. 387 U.S. 1, 19 (1967).

52. 397 U.S. 358, 90 S.Ct. 1068 (1970).

53. 403 U.S. 528, 91 S.Ct. 1976 (1971).

54. 421 U.S. 519 (1975).

55. 442 U.S. 707 (1979).

56. 467 U.S. 253 (1984).

57. 469 U.S. 325 (1985).

58. 492 U.S. (1989).

59. *McKeiver v. Pennsylvania*, 403 U.S. 528 (1971), at 538.

60. *Schall v. Martin*, 467 U.S. 253 (1984).

61. *New Jersey v. T.L.O.*, 469 U.S. 325 (1985).

62. Ibid., p. 538.

63. For differing views of juvenile justice legal policy, see H. Ted Rubin, *Behind the Black Robe—Juvenile Court Judges and the Court* (Beverly Hills, Calif.: Sage, 1985).

64. Sandra Evans Skouron, Joseph Scott, and Francis Cullen, "The Death Penalty for Juveniles: An Assessment of Public Support," *Crime and Delinquency* 45:562–76 (1989); also Dinah Robinson and Stephen Otis, "Patterns of Mitigating Factors in Juvenile Death Penalty Cases," *Criminal Law Bulletin* 28:246–62 (1992).

65. Davis, *The Rights of Juveniles*, pp. 7–12.

66. See Jay S. Albanese, *Dealing with Delinquency—The Future of Juvenile Justice* (Chicago: Nelson-Hall, 1992), p. 122.

67. See Barry Feld, "The Juvenile Court Meets the Principle of the Offense: Legislative Changes in Juvenile Waiver Statutes," *Journal of Criminal Law and Criminology* 78:471 (1987).

V CONTROLLING JUVENILE OFFENDERS

▪ ▪

Controlling juvenile delinquency is a complex task. While adults who violate the law are subject to clearly defined sanctions, the *parens patriae* philosophy demands that the state always consider the best interests of the child when controlling juvenile behavior. The line between treatment and punishment, however, is often a narrow one. When do the efforts of people truly desiring to help troubled youngsters actually become a crushing burden on them? Is it possible that the doctrine of *parens patriae* goes too far? These are questions that constantly perplex juvenile justice policymakers. Is it possible to create a system in which troubled juveniles are helped using the least restrictive alternatives possible, while at the same time serious juvenile offenders are restrained? Should we be more punitive than we have been, or should we employ even greater compassion and understanding? Or does the answer lie somewhere in between?

Part V contains three chapters devoted to the process and policies used to control juvenile offenders. Chapter 15 deals with police handling of delinquent and status offenders. It contains information on the police role, the organization of police services, and prevention efforts. It explores the power of a police officer to take a child into custody and the rights of the child when arrested and outlines the applicability of *Miranda v. Arizona* to the juvenile process. This chapter also points out how the U.S. Supreme Court has expressly found that juveniles fall within the protection of the Fourth Amendment. Chapter 16 is concerned with the important topic of early court processing. It describes such current issues as diversion programs, removal of minor offenders from secure detention facilities, and the transfer of youths to adult courts. The "transfer of jurisdiction" issue, often called waiver, remand, or removal to the criminal court, is a unique statutory process. Chapter 17 discusses the equally important topic of juvenile trial and disposition. It considers the role of the prosecutor, the juvenile court judge, and the defense attorney at adjudication and disposition. Since juveniles, as well as adults, are entitled to fair trials, this chapter concerns itself with a detailed analysis of the landmark constitutional decisions on juvenile justice. Next, it deals with disposition and sentencing—the key element in the juvenile process.

After reading these chapters, the student should have an understanding of how society has attempted to control juvenile offenders, beginning with the prejudicial process and concluding with the disposition. ▪

POLICE WORK
WITH JUVENILES

The modern juvenile justice system is the primary source of efforts to control juvenile crime. Other segments of society—the family, the political system, the schools, and religious institutions—play a role, but social control rests mainly with the juvenile justice system. As its law enforcement and social control arm, the police, therefore, become the frontline agency that deals with the prevention and control of juvenile delinquency.

Traditionally, the primary responsibility of the police has been to protect the public. In the minds of most citizens, that is still their most important responsibility. From the vast array of films, books, and TV shows that depict the derring-do of police officers in the field, the public has obtained an image of "crime fighters" who "always get their man." Since the tumultuous 1960s, the public has become increasingly aware that the reality of police work is quite a bit different from its fictional glorification. When police departments failed to bring the crime rate down despite massive government subsidies, when citizens complained of civil rights violations, and when tales of police corruption became widespread, it was evident that a crisis was imminent in American policing.

During the 1980s and early 1990s, a new view of policing emerged around the nation. Rather than foster the view of the police officer as a hell-bent-for-leather crime fighter who only tracks down serious criminals or stops armed robberies in progress, police departments adopted the concept that the police role should be to maintain order in the community, interact with citizens, and be a visible and accessible component of the community. The argument is that police efforts can only be successful if they are conducted in partnership with concerned and active citizens. This movement is referred to as **community policing.**[1]

Interest in the community policing concept does not mean that the crime-control model of law enforcement is past history. An ongoing effort is being made to improve the crime-fighting capability of police agencies, and there are some indications that the effort is being rewarded. Recent research indicates that aggressive, formal action by the police can help reduce the incidence of repeat offending.[2] And technological innovations, such as fingerprint-reading computers, may bring about greater police efficiency. Nonetheless, after twenty-five years of attempting to improve police effectiveness through a combination of policy and technical advancement, little evidence exists that adding police or improving their skills has a major impact on their crime-fighting success.[3]

During this era in which experts are rethinking the basic police role, the relationship between police and juvenile offenders has become quite critical. Because police officers represent the authority of the community, even the most casual meeting between a police officer and a child can have a profound effect on the youth's future. How the child reacts to this authority may depend on the police officer's response to the child's behavior. This more often than not depends on the officer's personal biases and values, as well as his or her role orientation and attitudes toward police work. Working with juvenile offenders may be especially perplexing for police officers since the need to help young people and guide them away from a criminal career may seem to be in conflict with the traditional police duties of crime prevention and order maintenance. In addition, the police are faced with a nationwide adolescent drug problem, increases in the violent crime arrest rate for teens, and renewed gang activity. While efforts are being made to improve adult crime control efforts of the police, it may also be necessary to increase specialized services for juveniles.

This chapter focuses on police work in juvenile justice and delinquency prevention. It covers the role and responsibilities of the police; the history of policing juveniles; the organization and management of police-juvenile operations; the legal aspects of police work, including custodial interrogation, search and seizure, and lineups; the concept of police discretion; and the relationship between the police and community efforts to prevent crime.

THE ROLE OF THE POLICE IN HANDLING JUVENILE OFFENDERS

How do juvenile officers spend their time and what roles do they perform in the overall police and criminal justice system? **Juvenile officers** either operate alone as specialists within a police department or as part of the juvenile unit of a police department. Their role is similar to that of officers working with adult offenders—to intervene if the actions of a citizen produce public danger or disorder. Most officers regard the violations of juveniles as nonserious unless they are committed by a chronic troublemaker or involve significant damage to persons or property. Juveniles who misbehave are often ignored or treated informally. Police encounters with juveniles are generally the result of reports made by citizens, and the bulk of such encounters pertain to matters of minor legal consequence.[4]

Of course, police must also deal with serious juvenile offenders whose criminal acts are similar to those of adults, but these are only a small minority of the offender population. Thus, police who deal with delinquency must concentrate on being peacekeepers and crime preventers.[5]

Handling juvenile offenders can produce major **role conflicts** for the police. They may find what they consider their primary duty, **law enforcement,** undercut by the need to aid in the rehabilitation of youthful offenders. A police officer's actions in cases involving adults are usually controlled by the rule of criminal law and his or her own personal judgment, or **discretion.** In contrast, a case involving a juvenile often demands that the officer consider the "best interests of the child" and how the officer's actions will influence the child's future life and well-being. Consequently, police are much more likely to use informal procedures with juvenile offenders than with adults. It is estimated that between 30 and 40 percent of all juveniles arrested by police are handled informally within the police department or referred to a community service agency (see Figure 15.1). These informal dispositions are the result of the police officer's discretionary authority, discussed later in this chapter.[6]

Many officers dislike getting involved in juvenile matters, probably because most juvenile crimes are held in low regard by fellow police officers.[7] Juvenile detectives are sometimes referred to as the "Lollipop Squad" or "Diaper Dicks." The field of juvenile law is often referred to as "Kiddie Court." Arresting a 12-year-old girl for shoplifting and bringing her in tears to the police station is not considered the way to win respect from one's peers.

Police intervention in these disorder situations is difficult and frustrating. The officer often encounters hostile or belligerent behavior. Overreaction by the officer creates the possibility of a major violent incident. Even if the officer succeeds in quieting or dispersing the crowd, the problem will probably reappear the next day, often in the same place.[8]

Role conflicts are often exacerbated because most police-juvenile encounters involve confrontations brought about by loitering, disturbing the peace, and

FIGURE 15.1

To understand how police deal with juvenile crime, picture a funnel, with the result shown here. For every 500 juveniles taken into custody, a little over 60 percent are sent to the juvenile court and almost 33 percent are released.

Source: Timothy J. Flanagan and Kathleen Maguire, eds., *Sourcebook of Criminal Justice Statistics 1991* (Washington, D.C.: U.S. Department of Justice, Bureau of Justice Statistics, 1992), p. 467.

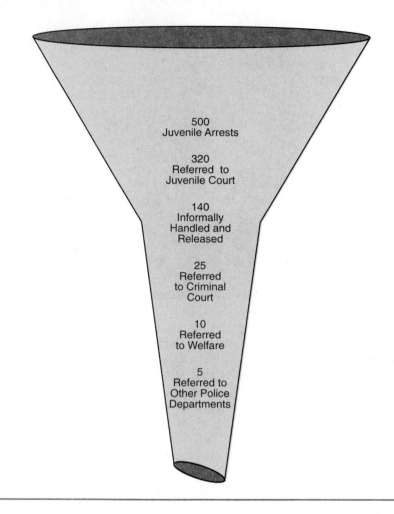

500
Juvenile Arrests

320
Referred to
Juvenile Court

140
Informally
Handled and
Released

25
Referred
to Criminal
Court

10
Referred
to Welfare

5
Referred to
Other Police
Departments

rowdiness, rather than by serious law violations. Dealing with youth problems brings little of the rewards or job satisfaction desired by police officers.

What role should the police take in mediating problems with youths—hardline law enforcement or social service-oriented delinquency prevention? The International Association of Chiefs of Police sees the solution as lying somewhere in between: "Most police departments operate juvenile programs that combine the law enforcement and delinquency prevention roles, and the police should work with the juvenile court to determine a role that is most suitable for the community."[9] In fact, police officers may also act as juvenile prosecutors in some rural courts when attorneys are not available. Thus, the police-juvenile role extends from the on-street encounter to the station house to the juvenile court. It seems that for juvenile matters involving minor criminal conduct or incorrigible behavior, the police ordinarily select the "least restrictive alternative" course of action. Such courses include nonintervention, temporary assistance, and referral to community agencies. Serious juvenile crime, on the other hand, requires that the police investigate, arrest, and even detain youths while providing constitutional safeguards similar to those available to adult offenders.

HISTORY OF POLICING JUVENILES

The origin of U.S. police agencies can be traced to early English society.[10] Before the Norman conquest of England, individuals were responsible for aiding neighbors and protecting each other from thieves and warring groups. This was known as the pledge system. People were entrusted with policing their own minor problems. By the thirteenth century, the watch system was created to help patrol England's larger communities. This was followed by the establishment of the constable, who was responsible for dealing with more serious crimes. By the seventeenth century, the constable, the justice of the peace, and the night watcher formed the nucleus of the local police system.

When the industrial revolution brought thousands of people from the countryside to work in English urban factories, the need for police protection increased. As a result, the first organized police force was established in London in 1829. The early "bobbies," as they were called, were often corrupt, unsuccessful at stopping crime, and influenced by the wealthy for personal political gain.[11]

By the mid-nineteenth century, children began to emerge as a distinguishable group. The Poor Laws, the apprenticeship movement, and the restricted family structure, as described in Chapter 13, all affected the juvenile legal system. When children violated the law, they were often treated in the same way as adult offenders. But even at this stage, a belief existed that the enforcement of criminal law should be applied differently to children.

Law enforcement in colonial America followed the English model. In the colonies, the local sheriff became the most important police official. By the mid-1800s, formal police departments were created in such cities as Boston, New York, and Philadelphia. Police work was primitive, officers patrolled on foot, and conflict often arose between untrained officers and the public.

During the latter portion of the nineteenth century, the problems of how to deal effectively with growing numbers of unemployed, undisciplined, and homeless youths increased. Twentieth-century groups, such as the Wickersham Commission of 1931 and the International Association of Chiefs of Police, became the leading voices for police reform.[12] Their efforts resulted in the creation of specialized police units, known as delinquency control squads.

The most famous police reformer of the 1930s was August Vollmer. As the police chief of Berkeley, California, Vollmer instituted numerous professional reforms, including university training, modern management techniques, prevention programs, and juvenile aid bureaus.[13] These bureaus were generally the first organized special police services for juvenile offenders.

Beginning in the 1960s, police work experienced turmoil, crises, and constant reformation. The U.S. Supreme Court handed down decisions designed to control police operations and procedures. Civil unrest produced growing tensions between police and the public. Urban police departments were unable to handle the growing crime rate. With federal funding from the LEAA, hundreds of new police programs were developed, police operations greatly influenced, and police services for children further enhanced. Even the police role seemed to change from one where the police were simply crime fighters to one marked by a greater awareness of community issues and crime prevention. This resulted in the emergence of the community policing concept, which is discussed at the end of this chapter.

By the 1980s, most urban police departments recognized that juvenile delinquency required special attention, although the degree of commitment to this approach varied from one department to another.

The role of the juvenile police officer (one assigned to juvenile work) has taken on added importance, particularly with the increase in violent juvenile and gang-related crime. Today, the majority of the nation's urban law enforcement agencies have specialized juvenile police programs. Typically, such programs involve (1) prevention (police athletic league, DARE, and community relations), and (2) law enforcement work (juvenile court, school policing, or gang control).[14]

In sum, specialized police work with children goes back to the first juvenile court in 1899 in Illinois.[15] While public interest in juvenile delinquency has focused less on police practices with juveniles than on the juvenile court process itself, law enforcement agents continue to be the front-end of the juvenile justice system. They are the primary referral source for juvenile law violators; they exercise discretion as to whether to arrest a youth; and they often determine whether an arrested youth should be diverted to a community agency or referred to court.

ORGANIZATION OF POLICE SERVICES FOR JUVENILES

The problem of juvenile delinquency and youth crime used to receive little attention from most municipal police departments. Even when juvenile crime was increasing during the 1960s, 1970s, and 1980s, police resources were generally geared to adult offenders. However, the alarming increase in serious juvenile crime in the past few years has made it obvious that the police can no longer neglect youthful antisocial behavior. They need to assign resources to the problem and have the proper organization for coping with it. The theory and

The number of police officers assigned to juvenile work has increased in recent years. Today, even relatively small departments may have an officer who specializes in juvenile crime.

Part V Controlling Juvenile Offenders

practice of police organization have recently undergone many changes, and as a result, police departments are giving greater emphasis to the juvenile function.

The organization of juvenile work depends on the size of the police department, the kind of community in which the department is located, and the amount and quality of resources available in the community. Today, most police agencies recognize that juvenile crime requires special attention.

The police who work with juvenile offenders usually have special skills and talents that go beyond those generally associated with regular police work. In large urban police departments, juvenile services are often established through a special unit. Ordinarily this unit is the responsibility of a command-level police officer. The unit commander assigns officers to deal with juvenile problems throughout the police department's jurisdiction. Police departments with very few officers have little need for an internal division with special functions. Most small departments make one officer responsible for handling juvenile matters for the entire community.

In either large or small departments, it cannot be assumed that only police officers assigned to work with juveniles will be involved in handling juvenile offenses. When officers on patrol encounter a youngster committing a crime, they are responsible for dealing with the problem initially. However, they generally refer the case to the juvenile unit or the juvenile police officer to follow up. In working with adult offenders, most police officers are concerned primarily about the type of offense the suspect has committed. When working with young people, the juvenile officer is concerned with what to do in cases that cannot be handled with on-the-scene referrals to families or social agencies.[16]

The number of police officers assigned to juvenile work has increased in recent years. The International Association of Chiefs of Police found that approximately five hundred departments of the fourteen hundred surveyed in 1960 had juvenile units. By 1970, the number of police departments with a juvenile specialist had doubled. Today, even relatively small departments have a juvenile specialist.[17] Figure 15.2 illustrates the major elements of a police department organization dealing with juvenile offenders.

Most juvenile officers are appointed after they have had some general patrol experience. A desire to work with juveniles and a basic understanding of human

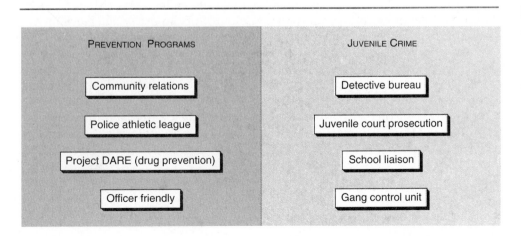

Typical urban police department organization chart with juvenile justice component

behavior are generally considered essential for the job.[18] Juvenile officers should have an aptitude for working with young people.[19]

POLICE AND THE RULE OF LAW

While serving as a primary source of referral and diversion of youth from juvenile court, the police are simultaneously required to investigate criminal activity and take children into custody in appropriate cases. Their actions are controlled by statute, constitutional case law, and judicial review. The following methods of police investigation and control in dealing with juvenile offenders are discussed below: (1) the arrest procedure; (2) search and seizure; (3) custodial interrogation; and (4) juvenile lineups.

The Arrest Procedure

Judicial limitations on police discretion in the investigation of offenses involving juveniles are similar to the limitations applied to adult offenders. When a juvenile is apprehended, the police must decide whether to release the child or refer him or her to the juvenile court. Cases involving serious crimes against property or persons are often referred to court. On the other hand, minor disputes between juveniles, school and neighborhood complaints, petty shoplifting cases, runaways, and assaults and batteries of minors are often diverted from court action.

Most states require that the law of **arrest** is the same for both adults and juveniles. To make a legal arrest, an officer must have **probable cause** to believe that an offense took place and that the suspect is the guilty party. Probable cause is usually defined as falling somewhere between a mere suspicion and absolute certainty. In misdemeanor cases, the police officer must personally observe the crime to place a suspect in custody. For a felony, police officers may arrest if they have probable cause to believe the crime has occurred and the person has committed it, as well as if they observe the offense.

The main difference between arrests of adult and juvenile offenders is the broader latitude police have to control youthful behavior. Police can arrest youths for status offenses, such as truancy, running away, and possession of alcohol; adults would be immune to arrest for such acts. Most existing juvenile codes, for instance, provide broad authority for the police to take juveniles into custody.[20] Such statutes are designed to give the police the authority to act *in loco parentis*. According to Samuel Davis, the broad power granted to police is consistent with the notion that a juvenile is not arrested but "taken into custody," which implies a protective and not a punitive form of detention.[21] Once a juvenile is formally arrested, however, the constitutional safeguards of the Fourth and Fifth Amendments available to adults are applicable to the juvenile as well.

Section 13 of the Uniform Juvenile Court Act, created by the National Conference of Commissioners on Uniform State Laws, is an excellent example of the statutory provisions typically used in state codes regarding juvenile arrest procedures.

Section 13.[taking into custody.]
(a) A child may be taken into custody:
    (1) pursuant to an order of the court under this Act;
    (2) pursuant to the laws of arrest;

(3) by a law enforcement officer [or duly authorized officer of the court] if there are reasonable grounds to believe that the child is suffering from illness or injury or is in immediate danger from his surroundings, and that his removal is necessary; or

(4) by a law enforcement officer [or duly authorized officer of the court] if there are reasonable grounds to believe that the child has run away from his parents, guardian, or other custodian.

(b) The taking of a child into custody is not an arrest, except for the purpose of determining its validity under the constitution of this State or of the United States.[22]

Search and Seizure

Do juveniles have the same constitutional right to be free from unreasonable **search and seizure** as adults? In general, a citizen's privacy is protected by the Constitution's Fourth Amendment, which states:

The right of the people to be secure in their persons, houses, papers, and effects, against unreasonable searches and seizures, shall not be violated, and no warrants shall issue, but upon probable cause, supported by oaths or affirmation, and particularly describing the place to be searched, and the persons or things to be seized.

Most courts in state jurisdictions have held that the Fourth Amendment ban against unreasonable search and seizure applies to juveniles in delinquency proceedings and that illegally seized evidence is inadmissible in a juvenile trial. To exclude incriminating evidence, a child's attorney makes a pretrial motion to suppress the evidence—the same procedure that is used in the adult criminal process. Virtually all lower court decisions that have considered this issue have mentioned this view. In *State v. Lowry*, the court stated:

Is it not more outrageous for the police to treat children more harshly than adult offenders, especially when such is violative of due process and fair treatment? Can a court countenance a system, where, as here, an adult may suppress evidence with the usual effect of having the charges dropped for lack of proof, and on the other hand a juvenile can be institutionalized—lose the most sacred possession a human being has, his freedom—for "rehabilitative" purposes because the Fourth Amendment right is unavailable to him?[23]

A full discussion of search and seizure is beyond the scope of this text, but it is important to note that the Supreme Court has ruled that police may stop a suspect and search for and seize evidence without a search warrant under certain circumstances. A person may be searched after a legal arrest but then only in the immediate area of the suspect's control: for example, after an arrest for possession of drugs, the pockets of a suspect's jacket may be searched;[24] an automobile may be searched if there is probable cause to believe a crime has taken place;[25] a suspect's outer garments may be frisked if police are suspicious of his or her activities;[26] and a search may be conducted if a person volunteers for the search.[27] These rules are usually applied to juveniles as well as to adults. However, two differences between adult and juvenile law make it somewhat easier for police to conduct searches of suspected delinquent offenders. First, juveniles can be arrested for *status offenses,* such as curfew violations or truancy, and police can legally search them after such an arrest is made. Furthermore, most courts have upheld the right of parents to give police permission or the right to search the rooms and possessions of their minor children.[28] However, a child's

The case of *New Jersey v. T.L.O.* allowed police and school officials to search students without probable cause that a crime has been committed. The legality of school locker searches has not been as clearly defined.

consent to search his home because he believed drugs were in his parent's bedroom was declared invalid after the court held that he did not possess sufficient maturity to agree to the search.[29] Cases involving a child's consent are often difficult to decide because the court is required to evaluate if the child knew or understood what the consequences of his or her consent would be.

Search and Seizure in Schools

One major issue of search and seizure in juvenile law is the right of school officials to search students and their possessions on school grounds and turn over evidence to the police. Searches of students' persons or lockers become necessary when it is believed that students are in the process of violating the law. Drug abuse, theft, assault and battery, and racial conflicts in schools have increased the need to take action against troublemakers. School administrators have questioned students about their illegal activities, conducted searches of students' persons and possessions, and reported suspicious behavior to the police.

In the 1985 landmark decision, **New Jersey v. T.L.O.,** the Supreme Court helped clarify one of the most vexing problems of school searches: whether the Fourth Amendment's prohibition against unreasonable searches and seizures applies to school officials as well as police officers.[30] In this important case, set out in the accompanying Focus on Delinquency, the Court found that students are in fact constitutionally protected from illegal searches but that school officials are not bound by the same restrictions as law enforcement agents. While police need "probable cause" before a search can be undertaken, educators can legally search students when there are reasonable grounds that the students have violated the law or broken school rules. In creating this distinction, the Court recognized the needs of school officials to preserve an environment conducive to education and to secure the safety of their students.

One of the most significant questions left unanswered by *New Jersey v. T.L.O.* is whether teachers and other school officials can search school lockers and desks. Here, the law has been controlled by state decisions, and each jurisdiction may create its own standards. Some allow teachers a free hand in opening lockers and desks.[31] However, not all school districts allow warrantless searches, holding as New Jersey did in *State v. Engerud:*

[W]e are satisfied that in the context of this case the student had an expectation of privacy in the contents of his locker. . . . For the four years of high school, the school locker is a home away from home. In it the student stores the kind of personal "effects" protected by the Fourth Amendment.[32]

These and other lower court decisions have helped establish, limit, and define the scope of the school's authority to search lockers and desks.[33]

However, faced with increased crime by students in public schools, particularly illicit drug use, school administrators today are inclined to enforce drug control statutes and administrative rules.[34] Some urban schools are using breathalyzers, drug-sniffing dogs, hidden video cameras, and routine searches of students' pockets, purses, lockers, and cars.[35] In general, courts consider such searches permissible when they are not overly offensive and where there are reasonable grounds to suspect that the student may have violated the law.[36] School administrators are walking a tightrope between students' constitutional right to privacy and school safety.[37]

Of the eighteen reported cases decided by state appellate courts that applied the *T.L.O.* standard since 1985, the intervention by school officials was upheld in fifteen.[38] The apparent basis for the opinions was the court's interest in preserving safety in the school system. As Judge White in *T.L.O.* stated:

Maintaining order in the classroom has never been easy, but in recent years, school disorder has often taken particularly ugly forms: drug use and violent crime in the schools have become major social problems. Annual surveys show over three million crimes occur on school campuses in America.[39]

Faced with this crisis, state courts have not hesitated to lessen the applicability of the Fourth Amendment in a school setting.

In summary, the critical issue with regard to the rights of the child and school searches is the extent of the student's Fourth Amendment protection against unreasonable search and seizure as compared with the extent of the school's authority to conduct searches and the duty of educators to protect other students. Have children lost some of their constitutional rights at the schoolhouse gate as a result of the *T.L.O.* decision?

New Jersey v. T.L.O.

FACTS

On March 7, 1980, a teacher at Piscataway High in Middlesex County, New Jersey, discovered two girls smoking in a lavatory. Because this was in violation of school rules, he reported the incident to the principal's office, and the girls were summoned to meet with assistant vice principal Theodore Choplick, who questioned them about their behavior. When one of the girls, T.L.O., claimed she had done nothing wrong, the assistant vice principal demanded to see her purse. When he examined it, he found a pack of cigarettes and also noticed a package of cigarette rolling papers, which are generally associated with the use of marijuana. He then searched the purse thoroughly and found some marijuana, a pipe, a substantial amount of money, a list of students who owed T.L.O. money, and letters implicating her in marijuana dealing. Choplick then informed both T.L.O.'s mother and the police about the evidence he uncovered. Later at the police station, T.L.O. confessed to dealing drugs on campus.

Based on her confession and the evidence recovered from her purse, the state proceeded against T.L.O. in the juvenile court. Her motion to suppress the evidence taken during the school search was rejected by the trial court on the grounds that school officials could search students if they had reasonable cause to believe that the search was necessary to maintain school discipline or enforce school policies; consequently, T.L.O. was found delinquent and sentenced to a year's probation. T.L.O.'s subsequent appeal of the decision was eventually upheld by the New Jersey Supreme Court on the grounds that Choplick's search of T.L.O.'s purse was not justified under the circumstances of the case. The state appealed to the U.S. Supreme Court.

DECISION

The Supreme Court held that the prohibitions against illegal search and seizure apply to school as well as law enforcement officials. Teachers are not merely substitute parents but agents of the state who are required to carry out state policy and law. Students do not give up their constitutional rights when they walk on school property. However, school officials also have to maintain an atmosphere that is conducive to learning. A balance must be achieved between a student's right to privacy and the school's need to provide a safe, secure environment. Therefore, the Court ruled that teachers do not need to obtain a warrant before searching a student who is under their authority. In addition, the search need not be based on probable cause to believe that a crime has taken place; rather the legality of the search of a student should depend simply on its reasonableness, considering the scope of the search, the age and sex of the student, and the behavior that prompted it to be made. Of considerable importance is the fact that school searches were found to be justified if a student was suspected of violating the law or of violating school rules. Considering this standard, the search of T.L.O. was found to be justified, since the report of her smoking created a reasonable suspicion that she had cigarettes in her purse and the discovery of the rolling papers then gave rise to a reasonable suspicion that she was in possession of marijuana.

SIGNIFICANCE OF THE CASE

By giving teachers and other school officials the right to search students if they are suspected of being in violation of school rules, the Court established a significant difference between the due process rights of adults and juveniles. An adult could not be legally searched by an agent of the government under the same circumstances under which T.L.O. was searched. Thus, the *T.L.O.* decision is in keeping with the judicial philosophy espoused in cases such as *Schall v. Martin* and *McKeiver v. Pennsylvania*, which find that juveniles, for their own protection, may be denied certain constitutional safeguards available to adults.

As a practical matter, *New Jersey v. T.L.O.* opens the door for greater security measures being taken on school grounds. It represents the Court's recognition that the nation's educational system is under siege and that educators need greater freedom to maintain school security. Underlying the decision is a recognition of the inherent rights of the mass of law-abiding students to receive an education unimpeded by the disruptive activities of a few troublemakers. ■

Source: New Jersey v. T.L.O., 105 S.Ct. 733 (1985).

Custodial Interrogation of Juveniles

Parents are usually contacted immediately after a child is taken into custody. In years past, the police often questioned juveniles without their parents or even an attorney present. Any incriminatory statements or confessions that the juveniles made could be used in evidence at their trials. However, in 1966, the landmark Supreme Court case **Miranda v. Arizona** placed constitutional limitations on police interrogation procedures used with adult offenders. *Miranda* held that persons in police custody must be told that:

■ They have the right to remain silent.
■ Any statements they make can be used against them.
■ They have the right to counsel.
■ If they cannot afford counsel, it will be furnished at public expense.[40]

These *Miranda* warnings, which secure the adult defendant's Fifth Amendment privilege against self-incrimination, have been made applicable to children taken into custody. The Supreme Court case of *In re Gault* stated that constitutional privileges against self-incrimination are applicable in juvenile cases as well as in adult cases. Because *In re Gault* implies that *Miranda v. Arizona* applies to **custodial interrogation** of juvenile offenders in the pre-judicial stage of the juvenile process, state court jurisdictions apply the requirements of *Miranda* to juvenile proceedings as well. Since *Gault* in 1967, virtually all of the courts that have ruled on the question of the *Miranda* warning have concluded that the warning does apply to the juvenile process.

One difficult problem associated with the custodial interrogation of children has to do with their waiver of *Miranda* rights: under what circumstances can juveniles knowingly and willingly waive the rights given them by *Miranda v. Arizona* and discuss their actions with police without benefit of lawyer? Is it possible for a youngster, acting alone, to be mature enough to appreciate the right to remain silent?

Most courts have concluded that parents or attorneys need not be present for children to effectively waive their rights.[41] In a frequently cited California case, *People v. Lara,* the court said that the question of a child's waiver is to be determined by the **totality of the circumstances doctrine.[42]** This means that the validity of a waiver rests not only on the age of the child but also on a combination of other factors, including: the education of the accused; the accused's knowledge of the charge and of the right to remain silent and have an attorney present; whether the youth was allowed to consult with family or friends; whether the interrogation took place before or after charges were placed; the method of interrogation; and whether the accused refused to give statements on prior occasions.[43]

The general rule is that juveniles can intentionally waive their rights to protection from self-incrimination, but the validity of this waiver is determined by the circumstances of each case. For example, in *New Hampshire v. Benoit,* a child's custodial statements were considered inadmissible because the child had not been told of the possibility that the statements could be used against him if he were tried as an adult.[44]

In addition, a number of states, recognizing the inability of children to comprehend their legal rights, have demanded by law that a parent or attorney be present when a juvenile is questioned by police; this is referred to as the "interested adult rule."[45]

FOCUS ON DELINQUENCY

Fare v. Michael C.

FACTS

Michael C. was implicated in the murder of Robert Yeager, which occurred during a robbery of Yeager's home. A small truck registered in the name of Michael's mother was identified as having been near the Yeager home at the time of the killing, and a young man answering Michael's description was seen by witnesses near the truck and near the home shortly before Yeager was murdered.

On the basis of this information, the police of Van Nuys, California, arrested Michael at approximately 6:30 P.M. on February 4. He was then 16 ½ years old and on probation to the juvenile court. He had been on probation since the age of 12. Approximately one year earlier, he had served a term in a youth corrections camp under the supervision of the juvenile court. He had a record of several previous offenses, including burglary of guns and purse snatching, stretching back over several years.

When Michael arrived at the Van Nuys station house, two police officers began to interrogate him. No one else was present during the interrogation. The conversation was tape-recorded. One of the officers initiated the interview by informing Michael that he had been brought in for questioning in relation to a murder. The officer fully advised him of his *Miranda* rights. The following exchange then occurred:

Q: Do you understand all of these rights as I have explained them to you?
A: Yeah.
Q: Okay, do you wish to give up your right to remain silent and talk to us about this murder?

A: What murder? I don't know about no murder.
Q: Do you want to give up your right to have an attorney present here while we talk about it?
A: Can I have my probation officer here?
Q: Well, I can't get a hold of your probation officer right now. You have a right to an attorney.
A: How do I know you guys won't pull no police officer in and tell me he's an attorney?
Q: Your probation officer is Mr. Christiansen.
A: Yeah.
Q: Well I'm not going to call Mr. Christiansen tonight. There's a good chance we can talk to him later, but I'm not going to call him right now. If you want to talk to us without an attorney present, you can. If you don't want to, you don't have to. But if you want to say something, you can, and if you don't want to say something, you don't have to. That's your right. You understand that right?
A: Yeah.
Q: Okay, will you talk to us without an attorney present?
A: Yeah, I want to talk to you.

Michael thereupon proceeded to answer questions. He made statements and drew sketches that incriminated him in the Yeager murder.

Largely on the basis of Michael's incriminating statements, probation authorities filed a petition in juvenile court alleging that he had murdered Robert Yeager and that he should be made a ward of the juvenile court.

continued on next page

This doctrine requires that the police explain the *Miranda* warning to the juvenile in the presence of a parent or someone acting *in loco parentis* for the child. Then, the adult must have the opportunity to consult with the child so that the child understands the rights and their significance. Most courts using this rule require that the adult present during the interrogation must be acting in the child's interest and not in any official capacity, such as a youth service employee, court social worker, or probation officer.

In a 1989 Massachusetts case dealing with this problem, the court acted to protect the rights of the juvenile by holding that no other minor, not even a relative, can act as an interested adult. In *Commonwealth v. Guyton*, Guyton's sister,

FOCUS ON DELINQUENCY

The California Supreme Court reversed the conviction, holding that Michael's request to see his probation officer negated any possible willingness on his part to discuss his case with the police and thereby invoked his Fifth Amendment privilege.

DECISION

Michael alleged that statements had been obtained from him in violation of *Miranda* because his request to see his probation officer at the outset of the questioning invoked his Fifth Amendment right to remain silent, just as if he had requested the assistance of an attorney. Accordingly, Michael argued that since the interrogation did not cease until he had a chance to confer with his probation officer, the statements and sketches could not be admitted against him in the juvenile court proceedings.

The Supreme Court reversed and remanded in an opinion by Justice Harry Blackmun. The *Miranda* rule that prior to interrogation the state must warn the accused of the right to an attorney and of the right to remain silent unless an attorney is present "has the virtue of informing police and prosecutors with specificity as to what they may do in conducting custodial interrogation, and of informing courts under what circumstances statements obtained during such interrogation are not admissible," the Court said. In this case, the California court had significantly extended the rule, it continued, and had ignored the basis of the *Miranda* rule, which is the "critical position" lawyers occupy in our legal system. Probation officers frequently are not trained in the law, and moreover they are employees of the state, duty bound to report wrongdoing by the juvenile. "In these circumstances," the Court said, "it cannot be said that the probation officer is able to offer the type of independent advice that an accused would expect from a lawyer retained or assigned to assist him during questioning."

The Court also rejected the contention that the youth's request constituted a request to remain silent. On the basis of the record, his replies show that he "voluntarily and knowingly waived his Fifth Amendment rights."

SIGNIFICANCE OF CASE

The *Fare v. Michael C.* case applied the "totality of the circumstances" approach to the interrogation of juveniles. The question of whether the accused waived his rights is one of substance, not form. Did the defendant knowingly and voluntarily waive the rights delineated in *Miranda?* The juvenile court was originally correct. The transcript of the interrogation took care to ensure that Michael understood his rights. The police fully explained that he was being questioned in connection with a murder. They informed him of all the rights delineated in *Miranda* and ascertained that he understood them. Nothing indicates that Michael failed to understand what the officers told him. Moreover, after his request to see his probation officer had been denied and after the police officer once more had explained his rights to him, he clearly expressed his willingness to waive his rights and continue the interrogation.

In addition, the Court held that the *Miranda* rule should not be extended to include a juvenile's request to see his or her probation officer. Such a request does not have the same effect as the request to see a lawyer. ■

Source: Fare v. Michael C., 442 U.S. 23, 99 S.Ct. 2560 (1979).

who was three weeks short of her eighteenth birthday, was acting *in loco parentis* for the brother while their mother was away, and the Court ruled that she could not act as an interested adult.[46] On the other hand, some courts have recognized that the interested adult need not be a parent but may be a relative, such as the juvenile's grandfather.[47] Usually, the one exception to the application of the interested adult rule is when the child is over age 14 and the circumstances demonstrate a high degree of intelligence, experience, and knowledge on the part of the child. Only then may child act alone.

The waiver of *Miranda* rights by a juvenile is probably one of the most controversial legal issues often addressed in the state courts. It has also been the subject of federal constitutional review, discussed above.

Supreme Court Interpretations of *Miranda* to Juvenile Proceedings

The Supreme Court has attempted to clarify children's rights when they are interrogated by the police in two cases, ***Fare v. Michael C.*** and *California v. Prysock.* In *Fare v. Michael C.,* the Court ruled that a child's asking to speak to his probation officer was not the equivalent of asking for an attorney; consequently, admissions he made to the police absent legal counsel were held to be admissible in court.[48] (Because of the importance of this case, it is set out in the Focus on Delinquency titled "*Fare v. Michael C.*") And in *California v. Prysock*, the Court was asked to rule on the adequacy of a *Miranda* warning given Randall Prysock, a youthful murder suspect.[49] After reviewing the taped exchange between the police interrogator and the boy, the Court upheld Prysock's conviction when it ruled that even though the *Miranda* warning was given in slightly different language and out of exact context, its meaning was plain and easily understandable, even to a juvenile.

Taken together, *Fare* and *Prysock* make it seem indisputable that juveniles are at least entitled to receive the same *Miranda* rights as adults and ought to be entitled to even greater consideration to ensure that they understand their legal rights.

Miranda v. Arizona is an historic and often symbolic decision that continues to effect the rights of all suspects, adults and children, placed in custody.[50] The following Case in Point exemplifies the extent to which *Miranda* can be applied in the juvenile justice system.

Identification from Lineups

Another important issue arises in the early police processing of juvenile offenders. Should the constitutional safeguards established for adult offenders to protect them during lineups and other forms of identification be applied to juvenile proceedings? In *United States v. Wade*, the Supreme Court held that the accused has a right to have counsel present at postindictment lineup procedures and that pretrial identification is inadmissible when the right to counsel is violated.[51] The Court further clarified this issue in *Kirby v. Illinois*, holding that the defendant's right to counsel at pretrial identification proceedings goes into effect only after the complaint or the indictment has been issued.[52] Based on these decisions, courts have ruled that juveniles also have constitutional protection during lineup and identification procedures. They have a right to counsel at a police lineup once they are charged with a delinquent act, and if this right is violated, the pretrial identification is excluded. For example, in the case of *In re Holley*, a juvenile accused of rape did not have counsel during the lineup identification procedure. In reversing Holley's conviction, the appellate court said the absence of counsel during Holley's lineup precluded a fair trial.[53] State courts have generally followed the mandate of the Supreme Court and applied its holdings to juvenile delinquency proceedings.

Today, almost as much procedural protection is given to children in the juvenile justice courts as to adults brought to the criminal courts. However, the authority of the police to deal with juvenile misconduct under most juvenile codes is ordinarily broader than with adults. Therefore, no aspect of the police role is more important than its reliance on juvenile officers being granted a reasonable amount of discretion in the handling of juvenile problems. When should a police

You are a juvenile court prosecutor faced with the responsibility of assessing the admissibility of evidence in juvenile cases. Defendant Kevin W., age 16 years and 9 months, was convicted of attempted second-degree murder and burglary of a convenience food store. After shooting the clerk, he fled the scene, leaving behind a friend who had accompanied Kevin but refused to enter the store.

One of the police officers who arrived at the scene was Kevin's father, Sergeant W. Knowing his son was supposed to be with the friend, Sergeant W. went home, found his son, and questioned him in the presence of the defendant's mother and brother. At this time, Sergeant W. did not advise his son of his *Miranda* rights. Kevin admitted that he had shot the victim and told his father where the gun was hidden.

Later at the police station, Kevin, while in the process of confessing to other police officers and having been informed of his rights, was interrupted by his father, who recommended that the boy say nothing further without speaking with an attorney. The defendant then invoked his right to remain silent.

On appeal, Kevin contends that the statements made to his policeman father should have been suppressed as the product of a custodial interrogation without the benefit of *Miranda* warnings. He argues that his confession was involuntary by reason of the fact that the officer was his father and further that his home was a custodial setting requiring the application of *Miranda* protection.

On the other hand, the state pointed out that the physical setting in which the statements were made was not coercive and the questioning very brief. In addition, the fact that the father was in uniform when he questioned his son did not necessarily constitute custodial activity. Although Sergeant W.'s investigation focused on his son, *Miranda* warnings are not required merely because the questioned person is a suspect. Only when the accused is "in custody" and deprived of his freedom in a significant way does *Miranda* apply.

Do you believe that Kevin's confession to his policeman father was voluntary and, therefore, not of a custodial nature requiring the application of *Miranda v. Arizona?*

officer act to assist a juvenile in need against his or her will? Should a summons be used in lieu of arrest? Under what conditions should a juvenile be taken into protective custody? The following sections describe the factors that influence police discretion and review the policies and programs for its control.

POLICE WORK WITH JUVENILES: DISCRETIONARY JUSTICE

When police officers confront a case involving a juvenile offender, they are forced to use their personal discretion to choose an appropriate course of action. Police discretion is defined as selective enforcement of the law by duly authorized police agents. Roscoe Pound defined discretion as the authority conferred by law to act in certain conditions or situations in accordance with an official's or agency's own considered conscience or judgment.[54] Discretion operates in the twilight zone between law and morals. According to Kenneth Davis, discretion gives officers a choice among possible courses of action within the effective limits on their power.[55] Joseph Goldstein has termed the exercise of police discretion a prime example of **low-visibility decision making** in the criminal justice system.[56] Low-visibility decision making refers to decisions made by public officials in the criminal or juvenile justice systems that the public is not in a position to understand, regulate, or criticize.

Police discretion is probably one of the most controversial and important of all police practices. Discretion exists not only in the police area but also in prosecutorial decision making, judicial judgments, and corrections. Discretion results in the law being applied differently in similar situations. For example, two teenagers are caught in a stolen automobile; one is arrested, the other is released. Two youths are drunk and disorderly; one is sent home, the other is booked and sent to juvenile court. A group of youngsters are involved in a gang fight; only a few are arrested, the others are released.

Regardless of what enforcement style they employ, police officers in both the adult and juvenile systems use a high degree of personal discretion in carrying out their daily tasks. In particular, much discretion is exercised in juvenile work because of the informality that has been built into the system to individualize justice. According to Victor Streib, arbitrary discretion is a characteristic of the informal juvenile system.[57] Furthermore, Streib says, police intake officials, prosecutors, judges, and correctional administrators make final, largely unreviewed decisions about children that are almost totally unsupervised in any meaningful way.

The daily procedures of juvenile personnel are not subjected to administrative scrutiny or judicial review, except when they clearly violate a child's constitutional rights. As a result, discretion sometimes deteriorates into discrimination, violence, and other abusive practices on the part of the police. As Herbert Packer has stated, the real danger in discretion is that it allows the law to discriminate against precisely those elements in the population—the poor, the ignorant, the unpopular—who are the least able to draw attention to their plight and to whose sufferings the vast majority of the population is not responsive.[58]

The problem of discretion in juvenile justice is one of two extremes. Too little discretion ties the hands of decision makers and does not provide flexibility in dealing with individual juvenile offenders. Guidelines and controls are needed to structure the use of discretion.

The first contact a child usually has with the juvenile justice system is with the police, and studies indicate that a large majority of police decisions at this initial contact involve discretion. Paul Strasburg found that only about 50 percent of all children who come in contact with the police ever get past this initial stage of the juvenile justice process.[59]

In a classic study, Nathan Goldman examined the arrest records for over one thousand juveniles from four communities in Pennsylvania to determine what factors operated in police referrals of juveniles to the court.[60] He concluded that over 64 percent of police contacts with juveniles were handled informally without court referral. In another early effort, Irving Piliavin and Scott Briar observed the behavior of thirty officers in the juvenile bureau of a large industrial city. Their study documented further the informality of police discretion in the initial arrest decision.[61] In 1966, Donald Black and Albert Reiss recorded descriptions of 280 encounters between juveniles and the police in efforts to discover discriminatory decision making. They found an unusually low arrest rate.[62] The FBI generally estimates that about one-third of all juvenile arrests involve interdepartmental handling of the case rather than juvenile court referral.[63]

The latest research on how the police handle juvenile arrests is illustrated in Figure 15.3. Notice that the largest proportion in this 1990 study by the Office of Juvenile Justice and Delinquency Prevention (nearly two-thirds) was referred to the juvenile court system.

These studies indicate that the police use a large amount of discretion in their decisions regarding juvenile offenders. Research generally shows that differential decision making goes on without clear guidance and uniformity. Figure 15.4 illustrates the alternatives in the police-juvenile decision-making process.

Factors Affecting Police Discretion

How does a juvenile officer decide what to do about a child who is apprehended? As might be expected, the seriousness of the crime, the situation in which it occurred, and the legal record of the juvenile have been found to significantly affect decision making. Police are much more likely to take formal action if the crime is serious and has been reported by a victim who is a respected member of the community and if the offender is well known to them.[64] However, these

■■ FIGURE 15.3

Police dispositions of juvenile offenders taken into custody, 1990

Source: Office of Juvenile Justice and Delinquency Prevention, *Arrests of Youth, 1990* (Washington, D.C.: U.S. Department of Justice, January 1992), p. 5.

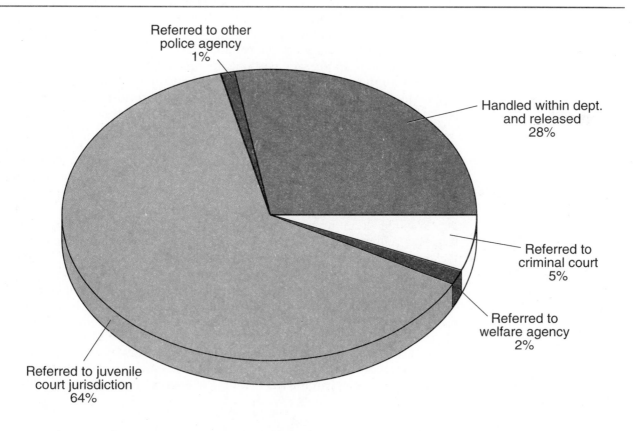

Referred to other police agency
1%

Handled within dept. and released
28%

Referred to criminal court
5%

Referred to welfare agency
2%

Referred to juvenile court jurisdiction
64%

Ladder of police-juvenile
decision making

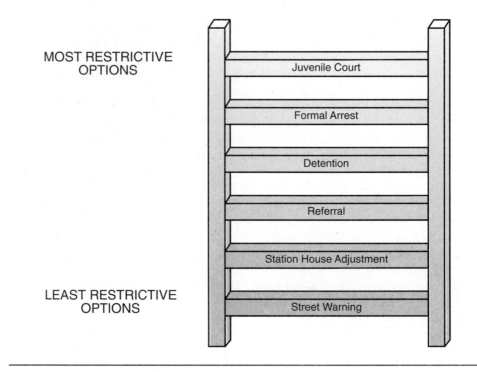

MOST RESTRICTIVE
OPTIONS

Juvenile Court

Formal Arrest

Detention

Referral

Station House Adjustment

LEAST RESTRICTIVE
OPTIONS

Street Warning

factors are not the only ones that have been found to influence discretion. Some
other important influences are discussed below.

The general environment in which the officer works effects the decision. For
instance, some officers work in communities that tolerate a fair amount of
personal freedom. In liberal environments, the police may be inclined to release
children into the community rather than arrest them. Other officers may work
in extremely conservative communities that expect a no-nonsense approach to
police behavior. Here, police may be more inclined to arrest a child.

The policies, practices, and customs of the local police department also provide
a source of environmental influence. Juvenile officers may be pressured to make
more arrests or to refrain from making arrests under certain circumstances.
Directives and orders instruct officers to be alert to certain types of violations on
the part of juveniles. The chief of police and political officials of a community
might initiate policies governing the arrest practices of the juvenile department.
For example, local merchants may complain that youths congregating in a
shopping center's parking lot are inhibiting business. Police may be called on to
make arrests in order to get the point across that loitering will not be tolerated.
Under other circumstances, a more informal warning might be given. Similarly, a
rash of deaths caused by teenage drunk driving may galvanize the local media to
demand police action. The mayor and police chief, sensitive to possible voter
dissatisfaction, may therefore demand that formal police action be taken in cases
of drunk driving.

Another source of influence is the pressure that individual superiors, such as
police supervisors, exert. The sergeant, for example, may initiate formal or
informal directives regarding the handling of youths in a given community. Some

supervising officers may believe that it is important to curtail disorderly conduct, drinking, or drug use. In addition, certain officers are influenced by the way their peers handle discretionary decision making.

A final environmental factor affecting the performance of officers is their perception of community alternatives to police intervention. Police officers may use arrest because they believe that nothing else can be done and that arrest is the best possible example of good police work. On the other hand, juvenile officers may be apt to refer a large number of juveniles to social service agencies, particularly if they believe that a community has a variety of good resources.

Situational Influences

In addition to the environment, a variety of situational factors effect a police officer's decisions. Situational influences are those attached to a particular crime. It is difficult to identify every factor influencing police discretion, but a few stand out as having major significance. Studies show that police officers rely heavily on the demeanor of a child in making decisions. In other words, the child's attitude and appearance play a serious role in the decision-making process. Goldman discovered that community attitudes, political pressures, and the bias of the individual police officer may also influence whether an offender is arrested, taken into custody, or released.[65] Aaron Cicourel found that the decision to arrest is often based on information regarding the offender's overall demeanor, including dress, attitude, speech, and level of hostility toward the police.[66] Piliavin and Briar found that police perceptions of the attitudes of offenders toward the police, the law, and their own behavior were the most important factors in the decision to process or release an offender.[67]

Most studies conclude that whether the decisions involve juvenile or adult offenders, the following variables are important to decisions made by police officers:

- The attitude of the complainant
- The type and seriousness of the offense
- The race and sex of the offender
- The age of the offender
- The attitude of the offender
- The history of the offender's prior contacts with the police
- In the case of a child, the perceived willingness of the parents to assist in disciplining the child and solving the problem
- The setting or location in which the incident occurs
- In the case of a child, whether the child denies the actions or insists on a court hearing
- The likelihood that a child can be serviced by a referral agency in the community

POLICE DISCRETION

Race

Do police allow racial, gender, or class bias to affect their decisions on whether to arrest youths? A great deal of debate has been generated over this very critical

Race, gender and class may all influence the decision to take a suspect into custody or release them with a warning.

issue. Some experts believe that police decision making is deeply influenced by the offender's personal characteristics, while others maintain that crime-related variables are actually more significant.

One suspected source of police bias is racial discrimination. It has long been charged that police are more likely to act formally with black suspects and use their discretion to benefit whites.[68] However, clear-cut proof that police officers act in a generally biased fashion has not been established. A number of well-respected studies by Robert Terry, Donald Black, and Albert Reiss and by Richard Lundman found that police are more likely to take offense and demeanor into account than race.[69] Polite, respectful youths were more likely to get the benefit of police discretion, whether they were African-American or white, than youths who displayed a "bad attitude." These findings are supported by T. Edwin Black and Charles Smith's national assessment of juvenile justice processing, which found that there was no difference in the proportion of African-Americans and whites arrested and referred to court, regardless of the nature of the offense.[70] However, it should be noted that Black and Smith found that Hispanics and other racial or ethnic minority groups had a greater chance for court referral than either black or white youths.

Some research efforts do show that police discriminate against black youths, most notably studies conducted by Terence Thornberry, Dale Dannefer, and Russell Schutt and by Jeffrey Fagan and his associates.[71] However, even research supportive of police discrimination does not indicate that it is overt and unidimensional. For example, Fagan and his associates found that police are more likely to formally process minorities except for crimes of violence, where the pattern is reversed and white offenders are referred to juvenile court at a higher rate.[72]

David Griswold states: "The preponderance, as well as the strength, of the evidence leans toward a view that the police do not discriminate against minorities and that factors other than race weigh most heavily in the police decision-making process."[73]

On the other hand, Donna Bishop and Charles Frazier find that race has a direct effect on decisions made at several processing junctures on the juvenile justice process.[74] Their recent research examines the effect of a juvenile's race in a cohort group of over fifty thousand youths in a large southern city where decisions were made from intake to disposition. According to Bishop and Frazier, African-Americans are more likely to be recommended for formal processing, referred to court, adjudicated delinquent, and given harsher dispositions than comparable whites. In the arrest category, specifically, being African-American increases the probability of formal police action by 11 percent.[75]

One of the most significant recent research efforts on differential processing of minorities is a report from the National Coalition of State Juvenile Justice Advisory Groups.[76] The report points out that minority youth, particularly African-Americans and Hispanics, are overrepresented at various stages of the juvenile justice system. The coalition suggests two possible explanations for this disparity; (1) differential rates in arrest, incarceration, and even release are the result of a racist system, and (2) the differential rates are the result of greater involvement by minorities in juvenile crime.[77] In either case, according to the report, to rectify this imbalance, there is an urgent need to alter the social structure of society by improving the educational system, creating more job opportunities, and providing more services for families. The report also recommends that the Office of Juvenile Justice and Delinquency Prevention examine police surveillance and apprehension procedures to determine why minority youths are at a greater risk of being handled differently and to reduce or eliminate any subtle discrimination that may exist in the early stages of the juvenile process.[78]

Another study released in 1992 by the National Council on Crime and Delinquency revealed an equally significant over-representation by black youths at every point in the California juvenile justice system. While making up less than 9 percent of the state youth population, African-Americans accounted for 19 percent of juvenile arrests. The causes for the racial and ethnic disparity included: (1) institutional racism, (2) environmental factors, (3) family dysfunction, (4) cultural barriers, and (5) and school failure.[79]

In sum, what we know is:

1. Some researchers have concluded that the police discriminate against African-American and other minority youths;
2. Some researchers do not find evidence of discrimination;
3. Racial disparity is most often seen at the arrest stage but probably exists at other processing points;
4. The higher arrest rates of minorities are more likely the result of interpersonal, family, community, and organizational differences; and
5. Higher arrest rates often result from police discretion with juveniles, street-crime visibility, and high crime rates within a particular group. Such factors, however, may also be linked to a general societal discrimination.

Further research is needed to document what appear to be findings of disproportional arrests of minority juvenile offenders.

Gender

Disagreement also exists over police handling of female offenders. Some experts favor the **chivalry or paternalism hypothesis,** which holds that police are more likely to act paternally toward young girls. Others believe that police may be *more* likely to arrest female offenders because their actions violate police officers' cherished stereotypes of the female.

Research by Christy Visher shows that police take race and age into account when arresting females but that these factors are less important for male arrests.[80] Visher finds that chivalry does indeed play a role in female arrests: younger girls who do not meet police officers' role expectations are more likely to be arrested than their older, more contrite sisters. Meda Chesney-Lind has found that female status offenders may be the victims of police discrimination; she concluded that adolescent girls are often arrested for less serious offenses than boys.[81] Again, disagreement exists over the extent of police gender bias. Merry Morash found that young boys who engage in "typical" male delinquent activities are much more likely to develop police records than females.[82] And Black and Smith's national assessment study found that "the sex of the offender alone appears to have no influence on whether an offender, after being arrested, is referred to the court."[83]

Bishop and Frazier revisited the issue of gender bias in a 1992 study. They found that the historical patterns of gender bias continue: both female status offenders and male delinquents are differently disadvantaged in the juvenile justice system.[84]

In sum, what many of these studies imply is:

1. Police bias favors females with regard to acts of delinquency.
2. Females seem to be referred to juvenile court for status offenses more often than males.
3. The chivalry or paternalism theory seems to apply where females are less likely than males to be arrested for person- and property-oriented crimes.
4. Some research indicates that males and females receive similar treatment from the police.
5. Evidence exists that the police and most likely the juvenile courts have applied a double standard in dealing with male and female juvenile offenders.

To a large degree then, current research findings seem inconclusive regarding the degree of differential treatment of females by the police in the juvenile justice system, except where police are unwilling to process females for criminal acts and discriminate against them regarding status offenses.

Organizational Bias

Even when police officers may not be discriminating on an individual level, the policies being used in some departments may result in biased law enforcement practices. Research conducted by a number of police experts, including Douglas Smith, has found that police departments can be characterized by their professionalism and degree of bureaucratization.[85] Departments that are highly bureaucratized and at the same time unprofessional are the ones most likely to be insulated from the community they serve (Smith labels these departments "militaristic"). According to Smith, isolation can result in the introduction into the social control process of bias toward minorities and the socially disadvantaged.

The direction of organizational policy may be fueled by the perceptions of police decision makers. A number of experts have found that law enforcement administrators have a stereotyped view of the urban poor as troublemakers who must be kept under control.[86] Consequently, lower-class neighborhoods experience much greater police scrutiny than middle-class areas, and their residents stand a proportionately greater chance of arrest and official processing. [87] Merry Morash concludes that if they fit the "common image"—for example, males, who hang with a tough crowd—youths significantly increase their chance of arrest and being officially labeled.[88]

This relationship has been explored in some important recent research. Robert Sampson, making use of both self-reports and official data, found that teenage residents of neighborhoods with low socioeconomic status had a significantly greater chance of acquiring police records than youths living in higher socioeconomic-status areas, regardless of the actual crime rates in these areas. Furthermore, Sampson found that this relationship held up after sex, individual income, race, gang membership, and delinquent peers were controlled.[89] Sampson found that when it came time to officially process arrested youth to the juvenile court, the decision was significantly related to the individuals' socioeconomic status.

This research indicates that while police officers may not discriminate on an individual level, departmental policy that focuses attention on lower-class areas may result in class and racial bias in the police processing of delinquent youth.

Considerations of race, economic status, or gender should not determine how the police exercise their authority.[90] Because the police retain a large degree of discretionary power, the ideal goal of nondiscrimination is often difficult to achieve in actual practice. However, the formulation and implementation of policy guidelines in the juvenile area eliminating bias and unfettered police discretion are not beyond our control.

Controlling Police Discretion

A number of leading organizations have suggested the use of guidelines to control police discretion. The American Bar Association (ABA) states, "Since individual police officers may make important decisions affecting police operations without direction, with limited accountability and without any uniformity within a department, police discretion should be structured and controlled."[91] The ABA notes further, "There is almost a unanimous opinion that steps must be taken to provide better control and guidance over police discretion in street and station house adjustments of juvenile cases."[92]

One of the leading exponents of police discretion is Kenneth Culp Davis, who has done much to raise the consciousness of criminal justice practitioners about discretionary decision making. Davis recommends controlling administrative discretion through (1) the use of statutorial definition, (2) the development of written policies, and (3) the recording of decisions by criminal justice personnel.[93] Narrowing the scope of juvenile codes, for example, would limit and redefine the broad authority police officers currently have to take children into custody for criminal and noncriminal behavior. Such practices would provide fair criteria for arrests, adjustment, and police referral of juvenile offenders and would help eliminate largely personal judgments based on the race, attitude, or demeanor of the juvenile. Discretionary decision making in juvenile police work can be understood by analyzing the following Case in Point and by examining Figure 15.5.

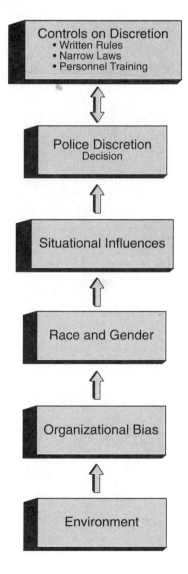

■■ FIGURE 15.5

Discretionary justice with juveniles

CASE IN POINT

You are a newly appointed police officer assigned to a juvenile unit of a medium size urban police department.

Wayne W. is a 14-year-old white boy who was caught shoplifting with two friends of the same age and sex. Wayne attempted to leave a large department store with a twelve-dollar shirt and was apprehended by a police officer in front of the store.

Wayne seemed quite remorseful about the offense. He said several times that he did not know why he did it and that he had not planned the act. He seemed upset and scared and, while admitting the offense, did not want to go to court.

Wayne had three previous contacts with the police: one for malicious mischief when he destroyed some property, another involving a minor assault of a boy, and a third involving another shoplifting charge. In all three cases, Wayne promised to refrain from ever committing such acts again, and as a result, he was not required to go to court. The other shoplifting involved a small baseball worth only three dollars.

Wayne appeared at the police department with his mother because his parents are divorced. She did not seem overly concerned about the case and felt that her son was not really to blame. She argued that he was always getting in trouble and she was not sure how to control him. She blamed most of his troubles with the law on his being in the wrong crowd.

The store had left matters in the hands of the police and would support their decision.

The other two boys did not steal anything and claimed that they had no idea that Wayne was planning anything when they entered the store. Neither had any criminal record.

Should Wayne be sent to court for trial? What other remedy might be appropriate?

POLICE WORK AND DELINQUENCY PREVENTION

If the police are to effectively provide services to children and enforce the law, they need to develop programs and relationships with social service systems. Then they can play an important role in implementing policies to control and prevent delinquency. Since the police decide what happens to a juvenile taken into custody, it is essential that they work closely with social service groups on a day-to-day basis. In addition, the police need to assume a leadership role in identifying the needs of children in the community and helping the community provide for such needs. In helping develop **delinquency prevention** programs, the police need to work closely with such organizations as youth service bureaus, the schools, recreational facilities, welfare agencies, and employment programs.[94]

Using **community services** to deal with delinquent and nondelinquent children has many advantages. Such services allow children to avoid the stigma of being processed by a police agency. They also improve the community's awareness of the need to help children, and through involvement of local residents, they give a greater recognition to the complexity of the delinquent's

It is common for police departments to provide delinquency prevention services. DARE, a national drug prevention initiative, is conducted by local police in the public schools.

problem, thus developing a sense of public responsibility and support for such programs. Another advantage of using community services is that they make it possible to restrict court referral by the police to cases involving serious crime.

One of the most important institutions playing a role in delinquency prevention is the school. Linking the school with the police in the community is one way to help prevent delinquency. Liaison programs between the police and the schools have been implemented in many communities throughout the United States. Liaison officers from schools and police departments have played a leadership role in developing recreational programs for juveniles. In some instances, they have actually operated such programs. In others, they have encouraged community support for recreational activities, including Little League baseball, athletic clubs, camping programs, police athletic programs, and scouting programs.

One prominent example of a successful police-community prevention effort is the privately funded **TOP program** in Rochester, New York. TOP stands for Teens on Patrol. Each summer, about one hundred youths are hired to patrol the city's parks and recreational areas. The young people help keep the parks "cool" and also learn a lot about police officers. A number of TOP graduates have gone on to become police officers.[95] The Focus on Delinquency titled "Project DARE" describes a well-respected and effective effort by a local police department to prevent teenage drug abuse. DARE projects, which were mentioned in Chapter 12, have been adopted by hundreds of police departments throughout the country.

COMMUNITY POLICING IN THE 1990S

One of the most important changes in American law enforcement is the emergence of the community policing model of crime prevention. This concept is based on the premise that police departments do not make efficient crime-fighting organizations when they operate independently. However, if they gain the trust and assistance of concerned citizens, they can carry out their duties more effectively. Therefore, the main police role should be to increase feelings of community safety and encourage area residents to cooperate with their local police agencies.[96]

Advocates of community policing regard the approach as useful in juvenile justice for a number of reasons:

1. Moving police officers from a position of anonymity in the patrol car to *direct* engagement with a community gives them more immediate *information* about problems unique to a neighborhood and insights into their solutions.
2. Freeing officers from the emergency response system permits them to engage more directly in *proactive crime prevention.*
3. Making operations more visible to the public *increases police accountability to the public.*
4. *Decentralizing* operations allows officers to develop a greater familiarity with the specific workings and needs of various neighborhoods and constituencies in the community and to adapt procedures to accommodate those needs.
5. Encouraging officers to view *citizens as partners* improves relations between police and the public.
6. Moving decision making and discretion downward to patrol officers places more authority in the hands of the people who best know the community's problems and expectations.[97]

The community policing model has been translated into a number of different policy initiatives. It has encouraged police departments around the country to get patrol officers out of patrol cars, where they were viewed as faceless strangers insulated from the community, and into the streets via **foot patrol.** Hundreds of experimental programs have been implemented around the country, and evaluation by the National Neighborhood Foot Patrol Center at Michigan State University indicates they are highly successful.[98]

In addition, the police have encouraged and worked with citizen groups to create neighborhood watch and crime prevention groups. The Police Foundation, a nonprofit organization that conducts research on police issues, has reviewed such efforts in Houston and Newark and found them to be effective methods of increasing citizen cooperation.[99] One of the most well-known programs is the Philadelphia block watch program, which cooperates with the police in a number of different delinquency control and victim-aid projects.[100] Another is the *innovations neighborhood-oriented policing* (INOP) approach. The main objectives of the INOP program are to foster community policing initiatives and implement drug reduction efforts at juvenile and adult levels.[101]

In sum, important efforts have been made by local police departments to involve citizens in the process of delinquency control. While little clear-cut evidence exists that these efforts can lower crime rates, they seem to be effective methods of improving perceptions of community safety and the quality of community life while involving citizens in the wider juvenile justice network. Under the community policing philosophy, juvenile prevention programs may become more effective crime-control measures.

Project DARE

Police departments around the country have been allocating resources to delinquency prevention programs. One of the most well known is **Project DARE** in Los Angeles. DARE, an acronym for Drug Abuse Resistance Education, is a joint project of the Los Angeles Police Department and the Los Angeles Unified School District. It is designed to equip elementary school children with the skill to resist peer pressure to take drugs. The program is carried out by experienced officers who bring their "street smarts" into the classroom. The curriculum they teach is organized into seventeen classroom sessions that are summarized below:

1. **Practices for personal safety.** The DARE officer reviews common safety practices to protect students from harm at home, on the way to and from school, and in the neighborhood.
2. **Drug use and misuse.** Students learn the harmful effects of misused drugs as depicted in a film, *Drugs and Your Amazing Mind.*
3. **Consequences.** The focus is on the consequences of using or choosing not to use alcohol, marijuana, and other drugs. If students are aware of those consequences, they can make better informed decisions regarding their own behavior.
4. **Resisting pressures to use drugs.** The DARE officer explains different types of pressure that friends and others exert on students to get them to try alcohol or drugs, ranging from friendly persuasion and teasing to threats.
5. **Resistance techniques: ways to say no.** Students rehearse the many ways of refusing offers to try alcohol or drugs—simply saying no and repeating it as often as necessary; changing the subject; walking away or ignoring the person. They learn that they can avoid situations where they might be subjected to such pressure and can hang around with nonusers.
6. **Building self-esteem.** Poor self-esteem is one of the factors associated with drug misuse. How the students feel about themselves results from positive and negative feelings and experiences. They learn to see their own positive qualities and discover ways to compliment others.
7. **Assertiveness: a response style.** Students have certain rights—to be themselves, to say what they think, to say no to offers of drugs. They must assert those rights confidently without also interfering with others' rights.
8. **Managing stress without taking drugs.** Students learn to recognize sources of stress in their lives and to develop techniques for avoiding or relieving it, including exercise, deep breathing, and talking to others. Using drugs or alcohol to relieve stress causes new problems.
9. **Media influences on drug use.** The DARE officer reviews strategies used in the media to encourage tobacco and alcohol use, including testimonials from celebrities and pressure to conform.
10. **Decision making and risk taking.** Students learn the difference between bad risks and reasonable risks, how to recognize the choices they have, and how to make a decision that promotes their self-interest.
11. **Alternatives to drug abuse.** Drug and alcohol use is not the only way to have fun, to be accepted by peers, or to deal with feelings of anger or hurt.
12. **Alternative activities.** Sports or other physical fitness activities are good alternatives. Exercise improves health and relieves emotional distress.
13. **Officer-planned lessons.** The class period is spent on a special lesson devised by the DARE officer.
14. **Role modeling.** A high school student selected by the DARE officer visits the class, providing students with a positive role model. Students learn that drug users are in the minority.
15. **Project DARE summary.** Students summarize and assess what they have learned.
16. **Taking a stand.** Students compose and read aloud essays on how they can respond when they are pressured to use drugs and alcohol. The essay represents each student's "DARE Pledge."
17. **Assembly.** In a schoolwide assembly, planned in concert with school administrators, all students who participated in Project DARE receive certificates of achievement. ∎

Source: William DeJong, "Project DARE: Teaching Kids to Say 'No' to Drugs and Alcohol," *National Institute of Justice Reporter,* March 1986, pp. 1–5.

SUMMARY

As society has become more complex and rates of delinquency and noncriminal behavior have soared, the police have become more important than ever to the juvenile justice system. It is almost always the police officer who has the initial contact with the large number of young people committing antisocial acts, so the importance of the juvenile police officer cannot be overemphasized.

Numerous factors influence the decisions that the police make about juvenile offenders. They include the seriousness of the offense, the harm inflicted on the victim, and the likelihood that the child will break the law again.

The recruitment, selection, and training of juvenile police officers is essential to good police organizations. Police work with children includes the legal aspects of arrest, custodial interrogation, and lineups. Through the *Miranda v. Arizona* decision, the U.S. Supreme Court established an affirmative procedure for custodial interrogation and police investigations. Such practices are applicable to juvenile suspects. Search and seizure procedures, lineups, and other police procedures are also subject to court review. One important issue is police discretion in dealing with juvenile offenders. Discretion is a low-visibility decision made in the administration of adult and juvenile justice. Discretionary decisions are made without guidelines or policy statements from the police administrator. Discretion is essential in providing individualized justice, but such problems as discrimination, unfairness, and bias toward particular groups of children must be controlled.

KEY TERMS

community policing
juvenile officers
role conflicts
law enforcement
discretion
arrest
probable cause
search and seizure
New Jersey v. T.L.O.
Miranda v. Arizona

custodial interrogation
totality of the circumstances doctrine
Fare v. Michael C.
low-visibility decision making
chivalry or paternalism hypothesis
delinquency prevention
community services
TOP program
foot patrol
Project DARE

QUESTIONS FOR DISCUSSION

1. The term *discretion* is often defined as selective decision making by police and others in the juvenile justice system who are faced with alternative modes of action. Discuss some of the factors affecting the discretion of the police when dealing with juvenile offenders.

2. What role should police organizations play in delinquency prevention and control? Is it feasible to expect police departments to provide social services to children and families? How should police departments be better organized to provide for the control of juvenile delinquency?

3. What qualities should a police juvenile officer have? Should a college education be a requirement?

4. In *New Jersey v. T.L.O.*, the Supreme Court held that prohibitions against illegal search and seizure apply to school as well as law enforcement officials. As a practical matter, will this decision give rise to overused safety and security measures in our school systems?

5. In light of the traditional and protective role assumed by law enforcement personnel in juvenile justice, is there any reason to have a *Miranda* warning for children taken into custody?

6. Can the police and community be truly effective in forming a partnership to reduce juvenile delinquency? Discuss the role of the juvenile police officer in preventing and investigating juvenile crime.

NOTES

1. Herman Goldstein, "Toward Community-Oriented Policing: Potential Basic Requirements and Threshold Questions," *Crime and Delinquency* 33:630 (1987).

2. Lawrence Sherman and Richard Berk, "The Specific Deterrent Effects of Arrest for Domestic Assault," *American Sociological Review* 49:261-72 (1984).

3. Craig Uchida and Robert Goldberg, *Police Employment and Expenditure Trends* (Washington, D.C.: Bureau of Government Statistics, 1986).

4. Donald Black and Albert J. Reiss, Jr., "Police Control of Juveniles," *American Sociological Review* 35:63 (1970); Richard Lundman, Richard Sykes, and John Clark, "Police Control of Juveniles: A Replication," *Journal of Research on Crime and Delinquency* 15:74 (1978).

5. American Bar Association, *Standards Relating to Police Handling of Juvenile Problems* (Cambridge, Mass.: Ballinger, 1977), p. 1.

6. FBI, *Uniform Crime Reports 1991* (Washington, D.C.: Government Printing Office, 1990). Over 40 percent of police-juvenile contacts are referred to juvenile court; see also David Huizinga and Finn Esbensen, "An Arresting View of Juvenile Justice," *National School Safety Center Journal*, Spring 1992, pp. 13-17.

7. For a discussion of police values and roles, see Michael Brown, *Working the Street: Police Discretion and the Dilemmas of Reform* (New York: Russell Sage, 1981).

8. Samuel Walker, *The Police of America* (New York: McGraw-Hill, 1983), p. 133.

9. R. Kobetz and B. Borsage, *Juvenile Justice Administration* (Gaithersburg, Md.: IACO, 1973), p. 112.

10. This section relies on such sources as Malcolm Sparrow, Mark Moore, and David Kennedy, *Beyond 911, A New Era for Policing* (New York: Basic Books, 1990); Daniel Devlin, *Police Procedure, Administration, and Organization* (London: Butterworth, 1966); Robert Fogelson, *Big City Police* (Cambridge: Harvard University Press, 1977); Roger Lane, *Policing the City, Boston 1822-1885* (Cambridge: Harvard University Press, 1967); Roger Lane, "Urban Police and Crime in Nineteenth-Century America," in Norval Morris and Michael Tonry, eds., *Crime and Justice*, vol. 2, (Chicago: University of Chicago Press, 1980), pp. 1-45; J. J. Tobias, *Crime and Industrial Society in the Nineteenth Century* (New York: Schocken Books, 1967); Samuel Walker, *A Critical History of Police Reform: The Emergence of Professionalism* (Lexington, Mass.: Lexington Books, 1977); idem, *Popular Justice* (New York: Oxford University Press, 1980); President's Commission on Law Enforcement and the Administration of Justice, *Task Force Report: The Police* (Washington, D.C.: Government Printing Office, 1967), pp. 1-9.

11. See generally Walker, *Popular Justice*, p. 61.

12. Law Enforcement Assistance Administration, *Two Hundred Years of American Criminal Justice* (Washington, D.C.: Government Printing Office, 1976).

13. See August Vollmer, *The Police and Modern Society* (Berkeley: University of California Press, 1936).

14. "Police Departments, 1991 National Survey," *Law Enforcement Technology*, October 1991.

15. See O. W. Wilson, *Police Administration*, 2d ed. (New York: McGraw-Hill, 1963).

16. National Advisory Commission on Criminal Justice Standards and Goals, *Task Force Report on Juvenile Justice and Delinquency Prevention* (Washington, D.C.: Law Enforcement Assistance Administration, 1976), p. 245.

17. Ibid.

18. National Advisory Commission on Criminal Justice Standards and Goals, *Task Force Report on Juvenile Justice and Delinquency Prevention*, p. 258.

19. American Bar Association, *Standards Relating to Police Handling of Juvenile Problems*, p. 109.

20. Linda Szymanski, *Summary of Juvenile Code Purpose Clauses* (Pittsburgh: National Center for Juvenile Justice, 1988); see also, for example, GA Code Ann. 15; Iowa Code Ann. 232.2; Mass. Gen. Laws, ch. 119, 56.

21. Samuel M. Davis, *Rights of Juveniles—The Juvenile Justice System* (New York: Clark-Boardmen, revised June 1989), Sec. 3.3.

22. National Conference of Commissioners on Uniform State Laws, *Uniform Juvenile Court Act* (Chicago: National Conference on Uniform State Laws, 1968), Sec. 13.

23. *State v. Lowry*, 230 A.2d 907 (1967).

24. *Chimel v. Cal.*, 395 U.S. 752, 89 S.Ct. 2034 (1969).

25. *United States v. Ross*, 456 U.S. 798, 102 S.Ct. 2157 (1982).

26. *Terry v. Ohio*, 392 U.S.1, 88 S.Ct. 1868 (1968).

27. *Bumper v. North Carolina*, 391 U.S. 543, 88 S.Ct. 1788 (1968).

28. See, for example, *Vandenberg v. Superior Court*, 8 Cal.App.3d 1048, 87 Cal.Rptr. 876 (1970).
29. See *"Davis v. State," Criminal Law News*, 9:1 (1992).
30. 469 U.S. 325 (1985).
31. *People v. Overton*, 24 N.Y.2d 522, 301 N.Y.S.2d 479, 249 N.E.2d 366 (1969); see also Brenda Walts, *"New Jersey v. T.L.O.:* Questions the Court Did Not Answer about School Searches," *Law and Education Journal* 14:421 (1985).
32. 94 N.J. 331(1983).
33. *In re Donaldson*, 75 Cal.Rptr. 220 (1969); *People v. Bowers*, 77 Misc.2d 697, 356 N.Y.S.2d 432 (1974); *In re W.*, 29 Cal.App.3d 777, 105 Cal.Rptr. 775 (1973); *Comm. of Pa. v. Dingfelt*, 227 Pa.Supr.380, 323 A.2d 145 (1974).
34. See D. A. Walls, "New Jersey v. T.L.O.: The Fourth Amendment Applied to School Searches," *Oklahoma Univeristy Law Review* 11:225-41 (1986); also Robert Shepherd, Jr., "Juvenile Justice—Search and Seizures Involving Juveniles," *American Bar Association Journal on Criminal Justice* 5:27-29 (1990).
35. K. A. Bucker; "School Drug Tests: A Fourth Amendment Perspective," *University of Illinois Law Review* 5:275 (1987).
36. See J. Hogan and M. Schwartz, "Search and Seizure in the Public Schools," *Case and Comment* 90: 28-32 (1985); see also M. Meyers, "T.L.O. v. New Jersey—Officially Conducted School Searches and a New Balancing Test," *Juvenile Family Journal* 37:27-37 (1986).
37. For an interesting article suggesting that school officials should not be permitted to search students without suspicion that each student searched has violated the drug or weapons law, see J. Braverman, "Public School Drug Searches," *Fordham Urban Law Journal* 14:629-84 (1986).
38. J. M. Sanchez, "Expelling the Fourth Amendment from American Schools: Students' Rights Six Years after T.L.O.," *Law and Education Journal* 21:381-413 (1992).
39. 469 U.S., at 339; see also National School Safety Center, *School Safety Update* (Malibu, Calif.: Pepperdine University, 1991); U.S. Department of Justice, *School Crime—A National Victimization Survey* (Washington, D.C.: Bureau of Justice Statistics, 1991).
40. 384 U.S. 436, 86 S.Ct. 1602 (1966).
41. *Commonwealth v. Gaskins*, 471 Pa. 238, 369 A.2d 1285 (1977); *In re E.T.C.*, 141 Vt. 375, 449 A.2d 937 (1982).
42. 67 Cal.2d 365, 62 Cal.Rptr. 586, 432 P.2d 202 (1967).
43. 399 F.2d 467 (5th Cir.1968).
44. 490 A.2d 295 (N.H.1985).
45. See, for example, *In re E.T.C.*, 141 Vt. 375, 449 A.2d 937 (1982).
46. 405 Mass. 497 (1989).
47. *Commonwealth v. McNeil*, 399 Mass. 71 (1987).
48. 442 U.S. 23, 99 S.Ct. 2560 (1979).
49. 453 U.S. 355, 101 S.Ct. 2806 (1981).
50. See, for example, Larry Holtz, "Miranda in a Juvenile Setting—A Child's Right to Silence," *Journal of Criminal Law and Criminology* 79:534-56(1987).
51. 388 U.S. 218, 87 S.Ct. 1926 (1967).
52. 406 U.S. 682, 92 S.Ct. 1877 (1972).
53. 107 R.I. 615, 268 A.2d 723 (1970).
54. See Roscoe Pound, "Discretion, Dispensation, and Mitigation: The Problem of the Individual Special Case," *New York University Law Review* 35:936 (1960).
55. Kenneth C. Davis, *Discretionary Justice: A Preliminary Inquiry* (Baton Rouge: Louisiana State University Press, 1969); see also M. Ted Rubin, *Juvenile Justice: Police, Practice and Law* (Santa Monica, Calif.: Goodyear, 1979).
56. Joseph Goldstein, "Police Discretion Not to Invoke the Criminal Process: Low-Visibility Decisions in the Administration of Justice," *Yale Law Journal* 69:544 (1960).
57. Victor Streib, *Juvenile Justice in America* (Port Washington, N.Y.: Kennikat, 1978).
58. Herbert Packer, *The Limits of the Criminal Sanction* (Palo Alto, Calif.: Stanford University Press, 1968).
59. See Paul Strasburg, *Violent Delinquents: Report to Ford Foundation from Vera Institute of Justice* (New York: Monarch, 1978), p. 11; see also Robert Terry, "The Screening of Juvenile Offenders," *Journal of Criminal Law, Criminology, and Police Science* 58:173-81 (1967).
60. Nathan Goldman, *The Differential Selection of Juvenile Offenders for Court Appearance* (Washington, D.C.: National Council on Crime and Delinquency, 1963).
61. Irving Piliavin and Scott Briar, "Police Encounters with Juveniles," *American Journal of Sociology* 70:206-14 (1964); Theodore Ferdinand and Elmer Luchterhand, "Inner-City Youth, the Police, Juvenile Court, and Justice," *Social Problems* 8:510-26 (1970).
62. Black and Reiss, "Police Control of Juveniles"; see also Richard J. Lundman, "Routine Police Arrest Practices," *Social Problems* 22:127-41 (1974).
63. FBI, Crime in the U.S.: *Uniform Crime Reports*, 1989 (Washington, D.C.: Government Printing Office, 1989), p. 240.
64. Douglas Smith and Christy Visher, "Street-Level Justice: Situational Determinants of Police Arrest Decisions," *Social Problems* 29:167-78 (1981).
65. Goldman, *The Differential Selection of Juvenile Offenders*, p. 25; Norman Werner and Charles Willie, "Decisions of Juvenile Officers," *American Journal of Sociology* 77:199-214 (1971).
66. See Aaron Cicourel, *The Social Organization of Juvenile Justice* (New York: Wiley, 1968).
67. Piliavin and Briar, "Police Encounters with Juveniles," p. 215.
68. Dale Dannefer and Russel Schutt, "Race and Juvenile Justice Processing in Police and Court Agencies," *American Journal of Sociology* 87:1113-32 (1982);

Smith and Visher, "Street-Level Justice: Situational Determinants of Police Arrest Decisions."

69. Terry, "The Screening of Juvenile Offenders;" Black and Reiss, "Police Control of Juveniles;" Lundman, "Routine Police Arrest Practices."

70. T. Edwin Black and Charles Smith, *A Preliminary National Assessment of the Numbers and Characteristics of Juveniles Processed in the Juvenile Justice System* (Washington, D.C.: Government Printing Office, 1980), p. 39.

71. Terence Thornberry, "Race, Socioeconomic Status, and Sentencing in the Juvenile Justice System," *Journal of Criminal Law and Criminology* 70:164-71 (1979); Dannefer and Schutt, "Race and Juvenile Justice Processing in Court and Police Agencies"; Jeffrey Fagan, Ellen Slaughter, and Eliot Hartstane, "Blind Justice? The Impact of Race on the Juvenile Justice Process," *Crime and Delinquency* 33:224-58 (1987).

72. Fagan, Slaughter, and Hartstane, "Blind Justice? The Impact of Race on the Juvenile Justice Process," pp. 237-38.

73. David Griswold, "Police Discrimination: An Elusive Question," *Journal of Police Science and Administration* 6:65-66 (1978).

74. Donna M. Bishop and Charles E. Frazier, "The Influence of Race in Juvenile Justice Processing," *Journal of Research in Crime and Delinquency* 25:242-261 (1988).

75. Ibid., p. 258.

76. National Coalition of State Juvenile Justice Advisory Groups, *A Delicate Balance* (Bethesda, Md.: National Coalition of State Juvenile Justice Advisory Groups, 1989).

77. Ibid., p. 4.

78. Ibid., p. 2. While not specifically dealing with juveniles, the issue of differential processing for young black males is addressed in the following study that found that nearly one of every four black men in their twenties is caught up in the criminal justice system: Marc Mauer, *Young Black Men and the Criminal Justice System* (Washington, D.C.: The Sentencing Project, 1990).

79. National Council on Crime and Delinquency, *The Over-Representation of Minority Youth in the California Juvenile Justice System* (San Francisco: NCCD, 1992).

80. Christy Visher, "Arrest Decisions and Notions of Chivalry," *Criminology* 21:5-28 (1983).

81. Meda Chesney-Lund, "Judicial Enforcement of the Female Sex Role: The Family Court and Female Delinquency Issues," *Criminology* 8:51-71 (1973); idem, "Young Women in the Arms of Law," in L. Bowker, ed., *Women, Crime and the Criminal Justice System*, 2d ed. (Lexington, Mass.: Lexington Books, 1978).

82. Merry Morash, "Establishment of a Juvenile Record The Influence of Individual and Peer Group Characteristics," *Criminology* 22:97-112 (1984).

83. Black and Smith, *Juveniles Processed in the Juvenile Justice System*, p. 37.

84. Donna Bishop and Charles Frazier, "Gender Bias in Juvenile Justice Processing: Implications of the JJDP Act," *Journal of Criminal Law and Criminology* 82:1162-86 (1992).

85. Douglas Smith, "The Organizational Context of Legal Control," *Criminology* 22:19-38 (1984).

86. John Irwin, *The Jail: Managing the Underclass in American Society* (Berkeley: University of California Press, 1985).

87. Morash, "Establishment of a Juvenile Record: The Influence of Individual and Peer Group Characteristics."

88. Ibid.

89. Robert Sampson, "Effects of Socioeconomic Context of Official Reaction to Juvenile Delinquency," *American Sociological Review* 51:876-85 (1986).

90. Institute of Judicial Administration and American Bar Association, Juvenile Justice Standards Project, *Standards Relating to Police Handling of Juvenile Problems*, (Cambridge, Mass.: Ballinger, 1977), Standard 2.1.

91. American Bar Association, *Standards of Criminal Justice: Standards Relating to Urban Police Function* (New York: Institute of Judicial Administration, 1972), Standard 4.2, p. 121.

92. Ibid., p. 45.

93. Kenneth C. Davis, *Police Discretion* (St. Paul: West, 1975).

94. Sherwood Norman, *The Youth Service Bureau—A Key to Delinquency Prevention* (Hackensack, N.J.: National Council on Crime and Delinquency, 1972), p. 8.

95. Karin Lipson, "Cops and TOPS: A Program for Police and Teens That Works," *Police Chief* 49:45-46 (1982).

96. For an analysis of this position, see George Kelling and James Q. Wilson, "Broken Windows: The Police and Neighborhood Safety," *Atlantic Monthly* 249:29-38 (1982).

97. U.S. Department of Justice, "Community Policing," *National Institute of Justice Journal*, 225:1-32 (1992).

98. Robert Trojanowicz and Hazel Harden, *The Status of Contemporary Community Policing Programs* (East Lansing: Michigan State University Neighborhood Foot Patrol Center, 1985).

99. Police Foundation, *The Effects of Police Fear Reduction Strategies: A Summary of Findings from Houston and Newark* (Washington, D.C.: Police Foundation, 1986).

100. Peter Finn, "Block Watches Help Crime Victims in Philadelphia," *NIJ Reports*, December 1986, pp. 2-10.

101. James Q. Wilson, "Drugs and Crime," in Michael Tonry and James Q. Wilson, ed., *Crime and Justice—A Review of Research*, vol. 13 (Chicago: University of Chicago Press, 1990).

PRETRIAL PROCEDURES

One of the most important stages in the juvenile process is the time between the child's arrest and the adjudicatory hearing. After the juvenile has been taken into police custody, decisions as to the disposition of the case need to be made under police and judicial discretionary authority. By this point, the child has been informed of his or her right to counsel and right to remain silent during questioning. In addition, the child's parents have probably been notified. At this time, the child may be faced with involuntary placement in a detention or shelter care facility. Detention, even if only for a short period, may have a serious effect on the child. For children who are confined unnecessarily, it may contribute to future antisocial and delinquent behavior.

During this period, the child either retains an attorney or is assigned counsel by the court. In addition to detention, the juvenile, the family, and the attorney must also consider diversion, bail, plea bargaining, and, in serious cases, transfer of the child to adult court. The family may seek to work with the police department and the courts to avoid formal judicial proceedings and to get help through a diversion program. Or after an interview, the intake probation officer in the court may recommend that no further action be taken against the juvenile. Alternatively, the juvenile might be supervised by the intake section of the court without a judicial determination.

If the decision is to file a petition initiating formal judicial action against the juvenile, the child's attorney will seek pretrial release through bail or some other release measure and possibly enter into plea bargaining discussions.

Thus, the period between arrest and adjudication is one of the most critical points in the juvenile justice system. Because the steps in this process are so important, this chapter will examine how the child is handled during this period. First, we will look at the detention system, which takes children out of the community before either their adjudication, disposition, or treatment. Then we discuss intake in the juvenile court. Intake procedures serve as a means of screening and diverting certain juvenile offenders from juvenile proceedings. Lastly, the chapter will examine bail and plea bargaining for children, diversion, and waiver to the adult court.

THE CONCEPT OF DETENTION

Detention is the temporary care of children in physically restricted facilities pending court disposition or transfer to another agency.[1] Traditional detention facilities for children are designed as secure environments. The approximately five hundred secure detention facilities operating around the United States have locked doors, high fences or walls, screen or bars, and other obstructions designed to prevent detainees from leaving the facility at will.

Detention facilities of this kind normally handle juveniles at different stages of the juvenile justice process. Some juveniles are kept in detention to await their court hearings. Others have had a trial but have not been sentenced or are awaiting the imposition of their sentences. A third group of children are those whose sentences have been imposed but who are awaiting admittance to a correctional training school. Thus, as the American Bar Association states, "the term 'pre-trial detainee' is inaccurate to describe the many juveniles in detention whose cases have already been adjudicated but whose disposition remains unimplemented."[2]

Detention is the temporary housing of children in physically restricted facilities pending court hearings or transfer to another agency such as the state Department of Mental Health.

There are other types of residential care programs that should be distinguished from detention. **Shelter care,** for example, is the temporary care of children in physically unrestricting facilities. The secure detention facility is normally used for children who have been charged with delinquent acts. Shelter care programs, including receiving homes, group homes, foster care homes, and temporary care facilities, are normally used for dependent and neglected children and status offenders who may be runaways or truants or who are often the victims of sexual and physical abuse.[3]

Regardless of its form, detention should not be viewed as a form of punishment. A juvenile is normally not a sentenced offender when placed in detention. In other words, a detention facility is not to be used as a permanent correctional facility. It provides temporary care for children who require secure custody.

Most experts in juvenile justice advocate that detention be limited to alleged delinquent offenders who require secure custody for the protection of themselves and others. In the past, however, children who were neglected and dependent, as well as status offenders, were placed in secure detention facilities. To remedy this situation, a national effort has been ongoing to remove status offenders and neglected children from detention facilities that also house juvenile delinquents. In addition, alternatives to detention centers—for example, temporary foster homes, detention boarding homes, and programs of neighborhood supervision—have been developed in numerous jurisdictions. They enable youths to live in private homes while the courts dispose of their cases. New types of residential facilities also are being created. Young persons who cannot return home are being held in dormitories and multiple-resident dwellings.[4] Efforts have also been made to improve services in existing secure detention facilities. Such programs as reception and diagnosis, community contact involving legal services and family visiting, and counseling, recreational, and educational services are important aspects of secure detention in some jurisdictions.

Detention Trends

In 1975, about eleven thousand youths were housed in detention centers on a given day. Despite ten years of effort to curb the use of detention, about fifteen thousand youths were in detention centers on a given day in 1985. There were also about four hundred thousand admissions to detention facilities during that year.

Since 1985, the number of youth held in short-term detention facilities has *increased* by about 15 percent, or over 18,500 children on a daily basis. About 500,000 admissions occur each year, of which 240,000 involve delinquency and 22,000 are status offense cases. In addition, the number of minority children (African-Americans and Hispanics) held in detention facilities has increased nearly 30 percent, which has caused considerable concern among juvenile justice professionals.[5] (See Figure 16.1.)

Juveniles often stay in detention facilities at some point between referral to court and case disposition. In 22 percent of delinquency cases (approximately 260,000) in 1989, authorities detained the juvenile prior to disposition. The use of detention in delinquency cases increased about 15 percent from 1985 to 1989.

The detention rate in cases involving property offenses increased 4 percent, while detention of youths involved in drug cases increased 71 percent. Nearly

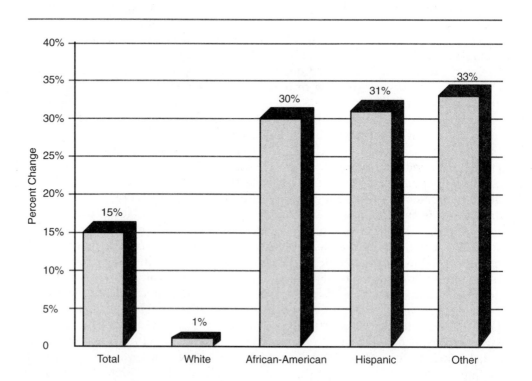

FIGURE 16.1

Increase in the number of juveniles in short-term public facilities: 1985–1987

Source: "Growth in Minority Detentions Attributed to Drug Law Violators," *Juvenile and Family Court Newsletter,* 20 (1990).

Part V Controlling Juvenile Offenders

half of the detentions in 1989 involved youths charged with property offenses (120,000).

Among cases involving male juveniles, the use of detention increased from 21 percent in 1985 to 23 percent in 1989. Among drug cases involving males, the detention rate climbed from 22 percent to 38 percent. Females were detained in only 18 percent of cases in both 1985 and 1989.

The use of detention in cases involving minority juveniles exceeded the detention rate for white juveniles in 1989 (28 percent and 19 percent, respectively). Significant racial differences occurred in the increased use of detention for drug-law violators. From 1985 to 1989, the use of detention for drug cases involving white youths increased slightly, while detention for drug cases involving minority youths increased from 33 percent to 55 percent.[6]

Juvenile detention was used in sixty-five hundred petitioned status offense cases in 1989. The use of detention for such cases declined from 17 percent (12,900 of 77,400 cases) in 1985 to 8 percent (6,500 of 76,700 cases) in 1989. Detention was least likely in truancy cases (2 percent) and most likely in runaway cases (21 percent). Runaways also accounted for the largest group of detained status offenders. Of the estimated sixty-five hundred petitioned status offense cases resulting in detention in 1989, 38 percent involved a youth charged as a runaway.[7]

With regard to the personal characteristics of children admitted to detention, the Office of Juvenile Justice and Delinquency Prevention found that the typical delinquent was male, over 15, and charged with a property crime, while the typical status offender was female, under 16, and a runaway.[8] (See Figures 16.2 and 16.3.)

These national and local increases and changes are occurring at a time when the overall population of juvenile offenders is decreasing. Experts believe the steady increase in detention use may result from (1) a rise in serious crime by juveniles; (2) a growing link to drug-related crimes; and (3) the involvement of younger children in the juvenile justice system.[9]

Thus, detention of youth continues to be a major issue in the juvenile justice system, and reducing its use has not been an easy task.

Preadjudication Detention

The majority of children taken into custody by the police are released to their parents or guardians. Some are detained overnight in a detention facility until their parents can be notified of the arrest. Police officers normally take a child to a place of detention only after other alternatives have been tried. Many juvenile courts in large urban areas have staff members, such as intake probation officers, on duty twenty-four hours a day to screen detention admissions.

Ordinarily, children who are apprehended for juvenile delinquency are detained if they are inclined to run away while awaiting their trials, if it appears that they will commit an offense dangerous to themselves or the community, or if they are violators from other jurisdictions. For example, in an analysis of detention decisions in a single county in Alabama, Belinda McCarthy found that juveniles were indeed being detained because they were a threat to the community, because their own safety was endangered, and because they tended

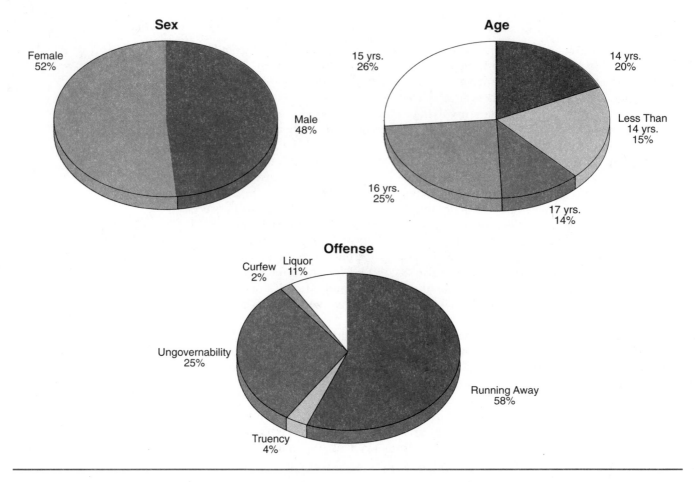

Sex

Female 52%

Male 48%

Age

15 yrs. 26%

14 yrs. 20%

Less Than 14 yrs. 15%

17 yrs. 14%

16 yrs. 25%

Offense

Curfew 2%

Liquor 11%

Ungovernability 25%

Running Away 58%

Truency 4%

■■**FIGURE 16.2**

Characteristics of youth
detained in status offense
cases

Source: Howard N. Snyder, *Growth in
Minority Detentions Attributed to Drug
Law Violators* (Washington, D.C.: U.S.
Department of Justice, Office of Justice
Programs, 1990), pp. 3 and 5.

to commit more serious crimes; offender race, class, and gender did not play a
role in detention decision making.[10]

However, the criteria used in deciding whether a child should be placed in
detention are far from clear; each jurisdiction handles detention decisions
differently. In fact, a recent study by Charles Frazier and Donna Bishop employing data on all juveniles processed in a single state over a two-year period failed
to uncover any pattern that could help explain how detention decisions were
made.[11] Frazier and Bishop concluded that detention decisions were based solely
on judicial discretion. Similarly, a recent study of New York state's juvenile
offender law in Westchester County, New York, also concluded that detention
decisions lack the clearly defined statutory criteria needed to reduce the number
of youths admitted to secure detention facilities.[12]

Today, many courts are striving to implement the recommendations of the
National Council on Crime and Delinquency and other standard-setting groups
that suggest that youth should be detained only if they are (1) likely to commit
a new offense, (2) present a danger to themselves or the community, or (3) are
likely to run away or fail to appear at subsequent court hearings.[13]

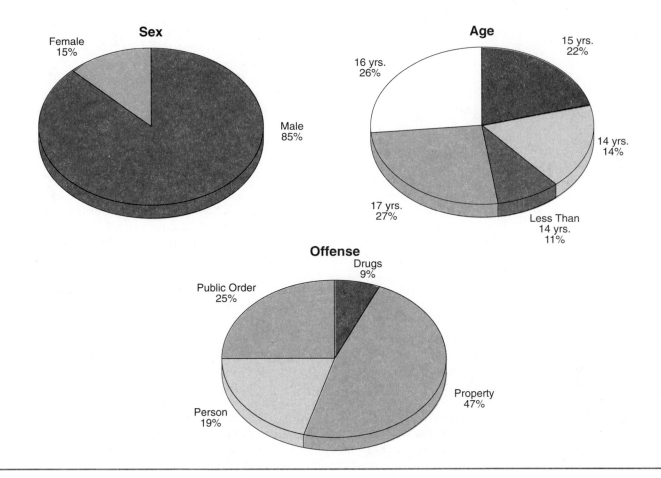

Sex

Female 15%

Male 85%

Age

15 yrs. 22%

16 yrs. 26%

14 yrs. 14%

17 yrs. 27%

Less Than 14 yrs. 11%

Offense

Drugs 9%

Public Order 25%

Property 47%

Person 19%

■■ FIGURE 16.3

Characteristics of youth detained in delinquency cases

Source: Howard N. Snyder, *Growth in Minority Detentions Attributed to Drug Law Violators* (Washington, D.C.: U.S. Department of Justice, Office of Justice Programs, 1990), pp. 3 and 5.

Right to Detention Hearings

A child who is placed in a detention facility or shelter care unit should not be kept there longer than twenty-four hours. Most jurisdictions require the filing of a formal petition against the child invoking the jurisdiction of the juvenile court within the twenty-four-hour period.

To detain a juvenile, there must be clear evidence of probable cause to believe that the child has committed the offense and that he or she will flee the area if not detained. Furthermore, once a child has been detained and a petition filed, the child should not continue in detention without a **detention hearing.**[14] Although the requirements for detention hearings vary considerably among the states, most jurisdictions require that they occur almost immediately after the child's admission to a detention facility and provide the youth with notice and counsel.

The probation department of the juvenile court may help the judge decide whether or not to keep a child in detention when the police file a petition. Usually a probation officer in the intake department assists the court in making a decision about the child's release.

In sum, the ultimate decision to detain or release depends on the nature of the children's actions, whether they are a danger to themselves or others, and whether their parents or lawful guardians can be reached quickly to take them home. If children are to be kept longer than twenty-four hours, a formal petition must be filed against them and their parents must be notified so the children can possibly be released in their custody.

Detention Problems

Detention has long been criticized because it entails placing children who have not yet been found to be delinquent in an often harsh environment that is more often than not lacking in any rehabilitative services. As one national survey of detention conditions put it: "the custody was a matter of lock and key, and the instructive experience was more the exception than the rule. . . . Repeatedly, detention emerged as a form of punishment without conviction—and often without crime."[15]

In addition, critics charge that the discretion used when selecting youths for detention often works against the poor and minorities. A study by the Humphrey Institute of Public Affairs found that minority youths are placed in secure detention facilities at a rate three to four times higher than white youths; during the three-year period studied (1979 to 1982), the overrepresentation became increasingly more pronounced.[16] Other researchers also report that differential detention rates are produced by economic, family, and community forces. For example, of almost twenty-five hundred cases taken from the juvenile court records of six New Jersey counties, researchers Russell Schutt and Dale Dannefer found that detention decisions favor protecting some classes of juveniles rather than ensuring them due process.[17] For example, African-American and Hispanic juveniles were quite likely to be detained even if they lived with two parents, but white juveniles were subject to detention if they lived with one parent only.

New Approaches to Detention

Efforts have been ongoing to improve the process of detention and to better detention conditions. The Juvenile Detention Committee of the American Correctional Association has developed standards for detention that establish fair and uniform positive expectations for its use. These standards state that:

Juvenile detention is the temporary and secure custody of children accused or adjudicated of conduct subject to the jurisdiction of the family/juvenile court who require a physically restricting environment for their own or the community's protection while pending legal action. Further, juvenile detention should provide and maintain a wide range of helpful services that include, but are not limited to, the following: education, visitation, private communications, counseling, continuous supervision, medical and health care, nutrition, recreation, and reading. To advise the court on the proper course of action required to restore the child to a productive role in the community, detention should also include or provide a system for clinical observation and diagnosis that compliments the wide range of helpful services.[18]

Some evidence indicates that preadjudicatory facilities are meeting this goal. The consensus of professional opinion today is that juvenile detention centers should be reserved for those youth who present a clear and substantial threat to the community. As a result, attention is being focused on the development of new approaches to detention care, such as day resource centers, detention alternative programs, and family shelters.[19] In Tennessee and Michigan, for example, nonsecure holdover facilities are being used to service juveniles for a limited period. In Utah, special intake programs are used to screen children to locate more secure housing whenever possible.

In addition, many pretrial detention centers are providing extensive education programs. The Spofford Juvenile Center in the Bronx, New York, is the only pretrial detention center in New York with an educational program approved by the state.[20] The center's instructional program includes a five-and-a-half-hour day, with a curriculum of reading and language arts, math, social studies, science, health and safety education, library skills, physical education, art, and music. Because students remain in detention for varying lengths of stay, the curriculum is organized in short modules so that students whose stays are brief can still complete a body of work. The Los Patrinos Juvenile Hall School in Downey, California, also operates with a highly transient population. Yet, it has been successful in offering comprehensive instruction in basic academic subjects and technological and functional living skills. It emphasizes helping students to develop positive self-concepts and improved relationships with others.[21] In New Hampshire, young people spend an average of twenty-one days in the ADC (Awaiting Disposition of the Court) Unit. The unit's on-site educational program employs a nontraditional, holistic learning approach designed to generate student opinions, cultivate discussions, and stimulate responses. The prime curriculum variable is the "Weekly Theme." Several educational themes or modules have been designed both to provide factual information and to promote student discussions on a variety of topics, including U.S. history, basic psychology, and family problems.[22]

Undoubtedly, juveniles pose special detention problems. But some efforts are being made to improve programs and reduce pretrial detention use, especially in secure settings. Of all the problems associated with detention, however, none is as critical as the issue of placing youths in adult jails, a practice that is addressed in the following section.

Detention in Adult Jails

One of the most significant problems with detention is placing youngsters under 18 in adult jails. This is usually done in rural areas where no other facility exists. Almost all experts in the field of juvenile justice agree that placing children under the age of 18 in any type of jail facility should be prohibited. Juveniles in adult jails can become the victims of other inmates, of the staff, and of their own hands.

The placement of juveniles in jails is also particularly distressing when the sorry state of the nation's jails is considered. Juveniles detained in adult jails often live in squalid conditions and are subjected to physical and sexual abuse. A federally sponsored study found that children confined in adult institutions were eight times as likely to commit suicide as those placed in detention centers exclusively for juveniles and have a 4.5 percent higher rate of suicide than children in the general population.[23] Over the years, jails have been the least progressive of all correctional institutions in the United States. Most jails were

The detention of juveniles in adult jails continues to be a significant social problem. Federal initiatives have helped to reduce, though not yet to eliminate, the practice.

constructed in the nineteenth century; few have been substantially improved in the twentieth century, and many are in poor physical condition. Many jails throughout the nation are overcrowded, have no rehabilitation programs, provide little or no medical attention, and make no effort to provide adequate plumbing, ventilation, or heating. Many are fire hazards. Courts throughout the nation have ruled that conditions in certain jails make incarceration there a cruel and unusual punishment, a violation of the Eighth and Fourteenth Amendments of the U.S. Constitution. Regardless of the conditions, the argument can be made that jailing juveniles with adults must be viewed as cruel and unusual punishment, considering their status.

Until a few years ago, the placement of juveniles in adult facilities was common. According to a study by the Community Research Center at the University of Illinois, 479,000 juveniles were admitted to adult jails in 1979. Of these, 20 percent were status offenders whose "crimes" included running away or underage drinking. Some 4 percent (over nineteen thousand youths) were jailed without having committed an offense of any sort; 9 percent were 13 years old or younger.[24] Efforts at changing this situation are discussed below.

Removing Youths from Adult Jails

The impetus for removing juveniles from adult jails comes from the Office of Juvenile Justice and Delinquency Prevention. In 1989, the Juvenile Justice and Delinquency Prevention Act (JJDPA) of 1974 was amended to require that the states remove all juveniles from adult jails and lockups. According to federal guidelines, all juveniles in state custody must be separated from adult offenders or the state could lose federal juvenile justice funds. The OJJDP defines separation as the condition in which juvenile detainees have either totally independent facilities or shared facilities that are designed so that juveniles and adults neither have accidental contact nor share programs or treatment staff.[25]

Much debate has arisen over whether the initiative to remove juveniles from adult jails has succeeded. It is still not known how many youths are being held in adult facilities. Some indications are that the numbers have declined significantly from the almost half a million a year recorded in 1979. Today, federal agencies estimate that about seventeen hundred juveniles are being held in adult jails on any given day, and about fifty-three thousand are held in adult jails or lockups some time during the year; about thirty states (75 percent) are in substantial compliance with federal guidelines. According to a 1990 report of juveniles in custody, the average daily population of juveniles held in adult jails declined nearly 18 percent (from seventeen hundred to fourteen hundred) between 1980 and 1989.[26]

Despite such assurances, these figures do not include youths held in urban jails for under six hours or in rural ones for under twenty-four hours, youths transferred to the criminal court, youths in four states that do not cooperate with the federal jail removal initiative, or youths in states that consider anyone over 16 or 17 to be an adult. The Community Research Center in Champaign, Illinois, which monitors the jailing of delinquent youths, believes that a more accurate estimate is that about two hundred thousand youths are still being jailed with adults each year.[27] Other researchers, on the other hand, still believe that close to half a million youths are detained in adult preadjudicatory facilities (jails or lockups) each year.[28] National trends in juvenile detention rates suggests that the actual number of detainees may have occasionally decreased over the last decade, but the length of time juveniles are held in jails and other secure facilities has increased.

Eliminating the confinement of juveniles in adult institutions continues to be a difficult and ongoing task. In a recent comprehensive study of the jailing of juveniles in Minnesota, Ira Schwartz found that even in a state recognized nationally for juvenile justice reform, the rate of admission of juveniles to adult jails remains unacceptably high.[29] His research also revealed that while the rate of admission was not related to the *seriousness* of the offense, minority youth spent greater amounts of time in jail for the same offenses than white offenders.[30]

In his report, Schwartz suggests that: (1) government enact legislation prohibiting the confinement of juveniles in jail; (2) appropriate juvenile detention facilities be established; (3) funds be allocated for such programs; (4) racial disparity in detention be examined; and (5) responsibility for monitoring conditions of confinement be fixed by statutes and court decisions.[31]

There are some promising trends. California, for example, passed legislation ensuring that no minor under juvenile court jurisdiction can be incarcerated in any jail after July 1, 1989.[32] And in the landmark federal court case, *Hendrickson v. Griggs,* the court found that Iowa had not complied with the juvenile jail removal mandate of the Juvenile Justice and Delinquency Prevention Act and ordered local officials to develop a plan for bringing the state into conformity with the law.[33] As a result, states will face increasing legal pressure to meet jail removal requirements in the future.

Because the actual number of juvenile detainees in adult jails is uncertain, it remains a difficult job to monitor progress in this area. With federal help, however, some progress appears to have been made in removing juveniles from adult facilities, but thousands each year continue to be held in close contact with adults, and thousands more are held in facilities that, though physically separate, put them in close proximity to adults. To the youths held within their walls, there may appear to be little difference between the juvenile detention facilities and the adult jail.

DEINSTITUTIONALIZATION OF STATUS OFFENDERS

One of the most important juvenile justice policy initiatives of the past two decades has been the removal of status offenders from secure detention facilities that also house delinquents. Along with removing all juveniles from adult jails, the OJJDP has made deinstitutionalization of status offenders a cornerstone of its policy.

The purpose of removing status offenders from secure detention facilities is both to reduce their interface and personal relationships with serious delinquent offenders and to insulate them from the stigma and negative labels associated with being a detainee in a locked facility. **Deinstitutionalization** has its roots in labeling theory, which views the experience of being labeled a delinquent as a primary cause of delinquent careers, and the conflict perspective, which holds that those chosen for sanctions will most likely be social and political outcasts. To counteract the effects of labeling, stigma, and delinquent learning opportunities, nonsecure alternatives—counseling, after-school programs, shelter care, and foster care—have been developed for nondelinquent youths.

The national effort seems to be paying important dividends. About fifteen years ago, forty-nine hundred status offenders were in some sort of public secure confinement; in the early 1980s, this number dropped to about twenty-five hundred. Since then, the number of status offenders being held in some sort of secure confinement has remained stable at approximately twenty-five hundred.[34]

Evaluating DSO

Over a decade ago, the OJJDP funded a national **Deinstitutionalization of Status Offenders Project (DSO)** to demonstrate the feasibility of removing status offenders from secure lockups and to evaluate the effects of deinstitutionalization.[35]

Since their inception, the DSO programs netted mixed results. One problem was the definition of status offenders. Some areas limited their programs to "pure" status offenders, who had no record of prior delinquency involvement, while others included "mixed offenders," those with a record of prior delinquency. The evaluation found that the pure status offender was relatively rare; most current status offenders had prior delinquent experiences. Another problem was "net widening." Because a new program was available, police were more willing to send youths to the juvenile court rather than handle the case themselves. Thus, the number of youths processed to court *increased* in a number of cities, impeding the antilabeling, antistigma aspects of the program.

Another problem was uncovered by M. A. Bortner, Mary Sutherland, and Russ Winn, who examined a midwestern community before and after it attempted to comply with deinstitutionalization of status offenders. One disappointing finding was that there was very little overall change in the processing of status offenders. Of greater concern was the fact that black status offenders were detained more often than whites and that their detention rates actually increased after the DSO effort had been implemented. On a more positive note, the researchers found that after the deinstitutionalization effort was undertaken, the use of formal hearings and severe dispositions for both black and white youths dropped substantially.[36]

Anne Schneider has conducted the most comprehensive evaluation of DSO programs on a national level. She found that the DSO programs were successful overall in significantly reducing—but not eliminating—the number of status offenders held in secure detention and the number of status offenders institutionalized after trial. However, the recidivism rate was unaffected by the DSO project, and in some sites, it actually increased. That is, status offenders placed in nonsecure facilities, separate from delinquents, were sometimes more likely to commit repeat offenses than those held in secure detention centers.[37]

This finding suggests that removing status offenders from detention is not a panacea for preventing juvenile crime. While removal did not reduce crime, however, it was as effective as secure detention. Because shelter and foster care is much less expensive than maintaining a secure detention facility, removal at least can be a more cost-effective juvenile justice policy.

According to Federle and Chesney-Lind, the deinstitutionalization movement of the JJDPA has also meant that girls have been put instead into mental health and child welfare programs. They conclude that the system appears to be perpetuating the paternalism that has historically characterized juvenile justice.[38] Thus, the debate over the most effective way to handle juvenile status offenders continues, especially when it comes to the concept of deinstitutionalization.

The Intake Process

When the police believe a child needs a court referral, the child becomes involved in the intake division of the court. The term **intake** refers to the screening of cases by the juvenile court system. The child and his or her family are screened by intake officers, who are often probation staff members, to determine whether the child needs the services of the juvenile court. Intake officers may (1) send the youth home with no further action, (2) divert the child to a social agency, (3) petition him or her to the juvenile court, or (4) file a petition and hold the child in detention. The intake process reduces demands on limited court resources, screens out cases that are not within the court's jurisdiction, and obtains assistance from community agencies when court authority is not necessary for referral.

Juvenile court intake is now provided for by statute in the majority of states.[39] Also, most of the model acts and standards in juvenile justice suggest the development of juvenile court intake proceedings.[40]

Intake procedures are desirable for the following reasons:

- Filing complaints against children in a court may do more harm than good, because rehabilitation often fails in the juvenile court system.
- Processing children in the juvenile court labels them as delinquent, stigmatizes them, and thus reinforces their antisocial behavior.
- Nonjudicial handling of children gives them and their families an opportunity to work voluntarily with a social service agency.

- Intake screening of children helps conserve already overburdened resources in the juvenile court system.
- Intake screening allows juvenile courts to enter into consent decrees with juveniles without filing petitions and without formal adjudication. (The consent decree is basically a court order authorizing disposition of the case without a formal finding of delinquency. It is based on an agreement between the intake department of the court and the juvenile who is the subject of the complaint.)[41]

Notwithstanding all of its advantages, intake also has some problems. First, because half of all juveniles who are arrested and brought to court are handled nonjudicially, intake sections are constantly pressured to provide available services for a large group of children. Intake programs also need to be provided twenty-four hours a day in many urban courts so dispositions can be resolved quickly on the day the child is referred to court. Second, poorly qualified employees in intake are a serious flaw in many court systems.

A third problem is that although almost three-quarters of all state juvenile court systems provide intake and diversion programs, the criteria and procedures for selecting children for such nonjudicial alternatives have not been established. Normally, the intake probation officer undertakes a preliminary investigation to obtain information about the child and the family prior to making a decision. Written guidelines are needed to assist intake personnel in their duties and to alert juveniles and their families to their procedural rights. Some jurisdictions have attempted to provide guidelines for intake decision making. Those used to determine whether a juvenile case is suitable for adjustment or whether court jurisdiction should be invoked include: (1) age of the child; (2) conduct; (3) prior or pending juvenile complaints; (4) the substantial likelihood that the child will cooperate with the adjustment process; and (5) the substantial likelihood that the child can receive and is in need of appropriate services without court intervention.

Finally, a number of legal problems are associated with the intake process. Among them are whether the child has a right to counsel at this stage, whether the child is protected against self-incrimination at intake, and to what degree the child needs to consent to nonjudicial disposition as recommended by the intake probation officer.

Changing the Intake Process

Since the intake process is so critical, it has been undergoing changes in various jurisdictions. One important trend in the intake process has been the influence of prosecutors on decision making. The traditional intake process was controlled by probation personnel whose decisions influenced heavily the presiding juvenile court judge's concept of which cases should be handled formally and which should be settled without court action.

The traditional role of intake, which has been to dispense the least incursive amount of rehabilitative justice, is being replaced in some jurisdictions by a prosecutor who may be more concerned with protecting the public and controlling offenders. Some states, such as Florida, now require that the intake officers get approval from the prosecutor before either accepting or rejecting a delinquency petition. Other states, such as Maryland and California, allow the complaining party to appeal petitions rejected by intake officers to the prosecutor, while in Colorado and Washington, prosecutorial screening of cases eliminates any significant probation intake role.[42]

The county's chief legal officer, the district attorney, is now playing a greater role in the juvenile court process. There is evidence of a shift from the rehabilitation model to the due process approach in juvenile justice. As Ted Rubin puts it: "The prosecutor's authority in the juvenile intake process is likely to develop into a controlling one, stimulated by the prosecutor's public protection image, the increased interest in handling juveniles according to offense and prior record, and diminished confidence in the ideal of rehabilitation."[43] A more detailed analysis of the role of the prosecutor is found in Chapter 17.

DIVERSION

One of the most important alternatives chosen at intake is nonjudicial disposition, or, as it is variously called, nonjudicial adjustment, handling or processing, informal disposition, adjustment, or diversion. **Diversion** is the most common term used to refer to screening out children from the juvenile court without judicial determination.

Numerous national groups, commentators, lawyers, and criminal justice experts have sought to define the concept of diversion since its inception in the mid-1960s. We suggest that juvenile diversion is the process of placing youths suspected of law-violating behavior into treatment-oriented programs prior to formal trial and disposition in order to minimize their penetration into the justice system and thereby avoid any potential stigma and labeling.

Diversion implies more than simply screening out cases that are trivial or unimportant and for which no additional treatment is needed. *Screening* involves abandoning efforts to apply any coercive measures to a defendant.[44] In contrasts, *diversion* encourages an individual to participate in some specific program or activity by express or implied threat of further prosecution. Juvenile justice experts define diversion as "the channeling of cases to noncourt institutions in instances where these cases would ordinarily have received an adjudicatory hearing by a court."[45] Whatever definition is used, diversion generally refers to formally acknowledged and organized efforts to process juvenile and adult offenders outside the justice system.[46]

Diversion has become one of the most popular reforms in juvenile justice since it was recommended by the President's Crime Commission in 1967. Arguments for the use of diversion programs contend that:

1. It keeps the juvenile justice system operating; without it, the system would collapse from voluminous caseloads;
2. It is preferable to dealing with the inadequate juvenile justice treatment system;
3. It gives legislators and other government leaders the opportunity to reallocate resources to programs that may be more successful in the treatment of juvenile offenders;
4. Its costs are significantly less than the per capita cost of institutionalization; and
5. It helps youths avoid the stigma of being labeled a delinquent, which is believed to be an important factor in developing a delinquent career.[47]

Police-based diversion models include family crisis intervention projects, referral programs, and youth service bureaus. In addition, court-based diversion models have been used extensively for status offenders, minor first offenders, children involved in family disturbances, and children involved in such offenses as shoplifting or minor assault and battery. Court-based diversion programs include intervention projects involving employment, referral for educational programs, and placement of juveniles who are involved with drugs in drug-related programs.[48]

Most court-based diversion programs employ a particular formula for choosing youths for diversion. Such criteria as being a first offender, nonviolent, or status offender, and drug or alcohol dependent are used to select clients. In some instances, youths will be asked to partake of services voluntarily in lieu of a court appearance. In other programs, prosecutors will agree to defer a case until a youth has successfully completed a treatment program and to then dismiss all charges. Finally, some programs can be initiated by the juvenile court judge after the case has been brought to his or her attention at an initial hearing.[49]

In summary, diversion programs have been created to remove nonserious offenders from the formal justice system to provide them with nonpunitive treatment services and help them avoid the stigma of a delinquent label.

ISSUES IN DIVERSION: WIDENING THE NET

Diversion has been viewed as a promising alternative to official procedures, but over the years its basic premises have been questioned by a number of experts.[50] The most damaging criticism has been that diversion programs, rather than limiting stigma and system penetration, actually involve children in the justice system who previously would have been released without official notice. This phenomenon is referred to as **widening the net.** Various studies indicate that police and court personnel are likely to use diversion program services for youths who ordinarily would have been turned loose at the intake or arrest stage.[51] For example, in an analysis of diversion programs in Florida, Charles Frazier and John Cochran found that after controlling for such social and legal variables as race, sex, age, offense severity, and prior record, diverted youths experienced at least as much involvement with the juvenile justice system as did youths who were not selected for diversion.[52] Similarly, after reviewing existing research on the effectiveness of employing diversion with status offenders, Dennis Anderson and Donald Schoen found little evidence that diversion programs have met their stated goals. They conclude that while diversion should not be dismissed as an "unrealistic or harmful fad," neither should it be judged as a "satisfactory approach to juvenile delinquency."[53] Thus, the youths in diversion programs may not be "saved" from a more serious delinquency label, nor are they freed from significant intrusion in their lives.

Why does net widening occur? One explanation is that police and prosecutors find diversion a more attractive alternative to both official processing and outright release—diversion helps them resolve the conflict between doing too much or too little. Second, many local diversion programs have been funded by outside money (federal, state, or private). Local officials, worried that support will be dropped if client quotas are not maintained, beg police and court officials for a few "warm bodies." Police and judges who are reluctant to give up control of offenders they feel need more formal treatment, refer youths whom they might have released with a warning in the past. As Sharla Rausch and Charles Logan put it:

In essence, the diverted population was drawn from a pool of offenders who, prior to the implementation of diversion programs, would probably have been released or left alone. The effect of such a policy has been to expand control over a larger, less seriously involved sector of the juvenile population.[54]

Similarly, Frazier and Cochran found that net widening may actually have a benign origin, since diversion staff members often have social service backgrounds: "Most staff believed that the more attention given a youth and the longer the period of time over which the attention was given, the better the prospects for a successful outcome.[55]

Diversion has also been criticized as ineffective and unproductive. That is, youths being diverted make no better adjustment in the community than those who go through official channels. However, not all delinquency experts are critical of diversion. Arnold Binder and Gilbert Geis claim that there are many benefits to diversion that more than balance its negative qualities.[56] They challenge the net-widening concept as being naive—how do we know that diverted youths would have had less interface with the justice system if diversion didn't exist? They suggest that even if juveniles had escaped official labels for their current offense, it may be inevitable that they would eventually fall into the hands of the police and juvenile court. They also point out that the rehabilitative potential of diversion should not be overlooked.

Although diversion programs are not the panacea their originators believed them to be, at least they offer an alternative to official processing. They can help the justice system devote its energies to more serious offenders while providing counseling and other rehabilitative services to needy youths.

In summary, an examination of the history of diversion indicates that most programs widen the net of the justice system and their ability to reduce recidivism remains uncertain. According to Mark Ezell, the central theme in the juvenile court movement is the endless search for effective alternatives.[57] Juvenile diversion programs are intended to be an alternative to the traditional process. Providing treatment services for nonserious young offenders who voluntarily enter a diversion program is exemplified by the following Case in Point.

■ ■ ■ ■ ■ ■ ■ ■ ■ ■ ■ ■ ■ ■ ■

CASE IN POINT

You are the intake worker assigned to the local juvenile court.

Charles is a 13 year old who was arrested for shoplifting in a department store. He was before the juvenile court for trial and disposition on his first delinquency offense. Charles comes from a broken home. He lives with his mother and three younger siblings in a public housing project. His parents are separated, and Charles hasn't seen his father in over a year. Charles is in the eighth grade, seems bright, but frequently fights in school. The school report indicates that Charles is a sad, lonely child with a hot temper.

The intake worker and defense attorney indicate that Charles wants to remain at home, and both recommend closing the delinquency case. The prosecutor and arresting police officer feel that Charles is an aggressive, acting-out youth whose behavior is unpredictable and who is in need of juvenile court supervision.

Do you believe that Charles would benefit from a diversion program?

How would you assess the juvenile court's role in this type of case?

The Petition

A **complaint** is the report that the police or some other agency makes to the court to initiate the intake process. Once the agency makes a decision in intake that judicial disposition is required, a formal petition is filed. The **petition** is the formal legal complaint that initiates judicial action against a juvenile charged with actions alleging juvenile delinquency or noncriminal behavior. The petition also includes such basic information as the name, age, and residence of the child, the parents' names, and the facts alleging the child's delinquency. The police officer, a family member, or a social service agency can bring a petition. If, after being given the right to counsel, the child admits the allegation in the petition, an initial hearing is immediately scheduled for the child to make the admission before the court, and information is gathered to develop a treatment plan.

If the child does not admit to any of the facts in the petition, a date for a scheduled hearing on the petition is set. This hearing, whose purpose is to determine the merits of the petition, is similar to the adult trial. Once a hearing or adjudication date has been set, the probation department, which is the agency providing social services to the court, is normally asked to prepare a social study report. This report, often known as the predisposition report, collects relevant information about the child and recommends treatment and service.

When a date has been set for the hearing on the petition, parents or guardians and other persons associated with the petition, such as witnesses, the arresting police officer, and victims, are notified of the hearing. On occasion, the court may issue a summons—a court order requiring the juvenile or others involved in the case to appear for the hearing. The statutes or the juvenile code in a given jurisdiction govern the contents of the petition. Some jurisdictions, for instance, require that a petition be filed on information and belief of the complainant alone. Others require that the petition be filed under oath or that an affidavit accompany the petition. Some jurisdictions authorize only one official, such as a probation officer or prosecutor, to file the petition. Others allow numerous officials, including family and social service agencies, to set forth facts in the petition.

Bail for Children

Bail is money or some other security provided to the court to ensure the appearance of a defendant at every subsequent stage of the justice process. Its purpose is to obtain the release from custody of the person charged with the crime. Once the amount of bail is set by the court, the defendant is required to pay a percentage of the entire amount in cash or securities or to pay a professional bail bonding agency to submit a bond as a guarantee for returning to court. If a person is released on bail but fails to appear in court at the stipulated time, the bail deposit is forfeited. The person, if apprehended, is then confined in a detention facility until the court appearance.

With a few exceptions, persons other than those accused of murder are entitled to reasonable bail, as stated in the Eighth Amendment of the U.S. Constitution. There is some controversy today about whether a constitutional right to bail exists or whether the court can impose excessive bail resulting in a person's confinement. In most cases, a defendant has the right to be released on

Most jurisdictions refuse
juveniles the right to bail
on the grounds that juve-
nile proceedings are civil
and not criminal and that
detention is for the pur-
pose of treatment and not
punishment.

reasonable bail. Many jurisdictions require a bail review hearing by a higher court when a person is detained because the initial judge sets excessive bail.

Whether a defendant will appear at the next stage of the juvenile or criminal proceeding is a key issue in determining bail. Bail cannot be used to punish an accused, nor can it be denied or revoked simply at the discretion of the court. Many experts believe that money bail is one of the worst aspects of the criminal justice system. It has plagued the system for decades. It is discriminatory because it works against the poor. It is costly because the government must pay to detain offenders who are unable to pay bail and who could otherwise be in the community. It is believed that people who await trial in jail have a higher proportion of subsequent convictions than people who are released on bail. The detention of individuals who cannot pay has a dehumanizing effect on them.

Over the years, few people have realized that the same issues are involved in the detention of juveniles. Juvenile detention prior to adjudication is one of the most serious problems facing the juvenile justice system. Large numbers of juveniles are incarcerated at this critical stage. Poor conditions exist in the detention facilities where they are held, and there are harmful aftereffects of the detention process.

Despite these facts, many states refuse juveniles the right to bail. They argue that juvenile proceedings are civil, not criminal, and that detention is rehabilita- tive, not punitive. In addition, juveniles do not need a constitutional right to bail because statutory provisions allow children to be released in parental custody.

Furthermore, it is suggested that detention facilities and the number of children in them should be reduced instead of developing a bail program.

In view of the recognized deficiency of the adult bail system, some experts believe that alternative release programs should be developed for the juvenile justice system. These programs include release on recognizance, release to a third party, and the use of station house summonses or citation programs in lieu of arrest.

Some states do provide bail programs for children. Bail is used only to ensure the presence of the accused at trial. A presumption exists that the accused should be released solely on this promise. Mark Solar points out that state juvenile bail statutes are divided into three categories: (1) those guaranteeing the right to bail; (2) those which grant the court discretion to give bail; and (3) those that deny a juvenile the right to bail.[58] The consensus generally is that allowing bail for juveniles is in conflict with the *parens patriae* concept and rehabilitation goals of the juvenile justice system.

There is no agreement among jurisdictions, however, on whether a child has the constitutional right to be released on bail. The U.S. Supreme Court has never decided the issue of whether juveniles have a constitutional right to bail. Some courts have stated that bail provisions do not apply to juveniles. Others rely on the Eighth Amendment or on state constitutional provisions or statutes and conclude that juveniles do have a right to bail.

In a bail hearing for a child, the court reviews such factors as the charge, the history of the parents' ability to control the child's behavior, the child's school participation, psychological and psychiatric evaluations, the child's desire to go home, and the parents' interest in continuing to take care of the child while awaiting the trial.

Preventive Detention

An issue closely related to bail is **preventive detention.** This refers to the practice of keeping a person in custody before trial because of his or her suspected danger to the community. Proponents argue that preventive detention can save the victim of crime from any additional trouble from an offender released on bail and also protect potential new victims from harm. Opponents hold that preventive detention statutes deprive offenders of their freedom since guilt has not been proven in the case at hand. It is also unfair, they claim, to punish people for what judicial authorities believe they may do in the future, since it is impossible to predict accurately who will be dangerous. Moreover, because judges are able to use unchecked discretion in their detention decisions, an offender could unfairly be deprived of freedom without legal recourse.

Though the Supreme Court has upheld preventive detention of adults, most state jurisdictions allow judges to deny bail to adult offenders only in cases involving murder (capital crimes), when the offenders have jumped bail in the past, or when they have committed another crime while on bail. However, every state allows preventive detention of juveniles. The reason for this discrepancy hinges on the legal principle that while adults have the right to liberty, juveniles have a right to custody. Therefore, it is not unreasonable to detain youths for their own protection. On June 4, 1984, the Supreme Court dealt with this issue in ***Schall v. Martin,*** when it upheld New York State's preventive detention statute. The Court concluded that there was no indication in the statute that preventive detention was used as punishment.[59] Because of the importance of this case, it is set out in the Focus on Delinquency titled *"Schall v. Martin."*

FOCUS ON DELINQUENCY

Schall v. Martin

FACTS

Gregory Martin was arrested in New York City on December 13, 1977, on charges of robbery, assault, and criminal possession of a weapon. Since he was arrested at 11:30 P.M. and lied about his residence, Martin was kept overnight in detention and brought to juvenile court the next day for an "initial appearance" accompanied by his grandmother. The family court judge, citing possession of the loaded weapon, the false address given to police, and the lateness of the hour the crime occurred (as evidence of a lack of supervision), ordered him detained before trial under section 320.5(3)(6) of the New York State code. Section 320.5 authorizes pretrial detention of an accused juvenile delinquent if "there is a substantial probability that he will not appear in court on the return date or there is a serious risk that he may before the return date commit an act which if committed by an adult would constitute a crime." Later at trial, Martin was found to be a delinquent and sentenced to two years' probation.

Martin's attorneys filed a habeas corpus petition (demanding his release from custody) while he was in pretrial detention. Their petition charged that his detention denied him due process rights under the Fifth and Fourteenth Amendments. Their suit was a class action in behalf of all youths subject to preventive detention in New York. The New York appellate courts upheld Martin's claim on the grounds that because most delinquents are released or placed on probation, it was unfair to incarcerate them before trial. The prosecution brought the case to the U.S. Supreme Court for final judgment.

DECISION

The Supreme Court upheld the state's right to place juveniles in preventive detention. It held that preventive detention serves the legitimate objective of protecting both the juvenile and society from pretrial crime. Pretrial detention need not be considered punishment merely because the juvenile is eventually released or put on probation. And after all, there are procedural safeguards, such as notice and a hearing, and a statement of facts that must be given to juveniles before they are placed in detention. The Court also found that detention based on prediction of future behavior was not a violation of due process. Many decisions are made in the justice system, such as the decision to sentence or grant parole, that are based in part on a prediction of future behavior, and these have all been accepted by the court as legitimate exercises of state power.

SIGNIFICANCE OF THE CASE

Schall v. Martin establishes the right of juvenile court judges to deny youths pretrial release if they perceive them to be "dangerous." However, the case establishes a due process standard for detention hearings that includes notice and a statement of substantial reasons for the detention. ■

Source: *Schall v. Martin,* 104 S.Ct. 2403 (1984).

In a recent study of the effect of *Schall,* the American Bar Association concluded that continued refinement of the detention screening process is needed to achieve the twin goals of public safety and protection of the juvenile offenders' constitutional rights.[60] Because preventive detention may attach a stigma of guilt to a child presumed innocent, the practice remains a highly controversial one.

THE PLEA AND PLEA BARGAINING

In the adult criminal justice system, the defendant normally enters a plea of guilty or not guilty. More than 90 percent of all adult defendants plead guilty before the trial stage. A large proportion of those pleas involve what is known as plea bargaining. **Plea bargaining** is the exchange of prosecutorial and judicial concessions for guilty pleas.[61] It permits a defendant to plead guilty in exchange for a less serious charge on an agreement by the prosecutor to recommend a reduced sentence to the court.

Few juvenile codes require a guilty or not guilty plea when a petition is filed against a child in juvenile court. In most jurisdictions, an initial hearing is held at which the child either submits to a finding of the facts or denies the petition.[62] When the child admits to the facts, the court determines an appropriate disposition and treatment plan for the child. If the allegations in the petition are denied, the case normally proceeds to the trial or adjudication stage of the juvenile process. When a child enters no plea, the court imposes a denial of the charges for the child.

A high percentage of juvenile offenders enter guilty pleas or admissions in the juvenile court. How many of these pleas involve plea bargaining between the prosecutor or probation officer and the child's attorney is unknown. In the past, it was believed that plea bargaining was unnecessary in the juvenile justice system because there was little incentive for either the prosecution or defense to bargain in a system that does not have jury trials, criminal labels, or long sentences. In addition, since the court must dispose of cases in the best interests of the child, plea negotiation seemed unnecessary. Consequently, there has long been a debate among experts over the appropriateness of plea bargaining in the juvenile justice system. The arguments in favor of plea bargaining include lower court costs and efficiency. Others believe that it is an invisible, unfair, unregulated, and unethical process. When used, experts believe the process requires the highest standards of good faith by the prosecutor in the juvenile and adult system.[63]

In recent years, however, with concern about violent juvenile crime, attorneys have begun to see advantages to negotiating a plea rather than accepting the so-called good interests of the court regarding the child's offense. The extension of the adversary process for children has led to an increase in plea bargaining, creating an informal trial process that parallels the adult system. Other factors in the trend toward juvenile plea bargaining include the use of prosecutors rather than probation personnel and police officers in juvenile courts and the ever-increasing caseloads in such courts.

Plea bargaining negotiations generally involve the reduction of a charge, the changing of the proceedings from delinquency to a status offense, the elimination of possible waiver proceedings to the criminal court, and suggested agreements between the government and defense regarding dispositional programs for the child. In states where youths are subject to long, mandatory sentences, reduction of the charges may have a significant impact on the outcome of the case. And in states where youths may be waived to the adult court for committing certain serious crimes, a plea reduction may result in the juvenile court maintaining jurisdiction.

Although little clear evidence exists of how much plea bargaining there is in the juvenile justice system, it is apparent that such negotiations do take place and seem to be increasing. In one of the most comprehensive studies of juvenile plea negotiation in juvenile court, Joseph Sanborn found that about 20 percent of the cases processed in Philadelphia resulted in a negotiated plea. Most were for reduced sentences, most typically probation in lieu of incarceration, or if an institutional sentence could not be avoided, the juvenile was assigned to a less restrictive environment. Sanborn found that plea bargaining was a very complex process in juvenile court, depending in large measure on the philosophy of the judge and court staff; in general, he found it to be a device that has greater benefit for the defendants than for the court itself.[64] (See the Focus on Delinquency titled "Pleading Guilty in Juvenile Court.")

In summary, the majority of juvenile court cases that are not adjudicated seem to be the result of open admissions rather than actual plea bargaining. Unlike the adult system, where almost 90 percent of all charged offenders are involved in some plea bargaining, there is less plea bargaining in the juvenile court since such common incentives as dropping multiple charges or substituting a misdemeanor for a felony are unlikely. Nonetheless, plea bargaining is firmly entrenched in the juvenile process. Any plea bargain, however, must be entered into voluntarily and knowingly; otherwise, the conviction may be overturned on appeal.

TRANSFER TO THE ADULT COURT

One of the most significant actions that occurs in the early court processing of a juvenile offender is the **transfer** process. Otherwise known as **waiver, bindover,**

FOCUS ON DELINQUENCY

Pleading Guilty in Juvenile Court

While the nature and extent of plea bargaining in the adult court system is well documented, pleading guilty in juvenile court has remained a "low visibility" practice. Recent research by Joseph Sanborn sheds more light on the role of plea negotiation in the juvenile justice system.

Sanborn conducted a survey of all state's jurisdictions and the District of Columbia in order to identify legislative and judicial recognition of juvenile plea bargaining. He also observed practices in three juvenile courts and interviewed personnel in order to illustrate the bargaining process.

Sanborn found that forty states recognize plea negotiations in juvenile court and apply some type of control over the guilty plea process. Twenty-five have formulated rules that control juvenile plea negotiations. Thirteen states have passed legislation that details a judge's obligations when a juvenile pleads guilty; another three states regulate the practice through appellate court ruling. Only ten states have not addressed the issue of juvenile plea negotiations.

Though most states now address juvenile court pleas, the amount of regulation still varies widely. Most but not all jurisdictions that recognize plea bargaining in juvenile

court require judges to remind defendants that they are giving up constitutional rights, warn them of possible sentencing outcomes, determine if the plea was voluntary, and establish if there was a factual basis for the plea. Only Delaware and California require that judges discuss all these issues with young defendants.

Sanborn's observation and interview data indicates that there are ecological differences in the way the plea bargaining process is carried out. Urban courts may be more likely to institute formal procedures, while suburban and rural courts conduct plea negotiations informally.

Sanborn concludes that as the juvenile court becomes more formal and punitive, it is essential for juvenile courts to institute more formal and rigorous proceedings in order to insure that admissions are not later lost on appeal. Fairness dictates that youths, some of whom face long incarceration sentences, understand precisely what they are doing and the implication of pleading guilty for both current and future considerations. ■

Source: Joseph Sanborn, "Pleading Guilty in Juvenile Court: Minimal Ado about Something Very Important to Young Defendants," *Justice Quarterly* 9:126–50 (1992).

Waiver is controversial because it can eventually lead to the incarceration of an adolescent in a facility which also houses experienced adult offenders.

or **removal,** this process involves transferring a juvenile from the juvenile court to the criminal court. Most state statutes allow for this kind of transfer.

Historically, the American justice system has made a fundamental distinction between children and adults. The juvenile justice system emphasizes rehabilitation, and the criminal justice system emphasizes deterrence, punishment, and social control. Proponents of the transfer process claim that children who commit serious, chronic offenses and who may be hardened offenders should be handled by the criminal court system. In fact, so the argument goes, these children cannot be rehabilitated. Even such well-regarded institutions as the National Council of Juvenile and Family Court Judges have made it their stated policy to favor transfer.[65] Unless a waiver policy exists, children may feel immune from "real" punishment.

Opponents suggest that the transfer process is applied to children unfairly and is a halfhearted effort at implementing the treatment philosophy of the juvenile court. Furthermore, some children tried in the adult criminal court may be incarcerated under conditions so extreme that they will be permanently damaged. Another serious disadvantage of transferring a child is the stigma that may be attached to a conviction in the criminal court. Labeling children as adult offenders early in life may seriously impair their further educational, employment, and other opportunities.

In reality, however, some juveniles take advantage of decisions to transfer them to the adult court. Often, although the charge against a child may be considered serious in the juvenile court, the adult criminal court will not find it so, and a child will have a better chance for dismissal of the charges or acquittal after a jury trial.

Today, all states allow juveniles to be tried as adults in criminal courts in one of three ways:

1. *Concurrent jurisdiction.* The prosecutor has the discretion of filing charges for certain offenses in either juvenile or criminal court.

2. *Excluded offenses.* The legislature excludes from juvenile court jurisdiction certain offenses that are either very minor, such as traffic or fishing violations, or very serious, such as murder or rape (offense-based waiver).

3. *Judicial waiver.* The juvenile court waives its jurisdiction and transfers the case to criminal court (this procedure is also known as "binding over" or "certifying" juvenile cases to criminal court).

Today, twelve states authorize prosecutors to bring cases in the juvenile or adult criminal court at their discretion; thirty-six states exclude certain offenses from juvenile court jurisdiction; and forty-eight states, the District of Columbia, and the federal government have judicial waiver provisions.[66]

Statutory Criteria in Transfer

Statutes set the standards for transfer procedures. Age is of particular importance. Some jurisdictions allow for transfer between the ages of 14 and 17. Others restrict waiver proceedings to mature juveniles and specify particular offenses. In a few jurisdictions, any child can be sentenced to the criminal court system, regardless of age. For example, Massachusetts law states that only juveniles between the ages of 14 and 17 are eligible for transfer and that a child can be transferred only if he or she has (1) previously been committed to the Department of Youth Services and the present offense is punishable by imprisonment or (2) has committed an offense invoking infliction or threat of serious bodily harm.[67] If the above conditions are met, a transfer hearing must be held to determine whether it is in the public interest to transfer the child. The court must consider the seriousness of the alleged offense; the child's family, school, and social history; the general protection of the public; the nature of past treatment efforts for the child; and the likelihood of the child's rehabilitation in the juvenile court.

More than thirty states have amended their waiver policies to automatically exclude certain offenses from juvenile court jurisdiction. For example, Indiana excludes cases involving 16- and 17-year-olds charged with kidnapping, rape, and robbery (if a weapon was used or bodily injury occurred); in Illinois, youths 15 to 16 who are charged with murder, aggravated or sexual assault, or armed robbery with a firearm are automatically sent to criminal court; in Pennsylvania, any child accused of murder, regardless of age, is tried before the criminal court.[68] While about half of these jurisdictions automatically exclude serious crimes, such as murder or rape, from the juvenile court, the rest use exclusion to remove minor traffic offenses and public ordinance violations, which are then handled by lower criminal courts. Nonetheless, the trend has been to exclude serious violent offenses from juvenile court jurisdictions, a response to the growing recognition of the chronic offender program.

In a minority of states, statutes allow prosecutors to file particularly serious cases either in the juvenile court or the adult court at their own discretion; this is called **concurrent jurisdiction.**[69]

A few states do not waive juveniles to the adult court. Nebraska has concurrent jurisdiction for all felonies. It allows the prosecuting attorney to choose between bringing the case to either juvenile court or adult court. New York gives original jurisdiction for serious cases to the adult court and allows waiver to the juvenile court at the judge's discretion. Most statutes consider age and/or seriousness of the offense as the basis for removing the child from the juvenile court[70] (see Tables 16.1 and 16.2).

■■ TABLE 16.1   Age for Waiver to the Adult Court

FORTY-EIGHT STATES, THE DISTRICT OF COLUMBIA, AND THE FEDERAL
GOVERNMENT HAVE JUDICIAL WAIVER PROVISIONS

YOUNGEST AGE AT WHICH JUVENILE MAY BE TRANSFERRED TO CRIMINAL COURT BY JUDICIAL WAIVER	STATES
No specific age	Alaska, Arizona, Arkansas, Delaware, Florida, Indiana, Kentucky, Maine, Maryland, New Hampshire, New Jersey, Oklahoma, South Dakota, West Virginia, Wyoming, federal districts
10 Years	Vermont
12	Montana
13	Georgia, Illinois, Mississippi
14	Alabama, Colorado, Connecticut, Idaho, Iowa, Massachusetts, Minnesota, Missouri, North Carolina, North Dakota, Pennsylvania, South Carolina, Tennessee, Utah
15	District of Columbia, Louisiana, Michigan, New Mexico, Ohio, Oregon, Texas, Virginia
16	California, Hawaii, Kansas, Nevada, Rhode Island, Washington, Wisconsin

Note: Many judicial waiver statutes also specify offenses that are waivable. This chart lists the states by the youngest age for which judicial waiver may be sought without regard to offense.

Source: Linda A. Szymanski, *Waiver/Transfer/Certification of Juveniles to Criminal Court: Age Restrictions: Crime Restrictions* (Pittsburgh: National Center for Juvenile Justice, February 1987).

Thus, the waiver process is a statutory one, and the criteria that affect the decision to transfer the child to the criminal court are found in each of the state juvenile court acts. Many states, however, favor keeping children in juvenile court rather than transferring them to criminal court. The ineffectiveness of the criminal justice system is itself an adequate argument for keeping children in juvenile court.

DUE PROCESS IN TRANSFER PROCEEDINGS

Since 1966, the U.S. Supreme Court and other federal and state courts have attempted to ensure fairness in the waiver process by handing down decisions that spell out the need for due process. Two Supreme Court decisions, **Kent v. United States** (1966) and **Breed v. Jones** (1975), are set out in the Focus on Delinquency entitled "Due Process and the Waiver Decision" because of their significance.[71] The *Kent* case declared a District of Columbia transfer statute unconstitutional and attacked the subsequent conviction of the child by granting him specific due process rights. In *Breed v. Jones*, the Supreme Court declared that the child was granted the protection of the double-jeopardy clause of the Fifth Amendment after he was tried as a delinquent in the juvenile court.

■■ TABLE 16.2 Legislative Waiver Based on Offense

CURRENT OFFENSE	STATES[a]
Murder[b]	California, Delaware, Georgia, Indiana, Kentucky, Maine, Minnesota, New Jersey, New Mexico, South Carolina, Virginia, West Virginia
Robbery or armed robbery	California, Delaware, Georgia, New Jersey, New Mexico, South Carolina, Virginia, West Virginia
Kidnapping	California, Georgia, Minnesota, New Jersey, West Virginia
Rape	California, Delaware, Georgia, Minnesota, New Jersey, New Mexico, South Carolina, Virginia, West Virginia
Burglary or aggravated burglary	Georgia, Minnesota, New Mexico, South Carolina
Aggravated assault	South Carolina
Other[c]	Connecticut, Florida, Georgia, Hawaii, Indiana, Kentucky, Maine, Maryland, Massachusetts, Minnesota, New Jersey, North Carolina, Virginia, West Virginia

[a]Not all states specify particular offenses serving as the basis for waiver decisions (i.e., some statutes prescribe "any" offense or "felonies" as justifying waivers). Some states are included in this list more than once because they stipulate a number of offenses eligible for waiver.
[b]In some states (e.g., Georgia, Kentucky, Maryland, and North Carolina) the specification is for "capital" offenses.
[c]This category includes offenses such as "Class A, B, or C felonies," "personal violence," "aggravated felonies," or simply "felonies."

Source: Barry C. Feld, "The Juvenile Court Meets the Principle of the Offense: Legislative Changes in Juvenile Waiver Statutes," *Journal of Criminal Law and Criminology* 78:505–8 (1987).

Today, as a result of *Kent* and *Breed*, states that have transfer hearings provide specific requirements for transfer proceedings in their juvenile code. For the most part, when a transfer hearing is conducted today, due process of law requires there be: (1) a legitimate transfer hearing, (2) sufficient notice to the child's family and defense attorney, (3) the right to counsel, and (4) a statement of the reason for the court order regarding transfer. These rights recognize what *Kent v. United States* indicated: namely, that the transfer proceeding is a critically important action in determining the statutory rights of the juvenile offender.

YOUTHS IN ADULT COURT

The issue of waiver is an important one. Waiver is attractive to conservatives because it jibes with the get-tough policy currently popular in the juvenile justice system. Liberals oppose its use because it is in contradistinction to the rehabilitative ideal. Some conservative thinkers have argued that the increased use of waiver can help get violent, chronic offenders off the streets. Barry Feld suggests that waiver to adult court should be mandatory for juveniles committing serious, violent crimes.[72] He argues that mandatory waiver would coincide with the currently popular just-deserts sentencing policy and eliminate potential bias and disparity in judicial decision making. A recent detailed analysis by Feld of legislative changes in juvenile waiver statutes indicates that the nature of the

FOCUS ON DELINQUENCY

Due Process and the Waiver Decision

KENT V. UNITED STATES

FACTS

Morris Kent was arrested at the age of 16 in connection with charges of housebreaking, robbery, and rape. As a juvenile, he was subject to the exclusive jurisdiction of the District of Columbia Juvenile Court. The District of Columbia statute declared that the court could transfer the petitioner "after full investigation" and remit him to trial in the U.S. District Court. Kent admitted his involvement in the offenses and was placed in a receiving home for children. Subsequently, his mother obtained counsel, and they discussed with the social service director the possibility that the juvenile court might waive its jurisdiction. Kent was detained at the receiving home for almost one week. There was no arraignment, no hearing, and no hearing for petitioner's apprehension. Kent's counsel arranged for a psychiatric examination, and a motion requesting a hearing on the waiver was filed. The juvenile court judge did not rule on the motion and entered an order stating, "After full investigation, the court waives its jurisdiction and directs that a trial be held under the regular proceedings of the criminal court." The judge made no finding and gave no reasons for his waiver decision. It appeared that the judge denied motions for a hearing, recommendations for hospitalization for psychiatric observation, requests for access to the social service file, and offers to prove that the petitioner was a fit subject for rehabilitation under the juvenile court.

After the juvenile court waived its jurisdiction, Kent was indicted by the grand jury and was subsequently found guilty of housebreaking and robbery and not guilty by reason of insanity on the charge of rape. Kent was sentenced to serve a period of thirty to ninety years on his conviction.

DECISION

The petitioner's lawyer appealed the decision on the basis of the infirmity of the proceedings by which the juvenile court waived its jurisdiction. He further attacked the waiver on statutory and constitutional grounds, stating: "(1) no hearing occurred, (2) no findings were made, (3) no reasons were stated before the waiver, and (4) counsel was denied access to the social service file." The U.S. Supreme Court found that the juvenile court order waiving jurisdiction and remitting the child to trial in the district court was invalid. Its arguments were based on the following:

■ The theory of the juvenile court act is rooted in social welfare procedures and treatments.
■ The philosophy of the juvenile court, namely *parens patriae*, is not supposed to allow procedural unfairness.
■ Waiver proceedings are critically important actions in the juvenile court.
■ The juvenile court act requiring full investigation in the District of Columbia should be read in the context of constitutional principles relating to due process of law. These principles require at a minimum that the petitioner be entitled to a hearing, access to counsel, access by counsel to social service records, and a statement of the reason for the juvenile court decision.

SIGNIFICANCE OF THE CASE

This case examined for the first time the substantial degree of discretion associated with a transfer proceeding

continued on next page

offense dominates the waiver decision, rather than the real needs of the offender. According to Feld, the waiver of a serious juvenile offender into the adult system on the basis of his offense, rather than an individualized evaluation of the youth's amenability to treatment or dangerousness, is both an indication of and a contributor to the substantive and procedural criminalization of the juvenile court.[73]

FOCUS ON DELINQUENCY

in the District of Columbia. Thus, the Supreme Court significantly limited its holding to the statute involved but justified its reference to constitutional principles relating to due process and the assistance of counsel. In addition, it said that the juvenile court waiver hearings need to measure up to the essentials of due process and fair treatment. Furthermore, in an appendix to its opinion, the Court set up criteria concerning waiver of the jurisdictions. These are:

- The seriousness of the alleged offense to the community
- Whether the alleged offense was committed in an aggressive, violent, or willful manner
- Whether the alleged offense was committed against persons or against property
- The prosecutive merit of the complaint
- The desirability of trial and disposition
- The sophistication and maturity of the juvenile
- The record and previous history of the juvenile
- Prospects for adequate protection of the public and the likelihood of reasonable rehabilitation

BREED V. JONES

FACTS

In 1971, a petition in the juvenile court of California was filed against Jones, who was then 17, alleging that he had committed an offense that, if committed by an adult, would constitute robbery. The petitioner was detained pending a hearing. At the hearing, the juvenile court took testimony and found that the allegations were true and sustained the petition. The proceedings were continued for a disposition hearing, at which point Jones was found unfit for treatment in the juvenile court. It was ordered that he be prosecuted as an adult offender. At a subsequent preliminary hearing, the petitioner was held for criminal trial, an information was filed against him for robbery, and he was tried and found guilty. He was committed to the California Youth Authority, over objections that he was being subjected to double jeopardy.

Petitioner Jones sought an appeal in the federal district court on the basis of the double-jeopardy argument that jeopardy attaches at the juvenile delinquency proceedings. The writ of habeas corpus was denied.

DECISION

The U.S. Supreme Court held that the prosecution of Jones as an adult in the California Superior Court, after an adjudicatory finding in the juvenile court that he had violated a criminal statute and a subsequent finding that he was unfit for treatment as a juvenile, violated the double-jeopardy clause of the Fifth Amendment of the U.S. Constitution as applied to the states through the Fourteenth Amendment. Thus, Jones's trial in Superior Court for the same offense as that for which he was tried in the juvenile court violated the policy of the double-jeopardy clause, even if he never faced the risk of more than one punishment, since double jeopardy refers to the risk or potential risk of trial and conviction, not punishment.

SIGNIFICANCE OF THE CASE

The *Breed* case provided answers on several important transfer issues: (1) *Breed* prohibits trying a child in an adult court when there has been a prior adjudicatory juvenile proceeding; (2) probable cause may exist at a transfer hearing, and this does not violate subsequent jeopardy if the child is transferred to the adult court; (3) because the same evidence is often used in both the transfer hearing and subsequent trial in either the juvenile or adult court, a different judge is often required for the different hearing. ■

Sources: Kent v. United States, 383 U.S. 541, 86 S.Ct. 1045, 16 L.Ed.2d 84 (1966); *Breed v. Jones*, 421 U.S. 519, 95 S.Ct. 1779 (1975).

In a similar fashion, the trend has been toward giving original jurisdiction for serious juvenile crimes to the adult courts and then allowing judges the power to waive deserving cases back to the juvenile court. However, youths cannot be placed in adult correctional facilities until they reach their sixteenth birthday.

Because of the popularity of waiver, the number of youths processed in adult courts has become significant. A federally sponsored survey in the early 1980s

Offense characteristics of delinquency cases waived to criminal court, 1989

Source: Howard N. Snyder, Melissa H. Sickmund, Ellen H. Nimick, Terrence A. Finnegan, Dennis P. Sullivan, Rowen S. Poole, and Nancy J. Tierney, *Juvenile Court Statistics, 1989* (Pittsburgh: National Center for Juvenile Justice, 1992), p. 21.

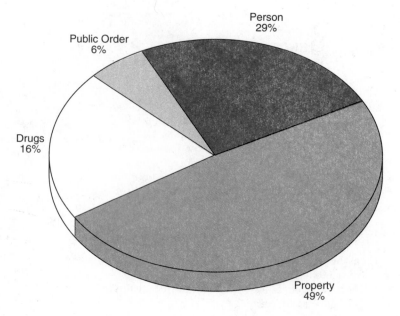

Cases Waived: 16,000

found that in a single year, nine thousand juveniles were waived to adult courts, two thousand were prosecuted as adults because of concurrent jurisdiction, and thirteen hundred were prosecuted as adults because the offenses they committed were excluded from juvenile court jurisdiction. In addition, since twelve states use low juvenile court maximum age limits, about 250,000 16- and 17-year-olds are handled by adult court each year. The study also found that (1) most waived youths are charged not with violent crimes but with property and public order (drug, alcohol) offenses; (2) most of the youths tried in adult courts are convicted or plead guilty; (3) youths are more likely to receive a probation sentence than confinement (but 46 percent of youths judicially waived were sent to adult correctional facilities); and (4) youths convicted as adults and sentenced to confinement do more time than they would have under juvenile court disposition. While the report does not recommend abolition of waiver, it suggests that juveniles should always be kept out of adult correctional facilities and be treated as juveniles as long as possible.

In 1989 (the latest available data), sixteen thousand delinquency cases were waived to criminal court, or 2.7 percent of all processed delinquency cases (see Figure 16.4). Between 1985 and 1989, the number of cases waived increased over 75 percent.[74]

DEBATING THE WAIVER CONCEPT

Despite the increased use of waiver, the efficacy of transferring youths to the adult court has been questioned. One alleged shortcoming is that the actual treatment of delinquents in adult court is quite similar to what they might have received had they remained in the custody of juvenile authorities; therefore, why transfer them? For example, New York's law has been criticized on the grounds that 70 percent of children arraigned in adult courts are waived to juvenile court, wasting both time and money; 40 percent of juveniles tried in adult court are sentenced to probation; and only 3 percent of the juvenile offenders tried in adult court received longer sentences than they could have been given in juvenile court.[75]

Other critics view transfer as adding undue burdens to youthful offenders. Research conducted by Cary Rudman, Eliot Hartstone, Jeffrey Fagan, and Melinda Moore compared case outcomes of a group of waived violent juvenile offenders to a control group of offenders with similar case characteristics retained in juvenile court. Using data from four jurisdictions, the researchers found that it took two and a half times as long (246 days verses 98 days) to process a waiver case than one that was retained in juvenile court.[76] During most of this added time, the juvenile was held in a detention center. The study also found that waived youths were treated quite harshly by the adult justice system: 90 percent were convicted; all convictions were to the top offense charged, indicating they engaged in relatively little plea negotiation; 90 percent of convicted youth were incarcerated (73 percent in prison and 18 percent in jail); and youths convicted in adult court received sentences five times longer than those retained in the juvenile court. With regard to the latter issue, youths convicted in adult courts received sentences averaging 247 months for murder and 171 months for rape; in comparison, juvenile courts sentenced offenders to 55 months for murder and 16 for rape. The research effort concluded that transferring youths to the adult court did indeed fulfill the get-tough role for which it was designed. However, it also found that program services for waived youths were lacking and that delinquencies will eventually come back to haunt society when waived youngsters are eventually released from prison without receiving adequate treatment.

The severe sentences given to waived youth have been substantiated by a federally sponsored survey of waiver in twelve urban jurisdictions, including Seattle, Miami, Chicago, and Denver. Of the 344 cases sent to criminal court, 66 percent resulted in a finding of guilt, and 77 percent of the convicted juveniles were sentenced to jail or prison for an average of 6.8 years. These figures indicate that juveniles are receiving somewhat longer prison sentences than adults get for comparable crimes.[77]

More serious are the objections raised by M. A. Bortner, whose research led to the conclusion that the transfer decision may be motivated by administrative and political considerations.[78] Bortner studied the records of 214 youths remanded to adult court in a western county. There was little evidence that the waived youths were any more dangerous or unruly than youths treated by the juvenile court. Nor was there any evidence that their transfer enhanced public safety. By turning a small portion of their clientele over to the adult court and by portraying these youths as the most dangerous, the juvenile court authorities were able to show that they were concerned for public safety while at the same time keeping control over the vast majority of youths in their jurisdiction and deflecting criticism of their entire juvenile justice operations. Critics see the new methods of dealing with offenders as inefficient, ineffective, and philosophically out of step with the original concept of the juvenile court. Supporters view them as a means of getting the most serious, chronic juvenile offenders off the streets for long periods, while ensuring that rehabilitation plays a lesser role.

Another question raised by critics is whether or not transfers to the adult court are carried out fairly and equitably. One warning sign is the fact that minorities are waived at a rate that is greater than their representation in the population. Jeffery Fagan and his associates have identified the existence of such racial disparity in decision making from apprehension through the commitment stage.[79]

Using prosecutorial discretion to determine whether to proceed in the juvenile or the criminal justice system is also a much maligned practice. (See Table 16.3 for a listing of the many factors influencing the waiver decision.) While most states decide to waive a child by a judicial hearing, a few jurisdictions allow the prosecutor to determine jurisdiction by filing a complaint in the juvenile or adult court. In other jurisdictions, where the juvenile court may have no jurisdiction over certain crimes, the prosecutor can control which court hears the case by the charge filed against the child. Such an approach eliminates the requirement of a waiver hearing but leaves a great deal of discretion in the hands of the prosecutor.[80]

A recent analysis of juvenile waiver by Frank Zimring argues that despite its faults, waiver is superior to alternative methods for handling the most serious juvenile offenders.[81] The major argument for waiver rests in the premise that the modern juvenile court is still preferable to the criminal justice system. As a consequence, certain cases will always occur in which the minimum criminal penalty is greater than that available to the juvenile court.

In sum, the trend has been to increase the flow of juvenile cases to adult courts. This policy change can be attributed to the get-tough attitude toward the serious, chronic juvenile offender. A number of important questions have been raised about the fairness and propriety of this method of handling serious juvenile cases. The big question is, what is accomplished by treating juveniles like adults? The following Case in Point considers the question of waiver.

The issue of waiver has become critical in recent years because transfer to the adult court is viewed as an efficient means of dealing with the violent and chronic juvenile offender. The seriousness of the offense plays a significant role in determining juvenile waiver, as do the number and the nature of prior offenses and prior treatment.[82] Waiver is also a refutation of the child's right to be treated in the juvenile justice system.[83]

■■ **TABLE 16.3**   Factors Influencing Waiver from Juvenile Court to Adult Court

OFFENSE	Seriousness of offense Person or property offense Violent crime
JUDICIAL POLICY	Merit of complaint Feasibility of trial
OFFENDER	Maturity of child Record of previous history Amenability for treatment

You are a newly appointed judge whose jurisdiction embraces criminal cases heard in the lower criminal court.

One week after his twelfth birthday, Dexter G., an honor student with a strict religious education, had his first contact with the justice system.

Dexter was arrested and charged with criminal homicide after he allegedly took his father's rifle, aimed from a third-floor bedroom window, and shot 8-year-old James once in the head as he rode along on his bicycle. James died instantly. Dexter was subsequently released to the custody of his parents.

The law of this jurisdiction requires that all persons charged with murder, regardless of age, stand trial as an adult in criminal court. If convicted of murder, Dexter could be sentenced to life imprisonment without parole. The state's Juvenile Court Act has a waiver provision that permits the criminal court judge to transfer the case to juvenile court if the child is under 17 and if the accused demonstrates that he is amenable to treatment and rehabilitation.

Dexter is a healthy youth with above-average intelligence and no apparent psychological problems. He has shown no emotion or remorse regarding the killing. Psychiatrists who examined Dexter indicate that the boy said he was "playing hunter" when the rifle accidently discharged.

If you were the judge, would you transfer the case to the juvenile court for jurisdiction? What criteria would you use in making this decision?

■ ■ ■ ■ ■ ■ ■ ■ ■ ■ ■ ■ ■ ■ ■

SUMMARY

Many important decisions about what happens to a child may occur prior to adjudication. Detention in secure facilities for those charged with juvenile delinquency and involuntary placement in shelter care for those involved in noncriminal behavior place a severe limitation on the rights of the child and the parents. There has been a major effort in the past few years to remove juveniles from detention in adult jails and to make sure that status offenders are not placed in secure pretrial detention facilities.

Most statutes ordinarily require a hearing on detention if the initial decision is to keep the child in custody. At a detention hearing, the child has a right to counsel and is generally given other procedural due process safeguards, notably the privilege against self-incrimination and the right to confront and cross-examine witnesses. In addition, most state juvenile court procedures provide criteria to be used in deciding whether to detain a child. These include (1) the need to protect the child, (2) the likelihood that the

child presents a serious danger to the public, and (3) the likelihood that the child will return to court for adjudication.

The intake stage is essentially a screening process to decide what action should be taken regarding matters referred to the court. The law enforcement officer is required to make hard decisions about court action or referral to social agencies. In addition, it is important for law enforcement agencies and the juvenile courts to have sound working relationships. Their objective is basically similar: the protection of the child and the community.

Throughout the early court stage of the juvenile process, the issue of discretion plays a major role. In the last decade, juvenile justice practitioners have made efforts to divert as many children as possible from the juvenile courts and place them in nonsecure treatment programs. Critics charge that diversion programs actually involve more youths in the justice system than would be the case had the programs not been in operation, a concept referred to as widening the net. Moreover, the effectiveness of diversion as a crime-reducing policy has been questioned.

Those who are held for trial are generally released to their parents, on bail, or through other alternatives, such as on recognizance. Since the juvenile justice system, like the adult system, is not able to try every child accused of a crime or a status offense due to personnel limitations, diversion programs seem to hold a better hope for the prevention and control of delinquency. As a result, such subsystems as diversion, statutory intake proceedings, some amount of plea bargaining, and other informal adjustments are essential ingredients in the administration of the juvenile justice system.

An issue related to bail is preventive detention, which refers to the right of a judge to deny persons release before trial on the grounds that they may be dangerous to themselves or others. Advocates of preventive detention argue that dangerous juvenile offenders should not be granted bail and pretrial release since they would then have an opportunity to intimidate witnesses and commit further crimes. Opponents retaliate that defendants are "innocent until proven guilty" and therefore should be allowed freedom before trial.

In addition to normal juvenile justice processing, thousands of other youngsters are transferred to the adult court because of the serious nature of their crimes. This process, known as waiver, is an effort to remove serious offenders from the juvenile process and into the more punitive adult system. Recent research indicates that waived youth are quite likely to receive incarceration sentences.

Prior to the first modern juvenile court in Illinois in 1899, juveniles were tried in adult criminal courts. However, the juvenile court system did recognize that certain crimes required that children be tried as adults. Today, virtually all jurisdictions provide by statute for waiver or transfer of juvenile offenders to the criminal courts.

KEY TERMS

detention
shelter care
detention hearing
deinstitutionalization
Deinstitutionalization of Status Offenders Project (DSO)
intake
diversion
widening the net
complaint
petition

bail
preventive detention
Schall v. Martin
plea bargaining
transfer
waiver
bindover
removal
concurrent jurisdiction
Kent v. United States
Breed v. Jones

QUESTIONS FOR DISCUSSION

1. Why has the use of jails and detention facilities for children been considered one of the greatest tragedies in the juvenile justice system?
2. Processing juvenile cases in an informal manner—that is, without filing a formal petition—is common in the juvenile court system. Describe some methods of informally handling cases in the juvenile court.
3. The use of diversion programs in the juvenile justice system has become common as an effort to channel cases to noncourt institutions. Discuss the advantages and disadvantages of diversion. Describe diversion programs and their common characteristics.
4. What is the purpose of bail? Do children as well as adults have a constitutional or statutory right to bail? What factors are considered in the release of a child prior to formal adjudication?
5. Under extraordinary circumstances, once juvenile proceedings have begun, the juvenile court may seek to transfer a juvenile to the adult court. This is often referred to as a transfer proceeding. Is such

a proceeding justified? Under what conditions? Does the juvenile court afford the public sufficient protection against serious juvenile offenders?

6. Explain the meaning of preventive detention. Is such a concept in conflict with the fundamental principle of presumption of innocence?

NOTES

1. National Council on Crime and Delinquency, *Standards and Guides for the Detention of Children and Youth* (New York: NCCD, 1961), p. 1.
2. American Bar Association, *Standards Relating to Interim Status of Juveniles* (Cambridge, Mass.: Ballinger, 1977), p. 4.
3. National Council on Crime and Delinquency, *Standards and Guides for the Detention of Children and Youth*, p. 12.
4. See Community Research Associations, *Michigan Holdover Network—Short-Term Detention Strategies* (Washington, D.C.: U.S. Department of Justice, 1986).
5. "Growth in Minority Detentions Attributed to Drug Law Violators," *Juvenile and Family Court Newsletter,* 20:3 (1990). See also National Council on Crime and Delinquency, *Recommendations on Juvenile Detention* (San Francisco: NCCD Council of Judges, March 1, 1989); Jeffrey Butts and Melissa Sickmund, *Offenders in Juvenile Court, 1989* (Washington, D.C.: U.S. Department of Justice, 1992), pp. 5 and 6; Barry Krisber, Robert Decomo, Norma C. Herrera, Marth Steketee & Sharon Roberts, *Juveniles Taken Into Custody,* (San Francisco: NCCD, 1992), p. 16; American Correctional Association, *National Juvenile Detention Directory* (Baltimore, Md.,:ACA, 1992).
6. Jeffrey Butts and Melissa Sickmund, *Update on Statistics, Offenders in Juvenile Court, 1989* (Washington, D.C.: U.S. Department of Justice, 1991), p. 5.
7. Ibid., p. 6.
8. Howard Snyder, *Update on Statistics, Growth in Minority Detentions Attributed to Drug Law Violators* (Washington, D.C.: U.S. Department of Justice, 1990), p. 2; also Howard Snyder, *Juvenile Court Statistics, 1989* (Pittsburgh: National Center for Juvenile Justice, 1992), p. 9.
9. Edward J. Loughran, "How to Stop Our Kids from Going Bad," *Boston Globe,* 11 February 1990.
10. Belinda McCarthy, "An Analysis of Detention," *Juvenile and Family Court Journal* 36:49–50 (1985).
11. Charles Frazier and Donna Bishop, "The Pretrial Detention of Juveniles and Its Impact on Case Dispositions," *Journal of Criminal Law and Criminology* 76:1132–52 (1986).
12. L. Rosner, "Juvenile Secure Detention," *Journal of Offender Counseling Services and Rehabilitation* 12:57–76 (1988).
13. National Council on Crime and Delinquency, *Standards and Guides for Detention for Children and Youth,* p. 1; also Michael McMillan, "Bringing Flexibility to Juvenile Detention: The Minimum Security Approach," *Corrections Today* 49:44–48 (1987).
14. American Bar Association, *Standards Relating to Interim Status of Juveniles,* p. 86; see also Claudia Worrell, "Pretrial Detention of Juveniles: Denial of Equal Protection Marked by the *Parens Patriae* Doctrine," *Yale Law Review* 95:174–93 (1985).
15. Edward Wakin, *Children without Justice—A Report by the National Council of Jewish Women,* (New York: National Council of Jewish Women, 1975), p. 43; also Ira M. Schwartz, (In) Justice for Juveniles—Rethinking the Best Interests of the Child (Lexington, Mass.: D.C. Heath, 1989), Chap. 3.
16. Hubert H. Humphrey Institute of Public Affairs, *The Incarceration of Minority Youth* (Minneapolis: Humphrey Institute, 1986); see also Katherine Hunt Federle and Meda Chesney-Lind, "Special Issues in Juvenile Justice: Gender, Race and Ethnicity," in Ira Schwartz, ed., *Juvenile Justice and Public Policy* (New York: Lexington Books, 1992), Chap. 9.
17. Russell Schutt and Dale Dannefer, "Detention Decisions in Juvenile Cases: JINS, JDs and Genders," *Law and Society Review* 22:509–20 (1988).
18. S. Smith and D. Roush, "Defining Juvenile Detention Goals: ACA Committee Takes the Lead," *Corrections Today* 51:220–21 (1989).
19. I. Schwartz, G. Fishman, R. Hatfield, B. A. Krisberg, and Z. Eisikovitz, "Juvenile Detention: The Hidden Closets Revisited," *Justice Quarterly* 4:219–35 (1987); John Criswell, "Juvenile Detention Resource Centers: Florida's Experience Provides a Model for Nation in Juvenile Detention," *Corrections Today* 49:22–26 (1987).
20. *Learning behind Bars: Selected Educational Programs from Juvenile Jail and Prison Facilities* (Laurel, Ind.: Correctional Education Association, 1989), p. 5.
21. Ibid., p. 10.
22. Ibid., p. 13.
23. Office of Juvenile Justice and Delinquency Prevention News Release, 4 January 1981. According to national census of 1989, the suicide rate for children in jails is four to six times higher than in public juvenile detention centers.
24. Reported in "Juveniles in Our Nation's Jails," *Criminal Justice Newsletter,* 14 February 1983, p. 8. These youths could have been held separately from adult offenders, although in the same facility.

25. "OJJDP Helps States Remove Juveniles from Jails," *Juvenile Justice Bulletin*, (Washington, D.C.: U.S. Department of Justice, 1990).

26. "Qualities of Best Plans for Rural 'Jail Removal' Described," *Criminal Justice Newsletter*, 15 April 1987; Also Krisberg, et al., *Juveniles Taken into Custody*, 1990 Report, p. 46.

27. Community Research Associates, *The Jail Removal Initiative: A Summary Report* (Champaign, Ill. 1987).

28. Charles Frazier, *Preadjudicatory Detention—From Juvenile Justice: Policies, Programs and Services* (Chicago: Dorsey Press, 1989), pp. 143–68.

29. Ira Schwartz, Linda Harris, and Lauri Levi, "The Jailing of Juveniles in Minnesota," *Crime and Delinquency* 34:131 (1988).

30. See, generally, Ira Schwartz, ed., "Children in Jails," *Crime and Delinquency* 34:131–228 (1988).

31. See Schwartz, Harris, and Levi, "The Jailing of Juveniles in Minnesota," p. 134.

32. David Steinhart, "California Legislation Ends Jailing of Children—the Story of a Policy Reversal," *Crime and Delinquency* 34:150 (1988).

33. See Henry Swanger, "*Hendrickson v. Griggs*—a Review of Legal and Policy Implications for Juvenile Justice Policymakers," *Crime and Delinquency* 34:209 (1988); *Hendrickson v. Griggs,* 672 F.Supp. 1126 (N.D. Iowa 1987).

34. "Assessing the Effects of the Deinstitutionalization of Status Offenders," *Juvenile Justice Bulletin* (Washington, D.C.: U.S. Department of Justice, 1990), p. 1.

35. Solomon Kobrin and Malcolm Klein, *National Evaluation of the Deinstitutionalization of Status Offender Programs, Executive Summary* (Washington, D.C.: U.S. Department of Justice, 1982); see also I. Spergel, F. Reamer, and J. Lynch, "Deinstitutionalization of Status Offenders: Individual Outcome and System Effects," *Journal of Research in Crime and Delinquency* 4:32 (1981).

36. M. A. Bortner, Mary Sutherland, and Russ Winn, "Race and the Impact of Juvenile Institutionalization," *Crime and Delinquency* 31:35–46 (1985).

37. Anne L. Schneider, *The Impact of Deinstitutionalization on Recidivism and Secure Confinement of Status Offenders* (Washington, D.C.: U.S. Department of Justice, 1985). For a similar view, see Susan Datesman and Mikel Aickin, "Offense Specialization and Escalation among Status Offenders," *Journal of Criminal Law and Criminology* 75:1246–75 (1984).

38. Duran Bell and Kevin Lang, "The Intake Dispositions of Juvenile Offenders," *Journal of Research in Crime and Delinquency* 22:309–28 (1985); also see Federle and Chesney-Lind, "Special Issues in Juvenile Justice: Gender, Race, and Ethnicity," p. 189.

39. American Bar Association, *Standards Relating to Juvenile Probation Function* (Cambridge, Mass.: Ballinger, 1977), p. 25.

40. National Council on Crime and Delinquency, *Standard Family Court Act*, p. 12; William Sheridan, *Model Acts for Juvenile and Family Courts*, p. 13; National Conference on Commissioners on Uniform State Laws, *Uniform Juvenile Court Act*, p. 9.

41. American Bar Association, *Standards Relating to Juvenile Probation Function*, p. 53.

42. Ted Rubin, "The Emerging Prosecutor Dominance of the Juvenile Court Intake Process," *Crime and Delinquency* 26:299–318 (1980).

43. Ibid., p. 318.

44. National Advisory Commission on Criminal Justice Standards and Goals, *Courts* (Washington, D.C.: Government Printing Office, 1967), p. 20.

45. Paul Nejelski, "Diversion: The Promise and the Danger," *Crime and Delinquency Journal* 22:393–410 (1976); Kenneth Polk, "Juvenile Diversion: A Look at the Record," *Crime and Delinquency* 30:648–59 (1984).

46. President's Commission on Law Enforcement and Administration of Justice, *Task Force Report: Juvenile Delinquency and Youth Crime* (Washington D.C.: Government Printing Office, 1967).

47. Ibid.

48. Polk, "Juvenile Diversion: A Look at the Record," pp. 648–59.

49. See Raymond T. Nimmer, *Diversion—The Search for Alternative Forms of Prosecution* (Chicago: American Bar Foundation, 1974); see also Mark Ezell, "Juvenile Arbitration: Net-Widening and Other Unintended Consequences," *Journal of Research in Crime and Delinquency* 26:358–77 (1989).

50. Edwin E. Lemert, "Diversion in Juvenile Justice: What Hath Been Wrought," *Journal of Research in Crime and Delinquency* 18:34–46 (1981).

51. Don C. Gibbons and Gerald F. Blake, "Evaluating the Impact of Juvenile Diversion Programs," *Crime and Delinquency Journal* 22:411–19 (1976); Richard J. Lundman, "Will Diversion Reduce Recidivism?" *Crime and Delinquency Journal* 22:428–37 (1976); B. Bullington, J. Sprowls, D. Katkin, and M. Phillips. "A Critique of Diversionary Juvenile Justice," *Crime and Delinquency* 24:59–71 (1978); Thomas Blomberg, "Diversion and Accelerated Social Control," *Journal of Criminal Law and Criminology* 68:274–82 (1977); Sharla Rausch and Charles Logan, "Diversion from Juvenile Court, Panacea or Pandora's Box," in J. Klugel, ed., *Evaluating Juvenile Justice* (Beverly Hills, Calif.: Sage, 1983), pp. 19–30.

52. Charles Frazier and John Cochran, "Official Intervention, Diversion from the Juvenile Justice System, and Dynamics of Human Services Work: Effects of a Reform Goal Based on Labeling Theory," *Crime and Delinquency* 32:157–76 (1986); see also Charles Frazier and Sara Lee, "Reducing Juvenile Detention Rates or Expanding the Official Control Nets: An Evaluation of a Legislative Reform Effort," *Crime and Delinquency* 38:204–14 (1992).

53. Dennis Anderson and Donald Schoen, "Diversion Programs: Effect of Stigmatization on Juvenile/Status Offender," *Juvenile and Family Court Journal* 36:13–25 (1985).

54. Rausch and Logan, "Diversion from Juvenile Court," p. 20.

55. Frazier and Cochran, "Official Intervention," p. 171.

56. Arnold Binder and Gilbert Geis, "Ad Populum Argumentation in Criminology: Juvenile Diversion as Rhetoric," *Criminology* 30:309–33 (1984).

57. Mark Ezell, "Juvenile Diversion: The Ongoing Search for Alternatives," in Ira M. Schwartz, ed., *Juvenile Justice and Public Policy* (New York: Lexington Books, 1992), pp. 45–59.

58. Mark Soler, James Bell, Elizabeth Jameson, Carole Shauffer, Alice Shotton, and Loren Warboys, *Representing the Child Client* (New York: Matthew Bender, 1989), Sec. 5.03b.

59. 467 U.S. 253, (1984).

60. James Brown, Robert Shepherd, and Andrew Shookhoff, *Preventive Detention after Schall v. Martin* (Washington, D.C.: American Bar Association, 1985); see also Michael O'Rourke, "Juvenile Justice—Preventive Detention of Juveniles: Have They Held Your Child Today: Schall v. Martin," *Southern Illinois University Law Journal* 4:315–33 (1985).

61. Albert W. Alschuler, "The Prosecutor's Role in Plea Bargaining," *University of Chicago Law Review* 36:50–112 (1968); see also Joyce Dougherty, "A Comparison of Adult Plea Bargaining and Juvenile Intake," *Federal Probation* (June 1988):72–79.

62. Sanford Fox, *Juvenile Courts in a Nutshell* (St. Paul: West, 1984–1985), pp. 154–56.

63. See Darlene Ewing, "Juvenile Plea Bargaining: A Case Study," *American Journal of Criminal Law* 6:167 (1978); Adrienne Volenik, *Checklists for Use in Juvenile Delinquency Proceedings* (Chicago: American Bar Association, 1985); Bruce Green, "Package Plea Bargaining and the Prosecutor's Duty of Good Faith," *Criminal Law Bulletin* 25:507–50 (1989).

64. Joseph Sanborn, "Plea Negotiations in Juvenile Court" (PhD. diss., State University of New York at Albany, 1984).

65. The National Council of Juvenile and Family Court Judges, "The Juvenile Court and Serious Offenders," *Juvenile and Family Court Journal* 35:13 (1984).

66. Bureau of Justice Statistics, *Report to the Nation on Crime and Justice* (Washington, D.C.: Government Printing Office, 1988) p. 79.

67. Mass.Gen.Laws Ann. ch. C.119, 61.

68. Ind. Code Ann. 31-6-2(d) 1987; Ill.Ann.Stat. Ch. 37 Sec. 805 (1988); Penn. Stat. Ann. Title 42 6355(a) (1982).

69. Joseph White, "The Waiver Decision: A Judicial, Prosecutorial or Legislative Responsibility," *Justice for Children* 2:28–30 (1987).

70. Linda A. Szymanski, *Statutory Waiver Criteria* (Pittsburgh: National Center For Juvenile Justice, October 1989).

71. 383 U.S. 541, 86 S.Ct. 1045, 16 L.Ed.2d 84 (1966); 421 U.S. 519, 95 S.Ct. 1179, 44 L.Ed.2d 346 (1975).

72 Barry Feld, "Delinquent Careers and Criminal Policy," *Criminology* 21:195–212 (1983).

73. Barry Feld, "The Juvenile Court Meets the Principle of the Offense: Legislative Changes in Juvenile Waiver Statutes," *Journal of Criminal Law and Criminology* 78:471–534 (1987); see also Paul Marcotte, "Criminal Kids," *American Bar Association Journal* 76:60–66 (1990).

74. Donna Hamparian, et al., *Major Issues in Juvenile Justice* (Washington, D.C.: U.S. Department of Justice, 1982), pp. 18–21; see also Snyder, et al., *Juvenile Court Statistics, 1989*, p. 7.

75. Richard Allinson and Joan Potter, "Is New York's Tough Juvenile Law a Charade?" *Corrections* 9:40–45 (February 1983).

76. Cary Rudman, Eliot Hartstone, Jeffrey Fagan, and Melinda Moore, "Violent Youth in Adult Court: Process and Punishment," *Crime and Delinquency* 32:75–96 (1986).

77. "Study Finds Strict Handling of Youths Sent to Adult Court," *Criminal Justice Newsletter*, 15 May 1987.

78. M. A. Bortner, "Traditional Rhetoric, Organizational Realities: Remand of Juveniles to Adult Court," *Crime and Delinquency* 32:53–73 (1986).

79. Jeffrey Fagan, Martin Forst, and T. Scott Vivona, "Racial Determinants of the Judicial Transfer Decision: Prosecuting Violent Youth in Criminal Court," *Crime and Delinquency* 33:359–86 (1987); also J. Fagan, E. Slaughter, and E. Hartstone, "Blind Justice: The Impact of Race on the Juvenile Justice Process," *Crime and Delinquency* 53:224–58 (1987); J. Fagan and E. P. Deschenes, "Determinants of Judicial Waiver Decisions for Violent Juvenile Offenders," *Journal of Criminal Law and Criminology* 81:314–47 (1990).

80. Soler, et al., *Representing the Child Client.*

81. Frank Zimring, "Treatment of Hard Cases in American Juvenile Justice: In Defense of the Discretionary Waiver," *Notre Dame Journal of Law, Ethics and Policy* 5:267–80 (1991).

82. F. W. Barnes and R. S. Franz, "Questionably Adult: Determinants and Effects of the Juvenile Waiver Decision," *Justice Quarterly* 6:117–35 (1989).

83. See the interesting case of *Toomey v. Clark*, 876 F.2d 1433 (9th Cir., 1989), where the juvenile court's consideration of criteria involving petitioner's pregnancy in its decision to decline jurisdiction was not sex discrimination and a violation of the equal protection clause.

CHAPTER

17

OUTLINE

THE JUVENILE
TRIAL AND
DISPOSITION

The development of the juvenile court and the separate process for handling children resulted from reform movements of the nineteenth and early twentieth centuries. The strategic role played by the juvenile court in setting juvenile justice policy has already been described. Throughout its history, the juvenile court has played a major role in helping to care for troubled youths who come before it. In fact, its influence is probably greater than that of the adult court because it is also charged with the care and treatment of offenders and not merely their punishment and control.[1] Therefore, the court and its representatives must consider their actions carefully, because a wrong decision can have long-term consequences for young offenders.

Compounding the problem is the magnitude of cases handled by the nation's juvenile courts each year. The latest study (1989) found that the nation's juvenile courts petitioned and formally processed an estimated 591,000 delinquency offense cases and 77,000 status offense cases (see Figure 17.1). This estimate does not take into account the hundreds of thousands of informally handled or nonpetitioned cases adjusted or diverted by the courts. Compared to 1985, petitioned delinquency cases increased by over 15 percent and status offense cases decreased by 1 percent in 1989 (latest data). (See Table 17.1) Thus, the nation's juvenile court system remains faced with dealing with an enormous number of youths who need care, protection, treatment, and control.

This chapter describes the adjudication stage of the juvenile justice process. About 60 percent of all formally processed cases, or 350,000 youths, are adjudicated as delinquent while 63 percent of the petitioned status offense cases (48,000 youths) are involved in adjudication.[2] The term *adjudication* refers to the trial stage of the juvenile court proceedings. This chapter initially explores the role of the important legal actors in the trial and disposition—the juvenile court prosecutor, the judge, the defense attorney, and the probation officer. In addition, it looks at the constitutional and due process rights of the child at the trial—particularly those rights dealing with counsel and trial by jury—through a detailed analysis of landmark U.S. Supreme Court decisions. Various procedural rules that govern the adjudicatory and dispositional hearings are also reviewed. The chapter concludes with a discussion of dispositional alternatives and trends in sentencing that effect juvenile dispositions.

THE PROSECUTOR IN THE JUVENILE COURT

The **juvenile prosecutor** is the government attorney responsible for representing the interests of the state and bringing the state's case against the accused child. Depending on the level of government and the jurisdiction, the prosecutor can be called a district attorney, a county attorney, a state attorney, or a United States attorney. He or she is a member of the bar and becomes a public prosecutor through political appointment or popular election.

Ordinarily, the juvenile prosecutor is a staff member of the local prosecuting attorney's office. If the office of the district attorney is in an urban area and of sufficient size, the juvenile prosecutor may work exclusively on juvenile and other family law matters. If the caseload of juvenile offenders is small, the juvenile prosecutor may also have criminal prosecution responsibilities.

Juvenile Court Processing of Delinquency Cases, 1989

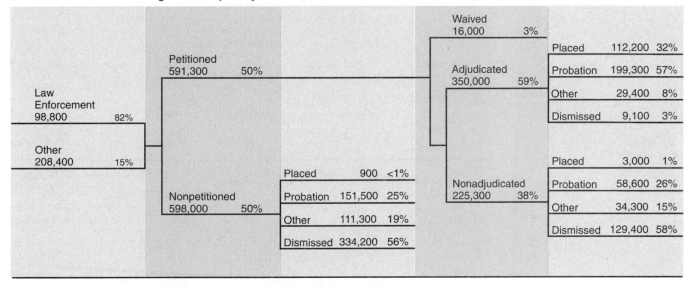

Juvenile Court Processing of Petitioned Status Offense Cases, 1989

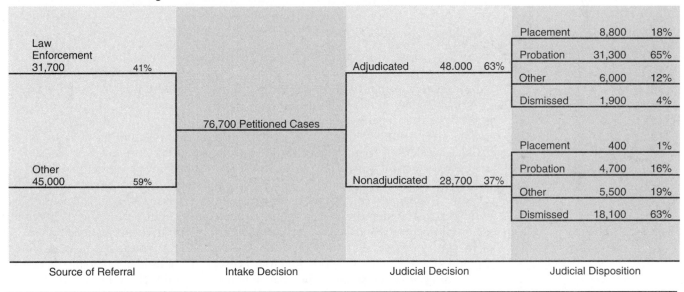

| Source of Referral | Intake Decision | Judicial Decision | Judicial Disposition |

FIGURE 17.1

Dispositions by juvenile courts for delinquency and status offense cases

Source: Jeffrey Butts and Melissa Sickmund, *Offenders in Juvenile Court, 1989* (Washington, D.C.: OJJDP, 1992), p. 4–6.

For the first sixty years of its existence, the juvenile court did not include a prosecutor as a representative of the state in court proceedings.[3] The concept of advocacy and the adversary process were seen as inconsistent with the philosophy of diagnosis and treatment in the juvenile court system. The court followed a social service helping model with informal and noncriminal proceedings believed to be in the best interests of the child.

■■ TABLE 17.1   Petitioned Delinquency and Status Offense Cases, 1985–1989

PERCENT CHANGE IN DELINQUENCY CASES PETITIONED, 1985–89

OFFENSE	NUMBER OF CASES		PERCENT CHANGE
	1985	1989	
Delinquency	515,300	591,300	15%
Person	96,800	113,200	17
Property	294,000	324,500	10
Drugs	33,300	47,800	44
Public Order	91,200	105,800	16

PERCENT CHANGE IN PETITIONED STATUS OFFENSE CASES

OFFENSE	NUMBER OF CASES		% CHANGE
	1985	1989	
Status	77,400	76,700	−1%
Runaway	17,100	11,800	−31
Truancy	22,700	20,900	−8
Ungovernable	16,700	11,000	−34
Liquor	15,600	24,400	57

Source: H. Snyder, M. Sickmund, E. Nimick, T. Finnegan, D. Sullivan, R. Poole, and N. Tierney, *Juvenile Court Statistics, 1989* (Pittsburgh: National Center for Juvenile Justice, 1992), pp. 20 and 50.

As we know, these views changed dramatically with the Supreme Court decisions of *Kent v. United States, In re Gault,* and *In re Winship,* which ushered in an era of greater formality and due process rights for children in the juvenile court system.[4] Today, almost all jurisdictions require by law that a prosecutor be present in the juvenile court.

The prosecutor's role in juvenile court is expanding. A number of states have passed legislation giving prosecutors control over intake and waiver decisions. Some have passed concurrent jurisdiction laws that allow prosecutors to decide where to bring serious juvenile cases. In some jurisdictions, it is the prosecutor and not the juvenile court judge who is entrusted with making the critical decision of whether to transfer the case to adult court. Consequently, the role of juvenile court prosecutor has become a critical element of the juvenile justice process.

In the words of the American Bar Association, "An attorney for the state, hereinafter referred to as the juvenile prosecutor, should participate in every proceeding of every stage of every case subject to the jurisdiction of the family court in which the state has an interest."[5] Including a prosecutor in juvenile court balances the interests of the state, the defense attorney, the child, and the judge in their respective roles. The independence of their respective functions and responsibilities is preserved.

The Legal Duties of the Juvenile Prosecutor

A prosecutor enforces the law, represents the government, maintains proper standards of ethical conduct as an attorney and court officer, participates in programs and legislation involving legal changes in the juvenile justice system, acts as a spokesperson for the field of law, and takes an active role in the community in preventing delinquency and protecting the rights of juveniles. Of these responsibilities, representing the government while presenting the state's case to the court is the prosecutor's most frequent task. In this regard, the prosecutor has many of the following duties:

- Investigate possible violations of the law
- Cooperate with the police, intake officer, and probation officer regarding the facts alleged in the petition
- Authorize, review, and prepare petitions for court
- Play a role in the initial detention decision
- Represent the case in all pretrial motions, probable cause hearings, and consent decrees
- Represent the state at transfer hearings
- Recommends if necessary, physical or mental examinations for children brought before the court
- Seek amendments or dismissals of filed petitions if appropriate
- Represent the state at the adjudication of the case
- Represent the state at the disposition of the case
- Enter into plea-bargaining discussions with the defense attorney
- Represent the government on appeal and in habeas corpus proceedings
- Be involved in hearings dealing with violation of probation

The power to initiate formal petitions against a child is key to prosecutorial responsibility. The ability either to initiate or to discontinue delinquency or status offense allegations represents the control and power a juvenile prosecutor has over a child. Prosecutors have broad discretion in the exercise of their duties. Because due process rights have been extended to juveniles, the prosecutor's role in the juvenile court has in some ways become similar to the role of the prosecuting attorney in the adult court. In the case of *State v. Grayer*, for example, a Nebraska court upheld the validity of the discretionary power of the juvenile prosecutor to decide whether to prosecute the child as a juvenile or as an adult.[6]

Such an approach demonstrates the judicial movement toward developing procedures for juveniles that are similar to those for adult offenders. However, it is important for the juvenile prosecutor not only to represent the government but also to remain cognizant of the philosophy and purpose of the juvenile court.

The Complex Role of Juvenile Prosecution

While it seems evident that prosecutors are beginning to play an ever-expanding role in juvenile courts, the actual impact of their presence may be open to debate. Research by John Laub and Bruce MacMurray conducted in the juvenile court in Boston indicates that prosecutors may find their roles to be rather limited in controlling juvenile court policies.[7] Laub and MacMurray found that prosecutors are considered "outsiders" whose adversarial ideas are not appreciated by juvenile court personnel. Some judges believe that the voice of law and order has a limited role in the juvenile court and that if district attorneys actively pursue such conservative policies as binding children over to the adult court, they will be committing "political suicide." Similarly, the researchers found that these district attorneys do not relish their juvenile court assignments and consider juvenile cases to be "garbage cases."[8]

Laub and MacMurray found that juvenile court personnel are not open to the idea of having the prosecutor play an important role in the processing of cases or introducing an adversarial system within its confines. They suggest that the prosecutor has to be perceived as being an insider or part of the team before he or she can begin to have an important influence on juvenile court operations.

To develop the role played by the prosecutor in juvenile court, some states have attempted to draw up general policy guidelines or principles for juvenile prosecution based on the recent Prosecution Standards issued by the National District Attorneys Association.[9] In Standard 19.2 (Juvenile Delinquency), the prosecutor is an advocate of the state's interest in juvenile court. The state's interest includes: (1) the protection of the community from the danger of harmful conduct by the restraint and rehabilitation of juvenile offenders and (2) the concern shared by all juvenile justice system personnel, as *parens patriae*, with promoting the best interests of the child. The prosecutor also has a duty to seek justice in juvenile court by insisting upon fair and lawful procedures. This entails ensuring, for example, that baseless prosecutions are not brought, that all juveniles receive fair and equal treatment, that liberal discovery of the state's case is available to defense counsel, that exculpatory evidence is made available to the defense counsel, and that excessively harsh dispositions are not sought. It also entails overseeing police investigative behavior to ensure its compliance with the law. This standard is discussed further in the following Focus on Delinquency.

Because children are committing more serious crimes today and the courts have granted juveniles constitutional safeguards, the prosecutor is likely to play a more significant role in the juvenile court system than in the past. According to a recent analysis by Shine and Price, the prosecutor's involvement will promote a due process model that should result in a fairer, more just system for all parties. But they also point out that prosecutors need more information on such issues as: (1) how to identify repeat offenders; (2) how to determine which programs are most effective; (3) how early childhood experiences relate to delinquency; (4) how immigrant groups are absorbed into local populations; and (5) what measures can be used in place of secure placements without reducing public safety.[10]

THE JUVENILE COURT JUDGE

The **judge** is the central character in a court of juvenile or family law. His or her responsibilities are quite varied and have become far more extensive and complex in recent years. Following *Kent* and *Gault*, new legal rulings have probed the basic legal aspects of the juvenile justice system. In addition, juvenile cases are far more complex today and represent issues involving social change, such as truancy, alcoholism, the use of drugs by children, juvenile prostitution, and violent juvenile crime. Such cases involve problems of both public safety and individualized treatment for children.

Juvenile or family court judges perform the following functions:

■ Rule on pretrial motions involving such legal issues as arrest, search and seizure, interrogation, and lineup identification
■ Make decisions about the continued detention of children prior to trial
■ Make decisions about plea-bargaining agreements and the informal adjustment of juvenile cases

National District Attorneys Association Prosecution Standard 19.2 Juvenile Delinquency

INTRODUCTION

Excellence in criminal prosecution demands excellence in all areas—including both adult and juvenile justice. Whether in response to the formalization of juvenile court procedures or increased interest in juveniles and the crimes they commit, America's prosecutors are playing a larger role in the juvenile justice system.

A. General Responsibilities of a Juvenile Prosecutor

1. Appearance of Prosecutor. The prosecutor should appear as an attorney for the state in all hearings concerning a juvenile accused of an act that would constitute a crime if he or she were an adult ("a delinquent act"). This includes but is not limited to hearings for: detention, speedy trial, dismissal, entry of pleas, trial, waiver, disposition, revocation of probation or parole status, and any appeal from or collateral attacks upon the decisions in each of these proceedings.

2. Primary Duty. The primary duty of the prosecutor is to seek justice while fully and faithfully representing the interests of the state. While the safety and welfare of the community, including the victim, is their primary concern, prosecutors should consider the special interests and needs of the juvenile to the extent they can do so without compromising that concern.

3. Personnel and Resources. Chief prosecutors should devote specific personnel and resources to fulfill their responsibilities with respect to juvenile delinquency proceedings, and all prosecutors' offices should have an identified juvenile unit or attorney responsible for representing the State in juvenile matters. Additionally, the prosecutor for juvenile cases should have adequate staff support to the extent possible given office resources including: clerical and paralegal personnel, interns, investigators, and victim/witness coordinators.

4. Qualifications of Prosecutor. Training and experience should be required for juvenile delinquency cases. Chief prosecutors should select prosecutors for juvenile court on the basis of their skill and competence including knowledge of juvenile law, interest in children and youth, education, and experience. While the unit chief, if any, must have criminal trial experience, assistant prosecutors assigned to the unit should also have prior criminal trial experience, assistant prosecutors assigned to the unit should also have prior criminal trial experience, if possible. Entry-level attorneys in the juvenile unit should be as qualified as any entry-level attorney, and receive special training regarding juvenile matters.

5. Cooperation. To the extent possible, prosecutors should cooperate with others in the juvenile justice system to promote speedy trials and efficient case processing. ■

Source: National District Attorney's Association, *Prosecution Standard 19.2, Juvenile Delinquency* (Alexandria, Va.: NDAA, 1992).

■ Handle bench and jury trials, rule on the appropriateness of conduct, settle questions of evidence and procedure, and guide the questioning of witnesses
■ Assume responsibility for holding dispositional hearings and deciding on the treatment accorded the child
■ Handle waiver proceedings
■ Handle appeals where allowed by statute and where no prior contact has been made with the case[11]

Judge Benjamin Lindsay presided over juvenile court in Denver, Colorado from 1900 to 1927.

In addition, judges often have extensive control and influence over other service agencies of the court: probation, the court clerk, the law enforcement officer, and the office of the juvenile prosecutor. Of course, courts differ organizationally and procedurally. Larger courts have more resources to handle the volume of juvenile cases. They may have unique approaches to juvenile problems, including specialized offender caseloads, such as drug users; diversion programs; and a whole host of special social services. Smaller courts have no more than a judge, a clerk, and a probation staff.

Juvenile court judges exercise considerable leadership in developing services and solutions to juvenile justice problems. In this role, juvenile court judges must respond to the external pressures the community places on juvenile court resources. In fact, research indicates that juvenile court decision making may be influenced more by the needs of the outside community than by the particular philosophy or views of the presiding judge.[12]

According to Judge Leonard Edwards of the Santa Clara, California, Superior Court, who has extensive experience in juvenile and family law, "The juvenile judge must take action to ensure that the necessary community resources are available so that the children and families which come before the court can be well-served." This may be the most untraditional role for the juvenile court judge, but it may also be the most important.[13]

Selection and Qualifications of Juvenile Court Judges

A variety of methods are used to select juvenile court judges.[14] In some jurisdictions, the governor simply appoints candidates chosen by a screening board. In other states, judges are chosen in popular partisan elections, while in others, judges run for office without party affiliation. In three states—

Connecticut, Virginia, and South Carolina—the state legislature appoints judges. About a dozen states have adopted the **Missouri Plan,** which involves (1) a commission to nominate candidates for the bench; (2) an elected official, usually the governor, to make appointments from the list submitted by the commission; and (3) subsequent nonpartisan and uncontested elections in which incumbent judges run on their records (usually every three years).

In some jurisdictions, juvenile court judges handle family-related cases exclusively. In others, they handle criminal and civil cases as well. Traditionally, juvenile court judges have been relegated to a lower status than other judges, with less prestige, responsibility, and salary. Judges assigned to juvenile courts have not ordinarily been chosen from the highest levels of the legal profession. Such groups as the American Judicature Society have noted that the field of juvenile justice has often been shortchanged by the appointment of unqualified judges and staff. In some jurisdictions, particularly major urban areas, juvenile court judges may be of the highest caliber, but many courts throughout the nation continue to function with mediocre judges. As the Advisory Council of Judges of the National Council on Crime and Delinquency states, "Juvenile court has been brilliantly conceived; its legal and social facets are not antithetical, but the preservation of equilibrium between them, which is the key to their successful fusion, depends upon the legal knowledge, social perspective, and eternal vigilance of *one person, the judge*".[15] Judge Maurice Cohill, former judge of the Juvenile Court of Allegheny County, Pennsylvania, put it most succinctly when he said, "In terms of sheer human impact, the juvenile court is the most important court in the land."[16]

Inducing the best-trained individuals to accept juvenile court judgeships is a very important goal. Where the juvenile court is part of the highest general court of trial jurisdiction, the problem of securing qualified personnel is not as great. However, if the juvenile court is of limited or specialized jurisdiction and has the authority to try only minor cases, it may attract only poorly trained and poorly qualified personnel. Lawyers and judges who practice in juvenile court receive little respect from their colleagues. The term "kiddie court" is often used to describe juvenile court. The juvenile court has a negative image to overcome, because even though what it does is of great importance to parents, children, and society in general, it has been placed at the lowest level of the judicial hierarchy. One group that has struggled to upgrade the juvenile court judiciary is the **National Council of Juvenile and Family Court Judges.** Located in Reno, Nevada, this organization sponsors research and continuing legal education efforts designed to help judges master their field of expertise. Its research arm, the National Center for Juvenile Justice in Pittsburgh, also offers assistance to courts in developing information processing and statute analysis methods; it also provides legal consultation to judicial groups. Some juvenile practitioners have even created their own bar association to support child advocacy programs.

THE DEFENSE ATTORNEY

Through a series of leading Supreme Court decisions, the right of a criminal defendant to have counsel at state trials has become a fundamental right in the criminal justice system.[17] Today, state courts must provide counsel to indigent defendants who face the possibility of incarceration.

The American Bar Association (ABA) has described the responsibility of the legal profession to the juvenile court in Standard 2.3 of its *Standards Relating to Counsel for Private Parties*. The ABA states that legal representation should be provided in all proceedings arising from or related to a delinquency or in-need-of-supervision action—including mental competency, transfer, postdisposition, probation revocation and classification, institutional transfer, and disciplinary or other administrative proceedings related to the treatment process—that may substantially effect the juvenile's custody, status, or course of treatment.[18]

Over the past two decades, the rules and procedures of criminal and juvenile justice administration have become extremely complex. Specialized knowledge is essential for the adversary process to operate effectively. Today, preparation of a case for juvenile court often involves detailed investigation of a crime, knowledge of court procedures, use of rules of evidence, and skills in trial advocacy. Prosecuting and defense attorneys both must have this expertise, particularly when a child's freedom is at stake. The right to counsel in the juvenile justice system is essential if children are to have a fair chance of presenting their cases in court.

In many respects, the role of **defense attorneys** in the juvenile process is similar to the one they play in the criminal and civil areas. Defense attorneys representing children in the juvenile court play an active and important part in virtually all stages of juvenile proceedings. For example, the lawyer helps to clarify jurisdictional problems and to decide whether there is sufficient evidence to warrant filing a formal petition at intake. The defense attorney also helps outline the child's position regarding detention hearings and bail and explores the opportunities for informal adjustment of the case. If no adjustment or diversion occurs, the attorney represents the child at adjudication, presenting evidence and cross-examining witnesses to see that the child's position is made clear to the court. Defense attorneys also play a critically important role in the dispositional hearing. They present evidence bearing on the treatment decision and help the court formulate alternative plans for the child's care. Finally, defense attorneys pursue any appeals from the trial, represent the child in probation revocation proceedings, and generally protect the child's right to treatment.

In some cases, a **guardian *ad litem*** may be appointed by the court. The guardian *ad litem* is an attorney appointed by the court "to promote and protect the interests of a child involved in a judicial proceeding, through assuring representation of those interests in the courts and throughout the social services and ancillary service systems."[19] While nominally used in abuse, neglect, and dependency cases, the guardian *ad litem* may be appointed in delinquency cases where there is a question of a need for a particular treatment (for example, placement in a mental health center) and the offender and his or her attorney resist placement. The guardian *ad litem* may advocate for the commitment on the grounds that it is in the child's "best interests."[20]

CASA (Court Appointed Special Advocates) programs also advise the juvenile court about child placement. The CASA programs (*casa* is spanish for "home") have demonstrated that volunteers can investigate the needs of children and provide a vital link between the judge, the attorneys, and the child in protecting the juvenile's right to a safe placement.[21]

Public Defender Services for Children

To satisfy the requirement that indigent children and their families be provided with counsel at the various stages of the juvenile justice process, the federal government and the states have had to expand **public defender** services. Three primary alternatives exist for providing children with legal counsel in the juvenile court today: (1) an all-public defender program, (2) an appointed private counsel system, and (3) a combination system of public defenders and appointed private attorneys.

The public defender program is a statewide program organized by legislation and funded by the government to provide counsel to children at public expense. This approach brings to juvenile proceedings the expertise of lawyers who spend a considerable amount of time representing juvenile offenders every day. Defender programs generally provide separate office space for juvenile court personnel as well as support staff and training programs for new lawyers.

In many rural areas, individual public defender programs are not available, and defense services are offered through appointed private counsel. Private lawyers are assigned to individual juvenile court cases and receive compensation for the time and services they provide to the child and the family. When private attorneys are used in large urban areas, they are generally selected from a list established by the court, and they often operate in conjunction with a public defender program. A system of assigned counsel used by itself suffers from such problems as unequal case assignments, inadequate legal fees, and lack of supportive or supervisory services.

Even though public defense services for children have grown in recent years, a major concern is continued provision of quality representation to the child and the family at all stages of the juvenile process. In some jurisdictions today, counsel is available to children in only part of the juvenile proceedings. In other jurisdictions, children are not represented in persons-in-need-of-supervision or neglect cases. Often public defender agencies and the assigned counsel system are understaffed and lack adequate support services. Representation should be upgraded in all areas of the juvenile court system.

Although juvenile court practice has not traditionally been viewed by the bar with the same esteem as a lucrative corporate practice or adult trial work, defense attorneys must meet the same high standards for competency and professional responsibility when representing a child in the juvenile justice system.

Do Lawyers Make a Difference in Juvenile Court?

A number of studies in the early 1980s found that having an attorney either makes no difference in juvenile cases or actually results in more damaging dispositions for clients.[22] Juveniles represented by an attorney are more likely to receive institutional sentences than those who waive their right to counsel. While not all research efforts arrive at this conclusion, sufficient evidence exists that at least in some jurisdictions, legal representation may not be in a juvenile's best interests.

One possible reason for this surprising finding is that only the most serious juvenile offenders request counsel, and these youths also have the greatest likelihood of receiving an institutional sentence. Another view is that counsel in juvenile court functions in a nonadversarial capacity, furthering the interests of the juvenile court rather than those of the client. Joseph Sanborn found quite a bit of role confusion in the three juvenile courts he studied. He found that some juvenile court personnel believed that the lawyers' role should be one of a fighting advocate for their client, while others viewed lawyers as guardians who

There is some question about the effectiveness of attorneys in juvenile court. Some research suggests that retaining counsel actually results in tougher dispositions.

helped guide juveniles through the treatment process.[23] Some of those Sanborn interviewed felt that attorneys should fight to prove their clients innocent during the trial stage but that once delinquency was established, they should revert to the guardian role in order to obtain the best treatment possible for their clients. In a case in which the judge believes that a child needs placement in a secure facility, the attorney may help convince the client that placement is in his or her best interest, rather than use all means to block the incarceration.[24] Still another explanation is that because juvenile defense work is generally a low-paid, low-prestige aspect of the law, the services children receive are less than adequate.

The Problems of Juvenile Defense Work

The problem of legal counsel in juvenile court has been confirmed by a New York study of juvenile defense work. The study, sponsored by the New York State Bar Association, found significant deficiencies in the quality of legal care given youths by their court-appointed lawyers. In 45 percent of the almost two hundred cases studied, the representation was considered inadequate, and in another 47 percent, it appeared that the lawyer had done little or no preparation on the case.

The study also found that lawyers representing children had little knowledge of the statutes governing juvenile law and were also unfamiliar with social services available to children. There were frequent instances of insensitivity to the client's feelings, particularly in cases involving sexual issues or abuse.[25] Based on such information, improved legal services for indigent juveniles may be a tough goal to achieve.

On the other hand, Sanford Fox claims: "Few of the rights granted children in the juvenile justice system would have much real meaning without an attorney to assert them or to advise the child when it is in his best interests to waive them."[26] However, Fox's statement has relevance only when counsel uses the full power of the law to protect the client's best interests. With the increase in serious crimes by juveniles and harsher sentences, appropriate procedural safeguards, such as the right to counsel, are essential elements of the juvenile justice system.

In one of the most comprehensive empirical examinations to date on right to counsel, Barry Feld analyzed variations in the rates of representation and the impact of counsel on juvenile delinquency and status proceedings in Minnesota in 1986.[27] Feld reported that overall, only 45.3 percent of juveniles in Minnesota received the assistance of counsel. In counties with high rates of representation, 94.5 percent of juveniles had counsel; in counties with medium rates, 46.8 percent had counsel; and in counties with low rates, only 19.3 percent had counsel.[28] The seriousness of the offense increases the likelihood of representation, while many juveniles who commit petty offenses go unrepresented because they waive their right to counsel.

Feld's findings confirm previous research in this area: youths with lawyers receive more serious sentencing dispositions. Almost twice as many youths were removed from their homes and institutionalized in the high-representation counties as in areas where there is low representation. Feld's study provides support for the existence of "varieties of juvenile justice" and suggests that administrative criteria and sentencing guidelines should be used to structure dispositional practices in the juvenile court.[29] Feld acknowledges the punitive nature of today's juvenile court and argues that the state must provide appropriate due process protection in this more formal legalistic system.[30]

Based on research, it appears that a great deal of variation still exists in the extent to which juveniles are represented by counsel at adjudication or dispositional hearings in the juvenile court system.[31] The major reasons for this seem to be:

1. Some juveniles are not advised of their right to counsel.
2. Some defense attorneys do not appear at the hearing.
3. Pleas of guilty are entered without full explanation.
4. Juveniles waive their right to counsel, often at the encouragement of parents or some public officer.
5. Parents are unwilling to retain an attorney.
6. Public defender services are inadequate.

According to some child advocates, juvenile offenders should have an unwaivable right to counsel. But many judicial personnel agree that providing every juvenile with legal counsel would seriously impede the work of the juvenile court. In spite of *Gault*, now almost thirty years old, there remain serious questions about the real extent and quality of legal representation. According to Feld, it appears that *Gault*'s promise of counsel remains unkept for most juveniles in most states.[32]

ADJUDICATION

At the **adjudication** stage of the juvenile process, a hearing is held to determine the merits of the petition claiming that a child is either a delinquent youth or in need of court supervision. The judge is required to make a finding on the evidence in the case and arrive at a judgment. Adjudication is comparable to an adult trial. Rules of evidence in adult criminal proceedings are generally applicable, and the standard of proof used—"beyond a reasonable doubt"—is similar to that in adult trials. The majority of juvenile cases do not reach the adjudicatory state, but serious delinquency cases based on violations of the criminal law, situations where children deny any guilt, cases of repeat offenders, and cases where children are a threat to themselves or the community often do reach this stage.

Much of the controversy over the adjudication process has centered on whether juveniles have been accorded fair procedures. State juvenile codes vary with regard to the basic requirements of due process and fairness. Most juvenile courts have bifurcated hearings—that is, separate hearings for adjudication and disposition. At disposition hearings, evidence can be submitted that reflects nonlegal factors, such as the child's home life, relationships, and background. While there has not been sufficient research on hearing fairness, there are some indications that minorities may be handled with disproportionate harshness at disposition.[33]

Edmund McGarrell's study of juvenile court data for 1985 and 1989 indicated that minority youths are more likely to be referred to and petitioned in court, detained, and placed away from the home after adjudication.[34] McGarrell speculates that this trend may be partially attributed to the increase in minority drug offenders. However, what sometimes seems to be racial or ethnic bias may actually be a result of legal or socially relevant factors, such as the willingness to plea-bargain, the seriousness of the crime, school performance, and so on.

At present, most state juvenile codes provide for specific rules of procedure and a finding at adjudication. These rules require that a written petition be submitted to the court, ensure the right of a child to have an attorney, provide that the adjudication proceedings be recorded, allow the petition to be amended, and provide that a child's plea be accepted. Where the child admits to the facts of the petition, the courts generally seek assurance that the plea is voluntary. If plea bargaining is used, prosecutors, defense counsel, and trial judges take steps to ensure the fairness of such negotiations.

At the end of the adjudication hearing, most juvenile court statutes require the judge to make a factual finding on the legal issues and evidence reviewed in the child's hearing. In the criminal court, this finding is normally an entry of judgment involving a verdict. In the juvenile court, the juvenile court judge normally (1) makes a finding of fact that the child or juvenile is not delinquent or in need of supervision, (2) makes a finding of fact that the juvenile is delinquent or in need of supervision, or (3) dismisses the case because of insufficient or faulty evidence. In some jurisdictions, informal alternatives are used, such as filing the case with no further consequences or continuing the case without a finding. These alternatives involve no determination of delinquency or noncriminal behavior. Because of the philosophy of the juvenile court of treatment and rehabilitation, a delinquency finding is not the same thing as a criminal conviction. The disabilities associated with conviction, such as disqualifications for employment, entrance into the military service, or involvement in politics, are not created by an adjudication of delinquency.

Consequently, there are still some significant differences between adult and juvenile proceedings. For instance, only a small proportion of states entitle juveniles to jury trials. And in almost all jurisdictions, juvenile trials are closed to the public.[35]

Constitutional Rights at Trial

In addition to state juvenile code requirements, the U.S. Supreme Court has mandated the application of constitutional due process standards to the juvenile trial. The term *due process* is mentioned in the Fifth and Fourteenth Amendments to the U.S. Constitution. It refers to the need in our legal system for rules and procedures that protect individual rights. Having the right to due process means that no person can be deprived of life, liberty, or property without such protections as legal counsel, an open and fair hearing, an opportunity to confront those making accusations against him or her, and so on. Basically, due process is intended to guarantee that fundamental fairness is available to every citizen.

For many years, children were deprived of their due process rights because the *parens patriae* philosophy governed their relationship to the juvenile justice system. Such rights as having counsel and confronting one's accusers were forbidden. Why should children need protection from the state when the only issue was their treatment, care, and protection? This view changed in the 1960s when, under the leadership of Chief Justice Earl Warren, the U.S. Supreme Court recognized the problems inherent in the juvenile justice system and began to grant due process rights and procedures to minors. As a result of Supreme Court activism, a child is now entitled to many of the same due process rights as an adult. As Justice Hugo Black stated in the landmark 1967 case *In re Gault:*

When a person, infant or adult, can be seized by the state, charged and convicted, for violating a state criminal law, and then ordered by the state to be confined for six years,

Most juvenile trials are bench trials held before a judge alone. Though not unknown, there is no Constitutional right to a jury trial in juvenile court.

Gerald Gault's (center) successful appeal to the Supreme Court revolutionized the legal rights of young offenders.

I think the Constitution requires that he be tried in accordance with the guarantees of all the provisions of the Bill of Rights, made applicable to the states by the Fourteenth Amendment. Appellants are entitled to these rights not because fairness, impartiality and orderliness, in short, the essentials of due process, require them, and not because they are the procedural rules which have been fashioned from the generality of due process, but because they are specifically and unequivocably granted by provisions of the Fifth and Sixth Amendments which the Fourteenth Amendment makes applicable to the states.[36]

The Warren Court set forth the role of due process in juvenile justice through major decisions made during the 1960s, beginning with *Kent v. United States,* decided in 1966.[37] In *Kent,* the court held that a transfer proceedings was a critically important stage in the juvenile process and must hold to at least minimal due process and fair treatment standards as required by the Fourteenth Amendment. This case was detailed in Chapter 15.

In the landmark case of *In re Gault,* the Supreme Court further articulated the basic requirements of due process that must be satisfied in juvenile court proceedings. It held that in an adjudicatory hearing:

■ The child must be given adequate notice of the charges.
■ The child and the parent must be advised of the right to be represented by counsel.
■ The child has a constitutional privilege against self-incrimination.
■ The child has the right of confrontation and sworn testimony of witnesses available for cross-examination.[38]

Because of the importance of the *Gault* case, it is set out in the following Focus on Delinquency.

FOCUS ON DELINQUENCY

In re Gault

FACTS

Gerald Gault, 15 years of age, was taken into custody by the sheriff of Gila County, Arizona, because a woman complained that he and another boy had made an obscene telephone call to her. At the time, Gerald was under a six-month probation as a result of being found delinquent for stealing a wallet. Because of the verbal complaint, Gerald was taken to the children's home. His parents were not informed that he was being taken into custody. His mother appeared in the evening and was told by the superintendent of detention that a hearing would be held in the juvenile court the following day. On the day in question, the police officer who had taken Gerald into custody filed a petition alleging his delinquency. Gerald, his mother, and the police officer appeared before the judge in his chambers. Mrs. Cook, the complainant, was not at the hearing. Gerald was questioned about the telephone calls and was sent back to the detention home and then subsequently released a few days later.

On the day of Gerald's release, Mrs. Gault received a letter indicating that a hearing would be held on Gerald's delinquency a few days later. A hearing was held, and the complainant again was not present. There was no transcript or recording of the proceedings, and the juvenile officer stated that Gerald had admitted making the lewd telephone calls. Neither the boy nor his parents were advised of any right to remain silent, the right to be represented by counsel, or any other constitutional rights. At the conclusion of the hearing, the juvenile court committed Gerald as a juvenile delinquent to the state industrial school in Arizona for the period of his minority.

This meant that, at the age of 15, Gerald was sent to the state school until he reached the age of 21 unless discharged sooner. An adult charged with the same crime would have received a maximum punishment of no more than a fifty dollar fine or two months in prison.

DECISION

Gerald's attorneys filed a writ of habeas corpus, which was denied by the Superior Court of the state of Arizona. That decision was subsequently affirmed by the Arizona Supreme Court. On appeal to the U.S. Supreme Court, Gerald's counsel argued that the juvenile code of Arizona under which Gerald was found delinquent was invalid because it was contrary to the due process clause of the Fourteenth Amendment. In addition, Gerald was denied the following basic due process rights: (1) notice of the charges with regard to their timeliness and specificity, (2) right to counsel, (3) right to confrontation and cross-examination, (4) privilege against self-incrimination, (5) right to a transcript of the trial record, and (6) right to appellate review. In deciding the case, the Supreme Court had to determine whether procedural due process of law within the context of fundamental fairness under the Fourteenth Amendment applied to juvenile delinquency proceedings in which a child is committed to a state industrial school.

The Court, in a far-reaching opinion written by Justice Abe Fortas, agreed that Gerald's constitutional rights had been violated. Notice of charges was an essential ingredient of due process of law, as was the right to counsel, the right to cross-examine and to confront witnesses, and the privilege against self-incrimination. The questions of appellate review and a right to a transcript were not answered by the Court in this case.

SIGNIFICANCE OF THE CASE

The *Gault* case established that a child had the procedural due process constitutional rights listed above in delinquency adjudication proceedings where the consequences were that the child could be committed to a state institution. It was confined to rulings at the adjudication stage of the juvenile process.

However, this decision was significant not only because of the procedural reforms it initiated but also because of its far-reaching impact throughout the entire juvenile justice system. *Gault* instilled in juvenile proceedings the development of due process standards at the pretrial, trial, and post-trial stages of the juvenile process. While recognizing the history and development of the juvenile court, it sought to accommodate the motives of rehabilitation and treatment with children's rights. It recognized the principle of fundamental fairness of the law for children as well as for adults. Judged in the context of today's juvenile justice system, *Gault* redefined the relationships between juveniles, their parents, and the state. It remains the single most significant constitutional case in the area of juvenile justice. ■

Source: In re Gault, 387 U.S. 1; 87 S.Ct. 1248 (1967).

FOCUS ON DELINQUENCY

In re Winship and *McKeiver v. Pennsylvania*

STANDARD OF PROOF: IN RE WINSHIP

Following the *Gault* case came *In re Winship*. This case expressly held that a juvenile in a delinquency adjudication must be proven guilty beyond a reasonable doubt.

FACTS

Winship, a 12-year-old boy in New York, stole $112 from a woman's pocketbook. The petition that charged Winship with delinquency alleged that this act, if done by an adult, would constitute larceny. Winship was adjudicated a delinquent on the basis of a preponderance of the evidence submitted at the court hearing. During a subsequent dispositional hearing, Winship was ordered placed in a training school in New York state for an initial period of eighteen months, subject to extensions of his commitment until his eighteenth birthday—six years in total. The New York State Supreme Court and the New York Court of Appeals affirmed the lower court decision, sustaining the conviction.

DECISION

The problem in the case was whether Section 744(b) of the New York State Family Court Act was constitutional. This section provided that any determination at the conclusion of an adjudicatory hearing must be based on a preponderance of the evidence. The judge decided Winship's guilt on the basis of this standard and not on the basis of proof beyond a reasonable doubt, which is the standard in the adult criminal justice system. The issue in the case was whether proof beyond a reasonable doubt was essential to due process and fair treatment for juve-

niles charged with an act that would constitute a crime if committed by an adult.

SIGNIFICANCE OF THE CASE

Although the standard of proof beyond a reasonable doubt is not stated in the Constitution, the U.S. Supreme Court said that *Gault* had established that due process required the essentials of fair treatment, although it did not require that the adjudication conform to all the requirements of the criminal trial. The Court further said that the due process clause recognized proof beyond a reasonable doubt as being among the essentials of fairness required when a child is charged with a delinquent act. The state of New York argued that juvenile delinquency proceedings were civil in nature, not criminal, and that the preponderance of evidence standard was therefore valid. The U.S. Supreme Court indicated that the standard of proof beyond a reasonable doubt plays a vital role in the American criminal justice system and ensures a greater degree of safety for the presumption of innocence of those accused of a crime.

Thus, the *Winship* case required proof beyond a reasonable doubt as a standard for juvenile adjudication proceedings and eliminated the use of lesser standards such as a preponderance of the evidence, clear and convincing proof, and reasonable proof.

RIGHT TO A JURY TRIAL: MCKEIVER V. PENNSYLVANIA

One of the most controversial issues in the areas of children's rights at adjudication involves the jury trial.

continued on next page

The *Gault* decision reshaped the constitutional and philosophical nature of the juvenile court system. As a result, those working in the system—judges, social workers, attorneys, and so on—were faced with the problem of reaffirming the rehabilitative ideal of the juvenile court while ensuring that juveniles received proper procedural due process rights. Prior to the *Gault* decision, only a few states required that juveniles have assistance of counsel. Now, according to Linda

FOCUS ON DELINQUENCY

Although the Sixth Amendment guarantees to the adult criminal defendant the right to a jury trial, the Supreme Court had not seen fit to grant this right to juvenile offenders. In fact, the U.S. Constitution is silent on whether all defendants, including those charged with misdemeanors, have a right to a trial by jury. In the case of *Duncan v. Louisiana*, the Supreme Court held that the Sixth Amendment right to a jury trial applied to all adult defendants accused of serious crimes. However, no mention was made of the juvenile offender.

The case of *McKeiver v. Pennsylvania* deals with the right of the juvenile defendant to a jury trial.

FACTS

Joseph McKeiver, age 16, was charged with robbery, larceny, and receiving stolen goods, all of which were felonies under Pennsylvania law. McKeiver was subsequently declared delinquent at an adjudication hearing and placed on probation after his request for a jury trial was denied.

In another case, Edward Terry, age 15, was charged with assault and battery on a police officer, misdemeanors under Pennsylvania law. He was declared a juvenile delinquent after an adjudication following a denial of his request for trial by jury.

In an unrelated case in North Carolina, a group of juveniles were charged with willful, riotous, and disorderly conduct, declared delinquent, and placed on probation. Their request for a jury trial was denied.

The Supreme Court heard all three cases together on the single issue of whether a juvenile has a constitutional right to a jury trial in the juvenile court system.

DECISION

The court was required to decide whether the due process clause of the Fourteenth Amendment guarantees the right to a jury trial in the adjudication of a juvenile court delinquency case. It answered in the negative, stating that the right to a jury trial guaranteed by the Sixth Amendment and incorporated in the Fourteenth Amendment is not among the constitutional safeguards that the due process clause requires at delinquency adjudication hearings. The Court's reasons were as follows:

■ A jury trial is not a necessary component of accurate fact-finding, as are the procedural requirements stated in the *Gault* case.
■ Not all the rights constitutionally assured to an adult are to be given to a juvenile.
■ Insisting on a jury trial for juvenile offenders could fully turn the adjudication into an adversary process.
■ Insisting on a jury trial would not remedy the problems associated with the lack of rehabilitation in the juvenile court.
■ The preferable approach would be to allow states to experiment and adopt for themselves a jury trial concept in their individual jurisdictions.
■ The jury trial, if imposed in the juvenile court, would certainly result in a delay, formality, and the possibility of a public trial, which at this point is not provided in most jurisdictions.

SIGNIFICANCE OF THE CASE

The *McKeiver* case temporarily stopped the march toward procedural constitutional due process for juvenile offenders in the juvenile justice system. The majority of the Court believed that juvenile proceedings were different from adult criminal prosecutions. The case also emphasized the fact that, as Justice Blackmun said, jurisdictions are free to adopt their own jury trial position in juvenile proceedings. The Court further noted that the majority of states denied a juvenile the right to a jury trial by statute. Thus, the Court believed that granting the juvenile offender the right to a jury trial would hinder rather than advance the system of juvenile justice in the United States. ■

Source: In re Winship, 397 U.S. 358, 90 S.Ct. 1068 (1970); *McKeiver v. Pennsylvania*, 403 U.S. 528, 91 S.Ct. 1976 (1971).

Szymanski of the National Center for Juvenile Justice, virtually all states provide counsel in one form or another at various stages of the juvenile proceedings.[39]

Following the *Gault* case, the Supreme Court decided *In re Winship* in 1970. This case considered the problem of the quantum of proof required in juvenile delinquency adjudications.[40] Prior to *Winship*, most juvenile courts judged the sufficiency of evidence in juvenile matters by applying a preponderance of the evidence, or clear and convincing evidence, test. In *Winship,* the Court rejected the idea that the juvenile system was a civil system and held that the Fourteenth Amendment due process clause required that delinquency charges in juvenile court be proved beyond a reasonable doubt.

Although the traditional juvenile court was severely altered by *Kent, Gault,* and *Winship,* the trend for increased rights for juveniles was somewhat curtailed by the Supreme Court's decision in *McKeiver v. Pennsylvania* (1971). In *McKeiver,* the Court held that trial by jury in a juvenile court's adjudicative stage is not a constitutional requirement.[41] This decision, however, does not prevent states from giving the juvenile a trial by jury as a state constitutional right or by state statute. In the majority of states, a child has no such right, while a small number of jurisdictions do grant it.

In re Winship and *McKeiver v. Pennsylvania,* major decisions signaling the Supreme Court's determination to evaluate the adjudicatory rights of juvenile offenders, are highlighted in a following Focus on Delinquency.

Once an adjudicatory hearing has been completed, the court is normally required to enter a judgment against the child. This may take the form of declaring the child delinquent, adjudging the child to be a ward of the court, or possibly even suspending judgment so as to avoid the stigma of a juvenile record. After a judgment has been entered in accordance with the appropriate state statute, the court can begin its determination of possible dispositions for the child.

DISPOSITION

The stage of the juvenile justice process after adjudication is called **disposition.** It is the sentencing step of the juvenile proceedings. At this point, the juvenile court orders treatment for the juvenile to prevent further delinquency. Adrienne Volenik claims that it is here where the original child-saving philosophy of the juvenile court can come into play.[42]

Disposition is the most important phase of juvenile proceedings.[43] Paul Piersma and his associates describe the disposition as the heart of the juvenile process.[44] Lindsay G. Arthur, who has spent many years working on behalf of the National Council of Juvenile and Family Court Judges, speaks about the importance and the philosophy of disposition:

A disposition is not simply a sentencing. It is far broader in concept and in application. It should be in the best interest of the child, which in this context means effectively to provide the help necessary to resolve or meet the individual's definable needs, while, at the same time, meeting society's needs for protection.[45]

The dispositional process has not received much attention from the courts. None of the Supreme Court decisions dealing with juvenile justice refers to its significance. Consequently, according to most legal documents, one of the most important issues in the disposition is the lack of proper procedure and due process for the child. In most jurisdictions today, adjudication and disposition hearings are separated, or bifurcated. In addition to a separate dispositional hearing, a child is generally accorded the right to counsel.

The Supreme Court has not ruled on the right to counsel at disposition, but counsel's participation is generally allowed either by state statute or by general practice. Defense counsel often represents the child, helps the parents understand the court's decision, and influences the direction of the disposition. Others involved at the dispositional stage include representatives of social service agencies, psychologists, social workers, and probation personnel. Their information about the child's background often may be disputed at the disposition, and many states now allow cross-examination at this stage of the juvenile process.

Another important issue at the dispositional hearing is the need to obtain information about the child in order to formulate the treatment plan. In determining the type of disposition to be imposed on the child, juvenile court statutes often require the completion of a **predispositional investigation.** Fox describes the needs and purposes of this report:

> Individualized justice is often taken to be the most salient characteristic of juvenile court dispositions. In order to have the disposition conform to this ideal, the juvenile court judge requires information about each particular child. This is usually provided by an investigation, usually performed by a member of the probation staff, and report, known as the social study or disposition report.[46]

The predisposition report in the juvenile court is similar to the presentence report in the adult criminal justice system. Its use at the adjudication may result in prejudicial error against the child and often results in a mistrial. However, social service information is often used at the intake phase of the juvenile process as well as at the disposition. In some jurisdictions, statutes mandate completion of a predisposition report, particularly before a child can be placed in a youth program.

The Predisposition Report

After the child has admitted to the allegations in the petition or after the allegations have been proved in a juvenile trial, the judge normally orders the probation department to complete a predisposition report. Investigating and evaluating the child coming before the court for juvenile disposition are two of the most important tasks of juvenile probation officers. The predisposition report has a number of purposes:

- ■ It helps the judge decide which disposition is best for the child.
- ■ It aids the juvenile probation officer in developing treatment programs where the child is in need of counseling or community supervision.
- ■ It helps the court develop a body of knowledge about the child that can aid others in treating the child.
- ■ It serves as a source of basic information for systematic research in juvenile justice.

The style and content of predisposition reports vary among jurisdictions and also among juvenile probation officers within the same jurisdiction. The requirements for the use of the report, the sources of dispositional information, the techniques for obtaining it, and the conditions of its distribution vary among jurisdictions and are based on rules of law and procedure.

Some juvenile court probation departments require voluminous reports covering every aspect of the child's life. Other jurisdictions require information about the basic facts of the case and only limited information about the child's background. Individual officers bring their personal styles and educational backgrounds to bear on the development of the report. The probation officer who is a trained social worker, for example, might stress the use of psychological data, while the probation officer who is a lawyer might concentrate on the child's prior record and how dangerous the child is to him- or herself and to the community.

Sources of dispositional data include questioning the juvenile as well as collecting information about the child from family and school officials. In addition, the results of psychological testing, psychiatric evaluations, and intelligence testing may be relevant to the predispositional report. Furthermore, the probation officer might include information about the juvenile's feelings and attitudes regarding the present situation.

Some state statutes make the predisposition report mandatory. Other jurisdictions require the report only when there is a probability that the child will be institutionalized. In Massachusetts, for example, the law reads that "in every case of a delinquent child, a probation officer shall make a report regarding the character of such child, his school record, home surroundings, and previous complaint, if any.[47] Some appellate courts have reversed orders institutionalizing children where the juvenile court did not use a predisposition report in reaching its decision.

Access to predisposition reports is an important legal issue. The Supreme Court ruled in the case of *Kent v. United States* that the child and counsel must be given access to the social service report at transfer proceedings.[48] The National Advisory Commission on Criminal Justice Standards and Goals recommends that no dispositional decision be made on the basis of facts or information in a report if they have not previously been disclosed to the defense attorney for the child and to the prosecutor representing the state.[49] According to Robert Shepherd, Jr., of the American Bar Association, this is also an excellent time for the defense attorney to bring to the probation officer's attention any favorable information regarding the child.[50]

In the final section of the predisposition report, the probation department recommends a disposition to the presiding judge. This is a very critical aspect of the report, since it has been estimated that the court follows more than 90 percent of all probation department recommendations. Thus, it is essential that the purpose of the report, which is to determine the care or treatment plan the child needs and not to prove or disprove the child's innocence or guilt, be accomplished.

Types of Juvenile Court Dispositions

Historically, the juvenile court has had broad discretionary power to make dispositional decisions after adjudication. The major categories of dispositional choices include: (1) community release, (2) out-of-home placements, (3) fines or restitution, (4) community service, and (5) institutionalization. A more detailed list of the numerous possible dispositions open to the juvenile court judge follows:[51]

■ *Informal consent decree.* In minor or first offenses, an informal hearing is held, and the judge will ask the youth and his or her guardian to agree to a treatment program, such as counseling. No formal trial or disposition hearing is held.

- *Probation.* A youth is placed under the control of the county probation department and asked to obey a set of probation rules and participate in a treatment program.
- *Home detention.* A child is restricted to his or her home in lieu of a secure placement. Rules include regular school attendance, curfew observance, avoidance of alcohol and drugs, and notification of parents and the youth worker of the child's whereabouts.
- *Court-ordered school attendance.* If truancy was the problem that brought the youth to court, a judge may order mandatory school attendance. Some courts have established court-operated day schools and court-based tutorial programs staffed by community volunteers.
- *Financial restitution.* A judge can order the juvenile offender to make financial restitution to the victim. In most jurisdictions, restitution is part of probation (see Chapter 18), but in a few states, such as Maryland, restitution can be a sole order.
- *Fines.* Some states allow fines to be levied against juveniles age 16 and over.
- *Community service.* Courts in many jurisdictions require juveniles to spend time in the community working off their debt to society. Community service orders are usually reserved for victimless crimes, such as possession of drugs, or crimes against public order, such as vandalism of school property. Community service orders are usually carried out in schools, hospitals, nursing homes, and so on.
- *Outpatient psychotherapy.* Youths whose behavior is bizarre and disorganized may be required to undergo therapy at a local mental health clinic.
- *Drug and alcohol treatment.* Youths with drug- or alcohol-related problems may be allowed to remain in the community if they agree to undergo drug or alcohol therapy.
- *Commitment to secure treatment.* In the most serious cases, a judge may order an offender put in a long-term treatment center, referred to as training schools, camps, ranches, homes, and so on. These may be either state- or privately run institutions, usually located in remote regions of the state. Training schools provide educational, vocational, and rehabilitation programs in a secure environment (see Chapter 19).
- *Commitment to a residential community program.* Youths who commit crimes of a less serious nature but still need to be removed from their homes can be placed in community-based group homes or halfway houses. They attend school or work during the day and live in a controlled, therapeutic environment at night.
- *Foster home placement.* Foster homes are usually used for dependent or neglected children and status offenders. Judges are today placing delinquents with insurmountable problems at home in state-licensed foster care homes.

The authority to order dispositional alternatives generally stems from the juvenile code. Most state statutes allow the juvenile court judge to select whatever disposition is best suited to the child's needs. In addition to the above dispositions, some states go so far as to grant the juvenile court the power to order parents into treatment or suspend a youth's driver's license.

On the other hand, state juvenile codes can have specific prohibitions that limit the judge's discretionary power. For instance, twenty-one states prohibit confining children in adult institutions.[52] Some states use a minimum age as a criteria for institutional placement, while others limit placement in such facilities to felony offenders only. In certain states, the juvenile court determines commitment in a specific institution, while in others, the youth corrections agency determines where the child will be placed. In other words, there is almost an infinite number of statutory variations to the dispositional process.

Standard 2.1 of the IJA-ABA Juvenile Justice Standards, Standards Relating to Dispositions, articulates the basic policy of seeking the least restrictive alternative in dispositional decision making. In choosing among statutorily permissible dispositions, "the court should employ the least restrictive category and duration of disposition that is appropriate to the seriousness of the offense, as modified by the degree of culpability indicated by the circumstances of the particular case, and by the age and prior record of the juvenile." The imposition of a particular disposition should be accompanied by a statement of the facts relied on in support of the disposition and the reasons for selecting the disposition and rejecting less restrictive alternatives.[53] The following Case in Point explores the disposition process.

■■■■■■■■■■■■■■

CASE IN POINT

You are a family court judge at a dispositional hearing faced with making a difficult sentencing decision.

John M. was arrested at the age of 16 for robbery and rape. As a juvenile offender, he was subject to the jurisdiction of the juvenile division of the state family court. After a thorough investigation by the police department, the prosecutor formally filed a petition against John for the alleged offenses. Subsequently, John's mother obtained counsel for him. When the prosecutor suggested that the court might consider transferring the case to the adult court, John admitted his involvement in the offenses and was sent home pending plans for disposition.

At the dispositional hearing, the probation officer reported that John was the oldest of three siblings living in a single-parent home. He has had no contact with his father for over ten years. Psychological evaluation showed hostility, anger toward females, and great feelings of frustration. His intelligence was below average, and his behavioral and academic records were poor. In addition, John seemed to be involved with a local youth gang, although he denied any formal association with the group. This is John's first formal petition in the family court. Previous contact was limited to an informal complaint for disorderly conduct at the age of 13, which was dismissed by the court's intake department. John verbalizes superficial remorse for his offenses.

To the prosecutor, John seems to be a youth with poor controls who is likely to commit future crimes. The defense attorney and court staff see the need for program planning to meet John's needs. As the judge, you recognize the seriousness of the crimes committed by John and have at your disposal a wide range of court services that might help in John's rehabilitation. No one can predict or assess John's future behavior and potential dangerousness.

What disposition would you order? The Family Court Act lists ten dispositional alternatives for juvenile delinquents: the most severe is commitment to training school; the others are community-level alternatives.

How Juvenile Court Handles Special Groups

Violent Crime

Violent crime by a juvenile involves such actions as criminal homicide, violent sex offenses, robbery, and aggravated assault. About 6 percent of the youths referred to juvenile court are charged with these crimes, and approximately 77 percent are handled formally by the courts.[54] Most youths charged with violent offenses are male, and older juveniles account for a significant share of the violent offenses referred to the juvenile courts.

The response of the juvenile court system to violent crime by young people occurs at the main decision-making points: (1) detention; (2) decision to file a petition for adjudication; and (3) disposition. Generally, youths referred for violent offenses are twice as likely to be detained as those referred for nonviolent offenses. This is because they are often considered a threat to themselves or the community. According to the Office of Juvenile Justice and Delinquency Prevention, an informal adjudicatory hearing is requested in 65 percent to 90 percent of the violent crime cases.[55]

Youths referred to court for violent crimes are five times as likely as nonviolent offenders to be transferred to adult criminal courts and twice as likely to be placed in a residential facility. This analysis suggests that juvenile courts act seriously against violent juveniles, but it leaves unanswered the question of whether such disposition decisions protect the community and also respond to a juvenile offender's needs.[56]

Drug and Alcohol Offenses

The juvenile courts saw an increase in drug and alcohol cases from 1985 through 1988.[57] Even though the data (see Chapter 11) show an overall stabilization in adolescent drug use, the juvenile courts have been faced with a progressively larger caseload of children involved with drugs and alcohol. For example, the National Center for Juvenile Justice found that from 1985 to 1988, while drug case rates for white juvenile offenders decreased by 15 percent, the drug case rate for minorities increased over 88 percent. This same study also found that drug and alcohol use increase with age and that rates for 16- and 17-year-olds were substantially higher than for younger children. In addition, in its annual report, *The State of Criminal Justice,* the American Bar Association also found that arrest increases for drug offenders have been significantly higher for minority juvenile offenders than for whites.[58]

Generally, during the late 1980s, drug cases were handled with increasing severity by the juvenile courts. This meant they were more likely to be handled formally, and juvenile offenders were also more likely to be placed outside the home. Unlike drug cases, the majority of alcohol cases during 1985 to 1988 were handled informally. However, a distinction was often made between drinking versus driving under the influence. Juveniles who had been driving under the influence were often petitioned and placed in a residential facility or on probation, and their cases were less likely to be dismissed than those involving just drinking.[59]

In addition to decision making by the juvenile courts about such crimes, many state legislatures have passed "abuse and lose" statutes to deter juveniles from abusing alcohol and drugs.[60] This type of legislation provides that individuals under a given age lose their driver's license if they are convicted of an alcohol or drug abuse offense. Since substance abuse is a significant cause of traffic accidents, states are likely to support such laws as a way of dealing with accidents caused by juveniles.

THE CHILD'S RIGHT TO APPEAL

Juvenile court statutes normally restrict appeals to cases where the juvenile seeks review of a "final order" or a final judgment.[61] Paul Piersma and his associates define a final order as one that ends the litigation between two parties by determining all their rights and disposing of all the issues.[62] The **appellate process** gives the juvenile the opportunity to have the case brought before a reviewing court after it has been heard in the juvenile or family court. Today, the law does not recognize a federal constitutional right of appeal in juvenile or adult criminal cases. In other words, the U.S. Constitution does not require any state to furnish an appeal to a juvenile charged and found to be delinquent in a juvenile or family court. Consequently, appellate review of a juvenile case is a matter of statutory right in each jurisdiction. However, the majority of states do provide juveniles with some method of statutory appeal.

The appeal process was not always part of the juvenile law system. For example, J. Addison Bowman found that in 1965, few states extended the right of appeal to juveniles.[63] According to the President's Commission on Law Enforcement and Administration of Justice, appellate review was equally limited in 1967:

By and large, the juvenile court system has operated without appellate surveillance. . . . Two factors contribute substantially to the lack of review. The absence of counsel in the great majority of cases in the first . . . . The other important factor is the general absence of transcripts of juvenile proceedings.[64]

Even in the *Gault* case in 1967, the Supreme Court refused to review the Arizona juvenile code, which provided no appellate review in juvenile matters. It further rejected the right of a juvenile to a transcript.[65]

Today, however, most jurisdictions that provide a child with some form of appeal also provide for counsel and for the securing of a record and transcript, which are crucial to the success of any appeal. Since adult criminal defendants have both a right to counsel at their initial appeal and a right to a stenographic transcript of trial proceedings, it would violate equal protection if juveniles were denied the same rights.

Since juvenile appellate review is a matter of statutory right, each jurisdiction determines for itself what method or scope of review will be used. There are two basic methods of appeal: the direct appeal and the collateral attack. The direct appeal normally involves an appellate court review to determine whether the rulings of law and the judgment of the court based on the evidence presented at the trial were correct. This approach is laid out in Section 59 of the Uniform Juvenile Court Act of the National Conference of Commissioners on Uniform State Law: "The appeal of the finding should be heard upon the files, records, and minutes or transcripts of the evidence of the juvenile court, giving appreciable weight to the findings of the juvenile court."[66] A similar approach is suggested by the National Advisory Commission on Criminal Justice Standards and Goals: "The appeal should be heard upon the files, records, and transcript of the evidence of the family court."[67]

A broader review procedure, which is a form of direct review, is the *de novo* review. A **trial *de novo*** is a complete retrial of the original case based on the original petition. All evidence produced at the first trial can be resubmitted, as can additional evidence. The trial *de novo* appeal is limited to only a few jurisdictions in the nation. It is usually encountered when a juvenile is originally tried in a court of very limited jurisdiction and in some administrative proceedings before masters or referees.

The second major area of review involves the collateral attack of a case. The term *collateral* refers to a secondary or indirect method of attacking a final judgment or order of the court. Instead of appealing the original juvenile trial because of errors, prejudice, or lack of evidence, collateral review uses extraordinary legal writs to challenge the lower court position. Two such procedural devices include the **writ of habeas corpus** and the **writ of certiorari.** The habeas corpus writ, known as the "Great Writ," refers to a procedure for determining the validity of a person's custody. In the context of the juvenile court, it is used to challenge the custody of a child in detention or in an institution. The writ of certiorari is an order from a higher to a lower court commanding that the case be brought forward for review. This writ is often the method by which the Supreme Court exercises its discretionary authority to hear cases regarding constitutional issues. Even though there is no constitutional right to appeal a juvenile case and each jurisdiction provides for appeals differently, juveniles have a far greater opportunity for appellate review today than in years past.

Trends in Juvenile Sentencing

For most of the juvenile court's history, disposition was based on the presumed needs of the child. Although such critics as David Rothman and Anthony Platt have challenged the motivations of early reformers in championing rehabilitation, there is little question that the rhetoric of the juvenile court has promoted that ideal.[68] For example, Joseph Goldstein, Anna Freud, and Albert Solnit in their classic work, *Beyond the Best Interest of the Child,* say that placement of children should be based on the **least detrimental alternative** available in order to foster the child's growth and development.[69] This should be the goal whether the children are delinquents or status offenders or are neglected, abandoned, or abused.

Views of juvenile sentencing have changed in the late 1980s and early 1990s. In Chapter 16, we discussed the changes in transfer policy that make it easier to waive children to the adult court. These changes are evidence of concern about how to handle the chronic juvenile offender. On the other hand, we have also noted a trend to deinstitutionalize status offenders and prohibit their incarceration with delinquent youths. Yet, as we shall see below, many states have imposed requirements for greater proportionality and determinacy in juvenile disposition.

Determinate versus Indeterminate Sentencing

Traditionally, states have used the **indeterminate sentence** in juvenile court. In about half of the states, this means having the judge simply place the offender with the state department of juvenile corrections until correctional authorities consider him or her ready to return to society or until the youth reaches his or her legal majority. The majority of states, including Missouri, Texas, and West Virginia, consider 18 to be the age of release; others, such as Michigan and Tennessee, peg the termination age at 19; a few, including Kansas, Montana, Ohio, South Carolina, South Dakota, Utah, Virginia, and Wyoming, can retain youths until their twenty-first birthday.[70] In practice, few youths remain in custody for the entire statutory period; children are usually released if their rehabilitation has been judged by the youth corrections department, judge, or parole board to have progressed satisfactorily. This practice is referred to as the **individualized treatment model**—each sentence must be tailored to the individual needs of the child.

Another form of the indeterminate sentence allows judges to specify a maximum term that can be served. For example, in Alabama, Alaska, North Dakota, and Colorado, youths can be sentenced to a maximum of not more than two years in a institution; in Maryland, New Jersey, and Pennsylvania, the maximum sentence is three years.[71] Youths may also be released from incarceration in these jurisdictions if the corrections department considers them to be rehabilitated or they reach the automatic age of termination (usually 18 or 21). In most of the twelve states that signify a maximum sentence, the court may extend the sentence for one or two years, depending on the youth's progress in the institutional facility.[72]

A number of states have changed their sentencing policies in an effort to toughen up on juvenile offenders. Some, including Arizona, Georgia, Minnesota, and California, have changed from indeterminate to determinate sentencing in juvenile court. This means sentencing juvenile offenders to a fixed term of years that must be served in its entirety. Virginia and Tennessee have enacted provisions allowing determinate commitments of youth adjudicated for certain serious offenses. Arizona, for example, allows the state juvenile corrections agency to set standards for release by creating guidelines based on offense conditions that are applied during the intake process.[73] California, Colorado, Delaware, Georgia, Connecticut, and Pennsylvania are among the states that have passed laws creating **mandatory sentences** for serious juvenile offenders. For example, Delaware law provides a one-year mandatory sentence for a juvenile who commits any two felony acts during a one-year period; if a previously adjudicated delinquent commits three felonies within a three-year period, he or she receives a mandatory three-year sentence.[74] Juveniles receiving mandatory sentences are usually institutionalized for the full sentence and not eligible for early parole. Pennsylvania passed legislation in 1986 that set up a statewide depository for fingerprints and photographs of dangerous juvenile offenders and youths aged 15 to 17 who are repeat violent offenders.[75]

New York's juvenile code gives the adult court original jurisdiction over cases involving 14- and 15-year-olds who commit serious violent felonies and over cases of 13-year-olds who commit murder.[76] If there are mitigating circumstances—for example, if the offender had a small role in the crime—the adult court judge can waive the case back to the juvenile court. Known as New York's Juvenile Offender Law, this controversial statute reduced the age of criminal responsibility for direct prosecution of youths committing certain offenses in the adult courts and authorized lengthy periods of incarceration. In addition, New York's Designated Felony Act allows the juvenile court judge to sentence children who commit murder, arson, or kidnapping to a sentence of five years in a juvenile institution.[77] The sentence can be renewed annually until the offender reaches 21. For less serious felony offenses, the judge can impose a three-year sentence, annually renewable.

Probably the best-known effort to reform sentencing in the juvenile court is the state of Washington's **Juvenile Justice Reform Act of 1977.** This act created a mandatory sentencing policy requiring juveniles ages 8 to 17 who are adjudicated delinquent to be confined in an institution for a minimum time.[78] The legislative intent of the act was to make juveniles accountable for criminal behavior and to provide for punishment commensurate with the (1) age, (2) crime, and (3) prior history of the offender. Washington's tough approach to juvenile sentencing is based on the principle of "proportionality." How much time a youth must spend in confinement is established by the Juvenile Dispositions Standards Commission based on the above three criteria. The introduction of such mandatory sentencing procedures standardizes juvenile dispositions and reduces disparity in the length of sentences, according to advocates of a "get-tough" juvenile justice system.

Evaluating Tough Sentencing Laws

Can such statutory changes in juvenile sentencing statutes have positive outcomes for the operation of the juvenile justice system? One reason for optimism has been the rather dramatic changes brought about in the state of Washington by the passage of the Juvenile Justice Reform Act of 1977. Research by Tom Castellano found that within two years of its passage, there was a high degree of compliance with its provisions.[79] The law has moved Washington's juvenile justice system away from informality and disparity toward the procedural regularity found in the adult system.

Castellano concludes that liberals should be able to cheer the due process rights afforded to offenders, the proportionality that now exists in sentencing, and the fact that under the new code, status offenders no longer can be incarcerated with delinquents. In fact, he disputes the charge that the reform act is a get-tough approach.

Conservatives can be equally satisfied that under the new law, serious offenders are given sterner sentences than they may have received earlier; over 90 percent of the serious juvenile offenders who come before the court are removed from the community, and many receive sentences ranging from two to four years.

On the other hand, not all statutory changes have had the desired effect. For instance, while New York's Juvenile Offender Law requires that juveniles accused of violent offenses be tried in criminal court and provides serious penalties comparable to those for adults, Simon Singer and David McDowall conclude that the law's aim of deterring juvenile crime has not been achieved.[80] Since the law lowered the age of criminal responsibility and included family court jurisdiction, many youths ended up receiving lighter sentences than they would have in the family court.

At the time it was enacted, the New York law was considered to be among the toughest in the nation pertaining to crimes committed by juveniles ages 13, 14, and 15. Yet, data through 1991 substantiates the findings of Singer and McDowall that indicate that more arrests under the law result in outright dismissal than in any other single disposition.[81]

■■ FIGURE 17.2

Juvenile sentencing
approaches

Sources: Texas Youth Commission,
*Juvenile Sentencing in the United States—
A Survey* (Austin: Texas Youth
Commission, 1991); Bureau of Justice
Statistics, *Report to the Nation on Crime
and Justice* (Washington, D.C.:
Department of Justice, 1988).

The growing realization that the juvenile crime rate has stabilized may slow the tide of legislative change in juvenile justice. What is more likely is that states will continue to pass legislation making it easier to transfer youths to the adult court or giving the adult court original jurisdiction over serious cases. Thus, rather than toughening juvenile law for everyone, society may focus on the few more serious cases.

A 1990 survey of all the states found that about one-third have a mixture of determinacy and indeterminacy in their sentencing statutes, while only 37 percent maintain the traditional juvenile sentencing model of little or no determinacy.[82] Figure 17.2 illustrates the common sentencing approaches. Thus,

	LENGTH OF STAY DETERMINED BY:	PHILOSOPHY/ PURPOSE:
INDETERMINATE approx. 37% of jurisdictions	Executive	Least Restrictive Alternative
INDETERMINATE AND DETERMINATE approx. 33% of juridictions	Executive/Judicial	Treatment/ Justice and Accountability
DETERMINATE approx. 17% jurisdictions	Judicial/Legislature	Justice/Punishment
COMBINATION OF: Indeterminate/ Determinate Serious Felonies Capital Punishment approx. 30% of jurisdictions	Mixed	Mixed

treatment seems to be a guiding principle in juvenile sentencing, although other purposes are clearly evident and the distinction between the juvenile and adult systems is decreasing. As Lloyd Ohlin suggests: "Our society is unwilling to sustain the levels of repression and incarceration needed to make more limited incremental gains in crime control."[83] Thus, juvenile sentencing will probably remain wedded to the *parens patriae* philosophy, even if states pass legislation to incarcerate some very serious offenders.

The Future of Juvenile Sentencing and Serious Crime

During the past decade, the treatment-oriented philosophy has taken a back seat to the development of more formal and punitive approaches toward juveniles charged with serious crimes. This pattern can be observed most clearly in studying statutory sentencing changes regarding the placement of children in secure settings. Although more than half the states still use indefinite sentencing, the trend is toward more determinate and fixed sentences.

Rita Kramer, author of *At a Tender Age: Violent Youth and Juvenile Justice,* calls for swift and sure sanctions, particularly for violent and repeat offenders. According to Kramer, placing juvenile offenders in a secure institution for a definite period of time should be the response to their acts of violence.[84]

A number of prominent national organizations have also recommended the use of tougher mandatory sentences. For example, the American Bar Association has developed standards that affect the disposition process. Stanley Fisher notes that these standards point to a shift in juvenile court philosophy from the traditional approach of rehabilitation to the concept of just deserts.[85] The standards recommend that juveniles receive determinate or flat sentences without the possibility of parole, rather than the indeterminate sentences that most of them now receive.

The standards further recommend that punishment be classified into three major categories: nominal, conditional, and custodial. *Nominal sanctions* consist of reprimands, warnings, or other minor actions that do not affect the child's personal liberty. *Conditional sanctions* include probation, restitution, and counseling programs. *Custodial sanctions,* which are the most extreme, remove the juvenile from the community into a nonsecure or secure institution. Other juvenile justice standards projects, such as the controversial model developed by the Rose Foundation, also recommend toughening sentences.[86] According to the National Conference of State Legislatures, nine states have already adapted the minimum/maximum sentencing pattern often used in the adult criminal justice system.[87] Also, more than half the states provide dispositional guidelines to assist in determining the juvenile's length of confinement. Thus, the "just deserts" or justice model described in Chapter 14 seems to be the current and most likely the preferred future approach for handling serious juvenile offenders.

Death Penalty for Children

The most controversial of all sentences, adult or juvenile, continues to be the death penalty. The execution of minor children has not been uncommon in our nation's history. Victor Streib, a law professor and leading expert on the death penalty for children, claims that 336 persons have been executed since 1642 for juvenile crimes. This represents about 2 percent of the total of more than eighteen thousand executions since colonial times. Given this, it is not so shocking that in 1992, there were about thirty-three people on death row who had committed their crimes while still teenagers but were waived to adult court for trial and sentencing. According to Streib, all thirty-three juvenile offenders on death row are male and had been convicted and sentenced to death for murder.[88]

Of the thirty-seven states that have laws authorizing **capital punishment,** twenty-two allow the death penalty for crimes committed by people under 18. The U.S. Supreme Court had a chance to resolve this issue in the 1982 case of *Eddings v. Oklahoma,* but it refused to do so.[89] The case involved a 16-year-old boy who killed a highway patrol officer. While the Court overturned his sentence, it did so on the grounds that the trial court had failed to consider his emotional state and troubled childhood when dispensing the death penalty. The Court did not deal with the issue of whether age alone could prohibit a person from being executed. In 1988, however, the Court prohibited the execution of persons below age 16 in the narrowly interpreted case of *Thompson v. Oklahoma.* Some justices endorsed the idea that a child should be presumed to be less responsible than an adult when he or she commits a criminal homicide. This decision left unanswered the issue of whether the Constitution prohibits the use of the death penalty for juveniles who were 16 or 17 years old when they committed their crimes.[90]

The Supreme Court finally confronted the highly emotional question in 1989 in the cases of **Wilkins v. Missouri** and **Stanford v. Kentucky.**[91] Wilkins was 16 when he committed murder, while Stanford was 17. The constitutional question raised by these two cases is basically the same as in the *Thompson* case: at what age does the Eighth Amendment ban the death penalty as punishment, no matter what the crime? Critics of the death penalty believed that there was a consensus against executing young people in the United States. Supporters of capital punishment argued that juveniles after age 16 should be held fully responsible for murder. The Supreme Court concluded that states were free to impose the death penalty for murderers who committed their crimes while age 16 or 17. According to the majority opinion written by Justice Scalia, society has not formed a consensus that the execution of such minors constitutes a cruel and unusual punishment in violation of the Eighth Amendment.

Today, the death penalty stands for people who have committed capital crimes while still in their minority, and a number of executions of such offenders have already taken place. Of the 111 juvenile death sentences imposed since 1973, five have been carried out. (It should be noted, however, that by the time of their execution, the offenders had passed through their teens, since the trial and appeal process consumed many years.)

Those who oppose the death penalty for children, led by Streib, find that it has little deterrent effect on youngsters who are impulsive and do not have a realistic view of the destructiveness of their misdeeds or their consequences. Streib and his associates maintain that the execution of a person who is a child at the time of the crime is cruel and unusual punishment because (1) the condemnation of children makes no measurable contribution to the legitimate goals of punishment, (2) condemning any minor to death violates contemporary standards of decency, (3) the capacity of the young for change, growth, and rehabilitation makes the death penalty particularly harsh and inappropriate, and (4) both legislative attitudes and public opinion reject juvenile executions.[92] Supporters of the death penalty hold that people, regardless of their age, can form criminal intent and therefore should be responsible for their actions. If the death penalty is legal for adults, they argue, then it can also be used for children who commit serious crimes.

CONFIDENTIALITY IN JUVENILE PROCEEDINGS

Along with the rights of juveniles at adjudication and disposition, the issue of **confidentiality** in juvenile proceedings has also received attention in recent years. The debate centers around whether the traditional approach of privacy for juveniles in the interest of their rehabilitation is preferred over the current cry for open proceedings that might increase public protection.[93] Confidentiality in the juvenile court deals with two areas: (1) open versus closed hearings and (2) privacy of juvenile records. Considered by many to be a basic tenant of juvenile justice philosophy, the issue of complete confidentiality has lost some of its credibility, as many legislatures have broadened access to juvenile records.

Open versus Closed Hearings

Generally, juvenile trials are closed to the public and press, and the names of the offenders kept secret. The Supreme Court has ruled on the issue of privacy in three important decisions. In *Davis v. Alaska,* the Court concluded that any injury resulting from the disclosure of a juvenile's record is outweighed by the right to completely cross-examine an adverse witness.[94] The *Davis* case involved an effort to obtain testimony from a juvenile probationer who was a witness in a criminal trial. After the prosecutor was granted a court order preventing the defense from making any reference to the juvenile's record, the Supreme Court reversed the state court, claiming that a juvenile's interest in confidentiality was secondary to the constitutional right to confront adverse witnesses.

The *Davis* case was a decision of evidentiary significance, whereas the decisions in two subsequent cases, **Oklahoma Publishing Co. v. District Court** and **Smith v. Daily Mail Publishing Co.,** balanced juvenile privacy with freedom of the press. In the *Oklahoma* case, the Supreme Court ruled that a state court was not allowed to prohibit the publication of information obtained in an open juvenile proceeding.[95] The case involved an 11-year-old boy suspected of homicide who appeared at a detention hearing and of whom photographs were taken and published in local newspapers. When the local district court prohibited further disclosure, the publishing company claimed that the court order was a restraint in violation of the First Amendment, and the Supreme Court agreed. The *Smith v. Daily Mail* case involved the discovery and subsequent publication by news reporters of the identity of a juvenile suspect in violation of a state statute prohibiting publication. The Supreme Court, however, declared the statute unconstitutional because it believed that the state's interest in protecting the child's identity was not of such a magnitude as to justify the use of such a statute.[96] Therefore, if newspapers lawfully obtain pictures or names of juveniles, they may publish them. Based on these decisions, it appears that the Supreme Court favors the constitutional rights of the press over the right to privacy of the juvenile offender.

None of the decisions, however, gave the press complete access to juvenile trials. Today, some jurisdictions still bar the press from juvenile proceedings unless they show at a hearing that their presence will not harm the youth. In other words, when states follow a *parens patriae* philosophy, ordinarily the public and press are excluded, but the court has discretion to permit interested parties to observe the hearings.

Privacy of Records

For most of the twentieth century, juvenile records were kept confidential by case, law, or statute. The general rule was that juvenile court records—both legal and social—were confidential information.[97] Today, however, the record itself or information contained in it can be opened by court order in many jurisdictions by statutory exception. The following groups can ordinarily gain access to juvenile records: (1) law enforcement personnel; (2) the child's attorney; (3) the parents or guardians; (4) military personnel; (5) and public agencies, such as schools, court organizations, and correctional institutions.[98]

Some states also allow a juvenile adjudication for a criminal act, such as rape, to be used as evidence in a subsequent adult criminal proceeding for the same act to show predisposition or criminal nature.[99] In addition, a juvenile's records may be used during the disposition or sentencing stage of an adult criminal trial in some states.[100] A major problem in dealing with juvenile offenders is the lack of information about serious crimes committed before the age of 18. Many first-time adult offenders committed numerous crimes as juveniles, and evidence of these crimes may not be available or relevant to sentencing for the adult offenses. To address this problem, the Department of Justice recently authorized the FBI to accept juvenile records from the states for inclusion in the national criminal records system.[101] States are urged to enact statutes to provide that juvenile convictions are relevant factors for adult sentencing. According to such experts as Ira Schwartz, the need for confidentiality today to protect juveniles is far less than the need to open up the courts to public scrutiny and accountability.[102] The problem of confidentiality of juvenile records will become more acute in the future as computerization makes them both more durable and accessible.[103]

■ ■ ■ ■ ■ ■ ■ ■ ■ ■ ■ ■ ■ ■ ■ ■

SUMMARY

This chapter described two major aspects of the juvenile justice system, adjudication and disposition. Most jurisdictions have a bifurcated juvenile code system that separates the adjudication hearing from the dispositional hearing. Juveniles alleged to be delinquent, as well as children in need of supervision, have virtually all the rights given a criminal defendant at trial—except possibly the right to a trial by jury. In addition, juvenile proceedings are generally closed to the public.

The types of dispositional orders that the juvenile court gives include dismissal, fine, probation, and institutionalization. The use of such dispositions has not curtailed the rising rate of juvenile crime, how-

ever. As a result, legislatures and national commissions have begun to take a tougher position with regard to the sentencing of some juvenile offenders. The traditional notion of rehabilitation and treatment as the proper goals for disposition is now being questioned, and some jurisdictions have replaced it with proportionality in sentencing procedures. Many juvenile codes do require that the court consider the "least restrictive" alternative before removing a juvenile from the home.

The predisposition report is the primary informational source for assisting the court in making a judgment about a child's care and treatment.

Once a juvenile is found delinquent or in need of supervision, the juvenile court is empowered through the dispositional process to make fundamental changes in the child's life. In recent years, a number of states have made drastic changes in juvenile sentencing law, moving away from the pure indeterminate sentence and embracing more structured, determinate forms of disposition. If there is any chance for juvenile crime to be reduced in the future, it may well depend on fair, just, and effective disposition.

Lastly, many state statutes require closed hearings and privacy of juvenile records in juvenile proceedings to protect the child from public scrutiny and provide a greater opportunity for rehabilitation. But this approach may be inconsistent with the public's recent interest in taking a closer look at the juvenile justice system.

KEY TERMS

juvenile prosecutor
judge
Missouri Plan
National Council of Juvenile and Family Court
   Judges
defense attorneys
guardian *ad litem*
CASA
public defender
adjudication
disposition
predispositional investigation
appellate process
trial de novo

writ of habeus corpus
writ of certiorari
least detrimental alternative
indeterminate sentence
individualized treatment model
mandatory sentences
Juvenile Justice Reform Act of 1977
capital punishment
Wilkins v. Missouri
Stanford v. Kentucky
confidentiality
Oklahoma Publishing v. District Court
Smith v. Daily Mail Publishing Co.

NOTES

1. Barry Krisberg, *The Juvenile Court: Reclaiming the Vision* (San Francisco: National Council on Crime and Delinquency, 1988).
2. Howard N. Snyder, Melissa H. Sickmund, Ellen H. Nimick, Terrence A. Finnegan, Dennis P. Sullivan, Rowen S. Poole, and Nancy J. Tierney, *Juvenile Court Statistics, 1989* (Pittsburgh: National Center for Juvenile Justice, 1992), pp. 7 and 45.
3. U.S. Department of Justice, *Prosecution in the Juvenile Courts* (Washington, D.C.: Government Printing Office, 1973), p. 9.
4. 383 U.S. 541, 86 S.Ct. 1045, 16 L.Ed.2d 84 (1966); 387 U.S. 1, 87 S.Ct. 1428, 18 L.Ed.2d 527 (1967); and 397 U.S. 358, 90 S.Ct. 1068, 25 L.Ed.2d 368 (1970).
5. American Bar Association, *Standards Relating to Juvenile Prosecution* (Cambridge, Mass.: Ballinger, 1977), p. 13; Robert Shepard, Jr. "The Prosecutor in the Juvenile Court," *ABA Journal on Criminal Justice* 32:36–40 (1968).
6. 191 Neb. 5231 (1974).

7. John Laub and Bruce MacMurray, "Increasing the Prosecutor's Role in Juvenile Court: Exceptions and Realities" (unpublished research report, Boston: Northeastern University, 1987).
8. Ibid., p. 11.
9. National District Attorneys Association, *Prosecution Standard 19.2, Juvenile Delinquency* (Alexandria, Va.: NDAA, 1992).
10. James Shine and Dwight Price, "Prosecutor & Juvenile Justice: New Roles and Perspectives," in Ira Schwartz, ed., *Juvenile Justice and Public Policy* (New York: Lexington Books, 1992), pp. 101–33.
11. F. Eastman, "Procedures and Due Process," *Juvenile and Family Court Journal* 35:36 (1983).
12. Yeheskel Hasenfeld and Paul Cheung, "The Juvenile Court and a People-Processing Organization: A Political Economy Perspective," *American Journal of Sociology* 90:801–24 (1985).

13. Leonard P. Edwards, "The Juvenile Court and the Role of the Juvenile Court Judge," *Juvenile and Family Court Journal* 43:3–45 (1992).

14. See Sari Escovitz with Fred Kurland and Nan Gold, *Judicial Selection and Tenure* (Chicago: American Judicature Society, 1974), pp. 3–16.

15. National Council of Juvenile and Family Court Judges, "Juvenile and Family Justice," *Juvenile and Family Court Journal* Volume 1, #3, 1992, p. 15.

16. National Council of Juvenile and Family Court Judges *Annual Report, 1991* (Pittsburgh: National Center for Juvenile Justice, 1991).

17. 287 U.S. 45, 53 S.Ct. 55, 77, L.Ed.2d 158 (1932); 372 U.S. 335, 83 S.Ct. 792, 9 L.Ed.2d 799 (1963); and 407 U.S. 25, 92 S.Ct. 2006, 32 L.Ed.2d 530 (1972).

18. American Bar Association, *Standard Relating to Counsel for Private Parties* (Cambridge, Mass.: Ballinger, 1977).

19. Howard Davidson, "The Guardian ad Litem: An Important Approach to the Protection of Children," *Children Today* 10:23 (1981); see also Daniel Golden, "Who Guards the Children?" *Boston Globe Magazine*, 27 December 1992, p. 12.

20. Eastman, "Procedures and Due Process," p. 32.

21. Office of Juvenile Justice and Delinquency Prevention, *CASA: Court Appointed Special Advocate for Children*, Juvenile Justice Bulletin (Washington, D.C.: Department of Justice, 1992).

22. S. H. Clarke and G. G. Koch, "Juvenile Court: Therapy or Crime Control and Do Lawyers Make a Difference?" *Law and Society Review* 14:263–308 (1980); Charles Thomas and Ineke Marshall, "The Effect of Legal Representation on Juvenile Court Dispositions" (Paper presented at the Southern Sociological Society, 1981); David Duffee and Larry Siegel, "The Organization Man: Legal Counsel in Juvenile Court," *Criminal Law Bulletin* 7:544–53 (1971).

23. Joseph Sanborn, "The Defense Attorney's Role in Juvenile Court: Must Justice or Treatment (or Both) Be Compromised?" (Paper presented at the Academy of Criminal Justice Sciences, St. Louis, 15–19 March 1987), p. 32; also Randy Hertz, Martin Guggenheim, and Anthony Amsterdam, *Trial Manual for Defense Attorneys in Juvenile Court* (Chicago: American Law Institute-American Bar Association, 1991).

24. Sanborn, "The Defense Attorney's Role in Juvenile Court," p. 8.

25. Jane Knitzer, *Law Guardians in New York State* (New York: New York State Bar Association, 1985); David Hechler, "Lawyers for Children: No Experience Necessary," *Justice for Children* 1:14–15 (1985).

26. Sanford Fox, *Juvenile Courts* (St. Paul: West, 1984), p. 162.

27. Barry C. Feld, "The Right to Counsel in Juvenile Court: An Empirical Study of When Lawyers Appeal and the Difference They Make," *Journal of Criminal Law and Criminology* 79:1187–1346 (1989).

28. Ibid., pp. 1217–18; for concern about the availability of counsel in the adult courts, see also Stephen Bright, Stephen Kinnard, and David Webster, "Keeping Gideon from Being Blown Away," *Criminal Justice Journal of the American Bar Association* 4:10–14 (1990).

29. Feld, "The Right to Counsel in Juvenile Court," p. 1318.

30. Ibid., p. 1346.

31. See Steven Clark and Gary Koch, "Juvenile Court: Therapy or Crime Control and Do Lawyers Make a Difference?" *Law and Society Review* 14:263–308 (1980); David Aday, "Court Structure, Defense Attorney Use, and Juvenile Court Decisions," *Sociological Quarterly* 27:107–19 (1986); James Walter and Susan Ostrander, "An Observational Study of a Juvenile Court," *Juvenile and Family Court Journal* 33:53–69 (1982); Barry Feld, "In re Gault Revisited: A Cross-State Comparison of the Right to Counsel in Juvenile Court," *Crime and Delinquency* 34:392–424 (1988).

32. Barry C. Feld, "The Punitive Juvenile Court and the Quality of Procedural Justice: Dysfunctions between Rhetoric and Reality," *Crime and Delinquency* 36:443–65 (1990).

33. Jeffrey Fagan, Ellen Slaughter, and Eliot Hartstone, "Blind Justice? The Impact of Race on the Juvenile Justice Process," *Criminal Delinquency* 33:224–58 (1987).

34. Edmund McGarrel, "Trends in Racial Disproportionality in Juvenile Court Processing: 1985–1989," *Crime and Delinquency* 39:29–48 (1993).

35. See Institute of Judicial Administration, American Bar Association Joint Commission on Juvenile Justice Standards, *Standards Relating to Adjudication* (Cambridge, Mass.: Ballinger, 1980).

36. 387 U.S. 1 (1967), 19.

37. 383 U.S. 541 (1966).

38. 387 U.S. 1 (1967).

39. Linda Szymanski, *Juvenile Delinquents' Right to Counsel* (Pittsburgh: National Center for Juvenile Justice, 1988).

40. 397 U.S. 358, 90 S.Ct. 1068 (1970).

41. 403 U.S. 528 (1971).

42. Adrienne E. Volenik, *Checklist for Use in Juvenile Delinquency Proceedings* (Washington, D.C.: American Bar Association, 1985), p. 42.

43. See, generally, R. T. Powell, "Disposition Concepts," *Juvenile and Family Court Journal* 34:7–18 (1983).

44. Paul Piersma, Jeanette Ganousis, and Prudence Kramer, "The Juvenile Court: Current Problems, Legislative Proposals, and a Model Act," *St. Louis University Law Review* 20:43 (1976); Robert Shepherd, Jr., "Preparing for the Juvenile Disposition," *American Bar Association Criminal Justice Journal* 7:35–36 (1993).

45. See Lindsay Arthur, "Status Offenders Need a Court of Last Resort," *Boston University Law Review* 57:63–64 (1977).

46. Sanford Fox, *Juvenile Courts in a Nutshell* (St. Paul: West, 1984), p. 221.

47. Mass.Gen.Laws Chap. 119, 57.

48. *Kent v. United States,* 383 U.S. 541, 86 S.Ct. 1045 (1966).

49. National Advisory Commission on Criminal Justice Standards and Goals, *Report of the Task Force on Juvenile Justice and Delinquency Prevention* (Washington, D.C.: Government Printing Office, 1976), p. 445.

50. See Shepherd, "Preparing for the Juvenile Disposition," p. 36.

51. This section is adapted from Jack Haynes and Eugene Moore, "Particular Dispositions," *Juvenile and Family Court Journal* 34:41–48 (1983); see also Grant Grissom, "Dispositional Authority and the Future of the Juvenile Justice System," *Juvenile and Family Court Journal* 42:25–34 (1991).

52. Criminal Justice Program of National Conference of State Legislatures, *Legal Dispositions and Confinement Policies for Delinquent Youth* (Denver: National Conference of State Legislatures, July 1988), p. 3; see also American Bar Association Institute of Judicial Administration Standards on Juvenile Justice Standards Relating to Dispositions, (Cambridge: Ballinger Press, 1977), 2.1.

53. See American Bar Association Institute of Judicial Administration Standards on Juvenile Justice, *Standards Relating to Dispositions,* (Cambridge: Ballinger Press, 1977), 2.1.

54. Office of Juvenile Justice and Delinquency Prevention, *The Juvenile Court's Response to Violent Crime* (Washington, D.C.: Department of Justice, 1989), pp. 1–5.

55. Ibid., p. 1.

56. See "The Young and Violent," Wall Street Journal, 23 September 1992, p. A14.

57. See Melissa Sickmund, *Juvenile Court Drug and Alcohol Cases: 1985–88* (Washington, D.C.: Department of Justice, 1991), p. 1.

58. American Bar Association, *The State of Criminal Justice—An Annual Report* (Chicago: ABA, 1993), p. 11.

59. Sickmund, *Juvenile Court Drug and Alcohol Cases,* p. 9.

60. Michael Vaughn, Victor Kappeler, and Rolando V. Del Carmen, "A Legislative and Constitutional Examination of Abuse and Lose: Juvenile Driving Statutes," *American Journal of Criminal Law* 19:411–33 (1992).

61. Fox, *Juvenile Courts in a Nutshell,* pp. 254–55.

62. Paul Piersma, Jeanette Ganousis, Adrienne E. Volenik, Harry F. Swanger, and Patricia Connell *Law and Tactics in Juvenile Cases* (Philadelphia: American Law Institute-American Bar Association, Committee on Continuing Education, 1977), p. 397.

63. See J. Addison Bowman, "Appeals from Juvenile Courts," *Crime and Delinquency Journal* 11:63–77 (1965).

64. President's Commission on Law Enforcement and Administration of Justice, Task Force Report, *Juvenile Delinquency and Youth Crime* (Washington, D.C.: Government Printing Office, 1967), p. 115.

65. 387 U.S. 1 (1967).

66. National Conference of Commissioners on Uniform State Laws, *Uniform Juvenile Court Act,* 59 (Philadelphia: American Law Institute, 1968).

67. National Advisory Commission on Criminal Justice Standards and Goals, *Report of the Task Force on Juvenile Justice and Delinquency Prevention,* p. 428.

68. See Anthony Platt, *The Child Savers: The Invention of Delinquency* (Chicago: University of Chicago Press, 1969); David Rothman, *Conscience and Convenience: The Asylum and the Alternative in Progressive America* Boston: Little, Brown, 1980).

69. See Joseph Goldstein, Anna Freud, and Albert Solnit, *Beyond the Best Interests of the Child* (New York: Free Press, 1973).

70. Martin Forst, Bruce Fisher, and Robert Coates, "Indeterminate and Determinate Sentencing of Juvenile Delinquents: A National Survey of Approaches to Commitment and Release Decision Making," *Juvenile and Family Court Journal* 36:1–12 (1985).

71. Ibid., p. 7.

72. Ibid., p. 9.

73. Ibid.

74. Del.Code Ann. Title 10, 937(c) (1977).

75. "Pennsylvania to Build Central Data Base of Juvenile Records," *Criminal Justice Newsletter,* 16 January 1987, p. 1.

76. N.Y.Fam.Ct.Act 753 (1978); also see New York State Laws of 1976, Chap. 878.

77. Ibid., 753a (1978).

78. See Washington Juvenile Justice Act of 1977, Chap. 291; Wash. Rev.Code Ann. Title 9A, Sec. 1–91 (1977).

79. Thomas Castellano, "The Justice Model in the Juvenile Justice System: Washington State's Experience" (Paper presented at the Academy of Criminal Justice Sciences, St. Louis, 15–18 March 1987).

80. Simon Singer and David McDowall, "Criminalizing Delinquency: The Deterrent Effects of NYJO Law," *Law and Society Review* 22:Sections 21–37 (1988).

81. New York State Division for Youth, *Research Focus on Youth-Juvenile Offenders,* Vol. 2, No. 1 (1992).

82. Texas Youth Commission, *Juvenile Sentencing in the United States—A Survey* (Austin: Texas Youth Commission, 1991).

83. Lloyd Ohlin, "The Future of Juvenile Justice," *Crime and Delinquency* 29:467 (1983).

84. See Rita Kramer, *At a Tender Age: Violent Youth and Juvenile Justice* (New York: Holt, 1988); also Rita Kramer, "Juvenile Justice Is Delinquent," *Wall Street Journal,* 27 May 1992, p. 34.

85. Stanley Fisher, "The Dispositional Process under the Juvenile Justice Standards Project," *Boston University Law Review* 57:732 (1977).

86. Alan Breed, "Reforming Juvenile Justice: A Model or Ideology?" *Juvenile Justice Digest* 15 (April 6, 1987).

87. See Criminal Justice Program of National Conference of State Legislatures, *Legal Dispositions and Confinement Policies for Delinquent Youth,* p. 5.
88. Victor Streib, *Death Penalty for Juveniles* (Bloomington: Indiana University Press, 1987); see also Paul Reidinger, "The Death Row Kids," *American Bar Association Journal* (April 1989):78; Victor Streib, *The Juvenile Death Penalty Today: Present Death Row Inmates under Juvenile Death Sentences* (Cleveland: Cleveland State University, 25 August 1992).
89. 455 U.S. 104 (1982).
90. Steven Gerstein, "The Constitutionality of Executing Juvenile Offenders, *Thompson v. Oklahoma,*" *Criminal Law Bulle.in* 24:91–98 (1988); also 108 S.Ct. 2687 (1988).
91. 109 S.Ct. 2969 (1989); for a recent analysis of the *Wilkins* and *Stanford* cases, see Note, "*Stanford v. Kentucky* and *Wilkins v. Missouri*—Juveniles, Capital Crime, and Death Penalty," *Criminal Justice Journal* 11:240–66 (1989).
92. Victor Streib, "Excluding Juveniles from New York's Impendent Death Penalty," *Albany Law Review* 54:625–79 (1990).
93. Paul R. Kfoury, *Children before the Court: Reflection on Legal Issues Affecting Minors* (Boston: Butterworth, 1987), p. 55.
94. 415 U.S. 308 (1974).
95. *Oklahoma Publishing Co. v. District Court,* 430 U.S. 97 (1977).
96. *Smith v. Daily Mail Publishing Co.,* 443 U.S. 97 (1977).
97. Linda Szymanski, *Confidentiality of Juvenile Court Records* (Pittsburgh: National Center for Juvenile Justice, 1989).
98. Ibid.
99. *Houser v. Georgia,* 326 S.E. 2d 513 (1985).
100. *Hayden v. South Carolina,* 322 S.E.2d 14 (1984).
101. "Combatting Violent Crime—Providing for Use of Juvenile Offense Records in Adult Sentencing, *Criminal Law Reporter,* 12 August 1992.
102. Ira M. Schwartz, *(In) Justice for Juveniles: Rethinking the Best Interests of the Child* (Lexington, Mass.: D.C. Heath, 1989), p. 172.
103. See the case of *Alonzo M. v. City Dept. of Probation,* 532 N.E. 2d 1254 (1988), where a New York state statute forbade any reference, even to the family court, of charges that were not proven or were dismissed.

VI JUVENILE CORRECTIONS

■■

D espite efforts to decarcerate as many juveniles as possible, it sometimes becomes necessary to institutionalize youths who need care, custody, and control. A variety of methods have been developed to meet these goals, including community-based and secure treatment programs. Over the years there has been a massive effort to remove non-serious offenders from secure institutions and place them in small, community-based facilities. Yet thousands of youngsters are sent to secure, prison-like facilities each year.

Children in custody have become an American dilemma. Many incarcerated adult felons report that they were institutionalized as youths. Severe punishment seems to have little deterrent effect on teenagers—if anything, it may prepare them for a life of adult criminality. The juvenile justice system is caught between the futility of punishing juveniles and the public's demand that something be done about serious juvenile crime. Even though the nation seems to be in the midst of a punishment cycle, juvenile justice experts continue to press for judicial fairness, rehabilitation, and innovative programs for juvenile offenders.

The two chapters in Part VI describe the correctional treatment of juveniles in the community and in custody. Both approaches seek "the best interest of the child" and "the protection of the community." Although sometimes contradictory, these two major positions dominate the dispositional process.

Chapter 18 discusses efforts to treat juveniles while they remain in society. The most common community disposition employed by juvenile courts is probation. Theoretically, its goal is to rehabilitate the general offender by treatment, guidance, and supplementary programs while the child remains in the community.

Chapter 19 reviews the history and practices of the juvenile institution and discusses efforts to rehabilitate youths in custody. Most secure institutions are not equipped to provide successful treatment for serious juvenile offenders. They often have limited treatment and educational services, as well as antiquated physical plants. One can understand why the training school is under constant judicial scrutiny.

By reading these chapters you should be able to develop an understanding of how the juvenile justice system deals with children who need treatment and present a danger to themselves and others.

OUTLINE

JUVENILE
PROBATION AND
COMMUNITY
TREATMENT

After adjudication, the treatment needs of children found to be either delinquents or status offenders are evaluated by court personnel. Since prevailing juvenile court philosophy demands that children be subject to the least restrictive disposition alternative possible, this usually means a period of community-based corrections.

Community treatment refers to a wide variety of efforts to provide care, protection, and treatment for children in need. These efforts include probation, a variety of treatment services such as social casework, group work, the use of volunteers in probation, as well as **restitution** and other appropriate programs. The term *community treatment* also refers generally to the use of nonsecure and noninstitutional residences, such as foster homes, small group homes, boarding schools or semi-institutional cottage living programs, forestry camps or outdoor camps, and nonresidential programs where youths remain in their own homes and receive counseling, education, family assistance, diagnostic services, casework services, or vocational training. Parole (aftercare) is often considered an extension of community treatment, but this will be discussed in the following chapter. In a broader sense, community treatment includes preventive programs, such as street work with antisocial gangs or early identification and treatment of predelinquents. Such programs are discussed in Chapters 10, 11, and 15.

This chapter discusses the concept of community treatment as a dispositional alternative for juveniles who have violated the law and who have been found delinquent by the juvenile court. Their hope for rehabilitation and the hope of society for resolving the problems of juvenile crime lie in the use of community treatment programs. Such programs are generally preferable to training schools because they are smaller, operate in a community setting, and offer creative approaches to treating the juvenile offender. Traditional institutions, on the other hand, are costly to operate and offer limited services.

First, this chapter discusses probation in detail. It examines new and important approaches for providing effective probation services to juvenile offenders. Next, it reviews restitution, which is being used in many jurisdictions to supplement probation supervision. It then traces the development of alternatives to incarceration, including community-based, nonsecure treatment programs. Juvenile court judges generally have considerable latitude regarding the use of the various community-based dispositional alternatives, and this chapter focuses on these programs.

JUVENILE PROBATION

Probation is the primary form of community treatment in the juvenile justice system. It ordinarily refers to a disposition. The child is placed and maintained in the community under the supervision of a duly authorized officer of the court. The term also denotes a status or process whereby the child on probation is subject to rules that must be followed and conditions that must be met in order for the child to remain in the community. *Probation* often refers to an organizational structure—a probation department (either an independent agency or one attached to a court) that manages, supervises, and treats children and carries out investigations for the court. Although the term has many other meanings too, *probation* usually refers to a legal disposition of nonpunitive type for delinquent youths and those in need of supervision, emphasizing maintenance in the community and treatment without incarceration.

Juvenile probation is based on the idea that the juvenile offender is not generally dangerous to the community and has a better chance of being rehabilitated within the community. Advocates of probation and community treatment suggest that the institutional experience can force juveniles to become further involved in antisocial behavior. Probation provides the child with the opportunity to be closely supervised by trained personnel who can help him or her reestablish forms of acceptable behavior in a community setting:

Probation is a desirable disposition in appropriate cases because (1) it maximizes the liberty of the individual while at the same time vindicating the authority of the law and effectively protecting the public from further violations of law; (2) it affirmatively promotes the rehabilitation of the offender by continuing normal community contacts; (3) it avoids negative and frequently stultifying effects of confinement, which often severely and unnecessarily complicate the reintegration of the offender into the community; (4) it greatly reduces the financial cost to the public of an effective correctional system.[1]

In practice, probation is a legal disposition, and only a judge can place a juvenile under an order of probation. Two methods are generally used. One is a straight order of probation for such a time and under such conditions as the judge deems proper. The other method involves ordering a child to be committed to an institution or department of youth services and then suspending the order and placing the child on probation. In the majority of jurisdictions, probation is a direct order and is exercised under wide statutory discretion. In particular, the conditions to be followed during the probationary period are subject to the court's discretion.

The Nature of Probation

A probation sentence involves a contract between the court and the juvenile. The court promises to hold a period of institutionalization in abeyance; the juvenile promises to adhere to a set of rules or conditions mandated by the court. If the rules are violated, and especially if the child commits another offense, the probation may be revoked. In that case, the contact between the court and the child is over, and the original commitment order may be enforced. The rules of probation vary, but they most typically involve such conditions as attending school or work, keeping regular hours, remaining in the jurisdiction, and staying out of trouble.

In the juvenile court, probation is often ordered for an indefinite period of time. Depending on the statutes of the jurisdiction, the seriousness of the offense, and the juvenile's adjustment on probation, children can remain under the court's supervision until the court no longer has jurisdiction over them, that is, when they reach their majority. New York limits probation to two years for a delinquent and one year for a status offender, extendable under exceptional circumstances. Florida mandates that probation last no longer than could a term of commitment to an institution.[2] State statutes determine if a judge can specify how long a juvenile can be placed under an order of probation.

In most jurisdictions, the status of probation is reviewed regularly to ensure that a child is not kept on probation needlessly. Generally, discretion lies with the probation officer to discharge the child if the child is adjusting to the supervision and treatment plan.

Since virtually all the states have adopted the Uniform Interstate Compact on Juveniles, the supervision of a juvenile probationer can be transferred from one state to another when it is necessary for a child to move from the original jurisdiction.[3] The compact provides jurisdiction over all nonresident children by allowing for the return of runaway children to their home state and for supervision of out-of-state children.

Historical Development

Although the major developments in juvenile probation have occurred in the present century, its roots go back much farther. In England, specialized procedures for dealing with youthful offenders can be found as early as 1820, when the magistrates of the Warwickshire quarter sessions adopted the practice of sentencing youthful criminals to prison terms of one day, then releasing them conditionally under the supervision of their parents or masters. This practice was developed further in Middlesex, Birmingham, and London, where probation supervision was first supplied by police officers, then by volunteer philanthropic organizations, and finally by public departments.[4]

In the United States, juvenile probation developed as part of the wave of social reform characterizing the latter half of the nineteenth century. Massachusetts took the first step toward development of a juvenile probation service. Under an act passed in 1869, an agent of the state board of charities was authorized to appear in criminal trials involving juveniles, to find them suitable homes, and to visit them periodically. These services were soon broadened and strengthened so that by 1890, probation had become a mandatory part of the court structure throughout the state.[5]

Probation made a central contribution to the development of the concept of the juvenile court. In fact, in some states the early supporters of the juvenile court movement accepted probation legislation as the first step toward achieving the benefits that the new court was intended to provide. The rapid spread of the juvenile court during the first decades of the present century encouraged the development of probation. The two closely related and to a large degree interdependent institutions sprang from the same dedicated conviction that the young could be rehabilitated and that the public was responsible for protecting them.

By the mid-1960s, juvenile probation had become a major social institution, large, complex, and touching the lives of an enormous number of children in the United States. Today, about four hundred thousand youths are being supervised on probation, and approximately half of those cases are formal probation orders where the juvenile was adjudicated a delinquent or status offender.[6] (See Figure 18.1.)

Organization and Administration

Juvenile probation systems are organized according to two main patterns. In the most common form, the juvenile court or a group of courts administers probation services. In the other, an administrative agency such as a state correctional agency, public welfare department, or a combination of such agencies, provides probation services to the court. The relationship between the court (especially the judge) and the probation staff, whether it is under the court or in a separate administrative agency, is an extremely close one.

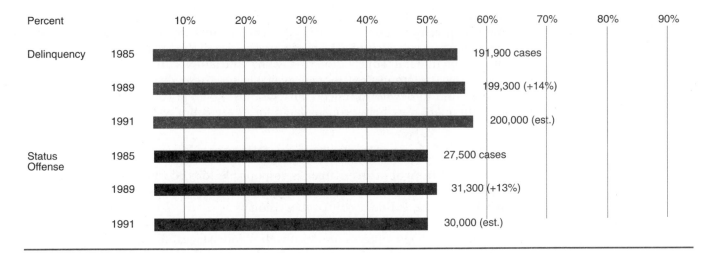

Percent		10%	20%	30%	40%	50%	60%	70%	80%	90%

Delinquency 1985 — 191,900 cases

1989 — 199,300 (+14%)

1991 — 200,000 (est.)

Status Offense 1985 — 27,500 cases

1989 — 31,300 (+13%)

1991 — 30,000 (est.)

■ ■ FIGURE 18.1

Delinquency and status offense cases placed on formal probation

Source: Howard Snyder, Melissa H. Sickmund, *Juvenile Court Statistics, 1989* (Pittsburgh: National Center for Juvenile Justice, 1992), pp. 24 and 57.

In the typical juvenile probation department, the leadership role of the chief probation officer is central to its effective operation.

Large probation departments include one or more assistant chiefs. Each of these middle managers is responsible for one aspect of probation service. One assistant chief might oversee training, while another might supervise and treat special offender groups, and still another might act as liaison with juvenile, police, or community service agencies. The probation officers who investigate and supervise juvenile cases are in direct and personal contact with the supervisory staff.

Each state has its own approach to juvenile probation organization. In some states—Massachusetts, for example—a statewide probation service exists, but actual control over departments is localized within each district court. New York, on the other hand, has in each of its counties a family court with exclusive original jurisdiction over children aged 16 or under; a single department handles probation for the five boroughs of the city of New York. In Maryland, the State Department of Juvenile Services provides probation services to the juvenile courts in each county. On the other hand, Wisconsin's probation program is administered by a county executive department, while in New Jersey, juvenile probation services are managed by judges. Thus, the administration of probation varies from one jurisdiction to another, and there is a considerable lack of uniformity in the roles, organization, and procedures of probation across the states.[7]

The National Center for Juvenile Justice found that, as of 1989, probation services are organized and administered exclusively by the local juvenile court or by the state administrative office of courts in twenty-four states and the District of Columbia. In another eleven states, probation administration is split between judicial and executive branch departments, while in ten states, it is handled exclusively at the state level by a state agency. In two states, county governments administer probation, and in three other states, the responsibility for probation is shared by county and state agencies.[8]

While it appears that juvenile probation services continue to be predominantly organized under the judiciary, recent legislative activity has been in the direction of transferring those services from the local juvenile court judge to a state court administrative office. Whether juvenile courts or state level agencies should administer juvenile probation services is debatable. In years past, the organization of probation services depended primarily on the size of the program and the number of children under its supervision. Today, the judicial-executive controversy is often guided by the amount of money available for these services. Because of this momentum to develop unified court systems, juvenile court services, including probation, are now being consolidated into state court systems.

Duties of Juvenile Probation Officers

The **juvenile probation officer** is responsible for the initial contact with the child, for continuing to process the case, and for providing services for the child while he or she is under court supervision.

According to the American Bar Association's standards for juvenile justice, juvenile probation officers are involved at four stages of the court process. At intake, they screen complaints by deciding to adjust the matter, refer to an agency for service, or refer to the court for judicial action. During the interim status or predisposition stage, they participate in release or detention decisions. At the postadjudication stage, they assist the court in reaching its dispositional decision. During postdisposition, they supervise juveniles placed on probation.[9]

At intake, the probation staff engages in preliminary explorations with the child and the family to determine whether court intervention is necessary or whether the matter can be better resolved by some other community service. If the child is placed in a detention facility, the probation officer helps the court decide whether the child should continue to be held or released pending the adjudication and disposition of the case.

■■■■■■■■■■■■■■

Probation orders typically involve treatment supervision which makes use of existing community based counseling and training programs.

The juvenile probation officer exercises tremendous influence over the child and the family by developing a **social investigation report** and submitting it to the court. This report is a clinical diagnosis of the child's problems and of his or her need for court assistance based on the child's social functioning. The report evaluates the child's personality and relationship to family, peers, and community in order to provide a future treatment plan. Professional investigative reports include analyses of children's perceptions of and feelings about their violations, their problems, and their life situations. They should shed light on the value systems that influence behavior. They will consider the degree of motivation to solve the problems that cause deviant behavior as well as the youths' physical, intellectual, and emotional capacity to change. These reports must examine the influence of family members and other significant persons in producing and possibly solving problems. Neighborhood and peer group determinants of attitudes and behavior also must be analyzed. All of this information must be brought together into a meaningful picture of a complex whole composed of the personality, the problem, and the environmental situation. This relationship must be considered in relation to the various possible alternative dispositions available to the court. Out of this, a constructive treatment plan must be developed.

Another important function of the juvenile probation officer is to provide the child with supervision and treatment in the community. The treatment plan is a product of the intake, diagnostic, and investigative aspects of probation. Treatment plans vary. Some children simply report to the probation officer and follow the conditions of probation. In other cases, the probation officer may need to counsel the child and family extensively or, more typically, refer them to other social service agencies, such as local mental health clinics and detoxification centers.

In sum, the juvenile probation officer's role requires a diversity of skills:

- Providing direct counseling and casework services
- Interviewing and collecting social service data
- Making diagnostic recommendations
- Maintaining working relationships with law enforcement agencies
- Using community resources and services
- Using volunteer case aides and probation officers
- Writing predisposition reports
- Working with families of children under supervision
- Providing specialized services, such as group work, behavior modification counseling, or reality therapy counseling
- Supervising specialized caseloads involving children on drugs or with special psychological or emotional problems
- Making decisions about the revocation of probation and its termination

Performance of all these functions requires a high-quality probation staff. Today, juvenile probation officers have legal or social work backgrounds or special counseling skills. Most jurisdictions require juvenile probation officers to have a background in the social sciences and a bachelor's degree. The probation officer's job is not an easy one. High caseloads often make the therapeutic goal difficult to achieve. Overseeing the probationer's compliance with the legal requirements of probation often becomes the short-term goal.

Conditions and Revocation of Juvenile Probation

Conditions of probation are rules and regulations mandating that a juvenile on probation behave in a particular way. They are important ingredients in the treatment plan devised for the child. Conditions can include restitution or reparation, intensive supervision, intensive probation counseling, participation in a therapeutic program, or participation in an educational or vocational training program. In addition to these specific conditions, state statutes generally allow courts to insist that probationers lead law-abiding lives during the period of probation, that they maintain a residence in a family setting, that they refrain from associating with certain types of people, and that they remain in a particular geographic area unless they have permission to leave.

Probation conditions vary, but they are never supposed to be capricious, cruel, or beyond the capacity of the juvenile to accomplish. Furthermore, conditions of probation should relate to the crime that was committed and to the conduct of the child. The juvenile probation process and the options designed to emphasize individual treatment are illustrated in Figure 18.2.

■■ **FIGURE 18.2**

The juvenile probation process

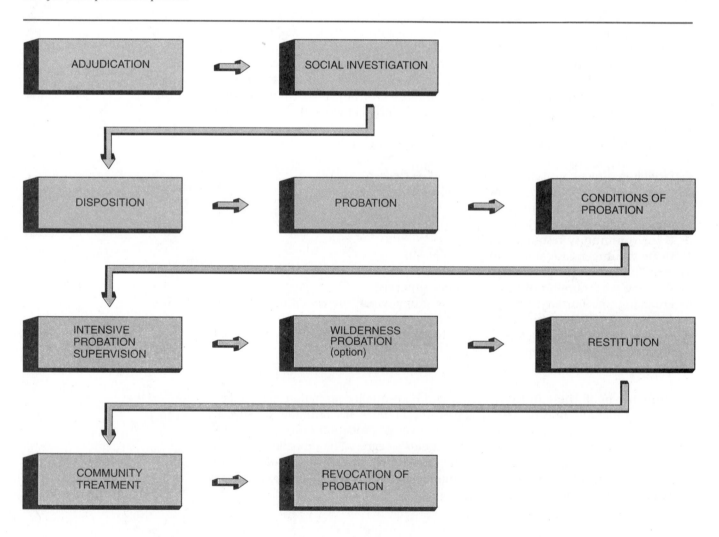

In recent years, appellate courts have invalidated probation conditions that were harmful and that violated the child's basic due process rights. Restricting a child's movement, insisting on a mandatory program of treatment, ordering indefinite terms of probation, and demanding financial reparation where this is impossible are all grounds for an appellate court review.

If a child violates the conditions of probation or breaks the law again, the court can **revoke** probation. The juvenile court ordinarily handles a decision to revoke probation upon recommendation of the probation officer. Today, as a result of Supreme Court decisions dealing with the rights of adult probationers, a juvenile is normally entitled to legal representation and a hearing when a violation of probation occurs.[10] This means that juveniles are virtually entitled to the same due process protections as adult probationers.

PROBATION INNOVATIONS

A number of recent innovations in probation services have impacted or may soon impact services for juvenile offenders. Although probation programs have varying rates of recidivism, experts claim they are generally more successful than placement in an institution. As a result, there has been a great deal of experimentation over the years with different probation techniques. Rule enforcement, guidance, and the use of community services remain the common ingredients for delinquency-reducing programs in probation.

Intensive Probation Supervision

One approach that has generated a great deal of enthusiasm is the **intensive supervision** model. This involves treating offenders who would normally have been sent to a secure treatment facility in very small caseloads that are given almost daily scrutiny.[11]

Numerous jurisdictions have adopted programs of intensive community supervision that have proven more successful than limited probation supervision. For example, Georgia, Oregon, and New Jersey have such programs, and the results seem encouraging.[12] The use of intensive probation as a mechanism for removing both children and adults from confinement no doubt will continue to grow. Even if intensive supervision is found to be no more effective in reducing recidivism than more restrictive correctional interventions, its demonstrated cost benefits (it costs about one-third that of confinement) make it an attractive alternative to traditional forms of treatment, such as confinement.[13]

A recent study by Richard Wiebush that examined the eighteen-month recidivism rate of juvenile felony offenders placed into an intensive supervision program showed that the intensive community supervision was clearly an effective alternative to incarceration.[14] At the same time multifaceted intervention for juvenile probationers (social skills, counseling, and outdoor adventure programs) may be no more effective than "standard" or "regular" probation services.[15] The need is obvious for continued research to determine what programs with what characteristics work for what types of juvenile offenders.

In sum, the results of certain juvenile intensive probation supervision program (JIPS) in different jurisdictions indicate that such programs may cause fewer youths to reenter the juvenile justice system.[16] Other research, however, shows marginal benefits. Today, JIPS components can be found in most metropolitan juvenile probation departments in all major regions of the country and are used as a true alternative to incarceration or other forms of out-of-home placement.[17]

Use of Volunteers

The use of civilian volunteers to assist probation officers is another practice that has proliferated. For example, the juvenile court of Boulder County, Colorado, has provided an extensive volunteer program of delinquency prevention and treatment.[18] Local volunteers work with juvenile offenders, providing tutoring, group counseling, and job training. The variety of community treatment programs available today allows the court greater flexibility in disposing of children's cases.

Electronic Monitoring

Another program that has been used with adult offenders and is finding its way into the juvenile justice system is **house arrest,** which is often coupled with **electronic monitoring.** This program allows offenders sentenced to probation to remain in the community on the condition that they stay in their home during specific periods of time—for example, after school or work, on weekends, during evenings. These offenders may be monitored through random phone calls or visits, but some jurisdictions are experimenting with the use of computer-monitored electronic devices to keep track of their clients. Probationers are fitted with a unremovable monitoring device that alerts the probation department's computers if they leave their place of confinement.[19] While house arrest has not been extensively evaluated in terms of reducing recidivism, its cost, even with active electronic monitoring, is often less than half that of a stay in a detention facility. Two well-known programs, one in Indiana and the other in North Carolina, for instance, appear to operate safely and effectively as alternatives to institutionalization and have become a formal part of probation programming in these jurisdictions.

Joseph B. Vaughn conducted the most recent intensive and descriptive survey of juvenile electronic monitoring in 1989, involving eight programs in five different probation departments.[20] Vaughn found that all the programs adopted electronic monitoring to reduce institutional overcrowdedness and that most agencies reported success in reducing the number of days children spent in detention. In addition, the programs allowed the children who would otherwise be detained to remain in the home and participate in counseling, educational, or vocational activities under reasonable security. Of particular benefit to pretrial detainees was the opportunity to be placed in a natural environment with supervision. This provided the court with a much clearer picture of how the juvenile would eventually perform if given probation. On the other hand, Vaughn found that none of the benefits of the treatment objective in the programs had been empirically validated. The potential for modification in behavior and the duration of any personal changes remain unknown. Overall, the use of electronic monitoring is a new phenomenon, and Vaughn reports that it is too early to assess the impact of such programs on the juvenile justice system.

Wilderness Probation

Another technique that seems to be growing in popularity with probation departments is **wilderness probation.** These programs, staffed by probation officers and lay volunteers, involve youngsters in outdoor expeditions to give them a sense of confidence and purpose.[21] Such programs are used as alternatives to standard dispositions for children being supervised in the juvenile court. They provide an opportunity for certain youth to confront the difficulties in their lives while achieving positive personal satisfaction. Probation counseling and group therapy are all part of a structured program that is significantly different than a purely recreational field trip. The wilderness program in Douglas County, Nevada, for instance, serves between thirty and fifty youths in three different types of wilderness excursions every month.[22] These programs seem to be proving effective with both probationers and institutionalized youth (see Chapter 19 for a discussion of the Outward Bound programs).[23]

Balanced Probation

In recent years, some jurisdictions have turned to a **balanced probation** approach in an effort to enhance the success of probation.[24] Probation systems that integrate community protection, the accountability of the juvenile offender, competency, and individualized attention to the offender incorporate the treatment values of this balanced approach. Some of these juvenile protection programs offer renewed promise for community treatment. This approach has been implemented with some success in Deschutes County, Oregon, and Travis County, Texas.[25] These programs are based on the view that children incur an obligation whenever they commit an offense and are responsible for their actions. The probation officer establishes a program tailored to the special needs of the offender, while helping the youth accept responsibility for his or her own actions. According to Gordon Bazemore, a case can be made for the balanced approach because it specifies a distinctive role and unique objectives for the juvenile probation system.[26]

While these balanced-approach programs are still in their infancy and their effectiveness remains to be tested, they have caused immense interest because of their potential for relieving overcrowded correctional facilities and reducing the pain and stigma of incarceration. There seems to be little question that the use of these innovations and probation in general will increase in the years ahead, particularly since the juvenile court is uniquely organized to provide these programs. Not only can the probation officer do the individual therapy, but he or she can also make the above possibilities available to the juvenile offender.

RESTITUTION

Victim restitution is another widely used method of community treatment. In most jurisdictions, restitution is part of a probationary sentence and is administered by the county probation staff. In some jurisdictions, such as Oklahoma City and Prince George's County, Maryland, independent restitution programs have been set up by local governments, while in others, such as Covington, Louisiana, and Charleston, South Carolina, restitution is administered by a private nonprofit organization.[27]

Restitution itself can take several forms. A child can reimburse the victim of the crime or pay money to a worthy charity or public cause; this is referred to as **monetary restitution.** In other instances, a juvenile can be required to provide

Community-based restitution programs employ youth in public service jobs as an alternative to more punitive and restrictive sanctions.

some service directly to the victim **(victim service)** or to assist a worthwhile community organization **(community service restitution).**

Requiring children to pay the victims of their crimes is the most widely used method of restitution in the United States. Less widely used but more common in Europe is restitution to a community charity. In the past few years, numerous programs have been set up to enable the juvenile offender to provide service to the victim or to participate in community programs—for example, working in schools for retarded children and fixing up neighborhoods. In some cases, children are required to contribute both money and community service. Other programs emphasize employment and work experience.[28]

Restitution programs can be employed at various stages of the juvenile justice process. They can be part of a diversion program prior to conviction, a method of informal adjustment at intake, or a condition of probation.

Restitution has a number of justifications.[29] It provides the court with alternative sentencing options. It offers direct monetary compensation or service to the victims of a crime. It is rehabilitative, because it gives the juvenile the opportunity to compensate the victim and take a step toward becoming a productive member of society. It also relieves overcrowded juvenile courts, probation caseloads, and detention facilities. Finally, it has the potential for allowing vast savings in the operation of the juvenile justice system. Institutional placement costs currently are about twenty-five thousand to thirty thousand dollars annually per child, but restitution programs cost far less. Monetary restitution programs in particular may improve the public's attitude toward juvenile justice by offering equity to the victims of crime and ensuring that offenders assume the obligations of their actions.

Despite what seem to be its many advantages, some believe that restitution contributes to retribution rather than rehabilitation because it emphasizes justice for the victim and criminal responsibility for illegal acts. There is some concern that restitution creates penalties for juvenile offenders where none existed before.

The use of restitution is increasing around the nation. Many states—among them, Minnesota, Massachusetts, Arizona, and Oklahoma—have developed novel approaches to restitution. Legislation authorizing restitution programs has been passed in virtually all jurisdictions in the United States. In 1977, there were fewer than fifteen formal restitution programs around the United States; by 1985, formal programs existed in four hundred jurisdictions, and thirty-five states had statutory provisions that gave courts the authority to order juvenile restitution.[30] In 1990, all fifty states, as well as the District of Columbia, have statutory restitution programs in one form or another.[31]

A sample statute from the State Juvenile Code of North Carolina indicates the type of statutory language used for restitution programs, and the latitude given the juvenile court judge regarding this disposition.

North Carolina Restitution Statute
In the case of any juvenile who is delinquent, the judge may:
(2) Require restitution, full or partial, payable within a twelve-month period to any person who has suffered loss or damage as a result of the offense committed by the juvenile. The judge may determine the amount, terms, and conditions of the restitution. If the juvenile participated with another person or persons, all participants should be jointly and severally responsible for the payment of restitution; however, the judge shall not require the juvenile to make restitution if the juvenile satisfies the court that he does not have, and could not reasonably acquire, the means to make restitution.
(4) Order the juvenile to perform supervised community service consistent with the juvenile's age, skill, and ability, specifying the nature of the work and the number of hours required. The work shall be related to the seriousness of the juvenile's offense and in no event may the obligation to work exceed twelve months.[32]

An example of a successful restitution program is that developed in the Quincy, Massachusetts, district court. The **Alternative Work Sentencing Program, (Earn-It)** handles juveniles referred by the court, the county probation department, and the district attorney's office. The program brings the child together with the victim of the crime in order to develop an equitable work program. Program staff members determine the extent of the victim's loss and place the child in a paying job to earn the required restitution. Some children are placed in nonpaying community service jobs to work off court orders. By all indications, Earn-It has been a success. During its first year of operation, in 1975, the program returned thirty-six thousand dollars in restitution payments. Today, well over one hundred thousand dollars is returned to victims, the courts, and the community each year.[33]

While it is difficult to assess the impact of programs like Earn-It on a national level, a federal government evaluation of eighty-five projects over a two-year period found that they had collected $2,593,581 in monetary restitution and had assigned 355,408 community service hours and 6,052 victim service hours.[34]

Does Restitution Work?

How successful is restitution with juvenile offenders? Most attempts at evaluation have shown that it is a reasonably effective treatment alternative. For example, in an analysis of federally sponsored restitution programs, Peter Schneider and his associates found that about 95 percent of youths who received restitution as a condition of probation successfully completed their orders.[35]

Factors that related to success were: family incomes, good school attendance, few prior offenses, minor current offense, and size of restitution order. Schneider found that the youths who received restitution as a sole sanction (without probation) were those originally viewed by juvenile court judges as the better risks, and consequently, they actually had lower failure and recidivism rates than youths ordered to make restitution after being placed on probation.

In another more recent attempt to evaluate restitution, Anne Schneider conducted an in-depth analysis of four programs in Georgia, Oklahoma, Washington, D.C., and Idaho.[36] Schneider found that the program participants had lower recidivism rates than youths placed in control groups, such as regular probation caseloads. While Schneider's data indicate that restitution may reduce recidivism, the number of youths who had subsequent involvement in the justice system still seems high. For example, 49 percent of the juveniles in the Clayton County, Georgia, restitution program were petitioned to juvenile court within three years of completing the program, as compared to 60 percent of the probation group; in Washington, D.C., 53 percent of the juveniles ordered to make restitution and 63 percent of the probationers became recidivists.

In sum, the evidence indicates that most restitution orders are successfully completed and that youths who make restitution are less likely to become recidivists. (See the following Focus on Delinquency.) Existing programs meet the important twin goals of retribution and rehabilitation.[37] However, the number of repeat offenses committed by juveniles who made restitution suggests that by itself, restitution is not an answer to the delinquency problem.

Critique of Restitution

The success of Earn-It and similar programs has encouraged the development of restitution programs in other communities. However, certain problems remain. Offenders often find it difficult to make monetary restitution without securing new or additional employment. This need, charges William Staples, makes restitution seem almost absurd at a time when unemployment rates for youth are "tragically high."[38] Since most members of such programs have been convicted of a crime, many employers are reluctant to hire them. Problems also arise when offenders who need jobs suffer from drinking, drug, or emotional problems. Public and private agencies are likely sites for community service restitution, but their directors are sometimes reluctant to allow delinquent youths access to their organizations.

Thus, even voluntary charitable work is difficult to obtain. To compensate for this problem, some programs find job opportunities for clients. However, Staples claims that this can cause some youths to view restitution programs as an employment office: "committing a crime can become, for some, the only means of obtaining a job."[39]

Another criticism directed at restitution programs is that they involve **widening the net** of social control. Some critics claim that those given restitution orders would not have received more coercive treatment under any circumstances and that therefore, instead of an alternative to incarceration, restitution has become an extra burden on some offenders.[40]

Beyond these problems, some juvenile probation officers view restitution programs as a threat to their authority and to the autonomy of their organizations. It is interesting to note that courts believe police officers view restitution

Restitution in Utah

The statewide Utah Juvenile Court operates a structured juvenile restitution program. In the majority of restitution cases, youths make restitution directly in the form of financial payments. Others may be ordered to participate in community service programs to earn money to make restitution. In 1988, financial or community service restitution was used in approximately 30 percent of petitioned cases and 10 percent of nonpetitioned cases.

Under state law, the Utah Juvenile Court may order youths to repair, replace, or make restitution for victims' property and other losses. Probation officers are authorized to develop restitution or community service plans even in cases where youths are not formally brought before the court by petition. In such cases, consent agreements are signed by youths and their parents, and restitution is often paid directly to the victims.

An innovative feature of Utah's approach to juvenile restitution, established by state law in 1979, permits the court to withhold a substantial portion of fines paid by juveniles to underwrite a work restitution fund. The fund allows juveniles otherwise unable to pay restitution to work in community service projects in the private or public sector to earn money to compensate their victims. The juveniles' earnings are paid directly from the fund to the victims.

During the past decade, the use of restitution has increased in Utah. In 1980, court-ordered restitution paid by juveniles and returned to victims was just under $250,000. By 1990, that amount had increased to more than $550,000.

RESULTS

More than thirteen thousand cases from Utah were studied to assess the association between the use of restitution and subsequent recidivism. Of the probationers ordered to pay restitution, 32 percent became recidivists within a year. In cases involving charges of burglary and theft, which represented the majority of all the cases, significantly fewer youths who were ordered to pay restitution became recidivists than those placed in probation alone. Formal probation cases involving juveniles charged with burglary had a recidivism rate of 31 percent when the disposition included restitution but 38 percent when probation alone was ordered. In the theft cases, the rates were 34 percent recidivism with restitution and 38 percent without it. Restitution combined with probation was consistently associated with lower recidivism rates than probation alone.

Overall, the results of the study suggest that the use of restitution is a significant factor in reducing recidivism among certain juvenile offenders. ■

Source: Administrative Office of the Courts, *Utah Juvenile Court: Restitution and Community Service Program* (Salt Lake City: Administrative Office of the Courts, 1991); also Jeffrey Butts and Howard Snyder, *OJJDP Update on Research, Restitution and Juvenile Recidivism* (Washington, D.C: Department of Justice, 1992), p. 4.

more positively than social workers because the police are quick to grasp the retributive nature of restitution.

Another problem restitution programs must deal with is the charge that they foster involuntary servitude. For the most part, the courts have upheld the legality of restitution even though it has a coercive element. Some people believe that restitution is inherently biased against indigent clients. A person who is unable to make restitution payments can have probation revoked and thus face incarceration. It is necessary to determine why payment has stopped and to suggest appropriate action for the court to take rather than simply treat nonpayment as a matter of law enforcement.

Finally, restitution orders are subject to the same abuses of discretion as traditional sentencing methods. The restitution orders one delinquent offender receives may be quite different than those given another similarly situated youth. To remedy this situation, a number of jurisdictions have been using restitution guidelines to control orders.

Restitution programs may be an important alternative in incarceration, benefiting the child, the victim, and the juvenile justice system. H. Ted Rubin, a leading juvenile justice expert, even advocates that courts placing juveniles in day-treatment and community-based residential programs also include restitution requirements in their orders and expect that these requirements be fulfilled during placement.[41]

However, all such programs should be evaluated carefully to answer such questions as what type of offenders would be most likely to benefit from restitution, when is monetary restitution more desirable than community service, what is the best point in the juvenile justice process to impose restitution, what is the effect of restitution on the juvenile justice system, and how successful are restitution programs. The evidence does indicate that restitution is inexpensive, avoids stigma, and helps compensate victims of crime.

PRIVATIZATION OF JUVENILE PROBATION

No discussion of innovative juvenile probation programs would be complete without mention of the private sector's role in correctional services.

Juvenile probation is a major component of the juvenile justice system and one that is finding its resources strained by growing caseloads. With juvenile courts placing more than 80 percent of adjudicated delinquents on some form of probation, these agencies represent the most significant area of juvenile corrections. Many juvenile probation programs, however, have been unable to maintain quality and cost-effective services. At the same time, the juvenile justice system is overwhelmed by such problems as drug use, youth gangs, school violence, and serious juvenile crime. To assist the juvenile courts in expanding their efforts and coping with these problems, the Office of Juvenile Justice and Delinquency Prevention has funded a $1.7 million Private Sector Probation Initiative Program.[42]

Its purpose is to have private companies and institutions offer probation services to selected juveniles. Under this program, a number of jurisdictions contract out probation services to private sources. In the Third Judicial District of Utah, for example, the private-public partnership offers a ninety-day intensive supervision program, with a significant reduction in recidivism rates. In Cleveland, Ohio, private-sector court services are provided to status offenders and delinquents at a cost per youth of eighty dollars, compared to twelve hundred dollars for public-sector probation services. Kenosha County, Wisconsin, contracted for central case management and weekend adventure programs, which has enabled the state to close one of its training schools. And San Francisco County was able to retain its status offender services by private contract when budget cuts threatened to eliminate them from the public sector.[43] What these programs demonstrate is that juvenile probation services can be improved by transferring some of the functions and responsibilities to the private sector. In the future, the private sector is expected to offer more juvenile justice services previously performed by government.

COMMUNITY-BASED PROGRAMS

To many juvenile justice experts, the institutionalization of even the most serious delinquent youths in a training school, reform school, or industrial institution is a great mistake. A period of confinement in a high-security juvenile institution usually cannot solve the problems that brought a youth into a delinquent way of life, and the experience may actually help to amplify delinquency once the youth returns to the community. Surveys indicate that about 30 percent to 40 percent of adult prison inmates had been juvenile delinquents and many have been institutionalized as youths. There is often little reason to believe that an institutional experience can have a beneficial effect or reduce recidivism.[44]

Because of the problems associated with institutional care, such influential policy-making bodies as the National Council of Juvenile and Family Court Judges, the National Council on Crime and Delinquency, and the American Bar Association have recommended that, whenever possible, treatment of serious offenders be community-based. While recognizing the problems presented by the chronic offender, these groups maintain that adequate security can be maintained in community-based programs.[45] Similar initiatives have been promoted by state governments.[46] For example, Florida requires its state correctional department to "develop nontraditional, innovative, and diversified commitment programs for youth."[47]

Since the early 1970s, Massachusetts has led the movement to keep juvenile offenders in the community. In the mid-1960s, its Department of Youth Services housed over one thousand youngsters in secure training schools. Under Jerome Miller, who became the commissioner of the department in 1969, Massachusetts closed most of its secure juvenile facilities and began a massive deinstitutionalization of juvenile offenders.[48] Today, twenty-five years after the institutions

■ ■ ■ ■ ■ ■ ■ ■ ■ ■ ■ ■ ■ ■ ■

Many communities maintain non-residential programs which are alternatives to the traditional justice system.

were closed, the Massachusetts Department of Youth Services operates a community-based correctional system. The vast majority of youths are serviced in nonsecure settings, while the relatively few committed youth are placed in some type of residential setting ranging from group and foster homes to secure facilities and forestry camps.

Initially, many of the early programs suffered from residential isolation and limited services. Over time, however, many of the group homes and unlocked structured residential settings were relocated in residential community environments and became highly successful in addressing the needs of juveniles presenting little or no security risk to themselves or others.

Roxbury Youthworks, an inner-city program in Boston, is such a private community-based agency controlling juvenile delinquency through a comprehensive range of resources that include: (1) evaluation and counseling at a local court clinic; (2) employment and training; (3) detention diversion; and (4) outreach and tracking to help youth reenter the community. Youthworks is one of twenty-four independent programs—both residential and nonresidential—contracted with by the state youth services department to provide intensive community supervision for almost 90 percent of all youths under its jurisdiction.[49]

There are other dramatic examples of jurisdictions that have attempted to reduce the need for high-security institutions to treat delinquent offenders. Similar to the Massachusetts experience, Vermont closed the Weeks School—the only training school in the state—in 1979 and moved to a noninstitutional system. As of 1985, Vermont did not operate a juvenile facility. In 1975, Pennsylvania removed youths from the Camp Hill Penitentiary, which had been used to house the most hard-core juvenile offenders. Three-quarters of the juvenile inmates were returned to programs in their home communities. The remainder were transferred for short periods to small, secure institutions, then released. In 1978, Utah established a system of seven community-based programs as an alternative to traditional institutionalization in the state's Youth Development Center. An evaluation comparing the recidivism rates of comparable groups showed higher rates of success for the alternative program.

Among the states with the lowest incarceration rates for juvenile offenders are Pennsylvania (76 per 100,000) and Utah (73 per 100,000). In neither of these states did the deinstitutionalization effort cause an increase in either the amount or the seriousness of juvenile crime.[50]

The deinstitutionalization movement is still alive. Most recently, Maryland closed its Montrose Juvenile Training School, a facility that had been in operation for nearly three-quarters of a century. Over two hundred youths were released from the school in less than a year. Many of them should not have been there in the first place since they had not committed serious or violent crimes. Nearly half of the youths were released with services and supervision in their own homes. Most of the others were safely placed in smaller, nonsecure residential programs.[51]

In the last two decades, we have seen a number of states reduce the use of institutionalization in favor of nonsecure facilities and community-based programs.[52] Recently, West Virginia, Oklahoma, Oregon, and Louisiana have either closed training schools or reduced the juvenile population in such institutions. Florida changed its system to emphasize community-based services as a result of a formal consent decree arising out of a federal court case. The following Case in Point highlights the need for such programs and the difficulty in obtaining services for children in the juvenile justice system.

CASE IN POINT

You are a juvenile corrections consultant doing a study to determine if dispositional decisions are meeting the needs of children in juvenile courts.

Jamie B., age 15, was adjudicated a juvenile delinquent. Placed on probation for one charge of shoplifting, he failed to report to the probation officer. Brought into the juvenile court on a second petition, namely being intoxicated and disruptive in public, Jamie admitted to having a substance abuse problem.

At the dispositional stage of the court process, Jamie's attorney asked the court to place him in a drug rehabilitation program. The judge suggested that such services could be obtained in a state training school since other less-restrictive dispositional alternatives were not available. Concluding that Jamie's behavior constituted a threat to the community and to his own welfare, the court committed the youth to a state training school for an indeterminate period of time not to exceed two years.

A wide variety of dispositional alternatives are listed in the juvenile code of this jurisdiction. Among these are: supervised probation; participation in a supervised day program; placement in a residential or nonresidential treatment program; and commitment to a state training school. The legislative preference for a community-based solution to Jamie's problem is reflected throughout the code. Jamie's lawyer challenges the dispositional decision, claiming that the commitment to a training school without first examining the appropriateness and availability of community-based services was judicial error.

Do you think the commitment order should be vacated and Jamie's case remanded for a new dispositional hearing?

Encouraging Community Corrections

A number of factors have affected the placement of juvenile offenders in nonsecure community-based facilities. At first, reformers, such as Jerome Miller, revealed the futility of exposing youths to the hardships of high-security institutions. Then in 1974, the Juvenile Justice and Delinquency Prevention Act tied the receipt of federal funds for juvenile justice programs to the removal of status offenders from institutions. Consequently, many states reformed their juvenile codes to support new community-based treatment programs and to remove status offenders from institutions. Most states now have provisions banning the institutionalization of status offenders with delinquents. In some states, however—for example, Missouri and Alaska—repeat status offenders may be placed in secure facilities, while in others—such as Connecticut and North Dakota—offenders cannot be held in public facilities but may be held in privately run institutions. A few states—Alabama and Ohio—allow status offenders to be institutionalized with delinquents if their behavior is so unruly that the court finds them unamenable to any other kind of treatment.[53]

The second factor fueling the deinstitutionalization movement was an effort to grant children the general right to services and, in particular, the legal **right to treatment.** This concept recognizes the principle that when the juvenile justice system places a child in custody, basic concepts of fairness and humanity suggest that the system supply the child with rehabilitation. The right to treatment (see Chapter 19) often meant providing counseling, education, adequate food and medical care, and so on. Consequently, the cost of maintaining youths in secure treatment facilities has skyrocketed. A national survey conducted in 1985 found that the average cost of maintaining one youth for one year was twenty-five thousand dollars.[54] In 1987, it was twenty-seven thousand dollars. In 1991, the cost was over thirty-thousand dollars and may reach forty thousand dollars per bed year in the future.[55] Considering these costs and the assumed ineffectiveness of institutional treatment, "the least restrictive alternative available" to treat juvenile offenders in many cases means placement in community-based programs.

A word of caution: while the movement to place juveniles in nonrestrictive, community-based programs continues, *the actual number of incarcerated youths has increased in recent years.* The population of juveniles held in secure public juvenile facilities increased 54 percent from twenty-nine thousand in 1977 to more than fifty-three thousand ten years later. Almost fifty-five thousand children are now held in secure public facilities.[56]

Also from 1977 to 1987, the number of children in halfway houses or group homes doubled, from eleven thousand to about twenty-one thousand.[57] Nonetheless, secure institutional programs still make up over 32 percent of public and private facilities and house 58 percent of the total juvenile population, in spite of all the emphasis placed on community corrections in the last two decades.[58] Community corrections truly has supplemented and not replaced institutionalization.

At the same time, the incentive is to privatize the system and develop a set of smaller, less intensive, and far cheaper alternatives for those children who would not present a significant risk to the community.

Residential Community Treatment

How are community corrections implemented with delinquent youths? In some cases, adjudicated children are placed under probation supervision, and the probation department maintains a residential treatment facility. Or placement can be made to the department of social services or juvenile corrections with the direction that the youth be placed in a residential nonsecure facility.

Residential programs can be divided into four major categories: (1) group homes, including boarding schools and apartment-type settings, (2) foster homes, (3) family group homes, and (4) rural programs.

Group homes are nonsecure, structured residences that provide counseling, education, job training, and family living. They are staffed by a small number of qualified persons, and they generally hold twelve to fifteen youngsters. The institutional quality of the environment is minimized, and children are given the opportunity for a close but controlled interaction and relationship with the staff. Children reside in the home, attend public schools, and participate in community activities in the area. Over the past two decades, extensive work has been done on group home settings. The following Focus on Delinquency illustrates two pioneering community-based residential treatment programs in the field of juvenile corrections that have served as models for many other programs. Unfortunately, these better known programs of the 1970s have not received as much attention today because of limited federal and state funding.

FOCUS ON DELINQUENCY

An Example of Residential Treatment Programs

THE HIGHFIELDS PROJECT

Highfields was a short-term residential nonsecure program for boys that began in 1950. Boys in the program were kept at Highfields, New Jersey, for periods of three or four months. They were permitted to leave the grounds under responsible adult supervision. They were also granted furloughs over weekends to visit their families and to continue to relate to the community. The youths lived in groups of no more than twenty boys in a large home on an estate. They also worked twenty to forty hours a week at a neuropsychiatric clinic. The most important treatment technique was peer pressure exerted through active participation in guided group interaction sessions.

The Highfields project was evaluated by using a controlled group of boys sent to Annandale, a juvenile reform school in the same state. One year after release, Highfields boys had a lower recidivism rate than Annandale boys. The Highfields project was considered as successful as any training school and was much less expensive to operate. However, the validity of the recidivism rates was questioned because of the difficulties associated with matching the control and treatment groups.

THE SILVERLAKE EXPERIMENT

The Silverlake experiment occurred in Los Angeles County in the mid-1960s. Like Highfields, this program provided a group home experience seeking to create a nondelinquent culture for male youths between the ages of 15 and 18. Seriously delinquent youths were placed in a large family residence in a middle-class neighborhood. Some of them attended local high schools, and many returned to their homes on weekends. Only twenty boys at a time lived in the residence. They were responsible for maintaining the residence and for participating in daily group interaction meetings. These sessions were the major formal treatment approach for implementing programs goals. The Silverlake program sought to structure a social system with positive norms by discussing the youths' problems and offering positive alternatives to delinquent behavior in the group sessions.

To evaluate the Silverlake experiment, experimental and control groups were selected at random from the youths participating in the program. There was no significant difference in the recidivism rates of the two groups tested, and it was unclear whether one program reduced recidivism more than the other. Since both control-group youths and treatment youths lived in the facility, the researchers concluded that the experimental group receiving guided group interaction and the control group were positively affected by the program. Recidivism rates twelve months after release indicated a general reduction in delinquent behavior on the part of participants. ■

Source: H. Ashley Weeks, *Highfields* (Ann Arbor: University of Michigan Press, 1956); LaMar T. Empey and Stephen Lubeck, *The Silverlake Experiment: Testing Delinquency Theory and Community Intervention* (Chicago: Aldine, 1971).

Foster care programs typically involve one or two juveniles who live with a family—usually a husband and wife who serve as surrogate parents. The juveniles enter into a close relationship with the foster parents and receive the attention, guidance, and care that they did not receive before. The quality of the foster home experience depends on the foster parents and their emotional relationship with the child. Foster care for adjudicated juvenile offenders has not been extensive in the United States. It is most often used for orphans or for children whose parents cannot care for them. Welfare departments generally handle foster placements, and funding has been a problem for the juvenile justice system. However, foster home services for delinquent children and status offenders have expanded as an approach in the area of community treatment.[59]

Family group homes combine elements of both foster care and group home placements. Children are placed in a private group home that is run by a single family rather than a professional staff. This model can help troubled youths learn to get along in family-type situations and at the same time help the state avoid the start-up costs and neighborhood opposition often associated with public institutions. Family group homes can be found in many jurisdictions throughout the United States.[60]

Rural programs include forestry camps, ranches, and farms that provide specific recreational activities or work in a rural setting. Individual programs handle from thirty to fifty children. Such programs have the disadvantage of isolating children from the community, but reintegration can be achieved if the child's stay is short and if family and friends can visit.

Most residential programs use group counseling techniques as the major treatment tool. Although group facilities have been used less often than institutional placements in the years past, there is definitely a trend toward developing community-based residential facilities.

Nonresidential Community Treatment

In **nonresidential programs,** youths remain in their homes or in foster homes and receive counseling, education, employment, diagnostic, and casework services. A counselor or probation officer gives innovative and intensive support to help the child remain at home. Family therapy, educational tutoring, and job placement may all be part of the program.

Nonresidential programs are often associated with the Provo program begun in 1959 in Utah and the Essexfields Rehabilitation Project started in the early 1960s in Essex County, New Jersey.[61] Today, the most well-known approach is **Project New Pride,** which has been replicated in a number of sites around the United States. The accompanying Focus on Delinquency describes the Project New Pride program.

CRITICISMS OF THE COMMUNITY TREATMENT APPROACH

The community treatment approach has limitations. Public opinion may be against community treatment, especially when it is offered to juvenile offenders who pose a real threat to society. Institutionalization may be the only answer for the violent young offender. Even if the juvenile crime problem abates, society may be unwilling to accept reforms that liberalize policies and practices in the field of juvenile corrections. For example, it is common for neighborhood groups to actively oppose the location of corrections programs in their community. The thought of a center for young drug users being located across the street can send shivers down the spine of many property owners.

Evaluations of recidivism rates do not show conclusively that community treatment is more successful than institutionalization. Some experimental programs indicate that young people can be treated in the community as safely and as effectively as children placed in an institution. However, commitment to an institution guarantees that the community will be protected against further

FOCUS ON DELINQUENCY

Project New Pride: An Example of a Nonresidential Program

One of the most well-known community-based treatment models is Project New Pride. Begun in Denver, Colorado, in 1973, it has been a model for similar programs around the country.

The target group for Project New Pride is serious or violent youthful offenders from 14 to 17 years old. They have at least two prior convictions for serious misdemeanors and/or felonies and are formally charged or convicted of another offense when they are referred to New Pride.

Will any hard-core offenders be accepted into New Pride? The only youths not eligible for participation are those who have committed forcible rape or are diagnosed as severely psychotic; New Pride believes this restriction is necessary in the interest of the safety of the community and of the youths themselves.

The project's specific goals are to work these hard-core offenders back into the mainstream of their communities and to reduce the number of rearrests. Generally, reintegration into the community means reenrolling in school, getting a job, or both.

1. *Schooling.* New Pride youths receive alternative schooling and are then reintegrated into the public school system or directed toward vocational training. Some youths get jobs and pursue a general equivalency diploma (GED). Some of them complete high school in the alternative school (certified by the public school system).

2. *Jobs.* New Pride places specific emphasis on vocational training. The staff recognizes that money is the key to independence for these youths, and the most socially acceptable way to get money is to work for it.

3. *Family.* Not only do the youths benefit from intensive counseling, but their families also have access to counselors. New Pride encourages family members to visit the project facility to observe the daily operations, involve themselves in their child's treatment, and get to know staff.

4. *Community.* New Pride community-based programs are extremely cost-effective when compared with the cost of placing a child in an institution. In Colorado and New Jersey, for example, it costs approximately twenty-eight thousand dollars per year to incarcerate a youth; the cost for placing a youth in Denver New Pride or the Juvenile Resource Center in Camden is approximately forty-five hundred dollars.

PROGRAM SERVICES

Each participant in New Pride has six months of intensive involvement and a six-month follow-up period, during which the youth slowly reintegrates into the community. During the follow-up period, the youth continues to receive as many services as necessary, such as schooling and job placement, and works closely with counselors.

Source: Project New Pride (Washington, D.C.: Government Printing Office, 1985).

crime, at least during the time of the child's placement. More research is essential to evaluate the success of community treatment programs.

Much of the early criticism of community treatment was based on poor delivery of services, shabby operation, and haphazard management, follow-up, and planning. In the early 1970s, when Massachusetts deinstitutionalized its juvenile correction system, there was a torrent of reports about the inadequate operation of community treatment programs. This was caused by the absence of uniform policies, different procedures in various programs, and the lack of accountability. The development of needed programs was hampered, and available resources were misplaced. Today's community treatment programs have generally overcome their early deficiencies and operate with more expertise than in the past. Innovative management techniques are also being applied today by many private-sector service providers, such as Associated Marine Institutes and the Northeastern Family Institute.[62] (See Chapter 19.)

It is also possible that the deinstitutionalization will result in increased use of pretrial detention for children, because judges fear that dangerous children will be treated leniently. Also, it may cause more children to be transferred to adult courts and subsequently to be committed to adult prisons. Finding out if this is actually happening is a difficult task, but law-and-order forces unquestionably are seeking to turn more children over to the adult system.[63]

On the other hand, community-based programs continue to present the most promising alternative to the poor results of reform schools for the following reasons:

(1) Some states, such as those previously mentioned, have found that residential and nonresidential settings produce comparable or lower recidivism rates.
(2) Community-based programs have lower costs and are especially appropriate for large numbers of nonviolent juveniles and those guilty of lesser offenses.
(3) Public opinion of community corrections remains positive. In choosing between two approaches, training schools or community-based programs, for all but the most violent or serious juvenile offenders, over 71 percent of the respondents in a recent public opinion survey indicated they favored a system that relied primarily on community-based services.[64]

As jurisdictions continue to face high rates of violent juvenile crime and ever-increasing costs for juvenile justice services, community-based programs will play an important role in providing rehabilitation of juvenile offenders and public safety.

Recidivism and Community-Based Programs

Has community treatment generally proven successful? Some concrete research efforts have shown this to be true. Lloyd Ohlin and his associates found that youths in nonsecure placements were less likely to become recidivists than those placed in more secure institutions.[65] However, other reviews of community corrections reached the opposite result. Dennis Romig's national survey of community treatment programs concluded that few were effective in helping youths, and Malcolm Klein's analysis showed that community corrections has many pitfalls.[66]

The dilemmas faced by community treatments are illustrated by the **Community Treatment Project (CTP)** of the California Youth Authority. The purpose of the project was to determine whether intensive supervision of juveniles in the community would be more successful than the normal program of institutionalization.[67] The project, established in 1961, served as a model in juvenile justice for more than two decades. The study took children committed from the juvenile courts of Sacramento, Stockton, San Francisco, and Modesto and classified them according to a measure of interpersonal maturity. The children were divided into a control group treated in a traditional institutional program. Those in the experimental group were placed in a community institution for eight months.

Individual treatment plans were developed for each child in the experimental group. Certain types of youths did especially well; others did not respond to community treatment.

Numerous researchers have examined the data from the California Community Treatment Project.[68] On the whole, recidivism rates seemed to be lower for those in community treatment than for those in traditional programs. However, in an important analysis, Paul Lerman showed that the original CTP success was more a function of the way recidivism rates were computed than the actual success of the program. While youths in the CTP were as likely to commit new crimes and get arrested as those in the comparison groups, their control agents were less likely to bring formal action against them. What appeared to be a change in the behavior of clients was actually a result of change in the behavior of their supervisors. Lerman found that the CTP project was no more effective than traditional institutionalization, nor was it any more cost-effective. Although the track record of community-based corrections is still debatable, many states continue to make a successful transition from large institutions to community-based programs.

The greatest advantage of community corrections continues to be its cost. A national survey of the costs of treating youths found that the average annual expenditure per child in a training school was forty-thousand dollars, while a community-based program may cost half as much. If community-based correction were only equally successful as secure institutional care, it could be justified on the basis of savings to the taxpayer alone.[69]

■■■■■■■■■■■■■■■■

SUMMARY

Community treatment represents efforts by the juvenile justice system to keep offenders in the community and spare them the pains and stigma of incarceration in a secure facility. The primary purpose of community treatment is to address the individual needs of juveniles in a home setting, employing any combination of educational, vocational, counseling, or employment-related services.

The most widely used method of community treatment is probation. Approximately four hundred thousand youths are currently on probation. They must obey rules given to them by the court and partake in some sort of treatment program. Probation officers monitor their behavior in the community. If rules are violated, youths can have their probation revoked and suffer more punitive means of control, such as secure incarceration.

Probation departments have developed restitution programs as a type of community treatment. These involve having the delinquents either reimburse the victims of their crimes or do community service. While these programs appear successful, critics accuse them of widening the net of social control over young offenders.

Other forms of community treatment are day programs and residential community programs. The former allow youths to live at home while receiving treatment in a nonpunitive community-based center; the latter require that youths reside in group homes while receiving care and treatment.

Despite criticisms, the cost savings of community treatment, coupled with its benign intentions, are likely to keep these programs growing. They are certainly no worse than secure institutions. Massachusetts, Maryland, Pennsylvania, Florida, and Utah are examples of states that have moved to deinstitutionalization.

KEY TERMS

QUESTIONS FOR DISCUSSION

1. Would you want a community treatment program in your neighborhood?
2. Is "net widening" a real danger, or are treatment-oriented programs simply a method of helping troubled youths?
3. If a youngster violates the rules of probation, should he or she be placed in an institution?
4. Is juvenile restitution fair? Should a poor child have to pay back a wealthy victim, such as a store?
5. What are the most important advantages to community treatment for juvenile offenders?
6. What is the purpose of juvenile probation? Identify some conditions of probation and discuss the responsibilities of the juvenile probation officer.
7. Discuss the recent trends in community treatment of juvenile offenders.

NOTES

1. American Bar Association, *Standards Relating to Probation*, Standard 1.2 (New York: Institute of Judicial Administration, 1968), p. 10; see also Dean J. Champion, *Probation and Parole in the United States*, (Columbus, Ohio: Merrill, 1990), Chap. 11.
2. Sanford Fox, *Juvenile Courts* (St. Paul: West, 1984), pp. 227–28.
3. See Ralph Brendes, "Interstate Supervision of Parole and Probation," in Robert Carter and Leslie Wilkins, eds., *Probation, Parole, and Community Corrections* (New York: Wiley, 1970).
4. George Killinger, Hazel Kerper, and Paul F. Cromwell, Jr., *Probation and Parole in the Criminal Justice System* (St. Paul: West, 1976), p. 45.
5. National Advisory Commission on Criminal Justice Standards and Goals, *Corrections* (Washington, D.C.: Government Printing Office, 1983), p. 75.
6. Bureau of Justice Statistics, *Report to the Nation on Crime and Justice*, 2d ed. (Washington, D.C.: Government Printing Office, 1988), p. 95. See also Howard N. Snyder, Melissa H. Sickmund, Ellen H. Nimick, Terrence A. Finnegan, Dennis P. Sullivan, Rowen S. Poole, and Nancy J. Tierney, *Juvenile Court Statistics, 1989* (Pittsburgh: National Center for Juvenile Justice, 1992).
7. Patricia Torbet, *Organization and Administration of Juvenile Services* (Pittsburgh: National Center for Juvenile Justice, September 1989).
8. *Ibid.*
9. American Bar Association, *Standards Relating to Juvenile Probation Function* (Cambridge, Mass.: Ballinger, 1977), p. 124.
10. See *Morrissey v. Brewer*, 408 U.S. 471, 92 S.Ct. 2593, 33 L.Ed.2d 484 (1972); and *Gagnon v. Scarpelli*, 411 U.S. 778, 93 S.Ct. 1756, 36 L.Ed.2d 655 (1973).
11. See, generally, James Byrne, "The Control Controversy: A Preliminary Examination of Intensive Probation Supervision Programs in the United States," *Federal Probation* 50:4–16 (1986).

12. For a review of these programs, see James Byrne, ed., *Federal Probation* 50:2 (June 1986); see also Emily Walker, "The Community Intensive Treatment for Youth Program: A Specialized Community-Based Program for High-Risk Youth in Alabama," *Law and Psychology Review* 13:175–99 (1989).

13. Edward Latessa, "The Cost Effectiveness of Intensive Supervision," *Federal Probation* 50:70–74 (1986); see also John Ott, "Bibliotherapy as a Challenging Condition to the Sentence of Juvenile Probation," *Juvenile and Family Court Journal* 40:63–67 (1989).

14. Richard G. Wiebush, "Juvenile Intensive Supervision: The Impact on Felony Offenders Diverted from Institutional Placement," *Crime and Delinquency* 39:68–89 (1993).

15. H. Preston Elrod and Kevin I. Minor, "Second Wave Evaluation of a Multi-Faceted Intervention for Juvenile Court Probationers," *International Journal of Offender Therapy and Comparative Criminology* 36:249–61 (1992).

16. S. H. Clarke and A. D. Craddock, *Evaluation of North Carolina's Intensive Juvenile Probation Program* (Chapel Hill, N.C.: University of North Carolina Institute of Government, 1987).

17. T. L. Armstrong, *National Survey of Juvenile Intensive Probation Supervision* (Washington, D.C.: Department of Justice, Criminal Justice Abstracts, 1988); see also National Council on Crime and Delinquency, *Juvenile Intensive Probation Programs—The State of the Art* (San Francisco: NCCD, 1991).

18. "Volunteers in Probation," *Newsletter of the National Information Center on Volunteerism.*

19. Richard Ball and J. Robert Lilly, "A Theoretical Examination of Home Incarceration," *Federal Probation* 50:17–25 (1986); Joan Petersilia, "Exploring the Option of House Arrest," *Federal Probation* 50:50–56 (1986); Annesley Schmidt, "Electronic Monitors," *Federal Probation* 50:56–60 (1986); Michael Charles, "The Development of a Juvenile Electronic Monitoring Program," *Federal Probation* 53:3–12 (1989).

20. Joseph B. Vaughn, "A Survey of Juvenile Electronic Monitoring and Home Confinement Programs," *Juvenile and Family Court Journal* 40:1–36 (1989).

21. Robert Callahan, "Wilderness Probation: A Decade Later," *Juvenile and Family Court Journal* 36:31–35 (1985).

22. "Wilderness Programs in Probation," *Juvenile and Family Court Newsletter* vol. 19 (1989), p. 5.

23. Steven Flagg Scott, "Outward Bound: An Adjunct to the Treatment of Juvenile Delinquents: Florida's STEP Program," *New England Journal on Criminal and Civil Confinement* 11:420–37 (1985).

24. Dennis Mahoney, Dennis Romig, and Troy Armstrong, "Juvenile Probation: The Balanced Approach," *Juvenile and Family Court Journal* 39:1–59 (1988).

25. *Ibid.,* also Charles McGee, "Measured Steps toward Clarity and Balance to Juvenile Justice System," *Juvenile and Family Court Journal* 40:1–24 (1989).

26. Gordon Bazemore, "On Mission Statements and Reform in Juvenile Justice: The Case of the Balanced Approach," *Federal Probation* 61:64–70 (1992).

27. Anne L. Schneider, ed., *Guide to Juvenile Restitution* (Washington, D.C.: Department of Justice, 1985); Anne Schneider and Jean Warner, *National Trends in Juvenile Restitution Programming* (Washington, D.C.: Government Printing Office, 1989).

28. Gordon Bazemore, "New Concepts and Alternative Practice in Community Supervision of Juvenile Offenders: Rediscovering Work Experience and Competency Development," *Journal of Crime and Justice,* 14:27–45 (1991); also Jeffrey Butts and Howard Snyder, *Restitution and Juvenile Recidivism* (Washington, D.C.: Department of Justice, 1992).

29. See Anne Newton, "Sentencing to Community Service and Restitution," in *Criminal Justice Abstracts* (Hackensack, N.J.: National Council on Crime and Delinquency, September 1979), pp. 435–68.

30. Anne Schneider, "Restitution and Recidivism Rates of Juvenile Offenders: Results from Four Experimental Studies," *Criminology* 24:533–52 (1986).

31. Linda Szymanski, *Juvenile Restitution Statutes* (Pittsburgh: National Center for Juvenile Justice, 1988).

32. N.C. Gen.Laws 7A, 649.

33. Descriptive materials can be obtained from the Earn-It Program, District Court of East Norfolk, Quincy, MA 02169. The Quincy District Court Probation Department was extremely helpful in providing information about this program, January 1993; see also Jean Warner, Vincent Burke, and Anne L. Schneider, *Directory of Juvenile Restitution Programs* (Washington, D.C.: National Criminal Justice Reference Service, 1987).

34. Peter Schneider, "Research on Restitution: A Guide to Rational Decision Making," in Anne L. Schneider, ed., *Guide to Juvenile Restitution* (Washington, D.C.: Department of Justice, 1985), p. 137.

35. Peter Schneider, William Griffith, and Anne Schneider, *Juvenile Restitution as a Sole Sanction or Condition of Probation: An Empirical Analysis* (Eugene, Ore.: Institute for Policy Analysis, 1980).

36. Anne Schneider, "Restitution and Recidivism Rates."

37. Burt Galaway, "Restitution as Innovation or Unfilled Promise," *Federal Probation* 52:3–15 (1989).

38. William Staples, "Restitution as a Sanction in Juvenile Court," *Crime and Delinquency* 32:177–85 (1986).

39. Ibid., p. 183.

40. Barry Krisberg and Jame Austin, "The Unmet Promise of Alternatives to Incarceration," *Crime and Delinquency* 28:374–409 (1982).

41. H. Ted Rubin, "Fulfilling Juvenile Restitution Requirements in Community Correctional Programs," *Federal Probation* 52:32–43 (1988).

42. "Privatizing Juvenile Probation Services: Five Local Experiences," *National Institute of Justice Reports* (Wash-

ington, D.C.: Office of Justice Programs, December 1989), p. 10; see also Yitzhak Bakal and Harvey Lowell, "The Private Sector in Juvenile Corrections," in Ira Schwartz, ed., *Juvenile Justice and Public Policy* (New York: Lexington Books, 1992), p. 196.

43. "Privatizing Juvenile Probation Services," p. 12.

44. Bureau of Justice Statistics, *Report to the Nation on Crime and Justice* (Washington, D.C.: Government Printing Office, 1988), pp. 44–45.

45. National Council of Juvenile and Family Court Judges, "The Juvenile Court and Serious Offenders," *Juvenile and Family Court Journal* 35:16 (Cambridge, Ma.: 1984); also American Bar Association, Institute of Judicial Administration, *Standards on Probation*, 1980.

46. Robert Pierce, *Juvenile Justice Reform: State Experiences* (Denver: National Conference of State Legislatures, 1989).

47. Fla. Stat.Ann. 959.011 (West Supp., 1983).

48. Commonwealth of Massachusetts, *Department of Youth Services Annual Report of 1978* (Boston: State Purchasing Agency, 1978).

49. "Roxbury Agency Offers a Map for Youths at the Crossroads," *Boston Globe*, 18 February 1990, p. 32.

50. National Council on Crime and Delinquency, *Juvenile Justice: Tough Enough* (San Francisco: National Council on Crime and Delinquency, n.d.), p. 10.

51. Jeffrey Butts, *Youth Corrections in Maryland: The Dawning of a New Era* (Ann Arbor, Mich.: Center for Study of Youth Policy, University of Michigan, 1988).

52. J. Blackmore, M. Brown, and B. Krisberg, *Juvenile Justice Reform—The Bellwether States* (Ann Arbor, Mich.: Center for Study of Youth Policy, University of Michigan, 1988).

53. W. N. Paul and H. S. Watt, *Deinstitutionalization of Status Offenders: A Compilation and Analysis of State Statutes* (Denver: State Legislative Leaders Foundation, 1980), pp. 54–57.

54. Bureau of Justice Statistics, *Children in Custody, 1985* (Washington, D.C.: Government Printing Office, 1986).

55. Bureau of Justice Statistics, *Children in Custody Series, 1975–85 Census of Public and Private Juvenile Detention, Correctional, and Shelter Facilities* (Washington, D.C.: Department of Justice, May 1989), p. 2; see also, Bakal and Lowell, "The Private Sector in Juvenile Corrections," p. 204.

56. Bureau of Justice Statistics, *Children in Custody Series, 1975–85 Census;* also Bureau of Justice Statistics, *Children in Custody, Public Juvenile Facilities, 1987* (Washington, D.C.: Department of Justice, 1989); Office of Juvenile Justice and Delinquency Prevention, *National Juvenile Custody Trends 1978–89* (Washington, D.C.: Department of Justice, 1992).

57. Ibid., p. 2.

58. Ibid., p. 2.

59. See E. Lawder, R. Andrews, and J. Parson, *Five Models of Foster Family Group Homes, Report of Child Welfare League of America* (New York: Child Welfare League, 1974); Yitzhak Bakal, *Closing Correctional Institutions* (Lexington, Mass.: D.C. Heath, 1973); Andrew Rutherford and Osman Berger, *Community-Based Alternatives to Juvenile Incarceration* (Washington, D.C.: Government Printing Office, 1976), pp. 10–35.

60. Joseph Rowan and Charles Kehoe, "Let's Deinstitutionalize Group Homes," *Juvenile and Family Court Journal* 36:1–4 (1985).

61. Lamar Empey and Maynard Erickson, *The Provo Experiment* (Lexington, Mass.: D.C. Heath, 1972); Paul Pilnick, Albert Elias, and Neale Clapp, "The Essexfields Concept: A New Approach to the Social Treatment of Juvenile Delinquents," *Journal of Applied Behavioral Sciences* 2:109–21 (1966).

62. Associated Marine Institutes is a private provider of social services for delinquent youth in seven states, while Northeastern Family Institute operates community-based programs in five states. They bid competitively to provide services to the states.

63. Barry Krisberg and Ira Schwartz, "Rethinking Juvenile Justice," *Crime and Delinquency* 29:333–64 (1983); see also Ira Schwartz, Shenyang Guo, and John Kerbs, "The Impact of Demographic Variables on Public Opinion Regarding Juvenile Justice: Implications for Public Policy," *Crime and Delinquency* 39:5–28 (1993).

64. Ira Schwartz, *Juvenile Justice and Public Policy* (New York: Lexington Books, 1992), p. 217.

65. Lloyd Ohlin, Alden Miller, and Robert Coates, *Juvenile Correctional Reform in Massachusetts* (Washington, D.C.: Government Printing Office, 1976).

66. Dennis Romig, *Justice for Our Children* (Lexington, Mass.: Lexington Books, 1978); Malcolm Klein, "Deinstitutionalization and Diversion of Juvenile Offenders: A Litany of Impediments," in Norval Mom's and Michael Tonry, eds., *Crime and Justice*, vol. 1 (Chicago: University of Chicago Press, 1979), pp. 145–201.

67. Marguerite Q. Warren, "The Community Treatment Project: History and Prospects," *Law Enforcement Science and Technology*, ed. S. A. Yafsky. Proceedings of the First National Symposium on Law Enforcement Science and Technology (Washington, D.C.: Thompson, 1967), p. 191.

68. See Paul Lerman, "Evaluating the Outcome of Institutions for Delinquents," *Social Work Journal* 13:68–81 (1968); Paul Lerman, *Community Treatment and Social Control* (Chicago: University of Chicago Press, 1975).

69. S. Lerner, *Good News about Juvenile Justice: The Movement away from Large Institutions and toward Community-Based Services* (Bolinas, Calif.: Ittleson Family Foundation, 1990).

INSTITUTIONS FOR JUVENILES

If, after a dispositionary hearing, the juvenile court judge finds that community treatment is inadequate to deal with the special needs of a delinquent child, the child may be referred to the state department of youth services for a period of confinement in a state-run treatment center. Or where appropriate, the child may be referred to a privately run treatment program that specializes in dealing with a particular social problem (for example, drug abuse or violent juvenile crime). Such programs are often long-term facilities that hold adjudicated delinquents in environments that limit access to the community.

Today, correctional institutions operated by federal, state, and county governments are generally classified as secure and nonsecure facilities. Secure facilities contain the movement of residents through staff monitoring, locked entrances and exits, and interior fence controls. Nonsecure institutions, on the other hand, generally do not restrict the movement of the residents and allow much greater freedom of access in and out of the facility.[1]

There has been a general movement in the past twenty years toward the use of fewer and smaller secure facilities, on the theory that these programs allow more freedom and a greater chance of rehabilitating young offenders than do large bureaucratic institutions. States such as Utah and Vermont have for the most part closed their large training schools and now rely on smaller institutions of less than forty youths. Violent youths and chronic serious offenders are placed in a few small, high-security treatment units.

This approach uses a diverse network of community-based programs that allow for specialized individual treatment and are generally offered by private providers under contract with the state.[2] One of the most talked about of these private-sector programs is the **Paint Creek Youth Center** (PCYC) in Bainbridge, Ohio. Since its beginning several years ago, PCYC has been the focus of

Some juvenile correctional facilities are bleak and dehumanizing.

considerable discussion within the juvenile justice community because it offers an alternative to traditional public correctional services. In a small, open setting, PCYC combines proven program components, including a highly structured environment, intensive aftercare, low client-staff ratio, job training and work experience, and many other comprehensive services.[3]

Beyond the secure and nonsecure classifications, there are at least six different categories of juvenile correctional institutions in the United States: (1) detention centers that provide restrictive custody pending adjudication or disposition, (2) shelters that offer nonrestrictive temporary care, (3) reception centers that screen juveniles placed by the courts and assign them to an appropriate facility, (4) training schools or reformatories that are for adjudicated youths needing a long-term, secure setting, (5) ranch or forestry camps that provide special, long-term residential care in a less restrictive setting, and (6) halfway houses or group homes where juveniles are allowed daily contact with the community.[4] Youth correctional systems often incorporate virtually all of these programs. (See Figure 19.1.)

Many experts believe that institutionalizing young offenders generally does more harm than good. It exposes them to prison-like conditions and to more experienced delinquents without giving them the benefit of constructive treatment programs. In contrast, offenders in the less costly community-based programs often have recidivism rates at least as low as (if not lower than) those

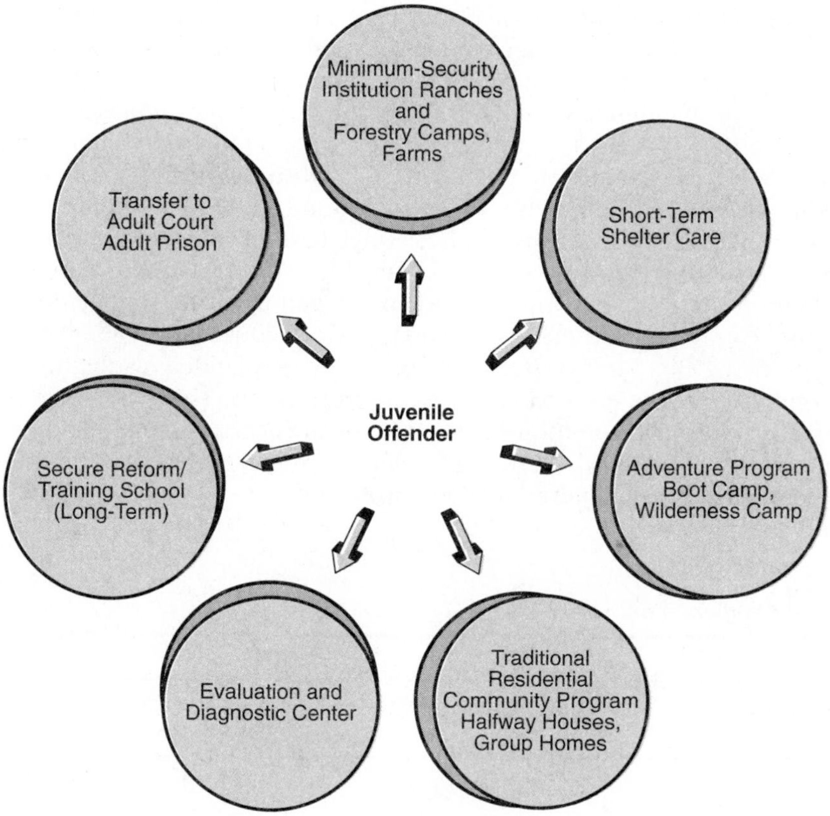

■■FIGURE 19.1

Institutional options for adjudicated youth

in institutions. Nonetheless, secure treatment in juvenile corrections is still being used extensively around the country, and the populations of these facilities are continuing to grow.

In this chapter, we analyze the current state of secure juvenile corrections. A brief history of juvenile corrections is undertaken, and then discussion turns to such issues as the extent of correction, the juvenile client, life in institutions, and treatment issues.

THE HISTORY OF JUVENILE INSTITUTIONS

Until the early 1800s, juvenile offenders as well as neglected and dependent children were confined in adult prisons. Physical conditions in these institutions were horribly punitive and inhumane, a fact that led social reformers to create a separate court system in 1899 and eventually to open correctional facilities solely for juveniles.[5] These early juvenile institutions were industrial schools modeled after adult prisons but designed to protect children from the evil influences in adult facilities. The first was the New York House of Refuge, established in 1825.

Not long after this, states began to establish **reform schools** for juveniles. Massachusetts was the first to open a state reform school—the Lyman School for Boys in Westborough—in 1846. New York opened the State Agricultural and Industrial School in 1849, and Maine opened the Maine Boys' Training School in 1853. By 1900, thirty-six states had reform schools.[6] While it is difficult to precisely measure the total population of these institutions, Margaret Werner Cahalan has impressively reviewed historical corrections statistics in the United States. She found that by 1880, there were approximately 11,468 youths in correctional facilities, a number that more than doubled by 1923 (see Table 19.1).[7] Early reform schools were generally punitive in nature and were based on the concept of rehabilitation or reform through hard work and discipline.

In the second half of the nineteenth century, emphasis shifted from the massive industrial schools to the **cottage system.** Juvenile offenders were housed in a series of small cottages in a compound, each one holding twenty to forty children. Each cottage was run by cottage parents, who attempted to create a home-like atmosphere. It was felt that this would be more conducive to rehabilitation than the rigid bureaucratic organization of massive institutions.

The first cottage system was established in Massachusetts in 1855, the second in Ohio in 1858.[8] The system was generally applauded as being a great improvement over the earlier industrial training schools. The general feeling was that by moving away from punishment and toward rehabilitation, diagnosis, and treatment, not only could known offenders be rehabilitated but crime among dependent and unruly children could be prevented.[9]

■■ **TABLE 19.1**   Youths in Correctional Facilities, 1880–1980

	1880	1890	1904	1910	1923	1980
Number	11,468	14,846	23,034	25,038	27,238	59,414
Per 100,000 population aged 10–20	97	100	126	125	125	136

Source: Margaret Werner Cahalan, *Historical Corrections Statistics in the United States, 1850–1984* (Washington, D.C.: Department of Justice, 1986), pp. 104–5.

Twentieth-Century Developments

The early twentieth century witnessed important changes in the structure of juvenile corrections. Because of the influence of World War I, reform schools began to adopt military styles. Living units became barracks; cottage groups, companies; housefathers, captains; and superintendents, majors or colonels. Military-style uniforms became standard.

As the number of juvenile offenders increased, the forms of institutions varied to include forestry camps, ranches, and educational and vocational schools. Beginning in the 1930s, for example, camps became a part of the juvenile correctional system. Modeled after the camps run by the Civilian Conservation Corps, the juvenile camps centered on conservation activities, outdoor living, and work as a means of rehabilitation.

Los Angeles County was the first to use camps during this period.[10] Southern California had problems with transient youths who came to California with no money and then got into trouble with the law. Rather than filling up the jails, the county placed these offenders in conservation camps, paid them small wages, and then released them when they had earned enough money to return home. When the camps proved more rehabilitative than training schools, California established forestry camps in 1935 especially for delinquent boys, and the idea soon spread to other states.[11]

Also during the 1930s, efforts at reforming the juvenile correctional institution were taken under the U.S. Children's Bureau. The bureau conducted studies and projects to determine the effectiveness of the training school concept. Little was learned from these early programs because of limited funding and bureaucratic ineptitude, and the Children's Bureau failed to achieve any significant change in the juvenile correctional field. But such efforts recognized the important role of positive institutional care in delinquency prevention and control.[12]

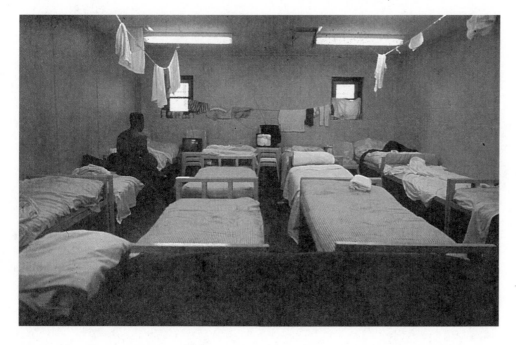

The rise in the correctional population has caused many juvenile institutions to suffer from overcrowding.

Another innovation came in the 1940s, with the American Law Institute's Model Youth Correction Authority Act. This act emphasized the use of reception-classification centers. California was the first to try out this new idea, opening the Northern Reception Center and Clinic in Sacramento in 1947. Today, there are many such centers scattered around the United States.

Since the 1970s, the major change in institutionalization has been the effort by the federal government to remove status offenders from institutions housing juvenile delinquents. This initiative also includes removing status offenders from secure pretrial detention centers and removing all juveniles from contact with adults in jails.

This **"decarceration"** policy mandates that courts use the **least restrictive alternative** in providing services for status offenders. This means that a noncriminal child should not be put in a secure facility if a community-based model will do. In addition, the federal government prohibits states from putting status offenders in separate custodial care facilities that are similar in form and function to those used for delinquent offenders. This is to prevent states from merely shifting their institutionalized population around so that one training school houses all delinquents and another houses all status offenders, but actual conditions remain the same.

The decarceration movement has had some dramatic results. At the end of 1977, some 3,376 status offenders were being held in public short- and long-term institutions; by 1985, the number declined to 2,293, and in 1989 (the latest available data), the figure stood at 2,245.[13] This decline may signify a shift in court policy and judicial decision making; judges may be more likely to encourage prosecutors to charge youths with delinquency rather than status offenses. Or as Paul Lerman warns, removing status offenders from secure public institutions may mean involving them in privately administered mental health and/or community-based programs.[14] According to Lerman, it is difficult to determine whether federal initiatives have resulted in a decline in the custodial population or merely a shift in its whereabouts.

JUVENILE INSTITUTIONS TODAY

There are approximately eleven hundred public and twenty-two hundred private juvenile facilities in operation around the United States, holding a one-day count of approximately ninety-four thousand youths (the latest available data).[15] In 1985, there were 1,040 public and 1,996 private juvenile facilities, with 83,402 juveniles in custody. Overall, the number of youth and institutions has increased by about 9 percent in this period, possibly due to a "get tough" policy with juvenile offenders (see Figure 19.2).

The majority of these institutions are small, nonsecure facilities holding less than twenty youths. However, there are also about seventy facilities that house over two hundred juveniles. While about 80 percent of the public institutions can be characterized as "closed" and secured, only 20 percent of private facilities are high-security.

Public institutions for juveniles can be administered by any number of state agencies: child and youth services; mental health, youth conservation, health, and social services; corrections; and child welfare. Social service departments administer juvenile institutions in twenty states and the District of Columbia, while corrections agencies have this responsibility in fourteen states and youth

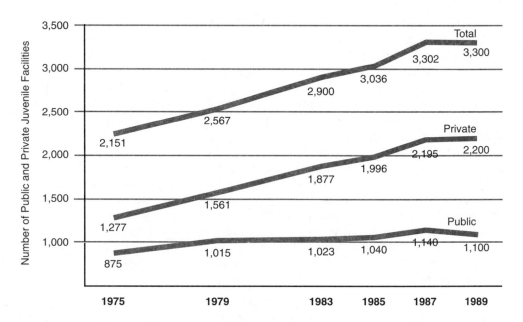

FIGURE 19.2

Growth in institutional care, 1975 to 1989

Source: Bureau of Justice Statistics, *Children in Custody 1975–85* and *Fact Sheet 1987* (Washington, D.C.: Department of Justice, 1989); Office of Juvenile Justice and Delinquency Prevention, *National Juvenile Custody Trends 1978–89* (Washington, D.C.: Department of Justice, 1992).

services departments in thirteen states. In three jurisdictions, delinquent institutions are administered by a specialized department of family and children's services.[16] Recently, a number of states have created separate youth service organizations and removed juvenile corrections from an existing adult corrections department or mental health agency. Virginia, for instance, created a Department of Youth Services in July 1990, while Arizona's juvenile corrections program has become an independent agency after it split from the Department of Corrections.[17] The institutions in some states fall under a centralized corrections system that covers adults as well as juveniles. Other states operate separate adult and juvenile systems. Maryland has enhanced its juvenile corrections program by the creation of its Juvenile Services Agency, whose director reports directly to the governor. It has eighteen hundred employees and an $87 million budget. In 1988, the agency served over twenty-nine thousand juveniles. It operates a secure facility, five youth centers, and four detention centers. These facilities are augmented with contractual residential and nonresidential programs for troubled youths as well as a variety of community-based services.[18]

Administrative Structures

A wide diversity of administrative arrangements characterize the organization of institutional juveniles corrections in the United States today. According to experts, there is a preference for a single statewide department of juvenile corrections.[19] This form of organization seems best able to carry out the courts' dispositions, appropriate monies, and implement effective institutional programs for children.

For the most part, institutional administration is not an easy task. It must cover financial management and program planning. The quality of administration often determines the effectiveness of a particular facility.

The physical plants of juvenile institutions across the nation vary tremendously. Many of the older training schools are tremendously outdated. Older facilities still tend to place juvenile offenders in a single building.[20] More acceptable structures today include a reception unit with an infirmary, a security unit, and dormitory units or cottages. Planners have concluded that the most effective design for training schools is to have facilities located around a community square. The facilities generally include a dining hall and kitchen area, a storage warehouse, academic and vocational training rooms, a library, an auditorium, a gymnasium, a laundry, maintenance facilities, an administration building, and other basic facilities, such as a commissary, a barbershop, and a beauty shop.

Physical conditions of individual living areas vary widely, depending on the type of facility and the progressiveness of its administration. In the past, most training school conditions were appalling, with children living in unbelievable squalor. Today, most institutions provide children with toilet and bath facilities, beds, desks, lamps, and tables. Following the recommendations of various standards, new facilities usually provide single rooms for each individual. A national survey described the typical juvenile institution:

Institutions for the delinquent child usually have vastly different characteristics than those holding adults. Often they are located on a campus spreading over many acres. The housing units provide quarters for smaller groups invariably less than sixty and frequently less than twenty. Often they also provide apartments for cottage staff. Dining frequently is a function of cottage life, eliminating the need for the large, central dining rooms. Grills seldom are found on the cottage doors and windows, although sometimes they are covered by detention screens. Security is not the staff's major preoccupation.[21]

Most experts recommend that juvenile facilities have indoor and outdoor leisure areas, libraries, academic and vocational education spaces, chapels, facilities where youths can meet with their visitors, a reception and processing room,

The security measures used in some closed juvenile institutions may be similar to those used in adult facilities.

security fixtures (which, when necessary, are normal in appearance), windows in all sleeping accommodations, and fire safety equipment and procedures.

Another approach has been the coeducational training school, which lessens the shock of being separated from society in a single-sex institution. However, Clemens Bartollas and Christopher Sieverdes's evaluation of coed training schools found that residents still felt "scared" within them and were victims of sexual and physical violence.[22]

The physical conditions and architecture of secure facilities for juveniles have come a long way from the training schools of the turn of the century. However, many administrators and state legislators have not yet realized that more modernization is necessary to meet even minimum compliance with national standards for juvenile institutions. Correctional administrators have described conditions as horrendous, and health officials have cited institutions for pollution by vermin, rodents, asbestos, and so on.[23] While some positive changes have taken place, there are still enormous problems to overcome.

At the heart of over twenty years of child advocacy, legal efforts continue to: (1) establish procedures to protect the rights of children in institutions; (2) reduce the number of institutionalized juveniles nationwide; and (3) improve the treatment of incarcerated youth, including providing for adequate medical and educational programs.[24]

Trends in Juvenile Corrections

There is little question that tremendous variation exists among the states in the use of juvenile correction. California is by far the leading state in both its use and variety of juvenile correctional facilities. It alone houses almost 20 percent of all residents of public and private facilities (about sixteen thousand currently).[25] The California incarceration rate for juveniles is over 540 per 100,000 juveniles in the population. In contrast, Texas holds almost 4,200 youths in public and private facilities and has an incarceration rate of about 235 per 100,000. New York, another populous state, has almost 5,400 youths in custody and averages an incarceration rate of 350 per 100,000 population.[26] In 1989, the national average was 367 juveniles per 100,000 in public custody. These numbers indicate that states address the problems of institutional care in different ways (see Table 19.2).[27]

One major problem facing the juvenile correctional system is overcrowding. Many juvenile institutions contain more residents than they are designed to hold. Overcrowding—and its attendant problems—is one reason that some states, including Idaho, Utah, and Connecticut, have made determined efforts to close

■■ TABLE 19.2   National Trends in Juvenile Corrections

	1979	1989	% CHANGE
Juveniles in Custody	71,922	93,945	+ 30%
Overall Custody Rate per 100,000	251	367	+ 46%
Admission Rate per 100,000	2,220	2,974	+ 34%
Total Expenditures	1,307,684	2,860,818	Over 100%
Total Number of Juvenile Institutions	2,200	3,267	+ 42%

Sources: Office of Juvenile Justice and Delinquency Prevention, *National Juvenile Custody Trends 1978–1989* (Washington, D.C.: Department of Justice, 1992); also Barbara Allen Hagen, *Public Juvenile Facilities—Children in Custody, 1989* (Washington, D.C.: Department of Justice, 1991).

public facilities and house most of their juvenile populations in small, privately run facilities. Colorado, West Virginia, Oregon, Pennsylvania, and North Dakota also are attempting to reduce their secure populations and rely more heavily on community-based programs.

Changes also occurred in the juvenile institutions of Arizona and Arkansas. The impetus for change in Arizona was a class-action lawsuit brought on behalf of minors confined in the Catalina Mountain Juvenile Institution that challenged the inadequate conditions of confinement at the institution. In Arkansas, an investigation into abuses at the state's two training schools led to reductions in that state's juvenile correctional population.[28]

Overcrowding has made some states reluctant to increase the number of juvenile residents in their publicly run facilities. Another reason for the reluctance is the enormous expense involved. The average cost of housing one resident for one year in 1989 was twenty-seven thousand dollars. New York ($54,000), Rhode Island ($78,000), Connecticut ($45,000), Idaho ($43,100), Minnesota ($39,100), and Oklahoma ($43,000) were among the top states in the cost of housing juveniles. Pennsylvania averaged forty-four thousand dollars per juvenile resident. Costs range from a low of $16,500 to a high of $78,000.[29]

Today, the average cost to house one resident for one day is about $75 and can be as high as $125 per day in the Northeast, where operating costs are substantially greater than other parts of the country.[30] In addition, the cost of constructing a thirty- to forty-bed secure treatment facility for juvenile offenders can be $6 million or more, or fifty thousand to sixty thousand dollars per juvenile per year, compared to an operating cost of five thousand to ten thousand dollars per year in most delinquency prevention programs.

PROFILE OF THE INSTITUTIONALIZED JUVENILE

The best source of information on institutionalized youths is the federal government's *Children in Custody* (CIC) series. This survey provides timely information on the number and characteristics of children being held in public and private facilities around the nation.

Other excellent references are the Office of Juvenile Justice and Delinquency's *National Juvenile Custody Trends* and the *Corrections Compendium*.

The latest information indicates that about ninety-four thousand youths were being held in all types of facilities as of 1989 (see Figure 19.3).[31] Of these, approximately sixty-six thousand were long-term commitments, sixteen thousand were preadjudication detainees, and the remaining ten thousand youths were admitted voluntarily to receive some type of treatment (mostly in private institutions). The census also found that over sixty-three thousand juveniles were confined for delinquent acts, eleven thousand as a result of status offenses, and eighteen thousand were nonoffenders.[32]

The number of youths in public facilities remained virtually unchanged between 1980 and 1985 (about 50,000) but increased 8 percent between 1985 and 1989 (56,103). Private-sector institutions experienced an increase of approximately 10 percent between 1983 and 1985 (from thirty-one thousand to thirty-four thousand), as well as another 10-percent increase from 1985 to 1989 (from thirty-four thousand to thirty-eight thousand).[33]

The data suggest that after a decade of decarceration efforts, the number of youths in some form of incarceration has increased, a trend that reflects the

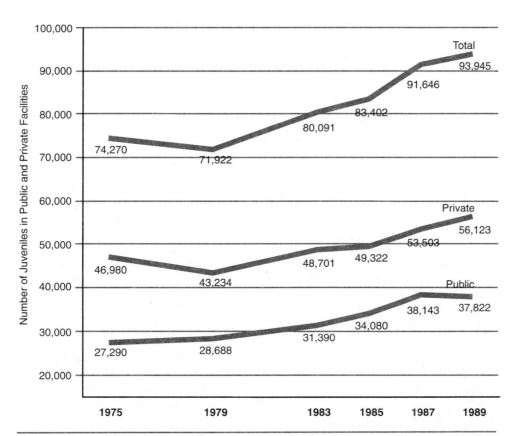

FIGURE 19.3

Rate for incarcerated children, 1985 to 1989

Source: Bureau of Justice Statistics, *Children in Custody 1975–85* and *Fact Sheet 1987* (Washington, D.C.: U.S. Department of Justice, 1989); Office of Juvenile Justice and Delinquency, *National Juvenile Custody Trends 1978–89* (Washington, D.C.: Department of Justice, 1992).

dominance of a conservative, control-oriented policy. Even the effort to remove status offenders from secure public facilities has slowed; the number of incarcerated status offenders stood at 2,200 in 1989.

The Hidden Correctional System

While the number of institutionalized youths appears to be on the increase, the CIC data may reveal only the tip of the correctional iceberg. For example, the data does not include many of the minors who are incarcerated after they are waived to adult courts or who have their cases tried there because of exclusion statutes. Most states do place underage juveniles convicted of adult charges in youth centers until they reach their majority, whereupon they are transferred to an adult facility. In addition, as Ira Schwartz and his colleagues point out, there is a "hidden" system of juvenile control that places wayward youths in private mental hospitals and substance-abuse clinics for behaviors that could easily have brought them a stay in a correctional facility or community-based program. Schwartz found that in a single year (1983), Minneapolis hospitals admitted more than two thousand teenage psychiatric patients for an average stay of thirty-eight days; the numbers of admissions doubled between 1976 and 1983.[34]

This "hidden system" is an important community resource for mentally ill children and substance-abuse offenders. During the past few years, fourteen states have made changes in their laws relative to the civil commitment of children. Wyoming, for example, created the State Hospital Juvenile Treatment Program and allowed any adjudicated delinquent or person in need of supervision to be committed to the program. Montana established a Youth Treatment Center for the care of seriously mentally ill children between the ages of 12 and 18, including those who committed delinquent acts. Michigan and Nebraska have enacted similar comprehensive statutes addressing the placement needs of minors. Other states, such as North Dakota and Missouri, are easing admission procedures for juvenile drug users in order to expand treatment options for them.

These efforts suggest that the number of institutionalized children may be far greater than is reported in the CIC surveys. Undoubtedly, private-sector juvenile corrections in the form of contract services or other institutional support has become a significant part of the juvenile justice system.[35]

Personal Characteristics

The data from the *Children in Custody* report gives some personal background information on children in custody. The "typical" resident is a 15- to 16-year-old white male who is incarcerated for an average stay of approximately five months in a public facility or six months in a private one. Almost 80 percent of all the residents in public and private facilities were male and about 20 percent were female.

With regard to racial characteristics, over 50 percent of all juveniles held in custody were white, 34 percent were African-American, and 12 percent were Hispanic. Also, private and public facilities differed widely in the racial makeup of the youth they held. Over 63 percent of those in private institutions were white, while over 54 percent of the juveniles held in public facilities were African-American or Hispanic. Only about 34 percent of the juveniles held in private settings were of minority origin. While the number of white juveniles held in public facilities decreased slightly between 1985 and 1989, the number of black and Hispanic juveniles increased by 15 and 20 percent, respectively.

Today, black and Hispanic juveniles constitute about 37 percent and 13 percent, respectively, of the juvenile population, while white youths are about 48 percent.[36] Because of these changing social patterns, a juvenile in a public facility today is most likely an African-American male between 14 and 17 years of age who is held for a delinquent offense, such as a property crime. On the other hand, a juvenile in a private facility is more likely to be a white male between 14 and 17 who is held for a nondelinquent act, such as running away or truancy.

While the data shows that a majority of juvenile correctional inmates are white, recent research by Barry Krisberg and his associates found that minority youths are incarcerated at a rate three to four times that of white youths and that this overrepresentation is not a result of differentials in their arrest or crime rates. Of equal importance, minorities are more likely to be confined in secure public facilities rather than in open private facilities that may provide more costly and effective treatment. The authors found that racial disparity in juvenile disposition was a growing problem that demands immediate public scrutiny.[37] Today, about 60 percent of the juveniles in custody belong to racial or ethnic minorities.

Most juveniles committed to institutions were between 14 and 17 years old. Private facilities tend to house younger youths, while public institutions provided custodial care for older children, including a small percentage between 18 and 21 years old (see Table 19.3). The number of juveniles held in public facilities increased 17 percent in 1985 and 5 percent in 1987. Coupled with a decline in

■■TABLE 19.3 Demographic Characteristics and Adjudication Status of Juveniles Held in Public Juvenile Facilities, 1983, 1985, 1987, and 1989

	NUMBER OF JUVENILES			
	1983	**1985**	**1987**	**1989**
Total	48,701	49,322	53,503	56,123
Sex				
Male	42,182	42,549	46,012	49,443
Female	6,519	6,773	7,491	6,680
Race and ethnicity				
White	27,805	29,969	24,631	22,201
Black and Hispanic	23,747	24,820	28,890	33,922
Other	1,104	1,084	0	0
Age on census date				
9 years and under	42	60	73	45
10—13 years	3,104	3,181	2,675	3,276
14–17 years	39,571	40,640	42,802	44,894
18–20 years	4,804	5,409	6,955	7,908
21 years and over	86	32	0	
Adjudication status				
Detained	13,156	14,474	11,566	17,612
Committed	35,178	34,549	38,522	38,209
Voluntarily admitted	367	299	535	302

Source: Bureau of Justice Statistics, *Children in Custody 1975–85* and *Fact Sheet 1987* (Washington, D.C.: U.S. Department of Justice, 1989) (data for 1987 computed from *Fact Sheet*); Barbara Allen-Hagen, *Children in Custody—Public Juvenile Facilities, 1989* OJJDP update (Washington, D.C.: U.S. Dept of Justice, 1991).

the overall juvenile population, this means a greater proportion of the juvenile population apparently is being held in custody.

What did juvenile offenders have to do in order to wind up in a correctional facility? Contrary to popular belief, the great majority of residents were not committed for violent crimes. Most incarcerated youths were property offenders. In fact, the number of nondelinquents committed to public and private institutions—including status offenders, neglected, dependent, and emotionally disturbed youths—was greater than the number of youths committed for violent acts. The image of the incarcerated delinquent as a violent menace to society is somewhat misleading.

Institutional Adjustment

More than a decade ago, shocking exposés of the treatment of institutionalized children focused public attention on the problems of juvenile corrections. Today, some critics believe that the light of public scrutiny has moderated conditions within training schools. There is now greater professionalism among the staff, and staff brutality seems to have diminished. Status offenders and delinquents are for the most part held in separate facilities. Finally, confinement length is shorter and programming has increased.

Despite such improvements, the everyday life of male inmates still reflects institutional values. Clemens Bartollas, S. J. Miller, and Simon Dinitz have identified an inmate value system that in many ways resembles the "inmate social code" found in adult institutions. The general code revolves around the following principles:

- Exploit whomever you can.
- Don't play up to staff.
- Don't rat on your peers.
- Don't give in to others.[38]

In addition to these general rules, there were separate norms for black inmates—"exploit whites," "no forcing sex on blacks," "defend your brother"—and for whites—"don't trust anyone," "everybody for himself."

The male inmate code still seems to be in operation. More recent research conducted in five juvenile institutions confirmed the notion that residents formed cohesive groups and adhered to an informal inmate culture in an effort to "do time" gracefully.[39] The more serious the youth's delinquent record and the more secure the institution, the greater the adherence to the inmate social code.

Today, male delinquents are more likely to form allegiances with members of their own racial group and attempt to exploit others less favored. They also scheme to manipulate staff and take advantage of weaker peers. However, in institutions that are treatment-oriented and where staff-inmate relationships are more intimate, residents are less likely to adhere to a negativistic inmate code.

Culture of the Female Offender

Females have traditionally been less involved in criminal activities than males. As a consequence, the number of females in institutions has been lower than the number of males. However, the growing involvement of girls in criminal behavior and the feminist movement have drawn more attention to the female juvenile offender. This attention has revealed a double standard of justice. For example, girls are more likely than boys to be incarcerated for status offenses, such as truancy, running away, and sexual misconduct. Institutions for girls are generally more restrictive than those for boys. They have fewer educational and vocational programs and fewer services. They also do a less-than-adequate job of rehabilitation. It has been suggested that this double standard operates through a chivalrous male justice system that seeks to "protect" young girls from their own sexuality.[40]

Over the years, the number of females held in public institutions has generally declined. This represents the continuation of a long-term trend to remove girls, many of whom are nonserious status offenders, from closed institutions and place them in less restrictive private or community-based facilities. So while a majority of males are today housed in private facilities, most female delinquents reside in private facilities.

In the past few years, overall admissions of females have increased about 18 percent. Female admissions to private institutions specifically have risen rapidly, increasing about 96 percent in 1989, compared with a continuous decline in public institution admissions. Generally, about 35 percent of incarcerated female juveniles are in private facilities, while half that number are in public facilities.[41] See Figure 19.4 for a comparison of the rates of growth in female and male admissions from 1979 to 1989.

Institutionalized girls are often runaways seeking to escape intolerable home situations that can involve abusive or incestuous relationships. Some are pregnant and have no means of support. Only a few are true delinquents. Many are

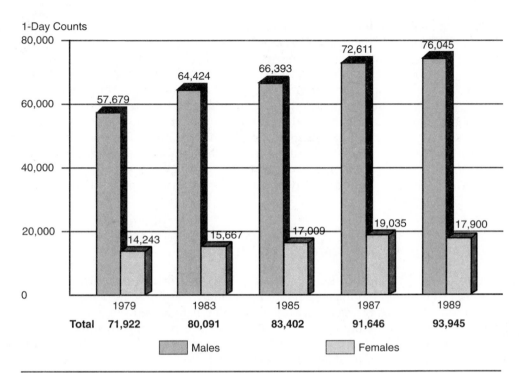

1-Day Counts

■■FIGURE 19.4

U.S. public and private juvenile facilities: One-day counts, 1979–1989

Sources: Barry K. Risberg, Robert DeComo, Norma C. Herrera 1979–1989 Census of Public and Private Juvenile Detention, Correctional and Shelter Facilities; and the U.S. Bureau of the Census population estimates.

the "throwaways" of society—those whom nobody wants. Recent studies also estimate that up to three hundred thousand or more female adolescents are involved in prostitution nationally.[42] This number continues to grow because the number of runaways keeps increasing.

The same double standard and inequality that bring a girl into an institution continue to exist once she is in custody: there, she receives training in "womanly arts" and is incarcerated for a longer term than most males receive. Institutional programs for girls tend to be strongly oriented toward the reinforcement of traditional roles for women. How well these programs rehabilitate girls and ready them for life in a quickly changing society is questionable.

Often many of the characteristics of juvenile female offenders are similar to those of their male counterparts. These include poor social skills, low self-esteem, and poor home environment. Other problems are more specific to the female juvenile offender, such as sexuality issues, victimization, educational and vocational inequity, and the lack of placement options.

Although there is a recent movement toward the use of coed institutions for juveniles, most girls remain incarcerated in antiquated, single-sex institutions that are usually isolated in rural areas and rarely offer adequate rehabilitative services. Results of a recent federally sponsored survey of training schools across the nation revealed a definite pattern of inequality in services for boys and girls.[43]

Several factors account for the different treatment of girls. One is sexual stereotyping by administrators, who feel that "girls should be girls" and that teaching them "appropriate" sex roles in prison will help them adjust on the outside. These beliefs are often held by the staff as well. Many of them have only a high-school education, as well as rigid and highly sexist ideas of what is appropriate behavior for adolescent girls. Girls' institutions tend to be smaller and less filled than boys' institutions. As a result, they simply do not have the money to offer as many varied programs and services as do the larger male institutions.[44]

In general, it appears that society is more concerned about girls who act out and less concerned about their rehabilitation because the crimes they commit are not serious. These attitudes get translated into fewer staff, less modern buildings, and poorer vocational, educational, and recreational programs than those found in boys' institutions. Ilene Bergsmann points out that little time and effort have been devoted to the female offender in the last century. She concludes that differential treatment of females and males in the juvenile justice system begins with the schools, continues with law enforcement, and is perpetuated by the correctional system.[45]

CORRECTIONAL TREATMENT FOR JUVENILES

Nearly all juvenile institutions use some form of treatment program for the children in custody—counseling on an individual or group basis, vocational and educational training, recreational programs, and religious counseling. In addition, most institutions provide medical and dental health programs of some kind, as well as occasional legal service programs. Generally, the larger the institution, the greater the number of programs and services offered.

The purpose of these various programs is to rehabilitate the youths within the institutions—to reform them into well-adjusted individuals and send them back into the community to be productive citizens. Despite generally good intentions, however, the goal of rehabilitation has rarely been attained. National statistics show that a significant number of juvenile offenders commit more crimes after release from incarceration.

One of the most common problems is a lack of well-trained staff members to run programs. Budgetary limitations are a primary concern when it comes to planning for institutional programs. It costs a minimum of twenty-seven thousand dollars per year to keep a child in an institution—a staggering amount that explains why institutions generally do not employ large staffs of professionals.

It is also not clear which programs provide the most effective treatment. Some often-cited studies indicate that few of the treatment programs presently being used in juvenile institutions are effective in preventing future delinquency.

The most glaring problem with treatment programs is that they are not being used effectively.[46] While the official goals of many institutions may be treatment and rehabilitation, the actual programs may center around security, control, and punishment. Whether juveniles who respond to a structured setting should be released without knowing if they have been really rehabilitated is exemplified in the situation outlined in the following Case in Point.

Individual Treatment Techniques—Past and Present

One common treatment approach is **individual counseling.** It is estimated that over 90 percent of juvenile institutions use this approach to some extent.[47] This is not surprising, since psychological problems such as depression are a real and present problem in juvenile institutions.[48] Individual counseling does not attempt to change a youth's personality. Rather, it attempts to help individuals

CASE IN POINT

You are an aftercare worker responsible for evaluating and recommending the release of juveniles from institutional confinement.

William G. was 15 and a half years old when he was committed for eighteen months to a secure juvenile institution after being adjudicated delinquent for breaking and entering and larceny. William resided with his aunt and uncle and two cousins. His mother died three years ago, and he has had no contact with his father for ten years. Initial psychological testing indicated that William was a hostile, angry youth with borderline intelligence, poor controls, and no guilt. The psychiatrist believed that William was likely to commit crime in the future. Considering the fact that William was before the juvenile court on two prior occasions (for truancy and drug use), he seemed like a youth out of control.

Recent evaluations of William's institutional progress are in marked contrast to his behavior while living in the community. He has been cooperative and personable and has maintained a positive attitude during his twelve months at the institution. William seems to have benefited from the structural controls and constant monitoring offered in such a setting. On the other hand, he does require special education, but because of his poor and inconsistent school record, the public school system is reluctant to take him back.

William is approaching his seventeenth birthday. The prosecutor's office and institutional personnel recommend that William complete his sentence. William's attorney suggests that the youth is ready for some form of residential placement.

How would you decide William's case?

What programs are needed to meet his needs?

Can both the doctrine of *parens patriae* and public protection be served here?

---

understand and solve their present adjustment problems. The advantage of individual counseling is that institutions can use it superficially with counselors who may not be professionally qualified.

Highly structured counseling can be based on psychotherapy or psychoanalysis. **Psychotherapy** is an outgrowth of Freudian psychoanalytic techniques and requires extensive analysis of the individual's past childhood experiences. An effective therapist attempts to help the individual solve conflicts and make a more positive adjustment to society through altering negative behavior.

Although individual counseling and psychotherapy are used extensively in institutions and may work well for certain individuals, there is little indication that these treatments are even marginally effective. In a review of ten such programs, Dennis Romig reported that eight had completely negative results.[49]

Another highly utilized treatment approach for delinquents is **reality therapy**.[50] This approach, developed by William Glasser, emphasizes the present behavior of offenders by making them completely responsible for their actions. Glasser feels that a psychoanalytical emphasis on the past may lead children to excuse present and future misbehavior by encouraging them to think of themselves as sick and unable to change their actions. The success of reality therapy depends greatly on the warmth and concern of the individual counselor. Unfortunately, many institutions rely heavily on this type of therapy because they assume that highly trained professionals are unnecessary. Actually, a skilled therapist is essential. The individual must be knowledgeable about the complexity of personalities and be able to deal with any situation that may come up in the counseling.

The object of reality therapy is to make individuals more responsible people. This end is accomplished by giving them confidence and strength through developing their ability to follow a set of expectations as closely as possible.

Behavior modification, another method of treatment, is used in almost three-quarters of all institutions.[51] It is based on the theory that all behavior is learned and that present behavior can be shaped through a system of rewards and punishments. This type of program is easily used in an institutional setting that offers points and privileges as rewards for such behaviors as work, study, or the development of skills. It is a reasonably effective technique, especially when a contract is formed with the youth to modify certain behaviors. When youths are aware of what is expected of them, they plan their actions to meet these expectations and then experience the anticipated consequences. In this way, they can be motivated to change. Behavior modification is effective in controlled settings, where a counselor can manipulate the situation, but once the youth is back in the real world, it becomes difficult to use.

In general, effective individual treatment programs are built around the following specific counseling techniques: (1) psychotherapy, (2) reality therapy, and (3) behavior modification. Other less formal approaches include personal growth counseling, substance-abuse treatment, assertion training, and self-image and ego development counseling.

Group Treatment Techniques

Group therapy is more economical than individual therapy because one therapist can handle more than one individual at a time. Also, the support of the group is often highly valuable to the individuals in the group, and individuals derive hope from other members of the group who have survived similar experiences. Another advantage of group therapy is that a group can often solve a problem more effectively than an individual.[52]

There are some disadvantages to group therapy. For one, it provides less individualized attention. Some individuals may be different from the other group members and need more highly individualized treatment. Others may be shy and afraid to speak up in the group and thus fail to receive the benefits of the group experience. Some individuals may dominate group interaction, and the leader may be ineffective in handling this situation. Finally, group condemnation may seriously hurt rather than help a child.

More than any other group treatment technique, group psychotherapy probes into the personality and attempts to restructure it. Relationships in these groups tend to be quite intense. The group is used to facilitate expression of feelings, to solve problems, and to teach members to empathize with one another.

Unfortunately, the components necessary for an effective group psychotherapy situation, such as personal interaction, cooperation, and tolerance, are in direct conflict with the antisocial, antagonistic, and exploitive orientation of delinquents. This type of technique is often effective when the members of the group are there voluntarily, but institutionalized delinquents are often forced to attend.

Guided group interaction (GGI) is a fairly common method of group treatment. It is based on the theory that through group interactions, a delinquent can begin to realize and solve personal problems. A group leader facilitates interaction among group members, and a group culture develops. Individual members can be mutually supportive and can help develop more acceptable behavior. Guided group interaction was an instrumental factor in the success of programs at Highfields, New Jersey, and Provo, Utah.[53] In the 1980s, a version of GGI called **Positive Peer Culture (PPC)** became popular in juvenile corrections. PPC programs use groups in which peer leaders get other youths to conform to conventional behaviors. The rationale for PPC is that if negative peer influence can encourage youths to engage in delinquent behavior, then positive influences can help them conform.[54]

Milieu therapy seeks to make all aspects of an inmate's environment a part of his or her treatment and to minimize differences between the custodial staff and the treatment personnel. It also emphasizes peer influence in the formation of constructive values. Milieu therapy attempts to create an environment that encourages meaningful change, increased growth, and satisfactory adjustment. This is often accomplished through peer pressure to conform to group norms.

One early type of milieu therapy based on psychoanalytic theory was developed in Chicago during the late 1940s and early 1950s by Bruno Bettleheim.[55] This therapy attempted to create a conscience, or superego, in delinquent youths by getting them to depend on their therapists to a great extent and then threatening them with loss of the loving and caring relationship if they failed to control their behavior.

Today, institutional group counseling often focuses on drug and alcohol group counseling, self-esteem development groups, and role-model support sessions. In addition, because juveniles are entering the system considerably more violent than in years past, group sessions are used in dealing with appropriate expressions of anger and rage and methods to understand and control such behavior.

Vocational, Educational, and Recreational Programs

In addition to individual and group treatment programs, most institutions use vocational and educational treatment programs designed to teach juveniles skills that will help them adjust more easily when they are released into the community. Educational programs for juveniles are required in long-term facilities because children must go to school until they are of a certain age. Since educational programs are an important part of social development and have therapeutic value in addition to their instructional values, they are an essential part of most treatment programs. What takes place through education is related to all other aspects of the institutional program—the work activities, cottage life, recreation, and clinical services.

Educational programs are probably some of the best-staffed programs in training schools, but even at their best, most are inadequate. Training programs must contend with a myriad of problems. Many of the youths coming into these institutions are mentally retarded or have low IQs or learning disabilities. As such, they are educationally handicapped and far behind their grade levels in basic academic areas. Most of these youths dislike school and become bored with any type of educational program. Their boredom often leads to acting out and subsequent disciplinary problems.

Ideally, institutions should allow the inmates to attend a school in the community or offer programs that lead to a high school diploma or GED certificate. Unfortunately, not all institutions offer these types of programs. Ironically, more secure institutions, because of their large size, are more likely than group homes or day-treatment centers to offer supplemental educational programs, such as remedial reading, physical education, and tutoring. Some more modern educational programs offer computer learning and programmed learning modules.

Vocational training has long been used as a treatment technique for juveniles. Early institutions were even referred to as industrial schools. Today, vocational programs in institutions are varied. Programs offered include auto repair, printing, woodworking, mechanical drawing, food service, beauty shop techniques, secretarial training, and data processing. One obvious problem here is sex-typing, and the recent trend has been to allow equal access to all programs offered in institutions that house girls and boys. This is more difficult in single-sex institutions, because funds often cannot be found to offer all types of training.

Vocational programs for youths that include job placement, vocational training, alone, do not positively affect juvenile delinquency. Youths need skills that will give them hope for advancement.

The Ventura School for Female Juvenile Offenders under the California Youth Authority has been a pioneer with the work placement concept. Private industry contracts with the youth authority to establish businesses on the institution's grounds. The businesses hire, train, and pay scale wages for work. Wages are divided into a victim's restitution fund, room and board fees, and forced savings, and a portion is given to the juvenile to purchase canteen items. Trans World Airlines (TWA), for example, has established a ticket reservation center on school grounds. The center handles the overflow phone calls from Los Angeles. Many juveniles have been trained and a significant number have been employed by TWA or travel agencies upon their release. Ventura also has a program that involves private industry in the manufacture of uniforms at the school, particularly for the petroleum industry. The development of these skills are often marketable to employers in need of trained workers.[56]

Recreational activity is also an important way to help relieve adolescent aggressions, as evidenced by the many diversionary and delinquency prevention programs that focus on these activities as the primary treatment technique. A recreation program should include active and sedentary activities, both indoor and outdoor, for teams and individuals. Adequate equipment and supplies should be provided for a comprehensive program. In the case of nonsecure facilities, maximum use of recreational facilities in the community—swimming pools, parks, bowling lanes, and gymnasiums—should be made.

Treating Chronic Delinquents

Treating the **chronic juvenile offender** has become a major concern in recent years. While significant efforts are being made to deinstitutionalize and decarcerate the nonserious and status offender, the question remains what to do with the more serious juvenile delinquent who commits such crimes as rape or robbery. One answer has been to ease waiver rules and standards so that younger children can be transferred to the adult court. A number of states have created concurrent jurisdiction laws, which enable prosecutors to choose whether to bring a case to the adult court or juvenile court.

Another approach has been to incarcerate serious offenders in intensive juvenile treatment programs, where their problems can be dealt with while they are isolated both from society and from other juvenile offenders. This policy received impetus from a controversial book by Charles Murray and Louis B. Cox, *Beyond Probation*.[57] Murray and Cox compared chronic delinquents sent to traditional Illinois training school programs with those in an innovative community-based program, the Unified Delinquency Intervention Services. They discovered a **suppression effect,** a reduction in the number of arrests per year of the incarcerated youths. Moreover, the suppression effect for youths sent to training school was higher than for those in less-punitive treatment programs. Murray and Cox concluded that the juvenile justice system must choose which policy alternative its programs are aimed at achieving: prevention of delinquency or the care and protection of needy youths. If the former is a proper goal for the juvenile justice system, then institutionalization or the threat of institutionalization is desirable.

Similarly, Andrew Vachss and Yitzhak Bakal argue that a secure treatment center is necessary to deal with what they call **life-style violent juveniles.**[58] If secure placements were not available, there would be (1) increased use of waiver; (2) a dangerous mixing of offender types within an institutional setting (that is, nonviolent youths would become exposed to more serious offenders); (3) collapse and failure of alternative programs, because they would become contaminated by chronic offenders; and (4) the continuing problems of a system that returns dangerous juveniles to communities in far more dangerous condition and at the same time continues to incarcerate nondangerous juveniles within its "programs."[59]

Specialized Programs

Many states have set up specialized programs to deal with the chronic, violent offender. These efforts have been aided and funded by the federal government's Violent Juvenile Offender program, which tests innovative strategies for reintegrating chronically violent offenders back into the community.[60]

Another approach that seems to show promise is the outdoor education and training programs (known collectively as **Outward Bound** programs). Two of these programs are described in the following Focus on Delinquency.[61]

According to Castellano and Soderstrom, very little is known about the effects of wilderness stress-challenge programs on juvenile recidivism. In a study of the Spectrum Wilderness Program in Illinois, the authors found that successful completion of the program often resulted in arrest reductions that began immediately and lasted for about one year. While overall results were mixed, the authors conclude that such programs are promising alternatives to traditional juvenile justice placements.[62]

While incarcerating the serious offender does have the near-term advantage of incapacitating a threat to the community, what are the long-term consequences? According to Murray and Cox, there is a "suppression effect" on the future arrests. However, not all research supports this contention. Donna Hamparian and her associates found that institutionalizing chronic offenders actually increased both arrest probability and the seriousness of future crimes.[63] Hamparian states:

The most obvious conclusion to draw is that the less intrusive the intervention, the better for all concerned. "Getting tough" seems to simply increase the velocity from one arrest to the next. Institutionalization may just promote some careers since there is little left to lose.[64]

Juvenile Rehabilitation Strategies: Wilderness Programs

Camping or wilderness adventure has usually played a peripheral role in juvenile rehabilitation programs. In the 1930s, the Chicago Area Project developed a summer camping component as part of its delinquency prevention efforts. Many states rotated selected wards from the state training schools through forestry camps, where they worked in fire crews or at maintaining trails. The difference with these newer programs is that the outdoor education component has now assumed a central role. Two well-established and respected programs using these concepts are VisionQuest and the Associated Marine Institutes. Many more use similar techniques.

VISIONQUEST

VisionQuest, a for-profit contractor with headquarters in Tucson, Arizona, is probably the largest program of its type, with annual commitments in excess of five hundred delinquent youths. VisionQuest typically takes youths committed directly by juvenile courts in Pennsylvania, California, and several other states. The length of stay is usually between one year and eighteen months.

To enter the program, each candidate youth must agree to (1) abstain from drugs and sex during his or her commitment, (2) not run away, and (3) complete at least two impact programs, which can include residence in a wilderness camp, cross-country travel on a wagon train, or voyaging on a sailing vessel. In addition to its impact programs, VisionQuest conducts counseling sessions with other family members while a youth is in the program and operates several group homes that facilitate reentry into the community. While they are on the wagon train or in wilderness camp, each youth is assigned to a small group (tepee) of about eight other youths and two junior staff. Each wagon train or wilderness camp consists of about thirty to forty-five youths and a similar number of staff. Junior staff members sleep in the tepees with the juveniles and are off duty two days in every seven.

In addition to the wagon trains and sailing programs, VisionQuest is also known for its confrontational style. Committed youths are not allowed to slide by and just "do time." Rather, an individual program is worked out to ensure that each youth is challenged intellectually, phys-

ically, and emotionally. When juveniles do not perform up to expectations or begin to "act out," they are "confronted" by one or more senior staff members in an attempt to get them to deal with whatever issues underlie the poor behavior.

ASSOCIATED MARINE INSTITUTES

Associated Marine Institutes (AMI) is the parent agency for a group of nonprofit programs (institutes) located in Florida that use various marine projects as a means of motivating and challenging delinquent youths. Most of AMI's programs are nonresidential, picking up participating youths in the morning and returning them home in the evening, five days a week. During a typical stay of six months in the program, a participating youth will attend remedial classes, learn scuba diving and related safety procedures, study marine biology, and participate in some constructive work project, such as refurbishing an old boat or growing ground cover for some commercial site.

AMI also operates a long-term residential program at Fisheating Creek in south-central Florida. In this program, boys committed by the Dade County Juvenile Court spend six months to a year in an isolated work camp. During the first phase, their living conditions are extremely primitive, and their working conditions are rather hard (digging out stumps to clear an airstrip). Graduation to Phase 2 earns participants the right to sleep in air-conditioned quarters and have better work assignments. The last two phases of the program are spent in one of the nonresidential institutes near their home.

One of the distinctive characteristics of the nonprofit AMI is its heavy reliance on the capitalist spirit. Employee performance is periodically assessed by computerized measures (such as GEDs obtained, program completion rate, or subsequent recidivism rate) applied to all of the youths. End-of-the-year staff bonuses, based on these performance measures, can exceed 10 percent of regular salary. Committed youths can also earn money by participating in various work projects, such as clearing brush, that AMI has contracted to undertake. ■

Source: Adapted from Peter Greenwood and Franklin Zimring, *One More Chance* (Santa Monica, Calif.: Rand Corp., 1985), pp. 41–42.

Hamparian's results are evidence that secure treatment for violent chronic offenders may not be the answer to halting serious delinquency.

Similarly, Martin Forst, Jeffrey Fagan, and T. Scott Vivona suggest that the public protection benefits of transfer statutes that result in the placement of chronic juvenile offenders in secure institutions may be offset by the social costs of imprisonment. According to the authors, the increased exposure of juveniles to violence in secure adult facilities may increase the chances that they will exhibit violent behavior upon release.[65]

Correctional **boot camps** are also being developed for juvenile offenders. Boot camps combine the "get tough" elements of adult programs with education, substance abuse treatment, and socialization skills training. The American Correctional Association's Juvenile Project has studied the concept and sees merit in well-run boot camp programs, provided they incorporate the following elements: (1) a focus on concrete feelings and increasing self-esteem, (2) discipline through physical conditioning, and (3) programming in literacy, as well as academic and vocational education.[66]

In the future, juvenile corrections agencies may implement shock incarceration programs. These feature high-intensity military discipline and physical training for short periods of time. The expectation is that the offender will be "shocked" into going straight. These programs are now being used with young adult offenders and juveniles who have been waived to the adult system in Mississippi, Kansas, Florida, Georgia, and other jurisdictions.

How Effective Is Treatment?

Without question, the primary justification for incarcerating juvenile offenders is the hope that they will one day be rehabilitated and become productive members of society. If successful rehabilitation were not the ultimate goal of juvenile corrections, the use of residential facilities would be an expensive exercise in futility. In fact, the concept of rehabilitation has received significant criticism for the past twenty years. Several reviews of correctional treatment for juveniles (and adults) have concluded that the occasionally successful rehabilitation effort was a rare exception to the general rule of failure; when rehabilitation efforts worked, it was in special settings with hand-picked offenders. All too often treatment efforts seem misguided and poorly planned, staffed, and funded. And while high hopes may have been held out for a particular treatment modality, those who implement it often fail to take into account the background of their clients, which is frequently marked by emotional trauma and low self-esteem.

Can the treatment of youthful offenders by the juvenile correctional system be written off as a lost cause? Those who favor the treatment philosophy believe it is still too early to close the book on rehabilitation and that even partial success is still better than the alternative. While no single program may be able to help all delinquents, and though some hard-core offenders may be immune to all efforts to rehabilitate them, even the most die-hard antirehabilitation foe would grant that many programs provide effective treatment to a great number of clients. For example, a national review of delinquency prevention projects by the Rand Corporation found that some innovative programs featuring outdoor work projects have produced dramatic results with even hard-core delinquents.[67] And some studies, including a recent review by Carol Garrett, indicate that the success of juvenile treatment may be greater than previously believed.[68]

Boot camps are a newly emerging alternative in juvenile corrections. Short term "shock" incarceration may build self-esteem and discipline at a relatively low cost. Youths in the Vision-Quest program engage in camping and physical activities.

Garrett reviewed the findings of 111 methodologically sound juvenile corrections studies conducted between 1960 and 1983. They included programs that stressed either psychological counseling, behavior modification, life-skill improvement, or other treatments (for example, the use of megavitamins). Her conclusion: institutional treatment can work. While there was no clear-cut evidence that one particular treatment strategy was the most effective, the great majority showed change in a positive direction. And while Garrett does not conclude that successful correctional treatment alone can prevent delinquency, she does find it has important consequences for the psychological adjustment of offenders and their improved academic achievement.

On the other hand, an analysis of juvenile correctional treatment research between 1975 and 1984 by Steven Lab and John Whitehead indicates that treatment has little impact on recidivism.[69] The authors report that the state of the evidence concerning correctional treatment presents a vast disparity in opinion regarding whether treatment actually works.

One of the real problems with obtaining effective treatment involves adapting programs to the changing character of the juvenile offender population. In response to changes in race, gender, age, and even offenses over the last twenty years, changes must be made in program goals. For example, competency-based education, employment skills, and public service programs may be more relevant today than traditional counseling programs.

Another effort to improve treatment results is by developing valid objective classification systems in juvenile corrections. Susan Guarino-Ghezzi and James Byrne have identified a classification model for structured decision making in this area. Using classifications for risk, treatment, and control, these researchers believe a hierarchy of sanctions could increase accountability and control in juvenile justice policy making and lead to the development of more effective treatment programs in the future.[70]

The literature on the current state of treatment in correctional programs, particularly for chronic and violent youths, concludes that many approaches have been tried but little definitive knowledge has resulted from these programs. It is clear that traditional, large training schools are expensive and counterproductive and that more attention should be focused on evaluating different treatment approaches, intensive services, and community-based sanctions, as described in Chapter 18.

THE LEGAL RIGHT TO TREATMENT

The goal of placing children in institutions is basically to prepare them for a positive adjustment in the community. Therefore, lawyers in the field of juvenile justice claim that children in state-run institutions have a legal **right to treatment.**

The concept of a right to treatment was first introduced to the mental health field in 1960 by Morton Birnbaum.[71] He theorized that individuals who are deprived of their liberty because of a mental illness serious enough to require involuntary commitment are entitled to treatment to correct that condition. People for whom treatment is not provided are entitled to be released from the institution.[72]

FOCUS ON DELINQUENCY

Nelson v. Heyne

FACTS

In a class civil rights action on behalf of juvenile inmates of the Indiana Boys' School, a state institution, a complaint to the district court alleged that defendants' (Robert Heyne, commissioner of corrections; Robert Hardin, director of the Indiana Youth Authority; and Alfred Bennett, superintendent of Indiana Boys' School) practices and policies at the school violated the Eight and Fourteenth Amendment rights of the juveniles under their care. The alleged practices included the use of corporal punishment, solitary confinement for periods ranging from five to thirty days, intramuscular injections of tranquilizing drugs, and censorship of inmate mail.

The school itself was a medium-security state correctional institution for boys 12 to 18 years of age, where about one-third were noncriminal offenders. The average length of stay at the institution was about six and a half months, and although the school's maximum capacity was under three hundred boys, the usual population was about four hundred. The counseling staff included twenty persons, three of whom were psychologists with undergraduate degrees, and one part-time psychiatrist who spent four hours a week at the institution. The medical staff included one part-time medical physician, one registered nurse, and one licensed practical nurse.

The district court in this case found that it had jurisdiction over the case and thereafter held that the use of corporal punishment and the method of administering tranquilizing drugs by the defendants constituted cruel and unusual punishment in violations of the plaintiffs' Eighth and Fourteenth Amendment rights. In a separate judgment, the court found that the juveniles had a right to an affirmative treatment and that the school had not satisfied the minimal constitutional and statutory standards required. The defendants appealed on January 31, 1974, before the final relief was granted. The Seventh Circuit of the U.S. Court of Appeals granted review.

DECISION

In *Nelson v. Heyne*, the circuit court dealt with the issue of a juvenile's constitutional affirmative right to treatment within a closed institution. Specifically, the questions were (1) whether the practices alleged by the defendants were violations of the cruel and unusual punishment clause of the Eighth Amendment and (2) whether defendants had a constitutional right to rehabilitative treatment, and if so, whether the treatment as provided by the school was adequate. The court discussed the practices of

continued on next page

Not until 1966 did any court acknowledge any such right to treatment. That year, in *Rouse v. Cameron*, the District of Columbia Circuit Court of Appeals held that mentally ill individuals were entitled to treatment, an opinion based on interpretation of a District of Columbia statute.[73] Although the court did not expressly acknowledge a constitutional right to treatment, it implied that it could have reached the same decision on constitutional grounds:

Had appellant been found criminally responsible, he could have been confined a year, at most, however dangerous he might have been. He has been confined four years and the end is not in sight. Since this difference rests only on need for treatment, a failure to supply treatment may raise a question of due process of law. It has also been suggested that failure to supply treatment may violate the equal protection clause. . . . Indefinite confinement without treatment of one who has been found not criminally responsible may be so inhumane as to be "cruel and unusual punishment."[74]

The constitutional right to treatment suggested by the *Rouse* decision was further recognized in 1971 in *Wyatt v. Stickney.*[75] This case was particularly important

FOCUS ON DELINQUENCY

corporal punishment in light of the cruel and unusual punishment standard suggested in *Furman v. Georgia*, 408 U.S. 238, 279 (1971). By that standard, punishment is excessive if it is unnecessary, and it is unnecessary if less severe punishment would serve the same purpose.

Although the court did not find corporal punishment to be cruel and unusual per se, it did find that on the basis of undisputed expert testimony the beatings as applied were unnecessary and therefore excessive, thus violating the Eighth Amendment proscription against cruel and unusual punishment. The court next looked at the school's practice of administering tranquilizing drugs "to control excited behavior" without individual medical authorization and without first trying oral medication. Based on expert testimony at trial that established the possible serious side effects of these drugs, the court rejected the school's assertion that the use of drugs was not punishment. After stressing the need to balance the school's desire to maintain discipline with the child's right to be free from cruel and unusual punishment, the court held that the school's interest in reforming juveniles through the use of drugs in maintaining a rehabilitative atmosphere did not justify the cruel and unusual dangers resulting from poorly supervised administration of tranquilizing drugs.

Turning to the crucial holding by the district court that incarcerated juveniles have an affirmative right to rehabilitative treatment, the Seventh Circuit Court of Appeals noted that the Supreme Court has assumed, although it has not explicitly stated, that the state must provide treat- ment for incarcerated juveniles. In light of this, the court looked at several recent cases concerning the impact of the *parens patriae* doctrine on this right, most notably the case of *Martarella v. Kelly*, 349 F. Supp. 575 (S.D.N.Y.1972), in which the court found a clear constitutional right to treatment for juveniles based on the Eighth and Fourteenth Amendments. The appellate court agreed then with the lower court that the juveniles did indeed have a constitutional as well as a statutory right to rehabilitative treatment. Last, the court held that the Quay system of behavior classification used by the school was not treatment. Subsequently the case was remanded to allow the lower court to determine the "minimal standards of care and treatment for juveniles" needed to provide them with their "right to 'individualized' care and treatment."

SIGNIFICANCE OF THE CASE

Nelson v. Heyne is the first federal appellate court decision affirming that juveniles have a constitutional as well as a statutory right to treatment. It is also the first to hold that federal judges can require standards by which to judge minimal adherence by institutions to individualized treatment. ■

Source: Nelson v. Heyne, 491 F.2d 353 (7th Cir. 1974).

because it held that involuntary commitment without rehabilitation was a denial of due process of law. There is an "unquestionable . . . constitutional right" for those in noncriminal custody "to receive such individual treatment as will give each of them a realistic opportunity to be cured or to improve his or her mental condition."[76]

Of greater significance, however, is the U.S. Supreme Court's decision in the case of *O'Connor v. Donaldson* in 1975.[77] This case concerned the right to treatment of persons involuntarily committed to mental institutions. The court concluded that, except where treatment is provided, a state cannot confine persons against their will if they are not dangerous to themselves or to the community. In his concurring opinion, however, Chief Justice Warren Burger rejected the idea that a state has no authority to confine a mentally ill person unless it provides treatment. He also denied that commitment is the *quid pro quo* for treatment.

The right to treatment argument has expanded to include the juvenile justice system. One of the first cases to highlight this issue was *Inmates of the Boys'*

Training School v. Affleck in 1972.[78] This case analyzed conditions that allegedly violated juvenile constitutional rights to due process and equal protection and that constituted cruel and unusual punishment. *Affleck* was one of the first cases to describe some of the horrible conditions existing in many of the nation's training schools. The court argued that rehabilitation is the true purpose of the juvenile court and that without that goal, due process guarantees are violated. It condemned such devices as solitary confinement, strip cells, and the lack of educational opportunities and held that juveniles have a statutory right to treatment. The court also established the following minimum standards for all juveniles confined in training schools:

- A room equipped with lighting sufficient for an inmate to read by until 10 P.M.
- Sufficient clothing to meet seasonal needs
- Bedding, including blankets, sheets, pillows, pillow cases, and mattresses, to be changed once a week
- Personal hygiene supplies, including soap, toothpaste, towels, toilet paper, and toothbrush
- A change of undergarments and socks every day
- Minimum writing materials: pen, pencil, paper, and envelopes
- Prescription eyeglasses, if needed
- Equal access to all books, periodicals, and other reading materials located in the training school
- Daily showers
- Daily access to medical facilities, including provision of a twenty-four-hour nursing service
- General correspondence privileges[79]

These minimum requirements were expanded in *Martarella v. Kelly,* which analyzed juvenile treatment facilities and the confinement of persons in need of supervision in New York. The court held that failure to provide these juveniles with adequate treatment violated their right to due process and to be free from cruel and unusual punishment.[80]

In 1974, the case of **Nelson v. Heyne** was heard on appeal in the Seventh Circuit Court of Appeals in Indiana. Because of its significance for the right to treatment issue, the case is outlined in the Focus on Delinquency titled *"Nelson v. Heyne."*

In **Morales v. Turman,** the court held that all juveniles confined in training schools in Texas have a constitutional right to treatment. The court established numerous criteria for assessing placement, education skills, delivery of vocational education, medical and psychiatric treatment programs, and daily living conditions.[81]

The *Morales* case marked a historic step in the effort to extend the civil rights of children in institutions. This landmark case challenged conditions and practices in all five juvenile training schools in Texas. **Morales v. Turman** has had a national impact, establishing benchmark standards for the treatment of detained juveniles, including access to medical and psychiatric care, and meaningful education and appropriate disciplinary treatment.

In a more recent case in New York, *Pena v. New York State Division for Youth,* the court held that the use of isolation, hand restraints, and tranquilizing drugs at Goshen Annex Center was punitive and antitherapeutic and therefore violated the Fourteenth Amendment right to due process and the Eighth Amendment right to protection against cruel and unusual punishment.[82]

Current Status of the Right to Treatment

Although the U.S. Supreme Court has not yet ruled that juveniles have a constitutional right to treatment, the cases described above have served as a basis for many substantive changes in the juvenile justice system, most notably in the improvement of physical conditions in juvenile institutions and in the judiciary's recognition that it must take a more active role in the juvenile justice system.

The principle theories used by the courts for the right to treatment doctrine include: (1) arguments under the due process clause of the Fourteenth Amendment; (2) the use of the Eighth Amendment's prohibition against cruel and unusual punishment; (3) and the application of state statutory or constitutional provisions where rehabilitation is the purpose for which the juvenile offender has been confined.

However, the right to treatment has not been advanced in all instances, and the case law does not totally accept a legal right to treatment for juvenile offenders. For example, in *Ralston v. Robinson,* the Supreme Court rejected a youth's claim that he should continue to be given treatment after he was sentenced to a consecutive term in an adult prison for crimes committed while in a juvenile institution.[83] In reaching its decision, the Court rejected the concept that every juvenile offender, regardless of the circumstances, can benefit from treatment. In the *Robinson* case, the offender's proven dangerousness outweighed the possible effects of rehabilitation.

Similarly, in *Santana v. Callazo,* the influential U.S. First Circuit Court of Appeals rejected a suit brought by residents at the Maricao Juvenile Camp in Puerto Rico on the grounds that the administration had failed to provide them with an individualized, comprehensive rehabilitation plan or adequate treatment. The circuit court concluded that it was a legitimate exercise of state authority to incarcerate juveniles solely to protect society from them and that therefore the offender does not have a right to treatment per se. However, courts can evaluate each case individually to determine whether the youth is receiving adequate care.[84]

The *Callazo* case also considered the constitutionality of putting juveniles in isolation in detention facilities. After the U.S. Supreme Court denied a writ of certiorari, the lower court subsequently found that isolation practices can be considered constitutional where they are part of an overall custody and treatment plan for juvenile offenders.[85]

The future of the right to treatment for juveniles is somewhat uncertain. The courts have not gone so far as to order the creation of new programs, nor have they decided what constitutes minimal standards of specific individual treatment. However, federal courts have continued to hear on a case-by-case basis complaints that treatment is not up to minimal standards or that inappropriate disciplinary methods were being used. In one such case, *Gary H. v. Hegstrom,* a federal judge ruled that isolation punishments at the McClaren School for Boys in Oregon were excessive and that residents were being denied their right to treatment.[86]

The circuit court of appeals affirmed the lower court's judgment regarding the existence of unconstitutional conditions at the school and ordered due process hearings prior to confinement in excess of twenty-four hours and minimum sanitary, health, educational, and medical resources for the residents. But the wholesale adoption of various professional association standards for model institutions was not constitutionally mandated. The court also held that it was not appropriate to mandate dispositions that were so costly that other children be deprived of services. Some experts believe that a case like *Hegstrom* may eventually reach the Supreme Court and provide an avenue for a definite decision on the right to treatment. Thus far, minimum standards of care and treatment have been mandated on a case-by-case basis, but some courts have limited the constitutional protections regarding the right to treatment. In light of the new hard-line approach to juvenile crime, it does not appear that the courts will be persuaded to expand this constitutional theory further.

CHILDREN IN INSTITUTIONS

Struggle for Basic Rights

Several court cases and a large amount of publicity have led a number of federal and state groups to develop standards for the juvenile justice system, including its institutions.[87] The most comprehensive standards are those of the Institute of Judicial Administration-American Bar Association's joint project on juvenile justice standards; the American Correctional Association; and the National Council on Crime and Delinquency. These standards provide appropriate guidelines for conditions and practices in juvenile institutions. They call on juvenile corrections administrators to maintain a physically safe and healthy environment for incarcerated youths.

Today, state-sponsored brutality has been for the most part outlawed. The use of restraints, solitary confinement, and even medication for unruly residents has certainly not been completely eliminated. The courts, however, have consistently ruled that corporal punishment in any form, other than for one's own protection, is constitutionally unacceptable and violates standards of decency and human dignity.

Disciplinary systems are an important part of any institutional program. Most institutions maintain disciplinary boards that regulate and hear appeals by juvenile inmates on their disciplinary procedures. The case of *Wolff v. McDonnell* focused on due process requirements for disciplinary proceedings in adult institutions.[88] To provide the same rights for juveniles, several sets of standards have recommended similar rules and regulations governing juvenile institutional boards, including notice, representation by counsel, and the right to a written record of proceedings and decision. Many state court decisions involving children have affirmed the principles in *Wolff v. McDonnell.*

Isolation or "administrative segregation" is also an issue that has been subject to court review. The leading case, **Lollis v. New York State Department of Social Services,** concluded that confining a female status offender to a small room for a two-week period was unconstitutional.[89] Virtually all courts have generally reached similar conclusions. If juveniles are confined under such conditions, it is only if they are a serious threat to themselves or others, and even then they should be released as soon as possible.

In the past twenty years, there has been considerable litigation over conditions of confinement. Most of the litigation results from the violations of the constitutional rights of the residents and has become the basis for institutional reform.[90]

JUVENILE AFTERCARE

Aftercare in the juvenile justice system is the equivalent of parole in the adult criminal justice system. When juveniles are released from an institution through an early-release program or after completing their sentences, they may be placed in an aftercare program of some kind. The feeling is that children who have been institutionalized should not be abruptly returned to the community without proper help and supervision. Whether individuals who are in aftercare as part of an indeterminate sentence remain in the community or return to the institution for further rehabilitation depends on their actions during the aftercare period.

In a number of jurisdictions, the early release of juveniles resembles the adult parole process. A paroling authority that may be an independent body or part of the corrections department or some other branch of state services makes the release decision. Like adult parole, juvenile aftercare authorities look at the youth's adjustment within the institution, whether he or she is chemically dependent, what the crime was, and so on.

Some authorities are even making use of **parole guidelines** first developed with adult parolees. Each youth who enters a secure facility is given a recommended length of confinement that is explained at his or her initial interview with parole authorities. The stay is computed on the basis of the offense record influenced by aggravating and mitigating factors. The parole authority is not required to follow the recommended sentence but instead uses it as a tool in making decisions.[91] Whatever approach is used, several primary factors are considered by virtually all jurisdictions when recommending a juvenile for release. They are (1) institutional adjustment, (2) length of stay and general attitude, and (3) likelihood of success in the community.

Risk classifications have also been designed to help parole officers make decisions about which juveniles will receive aftercare services.[92]

Supervision

One purpose of aftercare is to give an individual some extra assistance during the readjustment period in the community. The institutionalized minor is likely to have a difficult time coping with life in the community after release. The experience of being in the institution generally has negative effects. First, the minor's activities have been tightly regimented for some time; once such restraints are removed, the youth may not find it easy to make independent decisions. Second, peers in the institution may have convinced the minor that he or she has been scapegoated by an unforgiving society. Furthermore, the community itself may view the returning minor with a good deal of prejudice; adjustment problems may reinforce a preexisting need to engage in bad habits or deviant behavior.

Juveniles in aftercare programs are supervised by a parole caseworker or counselor whose job is to provide surveillance by maintaining contact with the juvenile, to make sure that a corrections plan is followed, and to show interest and caring in order to help prevent further mistakes by the juvenile. The counselor also keeps the youth informed of available services that may assist in reintegration and counsels the youth and his or her family on the possible reason for the original problems.

Unfortunately, aftercare caseworkers, like probation officers, often carry such large caseloads that their jobs are next to impossible to do adequately.

Research has generally questioned the effectiveness of traditional juvenile parole programs (those involving casework and individual or group counseling). In one of the most impressive research efforts on the effectiveness of juvenile parole, Patrick Jackson randomly assigned subjects from the California Youth Authority to parole or outright discharge.[93] He found that youths under formal parole supervision were actually more likely to become reinvolved in serious offenses than those simply discharged and left on their own. However, there was relatively little difference between the two groups with respect to the chance of being arrested or serving time in another institution. Jackson found that the longer a person was retained on parole, the greater the chance of his or her being rearrested. Thus, Jackson finds that there are few beneficial elements of parole supervision and many potentially harmful side effects.

Despite the less-than-encouraging results of the Jackson research, there are indications that juvenile aftercare can be very effective if it is combined with innovative treatment efforts. For example, the Violent Juvenile Offender program discussed earlier used short-term incarceration with intensive follow-up in what appears to be a successful rehabilitory effort. Jeffery Fagan and his colleagues found that highly structured efforts to reintegrate youths into society can have better results than previously thought possible.[94] The Albuquerque (New Mexico) Girls Reintegration Center is an excellent example of a successful community-based program that prepares female juvenile offenders for their eventual release to their home community.[95] The program provides participants with positive role models, involvement in community activities, and realistic school and work experience.

Aftercare Revocation Procedures

A final issue in aftercare for juveniles concerns revocation procedures. Although adult parolees have been entitled to certain procedural rights in revocation proceedings since 1972, the Supreme Court has not yet extended the same rights to juveniles.[96] However, most states have extended these rights to juveniles on their own initiative. In addition, appellate courts that have considered juvenile aftercare revocation procedures have found that juveniles are entitled to the same due process as adult offenders. To avoid revocation, a juvenile parolee must meet the following conditions, among others: adhere to a reasonable curfew set by youth worker or parent; refrain from associating with persons whose influence would be detrimental, including but not limited to persons convicted of crimes or persons of a known criminal background; attend school in accordance with the law; abstain from drugs; abstain from alcohol; report to the youth worker when required; refrain from acts that would be crimes if committed by an adult; refrain from operating an automobile without permission of the youth worker or parent; refrain from being habitually disobedient and beyond the lawful control of parent or other legal authority; and refrain from running away from the lawful custody of parent or other lawful authority.

Certain procedural safeguards have been set up to ensure that revocation of juvenile parole is handled fairly:

1. Parolee must be notified of the specific conditions of parole.
2. Parolee must receive notice of allegations.
3. Parolee has the right to legal counsel at state expense if necessary.
4. Parolee has the right to confront and cross-examine witnesses.
5. Parolee has the right to introduce documentary evidence and witnesses.
6. Parolee has the right to a hearing before an independent hearing officer who shall be an attorney but not an employee of the revoking agency.

The use of these procedures has led to sound administrative decision making and adequate constitutional safeguards for juveniles in revocation hearings.

SUMMARY

The juvenile institution was developed in the mid-nineteenth century as an alternative to placing youths in adult prisons. Youth institutions developed over the years from large, closed institutions to today's open, cottage-based education- and rehabilitation-oriented institutions. Most institutions for youths feature libraries and recreational facilities and are low-security.

The juvenile institutional population has increased in recent years to more than ninety thousand residents, despite efforts to decarcerate status offenders and petty delinquent offenders. Although there has been a shrinking youth population and a stabilization in juvenile arrest rates, there appears to be evidence of higher rolls of incarceration in the future. In addition, increasing numbers of youths are being "hidden" in private mental centers and drug-treatment clinics.

Most institutions maintain intensive treatment programs featuring individual or group therapy. Although a wide variety of techniques are used around the nation, little evidence has been found that any single method is effective in reducing recidivism. Yet, the philosophy of treatment and rehabilitation remains an important goal of juvenile practitioners.

The chronic offender has come to be recognized as a major social problem. A number of states have set up intensive programs to deal with these hard-core offenders.

The right to treatment is a major issue in juvenile justice. This refers to legal decisions that mandate that a child cannot simply be warehoused in a correctional center and must be provided with proper care and treatment to aid rehabilitation. What constitutes proper care is still debated, and recent federal court decisions have backed off from holding that every youth can be rehabilitated. Gender is also a factor in access to treatment resources: institutions for females generally have fewer vocational and educational programs than those exclusively for male delinquents.

Most institutions have a standard set of rules and discipline. There have been many exposés of physical brutality in youth institutions, and courts have sought to restrain the use of physical punishment on inmates.

Most juveniles released from institutions are placed on juvenile parole or aftercare. There is little evidence that this type of community supervision is actually more beneficial than simply releasing youths on their own. Many jurisdictions are having success with community halfway houses and reintegration centers.

KEY TERMS

Paint Creek Youth Center
reform schools
cottage system
"decarceration"
least restrictive alternative
individual counseling
psychotherapy
reality therapy
behavior modification
group therapy
guided group interaction (GGI)
Positive Peer Culture (PPC)

chronic juvenile offender
suppression effect
life-style violent juveniles
Outward Bound
boot camps
right to treatment
Nelson v. Heyne
Morales v. Turman
Lollis v. New York State Department of Social Services
aftercare
parole guidelines

QUESTIONS FOR DISCUSSION

1. Should status offenders ever be institutionalized with delinquents? Are they really different?
2. What kinds of programs would you implement in a juvenile correctional center?
3. Do you believe that juveniles have a right to treatment? Should all offenders receive psychological counseling? What court decisions give credence to your position?
4. Is the use of physical punishment ever warranted in a juvenile institution? If not, how do you reconcile the fact that the Supreme Court has upheld the use of corporal punishment in public schools?
5. Identify and explain the current problems and issues in juvenile corrections. What possible solutions might you suggest?
6. In light of the extensive use of incarceration for juvenile offenders, do you think the trend toward determinate sentences for serious juvenile crime is desirable? Isn't such an approach in direct conflict with our decarceration policy?
7. How should society deal with the chronic juvenile offender? Is incarceration the only practical solution?
8. What is meant by the "legal right" to treatment? Do juveniles have such a right? Discuss the meaning of the cases dealing with this issue.

NOTES

1. Bureau of Justice Statistics, *Children in Custody 1975– 85—Census of Public and Private Juvenile Detention, Correctional and Shelter Facilities* (Washington, D.C.: Department of Justice, 1989), p. 4.
2. Edward Loughran, "Juvenile Corrections: The Massachusetts Experience." In *Reinvesting Youth Corrections Resources: A Tale of Three States,* ed L. Eddison (Minneapolis: Un. of Minnesota, Hubert Humphrey Institute of Public Affairs, 1987) p. 11–18.
3. Office of Justice Programs, *Private Sector Corrections for Juveniles—Paint Creek Youth Center* (Washington, D.C.: Office of Juvenile Justice and Delinquency Prevention, 1988).
4. Office of Justice Programs, *Children in Custody 1975–85* (Washington, D.C.: Department of Justice, 1989), p. 4.
5. For a detailed description of juvenile delinquency in the 1800s, see J. Hawes, *Children in Urban Society: Juvenile Delinquency in Nineteenth Century America* (New York: Oxford University Press, 1971).
6. D. Jarvis, *Institutional Treatment of the Offender* (New York: McGraw-Hill, 1978), p. 101.
7. Margaret Werner Cahalan, *Historical Corrections Statistics in the United States, 1850–1984* (Washington,D.C.: Department of Justice, 1986), pp. 104–5.
8. Clemons Bartollas, Stuart J. Miller, and Simon Dinitiz, *Juvenile Victimization: The Institutional Paradox* (New York: Wiley, 1976), p. 6.
9. LaMar T. Empey, *American Delinquency—Its Meaning and Construction* (Homewood, Ill.: Dorsey, 1978), p. 515.
10. Edward Eldefonso and Walter Hartinger, *Control, Treatment, and Rehabilitation of Juvenile Offenders* (Beverly Hills, Calif.: Glencoe, 1976), p. 151.
11. Ibid., p. 152.
12. M. Rosenthal, "Reforming the Justice Correctional Institution: Efforts of U.S. Children's Bureau in the 1930s," *Journal of Sociology and Social Welfare* 14:47–73 (1987).
13. Bureau of Justice Statistics, *Fact Sheet on Children in Custody* (Washington, D.C.: Department of Justice, 1989); also Barbara Allen-Hagen, *Public Juvenile Facilities— Children in Custody, 1989* (Washington, D.C.: Office of Juvenile Justice and Delinquency Prevention, 1991).
14. Paul Lerman, "Child Welfare, the Private Sector, and Community-Based Corrections," *Crime and Delinquency* 30:5–38 (1984).
15. Data in this and the following section comes from the federal government's *Children in Custody* series, published biennially by the U.S. Department of Justice's Bureau of Justice Statistics. (*Fact Sheet on Children in Custody, 1989.*)
16. Patricia Torbet, *Organization and Administration of Juvenile Services: Probation, Aftercare, and State Delinquent Institutions* (Pittsburgh: National Center for Juvenile Justice, September 1989), p. 4.
17. Ibid.
18. L. Rossi, "Maryland's Juvenile Services Agency: Giving Youths a Chance to Change," *Corrections Today* 51:130 (1989).
19. American Bar Association, Project on Standards for Juvenile Justice, *Standards Relating to Corrections Administration* (Cambridge, Mass.: Ballinger, 1977), Standard 2.1.
20. American Bar Association, Project on Standards for Juvenile Justice, *Standards Relating to Architecture of Facilities*, Standard 5.1, Commentary (Cambridge, Mass.: Ballinger, 1977), p. 50.

21. National Advisory Commission on Criminal Justice Standards and Goals, *Corrections* (Washington, D.C.: Government Printing Office, 1973), p. 348.

22. Clemens Bartollas and Christopher Sieverdes, "Coeducational Training Schools: Are They a Panacea for Juvenile Corrections?" *Juvenile and Family Court Journal* 34:15–20 (1983).

23. Cited in Alan Breed and Barry Krisberg, "Is There a Future?" *Corrections Today* 48:14–26 (1986).

24. "My Twenty Years of Child Advocacy," *Youth Law News,* 6:3 (1990).

25. Office of Justice Programs, *Children in Custody, 1989* (Washington, D.C.: Department of Justice, 1991), p. 10.

26. Ibid; p. 13; see also Office of Juvenile Justice and Delinquency Prevention, U.S. Department of Justice, *Children in Custody,* Public Juvenile Facilities, 1987. Reported in *Juvenile Justice Bulletin,* October 1988, p. 2.

27. Office of Juvenile Justice and Delinquency Prevention, *National Juvenile Custody Trends 1978–89* (Washington, D.C.: Department of Justice, 1992); "Survey on Juvenile Corrections," *Corrections Compendium* vol. 17, July 1992.

28. Breed and Krisberg, "Is There a Future?"; Terry Demchak, "Changes Anticipated in Arizona and Arkansas Juvenile Institutions," *Youth Law News* 10:8–10 (December 1989).

29. Edward Loughran, "How to Stop Kids from Going Bad," *Boston Globe,* 11 February 1990, p. A21.

30. Bureau of Justice Statistics, *Fact Sheet on Children in Custody,* p. 1.

31. Data is from Bureau of Justice Statistics, *Fact Sheet on Children in Custody: Public and Private Juvenile Facilities, 1989* (Washington, D.C.: Government Printing Office, 1989). See also Barbara Allen-Hagen, "Children in Custody," *Public Juvenile Facilities, 1989 OJJDP update* (Washington, D.C.: U.S. Department of Justice, 1991).

32. Office of Juvenile Justice and Delinquency Prevention, U.S. Department of Justice, "More Juveniles Held in Public Facilities," *Children in Custody,* (Washington, D.C.: U.S. Department of Justice/Bureau of Justice Statistics, September 1989), p. 2.

33. Ibid.; also see David Shichor and Clemens Bartollas, "Comparison of Private and Public Placements" (unpublished paper, California State University, San Bernadino, 1990), which calls for a nationwide effort to evaluate private placements for juvenile offenders.

34. Ira Schwartz, Marilyn Jackson-Beck, and Roger Anderson, "The 'Hidden' System of Juvenile Control," *Crime and Delinquency* 30:371–85 (1984).

35. Rebecca Craig and Andrea Paterson, "State Involuntary Committment Laws: Beyond Deinstitutionalization," *National Conference of State Legislative Reports* 13:1–10 (1988).

36. Bureau of Justice Statistics, U.S. Department of Justice, "More Juveniles Held in Public Facilities," from *Children in Custody* (Washington, D.C.: U.S. Department of Justice/ Bureau of Justice Statistics, September 1989), p. 1.

37. Barry Krisberg, Ira Schwartz, G. Fishman, Z. Eisikovits & E. Gitman, "The Incarceration of Minority Youth," *Crime and Delinquency* 33:173–205 (1987).

38. Bartollas, Miller, and Dinitz, *Juvenile Victimization.*

39. Christopher Sieverdes and Clemens Bartollas, "Security Level and Adjustment Patterns in Juvenile Institutions," *Journal of Criminal Justice* 14:135–45 (1986).

40. Several authors have written of this sexual double standard. See E. A. Anderson, "The Chivalrous Treatment of the Female Offender in the Arms of the Criminal Justice System: A Review of the Literature," *Social Problems* 23:350–57 (1976); G. Armstrong, "Females under the Law: Protected but Unequal," *Crime and Delinquency* 23:109–20 (1977); M. Chesney-Lind, "Judicial Enforcement of the Female Sex Role: The Family Court and the Female Delinquent," *Issues in Criminology* 8:51–59 (1973) and "Juvenile Delinquency: The Sexualization of Female Crime," *Psychology Today* 19:43–46 (July 1974); Allan Conway and Carol Bogdan, "Sexual Delinquency: The Persistence of a Double Standard," *Crime and Delinquency* 23:13–135 (1977); M. Chesney-Lind, *Girls, Delinquency and the Juvenile Justice System* (San Francisco: Brooks/Cole, 1991).

41. OJJDP, *National Juvenile Custody Trends,* p. 2.

42. Patricia Hersch, "Coming of Age on City Streets," *Psychology Today,* January 1988, p. 28; Daniel Campagna and Donald Puffengerger, *The Sexual Trafficking in Children: An Investigation of the Child Sex Trade* (Dover, Mass.: Auburn House, 1988).

43. "A Look at Juvenile Female Offenders," *Juvenile Corrections and Detention Newsletter* 2:6 (1988).

44. For a historical analysis of a girls' reformatory, see Barbara Brenzel, *Daughters of the State* (Cambridge: MIT Press, 1983).

45. Ilene R. Bergsmann, "The Forgotten Few Juvenile Female Offenders," *Federal Probation* 53:73–79 (1989).

46. For an interesting article highlighting the debate over the effectiveness of correctional treatment, see John Whitehead and Steven Lab, "Meta-Analysis of Juvenile Correctional Treatment," *Journal of Research in Crime and Delinquency* 26:276–95 (1989).

47. Robert D. Vinter, ed., *Time Out: A National Study of Juvenile Correction Programs* (Ann Arbor, Mich.: National Assessment of Juvenile Corrections, 1976), pp. 20–53.

48. Louise Sas and Peter Jaffe, "Understanding Depression in Juvenile Delinquency: Implications for Institutional Admission Policies and Treatment Programs," *Juvenile and Family Court Journal* 37:49–58 (1985–1986).

49. Dennis A. Romig, *Justice for Our Children: An Examination of Juvenile Delinquent Rehabilitation Programs* (Lexington, Mass.: Lexington Books, 1978), p. 81.

50. See, generally, William Glasser, "Reality Therapy: A Realistic Approach to the Young Offender," in Robert

Schaste and Jo Wallach, eds., *Readings in Delinquency and Treatment* (Los Angeles: Delinquency Prevention Training Project, Youth Studies Center, University of Southern California, 1965); see also Richard Rachin, "Reality Therapy: Helping People Help Themselves," *Crime and Delinquency* 16:143 (1974).

51. See Helen A. Klein, "Towards More Effective Behavior Programs for Juvenile Offenders," *Federal Probation* 41:45–50 (1977); Albert Bandura, *Principles of Behavior Modification* (New York: Holt, Rinehart & Winston, 1969); H. A. Klein, "Behavior Modification as Therapeutic Paradox," *American Journal of Orthopsychiatry* 44:353 (1974).

52. See J. N. Yong, "Advantages of Group Therapy in Relation to Individual Therapy for Juvenile Delinquents," *Corrective Psychiatry and Journal of Social Therapy* 17:37 (1971).

53. See LaMar T. Empey and Steven Lubeck, *The Silverlake Experiment* (Chicago: Aldine, 1971); H. Ashley Weeks, *Youthful Offenders at Highfields* (Ann Arbor, Mich.: University of Michigan Press, 1958); LaMar T. Empey and J. Rabow, "The Provo Experiment in Delinquency Rehabilitation," *American Sociological Review* 26:679 (1961).

54. Larry Brendtero and Arlin Ness, "Perspectives on Peer Group Treatment: The Use and Abuses of Guided Group Interaction/Positive Peer Culture," *Child and Youth Services Review* 4:307–24 (1982).

55. Bruno Bettleheim, *The Empty Fortress* (New York, Free Press, 1967).

56. See *California Youth Authority Newsletter*, Ventura School for Juvenile Female Offenders (Ventura, Calif.: California Youth Authority, 1988).

57. Charles Murray and Louis B. Cox, *Beyond Probation* (Beverly Hills, Calif.: Sage, 1979).

58. Andrew Vachss and Yitzhak Bakal, *The Life-Style Violent Juvenile* (Lexington, Mass.: Lexington Books, 1979).

59. Ibid., p. 11.

60. Robert Mathias, Paul DeMuro, and Richard Allinson, eds., *Violent Juvenile Offender* (San Francisco: National Council on Crime and Delinquency, 1984).

61. Peter Greenwood and Franklin Zimring, *One More Chance, The Pursuit of Promising Intervention Strategies for Chronic Juvenile Offenders* (Santa Monica, Calif.: Rand Corp., 1985).

62. See Thomas Castellano and Irina Soderstrom, "Therapeutic Wilderness Programs and Juvenile Recidivism: A Program Evaluation," *Journal of Offender Rehabilitation* 17:19–46 (1992); Troy Armstrong, ed., *Intensive Interventions in High Risk Youth: Approaches in Juvenile Probation and Parole* (New York: Willow Tree Press, 1991).

63. Donna Martin Hamparian, Joseph Davis, Judith Jacobson, and Robert McGraw, *The Young Criminal Years of the Violent Few* (Washington, D.C.: Department of Justice, 1985), p. 8.

64. Donna Hamparian, Richard Schuster, Simon Dinitz, and John Conrad, *The Violent Few* (Lexington, Mass.: Lexington Books, 1975).

65. Martin Forst, Jeffrey Fagan, and T. Scott Vivana, "Youth in Prisons and Training Schools: Perceptions and Consequences," *Juvenile and Family Court Journal* 40:1–15 (1989).

66. William J. Taylor, "Tailoring Boot Camps to Juveniles," *Corrections Today* July 1992, p. 124.

67. Greenwood and Zimring, *One More Chance*.

68. Carol Garrett, "Effects of Residential Treatment on Adjudicated Delinquents: A Meta-Analysis," *Journal of Research in Crime and Delinquency* 22:287–308 (1985).

69. S. Lab and J. Whitehead, "Analysis of Juvenile Correctional Treatment," *Crime and Delinquency* 34:60–83 (1988).

70. Susan Guarino-Ghezzi and James Byrne, "Developing a Model of Structured Decision Making in Juvenile Corrections: The Mass Experience," *Crime and Delinquency* 35:270–303 (1989).

71. Morton Birnbaum, "The Right to Treatment," *American Bar Association Journal* 46:499 (1960).

72. Discussed in Adrienne Volenik, "Right to Treatment: Case Developments in Juvenile Law," *Justice System Journal* 3:292–307 (1978).

73. 373 F.2d 451 (D.C.Cir. 1966).

74. Ibid., p. 453.

75. 325 F. Supp. 781 (1971); see also Note, "*Wyatt v. Stickney*—A Constitutional Right to Treatment for the Mentally Ill," *University of Pittsburgh Law Review* 34:79–84 (1972).

76. 325 F. Supp. 373, 784 (1972).

77. 422 U.S. 563 (1975).

78. 346 F. Supp. 1354 (D.R.I. 1972).

79. Ibid., p. 1343.

80. 349 F. Supp. 575 (S.D.N.Y. 1972).

81. 383 F. Supp. 53 (E.D. Texas 1974).

82. 419 F. Supp. 203 (S.D.N.Y. 1976).

83. 102 S.Ct. 233 (1981).

84. 714 F.2d 1172 (1st Cir. 1983).

85. 466 U.S. 974 (1984), writ of certiorari denied.

86. 831 F.2d 1430 (1987); see also David Lambert, "Children in Institutions," *Youth Law News* 8:10–14 (1987).

87. Harry Swanger, Mark Soler, Alice Shotton, James Bell, Elizabeth Jameson, Carole Shauffer, Loren Warboys, Susan Burrell and Claudia Wright, "Juvenile Institutional Litigation," *Clearinghouse Review* 11:219–21 (1977). Swanger reports that the National Juvenile Law Center in St. Louis has been involved in litigation since 1972 that has sought and obtained reform of such practices as solitary confinement, disciplinary procedures, corporal punishment, forced drugging, and of institutional rules. Examples of the litigation include the following cases: *Nelson v. Heyne*, 355 F. Supp. 451

(N.D. Ind. 1972); *Inmates v. Affleck,* 346 F. Supp. 1354 (D.R.I. 1972); *Morales v. Turman,* 383 F. Supp. 53 (E.D. Tex. 1974). See also Mark Soler, *Representing the Child Client* (New York: Bender & Co., 1988), Release #9, 1993.

88. 418 U.S. 539 (1974).

89. 322 F. Supp. 473 (1970).

90. For extensive analysis of juvenile law, see Samuel Davis, *Rights of Juveniles, the Juvenile Justice System* (New York: Clark Boardman, 1993); also Joseph Senna and Larry Siegel, *Juvenile Law—Cases and Comments* (St. Paul: West, 1992).

91. Michael Norman, "Discretionary Justice: Decision Making in a State Juvenile Parole Board," *Juvenile and Family Court Journal* 37:19–26 (1985–1986).

92. James Maupin, "Risk Classification Systems and the Provisions of Juvenile Aftercare," *Crime and Delinquency* 39:90–105 (1993).

93. Patrick Jackson, *The Paradox of Control: Parole Supervision of Youthful Offenders* (New York: Praeger, 1983).

94. Jeffrey Fagan, Cary Rudman, and Eliot Hartstone, "Intervening with Violent Juvenile Offenders: A Community Reintegration Model," in Robert Mathias, Paul DeMuro, and Richard Allinson, eds., *Violent Juvenile Offenders* (San Francisco: National Council on Crime and Delinquency, 1984), pp. 207–31.

95. "Girls Reintegration Center—Albuquerque, New Mexico," *Juvenile and Corrections Newsletter* 2:6 (1988).

96. See *Morrissey v. Brewer,* 408 U.S. 471, 92 S.Ct. 2593, 33 L.Ed.2d 484 (1972). Upon revocation of adult parole, a defendant is entitled to the due process rights of (1) a hearing, (2) written notice of charges, (3) knowledge of evidence against him or her, (4) opportunity to present and cross-examine witnesses, and (5) a written statement of reasons for parole revocation. Most jurisdictions require that these procedures be applied to juveniles.

AMERICAN DELINQUENCY

■■

In this text, the authors have reviewed in great detail the current knowledge of the nature, cause, and correlates of juvenile delinquency and society's efforts to bring about its elimination and control. We have analyzed research programs, theoretical models, governmental policies, and legal cases. Taken in sum, this information presents a rather broad and complex picture of the youth crime problem and the most critical issues confronting the juvenile justice system. Delinquents come from a broad spectrum of society; kids of every race, gender, class, region, family type, and culture are involved in delinquent behaviors. To combat youthful law violations, society has tried a garden variety of intervention and control strategies: tough law enforcement; counseling, treatment and rehabilitation; provision of legal rights; community action; educational programs; family change strategies. Yet, despite decades of intense effort and study, it is still unclear why delinquency occurs and what, if anything, can be done to control its occurrence. One thing is for certain, juvenile crime is one of the most serious domestic problems faced by Americans.

Though uncertainty prevails, it is possible to draw some inferences about youth crime and its control. After reviewing the material contained in this volume, certain conclusions seem self-evident. Some involve social facts; that is, particular empirical relationships and associations have been established that have withstood multiple testing and verification efforts. Other conclusions involve social questions; there are issues that need clarification, and the uncertainty surrounding them has hampered progress in combating delinquency and treating known delinquents.

To sum up, we have assembled some of the most important social facts in this volume and some of the most important social questions that still remain to be answered. They are the focus for juvenile justice in the last decade of the twentieth century.

1. **The statutory concept of juvenile delinquency is in need of review and modification.** Today, the legal definition of a juvenile delinquent is a minor child, usually under the age of 17, who has been found to have violated the criminal law (juvenile code). The concept of juvenile delinquency occupies a legal position falling somewhere between criminal and

civil law in most jurisdictions. Some states, for example, end juvenile court jurisdiction at age 18, while others treat juveniles as adults when they are younger, such as 16 or 17 years of age. Serious consideration must be given to a redefinition of the jurisdictional aspects of juvenile criminality and the future of the juvenile court system.

2. **The concept of the status offender (PINS, CHINS, and MINS) needs to be clarified.** When a child is subject to state authority because of school truancy, incorrigibility, or being a runaway, such behavior is considered noncriminal but consistent with the **parens patriae** philosophy of giving the state jurisdiction to protect the best interest of the child. Separating the status offender from the juvenile delinquent avoids the stigma associated with the delinquency label. However, reforming the treatment for status offenders, as well as the possibility of eliminating the juvenile court's jurisdiction over such behaviors, need to be evaluated.

3. **Measuring juvenile delinquency requires that all methods of data collection be evaluated, including official statistics from the Uniform Crime Reports, self-report studies, victimization data, juvenile court data and information from the Children in Custody Series.** Official statistical information dealing with juvenile delinquency rates in the United States indicate that about 1.5 million youths were arrested by the police in 1992. Uniform Crime Report data indicates that the number of juveniles arrested has declined for more than a decade. While the general public has been skeptical of this conclusion, national crime survey data and victimization reports also agree that delinquency rates have either declined or stabilized. However, the disturbing news is that young people are committing proportionally more criminal behavior than those in any other age category. Today the public favors adjudicating juveniles who commit serious crimes in the adult courts.

4. **Substance abuse is closely associated with juvenile crime and delinquency.** Today, there is great uncertainty about the trends in teenage substance abuse. Although the total number of arrests involving legal minors has declined, those held for substance abuse have increased significantly. Surveys of arrested juveniles indicate sizable numbers of young people are involved with drugs and alcohol throughout the United States. Most efforts in the juvenile justice system to treat young offenders involved with substance abuse seem to be unsuccessful. Traditional prevention efforts and education programs have not had encouraging results.

5. **The chronic violent juvenile offender is a serious social problem for society and the juvenile justice system.** Official crime data indicates that the juvenile violence rate is at an all-time high. Chronic male delinquent offenders commit a disproportionate amount of violent behavior including a significant amount of the most serious juvenile crimes, such as homicides, rapes, robberies, and aggravated assaults. Many chronic offenders become adult criminals and eventually end up in the criminal court system. How to effectively deal with chronic juvenile offenders and drug users remains a high priority for the juvenile justice system.

Chronic juvenile delinquency has unquestionably become a major concept within the field. The best approach to dealing with chronic offenders remains uncertain, but concern about such offenders has shifted juvenile justice policy toward a punishment-oriented philosophy.

6. **There is basic disagreement in the juvenile justice system over the relationship between social class and juvenile crime.** In addition, there is uncertainty as to the relationship between race and juvenile delinquency. While some experts believe that class position influences crime rates, others disagree that lower class structure predetermines juvenile delinquent behavior. Furthermore, the existing data does not conclusively suggest that racial differences in the crime rate can be explained by an association between race, class, and antisocial behavior. Thus, research continues to be needed to determine what the true relationship is between these variables.

7. **No single scientific theory adequately explains the problem of juvenile delinquency.** Despite years of social research, no theory or combination of theories provides conclusive insight into the onset and location of delinquency and the causation of youth crime. While social psychological theories, such as those involving learning and social control, can help us better understand why some youths become delinquent and criminal, they fail to fully account for differences in delinquency rates across ecological areas, ranging from neighborhoods within a city to different regions throughout the country. These theories also fail to explain important individual differences between children who commit crime in high crime areas and those who do not.

8. **The life course perspective is becoming an emerging force in the study of delinquency.** Delinquency experts are now researching such issues as the onset, escalation, termination and continuation of a delinquent career. Growing evidence suggests that factors which emerge over the life course influence behavior choices. This evidence explains the influence of peers, education and family on delinquent behavior.

9. **Environmental influences, such as family relationships, affect patterns of behavior.** Over the years, family relationships have long been linked to the problem of juvenile delinquency by many experts. Broken homes, for instance, are not in and of themselves a cause of delinquency, but some evidence indicates that single-parent households are more inclined to produce delinquency-promoting behavior. In addition, there seems to be a strong association in family relationships between child abuse and delinquency. Cases of abuse and neglect have been found in every level of the economic strata, and a number of studies have linked child abuse and neglect to juvenile delinquency. While the evidence is not conclusive, it does suggest that a strong relationship exists between child abuse and subsequent delinquent behavior. Some experts believe a major effort is needed to reestablish parental accountability and responsibility.

10. **Female delinquency has become a serious topic of concern to experts in the juvenile justice system.** The nature and extent of female delinquent activities changed in the late 1980s, and it now appears that girls are engaging in more frequent and serious illegal activity in the 1990s. Female crime rates have increased in recent years, and the nature of female juvenile delinquency and youth crime is now similar in some respects to that of male delinquency.

11. **Juvenile gangs have become a serious and growing problem in many major metropolitan areas throughout the United States.** Ethnic youth gangs, mostly males aged 14 to 21, appear to be increasing in such areas as Los Angeles, Chicago, Boston, and New York. Sound empirical data on what

causes gang delinquency is currently unavailable. One view of gang development is that such groups serve as a bridge between adolescence and adulthood in communities where adult social control is not available. Another view suggests that gangs are a product of lower-class social disorganization and that they serve as an alternative means of advancement for poorly motivated and uneducated youth. Today's gangs are more often commercially than culturally oriented, and profit from the drug trade is generally a significant motive for gang behavior. Violent crime often results from such activity.

12. **Many of the underlying problems of youth crime and delinquency are directly related to education.** Numerous empirical studies have confirmed that lack of educational success is an important contributing factor in delinquency. Today, young people spend considerable time in school. Educational institutions are obviously one of the primary instruments of socialization. Since a great deal of delinquent activity takes place on school grounds and since dropping out of school is associated with antisocial behavior, experts generally agree that children who are unsuccessful in school are more likely to commit delinquent acts. School-based crime control projects have not been very successful, and a great deal more effort is needed in this critical area of school-delinquency prevention control.

13. **An analysis of the history of juvenile justice over the past 100 years shows how our policy regarding delinquency has gone through cycles of reform.** Many years ago, society primarily focused on the treatment of youth who committed criminal behavior often through no fault of their own. Today, society is concerned with the control of serious juvenile offenders and the development of firm sentencing provisions in the juvenile courts. These cycles represent the shifting philosophies of the juvenile justice system.

14. **Today, no single ideology or view dominates the direction, programs, and policies of the juvenile justice system.** Throughout the past decade, numerous competing positions regarding juvenile justice have emerged. As the liberal program of the 1970s has faltered, more restrictive sanctions have been imposed. The "crime control" position seems most formidable today. However, there remains a great deal of confusion over what the juvenile justice system does, what it should do, and how it should deal with youthful antisocial behavior.

15. **Today's problems in the juvenile justice system can often be traced to the uncertainty of its founders, the "child savers."** Such early twentieth-century groups formed the juvenile justice system on the misguided principle of reforming wayward youth and remodeling their behavior. The "best interest of the child" standard has long been the guiding light in juvenile proceedings, calling for the strongest available rehabilitative services. Today's juvenile justice system is often torn between playing the role of social versus crime control agent.

16. **In recent years, the juvenile justice system has become more legalistic by virtue of U.S. Supreme Court decisions that have granted children procedural safeguards in various court proceedings.** The case of *In re Gault* of the 1960s motivated state legislators to revamp their juvenile court legal procedures. Today, the Supreme Court is continuing to struggle with making distinctions between the legal rights of adults and minors. Recent Court decisions that allowed children to be searched by teachers and

denied their right to a jury trial showed that the Court continues to recognize a legal separation between adult and juvenile offenders.

17. **Despite some dramatic distinctions, juveniles have gained many of the legal due process rights adults enjoy.** Among the more significant elements of due process are the right to counsel, evidence efficiency, protection from double jeopardy and self-incrimination, and the right to appeal. The public continues to favor providing juveniles with the same due process and procedural guarantees accorded to adults.

18. **The death penalty for children has been upheld by the Supreme Court.** According to the *Wilkins v. Missouri* and *Stanford v. Kentucky* cases in 1989, the Supreme Court concluded that states are free to impose the death penalty for murderers who commit their crimes while age 16 or 17. According to the majority decision written by Justice Antonin Scalia, society has not formed a consensus that such executions are a violation of the cruel and unusual punishment clause of the Eighth Amendment.

19. **One of the most significant changes in American law enforcement has been the emergence of community policing in the field of delinquency prevention.** Community participation and cooperation, citizen crime prevention programs, and education programs such as Project DARE (drug education) have become a mainstay of law enforcement in the 1980s and early 1990s and have had a particularly significant impact on improving perceptions of community safety and the quality of community life in many areas.

20. **The use of detention in the juvenile justice system continues to be a widespread problem.** After almost two decades of work, virtually all jurisdictions have passed laws requiring that status offenders be placed in shelter care programs rather than detention facilities. Another serious problem related to the use of juvenile detention is the need to remove young people from lockups in adult jails. The Office of Juvenile Justice and Delinquency Prevention continues to give millions of dollars in aid to encourage the removal of juveniles from such adult lockups. But eliminating the confinement of children in adult institutions remains an enormously difficult task in the juvenile justice system.

21. **The use of waiver, bind-over, and transfer provisions in juvenile court statutes has been growing.** This trend has led toward a criminalization of the juvenile system. Since there are major differences between the adult and juvenile court systems, transfer to an adult court exposes youths to more serious consequences of their antisocial behavior and is a strong recommendation of those favoring a crime-control model. Waiver of serious offenders is one of the most significant developments in the trend to criminalize the juvenile court.

22. **The role of the attorney in the juvenile justice process requires further research and analysis.** Most attorneys appear to be uncertain whether they should act as adversaries or advocates in the juvenile process. In addition, the role of the juvenile prosecutor has become more significant as a result of new and more serious statutory sentencing provisions, as well as legal standards promulgated by such organizations as the American Bar Association and the National District Attorneys Association.

23. **Juvenile sentencing procedures now reflect the desire to create uniformity and limited discretion in the juvenile court, and this trend is likely to continue.** Many states have now developed such

programs as mandatory sentences, sentencing guidelines, and limited-discretion sentencing to bring uniformity into the juvenile justice system. As a result of the public's fear about serious juvenile crime, legislators have amended juvenile codes to tighten up juvenile sentencing provisions.

24. **In the area of community sentencing, new forms of probation supervision have become commonplace in recent years.** Intensive probation supervision, balanced probation, wilderness probation, and electronic monitoring have become important community-based alternatives over the last few years. Probation continues to be the single most significant intermediate sanction available to the juvenile court system.

25. **Victim restitution is another widely used and programatic method of community treatment in today's juvenile justice system.** In what is often referred to as monetary restitution; children are required to pay the victims of their crimes or in some instances provide some community service directly to the victim. Restitution provides the court with an important alternative sentencing option and has been instituted by statute in virtually every jurisdiction in the country.

26. **Deinstitutionalization has become an important goal of the juvenile justice system.** The Office of Juvenile Justice and Delinquency Prevention has provided funds to encourage this process. In the early 1980s, the deinstitutionalization movement seemed to be partially successful. Admissions to public juvenile correctional facilities declined in the late 1970s and early 1980s. In addition, the number of status offenders being held within the juvenile justice system was reduced. However, the number of institutionalized children in recent years has increased, and the deinstitutionalization movement has failed to meet all of its optimistic goals.

27. **The number of incarcerated youths continues to rise despite declining arrest rates.** Today, there are over 93,000 youths in some type of correctional institution. The juvenile courts seem to be using the most severe of the statutory dispositions, that is, commitment to the juvenile institution, rather than the "least restrictive statutory alternative." In addition, there seems to be a disproportionate number of minority youths incarcerated in youth facilities. The minority incarceration rate is almost four times greater than that for whites and minorities seem to be placed more often in public than in private treatment facilities. The overall organization of the juvenile justice system in the United States is changing. Early on, institutional services for children were provided by the public sector. Today, private facilities and programs service a significant proportion of juvenile admissions. In the next decade, many more juvenile justice systems will most likely adopt privatization of juvenile correctional services.

28. **Despite the growth of alternative treatment programs such as diversion, restitution, and probation, the number of children under secure institutional care has increased, and the success of such programs remains very uncertain.** Nearly all juvenile institutions utilize some form of treatment program for the children in their care. Despite generally positive intentions, the goal of rehabilitation in an institutional setting is very difficult to achieve and rarely attained. Reforms in state juvenile institutions often result from class action lawsuits filed on behalf of incarcerated youth such as the recent case of *Johnson v. Upchurch* in Arizona in 1993.

29. **The future of the legal right to treatment for juveniles remains uncertain.** The appellate courts have established minimum standards of care and treatment on a case-by-case basis, but it does not appear that the courts can be persuaded today to expand this constitutional theory to mandate that incarcerated children receive adequate treatment. Eventually, this issue must be clarified by the Supreme Court.

A serious crisis exists in the U.S. juvenile justice system. How to cope with the needs of large numbers of children in trouble remains one of the most controversial and frustrating issues in our society. The magnitude of the problem is such that over 1.5 million youths are arrested each year; over 1.3 million delinquency dispositions and one million status offense cases are heard in court; and drug abuse is a significant factor in more than 60 percent of all the cases referred to the juvenile courts. Today, the system and the process seem more concerned with crime control and more willing to ignore the rehabilitative ideal. Perhaps the answer lies outside the courtroom in the form of greater job opportunities, improved family relationships, and more effective education. Much needs to be done in delinquency prevention.

GLOSSARY

acquittal Release or discharge, especially by verdict of a jury.

action Lawsuit; a proceeding taken in a court of law. Actions are either civil (to enforce a right) or criminal (to punish an offender).

addict A person with an overpowering physical and psychological need to continue taking a particular substance or drug by any means possible.

addiction-prone personality The view that the cause of substance abuse can be traced to a personality which has a compulsion for mood altering drugs.

adjudicated Having been the subject of completed criminal or juvenile proceedings and having been convicted or declared a delinquent, a status offender, or a dependent.

adjudication (juvenile) Juvenile court decision, terminating a hearing, that the juvenile is a delinquent, a status offender, or a dependent or that the allegations in the petition are not sustained.

adjudicatory hearing In juvenile proceedings, the fact-finding process wherein the juvenile court determines whether there is sufficient evidence to sustain the allegations in a petition.

adjustment Settlement or bringing to a satisfactory state so that parties are agreed without official intervention of the court.

adversary system Procedure used to determine truth in the adjudication of guilty or innocence, which pits the defense (advocate for the accused) against the prosecution (advocate for the state), with the judge acting as arbiter of the legal rules. Under the adversary system, the burden is on the state to prove the charges beyond a reasonable doubt. This system of having the two parties publicly debate has proved to be the most effective method of achieving the truth regarding a set of circumstances. (Under the accusatory, or inquisitorial, system that is used in continental Europe, the charge is evidence of guilt that the accused must disprove; the judge takes an active part in the proceedings.)

affidavit Written statement of fact, signed and sworn to before a person having authority to administer an oath.

aftercare Supervision given children for a limited period of time after they are released from a training school but still under the control of the school or of the juvenile court.

age of onset Age at which youths begin their delinquent careers. Early onset of delinquency is believed to be linked with chronic offending patterns.

aggregate measures Data collected on groups of people rather than individuals. A good example of aggregate data is the Uniform Crime Reports index crimes; though the number of criminal incidents that occur in a given area can be counted, little data is provided on the offenders who commit them or the circumstances in which they occurred. Self-report surveys are usually considered individual-level data, since subjects' responses can be examined on a case-by-case basis.

aging out Refers to the phenomenon in which people spontaneously reduce the rate of their criminal behavior as they mature.

alienation Mental condition marked by normlessness and role confusion.

androgens Male sex hormones.

anesthetics Drugs such as PCP, which are used as nervous system depressants. Local anesthetics block nervous system transmissions; general anesthetics act on the brain to produce a generalized loss of sensation, stupor, or unconsciousness.

anomie Normlessness that is produced by rapidly shifting moral values. An anomic person has few guides to what is socially acceptable behavior. According to Merton, anomie is a condition that occurs when personal goals cannot be achieved by available means.

appeal Review of lower court proceedings by a higher court. There is no constitutional right to appeal. However, the "right" to appeal is established by statute in some states and by custom in others. All states set conditions as to type of case or grounds for appeal, which appellate courts may review. An appellate court does not retry the case under review. Rather, the transcript of the lower court case is read by the judges, and the lawyers for the defendant and for the state argue about the merits of the appeal—that is, the legality of lower court proceedings, instead of the original testimony. Appeal is more a process for controlling police, court, and correctional practices than for rescuing innocent defendants. When appellate courts do reverse lower court judgments, it is usually because of "prejudicial error" (deprivation of rights), and the case is remanded for retrial.

appellant Party who initiates an appeal from one court to another.

appellee Party in a lawsuit against whom an appeal has been taken.

arrest Taking of a person into the custody of the law, the legal purpose of which is to restrain the accused until he or she can be held accountable for the offense at court proceedings. The legal requirement for an arrest is probable cause. Arrests for investigation, suspicion, or harassment are improper and of doubtful legality. The police have the responsibility to use only the reasonable physical force necessary to make an arrest. The summons has been used as a substitute for arrest.

arrest warrant Written court order by a magistrate authorizing and directing that an individual be taken into custody to answer criminal charges.

atavistic According to Lombroso, the primitive physical characteristics that distinguish born criminals from the general population. Lombrosian theory holds that characteristics of criminals are throwbacks to animals or primitive people.

Augustus, John Individual credited with pioneering the concept of probation.

authoritarian Person whose personality revolves around blind obedience to authority.

bail Amount of money that has to be paid as a condition of pretrial release, normally set by a judge at the initial appearance. The purpose of bail is to ensure that people accused of crimes will return for subsequent proceedings. If they are unable to make bail, they are detained in jail.

Beccaria Eighteenth-century Italian philosopher who argued that crime could be controlled by punishments only severe enough to counterbalance the pleasure obtained from them.

behaviorism Branch of psychology concerned with the study of observable behavior rather than unconscious motives. It focuses on the relationship between particular stimuli and people's responses to them.

beyond a reasonable doubt Degree of proof required for conviction of a defendant in criminal and juvenile delinquency proceedings. It is less than absolute certainty but more than high probability. If there is doubt based on reason, the accused is entitled to the benefit of that doubt by acquittal.

biosocial The view that thought and behavior have both biological and social bases.

booking Administrative record of an arrest made in a police station. It involves listing of the offender's name, address, physical description, date of birth, employer, time of arrest and offense and the name of arresting officer. Photographing and fingerprinting of the offender are also part of booking. The *Miranda* warning is given again (the first time was at the scene of the arrest). In addition, the accused is allowed to make a telephone call.

burden of proof Duty of proving disputed facts on the trial of a case. The duty commonly lies on the person who asserts the affirmative of an issue and is sometimes said to shift when sufficient evidence is furnished to raise a presumption that what is alleged is true.

bourgeoisie In Marxist theory, the owners of the means of production; the capitalist ruling class.

capital punishment Use of the death penalty to punish transgressors.

career criminal Person who repeatedly violates the law and organizes his or her life-style around criminality. A chronic offender.

case law Law derived from previous court decisions; opposed to statutory law, which is passed by legislatures.

certiorari Literally, "to be informed of, to be made certain in regard to." The name of a writ of review or inquiry.

chancery court Court proceedings created in fifteenth-century England to oversee the lives of high-born minors who were orphaned or otherwise could not care for themselves.

child abuse Any physical, emotional, or sexual trauma to a child for which no reasonable explanation, such as an accident, can be found. Child abuse can also be neglecting to give proper care and attention.

child savers Nineteenth-century reformers who developed programs for troubled youth and influenced legislation creating the juvenile justice system. Today, some critics view them as being more concerned with the control of the poor than with their welfare.

chivalry hypothesis View that the low female crime and delinquency rates are a reflection of the leniency with which police treat female offenders.

choice theory The school of thought that holds that people will engage in delinquent and criminal behavior after weighing the consequences and benefits of their actions.

cholo Latino street youth culture.

chronic delinquent   Youth who has been arrested five or more times during his or her minority. This small portion of the offending population are believed to engage in a significant portion of all delinquent behavior.

chronicity   State of being a chronic recidivist.

classical theory   Theoretical perspective suggesting that (1) people have free will to choose criminal or conventional behaviors; (2) people choose to commit crime for reasons of greed or personal need; (3) crime can be deterred through fear of punishment.

clearance   Crime reported to the police that is "solved" by an arrest.

cocaine   The most powerful natural stimulant. Its use produces euphoria, laughter, restlessness, and excitement. Overdoses can cause delirium, increased reflexes, violent manic behavior, and possible respiratory failure.

cognitive theory   Study of the perception of reality; the mental processes required to understand the world we live in.

cohort study   Study utilizing a sample of people who share a single characteristic, such as place of birth, and whose behavior is followed over a period of time.

commitment   Action of a judicial officer ordering that an adjudicated and sentenced adult or adjudicated delinquent or status offender who has been the subject of a juvenile court disposition hearing be admitted to a correctional facility.

common law   Basic legal principles that developed in England and became uniform (common) throughout the country. Judges began following previous court decisions (precedent) when new but similar cases arose.

community facility (nonconfinement facility, adult or juvenile)   Correctional facility from which residents are regularly permitted to depart, unaccompanied by an official, to use community resources, such as schools or treatment programs, or to seek or hold employment.

community policing   Police strategy that emphasizes fear reduction, community organization, and order maintenance, rather than crime fighting.

concurrent sentences   Literally, running sentences together. The condition set for serving sentences of imprisonment for multiple charges. When people are convicted of two or more charges, they must be sentenced on each charge. If the sentences are concurrent, they begin the same day and are completed after the longest term has been served. (*See also* consecutive sentences.)

conduct norms   Behaviors that are expected of social group members. If group norms conflict with those of the general culture, members of the group may find themselves described as outcasts or criminals.

conflict theory   View that conflict among interest groups, especially those of opposing socioeconomic classes, is the main determinant of human behavior.

consecutive sentences   Literally, sentences that follow one another. Upon completion of one sentence, the other term of incarceration begins. (*See also* concurrent sentences.)

consent decree   Decree entered by consent of the parties. Not properly a judicial sentence but in the nature of a solemn contract or agreement of the parties that the decree is a just determination of their rights based on the real facts of the case, if such facts are proved.

containments   According to Reckless, internal and external factors and conditions that help insulate youths from delinquency-promoting situations. Most important of the internal containments is a strong self-concept, while external containments include positive support from parents and teachers.

constitutional law   Branch of public law of a state that maintains the framework of political and government authorities and functions in accordance with the state's constitution.

conviction   Judgment of guilt; verdict by a jury, plea by a defendant, or judgment by a court that the accused is guilty as charged.

co-offending   Committing criminal acts in groups. It is believed that a significant number of delinquent acts involve more than one offender.

correctional institution   Generic name for long-term adult confinement facilities that are often called prisons, federal or state correctional facilities, or penitentiaries, and for juvenile confinement facilities that are often called training schools, reformatories, boys' ranches, and the like.

correctional institution (juvenile)   Confinement facility having custodial authority over delinquents and status offenders committed to confinement after a juvenile disposition hearing.

corrections   Generic term that includes all government agencies, facilities, programs, procedures, personnel, and techniques concerned with the investigation, intake, custody, confinement, supervision, or treatment of alleged or adjudicated adult offenders, delinquents, or status offenders.

court   Agency of the judicial branch of government authorized or established by statute or constitution and consisting of one or more judicial officers that has the authority to decide on controversies in law and disputed matters of fact brought before it.

crack   Processed street cocaine. Its manufacture involves using ammonia or baking soda to remove the hydrochlorides and create a crystalline form of cocaine base which can then be smoked.

crime   Offense against the state; behavior in violation of law for which there is prescribed punishment.

crime control   Model of criminal justice that emphasizes the control of dangerous offenders and the protection of society. Its advocates call for harsh punishments as deterrents to crime, such as the death penalty.

criminal justice process   Decision-making process from the initial investigation or arrest by police to the eventual release of offenders and their reentry into society; the various sequential criminal justice stages through which offenders pass.

criminal justice standards Models, commentaries, or recommendations for the revision of criminal justice procedures and practices; for example, the American Law Institute's Model Penal Code, the American Bar Association's Standards for Criminal Justice, and the recommendations of the National Advisory Commission on Criminal Justice Standards and Goals.

criminal justice system Group of agencies and organizations—police, courts, and corrections—as well as the legislation and appellate courts responsible for the administration of criminal justice and crime control.

criminal law Body of law that defines criminal offenses, prescribes punishments (substantive law), and delineates criminal procedure (procedural law).

criminal sanction Refers to the right of the state to punish people if they violate the rules set down in the criminal code. The punishment is connected to commission of a specific crime.

criminology Study of the causes and treatment of criminal behavior, criminal law, and the administration of criminal justice.

critical criminology Branch of criminology that reviews and analyzes historical and current developments in law and justice in order to expose the interests of the power elite and ruling classes.

cross-sectional data Survey data that involves all age, race, gender, and income segments of the population measured simultaneously. Since people from every age group are represented, age-specific crime rates can be determined. Proponents believe that this is a sufficient substitute for the more expensive longitudinal approach that follows a group of subjects over time in order to measure crime rate changes.

culpable Implication of a wrongful act but one that does not involve malice. It connotes fault rather than guilt.

cultural deviance Condition that exists when obedience to subcultural norms conflicts with the rules and laws of the larger, general culture.

cultural transmission Concept that conduct norms are passed down from one generation to the next so that they become stable within the boundaries of a culture. Cultural transmission guarantees that group life-style and behavior are stable and predictable.

culture conflict Condition brought about when the rules and norms of an individual's subcultural affiliation conflict with the role demands of conventional society.

culture of poverty View that lower-class people form a separate culture with its own values and norms that are in conflict with conventional society; the culture is self-maintaining and ongoing.

dark figures of crime Incidents of crime and delinquency that go undetected by police.

degenerate anomalies According to Lombroso, the primitive physical characteristics that make criminals animalistic and savage.

deinstitutionalization Closing of institutions and moving inmates to community-based programs.

delinquency Juvenile actions or conduct in violation of criminal law and, in some contexts, status offenders.

delinquent Juvenile who has been adjudicated by a judicial officer of a juvenile court as having committed a delinquent act.

delinquent act Act committed by a juvenile for which an adult could be prosecuted in a criminal court. A juvenile who commits such an act can be adjudicated in a juvenile court or prosecuted in a criminal court if the juvenile court transfers jurisdiction.

dependency Legal status of juveniles over whom a juvenile court has assumed jurisdiction because the court has found their care by parents, guardians, or custodians falls short of a legal standard of proper care.

dependents Juveniles over whom a juvenile court has assumed jurisdiction because the court has found their care by parents, guardians, or custodians falls short of a legal standard of proper care.

desistance Phenomenon that relates to the decline in the crime rate as a person matures; synonymous with the aging-out process. Desisters are youths who spontaneously terminate their delinquent careers.

dessert-based sentences Principle of basing sentence length on the seriousness of the criminal act and not the personal characteristics of the defendant or the deterrent impact of the law. Punishment based on what people have done and not on what others may do or what they themselves may do in the future.

detached street workers Program that places social workers in the community in order to reach fighting gangs.

detective Police agent who is assigned to investigate crimes after they have been reported, to gather evidence, and to identify the perpetrator.

detention Temporary care of a child alleged to be delinquent who requires secure custody in physically restricting facilities pending court disposition or execution of a court order.

detention center Government facility that provides temporary care in a physically restricting environment for juveniles in custody pending court disposition.

detention facility (juvenile) Confinement facility having custodial authority over juveniles confined pending and after adjudication.

detention hearing In juvenile proceedings, a hearing by a judicial officer of a juvenile court to determine whether a juvenile is to be detained, to continue to be detained, or to be released while juvenile proceedings are pending in the case.

determinate sentence Involves "fixed" terms of incarceration, such as three years' incarceration. It is felt by many to be too restrictive for rehabilitative purposes; the advantage is that offenders know how much time they have to serve, that is, when they will be released.

deterrence Act of preventing a crime before it occurs by means of the threat of criminal sanctions.

developmental theory View that personal characteristics guide human development and influence and control behavior choices.

differential association Theory positing that criminal behavior is learned when an individual encounters an excess of definitions favoring law violations over those that support conformity to law; also learned in primary groups characterized by intimacy.

discretion Use of personal decision making and choice in carrying out operations in the criminal justice system. For example, police discretion can involve the decision to make an arrest, whole prosecutorial discretion can involve the decision to accept a plea bargain.

disposition For juvenile offenders, the equivalent of sentencing for adult offenders. The theory is that disposition should be more rehabilitative than retributive. Possible dispositions may be dismissal of the case, release of the youth to the custody of his or her parents, placement of the offender on probation, or sending him or her to an institution or state correctional institution.

disposition hearing Hearing in juvenile court conducted after an adjudicatory hearing and subsequent receipt of the report of any predisposition investigation to determine the most appropriate disposition of a juvenile who has been adjudicated a delinquent, a status offender, or a dependent.

district attorney County prosecutor who is charged with bringing offenders to justice and enforcing the laws of the state.

diversion Official halting or suspension of formal criminal or juvenile justice proceedings against an alleged offender at any legally prescribed processing point after a recorded justice system entry and the referral of that person to a treatment or care program administered by a nonjustice public agency or a private agency or the recommendation that the person be released.

dower Middle Ages custom of monetary compensation being given the groom by the bride's family before a marriage could take place.

drift According to Matza, the view that youths move in and out of delinquency and that their life-styles can embrace both conventional and deviant values.

Drug Enforcement Administration (DEA) Federal agency that handles enforcement of federal drug control laws.

due process Basic constitutional principle based on the concept of the primacy of the individual and the complementary concept of limitation on governmental power; a safeguard against arbitrary and unfair state procedures in judicial or administrative proceedings. Embodied in the due process concept are the basic rights of a defendant in criminal proceedings and the requisites for a fair trial. These rights and requirements have been expanded by appellate court decisions and include (1) timely notice of a hearing or trial that informs the accused of the charges against him or her; (2) the opportunity to confront accusers and to present evidence on the accused's own behalf before an impartial jury or judge; (3) the presumption of innocence under which guilt must be proven by legally obtained evidence and the verdict must be supported by the evidence presented; (4) the right of an accused to be warned of constitutional rights at the earliest stage of the criminal process; (5) protection against self-incrimination; (6) assistance of counsel at every critical stage of the criminal process; and (7) the guarantee that an individual will not be tried more than once for the same offense (double jeopardy).

ecological theory View that the interrelationship between people and their environment influences behavior.

ego identity According to Erikson, ego identity is formed when persons develop a firm sense of who they are and what they stand for.

electroencephalogram (EEG) Device that can record the electronic impulses given off by the brain, commonly called "brain waves."

emancipation Relinquishment of the care, custody, and earnings of a minor child and the renunciation of parental duties.

equipotentiality View that all people are equal at birth and are thereafter influenced by their environment.

exclusionary rule Principle that prohibits using evidence illegally obtained in a trial. Based on the Fourth Amendment "right of the people to be secure in their persons, houses, papers, and effects, against unreasonable searches and seizures," the rule is not a bar to prosecution, as legally obtained evidence may be available and may be used in a trial.

family court Court with broad jurisdiction over family matters, such as neglect, delinquency, paternity, support, and noncriminal behavior.

Federal Bureau of Investigation (FBI) Arm of the U.S. Justice Department that investigates violations of federal law, gathers crime statistics, runs a comprehensive crime laboratory, and helps train local law enforcement officers.

felony Criminal offense punishable by death or by incarceration in a state or federal confinement facility for a period whose lower limit is prescribed by statute in a given jurisdiction, typically one year or more.

finding of fact Court's determination of the facts presented as evidence in a case, affirmed by one party and denied by the other.

fine The court-imposed penalty requiring that a convicted person pay a specified sum of money.

focal concerns According to Walter Miller, the value orientations of lower-class cultures whose features include the need for excitement, trouble, smartness, fate, and personal autonomy.

free will View that people are in charge of their own destinies and are free to make personal behavior choices unencumbered by environmental controls.

general deterrence Crime-control policy that depends on the fear of criminal penalties. General deterrence measures, such as long prison sentences for violent crimes, are aimed at convincing the potential law violator that the pains associated with crime outweigh its benefits.

graffiti Inscription or drawing made on a wall or structure. Used by delinquents for gang messages and turf definition.

group home Nonconfining residential facility for adjudicated adults or juveniles or those subject to criminal or juvenile proceedings, intended to reproduce as closely as possible the circumstances of family life and, at minimum, provide access to community activities and resources.

guardian *ad litem* Court-appointed attorney who protects the interests of a child in cases involving the child's welfare.

habeas corpus Literally, "you have the body." A variety of writs whose objective is to bring a party before a court or judge. The function of the writ is to release the person from unlawful imprisonment.

halfway house Nonconfining residential facility for adjudicated adults or juveniles or for those subject to criminal or juvenile proceedings, intended to provide an alternative to confinement for persons not suitable for probation or in need of a period of readjustment to the community after confinement.

hallucinogens Drugs, either natural or synthetic, that produce vivid distortions of the senses without greatly disturbing the viewer's consciousness. Some produce hallucinations, and others cause psychotic behavior in otherwise normal people. *Hashish* (*hash*) is a concentrated form of marijuana made from unadulterated resin from the female plant.

hearing Presentation of evidence to the juvenile court judge, the judge's consideration of it, and the decision on disposition of the case.

helping professions Occupations such as social work, mental health, and family care that are dedicated to the health and welfare of the needy and indigent.

heroin The most dangerous commonly used drug made from the poppy plant. Users rapidly build a tolerance for it fueling the need for increased doses in order to feel a desired effect.

incarceration Putting a person in prison. The basic purposes of such confinement have been punishment, deterrence, rehabilitation, and integration into the community.

identity crisis Psychological state, identified by Erikson, in which youth face inner turmoil and uncertainty about life roles.

index crimes Crimes used by the FBI to indicate the incidence of crime in the United States and reported annually in the Uniform Crime Reports. They include murder and nonnegligent manslaughter, robbery, rape, aggravated assault, burglary, larceny, and motor vehicle theft.

indictment Written accusation returned by a grand jury that charges an individual with a specified crime after determination of probable cause. The prosecutor presents enough evidence to establish probable cause.

indigent Person who is needy and poor or who lacks the means to provide a living.

inhalants Vapors from lighter fluid, paint thinner, cleaning fluid, and model airplane glue sniffed to reach a drowsy, dizzy state sometimes accompanied by hallucinations.

inmate Person in a confinement facility.

innocents Youths who have never been apprehended for a delinquent act.

insanity Unsoundness of mind that prevents one from comprehending the consequences of one's acts or from distinguishing between right and wrong.

instrumental Marxist theory View that capitalist institutions such as the criminal justice system have as their main purpose the control of the poor in order to maintain the hegemony of the wealthy.

intake Process during which a juvenile referral is received and a decision is made to file a petition in juvenile court, to release the juvenile, to place the juvenile under supervision, or to refer the juvenile elsewhere.

intake unit Government agency or unit of an agency that receives juvenile referrals from police, other government agencies, private agencies, or individuals and screens them, resulting in closing of the case, referral to care or supervision, or filing of a petition to juvenile court.

interactionist perspective View that one's perception of reality is significantly influenced by one's interpretations of the reactions of others to similar events and stimuli.

interrogation Method of accumulating evidence in the form of information or confessions from suspects by police; questioning that has been restricted because of concern about the use of brutal and coercive methods and interest in protecting against self-incrimination.

interstitial Space that separates things. In criminology, a space or separation in the social fabric. An interstitial area encourages the formation of gangs.

investigation Inquiry into suspected criminal behavior for the purpose of identifying offenders or gathering further evidence to assist the prosecution of apprehended offenders.

jail Confinement facility, usually administered by a local law enforcement agency, that is intended for adults but sometimes also contains juveniles. It detains persons pending adjudication and persons committed after adjudication for sentences of a year or less.

judge Judicial officer who has been elected or appointed to preside over a court of law. The position is created by statute or by constitution, and the officer's decisions in criminal and juvenile cases can be reviewed only by a judge of a higher court.

judgment Statement of the decision of a court that the defendant is convicted or acquitted of the offense(s) charged.

judicial officer Any person exercising judicial powers in a court of law.

jurisdiction Every kind of judicial action; the authority of courts and judicial officers to decide cases.

just desserts Idea that penalties to be given to convicted offenders should be decided chiefly by reference to the seriousness of the offense and the number and seriousness of prior convictions.

juvenile courts Courts that have original jurisdiction over persons defined by statute as juveniles and alleged to be delinquents, status offenders, or dependents.

juvenile delinquency Participation in illegal behavior by a minor who falls under a statutory age limit.

juvenile justice agency Government agency or subunit thereof whose functions are the investigation, supervision, adjudication, care, or confinement of juveniles whose conduct or condition has brought or could bring them within the jurisdiction of a juvenile court.

Juvenile Justice and Delinquency Prevention Act of 1974 Federal law establishing an office of juvenile justice within the Law Enforcement Assistance Administration to provide funds for the control of juvenile crime.

juvenile justice process Court proceedings for youths within the "juvenile" age group that differ from the adult criminal process. Under the paternal (*parens patriae*) philosophy, juvenile procedures are informal and nonadversarial, invoked *for* the juvenile offender rather than *against* him or her; a petition instead of a complaint is filed; courts make findings of involvement or adjudication of delinquency instead of convictions; and juvenile offenders receive dispositions instead of sentences. Recent court decisions (*Kent* and *In re Gault*) have increased the adversarial nature of juvenile court proceedings. However, the philosophy remains one of diminishing the stigma of delinquency and providing for the youth's well-being and rehabilitation, rather than seeking retribution.

juvenile record Official record containing, at a minimum, summary information pertaining to an identified juvenile concerning juvenile court proceedings and, if applicable, detention and correctional processes.

labeling theory Theory that views society as creating deviance through a system of social control agencies that designate certain individuals as deviants. The stigmatized individual is made to feel unwanted in the normal social order. Eventually, the individual begins to believe that the label is accurate, assumes it as a personal identity, and enters into a deviant or criminal career.

latchkey children Children left unsupervised after school by working parents.

law Method for resolving disputes. A rule of action to which people obligate themselves to conform, via their selected representatives and other officials. The principles and procedures of the common law, as distinguished from those of equity.

law enforcement agency Federal, state, or local criminal justice agency whose principal functions are the prevention, detection, and investigation of crime and the apprehension of alleged offenders.

Law Enforcement Assistance Administration Unit in the U.S. Department of Justice established by the Omnibus Crime Control and Safe Streets Act of 1968 to administer grants and provide guidance for crime prevention policy and programs.

law enforcement officer Employee of a law enforcement agency who is an officer sworn to carry out law enforcement duties or a sworn employee of a prosecutorial agency who performs primarily investigative duties. Also called police officer.

law guardian Person with the legal authority and duty of taking care of someone and managing the property and rights of that person, if the person is considered incapable of administering the affairs personally.

learning disabilities Neurological dysfunctions that prevent people from learning up to their potential.

life course perspective A view of delinquency which holds that factors present at birth and events which unfold over a person's life time influence behavior. Life course theory focuses on the onset, escalation, desistance and amplification of delinquent behaviors. Delinquency has both individual and social roots.

lineup Pretrial identification procedure in which a suspect is placed in a group for the purpose of being identified by a witness.

mandamus Literally, "we command." A legal, not an equitable, remedy. When issued, it is an inflexible peremptory command to do a particular thing.

mandatory sentence Statutory requirement that a certain penalty shall be set and carried out in all cases on conviction for a specified offense or series of offenses.

manslaughter Voluntary (nonnegligent) killing; intentionally causing the death of another with reasonable provocation.

marijuana (Cannabis sativa) A plant grown throughout the world. The main active ingredient in marijuana is tetrahydrocannabinol or THC, a mild hallucinogen which alters sensory impressions and can cause drastic distortion in auditory and visual perception, even producing hallucinatory effects.

masculinity hypothesis View that women who commit crimes have biological and psychological traits similar to those of men.

medial model View that the justice system should help rehabilitate offenders rather than punish them. Advocates of the medial model liken criminality to a "disease" that can be "cured" through proper treatment.

mens rea Guilty mind; the mental element of a crime or the intent to commit a criminal act.

middle-class measuring rods According to Cohen, the standards with which teachers and other representatives of state authority evaluate lower-class youths. Because they cannot live up to middle-class standards, lower-class youths are bound for failure, which brings on frustration and anger at conventional society.

minor Person who is under the age of legal consent.

Miranda **warning** Result of two Supreme Court decisions [*Escobedo v. Illinois*, 378 U.S. 478 (1964) and *Miranda v. Arizona*, 384 U.S. 436 (1966)], that require police officers to inform individuals under arrest of their constitutional rights. Although aimed at protecting individuals during in-custody interrogation, the warning must also be given when the investigation shifts from the investigatory stage to the accusatory stage—that is, when suspicion begins to focus on an individual.

misdemeanor Offense punishable by a fine or by incarceration for not more than one year in a county jail. There is no uniform rule; an offense can be a misdemeanor in one jurisdiction and a felony in another.

Model Penal Code Generalized modern codification of that which is considered basic to criminal law, published by the American Law Institute in 1962.

moral entrepreneurs Interest groups that attempt to control social life and the legal order in order to promote their own personal set of moral values.

murder Intentionally causing the death of another without reasonable provocation or legal justification, or causing the death of another while committing or attempting to commit another crime.

National Council on Crime and Delinquency Private national agency that promotes efforts at crime control through research, citizen involvement, and public information efforts.

National Crime Survey Ongoing victimization study conducted jointly by the U.S. Justice Department and the Census Bureau that surveys victims about their experiences with law violation.

neurological Pertaining to the brain and central nervous system.

neutralization Ability to overcome social norms and controls. Neutralization theory holds that delinquents adhere to conventional values while "drifting" into periods of illegal behavior. In order to drift, delinquents must first neutralize legal and moral values.

nonjudicial disposition Rendering of a decision in a juvenile case by an authority other than a judge or court of law. Often an informal method used to determine the most appropriate disposition of a juvenile.

nonresidential program Program enabling youths to remain in their homes or foster homes while receiving services.

nonsecure setting Setting in which the emphasis is on the care and treatment of youths without the need to place constraints on them and to worry about the protection of the public.

Office of Juvenile Justice and Delinquency Prevention (OJJDP) Branch of the U.S. Justice Department charged with shaping national juvenile justice policy through the disbursement of federal aid and research funds.

official data Incidents of crime and delinquency that are recorded by police agencies.

official records Data kept by police, courts, and correctional agencies.

parens patriae Power of the state to act in behalf of the child and provide care and protection equivalent to that of a parent.

parole agency Correctional agency that may or may not include a parole authority and whose principal functions are the supervision of adults or juveniles placed on parole.

parole authority Person or correctional agency having the authority to release on parole adults or juveniles committed to confinement facilities, to revoke parole, and to discharge from parole.

parolee Person who has been conditionally released from a correctional institution prior to the expiration of his or her sentence and placed under the supervision of a parole agency.

part I offenses Eight index crimes whose incidence is reported to the FBI by local police.

part II offenses All other crimes other than part I offenses. Arrests for these crimes are reported to the FBI.

paternalism Male domination. A paternalistic family, for instance, is one in which the father is the dominant authority figure.

pathways The view that the path to a delinquent career may have more than one route, beginning with mild misconduct and escalating to serious crimes.

patriarchy Legal or social institution dominated or ruled by a male.

penalty Punishment meted out by law or judicial decision on the commission of a particular offense. It may be death, imprisonment, a fine, or loss of civil privileges.

persistence Refers to the offending patterns of youths who continue in a delinquent career despite repeatedly being apprehended and sanctioned by legal authorities.

person in need of supervision Person usually characterized as ungovernable, incorrigible, truant, and habitually disobedient.

petition Document filed in juvenile court alleging that a juvenile is a delinquent, a status offender, or a dependent and asking that the court assume jurisdiction over the juvenile or that the juvenile be transferred to a criminal court for prosecution as an adult.

petition not sustained Finding by a juvenile court in an adjudicatory hearing that there is insufficient evidence to sustain an allegation that a juvenile is a delinquent, a status offender, or a dependent.

plea-bargaining Discussion between the defense counsel and the prosecution by which the accused agrees to plead guilty for certain considerations. The advantage to the defendant may be in the form of a reduction of the charges, a lenient sentence, or, in the case of multiple charges, dropped charges. The advantage to the prosecution is that a conviction is obtained without the time and expense of lengthy trial proceedings.

police discretion Refers to the ability of police officers to enforce the law selectively. Police officers in the field have great latitude to use their discretion in deciding whether to invoke their arrest powers.

police officer style Refers to the belief that the bulk of police officers can be classified into ideal personality types. Popular style types include: supercops, who desire to enforce only serious crimes, such as robbery and rape; professionals, who use a broad definition of police work; service oriented, who see their job as that of a helping profession; avoiders, who do as little as possible. The actual existence of ideal police officer types has been much debated.

population All people who share a particular personal characteristic, for example, all high school students or all police officers.

positivism Branch of social science that uses the scientific method of the natural sciences and that suggests that human behavior is a product of social, biological, psychological, or economic forces.

precocious sexuality Sexual experimentation in early adolescence.

presentence report Investigation performed by a probation officer attached to a trial court after the conviction of a defendant. The report contains information about the defendant's background, education, previous employment family, his or her own statement concerning the offense, prior criminal record, interviews with neighbors or acquaintances, and his or her mental and physical condition (i.e., information that would not be made record in the case of a guilty plea or that would be inadmissible as evidence at a trial but could be influential and important at the sentencing stage). After conviction, a judge sets a date for sentenc-

ing (usually ten days to two weeks from date of conviction), during which time the presentence report is made. The report is required in felony cases in federal courts; in some states, it is optional at the discretion of the judge, while in others, it is mandatory before convicted offenders can be placed on probation. In the case of juvenile offenders, the presentence report is also known as a social history report.

primary deviance According to Lemert, deviant acts that do not help redefine the self and public image of the offender.

primogeniture Middle Ages practice of allowing only the family's eldest son to inherit lands and titles.

probable cause Reasonable ground to believe the existence of facts that an offense was committed and the accused committed that offense.

probation Sentence entailing the conditional release of a convicted offender into the community under the supervision of the court (in the form of a probation officer) subject to certain conditions for a specific time. The conditions are usually similar to those of parole. (Probation is a sentence, an alternative to incarceration; parole is administrative release from incarceration.) Violation of the conditions of probation may result in revocation of probation.

probation agency Also called probation department. Correctional agency whose principal functions are juvenile intake, the supervision of adults and juveniles placed on probation status, and the investigation of adults and juveniles for the purpose of preparing presentence or predisposition reports to assist the court in determining the proper sentence or juvenile court disposition.

probationer Person required by a court or probation agency to meet certain conditions of behavior; person who may or may not be placed under the supervision of a probation agency.

probation officer Employee of a probation agency whose primary duties include one or more of the probation agency functions.

problem behavior syndrome The belief that delinquency is one of many personal social problems which may also include substance abuse, depression, school failure and anomie.

procedural law Rules that define the operation of criminal proceedings. The methods that must be followed in obtaining warrants, investigating offenses, effecting lawful arrests, using force, conducting trials, introducing evidence, sentencing convicted offenders, and reviewing cases in appellate courts. Substantive law defines criminal offenses; procedural law delineates how the substantive offenses are to be enforced.

prosecutor Representative of the state (executive branch) in criminal proceedings; advocate for the state's case—the charge—in the adversary trial, for example, the attorney general of the United States, U.S. attorneys, attorneys general of the states, district attorneys, and police prosecutors. The prosecutor participates in investigations both before and after arrest, prepares legal documents, participates in obtaining arrest or search warrants, decides whether to charge a suspect and, if so, with which offense. The prosecutor argues the state's case at trial, advises the police, participates in plea negotiations, and makes sentencing recommendations.

prosecutorial agency Federal, state, or local criminal justice agency whose principal function is the prosecution of alleged offenders.

psychoanalytic (psychodynamic) Branch of psychology that holds that the human personality is controlled by unconscious mental processes developed early in childhood.

psychopath Person whose personality is characterized by lack of warmth and affection, inappropriate behavior responses, and an inability to learn from experience. While some psychologists view psychopathy as a result of childhood trauma, others see it as a result of biological abnormality.

psychotic Person who has lost control of his or her thoughts, moods, and feelings.

public defender Lawyer who works in a public agency or under private contractual agreement as defense counsel to indigent defendants.

random sample Sample selected on the basis of chance so that each person in the population has an equal opportunity to be selected.

rationale choice View that crime is a function of a decision-making process in which the potential offender weighs the potential costs and benefits of an illegal act.

recidivism Repetition of criminal behavior; habitual criminality. Recidivism is measured by (1) criminal acts that resulted in conviction by a court when committed by individuals who are under correctional supervision or who had been released from correctional supervision within the previous three years and (2) technical violations of probation or parole in which a sentencing or paroling authority took action that resulted in an adverse change in the offender's legal status.

referral to intake In juvenile proceedings, a request by the police, parents, or other agency or person that a juvenile intake unit take appropriate action concerning a juvenile alleged to have committed a delinquent act or status offense or to be dependent.

reform school Institution in which efforts are made to improve the conduct of those forcibly detained within. Educational and psychological services are employed to achieve this goal.

rehabilitation Restoring to a condition of constructive activity.

relative deprivation Condition that exists when people of wealth and poverty live in close proximity to one another. Some criminologists attribute crime rate differentials to relative deprivation.

release from detention Authorized exit from detention of a person subject to criminal or juvenile justice proceedings.

release on bail Release by a judicial officer of an accused person who has been taken into custody upon the accused's promise to pay a certain sum of money or property if he or she fails to appear in court as required. The promise may or may not be secured by the deposit of an actual sum of money or property.

release on own recognizance Release, by a judicial officer, of an accused person who has been taken into custody upon the accused's promise to appear in court as required for criminal proceedings.

release (pretrial) Procedure whereby an accused person who has been taken into custody is allowed to be free before and during trial.

residential child-care facility Dwelling other than a detention or shelter care facility that provides living accommodations, care, treatment, and maintenance for children and youths and is licensed to provide such care. Such facilities include foster family homes, group homes, and halfway houses.

residential treatment center Government facility that serves juveniles whose behavior does not necessitate the strict confinement of a training school, often allowing them greater contact with the community.

resource deprivation Effect of growing up under conditions lacking adequate care, custody, and material goods.

responsible Legally accountable for one's actions and obligations.

restitution Restoring of property, or a right, to a person who has been unjustly deprived of it. A writ of restitution is the process by which a successful appellant may recover something of which he or she has been deprived under a prior judgment.

revocation Administrative act performed by a parole authority that removes a person from parole or a judicial order by a court removing a person from parole or probation, in response to a violation on the part of the parolee or probationer.

rights of defendant Powers and privileges that are constitutionally guaranteed to every defendant.

right to counsel Right of the accused to assistance of defense counsel in all criminal prosecutions.

right to treatment Philosophy espoused by many courts that offenders have a statutory right to treatment. A federal constitutional right to treatment has not been established.

role diffusion According to Erikson, role diffusion occurs when youths spread themselves too thin, experience personal uncertainty, and place themselves at the mercy of leaders who promise to give them a sense of identity they cannot develop for themselves.

routine activities View that crime is a "normal" function of the routine activities of modern living. Offenses can be expected if there is a suitable target that is not protected by capable guardians.

runaway Juvenile who has been adjudicated by a judicial officer of a juvenile court as having committed the status offense of leaving the custody and home of his or her parents, guardians, or custodians without permission and failing to return within a reasonable length of time.

sample Limited number of persons selected for study from a population.

schizophrenia Type of psychosis often marked by bizarre behavior, hallucinations, loss of thought control, and inappropriate emotional responses. There are different types of schizophrenia: catatonic, which characteristically involves impairment of motor activity; paranoid, which is characterized by delusions of persecution; and hebephrenic, which is characterized by immature behavior and giddiness.

search and seizure U.S. Constitution protects against any search or seizure engaged in without a lawfully obtained search warrant. A search warrant will be issued if there is probable cause to believe that an offense has been or is being committed.

secondary deviance According to Lemert, deviant acts that redefine the offender's self and public image. Acts become secondary when they form a basis for self-concept, for example, when a drug experimenter becomes an addict.

secure setting Setting that places constraints on youths for care and treatment and for the protection of the public.

security and privacy standards Set of principles and procedures developed to ensue the security and confidentiality of criminal or juvenile record information in order to protect the privacy of the persons identified in such records.

sedatives Most commonly of the barbiturate family. Are able to depress the central nervous system into a sleeplike condition.

seductions of crime According to Katz, the view that crime provides thrills and excitement which make it attractive to adolescents.

selective incapacitation Policy of putting suspected chronic offenders behind bars for long periods of time. Advocates suggest that special laws be created to heavily penalize persistent offenders.

self-control theory According to Gottfredson and Hirschi, the view that the cause of delinquent behavior is an impulsive personality. Kids who are impulsive may find that their bond to society is weak and attenuated.

self-fulfilling prophecy Deviant behavior patterns that are a response to an earlier labeling experience. People act in synch with social labels, even if the labels are falsely bestowed.

self-report Research approach that requires subjects to reveal their own participation in delinquent or criminal acts.

sentence Sanction imposed by the court upon a convicted defendant, usually in the form of a fine, incarceration, or probation. Sentencing may be carried out by a judge, jury, or sentencing council (panel of judges), depending on the statutes of the jurisdictions.

sentence, indeterminate Statutory provision for a type of sentence to imprisonment, in which, after the court has determined that the convicted person shall be imprisoned, the exact length of imprisonment and parole supervision is fixed within statutory limits by a parole authority.

sentence, suspended Court decision postponing the pronouncing of sentence upon a convicted person or postponing the execution of a sentence that has been pronounced by the court.

shock probation Sentence that involves a short prison stay to impress the offender with the pains of imprisonment before he or she begins a probationary sentence.

short-run hedonism According to Cohen, the desire of lower-class gang youths to engage in behavior that will give them immediate gratification and excitement but that in the long run will be dysfunctional and negativistic.

skinhead Member of white supremacist gang, identified by a shaved skull and Nazi or Ku Klux Klan markings.

social bond Ties a person has to the institutions and processes of society. According to Hirschi, elements of the social bond include commitment, attachment, involvement, and belief.

social control Ability of social institutions to influence human behavior. Among the primary agencies of formal social control are the school and the justice system.

social disorganization Neighborhood or area marked by culture conflict, lack of cohesiveness, transient population, insufficient social organizations, and anomie.

socialization Process of human development and enculturation. Socialization is influenced by key social processes and institutions.

social process Operations of formal and informal social institutions. Elements of the social process include socialization within family and peer groups, the educational process, and the justice system.

social structure Fabric of society. Within the social structure are the various classes, institutions, and groups of society.

sociobiology Branch of science that views human behavior as being motivated by in-bred biological urges and desires. The urge to survive and preserve the species motivates human behavior.

sociopath Person whose personality is characterized by lack of warmth and affection, inappropriate behavior responses, and an inability to learn from experience. Used interchangeably with psychopath.

specific deterrence Crime-control policy that suggests that punishment should be severe enough to convince previous offenders never to repeat their criminal activity.

spontaneous remission Another term used for the aging-out process.

standard of proof Proof beyond a reasonable doubt—the standard used to convict a person charged with a crime. Many U.S. Supreme Court decisions have made the beyond a reasonable doubt standard a due process and constitutional requirement.

stare decisis "To stand by decided cases." The legal principle by which the decision or holding in an earlier case becomes the standard with which to judge subsequent similar cases.

status offender Juvenile who has been adjudicated by a judicial officer of a juvenile court as having committed a status offense.

status offense Act that is declared by statute to be an offense but only when committed by a juvenile. It can be adjudicated only by a juvenile court.

statutory law Laws created by legislative bodies to meet changing social conditions, public opinion, and custom.

steroids Anabolic steroids are drugs used to gain muscle bulk and strength for athletics and body building.

stigma Social disgrace or condemnation. Stigmatized persons feel they are outsiders or outcasts from society.

stimulants Synthetic drugs that stimulate action in the central nervous system. They produce an intense physical reaction: increased blood pressure, increased breathing rate, increased bodily activity, and elevation of mood. One widely used stimulant, amphetamines, produce psychological effects such as increased confidence, euphoria, fearlessness, talkativeness, impulsive behavior, and loss of appetite.

stop and frisk Practice of police officers who are suspicious of an individual to run their hands lightly over the suspect's outer garments to determine if the person is carrying a concealed weapon. Also called a "patdown" or "threshold inquiry," a stop and frisk is intended to stop short of any activity that could be considered a violation of Fourth Amendment rights.

stardom formations According to the Schwendingers, adolescent social networks whose members have distinct dress, grooming, and linguistic behavior.

strain Social psychological condition that is created when a person's social goals cannot be achieved by available legitimate means. Lower-class youths might feel strain because they are denied access to adequate educational opportunities and social support.

stratified Grouped according to social strata or levels. American society is considered stratified on the basis of economic class and wealth.

street crime Illegal acts designed to prey on the public through theft, damage, and violence.

structural Marxist theory View that the law and justice system is designed to maintain the capitalist system and that members of both the owner and worker classes whose behavior threatens the stability of the system will be sanctioned.

subculture Group that is loosely part of the dominant culture that maintains a unique set of values, beliefs, and traditions.

substantive criminal laws Body of specific rules that declare what conduct is criminal and prescribe the punishment to be imposed for such conduct.

subterranean values According to Sykes and Matza, the ability of youthful law violators to repress social norms.

summons Alternative to arrest usually used for petty or traffic offenses; a written order notifying an individual that he or she has been charged with an offense. A summons directs the person to appear in court to answer the charge. It is used primarily in instances of low risk, where the person will not be required to appear at a later date. The summons is advantageous to police officers because it frees them from spending time on arrest and booking procedures; it is advantageous to the accused in that he or she is spared time in jail.

surplus value Marxist view that the laboring classes produce wealth that far exceeds their wages and goes to the capitalist class as profits.

take into custody Act of the police in securing the physical custody of a child engaged in delinquency. Avoids the stigma of the word *arrest*.

tongs Chinese gangs.

totality of the circumstances Legal doctrine that mandates that a decision maker consider all the issues and circumstances of a case before judging the outcome. For example, before concluding whether a suspect understood his or her *Miranda* warning, a judge must consider the totality of the circumstances under which the warning was given. The suspect's age, intelligence, and competency may be issues that influence his or her understanding and judgment.

tracking Segregating youth in classes based on academic achievement and/or potential. Tracking is believed to be responsible for poor self-image and self-fulfilling prophecy.

training school Correctional institution for juveniles adjudicated to be delinquents or status offenders and committed to confinement by a judicial officer.

tranquilizers Have the ability to relieve uncomfortable emotional feelings by reducing levels of anxiety and promoting relaxation.

transfer hearing Preadjudicatory hearing in juvenile court for the purpose of determining whether juvenile court jurisdiction should be retained or waived over a juvenile alleged to have committed a delinquent act and whether he or she should be transferred to criminal court for prosecution as an adult.

transfer to adult court Decision by a juvenile court resulting from a transfer hearing that jurisdiction over an alleged delinquent will be waived and that he or she should be prosecuted as an adult in a criminal court.

transitional neighborhood Area undergoing a shift in population and structure, usually from middle-class residential to lower-class mixed use.

treatment Rehabilitative method used to effect a change of behavior in an inmate, juvenile delinquent, or status offender. It may be in the form of therapy programs or educational or vocational training.

triads Chinese self-help groups.

trial Examination of issues of fact and law in a case or controversy, beginning when the jury has been selected in a jury trial or when the first witness is sworn or the first evidence is introduced in a court trial and concluding when a verdict is reached or the case is dismissed.

Type I offenses   Another term for index crimes.

Type II offenses   All crimes other than index and minor traffic offenses. The FBI records annual arrest information for Type II offenses.

UCR   Abbreviation for the Federal Bureau of Investigation's uniform crime reporting program.

verdict   In criminal proceedings, the decision made by a jury in a jury trial or by a judicial officer in a court trial that a defendant is either guilty or not guilty of the offenses for which he or she has been tried.

victim   Person who has suffered death, physical or mental suffering, or loss of property as the result of an actual or attempted criminal offense committed by another person.

victim precipitated   Describes a crime in which the victim's behavior was the spark that ignited the subsequent offense, for example, the victim abused the offender verbally or physically.

victim survey   Crime-measurement technique that surveys citizens in order to measure their experiences as victims of crime.

waiver   Voluntary relinquishment of a known right.

wayward minors   Early legal designation for youths who violate the law because of their minority status. Wayward minor statutes have been converted into status offender laws.

widening the net   Phenomenon that occurs when programs created to divert youths from the justice system actually involve them more deeply in the official process.

writ of certiorari   Order of a superior court requesting that the record of an inferior court (or administrative body) be brought forward for review or inspection.

writ of habeas corpus   Judicial order requesting that a person detaining another produce the body of the prisoner and give reasons for his or her capture and detention. Habeas corpus is a legal device used to request that a judicial body review reasons for a person's confinement and the conditions of confinement. Habeas corpus is known as "the great writ."

writ of mandamus   Order of a superior court commanding that a lower court or administrative or executive body perform a specific function. It is commonly used to restore rights and privileges lost to a defendant through illegal means.

youthful offender   Person adjudicated in criminal court who may be above the statutory age limit for juveniles but who is below a specified upper-age limit for whom special correctional commitments and special record sealing procedures are made available by statute.

youth services bureau   Neighborhood youth service agency that coordinates all community services for young people and provides services lacking in the community or neighborhood, especially those designed for the predelinquent or the early delinquent.

EXCERPTS FROM THE U.S. CONSTITUTION

■■

Amendment I (1791)

Congress shall make no law respecting an establishment of religion, or prohibiting the free exercise thereof; or abridging the freedom of speech, or of the press; or the right of the people peaceably to assemble, and to petition the government for a redress of grievances.

Amendment II (1791)

A well regulated militia, being necessary to the security of a free state, the right of the people to keep and bear arms, shall not be infringed.

Amendment III (1791)

No soldier shall, in time of peace, be quartered in any house, without the consent of the owner, nor in time of war, but in a manner to be prescribed by law.

Amendment IV (1791)

The right of the people to be secure in their persons, houses, papers, and effects, against unreasonable searches and seizures, shall not be violated, and no warrants shall issue, but upon probable cause, supported by oath or affirmation, and particularly describing the place to be searched, and the persons or things to be seized.

Amendment V (1791)

No person shall be held to answer for a capital, or otherwise infamous, crime unless on a presentment or indictment of a grand jury, except in cases arising in the land or naval forces, or in the militia, when in actual service in time of war or public danger; nor shall any person be subject for the same offense to be twice put in jeopardy of life or limb; nor shall be compelled in any criminal case to be a witness against himself, nor be deprived of life, liberty, or property; without due process of law; nor shall private property be taken for public use without just compensation.

Amendment VI (1791)

In all criminal prosecutions, the accused shall enjoy the right to a speedy and public trial, by an impartial jury of the state and district wherein the crime shall have been committed, which district shall have been previously ascertained by law, and to be informed of the nature and cause of the accusation; to be confronted with the witnesses against him; to have compulsory process for obtaining witnesses in his favor, and to have the assistance of counsel for his defense.

Amendment VII (1791)

In suits at common law, where the value in controversy shall exceed twenty dollars, the right of trial by jury shall be preserved, and no fact tried by a jury shall be otherwise reexamined in any court of the United States, than according to the rules of common law.

Amendment VIII (1791)

Excessive bail shall not be required, nor excessive fines imposed, nor cruel and unusual punishment inflicted.

Amendment IX (1791)

The enumeration in the Constitution of certain rights shall not be construed to deny or disparage others retained by the people.

Amendment X (1791)

The powers not delegated to the United States by the Constitution, nor prohibited by it to the states, are reserved to the states respectively, or to the people.

Amendment XIV (1868)

Section I. All persons born or naturalized in the United States, and subject to the jurisdiction thereof, are citizens of the United States and of the state wherein they reside. No state shall make or enforce any law which shall abridge the privilege or immunities of citizens of the United States; nor shall any state deprive any person of life, liberty, or property, without due process of law; nor deny to any person within its jurisdiction the equal protection of the laws.

TABLE OF CASES

NAME INDEX

Blos, Peter, 247
Blumstein, Alfred, 85n.37, 86n.53
Boesky, Ivan, 101
Bonati, Lisa, 132nn.19,23, 133n.41
Bookin-Weiner, Hedy, 342n.104
Booth, Alan, 262n.35
Bordua, David, 149, 170n.21, 239n.48
Bortner, M. A., 238n.13, 520, 539,
    544n.36, 545n.78
Bouchard, T. J., 135nn.102,103
Bowman, J. Addison, 572
Brace, Charles, 429
Bracey, Dorothy, 307n.97
Brady, C. Patrick, 305n.30
Brady, Marianne, 238n.11
Braithwaite, John, 84n.23, 85n.31
Brandt, David, 135nn.111,123
Brannigan, Martha, 308n.132
Bray, James, 305n.30
Breed, Alan, 649nn.23,28
Bremmer, Robert, 438n.14
Brennan, William, 368
Brenzel, Barbara, 649n.44
Briar, Scott, 51n.4, 188, 209n.44, 492,
    495, 506n.67
Bright, Stephen, 582n.28
Britt, Chester, III, 86n.67
Broder, Paul, 134n.84
Bromberg, Walter, 247
Bronner, Augusta, 123, 137n.161, 244
Brooner, Robert, 410n.18
Brown, Larry, 24n.6
Brown, Michael, 505n.7
Browne, Angela, 284, 307nn.93,99
Brownfield, David, 49, 52n.48,
    85n.33, 195, 209n.61
Bruinsma, Gerben J. N., 208n.17
Buchanan, Christy Miller, 105,
    262nn.32,43
Bukoski, William, 373n.84
Bulger, James, 4, 12
Burger, Warren, 468, 641
Burgess, Ernest W., 144
Burgess, Robert, 181, 182,
    208nn.20,28, 290, 308n.126
Burke, Mary Jean, 208n.14
Burke, Vincent, 613n.33
Bursik, Robert, Jr., 86n.74, 150,
    170nn.13,20,31, 171n.35
Burt, Cyril, 243–44
Burton, Velmer, 25n.56
Butts, Jeffrey, 18, 25n.31, 613n.28,
    614n.51
Byrne, James, 84nn.15,22,
    170n.22,27,33, 612nn.11,12,
    639, 650n.70

C

Cahalan, Margaret Werner, 618, 648n.7
Callahan, Robert, 613n.21
Callahan, S., 262n.38
Calsyn, Donald, 136n.158
Campagna, Daniel, 649n.42
Campbell, Anne, 262nn.13,21, 324,
    341n.58
Carlson, Bonnie, 117, 136n.126
Carmen, Rolando V. Del, 583n.60
Carriger, Michael, 137n.173
Carroll, Leo, 170n.23
Cartwright, Desmond, 209n.42, 316
Caspi, Avshalom, 248, 262n.33
Castellano, Thomas, 132n.21, 575,
    583n.79, 635
Cernkovich, Stephen, 43, 52n.34,
    209n.62, 306n.68, 314, 340n.13
Chachere, J. Gregory, 118, 136n.133
Chaiken, Marcia, 397, 411n.51
Champion, Dean, 25n.58
Chaney, Edmund, 136n.158
Chard-Wierschem, Deborah, 132n.2,
    208n.1, 342n.97
Charles, Michael, 613n.19
Cheng, Yu-Teh, 52n.49
Chesler, Phyliss, 262n.24
Chesney-Lind, Meda, 84nn.4,7, 252,
    260, 261nn.1,2, 263nn.59,83,
    264n.88, 498, 521, 543n.16,
    544n.38, 649n.40
Cheung, Paul, 581n.12
Chilton, Roland, 149, 170n.21,
    305n.33
Chin, Ko-Lin, 333, 342n.80
Christenson, R. L., 356, 372n.58
Christiansen, Karl, 111, 135n.100
Cicourel, Aaron, 219, 495
Clark, David, 85n.38
Clark, John, 51n.31, 263n.72, 505n.4
Clark, Steven, 582n.31
Clarke, Ronald, 132nn.11,13,15
Clarke, S. H., 613n.16
Cleckley, Hervey, 121, 136n.149
Clinard, Marshall, 171n.75
Cloward, Richard, 83n.2, 164–65,
    171nn.70,72, 320, 335,
    341n.41, 411n.34, 455
Coates, Robert, 614n.65
Cobb, Michael, 263n.76
Cochran, John, 524, 525,
    545nn.52,55
Cohen, Albert K., 83n.2, 161–64,
    171nn.56,67, 335, 342n.87,
    350, 371n.25

Cohen, Jacqueline, 85n.37
Cohen, Lawrence, 85n.40, 98, 99,
    132nn.20,24
Cohen, Robyn, 410n.7, 411n.20
Cohen, Stanley, 221, 239n.42
Cohill, Maurice, 555
Coleman, John, 84n.3, 137n.172,
    262n.44
Collins, Patricia, 136n.130
Colvin, Mark, 233, 78
Conrad, John, 85n.44, 86n.58
Cook, John, 24n.6
Cook, Philip, 132n.13
Cooper, Sara, 424
Copp, Frank, 439n.24
Corbitt, Elizabeth, 238n.11
Cornblatt, Barbara, 135n.95
Cornell, Claire Pedrick, 282, 307n.81
Cornish, Derek, 132nn.11,13,15
Costa, Francis, 86n.71
Cowie, J., 245, 262n.20, 263n.46
Cowie, V., 245, 262n.20, 263n.46
Cox, Louis, 222, 239n.51, 635
Craddock, A. D., 613n.16
Creechan, James, 134n.91
Cressey, Donald, 122, 177, 179,
    208nn.7,9, 238n.27
Crimmins, Susan, 24n.11
Criswell, John, 543n.19
Cullen, Francis, 25nn.56,60, 209n.56,
    472n.64
Culliver, Concetta, 134n.83
Cunningham, Lea, 328, 342n.70
Curran, Deborah, 222, 239n.46
Curry, G. David, 316, 320, 340n.1,
    342nn.94,106
Curtis, Lynn, 342n.73
Czikszentmihalyi, M., 372n.53

D

Daldin, Herman, 307n.91
Dalton, Katharina, 247, 262n.29
Daly, Kathleen, 261n.2, 263n.83
Dannefer, Dale, 84nn.10,12, 496,
    506n.68, 507n.71, 516, 543n.17
Datesman, Susan, 24n.29, 544n.37
Davidson, Laura, 52n.37
Davies, Mark, 195, 209n.63, 411n.35
Davis, Dantrell, 4
Davis, Kenneth C., 492, 499, 507n.93
Davis, Samuel, 469, 472n.34, 482
Dawley, David, 341n.16
Dawson, Robert O., 472n.15
Decker, Scott, 87n.86

J

Jacklin, Carol, 249, 262nn.34,40
Jackson, Elton, 208n.14
Jackson, Lori, 134n.77
Jackson, Pamela Irving, 170n.23, 319, 341n.38
Jackson, Patrick, 51n.2, 645–46, 651n.93
Jackson-Beck, Marilyn, 649n.34
Jaffe, Jerome, 134n.74
Jaffe, Peter, 306n.47
James, William, 118
Jameson, Elizabeth, 472n.34
Janeksela, Galan, 12
Jang, Sung Joon, 209n.58, 210nn.78,79, 340n.10, 371n.14
Jarjoura, G. Roger, 85n.27, 357, 372n.59
Jeffrey, C. Ray, 133n.60
Jenkins, Patricia Harris, 372n.47
Jensen, Gary, 49, 52n.48, 84nn.5,8, 85n.30, 195, 209n.61, 221, 239n.38, 263n.72, 264n.86
Jerse, Frank W., 371n.13
Jessor, Richard, 75, 86nn.69,71
Joe, Tom, 84n.16
Johnson, Bruce, 68, 397, 402, 411n.51
Johnson, Charlotte, 134n.81
Johnson, E. H., 373n.85
Johnson, Joan, 52n.40
Johnson, Ray, 306n.54
Johnston, Lloyd, 24n.22, 51nn.24,25, 84n.9, 85nn.37,47
Johnston, Norman, 171n.45
Jou, Susyan, 63, 85n.34, 371nn.11,33
Junger-Tas, Josine, 209n.57

K

Kaiser, Gunther, 12, 340n.8
Kandel, Denise, 195, 208n.15, 209n.63, 341n.14, 411n.35
Kandel, Elizabeth, 134n.90
Kappeler, Victor, 583n.60
Kassenbaum, G., 411n.28
Katz, Jack, 97, 132n.16
Kay, Barbara, 209nn.46,47
Keenan, Kate, 86n.70
Kefauver, Estes, 9
Kehoe, Charles, 614n.60
Keilitz, Ingo, 134n.84
Keith, Bruce, 277, 304n.1, 306n.53

Kelley, Thomas, 20, 25nn.42, 49
Kelling, George, 507n.96
Kelly, Delos, 240n.88, 351, 371n.32, 372nn.38,41,42,43
Kempe, C. Henry, 282–83, 299, 307n.109, 308n.149
Kempf, Kimberly, 82, 87nn.82,88
Kendall-Tackett, Kathleen, 285, 307n.98
Kennedy, Leslie, 99, 132n.27
Kerner, H. J., 132n.2, 208n.1, 340n.8
Kerning, C. D., 239n.60
Kershner, J., 105
Kfoury, Paul, 471n.3, 584n.93
Kimbrough, Jackie, 373n.80
Kinnard, Stephen, 582n.28
Kistner, Janet, 308n.147
Kleiman, Mark A. R., 338, 342n.101
Klein, Dorie, 262n.23
Klein, Jody, 84n.12
Klein, Malcolm, 25n.32, 240n.86, 316, 318, 325, 328, 336, 341n.24, 342nn.64,70,73,89, 544n.35, 610, 614n.66
Klepper, Steven, 133n.34
Klockars, Carl, 240n.81, 411n.63, 412n.68
Klugel, J., 544n.51
Know, George, 358, 372n.63
Knutson, John, 307n.95
Kobrin, Solomon, 20, 25nn.32,53, 150, 170n.29, 544n.35
Koch, Gary, 582n.31
Kohfeld, Carol, 133n.33
Kohlberg, Lawrence, 119
Konopka, Gisela, 251, 263nn.47,50
Koppel, Herbert, 52n.44
Kornhauser, Ruth, 208nn.23,25
Kramer, Rita, 577, 583n.84
Kratcoski, Lucille, 263n.49
Kratcoski, Peter, 263n.49
Krisberg, Barry, 25nn.33,61, 234, 240nn.73,80,89, 342n.102, 581n.1, 613n.40, 614n.63, 626, 649nn.23,28
Krohn, Marvin, 84n.8, 85n.32, 86n.64, 132nn.2,19,23, 133n.41, 183, 195, 208nn.1,15,29,30, 209nn.58,64, 210nn.78,79, 273, 305n.25, 314, 340n.10, 341n.15, 342n.97, 371n.14, 411n.32
Kruttschnitt, Candance, 308n.136
Ksander, Margaret, 68

L

Lab, Steven, 24n.10, 639, 649n.46
Labouvie, Erich, 121
LaGrange, Randy, 52n.42, 194, 209n.60, 412n.71
Lambert, David, 650n.86
Land, Kenneth, 85n.40, 132n.24
Lander, Bernard, 149, 170n.21
Landis, Judson, 171n.78
Lang, Kevin, 544n.38
Lanza-Kaduce, Lonn, 84n.8
LaRosa, John, 68
Larson, Reed, 372n.53
Latessa, Edward, 613n.13
Laub, John, 69, 74, 79–81, 85nn.38,42, 86nn.51,52,63, 81, 278, 280, 305nn.36,41, 306nn.60,67,73, 551–52, 581n.7
Lawrence, Richard, 208n.31
LeBeau, James, 132n.21
Lee, Ruth, 263n.55
Lee, Sara, 545n.52
Leiber, Michael, 171n.47
Lemert, Edwin, 217–18, 238nn.14,17, 544n.50
Lenroot, Katherine, 439n.56
Leone, Peter, 373n.87
Lerman, Paul, 611, 620
Levi, Lauri, 544nn.29,31
Levin, Jack, 39
Levine, Murray, 264n.86
Lewis, Dorothy Otnow, 134n.77
Lewis, Oscar, 140, 170n.1
Liazos, Alexander, 371n.12, 373n.77
Lichter, Daniel, 24n.7, 306n.69
Lillard, Lee, 306n.71
Lilly, J. Robert, 613n.19
Lincoln, Alan Jay, 304n.2, 306n.77
Linz, Daniel, 136n.128
Lipson, Karin, 507n.95
Lishner, D., 210n.80, 373n.85
Liska, A. E., 210n.66
Litsky, Paul, 25n.61
Lizotte, Alan, 85n.32, 86n.64, 132n.2, 208n.1, 210nn.78,79, 340n.10, 342n.97, 371n.14, 411n.32
Loeber, Rolf, 75–76, 85n.45, 86n.70, 304n.2, 305n.26, 306n.66, 341n.60
Logan, Charles, 524–25, 544n.51, 545n.54
Lombroso, Cesare, 83n.1, 102, 242, 243, 244, 262nn.4,6

Long, John, 330, 342nn.86,91
Lonza-Kaduce, Lonn, 208n.29
Lorch, Elizabeth Pugzles, 136n.130
Lowell, Harvey, 613n.42
Lozovsky, David, 134n.74
Lubeck, Steven G., 371n.12
Lucan, Wayne, 412n.85
Lundberg, Emma, 439n.56
Lundman, Richard, 496, 505n.4,
    544n.51
Lykken, D. T., 135nn.102,103
Lyman, Donald, 137n.171, 262n.33
Lyon, Reid, 108, 134n.86

M

McCall, Robert, 137n.173
McCarthy, Belinda, 513, 543n.10
McCarthy, Bill, 97, 132n.18, 306n.57
Maccauley, J., 262n.42
Maccoby, Eleanor, 249, 262nn.34,40
McCord, Joan, 74, 86n.65, 128,
    137n.184, 278, 304n.3, 306n.56
McCord, William, 128, 137n.184
MacCoun, Robert, 398, 411nn.30,55,
    412n.89
McDermott, Joan, 49, 52n.45, 360,
    372nn.71,73
McDevitt, Jack, 39
McDill, E. L., 372n.70
McDonald, Lance, 309n.161
McDowall, David, 132n.2, 208n.1,
    575, 583n.80
McGahey, Richard, 170n.32
McGarrell, Edmund, 25n.61, 560,
    582n.34
McGee, Charles, 613n.25
McGee, Rob, 136n.148
McGee, Zina, 372n.68
McGlothlin, W., 411n.63
McGue, D. T., 135nn.102,103
McKay, Henry, 145–49, 170n.15, 275,
    317
McKinley, J. Charnley, 121
McKinney, J. D., 371n.23
McLanahan, Sara, 305n.42, 371n.34
McMillan, Michael, 543n.13
MacMurray, Bruce, 551–52, 581n.7
McNeill, Richard, 171n.39
McPartland, J. M., 372n.70
McPherson, Karla, 308n.123
McPherson, Susan, 309n.161
Mahan, Sue, 262n.27
Mahoney, Anne R., 238n.4, 239n.39
Mahoney, Dennis, 613n.24

Mannheim, Herman, 133nn.44,47
Manning, Peter, 239n.45
Marcotte, Paul, 545n.73
Markle, Gerald, 305n.33
Markman, Howard, 305n.27
Marshall, Chris, 25n.54
Marshall, Ineke, 25n.54
Martin, Lawrence, 19, 25n.45
Martin, LeRoy, 342n.66
Martin, Randy, 133n.43
Marx, Karl, 226–27
Mason, Robert, 308n.113
Massey, Charles, 371n.36
Massey, James, 132nn.19,23, 133n.41,
    195, 208n.30, 209n.64
Mathers, Richard, 209n.56
Mathias, Robert, 651n.94
Matsueda, Ross, 180, 208nn.13,21,
    223, 239nn.29,53
Matza, David, 177, 183–84, 208n.33,
    209nn.34,35,36, 219, 238n.25
Maughan, Barbara, 86n.70
Maume, David, 132n.28
Maxson, Cheryl, 328, 342n.70
Mednick, Sarnoff, 111, 134n.90,
    135nn.99,100,106, 137n.169
Meier, Robert, 62, 85n.29,
    239nn.56,59,62
Meltzer, Lynn, 108, 134n.88
Menacker, Julius, 372n.75
Menard, Scott, 124, 137n.174, 403,
    411n.29, 412n.70
Mennel, Robert, 425, 426, 438n.14,
    439nn.21,25,30
Merton, Robert, 153–55,
    171nn.40,41,45
Meseck-Bushey, Sylvia, 135n.97,
    306n.79
Messerschmidt, James, 258, 263n.84
Messner, Steven, 99, 132n.26,
    136n.136
Milich, Richard, 134n.71, 238n.11
Miller, Alden, 614n.65
Miller, Jerome, 603
Miller, Marc, 25n.41
Miller, S. J., 627
Miller, Walter, 159–61, 171nn.54,84,
    316, 317, 318, 341nn.17,
    21,27,29,48, 342n.72
Minor, Kevin I., 613n.15
Minton, Sophia, 424
Mischel, Walter, 117
Moffitt, Terrie, 108, 124, 134n.89,
    136n.148, 137nn.167,169,170,
    171, 262n.33

Monachesi, Elio, 121, 136n.153
Monopolis, Spyros, 410n.18
Monroe, Lawrence, 84n.25
Moore, Joan, 252, 263n.61, 319, 323,
    324, 330, 341nn.35,58, 342n.62
Moore, Mark, 338, 342n.101, 412n.75
Moore, Melanie, 356, 372n.58
Moore, Melinda, 84n.20, 539,
    545n.76
Morash, Merry, 220, 239n.35,
    263n.73, 499, 507nn.82,87
Morris, Norval, 85n.35, 132n.13,
    135n.99, 240n.86, 304n.2,
    306n.76, 340n.7, 341n.59,
    439n.25
Morris, Ruth, 252, 263nn.45,54
Morse, Barbara, 124, 137n.174
Mulvey, Edward, 68
Murcheson, C., 137n.159
Murphy, Patrick, 411n.30, 412n.89
Murray, Charles, 108, 134n.85, 222,
    239n.51, 635
Murray, Ellen, 133n.40, 209nn.46,47
Mutchnick, Robert, 133n.43
Muvihill, Donald, 342n.73

N

Nagin, Daniel, 86n.66, 133n.34
Nathan, John, 136n.130
Needle, Jerome, 342n.98
Neilson, Kathleen, 275, 305n.37
Newberger, Carolyn Moore, 307n.94
Newberger, Eli, 307n.94
Newman, Charles, 439n.23
Newman, Graeme, 24n.24, 132n.12
Niederhoffer, Arthur, 335, 342n.83
Nye, F. Ivan, 51nn.22,30, 62,
    84nn.5,24,25, 276, 280, 306n.65

O

Oakes, Jeannie, 352–53, 372nn.39,44
O'Brien, Robert, 99, 132n.25
O'Connor, Gerald, 239n.40
O'Connor, Sandra Day, 297
Odem, Mary, 246, 259–60, 435,
    439n.55
Ohlin, Lloyd, 83n.2, 164–65,
    171nn.70, 72, 320, 335,
    341n.41, 411n.34, 438n.15,
    455, 577, 583n.83, 610,
    614n.65
Olexa, Carol, 372n.37

Olsen, Virgil, 84n.25
O'Malley, Patrick, 24n.22, 51nn.24,25, 84n.9, 85nn.37,47
O'Neil, Joyce Ann, 411n.25
Orcutt, James, 208n.15
Osborn, Denise, 132n.22
Osborne, Lynn, 432, 439n.53
Osgood, D. Wayne, 51n.25, 85n.48, 86n.72, 262n.35
Oskamp, S., 136n.134
Ostrander, Susan, 582n.31
Ostrow, Miriam, 412n.86
Otis, Stephen, 472n.64
Ott, John, 613n.13

P

Packer, Herbert, 471n.10, 492
Padilla, Felix, 95–96, 132n.14, 165, 171nn.80,81, 319, 337, 341n.37, 342n.95
Padina, Robert, 412n.71
Paige, Karen, 262n.30
Park, Robert Ezra, 144
Parker, Robert Nash, 84n.21
Pasternack, Robert, 108, 134n.86
Paternoster, Raymond, 133nn.35,36, 223, 239n.52, 262n.3
Patterson, Gerald, 170n.11, 302, 306n.62, 309nn.163,164
Pauly, John, 233, 240n.78
Pelham, William, 134nn.71,81
Perry, David, 136n.125
Perry, Louise, 136n.125
Petersilia, Joan, 613n.19
Peterson, John, 25n.53
Piaget, Jean, 118
Pickett, Robert S., 439n.29
Pierce, Glenn, 36, 51n.16
Pierce, Robert, 614n.46
Piersma, Paul, 566, 572
Piliavin, Irving, 51n.4, 188, 209n.44, 492, 495, 506n.67
Pincus, Johnathan, 134n.77
Pink, William, 372n.38
Piper, Elizabeth, 52n.49, 84n.20
Platt, Anthony, 230, 240n.72, 431, 438n.13, 439nn.26, 583n.68
Pleck, Elizabeth, 438n.15, 439nn.18,20,42,43,50
Polk, Kenneth, 208n.4, 371nn.5,12, 25,30,35, 372nn.37,49,52
Pollack, Otto, 245, 262n.16

Pope, Carl, 84nn.12,19, 219, 239nn.30,31,33
Pottieger, Anne, 395, 403, 411nn.22,36,41,52
Pound, Roscoe, 491
Price, Dwight, 552, 581n.10
Puffengerger, Donald, 649n.42
Pugh, Meredith, 43, 52n.34, 209n.62, 314, 340n.13

Q

Quinney, Richard, 227, 239n.63, 240nn.71,72

R

Radosevich, Marcia, 84n.8, 208n.29
Raeder, Myrna, 308n.142
Rafter, Nicole Hahn, 133n.54
Rand, Alicia, 68
Rankin, Joseph, 275, 305nn.38,39
Rasmussen, Paul, 136n.125
Rausch, Sharla, 524–25, 544n.51, 545n.54
Ray, Melvin, 218, 238n.21
Reckless, Walter, 133n.40, 188–90, 209nn.46,47
Reed, M. D., 210n.66
Reidinger, Paul, 584n.88
Reinerman, Craig, 182, 208n.26
Reiss, Albert, 170nn.29,32,33, 188, 340n.7, 492–93, 496, 505n.4
Rendleman, Douglas, 420, 438nn.5,9,12
Reuter, Peter, 398, 411nn.30,55, 412n.89
Reynolds, Morgan, 132n.13
Rhenquist, William, 469
Rich, William, 134n.84
Richmond, F. Lynn, 371nn.25,30
Riley, David, 132n.11
Rivera, Ramon, 171n.79
Roberg, Roy, 261n.1
Roberts, Mary K., 209nn.55,61
Robey, Ames, 263n.55
Robinson, Dinah, 472n.64
Robinson, Paul, 306n.50
Rodick, J. Douglas, 306n.51, 340n.12
Roditi, Bethany, 134n.88
Rogers, D. E., 86n.69
Rogers, Joseph, 135n.97, 306n.79
Rogers, Willard, 170n.9
Roman, Deborah Decker, 136n.156

Romig, Dennis, 610, 613n.24, 614n.66, 631, 649n.49
Root, Maria, 307n.106
Rosen, Lawrence, 208n.3, 275, 305n.37
Rosenbaum, Alan, 306n.46
Rosenbaum, Jill Leslie, 306n.49
Rosenfeld, Richard, 149, 170n.27
Rosenthal, Margueritte, 439n.59
Rosenthal, Robert, 238n.10
Rosenwal, Richard, 263n.55
Rosner, Richard, 116
Ross, Robert, 25n.57
Rossi, A. S., 262n.36
Roszell, Douglass, 136n.158
Rothman, David, 24n.25, 434, 583n.68
Rouse, Martin, 25nn.37, 40
Rowan, Joseph, 614n.60
Rowe, David, 86n.67, 135nn.97,98, 281, 306n.79
Rubin, H. Ted, 472n.63, 544n.42, 602, 613n.41
Rudman, Cary, 539, 545n.76, 651n.94
Russell, Diana, 287, 307nn.100,105
Ryer, Charles, 309n.161

S

Sack, William, 308n.113
Sagatun, Inger, 309n.160
Salerno, Anthony, 439nn.23,49
Salert, Barbara, 87n.86
Salisbury, Harrison, 9, 24n.1
Sampson, Robert, 52n.37, 69, 74, 79–81, 84nn.15,22, 85n.42, 86nn.51,52,63, 81, 149, 170nn.22,26,27,33, 171n.38, 278, 280, 305n.36, 306nn.60,67,73, 499, 507n.89
Sanborn, Joseph, 530–31, 545n.64, 557, 582nn.23,24
Sanchez-Jankowski, Martin, 132n.14, 337, 342n.96
Sanders, Wiley B., 438n.8
Sarri, Rosemary, 51n.26, 84n.6
Saunders, Frank, 263n.56
Savitz, Lenoard, 171n.45
Scalia, Antonin, 469
Scarpitti, Frank, 171n.78, 209n.47
Schafer, Walter, 208n.4, 371nn.5,35, 372nn.37,49,52
Schauss, Alexander, 105
Scheurman, Leo, 150, 170n.29

Schlossman, Steven, 171n.82, 246, 259–60, 435, 439n.55
Schmidt, Annesley, 613n.19
Schmidt, Chester, 410n.18
Schneider, Anne, 521, 544n.37, 600, 613nn.27,30,33,34,36
Schneider, Peter, 599–600, 613n.34
Schoen, Donald, 524, 545n.53
Schoenthaler, Stephen, 106, 134nn.66, 69,70,73
Schoo, David, 4
Schoo, Sharon, 4
Schrag, Clarence, 171n.73, 209n.48
Schuessler, Karl, 122
Schulsinger, Fini, 137n.169
Schur, Edwin, 128, 215, 235, 239n.43, 240n.85
Schuster, Richard, 85n.44, 86n.58
Schut, Edwin, 137n.185
Schutt, Russell, 84nn.10,12, 496, 506n.68, 507n.71, 516, 543n.17
Schwartz, Ira, 19, 23, 25nn.33,43,55, 61,63, 342n.102, 457, 472n.14, 519, 543nn.15,16, 544nn.29,30,31, 545n.57, 581n.10, 584n.102, 614nn.63,64, 625, 649n.34
Schwartz, Joseph, 170n.28
Schwartz, Michael, 209n.48
Schwendinger, Herman, 170n.10, 228, 230, 232–33, 239n.67, 240nn.74,76,77, 263nn.79, 84, 439n.52
Schwendinger, Julia Siegel, 170n.10, 228, 230, 232–33, 239n.67, 240nn.74, 76,77, 263nn.79,84, 439n.52
Scott, Joseph, 25nn.56,60, 472n.64
Scott, Steven Flagg, 613n.23
Sederstrom, John, 157–58, 171n.51, 210n.74
Sedlak, Michael, 171n.82
Segal, Nancy, 135nn.98, 102
Selke, William, 240n.87
Sellin, Thorsten, 70, 85n.44, 86n.54, 132n.1, 133n.47, 158–59, 171n.52, 371n.17
Seng, Magnus, 307n.97
Senna, Joseph, 471n.10
Shannon, Lyle, 73, 85n.44, 86n.59, 348, 371n.15
Shantz, David, 133n.42
Sharer, Shanda Renee, 4
Shauffer, Carole, 472n.34

Shaw, Clifford, 145–49, 166, 170n.15, 275, 317
Shelden, Randall, 20, 25n.52, 78, 84n.7, 86n.75, 261n.1, 432, 439n.53
Sheldon, William H., 103
Sheley, Joseph, 372n.68
Shepherd, Robert, Jr., 568, 582n.44, 583n.50
Sheridan, William, 544n.40
Sherkat, Darren, 306n.63
Sherman, Lawrence, 505n.2
Shichor, David, 240n.88, 649n.33
Shine, James, 552, 581n.10
Short, James, 51nn.22,30, 62, 84nn.5,24, 25, 163, 171nn.67,79, 180, 209n.42, 313, 340n.9
Shotten, Alice, 472n.34
Shover, Neal, 68
Sickmund, Melissa, 18, 25n.31, 583n.59
Siegel, Larry, 209n.42, 239nn.57,68, 582n.22
Siegel, Leslie, 85n.38
Sieverdes, Christopher, 623
Silva, Phil, 137nn.167,170, 262n.33
Simcha-Fagan, Ora, 170n.28
Simon, Rita, 253, 255, 262n.6, 262n.23, 263nn.64,68
Simpson, John, 263n.85, 264n.87
Simpson, Sally, 263n.80
Singer, Simon, 49, 52n.46, 63, 85n.34, 264n.86, 371nn.11,33, 575, 583n.80
Skinner, B. F., 116
Skinner, William, 208n.30
Skogan, Wesley, 170n.33, 171n.37
Skovron, Sandra Evans, 25nn.56,60, 472n.64
Slater, E., 245, 262n.20, 263n.46
Slaughter, Ellen, 507nn.71,72, 545n.79, 582n.33
Slawson, John, 123, 137n.164
Small, John, 263n.55
Smart, Carol, 256, 263n.7
Smetena, Judith, 305n.44
Smith, Beverly, 428, 439n.39
Smith, Carolyn, 256, 263n.75, 273, 305n.25
Smith, Charles, 496, 507nn.70,83
Smith, Douglas, 52n.37, 62, 84n.12, 85nn.27,28, 262n.3, 498, 506n.64, 507n.85

Smith, Richard, 306nn.55,59
Smith, Robert, 472n.31
Snyder, Eloise, 239n.37
Snyder, Howard, 20, 25n.51, 74, 78, 85n.45, 86nn.61,76, 613n.28
Snyder, Phyllis, 19, 25n.45
Soderstrom, Irina, 635
Solar, Mark, 472n.34, 528, 545n.80
Somerville, Dora, 251, 263n.51
Sorrell, James, 116, 135n.120
Sparks, Richard, 51n.20
Speck, Richard, 109–10
Speckart, George, 411n.63, 412n.68
Spergel, Irving, 171n.74, 316, 324, 335, 341nn.26,36,54,59, 342nn.88,94,106
Spielvogel, Jackson, 438n.3
Spitzer, Stephen, 234, 239n.61, 240n.82
Sprafkin, Joyce, 136n.129
Sprague, John, 133n.33
Staples, William, 600, 613n.38
Stapleton, W. Vaughan, 342n.98
Stark, Rodney, 171n.36
Steffensmeier, Darrell, 51n.9, 85n.37, 256, 263n.76
Steffensmeier, Renee Hoffman, 256, 263n.76
Steinhart, David, 544n.32
Steinmentz, Suzanne, 307n.101
Stern, Susan, 209n.58
Stinchcombe, Arthur, 351, 354, 371n.31, 372n.50
Stone, Daryl, 320, 340n.1
Stone, Karen, 308n.117
Stone, Lawrence, 438nn.2,6
Stouthamer-Loeber, Magda, 86n.70, 137n. 171, 304n.2, 305nn.26,41, 306n.62
Strasburg, Paul, 492
Straus, Murray, 272, 279, 287, 289, 299, 304n.2, 306nn.64,77, 307nn.101,102, 103,104, 308nn.115,148
Streib, Victor, 492, 577, 584nn.88,92
Streifel, Cathy, 85n.37
Strodtbeck, Fred, 209n.42, 313, 340n.9
Sullivan, Dennis, 239nn.57,68
Sutherland, Edwin, 123, 137n.165, 171n.71, 177–81, 208nn.6,7,9
Sutherland, Mary, 544n.36
Sutton, John R., 436, 438n.17, 439n.57
Svikis, Dace, 410n.18

Swanger, Henry, 544n.33
Sykes, Gresham, 183–84, 208n.33, 209n.36, 239nn.55,64, 505n.4
Szymanski, Linda, 505n.20, 545n.70, 565, 582n.39, 584n.97, 613n.31

T

Takata, Susan, 322, 341n.50
Tamara, Hareven, 438n.14
Tangri, Sandra, 209n.48
Tannenbaum, Frank, 219, 238n.22
Tappan, Paul, 436
Tardiff, Kenneth, 99, 132n.26
Taussig, Cara, 309nn.162,165
Taylor, Carl, 165, 171n.80, 321, 324, 341nn.44,61
Tellegen, A., 135n.103
Templer, Donald, 410n.18
Tennenbaum, David, 122, 136n.157
Tennyson, Ray, 171n.79
Terry, Robert, 496, 507n.69
Thatcher, Robert, 135n.92
Thomas, Charles, 20, 25nn.50,54, 221, 239n.41
Thomas, Clarence, 469
Thomas, W. I., 83n.1, 244, 262n.14
Thome, P. R., 262n.42
Thompson, Carol, 68
Thompson, Kevin, 85n.30, 264n.86
Thornberry, Terence, 51n.3, 84n.11, 85nn.30,32, 86nn.55,64, 132n.2, 201–2, 208nn.1,15, 209n.58, 210nn.77,78,79, 314, 337, 340n.10, 341nn.15,60, 342n.97, 356, 371n.14, 372n.58, 394, 411n.32, 496, 507n.71
Thrasher, Frederick, 148, 170n.19, 315, 316, 317, 341n.23
Tifft, Larry, 51n.31, 239nn.57,68
Titchener, Edward, 118
Tittle, Charles, 62, 85nn.28,29, 133n.37, 208nn.14,17, 222, 239nn.46,54
Toborg, Mary, 412n.65
Toby, Jackson, 234, 240n.84, 350, 357, 371n.26, 372n.60
Tojanowicz, Robert, 507n.98
Tonry, Michael, 85n.35, 132n.13, 135n.99, 170nn.29,32,33, 240n.86, 304n.2, 306n.76, 340n.7, 341n.59, 438n.15, 439n.25, 507n.101, 614n.66

Tontodonato, Pamela, 81, 87n.87
Tracy, Paul, 84n.11, 85n.30, 86nn.55,57
Tracy, Sharon, 20, 25n.52
Traxler, Mary Pat, 276, 305n.43
Trickett, Alan, 132n.22
Trocki, Karen, 307n.100
Tromanhauser, Edward, 358, 372n.63
Tuck, Mary, 132n.11
Tumin, Melvin, 342n.73
Turnquist, Dawn, 307n.95
Tuthill, Richard, 424

U

Uchida, Craig, 505n.3

V

Vachss, Andrew, 635, 650n.58
Vallant, G. E., 411n.27
Van den Haag, Ernest, 132nn.4,12, 133n.29
Van Kammen, Wemoet, 86n.70
Van Voorhis, Patricia, 209n.56
Vasta, Ross, 52n.47
Vaughn, Joseph B., 596, 613n.20
Vaughn, Michael, 583n.60
Vaz, E., 263n.72
Vedder, Clyde, 251, 263n.51
Viano, Emilio, 239n.57
Vigil, James Diego, 317, 330, 333, 335, 336, 341nn.20,47, 342nn.62,81,85, 86,90,91
Villemez, Wayne, 62, 85n.28
Vinter, Robert D., 649n.47
Visher, Christy, 498, 506n.64, 507n.80
Vivona, T. Scott, 545n.79, 637
Volavka, Jan, 135n.99
Volenik, Adrienne, 471n.13, 566
Vollmer, August, 479
Von Hirsch, Andrew, 87n.85, 132n.12, 472n.27
Voss, Harwin, 59, 84nn.8,25, 355, 371n.3, 372n.55
Vuchnich, S., 170n.11

W

Waite, Linda, 306n.71
Waitrowski, Michael, 371n.36
Wakefield, James, 134n.70
Waldo, Gordon, 122

Walker, Samuel, 505n.8
Wall, J., 210n.80
Wallace, John, 411n.49
Wallace, Mel, 328, 342n.71
Wallace, Rodrick, 170n.3
Walsh, Adam, 47
Walter, James, 582n.31
Walters, Glenn, 135nn.101,109, 137n.181
Walters, James, 306nn.55,59
Walters, Richard, 117
Wang, Zheng, 342n.79
Warboys, Loren, 472n.34, 545n.58
Ward, David, 238n.27
Warner, Jean, 613nn.27,33
Warr, Mark, 181, 208n.22, 314, 340n.11
Warren, Earl, 561
Warren, Keith, 306n.54
Waternaux, Christine, 307n.94
Watson, John B., 116
Wattenberg, William, 263n.56
Watts, W. David, 412n.67
Webb, James, 170n.20
Webster, David, 582n.28
Webster-Stratton, Carolyn, 307n.109
Weeks, Ashley, 275
Weis, Joseph, 43, 51nn.5,6,32, 52n.36, 84n.5, 157–58, 171n.51, 198–99, 210n.74, 256, 263n.77
Weisheit, Ralph, 262n.27, 412n.68
Weitekamp, E., 132n.2, 208n.1
Weldon, Ward, 372n.75
Wellford, Charles, 222, 239nn.47,49
Wells, L. Edward, 275, 305n.38
Wells, Richard, 290, 308n.125
Werner, Norman, 506n.65
Wertham, Frederic, 9, 24n.18
West, D. J., 85n.44, 86nn.58,80, 280, 306nn.75,77, 340n.8, 349, 371n.16
Wharton, Robert, 308n.117
Wheeler, Etta, 281
Whitaker, Catherine, 52n.41
Whitcomb, Debra, 308nn.133,139
White, Helene Raskin, 77, 86n.73, 121, 171n.50, 194, 209n.60, 395, 411n.33, 412nn.68,71,73
White, Jennifer, 137n.170
White, Joseph, 545n.69
White, Thomas, 137n.181
Whitehead, John, 24n.10, 639, 649n.46

SUBJECT INDEX

■■

minor/status offense arrests by gender, 54, 55, 56

minor/status offense arrests by race, 57, 58, 59

serious arrests by age, 34, 35

use of, 32–33

Articulation hypothesis, 351

Asian gangs, 333

Associated Marine Institutes (AMI), 610, 636

At-risk youth, 11

Attention deficit disorder (ADD), 108, 109

B

Barbiturates, 383

Bail, 526–28

Balanced probation, 597

Balancing-of-the-interest approach, 293

Barrio, 317, 330

Barrio Gangs (Vigil), 336

Battered child syndrome, 282–83

Behavioral Science Institute, 59

Behavioral theory
description of, 116–17
role of media, 117–18
social learning theory, 116–17

Behavior modification, 632

Behavior syndrome, problem, 76–77

Best interests of the child, 12

Betrayal, sexual abuse and, 284

Beyond-control youngsters, 276

Beyond Delinquency (Murray and Cox), 222

Beyond Probation (Murray and Cox), 635

Bifurcated process, 450

Bindover. *See* Transfer of juveniles to adult court

Biosocial theory
biochemical factors, 105–6
contemporary, 104
definition of, 92, 104
description of, 101–12
diet and, 105–6
educational impact on delinquency and, 345
female delinquency and, 242–49
genetic influences, 108–12
neurological dysfunction and, 106–8
origins of, 102–3
summary of, 130

Boot camps, 637

Broken homes
family conflict versus, 277–78
impact of, 273–76

C

California
camps in, 619
community-based institutions in, 610–11
correctional institutions in, 623
probation in, 602
reception-classification centers in, 620

Cambridge-Somerville Youth Study, 128, 280

Cambridge study in delinquent development, 79

Camps, 608, 619

Canada, delinquency in, 12

Capitalism, Patriarchy, and Crime (Messerschmidt), 258

Capital punishment for children, 22, 100, 577–79

Carnegie Corp., 361

CASA (Court Appointed Special Advocates), 556

Causes of Delinquency (Hirschi), 190

Chancery court system, 420–21

Chicago Area Project, 148, 166, 339

Chicago Bar Association, 14

Chicago Intervention Network, 339

Child abuse
See also Sexual abuse
aftermath of, 285
alcohol and drug abuse and, 289–90
battered child syndrome, 282–83
causes of, 288–89
child protection system, 291–92
children attending court hearings, 294–96
delinquency and, 298–302
delinquency prevention and, 302–03
description of abusive parent, 289
difference between neglect and, 283–84
economic conditions and, 272–73
extent of, 285, 287–88
by gender, 54–56
historical view of, 281–82
legal issues, 296–98

legal processing of abuse cases, 291–92

number of reported cases, 287–88

origin of term, 283

by parents, 281

rights of parents, 291, 292

separation/removal of children from parents, 298

social class and, 290–91

state intervention, 291, 292–93

videotaping children's statements, 295–96

Child Abuse Prevention and Treatment Act, 291

Child Assistance Program (CAP), 167

Child care
in colonial America, 421–22
development of concern for, 418–21
in the 1800s, 422–23
in the Middle Ages, 416–17
in the 1600s and 1700s, 418
urbanization and, 423–24

Children
See also Child abuse; Sexual abuse
abduction of, 47–48
rights of, 14, 428, 466–68

Children in Custody (CIC) series, 624, 626

Children in Need of Supervision (CHINS), 437

Children's Aid Society, 205, 429

Children's Defense Fund, 272

Child Savers (Platt), 230, 431

Child-saving movement, 424–25, 431–33

Chivalry hypothesis, 245, 497

Choice theory
definition of, 92
development of, 93–94
educational impact on delinquency and, 345
family structure and delinquency and, 268
review of, 100–101

Cholo, 330

Chronic career offenders, 7

Chronic delinquents, 54
academic performance and, 348–49
categories of, 7
controlling, 461
Delinquency in a Birth Cohort, 70–73
drugs and, 402–3
predicting who will become, 70–71

tracking, 73–74
treating, 634–35
Chronic recidivists, 71
Classical criminology, 93
Clearance, 31–32
Cliques, 312, 324
Cocaine, 381–82
Cognitive theory, 118
Cohort studies
    child abuse and delinquency and
        use of, 299, 302
    Delinquency in a Birth Cohort
        (Wolfgang), 70–73
    research studies using, 71–73
Collateral review, 573
Colorado
    correctional institutions in, 624
    nonresidential community
        treatment programs in, 608,
        609
    probation in, 596
Comic books, impact of, 9
Community
    delinquency and change in the,
        150
    drug controlling programs, 407
    policing, 476, 501–3
Community-based institutions, 603–8
Community treatment
    community-based institutions,
        603–8
    criticisms of, 608–10
    definition of, 588
    nonresidential, 608
    privatization of probation, 602
    probation, 588–97
    residential, 606–8
    restitution, 598
Community Treatment Project (CTP),
    610–11
Complaint, 526
Comprehensive Employment Training
    Act, 204
Compulsory school attendance,
    365–67
Concurrent jurisdiction statutes, 532,
    533
Confidentiality in proceedings,
    579–80
Conflict
    criminology, 225
    effects of, on family, 271–73
    family/interfamily, 276–78
    subculture, 164
Conflict theory. *See* Social conflict
    theory

Conformity
    social adaptation, 153
    weak commitment to, 188
Connecticut
    community-based institutions in,
        605
    correctional institutions in, 623,
        624
Conscience and Convenience (Rothman),
    434
Containment theory, 188–90
Contemporary Woman and Crime, The
    (Simon), 255
Control theory, 175, 190–95
Co-offending, 313
Correctional institutions
    administrative structure of,
        621–23
    categories of, 617
    cost of, 624
    development of juvenile
        institutions, 428–30
    during the 1900s, 619–21
    early history of, 618
    hidden correctional system,
        625–26
    overcrowding in, 623–24
    profile of institutionalized
        juveniles, 624–25, 626–30
    statistics on, 618, 620, 621, 623,
        624–625, 627
    trends in, 623–24
Correctional treatment
    behavior modification, 632
    for chronic delinquents,
        634–35
    educational programs, 633–34
    effectiveness of, 637, 639
    general description of, 630
    group treatment techniques,
        632–33
    individual counseling, 630–31
    Outward Bound programs, 635,
        636
    psychotherapy, 631
    reality therapy, 631–32
    recreational programs, 634
    right to, 639–44
    specialized programs, 635–37
    vocational programs, 633–34
Corrections Compendium, 624
Cottage system, 618
Counseling, individual, 630–31
Court. *See* Juvenile court; Juvenile
    justice system
Crack, 382

Crime
    age and, 34–35, 63–67
    as choice, 125
    definitions for the types of, 30
    drug-crime connection, 31, 376,
        401–2, 403–4
    gangs and patterns of, 328
    gender and, 54–56, 255
    natural areas for, 145
    parental, 280–81
    patterns, 31–32
    prestige, 328
    rates, 36
    relationship of age and, 30–31
    in schools, 358–60
    seductions of, 97
    social class and, 60–63
    specialization, 77–78
    trends, 30–31, 36
    turning points in, 79–81
Crime and Human Nature (Wilson and
    Herrnstein), 95, 124, 125
Crime in the Making (Sampson and
    Laub), 79
Criminal atavism, 102
Criminality of Women, The (Pollak), 245
Criminal justice versus juvenile
    justice, 451–53
Criminal subculture, 164
Criminologists, role of, 8, 225
Critical criminology, 225
Crowds, 312
Cultural deviance theories
    culture conflict, 159
    delinquent subculture, 161–64
    description of, 143, 144, 157–59
    development of subcultures,
        158–59
    focal concern theory, 159–61
    middle-class measuring rods,
        162–64
    opportunity theory, 150, 164–65
    subculture of violence, 159
    summary of, 168
Cultural transmission, 146
Culture conflict, 159, 178
Culture of poverty, 140
Custodial interrogation by police,
    487–89

D

Dangerous classes, 424
DARE (Drug Abuse Resistance
    Education), 406–7, 501, 503

female delinquency and, 252–53, 259

group homes, 608

impact of, on delinquency, 273–81

learned delinquency and, 177

parental crime, 280–81

quality of parent-child relations, 278

siblings, 281

size, 280

social bond and, 190

social control theories and, 194

social process theories and, 268

social reaction theories and, 268

social structure and, 268

structure in the Middle Ages, 416–17

summary of theories on, 268

FBI, Uniform Crime Report, 29–30

Fear, role of, 150–51

Female delinquency

biosocial views of, 242–49

chivalry hypothesis, 245

early views of, 242, 243

gangs and, 252, 323–24

hormonal differences and, 248

liberal feminist theory and, 253–56

masculinity hypothesis, 244

menstruation and, 244, 245

power-control theory and, 259

precocious sexuality and, 245–46

premenstrual syndrome and, 247–48

profile of institutionalized females, 259–60, 628–30

psychology of sex and, 246–47

radical feminist views of, 256–59

sexuality and, 244–45, 248

socialization theories and, 249–53

summary of theories of, 260–61

Female Offender, The (Lombroso), 243

Feminist movement, female delinquency and

liberal views, 253–56

radical views, 256–59

Fifth Amendment, 561

First Amendment, 579

Five Hundred Delinquent Women (Glueck and Glueck), 251

Florida

community-based institutions in, 603, 604

probation in, 589

Focal concern theory, 159–61

Foot patrols, 502

Foster care programs, 607–8

Fourteenth Amendment, 518, 561, 562, 643

Fourth Amendment, 483, 485

Freebase, 381–82

Free speech, 367–68

Free will concept, 93

G

Gang(s)

See also Peers

African-American, 331

ages of members, 323

Anglo, 333–35

Asian, 333

breaking, 338

categories of, 321

clothing of, 327–28

communications in, 325–28

contemporary, 320–35

controlling, 337–39

criminality, 328

definitions of, 315, 316

detail, 337

drugs and, 399

drugs and reemergence of, 319

during the 1950s and 1960s, 318

during the 1970s, 318–19

ethnic and racial composition of, 328–35

extent of, 320

focal concern theory and, 159–61

formation of, 324

gender of members, 252, 323–24

group autonomy and, 163

group delinquency versus, 315

Hispanic, 330, 331–32

impact of, 38

leadership in, 324–25

location of, 321–22

near and youth, 315–17

neighborhood reactions, 322

reasons for, 335–37

reasons for increase in, 319

subcultures, 164–65

sweeps, 338

unit, 337

Gang, The (Thrasher), 317

Gender

aggression and, 249

of gang members, 252, 323–24

labeling theory and, 219–20

minor/status offenses arrests by, 54, 55, 56

police discretion and, 497–98

self-reported illegal behavior by, 55–56

Generalized modality of delinquency, 233

General Theory of Crime, A (Hirschi and Gottfredson), 195

Genetics

criminal behavior caused by, 108–12

drug use and, 395

Gentrified, 150

Georgia

probation in, 595

restitution in, 600

Germany, delinquency in, 12

Gestalt psychology, 118

Graffiti, gangs and use of, 325

Great Britain, delinquency in, 12

Group autonomy, 163

Group delinquency versus gangs, 315

Group homes, 606

Group psychotherapy, 632

Groups, near and youth, 315–17

Group therapy, 632

Group treatment techniques, 632–33

Guardian *ad litem*, 291, 292, 556

Guided group interaction (GGI), 633

Guns' N Roses, 10

H

Hallucinogens, 384

Hate crimes, 38, 39

Head Start, 204, 212

Hearings

abused children at, 294–96

detention, 449, 515–16

open versus closed, 579–80

Hearsay, 296

Heroin, 382

Highfields project, 607

Hindelang Research Center, 65

Hispanic gangs, 330, 331–32

Home Alone case, 4

Homicide, statistics on, 6

Hormonal differences, female delinquency and, 248

Hormonal levels, antisocial behavior and, 105

House arrest, 596

House of Reformation, 425

House of Refuge, 425, 618

Houses of refuge, 14

Humanistic psychology, 118

Human nature theory, 125, 130
Humphrey Institute of Public Affairs, 516

I

Idaho
    correctional institutions in, 623, 624
    restitution in, 600
Identity crisis, 115
Illinois
    Juvenile Court Act, 431, 432–33, 443
    transfer to adult court in, 533
Impulsive personalities, 196
In-court statements, child abuse cases and, 297–98
Indeterminate sentence, 573–74
Index crimes, 29
Indiana
    probation in, 596
    transfer to adult court in, 533
Individual counseling, 630–31
Individualized treatment model, 574
Informal consent decree, 568
Informal economic stage of delinquency, 233
Inhalants, 383
Inheritance theory, 102
In loco parentis, 368
Innovation, social adaptation, 153–54
Institute for Social Research (ISR), 41–42, 59, 64, 387, 388–89
Institute of Judicial Administration (IJA), 456–57, 644
Institutionalized juveniles, profile of, 624–25, 626–30
Institutions
    See also Correctional institutions
    community-based, 603–8
Instrumental theory, 232–33
Intake process, 449, 521–23
Integrated structural Marxist theory, 233–34
Integrated theories
    Elliott, 199–201
    interactional theory (Thornberry), 201–2
    social development theory (Weis), 198–99
    summary of, 207
Intelligence quotient (IQ)
    delinquency and, 122–25
    nurture theory and, 123

Intensive supervision model, 595–96
Interactional theory, 201–2
International Association of Chiefs of Police, 478, 479, 481
Interstitial area, 317
Interstitial group, 315
Intrafamily conflict, 276–78
Islands in the Stream (Sanchez-Jankowski), 337

J

Job Corps, 204
Jointure, 417
Judge, role of court, 552–55
Jukes: A Study in Crime, Pauperism, Disease, and Heredity, The (Dugdale), 102
Jukes in 1915, The (Estabrook), 102
Juvenile court
    defense attorney's role, 555–59
    judge's role, 552–55
    jurisdiction, 463–66
    number of cases before, 548
    prosecutor's role, 548–52
    structure of, 461–63
Juvenile delinquency
    conflict over treatment of, 21–23
    definition of, 6
    historical overview of, 11–13
    interdisciplinary study of, 8
    international, 12
    legal status of, 13
    statistics on, 6
    types of offenses, 4–5
    youth at-risk, 11
Juvenile Delinquency Prevention and Control (JDP) Act of 1968, 455
Juvenile delinquent(s)
    official versus unofficial, 28
    portrait of, 80
    relationship between victim and, 46–47, 49
    versus status offenders, 20
Juvenile Gangs in Context (Klein), 318
Juvenile institutions. *See* Correctional institutions
Juvenile Intensive Probation Supervision (JIPS) programs, 595–96
Juvenile justice
    American Bar Association standards, 456–57
    criminal justice versus, 451–53

definition of, 442–43
goals, 454–58
models of, 458, 459
shifting philosophies of, 458
Juvenile Justice and Delinquency Prevention Act (JJDPA)(1974), 442, 444, 456, 518, 605
Juvenile justice process, description of, 446–50
Juvenile Justice Reform Act of 1977, 575
Juvenile Justice Standards Project, 456–57
Juvenile justice system
    See also Pretrial procedures
    adjudication, 560–66
    confidentiality in proceedings, 579–80
    description of, 7, 444–46
    development of, 435–36, 442–44
    disposition, 566–70
    labeling theory and, 214–15, 219
    reforming the system, 436–37, 458
    right to appeal, 572–73
    sentencing, 573–77
    status offenders in, 16–17
    systems approach, 446
Juvenile officers, 477

K

Klikas, 324

L

Labeling
    description of theory, 213–23
    discrimination in, 219–20
    educational impact on delinquency and, 345
    effects of, 213–14, 215–17, 220–21
    evaluating the theory, 221–22
    future of, 222–23
    juvenile justice process and, 214–15, 219
    nature of crime and delinquency and, 215
    primary and secondary deviance, 217–18
    self-, 214
Latchkey children, 141
Latent delinquents, 115

Law enforcement, role of police and, 477
Law Enforcement Assistance Administration (LEAA), 455, 479
Law-violating youth groups, 314, 317
Learning disabilities (LDs), 107–8
Learning theory
    See also Social learning theories
    defintion of, 175
Least detrimental alternative, 573
Least restrictive alternative, 620
Legalization of drugs, 408
Legal status and responsibility, 13–14
Life course, 54
    educational impact on delinquency and, 345
    implications, 81–82
Life cycle of delinquency, 67, 69, 74–75, 78–79
Life history, 67
Life-styles of victims, impact of, 99
Life-style violent juveniles, 635
Lineup identifications, 490–91
Local school systems, 346
Longitudinal studies, age patterns and, 67
Los Patrinos Juvenile Hall School, 517
Louisiana
    community-based institutions in, 604
    restitution in, 597
    status offense laws in, 16
Lower-class culture conflict, focal concerns, 159–61
Low-visibility decision making, 492
Lyman School for Boys, 618
D-lysergic acid diethylamide-25 (LSD), 384

M

McGruff the Crime Dog, 406
McMartin Day Care Center, 292, 294
Maine, reform schools in, 618
Males, profile of institutionalized, 627–28
Mandatory sentences, 574
Marijuana, 376, 380–81
Marxist criminology, 225, 226–27
Marxist feminists, 256–57
Maryland
    community-based institutions in, 604

correctional institutions in, 621
    probation in, 591
    restitution in, 597
Masculinity hypothesis, 244
Massachusetts
    community-based institutions in, 603–4
    cottage system in, 618
    probation in, 591
    reform schools in, 618
    restitution in, 599
    transfer to adult court in, 533
Measuring methods for juvenile delinquency
    official data/statistics, 28–38
    self-report data, 28, 38–43
    victim surveys, 28, 43–45
Media, role of, 117–18
Medical model of crime, 93
Menopause, female delinquency and, 245
Menstruation, female delinquency and, 244, 245
Metallica, 10
Michigan, correctional institutions in, 626
Mid-City Project, 166
Middle-class delinquency, 62–63
Middle-class measuring rods, 162–64, 350
Milieu therapy, 633
Minimal brain dysfunction (MBD), 107
Minnesota
    correctional institutions in, 624
    Multiphasic Personality Inventory (MMPI), 121–22
    restitution in, 599
Minor child, definition of, 13
Minors in Need of Supervision (MINS), 437
Missouri
    community-based institutions in, 605
    correctional institutions in, 626
    Plan, 555
Mobilization for Youth (MOBY), 166, 339
Models of juvenile justice, 458, 459
Model Youth Correction Authority Act, 620
Monetary restitution, 597–98
Montana, correctional institutions in, 626
Moral and intellectual development theory, 118–19

Mortality rates, 6
Movies/films, impact of, 10
Multi-Service Family Life and Sex Education Program, 205
Music, impact of, 10

N

National Advisory Commission on Criminal Justice Standards and Goals, 19, 455–56, 568, 572–73
National Advisory Committee on Handicapped Children, 107
National Assessment study, gangs and, 320, 323, 324, 329, 337
National Association of State Alcohol and Drug Abuse, 391
National Center for Juvenile Justice, 15, 16, 406, 571, 591
National Center on Child Abuse and Neglect, 286, 287
National Coalition of State Juvenile Justice Advisory Groups, 497
National Commission on Excellence in Education, 361
National Committee for Prevention of Child Abuse (NCPCA), 287–88, 289, 290
National Conference of Commissioners on Uniform State Laws, 482, 572
National Conference of State Legislatures, 577
National Council of Juvenile and Family Court Judges, 532, 555, 603
National Council on Crime and Delinquency, 497, 514, 555, 603, 644
National Crime Victimization Survey (NCVS), 43–49, 65
National District Attorneys Association, 552, 553
National Household Survey, 387, 388
National Incidence and Prevalence of Child Abuse and Neglect Survey, 287, 290
National Institute of Drug Abuse (NIDA), 386, 387
National Institute of Justice, 320
National Institute of Mental Health, 118
National Juvenile Custody Trends, 624

revocation procedures and, 646
rights of minors and, 443, 466–68
right to treatment and, 641, 643
school crime and, 365
school discipline and, 369
search and seizure and, 483,
    485–86
University of Michigan, Institute for
    Social Research (ISR), 41–42,
    59, 64, 387, 388–89
Unraveling Juvenile Delinquency (Glueck
    and Glueck), 69
Upward Bound, 204
Utah
    community-based institutions in,
        604
    correctional institutions in, 623
    nonresidential community
        treatment programs in, 608
    restitution in, 601
Utilitarianism, 93

V

Vermont, community-based
    institutions in, 604
Victim
    relationship between offender and,
        46–47, 49
    restitution, 598
Victimization
    definition of, 45

lifetime likelihood of, 48–49
National Crime Victimization
    Survey (NCVS), 43–49
rates by age, 46
relationship between victim and
    offender, 46–47, 49
role of fear, 150–51
statistics, 45
Victims of Child Abuse Act, 296
Victim surveys, 28, 43–45
Violence
    juvenile justice system response to,
        571
    reasons for the increase in, 36–38
    in the schools, 358–60
    subculture of, 159
Violent Juvenile Offender program,
    635, 646
Virginia, correctional institutions in,
    621
VisionQuest, 636
Vocational treatment programs, 634

W

Wah Ching, 333
Waiver
    See also Transfer of juveniles to
        adult court
    debate over, 538–40
    factors influencing, 540

judicial, 533
of rights, 14
Washington D.C., restitution in, 600
Wayward minors, use of term, 14
Wellesley College, 257–58
West Virginia
    community-based institutions in,
        604
    correctional institutions in, 624
Wet nurses, 418
Wickersham Commission, 479
Widening the net
    definition of, 22
    diversion and, 236, 524–25
    restitution and, 236, 600
Wilderness probation, 596–97
Wisconsin
    probation in, 591, 602
    status offense laws in, 16
Women's movement, female
    delinquency and
    liberal views, 253–56
    radical views, 256–59
Writ of certioraria, 573
Writ of habeas corpus, 573
Wyoming, correctional institutions in,
    626

Y

Youth groups, 315–17
Youth service programs, 300, 337